EUROPE

SINCE 1914

ENCYCLOPEDIA OF THE AGE OF WAR
AND RECONSTRUCTION

EDITORIAL BOARD

SCRIBNER LIBRARY OF MODERN EUROPE

EUROPE
SINCE 1914
ENCYCLOPEDIA OF THE AGE OF WAR AND RECONSTRUCTION

Volume 1

Abortion to Chernobyl

John Merriman and Jay Winter

EDITORS IN CHIEF

CHARLES SCRIBNER'S SONS

An imprint of Thomson Gale, a part of The Thomson Corporation

THOMSON

GALE

Detroit • New York • San Francisco • New Haven, Conn. • Waterville, Maine • London • Munich

THOMSON

GALE

Europe since 1914: Encyclopedia of the Age of War and Reconstruction

John Merriman
Jay Winter
Editors in Chief

LIBRARY OF CONGRESS CATALOGING-IN-PUBLICATION DATA

Europe since 1914: encyclopedia of the age of war and reconstruction / edited by John Merriman and Jay Winter.
    p. cm. — (Scribner library of modern Europe)
    Includes bibliographical references and index.
    ISBN 0-684-31365-0 (set : alk. paper) — ISBN 0-684-31366-9 (v. 1 : alk. paper) — ISBN 0-684-31367-7 (v. 2 : alk. paper) — ISBN 0-684-31368-5 (v. 3 : alk. paper) — ISBN 0-684-31369-3 (v. 4 : alk. paper) — ISBN 0-684-31370-7 (v. 5 : alk. paper) — ISBN 0-684-31497-5 (e-book)
    1. Europe–History–20th century–Encyclopedias. 2. Europe–Civilization–20th century–Encyclopedias. I. Merriman, John M. II. Winter, J. M.
    D424.E94 2006
    940.503–dc22   2006014427

This title is also available as an e-book and as a ten-volume set with
Europe 1789 to 1914: Encyclopedia of the Age of Industry and Empire.
E-book ISBN 0-684-31497-5
Ten-volume set ISBN 0-684-31530-0
Contact your Gale sales representative for ordering information.

Printed in the United States of America
10 9 8 7 6 5 4 3 2 1

EDITORIAL AND PRODUCTION STAFF

Project Editors
Thomas Carson, Jennifer Wisinski

Art Editor
Joann Cerrito

Associate Editors
Andrew Claps, Pamela A. Dear

Editorial Support
Deirdre Blanchfield, Alja Collar, Angela Doolin, Carol Schwartz

Manuscript Editors
Jonathan G. Aretakis, John Barclay, Susan Barnett, Sylvia J. Cannizzaro,
Joanna Dinsmore, Ellen Hawley, Christine Kelley, John Krol, Mary Russell,
David E. Salamie, Linda Sanders, Jane Marie Todd

Proofreader
Carol Holmes

Indexer
Cynthia Crippen, AEIOU, Inc.

Text Design
Pamela A. E. Galbreath

Cover Design
Jennifer Wahi

Imaging
Randy Bassett, Lezlie Light, Dan Newell,
Christine O'Bryan, Kelly Quin

Permissions
Andrew Specht

Cartographer
XNR Productions (Madison, Wisconsin)

Manager, Composition
Mary Beth Trimper

Assistant Manager, Composition
Evi Seoud

Manufacturing
Wendy Blurton

Senior Developmental Editor
Nathalie Duval

Editorial Director
John Fitzpatrick

Publisher
Jay Flynn

CONTENTS

VOLUME 2

E

VOLUME 3

VOLUME 4

Q

R

S

VOLUME 5

T

INTRODUCTION

In 1914 most Europeans lived on the land; their families were larger and their life spans shorter than those of early-twenty-first-century Europeans. Life expectancy at birth was about fifty years for men, fifty-five for women. Approximately one in ten babies born in 1914 died before reaching its first birthday. These are figures associated with the Third World today. Over the course of the twentieth century, massive changes took place that made Europe overwhelmingly urban. In most of early-twenty-first-century Europe people live on average into their seventies for men and eighties for women. Family size has never been smaller.

The variation between European countries in terms of life changes and family size has diminished substantially. Partly because of the speed of technical change, partly because of the spread of information, teenagers in Moscow and Manchester dress alike; they listen to the same or similar music; they eat the same fast food. Europe has become a commercial entity even more than a political one.

THE END OF IMPERIAL EUROPE
In 1914, about half of the European continent was ruled by emperors or by kings with subject populations stretching around the globe. Germany was an empire; so was Austria-Hungary, Russia, and Turkey. These emperors ruled over multinational populations in or adjacent to Europe. Britain controlled a vast empire, as did France, though theirs was a republican form of government with an empire attached. Belgium held the Congo; Italy had Libya. Portugal had Angola and Mozambique, and Spain part of Morocco. Europe was imperial through and through.

Not so a century later. Every one of these empires disintegrated and virtually all these imperial holdings and dependencies have struggled for and gained their independence. One of the stories this encyclopedia tells is of the end of the European imperial project.

Where Is Europe? If Europe is no longer imperial in character in 2006, than what is it? Three questions may help open the way toward an answer. First, where is Europe, and where are its boundaries? This is a vexing political question, on which no consensus exists. There is in 2006 a European Union that spans twenty-five nations from Ireland to the Baltic states, but it leaves out Russia, the states that formerly made up Yugoslavia, and Turkey. So one answer is that Europe is described by the Atlantic Ocean to the west, by the Mediterranean to the south, and by the Arctic Ocean to the north. The eastern boundary is the problem and is likely to remain so. Where Europe ends on its eastern border is an issue that is likely to dominate European international affairs for the next century or more.

What Is Europe?   The second question asks about the nature of the political association that emerged slowly from the Second World War on. One answer to the question "What is Europe?" is that it is a loose federation of trading partners joined in an evolving European Union, whose populations are represented in a European Parliament, a Council of European states, and whose rights are defended in a European Court of Justice and a separate European Court of Human Rights.

Europe is a political project in the making. One way to visualize this enterprise is to see it as a series of concentric circles. At the core of Europe was the new Franco-German alliance, out of which the European Economic Community emerged. These two key countries had been devastated by the Second World War and were determined not to go back to the ugly years before and during the 1939–1945 conflict. Surrounding these two powers, central combatants in both world wars, a second circle of states joined France and Germany in the creation of a European union following the Treaty of Rome in 1958. Italy and the Benelux countries were there from the start. They were joined by Ireland, Denmark and Britain, then by Spain, Portugal, Austria, Sweden, and Finland. Norway voted to stay out. After 1989 and the collapse of the Soviet bloc, the European project moved east to embrace Poland, the Czech Republic, Hungary, Slovakia, the Baltic states, and Slovenia, and Cyprus. (Malta also joined the Union in 2004.)

By 2006, the European Union encompassed twenty-five states and a population of approximately five hundred million people. Discussions on further expansion continue, presenting the possibility of entry for other countries in eastern and southeastern Europe, including Turkey.

What kind of union is this? With some exceptions, it is an area within which there is a common currency, the euro, free movement of goods and capital, and the free movement of labor. It is not a political federation, since there is no generally recognized constitution. Attempts to write one have foundered on popular objections. In 2005, the citizens of the Netherlands and France rejected a draft constitution. In sum, Europe is a trading bloc with a commitment to democratic forms of government and to the defense of human rights. The history of the twentieth century is in part the story of how this came about.

Who Is a European?   If we can venture some preliminary answers to the two questions "Where is Europe?" and "What is Europe?," we still have to face a third, even thornier question: "Who is a European?" All people in the twenty-five states in the European Union can use a European passport alongside their national ones. But the definition of citizenship collides with the volatile and unpredictable phenomenon of immigration. Europeans control entry into the Union as a whole, but once an immigrant is admitted to one country, he or she can move around the Union at will to find work and a place to live. There are exceptions: Britain still controls its own immigration, separate from that of its European partners.

Underlying much of the controversy over immigration is the question of religion. Many of those seeking to build a life in Europe come from Turkey, North Africa, and the Middle East. Many, though not all, are Muslim. Given the upsurge in Islamic radicalism, especially after the attacks in the United States on 11 September 2001, the position of Muslims within Europe has been questioned time and again. Few will come out and say that Europe is a Christian project; the Holocaust shames into silence most people who believe this. But there is a reluctance to accept Turkey with its large Muslim population into Europe, even though Turkey was one of the first member states joining the Council of Europe in 1949.

Are Russians Europeans? Here too the question is yes and no. It is hard to imagine Europe without St. Petersburg. Who could describe European literature without Boris Pasternak or Alexander Solzhenitzyn, European music without Igor Stravinsky, European art without Wassily Kandinsky and Marc Chagall? Thus, outside of the sphere of international politics and international economic affairs, there is a Europe of the mind, of the spirit, that extends all the way to Vladivostok. In sum, Europe is at one and the same time a political project and a cultural idea. This encyclopedia sets out the basic information any informed person needs to have to understand both.

THE SHAPE OF EUROPEAN HISTORY SINCE 1914
It is tempting to divide twentieth-century European history into four parts:

1. The thirty years' war: 1914–1945

2. The thirty years' peace: 1945–1973

3. The end of the division of Europe: 1974–1991

4. The birth of the new Europe since 1992

Like any scheme, this one obscures critical dates in the middle of these periods—for instance, the onset of the world economic depression in 1929 or the period of revolt in 1968. But this rough four-part sketch does help us to see the way political and economic history has unfolded over the twentieth century. The two world wars were a coherent and catastrophic phase of European history. So too was the thirty-year period of rebuilding that took place in both Eastern and Western Europe. The Middle East war of 1973 and the oil crisis it left in its wake mark a period of economic instability and mass unemployment. These economic trends had profound implications for the Soviet bloc, which never competed successfully with the West, and which entered into discussions on European security in 1974 with the subject of human rights on the agenda. No one foresaw the speed and completeness of the collapse of the Soviet empire between 1989 and 1991, but its economic roots are now well known.

The end of the Cold War ushered in a new period in European history, in part symbolized by the Maastricht Treaty of 1992, which established a single European currency and in principle, a unified European economy. Achieving this goal is a daunting objective, but it does lay out some of the elements of the Europe that emerged in the first decade of the twenty-first century. There are three elements in this package. The first principle is that being a member of

Europe is a support for both domestic democratic institutions and domestic economic life. The second is that Europe is a project consistent with the sovereignty of individual states. The French are no less French because they are Europeans—they like to thumb their noses at European bureaucrats who know better than they do what is in their interests. And third, Europe is not just a project designed to promote a federation of democratic states and to facilitate the common economic development of the continent. It is also a project to make human rights the bedrock of civil society. To this end, countries that join Europe have to accept that the judgment of European courts is superior to the judgment of domestic courts. Where the two conflict, Europe wins. This is revolutionary and presents many possibilities for the future, similar to the experience of the emergent U. S. Supreme Court colliding with state courts in the late eighteenth and early nineteenth centuries. In the early twenty-first century Europe has two supreme courts—one for human rights law, and one for the rest, and both represent an achievement, a kind of unity, which was inconceivable in 1914.

The judicial construction of Europe is a precarious achievement. It is not at all clear how this political and economic entity will develop in the coming decades. But on one point we can reach agreement. A united or federated Europe in the twenty-first century is here to stay; there is no going back to the ideological or political divides of the twentieth century. Something new is in existence, the emergence of which is described in many parts of this encyclopedia.

In the course of the twentieth century, there was a shift in the focus of social movements. The Great War was fought to defend national boundaries and national honor. In the midst of it, a vast social revolution seized the initiative in Russia and gave birth to the Soviet Union. Other activists sought social justice in different ways, but by and large social movements focused on the transformative power of social class or nation: they were the vanguard of the future.

By the third quarter of the twentieth century, those ideas while still alive no longer had the same motivating, at times inspiring, force. Instead, after 1968, social movements dwelt less on nation and class than on human rights and civil society. Green movements emerged; so did movements for gay rights and for the rights of the homeless and the stateless. Young people were at the core of these causes, but they were not alone. The campaign for nuclear disarmament, which played a small, though not insignificant role, in détente, helped move public discourse away from what divided Europeans to what united them, which was overwhelmingly and primarily a hatred of war. Europeans know war in ways that most Americans do not, and out of that distinction comes much friction and misunderstanding of the one by the others.

CULTURAL HISTORY

One of the contrasts of *Europe since 1914* with *Europe 1789 to 1914* is in the space given to cultural history. There is more on this subject in the twentieth-century volumes than in the previous set. In part this is a function of the sources historians need to write their books. Political history requires archives, and many of these are either unavailable or, in 2006, are still governed by a thirty-year rule of confidentiality. Very contemporary history is very hard to write, since the sources are still in personal and private hands. In contrast, nineteenth-century political history is enriched enormously by vast archives out of which stories can be told with authority. To do the same for 1989, for example, will take decades.

In part the efflorescence of cultural practices in the twentieth century helps account for the shift in balance in the two encyclopedias we have jointly edited. The cinema, television, radio, the audio and video cassette, the Internet, have all created images on a scale which has multiplied the sources historians use to write their narratives of the past. Many of these media are constituent elements of our daily lives and thus are subjects of historical study themselves. And none of this leads to straightforward historical conclusions, just many more questions. Take film, for example. In some ways cinema describes the world in forms with which we can identify. But in other respects, film constructs the world we live in by giving us images—about race, gender, marriage, crime, to cite just a few— through which we understand where we are and who we are. And in other ways still, cinema totally distorts the world, cleans it up, for instance, makes war and violence thinkable, imaginable, do-able. The centrality of film for and in twentieth-century history clearly describes one facet of the past century that distinguishes it from earlier periods. But at the same time, it is the sheer volume of images—many of which are reproduced in this encyclopedia—that defines the twentieth century as a visual and visualized universe.

In the search for the cultural history of the twentieth century, we have sought the assistance of authors on both sides of the Atlantic. This is essential, since European history is now entirely transnational. Local and national histories continue to be written, but scholars are more sensitive than ever before of the ways in which Europe is a field of mass immigration and travel across national frontiers as well as within them. In 1914, many English and French town dwellers had never seen the sea. Now, nearly a century later, finding someone that landlocked would be difficult, though not impossible. In 1914 a person would have been considered mad for predicting that Indian cuisine would become a staple of the English diet, or that Chinese restaurants would dot every major European city, yet in 2006, both of these things are true.

Globalization is part of the reason why this is so, but it is unwise to claim that term for the turn of the twenty-first century alone. In 1914, there was the same volume of heavy capital flows, movements of goods and services, and transcontinental migration as in 2006. What the early twenty-first century has is speed, dizzying speed, but the processes are the same. In some ways, this encyclopedia describes Europe as having been at the core of two separate phases of globalization, divided by the convulsive violence of the two world wars. European culture is now globalized too, as anyone wandering around the music scene in Berlin, Paris, or London can attest.

DISRUPTION, UPHEAVAL, DISCONTINUITY

The nineteenth-century world was reconfigured by economic and social upheavals grouped under the umbrella term *industrialization*. In the twentieth century these changes accelerated, with new modes of mass production leading from the assembly line to robotics. Computer technology makes possible an extraordinary increase in productivity, to the extent that the service sector—what we now call the *information superhighway* and those who use it—has overwhelmed the manufacturing sector. In the twentieth century, there was thus a three-fold movement in the organization of work and in the location of the communities surrounding it. First came the move from the country and rural towns to cities; then came the shift from manufacture to the service sector; then came the appearance of postindustrial society, a place where old factories and storehouses turn into boutiques, museums, and Internet cafes.

Postindustrial Europe We must not forget that the move away from industrial production destroyed great urban centers and made unemployed and at times unemployable large sections of the population. In their place arrived millions of Asians, Africans, and Latin Americans who performed low-pay and low-skill jobs previously dominated by indigenous Europeans. In the late nineteenth century, the direction of migration was from east to west, across Europe and the Atlantic. In the twentieth century, the move was from south to north, which transformed the cultural and culinary life of Europe as well as changing the racial and ethnic composition of every European country.

Much of this movement was a result of a search for a way out of poverty, a search for a better life in Paris, Berlin, or London, as well as in many smaller towns. But at least as important in this migratory wave was the sheer number of people—certainly in the tens of millions—who moved out of terror, to escape persecution and war. Some were asylum seekers from outside Europe; others were Europeans persecuted by their own states, like Nazi Germany, or by successor states, like Serbia. Still others were expelled from homes in which they had lived for a millennium—Armenians from Anatolia, Greeks from Turkey, Turks from Greece, ethnic Germans from Czechoslovakia, and Jews from all parts of Continental Europe. The end of the two world wars brought staggering levels of social dislocation, as ethnic populations were sent packing from contested regions or left of their own volition.

And they were the lucky ones. One million Armenians died in the genocide perpetrated by the Turkish state from 1915 on. Here killing was individual, face-to-face murder, or the expulsion of an entire people into the Mesopotamian desert where they died from hunger, thirst, exposure to the elements, or at the hands of marauding bands of Kurds and Turks. The only crime committed by their victims was to be Armenian. Twenty-five years later, those Jews who were trapped in wartime Europe or who chose to stay were the target of the most staggering plan of industrial murder in history. Genocide succeeded in uprooting an entire world of Jewish life in Poland and the former Soviet Union. The Yiddish language lost its roots; six million people—including one million children—were exterminated. The Nazis found the reptilian heart of man, the English writer Martin Amis wrote, and built an Autobahn to get there. For many people, the application of industrial production to mass murder was a rupture in European history from which the very idea of Europe—or of humanity—could not and did not recover. For others it was the moment when the idea of Europe was redefined as a project based upon a commitment to universal human rights. This was the principle announced by the French jurist René Cassin on the steps of the Palais de Chaillot on 10 December 1948 to the United Nations assembled in Paris. What he declaimed was a Universal Declaration of Human Rights. A year later it was translated into a European Convention on Human Rights, with a court in Strasbourg to enforce it. Any nation wishing to adhere to the European Union must accept this document as an integral part of its own legal system.

The Cold War and the Nuclear Threat At the same time as the human rights project was formally launched as a foundational text of postwar Europe, the Cold War presented its diametrical opposite. In 1948 the democratic state of Czechoslovakia was taken over by the Communist Party. In the same year, the Soviet Union cut off supplies from the western zones of Germany occupied by France, Britain, and the United States, and Berlin, divided into four zones itself, but situated within Soviet-controlled eastern Germany. The U.S. airlift kept Berlin alive. A year later the Soviet Union announced that it possessed nuclear weapons and the Communist Party finally won its bloody thirty-year civil war for control of China. In 1950, the United Nations, after a Soviet walk-out from the Security Council, voted to send troops on a "police action" to Korea. Armed conflict with China loomed. The Cold War was on.

What made this episode in international history so important for Europe was that in short order, hundreds, then thousands of nuclear weapons were pointed not only at the USSR and the United States, but also at the heart of Europe. In the event of war, Europe would be completely destroyed. "They made a desert and called it peace," wrote the Roman historian Tacitus two thousand years ago. By the 1950s, the image of a nuclear desert spanning the entire European continent was no longer just a nightmare, but a real possibility, played out in war games by military planners all over the world.

The retreat from the edge of the precipice of total destruction is one of the dominant themes of the history of the second half of the twentieth century. It entailed complex diplomacy on the part of both European and extra-European powers. The most important of these were the Kennedy-Khrushchev exchanges of October 1962, which defused the explosive situation arising from the placement of Soviet missiles in Cuba. But for decades afterwards, millions of ordinary people remembered how near Europe was to nuclear catastrophe and joined mass movements to head it off. The economic costs of the nuclear arms race were staggering, and for the Soviet Union, crippling. It took the courage of the last major Soviet leader, Mikhail Gorbachev, to break the deadlock and thereby end the Cold War. The end of communism in Central and Eastern Europe, the collapse of the Soviet Union, and the bloody disintegration of Yugoslavia followed.

By the 1990s Europe was no longer faced with the insane possibility of mutually assured destruction. In its place came other worries—the emergence of radical Islam, the threat of biological and chemical warfare, waged not by nations but by groups of men and women from the Middle East and elsewhere determined to make Europeans see that what their governments do causes suffering in other parts of the world. Terrorism, a portmanteau for whatever anyone dislikes, became a reality in Russia, in Spain, in France, and in Britain.

Nearly a century after the outbreak of the 1914–1918 war, which ended four empires, took millions of lives, and unleashed some of the demons of the twentieth century, the institutions of war are with us still and have degenerated further. Europe is part of a world in which state-sponsored torture is commonplace. Whatever cruelties those who fought the Great War practiced, torture of prisoners was not one of them. The European Convention on Human Rights is a protection for some, but not everywhere and not for all. Europe in the early twenty-first century is a continent marked by both light and darkness. No one should see this encyclopedia, therefore, as a cavalcade of European progress. To be sure, Europeans today are taller, heavier, eat better, work shorter hours, and live longer than their antecedents one hundred years ago. But the same problems of inequality, of injustice, of the powers of the state, of violence of every kind, persist. In the year 2006, just as a century before, a Europe defined by peace and freedom is an idea in the making. No one can be sure of the outcome of these vast processes, but even to begin to understand them, historical knowledge is essential. This encyclopedia is a tool to help people imagine their own future by a thoughtful and informed reflection on the past century of European history. Without this tool (among many others) which open a window on European scholarship on both sides of the Atlantic Ocean, there is only prejudice and darkness.

BIBLIOGRAPHY

Bartov, Omer. *Hitler's Army: Soldiers, Nazis, and War in the Third Reich*. New York, 1992.

Brenan, Gerald. *The Spanish Labyrinth: An Account of the Social and Political Background of the Civil War*. Cambridge, U.K., 1943.

Browning, Christopher R. *Ordinary Men: Reserve Police Battalion 101 and the Final Solution in Poland*. New York, 1992.

Clendinnen, Inga. *Reading the Holocaust*. Cambridge, U.K., 1999.

Evans, Richard J. *The Third Reich in Power, 1933–1939*. New York, 2005.

Ferro, Marc. *The Great War, 1914–1918*. London, 1973.

Figes, Orlando. *A People's Tragedy: The Russian Revolution, 1891–1924*. London, 1996.

Fischer, Fritz. *Germany's Aims in the First World War*. New York, 1967.

Fitzpatrick, Sheila. *Everyday Stalinism: Ordinary Life in Extraordinary Times: Soviet Russia in the 1930s*. New York, 1999.

Fussell, Paul. *The Great War and Modern Memory*. New York, 1975.

Garton Ash, Timothy. *The Magic Lantern: The Revolution of '89 Witnessed in Warsaw, Budapest, Berlin, and Prague*. New York, 1990.

Hilberg, Raul. *The Destruction of the European Jews*. Chicago, 1961.

Hobsbawm, Eric. *The Age of Extremes: A History of the World, 1914–1991*. New York, 1996.

Judt, Tony. *Postwar: A History of Europe since 1945*. New York, 2005.

Kershaw, Ian. *Hitler*. London, 1991. First American ed., New York, 1999.

Laqueur, Walter. *Europe since Hitler*. London, 1970. Rev. ed., New York, 1982.

Mack Smith, Denis. *Mussolini*. New York, 1983.

Mazower, Mark. *Dark Continent: Europe's Twentieth Century*. New York, 1999.

Merriman, John M. *A History of Modern Europe*. Vol. 2. New York, 2004.

Milward, Alan S., George Brennan, and Federico Romero. *The European Rescue of the Nation-State*. Berkeley, Calif., 1992.

Neumann, Franz L. *Behemoth: The Structure and Practice of National Socialism, 1933–1944*. New York, 1944.

Paxton, Robert O. *Vichy France: Old Guard and New Order, 1940–1944*. New York, 1972.

Reynolds, David. *One World Divisible: A Global History since 1945*. New York, 2000.

Roberts, John M. *Twentieth Century: The History of the World, 1901 to 2000*. New York, 1999.

Rousso, Henry. *The Vichy Syndrome: History and Memory in France since 1944*. Cambridge, Mass., 1991.

Taylor, A. J. P. *English History, 1914–1945*. New York, 1965.

Thomas, Hugh. *The Spanish Civil War*. New York, 1961.

Weinberg, Gerhard L. *A World at Arms: A Global History of World War II*. Cambridge, U.K., 1994.

JOHN MERRIMAN, JAY WINTER

MAPS OF EUROPE SINCE 1914

The maps in this section illuminate some of the major events of European history in the twentieth and early twenty-first centuries, including World War I and World War II, the Holocaust, the breakup of Yugoslavia, and the formation of the European Union.

WWI in Europe

- Allies, 1918
- Central Powers
- Neutral nations
- Farthest advance by Central Powers
- 1914 border

ATLANTIC OCEAN

NORWAY

SWEDEN

Baltic Sea

DENMARK

North Sea

UNITED KINGDOM

London

NETH.

BELG.

Berlin

GERMANY

Eastern Front

RUSSIA

Paris

LUX.

Western Front

FRANCE

SWITZ.

Italian Front

Vienna

Budapest

AUSTRIA-HUNGARY

Black Sea

PORTUGAL

Lisbon

SPAIN

ITALY

Belgrade

MONT.

SERBIA

ROMANIA

BULGARIA

ALBANIA

Salonika Front

GREECE

Athens

Constantinople

OTTOMAN EMPIRE

Mediterranean Sea

0   250   500 mi.

0   250   500 km

Versailles Settlement

Newly-formed nations
Boundaries, 1923

ICELAND

ATLANTIC
OCEAN

NORWAY

SWEDEN

FINLAND

Christiania
(Oslo)

Stockholm

Helsinki
Tallinn
ESTONIA

Petrograd

Riga
LATVIA

Moscow

North
Sea

DENMARK
Copenhagen

LITH.

Danzig
East
Prussia
(Ger.)

Kaunas

UNION OF SOVIET
SOCIALIST REPUBLICS

IRISH
FREE
STATE

UNITED
KINGDOM

London

Amsterdam

NETH.

Berlin

Warsaw

Baltic Sea

Brussels

GERMANY

POLAND

BELG.

LUX.

Paris

Saar

Prague

Krakow

CZECHOSLOVAKIA

FRANCE

Bern

SWITZ.

Vienna

AUSTRIA

Budapest

HUNGARY

ROMANIA

Venice

Belgrade

Bucharest

Black Sea

ITALY

YUGOSLAVIA

BULGARIA

Rome

Sofia

PORTUGAL

ANDORRA

Madrid

Tirane

Constantinople

SPAIN

ALBANIA

GREECE

TURKEY

Lisbon

Tangier
(International
Territory)

Gibraltar

Athens

Spanish
Morocco

Mediterranean Sea

Moroooo (Fr.)

Tunisia
(Fr.)

Algeria
(Fr.)

N

0   200   400 mi.
0   200   400 km

WWII in Europe

- Axis Powers
- Maximum Axis Control
- Neutral countries
- Allied Powers
- Farthest German advance as of Dec. 1941
- 1937 borders

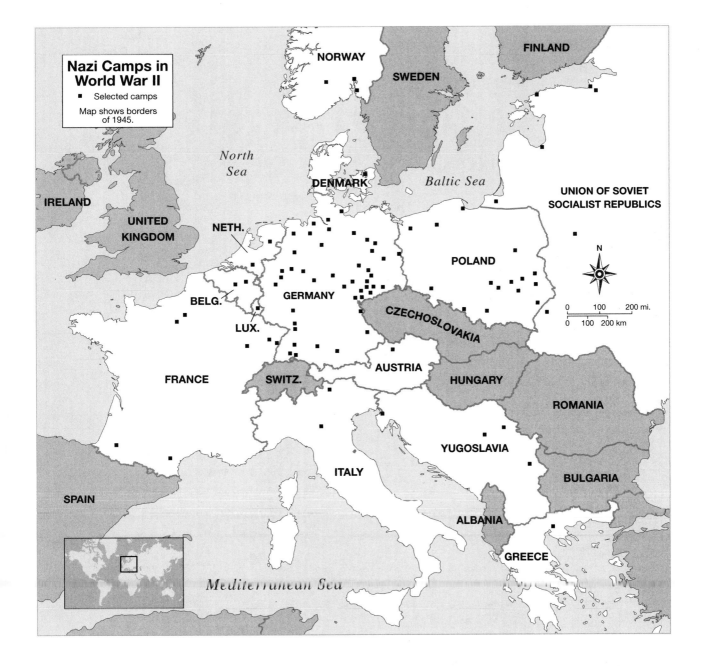

Nazi Camps in World War II

■ Selected camps

Map shows borders of 1945.

North Sea

IRELAND

UNITED KINGDOM

NETH.

BELG.

LUX.

FRANCE

SPAIN

NORWAY

SWEDEN

FINLAND

DENMARK

Baltic Sea

UNION OF SOVIET SOCIALIST REPUBLICS

GERMANY

POLAND

CZECHOSLOVAKIA

AUSTRIA

SWITZ.

HUNGARY

ROMANIA

YUGOSLAVIA

BULGARIA

ITALY

ALBANIA

GREECE

Mediterranean Sea

N

0   100   200 mi.
0   100   200 km

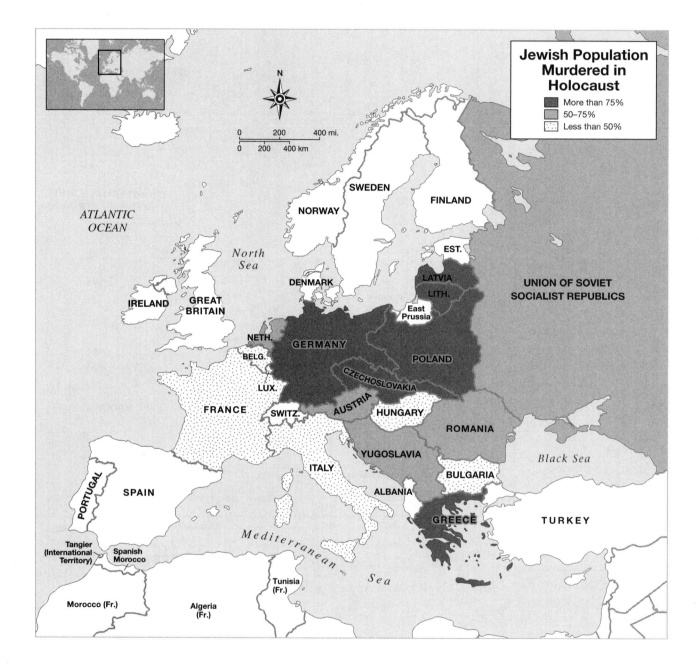

Post 1945 Europe

Communist nations — Iron Curtain
Non-Communist nations ⊛ Capital

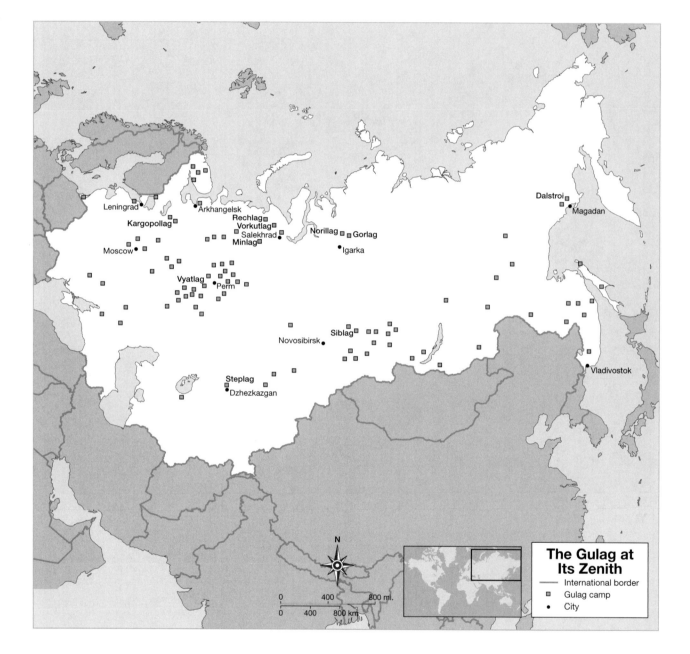

The Gulag at Its Zenith

Leningrad
Arkhangelsk
Kargopollag
Rechlag
Vorkutlag
Salekhrad
Minlag
Norillag
Gorlag
Igarka
Moscow
Vyatlag
Perm
Dalstroi
Magadan
Novosibirsk
Siblag
Steplag
Dzhezkazgan
Vladivostok

**The Gulag at
Its Zenith**

—— International border
▪ Gulag camp
● City

0   400   800 mi.
0   400   800 km

N

Yugoslavia Before the Breakup

International border
Republic border
Autonomous area border
National capital
Republic or autonomous area capital

AUSTRIA

HUNGARY

ITALY

ROMANIA

Ljubljana

Slovenia

Zagreb

Croatia

Vojvodina

Novi Sad

Belgrade

Bosnia and
Herzegovina

Sarajevo

Serbia

Montenegro

Priština

Kosovo

BULGARIA

Titograd

Skopje

Macedonia

ITALY

Adriatic Sea

N

ALBANIA

GREECE

0   40   80 mi.
0   40   80 km

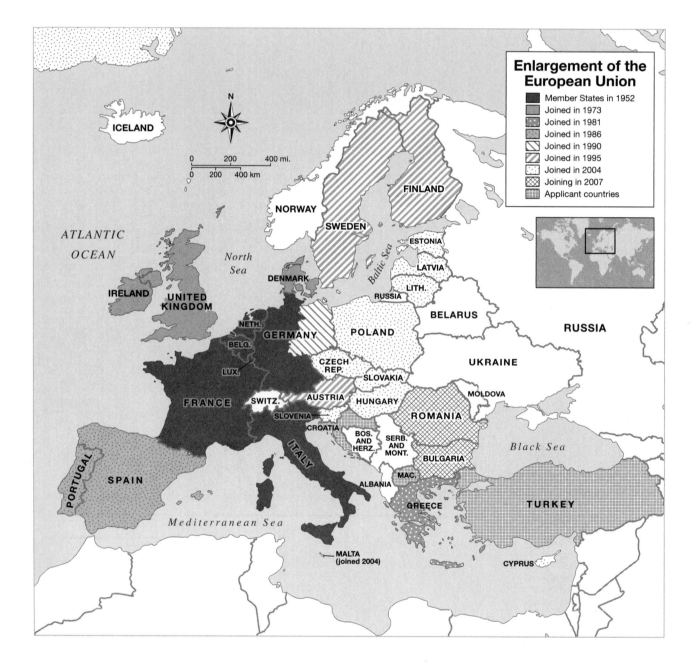

Enlargement of the European Union

- Member States in 1952
- Joined in 1973
- Joined in 1981
- Joined in 1986
- Joined in 1990
- Joined in 1995
- Joined in 2004
- Joining in 2007
- Applicant countries

CHRONOLOGY

The chronology is arranged by year from 1914 to 2005 and is organized under seven major headings that cover the encyclopedia's scope both thematically and over time. Most items listed below are discussed in the encyclopedia's articles and can be found by referring to the table of contents and the index. Because the section headings are not always mutually exclusive, certain events may be listed under more than one heading.

DATE	POLITICS AND DIPLOMACY	SCIENCE AND TECHNOLOGY	ECONOMY AND SOCIETY
1914	Assassination of Austrian archduke Francis Ferdinand in Sarajevo; Austrian ultimatum to Serbia; German "blank check"; alliances, aggression lead to war between Allies and Central Powers; Irish Home Rule becomes law	Typhoid vaccination and tetanus prophylactic reduces soldiers' risks of disease; British Henry Moseley develops atomic numbers	Austria-Hungary: War Production Law put into effect; emergency decrees passed in combatant nations
1915	Treaty of London	First use of gas in warfare; submarine warfare; dirigible airship; rehabilitation and plastic surgery developed; term "shell shock" coined	"Great Retreat" cripples Russian economy
1916	UK: David Lloyd George government, 1916–1922; Francis Joseph (Austria-Hungary) dies; Charles (Austria-Hungary), 1916–1918	Albert Einstein develops General Theory of Relativity	Germany: Hindenburg program for total war and Auxiliary Service Law; "Turnip Winter," 1916–1917; UK: Military Service Act; Russia: strikes
1917	Russia: Nicholas II abdicates; Corfu Agreement; France: Georges Clemenceau government, 1917–1920	Frenchman Paul Langevin develops sonar	Germany: food riots; France: strikes; France: income tax adopted; Russia: food riots, strikes; Bolshevik government decrees end of private land ownership

LITERATURE AND THE ARTS	INTELLECTUAL LIFE AND RELIGION	WAR AND ARMED CONFLICT	EUROPE AND THE WORLD	DATE
James Joyce, *Portrait of the Artist as a Young Man*, Henri Matisse, *Interior with Goldfish*; Wyndham Lewis founds Vorticist movement; Rupert Brooke, "1914: Peace"; Charles Péguy dies		Great War, 1914–1918; Schlieffen Plan; Plan XVII; Battle of Tannenberg; Battle of Masurian Lakes; Battle of the Marne; Austria's first invasion of Serbia; Battle of Ypres	German Togoland falls to British; British and French colonial subjects join war effort	*1914*
Franz Kafka, *Die Verwandlung*; Ezra Pound begins *The Cantos*, 1915–1960		Gallipoli invasion; Italy joins Allies; Western Front stalemate; Germans sink the *Lusitania*; Austrian occupation of Serbia	Armenian genocide; British fight Turks in Palestine and Mesopotamia; German Southwest Africa falls to British	*1915*
Tristan Tzara founds Dada	Ferdinand de Saussure, *Cours de linguistique générale* (posthumous)	Battle of Verdun; Battle of the Somme; Irish nationalist uprising; Battle of Jutland	German Cameroons fall to British	*1916*
Wilfred Owen, "Dulce et Decorum Est"; Marcel Duchamp, *Fountain*; Kasimir Malevich, *Suprematist Painting (Yellow Rectangle)*, 1917–1918; De Stijl founded		Germans declare unrestricted warfare; Russian February Revolution; Nivelle Offensive; US joins Allies; Kornilov Affair; French divisions mutinies; Russian October Revolution; Russian Civil War, 1917–1920	Balfour Declaration	*1917*

DATE	POLITICS AND DIPLOMACY	SCIENCE AND TECHNOLOGY	ECONOMY AND SOCIETY
1918	Treaty of Brest-Litovsk; collapse of German, Austro-Hungarian, and Ottoman empires; Germany: William II abdicates; German Republic declared; end of Great War; Poland, Czechoslovakia, Yugoslavia established		Germany: widespread strikes; Austria-Hungary: food riots; UK: food rationing; UK: Representation of the People Act; Alexandra Kollontai, *Communism and the Family*; influenza epidemic, 1918–1919
1919	Paris Peace Conference; Weimar Republic established; Comintern founded; *Fasci di Combattimento* founded; Treaty of Versailles; Hungary: Bela Kun founded; Hungarian Soviet Republic; France: "Blue Horizon" Chamber; League of Nations founded	John Alcock and Arthur Brown fly first trans-Atlantic non-stop flight; London-Paris international airmail established; Ernest Rutherford creates first nuclear reactions	France: 8-hour day; Sweden: 40-hour week
1920	Comintern's Twenty-One Conditions; Admiral Miklós Horthy Regent of Hungary, 1920–1944; Germany: Kapp Putsch; National Socialist German Worker's Party founded; French Communist Party founded; Czechoslovakia, Yugoslavia, Romania form Little Entente, 1920–1921; Estonia, Latvia, Lithuania gain independence from USSR; Treaty of Sèvres; Treaty of Trianon		John Maynard Keynes, *Economic Consequences of the Peace*; USSR: abortion legalized

LITERATURE AND THE ARTS	INTELLECTUAL LIFE AND RELIGION	WAR AND ARMED CONFLICT	EUROPE AND THE WORLD	DATE
John Singer Sargent, *Gassed,* 1918–1919; John Nash, *Over the Top,* 1918–1919	Oswald Spengler, *Der Untergang des Abendlandes,* 1918–1922; Lytton Strachey, *Eminent Victorians;* Bolshevik attack on the Russian Orthodox church	German spring offensive; Vittorio Veneto Offensive; German retreat; Great War ended	Post–World War I: German and Turkish colonies divided by Allies. British mandates: Iraq, Palestine, Tanganyika; French mandates: Syria, Lebanon, the Cameroons, Togoland; Belgian mandate: Ruanda-Urundi	*1918*
Walter Gropius founds Bauhaus school of design; Robert Wiene, *Das Kabinett des Dr. Caligari*	Karl Barth, *Der Römerbrief;* Sylvia Beach opens bookstore Shakespeare and Company (Paris)	Germany: Spartacist revolt; Karl Liebknecht and Rosa Luxemburg killed; Greece invades Turkey; Gabriele D'Annunzio seizes Fiume; Irish declare independence; Irish Republican Army founded; Russo-Polish War, 1919–1920; Hungarian-Romanian War	Indian protest against Rowlatt Acts	*1919*
Karel Čapek, *R.U.R.;* André Breton, *Les Champs Magnétiques*	Ernst Jünger, *In Stahlgewittern;* Joan of Arc canonized	Germany: Kapp Putsch; Greek-Turkish War, 1920–1923		*1920*

DATE	POLITICS AND DIPLOMACY	SCIENCE AND TECHNOLOGY	ECONOMY AND SOCIETY
1921	Irish Free State founded		USSR: New Economic Policy (NEP) instituted; Germany receives reparations bill
1922	USSR established; Ukraine, Byelorussia incorporated into USSR; Germany-USSR Rapallo meeting; Mussolini appoints prime minister	British archaeologists rediscover King Tutankhamen's tomb; Russian A. A. Friedmann postulates expanding universe	Austrian finances stabilized
1923	France occupies Ruhr; Treaty of Lausanne; Republic of Turkey established; President Mustafa Kemal (Atatürk) (Turkey), 1923–1938; Germany: Gustav Stresemann chancellor; Beer Hall Putsch; first government of Prime Minister Stanley Baldwin (UK), 1923–1924		Rampant inflation in Germany; *Rentenmark* introduced; Le Mans car race established
1924	V. I. Lenin dies; UK: Ramsay MacDonald forms first Labour Party government; assassination of Giacomo Matteotti; French *Cartel des Gauches*	Otto Rank, *Das Trauma der Geburt und seine Bedeutung für die Psychoanalyse*	Dawes Plan

LITERATURE AND THE ARTS	INTELLECTUAL LIFE AND RELIGION	WAR AND ARMED CONFLICT	EUROPE AND THE WORLD	DATE
Jaroslav Hašek, *The Good Soldier Schweik*, 1921–1923; Russian constructivist program published; Fernand Léger, *Le Grand Déjeuner*; Pablo Picasso, *Three Women at the Spring*	Ludwig Wittgenstein, *Tractatus Logio-Philosophicus*	Irish Civil War, 1921–1923; Nazi Sturmabteilung (SA) founded	Cairo Conference; Moroccan Revolt, 1921–1926	*1921*
James Joyce, *Ulysses*; BBC founded; T. S. Eliot, *The Wasteland*; Paul Klee, *Twittering Machine*; Adolf Loos, *Chicago Tribune* Tower design (unexecuted)			Egypt nominally gains independence from UK	*1922*
Darius Milhaud, *La Création du Monde*; Igor Stravinsky, *Les noces*; Wassily Kandinsky, *On White*; Rainer Maria Rilke, *Duineser Elegien*; Le Corbusier, *Vers une architecture*; Bela Bartók, *Dance Suite*	György Lukács, *Geschichte und Klassenbewusstein*; Edmund Husserl, *Erste Philosophie*, 1923–1924			*1923*
André Breton, *Manifeste du Surréalisme*; Arthur Honegger, *Pacific 231*; Thomas Mann, *Der Zauberberg*; Käthe Kollwitz, *Parents' Monument*, 1924–1932; E. M. Forster, *A Passage to India*; F. W. Murnau, *Der letzte Mann*				*1924*

DATE	POLITICS AND DIPLOMACY	SCIENCE AND TECHNOLOGY	ECONOMY AND SOCIETY
1925	President Paul von Hindenburg (Germany), 1925–1934; Locarno Agreements	Austrian Wolfgang Pauli develops exclusion principle	Adolf Hitler, *Mein Kampf*; Britain reestablishes gold standard; Italy: Operaio Nazionale Dopolavoro founded
1926	Nonfascist parties in Italy prohibited; Poland: Marshal Jozef Piłsudski coup; Germany joins League of Nations	Austrian Erwin Schrödinger develops Schrödinger equation; Ivan Pavlov, *Conditioned Reflexes*	UK: two-week general strike
1927	USSR: Joseph Stalin emerges as leader; Leon Trotsky expelled from Bolsheviks	Charles Lindbergh lands in France; Werner Heisenberg develops uncertainty principle; trans-Atlantic telephone service begins; Alfred Adler, *Menschenkenntnis*	Austria: general strike
1928	Kellogg-Briand Pact	Alexander Fleming identifies penicillin	USSR: First Five-Year Plan begins

LITERATURE AND THE ARTS	INTELLECTUAL LIFE AND RELIGION	WAR AND ARMED CONFLICT	EUROPE AND THE WORLD	DATE
Alban Berg, *Wozzeck*; Josephine Baker in Paris; Jean Cocteau, *L'Ange Heurtebise*; Sergei Eisenstein, *Battleship Potemkin*				*1925*
George Grosz, *The Pillars of Society*; Ernest Hemingway, *The Sun Also Rises*				*1926*
Virginia Woolf, *To the Lighthouse*; Hermann Hesse, *Der Steppenwolf*; Fritz Lang, *Metropolis*	Martin Heidegger, *Sein und Zeit*; André Gide, *Voyage au Congo*; Julien Benda, *La Trahison des clercs*	Austria: clash of demonstrators and police		*1927*
Kurt Weill and Bertolt Brecht, *Die Dreigroschenoper*; Vladimir Mayakovsky, *The Bedbug*; Virginia Woolf, *Orlando*; D. H. Lawrence, *Lady Chatterley's Lover*; Otto Dix, *War*, 1928–1932; William Butler Yeats, *The Tower*; Anton von Webern, *Symphony*	Manager Josémaría Escrivá de Balaguer y Albas founds Opus Dei		Iraq: Wahabi unrest	*1928*

DATE	POLITICS AND DIPLOMACY	SCIENCE AND TECHNOLOGY	ECONOMY AND SOCIETY
1929	Yugoslavia: King Alexander creates military dictatorship; Croatian Ustaša founded		Great Depression begins; Young Plan
1930	French withdraw from Rhineland	Briton Frank Whittle invents jet engine; Germany: BCG vaccine disaster	USSR: forced collectivization targeting kulaks; famine follows; France: fees abolished for secondary school
1931	UK: National Government formed; Spanish Republic founded	Austrian Kurt Gödel develops Gödel's proof	Proposed German-Austrian customs union opposed by France, Little Entente
1932	Chancellor Englebert Dollfuss (Austria), 1932–1934	Melanie Klein, *The Psychoanalysis of Children*	UK: George V broadcasts first royal Christmas address
1933	Adolf Hitler appointed chancellor; Enabling Act; Germany withdraws from the League of Nations		Germany: Jews purged from civil service; Law for the Protection of Hereditary Health; *Kraft durch Freude* founded; USSR: Second Five-Year Plan begins

LITERATURE AND THE ARTS	INTELLECTUAL LIFE AND RELIGION	WAR AND ARMED CONFLICT	EUROPE AND THE WORLD	DATE
Ludwig Mies van der Rohe, German (or Barcelona) Pavilion for the Exposición Internacional, Barcelona; László Moholy-Nagy, *Light Prop*; René Magritte, *Treachery of Images*; Alfred Döblin, *Berlin Alexanderplatz*; Robert Graves, *Good-Bye to All That*	Lateran Accord between Italy and Vatican; Virginia Woolf, *A Room of One's Own*; Rudolf Bultmann, "Der Begriff der Offenbarun im Neuen Testament"; José Ortega y Gasset, *La rebelión de las masas*			*1929*
Josef von Sternberg, *Der blaue Engel*; suicide of Vladimir Mayakovsky; Arnold Schoenberg, *Moses und Aron*, 1930–1932	Sigmund Freud, *Das Unbehagen in der Kultur*			*1930*
Salvador Dali, *The Persistence of Memory*; Fritz Lang, *M*			British Commonwealth formally founded	*1931*
Max Beckmann, *Departure*, 1932–1934; Aldous Huxley, *Brave New World*	Karl Barth, *Kirchliche Dogmatik*, 1932–1967; Emmanuel Mounier founds *Esprit*		Iraq gains independence from UK	*1932*
Robert Delaunay, *Rhythms without End* series		Germany secretly plans rearmament		*1933*

DATE	POLITICS AND DIPLOMACY	SCIENCE AND TECHNOLOGY	ECONOMY AND SOCIETY
1934	France: far right antiparliamentary riots; Chancellor Kurt von Schuschnigg (Austria), 1934–1938; Yugoslavia: Alexander I assassinated; Germany: Night of the Long Knives; German-Polish Nonaggression Pact; Bulgaria: coup d'état establishes royal-military dictatorship under King Boris III	Nazi laws allow forced sterilization	
1935		UK: Hugh Marriott and Alan Kekwick develop continuous drip blood transfusion	German Nuremberg Laws; USSR: Andrei Stakhanov praised for coal mining feat; first stretch of German Autobahn opens
1936	Popular Front government in France; Greece: General Ioannis Metaxas dictatorship; German-Japanese Anti-Comintern Pact; King George V (UK) dies; King Edward VIII abdicates; King George VI (UK), 1936–1952	UK: Leonard Colebrook develops sulfonamide drugs; BBC establishes television system	France: two weeks' paid vacation implemented; Stalin bans abortion; Germany: Four-Year Plan begins; John Maynard Keynes, *General Theory of Employment, Interest and Money*
1937	Italy joins Anti-Comintern Pact; Prime Minister Neville Chamberlain (UK), 1937–1940	UK: Alan Turing's hypothetical computer, the "Turing machine"; Germany: first successful helicopter flight	Volkswagen founded
1938	German-Austrian Anschluss; Munich Conference; Romania: King Carol II declares royal dictatorship	Germans Otto Hahn and Fritz Strassmann develop nuclear fission	Germany: *Kristallnacht*; USSR: Third Five-Year Plan begins

LITERATURE AND THE ARTS	INTELLECTUAL LIFE AND RELIGION	WAR AND ARMED CONFLICT	EUROPE AND THE WORLD	DATE
First All-Union Congress of Soviet Writers	Arnold Toynbee, *A Study of History,* 1934–1961	Brief civil war in Austria		*1934*
Louis-Ferdinand Céline, *Voyage au bout de la nuit*; Alfred Hitchcock, *The Thirty-Nine Steps*; Leni Riefenstahl, *Triumph des Willens*; Carl Orff, *Carmina Burana*	Leon Chwistek, *Limits of Science*		Italy invades Ethiopia	*1935*
Sergei Prokofiev, *Peter and the Wolf*	André Gide, *Retour de l'U.R.S.S.*	Spanish civil war, 1936–1939; German military occupation of Rhineland		*1936*
Pablo Picasso, *Guernica*; Piet Mondrian, "Plastic Art and Pure Plastic Art"; Jean Renoir, *La Grande Illusion*	Stephen Spender, *Forward from Liberalism*	Russo-Japanese conflict, 1937–1939		*1937*
Jean-Paul Sartre, *La Nausée*; Constantin Brancusi, Tîrgu-Jiu Complex, Romania; Marc Chagall, *White Crucifixion*	George Orwell, *Homage to Catalonia*	German occupation of the Sudetenland		*1938*

DATE	POLITICS AND DIPLOMACY	SCIENCE AND TECHNOLOGY	ECONOMY AND SOCIETY
1939	Spain: Nationalist Regime under Francisco Franco founded, 1939–1975; German-Italian Pact of Steel; Soviet-German Nonaggression Pact; World War II begins	UK: radar developed; John Desmond Bernal, *The Social Function of Science*; Swiss Paul Hermann Müller discovers insecticidal use of DDT; Germany: forced euthanasia performed; pure penicillin produced	
1940	French Third Republic ends itself; Vichy Regime established; Leon Trotsky dies; Moldavia made a republic within USSR; Estonia, Latvia, Lithuania incorporated into USSR; Atlantic Charter; Prime Minister Winston Churchill (UK), 1940–1945	Cave painting discovered in Lascaux, France	
1941	Independent state of Croatia founded under the Ustaše; Tripartite Pact		UK: conscription of unmarried women for war work; US: Lend-Lease Act; Germany: War Aid Service introduced
1942	Soviet-British-U.S. military alliance		Sir William Beveridge, *Social Insurance and Allied Services*; Germany: war economy restructured, increasing use of slave labor

LITERATURE AND THE ARTS	INTELLECTUAL LIFE AND RELIGION	WAR AND ARMED CONFLICT	EUROPE AND THE WORLD	DATE
Olivier Messiaen, *Mode de Valeurs et d'Intensités*		German occupation of Czechoslovakia; World War II, 1939–1945; Germany and USSR invade Poland; British and French "Phony War" on Germany; USSR invades Finland, occupies Estonia, Latvia, Lithuania		*1939*
Graham Greene, *The Power and the Glory,* Arthur Koestler, *Darkness at Noon*	Bertrand Russell, *An Inquiry into the Meaning and Truth*	Germany invades Norway, Denmark, Luxembourg, Belgium, the Netherlands, France; evacuation at Dunkirk; Battle of Britain; Italy invades Greece	Indochina War, 1940–1941	*1940*
Dmitri Shostakovich, *Seventh Symphony (Leningrad Symphony)*		Germany invades Greece, Yugoslavia, USSR; "Final Solution" increasingly implemented and systematized in East Europe; Yugoslav resistance strong under communist Tito; US enters war	Syria conquered by Allies; French mandate terminated	*1941*
Albert Camus, *L'Étranger*	C. S. Lewis, *The Screwtape Letters*	Wannsee conference; Allied invasion of North Africa, German occupation of Vichy France; Battle of Stalingrad, 1942–1943	Vichy France loses control of all African possessions	*1942*

DATE	POLITICS AND DIPLOMACY	SCIENCE AND TECHNOLOGY	ECONOMY AND SOCIETY
1943	Tehran conference; Mussolini's Italian Social Republic founded in Salò	Swiss Albert Hoffman creates LSD	France: *Service du travail obligatoire* instated
1944		German Wernher von Braun develops V-2 rocket; Dutchman Willem Kolff develops kidney machine	Bretton Woods Agreement; *Unione Donne Italiane* founded; Sweden: homosexuality decriminalized
1945	Yalta conference; German unconditional surrender; Potsdam conference; end of World War II; United Nations (UN) founded; Prime Minister Clement Attlee (UK), 1945–1951	Briton Arthur C. Clarke theorizes geosynchronous satellite	Millions of displaced people after the war; Nuremberg trials, 1945–1946; UK: Family Allowances Act
1946	France: provisional president Charles de Gaulle resigns; French Fourth Republic founded; Federal People's Republic of Yugoslavia founded; Churchill describes "Iron Curtain"		Baby boom, 1946–1964; UK: National Assistance Act, nationalization of the Bank of England
1947	Romanian People's Republic founded; Truman Doctrine; UN resolution concerning Israel and Palestine		US begins Marshall Plan; British abolishes fees for secondary school; France: Monnet Plan

LITERATURE AND THE ARTS	INTELLECTUAL LIFE AND RELIGION	WAR AND ARMED CONFLICT	EUROPE AND THE WORLD	DATE
Jean-Paul Sartre, *L'Être et le néant*; Jean Fautrier, *Otages* series		Allied victory in North Africa; Allied invasion of Italy; fall of Mussolini; Allies employ strategic bombing; French Conseil National de la Résistance founded		*1943*
	Dietrich Bonhoeffer dies	Allied invasion of Normandy; officers' plot against Hitler; Battle of the Bulge; Greek Civil War, 1944–1945, 1946–1949		*1944*
Evelyn Waugh, *Brideshead Revisited*; Roberto Rossellini, *Roma, città aperta*; Benjamin Britten, *Peter Grimes*	Maurice Merleau-Ponty, *Phénoménologie de la perception*	Liberation of concentration camps; Red Army captures Berlin; Germany surrenders unconditionally; United Nations founded	Sétif clash in Algeria; Indonesian War of Independence, 1945–1949	*1945*
George Orwell, *Animal Farm*	Karl Jaspers, *Die Schuldfrage*		Lebanon gains independence from France	*1946*
Albert Camus, *La Peste*; André Malraux, *La Psychologie de l'art*, 1947–1950, Germaine Richier, *The Storm*	Primo Levi, *Se questo è un uomo*; Antonio Gramsci, *Lettere dal carcere* (posthumous); Max Horkheimer and Theodor Adorno, *Dialektik der Aufklärung*; Polish exiles found anti-communist journal *Kultura*		India, Pakistan gain independence from UK; France at war in Indochina, 1947–1954	*1947*

DATE	POLITICS AND DIPLOMACY	SCIENCE AND TECHNOLOGY	ECONOMY AND SOCIETY
1948	Treaty of Brussels; Stalin expels Yugoslavia from Cominform; Communist coup in Czechoslovakia; Polish United Workers' Party founded	Soviet I. V. Michurin's theory of heredity shaped by environment	USSR blocks Berlin; US employs airlift to Berlin, 1948–1949; West German Deutschmark released, "economic miracle" begins; Organization for European Economic Cooperation founded
1949	North Atlantic Treaty Organization (NATO) founded; Council of Mutual Assistance (COMECON) founded; German Democratic Republic (east) divided from German Federal Republic (west); Christian Democrat Chancellor Konrad Adenauer (West Germany), 1949–1963; Italian Republic founded	USSR detonates its first atomic bomb	Simone de Beauvoir, *Le Deuxième Sexe*; Ludwig Erhard, West German economics minister, 1949–1963
1950	General Secretary Walter Ulbricht (East Germany), 1950–1971	Briton Alan Turing develops "Turing Test" for artificial intelligence	UK: nationalization of iron and steel, 1950–1951
1951	Prime Minister Winston Churchill (UK), 1951–1955		European Coal and Steel Community founded; Finnish abortion law liberalized
1952	Queen Elizabeth II (UK); European Defense Community, 1952–1954	UK develops nuclear weapons	First television channel in West Germany

LITERATURE AND THE ARTS	INTELLECTUAL LIFE AND RELIGION	WAR AND ARMED CONFLICT	EUROPE AND THE WORLD	DATE
Samuel Beckett, *En attendant Godot*, 1948–1952; Henri Matisse, Chapelle du Rosaire (Vence, France), 1948–1951; Vittorio De Sica, *Ladri di biciclette*; CoBrA expressionist group founded	Bertrand Russell, *Human Knowledge, Its Scope and Limits*		Israel founded; Burma, Ceylon gain independence from UK	*1948*
George Orwell, *1984*; Tatyana Yablonskaya, *Bread*; Eugène Ionesco, *La Cantatrice chauve*			Indonesia gains independence from The Netherlands	*1949*
European Broadcasting Union founded			Korean War, 1950–1953	*1950*
Henry Moore, *Reclining Figure*; Lucian Freud, *Interior in Paddington*	Hannah Arendt, *The Origins of Totalitarianism*		Libya gains independence from Italy	*1951*
Agatha Christie, *The Mousetrap*			Tunisian War of Independence, 1952–1956; Kenya: Mau Mau Revolt, 1952–1960	*1952*

DATE	POLITICS AND DIPLOMACY	SCIENCE AND TECHNOLOGY	ECONOMY AND SOCIETY
1953	Doctors' Plot; Joseph Stalin dies; Party Secretary Nikita Khrushchev (USSR), 1953–1964; transnational Christian Democrat Group (later known as European People's Party) founded		
1954		USSR: first nuclear energy reactor; Switzerland: European Center for Nuclear Research (CERN) founded	Britain ends wartime rationing; Briton Roger Bannister breaks the four-minute mile
1955	Warsaw Pact founded; Austria regains independence		USSR: abortion legalized again
1956	Premier Khrushchev (USSR), 1956–1964; Khrushchev's secret speech; Polish crisis over Władysław Gomułka, party leader 1956–1970; Hungary: Soviets crush Imre Nagy's reform movement		France: Poujadist revolt

LITERATURE AND THE ARTS	INTELLECTUAL LIFE AND RELIGION	WAR AND ARMED CONFLICT	EUROPE AND THE WORLD	DATE
Francis Poulenc, *Les dialogues des Carmélites*, 1953–1956; Jacques Tati, *Les Vacances de M. Hulot*	Roland Barthes, *Le Degré zero de l'écriture*; Czesław Miłosz, *The Captive Mind*; Ludwig Wittgenstein, *Philosophische Untersuchungen* (posthumous)	East German uprising	Moroccan War of Independence, 1953–1956	*1953*
Françoise Sagan, *Bonjour Tristesse*; Witold Lutoslawski, *Funeral Music in Memory of Béla Bartók*			Vietnam, Cambodia, Laos gain independence from France; Algerian War, 1954–1962; British troops agree to leave Egypt	*1954*
J. R. R. Tolkien, *The Lord of the Rings*; Luigi Nono, *Il canto sospeso*; Pierre Boulez, *Third Piano Sonata*, 1955–1957	Raymond Aron, *L'Opium des intellectuals*; Rudolf Bultmann lecture series, *History and Eschatology: The Presence of Eternity*	Cyprus conflict, 1955–1959		*1955*
Ingmar Bergman, *The Seventh Seal*; Richard Hamilton, *Just What Is It That Makes Today's Homes So Different, So Appealing?*; John Osborne, *Look Back in Anger*; Pier Luigi Nervi and Gio Ponti, Pirelli Tower (Milan); Alain Resnas, *Nuit et brouillard*		Soviet invasion of Hungary	Suez Canal crisis; Sudan gains independence from UK; Morocco, Tunisia gain independence from France	*1956*

DATE	POLITICS AND DIPLOMACY	SCIENCE AND TECHNOLOGY	ECONOMY AND SOCIETY
1957	Treaty of Rome	*Sputnik* launched; International Geophysical Year	European Economic Community (EEC or Common Market) founded
1958	French Fifth Republic founded	Integrated circuits invented	Minor recession, 1958–1959; Britian: Notting Hill clash between youths and West Indian immigrants; Exposition Universelle et Internationale de Bruxelles; UK: Campaign for Nuclear Disarmament founded
1959	President Charles de Gaulle (France), 1959–1969; Khrushchev visits United States	Soviet *Luna 1* launched	European Free Trade Area founded; West German SDP renounces Marxism
1960	American U-2 spy plane shot down over Soviet Union; Cyprus gains independence from UK	France develops nuclear weapons	

LITERATURE AND THE ARTS	INTELLECTUAL LIFE AND RELIGION	WAR AND ARMED CONFLICT	EUROPE AND THE WORLD	DATE
Boris Pasternak, *Dr. Zhivago*; Antoni Tàpies, *White Oval*	Richard Hoggart, *The Uses of Literacy*; Milovan Djilas, *The New Class: An Analysis of the Communist System*		Ghana gains independence from UK	*1957*
Karlheinz Stockhausen, *Kontakte*, 1958–1960			Guinea gains independence from France; Franco-Tunisian conflict, 1958–1961	*1958*
François Truffaut, *Les Quatre cents coups*; Federico Fellini, *La Dolce Vita*; Jean-Luc Godard, *À bout de soufflé*; Marguerite Duras, *Hiroshima mon amour*				*1959*
Situation exhibition, London; Alberto Giacometti, *Walking Man I–II*; Michel Butor, *Degrés*; Karel Reisz, *Saturday Night and Sunday Morning*; Yves Klein, *Leap into the Void*		Somalia gains independence from Italy; Madagascar, Central African Republic, Congo, Gabon, Cameroon, Niger, Chad, Dahomey, Togo, Mali, Senegal, Burkina Faso, Côte d'Ivoire, Mauritania gain independence from France; Zaire gains independence from Belgium; Nigeria gains independence from UK		*1960*

DATE	POLITICS AND DIPLOMACY	SCIENCE AND TECHNOLOGY	ECONOMY AND SOCIETY
1961	Berlin Wall constructed; Second Turkish Republic founded	First cosmonaut, Yuri Gagarin, orbits the earth	Adolf Eichmann Trial; contraceptive pill available
1962	Cuban Missile Crisis		*Der Spiegel* Affair
1963	U.S.-Soviet Nuclear Test Ban Treaty		De Gaulle vetoes British membership in EEC; Turkey associate of EEC; Frankfurt Auschwitz trial, 1963–1965
1964	Party Secretary Leonid Brezhnev (USSR), 1964–1982; Romanian Communist Party declared independent of USSR; Malta gains independence from UK	European Launcher Development Organization (ELDO) and European Space Research Organization (ESRO) founded	Birth rate begins decline

LITERATURE AND THE ARTS	INTELLECTUAL LIFE AND RELIGION	WAR AND ARMED CONFLICT	EUROPE AND THE WORLD	DATE
Bridget Riley, *Movement in Squares*	Pope John XXIII, *Mater et Magistra*; Walter Benjamin, *Illuminationen* (posthumous)	Organisation de l'Armée Secrète founded	Kuwait, Tanganyika, Sierra Leone gain independence from UK; Frantz Fanon, *Les Damnés de la terre*; Angolan War of Independence, 1961–1975; direct US involvement in Vietnam, 1961–1975	*1961*
Arman, *Chopin's Waterloo*; Anthony Caro, *Early One Morning*; David Hockney, Demonstrations of Versatility exhibit; Anthony Burgess, *A Clockwork Orange*; Benjamin Britten, *War Requiem*; The Beatles, "Love Me Do"	Second Vatican Council, 1962–1965; Claude Lévi-Strauss, *La Pensée sauvage*; Jürgen Habermas, *Strukturwandel der Öffentlichkeit*		Algeria gains independence from France; *pied-noir* refugees move to France; Burundi, Rwanda gain independence from Belgium; Uganda gains independence from UK	*1962*
Alexander Solzhenitsyn, *One Day in the Life of Ivan Denisovich*; Sigmar Polke, *Grid Pictures* series and *Fabric Pictures* series	Pope John XXIII, *Pacem in Terris*; Hannah Arendt, *Eichmann in Jerusalem: A Report on the Banality of Evil*; John Robinson, *Honest to God*; Roland Barthes, *Sur Racine*	Cypriot civil war; Italian anti-Mafia campaign in Sicily	Malaysia, Kenya, Zanzibar gain independence from UK; Guinea Bissau War of Independence, 1963–1974	*1963*
Joseph Beuys, *Fat Chair*; Sergio Leone, *A Fistful of Dollars*	Adam Schaff, *Language and Cognition*		Zambia, Malawi gain independence from UK; Mozambique War of Independence, 1964–1974	*1964*

DATE	POLITICS AND DIPLOMACY	SCIENCE AND TECHNOLOGY	ECONOMY AND SOCIETY
1965	Romanian leader Gheorghe Gheorghiu-Dej dies, succeeded by Nicolae Ceaușescu	First Soviet communications satellite launched	"Market socialism" reform in Yugoslavia; Spain: student protests
1966			Minor recession, 1966–1967
1967	Greece: military junta rules, 1967–1974	France: first electric plant using tidal movement opened	De Gaulle vetoes British membership in EEC again; EEC renamed European Community (EC); UK: renationalization of iron and steel; Jean-Jacques Servan-Schreiber, *Le Défi américain*
1968	Czechoslovakia: Prague Spring under Alexander Dubček; Brezhnev Doctrine		France: student protests and general strike; student protests in West Germany, Italy
1969	President Georges Pompidou (France), 1969–1974; Croatian Spring, 1969–1971; Chancellor Willy Brandt (West Germany), 1969–1974; Brandt promotes Ostpolitik		UK: "no fault" divorce legalized

LITERATURE AND THE ARTS	INTELLECTUAL LIFE AND RELIGION	WAR AND ARMED CONFLICT	EUROPE AND THE WORLD	DATE
Roger Hilton, *Two Nude Women*; Georges Perec, *Les choses*; Václav Havel, *The Memorandum*	Louis Althusser, *Pour Marx*		Maldives, Gambia, Lesotho gain independence from UK; Rhodesian War of Independence, 1965–1979	*1965*
Simone de Beauvoir, *Les Belles Images*; Krzystóf Penderecki, *Passio et mors Domini Nostri Jesu Christi secundam Lucam*; Gillo Pontecorvo, *La Battaglia di Algeri*	Jacques Lacan, *Écrits*; Enver Hoxha makes Albania the world's first atheist state		Botswana gains independence from UK	*1966*
The Beatles, *Seargent Pepper's Lonely Hearts Club Band*; Richard Long, *A Line Made by Walking*; Iannis Xenakis, *Metastasis*	Guy Debord, *La Société du spectacle*; Jacques Derrida, *La Voix et le phénomène, L'Écriture et la difference,* and *De la grammatologie*; Umberto Eco, *La struttura asserte*	Spain: ETA (Basque) begins using violence	South Yemen gains independence from UK	*1967*
Christo and Jeanne-Claude, *Wrapped Kunsthalle*, Bern, Switzerland; Jerzy Grotowski, *Towards a Poor Theatre*	Gabriel Marcel, *Être et avoir*; Pope Paul VI, *Humanae Vitae*	Soviet invasion of Czechoslovakia	Mauritius, Swaziland gain independence from UK; Equitorial Guinea gains independence from Spain	*1968*
Marcel Orphuls, *Le Chagrin et la pitié*; *Monty Python's Flying Circus*, 1969–1974		Northern Ireland civil insurgency begins		*1969*

DATE	POLITICS AND DIPLOMACY	SCIENCE AND TECHNOLOGY	ECONOMY AND SOCIETY
1970	West Germany recognizes Oder-Neisse line as Polish western border	West Germany: radio telescope installed; France: airport Turboclair fog-dissipation system	Italy: divorce legalized
1971	General Secretary Erich Honecker (East Germany), 1971–1989	Jane Goodall, *In the Shadow of Man*; Stephen Hawking theorizes miniature black holes	Collapse of gold standard; France: feminist party Choisir founded; Doctors without Borders founded
1972	Basic Treaty; Strategic Arms Limitation Treaty		Britain: nationwide coal miners' strike; environmental group Club of Rome founded; EC develops environmental policy
1973		France: TGV high-speed trains tested	Oil embargo; Britain, Ireland, Denmark join EC; France: worker management of Lip watch factory
1974	President Valéry Giscard d'Estaing (France), 1974–1981; new Yugoslav constitution		
1975	Francisco Franco dies; King Juan Carlos (Spain); Helsinki Accords	Merger of ELDO and ERSO as European Space Agency (ESA); Soviet supersonic Tu-144 cargo plane	France: abortion legalized; Iceland: 90 percent of women participate in Women's Strike
1976		Concorde jet in service	Margaret Papandreous's Union of Greek Women founded

LITERATURE AND THE ARTS	INTELLECTUAL LIFE AND RELIGION	WAR AND ARMED CONFLICT	EUROPE AND THE WORLD	DATE
				1970
Wim Wenders, *Die Angst des Tormanns beim Elfmeter*; Led Zeppelin, "Stairway to Heaven"; Heinrich Böll, *Gruppenbild mit Dame*			Bahrain, Qatar, United Arab Emirates gain independence from UK	*1971*
Stuart Brisley, *ZL 65 63 95C*; Josef Škvorecký, *The Miracle Game*; Bernardo Bertolucci, *Ultimo tango a Parigi*		Bloody Sunday in Northern Ireland; Palestinian terrorists kill Israeli hostages at Munich Olympics		*1972*
Michael Craig-Martin, *An Oak Tree*				*1973*
Alexander Solzhenitsyn, *Gulag Archipelago*; Anselm Kiefer, *March Heath*		Cyprus National Guard coup; Turkey invades Cyprus	Mozambique, Guinea Bissau gain independence from Portugal	*1974*
Lina Wertmüller, *Pasqualino Settebellezze*; Vladimir Voinovich, *The Life and Extraordinary Adventures of Private Ivan Chonkin*	Michel Foucault, *Surveiller et punir: Naissance de la prison*		Angola gains independence from Portugal	*1975*
The Sex Pistols, "Anarchy in the U.K."	Hélène Cixous, *Portrait de Dora*; Leszek Kołakowski, *Main Currents of Marxism*			*1976*

DATE	POLITICS AND DIPLOMACY	SCIENCE AND TECHNOLOGY	ECONOMY AND SOCIETY
1977	Charter 77; Eurocommunist declaration		German Red Army Faction kidnaps and murders Hanns-Martin Schleyer; Swedish Riksdag decrees acceptance of same-sex households
1978	Spain recognizes internal Basque communities	UK: first in vitro (test tube) baby born	Italy: abortion legalized; Italian Red Brigades kidnap and murder Aldo Moro; Martina Navratilova wins first Wimbeldon title
1979	Prime Minister Margaret Thatcher (UK), 1979–1990; U.S. refusal to sign SALT II; German Green Party founded	First *Ariane* launch	
1980	Tito dies, U.S. boycott of Moscow Olympics; coup in Turkey, martial law instated	Smallpox declared eradicated	Poland: worker self-management movement
1981	President François Mitterrand (France), 1981–1995; real choices, real debates, secrecy in Polish Communist Party elections	Switzerland: scanning tunneling microscope invented	Greece joins EC; noncommunist Polish trade union Solidarity recognized; international anti-nuclear demonstrations
1982	Chancellor Helmut Kohl (West Germany), 1982–1990; Spain: socialist government elected; Party Secretary Yuri Andropov (USSR), 1982–1984		Italy: rape made punishable by law

LITERATURE AND THE ARTS	INTELLECTUAL LIFE AND RELIGION	WAR AND ARMED CONFLICT	EUROPE AND THE WORLD	DATE
Renzo Piano and Richard Rogers, Centre Pompidou (Paris)	Jan Patocka dies; Bernard-Henri Lévy, *La barbarie à visage humain*		Djibouti gains independence from France	*1977*
	First Polish pope elected, John Paul II, 1978–2005			*1978*
Vladimir Menshov, *Moscow Does Not Believe in Tears*	Pierre Bourdieu, *La Distinction: Critique sociale du jugement*; Jean-François Lyotard, *La Condition postmoderne*		USSR invades Afghanistan, 1979–1989	*1979*
Frank Auerbach, *J. Y. M. Seated*		Bologna railroad station bombed; Italy: anti-Mafia campaign intensifies	Zimbabwe gains independence from UK	*1980*
Umberto Eco, *Il nome della rosa*	assassination attempt made against Pope John Paul II; Poland: first Catholic mass broadcast in thirty years	Polish martial law under General Wojciech Jaruzelski, 1981–1983		*1981*
Francis Bacon, *Study of the Human Body*; Wolfgang Petersen, *Das Boot*	Julia Kristéva, *Histoires d'amour*		Falkland Islands War	*1982*

DATE	POLITICS AND DIPLOMACY	SCIENCE AND TECHNOLOGY	ECONOMY AND SOCIETY
1983	Turkey: Prime Minister Turgut Özal, 1983–1989; West Germany: Green Party gains in parliamentary elections; Turkish Republic of Northern Cyprus founded but unrecognized except by Turkey	First *Spacelab* voyage	International anti-nuclear demonstrations
1984	Party Secretary Konstantin Chernenko (USSR), 1984–1985	Frenchman Luc Montagnier discovers HIV	UK: National Union of Mineworkers strike; France: SOS-Racisme founded; West Germany: commercial television channels introduced
1985	Party Secretary Mikhail Gorbachev (USSR), 1985–1991; Schengen Agreement	Members of the British Antarctic Expedition notice hole in ozone layer	USSR: *glasnost* and *perestroika* implemented; French intelligence agents sink Greenpeace ship *Rainbow Warrior*
1986	Swiss voters reject proposal to join UN; Single European Act	Soviet *Mir* space station launched	Soviet *Mir* space station launched
1987	Intermediate-Range Nuclear Forces Treaty		Klaus Barbie trial
1988		European scientists participate in Human Genome Project, 1988–2003	

LITERATURE AND THE ARTS	INTELLECTUAL LIFE AND RELIGION	WAR AND ARMED CONFLICT	EUROPE AND THE WORLD	DATE
I. M. Pei, Louvre pyramid (Paris), 1983–1988		Soviet Union shoots down Korean passenger jet		*1983*
Milan Kundera, *L'Insoutenable légèrté de l'être*; Akli Tadjer, *Les Ani du "Tassili"*				*1984*
Mehdi Charef, *Le Thé au harem d'Archimède*; Lasse Hallström, *My Life as a Dog*		Airports in Vienna and Rome bombed by Palestinian terrorists		*1985*
Claude Berri, *Jean de Florette*; Richard Rogers, Lloyd's Building (London)				*1986*
	Pope John Paul II visits the Roman Synagogue			*1987*
Pedro Almodóvar, *Mujeres al borde de un ataque de nervios*; Ismail Kadare, *The Concert at the End of Winter*; Louis Malle, *Au Revoir les enfants*; Vasily Pichul, *Little Vera*	USSR: Mikhail Gorbachev meets with Russian Orthodox Patriarch Pimen; Shroud of Turin carbon dated to 13th or 14th century		France: Matignon Accord concerning continuing conflict in New Caledonia	*1988*

DATE	POLITICS AND DIPLOMACY	SCIENCE AND TECHNOLOGY	ECONOMY AND SOCIETY
1989	Poland: Solidarity wins elections; East Germans emigrate west; fall of Berlin Wall; Romania overthrows and executes Ceauşescu; Czechoslovakian Communist leadership replaced by President Václav Havel; Yugoslavia: government allows free elections		
1990	German reunification; Chancellor Helmut Kohl (Germany), 1990–1998; Lithuania, Estonia, Latvia declared independent of USSR; President Lech Wałęsa (Poland), 1990–1995; President Boris Yeltsin (Russia), 1990–1999; reform and/or free elections in Albania, Bulgaria, Romania, Hungary; Prime Minister John Major (UK), 1990–1997	Tim Berners-Lee creates the Web at CERN; freshwater geothermal vents discovered at Lake Baikal	McDonald's opens in Moscow; German privatization agency Treuhand founded; privatization laws pass in Poland
1991	USSR breaks up; conservative-attempted coup; Gorbachev resigns; Commonwealth of Independent States founded; Slovenia, Croatia, Macedonia gain independence from Yugoslavia; new Bulgarian constitution	5,000-year-old "iceman" discovered in Alps	
1992	Bosnia-Herzegovina gains independence from Yugoslavia; Albanian democratic reform		Seville and Genoa international expositions; Russia: Yeltsin's "shock therapy" plan introduced; Euro Disney opens

LITERATURE AND THE ARTS	INTELLECTUAL LIFE AND RELIGION	WAR AND ARMED CONFLICT	EUROPE AND THE WORLD	DATE
ASTRA satellite broadcasting begins	Salman Rushdie, *The Satanic Verses*	Terrorists blow up US passenger airplane over Scotland		*1989*
	Leszek Kołakowski, *Modernity on Endless Trial*; Soviet "Freedom of Conscience" law		French, British participate in US-led Persian Gulf War	*1990*
M. C. Solaar, "Qui sème le vent récolte le tempo"				*1991*
Adolf Krischanitz, Kunsthalle (Vienna); Neil Jordan, *The Crying Game*		Bosnia: war and ethnic cleansing, 1992–1995		*1992*

DATE	POLITICS AND DIPLOMACY	SCIENCE AND TECHNOLOGY	ECONOMY AND SOCIETY
1993	Maastricht Treaty put into effect; EEC renamed European Union (EU); Velvet Revolution separates Czech Republic and Slovakia; Bosnia: Vance-Owen Peace Plan attempted; Russia: nationalist Vladimir Zhirinovsky State Duma success	Briton Andrew Wiles proves Fermat's Last Theorem	Euro planned; former Italian prime minister Giulio Andreotti accused of Mafia ties
1994	Prime Minister Silvio Berlusconi (Italy)		"Chunnel" links France and Britain
1995	Austria, Finland, Sweden join EU; President Jacques Chirac (France); Dayton Agreement		Sweden, Finland, Austria join the EU; Swiss bank controversy over funds of Jewish Holocaust victims
1996			First digital television channel in Germany; "Mad cow" disease scare
1997	Prime Minister Tony Blair (UK); Kyoto Protocol	Stephen Hawking concedes bet concerning naked singularities; Scottish team clones sheep Dolly	Diana, Princess of Wales, dies; UK: Labour Party "women only" lists increase number of female MPs; France: Maurice Papon trial, 1997–1998
1998	Chancellor Gerhard Schröder (Germany), 1998–2005; peace accord in Northern Ireland	Construction of International Space Station begins	France wins World Cup led by Zinedine Zidane; Russia defaults on international debts; Lisbon Expo '98; France: 35-hour week

LITERATURE AND THE ARTS	INTELLECTUAL LIFE AND RELIGION	WAR AND ARMED CONFLICT	EUROPE AND THE WORLD	DATE
Krzysztof Kieslowski, Trois Couleurs trilogy, *Bleu, Biały, Rouge*, 1993–1994; Andrzej Wajda, *The Ring of the Crowned Eagle*				*1993*
Yuri Mumin, *Window to Paris*	UK: first Anglican women priests ordained	IRA ceasefire; conflict in Chechnya, 1994–1996		*1994*
Christo and Jeanne-Claude, *Wrapped Reichstag, Berlin, 1971–95*; Michael Radford and Massimo Troisi, *Il Postino*; Lars Von Trier and Thomas Vinterberg's Dogme manifesto		NATO intervention in Bosnia		*1995*
Danny Boyle, *Trainspotting*	Potential schism between Russian Orthodox Church and Constantinople			*1996*
Roberto Benigni, *La vita è bella*; J. K. Rowling, *Harry Potter and the Philosopher's Stone*		IRA ceasefire; Albanian Civil War	Hong Kong to China	*1997*
Tom Tykwer, *Lola rennt*		Serbs force Albanians from Kosovo; Belfast Agreement		*1998*

DATE	POLITICS AND DIPLOMACY	SCIENCE AND TECHNOLOGY	ECONOMY AND SOCIETY
1999	Austria: Jörg Haider's Freedom Party joins the government		Euro launched; Turkey: Kurdish Workers' Party leader Abdullah Öcalan sentenced to death; France: José Bové attacks McDonald's
2000	President Vladimir Putin (Russia); Serbs overthrow Slobodan Milošević	International Space Station permanently occupied	Hanover Expo 2000; France: "Parité" law
2001	Prime Minister Silvio Berlusconi (Italy), 2001–2006	*Mir* space station abandoned	Immigration tightened after 11 September attacks on the US; Netherlands: same-sex marriages legally recognized
2002	EU begins work on constitution; Jean-Marie Le Pen second in French presidential election; Netherlands: Pim Fortuyn assassinated; Russia-NATO Council founded		Euro into circulation; Slobodan Milošević on trial for war crimes at the Hague
2003	Yugoslavia renamed Serbia-Montenegro	Concorde jet service discontinued	Belgium: same-sex marriages legally recognized; Russia: Yukos oil company scandal

LITERATURE AND THE ARTS	INTELLECTUAL LIFE AND RELIGION	WAR AND ARMED CONFLICT	EUROPE AND THE WORLD	DATE
Pedro Almodóvar, *Todo sobre mi madre*; Norman Foster, Reichstag Dome (Berlin)		NATO bombs Serbia; Chechen conflict renewed	Macao to China	*1999*
Zadie Smith, *White Teeth*; Marks Barfield Architects, London Eye; Arup Group, the Millennium Bridge (London)	Pope John Paul II visits Egypt and Israel; Jewish community center opens in Moscow			*2000*
Daniel Libeskind, Jüdisches Museum Berlin opens; Jean-Pierre Jeunet, *Le Fabuleux Destin d'Amélie Poulain*			European immigration laws tighten after 11 September attacks on the US	*2001*
	Catholic Church faces rising child sex-abuse scandal; rash of anti-Semitic attacks	Chechen rebels take hostages in Moscow theater		*2002*
Wolfgang Becker, *Good-Bye Lenin!*; Roman Polanski, *The Pianist*	Anglican Communion rocked by consecration of American homosexual Rev. V. Gene Robinson as bishop	Madrid terrorist attack	UK, Poland, Spain, Italy, and others back US invasion of Iraq; France, Germany, Russia protest	*2003*

DATE	POLITICS AND DIPLOMACY	SCIENCE AND TECHNOLOGY	ECONOMY AND SOCIETY
2004	Socialist Prime Minister José Luis Rodriguez Zapatero (Spain); EU expands by ten countries; Ukrainian Orange Revolution	American and Russian scientists produce super-heavy elements	Olympic Games held in Greece
2005			France: rioting by young West and North African men; violence worst seen in France since 1968

LITERATURE AND THE ARTS	INTELLECTUAL LIFE AND RELIGION	WAR AND ARMED CONFLICT	EUROPE AND THE WORLD	DATE
	Muslim headscarves banned in French schools; Orthodox Patriarch Bartholomew I accepts Pope John Paul II's apology for the sacking of Constantinople in 1204			*2004*
	Pope John Paul II dies; hundreds of thousands attend his funeral; Benedict XVI elected as his successor	Terrorist bombings in London transit system		*2005*

ABORTION. After World War I, Europe faced a recurrent anxiety common after most major conflicts: the fear of a severe drop in the birth rate. Demographic stagnation, already perceptible since the beginning of the century, made this perspective ominously plausible. Abortion and contraceptive means were strongly condemned and actively prohibited. Everywhere policies were organized to promote population growth. Legislation was enacted to repress the encouragement of the use of means of contraception and abortion as well as their advertisement (France, 1920; Belgium, 1923). However, the number of abortions did not decrease in the countries where this type of legislation was passed. In some countries (France, Belgium) in the hope of ensuring repression, abortion was no longer categorized as a "crime"—which would have led to a jury trial that ended, in 80 percent of the cases, in an acquittal. Instead, thanks to a procedural means ("correctionalization"), the prosecution took place before professional judges, who tended to be much less lenient. In France, for example, even if prosecutions remained relatively rare in the period from 1925 to 1935 (five hundred to one thousand cases a year), the rate of acquittal dropped to 19 percent. However, the numbers of abortions that were discovered and effectively prosecuted were small in comparison to the numbers of clandestine ones performed, which were estimated to be more than one hundred thousand cases a year. In fact abortion seemed to become more and more common and with fewer complications. The most commonly used method was the intrauterine injection.

Abortion was a matter for women, who had to seek out abortionists, nicknamed in French *"faiseuses d'anges"* ("angelmakers"). In some big cities there were private homes where provincial and foreign women came to obtain a clandestine termination of pregnancy. Brussels acquired an international reputation as a good place for finding "abortariums." In many newspapers, good addresses where "a return of the period" —in fact, a discreet abortion—might be obtained could easily be found.

In Protestant countries, women obtained the right to terminate pregnancy relatively early on. In the United Kingdom, the Offences against the Person Act of 1861 and the Infant Preservation Act of 1919 prohibited abortion except when the mother's health was in danger. In 1936, under the pressure of birth control advocates, the Abortion Law Reform Association came into being. In 1938 an important step was made in judge-made law that authorized abortion in the case of mental and physical distress. As early as 1938, Swedish women could obtain an abortion when the mother's life was in danger, in the case of a rape, or when the fetus was presenting serious malformations. The same right, with similar restrictions, was given to women in Switzerland in 1942 and in Finland in 1950. This legislation was made progressively more flexible, allowing more liberal practices in the 1970s.

Conservative and mostly authoritarian regimes prohibited any voluntary interruption of pregnancy. In the Soviet Union, prosecutions for abortion had stopped in 1917 and abortion was legalized in 1920, but was forbidden again under Stalin's rule in 1936. However, after the end of Stalin's regime, abortion was once again legalized (in 1955) and became the most widely practiced form of birth control through the remainder of the Soviet period and beyond. Under the Vichy regime in France, penal repression was reinforced when Marie-Louise Giraud, an angelmaker, was executed in 1943.

In the 1970s, the women's liberation movement transformed the female body into a public policy issue. The right of women for sovereignty over their bodies became a major demand, as illustrated by the feminist slogan "a baby, when I want, if I want." The debate became more and more political and also more passionate. In France, the number of clandestine abortions was estimated at about four hundred thousand a year in the mid-1970s, and women continued to die because of the conditions in which they took place. "Abortion tourism" was organized by the first birth control centers and by militant feminists: trips were planned to countries where abortion was authorized and where some new methods—for example, a method known as aspiration—were used. A more liberal attitude toward abortion was mostly the case in England (owing to the Abortion Act of 1967) and in Poland and the Netherlands, where abortion was not really legalized but was tolerated. Some centers dedicated to family planning first began to offer clients the necessary information to obtain abortions, and then, in the mid-1970s, started to provide abortions themselves. In the hope of forcing a public debate and a change in the legislation, some doctors revealed publicly both the number and the conditions in which they had provided abortions. Some were arrested, condemned, and imprisoned (as in the case of Willy Peers and Pierre-Olivier Hubinon in Belgium). In order to publicize further the state of affairs with regard to abortion, 343 notable French women (associated with the world of art, literature, press, and cinema, including Simone de Beauvoir, Catherine Deneuve, Marguerite Duras, Jeanne Moreau, Gisèle Halimi, Françoise Sagan, and others) signed a manifesto on 5 April 1971 in which they admitted having sought and obtained abortions. The signatories, who called for a depenalization of

abortion laws, created a furor in public opinion. Theoretically these women could have been prosecuted for having admitted their part in a "crime" but nothing happened. The result of this public acknowledgment was that ordinary women who might have been penalized were treated less harshly. Some trials took place in and benefited from important press coverage in France (for example, the Marie-Claire Chevalier case in 1971) or in Italy (the Gigliola Pierobon case in 1973). The impact of such trials was huge and precipitated reforms. In France, the Minister of Health, Simone Veil, in 1974, brought the debate to parliament and, in an exclusively male assembly, the discussion was tense and aggressive. At the end, a statute carrying the name of the pioneering minister ("la loi Veil") was passed in January 1975. Following some spectacular women's demonstrations in Italy, voluntary termination of pregnancy was legalized in May 1978, even though many doctors refused to perform abortions for reasons of conscience. In Belgium, abortion was decriminalized in 1990, after a constitutional crisis, when King Baudouin I refused to sign the act of parliament because of his religious convictions.

In the great majority of European countries, abortion is now available but with notable differences from one country to another in the conditions necessary to obtain it. The debate has switched from the principle of the availability of a legal abortion to the circumstances, the stage of pregnancy in which abortion is permissible, the cost of the intervention, parental consent for minors, and so on.

Some countries still have very restrictive laws (like Ireland, where abortion can only be obtained if the mother's health is in danger, leading some six thousand Irish women a year to seek abortions in the United Kingdom) or prohibit completely any voluntary interruption of pregnancy (the Republic of Cyprus, Malta). In Portugal, where the debate is especially divisive, a right-wing slogan claims that decriminalizing abortion is the equivalent of introducing the death penalty. In 2004 the odyssey of the *Borndiep,* a Dutch hospital boat nicknamed the "abortion boat," created a controversy: prohibited from putting into port, it stayed at sea in order to provide an abortion service to women who had boarded. Under Poland's former communist regime, abortion had been available on request since 1956, but by the end of 1980s, Catholic clergy started an offensive against it, claiming that abortion risked the genocide of the Polish people. Since 1993, abortion legislation in Poland has become among the most restrictive in Europe (abortion is only tolerated in the case of danger to the mother, of rape, or of malformation of the fetus). This change has led many Polish women to seek clandestine abortions.

The RU-486 pill, the so-called abortion pill, which makes it possible to abort without surgical intervention, was introduced on the French market in 1988. This pill is regulated under the same legal basis as abortion, and it has been legalized in most European countries since 1999 (with the notable exceptions of Portugal, Ireland, Malta, and Poland). The number of women seeking abortion who choose this new method is estimated at around 30 percent.

The right to obtain an abortion is regularly contested by religious authorities (Pope John Paul II compared it to the Holocaust and Pope Benedict XVI, from the outset of his pontificate, condemned any legislation tolerating it). Legal abortion is also challenged by medical personnel on grounds of conscience, by anti-abortion campaigns, by militants (though with less violence than is seen in the United States), and by various public initiatives, as well as in national parliaments, attempting to confer a legal status on the fetus.

See also **Divorce; Public Health; Sexuality.**

BIBLIOGRAPHY

Glendon, Mary Ann. *Abortion and Divorce in Western Law.* Cambridge, Mass., 1987.

Le Naour, Jean-Yves. *Histoire de l'avortement: XIX–XXe siècle.* Paris: 2003.

RÉGINE BEAUTHIER, VALÉRIE PIETTE

ACADEMIES OF SCIENCE. Elite national scientific organizations have been part of the social structure of modern science since its origins. By the twentieth century, academies of science had become a nearly ubiquitous feature of modern states. Although these bodies possess some common features, their organizational and functional differences provide an index of the various possible relationships among science, the state, and political ideologies in the modern era.

SCIENTIFIC ORGANIZATIONS BEFORE WORLD WAR I

Two enduring models were the Royal Society of London for the Promotion of Natural Knowledge, organized in 1660 and chartered in 1662, and the Royal Academy of Sciences of Paris, founded in 1666. These academies were forums for the examination and confirmation of results, increasingly through the scrutiny of written reports—the origins of what we now call peer review. They disseminated these reports and communications from corresponding members, for example, through the Royal Society's *Philosophical Transactions,* one of the earliest scientific journals.

The Royal Society had little connection with the state besides its name. Its fellows (FRS) received no governmental financial support. The society therefore depended on subscriptions and private donations, which meant that often amateurs were elected for reasons of patronage or prestige rather than scientific achievement. Although occasionally called upon to provide advice to the government on matters of scientific and technical import, the Royal Society was independent of state control.

By contrast, the Parisian academy was a designedly elitist state agency. Members—limited to six in each of (initially) five sections—received a modest annual stipend. The academy regularly advised the government on scientific and technological problems and served as a de facto patent court. The French academy developed a system of prizes for work in specified subjects—a way of subsidizing successful research but also of influencing its direction. Moreover, funds were sometimes provided for projects beyond the scope of individuals. Through the academy, the state promoted scientific talent but also enrolled that talent to achieve policy goals.

During the eighteenth century many European (and some new American) states established academies of science. (James E. McClellan lists more than sixty official academies in existence as of 1793; many of these were regional academies in France or academies based in small German and Italian states.)

Increasing specialization of the sciences in the nineteenth century complicated the organizational landscape. Research became more exclusively the domain of growing numbers of credentialed professionals. Likewise, the old categories of natural philosophy and natural history were differentiated into disciplines such as physics, geology, chemistry, and biology. This resulted in the creation of associations open to all working scientists (e.g., the British Association for the Advancement of Science) as well as professional societies for specific disciplines. Moreover, universities increasingly took on research functions. These changes challenged the traditional function of the academies; conversely, they took on new tasks of national representation in international scientific unions and conventions, such as those on measurements.

TWENTIETH-CENTURY ACADEMIES

In Great Britain nineteenth-century reform movements led to more rigorous, merit-based standards for Royal Society membership, and by the early twentieth century the title FRS regained its status as a crowning achievement of a scientific career. The Royal Society's *Transactions* and *Proceedings*—which eventually was split into several disciplinary series—remained premier scientific periodicals. The society also began to serve as a conduit for government research funds—for example, through several senior research professorships and a series of grants for students—and as a pool of expert advisors, particularly during the world wars. However, proposals to link it more closely to the state gained little traction.

In the French Academy of Sciences—the "Royal" appellation flickered in and out with various constitutional changes—the number of disciplinary sections increased to eleven during the nineteenth century, and its *Comptes Rendus* (published beginning in 1835) became the supreme general-subject French scientific journal. The scope of the prize system increased; in 1975 prizes in sixty-four different categories, worth a total of just over one million francs (mostly from donated endowments), were awarded. But by the mid-twentieth century the academy, with its membership restricted to a small pinnacle of the French scientific community, was widely perceived to be somewhat inflexible. Its function as an active promoter of research was largely supplanted by the National Center for Scientific Research (CNRS), founded as a consolidation of several previous government offices in 1939 to provide funds for a network of laboratories and direct research grants. Reforms in 1975 aimed at a younger overall membership and more active sponsorship of research, but little changed, and another round of reforms approved in 2003 aimed at similar ends.

The prime twentieth-century example of an academy as the agent of state policy was to be found in the Soviet Union. The Russian Academy of Sciences had been established in 1725—initially largely populated by foreign recruits—as part of Peter the Great's modernization efforts. After the Revolution of 1917 some Bolsheviks saw it as an indelibly bourgeois institution, but it was decided to use the expertise of a renamed Academy of Sciences of the USSR in furtherance of modernization and industrialization—ironically, continuing the tsarist heritage but taken to new lengths. The academy came to operate dozens of state-funded institutes—by 1939 fifty-eight laboratories and twenty museums—employing thousands of researchers. It is hardly surprising that the academy was buffeted by political tumult. By the late 1920s the initial tolerance of "bourgeois experts" met counterdemands that the academy become a more authentically "socialist" institution; some members were dismissed and many new members more inclined toward socialism were appointed. The academy also experienced the Great Purges of 1936–1939, though its institutional structures remained largely intact. Starting in the late 1930s as well, an adverse consequence of centralized state control was revealed in the pervasive anti-Mendelian influence exerted by Trofim Lysenko after he carried out a kind of coup d'état in the field of genetics. Soviet Academy institutes produced world-class research in many fields, particularly in mathematics, astronomy, and physics; however, junior scientists, especially, often chafed at the bureaucratic planning of science as though it were a kind of industrial production. The Soviet model was copied throughout the Eastern bloc after 1945, with previous elite national academies being transformed into planning bureaus for wide-ranging state laboratory networks.

Ideological conflicts and political divisions were also prominent in the history of scientific academies in Germany. The Saxon (founded 1846) and Bavarian (1759) academies, as well as those in Göttingen

(1751) and—until World War I—Vienna (1847) formed a "cartel" in 1893 but remained mutually independent. The Prussian Academy (founded 1700) and the new academy in Heidelberg (1909) joined later. The theoretically all-German Leopoldina Society of natural researchers, earlier peripatetic but based in Halle from 1878 on, was somewhat overshadowed by the state-based academies, particularly Prussia's. The German academies, like their British and French counterparts, served as honorific societies and published scholarly proceedings; unlike them, they also contained prominent sections for humanistic disciplines. Particularly in the humanities, several German academies were responsible for large-scale research endeavors, such as systematic editions of medieval historical documents and philological reference works. In the natural sciences, however, their sponsorship of research was indirect. State sponsorship of science was channeled through university laboratories, through grants provided by the Emergency Council for German Science (founded 1919, later renamed the German Research Society), and through the elite non-university research institutes of the Kaiser Wilhelm Society (founded 1911, later renamed the Max Planck Society), which had mixed governmental and private support.

The German academies faced co-optation under the Nazi state; after some temporizing, by the late 1930s they had mostly dismissed their "non-Aryan" members and instituted authoritarian internal leadership. These changes were revised after 1945, albeit differently in West and East. The West German academies largely reverted to previous patterns, with essentially only formal state affiliation. New academies in Mainz (1949) and Düsseldorf (1970) joined the Union of Academies (as the cartel had been renamed). In East Germany the Prussian Academy was renamed the Academy of Sciences of the German Democratic Republic and operated a network of laboratories on the Soviet model. After reunification this body was restructured yet again as the Berlin-Brandenburg Academy of Sciences. The Leopoldina tried—with considerable success—to maintain its status as an all-German society in the face of countervailing pressure from the GDR government.

Other European academies usually operated somewhere between the presence or absence of state control and between direct management of research or a predominantly honorific and editorial function. The Royal Academy of Sciences in Sweden, for example, managed several research institutes, but it also lost several functions during the course of the twentieth century: operation of the Natural History Museum (till 1965), environmental management of national parks (till 1967), and publication of the Swedish almanac (till 1972). The Swedish Academy gained a unique world prominence, however, through its custodianship of the Nobel Prizes in Physics and Chemistry, as well as (later) the Nobel memorial prize in Economics and the Crafoord Prize in Mathematics. Arguably its very location on the relative periphery of the academic world enabled it to take on this role as an international arbiter of scientific prestige.

See also **Purges; Science.**

BIBLIOGRAPHY

Crosland, Maurice. *Science under Control: The French Academy of Sciences 1795–1914.* Cambridge, U.K., and New York, 1992.

Frängsmyr, Tore, ed. *Science in Sweden: The Royal Swedish Academy of Sciences 1739–1989.* Canton, Mass., 1989.

McClellan, James E., 3rd. *Science Reorganized: Scientific Societies in the Eighteenth Century.* New York, 1985.

Paul, Harry W. *From Knowledge to Power: The Rise of the Science Empire in France, 1860–1939.* Cambridge, U.K., 1985.

Stimson, Dorothy. *Scientists and Amateurs: A History of the Royal Society.* New York, 1948.

Vucinich, Alexander. *Empire of Knowledge: The Academy of Sciences of the USSR (1917–1970).* Berkeley, Calif., 1984.

RICHARD H. BEYLER

ACTION FRANÇAISE. The most influential right-wing movement in twentieth-century France, the Action Française articulated a theory of "integral nationalism" that won adherents among intellectuals, Catholics, and members of the professional classes. Originating in the heyday of the Dreyfus affair in the 1890s, the movement denounced all foreigners, Jews, and republicans who identified with the egalitarianism of the French Revolution. Under the direction of Charles Maurras (1868–1952) and Léon Daudet (1867–1942), the Action Française held that the revolution of 1789 had ushered in an age of rampant disorder. France could be saved from further decline, Maurras argued, if it rejected the revolutionary tradition entirely and returned to the monarchical, corporatist, and Catholic society overthrown in 1789. Only those who were "integrally" French—those whose families could trace their French ancestry over several generations, whose ancestors espoused the Catholic faith, and who respected France's monarchist traditions—were truly French; all others—Protestants, Freemasons, and, most particularly, Jews—were "alien." Although the Action Française failed to restore the monarchy, it significantly influenced many intellectuals, eroded public confidence in the Third Republic, and provided the intellectual underpinnings of Vichy France's "national revolution."

From 1899 through 1914, the Action Française battled the Third Republic through scholarly discourse and direct political action. Reflecting the literary predisposition of Maurras, it used public lectures and erudite essays published in its monthly journal and, after 1908, the daily newspaper *Action française,* to call for a reorientation of intellectual values: France had to reject the revolutionary tradition and embrace in its stead an ideology of order, discipline, and hierarchy. At the same time, the movement orchestrated abrasive assaults on the republic and its defenders. Daudet developed an earthy rhetoric of public insult; and the more youthful supporters of integral nationalism, known as the *camelots du roi* (the king's street vendors, for their role in selling the newspaper), brawled with their republican adversaries and disrupted the lectures of professors most closely identified with the Dreyfusard cause. In the nationalist atmosphere of World War I, the movement enjoyed unprecedented success that carried over into the early 1920s. Its emphasis on hierarchy and obedience to legitimate authority, its repudiation of the French Revolution, and its identification of Catholicism as integral to true French identity made it attractive to many Catholics. That Maurras was agnostic was an inconvenient fact overlooked until 1926 when the Vatican, concerned that an ideology defined by an avowed agnostic represented a danger to the Catholic faith, condemned the movement and threatened with excommunication any Catholics who continued to support it.

After 1926 the movement, having abandoned most of its rabble-rousing prewar spirit, also lost many former adherents to the more overtly fascist leagues that emerged in the interwar years. In February 1934, when massive right-wing demonstrations threatened to topple the republic, the Action Française remained aloof. This political timidity prompted many erstwhile allies to support groups more inclined to fight the republic in the streets. The ideological influence of the Action Française remained significant, however. In the aftermath of military defeat in 1940, Marshal Philippe Pétain (1856–1951) promoted a domestic agenda largely inspired by Maurrassian ideas: the Vichy regime abolished parliament, persecuted Jews, excluded Protestants and Freemasons from positions of economic or cultural influence, and championed a return to the land reminiscent of old regime France. Proudly Pétainist, the Action Française nevertheless rejected any collaboration with the enemy. Some former supporters of the Action Française broke with Maurras on this point and became outright collaborationists; others, inspired by the nationalist spirit of the Action Française, joined the Resistance; but the movement remained one of Pétain's most loyal allies from 1940 through 1944. In 1945 Maurras was sentenced to life in prison for his support of Vichy.

Integral nationalism resembled or prefigured fascism in several ways. It denounced the liberal tradition of the French Revolution; championed a virulent nationalism that blamed foreigners for all of France's ills; and excoriated the Jews. But its authoritarian monarchism was not comparable to the cult of a charismatic leader characteristic of true fascist movements, and the movement lacked a will to power, preferring only to prepare the intellectual preconditions of a coup d'état. This emphasis on the centrality of intellect won it many supporters in French intellectual circles, but undermined any instinct to seize power.

The Action Française provided the ideological foundations of Vichy and, in the late twentieth and early twenty-first centuries, of Jean-Marie Le Pen's National Front, which has jettisoned the monarchism of the earlier movement but has retained the rhetorical virulence and xenophobic nationalism of the Action Française.

See also **Anti-Semitism; Fascism; Maurras, Charles.**

BIBLIOGRAPHY

Sternhell, Zeev. *Neither Right nor Left: Fascist Ideology in France.* Translated by David Maisel. Berkeley, Calif., 1986.

Weber, Eugen. *Action Française: Royalism and Reaction in Twentieth-Century France.* Stanford, Calif., 1962.

Winock, Michel. *Nationalism, Anti-Semitism, and Fascism in France.* Translated by Jane Marie Todd. Stanford, Calif., 1998.

MARTHA HANNA

ADAMS, GERRY (b. 1948), Irish republican.

By far the most significant Irish republican since Eamon de Valera and Michael Collins, Gerry Adams was born in the Lower Falls area of West Belfast to parents whose families had a history of involvement in Irish republicanism. The family moved to the new public housing estate of Ballymurphy in the early 1950s. His secondary education was at St. Mary's Grammar School, a Christian Brothers establishment. He left school at the age of fifteen and got a job as a barman.

Adams joined the Irish Republican Army (IRA) in 1965, a fact that he continues to deny. At this time the chief of staff of the IRA, the Dubliner Cathal Goulding, was taking the organization in a left-wing direction. Although many traditional republicans in Belfast resisted this move, Adams was sympathetic. Adams and other republicans were active in the civil rights movement, launched in 1967, aimed at ending the anti-Catholic discrimination practiced by the Unionist regime at Stormont. However, the civil rights marches were opposed by the supporters of the loyalist, Protestant fundamentalist Ian Paisley, leading to increasing sectarian tension. The outbreak of serious sectarian violence in Belfast in August 1969 allowed the traditionalists to assert themselves against Goulding, whom they accused of letting down defenseless Catholic communities. The IRA split into Provisional and Official sections and, after some initial hesitation because of the rabid anticommunism and conservatism of many of its founding members, Adams threw in his lot with the Provisionals.

He soon emerged as a leading member of the IRA in Ballymurphy and became the officer commanding the Provisional's second battalion in the city. He was interned in 1971 but released in July 1972 to be part of an IRA delegation that met the British secretary of state for Northern Ireland, William Whitelaw, for secret talks in London. He was adjutant of the Belfast IRA on Bloody Friday, 21 July 1972, when the organization exploded twenty-six bombs throughout the city, killing nine people. Arrested in July 1973, he did not emerge from prison until 1977. In "Cage 11" of the Long Kesh prison, he was the key figure in a rethinking of republican military and political strategy that resulted in a commitment to a "long war." For Adams the "long war" could take up to two decades and would necessitate developing the political arm of the republican movement. He spoke of the need for "active republicanism" that would entail social and political involvement to ensure that republicans were not isolated around a purely militarist approach. He was a severe critic of the southern-based leadership of the movement for agreeing to a cease-fire with the British in 1975, and from the mid-1970s he and his supporters set out to take over the movement.

The northerners were greatly assisted by the hunger strikes of 1980–1981, when Bobby Sands and nine of his comrades died in a struggle to obtain the status of political prisoners. Sands was elected to the Westminster Parliament in a by-election in 1981, and in 1982 Sinn Féin, the political arm of the movement, made its first major breakthrough in the elections for the Northern Ireland Assembly, winning just over 10 percent of the vote. In 1983 Adams, who was now president of Sinn Féin, won the West Belfast seat at Westminster. From the early 1980s he was convinced that the military struggle with the British was in stalemate and that republicans needed to build alliances with John Hume's Social Democratic and Labour Party (SDLP) and the Fianna Fail Party in the Irish Republic. Such a pan-nationalist front would then, with the support of Irish America, pressure Britain for a radical change in its Northern Ireland policy. However, the prerequisite for such an alliance was an IRA ceasefire.

The Anglo-Irish Agreement signed by the Irish prime minister Garret Fitzgerald and the British prime minister Margaret Thatcher in 1985 convinced John Hume that Britain was now "neutral" on the constitutional future of Northern Ireland.

Republicans did not agree and the violence continued, leading to the breakdown of talks between Sinn Féin and the SDLP in 1988. However, contacts between Hume and Adams continued.

The collapse of the Berlin Wall in 1989 and a radically different international environment assisted Adams's strategy. In 1992 he and John Hume sketched out the basis for a settlement. However, the 1993 British/Irish Downing Street Declaration did not include a key element of "Hume-Adams"—Britain's commitment to act as a "persuader" of Unionists toward a united Ireland. Despite this omission, Adams was able to persuade the IRA to declare a cease-fire in August 1994. Although this broke down temporarily in 1996, it was reinstated when Tony Blair's Labour Party won the 1997 general election. With the strong support of President Clinton, the historic Good Friday Agreement of 1998 saw the Ulster Unionist Party led by David Trimble agree to share power with Sinn Féin, provided the IRA decommissioned all its weapons.

A section of the republican movement had begun to criticize Adams for betraying republican ideals by agreeing to a partitionist settlement. Its members set up the Real IRA and carried out the bombing of Omagh in August 1998, with the loss of twenty-nine lives. However, Adams's "peace strategy" allowed Sinn Féin to overtake the SDLP to become the largest nationalist party in Northern Ireland and a significant political force in the Republic of Ireland. His reluctance to finally break with the paramilitarism that had given Sinn Féin so much political leverage in the past led to repeated crises of the institutions created by the agreement, while at the same time strengthening the more inflexible Unionists led by Ian Paisley's Democratic Unionist Party.

See also **IRA; Ireland; Northern Ireland; Paisley, Ian; Sinn Féin.**

BIBLIOGRAPHY

English, Richard. *Armed Struggle: The History of the IRA.* London, 2003.

Moloney, Ed. *A Secret History of the IRA.* London and New York, 2002.

Patterson, Henry. *The Politics of Illusion: A Political History of the IRA.* London and Chicago, 1997.

HENRY PATTERSON

ADENAUER, KONRAD (1876–1967), first chancellor of West Germany.

Konrad Herman Joseph Adenauer was twenty-two years old at the death of Otto von Bismarck (1815–1898), sixty-nine at the death of Adolf Hitler (1889–1945), and eighty-seven when he resigned from the chancellery. He was the youngest mayor of Cologne and the oldest chancellor of Germany. His role as patriarch indelibly stamped the history of the Federal Republic of Germany.

The third child of a large Rhineland family with western European leanings, Adenauer received a liberal, humanist Catholic education. His ideas of nation and state can probably be attributed to his father, a noncommissioned officer in the Prussian army. In spite of modest circumstances, Adenauer studied law and economics at Freiburg and Munich. He completed his studies in Bonn, where he was appointed a judge. His 1904 marriage to Emma Weyer, a Cologne socialite, ensured him a brilliant career as a public servant. From the position of deputy in 1906, he rose to become the mayor of Cologne in 1916 at the age of forty. With the addition of the Rhineland to western Prussia, Adenauer became a member of the Prussian administration. His ambition to turn Cologne into a metropolitan center of economic and cultural commerce with its neighbors was hampered by World War I and then by the seven-year-long British occupation. In opposition to separatist movements, he hoped to detach his Catholic Rhineland from the Prussian state while remaining within the German Reich. During the period between the wars, he attained national political status. He was president of the Prussian State Council (1920–1933), and he was one of the national leaders of the Zentrum (Center), the Roman Catholic party of which he had been a member since 1906. Within it, he represented the republican majority that supported the Weimar regime. A devout Catholic, he was an advocate of decentralization and a partisan of the moderate, interdenominational Liberal Party. As such, he was relieved of his duties as mayor by the Nazis in March of 1939, and he was interned several times from then until 1945.

After the war, Adenauer emerged as one of the principal figures of German reconstruction. (He

Konrad Adenauer (right) with Winston Churchill, London, December 1951. ©Bettmann/Corbis

was named mayor of Cologne by the U.S. government in 1945, but was removed by the British.) He devoted himself to the formation of an interdenominational party, the Christian Democratic Union, which was founded in June 1945. He was president of this party from 1950 until 1966, and he remained honorary president until the end of his life. Meanwhile, he participated in the legislative process of the new Germany. He was the first president of the Parliamentary Council in 1948 and a member of the Bundestag until his death. Through his role in the development of the Basic Law (8 May 1949) and in the choice of Bonn as the capital, followed by his election as the first chancellor of the Federal Republic of Germany (FRG) on 15 September 1949, his own political career became indistinguishable from the postwar history of Germany itself.

Adenauer's first goal was to recover the sovereignty of the West German state and an equality of its rights in relation to the occupying powers. To accomplish this, he assumed the office of minister of foreign affairs from 1951 to 1955. The results of this aim quickly followed: in November 1949 the

Petersburg Agreement with the occupying powers, which allowed for Germany to have an independent foreign policy; in 1951 the conclusion of the Ruhr Statute; in 1952 the lifting of the occupation statute with passage of the German Treaty (Deutschlandvertrag); and in 1957 the reintegration of the Saarland into the Federal Republic of Germany. This strategy entailed that the FRG should pay the debts of Nazi Germany. A reparations treaty with Israel was concluded in 1952. In 1953 the London Debt Agreement was signed, and laws were passed for the indemnification of victims of Nazism and the integration of German refugees. After the passage of amnesty laws, denazification passed into its second stage.

Adenauer's second aim was to position the new republic firmly within the "free world" and to ensure its security in the face of the Soviet threat (the Cold War). The war in Korea helped the "Allies' Chancellor" (according to his rival Kurt Schumacher [1895–1952]) to make Germany a military partner of the United States in spite of the public's reluctance. In addition, the FRG became a member of NATO in 1955. Adenauer refused any accommodation with the Soviet Union, even a 1952 proposal from Joseph Stalin (1879–1953) on the reunification of the two Germanys, but during his 1956 trip to the Soviet Union, he did reestablish diplomatic relations in exchange for the return of the remaining German POWs of World War II.

His third aim was to make the FRG an engine for the building of Europe as a means to international recognition, albeit at the cost of giving up any exclusive sovereignty. Adenauer advocated the participation of Germany in numerous European institutions (the Council of Europe, 1950; the European Coal and Steel Community, 1951; and the European Economic Community, 1957). He also worked toward the reconciliation of Germany with its traditional enemy, France. The warming of relations with France under Charles de Gaulle (1890–1970) benefited greatly from a weakening of ties with the United States and led to the Elysée Treaty of 1963.

Adenauer's strategy was supported by the economic expansion of the 1950s (the *Wunderwirtschaft*) and social changes (such as the adoption in 1951 of the policy of codetermination, whereby union leaders sit on companies' boards of directors, and pension reform in 1957) that contributed to the creation of the German market economy, in large part the work of his finance minister, Ludwig Erhard (1897–1977). Thus Adenauer, the great tactician, accustomed to a petit bourgeois way of life and at times abrupt, became the incarnation of "chancellor democracy" (*Kanzlerdemokratie*).

His fourth aim concerned the solution to the delicate question of a divided Germany. Adenauer's project of creating a prosperous, secure, and integrated Germany capable of luring East Germany onto the path toward unification had failed. His only consolation was that the 1954 treaty did not make the separation official. This failure cast a shadow over the end of the "Adenauer era"; he was even sometimes accused of being a "traitor to the national cause." Moreover, his lack of reaction to the building of the Berlin wall (13 August 1961), his indecisive candidacy for the presidency of the republic (1959), and the *Spiegel* affair in 1962 (involving revelations of Germany's military unpreparedness) all eroded his popularity. The result was the formation of a coalition government with the Free Democrats and his resignation on 15 October 1963. He devoted himself to his memoirs until his death in 1967 at his Rhöndorf estate.

Even though Adenauer is considered the founding father of the German Republic, his role is still debated: Did he determine the fate of Germany or simply follow the course of history? Even though the Allies made the major decisions, Adenauer was able to alter the status of Germany that had been decreed at Yalta. For the first time in history, thanks to him, Germany was schooled in the effectiveness of the parliamentary system. But his intra-German policy also led to an impasse. Did he put in place a workable concept of unification that was not simply reducible to an all-or-nothing politics in regard the Soviet Union? He was more a founding father than a providential figure, and in the end he was unable to make his fellow citizens understand the conditions and limitations of the birth of the new Germany.

See also **Christian Democracy; Economic Miracle; Germany.**

BIBLIOGRAPHY

Primary Sources

Adenauer, Konrad. *Memoirs.* Translated by Beate Ruhm von Oppen. Chicago, 1966.

Secondary Sources

Granieri, Ronald J. *The Ambivalent Alliance: Konrad Adenauer, the CDU/CSU, and the West, 1949–1966.* New York, 2003.

Krekel, Michael. *Konrad Adenauer: Profiles of the Man and the Politician.* Bad Honnef, Germany, 1999.

Schwarz, Hans-Peter. *Konrad Adenauer: A German Politician and Statesman in a Period of War, Revolution, and Reconstruction.* Translated by Louise Wilmot. Providence, R.I., 1995.

Williams, Charles. *Adenauer: The Father of the New Germany.* London, 2000.

FABIEN THÉOFILAKIS

ADORNO, THEODOR (1903–1969), German philosopher.

Born in Frankfurt am Main, Theodor Adorno studied philosophy there during the 1920s, when he became acquainted with future members of the Institute for Social Research such as Max Horkheimer, Leo Lowenthal, and Walter Benjamin. A youthful friendship with the writer and critic Siegfried Kracauer proved to be a major intellectual influence. When Adorno was fifteen, he and Kracauer read Immanuel Kant's *Critique of Pure Reason* together, an experience that the philosopher later described as an important turning point in his early development.

Having met Alban Berg in Frankfurt at a stunning 1924 production of Berg's opera *Wozzeck*, Adorno was so inspired that he decided, then and there, to travel to Vienna to study "modern music" (*neue Musik*) firsthand. Although he and the composer Arnold Schoenberg never hit it off, Adorno profited greatly from his contact with Berg. Adorno went on to become a major philosophical interpreter of the Vienna school music, despite Schoenberg's pronounced antipathy. "I could never really stand him," the composer once indelicately opined.

For Adorno, the integrity of Schoenberg's music—above all, middle-period Schoenberg, the master of "dissonance"—lay in its staunch refusal to provide ideological window dressing for a social world in which relations among persons were increasingly dominated by relations among things or commodities. The virtue of atonal composition was that it steadfastly resisted the idea of music as "consolation": sugarcoating for a "totally administered world." In Adorno's view, the rejection of harmony in favor of dissonance allowed "New Music" to unflinchingly articulate the language of social suffering. Under late capitalism, music, like all art, had become the flaccid blandishment of an all-encompassing consumer society. It had, in essence, become a "decorative" accompaniment to department store shopping. In Adorno's view, the colonization of composition by the "culture industry" was a tangible sign of the all-encompassing march of "total administration." Schoenberg's virtue as a composer was that he "declared his independence from this type of art. . . . His music systematically denied the claim that the universal and the particular had been reconciled."

Adorno was also a pioneer in the field of the "sociology of music," the study of how musical experience is influenced and shaped by social and economic forces. He set forth his views in a number of pioneering articles written for the Frankfurt school's journal, the *Zeitschrift für Sozialforschung.* Drawing on a long-standing German tradition dating back to Arthur Schopenhauer, Richard Wagner, and Ernst Bloch, as well as on Walter Benjamin's theological messianism, Adorno endowed serious music with a "redemptory" function. He believed that, in an era where philosophy, qua positivism, had been reduced to a handmaiden of the empirical sciences, only authentic works of art retained the capacity to "call things by their proper names." He argued that the nonconceptual character of classical composition—the fact that it communicated via the nonideational language of harmony and sound—endowed it with the ability to transcend the narrowly utilitarian orientation of bourgeois society and give voice to noumenal truth.

Drawing on Marx's notion of "commodity fetishism" as viewed through the prism of Georg Lukács's 1923 Marxist classic, *History and Class Consciousness,* Adorno depicted the commodification of modern musical experience. As a result of that commodification, music's utopian potential

Theodor Adorno, 1958. GETTY IMAGES

was increasingly diminished. Like other realms of social existence, music, too, had become subject to the all-encompassing dictates of the laws of supply and demand. Amid the forlorn cultural landscape of a burgeoning consumer society, musical taste had been reduced to a manifestation of conspicuous consumption. As Adorno argued in "The Fetish Character of Music and the Regression of Listening" (1938), "the listener really worships the money he pays for a ticket to the Toscanini concert." Under conditions of advanced capitalism, ends and means had been reversed, as commodification increasingly supplanted music's critical and utopian functions.

The Frankfurt school fled Germany shortly following Hitler's 1933 seizure of power. Adorno, conversely, remained in Germany until 1935, in the mistaken belief that the Nazi revolution might prove short-lived. In 1935 he emigrated to Oxford, where he completed *Against Epistemology: A Metacritique,* an important critique of Edmund Husserl's idealism. Following the precepts of ideology criticism, Adorno argued that the fashionable search for "essences," as it emerged, for example, in Husserl's idea of *Wesenschau* (the "intuition of essences"), masked social contradictions with a deceptive veneer of ideational harmony. Only a philosophy that rejected premature claims to "reconciliation" remained adequate to the lacerated state of contemporary social relations.

In 1938 Adorno left Oxford for New York. It was at this point that he became an integral member of the Frankfurt school in exile. He and Max Horkheimer established a close working relationship. Increasingly, critical theory's original methodological program of "interdisciplinary materialism," according to which philosophy would play a leading role in directing the research orientation of the various social sciences, seemed outmoded—especially in light of the ever-darkening European political situation. Horkheimer had felt burdened by his organizational responsibilities as the Frankfurt Institute's director and had always fantasized about writing a major study of "dialectics." Once Adorno emigrated to the United States, the prospect of writing a collaborative study materialized. In 1941 the two men repaired to Pacific Palisades, California, to write *Dialectic of Enlightenment*—one of critical theory's major intellectual statements.

Although the authors insisted that the book was jointly dictated, its approach was clearly Adornian in inspiration. In light of the ongoing European catastrophe—as they began writing, three-quarters of continental Europe lay under Nazi jackboots—Marx's progressive philosophy of history seemed naïve and untenable. In *Dialectic of Enlightenment* Horkheimer and Adorno outlined an alternative philosophy of history adequate to the realities of the contemporary political situation.

But this goal entailed a major reformulation of critical theory's mission statement. Whereas Horkheimer's original program remained fully indebted to the precepts of Enlightenment reason, *Dialectic of Enlightenment* reversed this orientation. Following Adorno's lead, the authors traced the origins of totalitarianism to the eighteenth-century ideal of a totally enlightened society. Instead of seeking Nazism's ideological origins in the rise of irrationalism (historicism, Friedrich Nietzsche, and *Lebensphilosophie*), they discovered its intellectual basis, counterintuitively, in modern

positivism. Following Nietzsche, they reasoned that a methodological approach such as positivism, for which ultimate value choices were an arbitrary posit—a question of faith or belief—could provide no compelling arguments against mass murder. The Nazis had merely drawn the logical conclusions from the triumph of bourgeois "instrumental reason." Whereas nineteenth-century observers as diverse as Marx and Herbert Spencer could still view human history via the narrative of progress, Horkheimer and Adorno, following Oswald Spengler, perceived it as essentially a tale of decline.

Another risky feature of their argument—also following Nietzsche—was the indictment of reason as a source of domination *simpliciter*. Marx had referred to logic, with its uncanny capacity to make dissimilar things similar, as the "money of the mind." *Dialectic of Enlightenment* stood Hegel back on his head (after Marx, in *Das Kapital*, claimed to have righted him) by contending that the "domination of nature" was at the heart of the program of Western reason. For obvious reasons, this conclusion lent the book's argument a type of conceptual impotence. For if reason were merely a handmaiden of social domination, what means lay at humanity's disposal to set things right? Here, too, Adorno's guiding hand was detectable. For with this indelicate rejection of reason, the only apparent solution was a quasi-religious reverence for inarticulate nature—a mythical, prelapsarian state prior to the corruptions and divisions of instrumental reason.

The approach perfected in *Dialectic of Enlightenment* became the basis for Adorno's major postwar philosophical works, such as *Negative Dialectics* (1966). There Adorno claimed that philosophy's "original sin" was its desire to grasp the nonconceptual—Being—via conceptual means. He thereby proclaimed the very project of philosophical understanding, going back to Plato, to be a false start. The rationalist goal of trying to make Being intellectually comprehensible possessed a type of primordial illegitimacy, he argued. For, by definition, it subjected Being or things to standards that were alien to their nature. In this way, Adorno stealthily reprised Friedrich Schelling's well-nigh anti-intellectual critique of Hegel's "pan-logism"—the imperialism of the *logos*. Still, one had the feeling that, despite its manifest brilliance, Adorno's project ended up in the intellectual cul-de-sac of a self-flagellating misology, or hatred of reason.

His other major work of the 1960s, *Aesthetic Theory* (published posthumously in 1970), was intended as a partial solution to *Negative Dialectics'* pessimism. Given philosophy's complicity in the Enlightenment project, the task of exposing social suffering fell to works of art. Art's utopian function lay in its "uselessness." Thereby, it defied the instrumentalist credo of bourgeois society. Yet, because art forms like music and painting were "speechless" or nonlinguistic, aesthetic theory was needed to render their contents in a conceptually meaningful fashion. Adorno had intended to write a moral philosophy before he died, in which case his major works (*Negative Dialectics* and *Aesthetic Theory*) would have paralleled the topics treated by Kant's three *Critiques*.

See also **Frankfurt School.**

BIBLIOGRAPHY

Primary Sources

Adorno, Theodor. *Negative Dialectics.* Translated by E. B. Ashton. New York, 1973.

———. *Philosophy of Modern Music.* Translated by Anne G. Mitchell and William V. Blomster. New York, 1973.

———. *Minima Moralia: Reflections from Damaged Life.* Translated by E. F. N. Jephcott. London, 1978.

Secondary Sources

Buck-Morss, Susan. *The Origin of Negative Dialectics.* New York, 1977.

Jay, Martin. *Adorno.* Cambridge, Mass., 1984.

RICHARD WOLIN

AFGHANISTAN. Modern Afghanistan owes its existence to the Great Powers' nineteenth-century imperialist rivalry, known as the Great Game. As Russia was pushing toward the warm waters of the Indian Ocean and Britain was consolidating its domination over India, in order to avoid direct confrontation they created Afghanistan as a buffer state between them. When World War I broke out, Afghanistan stayed neutral because Russia and Britain were allies and bound by the 1907 convention, which assigned Afghanistan to the British sphere of influence and mandated that its foreign policy be directed from New Delhi. In 1915 Germany attempted to undermine British control over India by sending two expeditions to Kabul to seek the support of Amir Habibullah (1872–1919) in instigating mass uprisings among the border tribes, which would tie up the Indian army for the rest of the war. Germany thus joined the Great Game as a third player and preserved that position even after it lost the war in Europe.

REFORM IN AFGHANISTAN
It was, however, revolutionary Russia that represented a real threat to the British by recognizing Afghanistan as a sovereign state and using it as a pawn in an attempt to penetrate India with the connivance of the reformist Ghazi Amir Amanullah (1892–1960), who hoped to modernize his country with the help of anti-British powers. Expecting Soviet assistance to arrive soon, in May 1919 he ordered his troops and armed tribesmen to cross the Durand Line, the boundary established in 1893 between Afghanistan and British India but contested by almost every subsequent Afghan government. The British stopped Amanullah, but in the resulting peace treaty had to recognize Afghanistan's full sovereignty. Amanullah initiated a number of radical reforms, which led to a conservative backlash that in 1929 forced him to flee. After a brief civil war, Amanullah's distant cousin Muhammed Nadir Shah (1883–1933) took the throne. He was assassinated in 1933 and succeeded by his son Zahir.

AFGHANISTAN UNDER ZAHIR SHAH
King Zahir Shah reigned from 1933 to 1973, during which time the country survived two major international crises, World War II and the partition of British India in 1947, but not the ramifications of the Cold War. During World War II, Afghanistan narrowly avoided Iran's fate, which was to be occupied by Allied troops in an attempt to forestall German penetration. German and Italian nationals, who had been in charge of most modernization projects, including the training of Afghan armed forces, were expelled under joint Anglo-Soviet pressure in 1941. A more serious crisis developed when British India was partitioned

into two independent states, Hindustan (India) and Pakistan. Because more than half of the Pashtuns, the largest ethnic group in Pakistan (accounting for 40 percent, compared to Tajik [30 percent], Hazara [10 percent], and Uzbek [9 percent]), lived across the Durand Line in India's Northwest Frontier Province (NWFP), where the Congress Party government voted in June 1947 to join Hindustan, the partition was bound to cause a serious crisis in Central Asia. In July, however, in a British-sponsored referendum the NWFP voted to join Pakistan, as did the tribal assemblies (*jirghas*) in its five tribal agencies, which had been established by the British inside the NFWP along the Durand Line. The Afghan government rejected the decision and refused to recognize both the popular vote and the Durand Line as an international boundary, insisting that the tribal agencies be treated like the roughly five-hundred native or princely states of British India that were given a third choice in the partition: independence. This would have created an independent Pashtunistan, which might or might have not soon joined Afghanistan.

Pakistan responded to the threat of Pashtunistan with a protracted trade blockade of Afghanistan, which affected gasoline imports. Deprived of imported gasoline, Afghanistan turned to the Soviet Union for economic and military assistance. With the United States backing Pakistan, Moscow offered in 1955 a $1.5 billion loan for development projects such as power plants and highways, including the Salang Pass Highway, which tunneled through the Hindu Kush, creating a year-round passage, which was crucial in a country without railroads. The king's cousin and from 1953 to 1963 the prime minister, Prince Daoud (1909–1978), was openly pro-Soviet and further antagonized Pakistan by stirring up pro-Pashtunistan uprisings in the border region. He was forced to resign and in 1964 the king initiated the drafting of a new constitution, which included a bill of rights for both men and women and a new legislature, in which for the first time women had guaranteed seats. However, the growth of leftist parties soon paralyzed the experiment in democracy and in 1973, while Zahir Shah was in Europe, Prince Daoud seized power with the help of military officers, abolished the monarchy, and became president. He first aligned himself with the communists (the People's Democratic Party of Afghanistan, PDPA) against Muslim traditionalists, but two years later he reversed course, dismissed the PDPA members from his government and changed the constitution to create a presidential, one-party political system.

THE COMMUNIST COUP AND THE MUJAHIDIN RESISTANCE

In April 1978 a handful of Afghan communists, supported by Soviet-trained army officers, launched a successful coup, during which President Daoud and his family were murdered. Daoud was succeeded by a communist government headed by Noor Muhammad Taraki (1917–1979), who enjoyed Soviet backing and initiated radical reforms. Taraki himself, however, was murdered in September the following year by his rival Hafizullah Amin (1929–1979) before the Soviets could intervene. The ensuing Soviet invasion of Afghanistan in the last days of 1979 led to a third shootout that cost the life of Amin and his supporters and brought power to another Soviet-backed leader, Babarak Karmal (1929–1996). Taraki and Amin had imposed radical reforms on the countryside—reforms that were designed to change overnight century-old Islamic and tribal customs regarding land tenure and the position of women in society and education—thereby quickly alienating the bulk of the population, which responded in the traditional way, with tribal warfare. The Soviet troops occupying Afghanistan were opposed by the guerrillas, or *mujahidin*, "those waging *jihad*." In 1986 Babrak Karmal was replaced by the more energetic Dr. Muhammad Najibullah (1947–1996), a physician who offered a more flexible strategy of negotiating with as well as fighting the insurgents while making gestures of respect toward Islam.

Without a sanctuary for the Afghan *mujahidin* and for Afghan refugees inside Pakistan, and international support, chiefly from the United States, resistance would have died out. Large-scale sovietization of the Afghan youth took place during this period, and an estimated eighty thousand Afghans were trained in the Soviet Union, including children of preschool age. In 1985, when the reformer Mikhail Gorbachev assumed power in the Soviet Union, he recognized that he needed to extricate his country from what had become a quagmire in

Ahmed Shah Masood, a leader of the *mujahidin* resistance to the Soviet occupation of Afghanistan, is shown here with his troops, May 1985. ©REZA; WEBISTAN/CORBIS

Afghanistan. In April 1988 negotiations started between the Najibullah government and the insurgents, who were represented by Pakistan, with both the Soviet Union and the United States acting as guarantors of the process. Under the terms of the agreement, the Soviet Union would withdraw its troops by April 1989 and refugees would be permitted to return home. The Soviet Afghan War lasted ten years and cost the lives of more than one million Afghans and as many as thirty thousand Soviet servicemen, as well as creating an estimated five million refugees. It served as an important catalyst for the fall of communism and the collapse of the Soviet superpower.

FROM TALIBAN TO THE U.S.-LED INVASION

After the Soviet withdrawal in 1989 and the capture of Kabul from Najibullah in 1992, the country descended into a new civil war. *Mujahidin* factions that had fought together against foreign invaders turned on each other in a struggle for control of the country until a new rival, the Taliban, took over. The Taliban recruited from among Muslim religious students, mostly Pashtuns, who studied in religious schools in Pakistan that were financed by Saudi Arabia. Between 1995 and 1997, Taliban forces conquered almost two-thirds of Afghanistan, including Kabul. They restored a semblance of order, but at the price of harsh enforcement of a deeply conservative interpretation sharia, or traditional Muslim law. Recognized only by Pakistan, Saudi Arabia, and the United Arab Emirates, the Taliban government permitted international terrorist organizations, including Al Qaeda, to maintain bases inside Afghanistan.

In spite of the UN resolutions demanding the closing of all Al Qaeda training camps and the handing over of its leader Osama bin Laden, the Taliban continued to harbor both, even after the 11 September 2001 attacks on the United

States. On 7 October, the United States and Britain invaded Afghanistan. Their ally on the ground was the Northern Alliance, composed of Afghanistan's minority tribes: Tajiks, Hazaras, Uzbeks, and Turkmen. By late November, Kabul was taken. Meanwhile, representatives of the major Afghan opposition and exile groups convened in Bonn under UN auspices. An interim government was established, presided over by a Durrani Pashtun, Hamid Karzai (b. 1957), until elections could be held. His presidency was confirmed by the traditional *Loya Jirga* (tribal grand assembly) the following June. Another *Loya Jirga* approved the new constitution in January 2004. Hamid Karzai was reelected in the first nationwide presidential election in October 2004, in which more than eight million voters, including women, participated. Parliamentary (250-seat) and provincial council elections were held in mid-September 2005, under relatively little intimidation by the Taliban, which had, nevertheless, become active again in some of the southern provinces. Outside Kabul, however, security remained a major problem because of frequent Taliban attacks and the interference of powerful warlords, who maintain large militia forces, while remnants of Al Qaeda remain in hiding on both sides of the Durand Line, despite the ongoing presence of U.S. (in 2006, twenty thousand) and UN (eight thousand) forces. During 2005 the number of Taliban and Al Qaeda attacks against teachers and administrations as well as roadside explosions increased and for the first time suicide terrorists struck in major Afghan cities including Kabul.

Although financial assistance exceeding several billion dollars was pledged by major industrialized countries, Afghanistan has little capacity or infrastructure with which to absorb it. After twenty-five years of continuous war, no industrial plant or bank remains intact; and agriculture is devastated to the extent that the only crop worth cultivating is the opium poppy for the production of heroin, of which Afghanistan is the world's leading illicit exporter. In late January 2006 representatives of Afghanistan, the United Nations, and more than sixty countries met in London and agreed on a five-year plan for Afghanistan's reconstruction and improved security, called the Afghanistan Compact, which succeeded the Bonn Agreement from late 2001. In early 2006 only about half of the financial aid of $9.5 billion pledged in 2001

had been delivered. Among the new goals are the disbanding of illegal militias by 2007, the creation of a competent Afghan police force, and of a national army of seventy thousand by 2010.

See also **British Empire; Cold War; Gorbachev, Mikhail; India; Pakistan; Russia; Soviet Union.**

BIBLIOGRAPHY

Adamec, Ludwig W. *Afghanistan's Foreign Affairs to the Mid-Twentieth Century: Relations with the USSR, Germany, and Britain.* Tucson, Ariz., 1974.

Arnold, Anthony. *Afghanistan: The Soviet Invasion in Perspective.* Stanford, Calif., 1981.

Cordovez, Diego, and Selig S. Harrison. *Out of Afghanistan: The Inside Story of the Soviet Withdrawal.* New York, 1995.

Dupree, Louis. *Afghanistan.* Princeton, N.J., 1973.

Fraser-Tytler, William Kerr. *Afghanistan: A Study of Political Developments in Central and Southern Asia.* London, 1953.

Girardet, Edward. *Afghanistan: The Soviet War.* London, 1985.

Gregorian, Vartan. *The Emergence of Modern Afghanistan: Politics of Reform and Modernization, 1880-1946.* Stanford, Calif., 1969.

Hauner, Milan, and Robert L. Canfield, eds. *Afghanistan and the Soviet Union: Collision and Transformation.* Boulder, Colo., 1989

Klass, Rosanna, ed. *Afghanistan: The Great Game Revisited.* New York, 1987.

Newell, Nancy Peabody, and Richard Newell. *The Struggle for Afghanistan.* Ithaca, N.Y., 1981.

Nyrop, Richard F., and Donald M. Seekins, eds. *Afghanistan: A Country Study.* Washington, D.C., 1986.

Rashid, Ahmed. *Taliban: Militant Islam, Oil, and Fundamentalism in Central Asia.* New Haven, Conn., 2000.

Roy, Olivier. *Islam and Resistance in Afghanistan.* Cambridge, U.K., 1990.

Rubin, Barnett R. *The Fragmentation of Afghanistan: State Formation and Collapse in the International System.* New Haven, Conn., 1995.

MILAN HAUNER

AFRIKA KORPS. The Afrika Korps was an expeditionary combat force of the German army that fought in North Africa from February 1941 until May 1943. Adolf Hitler ordered the establishment of a German expeditionary force in North Africa in January 1941, following Italian defeats in Tobruk and Benghazi, at the request of the Italians, who had refused an early German offer for military assistance. Originally known as Befehlshaber der deutschen Truppen in Libyen (Commander of the German Troops in Libya), from 21 February 1941 the unit was called the Deutsche Afrika-Korps. Hitler formed the Korps for strategic reasons; he had planned a campaign against Greece and feared the loss of the eastern Mediterranean and a severe weakening of his Axis ally. In addition, the occupation of North Africa was a major precondition for German supremacy in the Near and Middle East as envisaged in Hitler's long-range plans.

The Afrika Korps was led by General Erwin Rommel (1891–1944), a highly decorated World War I hero who served as military commander guarding Hitler's headquarters from 1938 and as commander of a tank division in 1940. The Afrika Korps itself in early 1941 consisted of the Wehrmacht's Fifteenth Tank Division and the Fifth Light Tank Division (later the Twenty-first Tank Division). Its forces were highly motorized and equipped with specific uniforms for desert warfare. The overall German-Italian military organization was gradually extended and renamed Panzergruppe Afrika in September 1941, Panzerarmee Afrika in February 1942, Deutsch-italienische Panzerkräfte Afrika in October 1942, and finally Heeresgruppe Afrika in January 1943, always under the command of Rommel. The actual Afrika Korps, which was led from August 1941 by other generals, then constituted only a part of these forces. Nevertheless its name is generally used for all of them, until the German forces became part of the First Italian Army in March 1943.

German troops landed in Libya on 8 February 1941. On 31 March 1941 they bombed the Suez Canal and attacked Cyrenaica, which was conquered by mid-April. British forces were weakened by a simultaneous attack by the Wehrmacht in southeastern Europe but regained their strength during the course of 1941. As a consequence of the German attack on the Soviet Union starting in June of 1941, the Afrika Korps was not reinforced during 1941, so it was not able to defend all of the gains it had made

in the spring of 1941. In November Rommel had to retreat to the earlier front line.

After German naval successes and the transfer of German Airforce Fleet 2 from the Soviet Union to the Mediterranean, Rommel on 21 January 1942 surprisingly again took the initiative and attacked British troops, and the Afrika Korps occupied Benghazi. But the advance was stopped because the Italian army had not been informed and did not participate in the offensive.

Supplied with information from broken U.S. diplomatic codes, Rommel was able to continue his offensive on 26 May. On 21 June 1942 his troops conquered the Tobruk area, where a decisive line for British logistics was cut. The Wehrmacht was able to capture twenty-eight thousand enemy soldiers and major supply stocks of the British army. Immediately thereafter the Afrika Korps entered northwestern Egypt as far as the village of El Alamein, almost one hundred kilometers west of Alexandria, where it was halted at the end of June by fierce British resistance. Rommel's next attack in the battle of Alam al-Halfa at the beginning of September failed. Since Hitler did not order the occupation of Malta as the Italians had suggested, the British Eighth Army was able to obtain excellent supplies, including new U.S. tanks, through the Royal Navy.

Rommel's new British counterpart General Bernard Law Montgomery, who could rely on airpower supremacy and excellent intelligence information, launched a counterattack on 23 October 1942 and overran the German positions on 2 November in a major tank battle at El Alamein. Thirty thousand Axis soldiers were captured. Meanwhile on 7–8 November in Operation Torch, the Allies landed to the rear of German troops in Morocco and Algeria. This took the German and Italian military totally by surprise. The German troops were quickly reinforced by 150,000 men but had to retreat from Libya, which was lost to the Germans at the end of January 1943, and into Tunisia. Rommel on 9 March was replaced by Colonel General Hans-Jürgen von Arnim. Since Hitler forbade any evacuation of troops, the Heeresgruppe Afrika surrendered with 275,000 men, among them the soldiers of the Afrika Korps, on 11 May 1943.

Panzer tanks of the Afrika Korps in the North African desert c. 1942. ©CORBIS

Hitler considered the North African theater of war a sideshow until November 1942, despite its strategic value, especially for Britain and the Royal Navy. Nevertheless considerable German forces were drawn from the European continent, especially after October 1942. German defeats occurred simultaneously in Stalingrad and North Africa.

The Afrika Korps has gained a major place in German and British memories of the war, especially due to the fact that in North Africa modern armies fought in a rather unusual environment. Already during the war Rommel was considered a brilliant operational performer, called the Desert Fox by his soldiers, among whom he was very popular; he was also admired to a certain extent by the British. His successes predominantly relied on his capability to surprise the enemy and on excellent logistical support. In June 1942 he was promoted to field marshal, the highest rank in the German army. The Afrika Korps was less implicated in German war crimes than units in other areas, although it took

some responsibility for the internment and forced labor of Tunisian Jews. Rommel's suicide on 14 October 1944, after the failure of the 20 July 1944 plot against Hitler, further bolstered his image as a military professional with a clean record.

See also **German Colonial Empire; World War II.**

BIBLIOGRAPHY

Baxter, Colin F. *The War in North Africa: 1940–1943: A Selected Bibliography.* Westport, Conn., 1996.

Boog, Horst, et al. *The Global War: Widening of the Conflict into a World War and the Shift of the Initiative, 1941–1943.* Translated by Ewald Osers. Vol. 6 of *Germany and the Second World War.* Oxford, U.K., 2001.

Mitcham, Samuel W. *Rommel's Desert War: The Life and Death of the Afrika Korps.* New York, 1982.

Porch, Douglas. *The Path to Victory: The Mediterranean Theater in World War II.* New York, 2004.

Schreiber, Gerhard, Bernd Stegemann, and Detlef Vogel. *The Mediterranean, South-east Europe, and North*

Africa, 1939–1941: From Italy's Declaration of Non-belligerence to the Entry of the United States into the War. Translated by Dean S. McMurry, Ewald Osers, and Louise Willmot. Vol. 3 of *Germany and the Second World War.* Oxford, U.K., 1995.

DIETER POHL

AGITPROP. Agitprop, short for *agitation and propaganda,* was a communist theatrical genre in interwar Europe, largely scripted and performed by amateurs, designed to inculcate communist values into the consciousness of workers. Its origins are debated; some scholars point toward medieval passion plays as a distant antecedent. Most, however, would agree that agitprop proper originated in Russia during the civil war (1918–1920) that followed the Bolshevik Revolution, when agit-trains carried acting troupes ("living newspapers"), pamphlets, and musicians to the largely illiterate Russian peasantry.

Agitprop's aesthetic called for scenes that were short, fast-paced, ideologically correct, current, and concrete. Whenever possible, they addressed local problems. Thus, excepting any so-called lead articles—pieces that addressed issues of interest to workers across the country—no central agency prepared the troupes' scripts. Troupes shared their work with each other. The scripts might speak to any aspect of working-class life or thought, including foreign policy, working-class organizations, and private concerns. Music and dance heightened scenes' agitational possibilities. Although pianos generally provided musical accompaniment, jazz bands were common. No musical style predominated; performances might include pastiches of both operatic arias and the most recent hits.

Costumes and other trappings were as simple as possible. Players often wore plain blue shirts matched with either black skirts or trousers and boots. Details indicated character types. For example, drunks wore red noses. As troupes prized mobility, simplicity was a point of principle; they used props only when necessary. Posters, however, were important to provide facts and figures to accompany performances. A characteristic of such work was its rejection of conventional forms as bourgeois, in favor of newer, supposedly proletarian forms. Here the troupes anticipated the style of Bertolt Brecht, interwar Germany's most important playwright.

Apart from the Soviet Union, agitprop theater was most important in Germany—the home of western Europe's most significant Communist Party—during the Weimar Republic, the period between the end of the First World War and the Third Reich. Agitprop arrived in Germany in 1927, when a Soviet troupe toured the country. The movement quickly became very popular. By 1930–1931, the Communist Party claimed approximately three hundred troupes.

German troupes were relatively small, having between six and twenty members. Most included women, but they were always outnumbered by men. Players tended to be young, often teenaged. Young workers probably joined such troupes to adopt a different personae, that is, to transform their identities from "mere" workers into representatives of the victorious revolutionary proletariat. The symbolic act of controlling their lives extended to the names the troupes adopted, such as Column Left, Curve Left, and the Red Megaphone. Agitprop theater was performed where workers lived and gathered: on the streets, in apartment courtyards, in bars, at sporting events, and at party-sponsored meetings. The most common issues addressed by the troupes included the Communist Party and Comintern (Communist International), development of the Soviet Union, religion and cultural reaction, the press, "social democratic treachery," unemployment, elections, and the police.

Communist music and literature in the 1920s and early 1930s conformed to rules similar to those of agitprop theater. The various national communist movements sponsored the writing of proletarian novels that would be cheap, gripping, and sharp. Soviet fiction of this period needed not only to be interesting but also politically acceptable and aesthetically progressive. Much of this work proved to be more politically appropriate than entertaining. It seems not to have engaged the expected proletarian audience.

This was also true in the West, where plots of such novels often centered around the growing class consciousness of urban workers who, having come to grasp their situations, affiliate with the Communist

Party. Other themes included the unmasking of political enemies to show their true natures. Generally these enemies were social democrats. Fascists and Nazis rarely emerged. This weakness certainly detracted from their purported realism.

Agitprop music included street singing of protest songs, as well as the performances of organized revolutionary choruses. Singers avoided the notion of art for art's sake, replacing it with a fully politicized repertoire. As Hanns Eisler, a prominent twentieth-century composer and collaborator of Bertolt Brecht, put it, "even our singing must represent struggle" (quoted in Durus, p. 4). Nevertheless, the movement struggled with, but never resolved, the question of whether classics could be rehabilitated or needed to be relegated to the past. A second debate addressed the costs and benefits of parodying contemporary hits. In Germany the Nazi Party came to power before these issues could be resolved. Indeed, like agitprop theater and agitational literature, agitprop music fell victim to the radical political shifts in Germany after the Nazi seizure of power.

See also **Brecht, Bertolt; Propaganda; Theater.**

BIBLIOGRAPHY

Bodek, Richard. *Proletarian Performance in Weimar Berlin: Agitprop, Chorus, and Brecht.* Columbia, S.C., 1997.

Durus. "Arbeitergesang und Agitprop." *Kampfmusik* (May 1931).

Mally, Lynn. *Revolutionary Acts: Amateur Theater and the Soviet State, 1917–1938.* Ithaca, N.Y., 2000.

Stourac, Richard, and Kathleen McCreery. *Theater as a Weapon: Workers' Theatre in the Soviet Union, Germany and Britain, 1917–1934.* London, 1986.

RICHARD BODEK

AGNELLI, GIOVANNI (1921–2003),
Italian industrialist.

Giovanni Agnelli, an industrialist born in Turin, Italy, on 12 March 1921, was known as Gianni Agnelli or "l'Avvocato" (the Lawyer). A leading figure in Italian economic, social, and sports life, he was the son of Edoardo (1892–1935) and grandson of Giovanni Agnelli (1866–1945), one of the founders of Fiat (Fabbrica Italiana Automobili Torino) in the early years of the twentieth century. After receiving a law degree he participated in World War II and in the struggle for the liberation of Italy.

When Edoardo died in an airplane accident in 1935 Gianni and his younger brother Umberto (1934–2004) became heirs to Italy's largest private enterprise. Upon the death of his grandfather in 1945 Gianni Agnelli became vice-chairman of Fiat; in 1963 he was named managing director and from 1966 (when he succeeded Vittorio Valletta [1883–1967]) until 1996 he was chairman of the company, after which he served as its honorary chairman. From 1974 to 1976 he was president of Confindustria, the Italian employers' organization. This association of Italian manufacturers demanded the strongest possible leadership because the student disturbances and the workers' unrest of those years had created an extremely sensitive political environment. In contrast to Valletta's managerial style, the collaboration among the government, the trade unions, and Confindustria developed into a cooperative system for managing fundamental economic choices.

Between 1966 and 1985 Gianni Agnelli's life was characterized by a continual battle, in which he was victorious, for the control and revival of Fiat. When the oil crisis of the 1970s struck the automobile sector Fiat faced ruin. Agnelli, however, did not lose his optimism, and under the banner of recovery he succeeded in establishing alliances with workers and trade unions, taking advantage of the mistakes of the latter to reduce their influence in the decision-making process of the company. In the 1980s he marketed an automobile, the Uno, whose popularity, due to its low cost and high gas mileage, made Fiat once more a profitable enterprise. By surrounding himself with the very finest managers (from Valletta to Vittorio Ghidella to Paolo Fresco) and establishing alliances with important Italian powers (Enrico Cuccia's Mediobanca [Financial bank]), he reformed Fiat's industrial policy in a manner consistent with international economic development. Supported by the managing director, Cesare Romiti, he relaunched Fiat, transforming it in just a few years into a holding company with branches in the fields of publishing and insurance.

In 1987 Fiat absorbed first Alfa Romeo and then in 1988 Ferrari, a company with which it had collaborated on a technical level since 1965 and with which it later established a joint participation agreement in 1969. Agnelli always closely followed the soccer team, Juventus, of which he was president from 1947 to 1953 (in 1955 his brother Umberto became its president). Agnelli held many positions. He chaired the financial enterprise Ifi (the Istituto Finanziario Industriale, a company founded by Giovanni Agnelli senior in 1927), the Exor Group, the Fondazione Giovanni Agnelli, and the publisher of the newspaper *La Stampa*; he was a member of the Board of Directors of Eurofrance, the International Advisory Council of the Chase Manhattan Corporation, and the Board of Trustees of the Solomon R. Guggenheim Foundation.

He was active in numerous international organizations, serving, for example, in the Bilderberg Advisory Group and on the International Advisory Board of the Council on Foreign Relations; he was also honorary chairman of the Council for the United States and Italy and vice-chairman of the Association for the European Monetary Union. In 1991 the president of the Republic of Italy, Francesco Cossiga (b. 1928), appointed Agnelli senator-for-life "for his outstanding contributions in the socioeconomic field." In the Senate from the Tenth to the Fourteenth Legislatures, Agnelli had the following assignments: member of the Autonomy Group from 30 May 2001 to 24 January 2003 and member of the Fourth Standing Committee of the Ministry of Defense from 22 June 2001 to 24 January 2003.

In politics Agnelli always distinguished himself for his ability to remain nonpartisan, his pragmatism, and his justified skepticism regarding the ability of Italian politics to reform itself and especially to maintain a middle-of-the-road course. This is the reason that, however proud he was to be Italian, as a magnate of industry he deemed it necessary to seek a stronger international identity for Italy's great industries and corporations. Moreover, he learned how to reconcile his patriotism with his nature as a true Europeanist. He supported the center-left Ulivo coalition (the Olive Tree Alliance) when sacrifices were necessary for Italy's admission as a full member of the European Monetary Union. Yet in the 2001 election campaign he supported the center-right politics of Silvio Berlusconi (b. 1936).

When he was diagnosed with cancer in 1996 Agnelli passed the chairmanship of Fiat to Romiti. His nephew, Giovannino Agnelli (son of Umberto and the intended chairman of Fiat), had been designated as his successor, but he died of cancer in 1997 at the age of thirty-three; Gianni Agnelli's forty-six-year-old son Edoardo committed suicide in 2000. In June 1998 Paolo Fresco (who had managed the alliance with General Motors, which held 20 percent of Fiat Auto with an option to buy it) was appointed chairman of Fiat and Gianni's twenty-two-year-old nephew John Elkann became director.

See also **Automobiles; Italy; Malaparte, Curzio.**

BIBLIOGRAPHY

Biagi, Enzo. *Il signor Fiat: Una biografia.* Milan, 1976.

Camerana, Oddone. *L'enigma del cavalier Agnelli e altri itinerari.* Milan, 1985.

Friedman, Alan. *Agnelli and the Network of Italian Power.* London, 1988.

Kline, Maureen. "Fiat Chairman Agnelli to End Era By Stepping Down." *Wall Street Journal,* 12 December 1995.

Ottone, Piero. *Gianni Agnelli visto da vicino.* Milan, 2003.

Pietra, Italo. *I tre Agnelli.* Milan, 1985.

Pochna, Marie-France. *Agnelli l'irresistibile.* Paris, 1989. Italian edition, *Agnelli l'irresistibile,* translated by Giorgio Arduin. Milan, 1990.

Tagliabue, John. "Agnelli Says He Will Retire from Fiat Post." *New York Times,* 12 December 1995.

Turani, Giuseppe. *L'Avvocato: 1966–1985, il capitalism italiano tra rinuncia e ripresa.* Milan, 1985.

Wallace, Charles P. "The Next Mr. Fiat?" *Fortune,* 14 October 1996.

MARIA TERESA GIUSTI

AGRARIAN PARTIES.

Agrarian parties emerged in Europe in the late nineteenth century. In the years between the world wars, these parties played a significant political and structural role in all parts of the Continent, including the northern and western countries, but their influence was especially strong in central and eastern Europe. On the eve of World War I, for example, a German agrarian league founded in 1893 succeeded in electing representatives to local government as well as to the Reichstag. Despite the greatly varied forms taken by agrarianism from one country to the next, it always sought to place agriculture and the defense of rural labor at the center of its political, economic, and social programs. The main agrarian issues were prices and tariffs, property relationships, and land reform. Even though supporters of agrarianism were often to be found in many different political and trade union organizations, the invariable goal of agrarian parties proper was to unite rural labor in a single structure with corporatist ambitions and to extend this base to other social strata, at first rural but eventually also urban.

RISE OF AGRARIAN POLITICS

During the interwar years the agrarian parties reached the apogee of their influence against a backdrop of crisis. The Polish Peasant Movement (PSL), founded in Galicia in 1895, emerged after the Armistice of 1918 as one of the country's four main political groupings, but it was undermined by factional fighting at the local level and repeated splits at the national one—notably involving the Galician branch, deemed to have fallen under the control of the clergy and the big landowners. In Romania, the Peasant Party enjoyed great success in the elections of 1919 thanks to an alliance with the nationalists, and its leader, Ion Mihalache, became minister of agriculture. But these gains came to naught. The party managed to reconfigure its ideology, proposing a fresh model of development—based on the thinking of the sociologist Virgil Madgearu—which, though founded on the primacy of agriculture, incorporated industrialization into its economic and social vision; this sharply distinguished the party's views from those of other agrarian groups such as the "poporanists" around Constantin Stere and the journal *Romanian Life,* who rejected the whole idea of an industrial economy. The Peasant Party nevertheless failed to hang on to power, and was swamped, like other political forces, by the nationalist and authoritarian dynamic that dominated Romania between the wars. Meanwhile a "Green International," headquartered in Prague and led by the Czechoslovakian

minister Mecir, sought but failed to combine the agrarian forces of several eastern European countries.

Agrarian parties emerged in almost every European country, even in some, such as France, where none had existed in earlier days. As Pierre Barral has shown, until World War I agrarian sentiments and projects were taken up and channeled in France by politicians (such as the moderate Jules Méline), by broader—governmental, socialist, or trade union—political forces, or even by institutions like the chambers of agriculture. Agrarianism was simply not central to French political and electoral preoccupations in either the city or the country. On the other hand, France differed sharply from Germany inasmuch as no organized anti-agrarian doctrine existed in that country. The situation was transformed, however, in the aftermath of World War I, when a "triple crisis" struck the French peasantry. The first aspect of this crisis was economic in character: as in other European countries, the 1920s ushered in a rapid fall in prices, notably in the price of wheat; second, the rural way of life came under threat from growing urbanization (as of 1931 more than 50 percent of the French population lived in urban areas); and third, the system of political and professional representation itself entered a critical time. The response was the founding in 1928 of the French Agrarian and Peasant Party, whose principal leaders were the teacher Fleurant, nicknamed "Agricola," and the lawyer Henri Noilhan. One agrarian candidate was successful in the legislative elections of 1932, eight in 1936. But the party was divided, and part of it seceded under Noihlan to form the more left-leaning Agrarian and Social Republican Party. It also had to confront the militant Peasant Defense movement, launched in 1928 by the journalist Henri Dorgères (Henri d'Halluin). Dorgères had an acid pen, he was a fearsome orator, and he believed firmly in direct action—a belief that led him, well before the advent of Poujadism (a movement of small business owners founded to protest sales taxes), to organize antitax protests at the grassroots level (notably at Bray-Sur-Somme in 1932) and to promote anti-"Red" actions in 1936–1937 intended to break both agricultural and industrial strikes. He was the best-known figure of French agrarianism. Dorgères's Peasant Defense became part of the Peasant Front at its foundation in 1934; the Front also included the Agrarian and Peasant Party and the National Union of Agricultural Trade Unions (UNSA), led by Jacques Le Roy Ladurie. But Dorgères and Peasant Defense were hobbled by their reputation for extremism and regularly accused of standing for "green fascism." To be fair, however—and appearances to the contrary notwithstanding, for his stage management of public rallies and general tactics certainly resembled the methods of nascent fascism—Dorgères embodied nothing worse than a blend of authoritarian nationalism and traditionalism. The issue of fascism remains central to any discussion of agrarian parties in the interwar years. A balanced analysis, while acknowledging areas of mutual influence between militant agrarians and some forms of fascism, will likely conclude that these should not be mistaken for fusion.

A telling example here is Claudius Heim, the "peasant general." Heim was the architect of the peasant revolt in Schleswig-Holstein, Germany, between January 1928 and October 1930; he was also the central figure in Ernst von Salomon's novel *Die Stadt* (1932; The city). The reasons for the revolt that began in 1928 were primarily economic, but questions of collective identity also played a part: the demonstrators felt that their professional and political organizations were incapable of defending them in any respect. They resorted to direct action (to prevent the seizure of their livestock) and terrorism in the form of assassinations. A more unusual tactic was their boycott of Neumünster, which lasted for nearly a year (1929–1930) and brought the town to the brink of financial ruin. Incarcerated in September 1929, Heim observed from a prison cell the first major success of the National Socialists, when they obtained 18.6 percent of the votes in the elections of 30 September 1930. Heim was fiercely independent and turned down the Nazis' offer to place him at the head of their electoral list. He had scant regard for Adolf Hitler, and he described Alfred Hugenberg, industrialist and founder of the German Nationalists, as "a faithful servant of international capitalism." The voters of Schleswig-Holstein were of a different mind, however, and in 1930, 27 percent of them gave their ballots to the National Socialists; in rural communes (less than two thousand inhabitants), moreover, the percentage of Nazi votes

was 35.1. By July 1932 these two percentages increased to 51 and 63.8 respectively. The fascists were thus able to turn surging agrarian frustration to their advantage and even to envelop it utterly in what Karl Dietrich Bracher calls the National Socialists' "agro-political apparatus" run by Richard Walter Darre, the ideologist of race and the peasantry who in 1934 was made "Reich peasant leader."

AGRARIANISM UNDER AUTHORITARIAN REGIMES AND POSTWAR ECLIPSE

The smothering of agrarian parties by fascist and authoritarian regimes was a widespread occurrence. Italy is a case in point. Immediately after World War I the agrarian movement was largely concentrated in the south of the country. It was not until the creation of the General Agricultural Confederation in April 1920 that the idea of a national agrarian party arose. The notion was buttressed by economic crisis and by land occupations that gave rise to a militarization of farmers under the aegis of the Upper Italian Association of Farmers. In the elections of 6 June 1921 the Agricultural Confederation ran some fifty candidates, of whom twenty-seven were successful. From this effervescence a formally constituted agrarian party emerged, its founding announced in Rome on 8 January 1922 by Angelo Parodi Delfino and Antonio Bartoli. When the Fascists came to power, however, the impetus was lost, and the main Italian agrarian forces found that they were fellow travelers of the regime rather than prime movers in their own right. Much the same pattern is discernible in the relationship between Vichy France and the Peasant Corporation. It is true that Jacques Le Roy Ladurie was appointed minister of agriculture, but Dorgères, for all that he eagerly offered his services, was not even invited to help draft a peasant charter and had to be satisfied with being one of nine general managers of the corporation. Peasant Defense never succeeded in becoming a counterweight to the influential UNSA.

Relative to their intentions, then, it must be concluded that the agrarian parties were a failure. They never succeeded in making their perspective the main axis of political life. Nor were they able to attract sufficient support to become truly representative organizations. It is hardly surprising, then, that the years after World War II saw the definitive eclipse of agrarian parties. In the Communist East they served as figureheads. In western Europe they were unable to regroup and in effect overwhelmed by competition from reinvigorated traditional agricultural trade unions. In France, for instance, it was the National Federation of Small Farmers (Fédération Nationale des Exploitants Agricoles) that marginalized the agrarian forces; this tendency was reinforced by the increasing influence among young agriculturalists of new organizations descended from Catholic Action. Later the emergence of far-reaching demands concerning the ecology or the defense of the land gave rise to new movements. But José Bové's Confédération Paysanne, for example, or the movement called Hunting, Nature, Fishing and Tradition (Chasse, Nature, Pêche et Tradition), which returned two members to the European Parliament in 1999, are a very far cry from the interwar agrarian organizations. On the other hand, there are clearer signs of continuity in central Europe, especially in postcommunist Poland.

See also **Agriculture; Land Reform.**

BIBLIOGRAPHY

Primary Sources

Dorgères, Henry. *Au temps des fourches.* Paris, 1975.

Salomon, Ernst von. *La ville.* Paris, 1933.

Secondary Sources

Barral, Pierre. *Les agrariens français de Méline à Pisani.* Paris, 1968.

Holmes, Kim R. "The Forsaken Past: Agrarian Conservatism and National Socialism in Germany." *Journal of Contemporary History* 17, no. 4 (October 1982): 671–688.

Hunt, James C. "The 'Egalitarianism' of the Right: The Agrarian League in Southwest Germany, 1893–1914." *Journal of Contemporary History* 10, no. 3 (July 1975): 513–530.

Le Bars, Michèle. "Le 'général paysan' Claudius Heim: Tentative de portrait." In *La Révolution conservatrice et les élites intellectuelles,* edited by Barbara Koehn, 115–140. Rennes, France, 2003.

Lewis, Gavin. "The Peasantry, Rural Change and Conservative Agrianism: Lower Austria at the Turn of the Century." *Past and Present* 81 (November 1978): 119–143.

Paxton, Robert O. *Le temps des chemises vertes: Révoltes paysannes et fascisme rural 1929–1939.* Paris, 1996.

Rogari, Sandro. "La crisi del ceto politico liberale la formazione del gruppo e del partito agrario." In *Partito politico dalla grande guerra al fascismo: Crisi dalla rappresentanza e riforma dello stato nell'età dei sistemi politici di massa: 1918–1925,* edited by Fabio Grassi Orsini and Gaetano Quagliariello, 531–550. Bologna, Italy, 1996.

Roger, Antoine. *Fascistes, communistes et paysans: Sociologie des mobilisations identitaires roumaines (1921–1989).* Brussels, 2002.

OLIVIER DARD

AGRICULTURE. The history of European agriculture in the era of industrialization and urbanization since the mid-nineteenth century is a history of an increasing loss of economic importance in every European national economy and at the same time a history of unprecedented success in increasing productivity. On the eve of World War I only 50 percent of the European population was dependent for a living on agriculture. An increasing number of people were attracted by the cities with their growing industry and new technical infrastructures. The new industries needed laborers. Also, a growing number of people emigrated from Europe to North and South America, Australia, and New Zealand.

Dramatic population growth paralleled rising per capita incomes. In many rural areas throughout Europe it was the first time in history that people had a real chance for a better life. In contrast to the situation in the United States or Canada, arable land and pastures in Europe were always a limited and valuable good. The system of agriculture was adapted to the natural and socioeconomic situation. The result was a complicated pattern of very different types of settlement structures and land use. Typical cultural landscapes dominated many regions of Europe: the *bocage,* or pastures framed by hedgerows, of Western Europe; the *dehesas* in Spain, areas with cork oak trees and pastures underneath, where large numbers of pigs can be raised; and extensively used grasslands, as in Hungary. Special cultures are still very typical of the unique diversity of agrarian landscapes in Europe. They include the cultivation of olive trees around the Mediterranean Sea, the use of terraced vineyards in the river valleys of Southern and Central Europe, and alpine pasture systems in the Alps, the Pyrenees, and other mountainous areas.

Until the 1950s woodlands in all forms had a very important additional role in rural economies. Woodland areas were the source for fuelwood and humus. Also, acorns, beechnuts, and fresh leaves were widely used, together with hay from the meadows, for feeding animals. In a long process that took more than half a century, this older type of fodder supply from nearby sources was replaced by mixed fodder and new forage plants like corn.

Animal-husbandry practices became ever more dependent on the knowledge of veterinary medicine as the scale of livestock breeding grew. Research from the emerging natural sciences—biology, entomology, and botany—helped to increase yields of crops and animal products. Industrial chemical insecticides were introduced in the first half of the twentieth century. One of the best-known was DDT. A Swiss chemist, Paul Hermann Müller (1899–1965), discovered the nature of DDT as an insecticide in 1939. First used against the mosquitoes that cause malaria, it was later deployed against other pests, such as the Colorado potato beetle, which was introduced in Europe in the first half of the twentieth century. The use of DDT increased the yields of many crops significantly until 1962, when Rachel Carson published her landmark book *Silent Spring*. Ten years later DDT was banned in the United States, and was then banned in Europe until the 1990s.

Chemical fertilizers were also introduced at the beginning of the twentieth century, when the use of natural saltpeter was replaced by the extraction of anhydrous ammonia from the air, a chemical process developed between 1905 and 1913 by the German scientists Fritz Haber (1868–1934) and Carl Bosch (1874–1940). The lack of organic matter in European soil had historically caused marginal yields and periodic harvest failure. This was no longer the case after the new applied chemistry emerged. Systematic plant breeding also contributed to higher yields. One of the early success stories of plant breeding was the dramatic increase of the sugar content of the sugar beet. Alterations of other crops, including cereals and potatoes, followed.

First attempts at the mechanization of agricultural production processes were made in the nineteenth century. Many of them failed due to the lack of appropriate power sources. The steam engine was only used for big plows. With the advent of the gasoline engine and later with the invention of the diesel engine, it was possible to mechanize nearly all these processes. The tractor became the universal engine for transporting agricultural goods. Despite all their advantages, however, tractors were too expensive for the majority of European farmers. For this reason agriculture was a latecomer in adopting innovations from science and technology until the 1950s. In the first half of the twentieth century modernized and highly mechanized big farms could frequently be found alongside small farms with no machines and no use of fertilizers and pesticides. Generally the use of specialized agricultural machinery was more evident in western and northern Europe than in eastern and southern Europe.

There were great differences in the socioeconomic situation of the rural population at the beginning of the twentieth century. The northern and western parts of Europe were dominated historically by small and more-or-less free farmers; in eastern Europe large areas were dominated by the estates of the landed elite, as in the eastern parts of the kingdom of Prussia and in Russia. Members of these aristocratic families played a very influential role in politics and the armed forces of these countries until later in the twentieth century.

There were different forms of tenancy and various titles of agrarian inheritance. The Mediterranean forms of tenancy, the *mezzadria* in Italy and the *métayage* in France, are distinctive. In these forms of tenancy, a tenant signed only short contracts with the owner, who made the farm buildings, the land, tools, and animals available to the tenant, who was thus a kind of farmworker. The tenant had to give one-half of the yields to the owner. The mezzadria system in Italy was dissolved after World War II.

In the northwestern parts of Europe the tenant signed longer contracts and had to pay money for the tenancy. At the beginning of the nineteenth century many feudal laws were dissolved, and the number of free farmers who were property owners in a modern sense increased in many countries. The titles of inheritance also were different. In some parts of Germany, for example, the whole farm with the land, fixtures, and livestock was given to the eldest or the youngest son. This title of inheritance was called *Anerbenrecht*. In those areas, as in northern and western Germany, the farms remained relatively large until the mid-twentieth century. In other regions, typically in southwestern Germany, another title of inheritance, the *Realteilungsrecht,* was predominant. In this case the farm was divided into equal parts for every child. This caused field patterns in which the arable land was typically scattered in small strips. Scattered villages with small farms and houses were also common. In those areas overpopulation was characteristic at the end of the nineteenth century.

Before 1914 agriculture became a part of a globalized economy. The advent of new agrarian suppliers, including the former colonies, lowered prices. In this situation most European countries tried to save their farmers through the use of protective tariffs. Only in some countries, like Great Britain, did the idea of a free market prevail. But the conflict between the free market and the protection of European agriculture by tariffs and treaties is still a live issue.

WORLD WAR I

World War I had a deep impact on European agriculture. Many farmers had to serve in the armies, and many of them never came back. In Germany alone two million of more than three million farmworkers and farmers had to leave their farms and villages for a long time. Yields of many crops decreased and feeding livestock became a serious problem. In many European countries bureaucracies were established to organize agricultural production and the distribution of agricultural goods. In Germany the Kriegsernährungsamt (war food department) was responsible for the food supply. But this office failed. Due to food shortages, harsh weather conditions, and the 1918–1919 influenza pandemic, 750,000 civilians died in Germany during the war.

The aftermath of the war was catastrophic. Some regions, such a northern France, were entirely destroyed. Many rural people had to leave their homelands in Greece and Turkey. Revolution, civil war in Russia, and the establishment and nation-building of many new countries in central and southeastern Europe caused huge problems for rural people. Germany lost 13 percent of its territory, mainly fertile agrarian regions such as Upper Silesia and western Prussia. Austria-Hungary was divided into several countries with different political and socioeconomic conditions underlying rural life.

INTERWAR PERIOD AND WORLD WAR II

European countries had to deal with the consequences of the war. Damaged farmland had to be restored, particularly in France and Belgium. In many countries an active agrarian-settlement policy was set up. The main goal was to ensure the food supply and to help former soldiers and unemployed industrial workers and their families. In 1919 the Reich Settlement Act of the young German democracy was formulated. Within the next years several thousand new farms were established. After the Treaty of Sèvres in 1920 and the subsequent war between Greece and Turkey hundreds of thousands of refugees had to be settled both in Greece and Turkey. With the assistance of the League of Nations a successful settlement program was initiated.

In the Soviet Union radical land reform and collectivization took place with incalcuable costs, both material and human. The kulak, or private farmer, was eliminated.

In 1939 Adolf Hitler (1889–1945) went to war in 1939 first against Poland with the idea of conquering Lebensraum (living space) for the German people. This objective was also an argument for the war against the Soviet Union in 1941. Influential agrarian politicians such as the secretary of agriculture, Herbert Backe (1896–1947), and the leading agricultural scientist Konrad Meyer (1901–1973) formulated plans and programs such as the *Generalplan Ost* for agrarian settlements of German farmers in the conquered areas. These plans were an integral part of the Holocaust and the agrarian exploitation of eastern Europe for the food supply of Germany during the war.

A DIVIDED CONTINENT AND A DIVIDED AGRICULTURAL HISTORY

The first years after World War II were characterized by hunger and devastation of wide parts of the agricultural economy. Millions of people, living in ruins in the cities or as refugees all over Europe, tried to survive on the produce of small garden plots or by dealing on the countless black markets.

The agricultural history of Europe in the decades following the 1940s can be seen as a part of the history of the Cold War. With the erection of the "Iron Curtain" Europe was divided until 1989 into two politically and ideologically separated parts.

A peasant stacks hay on her farm on a former World War I battlefield in France, 1922. ©BETTMANN/CORBIS

In Eastern Europe the traditional structure of landownership was fundamentally changed in every country. Land reform and waves of collectivization formed a new system of agriculture with big cooperative or state-owned farms. The traditional farmer on the small farm, who worked independently and within a rural community of other farmers, vanished as a socioeconomic type. These farmers became agricultural workers on big farms, controlled by a small number of executives with an academic background and membership in the Communist Party. It is quite clear that this development shaped rural villages. Ironically these deep changes preserved older settlement structures and the architectural heritage of the preindustrial period better than in Western Europe.

Western Europe went another way. In general, land ownership remained untouched. But with the foundation of the European Union in 1957 and the establishment of a "common agrarian policy" after the Stresa Conference in July 1958 agriculture was removed from the free market. Instead of trade and industry, European agriculture became a closed system intended to protect small farmers. Nevertheless the decades from the 1950s onward were a time of an unprecedented loss of farms and jobs in agriculture. As early as 1968 the Dutch politician and later Commissioner of the EU, Sicco Mansholt (1908–1995), published a plan in which he proposed to close most of the small farms. This plan caused many public protests. As of 2006 in Western Europe only 2.7 percent of all employees work in agriculture. In the area of the eastern enlargement of the EU the figure is 13 percent.

For the first time in history all aspects of agriculture were fully mechanized and modernized. Consequently yields increased by leaps and bounds.

Beginning in the 1970s the ecological consequences of highly industrialized agriculture increasingly became a controversial topic of public debate. In the 1980s organic farming became popular. With the "Slow Food" movement, which started in Italy in 1986, a new facet was added to criticisms of industrialized agriculture. The main idea is to preserve the diversity of traditional types of foodstuffs.

1989 AND ITS CONSEQUENCES

With the end of the Cold War in 1989 the situation of agriculture changed. The signature of this period is the triumph of capitalist agriculture. In all the eastern and southeastern countries formerly state-owned and collective farms were dissolved and sold to private owners or agrarian entrepreneurs from the West who ran huge farms with modern machinery.

Countries with very different agrarian traditions joined the EU over the course of several enlargements: in 1989 (former German Democratic Republic); 1995 (Austria, Sweden, Finland); and 2004 (Estonia, Latvia, Lithuania, Poland, Czech Republic, Slovakia, Hungary, Slovenia, Malta, and Cyprus). During these years the reform of the common agrarian market was one of the main political issues within the EU. It is believed that lowering subsidies and creating new political instruments should help to develop the rural peripheries of many European countries; protect agrarian landscapes with their historical, cultural, and ecological values; and lower tariff barriers. A fundamental change in agrarian policy was initiated in 2003 when agricultural subsidies were phased out as an economic strategy. Overproduction has diminished, but year after year the common agricultural policy comes under scrutiny. Its future is uncertain.

See also **Agrarian Parties; Common Agricultural Policy; European Union; France; Germany; Italy; Land Reform; Mad Cow Disease; World War I; World War II.**

BIBLIOGRAPHY

Alexander, Derek W., and Michael Drake. *Breaking New Ground: Fifty Years of Change in Northern Ireland Agriculture 1952–2002.* Belfast, 2002.

Almås, Reidar, et al., eds. *Norwegian Agricultural History.* Trondheim, 2004.

Blomme, Jan. *The Economic Development of Belgian Agriculture 1880–1980: A Quantitative and Qualitative Analysis.* Leuven, 1993.

Brown, Jonathan. *Agriculture in England. A Survey of Farming 1870–1947.* Manchester, U.K., and Wolfeboro, N.H., 1987.

Campbell, Bruce M., and Mark Overton. *Land, Labour and Livestock: Historical Studies in European Agricultural Productivity.* Manchester, U.K., and New York, 1991.

Campbell, Fergus J. M. *Land and Revolution: Nationalist Politics in the West of Ireland 1891–1921.* Oxford, U.K., and New York, 2005.

Chubarov, Alexander. *Russia's Bitter Path to Modernity: A History of the Soviet and Post-Soviet Eras.* New York, 2001.

Cleary, M. C. *Peasants, Politicians and Producers: The Organisation of Agriculture in France since 1918.* Cambridge, U.K., and New York, 1989.

Clout, Hugh. *After the Ruins: Restoring the Countryside of Northern France after the Great War.* Exeter, U.K., 1996.

Conquest, Robert. *The Harvest of Sorrow: Soviet Collectivisation and the Terror-Famine.* London, 1986.

Corni, Gustavo. *Hitler and the Peasants: Agrarian Policy of the Third Reich 1930–1939.* New York, 1990.

Davies, R. W., and Stephen G. Wheatcroft, eds. *The Years of Hunger: Soviet Agriculture 1931–1933.* New York, 2003.

Estók, János. *History of Hungarian Agriculture and Rural Life 1848–2004.* Budapest, 2004.

Farquharson, J. E. *The Plough and the Swastika: The NSDAP and Agriculture in Germany 1928–45.* Wayne, Pa. 1992.

Federico, Giovanni. *Feeding the World: An Economic History of Agriculture 1800–2000.* Princeton, N.J., 2005.

Fogel, Robert William. *The Escape from Hunger and Premature Death, 1700–2100: Europe, America and the Third World.* Cambridge, U.K., and New York, 2004.

Grigg, David. *The Transformation of Agriculture in the West.* Oxford, U.K., 1992.

Harding, Susan Friend. *Remaking Ibieca: Rural Life in Aragon under Franco.* Chapel Hill, N.C., 1984.

Heinzen, James W. *Inventing a Soviet Countryside: State Power and the Transformation of Rural Russia 1917–1929.* Pittsburgh, Pa., 2004.

Jones, Eric. *The European Miracle: Environments, Economies, and Geopolitics in the History of Europe and Asia.* 3rd ed. Cambridge, U.K., and New York, 2003.

Köll, Anu-Mai. *Peasants on the World Market: Agricultural Experience of Independent Estonia 1919–1939.* Stockholm, 1994.

Leigh, G. J. *The World's Greatest Fix: A History of Nitrogen and Agriculture.* Oxford, U.K., and New York, 2004.

Moeller, Robert G. *German Peasants and Agrarian Politics 1914–1924: The Rhineland and Westphalia.* Chapel Hill, N.C., 1986.

Offer, Avner. *World War I: An Agrarian Interpretation.* Oxford, U.K., and New York, 1989.

Orwin, Christabel S., and Edith H. Whetham. *History of British Agriculture, 1846–1914.* Hamden, Conn., 1964.

Perren, Richard. *Agriculture in Depression 1870–1940.* Cambridge, U.K., 1995.

Perry, P. J., ed. *British Agriculture 1875–1914.* London, 1973.

Robinson, Guy M. *West Midlands Farming, 1840's to 1970's: Agricultural Change in the Period between the Corn Laws and the Common Market.* Cambridge, U.K., 1983.

Sereni, Emilio. *History of the Italian Agricultural Landscape.* Translated with an introduction by R. Burr Litchfield. Princeton, N.J., 1997.

Simpson, James. *Spanish Agriculture: The Long Siesta, 1765–1965.* Cambridge, U.K., and New York, 1995.

Viola, Lynne, et al., eds. *The War against the Peasantry 1927–1930: The Tragedy of the Soviet Countryside.* New Haven, Conn., 2005.

Wilt, Alan F. *Food for War: Agriculture and Rearmament in Britain before World War II.* Oxford, U.K., and New York, 2001.

ANDREAS DIX

AIDS. Although cases of AIDS have been retrospectively identified, the disease only came to the attention of European societies in the early 1980s. At the beginning of that decade, gay men in North America and Western Europe began to die of immune system failures that made them especially vulnerable to ordinary infections, skin cancers, and gastric and respiratory diseases. At first the causes and nature of the disease were mysterious, but its recurring and variable features meant that by 1981 it had gained the name acquired immune deficiency syndrome (AIDS). Although it was initially thought to be particular to gay men, by 1982 it had begun to appear among hemophiliacs who had undergone blood transfusion. Within a few years the first cases caused by heterosexual intercourse and intravenous drug use were reported. By 1984 HIV (human immunodeficiency virus) had been isolated as the cause of AIDS.

The fact that the epidemic seemed at first mainly to affect gay men meant that to begin with it had a low political priority. Indeed, on the right of the political spectrum, the view that homosexuals had brought their fate upon themselves because of their supposedly promiscuous lifestyle was widespread. However, it rapidly became obvious that a public health crisis of enormous dimensions was unfolding, and governments of all types began to develop health education programs and advertising campaigns encouraging safer sex. Gay rights groups, however, became frustrated at the apparent slowness in the development of a cure and responded by chastising governments and the pharmaceutical industry for their apparent lack of urgency. However, by the mid-1990s drug therapies had achieved remarkable success against the disease, with the result that numbers of deaths fell dramatically. Thanks to these drug combinations, by the late 1990s AIDS did not necessarily develop in a patient following the acquisition of the HIV virus. HIV had become a manageable, if chronic, condition as long as there was access to remedial drugs. On a global scale, HIV and AIDS also seemed to be less of a European problem, with the vast majority of sufferers in sub-Saharan and southern Africa. As a result the epidemic fell somewhat below the political radar in Europe, or at least took on the aspect of a persistent but serious health problem rather than the apocalyptic crisis it had threatened to become in the early 1980s. By the early twenty-first century, however, drug-resistant strains of HIV had been identified as drug use spread following the collapse of communism and risk-taking sexual behavior became fashionable again in the West.

ORIGINS AND PROGRESS

AIDS is caused by the HIV virus. HIV belongs to a group of viruses that gradually attack and overwhelm the immune system and are known collectively as lentiviruses. There is some dispute about the origins of the epidemic, but it is probably the case that it was transmitted to humans from West

African apes, probably through the consumption of ape meat. The exact moment when AIDS appeared in Africa is also uncertain. Certain symptoms and diseases, which before the discovery of HIV were placed in different categories of pathology, have in some cases been retrospectively identified as AIDS. In addition, some blood samples given in the 1940s have been retested and discovered to be HIV-positive. Some theories suggest that AIDS can even be traced back to the nineteenth century. However, in 1998 the first definite case of HIV-1 infection was discovered by retrospective testing in a blood plasma sample taken in 1959 from a man living in what is now the Democratic Republic of Congo.

In 1999 it was discovered that chimpanzees suffered from a virus similar to HIV, known as SIV (simian immunodeficiency virus), and that this had somehow crossed species and mutated into HIV. Most authorities agree that SIV was probably transferred to humans through contact with simian blood during the killing, butchering, or eating of chimpanzee meat. However, another theory suggests that HIV was likely to have developed in the punitive and squalid labor camps common in central Africa under the colonial rule of Belgium and France in the late nineteenth century. In those camps, malnourished workers would have been likely to have eaten monkey meat, but any deaths from HIV-type infections would probably have been explained as the consequence of other more common infections or simple malnutrition. However, positive identification of the virus in past populations of humans and apes has been made. In 2003 the sub-type HIV virus known as HIV-2, which is much rarer and less infectious than the principal form of the virus, HIV-1, was identified as originating in Guinea-Bissau in West Africa in the 1940s. It was then held to have spread to Europe via the war for independence from Portugal that took place in that country between 1963 and 1974. It was later discovered that Portuguese veterans of that war had contracted HIV-2 at that time. Most authorities now accept that the worldwide epidemic of AIDS began sometime in the mid-1970s.

There were some identified cases of AIDS in the developed world before its discovery among gay men in the early 1980s. Indeed, it has been estimated that by 1980 there were between 100,000 and 300,000 undiagnosed cases of HIV across the world. However, those cases isolated and identified as a specific syndrome went largely unnoticed until common symptoms started to be observed among gay men in New York City, some of whom, it was noted, were suffering from severe bronchial pneumonia and other pulmonary infections that did not respond to drugs. These cases were first observed in March 1981, and by 1982 a similar syndrome began to be noticed in the United Kingdom. At first AIDS was seen as a specifically gay problem because it was transmitted through homosexual sex. The hysterical coverage in the British press in 1982 and 1983 labeled it a "gay plague" or a "gay cancer" while the early medical labels such as GRID (gay-related immune deficiency) reflected a similar preconception. However, it was clear by the end of 1982 that the virus could be transmitted in other ways, especially by blood transfusion. Cases of infections passed in this way began to appear in Europe at around this time. By late 1981 it was also obvious that the virus could be passed during heterosexual sex and through intravenous drug use. The HIV virus was identified by French scientists in May 1983 and in the following year was pinned down as the cause of the disease by an American team led by Robert Gallo.

In this early stage of the epidemic rates of reported infection remained low relative to the size of the European population, but this may have reflected underreporting of the disease especially in communist Eastern Europe. In 1984 there were 762 reported cases of AIDS in Europe, 108 of which were in the United Kingdom. However, the rate of infection was high, with the U.K. total more than doubling within the year. By 1993 there were an estimated 500,000 cases of adult HIV infection in Western Europe, 125,000 of which had progressed to AIDS. In Eastern Europe a further 50,000 were estimated to have the virus and 4,500 to have AIDS. By 2004 the numbers of adults and children living with AIDS in Central and Western Europe had risen to 600,000. In 2003 alone 73,974 new cases of HIV infection were diagnosed in Europe. By this time the countries with the fastest rates of infection, that is, with the largest increases in numbers of HIV diagnoses, were Portugal, Italy, and Spain. In 1999–2000

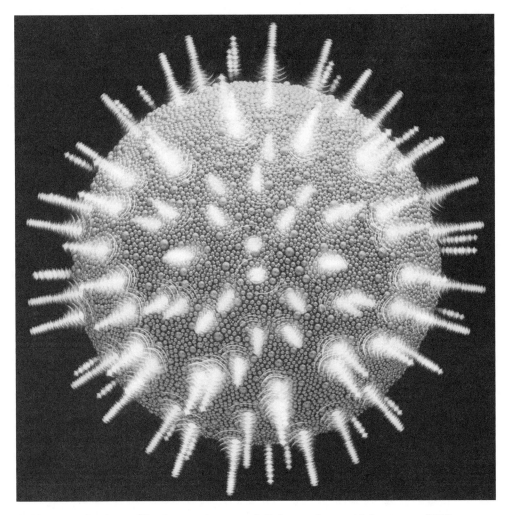

A microscopic view of the human immunodeficiency virus, which causes AIDS.
©MICHAEL FREEMAN/CORBIS

Portugal had an infection rate of 88.3 cases per million compared to the European average of 25, although the United Kingdom made up the largest proportion of new cases (39 percent in 2002). At the end of 2004 more than 2 million people across Europe and the countries of the former Soviet Union were infected with HIV/AIDS, some 5 percent of the global total of 39.4 million. Given the patchy nature of reporting the disease, especially in Eastern Europe, Italy, and Spain, the European figures are almost certainly an underestimate.

As the disease has spread it has lost its initial association with homosexual behavior. Except in Germany and the Netherlands, where homosexual behavior is still the chief source of transmission, by 1999 the majority of HIV infections in Western Europe were found to be the result of heterosexual sex. Of the 18,030 new cases reported in Western Europe in 2003 over half had contracted the virus through heterosexual contact, while only 30 percent were homosexual or bisexual men. Also, the gender profile of those with HIV has changed since the 1980s, with more women reporting HIV infection (37 percent of new diagnoses in Western Europe in 2003). There are, however, significant differences between Western and Eastern Europe in the profile of HIV-positive populations. The fall of communism in the Soviet Union and Eastern Europe after 1989 and its replacement by unregulated capitalism contributed to the collapse of health systems in those countries and has also led to increased drug use and a corresponding rise in HIV infection through needle sharing. While in

Western Europe most transmissions tend to take place through sexual contact, in Eastern Europe intravenous drug use has been the most common source of infection. By 2003 drug users in Western Europe accounted for 11 percent of infections, but in Eastern Europe 61 percent of those reporting from a transmission group had been infected through needle sharing. This type of infection is especially common in Russia, Romania, and Ukraine. In Romania an estimated 98,000 children had been infected by 1993, while in Ukraine, 1 percent of its population of around 48 million was HIV-positive in 2002.

POLITICAL RESPONSE
The initial response to AIDS was conditioned by the fact that it appeared to be a "gay plague." In Western Europe right-wing politicians jumped on the epidemic as an opportunity to point out the consequences of the permissive society. Perhaps because of this, it was gay groups who at first responded with the most effective types of health education and campaigning. Because they recognized that they were engaged in a virtual struggle for survival, gay groups also developed new kinds of confrontational activism that sought to pinpoint the failings of the state and the pharmaceutical industry.

At first AIDS seemed to some moralists to be some sort of divine punishment for supposed homosexual promiscuity. James Anderton, the chief constable of Greater Manchester and one of the most powerful policemen in the United Kingdom, observed in 1984 that AIDS was a simple consequence of the fact that homosexuals were "swirling around in a human cesspit of their own making." Similarly, the tabloid press in Western Europe reacted to the epidemic with a mixture of sensationalism and horror, especially when the first celebrity victims became known, such as the actor Rock Hudson, who died in 1985. The cultural climate produced by the epidemic also encouraged the Conservative government in its attack on the inheritance of 1960s "permissiveness." This trend was given legislative weight by the infamous Section 28 of the 1988 Local Government Act, which prevented local authorities from "promoting" homosexuality in schools as a "pretended family relationship." The actual effect of the

legislation was to undermine sex education efforts by limiting discussion of homosexuality, HIV transmission, and AIDS in schools.

In spite of such contradictory gestures, one of the principal results of the AIDS epidemic was the development of extensive health education schemes. While in Eastern Europe these tended to be organized by the state, in Western Europe in the early 1980s the most effective responses came from voluntary organizations and AIDS charities. There were also some efforts to curb dangerous drug use. Early efforts to encourage responsible needle use by intravenous drug users led to the establishment of needle exchanges in Amsterdam in 1984 and Dundee, Scotland, in 1986. In Eastern Europe compulsory blood screening programs were introduced. In Russia in 1993 over 20 million HIV tests were carried out. Compulsory tests for all foreign tourists, residents, and visitors were contemplated but have yet to be implemented. In Western Europe schemes to give out free condoms and sexual advice for gay men developed, while a series of television and cinema advertisements stressed the dangers of unprotected sex.

Gay groups developed a concerted response to the crisis. Some of this activism, such as that developed by ACT UP (AIDS Coalition to Unleash Power) in France after 1989 and Outrage in Britain during the 1990s built on an American model of confrontational "queer" activism. The main aim of AIDS activism like this was to confront what was seen as the ineffective policies of Western governments in the face of the AIDS epidemic. The strong implication of such campaigns was that because AIDS was primarily a problem among marginal groups such as gay men, immigrants, and drug users, governments and the medical establishment were dragging their feet over its solution. Medical programs were underfunded, according to ACT UP, and pharmaceutical companies were being ineffective in pursuing a vaccine. Their protests involved picketing drug companies, "die-ins," and battling the stigma associated with HIV status. ACT UP's slogan, meant to encourage a more open if not confrontational approach to the epidemic, was "Silence = Death." Other less confrontational and more health-oriented strategies emerged from the gay community and developed from organizations like the Terrence Higgins Trust, established in 1982 and named after one of the first gay men in Britain to die of AIDS. The trust, which is now the largest AIDS charity in Europe, is devoted to health and sex education among gay men and to preventing the spread of HIV infection.

The politics of AIDS did not only concern gay men, however. In the 1990s two major scandals over the transmission of contaminated blood erupted in Germany and France. In both cases it emerged that blood supply companies had been knowingly transfusing blood that was contaminated with the HIV virus. In Germany it was revealed in 1999 that the federal government had covered up 373 cases of HIV infection through contaminated blood that had occurred in the 1980s. In France the socialist government of Laurent Fabius was implicated in a similar scandal. In 1985 it was discovered that the national blood transfusion service (CNTS) had knowingly distributed HIV-infected blood to some 4,000 hemophiliacs. Fabius's government had also obstructed the introduction of an American test that would screen blood supplies because they wanted to promote a test being marketed by a French company. The head of the CNTS at the time received a prison sentence, but although the scandal rumbled on and Fabius was ordered to stand trial in 1998, he and his colleagues were eventually exonerated by the courts in the following year.

TREATMENT

By the mid-1990s the development of drugs that slowed the progress of the disease had eased the AIDS crisis. By 1997 deaths from the disease in Europe had begun to fall for the first time since the epidemic began. The success of these drug treatments has allowed many HIV-positive people to live with the virus and to prevent its development into the full immune-system failure that is associated with AIDS. One consequence of the success of these treatments is that AIDS has slipped down the political agenda and has come to be perceived as a primarily African problem. Sexual risk-taking is also back in fashion, as a general rise in all sexually transmitted diseases across Western Europe indicates.

Drugs that slowed down the progression of HIV to AIDS began to develop in the 1980s. The first efforts to treat AIDS focused on a cancer drug named AZT (azidothymidine). By the mid-1990s treatments that involved combinations of different anti-retroviral drugs (combination therapies) had proved effective in improving the condition even of those patients who had begun to develop AIDS. These drug therapies involved the combined use of protease inhibitors, fusion inhibitors, and reverse transcriptase inhibitors alongside AZT, which together slowed down the replication of the HIV virus. In many cases the effect was dramatic, allowing formerly bedridden hospital patients to return home. A further refinement on combination therapies was the development in 1999 of stronger so-called fusion inhibitor drugs. With the rise of these therapies HIV became a manageable condition and did not necessarily prevent patients from living normal lives. However, the high costs of combination drug therapies put these treatments beyond people outside Western European health systems. Although Glaxo Wellcome cut the price of AZT by 75 percent for mothers in developing countries in 1998, drugs that are routinely available to those in Western Europe are not necessarily accessible to poorer communities.

In addition, stories of new drug-resistant strains of HIV are circulating. Although strains of drug-resistant AIDS emerged in 1986 and have been reported periodically ever since, there is new concern that in the age of the Internet and combination therapies, promiscuous and unsafe gay sex is once more fashionable. However, the spread of unsafe sex is not merely a gay problem. In Western Europe the incidence of all sexually transmitted diseases (STDs) has increased enormously since the mid-1990s. This trend is particularly marked in the United Kingdom, where the incidence of all STDs (not including HIV infection) increased by 62 percent in the ten years up to 2004. Although AIDS has ceased to be the defining health crisis of the period, all the evidence suggests that it remains a chronic problem across Europe.

See also **Public Health; Venereal Disease.**

BIBLIOGRAPHY

Berridge, Virginia. *AIDS in the UK: The Making of a Policy, 1981–1994.* Oxford and New York, 1996.

Joint United Nations Programme on HIV/AIDS. *AIDS Epidemic Update 2004.* Geneva, 2004.

Mann, Jonathan M., and Daniel J. M. Tarantola. *AIDS in the World II: Global Dimensions, Social Roots, and Responses.* New York, 1996.

Smith, Raymond A., ed. *Encyclopedia of AIDS: A Social, Political, Cultural, and Scientific Record of the HIV Epidemic.* Chicago, 1998. Available at www.avert.org.

H. G. COCKS

AIRPLANES. *See* Aviation.

AKHMATOVA, ANNA (1889–1966), Russian poet.

Born Anna Andreyevna Gorenko, Anna Akhmatova, among the most renowned and beloved of twentieth-century Russian poets, was born near the southern Russian city of Odessa in 1889. Until her marriage to the poet Nikolai Gumilev in 1910, Akhmatova lived in Tsarskoe Selo and in Kiev; her father served first in the Russian imperial navy, later in the imperial civil service. Her poetry was to reflect the fate as well as the historical and spiritual experience of her generation in Russia, drawing a passionately engaged audience even during her many years as an outcast in the Soviet political system.

Making her poetic debut early in the twentieth century, Akhmatova was associated with a literary group whose members called themselves the Acmeists. These poets proclaimed their devotion to concrete, material, tactile images in their poetry, thus opposing themselves to the Russian symbolists, whose poetry they considered excessively weighed down by abstract themes and images as well as by a lack of clarity. Akhmatova's very first book of poetry, *Evening* (*Vecher*, 1912), evoked a strong positive critical response. Her second collection, *Rosary* (*Chyotki*, 1914), attracted a large readership as well as a considerable following of literary imitators. Her next books, *White Flock* (*Belaya staya*, 1917), *Plantain* (*Podorozhnik*, 1921), and *Anno domini MCMXXI* (1921), placed Akhmatova in the ranks of the most popular poets of her time in Russia.

Her work was greatly valued by such poetic authorities of her early years as Alexander Blok, Valery Bryusov, Fyodor Sologub, and Mikhail Kuzmin.

Characteristic of Akhmatova's poetry from its earliest stages was the representation of the emotional diary of a female heroine, ranging widely in type from the highly educated urbanite to the lowly circus performer, from the fine lady to the impoverished fishing girl. Each poem presents itself as a kind of photograph or sketch from a real-life history of visual and psychological verity, reproducing in minutest detail the specifics of furnishings, clothing, lighting, odor, gesture, and intonation. Akhmatova's work is also characterized by numerous direct and indirect references to the works of literary predecessors and contemporaries. Her poems are permeated with images and motifs that associate them not only with the poetry of Alexander Pushkin, Konstantin Batyushkov, Vasily Zhukovsky, Nikolai Nekrasov, Alexander Blok, Osip Mandelstam, Vladimir Mayakovsky, Marina Tsvetaeva, and others but also with Russian prose—above all with the works of Nikolai Gogol, Fyodor Dostoevsky, Andrei Bely, and Mikhail Bulgakov. "It could be that poetry itself is one great quotation," wrote Akhmatova.

From the middle of the 1910s, with her references to the beginning of World War I, Akhmatova's poems ever more frequently reflected the themes of current events. Indeed her poetry became a kind of testimonial to the many historical twists and turns of fate that were the lot of her contemporaries. Akhmatova took no part in the official Soviet literary life of the 1920s and 1930s. Her poetry during that period did not require either the agreement or the support of the new political system. During the 1920s Soviet journals and publishing houses gradually ceased to publish her work; by the end of the 1920s even private publishing houses found it impossible to publish her books and poetry despite all efforts. In the official Soviet press Akhmatova was increasingly the object of accusations that her poetry failed entirely to address the building of the new socialist society and the interests of the Soviet people, that it merely short-circuited in the realm of private interior life. When, in 1940, after an interval of almost fifteen years, a Leningrad publishing house released her poetry collection *From Six Books* (*Iz shesti knig*), a government decree banned the book from all government libraries and bookstores after only a few months. Akhmatova was accorded a short period of recognition under Joseph Stalin's rule during World War II, when major Soviet newspapers published her war poems. She was evacuated from Leningrad to Tashkent, where a book of her poetry was published in 1943. However, in August 1946 Akhmatova's poetry was subjected to vigorous ideological criticism in a special Communist Party decree, "On the Journals *Zvezda* and *Leningrad.*" Akhmatova was excluded from the Union of Soviet Writers and all copies of her books were destroyed directly at the printing presses. Within a few years her sole means of professional support was literary translation. Her poetry was no longer published, and school and university courses on the history of Russian literature referred to her only in negative terms. In 1949 she sought a compromise with the Soviet state: she wrote a cycle of poems entitled *In Praise of Peace* (*Slava Miru*) with the hope of easing the fate of her son, Lev Gumilev, who had been repeatedly arrested. The cycle was published, but even so her son was falsely found guilty of political crimes; he was released and rehabilitated only in 1957.

From the 1920s to the 1950s many other people close to Akhmatova were arrested, exiled, or died while unjustly imprisoned for political crimes. Her former husband Nikolai Gumilev was shot in 1921; one of her closest friends, Osip Mandelstam, was arrested in 1934. Her third husband, the art critic Nikolai Punin, died in a prison camp. At the end of the 1930s Akhmatova began work on her poem "Requiem" ("Rekviem"); in it, the fate and feelings of a mother whose son is arrested become a lyrical core around which she weaves the theme of the great tragedy that her contemporaries in the Soviet Union were forced to live through. She writes as if she were describing her own fate alone, but it was a fate she shared with millions of her compatriots. The poem was published in Munich in 1963, but even though Akhmatova's poetry had begun to appear again in her home country during the "thaw" period under Nikita Khrushchev (collections of old and new poetry came out in 1958, 1961, and 1965), "Requiem" would not be published in the Soviet Union until 1987, during Mikhail Gorbachev's perestroika.

In 1940 Akhmatova began writing one of her most significant works, "Poem without a Hero" ("Poema bez geroya"); she continued to work on it until the 1960s. Central to this work is the theme of evaluating one epoch from the perspective of another. On New Year's Eve the poet is visited by the spirits of figures from her literary youth. The theatrical, artistic, and literary St. Petersburg of 1913—on the eve of World War I and the Russian Revolution—is viewed through the prism of the eve of World War II and the wartime period itself. Akhmatova strives to create her own vision of the beginning of the twentieth century for her younger readers. She takes issue with other memoirists of the period about their representations of specific details of the period of her youth (for example, she asserts that Boris Pasternak's novel *Doctor Zhivago* paints an absolutely false picture), as well as with regard to hierarchies of cultural values and authorities, relations among literary figures, and so on. Akhmatova conveyed this vision of her epoch not only through her poetry but also through brief polemical memoirs, commentaries in her diaries, and numerous detailed stories for her young audience.

Her character and her fate provided both her own and a younger generation with an example of internal toughness and opposition in the face of the extreme difficulties of the life experienced by an independent artist during the years of war, revolution, and totalitarian Soviet control. In 1965 Oxford University awarded Akhmatova an honorary degree.

See also **Mandelstam, Osip; Mayakovsky, Vladimir; Terror; Tsvetaeva, Marina.**

BIBLIOGRAPHY

Haight, Amanda. *Anna Akhmatova: A Poetic Pilgrimage.* London, 1976.

Ketchian, Sonia I. *The Poetry of Anna Akhmatova: A Conquest of Time and Space.* Verse translated by F. D. Reeve. Munich, 1986.

Ketchian, Sonia I., ed. *Papers from the Akhmatova Centennial Conference at the Bellagio Study and Conference Center, June 1989.* Berkeley, Calif., 1993.

Polivanov, Konstantin, comp. *Anna Akhmatova and Her Circle.* Translated by Patricia Beriozkina. Fayetteville, Ark., 1994.

KONSTANTIN POLIVANOV

ALBANIA. Albania, today formally the Republic of Albania, is a small mountainous country situated on the Adriatic coast and bordered to the north by Serbia and Montenegro, to the east by the Former Yugoslav Republic of Macedonia, and to the south by Greece. When Albania first gained independence in 1913 it had a population of 800,000, which grew to 1 million in 1930, 1.4 million in 1955, 1.6 million in 1960, 2.7 million in 1981, and 3.3 million in 1991. Historically, ethnic Albanians have been divided into two major groups—the Gegs, mountaineers who lived in tribal clans in the part of the country north of the Shkumbin River, and the rural Tosks, who inhabited the southern areas. In the early part of the century, the tribal chiefs enjoyed the almost unlimited power of local feudal lords. However, during the interwar period King Zog (r. 1928–1939) managed to centralize power to an extent, and under the post–World War II communist regime suppressed the power of these chiefs altogether. Albania has a significant Greek minority, especially in the southeastern areas of the country. A large number of ethnic Albanians live outside of the borders of the country, in Italy, Greece, Turkey, and especially in Kosovo, a province of neighboring Serbia. Albanians speak two different dialects—the Geg dialect is spoken by two-thirds of the population, as well as Albanians in the neighboring Kosovo province, Montenegro, and Macedonia, while the Tosk dialect is spoken by the remaining third of the population. Ottoman rule had thwarted the development of a literary Albanian language, and a standardized Latin alphabet, which was originally adopted in 1908, was made official by the government in 1924. The interwar government also unsuccessfully tried to create an official language that combined the Geg and Tosk dialects. Under the rule of the communist leader Enver Hoxha (1908–1985), the Tosk dialect (which was Hoxha's native dialect) became the official language of the country.

Traditionally, there were three major religions in Albania—Islam, Eastern Orthodoxy, and Catholicism. Catholics lived primarily in the north, while the central part of the country was overwhelmingly Muslim and the southern part had an equal number of Muslims and Christians in the early 1920s. At end of World War II approximately 80 percent of the population was Muslim, 20 percent Orthodox, and a little less than 15 percent Roman Catholic. Until World War II the Albanian constitution guaranteed religious freedom and did not establish an official religion. Hoxha, considering religion to be a divisive force, launched an active campaign aimed at the eradication of organized religion in Albania by passing the Decree on Religious Communities, which subjugated all religious communities and institutions to the state. This decree nationalized church property, violently repressed the clergy, and outlawed the practice of religion. Realizing that Hoxha's campaign had met with limited success, in the mid-1980s his successor, Ramiz Alia (b. 1925), relaxed this virulently antireligious stance and in December 1990 revoked the ban on religious observance.

ECONOMIC RESOURCES AND TRENDS

From the beginning of independence Albanian statehood was thwarted by lack of economic development and severe poverty. In 1920 the country's lack of railroads and its insufficient roadways thwarted commerce. Furthermore, an underdeveloped educational system resulting from the ban on Albanian schools during Turkish rule hindered social and economic development. A small percentage of the population was educated in foreign schools and the development and nationalization of the school system was not achieved until the mid-1930s. Albania's economic situation largely dictated its political path, as it had to be dependent on outside powers for economic assistance. Between 1925 and 1939 Albania was subsidized and controlled by fascist Italy, which, among other measures, founded the Albanian National Bank and the Society for the Economic Development of Albania. Despite or perhaps due to Italian interference Albania remained an agricultural country with virtually no industrial development and its natural resources were untapped. Moreover, the Italians used their economic presence to gain political domination of Albania. Under communist rule Albania relied first on Yugoslavia, then the Soviet Union, and then China, for aid. However, beginning in 1976 the Albanian government followed an economic policy of "self-reliance," essentially autarky, and prohibited the acceptance of aid from any capitalist source. Through a series of five-year plans the government sought to increase productivity, exports, and self-sufficiency in food, but these measures did not meet with long-term success. By the mid-1980s Albania's economy was on the precipice of a major fall. In 1990, after the collapse of communism in Eastern Europe, the government moved toward decentralizing economic reform, but the measures proved to be insufficient and the economy collapsed. Between 1992 and 1996 the Albanian government implemented a macroeconomic stabilization program, which, with the help of strong leadership and popular compliance, brought about substantial economic progress. However, the national economy met with yet another significant setback when a network of pyramid schemes collapsed in 1997.

INDEPENDENCE

Albania was first recognized as an independent state in 1913 with the Treaty of Bucharest, which ended the Second Balkan War. It was organized under the protection of the Great Powers as a constitutional monarchy, and led by Prince William of Wied (1876–1945), a German army captain. As early as the summer of 1914 uprisings against the prince succeeded in divesting him of power. After the outbreak of World War I Albania fell into a state of political chaos. In September 1914 Prince William left Albania to fight with the German army on the eastern front.

During World War I Albania was occupied by at least seven foreign powers, and was used as a bargaining chip in the creation of wartime alliances. In 1914 Serbia and Montenegro occupied parts of northern Albania, Greece occupied southern Albania, and Italy occupied Vlorë. When Serbia was defeated in 1915, Austria-Hungary and Bulgaria occupied two-thirds of the country. Furthermore, the Great Powers partitioned Albania in the secret Treaty of London, promising land to Italy, Greece, Serbia, and Montenegro, leaving only a small autonomous state in the central regions that also would be under Italy's control. At the end of the war most of Albania was in Italian hands. However, the Albanians sent a delegation, which included members from Albanian émigré communities, to the Paris Peace Conference in order to oppose the partitioning of their country and regain their independence, which they managed to secure with the support of Woodrow Wilson (1856–1924). In 1920 Albania was admitted into

A young Albanian girl takes part in the celebration of International Children's Day at her government-run kindergarten in Tirana, 12 June 1968. ©BETTMANN/CORBIS

the League of Nations as a sovereign country and the Italians withdrew.

The early interwar period saw a power struggle for political control of Albania, primarily between the Orthodox bishop Fan S. Noli (1882–1965) and Ahmed Zogu (1895–1961), both members of the Popular Party. Noli was a western-minded liberal who had been educated at Harvard and had strong ties to the Albanian expatriate movement in the United States. Zogu, the son of a chief of a central Albanian Muslim tribe, was politically conservative. Both men held offices in the government formed by the Popular Party in 1921; Noli served as foreign minister and Zogu as internal affairs minister. However, they quickly came into conflict. In 1922 Zogu became premier and with his supporters organized the Government Party. In response, Noli and like-minded leaders organized the broadly based Opposition Party of Democrats. Even though Zogu's party won parliamentary elections in 1924, an assassination attempt and financial scandal caused him to flee to Yugoslavia, and Noli became prime minister. During his brief time in power, Noli tried to introduce parliamentary democracy and internal economic, social, and infrastructural reforms. However, Zogu, supported by Yugoslav forces to which he had promised territorial gains, regained power, causing Noli to flee to Italy.

In December 1924–January 1925, Albania was proclaimed a republic of which Zogu was elected president for a seven-year term. He ruled with a new constitution that gave him dictatorial powers supported by the military. In 1928 parliament was dissolved with its consent and the constitution was amended to make Albania a kingdom and name Zogu as King Zog I. King Zog began to resist Italian attempts to gain increasing political and economic control of Albania and in 1934 signed trade agreements with Yugoslavia and Greece. Nonetheless, in 1939, no longer able to resist Italian pressure, which aimed at full occupation and colonization of Albania, King Zog and his family fled to London. In April 1939 Albania was united with Italy and declared an autonomous constitutional monarchy with Italian King Victor Emmanuel III (r. Italy 1900–1946, r. Albania 1939–1943) at the helm. When Germany defeated Yugoslavia in 1941 it gave the province of Kosovo, as well as a Greek province that had a small Albanian minority, to Albania. In 1942 two Albanian resistance groups emerged. First came the National Liberation Front, which was organized by the Communist Party, and shortly after Balli Kombetar, which was strongly nationalist. In 1941 the Albanian Communist Party (ACP) was created with the assistance of Yugoslav communists. The supporters of the party came largely from European-educated urban intellectuals and the landless southern peasants. Despite Allied efforts to unite the two resistance groups, they fought openly with each other, and the increasing strength of the National Liberation Front led the Ballists to collaborate with the occupiers. Following the example of the Josip Broz Tito (1892–1980)–led Yugoslav partisans, the National Liberation Front convened the National Congress in May 1944 and created the Antifascist Council of National Liberation, the supreme legislative body, and forbade King Zog from returning to Albania. At the second meeting of the Antifascist Council in October 1944 a provisional government was created and was led by Hoxha, a young European-educated teacher of Muslim Tosk descent. Hoxha was a veteran of the Spanish civil war and a member of the National Liberation Front. Working alongside Hoxha, mainly in his shadow, was Mehmet Shehu (1913–1981), a prominent communist leader in the provisional government.

COMMUNISM

Albania established a communist regime largely under Yugoslav and Soviet tutelage. The communists consolidated control and created a one-party system. In January 1946 the People's Republic of Albania was declared. It was led by Hoxha, who served as party general secretary, prime minister, foreign minister, and commander in chief. Through repression and terror, his government eliminated all opposition and assumed full control of the economy. The internal-affairs minister, Koçi Xoxe (1917–1949), oversaw the purges of the opposition. In 1948, following Tito's split with Joseph Stalin (1879–1953), Hoxha in turn broke with Belgrade, changed the name of the ACP to the Albanian Party of Labor (APL), and entered into closer alliance with the Soviets, who gave Albania economic and military aid. In 1949 Xoxe was secretly tried and executed for being "pro-Yugoslav." Hoxha was a dogmatic Stalinist, and in the 1950s Albania became known as the most Stalinist regime in Eastern Europe. Albania avoided the destalinization process that swept throughout the region following Nikita Khrushchev's (1894–1971) denunciation of Stalin and instead pursued increased repression and centralization, key elements of which were the full collectivization of agriculture, the initiation of a cultural revolution, and the repression of religion. At the same time, Hoxha broke with Khrushchev and began forming an alliance with China, which also opposed the USSR's policies. China replaced the Soviet Union as Albania's source of economic and military aid. Cooperation between the two countries peaked in the 1960s and ended when China began to normalize relations with the United States in 1971. Albania increasingly moved into international isolation, extreme centralization, and internal repression marked by a series of purges in the 1970s. In 1980 Hoxha chose as his successor Ramiz Alia, who assumed responsibilities in 1983 and succeeded Hoxha as president and secretary of APL upon his death in 1985. In choosing Alia, Hoxha overlooked Shehu, who was found dead in 1981. The regime claimed he had committed suicide and denounced him as a spy. Some claim that Hoxha murdered Shehu because he opposed Hoxha's isolationist policies.

POSTCOMMUNISM

Despite Alia's efforts to reform and make his reforms appear democratic, discontent with the APL only grew. In July 1990 thousands of Albanians stormed foreign embassies in Tirana trying to flee the country. This "embassy incident" undercut the legitimacy of the Albanian regime and garnered unprecedented international attention to its problems. In response the regime moved toward liberal reforms and privatization. Largely under the pressure of students and liberal-minded intellectuals, Albania slowly began to move toward political pluralism. In December 1990 the first opposition party, the Albanian Democratic Party (ADP), was formed, and Sali Berisha (b. 1944), a cardiologist and public critic of the communist regime, was elected chair of the party in 1991. That same year multiparty elections were held for the first time since the 1920s. The ADP won 30 percent of parliamentary seats and the APL gained 67 percent, although Alia lost his seat. A few months later Albania passed an interim constitution and changed the name of the country to the Republic of Albania, which was declared to be a parliamentary state. The new republic was led by Prime Minister Fatos Nano (b. 1942), a moderate communist, and Alia as president. Popular protests and strikes forced the resignation of this government. In the 1992 elections the ADP took control of the government and Berisha became president. The government fell in 1997 largely due to corruption and the economic crisis brought on by the collapse of pyramid schemes. The socialists came back into power under President Rexhep Meidani (b. 1944). However, in the 2005 general election, the ADP won the majority in the parliament and Sali Berisha became prime minister. Albania in the twenty-first century continues to face many challenges on the road to democratization and economic reform.

See also **Communism; Hoxha, Enver; Italy; Kosovo; World War I; World War II; Yugoslavia.**

BIBLIOGRAPHY

Biberaj, Elez. *Albania in Transition: The Rocky Road to Democracy.* Boulder, Colo., 1998.

Clunies-Ross, Anthony, and Petar Sudar, eds. *Albania's Economy in Transition and Turmoil, 1990–1997.* Brookfield, Vt., 1998.

Fischer, Bernd J. *Albania at War, 1939–1945.* West Lafayette, Ind., 1999.

Hibbert, Reginald. *Albania's National Liberation Struggle: The Bitter Victory.* London and New York, 1991.

O'Donnell, James S. *A Coming of Age: Albania under Enver Hoxha.* Boulder, Colo., and New York, 1999.

Pipa, Arshi. *Albanian Stalinism: Ideo-Political Aspects.* Boulder, Colo., and New York, 1990.

Prifti, Peter R. *Socialist Albania since 1944: Domestic and Foreign Developments.* Cambridge, Mass., 1978.

Skendi, Stavro, ed. *Albania.* New York, 1956.

Stavrianos, L. S. *The Balkans since 1453.* New York, 2000.

Vickers, Miranda. *The Albanians: A Modern History.* London and New York, 1995.

Zickel, Raymond E., and Walter R. Iwaskiw. *Albania: A Country Study.* 2nd ed. Washington, D.C., 1994.

JOVANA L. KNEŽEVIĆ

ALBERT I (1875–1934; r. 1909–1934), king of Belgium.

Albert, son of Philip, Earl of Flanders, and Mary, Princess of Hohenzollern-Sigmaringen, was born in Brussels on 8 April 1875. The early death of Prince Leopold (1859–1869), the Earl of Hainaut and the son of King Leopold II (r. 1865–1909), raised the young prince to the first rank in the order of succession to the Belgian throne. Albert, King Leopold II's nephew, studied at the Military Academy and subsequently served a long term in the Grenadiers Regiment. In October 1900 in Munich, Prince Albert married Elizabeth (1875–1965), the Duchess of Bavaria and daughter of Duke Charles-Theodore and Maria Josepha, Infanta of Portugal. In the ophthalmological clinic founded by her father, Elizabeth had acquired elementary nursing skills, which she put to use during World War I. The royal couple gave birth to three children: the future Leopold III (1901–1983), the Duke of Brabant, who was king of Belgium from 1934 to 1951; Charles (1903–1983), the Earl of

Flanders and Regent of the kingdom from 1945 to 1950; and Marie-José (1906–2001), who was to marry Umberto, the Prince of Piedmont and, briefly, king of Italy (for about a month in 1946).

Albert, although long overshadowed by the figure of Leopold II, carefully prepared himself for his future royal responsibilities. In 1898 he undertook a first voyage to the United States, where he was profoundly impressed by the country's industrial development. In 1907 Leopold II made him Lieutenant General of the Kingdom, initiating him to national affairs. He also invited Albert to undertake a study trip to the Congo. Following Leopold II's death on 17 December 1909, King Albert made his solemn entry into Brussels, the national capital, on 23 December. His accession to the throne immediately aroused great enthusiasm, strengthened by the fact that the young king knew how to make himself popular: he went out to meet the crowd and shake people's hands; he showed his family and openly proclaimed his faith in modernity. The first few years of his reign were relatively calm. Belgium, a wealthy and prosperous nation, manifested its vitality by organizing large international exhibitions (in Brussels in 1910 and in Ghent in 1913), which were occasions for the royal couple to welcome a great number of foreign heads of state. In early 1914 the people of Belgium, placing an almost excessive trust in their country's neutrality, did not imagine that the nation would soon be plunged into war and be forced to take part in the conflict. Since the events of 1830 Belgium had taken no part in the various conflicts that shook Europe throughout the nineteenth century. On 23 July 1914 Austro-Hungary issued an ultimatum to Serbia. A few days later the news of the Austrian declaration of war spread rapidly. The Belgian neutrality and summer quietude were suddenly shattered by the German ultimatum demanding free passage of German troops across the national territory. If Belgium accepted, it would be granted compensation and protection; if it did not, war would be declared. The answer was to be given within twelve hours. King Albert, the chief secretary, and the government immediately gathered to voice Belgium's answer, a flat and irrevocable refusal. Belgium was invaded on 4 August 1914. On the same day, the houses of parliament met in an extraordinary session, in which King Albert made a speech that was to become an historic

landmark. On his way to parliament he crossed the city on his horse, in full military array, acclaimed by a delirious crowd voicing an unprecedented enthusiasm. As the epitome of Belgian unity in face of the German occupation, he was to take on the status of a national myth. On 5 August he personally took command of the armed forces, in accordance with the Belgian constitutional custom ("I am leaving Brussels to take my place at your head," he told the soldiers), and spent the four years of the conflict leading the troops. In October 1914, refusing to flee, he made what turned out to be the most important decision of the war, namely to stop the retreat of the Belgian army and hold his ground on Belgian soil along the Yser River. There, the Belgian army clung to and defended the last plot of national territory, resisting in the trenches and not yielding an inch. During the conflict, the royal couple took up residence in La Panne, at the seaside. Feeling that the royal family had a duty to set a perfect example, King Albert actually descended into the trenches to lead his army, and Queen Elizabeth became the soldiers' "White Angel," a devoted nurse caring for the soldiers wounded at the front. Before leaving Brussels, the queen opened the Royal Palace to make room for a hospital facility to provide first aid, which was to function throughout the war and which came to be known as the Royal Palace Ambulance. "Poor Belgium," the small heroic nation martyred by its occupiers, attracted the admiration of the whole world. This admiration was to focus on the figure of King Albert, the incarnation of the nation's suffering, pride, and victory. This enthusiasm was even strengthened by the contrast with his predecessor Leopold II, the end of whose reign had been marred by corruption and the Congo scandals. The contrast enhanced the image of Albert as a pure, knightly figure. The fact that he personally took command of the army also had significant consequences. More than once, he personally opposed pressure from the French and the English, who insisted that Belgium participate in large-scale Allied offensives. Albert, who did not believe that such attacks could be successful, was averse to wasting his soldiers' blood and reducing his small army, which he felt to constitute the last stronghold able to guarantee Belgium's independence. In this manner, he preserved the Belgian army from the bloodbaths of Verdun and the Marne. King

Albert waited until 1918 to launch an offensive that he considered to be feasible and which proved to be decisive. On 22 November, when the victorious army entered the liberated capital, with the king riding his horse at its head, popular joy was at its peak. In his famous throne speech to the parliament, the King paid a tribute to the Yser troops and announced the opening of a Dutch-speaking university and the introduction of universal male suffrage "because of the equality of all in suffering and endurance." After the war, the sovereign's activity focused on matters of national security, the interests of the colony, and scientific research. In 1919 he visited the United States, where his bravery during the war earned him a triumphant welcome. He returned to the Congo between 1928 and 1932. Fascinated by scientific and technological progress, the king had a keen interest in the development of railroads, aeronautics, and wireless communication (he actually installed a radio transmitter in an outbuilding in the Palace Gardens, and the first radio broadcast of a concert was transmitted from the Royal Palace). An active sportsman, he would regularly go mountain climbing, and it is during a solitary ascent at Marche-les-Dames that he fell to his death. The fatal accident struck the popular imagination and strengthened the King Albert myth even more. The sudden violent death of the king gave rise to the most extravagant rumors both in Belgium and abroad about the causes of his demise. In May 1934 a British colonel voiced before the House of Commons his opinion that King Albert had been murdered, and some people still credit the hypothesis of a murder or a suicide. The tragic death of King Albert, hero of the Yser and knight-king, has raised him to a privileged status in Belgium's collective memory.

See also **Belgium; World War I.**

BIBLIOGRAPHY

Thielemans, Marie-Rose, and Émile Vandewoude. *Le Roi Albert au travers de ses lettres inédites, 1882–1916.* Brussels, 1982.

van Kalken, Frans. "Albert Ier." In *Biographie nationale de Belgique,* edited by J. Balteau, M. Barroux, and M. Prevost. Brussels, 1957.

van Ypersele, Laurence. *Roi Albert: histoire d'un mythe.* Ottignes, Belgium, 1995.

VALERIE PIETTE

ALCOHOL. The production and consumption of alcoholic beverages have been characteristic features of European societies for centuries. Europe is the origin of beverage forms known the world over: distilled beverages such as gin, vodka, scotch, and cognac; wines that include champagne, Bordeaux, Burgundy, and Chianti; and beer styles such as lager, stout, and ale. Indeed, Europe has been the fount of the global flow of alcohol over the last several centuries, having exported both the taste for alcohol through worldwide emigration and colonization and the means of production through advanced knowledge of commercial viticulture, brewing, and distilling. Indigenous forms of alcohol have survived throughout the world together with these imported—and sometimes imposed—traditions, but nearly everywhere these European beverages and their many cousins, with their familiar brand names, have been associated with affluence, upward mobility, and a Western cultural outlook. The global market for alcoholic beverages totals about 780 billion dollars, and western European consumption accounts for 280 billion dollars, more than a third of the total. If alcohol is a factor in the global economy, it is also a factor in global health. The World Health Organization estimated for the year 2000 that alcohol consumption was a major factor in the global burden of disease, a measure of premature deaths and disability. Alcohol-related death and disability accounted for about 10 percent of the global burden of disease in developed countries, making it the third most important risk.

CULTURAL AND HISTORICAL FOUNDATIONS

Alcohol, of course, is no ordinary commodity. Its special character is recognized in myth and layers of symbolic association and cultural meaning that are not far below the surface even in the early twenty-first century. For the ancient Greeks, alcohol was an extraordinary gift of the gods, bestowed on humanity by Dionysus. Wine has played an important symbolic role in both Christian and Jewish rituals and traditions, and alcohol is closely linked to secular rituals of reciprocity and trust. Glimpses of this archaeology of meaning may still be seen—in toasts at dinner parties among family and friends; in the rituals of drinking together to conclude

FIGURE 1

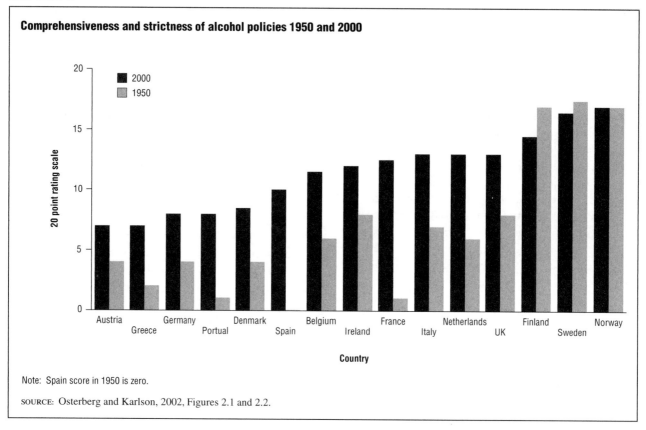

Comprehensiveness and strictness of alcohol policies 1950 and 2000

Note: Spain score in 1950 is zero.

SOURCE: Osterberg and Karlson, 2002, Figures 2.1 and 2.2.

important business dealings; in elaborate wedding ceremonies, which combine the convivial blessing of the couple and the sealing of the marriage contract; in the practice of alternate treating that confirms equality of status and solidifies social ties; and in the drinking bouts of young men—comrades in arms, teammates, fraternity brothers, or workmates—who test their ability to stand up to alcohol's powers, and thereby draw a circle of shared experience and trust around themselves.

Alcohol's duality as a food-drug is the foundation of its special cultural significance. Alcoholic beverages provide calories and refreshment; they nourish but also produce bodily harm. Alcohol is also an intoxicant—a source of pleasure and release but also of danger and disorder. Every society that has known the benefits of alcohol has also known its costs. For that reason, alcohol consumption is always closely regulated, both by formal institutional sanctions and, perhaps more importantly, by informal social controls that enforce standards of decorum through peer pressure, gossip, and ostracism. Together, they define who can drink,

when they can drink, with whom they can drink, and how they should behave.

Over time, alcohol has become available in increasing quantities to more and more people in European societies and around the world. The democratization of access to alcohol accelerated rapidly in European societies beginning in the late eighteenth and early nineteenth centuries. The intersection of the spread of rising wages and growing concentrations of people in towns and cities with the commercialization and industrialization of alcohol production and distribution made alcohol consumption more affordable, more frequent, and more visible. As a result, the discussion of the causes, consequences, and control of popular drinking behavior became a major public issue in the industrializing societies of Europe and North America. Led by middle-class Protestant reformers, temperance advocates in all these societies eschewed alcohol themselves and advocated greater controls on the drinking of others, particularly of the working men whose drinking, often boisterous and public, seemed a threat to the middle-class

FIGURE 2

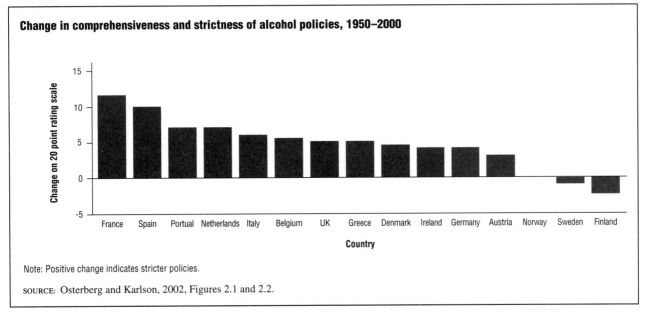

Change in comprehensiveness and strictness of alcohol policies, 1950–2000

Note: Positive change indicates stricter policies.

SOURCE: Osterberg and Karlson, 2002, Figures 2.1 and 2.2.

values of self-discipline, thrift, and domesticity upon which economic prosperity and social order were thought to depend. For the people doing the drinking, on the other hand, the consumption of alcohol was a first form of modern consumer satisfaction and a focal point for their leisure-time activities and limited opportunities for relaxation and socializing outside of work.

American prohibition in the 1920s was undoubtedly the global culmination and most extreme manifestation of the antialcohol sentiment that characterized leading sectors of Western societies in the nineteenth century. Its failure, and the collapse of the utopian expectations that had accompanied the "noble experiment," also put a definitive end to any remaining grand designs for comprehensive alcohol reform in Europe. In the early 2000s alcohol consumption is a fully integrated part of the modern consumer economy in ways that would have been unimaginable at the beginning of the twentieth century, when the battle against alcohol was about to be won. The notion that alcohol consumption is a fundamental obstacle to social integration and progress has almost universally been replaced by an acceptance of alcoholic beverages as part of the good life that Western economic development promised in the first place. Shaped by modern advertising, marketing, and packaging techniques, alcohol consumption is thoroughly normalized and domesticated, a part

of home life as well as public social life. From an economic standpoint, the production and distribution of alcohol and associated hospitality businesses make significant contributions to local and national economies. Despite long-term trends toward consolidation of ownership and production, the alcoholic beverages business remains relatively disaggregated and local compared to other global commodities. Producers and distributors are part of the social fabric of any local, regional, or national community and constitute one set of interests the state must balance in formulating alcohol policy.

The social context—and meaning—of drinking substantially changed over the course of the twentieth century. By the time of World War I, a transition was under way from the nineteenth-century era in which alcohol was widely considered an inferior consumer good associated with poverty and deprivation (even if a means of relief from them) to a world in which alcohol consumption was more universally recognized as a mark of affluence and drinking a means of partaking in a consumer society and demonstrating one's standing within it. The relative prosperity of the 1920s, and alcohol's association with the avant-garde, the Jazz Age, and the cosmopolitan life of the great European cities, helped change the tide. After World War II, alcohol consumption increased rapidly into the 1970s as European economies rebuilt and prospered.

HISTORIOGRAPHY AND INTERPRETATIVE PARADIGMS

While social observers have commented on European drinking habits for centuries, only since the 1970s have historians made alcohol a subject of sustained study. Beginning with Brian Harrison's *Drink and the Victorians* in 1971, historians have covered the major European countries, both explicating the history of alcohol production, consumption, and control as a subject in its own right and illuminating larger social, cultural, and political themes through the particularly revealing lens that alcohol provides. Their monographs have examined the role of alcohol in popular culture; the growth of the alcohol industry; the motives, methods, and accomplishments of temperance reformers; and the roles political parties and government agencies played in shaping alcohol policy. A substantial number of article-length studies extend and complement this work, and brief treatments of alcohol-related topics are more and more often included in wider studies as a means of illustrating particular issues in social and cultural history. The two-volume international encyclopedia *Alcohol and Temperance in Modern History* (2003) cites much of this literature. The Alcohol and Drugs History Society, founded in 1979 as the Alcohol and Temperance History Group, publishes the *Social History of Alcohol and Drugs: An Interdisciplinary Journal* (formerly *The Social History of Alcohol Review*) and maintains a useful Web site: http://historyofalcoholanddrugs.typepad.com.

Virtually all of this work by professional historians focuses on the nineteenth century (or earlier eras), with coverage typically ending with World War I. However, alcohol-related themes in twentieth-century Europe have received attention from other disciplines—sociology, public health, and medicine, for example—and much of this work does provide historical coverage, if not historical interpretation. Economic and business aspects of alcohol production, marketing, distribution, and consumption are also well documented.

Historians and policy analysts have distinguished three eras in modern efforts to conceptualize and manage the individual and social costs associated with alcohol consumption. The nineteenth century was the era of voluntary associations, the creation of temperance organizations, and the mobilization of middle-class sentiment in campaigns

of public education about the dangers of alcohol and efforts to persuade legislatures and state agencies to tighten alcohol controls. Temperance reformers, of course, saw much more harm than good in alcohol, linking it to poverty, urban squalor, and a host of contemporary social problems. They operated with two complementary theories about the ultimate source of problems with alcohol. Many proponents of alcohol control believed that alcohol was inherently debilitating, a threat to all who consumed it; others emphasized the moral failings and weak character of those who drank to excess, flaws they saw in some social groups more than others. (Some socialists and trade-unionists offered an alternative view: that problem drinking was the result of capitalist labor conditions.) The substantial mobilization of social energies around the "drink question" largely ended with World War I. Europe had other preoccupations after the war, and the closely watched failure of American prohibition seemed to confirm that a political solution to the drink question could not be achieved.

After the end of this period of public mobilization, alcohol concerns were left primarily to experts in the health professions. As in the United States, the "disease concept of alcoholism" gained ascendancy. The predominant theory about the source of problems with alcohol no longer blamed alcohol itself or the moral failings of drinkers; experts pointed instead to a predisposition in some individuals—a disease—whose manifestation was an inability to control alcohol consumption. The focus shifted from public policy measures that might influence the drinking behavior of the whole population, or substantial segments of it, to individuals susceptible to drinking problems and their appropriate treatment. In extreme cases, as in Nazi eugenics policy, treatment could mean sterilization rather than individual rehabilitation. This basic paradigm for explaining and managing problems with alcohol carried into the post–World War II welfare state, which generously supported therapeutic interventions to manage individual problems with alcohol. Meanwhile, under prevailing liberal economic policies and with the lowering of trade barriers within Europe, the business of producing, marketing, and distributing alcoholic beverages expanded largely unchecked by government intervention, and European alcohol consumption increased rapidly.

FIGURE 3

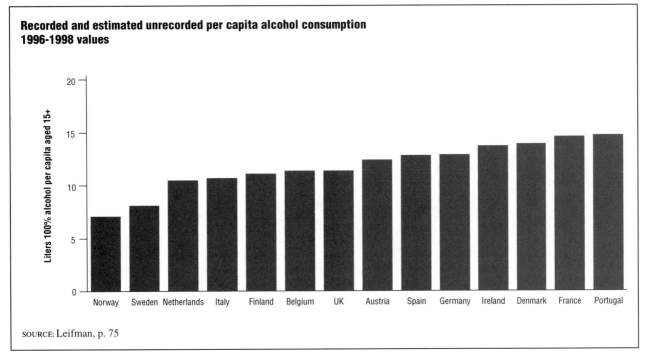

Recorded and estimated unrecorded per capita alcohol consumption 1996-1998 values

SOURCE: Leifman, p. 75

Beginning in the mid-1970s, a new public health focus emerged in European (and North American) discussions about alcohol. Epidemiological analyses underscored the collective social harm that was the correlate of the individual freedom to drink, and these discussions pointed again to general public policy solutions rather than just individual therapeutic ones. This movement has been called neo-prohibitionist because of its renewed focus on alcohol itself, rather than on the individual drinker, and on measures to limit aggregate supply and demand. The World Health Organization and the European Union have supported cooperative studies and strategies across the European states. Even within this public health paradigm there have been substantial debates about how to balance the interests of consumers and producers with the overall interests of the state and society. Alongside originally proposed prevention strategies aimed at reducing aggregate consumption on the theory that alcohol-related harm is directly correlated to the total volume of consumption in any given society (the so-called Lederman total consumption model), a variant perspective has emerged more recently that focuses on harm reduction and aims not primarily at reducing overall consumption but at mitigating risk.

TRENDS AND NATIONAL VARIATIONS IN ALCOHOL REGULATION

Even though debates about alcohol have not had the place on the social and political agenda they occupied before World War I, European societies have continued to adjust social policies regarding alcohol to balance the often conflicting interests between individual rights and social consequences, between economic benefits and social costs. In a survey of the evolution of alcohol control policies in fifteen western European countries since 1950, Esa Österberg and Thomas Karlson found a pattern of increasing government engagement. They developed a twenty-point rating scale to evaluate the strictness of formal alcohol controls in each society, considering such matters as drinking age, hours of distribution, marketing restrictions, excise taxes, drunk-driving laws, and educational initiatives.

Figure 1 compares the 2000 rating score to the 1950 rating score for each country in the study. The chart is ordered from left to right from the currently least restrictive (Austria) to the currently most restrictive (Norway). The three Scandinavian countries have had the most restrictive policies over the entire period, though they have become marginally less restrictive. Every other country has become more restrictive over the last half century, with the

FIGURE 4

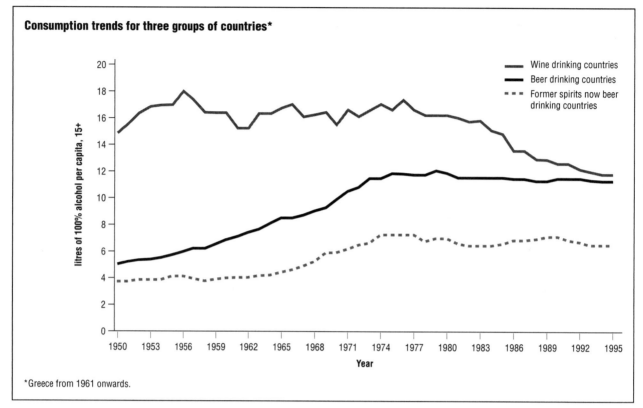

Consumption trends for three groups of countries*

*Greece from 1961 onwards.

biggest changes among the wine-producing countries (France, Greece, Italy, Portugal, and Spain)—these are also the areas where per capita consumption has declined the most. Figure 2 shows the total change in the rating scale for each country over the fifty-year study period.

Although increased social attention to alcohol issues is evident in these trends, the forms of state involvement in the alcohol realm have been changing, with fewer direct controls on production and retail—and hence consumer freedom—and more efforts to control outcomes through education programs and the regulation of drinking and driving. The effect has been less to limit supply and consumer choice than to educate consumers about responsible drinking and to set clearer limits on socially accepted behavior.

TRENDS AND NATIONAL VARIATIONS IN ALCOHOL CONSUMPTION

In the fifteen European societies covered in the European Comparative Alcohol Study (2002), aggregate per capita consumption rose rapidly and steadily from 1950 to the late 1970s, with a total

increase of more than 50 percent, from the equivalent of approximately eight liters of 100 percent alcohol per capita to slightly more than twelve. Since the late 1970s, per capita consumption has been in a gradual and unabated decline, falling from more than twelve to approximately eleven liters per capita by 1995. The overall growth is clearly associated with Europe's economic recovery, the spread of consumer values, and growing purchasing power. The gradual decline is associated with moderating influences associated with increasing awareness of alcohol's risks, the growing popularity of health and fitness as part of consumer culture, the marketing of newer, nonalcoholic beverages, and the breakdown—particularly in the wine-drinking cultures—of the close-knit traditional family, whose mealtimes together almost invariably involved alcohol consumption. Figure 3 provides a comparative profile of per capita consumption in the ECAS study countries.

Europe is often divided according to predominant beverage preference into wine-drinking, beer-drinking, and spirits-drinking regions. These preferences are rooted in national production

FIGURE 5

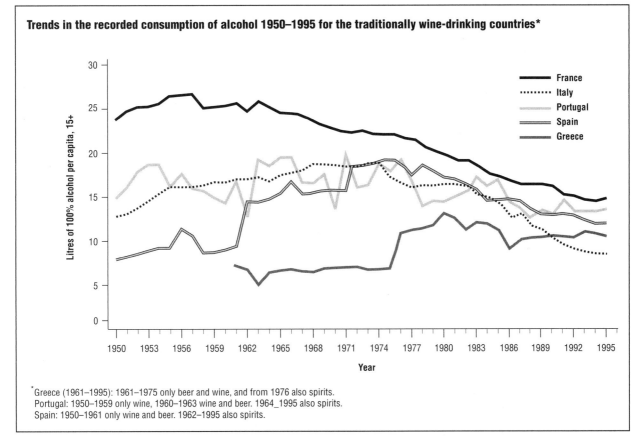

Trends in the recorded consumption of alcohol 1950–1995 for the traditionally wine-drinking countries*

France
Italy
Portugal
Spain
Greece

Litres of 100% alcohol per capita, 15+

Year

*Greece (1961–1995): 1961–1975 only beer and wine, and from 1976 also spirits.
Portugal: 1950–1959 only wine, 1960–1963 wine and beer. 1964_1995 also spirits.
Spain: 1950–1961 only wine and beer. 1962–1995 also spirits.

patterns, relative taxation and price, and long-standing consumer preferences, especially among the older generations. Among younger consumers, especially young professionals, these traditional patterns hold less sway. While these regional differences have receded in importance, they continue to be evident. In the 1950s consumption in seven of the fifteen study countries was dominated by a single beverage type that accounted for 75 percent or more of total consumption; by the 1990s, only one country (Italy) fit that description. Still, if the differences are less pronounced, they remain important. In the 1990s, a single beverage type accounted for 50 percent or more of total consumption in twelve of the fifteen study countries. Figure 4 depicts aggregate consumption trends in each of the three consumption groups.

The wine-producing and -consuming countries share a Mediterranean climate, a Catholic heritage, and drinking traditions that are deeply entwined in everyday life, especially at mealtimes. In general, per capita consumption is highest in these

countries, and drinking is an everyday occurrence. Women are more likely to consume alcohol regularly than in other regions, but even in the wine-drinking countries they drink much less often and consume smaller quantities than men. Young people are acculturated to drinking practices and behavioral expectations gradually and from an early age within extended family circles. Only recently have minimum drinking ages been established, generally sixteen. (In Italy and Spain, there is no age limit if a young person is accompanied by an adult.) Virtually all adults consume alcohol on occasion, if not daily, and very few people abstain from alcohol completely. It is in these countries, however, that per capita consumption has been declining, particularly in France, as awareness of the health risks of alcohol consumption has begun to balance appreciation for its benefits, especially among younger consumers. Overall, per capita consumption in the wine-drinking countries was fairly stable from 1950 through the late 1970s at an average of about sixteen liters of 100 percent alcohol per capita aged fifteen and over; consumption has fallen

FIGURE 6

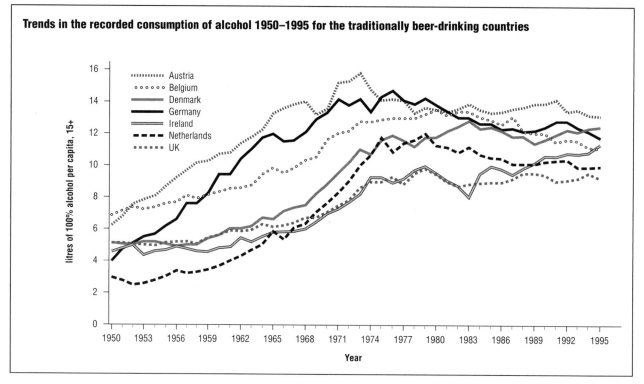

Trends in the recorded consumption of alcohol 1950–1995 for the traditionally beer-drinking countries

steadily since then, bottoming at twelve liters per capita in 1995, a 25 percent reduction. France dominates, with a long-term, steady decline from the mid-1960s level of twenty-five liters per capita to about fifteen liters per capita in 1995, a 40 percent reduction. Consumption has also fallen sharply in Italy, but only from the mid-1970s, when it stood at about nineteen liters per capita, decreasing to nine liters per capita in 1995, a 40 percent reduction. Figure 5 depicts the per capita consumption trend for each of the predominantly wine-drinking countries.

The predominantly beer-producing and -consuming countries include Austria, Belgium, Denmark, Germany, Ireland, the Netherlands, and the United Kingdom. Wine has become more popular over time in these countries, but beer is still the predominant beverage, accounting for 50 percent or more of all beverage consumption in each nation. The post–World War II consumption curves of all these countries look very similar, with steadily rising consumption from 1950 to the early 1970s and essentially stable consumption thereafter. Average per capita consumption in the beer-drinking countries more than doubled from 1950 to the early 1970s, increasing from five to twelve liters per

per capita, where it essentially remained through the mid-1990s. Per capita consumption is highest in the Austria, followed closely by Germany. Figure 6 shows per capita consumption trends in each of the predominantly beer-consuming countries.

The classic spirits-consuming countries in the ECAS study are Finland, Norway, and Sweden. In all three countries, at least 50 percent of total consumption was in the form of spirits in the early 1950s, but by the mid-1990s the role of spirits had been reduced by half. Beer, and to a lesser extent wine, have played increasing roles in these societies. The general trend since World War II shows stable consumption in the 1950s and early 1960s at about four liters per capita, then a rapid rise from the mid-1960s to the mid-1970s, with consumption reaching more than seven liters per capita, a 75 percent increase, and remaining generally stable at that level through the mid-1990s. Norway and Sweden conform to this general pattern, while Finland appears to be a special case, with a doubling of consumption in the early 1970s, from four to eight liters per capita, and an increase to nearly ten liters per capita in the early 1990s before a period of declining consumption began.

FIGURE 7

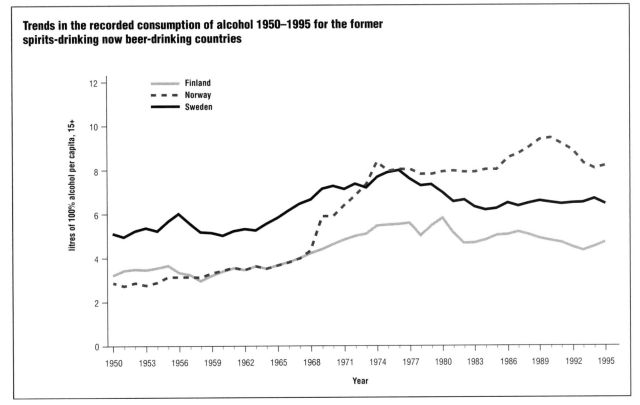

Trends in the recorded consumption of alcohol 1950–1995 for the former spirits-drinking now beer-drinking countries

Figure 7 charts per capita consumption trends for the traditional spirits-consuming countries.

SUMMARY

The production and consumption of alcoholic beverages have deep roots in European culture. Like all other societies that use alcohol, European societies have developed both formal institutional means and informal cultural norms to regulate the production and consumption of alcohol and to balance its benefits and risks. The nations of western Europe and North America experienced rapid changes in the availability of alcohol and the social context of drinking during the late eighteenth and early nineteenth centuries, and alcohol consumption was a focal point in discussions about how to create an orderly society that would mitigate the social problems and social conflicts connected with rapid industrialization and urbanization. During the interwar years, discussions about alcohol were less prominently a part of debates about the major issues of the day, though of course every society had to continue its own form of regulatory watch over production and consumption. In general,

however, alcohol issues moved from the public realm of policy debate to the private realm of therapeutic intervention in the lives of the most conspicuous problem drinkers. This shift of focus allowed the production and consumption of alcohol to gain an accepted role in the modern consumer economy, and especially after World War II the combination of rising prosperity, new marketing techniques, and older drinking traditions led to rapidly rising consumption—no longer associated with the grinding conditions of industrialization and urbanization but with the spread of middle-class lifestyles and consumer values and the integration of alcohol into the home. Of course all of these trends can be decomposed into many layers of continuities and innovations, regional variations, and differences according to gender, age, ethnicity, religion, and social class. More recently, a new consciousness of the global social consequences of relatively unconstrained alcohol has prompted increased government attention, within and across the countries of Europe, and the advance of public health perspectives to the forefront. Europe is no longer a growth market for alcoholic beverages, but neither is it a region where dramatic state interventions are likely. A modus vivendi has been struck among producers, consumers, and the state to create a realm for informed consumer choice within a framework that combines individual therapeutic interventions with public health perspectives to mitigate alcohol's associated risks. This is a Sisyphean labor, as the dialectic among production, consumption, and control is constantly evolving in every society that enjoys Dionysus's wonderful, terrible gift.

See also **Diet and Nutrition; Drugs (Illegal); Public Health.**

BIBLIOGRAPHY

Alcohol, Society, and the State. Toronto, 1981.

Barrows, Susanna, and Robin Room, eds. *Drinking: Behavior and Belief in Modern History.* Berkeley, Calif., 1991.

Blocker, Jack S. J., David M. Fahey, and Ian R. Tyrell. *Alcohol and Temperance in Modern History: An International Encyclopedia.* Santa Barbara, Calif., 2003.

Heath, Dwight B., ed. *International Handbook on Alcohol and Culture.* Westport, Conn., 1995.

Jellinek, E. M. "The Symbolism of Drinking; a Culture-Historical Approach." *Journal of Studies on Alcohol* 38 (1977): 852–866.

Müller, Richard, and Harald Klingemann, eds. *From Science to Action?: One Hundred Years Later—Alcohol Policies Revisited.* Dordrecht, Netherlands, 2004. See especially essays by Thomas Babor, Irmgard Eisenbach-Stangl, and Barbara Lucas.

Norström, Thor, ed. *Alcohol in Postwar Europe: Consumption, Drinking Patterns, Consequences, and Policy Responses in Fifteen European Countries.* Stockholm, Sweden, 2002. See especially essays by Håkan Leifman and Esa Österberg and Thomas Karlsson.

Roberts, James S. "Long-Term Trends in the Consumption of Alcoholic Beverages." In *The State of Humanity,* edited by Julian L. Simon, 114–120. Oxford, U.K., 1995.

JAMES S. ROBERTS

ALEXANDER OF YUGOSLAVIA. *See* Yugoslavia.

ALFONSO XIII (1886–1941), a member of the Bourbon Dynasty, ruled as king of Spain from 1886 until 1931.

Alfonso XIII was born king; his father, Alfonso XII (r. 1875–1885), died six months before his birth. Alfonso XIII's mother, Queen María Christina of Habsburg-Lorraine (1858–1929), ruled as regent until he reached his sixteenth birthday. Alfonso came to his majority in 1902 in the midst of the political crisis caused by the Spanish-American War of 1898, in which Spain lost the remnants of its overseas empire. "Regenerationist" intellectuals and republicans blamed the ruling monarchist parties for the defeat and many called for an end to the monarchy.

Like many of his contemporaries, Alfonso XIII became caught up in the regenerationist fervor of the period, and during the early years of his reign he sought to use his limited constitutional powers to spur reform in the political system and modernize the economy. Deeply imbued with the military traditions of his upbringing, he also longed to restore Spanish prestige in international relations, and he supported the escalation of military operations in Spain's Moroccan protectorate. In 1909 a call-up of reservists sparked a week of bloody riots and church burnings in Barcelona in what became known as the *semana trágica.*

Spain remained neutral in World War I, but it could not avoid the social dislocation caused by wartime inflation and scarcity. With an Austrian mother and an English queen (Alfonso had married Princess Victoria Eugenia of Battenberg [1887–1969] in 1906), Alfonso was deeply affected by the war. He became an advocate for prisoners of war on both sides of the conflict, acting as a conduit for inquiries and money on behalf of prisoners' families. By 1917, however, his government was struggling with socialist and anarchosyndicalist strike movements, Catalan separatism, and unrest in the army. Alfonso and his ministers responded by crushing strike movements and retreating from prewar promises of reform.

The army's colonial adventures in Morocco culminated in a disastrous defeat at Anual in 1921. The setback sparked a wave of recriminations in the press and parliament. This, coupled with a surge in anarchosyndicalist violence in Barcelona, convinced many generals that the politicians were incapable of fending off the forces of revolution. By 1923 Alfonso XIII had come to share this view, and he did nothing to oppose the coup d'état of General Miguel Primo de Rivera y Orbaneja (1870–1930) in September of that year.

With the king's blessing, Primo de Rivera suspended the constitution and set up a military "directorate" that soon grew into a dictatorship lasting from 1923 to 1930. Alfonso was never entirely comfortable with the dictatorship, and republican and dynastic politicians alike accused him of violating his oath to uphold the constitution. Primo de Rivera restored order in Barcelona and in the Moroccan protectorate but failed to create a political apparatus that could stand without the backing of the army. Faced with a deteriorating economy and growing popular opposition to his regime, Primo stepped down in 1930, leaving the king to attempt to restore constitutional government amid growing social unrest. The king named General Damaso Berenguer (1873–1953) to head a government charged with holding general elections under the old constitution of 1876, but many political leaders refused to participate on the grounds that the king's connivance with the dictatorship required either abdication or a new constitution that would rein in the power of the crown and the military.

In the municipal elections of 12 April 1931, held under Berenguer's successor, Admiral Juan Bautista Aznar (1860–1933), monarchist candidates were defeated by the republican-socialist coalition in almost all major cities and provincial capitals across Spain. Spontaneous demonstrations proclaimed the Second Republic in town squares, and republican and socialist leaders demanded the king's abdication. The leaders of the army and civil guard warned that they could not vouch for the loyalty of their troops if it came to a confrontation in the streets. Most of the king's ministers counseled against resistance, and the king himself quickly realized the seriousness of the defeat. On 14 April he suspended his prerogatives and left for Paris with his family. The king spent the years of the Republic in exile in France and Italy, hoping that the republican experiment would end with his eventual return to power. He supported the uprising against the Republic led by General Francisco Franco (1892–1975) in 1936, but Franco and his nationalist backers regarded the king as too imbued with liberal parliamentarianism and prevented the royal family's return to Spain. Alfonso died in Rome in 1941.

See also **Franco, Francisco; Primo de Rivera, Miguel; Spain.**

BIBLIOGRAPHY

Alvarez Junco, José, and Adrian Shubert. *Spanish History since 1808.* London, 2000.

Ben-Ami, Shlomo. *Fascism from Above: The Dictatorship of Primo de Rivera in Spain, 1923–1930.* Oxford, U.K., 1983.

Borràs Betriu, Rafael. *El rey perjuro: Don Alfonso XIII y la caída de la Monarquía.* Barcelona, 1997.

Boyd, Carolyn P. *Praetorian Politics in Liberal Spain.* Chapel Hill, N.C., 1979.

Carr, Raymond. *Spain, 1808–1975.* 2nd ed. Oxford, U.K., 1982.

Cortés-Cabanillas, Julián. *Alfonso XIII: Vida, confesiones, y muerte.* Barcelona, 1956.

Fernández Almagro, Melchor. *Historia del reinado de Don Alfonso XIII.* Barcelona, 1933.

Gómez-Navarro, José Luis. *El régimen de Primo de Rivera. Reyes, dictaduras, y dictadores.* Madrid, 1991.

González Hernández, María Jesús. *El universo conservador de Antonio Maura.* Madrid, 1997.

Gortázar, Guillermo. *Alfonso XIII, hombre de negocios.* Madrid, 1986.

Hall, Morgan C. *Alfonso XIII y el ocaso de la Monarquía liberal, 1902–1923.* Madrid, 2005.

Herr, Richard. *An Historical Essay on Modern Spain.* Berkeley, Calif., 1971.

Moreno Luzón, Javier. *El Conde de Romanones: Caciquismo y política liberal.* Madrid, 1998.

Noel, Gerald. *Ena, Spain's English Queen.* London, 1984.

Payne, Stanley G. *Politics and the Military in Modern Spain.* Stanford, Calif., 1967.

Petrie, Sir Charles. *King Alfonso XIII and His Age.* London, 1967.

Romero Salvadó, Francisco. *Twentieth Century Spain: Politics and Society in Spain, 1898–1998.* New York, 1999.

Seco Serrano, Carlos. *Alfonso XIII y la crisis de la Restauración.* 3rd rev. ed. Madrid, 1992.

————. *Alfonso XIII.* Madrid, 2001.

Shubert, Adrian. *A Social History of Modern Spain.* London, 1990.

Tusell, Javier, and Genoveva G. Queipo de Llano. *Alfonso XIII: El rey polémico.* Madrid, 2001.

Ullman, Joan Connelly. *The Tragic Week: A Study of Anticlericalism in Spain, 1875–1912.* Cambridge, Mass., 1968.

MORGAN C. HALL

ALGERIA. Algeria, North Africa's largest country, began the twentieth century as a political part of Europe. It was the only one of France's colonies to be declared "an integral part of French territory" and its history had become intimately tied to that of France. This unusually close colonial connection was broken only by one of the century's costliest wars of independence, which lasted from 1954 to 1962. France's attempt to maintain the colonial tie led it to join Britain in a disastrous final defense of European imperialism at Suez in 1956 and brought down the French state with the collapse of the Fourth Republic in 1958.

FRENCH ALGERIA TO 1954

By 1914 France had considered Algeria French for eighty-four years; Algeria's economy and political system were oriented toward and controlled by metropolitan France, and by the approximately 720,000 settlers from various parts of Europe and the Mediterranean. In 1889 the children of European settlers had been granted French citizenship; they came to be called *pieds noirs* (black feet, a term of uncertain origin). This population included the indigenous Jewish population of northern Algeria, to whom French citizenship had been granted in 1870, despite the protests of European settlers, among whom anti-Semitism was widespread. The European population had almost complete control of the country's most productive land, along with its industry, infrastructure, and other assets, and it occupied almost all of the middle- and high-ranking positions in public services and the professions.

The majority of Algeria's population, the indigenous Arabic- and Berber-speaking Muslims, numbering between four and five million, were excluded from French citizenship (although they were considered to hold French nationality) and thus from equal civic and political rights. Until 1944 they were subject to repressive legislation, called the *régime de l'indigénat* (native status code), enacted in 1881 as emergency legislation for civilian-ruled territory after the end of the military conquest, which had begun in 1830 with the fall of the city of Algiers. As a subjugated and socially and economically dislocated population, Algerian political participation was limited to token

representation in municipal and regional councils and in the colonial and national assemblies. Algeria's administration was directed by the Government General, a department of the French Ministry of the Interior, and although the civilian European population in most of the country was governed in much the same way as it would be in any part of France, the colony's tax base and labor force rested disproportionately on the disenfranchised and repressed Algerian population.

Algeria had been declared an integral part of France after the Revolution of 1848 overthrew the monarchy of King Louis-Philippe (r. 1830–1848) and briefly reinstated republican government. Although the Second Republic lasted only until 1851, Algeria's integral status, which the republic had proclaimed, was reaffirmed by all succeeding French governments for over a century. In 1870 settlers and their lobbyists blamed a major rebellion on the prevailing system of military rule. With the return of republican government once more in 1871, after the collapse of the Second Empire in the Franco-Prussian War (1870), civilian rule was affirmed in the colony, with local self-government by colonial municipalities and a civilian governor general. Only the Saharan territories in the south remained the exclusive domain of the military. The European population thus gained republican and democratic self-rule and extensions of their rights, which bolstered French sovereignty in Algeria against the claims of other European powers (especially Italy). In 1898 the colonial population was accorded its own colony-wide assembly, the *délégations financières,* which exercised budgetary autonomy for Algeria within the wider French state. At the same time, demands on the Muslim Algerian population continued to increase while their legal status and economic standing worsened. In 1911, partly in response to decrees making them subject to military conscription, some four thousand Algerians fled the country. Between 1914 and 1918, around 173,000 Muslim Algerians (including 87,500 volunteers) served in the French army in World War I; 25,000 Muslim and 22,000 European Algerians were killed.

The Algerian contribution to the war became a major justification for reform after 1918, and a series of proposals were made both by groups claiming to represent Algerians' interests, especially the Algerian Muslim Congress of 1936, and by liberal French politicians, notably the antifascist Popular Front government, which gained power in that same year. The great majority of colonial settlers and colonial lobbyists in Paris, however, not only feared losing their dominance in the colony but believed that French presence could be maintained only by force against what they called native xenophobia and resistance. Like Algerian nationalists later, the European Algerians never believed that equal coexistence was possible, and they saw every demand for Algerian rights as a threat to their very existence. The various reforms that were advanced from 1919 to 1944 and that were not blocked in parliament by the colonial lobby therefore had limited impact on the fundamental problems of the colonial system.

From World War I onward, Algerian workers began migrating to metropolitan France in large numbers, and it was among the emigrant laborers in Paris that a radical, populist nationalism demanding Algerian independence began. From its creation in 1926, this movement gained support among Algerians in France, and in 1936 the Algerian People's Party (PPA) that emerged from it set up branches in Algeria. On 8 May 1945, demonstrations marking the end of World War II turned into an aborted attempt at nationalist insurrection in parts of eastern Algeria and 103 Europeans were killed. Estimates of the number of Algerians killed in the resulting repression, both by the settlers' militia and by the regular army, navy, and air force, range from 1,500 to 45,000. PPA militants began to prepare for a war of independence.

WAR, INDEPENDENCE, AND DEVELOPMENT, 1954 TO 1978

The Algerian war of independence began with coordinated armed actions by the Front de Libération Nationale (FLN, National Liberation Front) on the night of 31 October 1954 and ended when a ceasefire was announced on 19 March 1962. In between, the war brought down the parliamentary fourth French republic in 1958 and brought about the creation of the presidential Fifth Republic and the return to power of Charles de Gaulle. It gave rise in 1961 to an attempted revolt by French generals, the threat of civil war in France, and the emergence of European terrorist groups opposed to decolonization.

France fought a counterinsurgency that became a massive campaign of territorial control, forcibly relocating around three million people from the countryside into resettlement camps under military supervision, creating free-fire zones across rural Algeria, destroying some eight thousand villages, and putting some two million French soldiers into the field against an Algerian liberation army of only twenty-one thousand men and women at its height in mid-1958. Some three hundred thousand Algerians were made refugees, and according to demographic calculations another three hundred thousand were killed. The sufferings of the Algerian population—which included internments, disappearances, systematic torture, summary executions, and rapes—came to be symbolized by the official Algerian figure of one and a half million martyrs. Officially termed "operations for the maintenance of order," however, the conflict was unrecognized as a war by France until 1999, and its consequences in both France and Algeria have been the focus of renewed scholarly and public debate since the early 1990s.

After 1962, independent Algeria initially stood out on the world stage as a staunch advocate of Third World assertiveness, Cold War nonalignment, and global anti-imperialism, and as an inspirational model of revolutionary liberation and state-led industrial development for the European as well as the African and Middle Eastern Left. Algeria's independence, which was recognized by France on 3 July 1962 and officially celebrated in Algeria on 5 July, brought to power a faction of the FLN that the army supported, one which had been organized on the Tunisian and Moroccan frontiers in the final years of the war and which emerged successfully from internal struggles with control of the provisional government and other armed factions.

The country's first president, Ahmed Ben Bella, consolidated a bureaucratic, single-party system, proclaimed Algeria's socialist orientation, and sought to marginalize potential rivals within the regime. Some of these, however, grouped around the minister of defense, Houari Boumedienne, and removed Ben Bella in a coup d'état on 19 June 1965. Algeria under Boumedienne nationalized major industries and embarked on an ambitious program of state-led industrial development, partnerships with the Soviet bloc, and diplomatic

French soldiers patrol the market area of Algiers, known as the Casbah, January 1957. The normally bustling streets have been emptied by a general strike called by independence leaders prior to UN discussions concerning the fate of Algeria. ©BETTMANN/CORBIS

support for independence struggles in Palestine, Western Sahara (against neighboring Morocco, with which Algeria fought a brief war in October 1963), Vietnam, and sub-Saharan Africa. In 1964 Algeria's national currency, the dinar, replaced the franc, and Algeria, alone of France's major former territories, remained outside forums such as the Francophonie, an intergovernmental organization of France and the former colonies. In 1971 Algeria nationalized its oil wells and pipelines, taking a 51 percent stake in all French-owned oil interests in the country.

In the 1960s and 1970s, despite these breaks with the former colonial power, thousands of French technical advisors and educational personnel worked in Algeria, partially replacing the skills that had been lost when the European population, which numbered almost one million, left the country in 1961 and 1962. Arabization and the

promotion of Islamic culture was, during the same period, heavily reliant on ideas and personnel from Egypt and the Middle East. More significantly, the economic independence that was projected to grow out of Algeria's so-called specific socialism was never realized, since its industrialization was dependent on the purchase of technology and expertise from Europe, financed by revenue from hydrocarbon exports. In addition, underinvestment in agriculture and other sectors meant that the development of Algeria's industrial production never had the anticipated effect of stimulating the rest of the economy and of creating, and growing to meet, expanding demands.

ALGERIA, EUROPE, AND THE MIDDLE EAST, 1979 TO 2004

After the death of Boumedienne in 1978, statist economic programs were abandoned, the private sector was encouraged, and middle-class consumption increased while much of the population lived in poverty. The country's basic dependence on imports and its reliance on a single export commodity—hydrocarbons—did not change. With proven reserves in 2004 of 11.87 billion barrels of oil and 4.739 trillion cubic meters of gas, and as the world's second-largest gas exporter, Algeria remains an important country for its northern neighbors.

Algeria entered a period of political uncertainty in the 1980s, when Islamist radicalism increased among the younger generation and the monolithic, ritualized nationalism of the postindependence period eroded without being replaced by steps toward political pluralism. The shift away from the 1970s' Third Worldism brought the country back into Euro-Atlantic, and especially the French and later the American, spheres of influence. Algeria became a strategically and economically significant part of Europe's southern Mediterranean "near abroad." The same period saw Algeria, along with much of the Arab world, realigning itself toward the Gulf states and the concomitant rise of a domestic Islamist politics linked to events in the Middle East: the Iranian revolution, the anti-Soviet war in Afghanistan, the development of Egyptian Islamism, the Palestinian *intifada* (the uprising against Israeli occupation in the West Bank and Gaza, from 1987 to 1993) and the Gulf War of 1990 and 1991. In the 1990s Algeria suffered a decade-long political crisis and Islamist insurgency, in which between one hundred thousand and two hundred thousand Algerians are believed to have been killed.

At the start of the twenty-first century, Algeria emerged from this crisis as a significant regional actor in European and American strategic and economic calculations, a sizable emerging market and major energy supplier, and an important near neighbor to Europe—especially to France but also to Spain, Germany, and the United Kingdom—in terms of trade, security, and migration. After 2001 Algeria also became an ally of what the United States called the global war on terror, one whose own recent historical experience exemplifies the complexities of the contemporary politics of globalization, economic adjustment, Islamism, security, terrorism, and democratization.

See also **Algerian War; Ben Bella, Ahmed; Colonialism; France; Immigration and Internal Migration; Suez Crisis.**

BIBLIOGRAPHY

Ageron, Charles Robert. *Modern Algeria: A History from 1830 to the Present.* Translated by Michael Brett. London, 1991.

Bennoune, Mahfoud. *The Making of Contemporary Algeria, 1830–1987: Colonial Upheavals and Post-Independence Development.* Cambridge, U.K., 1988.

Horne, Alistair. *A Savage War of Peace: Algeria, 1954–1962.* London, 1977.

Roberts, Hugh. *The Battlefield Algeria, 1988–2002: Studies in a Broken Polity.* London, 2003.

Ruedy, John. *Modern Algeria: The Origins and Development of a Nation.* Bloomington, Ind., 1992.

Schatz, Adam. "Algeria's Ashes." *New York Review of Books.* 18 July 2003.

Stora, Benjamin. *La Gangrène et l'oubli: La mémoire de la guerre d'Algérie.* Paris, 1991.

JAMES MCDOUGALL

ALGERIAN WAR. It was not until October 1999, nearly forty years after the end of hostilities, that French political authorities officially adopted the term *Algerian War.* It designates the period when Algerian nationalists were fighting the French army for control of the political future of their country (1954–1962). Among ordinary people in France and elsewhere, however, there was a general consensus from the start that *war* was the right word for the conflict. In Algeria, by contrast, it was often called a "revolution" (*thawra*) or a "national war of liberation."

From the outset, the various terms point to different agendas. To acknowledge a state of war leads one to examine the events in terms of the traditional characteristics of wars: armed troops and battles, but also two agents, each implicitly viewed, even at the time, more or less as a nation. Terms such as *national war of liberation* or *revolution*, conversely, describe the conflict in terms of its outcome, a break with the existing colonial order. The term *war* connotes progress whereas *national liberation* was conceived at the time more as a call to action than as a description of the conflicts. *Thawra* belongs to the same lexicon as the works of Frantz Fanon, one of the major theoreticians of the war; it stresses the importance of violence in the process of the Algerian people's liberation. In fact, Fanon

French soldiers arrest a suspected Algerian rebel, May 1956. ©BETTMANN/CORBIS

believed it was his duty to spearhead a "revolutionary violence," turning the violence of conquest against the colonial oppressor.

Taken together, all these terms grant a particular identity to the period between 1 November 1954 and 19 March 1962. The war began with a series of coordinated attacks throughout Algeria. The Front de Libération Nationale (FLN; National liberation front), a group unknown at the time, claimed responsibility. The declaration of war is thus identified and authenticated by the "proclamation" signed by the FLN and found at the sites of the attacks. As for the end of the war that had torn apart Algeria and metropolitan France for almost eight years, it is associated with the cease-fire decreed by the 1962 Évian Accords, which did not lead to a formal peace treaty.

Although these dates were deemed politically valid by French and Algerian authorities, historians have subjected them to a reconsideration. The first act of war has thus been pushed back to May 1945, and the end of the conflict could legitimately be placed in July 1962, when Algeria obtained its official independence.

THE FRENCH EMPIRE BEGINS TO CRUMBLE

France's prestige was damaged with the country's defeat by Germany in May 1940, and the Anglo-American landing in Algeria in November 1942 further undermined it in the eyes of its colonies. Two years later, the Provisional Government of the French Republic, led by General Charles de Gaulle (1890–1970), attempted to undertake reform in all its colonial territories. Although Algeria was already theoretically and juridically part of France, this limited spirit of change would affect it as well. About sixty thousand Algerian men, selected on a merit basis (law of 7 March 1944), were granted the right to vote in national elections without having to renounce their status as Muslims. The extension of the franchise to all "French Muslims of Algeria," as they were called, was delayed temporarily, but the path to full civic equality had been cleared.

Yet the promise of reform could not satisfy Algerian nationalists, whom the French had long repressed and treated with contemptuous mistrust. Although a moderate nationalist, Ferhat Abbas declared that he wanted "an autonomous republic in a federation with a new French republic, one that is anticolonialist and anti-imperialist." His followers, members of the movement Amis du Manifeste et de la Liberté (Friends of the manifesto and of freedom), joined with the more radical Parti du Peuple Algérien (PPA; Party of the Algerian people), which in May 1945 demanded the release from prison of their party leader, Messali Hadj, and asserted the Algerians' right to self-determination. They referred explicitly to the principles of the Atlantic and United Nations charters. Thousands demonstrated in North Constantine, in the region of Sétif, and in the town of Guelma, purposely choosing the day of the Allied victory over the Nazis. Repression was swift and riots led to the deaths of nearly one hundred European civilians. In the weeks that followed, punitive expeditions, disguised as safety measures to prevent unrest, were mounted, with hundreds of summary executions carried out by the French army, police, and above all, by European civilians organized into militias. Although an official report attempted to assess the extent of the repression and though historians also considered the question, the various estimates of the dead are still far apart. Nevertheless, there seems to be no doubt that at least several thousand Algerians were killed. May 1945 can thus be considered the beginning of a war that would not erupt full-scale until nearly a decade later.

RADICALIZATION OF ALGERIAN NATIONALISTS

While ostensibly working toward an appreciable amelioration of relations, the French in fact continued their century-long habits of neglect and humiliation, and the Algerian nationalists became radicalized. A legislative body, the Algerian Assembly, was established in September 1947, holding out the prospect of a representative government, a voice, and political weight for Algerians; but the seats were apportioned to maintain French domination. In addition, the first elections were marked by intimidation of nationalist parties and the results were thoroughly rigged.

For the most radical nationalists, it was obvious that Algerian reform could not be accomplished by legal means. The main nationalist organization, Le Mouvement pour le Triomphe des Libertés Démocratiques (MTLD; Movement for the triumph of democratic liberties), went through a period of crisis that culminated in 1954 with a splinter group opting for armed struggle.

At the time, the French Empire was roiling from the loss of Indochina after an eight-year war that had received little attention at home but had done serious damage to the armed forces. In the summer of 1954, the Geneva Accords consummated the victory of the Vietminh, while unrest marked the North African (Maghrib) protectorates. In Algeria, however, the situation seemed calm. An exceptionally large presence of French men and women—accounting for almost one million of Algeria's nine million inhabitants—seemed to constitute a bulwark against any radical change. In reality, the war would transform Algerian society and, albeit less dramatically, seriously alter French society.

"REBELLION" AND "MAINTAINING ORDER"
Officially, the few regiments that were sent to North Constantine and the Aurès in 1954 were only supposed to "maintain order," to provide backup in the repression of the nationalists, which, as usual, was entrusted primarily to the police. But it quickly proved necessary to modify the legal basis of intervention. A law passed in April 1955 decreed a state of emergency in several *arrondissements*, or districts, of Algeria. The French government authorized the police to take exceptional measures and extended the jurisdiction of military law, thus departing from common law in two respects. Authorities used their desire to wage an effective campaign against the so-called rebels or terrorists to justify these measures.

While each side was taking stock of the other and preparing to fight, a popular uprising on an unprecedented scale erupted in North Constantine on 20 August 1955, the second anniversary of the deposing of the Moroccan sultan by the French. European civilians as well as moderate Algerians became the targets of savage violence and the French army undertook a brutal repression. In this region, affected by confrontations since its conquest in the nineteenth century, the breach between French inhabitants and Algerians widened inexorably.

SPECIAL POWERS

When the state of emergency expanded to include the entire territory after the 20 August riots, that breach spread to the whole of Algeria. French authorities decided that such legalistic maneuvers were inadequate. A new government in France, headed by the socialist Guy Mollet and supported by political parties in favor of "peace in Algeria," asserted that victory on the ground was the precondition for any negotiations. In March 1956, the French legislature granted Mollet "special powers" to settle the Algerian question. Specific measures granted under the "state of emergency" were superseded by the principle of absolute executive power over all matters concerning Algeria. These special powers were to last six months and had to be renewed by every new government. At the same time, the government decided to send the entire cohort of draftees for the year 1956 to Algeria. Henceforth all young men could be deployed "to maintain order" in what French authorities described as a "police operation."

In providing the legal and conceptual framework for intervention in Algeria, the special powers shaped events in the ensuing years. They were extended to the French metropolis in the summer of 1957 and then systematically renewed by successive governments under the Fourth Republic and in the early years of the Fifth. This meant, first, that beyond the powers granted the executive branch, the governor in Algeria was accorded immense latitude. These special powers also gave the army significant prerogatives that, despite their provisional character (which was regularly reasserted), had considerable political consequences.

REIGN OF THE ARMY

Unrestricted, the French army launched a total war. Concerned about the impact on the general population, it created special administrative sections (SAS) designed to bring some measure of relief to even the most remote areas of the colony. The army also took charge of educating Algerian children, even using soldiers as primary schoolteachers, while others worked to improve the health of Algerians, notably through vaccination campaigns.

At the same time, the army advised an all-out war grounded in intelligence operations. Inspired by methods the colonial police had used in Indochina, the French army gradually adopted torture to extract by force information about "the rebellion" otherwise unobtainable because of the army's limited infiltration into Algerian society. Torture turned out to be particularly well adapted to a war largely rooted in terror. In addition, the suffering that French soldiers intentionally inflicted on people was a way to assert the power of the colonial authority over individuals and families, villages and political parties, and the Algerian people as a whole.

Violence spread all the more readily in Algeria because the army, given significant powers, had developed a new theory that located the war's epicenter outside traditional battlegrounds and within the general population. Obliged to adapt to the guerrilla tactics of the nationalist forces of the Algerian Armée de Libération Nationale (ALN; National army of liberation), the French army counterattacked by advocating counterrevolutionary actions relying on psychological warfare adapted to various groups implicated in the war, including the military, Algerian and European civilians, and underground guerrillas. It also employed unconventional combat methods such as indoctrination of the enemy, using torture, carrying out summary executions, and orchestrating "disappearances."

Thus, in the name of strategic imperatives, the army authorized illegal actions by ordinary soldiers, not just special forces trained to so act for reasons of state. The military had its own way of running the war, which involved repeated and regular violations of the law, to be approved after the fact by political authorities faced with a fait accompli. The interception in October 1956 of a Moroccan airplane carrying four leaders of the FLN is symptomatic in that regard. In stopping the plane, the army violated Moroccan sovereignty. The French government, informed only when the operation was already under way, covered up the incident and imprisoned the Algerian political leaders Ahmed Ben Bella, Mohammed Boudiaf, Hocine Aït Ahmed, and Mohammed Khider.

Algerian Army of Liberation soldiers stand in formation at their headquarters in the Atlas mountains, June 1957.
©BETTMANN/CORBIS

A few months later, faced with the proliferation of terrorist attacks in Algiers—a consequence of the FLN's new tactical orientation adopted after the so-called Soummam Congress in the summer of 1956—the task of maintaining order in the capital was handed over to French army paratroopers. To accomplish their mission, they systematically combed the Arab neighborhoods and practiced large-scale torture on arrested suspects, going so far as to kill one of the principal leaders of the FLN, Larbi Ben M'hidi. The army also resorted to kidnappings on a deplorable scale. At least three thousand people disappeared during the eight-month operation dismantling the nationalist networks in Algiers and those of their communist or left-wing liberal supporters.

Strengthened by their apparent victory after arresting or killing the major FLN leaders and putting an end to terrorist attacks, paratroopers added to their tough image a certified competence in "counterrevolutionary" warfare. This "Battle of Algiers" model spread across Algeria before being in part exported to France, especially to Paris.

The international community disapproved of the French actions in Algeria; the United States in particular pressed for an increased understanding of the nationalists' demands. In February 1958 the bombing of a Tunisian village, Sakkiet Sidi Youssef, gave the international community an opportunity to intervene in what France resolutely presented to the world as a strictly French affair. Aware of that international potential, the FLN sought support abroad for its cause and denounced French policy to the world and to the United Nations. By this juncture, French political authorities seemed largely beholden to the military for their strategy. In May 1958 the army helped bring down the French government, which it considered too soft on the Algerian issue.

CHARLES DE GAULLE

Charles de Gaulle, who returned to political office as prime minister in May 1958 and elected president in 1959, immediately had to contend with the high hopes placed in him. He also had to rein in the army, which from the beginning had been given a free hand. General Raoul Salan had come to acquire both political and military responsibilities throughout Algeria, but de Gaulle managed to remove him at the end of 1958.

Little by little, de Gaulle made his mark on Algerian policy. Like his predecessors, he continued to work simultaneously to secure a military victory and to win the confidence of the Algerian population, especially through a determined economic development policy. But this policy was paradoxical in that all-out war was being conducted even as French authorities were launching the most ambitious policy to modernize the country ever undertaken. That paradox attests to the fact that winning the hearts and minds of the Algerian population had become the principal stakes in the conflict. Since the FLN was an integral part of the general population, however, the French had a difficult time distinguishing between the war against the FLN and the war against the population at large.

The FLN, in fact, was considered to be within the population like "a fish in water." The military believed they had found the solution, proposing to separate out "the fish," a strategy that led to the establishment of huge internment camps where, within less than two years, some two million people, one-quarter of the Algerian population, were confined. Deprived of their homes, separated from their fields, work, and activities, people were condemned to miserable living conditions, which in the end undermined the French cause. At the same time, these camps clearly indicated France's desire to remodel the country entirely, to construct a new French Algeria, making use as necessary of the tactics of a war of conquest.

CHANGING AGENDAS

In this context, both sides had difficulty adopting a moderate stance. In Algeria, the FLN's elimination of moderates, like General Jacques Massu's repression of the liberals in 1957, indicated the growing radicalization of the war. As the years passed it seemed that cultural identity was becoming increasingly important; most Algerian residents would no doubt have said, as did the Algerian-born Nobel Prize winner Albert Camus, "I believe in justice, but will defend my mother before justice."

Although radicalization was less significant in metropolitan France, where there was more respect for freedom of expression, radicalism could be found in particular groups. Among Algerian workers, a fratricidal war put the supporters of the FLN at odds with the nationalists close to Messali Hadj, who belonged to the Mouvement National Algérien (MNA; National Algerian movement). In this power struggle within the Algerian camp, assassinations were committed on a daily basis, resulting in several thousands of victims. Algerians living in France, oppressed by French policies, were also involved in the war at home and obliged to contribute money and to hew the party line. By contrast, non-Algerians remained largely above the fray. Opinion polls gradually registered growing concern about the events in Algeria, and public opinion slowly came to favor greater autonomy, then self-determination, as de Gaulle's policies evolved step by step and he asked the French to validate them by referendum.

An infinitesimal minority in France chose to support the FLN by sheltering people or clandestinely channeling money to the movement. The discovery of one of these networks, headed by the philosopher Francis Jeanson, came as a shock to the French. But it showed that some people were capable of envisaging a different kind of relationship with the Algerians. While the trial of the Jeanson network made headlines, the position of the many French intellectuals who signed a declaration claiming that those in the military had the right to insubordination demonstrates that, in the fall of 1960, the war was becoming a disturbing feature of French life. Had not General de Gaulle talked of an "Algerian Algeria" the previous March? In November he even spoke of an "Algerian republic"; then, in April 1961, he offered the prospect of a "sovereign Algerian state."

By this time, in fact, negotiations with the Gouvernement Provisoire de la République Algérienne (GPRA; Provisional government of the Algerian Republic) were an admitted necessity. By staging mass protests the previous December during de Gaulle's visit to Algiers, the GPRA had

An Algerian woman forced by French authorities to remove her veil for an identity card photograph, 1960. ©Marc Garanger/Corbis

demonstrated that it alone could represent the Algerian people.

In April 1961, while negotiations toward Algerian sovereignty made halting progress, four prestigious generals—two of them were former commanders in chief in Algeria—organized a putsch. Although a failure, it revealed the level of bitterness that de Gaulle's policy incited among the professional military staff in Algeria as well as among the Europeans living there. Some joined a clandestine organization headed by General Salan with the goal of battling those they accused of abandoning French Algeria. The Organisation de l'Armée Secrète (OAS; Secret army organization) operated as a terrorist group, created networks of supporters

within France, and was responsible for numerous assassination attempts against de Gaulle himself— even after the war ended.

In 1958–1959, the war gradually extended to metropolitan France. Militants organized meetings against torture, students demonstrated against the war, and counterefforts were made to organize support for French policy. Algerians were increasingly viewed as the enemy and treated as such by the police and public institutions. From 1961 on, particularly in Paris, a curfew was imposed on them. On 17 October of that year, to protest this curtailing of freedom of assembly and association, Algerians in Paris and the surrounding suburbs marched at the behest of the FLN. The police responded with considerable force, arresting about half the demonstrators and killing dozens more.

Although its magnitude remained unknown, a massacre in the center of Paris could scarcely go unnoticed, and protests arose in the days that followed, in the city council of Paris and elsewhere. But gradually the massacre disappeared from the history of the war, wiped out in France by the deaths of nine participants at the hands of police during a left-wing demonstration in February 1962 against the OAS. It was part of a traditional protest by the French Left, who had united against "fascism" at the end of a war, though the various parties' positions during it were far more complex. The French Communist Party had initially voted for the special powers but distanced itself over time from the orientations of the other left-wing parties, the socialists and especially the radicals. The socialist Section Française de l'Internationale Ouvrière (SFIO; French branch of the workers' International) had played a key role in prosecuting the war and in instituting the increasingly harsh repressive measures, to such an extent that a minority eventually split off to establish the Parti Socialiste Autonome (Autonomous socialist party), later the Parti Socialiste Unifié (PSU; Unified socialist party). The antifascist movement gave cohesion to the Left while at the same time enabling it to support the major goals and orientation of de Gaulle's policy at the end of the war.

THE CEASE-FIRE AND THE CASUALTIES

In March 1962, the Évian Accords led to a progressive transfer of sovereignty. In Algeria the FLN had managed to position itself as the only qualified negotiator while, inside the party, a merciless battle for control raged among the leaders. Disregarding the principles Abane Ramdane had tried to establish during the founding Soummam Congress—namely, the primacy of Algerians living in Algeria over those living abroad and of political leaders over military ones—the formerly exiled army chiefs finally prevailed. Abane Ramdane, who would no doubt have become a key political leader in the new regime, was assassinated in December 1957 by his former comrades, and Colonel Houari Boumédienne, chief of the general staff of the Armée de Libération Nationale (the armed wing of the FLN) beginning in March 1960, managed to turn himself into the strongman of Algeria.

During negotiations with French authorities, past leaders were used for their symbolic value. Thus Ahmed Ben Bella was appointed president of the GPRA, even though he had been in a French prison since October 1956. But gradually the founding figures of Algerian nationalism were marginalized by the returning leaders. On 5 July 1962 Algeria was officially declared independent, ending 132 years of French rule.

The months following the cease-fire were especially bloody. The OAS undertook a radical scorched-earth policy while the *harkis* (Muslim auxiliaries in the French army) were hunted down, threatened, and sometimes summarily executed. The violence led a large number of European Algerians to flee the country and a smaller percentage of *harkis* relocated to France. Those remaining in Algeria had to face retribution, which in some cases culminated in massacres. As with many statistics relating to casualties in this war, the number of *harkis* killed is still uncertain. A low estimate would be ten thousand. As for the war itself, the Algerian leadership had always claimed "a million martyrs." That number was reevaluated by historians beginning in the 1960s and three hundred thousand victims suggested as a reliable estimate; nonetheless, the larger number was still used in Algeria at the beginning of the twenty-first century. Among French civilians, it is difficult to say how many were killed by the FLN and how many by the OAS. The only precise figures available are provided by the military: more than twenty-three thousand French people were killed in Algeria, one-third of them noncombat deaths. The number of noncombat deaths underlines the point that the French conscripts were not well prepared for this war. The awakening of the colonial dream was brutal.

See also **Algeria; Ben Bella, Ahmed; Camus, Albert; Colonialism; France; French Empire; Indochina; Vietnam War.**

BIBLIOGRAPHY

Ageron, Charles-Robert, ed. *La guerre d'Algérie et les Algériens.* Paris, 1997.

Connelly, Matthew. *A Diplomatic Revolution: Algeria's Fight for Independence and the Origins of the Post–Cold War Era.* Oxford, U.K., 2002.

Evans, Martin. *Memory of Resistance: The French Opposition to the Algerian War, 1954–62.* Oxford, U.K., 1997.

Harbi, Mohammed. *Le FLN: Mirage et réalité, des origines à la prise du pouvoir (1945–1962).* Paris, 1980.

Harbi, Mohammed, and Benjamin Stora, eds. *La guerre d'Algérie : 1954–2004, la fin de l'amnésie.* Paris, 2004.

Heggoy, Alf Andrew. *Insurgency and Counterinsurgency in Algeria.* Bloomington, Ind., 1972.

Horne, Alistair. *A Savage War of Peace: Algeria, 1954–1962.* London, 1977.

House, Jim, and Neil MacMaster. *Paris 1961: Algerians, State Terror, and Postcolonial Memories.* Oxford, U.K., forthcoming.

Jauffret, Jean-Charles. *Soldats en Algérie 1954–1962: Expériences contrastées des hommes du contingent.* Paris, 2000.

Meynier, Gilbert. *Histoire intérieure du F.L.N.: 1954–1962.* Paris, 2002.

Rioux, Jean-Pierre, ed. *La guerre d'Algérie et les Français.* Paris, 1990.

Stora, Benjamin. *Ils venaient d'Algérie. L'immigration algérienne en France, 1912–1992.* Paris, 1992.

RAPHAËLLE BRANCHE

ALLIES. *See* **World War I; World War II.**

ALMODÓVAR, PEDRO (b. 1951), Spanish filmmaker.

Pedro Almodóvar was born in the rural village of Calzada de Calatrava, in La Mancha, Spain. As a child, he was an avid reader and moviegoer with a remarkable imagination and a keen interest in playacting and theater, including the rituals of his local Catholic church.

Rather than attend film school or university, Almodóvar became a tremendous autodidact. His literary and cinematic tastes run from the decadent French poets of the nineteenth century to the British mystery writer Ruth Rendell, and to filmmakers as diverse as William Wyler (1902–1981) and Michelangelo Antonioni (b. 1912). After moving to Madrid in 1968, Almodóvar worked at the Spanish national telephone company Telefónica,

eventually earning enough money to purchase his first Super-8 camera. During the 1970s, Almodóvar became renowned for his amateur films in Madrid's burgeoning underground culture, whose growth was fueled by Spain's reversion to a more democratic government following General Francisco Franco's death in 1975.

Almodóvar made his first feature, *Pepi, Luci, Bom,* in 1980 with the actress Carmen Maura, who would star in several of his subsequent films. With Maura, Almodóvar inaugurated the practice of working with a kind of repertory of favorite actors, which he continued throughout his career. His earliest feature films perpetuate the gleefully anarchic feel of his Super-8 shorts, but by his third feature, *Dark Habits* (1983), he had already begun to integrate more serious themes and a tighter narrative and stylistic structure. *Dark Habits* also foregrounds one of Almodóvar's abiding obsessions: through a story of drugged-out nuns, Almodóvar began to develop his vision of the florid beauty and hypocrisy of the Spanish church. Much later, in *Bad Education* (2004), Almodóvar returned with a passion to this theme, with a story of sexual awakening and clerical perversion—it is this single word *pasión* (passion), in fact, that engulfs *Bad Education*'s final frame.

During the late 1980s, Almodóvar's films began to garner attention in and beyond Spain. His first international hit was the 1987 film *Women on the Verge of a Nervous Breakdown,* though many critics (including Almodóvar himself) consider his film from the previous year, *The Law of Desire* (1986), much more important. With *Women on the Verge, Tie Me Up! Tie Me Down!* (1989) and *High Heels* (1990), Almodóvar's signature "look" became firmly established. Almodóvar used a very wide 35-mm filmmaking format (1:85) in *Women on the Verge* and *High Heels,* to imitate classic American comedies filmed in CinemaScope, a significant departure from his hand-held Super-8 days. His filmmaking became synonymous with the use of kitsch and of vibrant, primary colors—red in particular—as well as strong background music and songs that convey key narrative and tonal elements. Some of the songs featured in Almodóvar's films over the years, many of them original, have become major hits in Europe.

Pedro Almodóvar with Gael Garcia Bernal on the set of Bad Education. CANAL+/TVE/THE KOBAL COLLECTION

Almodóvar's *All about My Mother* won the Academy Award for best foreign film.

For all the apparent stylistic and thematic coherence in his oeuvre, however, there are exceptions to every seemingly well-established "Almodóvarian" convention. While Almodóvar usually works in a highly stylized, exuberant mode, *What Have I Done to Deserve This?* (1984) is a morose and poignant social realist film. Likewise, while *Matador* (1985) and *Kika* (1993) are highly conceptual, abstract works, *The Flower of My Secret* (1995) is soft in tone, with a straightforward narrative that is unique among Almodóvar's films. For yet another contrast, consider *Bad Education* (2004), whose movement in and out of its story-within-a-story teases the viewer by simultaneously treading near the outlines of Almodóvar's own biography.

Perhaps the difficulty of pinning down Almodóvar can be best explained by the director himself: he has said that he does not consider himself a transgressive filmmaker, because transgression is already too strong an acknowledgment of the law. Instead of being anti-Franco, for instance, he simply does not acknowledge Franco's existence in the Spain he creates in his films. For Almodóvar, this radical sense of freedom is the only way to move toward the truth of contemporary human experience. Only thus can a master of artifice render humanity—and *pasión*—so real.

See also **Cinema; Spain.**

BIBLIOGRAPHY

Smith, Paul Julian. *Desire Unlimited: The Cinema of Pedro Almodóvar.* 2nd ed. London, 2000. The definitive book on Almodóvar for both scholars and popular readers.

Strauss, Frédéric, ed. *Almodóvar on Almodóvar.* Translated by Yves Baignères. London, 1996. Almodóvar considers this his "official bibliography" because it is primarily concerned with his films rather than his life.

Vernon, Kathleen, and Barbara Morris, eds. *Post-Franco, Postmodern: The Films of Pedro Almodóvar.* Westport, Conn., 1995. Essays that address the cultural context and reception of Almodóvar in Spain and abroad.

ANNE M. KERN

At the center of these films, too, is a woman or women. Almodóvar's depiction of women has evoked mixed reactions over the years; during Almodóvar's rise to international fame, several feminist film scholars decried what they considered hysterical female representations. But as with all his characters, Almodóvar dares us to see women as he sees them *cinematically*—that is, fetishized in their strength *and* their vulnerability, always larger than life.

In addition to the worldwide success of *Women on the Verge,* 1987 was a key year in Almodóvar's history because he and his brother Agustín established their own production company, El Deseo S. A. El Deseo ensured the aesthetic independence of Almodóvar's filmmaking, as well as certain formal continuities, made possible by a permanent staff at every level of production. Almodóvar also wrote or cowrote all his own films. In 2000

AL QAEDA. Al Qaeda ("the base") is an umbrella organization of Islamist terrorist groups founded by the Saudi millionaire Osama bin Laden in 1988. For well over a decade Western intelligence agencies remained largely unaware of its nature and activities, failing to see an underlying pattern in a series of attacks conducted throughout the 1990s and culminating in the 11 September 2001 attacks on the United States. Only after the attacks did the relationship between these events and their perpetrators become clear. While the United States and its allies have put together a better picture of Al Qaeda and launched an international effort to destroy it, the organization has proved remarkably and extremely flexible.

Al Qaeda developed out of the struggle to expel the Soviet Union from Afghanistan. In 1979 Soviet forces invaded the central Asian nation to prop up its Communist puppet regime. *Mujahidin*, or "holy warriors," flocked to Afghanistan from throughout the Muslim world but primarily from the Middle East and North Africa determined to assist an Islamic state in a holy struggle to resist the infidel. Eager to check Soviet expansion in the region, the United States backed the foreign fighters, supplying them with money, arms, and probably advisors as well. At the time, Washington foresaw no adverse consequence of arming, training, and equipping fighters who harbored a deep animosity toward non-Muslims. No one seems to have considered that the foreign fighters would form an organization after the Soviet withdrawal.

Osama bin Laden, son of a wealthy Saudi contractor, joined many young Arab men of his generation in Afghanistan. While he appears to have played a very minor role in the fighting, his wealth enabled him to recruit, train, and supply fighters for the insurgency. Elated by the *mujahidin* victory, which culminated in Soviet withdrawal, bin Laden founded Al Qaeda in 1988. Bin Laden and his associates wished to promote the teachings of Wahhabism—a brand of Islam common in Saudi Arabia—throughout the Muslim world. The Afghan war taught them that Islam faced ongoing threats from the non-Muslim world and that a small group of dedicated fighters possessed of an unshakable faith in their cause could accomplish a great deal in their defense of Islam, as they saw it. It was one minute to midnight, these Muslims believed, and unless they took steps to preserve Islam, westernized Muslim governments and the United States would destroy it.

Al Qaeda's religious convictions have defined its strategy and choice of targets as a terrorist organization. While not all Wahhabis espouse violence, those that support Al Qaeda consider jihad against their enemies acceptable. "Apostate" regimes in the Muslim world top this list of acceptable targets. Bin Laden believes that secular governments such as those of Egypt, Pakistan, and Iraq (led either by Saddam Hussein or the subsequently elected parliament) should be replaced by strict Islamic republics governed by sharia law. Only the Taliban, who seized power in Afghanistan after the Soviet withdrawal, seemed to fit bin Laden's definition of a legitimate Muslim government. That regime outlawed music, deprived women of any civil and most human rights, and conducted a reign of terror against its own people. Saudi Arabia became a primary Al Qaeda target during the first Gulf War. The monarchy turned down bin Laden's offer of an army of *mujahidin* to expel Saddam from Kuwait and invited a U.S.-led coalition onto Saudi soil.

The United States fell into Al Qaeda's crosshairs primarily because it hindered bin Laden's goals in the Muslim world. The United States supported most of the moderate Muslim regimes that he hated, funded and consistently backed the state of Israel, and defiled the sacred soil of Saudi Arabia with its troops. During the 1990s the United States suffered a series of terrorist attacks that it did not initially see as connected. In 1993 the Egyptian Ramzi Yousef planted a truck bomb in the garage of the World Trade Center, killing six and injuring more than one thousand. The blind Egyptian cleric Khalid Shaikh Mohammed probably planned the attack. In June 1996 terrorists bombed a U.S. military housing complex known as the Khobar Towers in Saudi Arabia, killing nineteen servicemen. Although an Al Qaeda connection to either attack has not been proven, analysts suspect that these terrorist incidents were part of a larger Al Qaeda campaign.

Any doubt about the organization's commitment to terrorism against the United States disappeared on 7 August 1998 when Al Qaeda destroyed the U.S. embassies in Nairobi, Kenya, and Dar es Salaam, Tanzania, killing 220 people. The previous February bin Laden had issued a *fatwa* (religious edict) proclaiming it a sacred duty for devout Muslims to kill

Americans whenever and wherever they could be found. The *fatwa* and the embassy bombings revealed important but disturbing truths about the nature of Al Qaeda terrorism: for bin Laden and his followers there was no such thing as an innocent civilian, and they would exercise no restraint in inflicting mass casualties on their enemies. Unfortunately, the U.S. response to the embassy bombings exacerbated the situation. The Clinton administration launched cruise missiles against Al Qaeda training camps in Afghanistan and a pharmaceutical factory in Khartoum, Sudan. The camps suffered little damage, and no evidence that the Sudanese plant produced chemical weapons (as was alleged at the time) has ever been produced. Innocent people died in the Sudan attack. Bin Laden and the Taliban regime with whom he now resided had every reason to believe that they had little to fear from American retaliation, which so far had been weak and ineffectual. Two years later Al Qaeda struck again, attacking the USS *Cole* in Aden harbor, Yemen. Seventeen U.S. sailors died, and again the United States did not respond effectively.

The embassy bombings and the attack on the *Cole* did, however, alert the United States to the growing Al Qaeda threat. Vigilance and good intelligence work foiled a number of plots planned for millennium celebrations in the United States. Border security apprehended suspects attempting to cross into Maine and Washington from Canada. However, as important as these successes were, they may also have made Americans complacent about the risk of foreign terrorism perpetrated within the United States. All successful attacks to date had occurred against U.S. targets abroad, a phenomenon Americans had faced since the early 1980s. Nothing bespoke this illusion of security more clearly than the absurd policy of screening baggage and passengers on foreign flights while treating them much more casually for domestic flights. The attacks on 11 September 2001 demonstrated how little the United States knew about Al Qaeda and how lax domestic security had become.

Since the attacks the United States has mounted a full-scale war on terrorism, a vague term used for political reasons for invading both Afghanistan and Iraq while improving homeland security and intelligence gathering. In the face of this concerted effort Al Qaeda has demonstrated both persistence and flexibility. This once

hierarchical organization with cells connected to central control by bin Laden has evolved into a flat network of loosely connected bodies receiving minimal direction and support from the main terrorist group.

The Madrid train bombings of 11 March 2004 and the London Underground bombings of 7 July 2005 were carried out by domestic terrorist cells constituted for a single operation and destroyed in the act of carrying it out. The group Al Qaeda in Iraq, founded by Abu Musab al-Zarqawi following the U.S. invasion, is only loosely connected to the parent organization, which does not control it.

As of 2006, Al Qaeda remains a serious threat as an umbrella organization linking an extensive network of cells and terrorist groups. The Western intelligence picture of the network remains incomplete, and the resolve of the terrorists seems unshaken. Every indication suggests that the United States and its allies will be contending with Al Qaeda for the foreseeable future.

See also **Islamic Terrorism; Terrorism.**

BIBLIOGRAPHY

Gunaratna, Rohan. *Inside Al Qae'da: Global Network of Terror.* New York, 2002.

Mockaitis, Thomas R., and Paul Rich, eds. *Grand Strategy in the War against Terrorism.* London, 2003.

TOM MOCKAITIS

ALSACE-LORRAINE. In 843, in Verdun, the grandsons of Charlemagne (king of the Franks, 768–814; and emperor of the West, 800–814) divided the Carolingian Empire into three parts. The western and eastern portions later became France and Germany, respectively, while between them, spreading from the North Sea to Italy, was the kingdom of Lotharingia, which soon fell apart. Alsace and Lorraine, a portion of Lotharingia, remained in Germanic hands until the seventeenth century, when Louis XIV (r. 1643–1715) was able to reunite a major portion of Alsace with the kingdom of France. Southern Alsace, notably the region of Mulhouse, was annexed only during the Revolution. This reunification allowed France to reach its "natural border" along a section of the Rhine.

Lorraine, where the population spoke French except in the Germanophone northeast, was more disputed. From the sixteenth century, reunification was gradual and only completed during the second half of the eighteenth century. The two provinces had scarcely any ties or sympathy for each other, and were only treated as a unit after they were annexed together by the victorious Germans after the war of 1870–1871. In fact, the two provinces were not united in their entirety. Only the major part of Alsace, less the region of Belfort, and the department of Moselle in the north of Lorraine, were involved in the annexation.

While the region's legislative deputies solemnly protested this "odious abuse of power," Alsace-Lorraine came to embody in some measure the achievement of German unity that was symbolized by the proclamation of the king of Prussia, William I (r. 1861–1888), as emperor of Germany at Versailles, on 18 January 1871. To reinforce the symbolism, Alsace-Lorraine became a *Reichsland* (territory of the empire) and common property of all the German states. For the French, reconquest of Alsace-Lorraine was the principal theme of revanchism (from the French word for revenge). But gradually, apart from nationalist groups such as La Ligue des Patriotes (Patriots' League) in the 1880s and the monarchist Action Française (French Action) at the beginning of the twentieth century, French public opinion did not favor a war to regain the lost provinces. However, the Alsace-Lorraine controversy prevented reconciliation between France and Germany and was a cause of discord in Europe.

The 1871 Treaty of Frankfurt stipulated that French inhabitants of the annexed territories would have the right, until 31 October 1872 to repatriate to France. Out of a population of 1.6 million, about 150,000 decided to exercise this right, among them a significant number of the political, cultural, economic, and military elites, especially in Alsace. Those who decided to stay did not necessarily accept annexation, and public opinion tended toward protest and dissatisfaction. At first the *Reichsland* was directly under the authority of Berlin through the *Statthalter* (representative) in Strasbourg. Despite strict rules—the German language was obligatory, for example, while French was prohibited—the *Reichsland* benefited

from a conciliatory policy on the part of German authorities. But confronted with persistent protests, the regime became far more rigid. After 1890 discord lessened as many Germans now settled in the two provinces. Unity with Germany had improved the region's prosperity and the young generation had never known anything except a German government. Rather than revert to France, many inhabitants of Alsace-Lorraine pressed for greater autonomy within the German Empire, and in 1911 obtained a new constitution. The population of Moselle clearly did not want to be the object of a confrontation between France and Germany; nevertheless, the climate was often tense in Alsace, as demonstrated in Saverne in 1913, when, after a young German lieutenant insulted Alsatian recruits, serious incidents took place between the civilian population and the German troops. The Alsatian Museum of Doctor Bücher in Strasbourg and the drawings of the artists Hansi (Jean-Jacques Waltz; 1873–1951) and Henri Zislin (1875–1958) are the best demonstrations of continued attachment to France and of a rejection of Germanization.

The outbreak of war in 1914 was in no way a consequence of the Alsace-Lorraine question, but once the battle was joined, reconquest of the two provinces became France's war aim par excellence. French troops' brief occupation of Mulhouse in August 1914 provoked an outburst of enthusiasm there. However, 250,000 soldiers of Alsace-Lorraine did fight in the German army, and for most of the next four years the "war map" was so favorable to Germany that it gave no thought to returning Alsace-Lorraine, which made a compromise for peace almost impossible. On the other hand, the United Kingdom only belatedly considered this restitution a priority. At the time of the armistice talks, France demanded the return of Alsace-Lorraine without waiting for a conclusion of the peace process. The French president Raymond Poincaré (1860–1934), prime minister Georges Clemenceau (1841–1929), and generals Ferdinand Foch (1851–1929) and Philippe Pétain (1856–1951) were welcomed in the liberated Alsace-Lorraine amid great enthusiasm, and the German "immigrants" were now expelled. Nonetheless, although secular French law was not imposed—especially in Alsace where religion, both

Catholic and Protestant, had particular importance—the relationship with the interior authorities, who scarcely recognized the Alsatian "exception," soon grew strained. An "autonomist" movement grew up until the 1930s, when it became pro-Nazi and lost its influence.

Victorious in 1940, Nazi Germany immediately annexed the former Alsace-Lorraine and named Robert Heinrich Wagner gauleiter (leader of a regional branch of the Nazi party) of Alsace and Joseph Bürckel gauleiter of Lorraine. From August 1942, the region's young men were drafted into the German army, giving birth after the war to the denomination of the "malgré nous"—the 130,000 young men of Alsace-Lorraine who later claimed to have been compelled against their will to serve in the German army, which was true for the great majority of them. Some twenty thousand never returned, especially from the Russian front, where they were killed in combat or died in prisoner-of-war camps such as the notorious Soviet camp of Tambov. In some cases prisoners were held by the Soviet authorities until years later (most were liberated by 1947, but the last of them only in 1955). The fate of some thirteen thousand remains unknown. Nazi reprisals against the French Resistance in Alsace were severe; many were sent to die in the Alsatian concentration camp of Schirmeck.

The Second World War put an end to the Alsace-Lorraine question. Lorraine was reunified, and Alsace was at last able to reconcile a deep French patriotism, expressed by a strong attachment to Gaullism, with a European calling—Strasbourg became the seat first of the Council of Europe (1948), and later of the European Parliament (1979). Although now entirely French, Alsace retains its unique character within the whole of France through its traditions, its way of life, and by the maintenance, at least in the country, of the local "dialect."

See also **Action Française; France; Germany; World War I.**

BIBLIOGRAPHY

Dollinger, Philippe, ed. *Histoire de l'Alsace.* Toulouse, France, 2001.

Le Marec, Bernard, and Gérard Le Marec. *L'Alsace dans la guerre: 1939–1945.* Paris, 1988.

L'Huillier, Fernand. *Histoire de l'Alsace.* Paris, 1974.

Mayeur, Jean-Marie. *Autonomie et politique en Alsace: La constitution de 1911.* Paris, 1970.

Moullec, Gaël. "De la Wehrmacht aux camps soviétiques: La tragédie des malgré nous (avis de recherches)." *L'histoire* 255 (June 2001).

Roth, François. *La Lorraine annexée (1870–1918).* Nancy, France, 1976.

———. "L'Alsace-Lorraine au début du XXe siècle." In *Encyclopédie de la Grande Guerre (1914–1918): Histoire et culture,* under the direction of Jean-Jacques Becker et Stéphane Audoin-Rouzeau. Paris, 2004.

Spindler, Charles. *L'Alsace pendant la guerre.* Strasbourg, 1925.

Vogler, Bernard. *Histoire politique de l'Alsace: De la Révolution à nos jours; Un panorama des passions alsaciennes.* Strasbourg, 1995.

JEAN-JACQUES BECKER

ALTHUSSER, LOUIS (1918–1990), French Marxist and social theorist.

Louis Althusser was perhaps the most influential Marxist thinker of his time, and during the 1960s and 1970s one of the most influential European thinkers in any tradition of social thought. Born in Algeria in 1918, Althusser moved with his parents to France in 1930. He spent much of the war in a German POW camp, where he was greatly impressed by a communist fellow prisoner. He joined the French Communist Party soon after the war, but, as an independent-minded intellectual, soon fell out with the party leadership. His most important achievements were to bring Marxist thought into creative dialogue with other traditions, and to revitalize Marxism as an openended research program that influenced philosophy, sociology, literary criticism, psychoanalysis, political science, anthropology, and gender and cultural studies. Above all, he was concerned to develop distinctively Marxist ways of analyzing cultural and political processes as a counterweight to widespread misreadings of Marxism as a form of economic determinism. His life ended in tragedy, and most of his last decade was spent in a psychiatric hospital.

Collections of essays that Althusser first published in the early 1960s were deeply controversial—partly because of his provocative declaration that he was an "anti-humanist." To understand what he meant by this, and why it was so shocking, one needs to know something of the context. By the 1950s it was clear to many on the political left that the great attempt at human liberation inaugurated by the revolution of October 1917 in Russia had been transformed into an oppressive bureaucratic dictatorship. Nikita Khrushchev (1894–1971) had briefly denounced the crimes of Joseph Stalin (1879–1953), but when Soviet tanks rolled in to suppress the reform movement in Hungary in 1956 it was clear that little had really changed. Marxist critics of the Soviet regime turned to early writings by Karl Marx as the basis for an outright moral condemnation of what had been done in the name of Marx. They found in those early writings a vision of human history as a long struggle toward an eventual realization of full human potential in a future socialist society. The Soviet state had become a living denial of that very vision, with its continued exploitation of an "alienated" population. Views such as this were developed by independent intellectuals, of whom the best known were Jean-Paul Sartre (1905–1980) and Maurice Merleau-Ponty (1908–1961), but they were also very influential within the French Communist Party itself. It was this "humanist" moral criticism of the Soviet "Stalinist" system that Althusser rejected, thus laying himself open to the charge that he was a closet Stalinist. In fact, his rejection of the humanist critique was motivated by his recognition of the need for a much deeper analysis and critique of what had gone so terribly wrong in the history of the communist movement. The moral critique, though fully justified, was not enough: it was necessary to rethink the whole Marxist legacy to try and explain why this had happened. To do this Althusser drew on two important traditions of thought that had developed independently of Marxism: structuralism and a distinctively French approach to understanding the history of science. The historians of science (notably Georges Canguilhem [1904–1995] and Gaston Bachelard [1884–1962]) had shown that scientific ideas form an interconnected network, or "problematic" that shapes the questions that are asked in each discipline. Scientific innovation thus involves wholesale transformations of problematics—scientific revolutions, in which older questions and patterns of thought are replaced by new ones.

Althusser applied these ideas to Marx's own intellectual life history, proposing that the earlier "humanist" view of history was prescientific. In Althusser's account, Marx soon came to see the limitations of his earlier philosophical narrative of human history, and proceeded to develop a new "scientific" conception based on empirical study. Major transformations in society should not be seen as inevitable outcomes of some underlying "telos" of history, but, rather, were the outcome of complex combinations of contingent circumstances and causes.

But if the idea of history as the unfolding of human potential had to be abandoned, what alternative view of history could be discerned in Marx's later writings? Althusser and his students read Marx's great economic work, *Capital,* for inspiration (and, in the process, set off a fashion for *Capital* reading groups all over Europe). However, the way they read *Capital* was very much shaped by the ideas and methods of the structuralists: anthropologist Claude Lévi-Strauss (b. 1908), linguist Ferdinand de Saussure (1857–1913), and psychoanalyst Jacques Lacan (1901–1981). While denying that he was a structuralist, Althusser shared much with them: looking for deep structures by a practice of "symptomatic" reading, understanding human consciousness and agency as the outcome of underlying sociocultural and psychological conditions, and seeing society itself as a complex set of structures, producing its effects independently of the will of human agents. The result of the study of *Capital* was a new and more rigorous definition of key Marxist ideas for thinking about economic life: the forces of production (raw materials, machinery, the division of labor and so on), and the social relations of production (relations of property and command) making up the "mode of production." But more significant was a new way of thinking about the place of economic activity within the wider society: here Althusser decisively rejected economic determinism in favor of a view of society as made up of a series of distinct "practices," including ideological (cultural), intellectual, and political practices as well as economic. Though the economy had great causal weight, the other practices had their own "relative autonomy," each playing its own part in producing the flow of historical events.

This notion of the relative autonomy of those noneconomic activities that had been assigned to the "superstructures" in classical Marxism was Althusser's way of addressing the key problem of twentieth-century European Marxism: how to understand the role of ideas and politics, of consciousness and agency in history. Marx had left a powerful legacy of economic theory, but only sketchy indications about these other topics: hence the widespread misrepresentation of Marxism as a kind of economic reductionism. In an essay written in 1968, the year of the "events" in Paris, Althusser developed his ideas further: ideology was to be understood in terms of the formation of individuals as "subjects" through their participation in social practices. The social locations of these practices were the "ideological state apparatuses" (ISAs): the schools, the family, trade unions, political parties, churches, and voluntary associations. These function by engaging individuals in practices that shape their sense of who they are in conformity to their destiny in society: as workers, mothers, professionals, obedient citizens. In other words, the ISAs play their part in reproducing the structure of social relations, and fitting human agents to their place in that structure. In this respect they complement by other means the disciplining and normalizing role of the central coercive institutions of the state (the "repressive state apparatuses": RSAs).

Although Althusser had, through these and other ideas, sparked off a huge renewal of Marxist thinking, his innovations were received much less enthusiastically by the student radicals of 1968. In seeming to deny a role for human agents in changing society, he had divorced theory from the urgent demands of practice. Althusser then embarked on a series of self-critical revisions of his ideas, never quite recapturing the originality of his earlier work. His insistence on recognizing the "relative autonomy" of cultural processes was taken further by poststructuralist students and followers such as Jacques Derrida (1930–2004) and Michel Foucault (1926–1984), who came to detach the analysis of cultural or "discursive" processes entirely from their economic underpinnings.

See also **Derrida, Jacques; Foucault, Michel; Merleau-Ponty, Maurice; Sartre, Jean-Paul.**

BIBLIOGRAPHY

Althusser, Louis. *For Marx.* Translated by Ben Brewster. London, 1969.

———. *Lenin and Philosophy and Other Essays.* Translated by Ben Brewster. London, 1971.

Benton, Ted. *The Rise and Fall of Structural Marxism.* New York, 1984.

Callinicos, Alex. *Althusser's Marxism.* London, 1976.

Elliott, Gregory. *Althusser: The Detour of Theory.* London, 1987.

Elliott, Gregory, ed. *Althusser: A Critical Reader.* Oxford, U.K., 1994.

Resch, Robert Paul. *Althusser and the Renewal of Marxist Social Theory.* Berkeley, Calif., 1992.

TED BENTON

AMERICANIZATION.

According to James Ceasar's *Reconstructing America: The Symbol of America in Modern Thought,* the term *Americanization* originated in the feeling among German immigrants of a growing estrangement of German Americans from their cultural roots back in Europe. But even if the word was not yet in use in the first half of the nineteenth century, the notion may well be traced back to the nation-building project that the United States began in the late eighteenth century. The United States had defined itself as an immigrant society and was faced with an influx of large numbers of people, at that time mainly from Europe but nevertheless of very diverse ethnic backgrounds. The task—according to the political elites in Washington and other vocal groups—was to turn the newcomers and also those who had already settled in the remote parts of the country farther west into "Americans," by which they meant active and loyal citizens. This pressure on the newcomers to become part of the existing society and to support its constitutional framework continued throughout the nineteenth century and evolved into a purposeful "Americanization" campaign in the early twentieth century.

THE RISE OF AMERICA AS A WORLD POWER

However, how the concept came to be generally understood in the twentieth century and is being understood in the early twenty-first century is an altogether different matter; for it shifted to the question of the impact that the United States is deemed to have outside its own national borders as an economic-technological, military-political, and cultural-intellectual power. This shift appears to be due not only to the successful internal nation building and consolidation of American society during the nineteenth century but also to its rise as an industrial nation. Before the beginning of the twentieth century, North America was viewed by many Europeans, but also by educated people in other parts of the world, as an untamed continent, populated by trappers, cowboys, and "Red Indians." Its economy was primarily agricultural. In European eyes, it was a faraway continent, largely self-sufficient and not in any tangible way immersed in the world economy and its global trading structures.

By the late nineteenth century, this image was no longer in tune with reality. During those years, the United States underwent a process of industrialization as rapid as that of other latecomers in Europe, notably imperial Germany. Its expanding manufacturing centers in Pennsylvania, Ohio, New York, and Michigan developed not only large capacities but also organizational infrastructures and practices of running an industrial enterprise that were highly innovative and, by the standards of the time, modern. Consequently, the United States began to appear in the rearview mirror of the great powers of Europe, whose imperialist politicians had more or less carved up the rest of the globe among themselves and now puzzled over the future role and socioeconomic dynamics of this "America" in world politics and the global economy. It certainly had the size and the material resources to compete with all of them. Its people were innovative, assertive, and smart enough to pose a major challenge.

It is probably no accident that the sense of facing a new competitor was particularly acutely felt in Britain, where debates on the future viability of its empire had become more heated after the turn of the twentieth century and in the wake of the poor performance of the British army in the Boer War in South Africa. Perceiving the course of world history in cyclical terms of the perennial rise and fall of great powers, writers and politicians in London wondered if the hegemonic position that the country had enjoyed in the nineteenth century would sooner or later have to give way to a global

American empire. This shift was seen not merely in political-military but also in technological-economic and sociocultural perspective and accounts for the success of a book that the British journalist William Stead published in 1902 under the title *The Americanization of the World*. By then other Europeans had similarly become more aware of the rise of the United States on the world stage and that it offered a model not only of modern industrial production and organization but also of political and constitutional ordering. Only now, some seventy years after its first appearance, did Alexis de Tocqueville's *Democracy in America* (1835, 1840) became more widely read in Europe. Even in Germany—a country that saw itself as an up-and-coming Great Power eager to challenge the older ones, and Britain in particular—people began to speak of an "American danger."

INDUSTRIAL MODELS AND CULTURAL INFLUENCES

One response to these developments was for Europeans to travel across the Atlantic to see the New World in person. The famous sociologist Max Weber, whose family had earlier on invested in American railroad stocks, was one of these visitors. In addition to academics, industrialists also took one of the modern ocean liners to study the American industrial system. This interest increased after the end of the Paris World Exhibition of 1900, where, in the American pavilion, visitors had been able to view the latest steel-cutting machinery and other technological developments. However, businessmen and engineers who traveled to the United States after the turn of the century were interested not merely in American technology but also in workshop organization and management techniques. In this connection they frequently tried to get an interview with Frederick Taylor and other apostles of the scientific management movement that promoted factory rationalization and the idea of incentives to both workers and entrepreneurs to change industrial practices and attitudes.

By 1914 these visitors would also go to Michigan to inspect Henry Ford's assembly lines and to learn about his ingeniously simple recipe of how to link the mass production of cars and other consumer durables to the creation of a mass consumer society. By not pocketing all the profits of rationalized production but by using the benefits of cost reduction and greater productivity to pay bonuses to his workers and to lower the price of his automobiles, Ford ensured that his cars, which had hitherto been beyond the financial means of the average family, became affordable. It was the beginning of mass motorization in America.

While some European industrialists were fascinated by Ford's innovations, others remained skeptical. They wondered about the transferability of Taylorism and Fordism to countries with different traditions, manufacturing practices, and employers' and workers' mentalities. Thus Renault cars in France and the Stuttgart electrical engineering firm of Robert Bosch began to experiment with ideas imported from America. But by 1913 the introduction of what became known as the "Bosch tempo" had run into so much resistance from the workforce in Stuttgart that the local metalworkers' union proclaimed a strike. It showed Bosch the cultural limits of "Americanization" and generated a good deal of schadenfreude among his more conservative colleagues, who had pointed to the differences between the American and German industrial systems and had predicted this kind of trouble.

From the start the Europeans, in confronting the question of Americanization, were therefore divided into two camps: those who were open to American ideas about how to manage a company and modern industrial system and others who rejected Fordism and Taylorism. This division applied not merely to factory organization but also to the structuring of the capitalist market. Thus the German steel industrialist August Thyssen became an early advocate of building large corporations that were capable of competing with American, French, or British steel trusts in a marketplace that was oligopolistically organized. Meanwhile many of his colleagues in the Ruhr region and elsewhere in Europe stuck to their preference for cartels, horizontal conglomerates of independent firms that fixed prices and laid down production quotas, thus trying to restrict competition.

These debates on the Americanization of European industry were disrupted by World War I and its chaotic aftermath. But when, from 1924 onward, the war-ravaged national economies of Europe began to stabilize and expand, interest in

American ideas revived. Once again European entrepreneurs, academics, and engineers—and this time also trade unionists—traveled across the Atlantic to inform themselves about American modernity. More than that, this time American industry itself came to Europe, either to establish its own production facilities in Britain, France, or Germany or to sign cooperation and patent agreements with individual companies. Thus Ford built factories in the British Midlands and Cologne, while General Motors took a stake in Opel cars in Germany and Vauxhall Motors in Britain. At the same time American and European chemical trusts increased their cooperation.

Next to rationalized American production that held out the promise of generating mass consumption, it was now also American popular culture and mass entertainment that reached Europe. Within a few years, Hollywood established a dominant position in the European movie business. Week after week millions of people would go to see one of the increasingly sophisticated products emerging from the dream factories, some 70 to 80 percent of which came from California. Jazz and new dance forms, such as the Charleston, were embraced as imports from America by mainly young people. However, just as in the case of Taylorism and Fordism, there was also rejection. The critics argued that what was flooding the market from across the Atlantic was cheap, primitive, and vulgar and threatened the allegedly superior and more refined cultural traditions of Europe.

The collapse of the world economy in 1929 put a heavy damper on the American challenge of the 1920s. Investments in Europe shrank as nations retreated behind protective tariff walls. Only Hollywood films continued to be imported, and for Hitler's propaganda minister Joseph Goebbels the products churned out in California provided a model for the building of a "counter-Hollywood" that would flood Europe with German films. Nor did the interest in the American manufacturing industry and its methods disappear in Europe. American firms such as Ford and General Motors continued to operate until the outbreak of World War II. And when Hitler decided to build a mass-produced Volkswagen (people's car) at Wolfsburg in Lower Saxony based on a design by Ferdinand Porsche, the latter traveled to the

United States to study American car manufacturing. By the late 1930s, not only German but also British and French industry had refocused their efforts away from civilian goods and on the rationalized production of military hardware.

AMERICANIZATION AFTER WORLD WAR II

Two factors revived the question of Americanization soon after the end of the global conflict in 1945: first, the United States was now unquestionably the hegemonic power of the West after the war had devastated large parts of Europe and greatly depleted the wealth of its nations; second, the United States had begun to learn a lesson from the perceived mistakes made after World War I. This time Washington, instead of retreating into isolationism, committed itself without delay to the reconstruction of Europe. It was a decision that was reinforced by the outbreak of the Cold War against the Soviet bloc. In 1945 and 1946 some Western Europeans still thought that it might be possible to find a "third way" between American capitalism and Soviet communism, but they quickly came to realize that economic self-interest and the need to protect themselves against a possible invasion by the Soviets led them to the side of the United States. They thus accepted Washington's leadership in the fields of politics and defense and also—albeit more grudgingly—in the field of economic reconstruction. The rebuilding of Western Europe with the help of the European Recovery Program (ERP, also known as the Marshall Plan) was tied to the broad acceptance of American ideas about organizing the postwar world economy. This world economy would be liberal-capitalist and required adapting the organizations of production and management to the American practices, including labor relations.

These practices were partly transmitted through study tours, funded by Marshall Plan productivity councils, which took European industrialists, academics, and trade unionists to the manufacturing centers of the East Coast and the Midwest. But there were also local programs and the example of American firms in Europe. Ford and General Motors resumed production at the former sites. American styling began to influence the body design of European cars—for example, of the Opel Kadett and Opel Kapitän models. Cooperation

The 1958 Opel Kapitän model reflected the influence of American automobile design and engineering technology. ©BETTMANN/CORBIS

with the big rubber trusts in Ohio led to the introduction of tubeless and whitewall tires. Marketing and packaging also became exposed to American ideas. However, as before World War II, Fordism was never just about modern machinery and rationalized assembly-line production. It was also about affordable prices, and if price tags even for a Volkswagen, a Citroën, or a Baby Austin were initially still out of reach for the average European consumer, manufacturers of mopeds, motorbikes, scooters, and "bubble cars" stepped into the breach. Mass motorization thus advanced in stages as people traded upward.

Yet, as in the 1920s, there was also resistance to these Americanizing trends. Among the entrepreneurs, the conservative coal and steel magnates, especially in the Ruhr region, were the most stubborn critics. Nor did many older generation consumers find it easy to accept lavish chrome grills on cars or Madison Avenue–style advertising billboards. What happened was that in many cases modern designs for automobiles, radios, gramophone combinations, or kitchen appliances either integrated the foreign with the indigenous or offered the old and the new side by side. Furniture provides a good example of this: while many people kept or, if lost in the war, repurchased traditional-style heavyset sideboards and settees, others, especially young people, opted for kidney-shaped tables, colorful curtains, and tubular steel sofa beds. Some of these latter designs, it is true, had first been developed by the Bauhaus movement until the Nazis forced its leading lights into exile. Now their designs returned to Europe transformed by the experience of the so-called Chicago Bauhaus. The key point to be made here is not only that European fascism and its aftermath had intensified the movement of people and ideas back and forth across the Atlantic but also that Europe's renewed exposure to America after 1945 resulted in a blending of foreign with native influences. It was a trend that could be observed all over Western Europe.

At the same time, the relative speed with which living standards rose dictated how quickly Fordism in both the productionist and consumerist sense proliferated. Nevertheless, even in those countries where material prosperity came at a slower pace, the images of consumerism that appeared on billboards, in newspapers ads, and in magazine articles helped to create desires and expectations. These in turn induced consumers to plan their next major acquisition, while the manufacturers came under pressure to respond to the popular quest for a better life.

There was yet another aspect to the growing presence of American ideas in the production and marketing of goods in Western Europe during the 1950s. Just as Fordist production reappeared, so did American popular culture and mass entertainment. If living standards rose too slowly to make the purchase of a car or washing machine immediately affordable, prices for movie theaters and rock or jazz concerts were within the reach of enthusiasts. Consequently, film stars such as Marlon Brando and James Dean or rock musicians such as Elvis Presley and Bill Haley achieved a similar status in many parts of Western Europe as they had first gained in the United States. This popular culture had a democratizing impact on the young people who began to see and listen to it. Gender relations began to change. Postwar social conventions and

behavior patterns were being challenged and slowly softened up. If many parents, family politicians, and churchmen were initially appalled by the arrival of American cultural imports, over time they, too, became more tolerant, partly because they came to recognize that the fears they had harbored of the moral and political dangers of American popular culture were exaggerated.

In these circumstances the expansion of consumerism and popular culture continued. Toward the end of the twentieth century, America was very present in Europe in many spheres of life, and resistance to it, which had remained quite vociferous, especially among the educated middle classes in the 1950s, had weakened. Still, Americanization never went so far as to obliterate indigenous traditions and practices. Wherever one traveled in Western Europe in the 1980s and 1990s, one could never mistake that one was in the United States rather than in Italy, Spain, France, Britain, Sweden, or Germany. The indigenous and the "American" had either come together in a peculiar new mix, or they existed side by side. It depended on the sphere of social reality whether the foreign element had succeeded in leaving a stronger or weaker mark on the original local product or practice.

ASSESSING AMERICAN INFLUENCES

The complexities of these interactions and negotiations between American industry and popular culture, on the one hand, and between the societies that came under the hegemonic influence of the Western superpower after World War I and even more directly and persistently after 1945, on the other, have not always been given full recognition by those social scientists and historians who turned their attention to the postwar processes of European reconstruction. At the one end of the spectrum of opinion were those scholars who viewed Americanization as a steamroller that flattened existing institutions, traditions, and practices, leading to a sprouting of purely American "plants" in its wake. Not surprisingly, this interpretation was soon countered by a school of thought that believed that the economies of Europe pulled themselves up by their own bootstraps and that not even the tangible aid given by the Marshall Plan had made much of a difference. Focusing on market structures and

McDonald's advertising sign, Paris, 1992. The appearance of the American fast-food chain in Paris was seen by many Europeans as a powerful symbol of unwanted Americanization and sparked protests at many levels of French society. ©CAROL HAVENS/CORBIS

labor relations, they had a point in that traditions proved noticeably resistant and durable in these spheres. The writings of the British economic historian Alan Milward were particularly influential here, as were the books of Werner Abelshauser in West Germany.

Other economic and business historians came along to undermine Milward's and Abelshauser's arguments and to demonstrate that American ideas and policies were powerful enough to wrench European entrepreneurs away from traditional behaviors and mindsets. Before long, the debate among those working with quantitative materials spilled over into questions of more intangible cultural patterns. Early cultural and literary historians still took the steamroller approach when they spoke of the "Coca-Colonization" of European culture. What came to be emphasized in the early twenty-first century were the subtle processes of encounter

and negotiation between two different industrial cultures and cultural systems more generally. As a result, economic and business history, in the past firmly wedded to hard statistical data, took a "culturalist turn" and is interested in less tangible shifts in entrepreneurial behavior. Similar developments have occurred in research on consumers and their responses to American imports. The experience of Japan in these fields has meanwhile also been made the subject of scholarship.

All this has created a wider acceptance of the notion that Americanization is a useful analytical tool for examining the structural and mental changes in postwar Europe (and Japan), but it also means that one has to consider a greater durability of indigenous structures and attitudes in some fields than the early steamroller interpretation of these processes had allowed for. Furthermore, it is thought important not only to look at changes at the macroeconomic and national level but also to take into account possible generational, class, and gender differences within a particular nation. These differences were probably more marked in the Americanization processes of Europe during the interwar years or in the 1950s. But they should also be borne in mind when testing the concept with regard to later decades, not least because it has become more difficult to delineate precisely what is American and what is not in a world that has become more interpenetrated economically and culturally.

See also **Automobiles; Cinema; Consumption; Fordism; Globalization; Industrial Capitalism; Jazz; Marshall Plan; Taylorism; Technology.**

BIBLIOGRAPHY

Berghahn, Volker R. *The Americanization of West German Industry, 1945–1973.* New York, 1986.

Ceasar, James. *Reconstructing America: The Symbol of America in Modern Thought.* New Haven, Conn., 1997.

Costigliola, Frank. *Awkward Dominion: American Political, Economic, and Cultural Relations with Europe, 1919–1933.* Ithaca, N.Y., 1984.

Fehrenbach, Heide, and Uta G. Poiger, eds. *Transactions, Transgressions, Transformations: American Culture in Western Europe and Japan.* New York, 2000.

Hogan, Michael J. *The Marshall Plan.* Cambridge, U.K., 1987.

Kroes, Rob. *If You've Seen One, You've Seen the Mall: Europeans and American Mass Culture.* Urbana, Ill., 1996.

Kuisel, Richard F. *Seducing the French: The Dilemma of Americanization.* Berkeley, Calif., 1993.

Pells, Richard H. *Not Like Us: How Europeans Have Loved, Hated, and Transformed American Culture since World War II.* New York, 1997.

Rosenberg, Emily. *Spreading the American Dream.* New York, 1982.

Saunders, Frances Stoner. *The Cultural Cold War.* New York, 1999.

Wagnleitner, Reinhold. *Coca-Colonization and Cold War.* Chapel Hill, N.C., 1994.

VOLKER R. BERGHAHN

AMSTERDAM. On the eve of the First World War Amsterdam was an extraordinarily full city. The population had roughly doubled since the mid-nineteenth century, to some 700,000, and continued to grow. Some new neighborhoods had been built during the 1870s, most notably the working class neighborhood De Pijp to the south of the city. Likewise, a number of wealthy commuter villages such as Bloemendaal and Hilversum had developed. These expansions, however, were not nearly enough to house the increasing population. Although Amsterdam's population growth slowed markedly during the twentieth century, the city was more than three times as large, geographically, in 2004 as it had been in 1914.

The first decades of the twentieth century saw new developments that, unlike the new neighborhoods of the late nineteenth century, were carefully managed by local governments. The first and largest new expansion, Plan Zuid, designed by the architect Henrick Petrus Berlage (1856–1934), was approved in 1917. It was one of the first such large-scale expansion plans in The Netherlands and had a great influence on similar projects in other cities. The plan also offered an opportunity to modernist architects such as Berlage and to the newly developed Amsterdam school of architecture. Compared to the rather stern modernism of Berlage's architecture, the Amsterdam School stands out for its curvy, Jugendstil-inspired style, which still dominates much of the southern half of the city. During the interwar years, the first garden cities were built. Farther away from the city center, these oases would offer the working classes a healthy living environment, with ample fresh air and green surroundings. To the north of the city, across the Het IJ waterway, neighborhoods arose with alluring names such as "garden village" and, to modern tastes at least, less appealing ones such as "concrete village."

Quantitatively, however, the greatest urban expansion took place after World War II. During the 1950s and 1960s, new residential areas were erected on all sides of the city, more than doubling the built surface. In the early 1970s, the Bijlmermeer district was constructed in the southeast of the city. The Bijlmer was seen by many at the time as the answer to the housing problems of the modern city, but the high-rise apartment blocks soon became notorious for housing criminals and drug addicts. Moreover, Amsterdam began to expand beyond its formal borders, as people moved to Amstelveen and other neighboring towns and commuted to Amsterdam. In the 1970s and 1980s, a new city, Almere, was built in the newly acquired land of the Flevopolder, housing much of the population spillover from the city. Throughout most of the twentieth century, however, Amsterdam continued to face a serious housing shortage, often leading to serious social tensions.

IMMIGRATION

Amsterdam was always an immigrant city, and it experienced a number of smaller and larger waves of immigration during the twentieth century. During the 1930s, numerous Jewish refugees from Germany came to Amsterdam, among them, in 1934, five-year-old Anne Frank. The quick and successful integration of the Frank family into Amsterdam's economy and society was not, however, entirely typical. Relations between the local Jewish community and newcomers were often tense, as were relations between newcomers and non-Jews. There has been continuing debate about the prospects of survival for the Netherland's roughly twenty-two thousand foreign Jews, the majority of whom lived in Amsterdam, during World War II. Foreign-born Jews were among the first to be deported and very few of them returned to Amsterdam after the war.

During the 1960s and 1970s, Moroccans and Turks moved to Amsterdam in considerable numbers, finding housing in often decrepit nineteenth-century housing blocks. Although initially immigrants consisted mainly of young men, family reunification eventually led to the establishment of sizable Turkish and Moroccan communities in Amsterdam. Relations between these immigrants, and their children and grandchildren, and the ethnically Dutch inhabitants of the city never were ideal and reached an absolute low in November 2004 when the film director Theo van Gogh, after releasing a controversial anti-Islamic film, was murdered by a fundamentalist Muslim of Moroccan descent.

After the independence of Surinam in 1975, numerous Surinamese came to Amsterdam. Because their arrival coincided with the building of the Bijlmermeer, where relatively cheap housing

was available in considerable quantities, the newly built neighborhood came to house the large Surinamese community.

While newcomers moved to the city, many among the native population were moving out. The ethnically Dutch moved out of the city, to Almere, Purmerend, Amstelveen, and other commuter cities. The places they left open in the city were filled partly by foreign immigrants and partly by the highly educated and affluent Dutch, many of them without children.

ECONOMY

The economic backbone of Amsterdam, and arguably its raison d'être, has long been its harbor. During the twentieth century, however, the relative importance of the Amsterdam harbor to the Dutch and European economies declined. The rise of Rotterdam, since the 1870s, as the region's most important harbor, gradually reduced the port of Amsterdam to a junior status. The port of Amsterdam declined but did not disappear altogether. Certain products, such as tobacco, cocoa, and timber, long continued to be landed in Amsterdam in considerable quantities.

Another important economic function of Amsterdam stemmed from its position as the nation's financial center. The Amsterdam stock exchange, built on the Rokin by Berlage in 1903, served as the main stock exchange in the Netherlands, and it attracted considerable financial and banking activity. It nevertheless employed but a fraction of the hundreds of thousands of people who lived in Amsterdam. During the first decades of the twentieth century, the city's considerable industrial activity employed the bulk of the population, but it was never a center of industry on the order of cities such as Enschede (textiles), Eindhoven (electronics), and Rotterdam. Still, metallurgy and textile manufacturing were prominent, offering employment to many of Amsterdam's residents.

The production of pharmaceutical drugs, cigars, and beer were typical industries for the city, but they did not retain their links to the city after the Second World War. The influx of Jewish textile workers, refugees from Nazi Germany, helped in the expansion of the textile industry, an expansion abruptly ended by the German invasion of May 1940. Another predominantly Jewish, Amsterdam-based

A residential development designed by Amsterdam-school architect Michael De Klerk and completed in 1920 includes housing, a school, and a post office. ©CHRISTIAN SARAMON/CORBIS

industry also deserves notice. The diamond processing industry formed a reasonably large part of the prewar labor market, and was notable as the first unionized industry in the Netherlands. Socialist politics in prewar Amsterdam, and in the Netherlands generally, owed a considerable debt to the diamond workers.

One industry that remained centered in Amsterdam throughout the twentieth century was printing and publishing. Most of the main newspapers were based in Amsterdam, and the many newspaper mergers during the twentieth century further strengthened the dominance of the city within the Netherlands. Publishing houses, like Dutch cultural life in general, remained very much an Amsterdam affair. This is also indicative of the position of Amsterdam within the Netherlands. The city was not a major industrial center and no longer the nation's main harbor or its seat of government. Among the "softer" industries, and

especially as the center of opinion-making and culture, its position remained dominant throughout the modern period.

From the 1960s onward, Amsterdam attracted large numbers of tourists. The city's liberal attitudes toward prostitution and illegal drugs were attractive to some, alluring the young and pleasure seekers from around Europe and the United States to the famous Red Light District and cannabis coffeehouses. Less visibly, the city also became an important attraction for older, more culturally inclined tourists. The relatively intact city center, the Rijksmuseum National Gallery with its unsurpassed collection of Dutch masters, and the Van Gogh museum were among the main attractions for the millions of tourists who visited the city annually during the second half of the twentieth century. This development contributed to the formation of a strongly service-oriented economy.

THE SECOND WORLD WAR

Compared to the other major Dutch city, Rotterdam, Amsterdam had a relatively easy start to the German occupation. The Luftwaffe bombarded Rotterdam, destroying much of the city and leaving more than two thousand dead. Amsterdam was hit, on 11 May 1940, leaving fifty-one people dead, but the devastation was not comparable to that experienced by Rotterdam. The fear that Amsterdam would be bombed in the manner of Rotterdam was one reason why the Dutch government capitulated. The city fell into German hands largely unscathed, and troops marched into Amsterdam unhindered and without meeting any significant resistance from the populace.

The fate of Amsterdam was to be far worse than some might have anticipated during those first weeks. Home, as it was, to the bulk of the Jewish population of the Netherlands, Amsterdam became the main theater of isolation, discrimination, and ultimately deportation of tens of thousands of people. This process was partly organized by the "Jewish council," led by eminent members of the Jewish community Abraham Asscher and David Cohen. The Jewish council proved to be a highly effective organ for organizing the genocide that followed. Careful to avoid an intensification of German aggression, the council supported cooperation and collaborated both with policies of isolation and, to some degree, administered the deportation. In the process of isolating and deporting the Jewish citizens of Amsterdam, the Germans could also count on a remarkably loyal civil service and especially a highly cooperative local police force.

That is not to say, however, that there was no resistance whatsoever. On 25 and 26 September 1941 members of the clandestine Communist Party instigated a general strike against the discrimination against Jews. The strike, and the demonstrations that came with it, made a great impression on the people of Amsterdam and the Netherlands and continues to be commemorated annually. Nevertheless, the strike was unsuccessful, and on 26 September German troops violently put an end to it. The importance of the strike for the Jewish population of Amsterdam was that it awakened, in some, a sense of duty to help. Children were smuggled out of the city and hidden. A minority of the Jewish community went into hiding with the aid of non-Jewish citizens. Still, the number of Jewish Amsterdamers who survived in hiding were far outnumbered by those who saw no other option but to report for deportation when so required. On 29 September 1943 the last razzia, or roundup, occurred, and the Jewish council was disbanded. Apart from those who remained in hiding, and a small minority who had escaped persecution through marriages, the eighty-thousand-strong Jewish population was gone. Only a handful returned after liberation.

As the occupation progressed, deprivation increased. Shortages of textiles, fuel, and shoes gradually developed from a nuisance into a severe problem. Economic hardship reached its peak in the winter of 1944–1945, when the combination of a train strike, German aggression, and the freezing of canals disabled the supplies of food to Amsterdam and other large cities. As food stocks ran dangerously low, a serious crisis ensued. Long lines of people took to the countryside to buy or barter food from farmers. Black market prices soared. Those who were socially and economically weak, notably the elderly who lacked the support of family or friends, fell victim to starvation. An eruption of infectious disease took even more lives. To avoid freezing, people ravaged their home interiors for firewood, as well as (perhaps primarily) the interiors of others. By the time of liberation, the "hunger winter," as it was known, had led to thousands of deaths in Amsterdam alone.

ART

Amsterdam had long been the center of art and culture in the Netherlands, and the twentieth century brought an intensification of this dominance. During the interwar years, Amsterdam boasted a lively cultural life, including painters of repute. The Concertgebouw was widely recognized as one of Europe's finer concert halls and housed an excellent orchestra. Still, Amsterdam's international appeal was limited. Although the once common view, that the Netherlands were particularly backward in things artistic during the interwar years, has been refuted, it is clear that the city could not compete with Paris, London, or Vienna as a cultural center. The relative importance of Amsterdam in the international cultural scene did increase markedly after the Second World War.

Special mention should be made of the Stedelijk Museum, or city museum. Founded in the late nineteenth century, the Stedelijk became a center of avant-garde art during the tenure of Willem Sandberg as director (1945–1962). Sandberg modeled the museum on New York's Museum of Modern Art and introduced a number of modern artists to the Dutch public, often to both their disgust and that of the press. The 1949 exhibition of members of the CoBrA group was groundbreaking, as were exhibitions of work by the artists of the movement called De Stijl (Dutch for "the style"), Pablo Picasso (1881–1973) and Joan Miró (1893–1983). Not only did Sandberg change a somewhat provincial local museum into an important center of modern art and develop a magnificent collection, he also did much to make modern, and especially abstract, art respectable (or even palpable) to Dutch audiences.

More generally, the 1950s and 1960s were an era of great cultural and artistic upheaval. Modern jazz found an audience among the bohemians, intellectuals, and artists of Amsterdam. Musicians moved to the city, not least because of the prevailing liberal atmosphere. In 1968 Paradiso, the city's main venue for pop and rock music, was established in a former church and proved able to attract many international stars. In 1973 the Bimhuis, a venue for jazz and improvised music, was opened, with a likewise international outlook. In combination with the Concertgebouworkest, Amsterdam became host to an exceptionally wide range of musical styles and genres.

REVOLUTION?
Amsterdam was never a politically quiet city. Before World War II, the city experienced considerable political upheaval especially during the years of economic hardship of World War I and the crisis years of the 1930s. Compared to the Netherlands at large, Amsterdam was (and remained) a city of left-wing sympathies. During World War I and the 1930s, when economic hardship struck the working classes, the city was rocked by rioting. Although communist and other revolutionary political movements were involved in agitating among the impoverished unemployed during these troubled times, much of the rioting of 1917 and 1934, when the biggest eruptions took place, had a more or less spontaneous character.

True revolutionary zeal developed after liberation from the Germans, albeit without ever posing a truly serious threat to the official, democratic political order. In the 1946 elections, the Communist Party gained so many seats that it was able to form a coalition with the Social Democrats, but in the longer run its following was too small to constitute much of a threat. In 1956, after the Soviet invasion of Hungary, the Communist Party office was besieged by an angry mob. Although it remained a radical voice in the city until the late 1980s, communism was not a particularly potent political force in postwar Amsterdam.

Nevertheless, Amsterdam did experience a considerable amount of militant left-wing activity in the years following liberation. The nation's capital city became the focal point of politically inspired unrest. During the early 1960s, a loose federation of young, highly heterodox activists began to rebel against the status quo. Cigarette smoking, which had only recently been found to cause cancer, became something to rebel against, along with the atomic bomb, NATO, and many other things. The demonstrations and other activities carried out by militants briefly united under the name Provo—an anarchist youth movement and also the name of an anarchist magazine (1965–1967)—elicited considerable police violence but were not initially seen as particularly threatening. This changed on 10 March 1966 when a smoke-bomb was thrown into the wedding parade of crown-princess Beatrix and her German husband, Claus von Amsberg, and shocked the nation.

The significance of Provo in the history of Amsterdam and the Netherlands stems to a large extent from demographic circumstances. The movement itself did not survive the mid-1960s, but it did inspire the baby boom generation that was then reaching adolescence. The sheer number of adolescents in the country, and their eagerness to come to Amsterdam, ensured that the counterculture would be there to stay. The city seemed engulfed with activism against the Vietnam War, against local policies, and against the establishment in general. Students occupied the university, people slept in the street, and marijuana was consumed in ample quantities. Amsterdam was gripped by the 1960s counterculture. The city changed visibly, but the true confrontations with the authorities were yet to come.

The hard clashes between activists and the authorities, interestingly, did not normally concern issues such as NATO or South African apartheid or other vexing issues, but city policies. The main trend in urban planning had been toward the spatial separation of urban functions, large-scale projects, and a more practical urban infrastructure. The Bijlmer, the Metro, the new city hall, and the opera theater rallied the cities' radicals to violent resistance. The postwar view of urban development, inspired by the likes of the Swiss-born architect and artist Le Corbusier, met little enthusiasm among the extreme Left in Amsterdam. Attempts to move people out of the overcrowded, badly maintained, and ill-planned old neighborhoods and into garden cities farther away seemed socially sound, but many people begged to differ.

The radical Left in the city opted rather for the "compact city" in which various urban functions (working, living, shopping) were to take place in the same space, and large projects and demolition were taboo. From 1970 onward, this movement was strengthened by an energetic and very vocal movement of squatters. Squatting in empty houses and other buildings was, under certain conditions, not illegal. Moreover, at first the squatters could count on considerable public sympathy. The image of the homeless squatter pitted against the heartless landlord was a heroic one, but squatters rapidly lost public sympathy due to the often violent confrontations with the police. The low point in this period was the coronation of Queen Beatrix on 30 April 1980, when she was once more confronted with an unruly city; squatters and the police spent the afternoon in seemingly endless and violent battle. During the later 1980s and 1990s squatting declined, although it never totally disappeared. Along with it, large-scale rioting against urban planners has been marginalized. This is at least partially the result of changed views on what Amsterdam should become. Many of the views of the radical Left on the use of the public space, most notably that of the compact city, have become incorporated into mainstream policies.

See also **Frank, Anne; Netherlands; 1968; World War II.**

BIBLIOGRAPHY

Mak, Geert. *Amsterdam: Brief Life of the City.* Translated by Philipp Blom. Cambridge, Mass., 2000.

Moore, Bob. *Victims and Survivors: The Nazi Persecution of the Jews in the Netherlands, 1940–1945.* New York, 1997.

Roegholt, Richter. *Amsterdam na 1900.* Amsterdam, 1993.

RALF FUTSELAAR

ANARCHISM. Throughout the nineteenth century there was a sense of shared values that linked the anarchist, the socialist, the Marxist, the syndicalist, and even the social reformer. Itinerant figures who crossed among parties, groups, and campaigns were probably more typical of this period than were dedicated, dogmatic one-party militants. Anarchism was therefore one aspect of an eclectic and varied political milieu. For example, one could cite the political biography of Madeleine Pelletier (1874–1939). She is best remembered for her campaigns for women's contraceptive rights, but the story of her changing political allegiances is revealing. While a teenager, Pelletier attended anarchist and feminist meetings. She joined a women's Masonic lodge in 1904 and enrolled in both a Republican group and a socialist organization in 1906. In the same vein, one could cite figures such as William Morris (1834–1896), Oscar Wilde (1854–1900), Georges Sorel (1847–1922), and Octave Mirbeau (1850–1917): all activists and writers whose political values defy the more precise descriptions that were to come into use during the twentieth century.

However, during the nineteenth century a number of tendencies developed that later came to be seen as distinctively anarchist. The most important of these related to the role of authority in the political process. While Marxists and Blanquists (followers of the veteran revolutionary Auguste Blanqui [1805–1881]) defended the idea of a temporary revolutionary dictatorship to guide oppressed people to a better society, anarchists stressed the need to start the construction of non-authoritarian structures immediately. From this point flowed a number of lesser, but still significant, differences. Marxists linked political processes to economic cycles; anarchists showed a more flexible or more naive faith in the imminent possibility of revolution in even the most adverse circumstances. Correspondingly, Marxists stressed the central political importance of the working class. Many nineteenth-century anarchists accepted this, but there remained skeptics who would also consider the political potential of the peasant community, or of artistic and literary circles. Marxists could defend colonialism as bringing primitive societies, based on irrational, archaic myths, into the world of modernity. Anarchists were often more skeptical about claims that a colonial state could guide such societies along a progressive path—although even they found it difficult to identify the native peoples of Africa or Asia as their equals. Another small, but telling, detail was an attitude to language. Marxists tended to demand that the workers' press should be written grammatically, with correct spelling and syntax. Anarchists were fascinated by the subversive potential of slang and some—such as the veteran French anarchosyndicalist propagandist Emile Pouget (1860–1931)—wrote columns of newspaper prose in the vivid, earthy tones of proletarian patois. Finally, some important economic issues distinguished the two strands.

EARLY TWENTIETH-CENTURY ANARCHISM
Twentieth-century anarchist history can be structured around four key dates: 1921, 1936, 1968, and 1999.

The separation and clarification of the loose strands of nineteenth-century leftist thought occurred between 1914 and 1917. The outbreak of World War I divided patriots from revolutionaries: significantly, even Peter Kropotkin (1842–1921), one of the greatest late nineteenth-century anarchist political philosophers, chose to back the western allies against Germany, seeing this as an alliance of liberal societies against authoritarian states. Few anarchist militants followed him, but many found themselves as isolated antiwar critics, cut off from all mass movements. The second great political division came in 1917: the Bolshevik Revolution.

The years after 1917 were unsettled. Following the slaughter that occurred during World War I and the censorship and repression of dissident leftist voices across Europe, the Bolshevik Revolution seemed like the answer to many prayers. Anarchist

responses ranged from the enthusiastic to the cautious, but very few made any immediate criticisms. Across Europe, the creation of communist parties divided and confused anarchists. Frequently, anarchists joined. In most cases, they then grew disillusioned with the ethics and practices of bolshevism. However, there was no single, stark turning point in European anarchists' analyses and attitudes regarding the communist state. The experience of Victor Serge (1890–1947), a Belgian-Russian militant with a record of anarchist activism in France and Spain, is a good example of the anarchist experience. He crossed into Soviet Russia in 1919. He was appalled by the grim, bureaucratic, authoritarian ethos of the Communist Party, but felt constrained to support it against its reactionary enemies. However, he continued to voice criticisms of the new regime. He was imprisoned in 1933 and then released and expelled from the Soviet Union in 1936 as a gesture by the Soviet government to the Popular Front coalitions in France and Spain. While Serge never returned to anarchism, his post-1936 criticisms of the Soviet Union, both in the form of pamphlets and astonishingly powerful novels, are some of the most eloquent libertarian analyses of communist society. Serge died in exile in Mexico.

The revolt in the port of Kronstadt (opposite Petrograd) in March 1921, was a key indication of the deep difference between anarchist and communist forms of organization and political philosophies. The ports' sailors and soldiers, previously militant communists, revolted against the dictatorship of the Communist Party and demanded more libertarian forms of political organization. Their revolt was put down by the Red Army under Leon Trotsky (1879–1940). A few desperate dissidents crossed the Gulf of Finland to spread the news about the crushing of the revolt, but few anarchists heard their message clearly. Instead, in each country, an awkward, emotionally charged argument continued sporadically over the 1920s. In many European countries (such as Germany and Great Britain), the new communist organizations effectively replaced the older syndicalist and anarchist groups. In Italy, the anarchosyndicalist USI (Unione Sindacale Italiana—Italian Syndicalist Union) retained some working-class presence, but was then crushed by Benito Mussolini's (1879–1940) dictatorship. In France, anarchosyndicalism only survived as a fractured tendency, maintaining a marginal existence within both the Socialist CGT (Confédération Générale de Travail) and the Communist CGTU (Confédération Générale de Travail unifiée) and—confusingly—also represented by the small CGTSR (Confédération Génerale de Travail Syndicaliste Révolutionnaire) after 1926.

Few of the pre–World War I anarchosyndicalist movements survived into the 1930s. One of the exceptions was the Swedish SAC (Sveriges Arbetares Centralorganisation—Central Organization of the Workers of Sweden), which, having drifted into moderate, reformist politics in the 1930s, and Cold War anti-Sovietism in the 1950s, is at the beginning of the twenty-first century experiencing a modest revival in its numbers. However, the most important of the remaining organizations was the Spanish CNT (Confederación Nacional del Trabajo—National Confederation of Labor), created in 1911. About half a million workers were members in 1931; it seems possible that late in 1936 there were more than a million, making the CNT the largest anarchist organization in history.

The trajectory of Spanish anarchism was central to the overall development of mid-twentieth-century anarchism. The CNT attracted the support of the most advanced workers in Spain (the textile factory workers of Barcelona), but it also attracted much support from the poor landless laborers of Andalusia and from intellectuals, artists, and writers. An anarcho-feminist organization, Mujeres Libres (Free Women) developed alongside it. In July 1936 a reactionary coup was launched by conservative generals terrified by the prospect of radical social reform. Its immediate consequence was the collapse of parliamentary government, and for a few brief months the tried and tested anarchist arguments became the common sense of democratic Spain. Workers' militias beat back soldiers and the police, preserving about two-thirds of Spain from the coup. The CNT effectively ran Barcelona, which, with more than a million inhabitants, was the biggest city in Spain. They also controlled much of Catalonia, Valencia, and Aragon. Peasants seized the land, expelled landowners and priests, and ran their own communities.

By 1937 the situation had changed. Italian and German military aid to the rebel generals made them into a much more serious fighting force. The more meager Russian military aid, often sent directly to the Spanish Communist Party, transformed it from a tiny far-left sect into a serious political force, uniting moderate Republicans, liberal officers, and committed militants. The CNT, by comparison, seemed almost alone in the world. Small anarchist groups revived across Europe, desperately attempting to provide solidarity and aid. But the anarchosyndicalists were outgunned: many joined the great wave of a half a million refugees who fled from Catalonia to France in January and February 1939, when the Spanish Republic was finally extinguished.

LATE TWENTIETH-CENTURY ANARCHISM

The next three decades were desperate times for anarchist movements. The political polarization typical of the Cold War left little room for libertarian thought. A few tiny anarchosyndicalist groups survived in France and Sweden; some libertarian magazines and papers continued. Significantly, Cornelius Castoriadis (1922–1997), a genuinely innovative Greek French thinker who moved closer to anarchist principles in this period, and who contributed much to the later revival of anarchist thought, never used the term *anarchist* to describe his own thinking. There was a type of generational renewal of anarchist principles: the next generation of militants were more likely to have drawn their inspiration from radical art movements, such as the surrealists, or from ecological ideals, rather than from the labor movement.

May 1968 began the breakdown of the rigid structures of Cold War politics. A new far-left emerged. It was sometimes as authoritarian, as worker-oriented, as the old communism, but sometimes more eclectic and more willing to draw inspiration from heterodox sources. It was significant that, for example, the participatory ideals of the women's liberation movement often resembled the older anarchist antiauthoritarian practices. Green activists were more inspired by Kropotkin's *Mutual Aid* (1902) than by Karl Marx's (1818–1883) *Capital*. But within this tapestry of new thinking, anarchism was just one strand among many. While there was some re-foundation of anarchist organizations, none of them ever acquired the status or the mass membership of the early twentieth-century groups.

After the death of Francisco Franco (1892–1975) and the reestablishment of democratic rule in Spain there was a widespread expectation that the CNT would revive as a powerful force in Spanish politics. This never happened. Instead, the movement split, with one tendency aggressively defending a legacy of syndicalist hyper-militancy (still known as "CNT"), while another, the CGT (Confederación General del Trabajo), adopting a self-consciously "pragmatic" stance. At the end of the twentieth century this second tendency was quite successful in recruiting disillusioned militants from communist and socialist trade unions, but often its explicitly anarchosyndicalist identity seems to have been diluted. Similar processes are at work in France, with two rival CNTs, plus a somewhat larger organization, SUD (Solidaires, Unitaires, et Démocratiques—Solidarity, Unity, and Democracy), with a rather distant, indirect link to the older anarchosyndicalist tradition.

Elsewhere anarchists have contributed to a diverse range of causes: antinuclear and antiwar activism, squatters' movements, animal rights, free schools, and solidarity campaigns. In such cases, anarchism has worked best as a strand of critical, independent thought, invigorating and radicalizing other movements. The movement's intellectual center of gravity seems to have moved across the Atlantic. After the intriguing postsurrealist utopianism of the Parisian Situationists, the most significant recent anarchist thinkers are mainly based in the United States. They include Noam Chomsky (b. 1928), Ursula le Guin (b. 1929), Murray Bookchin (b. 1921), and John Zerzan (b. 1943). They have proposed a variety of ideas: Chomsky has achieved a worldwide reputation as a critic of U.S. foreign policy, Le Guin is a gifted science fiction writer and a committed Daoist, Bookchin has synthesized ecological thinking with more traditional anarchist concerns, and Zerzan proposes an antiindustrial, antitechnological utopianism. There is some tension between European anarchist political culture, within which the legacy and ethos of anarchosyndicalism still commands respect, and the "post-leftist" ideas that circulate in the United States.

Antiglobalization—or "alternative globalization"—has become a key theme in contemporary anarchist political culture. The inspiration for this turn came from the Zapatista revolt in Chiapas in 1994 and from the street protests in Seattle, Washington, during the World Trade Organization meeting in 1999. While never simply and straightforwardly anarchist in character, this new wave of protest demonstrated close affinities to both the older ideals of the anarchosyndicalists and to an eclectic range of sympathies demonstrated by the late-twentieth-century and early-twenty-first-century anarchist thinkers.

See also **Anarchosyndicalism; Communism; Feminism; Labor Movements; Russian Revolutions of 1917; Socialism; Spanish Civil War.**

BIBLIOGRAPHY

Ackelsberg, Martha A. *Free Women of Spain: Anarchism and the Struggle for the Emancipation of Women.* Bloomington, Ind., 1991.

Avrich, Paul. *Kronstadt, 1921.* Princeton, N.J., 1970.

Baschet, Jerôme. *L'Etincelle Zapatiste: Insurrection indienne et résistance planétaire.* Paris, 2002.

Berry, David. *A History of the French Anarchist Movement, 1917–1945.* Westport, Conn., 2002.

Casanova, Julián. *De la calle al frente; el anarcosindicalismo en España (1931–1939).* Barcelona, 1997.

Gemie, Sharif. "The Ballad of Bourg-Madame: Memory, Exiles and the Spanish Republic Refugees of the 'Retirada.'" *International Review of Social History* 51 (2006): 1–40.

Graeber, David. "The New Anarchists." *New Left Review* 13 (2002): 61–73.

Kinna, Ruth. *Anarchism: A Beginner's Guide.* Oxford, U.K., 2005.

Levy, Carl. "Currents of Italian Syndicalism before 1926." *International Review of Social History* 45, no. 2 (2000): 209–250

Marshall, Peter. *Demanding the Impossible: A History of Anarchism.* London, 1993.

Serge, Victor. *Memoirs of a Revolutionary.* Translated by Peter Sedgwick. London, 1984.

SHARIF GEMIE

ANARCHOSYNDICALISM.

A hybrid doctrine born of the cross-fertilization of libertarian theory and radical labor practice, anarchosyndicalism had its roots in the unstable soil of nineteenth-century class conflict. By the 1890s, many anarchists accepted the trade union (*syndicat*) as the main organ of revolution and the embryo of future society, thus shedding their "purist" excesses of bomb-throwing "propaganda by the deed." Over time, this new "revolutionary" syndicalism itself evolved closer to reformist social democracy, despite the discourse of militant autonomy from party politics as pronounced in the Amiens Charter by France's General Confederation of Labor (CGT) in 1906. Yet the onset of World War I, plus the rise of worldwide communist parties, reopened the question of how (or whether) to pursue a class-based revolutionary agenda. Should workers follow "bourgeois" governments into war, thus serving as cannon fodder? Should they remain wary of party politics, or instead embrace newly proletarianized parties more worthy of their support? How far should they subordinate labor goals to political intentions, including the demands of a dictatorial party-state? If the late nineteenth century may be seen as the heyday of doctrinal debates within the anarchist and syndicalist movements, the twentieth century was the era of hard choices in revolutionary practice, including the roles to play in world wars, revolutions, and new communist and fascist regimes.

Scholars disagree on how far World War I marked a clear turning point for left-wing theory and practice, as for other features of European politics and culture. But few doubt that the war and its aftermath at least threatened to make anarchosyndicalism a reactionary vestige of the past, as Marxists and Leninists had long assumed. The term itself, apparently coined in Russia in 1907, entered more common leftist parlance in the 1920s, mostly in a pejorative fashion. For a new generation of militants, the war's boost to mass production and to the centralized power of bourgeois states made a similarly centralized, even "bolshevized," labor movement a necessary counterweight, even if it reduced unions to mere "transmission belts" from party leaders to the masses. In this altered context, anarchosyndicalists would have to shift gears, adopt new tactics, and win new constituencies if they hoped to remain relevant in the modern age.

WORLD WAR I AND THE RUSSIAN REVOLUTION

Socialists and syndicalists across Europe had once spurned bourgeois warfare as what Jean Jaurès called "the supreme diversion" from labor struggles. Yet in both belligerent camps the war created a spirit of "Sacred Union" that linked Left and Right in defense of the nations-in-arms—at least at first. By 1917, this unity began dissolving in mass strikes and antiwar protests, as a result of the war's huge toll in blood and gold, plus the heavy pressures even on factory workers behind the lines. Protests climaxed in the Russian Revolutions of 1917 and in widespread strikes from 1918 through 1920, thus surviving the Armistice, as gains even for the victors hardly justified the expenses. Neutral countries such as Spain were also engulfed by wartime inflation and postwar insurgency, which helped launch communist parties throughout the world.

Like their socialist comrades, anarchists and syndicalists were hardly united in their choices for or against Sacred Union. Although some anarchists published antiwar texts, others—notably Jean Grave, Peter Kropotkin, and Errico Malatesta—rallied to the Entente's fight against "Prussian militarism." France's CGT leaders later claimed only to have deferred to the masses in their failure to mobilize against the war. But despite these uncertainties, syndicalists were often the last to embrace national defense, the first to join strikes, and the most intent on radicalizing them beyond simple material demands. Anarchosyndicalists even hailed bolshevism as "a revolution of a syndicalist nature" (Pierre Monatte), with Russia's "soviets" the workers' councils of the future. And yet the attempted bolshevization of the international labor movement left syndicalists in and outside Russia unwilling to subordinate their goals to Soviet dictate; most refused to join or soon quit (or were expelled from) the new Third (Communist) International, especially by 1924.

VARIETIES OF SYNDICALISM: THE INTERWAR ERA

Although many prewar syndicalists remained on the far left, in or outside the Third International, after the war, others continued their prewar slide toward reformism, convinced that a "politics of presence" in bourgeois governments was the best way to make their voices heard. Such was the case for France's postwar CGT, which retained the majority of unionized members even after a schism parallel to the party split that created—and gave a majority to—the French Communist Party (PCF). On the left, the new CGTU (CGT Unitaire) rallied dissident as well as communist unionists, including renegades from the newly bolshevized PCF. But a sectarian fringe quit the CGTU to form the new CGTSR (CGT Syndicaliste Révolutionnaire) in 1926, led by self-styled libertarian purist Pierre Besnard.

Railroad worker and theoretician, author of several books on the spirit and vision of anarchosyndicalism, Besnard disliked the pejorative term and called for an updated, "rationalized" labor movement: "The period of revolutionary romanticism is finished!" Yet despite his acceptance of group organization and collective responsibility, Besnard's critics on the left called him an "apostle of schism" for creating the splinter group, and a utopian dreamer for proposing the six-hour day and a uniform wage for all. The CGTSR's aura also lay more in the past than the future: its Lyon Charter mirrored the old Amiens Charter (both were drafted by the same author, Victor Griffuelhes), and its international federation, which Besnard later headed (it was formed in Berlin in 1921, to rival the Moscow-based Profintern), took the name of the International Working Man's Association (IWMA), echoing the old First International of Pierre-Joseph Proudhon.

The IWMA also rallied small syndicalist groups across Europe, Asia, and Latin America; but its largest member—soon the world's largest syndicalist union—was Spain's National Confederation of Labor (CNT). Founded on the French model in 1911, and still openly libertarian in ethos, the CNT was one of the rare anarchosyndicalist bodies to gain and hold a majority of its nation's unionists after the post–World War I schisms. It was in Spain that anarchosyndicalism remained truest to its millenarian origins, including a sustained "bombist" streak, due both to the slow growth there of modern mass production and to the CNT's long years in clandestinity before and after the war. Teamed with the anarchist FAI (Iberian Anarchist Federation, founded in 1927), the CNT targeted rural areas with its program of land expropriation. Its diverse members included Marxists, social democrats, and "anarcho-Bolsheviks" who embraced Spain's Popular Front in 1936.

Against the purist Besnard (who likewise opposed France's own Popular Front), the CNT took ministerial posts in Spain's left-republican government and then faced the dilemma of how to exercise power without losing its identity in the "bourgeois" state. These CNT leaders also deferred their long-term antimilitarist and revolutionary agenda for the immediate defense of the republic in Spain's civil war. Still, Spain's example energized a generation of militants for whom bolshevism was no longer the sole extant revolution demanding their allegiance. Rank-and-file anarchists, inspired in part by regionalist aims, practiced worker self-management in communal collectives in Catalonia and elsewhere. But their libertarian goals collided with those of Spain's Soviet-sponsored Communist Party and the latter's own unions, as recounted in George Orwell's *Homage to Catalonia* (1938). These conflicts on the left hastened the right-wing military victory of Francisco Franco in 1939.

If not World War I and the Bolshevik Revolution, it was the rise of right-wing dictatorships, such as in Spain, that marked the long eclipse of anarchosyndicalism until its partial reemergence after 1945. Some syndicalists in Italy and elsewhere, especially those drawn from intellectual circles outside organized labor, rallied toward early fascism in hopes that a "national" socialism or syndicalism might offer a more genuinely radical or populist alternative to Marxism. Such "third-way" currents were transient but frequent experiments in the "nonconformist" politics of the interwar era. But whatever the anarchist echoes on the right, most anarchosyndicalists remained fierce libertarians, opposed to the dictatorships of either wing.

Before the fascists took power, Italy's anarchosyndicalists had joined in the wave of mass strikes and factory occupations of 1919 and 1920, alongside the "council communists" led by Antonio Gramsci (1891–1937) and his group at the journal *L'Ordine nuovo* (The new order), based in Turin. Occupying the factories was a tactic suited to the postwar recession, when surplus stocks erased employers' incentive to settle a strike. For syndicalists, factory councils also seemed more responsive to workers' goals—including eventual self-governance—than the centralized unions that were succumbing to Bolshevik dictate. Yet the communist Gramsci still dubbed syndicalism an "instinctive, elementary, primitive" reaction against bourgeois socialism. Just as communist parties were to dominate the unions, so unions were to dominate (or absorb) the factory councils, subordinating workers' control of production

Members of the anarchist militia of the Confederación Nacional del Trabajo (CNT; National Confederation of Labour) celebrate in Barcelona c. 1937. The CNT supported the republican Popular Front government during the Spanish civil war. ©HULTON-DEUTSCH COLLECTION/CORBIS

to the larger struggle against capitalism or for the defense of the Soviet state.

In postwar Germany, council communists also briefly recharged the prewar federalist current of local craft groups against the centralizing trend of socialist or communist unionism. But German unions typically offered more social services than syndicalists welcomed, put off by the implied threats to personal liberties; and these unions still prized the political struggle above labor radicalism, even after the republic's birth. Likewise in Britain, the wartime shop-steward movement, based especially in Scotland's skilled machine trades, faded before the union constants of welfare services, electoralism, and mass recruitment. Britain's Trades Union Congress adopted some features of prewar industrial syndicalism, where "one big union" merged industrial or transport sectors and straddled barriers between the skilled and unskilled. These unions also avoided the rupture that elsewhere created a communist wing; Britain's Communist Party was formed not by schism but by the fusion of small preexisting groups. Yet despite large strikes, especially among coal miners, high unemployment kept a lid on labor militancy. The mostly nonviolent General Strike of 1926 ended in a truce and a wage cut, much to radicals' dismay.

Under these circumstances, syndicalism's post-1914 fate hinged less on the structural changes beloved by Marxist technological determinists than on social and political contingencies: not mass production or capitalist concentration but recession, political schism, dictatorial coups, and renewed war. If syndicalist habits of direct action and wildcat strikes (the old "revolutionary gymnastics") endured longer than material conditions might seem to justify, they long rivaled the party discipline that privileged political ends, such as anticolonialism or antifascism, both before and after World War II. French anarchosyndicalists may have spurned the Popular Front, but they celebrated the strikes and factory sit-ins that followed the electoral victory in May and June of 1936. That same spirit excited new bursts of syndicalist militancy in the period from 1945 to 1947 and in 1968.

WORLD WAR II AND AFTER

Despite its huge toll in military and civilian casualties, World War II created far less social conflict than its predecessor, as both democracies and dictatorships secured mass support for national combat. Yet Vichy France was a special case, backed by many "national" syndicalists who had opposed the war, or championed appeasement, before 1939. These syndicalists also endorsed the regime's paternalist "Labor Charter" and its slogan that placed "Work" (although not mainly industrial work) alongside "Family" and "Country" as the highest social values. They further preferred collaboration with the Nazis to the political risks of the Resistance, with its large communist base, and to the social costs of mass production needed to win the war.

Indeed, many such views survived the Liberation, despite the change in circumstance, as grounds for syndicalist dissent from the communist-led "battle for production." Against communist productivism, or the party's role in coalition governments, French anarchists and Trotskyists were avid strikers in 1945 through early 1947, before the Cold War brought new schisms on the left. Besnard's CGTSR joined with Spanish anarchists in exile to form a new CNT, based again on the direct action principles of the 1926 Lyon Charter. Spain's anarchists had also joined the Maquis in southwestern France and then supported the CNT in clandestine strikes in Spain in 1947 and 1951. But despite such militancy, it was the communist and Christian wings of the labor movement that saw the most postwar growth across Western Europe, due both to their prominence in the wartime Resistance and to the eventual rise of prosperity, consumerism, and welfare-state politics. Many

syndicalists would then vest their revolutionary hopes in third-world peasants in lieu of Europe's bourgeois "new working class."

In the late 1960s, at the tail end of this prosperity surge, rose a new wave of protests that stressed qualitative issues of lifestyle as much as quantitative demands for economic concessions. University students took the lead in such strikes in France and elsewhere, while strikers in Italy posed issues of health, transport, lodging, and school, not just factory life. Although the economic reversals of the 1970s caused some of these currents to ebb, left-wing terrorism surged in both Germany and Italy, against union support for austerity policies and against the "historic compromise" by Italy's Communists and Christian Democrats in 1973. Eastern Europe's anti-Soviet protests also showed traces of what one might call "fin-de-siècle communitarian socialism" or "council democracy," all part of a broad anarchosyndicalist legacy. If purists deplored the eclecticism of these "new social movements," others hailed the proliferation of antiracist, antinuclear, pro-feminist and pro-ecology protests that spurned parliamentarianism for direct action or self-management (*autogestion*).

Since the 1970s, syndicalism is no longer the main site for anarchist activity, where the two strains were once nearly synonymous. In France, a group named for Bourses du travail founder Fernand Pelloutier (1867–1901) changed its newsletter's title from *L'Anarcho-Syndicaliste* to *L'Anarcho* (1973), thus letting the libertarian half of the group's hybrid identity trump the half rooted in the industrial age. Pelloutier's influence, renouncing the terrorist acts of an earlier day, had marked a step beyond romantic anarchism and toward syndicalist practicality. Is the movement now circling back to its origins, as the astronomer's term *revolution* suggests? Once reviled by Marxists as "pseudorevolutionary," anarchosyndicalism still privileges direct action over revolutionary politics, still prefers the élan of "active minorities" to the apathy of mass memberships, and scorns the electoral calculus by claiming a universal constituency beyond its small number of recruits. In the post-industrial era, the trade union is no longer the structural model for future society, nor work the central fact of human experience. Yet in the populist spirit of its forebears, Pierre-Joseph Proudhon (1809–1865) and Mikhail Bakunin (1814–1876), anarchosyndicalism may now speak not just for a subset of workers but for all "the people," across lines of gender, race, and class.

See also **Anarchism; Spanish Civil War.**

BIBLIOGRAPHY

Amdur, Kathryn E. *Syndicalist Legacy: Trade Unions and Politics in Two French Cities in the Era of World War I.* Urbana, Ill., 1986.

Berry, David. *A History of the French Anarchist Movement, 1917–1945.* Westport, Conn., 2002.

Gildea, Robert. "Anarchism." Chap. 6 in *The Past in French History.* New Haven, Conn., 1994.

Kern, Robert W. *Red Years/Black Years: A Political History of Spanish Anarchism, 1911–1937.* Philadelphia, 1978.

Launay, Michel. *Le syndicalisme en Europe.* Paris, 1990.

Sagnes, Jean, ed. *Histoire du syndicalisme dans le monde: Des origines à nos jours.* Toulouse, France, 1994.

Schecter, Darrow. *Radical Theories: Paths Beyond Marxism and Social Democracy.* Manchester, U.K., 1994.

Skirda, Alexandre. *Facing the Enemy: A History of Anarchist Organization from Proudhon to May 1968.* Translated by Paul Sharkey. Oakland, Calif., 2002.

Thorpe, Wayne. "Anarchosyndicalism in Inter-War France: The Vision of Pierre Besnard." *European History Quarterly* 26, no. 4 (1996): 559–590.

van der Linden, Marcel. "Second Thoughts on Revolutionary Syndicalism." *Labour History Review* 63, no. 2 (1998): 182–196.

Williams, Gwyn A. *Proletarian Order: Antonio Gramsci, Factory Councils, and the Origins of Communism in Italy, 1911–1921.* London, 1975.

KATHRYN E. AMDUR

ANDREOTTI, GIULIO (b. 1919), Italian politician.

Giulio Andreotti, born in Rome on 14 January 1919, was an Italian politician who was among the founders of the Christian Democratic Party (DC). He graduated from law school in 1941 with a specialization in canon law, and Pope Pius XII (r. 1939–1958) soon appointed the twenty-two-year-old Andreotti president of the Federazione Universitaria Cattolica Italiana (Italian Catholic University Federation). After the liberation of Rome (June 1944), he became the national delegate for Christian Democratic youth groups and in 1945 he participated in the National Council. He was elected to the Constituent Assembly the following year, and he ran successfully in every election to the Chamber of Deputies from 1948 to 1987. Twice elected to the European Parliament, he was appointed senator for life in 1991 by the president of the Italian Republic, Francesco Cossiga (b. 1928).

Andreotti's government career began in 1947 as undersecretary to the Office of the Prime Minister in Alcide De Gasperi's (1881–1954) fourth government, a post that he held through the eighth De Gasperi government (1953) and in the succeeding Giuseppe Pella (1902–1981) government. Andreotti was not only the premier's undersecretary but also the confidant of De Gasperi, who invited him to participate in highly sensitive meetings with Palmiro Togliatti (1893–1964) and Pietro Sandro Nenni (1891–1980) in the 1950s. He was never national secretary of the DC nor did he ever play a decisive role in the party with his majority wing, but more than anyone else he represented the quality and the continuity of Christian Democratic power in the state. From 1954 to 1968 he headed the ministries of interior, finance, treasury, defense, and industry. As leader of the DC deputies, he presided over the Chamber Committee on Foreign Affairs for the eighth legislature from December 1968 to February 1972. He became prime minister for the first time in 1972 (his was the shortest government of the Republic: it lasted only ten days) and on 26 June he formed his second coalition government (which lasted until June 1973) involving the DC, the Democratic Socialist Party (PSDI), and the Liberal Party (PLI), and with the outside support of the Republican Party (PRI). He returned to the Ministry of Defense in the Mariano Rumor (1915–1990) government of 1974, after which he headed the Office of Budget in the Aldo Moro (1916–1978) governments of 1974–1976. From July 1976 to 1978 he was premier of a one-party DC government that was formed thanks to the abstention of the Communist Party (PCI), the Socialist Party (PSI), the PSDI, the PRI, and the PLI during a period of emergencies created by economic crises and terrorism.

From 16 March 1978, the day that Moro was kidnapped, Andreotti led a new one-party government supported by the positive vote of even the Communists (although they had no share in the government), but not that of the PLI. After the resignation of his fifth government (31 March 1979) Andreotti did not hold any position in the executive branches of the governments that followed (Francesco Cossiga, 1979 and 1980; Arnaldo Forlani [b. 1925], 18 October 1980–26 May 1981; Giovanni Spadolini [1925–1994], 1981 and 1982; and Amintore Fanfani [1908–1999], 1 December 1982–29 April 1983). In Bettino Craxi's (1934–2000) government (4 August 1983) Andreotti became Minister of Foreign Affairs, a post that he also occupied in the second government of Craxi (1 August 1986–3 March 1987) and in those of Fanfani, Giovanni Goria (1943–1994), and Ciriaco De Mita (b. 1928). An expert in the geopolitical balance of power, he was particularly interested in relations with the Arab world. At the end of the 1980s, it was presumed that Andreotti had formed a secret political pact with Craxi and Forlani—the leaders of the most important parties of the government coalition, PSI and DC. The pact (called CAF, from the initials of the three) was presumably aimed at turning Italian policy in their favor.

In 1991 Andreotti formed the last government led by the DC, which collapsed because of the "Tangentopolis" (Bribesville) investigations. Andreotti was not involved in this scandal, but in the mid-1990s he was indicted by two prosecutors' offices, one in Perugia and the other in Palermo. The former accused him of complicity in the assassination of the journalist Carmine "Mino" Pecorelli (1928–1979), who supposedly blackmailed Andreotti about the written documents left by Aldo Moro. The trial began 11 April 1996 and ended 24 September 1999 with Andreotti's acquittal "for not having committed the crime." The prosecutor of Palermo, Giancarlo Caselli, requested of the Senate and received from it on 13 May 1993 authorization to begin proceedings against Andreotti for collusion with the Mafia. According to the judges, Andreotti allegedly showed favoritism toward the Mafia in the handling of work contracts in Sicily, using as a mediator Salvo Lima, the Christian Democratic Eurodeputy murdered by the Mafia in Palermo on 12 March 1992. The trial was based on the testimony of a few informants, among them Balduccio Di Maggio, who told of Andreotti's famously kissing Sicilian Mafia boss Totò Riina (in the Mafia underworld the gesture indicates a rapport of familiarity and mutual esteem). In the course of the proceedings that began 26 September 1995, the prosecution asked for fifteen years' imprisonment. The first-stage trial ended 23 October 1999 with acquittal for lack of evidence, but the prosecutor's office in Palermo appealed.

In a second-stage trial, the Court of Appeals in Palermo acquitted Andreotti on 2 May 2003 with a decision divided into two parts: although it recognized his ties to the Mafia up to 1980, the admissibility of the relevant evidence had expired under the statute of limitations; for the charge of criminal collusion with the Mafia the acquittal was absolute. On 30 October 2003 the Court of Cassation definitively acquitted Andreotti of the charge of complicity in the murder of Pecorelli and on 15 October 2004 it rejected both the appeal by the Public Prosecutor's Office of Palermo challenging the acquittal and a petition presented by the defense to cancel the statute of limitations for some of the evidence; finally, upholding the ruling of the Court of Appeals, it acquitted Andreotti of the charge of collusion with the Mafia.

At more than eighty years of age Andreotti returned to politics with a new group splintered off from the People's Party (PPI); in the 2001 political elections it presented itself as centrist but received only 2.4 percent of the votes, thus failing to reach the electoral threshold.

The author of several books on recent Italian history, Andreotti still retains his brilliant personality, intelligence, and political acumen, the fruit of experiences that have made him a perennial protagonist in Italian political life.

See also **Craxi, Bettino; Crime and Justice; Italy; Mafia.**

BIBLIOGRAPHY

Primary Sources

Andreotti, Giulio. *A ogni morte di papa: I papi che ho conosciuto.* Milan, 1980.

———. *Diari, 1976–1979. Gli anni della solidariet.* Milan, 1981.

———. *The U.S.A. Up Close: From the Atlantic Pact to Bush.* Translated by Peter C. Farrell. New York, 1992. Translation of *Gli USA visti da vicino.* Milan, 1989.

Secondary Sources

Cianciaruso d'Adamo, C. *Profilo di un Presidente: Giulio Andreotti, pilota della crisi.* Naples, 1979.

Lupo, S. *Andreotti, la mafia, la storia d'Italia.* Rome, 1996.

Robb, Peter. *Midnight in Sicily: On Art, Food, History, Travel, and La Cosa Nostra.* Boston, 1998.

MARIA TERESA GIUSTI

ANDROPOV, YURI (1914–1984), leader of the Soviet Union from 1982 to 1984.

Yuri Vladimirovich Andropov has entered history for three main reasons. The first concerns his duplicitous behavior as Soviet ambassador to Hungary during the uprising of 1956; the second his role in modernizing the Committee for State Security (KGB); and the third is associated with his brief tenure as leader of the Soviet Union between November 1982 and February 1984 when he launched a program of authoritarian modernization. These three phases of his public activity reflect facets of the man.

Andropov was born into the family of a railway worker in the Cossack village of Nagutskaya in the Stavropol region, although the family itself was not Cossack. He lost his parents early and was looked after by his stepfather. He went to school in Mozdok and then took on a number of jobs, including working on a barge on the Volga. At age eighteen he entered the Rybinsk Water Transport College. Rybinsk, a town in the Yaroslavl region, was renamed after him in 1984, although not for long. With the Great Terror in the mid-1930s thinning out political cadres, Andropov did not work in his specialty but began his political career as Komsomol boss in one of Rybinsk's major enterprises, from which he swiftly graduated to the post of first secretary of the Yaroslavl Komsomol organization by the age of twenty-four in 1938. While still in Rybinsk he married his first wife, Nina Engalycheva, with whom he had a son and daughter before they divorced after five years of marriage. He joined the Communist Party in 1939.

In 1940 Andropov was sent to the Karelo-Finnish republic as head of the newly formed region's Komsomol organization. It was while in the region's capital, Petrozavodsk, that he married for a second time, Tatyana Filippovna, with whom he had another son and daughter. With the onset of war he headed partisan activity in the occupied parts of the republic while remaining head of the Komsomol in the rest, and at this time he appears to have worked closely with the security services. In 1944 Andropov shifted over to party work, becoming second secretary of the Petrozavodsk party organization. At the same time he studied at Petrozavodsk State University and the Higher Party School in Moscow. By 1947 the thirty-three-year-old Andropov was second secretary of the republic's party organization. The chair of the Presidium of the Republic's Supreme Soviet at this time was the veteran communist Otto Kuusinen, one of the founders of the Finnish Communist Party and secretary to the Comintern's Executive Committee. Kuusinen was to exert enormous influence on Andropov's intellectual development and acted as a patron later.

In the early 1950s Andropov worked as an inspector and then head of a section in the Communist Party of the Soviet Union's (CPSU) Central Committee in Moscow and for a brief period in 1953 worked in the Ministry of Foreign Affairs dealing with communist countries before being sent to work in the Soviet embassy in Hungary, becoming ambassador in 1954. He was ruthless in suppressing the revolution in 1956 and went back on promises for safe passage for the ousted prime minister, Imre Nagy, after he had sought asylum in the Yugoslav embassy. Nagy was executed in 1958. Andropov was by no means the driving force of Soviet policy in this crisis, with Nikita Khrushchev directly following events and his envoys, Anastas Mikoyan and Mikhail Suslov, in Budapest. Andropov's tactical sophistication was apparent in ensuring that repression was balanced by concessions, and he prevented the full restoration of the Stalinist system by placing the relative moderate János Kádár as the new leader of the party. In due course Kádár came to head one of the more reformist communist systems known as "goulash communism."

Having handled the Hungarian crisis to Moscow's satisfaction, in 1957 Andropov was appointed head of the CPSU Central Committee's new department for relations with communist and workers' parties of socialist countries. The aim was to ensure that there would be no repetition of Hungarian events and to act as the successor to the Comintern and Cominform in organizing the world communist movement. He was elected a member of the Central Committee in 1961 and was a secretary of the Central Committee between 1962 and 1967. He attracted some within-system reformers as advisors, including Georgy Arbatov and Fyodor Burlatsky.

In 1967 he left the party apparatus to head the KGB, possibly as part of the attempt by conservatives like Suslov to ensure that Andropov would be disqualified from becoming party leader; there was an implicit rule that the head of the security services could not become general secretary of the party. As compensation he was made a candidate member of the Politburo at this time and a full member in 1973. Before his appointment the KGB had been involved in some scandalous show trials of dissidents—notably those of Joseph Brodsky in 1964 and Yuli Daniel and Andrei Sinyavsky in 1966—that had discredited the Soviet Union. Andropov's appointment was intended to ensure a rather more sophisticated approach to repression, which he delivered. He recruited more educated staff and transformed the image of the KGB into the incorruptible shield of the revolution amid the sea of late Brezhnevite corruption. It was this image that attracted the young Vladimir Putin to the KGB's service in 1975. By the skillful use of sanctions, heightened surveillance of those whom he considered "system destroyers," the abuse of psychiatry, and, in the case of Andrei Sakharov, internal exile, he effectively extinguished dissent as a coherent political force and thus destroyed precisely the class of people who could have acted as the bedrock of democratization later. He was not averse to the use of assassination abroad, as with the killing of the Bulgarian dissident Georgi Markov in London and alleged involvement in the attempted murder of Pope John Paul II in 1981.

On Suslov's death in February 1982 Andropov immediately left the KGB to replace him as the Central Committee secretary responsible for ideology. This provided the launch pad for his successful bid to replace Leonid Brezhnev as head of the party on the latter's death in November 1982. Andropov's speeches as leader signaled a degree of greater ideological flexibility and awareness of the problems facing the country, but his fundamental response was greater discipline, an anti-alcohol campaign, and some progressive personnel changes that bought Yegor Ligachev and Nikolai Ryzhkov into the Secretariat. In foreign policy he sought to use Western peace protesters to prevent the deployment of Cruise and Pershing missiles in Germany. As the architect of what some call the Second Cold War from 1979, relations with the West became as bad as at the height of the Cold War and brought the world to the brink of nuclear war, symbolized by the shooting down of South Korean flight KAL 007 on 1 September 1983. Andropov by then was ailing, kept alive by a dialysis machine. He recognized Mikhail Gorbachev's talents and clearly wished him to be his successor, an ambition that was fulfilled only after Konstantin Chernenko's brief leadership between February 1984 and March 1985. Andropov was an intelligent and relatively flexible leader, untainted personally by the corruption that swirled around him, but his tragedy was that his very success in defending the Soviet system from external threats and internal dissent destroyed the very sources of renewal that might have allowed the system to survive.

See also **Brezhnev, Leonid; Gorbachev, Mikhail; Soviet Union.**

BIBLIOGRAPHY

Primary Sources

Andropov, Yuri V. *Speeches and Writings.* 2nd enl. ed. Oxford, U.K., 1983.

Secondary Sources

Beichman, Arnold, and Mikhail S. Bernstam. *Andropov: New Challenge to the West.* New York, 1983.

Besançon, Alain. "Andropov and His Soviet Union." *Policy Review* 25, no. 1 (summer 1983): 21–23.

Brown, Archie. "Andropov: Discipline *and* Reform." *Problems of Communism* 32, no. 1 (January–February 1983): 18–31.

Ebon, Martin. *The Andropov File*. London, 1983.

Elliot, Iain. "Andropov Scrutinized." *Survey* 28, no. 1 (spring 1984): 61–67.

Heller, M. "Andropov: A Retrospective View." *Survey* 28, no. 1 (spring 1984): 46–60.

Medvedev, Roi. *Neizvestnyi Andropov*. Moscow, 1999.

Medvedev, Zhores. *Andropov: His Life and Death*. Oxford, U.K., 1984.

Steele, Jonathan, and Eric Abraham. *Andropov in Power*. Oxford, U.K., 1983.

Sturman, D. "Chernenko and Andropov: Ideological Perspectives." *Survey* 28, no. 1 (spring 1984): 9–21.

RICHARD SAKWA

ANNALES SCHOOL. In historiography, the name *Annales* refers to three interlinked phenomena: (1) a journal founded by Marc Bloch (1886–1944) and Lucien Febvre (1878–1956) that still exists in the early twenty-first century, "probably the world's most talked about and most influential scholarly journal devoted to historical studies" (Huppert, p. 873); (2) a "school," or, more precisely, a circle or network of French and French-speaking historians; and, finally, (3) a broad, heterogeneous movement that, under the impetus of the journal of the same name, has profoundly renewed the way of thinking and writing about history, especially since the end of World War II.

In 1929 Bloch and Febvre, both then professors at the University of Strasbourg, founded a new journal entitled *Annales d'histoire économique et sociale* (Annals of economic and social history) that was meant to compete, in France, with the traditional *Revue d'histoire économique et sociale* (Review of economic and social history), deemed too "placid" and too "juridical" in its approach, and, on the international level, with the *Vierteljahrschrift für Sozial- und Wirtschaftsgeschichte* (Quarterly for social and economic history), which had been discredited by the conduct of German scholars during World War I. In the diversity of its subject matter as well as its multidisciplinary perspective, which returned to an approach already practiced in the *Année sociologique* (Social science journal) of Émile Durkheim (1858–1917), the *Annales* went beyond the horizons of the dominant academic history to incorporate everything that might in one way or another enrich a history conceived as being "total," in the Durkheimian sense, or as a "synthesis," in the sense of Henri Berr (1863–1954).

While the earliest works of Bloch, Febvre, and their closest collaborators (notably Georges Lefebvre; 1874–1959), along with others such as the great Belgian historian Henri Pirenne (1862–1935) or the Austrian Jewish emigrant Lucie Varga (1904–1941), concentrated on particular problems in social history or on putting regional French or European history into a new perspective, with particular emphasis on the anthropological phenomenon of "mentalities," the arrival of Fernand Braudel (1902–1985) at the helm of the journal led, during the 1950s, to a methodological shift toward quantitative history and "long-term" studies modeled on the works of Braudel himself, notably *La Méditerranée et le monde méditerranéen à l'époque de Philippe II* (2 vols., 1949; *The Mediterranean and the Mediterranean World in the Age of Philip II*, 1972–1973) and *Civilisation matérielle, économie et capitalisme, XVe–XVIIIe siècle* (3 vols., 1967–1979; *Civilization and Capitalism, 15th–18th Century*, 1981–1983).

Owing to the institutional support that the *Annales* derived from its collaborators' prominence in the "Sixth Section" of the École Pratique des Hautes Études (known since 1975 as the École des Hautes Études en Sciences Sociales)—headed by Febvre, then by Braudel, then by Jacques Le Goff (b. 1924), François Furet (1927–1997), and so on—the intellectual approach associated with its name over the years took on the form of a true movement that quickly expanded beyond the borders of France. Along the way, and with successive generations, the "*Annales* paradigms," as the scholar Jacques Revel called it, changed. Following the dominance of "total" socioeconomic history and then the "history of mentalities," since the 1970s particular predilections for historical anthropology and then for "microhistory" have been evident. To be sure, sociology as a discipline has remained the most important auxiliary frame of reference, but the functionalism and structuralism of days past have been succeeded, under the impetus of Jacques Revel and Bernard Lepetit (1948–1996) in particular, by a strong antideterministic orientation entirely focused on "agents" and their mutual "conventions." In 1994 this "critical turn" was reflected in a reorganization of the editorial board and a new subtitle: *Annales. Histoire, sciences sociales.*

Among the many criticisms made of the *Annales,* especially noteworthy is the accusation that it was too exclusively limited to the distant past of the early modern period or the Middle Ages, or even antiquity, whereas the nineteenth and twentieth centuries—in short, the contemporary period, with its effects on the present—appeared only as a sort of poor relation: underrated and unappreciated. Looking more closely, however, this reproach is only partially justified. In fact, during the interwar years Bloch's and Febvre's *Annales* devoted many studies and even more summaries and reviews to current social, economic, and even political events—and thus, to economic crises, fascism, Nazism, and the Soviet regime. At the time it was founded, moreover, it was clear that the *Annales* was not solely addressed to academic readers but that it also targeted a readership of "men of action." This was echoed in countless articles on the business world, and the presence of several economists and bankers (Charles Rist, Alfred Pose) on the enlarged editorial board seems to underscore that the "spirit of the *Annales*" aimed to understand the past from the perspective of present concerns—and vice versa. It was only during the 1950s and 1960s—in other words, in the context of the Cold War—and when the journal itself became a "major multinational business," that this mooring in the present was to some extent lost. Other French journals have since more or less adopted an *Annales*-type approach in their respective fields: *Le mouvement social, Vingtième siècle,* and so forth, even though the issue of the relationship between "society" and the "political," between "structure" and "event," or between "long" and "short" term has remained one of the major topics of debate in historiography.

See also **Bloch, Marc; Braudel, Fernand; Febvre, Lucien.**

BIBLIOGRAPHY

Burke, Peter. *The French Historical Revolution: The Annales School, 1929–89.* Stanford, Calif., 1990.

Carrard, Philippe. *Poetics of the New History: French Historical Discourse from Braudel to Chartier.* Baltimore, 1992.

Clark, Stuart, ed. *The Annales School: Critical Assessments.* 4 vols. London, 1999.

Dosse, François. *New History in France: The Triumph of the "Annales."* Translated by Peter V. Conroy. Urbana, Ill., 1994.

Hunt, Lynn, and Jacques Revel, eds. *Histories: French Constructions of the Past.* Translated by Arthur Goldhammer and others; Ramona Naddaff, series editor. New York, 1995.

Huppert, George. "The '*Annales*' Experiment." In *Companion to Historiography,* edited by Michael Bentley, 873–888. London, 1997.

Stoianovich, Traian. *French Historical Method: The "Annales" Paradigm.* Ithaca, N.Y., 1976.

PETER SCHÖTTLER

ANSCHLUSS. Austria; World War II.

ANTI-AMERICANISM.

The amorphous term *anti-Americanism* is usually used to describe an irrational prejudice against or aversion to American politics, society, economy, and culture. *Americanism* is usually taken to mean democratic politics, liberal capitalism, mass production, consumerism and materialism, mass culture, and the expansion of these through an aggressive, even imperial foreign policy throughout the world. Anti-Americans do not normally extend their prejudice to individual Americans, although radical elements outside Europe, certainly those behind the terrorist attacks on the United States on 11 September 2001, have done so; in this sense anti-Americanism should be distinguished from anti-Semitism, to which it is often compared. Indeed many critics of anti-Americanism indict the American intellectual establishment itself—the universities, media, even mainline Protestant churches—as among its frontline purveyors.

European anti-Americanism is best defined as a discourse engaged in primarily by intellectuals that has been continuous since the United States was founded, contains persistent stereotypes, and at times has heavily influenced popular attitudes, diplomacy, and in some cases overall state policy. During the Enlightenment some critics believed that the American climate caused the physical deterioration of human beings and rendered cultural creativity impossible. Early America appeared to be a place where material prosperity had reached unusual heights and democracy developed to excessive proportions, making America a land of materialism and social uniformity. America was criticized for slavery and its treatment of Indians, while the Civil War elicited sympathy for the Confederacy as the defender of a more European-like social order. Later in the century a socialist-based critique of America as the land of predatory capitalism was added to the mixture; then followed the Spanish-American War, a shock to Europeans, some of whom saw in the United States a new expansionist imperial power now ripe for world conquest.

It was during the late 1920s that several classic texts of anti-Americanism were produced in France and Germany, building upon existing stereotypes listed above but further absorbing the unwelcome reality of mass production, rationalization, the assembly line, and unprecedented American financial power. Europeans also noted with unease the rapid population growth, racial mixture produced by immigration, and prosperity achieved by American Jews; this produced a tendency for existing anti-Semitic tropes to be married to anti-American ones, Uncle Sam being portrayed as Uncle Shylock. There was also widespread disillusionment with American diplomacy as exemplified by Woodrow Wilson and the negotiations for the Treaty of Versailles (1919), in which the American statesman announced a new humanitarian democratic order that the treaty failed to produce and that America then refused to underwrite. The memory of the American rescue of the Allies in World War I rapidly faded as America appeared greedy to collect debts from its allies and eager to extend loans to Europe to gain power and wealth for itself but unwilling to mix in European diplomacy in an effort to stabilize peace through the League of Nations. America quickly emerged as the primary threat to the interests of the new mass movements of fascism and communism, and a virulent anti-Americanism became part of the state doctrines of both Nazi Germany and Soviet Russia and their sympathizers: for the Nazis the United States was the land of racial intermixing and degeneracy and of unlimited Jewish power and influence; for the Soviet Union it was the home of untrammeled capitalism and imperialist warmongering. Paradoxically neither succeeded in impressing their anti-American doctrines on their populations over the long term; postwar Germany and postcommunist Russia have been among the least anti-American of European countries.

The Cold War muted anti-Americanism virtually everywhere in Western Europe except among Communist parties and significant numbers of fellow travelers with the parties on one or another issue. Communist parties carried on successful propaganda campaigns, for example, against McCarthyism, the espionage trial and 1953 executions of Julius and Ethel Rosenberg, and the atomic bomb, and the peace movement retained an appeal thereafter, opposing the deployment of American weapons in Europe through the 1980s in Germany and Britain. The Marshall Plan, instituted to foster European economic recovery after World War II and regarded by most Americans as an unprecedented act of humanitarian generosity, engendered opposition for its intrusive methods of influencing the policies of recipient nations, who were often humiliated by the necessity of accepting it. The Suez campaign of 1956, during which the British and the French sought to recapture the Suez Canal and preserve their colonial empires against American opposition, gave rise to renewed anti-Americanism in both countries. Only in France, however, did noncommunist anti-Americanism retain a certain salience throughout the postwar period, beginning with campaigns to prevent the introduction of Coca-Cola, continuing through efforts to prevent the import of American films and the "noxious" influence of Hollywood, and culminating with critiques of the Paris region Disneyland. French intellectuals condemned "Coca-Colonization" and believed that Hollywood used the power of the American state to crush the French film industry. Despite its status as America's oldest ally and its shared democratic values, France has consistently challenged American hegemony in Europe in quest of a leadership role for itself, while feeling increasingly defensive in the face of the

Spanish citizens protest U.S. policies during a visit by President Ronald Reagan, May 1985. ©Jacques Langevin/Corbis Sygma

growing preeminence of the English language and the growing popularity of American mass culture. It opposed Washington by developing its own nuclear deterrent and struggling for the allegiance of Germany. Charles de Gaulle would seem to have shared anti-American prejudices in his challenge to American foreign policy in the 1960s, and his policies have remained influential in France. His strong critique of the American bombardment of North Vietnam during the war there resonated among European populations if it was not reflected in their governments' policies, but he remained much more anticommunist than anti-American.

With the end of the Cold War the United States emerged as the sole remaining superpower, while its economy rode the new computer-based postindustrial revolution to new heights of prosperity. Renewed American emphasis on liberal capitalist values since the Reagan years came into conflict with European commitments to the

government-sponsored welfare state, while Washington vigorously promoted globalization and helped create a countermovement of protest that in France manifested itself in attacks on the ultimate symbol of American consumer-based imperialism, McDonald's. Finally, the military gap between Europe and America in terms of military power increased, and the management of crises in which Europe had a preeminent interest, whether the Gulf Wars, Bosnia, or Kosovo, remained dependent on Washington for settlement. Resentment of Washington as a "hyper-power" predated 11 September 2001, but that event and the American reaction to it gave rise to a renewed outburst of anti-Americanism in Europe, this time more in tune with European government polices and public opinions than ever in the past.

Europeans at first rallied to America after 11 September 2001, despite growing opposition to the George W. Bush administration's adoption of some controversial unilateral policies. Some public opposition appeared to the American attack on Afghanistan in October 2001, but European governments rallied and there remained preponderant public support. The March 2003 U.S. attack on Iraq in the name of preemptive war, however, was strongly opposed by European intellectuals and the public; whereas the British, Italian, Spanish, and most Eastern European governments backed Washington, the French and Germans pointedly did not, the French leading a counterchallenge that won the support of Russia and China and denied the United States the coveted support of the United States. In the aftermath of the Iraq invasion European favorable public opinion with regard to the United States declined to the lowest levels ever, and a majority of European publics even identified the United States as the principal threat to world peace. The collapse of Middle East peace negotiations and growing support in Europe for the Palestinian cause in the face of American support for the Israeli occupation gave rise to increased perceptions of inordinate Jewish or Israeli influence on American policy; helped by Islamist propaganda, the revived trope of a Zionist-American-imperialist design for world domination seemed increasingly to take hold. Meanwhile Europeans openly debated the extent to which the seeming new American unilateralist emphasis on military solutions to complex international problems was a temporary feature of American policy introduced by the Bush administration or a permanent change reflecting a new American drive to make over the world in its image.

Anti-Americanism has always been part of an internal European debate over modernization, industrialization, mass culture, and globalization, which Washington has always seemed to embody. As Europe seeks a new integrated identity it also seeks a means of differentiating itself from Washington and adapting these phenomena to its own culture and traditions. A certain level of anti-Americanism is an inevitable result of the size, strength, indeed simple "space" occupied by America in the world. America will always be resented somewhat for what it is, notwithstanding what it does. But Washington's policies still have a great deal to do with the growth of anti-Americanism, which in the period since 11

September 2001 appears to have effected a major transition from simple discourse or rhetorical prejudice to very lethal behavior.

See also **Cold War; Gulf Wars; Vietnam War.**

BIBLIOGRAPHY

Berman, Russell. *Anti-Americanism in Europe: A Cultural Problem.* Stanford, Calif., 2004.

Diner, Dan. *America in the Eyes of the Germans.* Princeton, N.J., 1996.

Hollander, Paul. *Anti-Americanism: Critiques at Home and Abroad, 1965–1990.* Oxford, U.K., and New York, 1992.

Roger, Philippe. *American Enemy: The History of French Anti-Americanism.* Translated by Sharon Bowman. Chicago, 2005. Translation of *L'ennemi américain: Généologie de l'anti-américainisme français.*

Ross, Andrew, and Kristin Ross. *Anti-Americanism.* New York, 2004.

Rubin, Barry, and Judith Colp Rubin. *Hating America.* New York, 2004.

Strauss, David. *Menace in the West: The Rise of French Anti-Americanism in Modern Times.* Westport, Conn., 1978.

IRWIN M. WALL

ANTICLERICALISM. Anticlericalism, understood as opposition to the clergy's powers and attitudes, and often colored by antireligious and/or anti-Catholic sentiment, is a reactive ideology of opposition. It therefore depends on the power and attitudes of the clergy and on how these are perceived. It has been most prevalent in those countries where, for centuries, the Roman Catholic Church has been the majority religion and a dominant political and cultural force.

There are two major forms of anticlericalism: political and social. Political anticlericals have traditionally opposed favored legal status for the clergy, and thus have wanted separation of church and state; they have opposed clerical control of public (and often private) education; they have opposed the retention in the hands of the clergy of substantial property and landholdings; and they have generally favored replacing Catholic clerical cultural and moral values with secular and humanistic values. Their aims have generally been amenable to legislation. Social anticlericals, on the other hand, are more concerned with the clergy's support of one class in preference to another. They have generally been proletarians, supporters of socialist and anarchist movements, and they have accused the clergy of favoring the upper classes, violating the Christian ethic of helping the poor. The social anticlericals have frequently been violent, believing that nothing less than a class revolution can change the clergy.

For the first half of the twentieth century, anticlerical conflict was a feature of the history of those countries that had been hotbeds of anticlerical tension in the eighteenth and nineteenth centuries, principally France, Italy, Spain, and Portugal, and thus these struggles were simply a continuation of those earlier centuries' conflicts. By midcentury, after the cataclysmic conflicts of the two world wars, and the Spanish civil war (1936–1939), anticlericalism was no longer a major issue. Other factors rendering traditional political and social anticlericalism quiescent were: the reforms of Vatican II (1962–1965), especially the proclamation of religious toleration, along with the acceptance of nonfavored status for the clergy; the declining numbers of clergy after the 1960s; and the rise in living standards, which tended to limit class conflict.

By the 1970s and 1980s a new anticlericalism arose, aimed at the clergy's attempts to prevent legislation dealing with sexual mores, particularly divorce, contraception, and most especially, abortion. However, because the clergy had lost their political power, opposition to the clergy's stands was nonviolent, and the general acceptance of democratic procedures confined the conflicts to the popular press and national legislatures. In addition to this new anticlericalism, a movement of lay Catholics wanting a larger role in the making of church policy, and therefore opposed to the clergy's traditional dominating role, added a distinctive element to these conflicts. Furthermore, new social anticlericals appeared in the form of traditional, conservative Catholics opposed to the clergy's support of proletarian movements, particularly in Third World countries. All of these movements and factors have yet to work themselves out in the twenty-first century.

The history of anticlerical movements in the twentieth century is best seen in the histories of the different countries.

FRANCE

In France, after a century and a half of anticlerical conflict, by 1914 the anticlericals had won most of their battles. In the Third Republic, through a series of legislation from 1879 to 1905, the clergy lost their favored status, including state salaries and property; the regular clergy were suppressed and forbidden to teach; and public education was out of clerical hands. Relations with the Vatican were broken off, and church and state were formally separated. But within a few years, the regular clergy were back in charge of their private schools, enrolling by the 1920s more than a fifth of French schoolchildren. This relaxation in the application of the laws was the result of World War I and the surge toward national unity, which did more than anything else to end the religious conflict. There were attempts to enforce the anticlerical legislation in the 1920s, largely because government leaders, usually Radical Party members, tried as they had in the past to use anticlericalism as a means of reviving weak coalition ministries. These attempts were unsuccessful. The Vatican helped to defuse tensions by abandoning its disapproving policies and pursued moderation with the government; and in a twist on the traditional conflict, French extremist clericals, led by Charles Maurras (1868–1952) and the Action Française attacked the Vatican for its accommodating policies and dredged up all of the anticlerical myths of the nineteenth century.

When France was defeated by Germany in 1940, clericals ascribed the defeat to the anticlerical secularism of the Third Republic, and the Vichy government annulled the anticlerical laws, and while some of the clergy backed the Vichy regime, many did not. With the end of World War II and the repeal of the Vichy laws, the need for national unity overrode the anticlerical conflict, even to the extent that religious schools received government subsidies in the new governments.

Anticlericalism after 1945 tended to be a matter of historical opposition, favored by communist, socialist, and some middle-class parties, rather than a response to actual circumstances. The numbers of clergy were in decline and were split between traditionalist and progressive groups. Freemasonry, the traditional vehicle of anticlericalism in France, was also in decline. Evidence of the quiescence of anticlerical conflict was the lack of widespread protest (and hence counterprotest) over the 1975 law permitting abortion.

ITALY

As in France, Italy's anticlerical conflicts had occurred largely in the nineteenth century, and laws restricting the clergy were on the books by 1914. However, they were not enforced, and the clergy lived much as they had before the legislation. One reason for this was that the anticlerical conflict was subordinated to the struggle for national unification, and despite papal opposition to the struggle, for it meant the loss of Rome and the Papal States, the Italian clergy were in favor of unification. The papacy and the Vatican were dominated by Italians, and the church was such an integral part of Italian history (and tourism) that once the anticlerical legislation was passed, the various governments saw no need to enforce it. By the time Italy entered World War I in 1915, the only major problem between church and state was the Roman Question—the refusal of the papacy to recognize the Italian state, and the papal decree that Catholics neither run nor vote for national office. The clergy had no fear of social anticlericalism, because church organizations provided most of the welfare for the poor.

By the end of the war in 1918, Pope Benedict XV (r. 1914–1922) rescinded the ban on Catholic voting, and the Popolare, a Catholic party, was founded. Despite the new party's favoring social welfare legislation, the Socialists considered it a bourgeois party, which they saw dominated by priests. An opportunity to prevent the rise of the Fascist Party of Benito Mussolini (1883–1945) by a Popolare-Socialist electoral union was prevented by both Socialist anticlericalism and the condemnation of such a union by the new pope, Pius XI (r. 1922–1939), after Mussolini had promised to end the Roman Question in favor of the papacy.

In the wake of political stalemate and growing fear of socialist revolutionary upheaval, Mussolini's Fascists won the king's support; and *il duce* became prime minister in 1922 and dictator within a few years. True to his promise, he negotiated an end to the Roman Question and signed the Lateran Pacts in 1929 with the pope's emissary. The anticlerical laws were nullified, but there was no outcry from anticlericals, now more concerned with opposing the Fascists. Despite some clerical support for the Fascists for Mussolini's aggressive foreign policy and conquests, there were enough clergy supporting the resistance movements so that when World War II ended there was no anticlerical conflict. The Socialist and Communist parties were more interested in economic reform than in raising the clerical issue, despite the Vatican's public support for the Christian Democratic Party for decades after 1945.

Agreements and legislation ended the privileged status of the clergy and updated the Lateran Pacts in the 1980s, and by the postwar constitution there were no subsidies for Catholic schools. Anticlericals protested the presence of crucifixes in public schools and government buildings, and these were removed, but there was no further anticlericalism. As in France and Spain, there were protests against the clergy's opposition to divorce, contraception, and abortion, but again, these were reactive stances on the part of the clergy.

SPAIN

Despite attempts by political anticlericals to legislate the Spanish clergy out of power during the nineteenth century, they were unsuccessful; but the clergy came to depend on middle- and upper-class support against anarchist violence by the end of the century, a phenomenon that was most clearly shown in the burning of churches in Barcelona in 1909. Anticlerical violence continued until a dictatorship was established under Primo de Rivera in 1923. But the clergy remained fearful, and all of the reformist groups—liberal democrats, socialists, and anarchists—called for anticlerical reforms, often making the clergy scapegoats for unsolvable national problems.

The opportunity came in 1931 with the ouster of the monarchy and the establishment of the Second Republic. The Republican-Socialist governing coalition legislated the end of clerical salaries, separated church and state, dissolved the Jesuits, and prohibited the regular clergy from teaching. More frightening to the clergy were anarchists and agents provocateurs who burned churches in

Madrid and southern Spain. A right-wing party, the Confederation of Autonomous Right-wing Parties (Confederación Española de Derechas Autónomas, or CEDA), was formed, which won power in 1933 in coalition with the ancient anticlerical party, the Radical Party. The anticlerical legislation was allowed to lapse, and where churches were burned, arsonists were jailed.

In the elections of February 1936, a Popular Front coalition of all the leftist parties was formed, and one of their electoral pledges was the implementation of the anticlerical legislation. When they won the election and began to enforce the legislation, there were more church burnings and some attacks on the clergy. Civil war erupted in July 1936 when the army rebelled against the government. This rebellion, backed by the conservative classes, including some clergy, led to an anticlerical fury unequaled in modern times. Nearly seven thousand priests, nuns, and religious brothers were killed, mainly by anarchists. Churches were burned or closed all over government-held Spain, and religious objects were destroyed, clerical graves profaned, and innumerable laypersons killed simply for having been practicing Catholics. This fury was over by the end of the first six months of the war, but those churches not destroyed remained closed until the end of the war and the victory of the Nationalists under General Francisco Franco (1892–1975) in 1939.

In the new Francoist Spain, the clergy were restored to power, but the anticlerical fury had spent itself. Under the heavy hand of the dictator, order was restored in Spain. In the 1960s a new form of anticlericalism appeared when younger clergy began supporting clandestine proletarian groups, and the Franco regime created a special prison for those priests. Basque priests who had opposed the Nationalists during the civil war and after were also imprisoned. When Franco died in 1975, all the priests were released, and in the spirit of Vatican II, the restored monarchy under King Juan Carlos I (r. 1975–) decreed religious toleration in the new constitution and later renounced the privileges of the concordat of 1953. As in France and Italy there were clerical protests against divorce and abortion legislation, but anticlericals ignored them.

OTHER COUNTRIES

In Portugal, the other Latin European country that was the scene of anticlerical conflict in the nineteenth century, anticlericals used the overthrow of the monarchy in 1910 to pass laws restricting the clergy; there were also a few instances of violence against priests.

But the problems facing the new republic were so great that anticlerical activity did not continue. National unity was needed and anticlericalism served only to divide. The military coup of 1917 established a dictatorship, ultimately in the hands of Antonio de Oliveira Salazar (1889–1970) after 1928, and all of the anticlerical laws were nullified.

In Poland and Ireland, both devout Catholic countries in the nineteenth and early twentieth centuries, the clergy supported movements for independence from the Soviet Union and Britain respectively, so that there was little anticlericalism in those countries, and despite gaining independence, nominally in the case of Poland until the Soviet Union lost control in the 1990s, and actually in Ireland by the 1930s, the clergy were still generally respected and were powerful. The only other European country in which action was taken against the clergy was Nazi Germany, but the moves of Adolf Hitler (1889–1945) were less anticlerical than they were anti-Catholic.

See also **Catholic Action; Catholicism.**

BIBLIOGRAPHY

Birmingham, David. *A Concise History of Portugal.* 2nd ed. Cambridge, U.K., 2003.

Callahan, William. *The Catholic Church in Spain, 1875–1998.* Washington, D.C., 2000. The single best study of the Spanish church.

Grew, Raymond. "Catholicism in a Changing Italy." In *Modern Italy: A Topical History since 1861,* edited by Edward R. Tannenbaum and Emiliana P. Noether, 254–273. New York, 1974.

McCarthy, Patrick. "The Church in Post-War Italy." In *Italy since 1945,* edited by Patrick McCarthy, 133–152. Oxford, U.K., 2000.

Sánchez, José. *Anticlericalism: A Brief History.* Notre Dame, Ind., 1972. Comprehensive study but now outdated.

Schapiro, J. Salwyn. *Anticlericalism: Conflict between Church and State in France, Italy, and Spain.* Princeton, N.J., 1967.

Sowerwine, Charles. *France since 1870: Culture, Politics, and Society.* New York, 2001.

Zeldin, Theodore. *France, 1848–1945.* Vol. 2: *Intellect, Taste, and Anxiety.* Oxford, U.K., 1977. Chapter on anticlericalism is the best for understanding the phenomenon in every country.

JOSÉ M. SÁNCHEZ

ANTICOMMUNISM. The Bolshevik Revolution of November 1917 heralded the prospect of the first communist state and with it a direct challenge to the established international political order. The Bolsheviks soon set about marshaling the two principal weapons at their disposal: firstly, the material resources of the Russian landmass, soon to be extended with the creation of the Union of Soviet Socialist Republics (USSR) in 1923; secondly, the universal ideology of Marxism-Leninism, which was to be projected and promoted throughout the world via newly organized communist parties and allied organizations in civil society. In the face of this challenge across several fronts, anticommunists represented a broad church involving a whole array of positions from left to right across the political spectrum. Disagreement over how much of a threat the communist movement actually represented, and whether communist ideology offered useful insights or should be rejected in toto, split anticommunist forces into distinguishable groups, which can be typified as the Socialists, the Liberals/Social Democrats, the Conservatives, the far Right, and the Left opposition.

RESPONSES TO THE BOLSHEVIK REVOLUTION

Prior to 1917 the perception that some form of collective action—involving concerted state intervention in the running of the national economy to ensure greater material equality and social justice—was essential (if not inevitable) was already prevalent within European politics. Even those who disagreed with its premises recognized socialism, as a kind of secular religion of modernity, to be the movement of the future. Its supporters occupied several different positions. In Germany and Austria the Social Democrats rejected revolution in favor of the reform of capitalism through legislation. To their left were the Democratic Socialists such as Jean Jaurès (1859–1914) in France and the Labour Party in Britain, who agreed with the democratic means but who remained committed to the end goal of a fully socialist socioeconomic system. In Britain the Liberal government of 1906–1910 also moved with this tide, introducing wide-ranging social legislation, though within the framework of private control of the economy. Conservatives too, recognizing the danger socialist-inspired reforms represented for traditional values and hierarchies, searched for ways to diffuse this movement through limited, controlled change. The Bolshevik seizure of power therefore added a new phase to an already long-running debate.

Among the Socialists, Social Democrats, and Liberals, hopes that bolshevism indicated another positive step in the general trend toward collectivism and social emancipation soon began to fade. Apologists for the Soviet regime—the so-called Fellow Travellers—would always remain, their belief in the inherent progressiveness of social revolution preventing them from rejecting completely the Soviet experiment. The British Fabian socialists Sidney Webb and Beatrice Webb, who published *Soviet Communism: A New Civilisation?* in 1935, were typical of this circle. Yet from the beginning the revolutionaries Vladimir Lenin (Vladimir Ilyich Ulyanov; 1870–1924) and Leon Trotsky (1879–1940) were vociferous in their critique of the failure of leftist parties to oppose World War I, and already in March 1919 the launch of the Comintern marked an assault on the Second International (later called the Socialist International). Throughout Europe and elsewhere, during 1920–1921 the Socialists and Social Democrats were deliberately split by revolutionary factions dividing off to form communist parties loyal to Moscow. In Germany and France these factions initially represented the majority, but in Italy, another country where hopes for insurrection were high, the Communists proved to be in the minority. The Socialists responded by reviving the Socialist International in 1923, but they were now politically on the defensive. These developments caused much long-term bitterness, and the fault line between Socialists and Communists was not helped by the latter referring to the former as class traitors.

The rise of fascism did eventually cause a tactical rapprochement in the form of the Popular Front from 1934 onward, but the purges of Soviet dictator Joseph Stalin (1879–1953), the ruthless tactics employed by Moscow during the Spanish civil war (1936–1939), and the signing of the Nazi-Soviet pact in 1939 ensured a complete break in trust between the two sides prior to World War II. The experience of Stalinism ensured that Socialist and Social Democratic parties and trade unions (pace Fellow Travellers) would prove to be a strongly anticommunist bulwark in West European politics up to the 1970s.

For conservatives, bolshevism was a major challenge to the established socioeconomic and moral order of the ruling classes. For the British and French the initial fear was that Germany would profit from the Russian withdrawal from World War I, and this strategic concern had far-reaching consequences. Firstly it justified the military intervention in Russia in 1918, which involved up to thirteen thousand French and forty-four thousand British soldiers fighting on the side of the White Russians against the Red Army. However, the failure to destroy bolshevism abroad militarily led to a determination to restore the forces of order by opposing further collectivism domestically. The result was an anticommunism that tended to indiscriminately gather all the forces of the Left under the same banner as a threat to the socioeconomic and moral order. Conservatives also recognized the need to oppose the leftist, modernist secular religion on the ideological plain with an alternative set of ideas. Communism was seen as an evil set of ideas that challenged all cultural hierarchies and moral values, and these, as the central framework of civilization, had to be defended at all costs. One of the main sources for this view was a revived interest in Christianity after 1917 and again after World War II as a form of "moral rearmament." The Catholic Church, aside from being a principal source of ideological inspiration, also became an important player within anticommunist politics. In 1919 the Vatican authorized the founding of the Popular Party in Italy as a means of channeling social discontent, especially in the countryside, away from the radical Left. Following the seizure of power by Benito Mussolini (1883–1945) and the settling of differences with the Vatican through the Lateran treaties, the church turned its attention abroad. Most

notably this led to the formation of Pro Deo, established by the Belgian Father Felix Morlion as a transnational network dedicated to opposing the worldwide influence of communism and a close partner of the U.S. Central Intelligence Agency (CIA) during the Cold War (1945–1989).

The wave of communist agitation following the end of World War I, which involved major industrial unrest in France, Germany, and Italy, and the successful (albeit brief) seizure of power in Hungary and Munich, posed a serious threat to corporate interests across Europe. As a result, industrialists mobilized their resources and channeled them into the most aggressive anticommunist force: fascism. In Italy the Confederation of Industry (Confindustria) was revitalized and reorganized to meet the new threat and was soon lending its considerable support to Mussolini. Major German industrialists such as Hugo Stinnes, Gustav Krupp, Fritz Thyssen, and Albert Voegler were all contributing to the National Socialists under Adolf Hitler (1889–1945) by the mid-1920s. The rise of the Right was caused by many factors, but a central reason was the perceived weakness of liberal democracy in the face of the communist challenge. Economic stagnation, acute following the Wall Street crash of 1929, confirmed the inability of parliamentarianism to deal with these structural difficulties. Between 1929 and 1936 France was run by fifteen different premiers in charge of twenty-two different cabinets. The European middle classes, seeking a counterrevolutionary force to stave off revolution and offer security, were attracted in many countries to the discourse of nationalist revival offered by the Right. Conservative authoritarian and autocratic governments, often centered around the monarchy and the nobility and strongly anticommunist, dominated the political scene in Poland, Hungary, Romania, and Yugoslavia during the 1920s and 1930s. By 1938 Czechoslovakia was the only remaining democratic regime in eastern Europe. In the contest between the major ideologies, democracy could not compete.

THE EFFECTS OF STALINISM

The brutalities of Stalinism had alienated many on the left, who as a result sought alternative paths to the socialist utopia. One pole was offered by Trotsky, whose opposition to Stalin forced him into exile and who founded the Fourth International in

1938 to promote the further development of "permanent revolution" through the strategy of the vanguard party. Trotskyites represented the Left opposition because of their contention that the Soviet Union was not the communist state it claimed to be. Others turned to anarchism. Originally supporters of the emancipatory potential offered by the Bolshevik Revolution, the crushing of the Kronstadt rebellion (1921) by Trotsky and Lenin, and the development of an oppressive Soviet bureaucratic state by Stalin confirmed for anarchists the original criticism of the Russian anarchist Mikhail Bakunin (1814–1876) against "the dictatorship of the proletariat." Although a minority view, the anarchist belief in an individual freedom bereft of the hypocrisies of liberalism did find resonance with many on the democratic left. Typical of this tendency was the British writer George Orwell (Eric Arthur Blair; 1903–1950), whose bitter rejection of both Stalinism and fascism led him to hope for the advancement of individual liberty via a revitalized democratic socialism. Thus the excesses of the 1930s led Orwell and others of a progressive bent to adopt a position of antitotalitarianism.

Yet as Hannah Arendt argued in *The Origins of Totalitarianism* (1951) and elsewhere, the challenge for modernity was to establish a politics that would avoid the complete subordination of the individual to the mass as expressed in extremity by communism, fascism, and Nazism. As a result antitotalitarianism was a label that could fit an array of political positions, from conservatism to democratic socialism. In 1944 the Austrian economist Friedrich Hayek published *The Road to Serfdom*, a call to revive classical libertarian liberalism that regarded all attempts to institute collectivism and state planning of the economy as inimical to personal freedom. Hayek also attacked the perversion of language through communist hijacking of terms such as "freedom" and "democracy," and emphasized the need to reclaim their original meaning. Although Keynesianism, which regarded state intervention in the economy as essential for stability, remained the norm in Western Europe up to the 1980s, Hayek laid the ground for a neoliberal revival that would ultimately succeed in placing the free market and individual choice as the natural antithesis to communism.

ANTICOMMUNISM AND THE COLD WAR

From 1941 to 1945 the grand alliance of the Soviet Union with the Western Allies placed the forces of communism and democratic anticommunism on the same side. Stalin even abandoned the Comintern in 1943 in the interests of wartime solidarity. The activities of communists in the wartime Resistance also raised the credibility and prestige of their cause after the debacles of the previous decade. Nevertheless, the adherence of communist parties to directives from Moscow was always going to be a political weak point in peacetime. The solidification of Soviet control over Eastern Europe during 1945–1948, and fears over how expansionist Stalin might actually be, created widespread apprehension and mistrust in the West. Developing a harder line toward Moscow therefore required controlling its proxy forces in domestic politics as well. The declaration of the Dutch Communist Party in the wake of the communist coup in Czechoslovakia (1948) that it would fight on the side of an invading Red Army placed postwar loyalties in stark relief. Responses from the state toward the communist parties varied according to national conditions. In the Netherlands the party remained legal, but "loyalty checks" were instituted for public service employees. In West Germany (the Federal Republic of Germany, or FRG) anticommunism became one of the central pillars of the divided country's identity, a position that translated in some quarters into right-wing sentiments that regarded the FGR as a bulwark against the atheist, Slavic "hordes" to the east. The Kommunistische Partei Deutschland was eventually made illegal in the FRG in 1956. In France and Italy the strength of the parties, polling around 25 percent of the vote and investing in a whole "countersociety" superstructure, made them more of a potent threat. But even here (as also in Belgium) the communist parties were excluded from government in 1947, and as support for them declined they were not to return as serious governing partners until the mid-1970s.

Above all, the anticommunist struggle after World War II was bound up with the ultimate struggle to reestablish and maintain both liberal democracy as a viable political model and capitalism as a stable economic system. In these circumstances, with fascism and Nazism a recent reality and communism a real threat, the European Recovery Program

(Marshall Plan) and the North Atlantic Treaty Organization (NATO), founded April 1949, were pivotal events in terms of confidence-building. These developments, which marked a direct involvement in and commitment to West European affairs by the United States, strengthened the forces of anticommunism and legitimized the (re)structuring of social, political, economic, and cultural life. Containment became the goal, both of Soviet expansionism abroad and communist advances at home. Once again, within this field different gradations of anticommunism existed, from the Social Democrats who argued that radical social reform was the best way to undermine support for the radical Left to conservatives who totally rejected the legitimacy of communism and sought to wipe it (and all its political kin) from the map.

During the Cold War, the anticommunist forces of the Left and the Right were often as opposed to each other as they were opposed to communism itself. Within domestic politics, however, the dominance of Keynesianism led to the further development of the welfare state and a consensus among Social and Christian Democrats toward managed collectivism and state intervention in the economy to ensure social equality and justice. Within society as a whole, the determination to ensure political and economic stability and the establishment of anticommunism as the norm led to a large-scale mobilization of material and intellectual forces. In some fields the methods of the Soviet Union were deliberately mimicked. In 1925 the All Union Society for Cultural Relations with Foreign Countries, or VOKS, had been created by Moscow to build and coordinate links between Soviet civil organizations and their counterparts abroad. A series of "fronts" had been developed, such as the International Union of Students, the World Federation of Democratic Youth, and the International Union of Journalists, to organize and utilize these groups for the benefit of Soviet foreign policy. After World War II similar anticommunist "fronts" were established to attract members away from the communist-dominated organizations. Examples are the World Assembly of Youth (WAY, founded in London, 1948), the International Federation of Journalists (Brussels, 1952), and the International Commission of Jurists (West Berlin, 1952). The trade unions were a crucial battleground

for this approach. Thus the anticommunist Force Ouvrière was established in France to oppose the powerful left-wing General Confederation of Labour (CGT), and in 1949 the communist-controlled World Federation of Trade Unions was undermined when Western nations split off to form the International Confederation of Free Trade Unions. In all these developments European and American anticommunists worked side by side, identifying themselves with the "Free West" against the totalitarian East.

In this battle of ideas the most interesting development was the founding of the Congress for Cultural Freedom (CCF), in West Berlin in June 1950, which aimed to establish a high-profile intellectual-cultural network opposed to the restrictions on freedom of thought and expression as proclaimed by Stalinism. The CCF was mainly a Euro-American coalition of conservatives, Social Democrats, and, crucially, former communists such as the British-Hungarian writer Arthur Koestler (1905–1983) and the Italian writer and politician Ignazio Silone (Secondo Tranquilli; 1900–1978). Not coincidentally, the CCF appeared in the same year as the publication *The God That Failed,* which collected the ruminations of six former communists (including Koestler and Silone) on their former "faith" and why they abandoned it. Apostates of communism such as Koestler were important figures in the anticommunist cause, their first-hand knowledge of the communist movement giving them a high-profile moral superiority and prestige. They also exuded intolerance of any who continued to profess respect for Marxism and its progeny, causing them naturally to gravitate to the conservative camp and to attack Fellow Travelers as much as they attacked the communists themselves. The CCF went on to refine a sociopolitical position known as the "End of Ideology," of which the foremost European proponent was Raymond Aron in *L'opium des intellectuels* (1955; *The Opium of the Intellectuals,* 1957). This was based on the claim that ideological thinking was passé, because a broad welfare state consensus within Western politics had opened up new possibilities for the improved technocratic management of modern society. In this way the advocates of the End of Ideology sought to reclaim the mantle of progress for democratic capitalism, symbolically leaving communism behind in the "dustbin of history."

An important player in this battle for supremacy and legitimacy between competing civil society organizations was the secret state. Because free institutions such as the CCF should be seen to arise spontaneously through the free will of active citizens, it was important to conceal any state involvement in their financing and management. The CIA was most closely involved with this strategy, providing most of the funding for the CCF, paying American trade unions to support their counterparts in Europe, and supporting a whole network of anticommunist institutions. Against the Soviet Union itself it funded guerrilla units in the Ukraine and the Baltic States (all penetrated by Soviet intelligence) and funded Radio Free Europe and Radio Liberty to broadcast across the Iron Curtain. But West European intelligence services also played a role, for instance with British support for WAY. Covert support (probably CIA) is also strongly suspected in the case of Paix et Liberté, a transnational anticommunist propaganda network based in Paris and with affiliates across Western Europe during the 1950s. By the early 1960s the need for a better understanding of communist theory and practice led the French, Dutch, and German intelligence services to create Interdoc, another transnational network that aimed to raise awareness of the dangers for the West of the "peaceful coexistence" strategy of Soviet premier Nikita Khrushchev (1894–1971). This determination of the intelligence services to remove the communist threat at all costs also led to more extreme activities, such as the "Gladio" network of irregular forces prepared to resist an invasion of the Red Army behind the lines, and the "Strategy of Tension" in Italy, which involved elements of the security service in acts of terrorism that were then blamed on the Left.

1968, DÉTENTE, AND THE END OF THE COLD WAR

At the end of the 1960s the anticommunist consensus was shattered by a new generation who saw it as no more than another method for sociopolitical control, and who saw the war in Vietnam as evidence that the anticommunist cause was unnecessarily violent and morally bankrupt. Significantly, the New Left movements that sprang up around 1968 rejected the monolithic power structures of both American-style corporate capitalism and Soviet-style centralized communism in equal measure, instead choosing a cross between the dissident Left (Che Guevara, Maoism, Trotskyism) and a radical libertarianism. The upheavals surrounding 1968 had two longer-term consequences. The first concerned the political forces released by these disparate groups, with their unorthodox take on the Cold War struggle. At the end of the 1970s, in the context of rising tensions between NATO and the Warsaw Pact, they coalesced around the antinuclear/peace movements and in transnational coalitions such as European Nuclear Disarmament (END). The second concerned the viability of the communist parties themselves. The 1968 phenomenon challenged the established order in both Western and Eastern Europe, as the movement for "Socialism with a Human Face" took hold in Czechoslovakia and Poland. Détente between the superpowers also loosened the international framework in which these parties could operate. The result was Eurocommunism, a reformist program of the largest communist parties in the West (France, Italy, Spain after 1975) that aimed both to connect with the new emancipatory movements and the expanding middle classes, and to create a strategic distance from Moscow.

Yet Eurocommunism's hoped-for breakthrough did not happen. Instead, the leftist dominance of West European politics during the 1970s and the rise of the antinuclear/peace movements triggered a reaction from the hard-line conservative Right. The high point for this reaction was the highly suspect assassination of the Italian premier Aldo Moro in 1978, at the moment when he was leading the Christian Democrats into a political "historic compromise" with the Communists. The electoral victory of Margaret Thatcher in Britain in 1979 (and the election of Ronald Reagan as president of the United States in 1980) was a significant moment in the polarization of Left and Right in Western European politics. The strength of the peace movement was enough to unsettle domestic politics in the Netherlands and West Germany and to challenge the defense strategy of NATO itself (which relied on the placement of medium-range nuclear missiles in these countries). Once again, as during the early Cold War, the Right used the excuse of a threatening Soviet Union to attack all of its actual or potential allies on the left in the same way. The claim of the Right, that a united stand against the Soviet Union based on the common security interests of NATO ultimately won the superpower contest, has some degree of merit. However, the anticommunist force in Europe that actually brought about the unraveling of the Eastern bloc regimes was the citizens of those regimes themselves, first through the Solidarity union in Poland from 1980 onward and then during 1988–1989 in Hungary, Czechoslovakia, and East Germany. The attempt of Soviet premier Mikhail Gorbachev (b. 1931) to reform the communist system from within met too much opposition from those who wanted to benefit from its fall, and anticommunism effectively came to an end as a meaningful concept with the dissolution of both the Soviet Communist Party and the Soviet Union itself in 1991. The parties across Europe either transformed themselves into Social Democratic–type movements as in Italy, joined forces with the Greens as in the Netherlands, or aimed for acceptance as part of the post–Cold War political landscape as in Hungary (and with some success). Forms of authoritarianism continue to be successful, as in Russia, and may well return elsewhere on the Continent. Anticollectivist and collectivist arguments, now couched in terms of neoliberalism and its discontents, will continue to dominate political discourse. Nevertheless, twenty-first-century Europe has lost the haunting specter of communism that defined its sociopolitical divisions for the previous hundred years.

See also **Antifascism; Cold War; Communism; Eurocommunism; Totalitarianism.**

BIBLIOGRAPHY

Aron, Raymond. *The Opium of the Intellectuals.* Translated by Terence Kilmartin. Garden City, N.Y., 1957.

Carew, Anthony. *Labour under the Marshall Plan: The Politics of Productivity and the Marketing of Management Science.* Manchester, U.K., 1987.

Caute, David. *68: The Year of the Barricades.* London, 1988.

Crossman, R. H. S., ed. *The God That Failed.* New York, 1950.

Delmas, Jean, and Kessler, Jean. *Renseignement et propagande pendant la guerre froide, 1947–1953.* Brussels, 1999.

Dorril, Stephen. *MI6: Fifty Years of Special Operations.* London, 2000.

Ganser, Daniele. *NATO's Secret Armies: Operation Gladio and Terrorism in Western Europe.* London, 2005.

Grémion, Pierre. *Intelligence de l'anticommunisme: Le congrès pour la liberté de la culture à Paris, 1950–1975.* Paris, 1995.

Hamilton, Alastair. *The Appeal of Fascism: A Study of Intellectuals and Fascism, 1919–1945.* New York, 1971.

Hobsbawm, Eric. *Age of Extremes: The Short Twentieth Century, 1914–1991.* London, 1994.

Kisatsky, Deborah. *The United States and the European Right, 1945–1955.* Columbus, Ohio, 2005.

Major, Patrick. *The Death of the KPD: Communism and Anti-Communism in West Germany, 1945–1956.* Oxford, U.K., 1997.

Mazower, Mark. *Dark Continent: Europe's Twentieth Century.* London, 1998.

Ruotsila, Markku. *British and American Anticommunism before the Cold War.* London, 2001.

Sassoon, Donald. *One Hundred Years of Socialism: The West European Left in the Twentieth Century.* London, 1996.

Scott-Smith, Giles. *The Politics of Apolitical Culture: The Congress for Cultural Freedom, the CIA, and Post-War American Hegemony.* London, 2002.

Tökes, Rudolf. *Eurocommunism and Détente.* New York, 1978.

Van den Dungen, Peter, ed. *West European Pacifism and the Strategy for Peace.* Houndmills, U.K., 1985.

GILES SCOTT-SMITH

ANTIFASCISM.

The intensity of contemporary debates over the legacy of antifascism are to no small degree the result of the fact that there is no consensus over the historical role of antifascism as a political and cultural movement. Unlike Italian fascism and German National Socialism, which were defeated and discredited militarily and politically in 1945, antifascism emerged from the war with its reputation enhanced by the aura of resistance movements and the Soviet victory. Postwar European communist parties and regimes, especially in the German Democratic Republic (GDR), drew their legitimacy from the sacrifices of heroes and martyrs who became the touchstone of state-sanctioned myths and rituals until 1989. While for some historians antifascism was marked by an extraordinary mobilization of the intellectuals in defense of culture and democracy, for others it was thoroughly corrupted by its association with communism.

Characteristically, two distinguished historians, both of them veterans of the antifascist movement, could retrospectively approach the subject from entirely opposing perspectives. British historian Eric J. Hobsbawm reprised the moment during the 1930s when the Left abandoned its sectarian illusions, recovered from its earlier defeats, challenged the half-hearted and insincere policies of appeasement, and welded together a broad coalition of conservatives, liberals, socialists, and communists in a variety of countries "against the common enemy." By contrast, the French historian François Furet claimed that antifascism was the new face of Stalinism: a cynical and effective doctrinal shift that allowed European communists to change overnight from dedicated Bolsheviks into champions of liberty, marching under the banner of democracy, humanity, and hatred of Adolf Hitler (1883–1945).

Both approaches are too restrictive both in scope and content. The ideology of antifascism varied greatly from the Comintern's official declarations linking fascism and monopoly capitalism to more diffuse moral pronouncements by intellectuals like novelists Romain Rolland or Heinrich Mann, the German exile writer. At its height in the mid-1930s, antifascism was the rallying cry of the Left, but given the abiding hostility of communists and socialists, it was also a "pragmatic compromise" cobbled together to meet the emergency of Hitler's rise to power. Antifascism mobilized genuine popular support for democratic currents while at the same time it caused a fatal blindness that allowed many Western intellectuals to sacrifice their judgment and lead "double lives" guided by a secret Stalinist *apparat*.

Though communist antifascism was attractive to varying degrees in different periods, it is necessary to more broadly include noncommunist antifascism and go beyond parties and organizations to include ideas, intellectuals, the press, everyday life, and religious movements. A more capacious approach would also include "an attitude or feeling of hostility toward fascist ideology and its propagators." It is therefore advisable to distinguish the official antifascism of the Comintern from local initiatives as well as from exile intellectuals and noncommunist resistance groups, which encompassed a much more complicated fiber of beliefs, convictions, hopes, emotions, attitudes. The three main phases of the history of antifascism considered below are: antifascism before the rise of Hitler (1920–1933); antifascism in the era of Hitler and Stalin (1934–1945); antifascism after fascism (1946–1989).

ANTIFASCISM BEFORE THE RISE OF HITLER

Though fascism demonstrated its brutality and violence against Italian socialists and communists in the years before the establishment of the Benito Mussolini (1883–1945) government in October 1922, it initially caused no great alarm for the Italian Communist Party (PCI) or the Soviet Union. The leader and founder of the party, Amedeo Bordiga, saw no fundamental distinction between bourgeois democracy and fascist dictatorship; convinced of the imminent collapse of capitalism, he consider the greater danger to lie in a Social Democratic government after the fall of the dictatorship. During 1922 the Alleanza del Lavoro, probably the first antifascist organization, emerged, a more or less spontaneous coalition of socialists, republicans, trade unionists, communists, and anarchists. Early antifascism was politically and philosophically diverse. At the forefront of the parliamentary opposition to Mussolini (until his death from a beating in 1926) was Giovanni Amendola, a brilliant journalist who protested the ban on opposition parties and coined the term "totalitarian" to describe Mussolini's system. Catholic, socialist, and communist opponents of the dictatorship formed the "Aventine Secession" (named after the protest of Gaius Sempronius Gracchus in ancient Rome), withdrawing from Parliament after the assassination of the reform Socialist Giacomo Matteotti in 1924. The following year, antifascists were suppressed, arrested, forced into exile and murdered. The voice of Italian liberalism, the philosopher Benedetto Croce, abandoned his initial support for Mussolini and issued his influential "Manifesto of the Antifascist Intellectuals" on 1 May 1925, calling for a "far deeper and more concrete understanding of the virtues of liberal laws and methods." After 1926, the PCI adopted the more nuanced position on the Italian dictatorship put forward by Antonio Gramsci (imprisoned by

Mussolini) and Palmiro Togliatti (the PCI leader in exile), which admitted that at least in its first years fascism had been a genuinely revolutionary movement.

While in Italy the communist underground remained the only clandestine movement that attracted any substantial popular support, exile antifascism was severely hampered by the nonparticipation of the communists. In 1927, the Concentrazione Antifascista (Antifascist Coalition) was created in Paris under the auspices of the Socialist Pietro Nenni. The most important antifascist exile organization was Giustizia e Libertà (Justice and Liberty), the political creation of Carlo Rosselli who conceived of a "liberal socialism" as an alternative to the divisions that fractured the organized Left in Europe. Many of the great writers of the antifascist movement, including Carlo Levi, Cesare Pavese, and Ignazio Silone, were prominent figures in the Italian exile community in Paris. By 1937, however, the Rosselli brothers (Carlo and Roberto) had been murdered and the exile antifascists were increasingly estranged from the situation in Italy.

Soviet foreign policy in the 1920s was highly ambivalent, continuing to maintain friendly relations with Mussolini and court the German nationalist Right, especially in the era of Soviet-German military rapprochement following the 1921 Treaty of Rapallo. In 1924 Joseph Stalin (1879–1953) announced the new policy of the Comintern: "Social Democracy is objectively the moderate wing of fascism.... These organizations do not negate, but supplement each other. They are not antipodes; they are twins." Throughout 1931 and 1932, communists and Nazis sometimes struck tactical alliances, as they did in the Berlin transport strike of November 1932. Even the International Congress against Fascism and War in Amsterdam, held in the summer of 1932, refrained from condemning Italy or Germany.

ANTIFASCISM IN THE ERA OF HITLER AND STALIN

Before 1934, Italian socialist exiles and Austrian and German Social Democrats were the most prominent opponents of both Mussolini and Hitler. Following the Reichstag Fire of 28 February 1933, some five thousand communists were arrested and the powerful German Communist Party (KPD),

with its 100,000 members and almost six million supporters, was dismantled. But as late as January 1934, the Red Army continued to maintain cordial relations with the German Reichswehr and a new commercial agreement with Germany was signed. Soviet leaders began to question, however, whether a new alliance with France and Britain might make more sense than the deteriorating Soviet-German connection.

In May 1935, the Soviet Union signed mutual assistance pacts with France and Czechoslovakia, signaling a turnabout. Events in France were already fuelling an upsurge in popular antifascist activism. The night of the nationalist "Leagues" in Paris on 6 February 1934 led to strong counterdemonstrations by the Left on 12 February (the day of the insurrection against Engelbert Dollfuss by the Social Democrats in Vienna), and to a joint antifascist declaration of the intellectuals signed by figures as diverse as the Surrealists André Breton, René Crevel, and Paul Eluard, the writer André Malraux, and the Radical philosopher Emile Chartier (known by the pseudonym Alain). At a Party Congress in June 1934, the French Communist leader Maurice Thorez told his followers, "It is not a question of choosing between communism and fascism, but between fascism and democracy." In the Loiret department, for example, there were only 200 active communists in 1930 but by 1935, more than 5,000 members had joined 77 local antifascist committees, reaching not only the workers' districts of the city of Orléans but rural villages where the Left had little influence. This is not to assert that pressure from below effected the doctrinal reversal of the French Communist Party on 27 July 1934 (the date of the unity of action pact signed by Communists and Socialists [SFIO]), but there is no question that the pact presaged the Comintern's Popular Front strategy announced at the Seventh Congress of the Comintern on 25 July 1935.

Georgi Dimitrov (1882–1949), who had become a hero during his trial on charges of conspiracy to burn the Reichstag in Leipzig, was installed as the new head of the Comintern, coinciding with its new strategy of a "broad people's antifascist front." Fascism was now defined as "the open terrorist dictatorship of the most reactionary, chauvinistic and most imperialist elements of

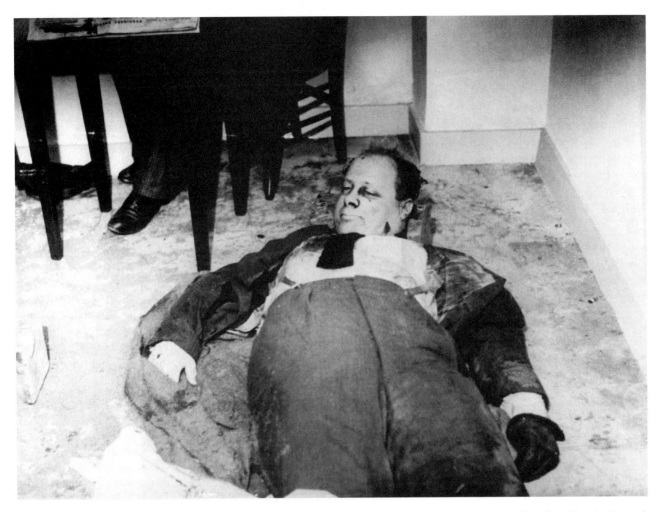

The body of Carlo Rosselli, 9 June 1937. One of the most prominent antifascist intellectuals and the founder of the Justice and Liberty organization, Rosselli was murdered by fascist operatives while in exile in France. ©HULTON-DEUTSCH COLLECTION/CORBIS

finance capital." The election of the Popular Front government in France in May 1936 cemented the alliance of the Left, increasing Communist representation in Parliament sevenfold and giving the Socialists 146 (from 97) seats. Conversely, tensions between industrial workers and the government of Leon Blum (1872–1950) during the 1936 strike wave and the overweening presence of Communists in the national antifascist organizations alienated local antifascists and caused a rapid decline in the grassroots movement.

German Social Democrats and communists in exile failed to produce a united front, but there were figures on both sides, including Willi Münzenberg and the Social Democrat Rudolf Breitscheid, who sought such an alliance. Münzenberg and his lieutenant, the talented Otto Katz, orchestrated spectacular international antifascist campaigns, cultural congresses, and committees to free Ernst Thälmann (who was imprisoned as a left-wing opponent of the regime). But the communists by no means dominated these genuinely mass campaigns. A comparison of communist and noncommunist publications among German exiles reveals that bourgeois-liberal writers published three times more than their communist colleagues. Antifascist culture in the 1930s was characterized by social inclusivity, political flexibility, and ideological imprecision, especially in defining who or what was "fascist."

Popular Front organizations embraced antifascists great and small, from commanding intellectual figures like Romain Rolland, André Gide, and Heinrich Mann, to the rank and file who attended Soviet dance recitals, lectures by the Archbishop of

Canterbury, or tea parties for Spain. Such innocuous activities frequently masked uncritical admiration for the Soviet Union's achievements and sometimes even turned a blind eye to its crimes. But in 1937, at the height of the Spanish civil war, support for the Soviet Union did not always necessarily entail an embrace of communism, nor did it always mean a rejection of liberalism. "For us in the 1930s," historian George Mosse recalled, "antifascism was both a political and cultural movement in its own right, and one could join the movement, admire the Soviet Union for its lonely stand against appeasement, and yet reject Communism and Bolshevism as systems as well as for their materialist views of history."

Antifascism was a complex mix of ideas, images, and symbols that ultimately divided the world into two hostile camps, and subordinated all political judgment to a Manichaean logic. In the struggle between "fascism" and its enemies, there could be no middle ground, no neutral space, and no noncombatants in a world divided between the forces of progress and decline, the friends and enemies of culture and civilization. The historian Richard Cobb, who lived in Paris during the 1930s, recalled that "France was living through a moral and mental civil war ... one had to choose between fascism and fellow traveling."

Not unconnected to its friend-enemy logic was the antifascist myth of "virile innocence," especially concerning masculine heroes. "Better the widow of a hero than the wife of a coward" was an oft-repeated slogan. The centerpiece of the myth of heroic innocence was the *Brown Book of the Reichstag Fire* (1933), one of the all-time bestsellers of world communism, "the Bible of the antifascist crusade." It offered a picture of the Nazi regime that not only masked the real defeat, but that became all too familiar: a regime devoid of popular support, resting on terror, conspiracy, and arson, orchestrated by a band of "feminized" homosexual degenerates, dope-fiends, torturers, and corrupt officials.

Many of the international volunteers who arrived in Spain during the heyday of antifascism during the Spanish civil war (1936–1939) truly felt that they belonged not to a nation or class, nor to a party or a movement, nor a doctrine or a metaphysics, but to a common humanity whose adherents all spoke the same Spartan language, shared the

same sacrifices, and were engaged in the same redemption of the world. The writer Milton Wolff, who joined the Abraham Lincoln Brigade composed of 3,000 American volunteers, wrote of his "Spanish Lesson": "He went to Spain in 1936 because he was an antifascist. He felt, although he did not know for sure, that if fascism were not stopped in Spain, it would sweep the world. He did not know beforehand what he was going to do when he got to Spain. Certainly he did not know anything about fighting or killing or dying; but he was a volunteer. In Spain he met a people who lived, slept and ate antifascism, who never tired of doing something about it." This rhetoric of innocence and the innocence of antifascist rhetoric may explain why antifascism remained so pure in the memory of its veterans. As George Orwell wrote in his classic *Homage to Catalonia* (1938), those illusions were in truth the correct "anti-Fascist" attitude that had been carefully disseminated largely in order to prevent people from grasping the real political nature of the civil war within the civil war.

For opponents of Hitler, the news of the non-aggression pact signed between Foreign Ministers Vyacheslav Molotov and Joachim von Ribbentrop on 23 August 1939 was a devastating blow. Though Stalin had already begun to withdraw from the Spanish conflict, though explorations of a possible rapprochement with Hitler continued throughout 1937, and though the British and French alliance never materialized, no one anticipated what simply seemed inconceivable. While the majority of communists quickly knuckled under and abandoned antifascism to pro-Sovietism, a minority of dissident intellectuals like Münzenberg, Manès Sperber, Arthur Koestler, Gustav Regler, Ignazio Silone, and Hans Sahl, broke ranks in order to remain antifascists. Forced to choose between loyalty to communism and opposition to Hitler, these writers understood that the "Machiavellian powers," as Sperber called them, had struck up a totalitarian alliance. Even the word *fascist* disappeared from the communist lexicon.

If the Hitler-Stalin pact all but destroyed the hopes of European antifascism, the invasion of the Soviet Union on 21 June 1941 partially revived them. But it is mistaken to assume the wartime policy of the Comintern, which was dissolved in May 1943, resumed the antifascist discourse of the Popular

Front era. Rather, Stalin rejected the idea that the Nazi-Soviet conflict was a "general anti-fascist war" and instead supported the creation of broad "national fronts" of all forces willing to oppose the Germans (with whom a separate peace might still be concluded). In the Soviet Union, "the great patriotic war" remained the national symbol and the national myth, even after communism's collapse.

ANTIFASCISM AFTER FASCISM

After World War II, antifascism became a "foundational myth" of the newly created "People's Republics" throughout Eastern Europe. What this meant was that Soviet rule could be cemented by celebrating the latter's victory over "fascism," while the abolition of private property could be justified by vigilance against "imperialism" and "militarism"—which during the Cold War meant West Germany and the United States. The new, postfascist German Democratic Republic (GDR) was built on a complex structure of legitimating myths, first and foremost that the German Communist Party had led a popular antifascist resistance movement against National Socialism that ultimately had resulted in the creation of the GDR. Antifascism was colored by its highly clichéd veneration of the heroes of the resistance, by the blood sacrifice of the Soviet Union, and by the martyrs whose noble deeds provided the basis for school textbooks, memorials, and rituals. Ernst Thälmann, the leader of the Communist Party who was imprisoned by Hitler in 1933 and died in Buchenwald concentration camp in 1944, was the object of an official sanctification that included countless poems, books, and films. More concretely, the antifascist German state dispensed broad amnesty and rehabilitation for the mass of former Nazi Party members and fellow travelers. The antifascist narrative allowed mass popular support for the Nazi Party and Hitler to be swept under the rug while the population could be collectively "immunized" against any association with the recently defeated Nazi regime. Collective memory in the GDR was "staged," "ritualized," and censored to present only the most schematic and authorized version of the history of antifascism. Especially during the 1950s, the German Communist Party was portrayed as the only leading and organized force of the antifascist resistance within Germany. The officially sanctioned history of German communism

failed (despite its eight bulky volumes) to mention the key figures of German antifascism who had fallen into disrepute, such as Münzenberg, and of course avoided any reference to the nearly three thousand German exiles who disappeared during Stalin's purges in the USSR.

Biography, in the Stalinist and post-Stalinist era, was destiny. The creation (and re-creation) of a curriculum vitae that included the "correct" antifascist past and the right landmarks of a personal itinerary was a sine qua non for success among the Party elite. The creation of a state-sanctioned myth of antifascism often produced collisions with the actual individuals and groups that had taken part in the very struggles so sanctimoniously commemorated. Among these, veterans of the Spanish civil war, though officially enshrined in the pantheon of heroes, were in fact frequently considered a major threat to official memory. Their familiarity with—indeed participation in—the military police in Spain, the repression of anarchists and the "Trotskyite" Marxist Party of Unification (POUM), and knowledge of what the writer Bodo Uhse called "the arrests over there" (in the Soviet Union), produced profound distrust among the party cadre. The Organization of Those Persecuted by the Nazi Regime (VVN) was abruptly dissolved in 1953 because of constant friction between its members and the GDR regime. Some members of another highly venerated group, the communist functionaries that had been interned in concentration camps like Buchenwald, were later revealed to have engaged in highly questionable behavior as "red Capos" (camp police). However, the experience of internment, Soviet exile, or Western exile did not lead to greater doubt among party members but instead reinforced loyalty to the cause and heightened distrust of comrades who might betray it.

From the outset, citizens who had taken part in the active "struggle against fascism" were given a higher standing in the official and administrative hierarchy of the GDR than those, like Jewish survivors of the Holocaust (or Jehovah's Witnesses), who were only reluctantly designated "victims of fascism." Ideological conformity was strictly enforced and communists who had spent time in the West came under suspicion. By the mid 1950s, the most prominent left-wing Jewish intellectuals—the philosopher Ernst Bloch, the literary critic Hans

Mayer, and the publicist Alfred Kantorowicz, who had voluntarily returned to the GDR—had gone over to the West. Beginning in 1948 and 1949, the Soviet Union inaugurated a campaign against prominent Jewish figures, beginning with the murder of the actor Solomon Mikhoels, a world-renowned figure in the Jewish Antifascist Committee. In August 1952, fifteen Soviet Jews, including five prominent Yiddish writers and poets, were secretly tried and executed for capital offenses, including treason, espionage, and bourgeois nationalism. In December of that year, the former Secretary General of the Czech Communist Party, Rudolf Salzmann Slansky, and thirteen others (including eleven Jews) were convicted of espionage in Prague. In 1951 the preparations began for an "anticosmopolitan" (a euphemism for anti-Semitic) trial in the GDR centering on Paul Merker, a member of the central committee of the Sozialistischen Einheitspartei Deutschlands (SED) who had been in exile in Mexico. Though the trial never took place due to Stalin's death, Merker was accused of being an agent of "imperialist intelligence" and "Zionism" for having written that the Jews should be compensated for their suffering at the hands of the Germans. The purges were a turning point in the East German attitude toward the Holocaust and Nazi anti-Semitism. Despite a few exceptions like Jurek Becker's novel *Jacob the Liar* (1969), the Holocaust remained a virtually taboo subject until the fall of the Berlin Wall in November 1989.

Official antifascism created a cult of state-sanctioned nostalgia and ex post facto legitimacy. Even the erection of the Berlin Wall in 1961 was justified as an "antifascist protective wall." Ironically, the institutionalized memory of antifascism not only disavowed the mass extermination of the Jews, the mass extermination of the Jews was a subject that transcended the "eternal" struggle between communism and fascism and thus threatened to destabilize the state ideology. Despite the efforts of well-intentioned scholars and contemporaries to disentangle authentic antifascist memory from the official rituals of state policy after 1989, the two were so entwined that not even the most careful craftsmanship could untie them. This is perhaps true of antifascism in the broader sense: though not all antifascists were implicated in communism and its crimes, antifascism as an ideology and as state

sanctioned memory could not be entirely dissociated from them.

See also **Anticommunism; Communism; Fascism; Molotov-Von Ribbentrop Pact.**

BIBLIOGRAPHY

Beetham, David, ed. *Marxists in the Face of Fascism: Writings by Marxists on Fascism from the Interwar Period.* Manchester, U.K., 1983.

Canali, Mauro. "Ignazio Silone and the Fascist Political Police." *Journal of Modern Italian Studies* 5, no. 1 (2000): 36–56.

Ceplair, Larry. *Under the Shadow of War: Fascism, Anti-Fascism, and Marxists, 1918–1939.* New York, 1987.

Copsey, Nigel. *Anti-Fascism in Britain.* London, 1999.

Diner, Dan. "On the Ideology of Antifascism." *New German Critique* 67 (Winter 1996): 123–132.

Epstein, Catherine. *The Last Revolutionaries: German Communists and Their Century.* Cambridge, Mass., 2003.

Fisher, David James. "Malraux: Left Politics and Anti-Fascism in the 1930s." *Twentieth Century Literature* 24, no. 3 (autumn 1978): 290–302.

Furet, François. *The Passing of an Illusion: The Idea of Communism in the Twentieth Century.* Translated by Deborah Furet. Chicago, 1999.

Gleason, Abbot. *Totalitarianism: The Inner History of the Cold War.* New York, 1995.

Grunenberg, Antonia. *Antifaschismus—ein deutscher Mythos.* Hamburg, Germany, 1993.

Herf, Jeffrey. *Divided Memory: The Nazi Past in the Two Germanies.* Cambridge, Mass., 1997.

Hewitt, Andrew. *Political Inversions: Homosexuality, Fascism, and the Modernist Imaginary.* Stanford, Calif., 1996.

Hobsbawm, Eric. *The Age of Extremes: A History of the World, 1914–1991.* New York, 1994.

Kantorowicz, Alfred. *Nachtbücher: Aufzeichnungen im französischen Exil 1935 bis 1939.* Edited by Ursula Büttner and Angelika Voß. Hamburg, Germany, 1995.

Koch, Stephen. *Double Lives: Spies and Writers in the Secret Soviet War of Ideas Against the West.* New York, 1994.

Koenen, Gerd. "Causal Nexus? Toward a Real History of Anti-Fascism and Anti-Bolshevism." *Telos* 114 (winter 1999): 49–67.

Koestler, Arthur. *The Invisible Writing.* New York, 1984.

Kriegel, Annie. "Sur l'antifascisme." *Commentaire* 50 (1990): 15–37.

McLellan, Josie. *Antifascism and Memory in East Germany: Remembering the International Brigades, 1945–1989.* Oxford, U.K., 2004.

Mosse, George L. *Confronting History: A Memoir.* Madison, Wis., 2000.

Nolan, Mary. "Antifascism under Fascism: German Visions and Voices." *New German Critique* 67 (winter 1996): 33–55.

Nothnagle, Alan L. *Building the East German Myth: Historical Mythology and Youth Propaganda in the German Democratic Republic, 1945–1989.* Ann Arbor, Mich., 1999.

Orwell, George. *Homage to Catalonia.* New York, 1952. Reprint, New York, 1980.

Oosterhuis, Harry. "The 'Jews' of the Antifascist Left: Homosexuality and Socialist Resistance to Nazism." *Journal of Homosexuality* 29, nos. 2/3 (1995): 227–257.

Payne, Stanley. "Soviet Anti-Fascism: Theory and Practice, 1921–1945." *Totalitarian Movements and Political Religions* 4, no. 2 (autumn 2003): 1–62.

Pugliese, Stanislao G. *Fascism, Anti-fascism, and the Resistance in Italy: 1919 to the Present.* Lanham, Md., 2004.

Regler, Gustav. *The Owl of Minerva: The Autobiography of Gustav Regler.* Translated by Norman Denny. New York, 1959.

Rubenstein, Joshua, and Valdimir P. Naumov, eds. *Stalin's Secret Pogrom: The Postwar Inquisition of the Jewish Anti-Fascist Committee.* Translated by Laura Ester Wolfson. New Haven, Conn., 2001.

Sperber, Manès. *Until My Eyes Are Closed with Shards.* Translated by Harry Zohn. New York, 1994.

Thorez, Maurice. *Son of the People.* London, 1938.

Traverso, Enzo. "Intellectuals and Anti-Fascism: For a Critical Historicization." *New Politics* 9, no. 4 (winter 2004): 91–103.

Wolff, Milton. "Spanish Lesson." In *Heart of Spain,* edited by Alvah Bessie. New York, 1952.

ANSON RABINBACH

ANTI-SEMITISM.

In the second half of the nineteenth century, more and more European countries enacted first-time legislation protecting Jewish rights. Despite this formal emancipation, the product of rising liberalism, Jews of the fin de siècle were confronted with a vigorous revival of anti-Semitism. Christian anti-Judaism, which was primarily religious in inspiration, had never been entirely free of racist tendencies. But around the turn of the century the racial component of Jew hatred started playing a more pronounced role and developed into the most important feature of modern anti-Semitism.

With the aid of social Darwinist and pseudo-biological arguments, anti-Semites began to view Jews as a distinct "race," which not even baptism could change. Whether a person had ancestors who belonged to the Jewish religion was key. If so, then Jewish identity was established for all time. Nationalists especially, who regarded Jews as a "state within a state," seized upon this biological weltanschauung to place Jews outside society.

In addition to the attempt to forge a "national identity," anti-Semites and anti-Semitic movements also used Jews as a screen on which to project their own anxieties. Jews represented the negative aspects of urbanization and industrialization and were regarded as champions of liberalism, capitalism, materialism, socialism, and above all bolshevism. Both aspects, the attempt to artificially create a national identity and the desire to construct an explanatory model for intractable social problems, again and again played a major role, alone or in combination, in twentieth-century anti-Semitism.

BOLSHEVISM AND ANTI-SEMITISM

The October Revolution of 1917 and the seizure of power by the Bolsheviks in Russia sent shockwaves around the world. Many feared political instability and economic loss. During World War I, on 30 August 1918, the Dutch diplomat Willem Jacob Oudendijk, the individual charged by the British with negotiating the evacuation of Britain's subjects from revolutionary Russia, declared:

> I consider that the immediate suppression of Bolshevism is the greatest issue now before the world, not even excluding the war which is still raging, and unless . . . Bolshevism is nipped in the bud immediately it is bound to spread in one form or another over Europe and the whole world as it is organised and worked by Jews who have no nationality, and whose one object is to destroy for their own ends the existing order of things. The only manner in which this danger could be averted would be collective action on the part of all powers. ("Withdrawal of Missions and Consuls," pp. 678–679)

The notion that bolshevism was "Jewish" was shared in the highest places. On 8 February 1920

Winston Churchill argued, in an article titled "Zionism versus Bolshevism" in the *Illustrated Sunday Herald,* that Jews were behind world revolutions everywhere:

> This movement among the Jews is not new. From the days of Spartacus-Weishaupt [the Illuminati founder Adam Weishaupt] to those of Karl Marx, and down to Trotsky (Russia), Bela Kun (Hungary), Rosa Luxembourg [*sic*](Germany), and Emma Goldman (United States), this worldwide conspiracy for the overthrow of civilisation and for the reconstitution of society on the basis of arrested development, of envious malevolence, and impossible equality, has been steadily growing.... It has been the mainspring of every subversive movement during the Nineteenth Century, and now at last this band of extraordinary personalities from the underworld of the great cities of Europe and America have gripped the Russian people by the hair of their heads and have become practically the undisputed masters of that enormous empire.

It is not surprising that the revolution held a strong appeal for parts of the Jewish population of tsarist Russia. Around the turn of the century some 5.2 million Jews lived there, accounting for 4.1 percent of Russia's population and almost half the world's Jews. They were the most oppressed population group in the tsarist empire, and the Bolsheviks initially presented themselves as a radical movement of emancipation. Jews were not the only ones to be so attracted. Other ethnic and national groups, such as Poles and Georgians, for example, were also "overrepresented" among the Bolsheviks.

The identification of bolshevism with Jewry is inaccurate: there were even more Jews among the Mensheviks and Social Revolutionaries than among the Bolsheviks. As well, Jews could be found among the staunchest opponents of bolshevism. It was a Jewish woman, the Social Revolutionary Fanya Kaplan, whose attempted assassination of Vladimir Ilich Lenin on 30 August 1918 left the Bolshevik leader seriously wounded. On the same day, another Jewish Social Revolutionary, the student Leonid Kannegisser, succeeded in killing Moisei Uritsky, the Petrograd chief of the Bolshevik secret police, the Cheka. Both events marked the beginning of the Red Terror. The equation of Jewry with bolshevism is further refuted by the fact that religious Jews were immediately confronted with the negative aspects of the revolution. The October Revolution, it is true, made anti-Semitism a punishable offense. At the same time, however, the Bolsheviks had declared a war on religion, thus also on Judaism.

In the period between the two world wars the whole of Europe saw the rise of nationalist movements that were nearly always anti-Semitic. The situation was particularly troubling in the newly created state of Poland (1918), where Jews accounted for 10 percent of the population. The frontier established in the Treaty of Riga between Poland and Russia in March 1921 left 38 percent of Poland's population composed of minorities, with Jews, Ukrainians, White Ruthenians, and Germans constituting the largest groups. At the time, Polish nationalists assumed that the integration of the Slavic Ukrainians and White Russians could be advanced by means of assimilation; Jews and Germans, on the other hand, were regarded as unsuited for integration.

Most Polish politicians were highly unsympathetic toward their minorities and tried to enforce an ethnically defined national identity. Stanislaw Grabski, the foreign policy spokesman for the Polish parliament and later minister of culture, explained, in a speech in Poznan in 1919: "We want to base our relationships on love, but there is one kind of love for countrymen and another for aliens. Their percentage among us is definitely too high.... The foreign element will have to see if it will not be better off elsewhere. Polish land for the Poles!" (Blanke, p. 89).

Both the Polish Catholic Church and the Camp of National Unity, the government party created in 1937, pursued aggressively anti-Semitic policies, and even more so after Hitler's advent to power in 1933 and the death of Marshal Józef Piłsudski in 1935. August Cardinal Hlond represented the cold and hostile attitude of the Vatican vis-à-vis the Jews. His pastoral letter of 1936 called for an economic boycott of Jewish shops and defined Jews as "freethinkers [who] constitute the vanguard of atheism, Bolshevism, and revolution" (Lendvai, p. 213).

The avowed aim of Polish nationalists was the expulsion of all Jews from Poland because in their eyes Jews could not be Poles. In 1938 the Polish ambassador to Germany, Józef Lipski, reporting a conversation he had had with Hitler, told Józef Beck, the Polish minister of foreign affairs: "That he [Hitler] has in mind an idea for settling the Jewish problem by way of emigration to the colonies in accordance with an understanding with Poland, Hungary, and possibly also Romania (at which point I told him that if he finds such a solution we will erect him a beautiful monument in Warsaw)" (Lipski, p. 411).

WEIMAR GERMANY

In the eyes of German nationalists, Jews, who comprised less than 1 percent of Germany's population, became the scapegoats for the lost war and the ensuing economic misery. The Spartacist uprising that broke out in Berlin in 1919 under the leadership of Karl Liebknecht (who was not Jewish) and Rosa Luxemburg only served to reinforce this perception. It quickly became clear that this revolt, like those of the other council republics (*Räterepubliken*) that had been proclaimed in the revolutionary year of 1919, was doomed to fail. German revanchist elements however, immediately seized upon this opportunity to agitate against "Jewish bolshevism."

But not only the council republics were seen as "Jewish." According to Germany's nationalists, the Weimar Republic, proclaimed on 9 November 1918, was also a "Jewish republic." On 24 June 1922 Walther Rathenau, Germany's foreign minister, was assassinated by members of one of the Freikorps. In World War I, Rathenau, himself an ardent nationalist, had been in charge of the German war economy. Nonetheless, many regarded him as a "Jewish politician favoring appeasement" (*"jüdischer Erfüllungspolitiker"*) who had betrayed Germany to the Allies. This murder marked a turning point in the political anti-Semitism of Germany, which from then on became increasingly more aggressive.

In the Weimar Republic, anti-Semitism did not only come from the right but also from the left. The Kommunistische Partei Deutschland (KPD, Communist Party of Germany) was not a party with an anti-Semitic worldview. On the contrary, until the November pogroms of 1938 it hardly paid any attention to the "Jewish Question." But in its attempt to attract the votes of workers and the petty bourgeoisie, the party did make use of anti-Jewish stereotypes by linking capitalism and Jewry. Oft-heard epithets were "stock market Jews," "Jewish finance capital," "Jewish racketeers," or "Jewish jobbers" (Haury, p. 282; author's translation).

An intense struggle took place in the Weimar Republic between the National Socialists (NSDAP) and the KPD to win over the proletariat and the middle classes. This struggle was carried on with variable success. Already in *Mein Kampf*, his autobiography and political manifesto, which was published in two volumes in 1925 and 1927, Adolf Hitler had written with satisfaction that from the very early years of the NSDAP "tens of thousands of Marxists were induced to make their way back to the *Volksgemeinschaft* [the folk community] to become fighters for an imminent and free German Reich" (vol. 2, p. 557; author's translation).

The nationalistically tinged anticapitalism of the Communist Party also made it easier for National Socialists to form temporary alliances with the KPD. The first time this came about was in the so-called Schlageter course. Launched in 1923 by the Comintern (Communist International) functionary Karl Radek, the Schlageter course was an attempt to wrest control of nationalistic feelings.

Albert Leo Schlageter had fought with the right-wing Freikorps. Charged with engaging in sabotage by the French occupying force, he was sentenced to death and executed on 26 May 1923. Karl Radek was a member of the presidium of the Executive Committee of the Comintern in charge of KPD's political instruction. On 20 June 1923, at a plenary session of the committee, Radek praised Schlageter as a "martyr to German nationalism" and a "courageous soldier of the counterrevolution." Radek, who was Jewish, declared: "If the people matters to the nation, then the nation will matter to the people."

This nationalist course reached its high point with an address by the KPD official Ruth Fischer to students on 25 July 1923. Fischer, herself of Jewish ancestry, proclaimed, with regard to Schlageter's death:

> You are protesting against Jewish capitalism, gentlemen? Whoever protests against Jewish capitalism, gentlemen, is already a class warrior, whether he knows it or not. You are against Jewish capital and want to bring down the stock exchange jobbers. That's all right. Stamp on the Jewish

capitalists, string them up from the lampposts, trample them underfoot. But, gentlemen, what do you think of major capitalists like Stinnes, Klöckner . . . ? (Haury, p. 283)

The KPD pursued an aggressive anticapitalist course that made no distinction between Jewish and non-Jewish capital on the one hand, but on the other did exploit anti-Semitic stereotypes. The Schlageter course lasted only a few months and was abandoned for the sake of Soviet foreign policy.

THE THIRD REICH

The alliances between the NSDAP and the KPD were short-lived and exclusively tactical in nature. With the Nazi assumption of power in 1933, German society was subjected to totalitarian control, and thousands of communists promptly disappeared into the concentration camps.

National Socialists endeavored to create an ethnically homogeneous nation by exploiting late-nineteenth-century racist thinking. Point four of the party program of the NSDAP of 24 February 1920 stated, unequivocally, that Jews could not be Germans: "None but members of the nation [*Volksgenossen*] may be citizens. None but those of German blood, whatever their creed, may be members of the nation. No Jew, therefore, may be a member of the nation" (author's translation). The National Socialists increasingly began referring to Jews as "bacillus," "bacteria," "parasites," or "poison."

Hitler's anti-Semitism was motivated not only by racism, antibolshevism, and anticapitalism; he also construed a connection with Christian anti-Semitism. In *Mein Kampf* he asserted:

> If, with the help of his Marxist creed, the Jew is victorious over the peoples of this world, his crown will be the dance of death of humanity and this planet will, as it did millions of years ago, move through the ether devoid of men. Eternal Nature inexorably avenges the infringement of her commands. Hence today I believe that I am acting in accordance with the will of the Almighty Creator: by defending myself against the Jew, I am fighting for the work of the Lord. (pp. 69–70)

Shortly after Hitler came to power, legislation was enacted excluding Jews from society. This legislation, which the overwhelming majority of the German population did nothing to protest, would become the immediate prelude to a genocide of unprecedented magnitude.

The Nuremberg Law for the Protection of German Blood and Honor banning marriage between Jews and non-Jews was passed on 15 September 1935. A November supplementary decree to the Reich Citizenship Law stated that all Jews, including quarter- and half-Jews, were no longer citizens of the Reich but *Staatsangehörige* (subjects of the state). The law deprived Jews of their basic rights as citizens, including the right to vote, and in 1936 Jews were excluded from all professional jobs.

During the night of 9–10 November 1938, the SS and the mob went on a rampage throughout Germany, Austria, and Sudetenland, attacking Jews wherever they could find them. During this so-called *Kristallnacht,* or the "Night of Broken Glass," hundreds of synagogues were destroyed and set on fire, thousands of Jewish residences and stores vandalized and looted. At least ninety-one people were murdered and many were mistreated. In the days thereafter more than thirty thousand male Jews were rounded up by the Gestapo and the SS and interned in the concentration camps of Buchenwald, Dachau, and Sachsenhausen. Most of them were only let go after they had signed a statement declaring themselves prepared to "emigrate."

From *Kristallnacht* it was but a small step to the so-called *Endlösung der Judenfrage* (the final solution of the Jewish question). Streamlining the mass murder of millions of Jews was the objective of the Wannsee Conference, held in Berlin on 20 January 1942 and chaired by Reinhard Heydrich, one of the main architects of the Holocaust (Shoah). The number of Jewish lives claimed by the Shoah has been put at approximately six million (the number cited by the U.S. Holocaust Memorial Museum).

It has been said that the history that led up to the Shoah had by and large been concealed from the German population. This is only partly true, not only because regular troops also had been involved in the preparations for the mass murders in the east, but more so because Hitler had openly alluded to the Holocaust early on. Looking back to World War I, he declared in *Mein Kampf,* with regard to what he characterized as a Jewish-led "Marxist delusion":

Anti-Semitic graffiti on a shop in the Jewish quarter of Vienna, 1938. ©HULTON-DEUTSCH COLLECTION/CORBIS

If, at the beginning and during the War, twelve or fifteen thousand of these Hebrews who were corrupting the nation had been forced to submit to poison-gas, just as hundreds of thousands of our best German workers from every social stratum and from every profession had to endure it in the field, then the millions of sacrifices made at the front would not have been in vain. On the contrary: If twelve thousand of these rogues had been eliminated in proper time probably the lives of a million decent men, who would have been of value to Germany in the future, might have been saved. (vol. 2, p. 772)

What is more, on 30 January 1939, in a speech to the Reichstag, he stated: "If the international Jewish financiers in and outside Europe should succeed in plunging the nations once more into a world war, then the result will not be the Bolshevizing of the earth, and thus the victory of Jewry, but the annihilation of the Jewish race in Europe."

The Germans began to make good on his threat almost immediately after the surprise attack on Poland on 1 September 1939. As of 23 November 1939 all Jews over the age of six had to wear a Star of David on the left side of their chest. Thousands of Jews perished at the hands of Einsatzgruppen in random killings in the open or died as a consequence of enforced ghettoization.

After the German invasion of the Soviet Union on 22 June 1941 the Einsatzgruppen went all out. The principal targets of these mobile killing squads, which were divided into smaller units called Einsatzkommandos and Sonderkommandos, were communist officers, officials, intellectuals, prisoners of war, Romanies (Gypsies), and Jews. In conjunction with collaborators and with the assistance of the Wehrmacht, they murdered approximately 1.5 million people, the vast majority of whom were Jews.

The desire to carry out the murders with greater efficiency led to the creation of the death camps. From 1941 to 1942 millions of Jews were being murdered with industrial methods by gassing in camps like Auschwitz, Chelmno, Belzec, Treblinka, Sobibor, and Majdanek. The Shoah was a German enterprise, but not all of the killers were German. Willing executioners came forward in Slovakia and Poland, the Baltic republics, Hungary and Croatia, Rumania and Ruthenia. In Paul Lendvai's words, "clerical and traditional Jew-hatred, economic jealousy, social protest, and nationalist resentment all help to explain the powerful current of indifference and the absence of any appreciable reaction when Hitler embarked on the 'final solution' of the Jewish Question in Eastern Europe" (p. 64).

In occupied western Europe as well, the Germans could count on cooperation rooted in ideological affinity or indifference to the fate of the Jews. In France the puppet government of Vichy (1940–1944), presided over by Marshal Philippe Pétain, an anticommunist and a national hero, collaborated with Nazi Germany. Jews were rounded up by the French police and sent to a transit camp in the Parisian suburb of Drancy, from which they were deported. In all, 75,000 French Jews died in the East (Hilberg, p. 339).

In the Netherlands, the Dutch civil service actively participated in the preparations for the deportation of Dutch Jewry. After Queen Wilhelmina and the cabinet fled the country, several permanent secretaries approved the "declarations of Aryan origin." Many Jews were betrayed by "ordinary Dutchmen" out of greed and personal enrichment. It was Dutch policemen who arrested the Jews. And it was the Dutch military police that guarded them in the Westerbork transit camp, from which they were deported to their deaths by Dutch railroad personnel. In all, one hundred thousand were murdered.

It is also difficult to maintain that the fate of the Jewish deportees was completely unknown in western Europe. Even a girl like Anne Frank, who lived in hiding, came to believe the worst. In a diary entry dated 9 October 1942, she writes: "If even in Holland it is this bad, how will they live in the far and barbarian regions where they are being sent? We assume that most of them will be killed. The English radio speaks of gassing. Maybe that is after all the quickest method of dying. I am completely upset" (p. 35).

ANTI-ZIONISM AND ANTI-SEMITISM

Shortly after the Holocaust, Jews were once again confronted with politically organized anti-Judaism, this time under the banner of anti-Zionism. In the 1950s purges took place in communist parties throughout the Eastern bloc. Such purges may be regarded as pseudo revolutions, the object being the political control of the population. The authorities next fell back on deeply ingrained anti-Jewish stereotypes. After all, only Jews could be "Zionists," and all Jews were suspected of "Zionism." In order to counter the charge of anti-Semitism the party cadres declared that they differentiated between good "hard working Jews" and poisonous "Jewish Zionists."

Officially Zionism was seen, as Joseph Stalin put it, as a "reactionary nationalist current, which found support in the Jewish bourgeoisie, the intelligentsia and the backward layers of the Jewish working class. The Zionists attempted to isolate the Jewish working masses from the common struggle of the proletariat" (p. 364). It was at the trial of the Hungarian foreign minister László Rajk in September 1949 that Zionism was first injected into the accusations against party members. Rajk was not Jewish but three of his codefendants were, as was Mátyás Rákosi, the ruthless party leader, who fondly described himself as "Stalin's best Hungarian disciple."

But nowhere in the Eastern bloc was "anti-Semitism after Auschwitz" more in evidence than in the eastern part of Germany, where the German Democratic Republic (GDR) was established under the auspices of the Soviet Union. From the very beginning, the East German communists of the Socialist Unity Party of Germany (SED), recognizing the necessity of legitimizing their "antifascist" state vis-à-vis the Federal Republic (West Germany), the allied countries of the Warsaw Pact, and its own population, embarked on a "national" course. This accounts for the extremely aggressive character of its nationalistic, "anticosmopolitan," and anti-Western campaigns.

Rudolf Slánský was a Jew and the general secretary of the Communist Party in Czechoslovakia. In 1952 Slánský and his so-called group were accused of "Zionist conspiracy." On 20 December 1952, the SED issued a proclamation with the "lessons from the trial against the group of plotters around Slánský." In the matter of anti-Jewish stereotypes, this proclamation showed strong affinities with the nationalist KPD traditions of the Weimar Republic. The proclamation contained the following statement from the Central Committee of the SED:

> Sailing under the Jewish-nationalistic flag, and disguised as a Zionist organization and as diplomats of the American vassal government of Israel, these American agents practiced their trade. The Morgenthau-Acheson plan which came to light at the Prague trial makes it abundantly clear that American imperialism organizes and supports its espionage and sabotage activities in the People's republics via the state of Israel with the assistance of Zionist organizations. ("Lehren aus dem Prozess," p. 51; author's translation)

The same proclamation accused the German communist Paul Merker of being an agent of Zionism who acted "in the same way as the criminals in Czechoslovakia." During his exile in Mexico between 1942 and 1946, Merker had taken the fate of the Jews to heart, demanding the German state pay restitution to Jewish Germans. The GDR neither acceded to this demand nor thanked him for his efforts. The proclamation stated:

> It can no longer be doubted that Merker is an agent of the U.S. financial oligarchy, whose demand for compensation for Jewish properties is only designed to infiltrate U.S. financial capital into Germany. That is the real reason for his Zionism. . . . He demands the displacement of German national wealth with the words: "The compensation for the harm that has been done to Jewish citizens will be given both to those who return and to those who want to stay abroad." Merker illicitly transformed the maximum profits squeezed out of German and foreign workers by monopoly capitalists into alleged property of the Jewish people. In reality "Aryanization" of this capital merely transferred the profits of "Jewish" monopoly capitalists to "Aryan" monopoly capitalists. (pp. 55–56)

The Arab-Israeli Six-Day War in June 1967 and the invasion of Czechoslovakia in 1968 by Soviet, East German, Polish, Hungarian, and Bulgarian army units marked the beginning of new anti-Zionist campaigns initiated by Moscow, East Berlin, and Warsaw. On 6 September 1968 the Nazi hunter Simon Wiesenthal published a report that demonstrated that the continuities between the GDR and the Third Reich even extended to personnel. The official stand of the entire Eastern bloc during the war was distinctly pro-Arab and anti-Israel. However, it struck Wiesenthal that the news service of the GDR was particularly biased and anti-Israel. Wiesenthal noticed that the use of words in the press and propaganda of the GDR deviated from the commentary of other Communist Party–led countries. Some utterances corresponded literally to remarks in former National Socialist newspapers and journals. It did not take very long for it to be confirmed that some of the regular contributors of the anti-Israel articles in the East German press were the same people who had written about the "Jewish peril" during the Third Reich.

On 14 July 1967, for example, a cartoon appeared in the *Berliner Zeitung*, depicting a flying Moshe Dayan, with his hands stretched out toward Gaza and Jerusalem. Next to him stood Adolf Hitler, shown in an advanced state of decomposition, encouraging Dayan with the words: "Carry on, colleague Dayan!" It was apparent to Wiesenthal that there were Nazis on the editorial staff of several East German newspapers and magazines (Wiesenthal, pp. 20, 26–38).

Despite its antifascist credo, the SED took no responsibility whatsoever for the German role in the Holocaust. On the contrary, the East German population subsequently was declared the victor and victim of "fascism," while the Holocaust itself received scant attention. In this way the GDR was able to avoid dealing with feelings of guilt. Latent anti-Jewish feelings were further reinforced by anti-Zionist campaigns rife with insinuations that Jews desired to infiltrate, sabotage, and exploit the East German state.

NATIONAL SOCIALISM AND COMMUNISM: SIAMESE TWINS?

In the early twenty-first century, overt anti-Semitism on the part of all authoritative political and social organizations is strictly taboo and thoroughly repudiated. Even so, at the beginning of the 1990s approximately 10 to 25 percent of the population in western industrialized countries harbored anti-Semitic sentiments (Haury, p. 123). The phrase *secondary anti-Semitism* came into use to refer to an

The cover of a c. 1940 French edition of the classic anti-Semitic text *The Protocols of the Elders of Zion.* Purporting to reveal Jewish plans for world domination, the text remained in wide circulation even after its authenticity was convincingly disputed in the 1920s. BRIDGEMAN ART LIBRARY

de Recherche et d'Études sur la Civilisation Européenne (GRECE) set the tone for the New Right throughout Europe. De Benoist has claimed to be neither right- nor left-wing, but his writings make clear that his overall philosophy combines elements of right-wing extremism and conservatism. The European New Right is not a homogeneous movement with a unified ideology. The typical supporter is anti-Western, antiliberal, anticommunist, anti-American, and, above all, antimulticultural. Although de Benoist has distanced himself from anti-Semitism, the arguments of his followers have not always been free from anti-Semitic overtones.

One of the most prominent examples of New Right agitation in Europe came to the fore in the so-called *Historikerstreit,* an academic controversy fought out in the German media in the middle of the 1980s. The *Historikerstreit* grew out of the New Right historian Ernst Nolte's claim that in the totalitarian troika of National Socialism, fascism, and Marxism-Leninism, National Socialism was a *reaction* to Stalinism. In Nolte's view, communism constituted the original and National Socialism a copy, more or less.

Nolte and his sympathizers perceived a causal connection between the mass murders of the Russian Revolution and the crimes of Nazi Germany. "Auschwitz," according to this reasoning, was a reaction born of fear, the fear that the destruction unleashed by bolshevism might spread and come to Germany. In other words, Stalin and his regime were partly responsible for the creation of the Third Reich. Hence, for Nolte, "Auschwitz" and the "gulag" were equally criminal, apart from, as he put it, the "technical procedure of gassing" (p. 45).

Indeed, at first glance there are similarities between the two political systems. What class was for Lenin and Stalin, race was for the Nazis. What capitalists were for the Communist Party, Jewry was for Hitler. For the Soviets the New Man was the proletarian. The Nazis rejected the proletarian in favor of the Aryan. In addition, Hitler and Stalin had concluded a nonaggression pact from which it could be deduced that the two dictators were "blood brothers." But opponents of this theory of totalitarianism contend that the equation of the

attitude that views "Auschwitz" as a blot on a nation's history (Germany, France, Poland, and so on), for which contemporary Jews then receive the blame. Often this inclination not to forgive Jews for "Auschwitz" is of a piece with the desire to deny the Holocaust or to "relativize" it. This relativization of the Holocaust is especially popular among adherents of a political-cultural movement known as the New Right, who resort to it frequently.

New Right intellectuals are attempting to bring about a cultural revolution by smashing taboos and turning the arguments on their head. This school of thought originated in France and was founded in 1968 by Alain de Benoist, whose Groupement two dictatorships as opposed to their comparison is highly problematical.

In National Socialism the principle of human inequality rooted in biology was raised to the level of dogma. In communism—to judge by its ideology, at least—the principle of equality was central. National Socialism was by definition German nationalist, whereas communism—again according to its ideology—was internationalist. Stalinism was not the essence but the perversion of communism. In National Socialism, however, doctrine and reality coincided. To put it in the words of the Italian writer and concentration camp survivor Primo Levi: "One can't imagine Nazism without gas chambers, but one can imagine Communism without camps."

The mass murder perpetrated by National Socialism was carried out meticulously, dutifully, "in an orderly fashion," and with industrial methods. Ideologically this genocide was a mixture of the rational and irrational. On the one hand, individuals often were relegated to the status of *Untermenschen*—subhumans—and employed as slave labor in German industries. On the other hand, they were the victims of a deeply antimodern irrationalism, a perverse nationalism, and a unique racial delusion whose roots stretched back to the nineteenth and early twentieth centuries. Both the quantity and the quality of National Socialism's organized mass murder made the Third Reich unique, despite similarities with Stalin's Soviet Union—all the more so because Hitler's assumption of power was legitimized by the electorate.

The views of Nolte and others not only were of historiographical interest but also served a political goal. In order to create a "post-Auschwitz national identity," Nolte and his sympathizers strove to "neutralize" Auschwitz by placing the Third Reich and Stalinism in the same box. Once accepted, it then becomes easier to take up the "Jewish part" in bolshevism. Taking it one step further, Nolte reasoned that it might be legitimate to argue that Hitler was entitled to intern German Jews as prisoners of war: had not Chaim Weizmann announced in September 1939 that Jews all over the world would fight on the side of England?

The assertion that National Socialism and communism were Siamese twins also sparked fierce discussions in France. There, the *Black Book of Communism* (*Livre noir du communisme*) by the ex-Maoist Stéphane Courtois, appeared in 1997. In it, the author concluded: "But the intransigent facts demonstrate that Communist regimes have victimized approximately 100 million people in contrast to the approximately 25 million victims of the Nazis" (p. 15). Courtois's opponents argued that this "history with a calculator" drew an inaccurate picture, inasmuch as executions, deliberate or accidental famines, along with epidemics were added up without differentiating among them. Moreover, many found that a comparison between communism and capitalism would have provided a more realistic picture than that between communism and National Socialism.

Nowhere in western Europe, however, was the political exploitation of the equation of communism and National Socialism more pronounced than in Germany. As a result of German unification in 1990, the country not only had to confront the legacy of East German communism; the unification also affected the way in which people started looking at the National Socialist past.

In January 2004 the vice president of the Central Council of Jews in Germany, Dr. Salomon Korn, ceased collaborating with the Stiftung Sächsische Gedenkstätten, the Saxon government agency that deals with the reconstitution of camps into museums. First used by the Nazis, some of these former concentration camps were subsequently taken over by the Soviet Union and the East German authorities. Korn was protesting the policy of implied moral equivalence that treated the political prisoners of the GDR and people persecuted by the Nazis as though they were the same. Some East German officials seemed to regard the Soviet Russian occupation of East Germany as a punishment for "Auschwitz," a punishment that might be said to have ended with the unification of the two Germanys. Korn even spoke about a "renationalization" of public commemorative policies.

Many agreed with Korn that the politics of equating communism, including its GDR variant, with National Socialism had started immediately after the fall of the Berlin Wall. As early as 1991, for example, a special brochure issued by the camp museum in Sachsenhausen near Berlin stated: "Sachsenhausen is first and foremost the scene of

National Socialist and SS crimes; but it is also a place where crimes were committed in the name of another ideology, with no less inexorable consequences. The creed of National Socialism and of communism was the same: the opponent must be destroyed."

Encouraged by an international climate in which the Third Reich was being equated with communism, the German Christian Democratic politician Martin Hohmann went one up on Ernst Nolte in breaking a taboo. Amid the celebrations of German Unity Day, 3 October 2003, he insinuated that Jews could just as well be regarded as a "nation of perpetrators" (*Tätervolk*) as Germans. After all, he argued, in the first phase of the Russian Revolution, which cost the lives of millions of people, many Jews were involved in terrorist activities.

Like Nolte, Hohmann attempted to articulate a post-Auschwitz national identity that, along with its anti-Semitic undertones, could be derived from the equation "communism equals National Socialism." With this it became much simpler to point to "Jewish guilt" and "national victimization." Vigorous protests and intense media attention in Germany led to Hohmann's expulsion from the party, but it was nonetheless clear that a considerable minority supported his views.

In the early twenty-first century such viewpoints can be found in many postcommunist countries in central and eastern Europe, where they are extremely popular and politically acceptable. Soviet rule and the struggle for national independence often are the main topics of history and politics. The German occupation, collaboration, and the Holocaust are treated as occurrences of secondary importance, while much of the criticism is directed at bolshevism, which continues to be associated with Jewry. This is especially true for the Baltic states, Poland, and Ukraine.

The president of Estonia, Arnold Rüütel, in 2005 refused to attend the commemorations of the sixtieth anniversary celebrations of the end of World War II in Moscow. He declared that we must do everything to see to it that the Holocaust and the "Holodomor," that is, the "Great Famine-Genocide" perpetrated by Stalin in the 1930s on the rural population of Ukraine, will never be repeated. Vaira Vike-Freiberga, the president of Latvia, did commemorate the Holocaust but at the same time lionized the men from Latvia who were "abused as cannon fodder" in the Waffen-SS. These soldiers are widely honored as national resistance fighters against bolshevism.

National conservative and New Right politicians throughout Europe applaud the equation of National Socialism and bolshevism. It remains to be seen, however, whether such a "positively differentiated" perception of anticommunist and anti-Semitic nationalists in the interbellum will not lead to increased anti-Semitism.

See also **Auschwitz-Birkenau; Babi Yar; Concentration Camps; Einsatzgruppen; Frank, Anne; Genocide; Holocaust; Kristallnacht; Nuremberg Laws; Slánský Trial; Warsaw Ghetto; Wiesenthal, Simon; Zionism.**

BIBLIOGRAPHY

Primary Sources

Courtois, Stéphane, et al. *The Black Book of Communism: Crimes, Terror, Repression.* Translated by Jonathan Murphy and Mark Kramer. London, 1999.

Frank, Anne. *Het Achterhuis. Dagboekbrieven. 12 Juni 1942– 1 Augustus 1944.* Amsterdam and Antwerp, 1957.

Hilberg, Raul. *The Destruction of the European Jews.* Rev. and definitive edition. New York and London, 1985.

Hitler, Adolf. *Mein Kampf.* 2 vols. Munich, 1940.

"Lehren aus dem Prozess gegen das Verschwörerzentrum Slánský." Beschluss des Zentralkomitees der Sozialistischen Einheitspartei Deutschlands. December 20, 1952. In Hermann Matern, *Über die Durchführung des Beschlusses des ZK der SED Lehren aus dem Prozess gegen das Verschwörerzentrum Slánský* 13, 48–70. Tagung des Zentralkomitees der Sozialistischen Einheitspartei Deutschlands May 13–14, 1953. Berlin, 1953.

Lipski, Józef. *Diplomat in Berlin 1933–1939: Papers and Memoirs of Józef Lipski, Ambassador of Poland.* Edited by Waclaw Jedrzejewicz. New York, 1968.

Nolte, Ernst. "Vergangenheit, die nicht vergehen will. Eine Rede, die geschrieben, aber nicht gehalten werden konnte." In *Historikerstreit: Die Dokumentation der Kontroverse um die Einzigartigkeit der national-sozialistischen Judenvernichtung,* 39–47. Munich, 1987.

Stalin, Jozef. *Werke.* Vol. 2. Berlin, 1950.

Wiesenthal, Simon. "Die gleiche Sprache: Erst für Hitler— jetzt für Ulbricht." Pressekonferenz von Simon Wiesenthal am 6. September 1968 in Wien. Eine Dokumentation der Deutschland-Berichte. Jüdisches

Dokumentationszentrum, Simon Wiesenthal Centre, Vienna.

"Withdrawal of Missions and Consuls." Sub enclosure. Report of the Netherlands Minister relating to conditions in Petrograd. In *Publications of the Department of State, Papers relating to the Foreign Relations of the United States. 1918. Russia.* Vol. 1, pp. 675–679. Washington, D.C., 1931.

Secondary Sources

Blanke, Richard. "The German Minority in Inter-war Poland and German Foreign Policy—Some Reconsiderations." *Journal of Contemporary History* 25 (1990): 87–102.

Brinks, Jan Herman. "The Dutch, the Germans, and the Jews." *History Today* 49, no. 6 (June 1999): 17–23.

Haury, Thomas. *Antisemitismus von links: Kommunistische Ideologie, Nationalismus und Antizionismus in der frühen DDR.* Hamburg, Germany, 2002.

Lendvai, Paul. *Anti-Semitism in Eastern Europe.* London, 1972.

JAN HERMAN BRINKS

ANTONESCU, ION. *See* Romania.

ANZIO, BATTLE OF.

If good inter-Allied planning and operational clarity were the harbingers of victory in Normandy, then it is chilling to reflect that they were absent from the contemporary Allied effort in the Mediterranean. Anzio has since become a byword for the near-failure of a promising amphibious landing. At the time, the consequences for the Italian campaign were grave, but it should also be borne in mind that Operation Shingle, the plan to land the U.S. Sixth Army Corps from the sea at Anzio, was launched in January 1944, four and a-half months before Operation Overlord in Normandy, where failure was not an option for the Anglo-American force. In 1944 Anzio was a small fishing village on the western Italian coast thirty-five miles due south of Rome and sixty miles behind the fighting lines, which ranged west to east across the Italian alps, centered on Monte Cassino.

The campaign stemmed from the feeling that by winter 1943 the Allied campaign in Italy had fallen far short of expectations. Both Lieutenant General Mark W. Clark's U.S. Fifth Army on the west coast and General Bernard L. Montgomery's British Eighth Army in the east had been fought to a standstill on the Gustav Line, in difficult terrain and atrocious weather. In a landscape that was a gift to its defenders, their battle-hardened German opponents proved especially stubborn, led by energetic and able commanders. The Allied advance stalled along a range of hills that dominated the approach up the Liri Valley to Rome. Although by no means the tallest of the hills, Monte Cassino with its associated abbey proved the linchpin of the German defensive system; the cratered landscape and shattered dwellings added to the Axis advantage, proving impassable to Allied vehicles, and allowing only foot soldiers and mules. With no means of outflanking the German defenders, the Allies turned to frontal assault, little realizing that the nature and duration of the fighting would match the worst experiences of the World War I western front. It was to outflank the Cassino defenders by sea and (possibly) seize Rome that Shingle was devised.

Generals Mark Clark and Harold Alexander, the Allied Fifteenth Army Group commander, had earlier discussed seaborne assaults as a way of turning German defense lines (as Patton had tried on a smaller scale in Sicily the previous August), and Clark had established his own amphibious-operations planning staff. Sideshows of this nature were exhaustively championed by Winston Churchill to the irritation of his military advisors, but by mid-December 1943 the necessary landing craft were already earmarked for the Normandy invasion and a simultaneous landing in southern France (Operation Dragoon, eventually delayed to August 1944), so the operational aim of another Italian seaborne assault had to be clear and the case overwhelmingly convincing; this was neither.

The attack, launched by nearly four hundred ships and assault craft, was designed to stretch the defenders at Cassino by diverting much-needed reserves to block an invasion to their rear. When Major General John P. Lucas's Anglo-American Sixth Corps landed on 22 January 1944, it achieved complete surprise. The British First

Division landed unopposed northwest of Anzio, the U.S. Third Division at Nettuno, to the east, and Anzio with its handy deep-water port was taken by U.S. Rangers. Within forty-eight hours Lucas had secured a beachhead seven miles deep, yet he was unsure what to do with his success. Clark's orders were to secure the beachhead, then advance to the Alban Hills—visible in the distance from the port—beyond which beckoned Rome, just thirty-five miles distant. Recalling the bloody landings at Salerno in September 1943, Clark warned Lucas privately not to stick his neck out and overextend his forces.

Alas for him, Lucas faced Albert Kesselring, a Luftwaffe field marshal with an unusually sure hand at land warfare, who did not oblige by pulling men back from Cassino as hoped but ordered his Fourteenth Army (under General von Mackensen) to counterattack with shock and speed. By the end of January, Mackensen had four divisions, a tank regiment, and two hundred guns in the area while the Luftwaffe achieved air parity, bombing every night. The flat open terrain beyond Anzio became the scene of vicious fighting, with every yard of the ground disputed and covered by German artillery. Both sides used dried river beds as make-shift trenches in what became a brief rerun of the World War I western front. Forewarned by intelligence from the British Ultra project just beforehand, a series of German attacks culminated in a near breakthrough, but by early April it was clear that fighting had reached an attritional stalemate. On 22 February Clark (at Alexander's urging) replaced Lucas with his deputy Truscott, Alexander describing the former Sixth Corps commander as "a broken reed" following a visit to the bridgehead.

Churchill was particularly critical, stating, "I had hoped we were hurling a wildcat on the shore, but all we got was a stranded whale." Instead of Anzio supporting the Cassino front, the Allies had to launch Operation Diadem (the fourth battle of Cassino in five months) on 11 May 1944 to rescue Anzio. The crushing land offensive of over a dozen divisions shattered the Gustav Line around Cassino, and as the Germans withdrew slowly northward via the Hitler Line, up the Liri Valley and Highway 6 to Rome, the Anzio force was able to seize its moment and break out.

Though specifically ordered to leave Rome alone, Clark entered the Eternal City, diverting forces that would have otherwise cut off the Anzio and Cassino defenders at Valmontone and brought about a swifter end to the Italian campaign. Clark, however, knew that Overlord was about to commence and wanted his moment of glory. He succeeded by making front-page news as the liberator of Rome on 5 June 1944, but D-day in Normandy eclipsed the Italian campaign thereafter. Later, a German military historian wrote that when the breakout from Anzio occurred in May 1944 it was felt that only a miracle would prevent another Stalingrad south of Rome and "General Clark provided that miracle."

The lost opportunities of Anzio aroused controversy that reverberates to this day. In Lucas, Clark clearly chose the wrong man for Anzio: He was not an inspiring commander when one was needed. Lucas had the opportunity to follow his own judgment but was faced with an impossible choice. Had he pushed on for Rome as intended, Kesselring would surely have crushed his slender force. Perhaps only Patton would have been rash enough to try and lucky enough to have succeeded. Yet Lucas's decision to stay and consolidate his position betrayed a timidity that Churchill, Alexander, and others vilified. Nevertheless, in his defense, Lucas had enough men at the bridgehead to prevent it from falling to the series of brutal German counterattacks.

With the operational aims far from clear, Shingle was surely mistimed. No senior commander emerges from Anzio with credit. Clark's decision to head for Rome rather than Valmontone is (to put it lightly) highly questionable. His superior, the patrician Alexander, was never one to give firm orders; he preferred to offer advice in a gentlemanly fashion, and his lack of grip may have contributed to the debacle. This gamble, that promised much but was probably never going to deliver, cost the Allies seven thousand killed and thirty-six thousand wounded, as well as forty-four thousand sick in the malaria-ridden water courses. Kesselring, who fought on for another eleven months, estimated German losses at forty thousand, including five thousand killed and 4,500 captured.

See also **D-Day; World War II.**

BIBLIOGRAPHY

Blumenson, Martin. *Anzio: The Gamble That Failed.* Philadelphia, 1963.

———. *United States Army in World War II: The Mediterranean Theater of Operations.* Vol. 3: *Salerno to Cassino.* Washington, D.C., 1969.

D'Este, Carlo. *Fatal Decision: Anzio and the Battle for Rome.* London, 1991.

Molony, C. J. C. *The Mediterranean and Middle East.* Vol. 5: *The Campaign in Sicily, 1943, and the Campaign in Italy, 3rd September 1943 to 31st March 1944.* London, 1973. Vol. 6: *Victory in the Mediterranean, Part 1: 1st April–4th June 1944.* London, 1984.

Trevelyan, Raleigh. *The Fortress: A Diary of Anzio and After.* London, 1956.

Zaloga, Steven J. *Anzio 1944: The Beleaguered Beachhead.* Oxford, U.K., 2005.

PETER CADDICK-ADAMS

APARTHEID. *Apartheid* is Afrikaans for separateness. From 1948 until 1990 apartheid was the government's official race policy in South Africa.

Apartheid is associated with 1948, when the National Party won elections. However, racial segregation was practiced long before 1948, just as in other European colonies. While after 1948, with the decline of European empires and liberation of colonies, racial segregation died away elsewhere, in South Africa apartheid in 1948 institutionalized what before were largely flexible social rules of racial segregation.

Apartheid's foundations were laid not only by social practice but also by the segregationist policies of British imperial rule. After the Anglo-Boer war (1899–1902) Boer generals negotiated with the British to craft a single "native policy" for South Africa. The British created the South African Native Affairs Commission (SANAC), which proposed far-reaching racial segregation with respect to land, labor, education, and politics. The 1910 Union government put the SANAC proposals into effect through laws designed to control the movement, settlement, and economic participation of blacks: the 1911 Mines and Works Act (created and regulated the category of black labor); the 1913 Natives' Land Act (provided for territorial separation of rural whites and blacks); the 1920 Native Affairs Act (proposed a system of government-appointed tribal district councils to govern blacks); and the 1923 Natives (Urban Areas) Act (regulated the presence of blacks in urban areas).

After 1948 the National Party aimed to preserve white Afrikaner power. Their apartheid meant "total segregation"—an all-white South Africa would be created by sending blacks to "homelands." In these ethnic "homelands" blacks supposedly could enjoy citizenship and civil rights, but could obtain no citizenship rights in "white" South Africa. However, economic realities dictated another story—the migrant labor system. White-owned mines, farms, and industries depended on cheap black labor. This created the strangeness and harshness of life under apartheid—black people, after being removed from "white" areas to "homelands," had to return to work in the white economy.

Many laws were enacted to give effect to total segregation and to regulate the continued presence of blacks in "white" areas. The first was the 1949 Prohibition of Mixed Marriages Act, followed by an amendment to the Immorality Act outlawing sexual relations between whites and individuals of any other race. 1950 saw the Population Registration Act, which defined *race* on the basis of physical appearance, and the Group Areas Act, which restricted racial groups to their own residential areas; and 1953 saw the Reservation of Separate Amenities Act, which mandated separate amenities on public premises and transport. Other laws were the much-contested Pass Laws (1952), which forced blacks, under threat of criminal penalty, to carry passbooks wherever they went, and the Prevention of Illegal Squatting Act (1951) and Bantu Authorities Act (1951), the first steps toward "separate development" as the apartheid architect Hendrik Frensch Verwoerd's (1901–1966) vision for South Africa later became known.

As apartheid grew, resistance grew. The South African Native National Congress was established in 1912 as a moderate organization focusing on the political and social conditions of black people. It was renamed the African National Congress (ANC) in 1923. Throughout the 1950s the apartheid government faced peaceful civic protest. The ANC, with groups from "colored," "indian," and "white" communities, staged a Defiance Campaign of peaceful resistance against apartheid laws. In 1956 the Women's March took place—20,000 women took to the streets to defy the Pass Laws. In 1955 the Freedom Charter was adopted at Kliptown during the Congress of the People. However, in December 1956 many leading activists were detained and charged with high treason. By 1961 the so-called Treason trial was over, with all the accused acquitted.

In 1959 the Pan-Africanist Congress was formed. Its first attack on apartheid was an anti–Pass Laws campaign that resulted in sixty-nine people being shot by police on 21 March 1960 at Sharpeville. In December 1961 the ANC turned to armed struggle, forming its military wing, Umkhonto weSizwe. In 1963 Nelson Mandela (b. 1918) and other antiapartheid activists were sentenced to lifelong imprisonment in the Rivonia trial. Now most of the ANC and PAC leadership was in jail or exiled, antiapartheid organizations were banned, and civil disobedience and dissent was criminalized. Nevertheless, resistance continued, even as repression grew more violent. In 1976 black children protested against apartheid "Bantu education" that forced them to be taught in Afrikaans, resulting in the Soweto uprisings of 16 June 1976, which were violently suppressed. Steve Biko (1946–1977), who created the South African Students' Organization in 1968, died in detention on 12 September 1977 after being brutally tortured by members of the security police.

Under the banner of the United Democratic Front, resistance to apartheid rule continued throughout the 1980s, through various forms of violent and nonviolent mass action. This era saw a series of states of emergency proclaimed and the widespread use of detention without trial and of assassination by the apartheid state against its opponents. Opposition to apartheid was not only internal to South Africa. The international community took a critical stance early on. With the establishment of the Republic of South Africa (1961) Verwoerd withdrew South Africa from the United Nations. The international community responded with a call for ecomonic, cultural, and other sanctions against South Africa.

Informally, apartheid ended on 2 February 1990, with the unbanning of antiapartheid organizations, the freeing of political prisoners, and the announcement that negotiations would commence

for a resolution of conflict. Apartheid came to an official end with the 1994 democratic elections and the adoption of an interim (1994) and final (1996) constitution. The Truth and Reconciliation Commission was one attempt to reflect publicly on the atrocities that occurred under apartheid. The legacy of apartheid lingers in South Africa and it will take many years for its effects to be addressed in any sense.

See also **Political Prisoners; Racism.**

BIBLIOGRAPHY

Asmal, Kader, Louise Asmal, and Ronald Suresh Roberts. *Reconciliation through Truth. A Reckoning of Apartheid's Criminal Governance.* Cape Town, 1996.

Dhansay, Hanifa. *Apartheid and Resistance.* Swaziland, 1996.

Lapping, Brian. *Apartheid: A History.* London, 1986.

Mandela, Nelson. *Long Walk to Freedom: The Autobiography of Nelson Mandela.* London, 1994.

Saunders, Christopher, ed. *Illustrated History of South Africa.* Cape Town, 1988.

KARIN VAN MARLE

APOLLINAIRE, GUILLAUME (Wilhelm Apollinaris de Kostrowitzky; 1880–1918), French poet, writer, and art critic.

Along with Blaise Cendrars (Frédéric Sauser; 1887–1961), Apollinaire is regarded as the inventor of modern French poetry. It was his *Alcools* collection, published in 1913, that raised him to the firmament of modern poetry. By defying classical meter without shunning it altogether, eliminating punctuation, and even drawing with words in his famous *Calligrammes* (1918), he invented for himself an entirely free style. However, this stylistic freedom is never a purely intellectual exercise because it is always deployed in the service of a deep lyricism that makes his work instantly recognizable.

The illegitimate son of an Italian soldier, Francesco d'Aspermont, Apollinaire was brought up by his mother, Angelica de Kostrowitzky, who came from the Polish population that emigrated to Italy following the 1866 uprising. In 1887 Guillaume, his mother, and his brother Albert settled in Monaco, where they lived until 1899.

Guillaume proved to be a brilliant pupil at the lycée, winning a series of prizes. In 1897 he composed some poems under the name of Guillaume Apollinaire for the first time. His first remarkable texts were written two years later while he was staying in Stavelot in the Belgian Ardennes. After this stay, Apollinaire settled in Paris, where he rejoined his mother. From 1899 to 1901, Apollinaire established some contacts in literary circles, published work in some small magazines and wrote some erotic opuscules in order to earn some money quickly. In 1901 and 1902 he made several visits to Germany, in particular the Rhine Valley. From there he brought back the *Rhénanes* (Rhenish) cycle (published in *Alcools*), for which his sources of inspiration were not only the German and French Romantics but also the experience of the poet with a capacity for wonder. With more and more of his work being published in well-known journals, Apollinaire also took an interest in the development of the modern art of his day. He associated with the fauvists, then the cubists, and became a figure in literary and artistic life in Montmartre. He posed at this time for many painters (Henri Rousseau, Pablo Picasso). His first published collection attested to this proximity to artistic circles. In fact, *L'enchanteur pourrissant* (1909), illustrated with woodcuts by André Derain (1880–1954), was commissioned by the art dealer Daniel-Henry Kahnweiler (1884–1979). His second work, *L'hérésiarque et Cie,* published the following year, came to notice and won three votes at the Goncourt prize. By the outbreak of the First World War, Apollinaire, as a poet who was celebrated on some sides and execrated on others—with his *Alcools* collection being slated by Georges Duhamel (1884–1966) in *Mercure de France* in 1913—was an established figure throughout Parisian literary and artistic circles.

The entry into the war in 1914 represented for Apollinaire "a farewell to an entire era." He had Russian nationality through his mother, and he enlisted as a foreign volunteer in the French army on 10 August 1914. On 5 December, his application for enlistment was accepted and he was assigned to the artillery. In November 1915 he requested a transfer to the infantry—a more dangerous section—and on 17 March 1916 he received a severe head wound. Meanwhile, he had been granted French nationality. Having recovered following major head surgery, he served in the censorship unit and was made a second lieutenant, then a first lieutenant.

During the war, he experienced two great loves, with Lou and Madeleine, who must have been the inspiration for some of his poems, as well as a remarkable romantic and erotic war correspondence:

> We are ready to die so that you may live
> in happiness
> The shells have burnt the flowers of lust
> And that flower
> which was growing in my heart and is called
> memory
> The ghost of that flower endures
> It is desire ... (Letter to Lou, 1 April 1915;
>   translated from the French)

In April 1918 *Calligrammes* was published. Apollinaire's war poems express a deep compassion for the soldiers, his fellows, and are sometimes permeated with an irony that is reminiscent of the British war poets, but they also reflect a strange fascination with war and cannot be interpreted as pacifist pleas. In fact, during the war, Apollinaire had intensified his stylistic innovations and lyricism of the prewar period (his first *Caligramme* dated from 15 June 1914), without changing them altogether.

Apollinaire, who coined the term *surrealism* (his play *Les mamelles de Tiresias* [The mammaries of Tiresias] of 1918 was subtitled "a surrealist drama") was to remain the main reference-point for the young French poets of the twentieth century, although André Breton (1896–1966) was later to criticize his patriotism. He died of Spanish influenza on 9 November 1918. According to the legend, partly forged by his friend and rival Blaise Cendrars, he was buried on 11 November during the Armistice celebrations. In fact, he was laid to rest two days later.

See also **Surrealism.**

BIBLIOGRAPHY

Primary Sources

Apollinaire, Guillaume. *Œuvres poétiques.* Paris, 1965.

———. *Œuvres en prose complètes.* 3 vols. Paris, 1993.

Secondary Sources

Bohn, Willard. *Apollinaire and the International Avant-Garde.* Albany, N.Y., 1997.

Boschetti, Anna. *La poésie partout: Apollinaire, homme-époque (1898–1918).* Paris, 2001.

NICOLAS BEAUPRÉ

APPEASEMENT.

Appeasement is a label used to describe the foreign policy of the British and French governments during the 1930s toward the aggressor nations of Germany, Italy, and Japan. The rise of Adolf Hitler saw Germany begin to challenge the rulings of the Treaty of Versailles (1919), while Japanese expansionism in China from 1931 threatened British and French imperial interests, and the Italians proved an ever-increasing threat in the Mediterranean and North Africa. Military chiefs in both Britain and France gloomily warned their political masters that they were in no position to fight a war on three fronts and this, as the British foreign secretary Edward Frederick Lindley Wood, 1st Earl of Halifax (1881–1959), conceded, placed a heavy burden on diplomacy while rearmament took place.

Appeasement has become synonymous with surrender, something apparently epitomized by the Munich agreement of September 1938. It was a view that quickly took hold from 1940 and, when coupled with the successes of the Axis war machine, encouraged a presumption that Hitler had planned and prepared for war, making the assumptions of British and French governments that the dictators could be bought off with concessions all the more foolish. The left-wing booklet by the pseudonymous Cato, *Guilty Men* (1940), published shortly after the Dunkirk Evacuation, ridiculed the British political establishment for its failure to foresee the dangers presented by the dictators and for failing to adequately rearm Britain. This "Guilty Men" thesis has proved itself to be enduring in the popular memory and forever tarnished the reputations of prime ministers Stanley Baldwin (1867–1947) and Neville Chamberlain (1869–1940). That France collapsed so quickly before the advancing German forces in May 1940 also ensured that French Third Republic's prewar diplomacy has been tarred with the brush of complacency and decadence.

Yet prior to these events, for many contemporaries appeasement was equated with realism. Britain showed a willingness to attempt to reach a general settlement for Europe during the mid-1930s. Although the specific details of a settlement differed from time to time, the main platform for such an agreement would involve a revision of the Treaty of Versailles (1919), a series of security pacts, and possibly limitations upon rearmament. The expectation was that by settling the outstanding grievances of the dictators they could be brought back into the international fold. In reality, Germany, while prepared for economic discussions and happy to make imprecise demands for a colonial deal alongside a desire to resolve issues in Eastern Europe, would not be drawn into an agreement.

DEFINING APPEASEMENT

Historians have debated about the nature of appeasement. Some have seen it as a policy specific to the period of the 1937–1939 Chamberlain government, where the personal quest of the prime minister to seek peace combined with a plethora of structural issues obliged Britain to seek a form of understanding with the fascist powers, Germany and Italy. Appeasement, it could be argued, was based upon apparently sound strategic reasons. Yet among the policy makers there was no unanimity about how to secure this understanding. Some, like foreign secretary Sir Anthony Eden (1897–1977), favored negotiations with Germany but were unwilling to sanction such discussions with the Italians. It would appear from Chamberlain's view that his motivations were driven by a belief that war with one or other of the dictators would cause the demise of the British Empire and allow Europe to be dominated by the Soviet Union.

Other historians have argued that appeasement was a broader phenomenon of the interwar era, arising from a need to seek to implement and sustain the Versailles peace settlement. Some, though, have questioned whether in actuality it was a form of traditional British foreign policy dating from the mid-nineteenth century—the idea of aiming to maintain the balance of power in Europe by negotiation because it was recognized that Britain was too weak both financially and militarily to intervene. The historical debate has been framed by the corresponding post-1945 Cold War and political climate: the Suez Crisis of 1956, the Czech Uprising of 1968, and the collapse of the Soviet Union. Since 1940 the British Conservative party, which Chamberlain led until shortly before his death, has sought to disassociate itself from appeasement. This occurred not least because many of the subsequent party leaders from Sir Winston

Which Backbone Shall I Lay Out for You This Morning My Lord? Cartoon by David Low from the London *Evening Standard*, 1 August 1938. British foreign secretary Lord Halifax is criticized for his lack of conviction regarding negotiations with Hitler. BRIDGEMAN ART LIBRARY

Churchill (1874–1965) to Edward Heath (1916–2005) had established their reputations as internal opponents of Chamberlain's foreign policy.

Historical revisionism only began in the late 1960s, helped in part by the official release of governmental records. The revisionists began to argue that the inability of the democracies to resist the advances of the dictator nations was the inevitable result of various constraints: military and economic weakness, world and public opinion, and the realization that war would prove too costly for the democracies and their empires. They also began to debate as to whether Hitler intended to provoke war. It was a long-held view that French foreign policy during the 1930s was a mere appendage of London's appeasement. In the last decades of the twentieth century, this assumption was challenged. The idea that France's Third Republic was moribund and in the final stages of a long decline has been dismissed and instead a more subtle appreciation of French

civil-military relations has emerged that stresses the limitations that political, economic, and strategic considerations placed on the policy makers. The French are portrayed as seeking to pursue their own foreign policy objectives after September 1938, which included enticing the British into a continental commitment so they could face the dictators together.

Appeasement was as much a state of mind as a specific strategic policy, which sought concession in preference to conflict as the democracies tried increasingly unsuccessfully to sustain the flawed Versailles settlement with rhetoric about collective security and self-determination. Sir Nevile Henderson (1882–1942), British Ambassador to Berlin 1937 to 1940, described appeasement as: "the search for just solutions by negotiation in light of higher reason instead of by the resort to force." The weight of scholarship in the area has shown that appeasement cannot be solely considered as a diplomatic experience, but needs to be examined in conjunction with the military, strategic, intelligence, domestic, and global perspectives. It has meant that historians have been warned to avoid using the term *appeasement* because it has been so all-embracing and subsequently too generalized. Central to the revisionist argument is that there was no alternative policy available; however, some historians have begun to question this assumption. The apparent task now for the counter-revisionists is, if they are to successfully undermine the argument that appeasement was the only option possible, to establish that there was a credible and viable alternative.

FINAL ATTEMPTS AT APPEASEMENT

The path toward war was conducted within the context of an impotent League of Nations, an isolationist United States, and a Bolshevik-run Soviet Union. The League clearly showed its failings by its inability to act over the Japanese invasion of Manchuria. Its mortality was confirmed by its inability to press the Italians into ending their invasion of Abyssinia in 1935–1936. Hitler came to power in 1933, and by the end of the year had already left the Geneva disarmament conference and the League of Nations. By 1934 German rearmament had recommenced.

The British response was to initiate a rearmament program in March 1935; however, it was conducted on the presumption that it must not jeopardize the long-term economic recovery of Britain or interfere with normal trade. The economy was the fourth arm of defense, a view widely subscribed to in Britain and France that economic strength would be essential to victory in any future conflict. Anglo-French-Italian cooperation had ensured that Austria had been safeguarded from Hitler's advances in 1934, but the Italian invasion of Abyssinia destroyed the Stresa front (a coalition between Britain, France, and Italy formed in 1935) and weakened Anglo-French relations. Hitler seized his opportunity and in March 1936 reoccupied the Rhineland, flouting both the Versailles and the Locarno treaties. The descent of Spain into civil war in 1936 saw the British and French attempt to isolate this to a regional conflict through a policy of nonintervention, which essentially meant turning a blind eye to the involvement of the Germans and Italians on the side of Francisco Franco (1892–1975).

Meanwhile, the Japanese were in full-scale conflict with the Chinese and threatening British interests in Shanghai. All this gave encouragement to those who felt it was necessary for the British to use diplomacy to detach the Germans and Italians. Attempts to resolve the concerns of Germany for a navy were made with the 1935 Anglo-German Naval Agreement, while sanctions were lifted from Italy in late 1936. During 1936 and 1937 the British increasingly felt that Germany might be pacified by a deal over the former German colonies confiscated at the end of World War I, but Hitler showed little real desire to reach a deal, and in reality was more interested in Eastern Europe, something the British and French were slow to appreciate. In March 1938 Germany sent troops into Austria. Although this action was condemned, many senior British figures felt that even at this stage Germany was merely seeking to resolve the inequities of the Treaty of Versailles. Similarly, too, the demands to absorb the Sudenten Germans into Germany provoked the Munich agreement of September 1938: the high point of appeasement. For the French, who had defense treaty obligations to the Czechoslovaks, this was a humiliating experience, and only thereafter did the threat from Hitler take precedence over France's internal problems in the making of policy.

APPEASEMENT ABANDONED

When in March 1939 German troops crossed the Sudeten border and violated the Munich agreement, Britain was obliged to abandon appeasement. A combination of parliamentary and public opinion forced Chamberlain's hand. The Territorial Army was doubled in size and conscription was introduced for the first time to enable Britain to send a field force to continental Europe. On 31 March 1939, Chamberlain broke with the traditions of recent foreign policy and offered a guarantee to the Polish nation. At the same time Anglo-French negotiations were begun, although reluctantly, with the Soviets about the possibility of a grand alliance against the dictators. Some contemporaries and historians are suspicious about whether Britain and France really abandoned appeasement in March. When it appeared that Britain might delay its declaration of war in September following the German attack on Poland, rumors spread that Chamberlain planned a second Munich. The reality could not be further from the truth. Chamberlain recognized in March

Neville Chamberlain (center) and Adolf Hitler consult a map of Europe during their negotiations over Czechoslovakia, October 1938. ILLUSTRATED LONDON NEWS LIBRARY/BRIDGEMAN ART LIBRARY

1939 that Britain had to prepare for the inevitability of war, no matter how horrid the prospect was. There were elements within the British government, in minor positions, like Richard Austen ("Rab") Butler (1902–1982) at the Foreign Office, who entertained hopes that perhaps Germany could be bought off with an economic deal; there was also a faction within the French government, centered around Georges Etienne Bonnet (1889–1973), that hoped to avoid war by further concessions, but neither group was in any position of significant influence. As soon as the German-Soviet Nonaggression Pact (also known as the Molotov-von Ribbentrop Pact) was announced on 23 August 1939, Chamberlain began preparing the personnel who would form the British war cabinet. The delay in declaring war was less about securing a new Munich than ensuring that the British went to war simultaneously with their ally, the French.

Since 1940 the perception of appeasement as an ill-conceived diplomatic policy has meant that the label has become entrenched in the political vocabulary of the world as a dirty word. Politicians, policy makers, and commentators have widely used it to criticize, or justify, political responses to diplomatic crises around the world: from Suez (1956) to the Vietnam War (1955–1975), to the Falklands Islands War (1982), to the First and Second Gulf Wars (1990–1991; 2003–).

See also **Baldwin, Stanley; Chamberlain, Neville; Molotov-Von Ribbentrop Pact; Munich Agreement; Sudetenland; World War II.**

BIBLIOGRAPHY

Adamthwaite, Anthony P. *France and the Coming of the Second World War, 1936–1939.* London, 1977.

Charmley, John. *Chamberlain and the Lost Peace.* London, 1989.

Jackson, Peter. *France and the Nazi Menace: Intelligence and Policy Making, 1933–1939.* Oxford, U.K., 2000.

Parker, R. A. C. *Chamberlain and Appeasement: British Policy and the Coming of the Second World War.* New York, 1993.

Watt, Donald. *How War Came: The Immediate Origins of the Second World War, 1938–1939.* London, 1989.

Young, Robert J. *In Command of France: French Foreign Policy and Military Planning 1933–1940.* Cambridge, Mass., 1978.

NICK CROWSON

ARAGON, LOUIS (1897–1982), French surrealist writer and Communist.

Louis Aragon, a prolific writer from the age of six, began his writing career thanks to an encounter with fellow medical student André Breton (1896–1966) at the height of World War I. United by a certain taste in literature, notably for the then obscure poet Le Comte de Lautréamont (1847–1870), and by their revolt against the massacres in the trenches, they were attracted to the iconoclastic fury of the Dada movement. In the aftermath of war, their rebellion took the form of surrealism, which sought to liberate the depths of the human psyche, particularly through the technique of automatic writing, and to bring about a revolution in everyday life. Aragon's most notable texts from his surrealist period are an account of his drifting through the French capital, *Le paysan de Paris* (1926; The peasant of Paris), and a collection of poems, *Le mouvement perpétuel* (1925; Perpetual motion).

In 1927 Aragon, along with Breton and others, joined the French Communist Party, then the only force opposed to French colonialism. Conflicts immediately erupted between the autonomy of the avant-garde and party discipline, between Aragon and Breton's bourgeois social origins and liberal attitudes (particularly regarding sexuality) and a "workerist" culture. Aragon broke with the surrealists, putting his writings in the service of the Communist "family" and choosing to write about "reality," both in his poetry and in novels. In 1931 he published "Front rouge," a virulent long poem that was seized by the authorities for its subversiveness. Breton and other surrealists supported Aragon's freedom of expression but attacked his loyalty to the Communist Party and "retrograde" realism.

During the 1930s, Aragon rallied to the theory of socialist realism, for example, in his novel *Les cloches de Bâle* (1934; The bells of Basel), and, following the Comintern's new Popular Front line of antifascist unity between Communist and non-Communist parties, developed the notion of a "national" literature that drew on the traditions of France in a progressive and antifascist way. In World War II, Aragon was a leader of the intellectual Resistance. His poetry of this period, clandestine for the most part, was written in a regular meter and was often addressed to his muse, the Russian novelist Elsa Triolet (1896–1970). These poems were more patriotic than communist, and some have passed into popular French culture, particularly as songs. At the Liberation, Charles de Gaulle hailed Aragon as a poet of the Resistance, but this prestige was tarnished by the settling of accounts between Resistance and collaborationist intellectuals during *l'épuration,* or purge. At the same time, the surrealists denounced his "chauvinism."

With the onset of the Cold War, Aragon, now a member of the central committee of the French Communist Party, was in the line of fire as a prolific author and director of the weekly journal *Les lettres françaises.* Revelations about the excesses of Stalinism—which the French Communist Party suppressed—led to disillusionment on Aragon's part, which he expressed indirectly in a long autobiographical poem, *Le roman inachevé* (1966; The unfinished novel). While increasingly vocal in his criticism, Aragon remained attached to communism and the Eastern bloc. As a result, he became more politically and culturally isolated: Aragon championed dissident East European writers as well as homegrown avant-garde movements, supported the student revolt of May 1968, and denounced the invasion of Czechoslovakia that same year, but was attacked by both non-Communists and by the conservative elements within the party leadership.

After the death of Elsa Triolet, the other side of Aragon's bisexuality became public, undermining the mythos surrounding the couple, whom the

Communists had promoted as a rival to Jean-Paul Sartre and Simone de Beauvoir. Aragon continued to experiment in his writing but never left the Communist Party: his last public declaration was in support of the Soviet invasion of Afghanistan in 1979. When he died in 1982, a year after being awarded the Legion of Honor by President François Mitterrand, the often bitter obituaries written about Aragon showed that he had remained a contentious and passionately divisive figure in French culture.

See also **Breton, André; Communism; Dada; Eurocommunism; Socialist Realism; Surrealism.**

BIBLIOGRAPHY

Bowd, Gavin. *L'interminable enterrement: Le communisme et les intellectuels français depuis 1956.* Paris, 1999.

Daix, Pierre. *Aragon, une vie à changer.* Expanded and updated version. Paris, 1994.

Kimyongür, Angela. *Socialist Realism in Louis Aragon's* Le Monde réel. Hull, U.K., 1995.

Ristat, Jean. *Avec Aragon: 1970–1982.* Paris, 2003.

GAVIN BOWD

ARCHITECTURE.

"Should there be a new style for the twentieth century?" This was the question many European architects had asked in a time of unprecedented social and technological change. But in spite of creative experiments, art nouveau chief among them, most architecture remained traditional as World War I began in 1914. The postwar world was distinctly different: old assumptions in politics and philosophy were aggressively discarded and new answers demanded. Architects responded with feverish attempts throughout the 1920s to devise a truly innovative approach that would suit modern conditions.

PATHS TO MODERNISM

In Germany the shattering effects of war led a younger generation of architects to shake themselves free from nineteenth-century ideological freight. A new mode emerged, expressionism. It was novel, yet rooted in prewar art nouveau and experiments with steel and glass in industrial buildings, including those of Peter Behrens (1868–1940), whose later IG Farben Dyeworks (1920–1924) was much admired. Expressionism was highly Romantic, borrowing forms from nature or the arts of the medieval German past. The 1919 Grosses Schauspielhaus interior, Berlin, by Hans Poelzig (1869–1936), engulfed theatergoers in what appeared an astonishing cavern of sharp stalactites. Here one sees close affinities to expressionism in contemporary painting and cinema. Erich Mendelsohn (1887–1953) was involved pre-1914 with the Blaue Reiter group of Munich painters and doodled expressionist designs that mostly went unbuilt. Einstein Tower, Potsdam (1919–1921), was an exception: a sketch come to life in a curvaceous, sculptural mass of concrete, as if the astronomical observatory were morphing into a living organism. Caught up in the politics of the hour, expressionists called for art and architecture to serve the masses, a goal taken up in 1919 by Walter Gropius (1883–1969) at the Weimar Bauhaus design school, where a medieval handicraft aesthetic at first prevailed before machine-inspired functionalism took over. Expressionism proved short-lived and produced few tangible monuments, but many subsequent twentieth-century architects found its creativity and giddy, nature-based experimentalism inspiring as an alternative to the machine aesthetic.

Whereas expressionism flourished in postwar Germany, the Italian avant-garde developed futurism, founded upon an anti-Romantic obsession with machines of speed and war. Futurist painting, sculpture, and music had already spawned countless shrill manifestos when Antonio Sant'Elia (1888–1916) wrote *Manifesto of Futurist Architecture* (1914), calling for a complete break with nineteenth century thinking and a rejection of classical, gothic, and other traditional styles. Monumentalism and heaviness should give way to lightness and energy, the airplane and the race car should provide inspiration. The futurist city would be as agile and dynamic as a shipyard; the futurist house would resemble a machine. As was the case for all futurists, Sant'Elia's tone was strident as he loudly proclaimed his hatred of the architecture of the past. When first starting out as an architect, he had been influenced by the Vienna Secession movement (headed by Joseph Maria Olbrich [1867–1908] and Otto Wagner [1841–1918]), but he soon turned away from decorative and ornamental approaches to the bare look of industrial facilities. In exquisite drawings exhibited as *Città Nuova* (1914) he envisioned a utopian city of the future where the machine aesthetic reigns triumphant. These illustrations uncannily predicted the coming form of the European city—but Sant'Elia did not live to see that future, as he died in battle in 1916.

The modernist architecture of the fledgling Soviet state in Russia was at first of a fantasy variety too, as the economic situation was desperate and little could be built. There were no clear lines between the dreams of architects, stage designers, and artists. The painter Vladimir Tatlin (1885–1953) conceived a colossal Monument to the Third International (1919–1920), a kind of reconceptualized Eiffel Tower in the form of an off-kilter dynamic spiral, exciting but entirely impractical. Tatlin's notions of constructivism were promulgated by the OSA (Union of Contemporary Architects) in 1925–1930, during which period a few constructivist buildings were actually erected. The culmination of this first phase of Soviet architecture came in 1931 with a competition for the Palace of the Soviets, Moscow. Architects from across Europe put forward some of the most exciting functionalist schemes ever proposed, including one by Le Corbusier (Charles-Éduoard Jeanneret, 1887–1965) for a parabolic arch that would support the main auditorium with suspended cables. It incorporated some of the dynamism of Tatlin. But the winning entry was anything but modernist—Boris Iofan's (1891–1976) overblown, stripped-classical wedding-cake skyscraper topped with a herculean statue of Vladimir Lenin (1870–1924). From here on, the government would sanction only a dull socialist realism style in art and architecture.

In Germany, the Bauhaus enshrined the "form follows function" approach, a reductivist mode that abolished ornament and historical reference and followed the cues of steel frames and plate glass, everything rectilinear and mechanical. Gropius was a key figure, but so too was his fellow countryman Ludwig Mies van der Rohe (1886–1969), one of the most influential architects of the twentieth century. The son of a stonemason, he worked under his father and later with Behrens but had no formal architectural training, thereby freeing him to experiment. The American architect Frank Lloyd Wright (1867–1959) briefly lived in Germany, and the young Mies was awed by an exhibition of his work in Berlin and the published *Wasmuth Portfolio* of Wright's architectural drawings (1910–1911). After a stint in the army, Mies participated in the visionary daydreaming of the early 1920s; his Glass Skyscraper drawings (1919–1921) pointed prophetically to the future in their embrace of the curtain wall—a non-loadbearing skin of glass that sheathes the steel skeleton inside. By 1926 Mies was in charge of the Deutscher Werkbund, an association of artists and designers that had been struggling to decide whether to stick with the medieval handicraft aesthetic of expressionism or plunge into functionalism.

Mies epitomized the latter camp, and under his leadership Deutscher Werkbund became a leading force in promoting the functionalist credo through its journal, *Die Form,* and a much-lauded housing estate in Stuttgart, the Weissenhofsiedlung (1927). Mies laid it out, and seventeen mostly young European architects contributed designs, including himself, Gropius, Le Corbusier, Behrens, and Poelzig. Here some half-million visitors experienced architectural modernism, often for the first time. Traditionalists decried the general white-walled starkness, and the flat-roofed aesthetic later found deliberate antithesis in the peaked medieval roofs of clay tile promulgated by the Nazis, who detested Deutscher Werkbund modernism as degenerate, left-wing internationalism. They never got around to demolishing the Weissenhofsiedlung, and it has been restored (1981–1987) as a major world monument of the modern movement. A museum is currently proposed for one house designed by Le Corbusier and his cousin Pierre Jeanneret (1896–1967), a shoe box elevated on their trademark piers or *pilotis* and marked by long "ribbon" windows. It epitomizes Le Corbusier's "Five Points of a New Architecture" as spelled out in 1926: *pilotis,* roof terrace, open plan, ribbon windows, and free-façade design. His Citrohan house also debuted here, a low-cost type assembled from standardized parts.

The Weissenhofsiedlung attracted wide attention to modernism and made Mies famous. The Weimar government chose him to design the German Pavilion for the International Exposition, Barcelona (1928–1929). The forward-looking and democratic nature of the Weimar regime was given visual expression through a compendium of functionalist concepts: a flat, cantilevered roof-slab resting on slender steel columns; wall planes carefully arranged to provide an open plan; generous use of floor-to-ceiling plate glass; a grid system organizing the whole. The stonecutter's son chose sumptuous materials, including green marble, golden onyx, and Roman travertine for a stunning look. The original pavilion was dismantled in 1930, but so important has it become as a leitmotif of twentieth-century modernism, it was re-created in 1983–1986 on its original site.

Like Gropius, Mies fled to America to escape the Nazis and advocated for modernism there. He was greeted warmly by an intelligentsia familiar with his work from the landmark 1932 Museum of Modern Art show in New York and accompanying book, *The International Style: Architecture Since 1922,* organized by art historians Philip Johnson (1906–2005) (later an important architect in his own right) and Henry-Russell Hitchcock (1903–1987). Love it or hate it, Mies van der Rohe's sleek, functionalist European modernism was taken up by corporate America post-1945. Late in life he built in Germany again: the Neue Nationalgalerie art museum, Berlin (1962–1968), has cruciform columns and a cantilevered roof harkening back to Barcelona. It forms part of the Kulturforum, the remaining buildings of which are by the architect Hans Scharoun (1893–1972), whose approach was very different from that of Mies: an exuberant sculpturalism in part derived from the expressionism Mies had sought in the 1920s to destroy. The rectilinear minimalism of Mies's museum could hardly be more different from Scharoun's Berlin Philharmonie Concert Hall (1956–1963) with its dramatic staggered terraces of seats under a soaring tentlike roof. Mies thought he had solved the central problem of twentieth-century architecture with his dictum, "Less Is More," but many subsequent architects have found this unsatisfactory—including the recent postmodernists, who declare, "Less Is a Bore."

Inspired by the cubist paintings of Mondrian as well as by Wright's *Wasmuth Portfolio,* a group of young Dutchmen created an architecture of extraordinary geometrical purity, De Stijl ("the style"). Their chief monument is the Schröder House, Utrecht, by Gerrit Rietveld (1888–1964), an odd intruder in a plain nineteenth-century neighborhood of brick rowhouses. Rietveld was a furniture designer whose cubistic *Red Blue Chair* of wooden

panels was painted in primary colors (1917–1918); he approached the design of the house in the same way, assembling cardboard models that showed walls, roof slabs, and balconies as free-flowing sculptural units that appear to slide past each other and that are picked out in whites, grays, or touches of red or yellow.

MODERNISM ASCENDANT

The iconic twentieth-century architect is Le Corbusier, a kind of grand impresario whose oversize pronouncements and astounding breakthroughs drew the attention of every practitioner—for admiration or vilification, depending on their views of his brand of modernism. So important is his body of work that plans were begun in 2004 to inscribe all of it on the prestigious UNESCO World Heritage List. To this day his urban planning ideas inspire anger among those who blame him for advocating, all too effectively, for the destruction of old urban centers. First put forth in drawings for a "Contemporary City for Three Million Inhabitants" (1922), his urbanistic schemes were later promulgated by CIAM (Congrès Internationaux d'Architecture Moderne), a kind of working group of top modernist architects from many European countries. It was founded in a meeting in Switzerland in 1928 (CIAM I). In subsequent gatherings there was much discussion of the problems of low-cost housing, part of the leftist agenda of the group. CIAM IV met on a cruise ship, SS *Patris II,* in 1933 and considered how European cities could be redesigned to render them less dense. The CIAM participant José Luis Sert (1902–1983) went on to consider the thorny issues in a book, *Can Our Cities Survive?* (1942). Codifying the *Patris* discussions was Le Corbusier's doctrinaire *Athens Charter* (1943)—the ship had been steaming toward Athens—that pointed the way to heavy-handed approaches in postwar urban redevelopment, specifically the tall apartment tower surrounded by windswept open space. CIAM continued to meet for many more sessions. The Swiss critic Sigfried Giedion (1888–1968) was especially influential. His *Space, Time and Architecture* (1941) soon became a classic theoretical text of modernism. The early CIAM meetings were important for achieving a critical mass in the nascent modernist movement and forging a functionalist consensus out of the myriad localized approaches of the 1920s. Postwar meetings grappled with what some increasingly perceived as functionalism's straitjacket.

Thanks in part to the tireless proselytizing of CIAM, modernism invaded every corner of Europe. In Sweden, Erik Gunnar Asplund (1885–1940) had already bridged nineteenth-century approaches and modernism: inspired by a pre–World War I trip to Italy, he embraced a simplified classicism. His City Library, Stockholm (1920–1928), was minimalist: a cube of reading rooms topped by a gigantic simple cylinder lighting the main hall with clerestory windows. He owed the concept to the eighteenth-century French rationalist Claude-Nicolas Ledoux (1736–1806). As chief architect of the Stockholm Exhibition in summer 1930, Asplund decisively introduced modernism to Scandinavia with constructivist-derived functionalism, including a tall skeletal mast brilliant with neon signs. The furniture and interior design there launched the great twentieth-century Swedish tradition of modernist innovation for everyday living. Asplund's classicism inspired his affable friend Alvar Aalto (1898–1976) in Finland. By 1928 Aalto had embraced modernism. His concrete Paimio Sanatorium, Turku (1929–1933), had tall, radiating wings among the pine trees, oriented toward sunlight and view. The small house called Villa Mairea, Noormarkku (1937–1939), synthesized classicism, functionalism, and the Finnish vernacular, with a special feeling for wood. Later Aalto would assist in post–World War II reconstruction of damaged cities, seeking to soften technological modernism and mass-produced housing designs with references to nature.

ARCHITECTURE AND IDEOLOGY

Totalitarianism darkened Europe as economies collapsed in the 1930s. Architecture played a critical role in Adolf Hitler's (1889–1945) plans for a reinvigorated Germany. A onetime Viennese watercolorist with a penchant for architectural subjects, Hitler saw the value of great public buildings in boosting national pride and signaling the permanence of his Thousand-Year Reich. His friend Paul Troost (1879–1934) had designed interiors for luxury ships and understood his Führer's lust for theatricality. Troost's Haus der Deutschen Kunst, Munich (1933–1937), was a museum for "pure" art, not the "degenerate" modernism then being purged. Its style became the official Nazi one: grandiose classicism, but simplified and rendered rigid and coldly sublime. The German architectural tradition of Karl Friedrich Schinkel (1781–1841) was married to a primitive Greek classicism. After Troost died, Albert Speer (1905–1981) took his place in Hitler's affections, conceiving a utopian rebuilding of Berlin as "Germania" with a preposterously oversized dome as its focus. Like Hitler, Speer saw Germany as a new Roman Empire dominating all of Europe and developed a suitably grandiose architecture, clad in stone. His built projects shared a megalomania, including the Zeppelinfeld Stadium, Nuremberg (1934–1937), for mass Nazi rallies and the Reich Chancellery, Berlin (1938), center of Hitler's cult of personality. Its echoing halls, one nearly five hundred feet long, were meant to instill awe in visiting dignitaries. Hitler's grim final days were spent in an underground bunker out back. Much of Speer's work was bombed to rubble during World War II, and he was later imprisoned for his role in organizing slave labor and death camps. He is the twentieth century's most controversial architect.

If the totalitarian regime in Germany rejected modernism, that in Italy was more receptive. Benito Mussolini (1883–1945) found an avid following among a young generation of architects, including the brilliant but short-lived Giuseppe Terragni (1904–1943), who helped found Gruppo 7 in 1926. Gruppo 7 was a gathering of Milanese modernists who pressed for what they called *Rationalismo*: anti-individualistic and pro-Fascist; embracing functionalism in design but tempering it with historical references to the glories of the Italian past. Terragni's Casa del Fascio, Como (1933–1936), a Fascist headquarters and community center, evolved through various conceptions into a harmonious and cubistic work of pure geometries and white walls stripped of any ornament. Its rationalist composition embodied in a gridlike reinforced concrete frame was apparently simple but actually quite complex, blending functionalist dicta with principles from the Roman past, including perfect proportions, an interior atrium, and marble cladding. It has won a legion of admirers. In time for Terragni's centennial in 2004 the New York architect Peter Eisenman (b. 1932) published *Giuseppe Terragni: Transformations, Decompositions, Critiques*, a book he had worked on for forty years that celebrated the subtleties of Casa del Fascio and Casa Giuliani-Frigerio, also in Como. Never built was Terragni's proposed monument to the poet Dante (1265–1321) (1938) in the Roman Forum, likewise a fusion of modernist rationalism with reference to the historical past, specifically the hypostyle halls of Egyptian temples, where columns stood as thickly as trees in a forest—only at the Danteum the columns were to have been of glass. World War II discredited fascism, but the ideas of Terragni later helped inspire postmodernism: Aldo Rossi (1931–1997) pioneered neo-rationalism in the 1960s, seeking to infuse history into the modernist vocabularies of concrete, glass, and steel, much as Terragni had done.

A RESTLESS SEARCH FOR ALTERNATIVES

No sooner had international style come to the fore in the 1930s than did some architects seek to refine or even replace it. At the same time they experimented with new materials, trying to develop novel aesthetic approaches based on the innate qualities and strengths of each. Concrete was arguably twentieth-century architecture's signature material; it was used on a scale previously undreamed-of and with great boldness. Properly speaking it is ferro-concrete, a combination of concrete with steel reinforcing bars or meshes that can be used in many clever ways to create rigid or shell-like structures that mark a complete break from the architecture of previous centuries. Early applications were frequently technological, as in the pre–World War I bridges of Swiss civil engineer Robert Maillart (1872–1940). After the war he introduced a series of exciting innovations, designing concrete bridges that were ever-lighter and free from visual reference to earlier masonry technologies, culminating with the Salginatobel Bridge, Schiers (1929–1930). It comprises one sweeping arch hundreds of feet above a rocky mountain gorge, the whole forming a seamless structural unit of hollow-box reinforced concrete. Engineers still travel from around the world to admire this aesthetic gem. Maillart's influence was huge, for example on the concrete "shell structures" of the Spanish-born Félix Candela (1910–1997) in Mexico. The European genius in concrete after Maillart was Pier Luigi Nervi (1891–1979) in Rome, who combined technical innovations with an unsurpassed feel for pure sculptural geometries. At Valentino Park, Turin (1947–1949), he built exhibition halls that span hundreds of feet in one leap. They are formed of poured concrete arches and, between them, precast shells pierced by window openings. He collaborated with Gio Ponti (1891–1979) on Italy's tallest building,

Pirelli Tower, Milan (1956–1958), its unusual lozenge-like plan and sleek surfaces an instant emblem of corporate sophistication in the postwar world (restored after being struck by an airplane in 2002). Ponti exemplifies the twentieth-century architect in the mold of Le Corbusier who participated in poetry, painting, writing, and design, all with a spirit of passionate exuberance. The magazine he edited for decades, *Domus* (meaning "house"), transmitted ideas of cutting-edge architecture and design to a wide readership in Europe and abroad. Like several top European architects, by the 1960s Ponti was designing buildings around the world.

For truthful expression of concrete as a structural material, all eyes were on Le Corbusier in the 1950s. With uncompromising rawness he allowed concrete to show at his Maisons Jaoul, Neuilly, France (1951–1955), much copied by younger architects in Europe and America. Exposed, rough concrete (*béton brut*), still showing the imprint of the wooden formwork into which it was poured, was likewise the keynote of his Unité d'Habitation, Marseilles (1946–1952) and other notable works of this period. A British husband-and-wife team, Alison (1928–1993) and Peter Smithson (1923–2003), greatly admired Le Corbusier's honesty and helped coin the term "new brutalism" in 1954 for any sort of tough, gritty functionalism, whether using *béton brut* or not. Their Hunstanton Secondary Modern School, Norfolk, completed that year, defined brutalism in England: the steel structure exposed to view and the whole complex resembling a gleaming-new industrial site, with a nod to Mies van der Rohe's recent Chicago work. (Later critics blasted it for a prison-like bleakness hardly appropriate for teaching children.) The Smithsons were active in Team 10, a group of young architects that broke away from CIAM and expressed appreciation for the rough new Britain of housing tracts and slum streets. At the *Economist* headquarters, London (1959–1964), the Smithsons offered a more refined approach, three small office towers rising above a pedestrian plaza and clad in fossiliferous Portland stone—a sensitive effort to resolve problems of urban site and scale.

In France, Jean Prouvé (1901–1984) was likewise among the important twentieth-century experimenters with situation-specific architectural design and the honest expression of materials, including unconventional ones. With no architectural training, he entered the field as an iron-worker, brainstorming with Le Corbusier and Jeanneret about portable housing units made of lightweight materials. His aluminum Tropical House (1949–1951), of small prefabricated pieces assembled on a grid system, was flown by airplane to the Congo as a demonstration of the possibilities for colonialist housing. At the same time he designed inexpensive homes for French citizens dislocated by war. Prouvé is a lodestar for recent architects who seek to use cheap materials in extraordinary ways, and Tropical House was retrieved from Africa in 2001 and taken on a celebratory tour of American museums.

Critiques of modernism coalesced in the 1970s into a definite revolt. It was called insensitive, inhumane, and authoritarian ("heroic" had a bad connotation to the counterculture). It had destroyed old neighborhoods for "urban renewal" and encouraged bland, box-like building. The high-rise apartment towers beloved of CIAM were singled out as especially awful to look at and live in, and many alternatives were put forward. In Britain, Team 10 member Ralph Erskine (1914–2005) designed Byker Wall, Newcastle (1969–1975), a multistory housing development that sought to diversify the modernist idiom (a complex, stepped profile; house-like shed roofs; brickwork of bold colors and patterns; varied balcony forms) and even engaged future residents in planning consultations in an effort to be democratic. Architects increasingly sought to avoid the bombast of the mid-twentieth-century "megastructure" by breaking up big compositions and paying sensitive attention to local context. The British architects Sir James Stirling (1926–1992) and Michael Wilford's (b. 1938) German museum, the Neue Staatsgalerie, Stuttgart (1977–1984) defined the emerging postmodern approach: the complex subdivided to render its scale more human and enlivened with brightly colored elements to engage the ordinary visitor; an abundance of witty allusions to the architecture of the past, from Rome and Schinkel to Le Corbusier and Aalto, all in a peppy pastiche; an embracing of the "complexity and contradiction" that American Robert Venturi (b. 1925) pinpointed as sadly

lacking in modernism. Stirling called his museum "representational *and* abstract, monumental *and* informal, traditional *and* high tech." These tensions and ironies crop up frequently throughout subsequent postmodernism.

ARCHITECTURE IN THE AGE OF GLOBALISM

At century's end architectural practice had gone global, with major firms routinely engaged in projects on many continents. Europe no longer enjoyed its old cultural preeminence. Perhaps sensing the shift, in the 1980s the French president, François Mitterrand (1916–1996), funded a series of architectural showpieces meant to demonstrate his nation's continuing greatness, the *Grands Projets*. Jean Nouvel (b. 1945) won rave reviews for his Institut du Monde Arabe (1987–1988): its south-facing wall forms a silvery metal-and-glass curtain suggestive of Islamic screens, with thirty thousand small, light-sensitive diaphragms that close like a camera lens to cut out sun glare—an innovative use of "smart" materials that respond to their environment. Another Mitterrand landmark was the Bibliothèque Nationale (1989–1997) by Dominique Perrault (b. 1953), four L-shaped glass towers each reminiscent of an open book and embracing a monumental central space. Paris has seen many important museums; previously, the Italian architect Renzo Piano (b. 1937) had collaborated with the Englishman Richard Rogers (b. 1933) on Centre Georges Pompidou (1971–1977), one of modern Europe's most recognizable buildings, visited by 160 million persons since it opened, five times the expected crowds. To keep the interior wide open for the display of art, the architects placed the steel support structure and mechanical systems on the outside, daringly exposed to view and color-coded for visual effect (blue=air ducts, green=water pipes, yellow=electricity), with escalators rising in clear plastic tubes.

In pursuit of ever-more-sweeping interior spaces, Rogers would go on to design London's Millennium Dome (1999), using a newly perfected technology, a mast-supported network of cables that suspend a tent-like roof. The Dome spans an incredible 738 feet, entirely free from interrupting supports. It improved upon the continental experiments of the German engineer Frei Otto (b. 1925), who collaborated with the architect Gunter

Behnisch (b. 1922) on the striking Olympic Stadium, Munich (1968–1972): tall steel poles supported spidery cables that held up complex, flowing tent roofs of polyester fabric coated in plastic. All these innovations were extremely novel, suggesting new avenues toward solving the old problem of enclosing generous space.

Worldwide attention was brought to bear on Berlin after the reunification of the city in 1990 and the relocation of the national government there from Bonn. In ruins since the days of Hitler, the former parliamentary building, the Reichstag, was restored by Sir Norman Foster (b. 1935), a London architect, in 1993–1999. Mindful of history, he preserved the graffiti left on the blackened walls by Soviet soldiers in 1945. His landmark glass dome, a strikingly contemporary note atop the more-than-century-old building, was lit from inside at night. It symbolizes the transparency of democratic governments. A mirrored cone occupies the center of the dome to enhance the daylighting of a spiraling pedestrian ramp. The much-honored Foster and Partners firm has worked in forty-eight countries. Their 850-foot Commerzbank Tower, Frankfurt (1997), was Europe's tallest building upon completion. Their breathtaking cable-stayed road bridge, the Millau Viaduct, France (2001–2005), is the tallest vehicular bridge in the world, with seven concrete piers each higher than the Eiffel Tower.

No longer are great European buildings necessarily designed by Europeans, as evinced by the fame of two recent museums by Americans. I. M. Pei (b. 1917) created a glass pyramid for the Louvre, Paris (1985–1989), a controversial intrusion of the modern into a historic complex. For the much-praised Guggenheim in Bilbao, Spain (1992–1997), the Californian Frank Gehry (b. 1929) conceived a fantastically complex, deconstructivist design clad in a shiny titanium skin. Critics heaped praise on it as boldly pointing the way to coming twenty-first-century approaches, which they predicted would be marked by increasing fragmentation and freedom. Daniel Libeskind's (b. 1946) annex to the Berlin Historical Museum and Peter Eisenman's Berlin Memorial to the Murdered Jews of Europe, both works by American architects, are two other striking cases in point.

Deconstructivism gained notoriety in the 1980s as a transatlantic alternative to both international style and postmodernism. It defined an architecture that seemed to have been wrenched violently apart, twisted, and contorted, its complex visual effects made possible by computer-aided design (CAD) software. The Viennese firm Coop Himmelb(l)au emerged as a leading practitioner. Their UFA Cinema Center, Dresden (1993–1998), is a movie theater entered through a weirdly tilted glass structure resembling a faceted crystal. The architect Rem Koolhaas (b. 1944) started out as a writer whose *Delirious New York* (1978) earned him fame as a visionary theorist with a radical, streetwise approach: forget trying to improve modern cities, he says, and instead embrace "the culture of congestion," the vibrant chaos of modern life. Subsequently he has gone on to develop a worldwide practice, and he won architecture's highest honor, the Pritzker Prize, in 2000. As the twenty-first century began, his status among young architecture students was cult-like, many calling him the greatest living architect. His firm, the Office for Metropolitan Architecture (OMA), has produced designs that defy categorization but are often classed with deconstructivism. They have inspired diverse reactions: admiration for their hip, intellectualized analysis of contemporary problems; dislike for their harsh, formless geometries and brash rawness.

OMA's largest executed planning project was a new city center for Lille, France (1988–2004), called Euralille, designed to accommodate commercial growth owing to the new Channel Tunnel linking France and Britain. Koolhaas embraces "bigness" and designed at a scale meant to be appreciated not on foot but from a hurtling high-speed train. Contrary to most contemporary thinkers, he favors big, signature buildings to capture the public imagination. Some saw in this a return to discredited principles of CIAM. Koolhaas's major building at Lille, erected on a tight budget, is the Grand Palais exhibition hall or Congrexpo (1994), nicknamed The Egg for its distinctive form, which is surfaced in black-pebbled concrete and corrugated plastic. He likes ovals, thinking back to New York and Wright's Guggenheim Museum, but here the oval embraces wild dissonance in its internal forms, shapes, and materials, the whole sometimes garish and vulgar, much like the modern cities Koolhaas so passionately admires. His followers are many, including the 2004

Pritzker Prize winner Zaha Hadid (b. 1950), born in Iraq but now a resident of London. Among her few built projects is the Bergisel Ski Jump, Innsbruck, Austria (1999–2002), a towering structure of pure sculptural drama.

At the dawn of the twenty-first century, London was the setting for some of the most dramatic architectural developments in Europe. Foster and Partners experimented with strange CAD forms, including the warped glass ovoid of London City Hall (1998–2002), which has no front or back. Its shape is precisely configured to minimize the area exposed to direct sunlight and reduce dependence upon air conditioning. Many European architects have lately embraced this kind of ecologically sustainable or "green" design. Also by Foster and Partners is the extraordinary-looking 30 St. Mary Axe, or Swiss Re Headquarters (1997–2004), nicknamed the Gherkin for its swelling, bullet-like form. Advertised as London's first ecologically friendly skyscraper, its round plan helps drive a system of natural ventilation via openings in the curving, glazed façade, so the building uses only half the energy of a typical office tower. The same firm collaborated with engineers and a sculptor on Millennium Bridge, a stylish footway over the Thames (1996–2000). It connects to a new museum, Tate Modern (1995–2000), by a Swiss firm, Herzog & de Meuron—a good example of the postmodern preference for historic preservation, as it occupies a former power plant. Piano began work in 2000 on what was planned to be the tallest building in Europe, 1,016-foot London Bridge Tower, so thin and crystalline it was instantly nicknamed the Shard when the drawings were unveiled. If completed, it will be an appropriate symbol of London's growing financial and cultural preeminence among European cities. Designed at the very end of the period 1914–2004, the Shard proposal intriguingly recalls Mies van der Rohe's Glass Skyscraper scheme of more than eighty years earlier, history coming full circle. For all the phases it has undergone and challenges it has faced, architectural modernism remains exciting and innovative in Europe, constantly seeking new approaches and new relevance for an everchanging world.

See also **France; Futurism; Germany; Italy; Nazism; Russia; Technology; United Kingdom.**

BIBLIOGRAPHY

Colquhoun, Alan. *Modern Architecture.* Oxford, U.K., and New York, 2002.

Curtis, William J. R. *Modern Architecture since 1900.* 3rd ed. Upper Saddle River, N.J., 1996.

Frampton, Kenneth. *Modern Architecture: A Critical History.* 3rd ed. London and New York, 1992.

Ghirardo, Diane. *Architecture after Modernism.* New York, 1996.

Giedion, Sigfried. *Space, Time and Architecture.* 5th ed. rev. Cambridge, Mass., 2003.

Placzek, Adolf K., ed. *Macmillan Encyclopedia of Architects.* New York and London, 1982.

Tzonis, Alexander, and Liane Lefaivre. *Architecture in Europe since 1968: Memory and Invention.* New York, 1992.

Yarwood, Doreen. *The Architecture of Europe: The Nineteenth and Twentieth Centuries.* Chicago, 1991.

W. BARKSDALE MAYNARD

ARENDT, HANNAH (1906–1975),
German-born American political philosopher.

Born in Hanover, Germany, Arendt began studying existentialism with Martin Heidegger in Marburg in 1924. Two years later, she relocated to Heidelberg, where she completed a dissertation on "St. Augustine's Doctrine of Love" under the direction of another existentialist, Karl Jaspers.

Although the Nazi electoral breakthrough did not occur until 1930, it seems that, upon finishing her dissertation, Arendt sensed the political catastrophe that would befall Germany four years hence. At this point she abandoned her philosophical interests and began research for a major study on the early-nineteenth-century Jewess and *salonnière* Rahel Varnhagen. Reflecting on this period in a 1962 interview, Arendt expressed strong misgivings about the attitudes of fellow German intellectuals. She had anticipated discrimination among common folk. But the anti-Semitism she encountered among academicians came as a shock. As she later opined, "Among intellectuals *Gleichschaltung* [the Nazi euphemism for the elimination of opponents] was the rule . . . I never forgot that. I left Germany dominated by the idea . . .: Never again! I shall never again get involved in any kind of intellectual business. I want nothing to do with that lot." Later in life, she preferred being identified as a "political thinker" rather than as a "philosopher."

Arendt emigrated to Paris in 1933, where she worked with Youth Aliya, helping Jewish children relocate to Palestine. Eight years later, she emigrated to the United States, where she taught at Brooklyn College, commented in journals on European politics, and worked for the Jewish publishing house Shocken. In 1951 her landmark study, *The Origins of Totalitarianism,* appeared: a sweeping attempt to account for the rise of political dictatorship as result of the breakdown of tradition and the rise of "mass society." Her methodological approach bore similarities to Alexis de Tocqueville's conclusions in *The Old Regime and the Revolution* (1856). Tocqueville had tried to explain the despotic turn taken by the French Revolution (under the Jacobins and then Napoleon) by analyzing the breakdown of the traditional "estates" and the social leveling initiated under the age of absolutism.

In the early 1950s, Arendt reconciled herself with her former mentor, Heidegger, who, during the early 1930s, had vigorously supported the Nazis. Yet, when she proudly sent him a copy of her pathbreaking study on totalitarianism, the philosopher demurred, claiming his English was not good enough to read it. Arendt and Jaspers also reestablished contact after the war. Their extensive correspondence, first published during the early 1990s, represents one of the most significant philosophical and political records of the twentieth century.

Arendt returned to political philosophy with the publication of *The Human Condition* (1958), which she had begun as a critical study of Marxism. Here, she reprised some of the Aristotelian thematics she had encountered thirty years earlier as a Heidegger protégé. Arendt argued that one of the debilities of modern politics was that it placed the concerns of "life"—the subaltern, biological ends of production and reproduction—at its center. Yet, from the standpoint of classical political philosophy, what distinguished humanity from the beasts was precisely its capacity to transcend the "life process" via cultural achievement and "great politics." In Arendt's view, politics—in the Greek sense of "political excellence"—meant "action," which she defined as the capacity for men and women

to distinguish themselves in public through speech and heroic deeds. In her view, one of the problems with modern politics was that it downplayed "action" in favor of "social" concerns. Thus, under the modern welfare state, the summum bonum became the (vulgar) material ends of the "life process" and little else.

Her antimodern prejudices were also evident in "Reflections on Little Rock," a 1959 article in which she criticized the civil rights movement. Arendt felt it was not the business of "politics" or "government" to meddle in "society"—even if, in the case at hand, inaction meant perpetuating segregation. Her distrust of "mass society" was so profound that, in *On Revolution* (1963), she toyed with the idea of eliminating universal suffrage as one way to keep the unwashed masses out of politics. Elsewhere, she praised "workers councils" (*Räte*) as contemporary embodiments of "action," despite their "social" origins—the fact that they emerged from the lowly sphere of "labor."

Understandably, Arendt's critics found her position rife with "aristocratic" prejudices. They argued that by belittling social concerns, she failed to appreciate modernity's vast democratic potential and import. Moreover, over the course of the twentieth century, our understanding of "rights" has progressively evolved, from civic to political to social rights (unemployment insurance, health care, pensions, safe working conditions, and so forth). Arendt's distaste for social questions and issues risked overlooking these gains insofar as they pertained to the "life cycle."

In 1963 Arendt published *Eichmann in Jerusalem.* Her contention that leaders of the Jewish councils of occupied Europe cooperated with the Nazis escalated into a major international controversy. Even if her accusations contained a measure of truth, Arendt seemed oblivious to the state of duress under which the Judenräte leaders operated. Often they found themselves in a no-win situation vis-à-vis the Nazis' deportation demands and did what they could to stall for time.

Arendt seemingly poured fuel on the fire by proposing her "banality of evil" thesis to describe Nazi henchmen like Eichmann. By using this phrase, Arendt sought both to expose the perpetrators' mediocrity and to highlight their bureaucratic approach to mass murder. Conversely, her detractors felt that, by employing this epithet, she appeared to downplay the sadistic brutality that distinguished the Nazi crimes.

In 1969 she wrote a text in honor of Heidegger's eightieth birthday in which she exonerated his Nazi behavior. Undoubtedly, her intended target was Theodor Adorno, who in 1964 wrote a trenchant Heidegger critique, *The Jargon of Authenticity,* and who had once claimed that Heidegger's philosophy was "fascist down to its innermost core." Parrying Adorno's accusations, Arendt suggested that Nazism was a "gutter-born phenomenon" and, as such, had nothing to do with the life of the mind. She also claimed that, as a philosopher, Heidegger possessed an ethereal understanding of politics and thus should not be held accountable for his actions. At this juncture, the Nobel laureate and Holocaust survivor Elie Wiesel could not help but weigh in, claiming that "Arendt was so arrogant that she thought she alone could decide who should be forgiven and who should not." Coincidentally, among New York intellectuals her unflattering nickname had been "Hannah Arrogance."

See also **Adorno, Theodor; Eichmann, Adolf; Nazism; Totalitarianism.**

BIBLIOGRAPHY

Primary Sources

Arendt, Hannah. *The Origins of Totalitarianism.* New York, 1951.

————. *The Human Condition.* Chicago, 1958.

————. *Eichmann in Jerusalem: A Report on the Banality of Evil.* New York, 1963.

Secondary Sources

Canovan, Margaret. *Hannah Arendt: A Reinterpretation of Her Thought.* Cambridge, U.K., 1992.

Wolin, Richard. *Heidegger's Children: Hannah Arendt, Karl Löwith, Hans Jonas, and Herbert Marcuse.* Princeton, N.J., 2001.

RICHARD WOLIN

ARISTOCRACY. Since the early 1980s historians have debated the importance and the role of the aristocracy in early-twentieth-century Europe.

This debate originated from the thesis advanced by Arno J. Mayer in a book titled *The Persistence of the Old Regime* (1981). Mayer argued both that aristocracy still dominated much of European political, social, and cultural life in 1914, and that this domination was a key cause of Europe's descent into war.

THE ARISTOCRACY IN 1914

Mayer's book was very useful in encouraging modern historians' attention to the aristocracy, which had hitherto been a neglected topic. Nor is his thesis without some virtue. In political terms, for instance, the Russian and Prussian aristocracies were in some ways more powerful in 1914 than a century before. Ironically, this was due to the retreat of absolute monarchy and the introduction of parliamentary institutions. Not merely did aristocrats often dominate upper houses, but the restricted franchise gave them great power in lower houses too. This allowed the aristocracy unprecedented opportunities to articulate and defend common interests, choose its own political leaders, and block legislation it disliked. Both Petr Arkadyevich Stolypin in Russia and Theobald von Bethmann Hollweg in Germany had reformist legislation wrecked by aristocratic intransigence in the years before 1914.

Mayer is also correct in pointing to the immense wealth and continuing prestige of some great magnate families, and to the continuing predominance of men of aristocratic origin in the armed forces and the diplomatic services of monarchical Europe. Nor is he wrong to argue that a sense that modernity was increasingly marginalizing the aristocracy was a source of pessimism, even cultural and political despair, for some aristocrats, and that this could sometimes feed into political radicalism (e.g., the British Conservatives' unconstitutional encouragement of Ulster rebellion from 1912 to 1914) or even into willingness to accept the "heroic remedy" of war as a solution to intractable domestic political crisis.

Nevertheless, Mayer takes his argument much too far. By 1914 landed wealth was well outstripped by financial, industrial, and commercial fortunes. To the extent that a small minority of the richest and most prestigious aristocratic families had consolidated their position at the core of the emerging European modern plutocracy, this was possible only because they had tapped into these new "industrial era" sources of wealth—always in the form of stocks and bonds, but often as owners of coal mines or urban property. Moreover even these untypical aristocratic families risked being marginalized as a mere leisure class and losing their traditional position at the core of political life as a true ruling elite. This had much to do with the increasing complexity of society and its management, which had spawned a swath of professional bureaucracies, politicians, and experts.

Even in the armed forces, in which officers of aristocratic origin remained very important, increasing professionalization greatly affected the mentalities of the military elites. As regards the decision to go to war in 1914, railway timetables and the logic of mass mobilization were at least as important as aristocratic values. Moreover, in the military context it is wrong to associate aristocracy with belligerence, and modernity with more pacific values. Young turks at the cutting edge of military modernity—Erich Ludendorff in Germany or Mikhail Tukhachevsky and Alexander Nemitz in Russia—were more wholehearted advocates of aggressive "total" war than aristocratic courtier generals desperate to sustain the traditional social order of which they were major beneficiaries.

This bears on the more general issue of aristocracy, modernity, and democracy. Particularly in the United States there is a strong tendency to automatically equate modernity with virtue, liberalism, and democracy. American identity to some extent always defined itself against an aristocratic "other" and therefore finds it easy to condemn aristocracy for the world's problems. Moreover to blame "premodern" aristocracy for many of the twentieth century's political disasters is very comforting because in the early twenty-first century aristocracy is dead, liberal democracy has triumphed, and therefore disaster is by definition a thing of the past. In reality matters were never so simple.

In Imperial Germany, for instance, the Junkers adapted very successfully to the pressures of modernity through a military professionalism that made the German army a model for the world, and by creating the world's first mass agrarian interest group, the Bund der Landwirte. There is unfortunately nothing unmodern about the latter's organizational sophistication, its ruthlessly single-minded pursuit of sectional interest, or its brilliant exploitation of popular self-interest and ethnonational prejudice. Moreover, the single most dangerous element in German foreign policy, namely the pursuit of Weltpolitik and naval power, had far more to do with new professional and industrial groups than with the aristocracy. The German naval lobby saw Junkers as an anachronism and itself as the epitome of modernity. Given the geopolitics of imperialism and the history of nineteenth-century liberalism, they had a point. Nor were these trends a merely German phenomenon. The French and American republics played an enthusiastic part in the imperialist expansion of Western power and territory. White settler democratic electorates yielded to no one in their racism or their hunger to expropriate native land. The land and culture of Algerian natives were better preserved under the military despotism of Napoleon III than under the Third Republic. In 1914 European aristocracy was not as powerful nor was its influence as baneful as Mayer argues. Nor was European modernity as virtuous. The coming of war was closely linked to the logic of imperialism, but neither the world war nor imperialism can simply be explained by the Primat der Innenpolitik (primacy of domestic politics), let alone by supposed aristocratic hegemony and wickedness.

World War I hastened the decline of the European aristocracy. Particularly in Germany and Britain, young male aristocrats suffered disproportionately heavy casualties partly because of their traditional role as officers but also perhaps because they saw the war unconsciously as a time to relegitimize their leading role in society through sacrifice for the national cause. In the less "national" and less modern Romanov and Habsburg empires, aristocratic self-sacrifice was less universal, depending much more on individual motivation and the differing traditions of military service from one aristocratic family to another.

THE ARISTOCRACY IN THE EUROPEAN PERIPHERY

The war destroyed the Russian and part of the Austrian aristocracy. Expropriated wholly in Transylvania and to a much lesser extent in

Czechoslovakia, the only place where the Habsburg aristocracy retained its prewar wealth and political influence was in the rump Hungarian state. In Hungary the aristocracy survived thanks to successful foreign (Romanian) intervention, which led to the victory of the counterrevolution in the Hungarian civil war and the overthrow of the Hungarian "Bolshevik" regime. Though the establishment of Admiral Miklós Horthy's regime was accompanied by a "white terror" against its socialist enemies, once Horthy was firmly in place the traditional aristocratic liberalism of the Hungarian elites reestablished itself.

The self-esteem and identity of the Hungarian traditional elites were linked to Hungary's ancient constitution, laws, and parliament, which the Hungarian aristocracy had defended for centuries against Habsburg absolutism. The aristocracy's role in the 1848 revolution also became part of its defining myth and added a modern twist to Hungarian elite liberalism. The Hungarian aristocracy was never democratic even by British aristocratic standards, but on the whole its traditions did distance it from the right-wing populism, anti-Semitism, and fascism that came to dominate much of eastern and central Europe in the 1930s.

Hungary can usefully be seen as part of Europe's peripheral "Second World," which stretched from Ireland and Iberia in the west, through Italy and the Balkans in the south, to the Habsburg and Romanov empires' territory in eastern Europe. Many features distinguished this periphery from Europe's "First World" core in Britain, France, Germany, and the Low Countries. For example, almost everywhere in the periphery society was poorer and more lawless, middle classes were much smaller, and property was less secure. In most countries, of all forms of wealth and property, the big estates were the most vulnerable to expropriation. In many cases traditional peasant resentment of the aristocracy had been exacerbated by the effect that market-oriented capitalism had on the way the aristocracy fenced off and exploited its forests and farms. Peasants deprived of access to common land or to the aristocracy's forests could be willing recruits for the socialist and anarchist movements that were beginning to spread their tentacles into rural areas, which the railways and growing literacy were making less inaccessible to urban "agitators."

It was therefore not unrealistic for large landowners in peripheral Europe to fear social revolution and the arrival of mass democracy in the first years of the twentieth century. Inevitably the disruption of society and radicalization of politics caused by World War I increased such fears. So too above all did the Russian Revolution of 1917, which resulted in the total expropriation of the Russian aristocracy and the death or exile of many of its members. Although the Bolsheviks ratified the expropriation of the landowners in 1917 and 1918, the peasantry had itself taken the initiative in this matter, frequently also burning down the manor houses though seldom murdering their occupants. Had democracy triumphed in Russia the Constituent Assembly would have expropriated the estates without compensation. Only successful military counterrevolution would have saved the property of the Russian aristocracy, as Admiral Horthy and General Francisco Franco subsequently did for their Hungarian and Spanish peers.

Responses to the threat of agrarian revolution differed across the European Second World. In the generation before 1914 the British government bought out most of the Anglo-Irish landowning class. This was crucial in averting social, though not national, revolution in the period from 1918 to 1923. Nevertheless the "Troubles" caused the destruction of some aristocratic houses and hastened the retreat of the Anglo-Irish aristocracy to England. Somewhat similar was the fate of the Baltic German aristocracy in newly independent Latvia and Estonia. A key justification for expropriation here was the avoidance of social revolution and the attractiveness of communism, which in 1917 and 1918 had strong support, particularly in Latvia. The key difference between the fate of the Baltic German and Anglo-Irish landlords was that the former did not have the immensely wealthy British taxpayer willing and able to buy them out on generous terms. In Romania too, the immediate postwar years saw radical land reform with minimal compensation, designed once again to remove the threat of social revolution. In terms of Barrington Moore Jr.'s famous thesis about the agrarian origins of democracy, fascism, and communism, the Baltic and Romanian land reforms are of great interest. Though these reforms were successful in undermining mass support for social revolution, they did not guarantee lasting democracy. In Romania in particular populist politics moved to the nationalist right of the political spectrum, with anti-Semitism at its core.

In Italy and Spain the landed aristocracy survived, though in both cases it did so in alliance with right-wing authoritarian regimes. In the immediate aftermath of World War I the liberal regimes of both Spain and Italy collapsed. The landowning class in northern Italy played an important role in funding and protecting fascist bands in order to terrorize increasingly rebellious agrarian labor and to save themselves (so many believed) from Russian-style social revolution. The traditional Italian elites then lived in relatively comfortable cohabitation with the fascist regime for a generation, their confidence, status, and interests being boosted by the survival of the key political institutions of the prefascist era—namely the monarchy, royal army, and diplomatic corps on the one hand, and the Vatican on the other. Fascist Italy then played an important role in ensuring Franco's victory in the Spanish civil war (1936–1939) and thereby saving the estates of the Spanish aristocracy. By 1936 it was not unrealistic for the aristocracy of, in particular, Andalusia to believe that only military counterrevolution would save its lands from expropriation. Extreme class conflict in parts of the Spanish countryside was probably not the most important reason why Spanish democracy collapsed in the 1930s, but it was a significant contributory factor.

THE ARISTOCRACY IN THE EUROPEAN CORE

Ultimately, however, Europe's future and aristocracy's role within it would be decided mostly in the Continent's First World core. By 1914 the British aristocracy was much weaker than it had been in 1850. British agriculture, unprotected by tariffs, had suffered severely in the four prewar decades. The great majority of the population now lived in towns. Financial, industrial, and commercial wealth far outstripped the proceeds from agriculture. A mass socialist party had emerged by 1914, and the House of Lords had lost most of its power in 1911. The long-term trends that underlay these developments continued in the interwar years. Nevertheless the British aristocracy remained very significant in political, cultural, and social terms, and some of its members were still extremely wealthy. Victory in World War I enhanced the legitimacy of monarchy, political system, and aristocracy alike, not least because the British aristocracy's sacrifices in the war had earned it respect. The collapse of the global capitalist economy in the 1930s split the socialist movement and resulted in fourteen years of what was in essence Conservative rule (1931–1945). Though the three prime ministers of the 1930s were not aristocrats, many of their key ministers were. Most famously, Winston Churchill, a scion of one of England's greatest aristocratic families, led the country to victory in World War II.

Victory in the war ensured that the swansong of the British aristocracy continued for some time after 1945. Even in the 1960s the head of one of Scotland's leading aristocratic families could serve as Britain's prime minister. By the end of Margaret Thatcher's era (1979–1990), however, aristocrats were marginalized even in the Conservative Party. British mass culture, influenced by American values, had become much less deferential and more self-confident. Education at the elite Eton College had become a positive disadvantage in public life.

The fate of the German aristocracy was less happy. Defeat in World War I and the fall of the German monarchies weakened the prestige of traditional elites, institutions, and values. Except to some extent in territory annexed by Poland, the German aristocracy nevertheless preserved its estates. Moreover the Weimar regime was actually quite generous in the protection it offered to large-scale agriculture. The great suffering caused by the British wartime blockade had convinced many Germans that agricultural self-sufficiency might be more than just a cover for Junker selfishness. Moreover the German army and diplomatic service remained aristocratic havens. Nevertheless most of the German aristocracy despised the Weimar Republic and were not unhappy to see it replaced by the Nazis. Key members of the aristocratic political and military elite, led by Franz von Papen, were instrumental in bringing Adolf Hitler to power, believing that the perks of office would undermine the radicalism of the Nazis and that the latter would be controllable by Germany's traditional elites.

Lord and Lady Mountbatten with Mohandas K. Gandhi, New Delhi, India, April 1947. The career of Lord Mountbatten exemplified the continuing ascendancy of the British aristocracy in the twentieth century. After serving as a naval officer in both world wars, he was named viceroy of India and oversaw negotiations on Indian independence. He subsequently served the government in a variety of positions until his assassination by members of the Irish Republican Army in 1979. ©HULTON-DEUTSCH COLLECTION/CORBIS

In Germany as in Italy it was only when the fascist regime was clearly losing the war that core elements in the traditional elite sought to overthrow it. The German conservatives, unlike in Italy, had no king through whom to remove the fascist leader, and many of them paid with their lives for the failure of the attempt to assassinate Hitler and assume power by coup d'état in 1944. There was symbolism in the fact that Hitler's would-be assassin was Count Claus von Stauffenberg, a member of the South German Catholic aristocracy. With few exceptions the Catholic, and above all Bavarian, aristocracy was not closely associated with fascism, unlike significant sections of the Protestant nobility. Nevertheless it is worth noting that many of the

key figures in the July assassination plot came from the cream of the Prussian aristocracy and that their opposition to Hitler was deeply rooted in Christian ethics and dated back to his first moments in power. Though it is nonsense to see most of the Protestant German aristocracy as long-term enemies of Nazism, the aristocracy was certainly not more pro-Nazi than the professional middle class or indeed the mass electorate. Given contemporary ideology and the balance of political forces in early-twenty-first-century Germany, it is often convenient, however, to pretend otherwise.

THE ARISTOCRACY IN POST-1945 EUROPE
World War II hugely weakened the German and European aristocracy. Everywhere in the Soviet

bloc the aristocracy was expropriated. Because the core of German aristocratic power and wealth lay in the territories that fell to communism, this in itself reduced the significance of the traditional elites in German life, even though unlike in Japan the victorious Western Allies did not expropriate the aristocracy in their German occupation zones. In addition, however, all significant sections of West German society after 1945 were determined to make a clean break with the past and had an unconditional commitment to democratic values.

Whereas the great majority of East German aristocrats fled to noncommunist parts of Germany, many Polish and Hungarian aristocrats lived on in their countries, with some individuals playing notable roles in cultural life and even in post-1989 politics. Some property was restored to aristocratic families after 1989, though this amounted to relatively little; some of the most spectacular acts of restitution occurred in the Czech Republic.

Interestingly, the postcommunist Czech Republic was more generous to its Habsburg-era aristocracy than Germany was to the former landowning class of Prussia, Saxony, and Mecklenburg, the great majority of whom were excluded from the restitution of property. Though legal (and indeed Russian) obstacles to restitution were cited, the widespread belief that the eastern aristocracy had been historical enemies of democracy and supporters of fascism facilitated this decision.

By 2000 the aristocracy was of minimal importance in Europe, though some heads of great aristocratic families were still extremely wealthy, especially in Britain, and a disproportionate number of aristocrats could still be found in the higher reaches of some European diplomatic services. The European monarchs and their families had mostly escaped from the traditional aristocratic social circle and had become part of the international world of celebrities, alternately fawned on and hounded by the paparazzi and their readership. Thus the restoration of the Bourbons in 1975 did not much enhance the role of aristocracy in Spain. Even royalty was finding it increasingly hard to compete in the European public imagination with the heroes of the screen and the sports stadium.

See also **Alfonso XIII; Bourgeoisie; Churchill, Winston; Diana, Princess of Wales; Franco, Francisco; Horthy, Miklós; Nicholas II; Working Class.**

BIBLIOGRAPHY

Cannadine, David. *The Decline and Fall of the British Aristocracy.* New Haven, Conn., 1990.

Cardoza, Anthony L. *Aristocrats in Bourgeois Italy: The Piedmontese Nobility, 1861–1930.* Cambridge, U.K., 1997.

Gibson, Ralph, and Martin Blinkhorn, eds. *Landownership and Power in Modern Europe.* London, 1991.

Lieven, Dominic. *The Aristocracy in Europe, 1815–1914.* Houndmills, U.K., 1992.

Malinowski, Stephan. *Vom König zum Führer.* Berlin, 2003.

Mayer, Arno J. *The Persistence of the Old Regime.* London, 1981.

Reif, Heinz. *Adel im 19. und 20. Jahrhundert.* Munich, 1999.

DOMINIC LIEVEN

ARMENIA. In the early twenty-first century the Armenian population worldwide is estimated at 5.6 million. In addition to about 3 million inhabitants of the Republic of Armenia, the diaspora includes about 1.25 million in the United States, 900,000 in the former Soviet Union, 375,000 in France, and 310,000 in the Middle East. Fewer than 50,000 Armenians inhabit Turkey, most in Istanbul.

At the turn of the twentieth century the Ottoman Empire was home to most of the world's Armenians; many lived in Constantinople and in the region known as Anatolia, the historical cradle of this Eastern Orthodox people. In 1914 the Turks estimated the number of Armenians to be 1.3 million, while the Armenian patriarchate put the population at 2.4 million. The Armenians comprised the largest and most trustworthy community in the Ottoman empire. In the second half of the nineteenth century Armenians supported efforts to democratize the empire and to spur economic development. The great massacres of 1894–1896 ordered by Sultan Abdul-Hamid II (r. 1876–1909), doubtlessly led to the birth of an Armenian nationalist movement, but did not in themselves undermine the allegiance of the Armenian people, as a whole, to the empire. The almost complete disappearance of Armenians from Turkey—that is, from Constantinople and the vast western part of

Armenian troops march out of Erivan, the Armenian capital, to meet Turkish forces, November 1920. ©BETTMANN/
CORBIS

historic Armenia (the Armenian Republic is situated in the east)—was the result of a genocide perpetrated, beginning in 1915, by the Young Turks, who had come to power in what remained of the Ottoman Empire. In addition to mass murder, the policy of the new Kemalist state forced thousands of surviving Armenians to emigrate at the end of World War I, during the Turkish war of independence conducted by Mustafa Kemal Atatürk (1881–1938).

The history of the Armenian people in the twentieth century is doubly tragic. Armenians were victims of the first modern genocide, which destroyed half to two-thirds of the entire community and, in addition, the survivors were cleansed from their historic lands. No other genocide in the twentieth century, moreover, so ensured the impossibility of survivors returning to the place where absolute extermination was the chosen method for elimination.

The story is still more tragic if one considers Turkey's persistent refusal to recognize the genocide as a historical fact. Denial frustrates mourning, keeps the events fresh, and perpetuates suffering. It also polarizes the communal memory concerning the great catastrophe of 1915–1917, often to such an extent that younger Armenians are deprived of the broader dimensions of their history.

From the horrific circumstances surrounding the genocide, however, one can discern an essential trait that helps illuminate the whole history of the Armenians. From their origins until 1914, they were an eastern people, but great numbers of them in the diaspora subsequently constituted a western community that adapted readily in countries where they were accepted. Armenians fully adapted to life in France and the United States, readily espousing the values and history of their adopted lands.

EARLY HISTORY

The Armenians originated in the valleys of the Euphrates and Arsanias (also known as the Murat) Rivers in Asia Minor, where they settled in the second millennium B.C.E. Their Indo-European language distinguished them from Semitic and African peoples. The Kingdom of Armenia was created about 330 B.C.E. Six hundred years later, in 313 C.E., after being conquered by the Romans, the Armenians converted to Christianity and, indeed, Armenia became the first officially Christian nation. Ruled first by the Byzantine Empire, then by the Ottoman Empire, the nation's long history indicates its people's ability to adapt and reconstitute state, kingdom, principality and, above all, church.

From the fifteenth century Armenians were under Turkish-Ottoman rule in the west and Persian domination in the east; a portion of Armenian lands fell to Russia in the nineteenth century. Through the centuries the Armenian Church, with a patriarchate established about 1540 in Constantinople, played an important role in maintaining a powerful feeling of union among the disparate Armenian enclaves. The church united almost the entire community, save minorities of about 10 percent Roman Catholic and 5 percent Protestant.

MASSACRES AND EXPULSION

Conditions for Armenians in the Ottoman Empire deteriorated considerably early in the twentieth century. The Hamidian massacres endangered the Armenian nationalist agenda and relations with the Turkish majority grew tense, especially with the arrival of Balkan refugees who perceived Armenians, because they were Christian, as the cause of all their misery. Extreme poverty was also an issue, the result of looting during the pogroms and significant taxation imposed on Armenians by the Sublime Porte, as the Ottoman government was known, to service foreign debt. Finally, Armenians increasingly became the scapegoats of the radical nationalism promulgated by the Young Turks who, after coming to power with the 1908 revolution, sought a solution in the eastern part of the empire to all the disasters that had befallen them in the west. The pan-Turkish dream sought unification of the Turkophone lands from Eastern Thrace to Siberia. Armenians densely populated the territory extending south to the Taurus Mountains and the province of Cilicia, north to the Caucasus,

west to near the center of Anatolia, and the east as far as Iran. They thus represented a major obstacle to this huge nationalist project. Moreover, when Ottoman defeats brought part of the Armenian population under Russian authority, those remaining in Turkey were increasingly viewed as the enemy within. Western efforts to protect the Armenian community by exerting various kinds of pressure on the Sublime Porte were not truly effective; on the contrary, they magnified the Turkish perception of the Armenians as traitors. The Armenian community could only look to itself, to its nascent political organization—the revolutionary Dashnak Party and the liberal Hintchak Party—as well as to timely and often crucial help from Christian missionaries and foreign-aid associations. But with a second wave of huge massacres in Cilicia in 1909, the situation deteriorated still further.

At about this time emigration to Europe and United States accelerated, an apparent response to the Ottoman persecutions and increasing poverty. On the eve of World War I there were positive developments in the Russian-controlled Armenian territories of Transcaucasia after a series of Russian military victories over the Ottoman armies. Russia dispensed a liberal domestic policy and, on an international plane, favored autonomy for a large part of Armenia—including the portion that had belonged to Turkey. Nevertheless, at a secret gathering at the beginning of World War I, Armenian leaders decided to declare loyalty to the states on which they depended. Their devotion to the nations in which they lived came before their claims of identity as a people.

Like almost all Orthodox Christians in eastern Europe, the Armenians were caught up in the torments and massacres of World War I. Some three hundred thousand from the Van and Erzurum provinces in Eastern Anatolia were evacuated at the beginning of the war by the Russians. Others settled in Transcaucasia, in the territory that would become the Armenian Republic, on the eastern border of historic Armenia. But Armenians who remained near the front lines were among the two hundred thousand civilians killed by the Turkish army during its 1916 offensive in Caucasia, according to Russian statistics. A number survived their deportation to camps in Mesopotamia and Syria, while an estimated fifty thousand Armenians were able to reach the environs of Aleppo, where they

Bread is distributed to starving refugees at a distribution center in Armenia, 1920. ©Bettmann/Corbis

endured miserable living conditions. About two hundred thousand others took refuge in Cilicia, counting on protection from the occupying French. But France, threatened by the Turks' progress in their war of independence, agreed on an armistice with Atatürk on 30 May 1920, and the next year signed a separate peace treaty that renounced claims on Cilicia.

The scale of extermination visited upon the Armenians in the years 1915 to 1917 wiped them entirely out of the heart of Anatolia, which henceforth became, according to Kemalist ideology, the historic cradle of Turk civilization. Only a small community survived in Istanbul. In 1927 the first Turkish census reported sixty-five thousand to seventy-seven thousand Armenians registered as inhabitants, their identity papers stamped "ermeni" (Armenian). Some six hundred thousand to seven hundred thousand Armenians escaped the genocide. The fate of the survivors varied.

After considerable hardships, Armenian refugees thereafter ended up in Aleppo, which became the central staging area for out-migration. The diaspora may be said to have begun here. Some Armenians went on to settle in Syria, Lebanon, Egypt, and Iraq; for others, Aleppo was a stepping-stone to the United States and France, the two most frequent western destinations. Still others moved to the Balkans, Greece, Romania, Bulgaria, and other countries.

However, Armenians were forbidden to return to Turkey, their former homeland. An agreement between Atatürk and the League of Nations, signed after the Lausanne Treaty, made this prohibition official. Hundreds of thousands of Armenians were thus declared stateless and were forced to seek a radically different way of life, disconnected from their past—apart from memories and photographs that enabled some to preserve family or community ties. Outside of Constantinople, it was rare for all members of an Armenian family to survive. During the genocide Turkish and Kurdish families captured Armenian women and orphans and forced them to convert to Islam. In addition, Armenians in Turkey under the Kemalist Republic were compelled to change their names and to adapt to Turkish manners and the Turkish way of life. They remained in Turkey but lost their Armenian identity.

THE ARMENIAN STATE

An Armenian state was nonetheless created at the end of World War I and, although it came under Soviet domination, would finally outlast the USSR. After the Bolshevik Revolution in October 1917 Armenians in Caucasia fought the Ottoman Empire in defense of Eastern Armenia. In January 1918 a Turkish offensive threatened Yerevan but the Armenian volunteers won several decisive battles, which turned out to be a prelude to the Armenian declaration of independence. Turkey recognized Armenia in the Caucasus with the signing of the Batoum Treaty on 4 June 1918.

The new state, neighbor to other Caucasian independent states such as Georgia and Azerbaijan, immediately found itself in a dramatic and dangerous situation. Its population of one million, including thirty thousand Muslims, was overwhelmed by three hundred thousand refugees living in unsanitary and nutritionally disastrous conditions. The population dropped by 20 percent in a year. Mobilization of public opinion and resources, particularly from the U.S. Near East Relief organization, which was already in action against the genocide, lent support. Progress was swift, with democratic reforms, enfranchisement of both men and women, free and compulsory education, and economic restructuring that included nationalization and agricultural modernization. British troops disembarked at Batoum to enable the republic to extend to the whole of Eastern Armenia—some forty-six thousand square kilometers—more land than the Armenians had ever occupied.

At the Paris Peace Conference, which began on 18 January 1919, the Armenian delegation presented a project for an Armenian mandate that extended from the Black Sea to the Mediterranean Ocean. This idea was turned down in favor of an independent Armenia that still had a surface area twice the size of the first state proclaimed in 1918. But the U.S. Senate's refusal to ratify the treaties, together with Atatürk's victorious war over the Allies, dashed Armenian hopes—especially those of the Dashnak Party, then in power in Yerevan.

SOVIET DOMINATION TO INDEPENDENCE

By 1920 the Armenian situation seemed hopeless. While Kemalist troops marched into the Kars and Ardahan provinces, Armenia's neighbors, the

A man searches coffins for the body of his brother following the 1988 earthquake in Armenia. ©MIROSLAV ZAJÍC/CORBIS

Azeris, launched an offensive against the Armenian Republic, where there was, in addition, Bolshevik-led unrest. In December 1920 the Dashnak government resigned the same day that Armenia was forced to sign the Treaty of Alexandropol. The new nation lost half its territory to Turkey and Azerbaijan, which gained the region of Nagorno Karabakh, in spite of the fact that 95 percent of the population of that region was Armenian. This represented a double defeat in that Armenia lost much of its territory to the Turks while being brought into the Soviet Union; in 1936 Armenia would be officially declared a Soviet Republic. Even so, Armenians retained their identity and preserved their culture, thanks in great part to the power of the Armenian Church, which the Soviet authorities failed to destroy.

But Stalinization had a profound influence on Armenia that only started to ebb after World War II.

In Joseph Stalin's "great patriotic war," declared against Nazi Germany in 1943, Armenians played conspicuous roles in the Soviet victory. In the aftermath of war, some one hundred thousand Armenians of the diaspora, especially those living in France, responded to an appeal to rejoin the republic. This did not work out as expected, however. While Armenians from France returned, many more emigrated to the United States. Soviet Armenia nevertheless flourished both economically and culturally, for the most part. The Armenian homeland consolidated what remained of its historic territory, enabling it to confront consecutive crises that arose with the collapse of the Soviet Union. A referendum on 21 September 1991 brought Armenia complete independence.

THE NEW REPUBLIC OF ARMENIA

Never reconciled to the loss of Nagorno Karabakh, in 1988 Armenians mobilized for reunification. The neighboring Azeris reacted violently, persecuting Armenians and organizing a pogrom in Sumgait in February 1988. As Soviet power was everywhere contested, an Armenian Committee of the Karabakh was formed, though its operation was hampered by a devastating earthquake on 7 December 1988 that killed some forty-five thousand Armenians. A major leader emerged, however. Levon Ter Petrosian (b. 1945), although imprisoned for a time, organized the Armenian National Movement after his release in June 1989. When this party won the elections in October 1990 he became president of the new Republic of Armenia.

The first years of Armenian independence were difficult and resulted in considerable out-migration. Military operations that aimed to reunite the Karabakh region did not succeed; and, although both parties signed a cease-fire in 1994, Armenia and Azerbaijan remained technically at war. A positive demographic change came with the arrival of Armenians from the "interior diaspora" of the former Soviet Union. Despite difficult relations with neighboring countries and tensions throughout the region, Armenians could hope that the twenty-first century would open a new phase in their nation's history as a European and democratic republic, contending with past and future, reunited after a diaspora in the wake of genocide and decades of Soviet rule.

Exiled Armenians, with the impossibility of returning to their homeland, were forced to live and think with an international perspective—at least for those who settled in Western Europe and the United States. Armenians in the diaspora identify themselves and are recognized as U.S. or French citizens. This should not paper over the significant hardships that emigres experienced, but it helps explain why European and U.S. Armenians did not return to the Republic of Armenia. However, Armenians worldwide preserve common values and a shared identity, the intangible but painful memory of genocide, the spiritual and financial connection to the Armenian Church, and consciousness of an old and prestigious history. Powerful associations energize and organize the contemporary Armenian identity. The Armenian General Benevolent Union, for example, operates worldwide. There are also numerous, often highly patriotic, organizations within the various countries of the diaspora that struggle to compel worldwide recognition of the Armenian genocide. This effort has achieved undeniable progress since the 1990s. At the turn of the twenty-first century travels and various research projects have enabled European Armenians to discover the history of their ancestors in Eastern Turkey and even to work with Turkish intellectuals to recover a culture that was often enough not monocultural but collective, beneficial to both peoples.

See also **Armenian Genocide; Atatürk, Mustafa Kemal; Turkey; World War I; World War II.**

BIBLIOGRAPHY

Avakian, Arra S., and Ara John Movesian. *Armenia: A Journey through History.* Fresno, Calif., 2000.

Bournoutian, George A. *A Concise History of the Armenian People: From Ancient Times to the Present.* 4th ed. Costa Mesa, Calif., 2005.

Hovannisian, Richard G. *Republic of Armenia.* 4 vols. Berkeley, Calif., 1971–1996.

Libaridian, Gerard. *Modern Armenia: People, Nation, State.* New Brunswick, N.J., 2004.

Miller, Donald E., and Lorna Touryan Miller. *Survivors: An Oral History of the Armenian Genocide.* Berkeley, Calif., and London, 1993.

Sargsyan, Gevorg. *From Crisis to Stability in the Armenian Power Sector: Lessons Learned from Armenia's Energy Reform Experience.* Washington, D.C., 2006.

Walker, Christopher J, ed. *Visions of Ararat: Writings on Armenia.* London and New York, 1997.

VINCENT DUCLERT

ARMENIAN GENOCIDE.

The destruction of the Eastern Armenians, carried out by the rulers of the Ottoman Empire during World War I, is a signal event in twentieth-century history. Signal because of its genocidal nature, which at the time had never been seen before and which, to borrow a phrase from journalist and scholar Samantha Power, ushered the world into the "age of genocides." Signal as concerns the will of a government, a state, and a people to destroy an ethnic group fully integrated into the empire, having contributed to its prosperity as well as its past splendor. Signal with respect to the inability of the civilized world, and the victorious Allied Powers in particular, to fully gauge the historical scope of the tragedy and to erect interstate barriers to prevent its repetition (in that the juridical arsenal that arose out of the Nuremberg trials and the United Nations Convention on the Prevention and Punishment of the Crime of Genocide arose only after the destruction of Europe's Jews). Signal as concerns the battle waged since the 1970s (and which rages still) for the events to be retroactively classified as a genocide—a vital step for a people still deprived of the means for mourning and remembering. Signal with respect to the New Turkey's denial of the reality of the destruction of the Armenians and the scale of the massacres themselves. Signal, finally, concerning the challenge posed to historians to mold their knowledge in such a way as to yield principles of reconciliation between peoples and the responsibility of humanity.

BEGINNINGS OF THE EXTERMINATION OF A MINORITY

Between one-half and two-thirds of the Armenians living along the outer reaches of the empire were exterminated, either directly in the central Anatolian regions where they were living, over the course of massive deportations to the south, or else after having arrived at their final destinations in Syria and Mesopotamia. This, the empire's preeminent minority group, reputed to be its most faithful, would ultimately lose more than a million of its members, massacred under horribly cruel conditions that revolted the diplomats and missionaries who witnessed the origins and execution of the destruction of a people identified solely by their religion—Christianity. Virtually all the survivors were forced into exile in order to end a conflict whose goal was a "war of national liberation" waged between 1919 and 1923, so called by General Mustafa Kemal, leader of the Nationalist Turks. Anatolia, where the majority of Armenians were concentrated, (including Constantinople and the great Aegean coastal cities like Smyrna [Izmir]), was emptied of its minorities in order to secure a firm foothold for the nation-state sought by this "Father of the Turks," Atatürk. According to the republic's first census in 1927, only 65,000 to 77,000 Armenians were to remain in Turkey, essentially all in Istanbul, out of a population estimated in 1882 of 2.4 million (based on figures provided by the Patriarchal Authority).

These facts are openly admitted by everyone, including numerous eyewitness testimonies, the trials that took place in Constantinople and Berlin between 1919 and 1921, and an abundance of historical studies of the period. The effects of this accumulated knowledge permit us to corroborate the number of victims, the specific means used to destroy persons and groups, and the methods employed to administer collective death. It also authorizes us to re-map the planning undertaken for the deportations and mass murders, to understand the workings behind the ethnic and national hatreds that formed the ideological wellsprings of destruction, and to establish once and for all the direct responsibility of the Young Turk government and the Ottoman state at war, as well as the role the Allied Powers played in abandoning the survivors and refusing all Armenian rights in Anatolia, a vast territory once called "Great Armenia."

The destruction of the Armenians was based on the development of a transnationalist ideology that arose out of the growing difficulties experienced by the Ottoman Empire during the second half of the nineteenth century. The empire, which had lost several of its rich European provinces during the first Balkan wars, was transformed into a bloody dictatorship erected against internal enemies.

The "Red" Sultan Abdul-Hamid II encouraged the exploitation of the Armenians, then ordered their widespread massacre. Unanimous protest on the part of Western public opinion, combined with the threat of armed intervention, ended up stopping an unprecedented murderous rampage responsible for the deaths of two hundred thousand victims. Regime change in 1908 and the outbreak of the Young Turk Revolution did little to change the course of the new Ottoman-Turk nationalism and its violence against minority groups. In 1909, several thousand Armenians were massacred in Constantinople, and twenty-five thousand perished in Cilicy while sailors from the Triple Entente stood by and watched.

The political and social situation for Armenians become even worse after the empire's losses in the Balkan wars of 1912. They became the primary obstacle to the rebirth of the nation sought by the Young Turks, who erected a military dictatorship founded on the ideological project of pan-Turkism on the eve of the outbreak of World War I. The influx into Anatolia of Ottoman Turk people fleeing the extreme violence of the Balkan wars rendered the continued existence of minority groups even more problematic, because they came to seem more and more like traitors and foreign agents. Violence against the Armenian population resumed after war broke out on the western front and increased even further when Turkish soldiers discovered that Russia had enlisted volunteers from the Armenian regions under its control. Faithful to the Russians on that side of the border, the Armenians were just as faithful within the empire, whose Young Turk army they loyally served.

But the loss to Russia at Sarikamis in January 1915 unleashed a conspiracy theory that styled the Armenians as enemy agents and furthermore allowed for the military disaster to be justified without questioning the responsibility of the Ottoman commanders. Inscribed as it was in the ultranationalist ideology of the army officers and Young Turk Committee of Union and Progress (CUP), the conspiracy theory legitimated the decision to eliminate the Armenians and ultimately furnished a society in decline with an easy causal explanation for the reverses suffered by the empire, which had been building up for years.

A PROCESS OF DESTRUCTION IN FIVE PHASES

In the first phase, immediately following the defeat at Sarikamis, massive reprisals against the Armenians occurred in the war-affected regions of Bitlis, Much, and Sasun. The survivors, stripped of all their possessions, reduced to a state of utter misery and extreme humiliation, were deported, along with the sizable community at Zaytun which had previously been sheltered from the massacres that had taken place at the end of the previous century. They were driven by road and on trains to the western edge of the Mesopotamian desert, either to Konya or Deïr-es-Zor. These initial acts prove that the Turkish populations were ready to avenge their own humiliations on an innocent minority transformed into agents of betrayal. They also showed how deportations were used as a complement to on-site extermination, especially when diplomats and missionaries were able to oppose the murders in situ. Simultaneously the numerous Armenian soldiers and officers of the Imperial Army were disarmed and executed. This marked the beginning of the second phase of the Armenian community's destruction—the elimination of the elite members of the military and public administration, despite how this was to have a profound affect on the empire's functioning and defense.

The third phase took place in the empire's capital on the evenings of 24–25 April 1915 and the days that followed. A sizable portion of the Armenian elites (23,405 people out of a community of 150,000) was swept up, tortured, deported to Angora, and there killed. Minister of the Interior Talat Pasha justified these arrests with reference to the uprising at Van and the intervention of Russian troops that evacuated 210,000 people threatened with annihilation. The protests of religious dignitaries and above all of ambassadors and diplomats, including those from Germany and Austria, dissuaded him from perpetrating additional acts of violence upon the Armenians of Constantinople.

The fourth phase, which was the most characteristic of the genocidal process, consisted of the commencement of the general deportation of the Armenians living in Anatolia, the cradle of their civilization. A "Provisional Deportation Law" was quickly promulgated on 27 May 1915, which did little more than give legal stamp to a fait accompli.

The law authorized the military authorities to take any action deemed necessary against "the populations of cities or villages suspected of espionage or treason" (article 2), without specifically mentioning the Armenians. However, the decree of 30 May, specifying how the law was to be applied, directly concerned Armenians "relocated to other places due to conditions of war and emergency policy needs" as well as the management of their land and other property. A legal framework was therefore established for a vast plan of deportation, which consisted of emptying all the empire's western and eastern provinces of their Armenian populations, who were to be driven by force to desert spaces extending between Mosul and Aleppo. This constituted the turntable of the deportation completed by the end of 1916. The deportation ended in the physical destruction of almost all of those displaced. Following the deportation of Armenians in the areas of Zaytun and Van, the plan turned to the larger populations constituting "Great Armenia," meaning one million Armenians from Trebizond on the Black Sea to Diyarbakir on the Syrian border, with Sivas on the west and Van to the east.

These communities, composed of both urbanites and villagers alike, already weakened by any number of previous massacres, generally made leaderless by the preliminary assassination of their notables, and traditionally respectful of Ottoman authority anyway, offered no resistance whatsoever. Only 150,000 Armenians managed to escape to the Russian-occupied Caucasus. Whole populations were then massacred en route, either by military units and police, by local populations of Turks and Kurds, or else by the actual coordinators of the deportations, the men of the Special Organization.

Eyewitness accounts repeatedly mention in particular rapes, physical mutilations, and the massacres of women, children, and newborn babies. Those who escaped death were forced to contend with severe hunger and thirst in the middle of summer with no means of sustenance whatsoever. The empire's western provinces, which were equipped with a railroad infrastructure, were also affected by the deportation orders, allowing three hundred thousand Armenians to be deported in just a few short months.

Despite this, some five hundred thousand Armenians escaped death by deportation, because the often primitive techniques visited upon them prevented their total extermination. Upon their arrival in Mesopotamia and Syria therefore, they were interned in camps resembling the antechambers of Hell, where they were herded into caves (Deïr-es-Zor), thrown into the Euphrates, and even burned alive in immense pits. Just fifty thousand managed to regroup outside Aleppo, primarily women and children who had somehow escaped forced Islamicization and slavery in Kurdish tribal villages. Throughout the rest of the empire the hunt for survivors, which was formally declared by the regime and which lasted until the final months of the war, was particularly focused on the elimination of orphaned children or, for those who were lucky enough, on forced conversion to Islam. This was because the Armenian Genocide, unlike the Nazis' Final Solution, did not call for the total extermination of all Armenians as persons. Conversion to Islam sufficed to suspend the genocidal process. The ideology that sustained it was therefore more ethnic, nationalist, and religious than fundamentally racist in nature.

All told, 1.2 million Armenians were exterminated either in situ, during the deportations, or in the camps. Another 100,000—mostly women and young girls—were abducted and converted to Islam, and 150,000 managed to survive the camps or to hide with Turkish, Kurdish, or Arab families. A small number, such as the 4,200 combatants in the battle at Musa Dagh, evacuated by the French vessel *Jeanne d'Arc* cruising near Alexandria, were saved by the Allied Powers. The Armenian minority simply no longer existed as such within the confines of the Ottoman Empire, save in highly reduced form in the two metropolises of Constantinople and Smyrna.

But the terror engendered by the genocide of their co-religionists, and the continuation of the massacres during Mustafa Kemal's war of national liberation, led to the exile of almost the entire population of survivors, who fled toward Europe and the United States. An additional two hundred thousand Armenians would reach the Caucasus region, future birthplace of the tiny Republic of Armenia. None of the survivors would ever return to their homelands, a situation that lends a unique quality to the Armenian Genocide: it is the only instance in which no reparations have been paid and which has never been granted any formal recognition.

The bodies of Armenians lie on the ground following a massacre by Turks, June 1919. ©BETTMANN/CORBIS

THE GENOCIDAL PLAN OF A REGIME AND A STATE

It is not possible in the early twenty-first century to demonstrate the genocidal nature of the Young Turk regime with reference to an infallible document, because the archives of the Ottoman Empire (those at least that survive in present-day Turkey) are inaccessible. Specialists prefer to discount Talât Paşa's telegrams published by Aram Andonian in 1920, based on the near total loss of the originals and due to the propaganda purposes behind their release. This does not mean, however, that they are fakes, as official Turkish history would have it. Their authenticity is easily verified when they are situated with respect to the reasonings put forth at the time and the general sequence of events, which evince the application of a plan to exterminate the empire's Armenian minority. Unlike tribunals, which require direct evidence to convict someone, historians bring to light explanatory systems that encompass all the facts and inscribe them in their broader contexts, resulting in the construction of a historical continuum that proves the existence of genocidal intentions that were actually carried out.

The destruction of the Eastern Armenians during World War I is verifiable on the one hand by the reality of previous massacres, which reveals the existence of powerful mechanisms designed to eliminate the empire's minority groups, exploit their members so as to psychologically and socially degrade them, and ultimately hand them over to Kurdish tribes, irregular troops, and Turkish activists. The great massacres of 1894–1896, followed by others in 1909–1912, constituted a profound shock to the Armenian community, which was stripped of its land, ancestry, and culture. These massacres alone contributed to the deaths of 300,000 people, the forcible conversion of 100,000 others, the abduction into slavery of 100,000 women and young girls, and the exile of approximately 200,000 Armenians. These prewar activities paved the way for the genocide of 1915 through their terrorist methods, ideological wellsprings, and in the numbers of their victims. An intent to commit genocide may also be corroborated with reference to the systematic official discourse used to transform the Armenians into internal enemies, scapegoats for military defeat, and imminent threats to the nation of Ottoman Turks. It is equally evident in the massive deportation orders and the role the Special Organization, directly attached to the Unionist Triumvirate, played in coordinating the massacres along the highways and in the camps. It becomes clear by studying the actions on the ground of the Ottoman authorities who took on the large part of the burden of the extermination itself, a systematic enterprise that proves that the destruction of the Armenians did not equate to a series of war crimes but was a deliberate plan to make this pre-eminent non-Muslim eastern minority group simply disappear, because it was an obstacle to the ethnic unification of the empire and the full establishment of the Young Turk dictatorship. The fact that the decision was made to mobilize forces for internal operations in an empire already militarily hobbled by the defeats it had suffered in 1915 points to the degree of importance placed on their success and the true nature of the hoped-for outcome. Finally, the sheer number of victims cannot be explained solely with reference to explosions of hatred against individuals being held responsible for military setbacks. With two-thirds of the population exterminated, the level of Armenian victims nearly reached that of the genocide of the Jews, but this across a large swath of territory and a very shortened time period, just one-and-a-half years (April 1915 to December 1916), although the extermination would continue until the end of the war and beyond. During this time, as the empire lost ground on numerous fronts, Armenians allied with the Russians took the advantage to carry out reprisals for the massacres against Muslim populations. Official Turkish history, in its battle to revise historical reality, no longer hesitates to qualify these acts as "genocidal."

The final historical proof that the Young Turk regime harbored genocidal intentions rests in the decision taken by its principal authorities, just prior to the empire's total collapse on 30 October 1918 and their flight aboard a German naval vessel, to proceed with the large-scale destruction of their archives. However, they failed to erase every trace of their criminal intentions, primarily because large amounts of evidence and testimony corroborating the process of extermination were collected from throughout the empire.

EVIDENCE-GATHERING AND TRYING THE GUILTY

As a great diplomatic power that was opening up to the powerful Western countries for the purposes of its development, the Ottoman Empire hosted large numbers of foreign diplomats throughout its various territories. Europeans and Americans also dominated the staffs of many of the charitable organizations and missions there. These men and women delivered horrifying accounts of how the Armenian annihilation was carried out. The Allied Powers' foreign consulates had the wherewithal to preserve these testimonies, out of humanitarian concern as well as for use as a weapon in wartime. Furthermore, communications in the same vein were gathered by numerous American consuls posted to the Ottoman Empire under the authority of U.S. ambassador Henry Morgenthau, as well as by German and Austrian diplomats and foreign nationals. The British "Blue Book," first published in 1916 and for many years accompanied by an introduction from Arnold Toynbee, furnished much-needed guarantees of objectivity. In the same year, the German pastor Johannes Lepsius, who had pleaded the Armenian cause directly to Talât Paşa in vain, made public his extensive *Report* (1918). In various other depositions, witnesses insisted that this was the deliberate destruction of a people. Thus for instance the German ambassador, Baron Hans von Wangenheim, on 7 July 1915 believed "the government is in fact pursuing the goal of annihilating the Armenian race throughout the Ottoman Empire."

The growing chorus of accusations emanating from international circles weighed heavily on the decision of the new Ottoman government formed after the fall of the Young Turks from power to try those responsible for the extermination. The trials held in Constantinople in 1919 and 1920 ended in stiff sentences, including the death penalty in absentia for the members of the Triumvirate. The trials also furnished an opportunity for compiling damning documentary proof that outlines specifically the roles played by the Young Turk Party and the Special Organization as well as to gather together the confessions of guilt. The work of two official investigatory commissions further reinforced these attempts to document and reflect. Yet the Allied Powers never sought to prosecute at the international level a process they themselves had recognized and denounced as terrifying in nature.

THE FAILURE OF ALLIES AND THE APATHY OF COMPATRIOTS

On 24 May 1915, even before the publication of the General Deportation Order, the Allies directed a solemn warning to the Young Turks: "In view of these new crimes of Turkey against humanity and civilization, the Allied governments announce publicly...that they will hold personally responsible [for] these crimes all members of the...government and those of their agents who are implicated in such massacres." The threat had no effect on the fate of the Armenians and was never carried out. The Allied governments did not seek to protect this population. Nor did they conduct trials within the confines of the Paris Peace Conference. The Treaty of Sèvres did, however, provide the necessary legal framework to pursue the authors of the crimes perpetrated by the Ottoman state against its Armenian citizens. But the preservation of Ottoman sovereignty and the trials being held in Constantinople diffused the early intentions of the occupiers to try the guilty themselves. Later on it was the Allies' will that flagged, as the geopolitical situation in that part of the world became increasingly complex. The collective renunciation allowed these tragic events to pass from European consciousness, which was only piqued from time to time by isolated protests coming from intellectuals such as the Austrian-Jewish novelist Franz Werfel, who wrote his book *Die vierzig Tage des Musa Dagh* (1933; Forty days in Musa Dagh) after having witnessed "the devastating spectacle of refugee children...maimed and eaten away by starvation" at Aleppo in 1929.

The fading from history of the destruction of the Armenians also ensued from the relations of force that eventually prevailed between Turkey and the Allies. As early as 1920 General Mustafa Kemal battled the Ottoman government established after the empire's defeat. The "Victor at the Dardanelles" laid the foundations of a nation-state within the sanctuary of Anatolia. This new regime completely distanced itself from the search for justice and truth that had at least in part characterized the empire on the eve of its defeat. The 24 July 1923 Treaty of Lausanne, which designated the Republic of Turkey victor and outlined its borders, declared a general amnesty that pardoned those found guilty in the trials in 1919–1920 and led to the destruction of the nascent archives of the extermination itself. Atatürk's regime instilled a veritable ideology of history that grounded the republic on an ethnocentric, state-sponsored nationalism. In reaction to this attempt by Mustafa Kemal to wipe the slate clean, the Armenian Dachnak Party declared a "special mission": select militants would execute the sentences levied in Constantinople by assassinating those convicted in the European capitals where they had taken refuge. Talat Pasha's murderer, Salomon Teilirian, was arrested in Berlin and tried in June 1921. Pastor Lepsius and General Liman von Sanders, former chief of the Fifth Ottoman Army, recognized the reality of the extermination by testifying at his trial. "Before the word itself was even known, [these juries] were to accuse Talaat of being the primary author of a genocide, by acquitting Teilirian" (Chaliand and Ternon).

The rise of the dictatorships, the dawn of the era of large-scale ideological confrontation, and widespread anti-Semitism throughout Europe would all contribute to the near-total disappearance of any and all references to these events of 1915, which failed therefore to become the springboard for anticipating the process of the destruction of the Jews of Europe.

THE BATTLE FOR CLASSIFICATION AS GENOCIDE

That being said, the Final Solution decreed against the Jews by the Nazis would lead to a major shift in how the events of 1915, and contemporary Armenian identity, came to be seen. The investigations into the genocide perpetrated during World War I, the indictments for crimes against humanity at the Nuremberg Trials in 1945–1946, and finally the formal definition of genocide itself, each led to an eventual revisiting of the history of the destruction of the Armenians and the historical as well as juridical terms used to classify it. On 9 December 1948 the United Nations Organization meeting in Paris unanimously adopted in plenary session the

Convention on the Prevention and Punishment of the Crime of Genocide. Is the extermination of the Armenians, which is indubitably a genocide in historical terms, also one in legal terms as well? In this instance history makes law—a fact that may even be verified with reference to the origins of the concept of genocide itself, such as it was developed for the United Nations Convention in 1943 by Raphael Lemkin. To choose to classify the Armenian genocide as such in legal terms therefore risks weakening its accusatory power, because it cuts it off from its historical foundations.

The grounds for the desire to obtain this classification nonetheless, which by the end of the 1980s had grown very strong among the Armenians in the diaspora and in the tiny Republic of Armenia in the Caucasus, is more directly related to the logic of politics and identity. The struggle for classification is clearly an Armenian response to Turkey's denial that the exterminations actually took place and its obstruction of the research needed to provide knowledge for the survivors to mourn by symbolically burying their parents, neighbors, friends, lovers, and fellow Christians—all of which presupposes that their extermination itself becomes known and recognized. Having the classification of genocide in hand was also a weapon for forcing the Turks (sovereign rulers over the lands where the destruction took place and of the state responsible for these murders) to admit the truth. In addition it was a means for writing the untold story of the Armenians, living and dead. This politics of memory carried out in the struggle for classification as genocide only began to produce tangible results as the twentieth century drew to a close. The first action taken was by the European Parliament, which on 18 June 1987 recognized that "the tragic events which took place from 1915–1917 against the Armenians residing in the territories of the Ottoman Empire constitute a genocide according to the definition laid out in the Convention for the Prevention and Punishment of the Crime of Genocide adopted by the United Nations General Assembly on 9 December 1948." The Parliament insisted, furthermore, on the "instigation of a political dialogue between Turkey and the delegated representatives of the Armenians" and condemned the avowed denials as "incontrovertible obstacles to the consideration of Turkey's eventual admission to the Community." Intense Turkish

diplomatic and political pressure failed to prevent the passage of similar acts of recognition by the legislatures of Russia (1995), Greece (1996), Belgium (1998), and finally Sweden, Italy, and France (2001). In April 2005, on the occasion of the ninetieth anniversary of the commencement of the genocide itself, the British House of Commons and the Polish Diet both adopted similar measures.

Armenian lobbying associations failed, however, to convince the United Nations to officially include the Armenian genocide in the legal briefs of the 1948 Convention. Despite strong support in the court of public opinion and the efforts of high-profile political figures, as of 2006 the U.S. administration and Congress continue to withhold their recognition and refuse to designate 24 April as an official Day of Commemoration. There, at least, Turkish diplomatic ultimatums continue to hold sway. These same pressures have provoked at times desperate acts on the part of militant Armenians who have sunk to engaging in terrorism to win their cause.

This radicalization of the struggle for genocidal classification has fed upon the intransigence of the Turkish positions taken with regard to this question, which are justified on the grounds of the need to defend Turkey from ideological and racist attacks.

THE DENIAL BY TURKEY AND HISTORY AS NATIONAL IDEOLOGY

When the Republic of Turkey was born in 1923, its founder, Mustafa Kemal, launched a project to completely reread history in order to construct a veritable teleology whose endpoint was the New Turkey itself. For this reason the question of denial can only be understood in relation to this conception of history, which largely predominates in the country even in the early twenty-first century. The denial of the genocide continues to mobilize political power, the state, and society in a quasi-unanimous defense of the nation threatened by these "Armenian allegations." The few independent historians in Turkey do their work under constant threat and are often sent into exile. Their attempts to organize professional conferences are prohibited by the government. The struggle against official historiography will continue to prove impossible so long as it is anchored at the highest levels of the state, claims leading academic experts as its adherents, and remains a part of decades of tradition.

Supported by Kemalist power, official Turkish historians established a counterhistory of the Ottoman Empire during World War I. The authors of this official literature minimized, relativized, and ultimately obscured the scale of the violence by foregrounding arguments to the effect that the size of the Armenian populations registered in the census and in the massacres was much lower than the numbers put forward by independent research; that the Kurds were the primary perpetrators of acts of violence; that other minorities were victims of massacres as well; that the Armenians were indeed prone to treason and simply had to be moved from the front-line areas; and that they were themselves responsible for numerous massacres. Some of this World War I counterhistory's authors even referred to the existence of an Armenian genocide against the Turks on the front line in the Caucasus region between 1917 and 1919—a commemorative monument was erected in 1999 at Igdir as a permanent challenge to the one that stands in Erevan in commemoration of the catastrophe of 1915. Those who maintain the suppression of the facts distance the Ottoman state from any criminal intentionality and deny any role played by the Turkish nation in the disappearance of the Anatolian Armenians. They attribute the massacres to a convergence of events stemming primarily (meaning exclusively) from the fact of the war itself and the extreme violence it inspired on the military fronts and in the empire's interior. The three hundred thousand Armenian dead would therefore be no more exceptional than the three million Turks lost to the world's first global conflict. Finally, they interpret the efforts to right the historical picture as evidence of a plot against Turkish national identity and ultimately against the existence of Turkey itself.

The source of the power this propaganda holds is to be found in the process that began during the republic's first years of existence, when Kemal relegated to historical discourse a determining role in the construction of the Turkish nation. The birth of Kemal's Turkey as a regional power and secular model imposed at best a silence concerning the facts, at worse an adherence to an official history

written by fiat from the top. The Armenians were alone responsible for their fate in World War I because of their agitations against the nation of Ottoman Turks. The revision of the rest of the story had already begun as early as 1916 when the Ottoman Empire published a "White Book" on the activities of Armenian Revolutionary Committees accused of seeking its defeat. After the war of independence, the New Turkey no doubt did in fact forge a permanent break with a regime that had pushed the Turks into corruption and defeat. But the gains won from the empire by "uprooting the Greek and Armenian populations of Anatolia" were recognized by the Turkish Historical Society founded in 1931. The Turkish bourgeoisie, newly formed out of the pillage of Armenian wealth, constituted from 1919 onward the social base for the war of independence itself. After World War II, Turkey strengthened its international position by joining the United Nations and then NATO, followed by its slow but steady efforts aimed at integrating with the European Union and forging a special alliance with Israel. In this way the country furnished itself with even more of the power it needed to defend its version of history, used to further its strategic interests, which are nonnegotiable in diplomatic and political terms. This state-centered line of reasoning has led Turkey to become the overseer of its national historians and to seek out foreign university specialists, primarily from the United States, ready to serve the cause of official history. Analysis of Turkish reactions to the ninetieth anniversary of the genocide's commencement proves the extent of their radicalization: Denouncing the "Armenian allegations" and those who propagate them has become a badge of nationalism and routine government practice. The moderate Islamic government of Recep Erdogan has played this radicalization card to the utmost, at the risk of amplifying an already heightened Islamic nationalism. Starting in April 2005 a major press campaign, accompanied by death threats and measures prohibiting his novels, took aim at the internationally renowned writer Orhan Pamuk. His crime was to have declared openly in a Swiss newspaper that "one million Armenians and 30,000 Kurds have been killed in Turkey." This new phase in the crusade against the genocide is in stark contrast to the gestures toward opening made during the so-called Özal era at the end of the 1980s, named for Turgut Özal, the prime minister and then president of Turkey who held power from 1983 until his mysterious death in April 1993. This reformist leader, profoundly religious but highly tolerant, and furthermore an economics professor educated in the United States, envisaged recognizing the genocide of 1915 and was headed toward a peaceful and political resolution of the Kurdish question as well.

CONCLUSION

In the early twenty-first century, beyond the stakes involved in the classification of genocide as such, the true question raised by the Armenian Genocide concerns the battle over history itself—over the history of the destruction of the Eastern Armenians certainly, but also and even more so over history as an independent field of inquiry, free of political threats and communal interests, capable of offering a more effective definition of genocide than the juridical norm. For history as a research activity identifies processes and causal mechanisms and writes accounts that go beyond what law is able to circumscribe. Historical knowledge can examine the mechanisms of Turkish denial and the uses of history already detailed here, and through their exposure lead the way toward getting past them. It can also reflect on the historical specificity of this genocide, on the differences between it and the other genocides of the twentieth century, and on the impediments to its full realization.

From this point forward, therefore, the goal would seem to be less about classifying the destruction of the Eastern Armenians, which is no doubt a genocide in historical terms, as it is to transform their story by inscribing it into that of the twentieth century as a whole. This is the meaning of the new age of historiography that is emerging in the twenty-first century and which is ensuring that the Armenian Genocide remains a continually relevant, indeed universal, fact. The sheer modernity of the words of U.S. Ambassador Henry Morgenthau and British Prime Minister Winston Churchill echoes loudly and painfully still: Morgenthau, when confronted with Talat Pasha's surprise that he, a Jew, was interested in the fate of Christians, responded: "You don't seem to realize that I am here not as a Jew but as American Ambassador," and Churchill maintained in his recollections that "in 1915 the Turkish Government began and ruthlessly carried out the infamous general massacre and deportation

of Armenians in Asia Minor.... The clearance of the race from Asia Minor was about as complete as such an act, on a scale so great, could well be.... There is no reasonable doubt that this crime was planned and executed for political reasons." These accusations expressed the highest of democratic values but fell upon deaf ears and were ultimately snuffed out. In order to render them louder and more inspiring in the future, it falls to us therefore to heighten humanity's historical conscience by raising its consciousness of events such as these and transmitting this knowledge to the greatest possible number.

See also **Armenia; Atatürk, Mustafa Kemal.**

BIBLIOGRAPHY

Primary Sources

Andonian, Aram. *Documents officiels concernant les massacres arméniens.* Paris, 1920.

Bryce, James, and Arnold Toynbee. *The Treatment of Armenians in the Ottoman Empire, 1915–1916* ("Blue Book"). Uncensored ed. Edited by Ara Sarafian. Princeton, N.J., 2000.

Davis, Leslie A. *The Slaughterhouse Province: An American Diplomat's Report on the Armenian Genocide, 1915–1917.* Introduction by Susan Blair. New Rochelle, N.Y., 1989.

Lemkin, Raphael. "Genocide: A New International Crime: Punishment and Prevention." *Revue internationale de droit penal* 10 (1946): 360–370.

———. "Genocide as a Crime under International Law." *American Journal of International Law* 41, no. 1 (1947): 145–151.

Lepsius, Johannes. *Le Rapport secret du Dr. Johannès Lepsius ... sur les massacres d'Arménie.* Paris, 1918. Reprint, 1987.

———. *Archives du génocide arménien: Recueil de documents diplomatiques allemands, extraits de Deutschland und Armenien (1914–1918).* Préface by Alfred Grosser. Paris, 1986.

Lepsius, Johannes, ed. *Deutschland und Armenien.* Potsdam, Germany, 1919.

Meynier, Gustave. *Les massacres de Diarbekir: Correspondance diplomatique du vice-consul de France 1894–1896.* Présentée et annotée par Claire Mouradian et Michel Durand-Meyrier. Paris, 2000.

Morgenthau, Henry. *Mémoires, suivis de documents inédits du département d'État.* Paris, 1919. Reprint, 1984

Toynbee, Arnold J. *The Treatment of Armenians in the Ottoman Empire, 1915–16.* Edited by James Bryce. London, 1916.

Wegner, Armin T. *Der Weg ohne Heimkehr: Ein Martyrium in Briefen.* Dresden, Germany, 1919.

Secondary Sources

Adalian, Roubel Paul. "The Armenian Genocide: Revisionism and Denial." In *Genocide in Our Time, an Annotated Bibliography with Analytical Introduction,* edited by Michael N. Dobkowski and Isidor Wallimann. Ann Arbor, Mich., 1992.

———. "Négationnistes et génocide arménien." In *Le Livre noire de l'humanité,* edited by Israel W. Charny. Toulouse, France, 2001.

Balakian, Peter. *The Burning Tigris: The Armenian Genocide and America's Response.* New York, 2003.

Chaliand, Gerard, and Yves Ternon. *Le génocide des Arméniens.* Brussels, 1984.

Dadrian, Vahakn N. "The Convergent Aspects of the Armenian and Jewish Cases of Genocide: A Reinterpretation of the Concept of Holocaust." *Holocaust and Genocide Studies* 3, no. 2 (1988): 151–169.

———. "Genocide as a Problem of National and International Law: The World War I Armenian Case and Its Contemporary Legal Ramifications." *Yale Journal of International Law* 14, no. 2 (summer 1989). Printed separately with two appendices and bibliography. 134 pp.

———. *History of the Armenian Genocide: Ethnic Conflict from the Balkans to Anatolia to the Caucasus.* Providence, R.I., and Oxford, U.K., 1995.

———. *Warrant for Genocide: Key Elements of Turko-Armenian Conflict.* New Brunswick, N.J., and London. 1999.

———. "The Armenian Question and the Wartime Fate of the Armenians as Documented by the Officials of the Ottoman Empire's World War I Allies: Germany and Austro-Hungary." *International Journal of Middle East Studies* 34, no. 1 (2002): 59–85.

Power, Samantha. *"A Problem from Hell": America and the Age of Genocide.* New York, 2002.

Trumpeter, Ulrich. *Germany and the Ottoman Empire, 1914–1918.* Princeton, N.J., 1969.

VINCENT DUCLERT

ARMIES. The armies that took the field in Europe at the outbreak of war in 1914 resembled nothing so much as a medieval knight's broadsword:

formidable in appearance but poorly balanced and poorly tempered, unable to hold an edge. Their structure reflected the nineteenth century's development as an age of systems: bureaucratization and administration, control and specialization. The dominant intellectual modes of everyday activity remained positivism and Darwinism. Both depended on structuring and classifying: understanding wholes through mastering parts.

WORLD WAR I

Continental Europe obtained its soldiers by general conscription systems. Two or three years of active service were followed by variously structured terms in the reserves. Even Britain, with its long-service army geared to extra-European deployment, was constrained to fill the ranks of its expeditionary force with reservists, to an average level of 50 percent in the infantry. On mobilization, everyone was expected to report for duty, take his place in the ranks, and march forward to victory. Patriotism and numbers would make up for any minor shortcomings in skills.

Reality proved far more grim. Peacetime training had been on the whole mechanical: perfunctory and superficial. Reservists quickly forgot most of what they learned. Perhaps that was to their advantage, because so much received wisdom proved irrelevant when confronting industrial-strength firepower. Leadership was equally deficient. The cadres of professional officers and noncommissioned officers, kept relatively small for economic and social reasons, were swamped by the influx of mobilized civilians that bloated armies to three and four times their strength in a matter of days. Their casualties were disproportionally heavy as they sought to inspire and instruct. Effectiveness declined correspondingly, especially at the small-unit level.

War ministries, general staffs, and senior officers had not been blind to their armies' flaws and shortcomings. Desperately seeking any advantage, no matter how small, armies before the war paid increasing amounts of attention to each other. In turn they tended to imitate each other, from details of organization and equipment to general patterns of training and doctrine. This produced comprehensive symmetry: a pitting of like against like that worked against decisions on the tactical and operational levels.

Europe's military planners sought to compensate at the levels of policy and strategy. Immediate mobilization in a crisis would be followed by immediate movement to the front, coordinated by elaborate, constantly revised schedules constructed around railroad networks. Generals of proven professional competence would exploit the opportunities gained by being first with the most.

Reality again proved unobliging. What the nineteenth-century Prussian military theorist Carl von Clausewitz (1780–1831) aphorized as "fog and friction" threw grit into the machinery of mobilization and concentration. Generals stumbled as blindly as captains through mazes of uncertainty. Within weeks not only had the battle lines become static, but prewar planning and artifice had reached a dead end.

The armies of World War I were saved by an unexpected event. Instead of, collapsing in the face of adversity, as widely expected before 1914, Europe made unprecedented human and material resources available to its governments and its generals. Societies developed "war cultures" sustaining and affirming their sacrifices. Predictably, armies responded by emphasizing mass warfare. They developed enough administrative competence in everyday matters to sustain compliance in their ranks. They adjusted their doctrines to what seemed endless supplies of shells and endless streams of replacements: blood and steel alike became cheap on all of the war's multiplying fronts.

The net result was the loss of millions of lives and the consumption of millions of tons of resources for nothing remotely resembling proportionate achievements. World War I was a long war relative only to prewar anticipation. By the standards of previous conflicts with similar stakes and matrices it proceeded at jazz tempo. Far from being the blinkered, obscurantist institutions of popular myth, the armies were almost obsessively flexible and innovative, if only from desperation as they sought to end the fighting at something resembling acceptable cost.

Signs of overstretch were clear by mid-1916, and armies responded by turning to technology. Increasing amounts of material were transported by internal-combustion engines. Trucks and tractors began replacing horses and mules even at the front. Operational technology developed in even

more spectacular fashion—not merely in the familiar areas of tanks and aircraft, but also in the traditional combat arms of the infantry and artillery. Light machine guns and portable mortars, new fire control techniques and improved munitions, reshaped the battlefield by 1918.

The new form of warfare did not involve replacing men with machines. Rather, it was both machine intensive and personnel intensive. Its most complete development was the all-arms "managed battle." Introduced by the French and British in the war's final months, it harmonized artillery firepower, direct and indirect air support, tanks to crush wire and boost morale, and infantry able to help itself by improvisation. The result was a pattern of lurching forward, regrouping, and lurching forward again, always at the price of heavy casualties. It nevertheless represented an exponential advance from 1915.

Adaptation to industrial war had a human aspect as well. The heavy, blunt methods of the war's early years fostered a sense of helplessness before technology that would find eloquent postwar expression in such films as Fritz Lang's *Metropolis* (1927). Traditional images of war had been pastoral. By 1918 the tropes had become mechanical, borrowing images from mines and factories to build on prewar fears of the machine as Moloch, devouring what remained of humans' sensibility. Simultaneously every man in uniform, whether the innocent German volunteers of 1914 commemorated in the myth of Langemarck, which had them singing as they charged into the British line, or the lemming-like privates depicted in so many British narratives of the Somme and Passchendaele, became a liability in warmaking.

That was only part of the story. Mass warfare produced victims. Machine warfare as it developed after 1916 nurtured warriors. Traditional images of the soldier were constructed around courage and discipline. Now in the British Expeditionary Force men from the Dominions acquired a positive reputation for being able to think, act, and cooperate on levels that were alien to their counterparts from the deferential societies of the British Isles. The German assault battalions and the Italian arditi (elite assault troops) developed as a means of institutionalizing imagination, initiative, and intelligence: establishing a community bonded in blood by the "front experience." The French army expected an infusion of the warrior spirit from African contingents as yet unenervated by materialism and introspection. Men such as the German writer Ernst Jünger (1895–1998) and his Italian counterpart Gabriele D'Annunzio (1863–1938) followed the opposite path, seeking to transcend the machine by interfacing with it. For more than a century Europe's armies had been constructed on the postulate that ordinary men could go to war, then resume their civilian lives, with a minimum of adjustment. That certainty, like so many others, was called into question by the experiences of World War I.

UNCERTAIN TRUMPETS: CONCLUSIONS DRAWN IN THE INTERWAR YEARS

Armies, even losing ones, usually find reasons to congratulate themselves once peace breaks out. World War I was an exception. The defeats had been catastrophic, the victories ugly. Europe's military establishments approached the future with a single emotion: never again—at least, not in the same way.

Public and political opinion favored such meta-alternatives as pacifism and disarmament. Armies sought more effective ways of warmaking. The German general Erich Friedrich Wilhelm Ludendorff (1865–1937) asserted that future war required permanent mobilization in peacetime of the state's entire human, moral, and material resources, under a leader with dictatorial power, with critics facing silence or incarceration. Closely examined, however, the wartime experiences of Europe's major belligerents indicated practical limits to national mobilization, no matter how extreme the threat. Neither military nor civilian bureaucracies had proven able to establish and implement priorities. No permanent balances were struck among the state's armed forces, or within them. Civilian needs continued to exist apart from the war effort. Total mobilization, in short, wherever attempted, seemed to have been more disruptive than productive—at best efficient rather than effective.

In contrast to pre–World War I symmetry, four distinct approaches to organizing war developed after 1918, each intended to avert another spiral into ineffective efficiency. The first reduced armies to a secondary role. It was based on paralysis: striking at the taproots of moral and material resources from war's developing third element, the air. Here

Britain took the institutional lead. It had embarked on a strategic air offensive as early as 1916 under the auspices of the Royal Navy. In the postwar years its independent Royal Air Force insisted that regular and repeated bombing attacks would disrupt production and undermine confidence no matter what the bombs hit. Warmaking from above was disproportionately attractive to British strategic planners and policy makers. It fit the prevailing concept of a limited-liability approach to Europe in a context of "imperial overstretch." It incorporated a high-tech dimension element that seemed unavailable to continental powers constrained to devote most of their spending to ground forces. Above all, it offered a "clean war" push-button alternative to the hecatombs whose sites of "memory and mourning" were metastasizing under the auspices of the Commonwealth War Graves Commission.

The second paradigm of interwar planning was management. Here France assumed pride of place, developing a centrally controlled grand matrix integrating foreign policy, defense budgets, military planning, and psychological conditioning designed to make the state's next war the focus of its people's consciousness and will. The army was conceptualized as a cadre force whose carefully crafted tables of organization allowed most of its active units to triple themselves immediately on mobilization. Fixed frontier defenses culminating in the Maginot Line, and a developing mobile force of motorized and light armored divisions, would shield the fatherland, while its national army prepared the massive offensive that would decide the war.

Plans for that offensive were predicated on the conviction that victory would not be easy. It would require coordinating the disparate elements of modern war, mobility, firepower, and battlecraft, to produce a whole greater than the sum of its parts. The "managed battle" and the "managed campaign" were not exercises in button-pushing. A French commander was not a bureaucrat but a symphony conductor, expected to bring his own touch to the "score" of the plan and the "players" executing it.

The managed battle was also expected to control and focus the application of France's limited resources, a contract to the continuous and costly improvisations of 1914–1917. The French army's self-defined benchmarks of interwar effectiveness were based on management: improving the training of reservists, the qualifications of senior officers, the structures of logistics, and the networks of communications. It was a system conditioned at all levels to think *inside* the box—and to compel an enemy to enter that box on the French army's terms.

The third approach to interwar warmaking emphasized shock. The German offensives of 1918, despite their limited strategic success, attracted significant postwar attention. Some Italian military planners considered reorganizing the kingdom's army into no more than a dozen or fifteen divisions. Kept at full strength, given state-of-the art equipment and cutting-edge training, unleashed offensively at the beginning of the next war, they would be Italy's insurance against another eleven battles of the Isonzo (1915–1917).

Projected costs and institutional conservatism inhibited the development of the concept. North of the Alps, however, a German army reduced to a hundred thousand men by the Treaty of Versailles (1919) was correspondingly willing to experiment with new ideas and new approaches. Flexibility was facilitated by the Reichswehr's nature as a long-service volunteer force, where routine and boredom were deadly sins. German soldiers' growing emphasis on mobility, maneuverability, and initiative also reflected an absence of alternatives. The Reichswehr faced a situation in which waging effective war against any likely enemy for any length of time was impossible. The underlying principle of its operational art was less to seek victory than to buy time for the diplomats to seek a miracle. That meant keeping the army as a force in being, not wearing it down in costly frontal attacks or hopeless last stands.

The Truppenamt, successor to the Versailles-banned German General Staff, grew increasingly convinced that the next war would be decided by campaigns of maneuver. The internal-combustion engine was a Reichswehr force multiplier from the beginning. The battalion of trucks assigned to each infantry division developed into an increasingly comprehensive mobile-war supplement to the cavalry that—by Allied fiat—made up almost a third of the army's combat strength. By 1929 theoretical training programs existed for still non-existent tank regiments. War games and maneuvers became increasingly abstract, postulating artificial force structures and troop levels whose doctrines were based on mobility, surprise, and flexibility. Officer training stressed thinking ahead of the enemy and taking risks against odds.

The rearmament, which began even in advance of the rise to power of Adolf Hitler (1889–1945), fleshed out materially a concept of war based on shock. This mechanization in reverse meant capacities were adjusted to doctrine rather than the other way around, in which machines determined their uses. As it developed, what those who faced it called *Blitzkrieg* was not built around a small professional force of the kind advocated across the Rhine by Charles de Gaulle 1890–1970) in *Vers l'armée de métier* (1934). Nor did it involve a homogenized mass army on the pattern of imperial Germany. Its offensives were carried out by a high-tech elite within a mass—a functional elite based not on Aryan race or Nazi ideology, but learned military skills. The elite faced traditional elite risks: overheating and overextension. These were, however, unlikely to become serious problems should "the craft of war" and "the art of policy" synchronize as they had done in the days of Otto von Bismarck (1815–1898) and Helmuth von Moltke (1800–1891).

It was in that context that the German army perceived common ground with Adolf Hitler. His repeated description of the Reich as resting on "two pillars," the German army and the Nazi movement, led the generals to take him at their interpretation of his word, assigning him the role of establishing political and diplomatic conditions for the Wehrmacht's killing stroke. But should shock fail to generate awe, should Germany's enemies fight on rather than negotiate or collapse, military overstretch was a looming possibility.

A fourth culture of war developed around ideology. The Red Army of the Soviet Union (USSR) was from its beginnings an ideological institution. Its roots were in the Russian Revolution's Red Guards. Throughout the Russian civil war (1918–1920) it depended on Communist enthusiasts to revitalize flagging zeal at times of crisis. As it took permanent form in the 1920s, the Red Army was structured to wage a future war that was not a contingency, but a given. The capitalist states surrounding the Soviet Union sought its destruction because of their own class dynamics. Preparing for war was thus a pragmatic imperative. The Red Army incorporated party members and accepted party supervision at all levels in order to develop and increase necessary ideological consciousness. It became a cutting-edge instrument of social and cultural modernization, mixing workers and peasants in a military community intended to produce New Soviet Men on assembly lines.

The direct success of this ambitious effort was decidedly limited. At the same time the Red Army's commanders increasingly perceived the operational limitations of politicized enthusiasm. A rising generation of technocrats such as Mikhail Tukhachevsky (1893–1937) called for the development of comprehensive military mechanization supported by a developed industrial base. Such a "New Model" army could export as well as defend the revolution. It could preempt wavering and suppress doubt by delivering early victories—won on enemy territory. It would validate the ideology that was the Soviet Union's ultimate source of legitimacy, creating enthusiasm not by compulsion or indoctrination, but directly: showing what the Soviet Union could do to its enemies. The modernizers insisted that mechanization Soviet-style vitalized rather than challenged the importance of the masses under arms. The projected strength of the mobilized Red Army in the 1930s was over 250 divisions—hardly a Praetorian elite. Nor did machines challenge the Red Army's revolutionary character. Only class-conscious proletarians could make optimum use of the material innovations created under communism.

The transformation of Tukhachevsky's mechanized mass vanguard of revolution into a hamstrung giant by the purges of Joseph Stalin (1879–1953) was a temporary phenomenon. The brute-force operations of 1942–1943 rapidly gave way to a way of war no less sophisticated than those of contemporary Western armies. The multiplication of mass by impulsion, however, retained its ideological matrix until the Soviet Union itself disappeared.

WORLD WAR II: A UNIVERSAL ARMY FOR A GLOBAL WAR

From September 1939 to December 1941, the debate over styles of soldiering seemed to have been definitively resolved in favor of the German model. In the course of becoming the master of Europe, Germany's army defied paralysis, confounded management, and trumped ideology. On the other side of the world, in the aftermath of Pearl Harbor a Japanese army cooperating closely with air and naval forces offered contrapuntal lessons in shock and awe as Japan conquered an empire on a shoestring.

So impressive were these victories that the rolling back and eventual crushing of the armies that won them is still widely considered remarkable. In particular what has been called "Wehrmacht penis envy" continues to inform much popular writing. Time and research have produced a more nuanced understanding. The defeat of France in June 1940 emerges as a consequence less of German mastery of a new way of war than of battles lost because of Allied miscalculation of Germany's operational intentions and Allied failure to match German operational effectiveness. Many German as well as French soldiers panicked on the battlefields of 1940. French military systems were sufficiently competent, and French strategic plans sufficiently sound that the alternative of a French victory parade down Unter den Linden in Berlin was a real possibility.

Beginning with the aborted invasion of Britain in 1940, the German army found itself forced into an increasingly random framework of improvisations. Its original bag of tricks emptied somewhere on the high road between Smolensk and Moscow. What remained was a material demodernization that fostered a psychological demodernization. Willpower and ferocity became not merely desirable but necessary force multipliers. Nazi ideology assumed a central role by explaining and justifying the sacrifices demanded of the ordinary soldier in terms of a racial war for Germany's survival. War and warmaking became ends in themselves—and correspondingly self-defeating.

The paradigm for armies in the World War II era was instead established by an unlikely outsider in the military sweepstakes. The United States' war effort was based on power projection and versatility. The United States dispatched significant forces everywhere in the world, in every theater except the Soviet. Even on the eastern front, Lend-Lease aid was vital to the Soviet war effort. U.S. infantry stormed a half-dozen European beaches. The

A German tank drives through dusty Ukrainian fields on the eastern front during World War II. ©CORBIS

United States committed entire divisions to South Pacific islands barely on the map in 1941, then built an infrastructure to sustain them. The United States committed a division-strength task force to the Burma campaign and sustained a military presence in the Aleutian Islands. Other combatants did some, or many, of these same things. No one did all of them.

The United States was correspondingly unique in creating nearly from scratch two entirely different armies. The one deployed in Europe was optimized for large-scale, high-tech ground combat, and modified everything from its divisional organizations to its standard tank in order to deal more effectively with a German opposition that never ceased to be formidable. In the Pacific, by contrast, army ground forces depended for deployment and sustainability on a navy that by 1945 possessed in addition to its ships one of the world's largest air forces, and in the U.S. Marine Corps a ground

component of more than a half-million of the war's most formidable fighting men.

Despite the differences between and among operational theaters, the U.S. Army waged a homogeneous global war, creating systems that proved successfully applicable everywhere in the world. It began with an assembly-line system for mass-producing divisions from nothing by taking small cadres from existing formations, then providing "fillers," draftees deliberately drawn from all quarters of the country, and training them to a common pattern.

Geared to produce effectiveness rather than excellence, this homogenization was a sharp contrast both to the British "artisanal" system that decentralized much training to regimental levels, and to the German practice of recruiting and reinforcing divisions from the same region. It also meant that a U.S. soldier could readily "find a home in the army." His new unit did things in essentially the same ways as his old one. Even the army's often-indicted system of individual replacement worked better than might have been expected because standard operating procedures developed, even in forward areas, to integrate new men.

Homogenization contributed to the U.S. Army's second distinguishing characteristic: flexibility. American soldiers at all levels in all theaters adapted effectively and comprehensively to the conditions they faced. The process was neither automatic nor uniform, but combat and support formations alike had high learning curves. The army began adjusting to the closely mixed woodland and pasture of the Normandy *bocage* within days of landing, and continued to match every German tactical or technical riposte until VE Day. On the other side of the world the army-dominated ground campaigns in New Guinea and the Philippines produced not merely formidably effective jungle-fighting divisions, but what might be called jungle/mechanized formations that combined motorized mobility and armored punch with the ability to operate away from road nets. America's "other army," the marines who carried the burden of the Central Pacific campaign, similarly adjusted from a light-infantry mentality first to the shock troop demands of atoll fighting, and then to the demands of extended ground campaigns in the Marianas Islands and on Okinawa.

Army practice regarding senior officers also facilitated flexibility. Patterns of appointment and removal, especially from mid-level and senior command positions, tended to replicate those of civilian management: produce or else. In contrast to Germany, where the number of senior officer slots at times exceeded the number of available generals, the relatively small number of divisions and equivalent large formations the United States fielded meant the army always had new candidates and fresh blood. With the arguable exception of the Soviet Union, the United States was the most ruthless combatant in relieving or reassigning generals and colonels in World War II. It began with Lieutenant General Walter Short, commanding the Hawaiian Department when Japan attacked Pearl Harbor. It continued in all theaters. A man might get two chances to repeat a mistake—seldom a third.

Flexibility was further influenced by technology. Most combatants excelled in weapons systems tailored to particular environments: the Spitfire fighter or the Panther tank. None came near to matching the United States in developing and producing general-purpose tools of war. The C-47 transport, the 2-ton truck, and the jeep were almost as central to the Soviet and British armed forces as to the Americans. Each of those designs, and most of their stablemates, could go anywhere. But the best example of global flexibility is an armored fighting vehicle. The often-criticized M-4 Sherman was no match individually for its Panther and Tiger rivals in the specific conditions of northwest Europe. But in its upgunned versions it was competitive. And neither of the German designs could have matched their United States counterparts under the conditions of Saipan, Okinawa, or Burma, where tanks played increasingly important roles.

The U.S. Army's third defining quality was sustainability. Modern war's bedrock is management: getting from here to there and then staying there, all without tripping over one's administrative feet. That was uniquely true for the United States, a geostrategic island. Nothing succeeds in war like excess. American management, civil and military, applied the excess. The U.S. Army was consistently able to fix and bypass German and Japanese forces, to keep campaigns moving when its counterparts were running out of gas or men. The replacement system kept fighting units up to strength, requiring neither reduction and disbandment on the late-war British pattern nor the grouping of clusters of survivors into ad hoc battle groups that was the Wehrmacht's preferred emergency solution, nor the erosion of divisions to cadres of survivors that was the Red Army's norm.

Sustainability was also a product of firepower. Former enemies and former allies remain quick to make the point that the U.S. armed forces won their war by brute force relentlessly applied. Saving blood by the sophisticated application of steel would seem to indicate virtuosity rather than awkwardness. The U.S. Army used its broad spectrum of available firepower to produce tactical environments that extended battle zones beyond defenders' capacities to respond, and to sustain offensives whose successes did not depend on obliging enemies such as the ones Germany faced from 1939 to 1942.

Each of the previous factors is linked with a fourth one: morale. Never in history did so many fight so far from home in a war not obviously theirs. American territory was not under direct attack. American civilians were not directly threatened. To the extent that the American soldier had a "worldview" of the war, it was as a job to be done, as quickly and completely as possible. United States battle casualties overall may have been low—risibly low by German or Soviet standards. Yet in both Europe and the Pacific, United States ground forces were willing to take, and continue taking, heavy losses for specific tactical objectives such as Aachen or Iwo Jima. American rifle companies in the European Theater of Operations (ETO) consistently took casualties of 200–300 percent, and kept coming. Marines climbed the cliffs of Peleliu when it was clear that the operation's purpose had evaporated. The records show desertion, straggling, hanging back—but no significant collective refusals of duty. Even the much-abused 5307th Composite Unit (Provisional), better known as Merrill's Marauders, as jerked around and as far from home as any unit the U.S. Army fielded, staggered forward as long as its survivors could stand up.

American soldiers are usually described as standing somewhat behind the Germans in operational virtuosity, and even further behind the Russians in hardihood. But the U.S. Army of 1945 had developed a high level of skill in stacking operational decks, systematically pitting its strengths against opponents' shortcomings. The U.S. Army, moreover, had demonstrated an ability to fight effectively under a far broader spectrum of conditions than any of its counterparts. The Grossdeutschland Division, or the Red Army guardsmen who held Stalingrad and stormed Berlin, might have adapted perfectly to Leyte or Iwo Jima—but they never faced that test. The U.S. Army did, and its universal soldiers passed with honors.

ARMIES FOR A COLD WAR

America's universal soldiers, like their Soviet and British counterparts, were self-identified as citizen soldiers. The existential warriors of Germany and the modernized samurai of Japan went down before civilians in uniform, who regarded their war experience as temporary; dues paid for a brighter future. The votes of soldiers and their families contributed significantly to the postwar election of a Labour government committed to a socialist Britain. When the United States government considered ways to thank its men and women in uniform, it developed economic rewards, such as a Veterans Administration program that provided low-cost home loans and a GI Bill offering what amounted to free vocational training and higher education to all veterans. Those programs and their counterparts, by democratizing the ranks of homeowners and professionals, laid the foundation of the United States as a self-defined middle-class society. Communist ideology, fear of punishment, revenge for unprecedented suffering at German hands, alike played limited roles in the Red Army's combat motivation. Instead, frontline soldiers increasingly hoped their sacrifices would bring about comprehensive reform: "communism with a human face." Instead their reward was a comprehensive Stalinist crackdown—a crackdown that structured armies' development for almost a half-century.

The Cold War's origins might be complex, but its essential paradigm was defined by the Soviet Union's enduring policy of maintaining a large conventional army, supported by national mobilization, on its frontier with Western Europe for the purpose of mounting a general offensive on the outbreak of war. A consistent mission, but one it was never summoned to execute, enabled the Soviet army to retain its World War II character for the remainder of its existence. Comprehensive mechanization produced consistent updates of equipment from small arms to main battle tanks. Chemical, biological, and nuclear weapons; missiles of all sizes and functions; made their respective appearances in inventories. Orders of battle were reconfigured and doctrines modified. Essentially, however, Soviet soldiers spent years and decades studying how to do essentially the same things more effectively.

Their focus shaped the West's response. Early Cold War thoughts of refighting the 1944–1945 Liberation Campaign foundered on a developing comprehension of the effects of nuclear weapons. The North Atlantic Treaty Organization (NATO) initially proposed to match Soviet numbers with its own. But plans for a ninety-division international army foundered on the refusal of a materially and morally exhausted Europe to devote the necessary resources to such a force. Instead NATO's armies developed in a context of nuclear deterrence and Mutual Assured Destruction.

Logic suggested that the Alliance needed no more than a "tripwire:" a token conventional capacity sufficient to trigger a nuclear exchange. A combination of factors, however, modified that syllogism significantly. First among these was an unwillingness at both the policy and the institutional levels to accept the implications of such fundamental military asymmetry. The West's armies might never be able to match Soviet numbers. But the West's heritage suggested an alternative: emphasizing the quality of its armies in all aspects from technology to doctrine to training to command and planning. That approach was encouraged by the Federal Republic of Germany's growing contributions to NATO. Included among them was a Wehrmacht legacy built around its interpretation of its post-Stalingrad experience in the Soviet Union. It encouraged consideration of developing NATO conventional forces able to play its clumsy, rigidly structured, Warsaw Pact opponent as a matador plays a bull, at best stopping the offensive in its tracks and at the worst buying time for the diplomats to avert nuclear Armageddon.

Quality was not an indefinite force multiplier. Numbers were necessary as well. Securing them remained a sticking point, particularly in societies increasingly sensitive to all forms of loss and suffering, and increasingly committed to nonmilitary priorities for government expenditure—above all, Europe's metastasizing network of social welfare programs. Britain, after a brief and unsatisfactory fling with National Service, reverted gratefully to its long-standing heritage of a small professional force whose personnel quality was expected to compensate for any shortfalls in numbers or equipment. France and West Germany accepted "social conscription," military service as an essential element of citizenship. The attempt to combine quality with conscription generated a spectrum of problems. The days of hut-two-three-four, salute it if it moves and paint it if it doesn't, were long past. The physical, intellectual, and psychological demands of high-tech war increasingly challenged even well-motivated draftees. Two years active service was barely enough time for conscripts to learn the fundamentals—and that term came under increasing fire for its length in newspapers and parliaments.

How far could the claims of citizenship be extended? That question became increasingly salient as the Cold War acquired a global dimension, piggybacking on the simultaneous process of decolonization. A British army incorporating a significant conscript element was the military keystone of a counterinsurgency campaign in Malay whose eventual success has obscured the insurgency's limited ethnic and ideological appeals, its correspondingly limited resources, and the trials and errors accompanying the military operations. In Indochina a French expeditionary corps, denied by law a metropolitan conscript element, waged what amounted to a low-end high-tech war, increasingly relying on warrior spirit as a force multiplier and in the process demodernizing to a point where, at the climactic battle of Dien Bien Phu, it committed an improvised mixture of individual battalions against the Viet Minh's organized divisions. The subsequent military and political debacle in Algeria owed something to a deployment of conscripts to what was legally part of France that was nevertheless widely seen as a breach of France's postwar social contract.

Cold War globalization's effects on homogenization, flexibility, sustainability, and morale were, however, best illustrated in Vietnam. After an initial series of disasters in Korea, the U.S. Army successfully and effectively deployed an essentially conscript force in an essentially conventional war, sustaining morale largely by a combination of limited tours of duty and limited operational commitment. An essentially similar force was dispatched to Vietnam fifteen years later, the product of the first peacetime mass army in America's history, sustained by a "selective service system" providing a sufficiently broad spectrum of alternatives and exemptions that it did not intrude significantly on a burgeoning population.

Initially that army proved as good, in its own terms, as anything the United States had fielded in a war's early stages since the Mexican War (1846–1848). It failed, however, to balance mass and technology. Numerical weakness relative to the enemy and the theater of operations generated an overreliance on firepower and air mobility that proved addictive to citizen conscripts on one-year tours. The consequent gridlock, a war that seemingly could neither be won nor lost, comprehensively eroded morale, both military and civilian. In Vietnam's aftermath the U.S. Army abandoned the human model so successful in World War II and accepted the leap in the dark of a volunteer

Soviet troops parade in Red Square, 1 May 1946.
The dramatic show of force was an annual May Day event in
the Soviet Union. ©Bettmann/Corbis

military. That decision, though reluctantly made
and reluctantly accepted, enabled the United
States to once again take the lead in developing a
defining army form. This time it was an army for
the Cold War.

The U.S. Army emerged from its post-Vietnam
reconfiguration as a combination of professionalism, technology, and numbers. The harsh lessons
of southeast Asia inspired a revitalization of its
officer and noncommissioned cadre, and an era of
innovation in doctrine. The increased military budgets of the Reagan administrations provided funding for a spectrum of new weapons systems, at a
time when the costs of technology were beginning
to exceed the willingness of other states to keep
pace. And American society provided a continuing
supply of motivated and capable recruits. Contrary
to some expectations—and to the experiences of

other states with professionalization—the volunteer army has remained closely tied to the civil
community. Over a quarter-century, a large number of middle- and working-class families have had
a child, a relative, a neighbor, or an acquaintance
who spent time in uniform and enjoyed a positive
experience. Many of these enlisted for no more
than a term or two, acquired skills, bonuses, or life
experience, then moved on. It was easy enough to
do at a time when America's guns were silent, when
the USSR's military arteriosclerosis was highlighted
in Afghanistan.

Thus untested, the U.S. Army did not comprehend its own proficiency until Iraq's invasion of
Kuwait in 1990. Many of the units deployed to
the Persian Gulf were scheduled for disbandment
as part of the "peace dividend" expected with the
disappearance of the Soviet Union. Before furling
their banners they eviscerated an Iraqi army widely
considered among the most capable in the world.
In a hundred hours of fighting the Americans lost
fewer than a hundred lives—in contrast to predictions of body bags that ran into the tens of thousands. While air and sea power played significant
roles, Operation Desert Storm was the valedictory
speech and the graduation dance of the Cold War
U.S. Army and its post-Vietnam cadres.

A MILITARY COUNTERREVOLUTION?

Beginning in the 1970s the comprehensive introduction of pathbreaking new technologies in the
U.S. armed forces led Soviet thinkers to postulate
the emergence of a "military-technical revolution."
The concept was taken up eagerly in the American
national security community. Eventually reified
into a complex hierarchy of "military technical
revolutions," "revolutions in military affairs," and
"military revolutions," the underlying premise
remained the same. Superiority in weapons systems and information/communications technology
would create a level of dominance enabling the
United States to control absolutely the pace and
the intensity of warmaking. Some proponents of
the concept spoke of "virtual war," and eventually
"bloodless war," as machines replaced men and
targets became other machines.

Apart from the Americans' dominating performance against Iraq, the notion of reconfiguring
armies in terms of small scale and high tech was

attractive to Western states seeking to reduce their military "footprints" in a post–Cold War environment. The new Russian Republic, sorting through a Soviet legacy that at the end provided neither mass nor quality, also opted for a "lean and mean" profile. By the mid-1990s the conscript soldier who had been the central element of twentieth-century armies was becoming vestigial. Germany steadily reduced its intakes of draftees, and provided increasingly broad alternative-service options. Even France traded its mythos of Republican citizens in arms for the new model of professionalism.

Cynics—or realists—might suggest that the restructuring of armies was more sham than substance, given the general unwillingness of states and societies actually to invest in the cutting-edge technologies that were central to military revolution. Nevertheless the new-style forces, enjoying the advantage of easy deployability, performed well enough in the peacekeeping and nation-building missions that dominated the twentieth century's final decade. And with the century's turn, the new order of armies seemed validated beyond question as U.S. forces effortlessly projected American power into the mountains of Afghanistan, then overran Iraq in less than a month without breaking the proverbial sweat.

Even before the 11 September 2001 attacks on New York and Washington, D.C., however, war's center stages had shifted. Between 1914 and 1990, globalization did not challenge Eurocentricity. The Rhine and the Vistula, the North German plain and the Fulda Gap, were the consistent focal points of policy, planning, and national interest. The American general who allegedly refused to ruin the army of the United States "just to win this lousy war" in Vietnam was a more profound strategist than perhaps he realized.

Non-Western armies correspondingly tended to follow Western models as far as possible. The heroic vitalism that led the Japanese to put bayonet attachments on their light machine guns owed less to Japan's cultural heritage than to the recognition that Japan must compensate for material inferiority with strength of will. The Chinese leader Mao Zedong (1893–1976) may have developed a three-stage model for revolutionary war, but the Chinese communists lost no time and spared no effort to reach the third stage of conventional operations as quickly as

possible. Even the Vietnamese model of comprehensive struggle (*dau tranh*) was arguably less an original way of warmaking than a means of mobilizing a population in numbers no Western expeditionary force could match. Israel too shed the unconventional aspects of its military system in favor of Western models.

The armies that emerged in the contexts of decolonization also reflected Western influences. India's became more British than its mentors had been, and in Pakistan too the British heritage survived to an extent often unrecognized. The Muslim Middle East combined British foundations and Soviet overlays in varying degrees of harmony. Whatever their shortcomings—and those could be spectacular—in regional mid-intensity conventional wars the armies built on these more or less ramshackle templates gave more satisfaction than is often understood or conceded. The successive thrashings administered by Israel inspired institutional reforms, but no paradigm shifts. Even the Iran of the Ayatollahs eventually rebuilt a conventional military capacity rather than place full trust in revolutionary Islamic forces such as the Islamic Revolutionary Guard Corps, the pasdaran.

Beneath the surface, change winds were blowing. The 1990s witnessed comprehensive challenges to state sovereignty and international law. An environment of policy entrepreneurship led to a corresponding erosion of the concept of legitimacy. In part the new environment was a consequence of unilateral action, whether by individual states like France in Africa, regional organizations such as NATO in the Balkans, or a hyperpower such as the United States anywhere it chose. In a deeper sense it reflected a general breakdown of international consensus as the Cold War's restraints eroded. In the final years of the twentieth century, conflicts increasingly tended to mutate, changing shapes, goals, and players in a multidimensional, kaleidoscopic fashion challenging and denying the linear, logical analysis that defines armies on the Western model.

That development was in part a response to the proven futility of engaging the West's armed forces on anything like their own terms. Ultimately, however, what the French philosopher Raymond Aron (1905–1983) called "polymorphous" warmaking reflects a synergy of internal dynamics often unclear to the participants themselves. In Bosnia and Haiti, in Iraq and Palestine, in Rwanda and Darfur, farragoes of political, nationalist, sectarian, and ethnic objectives have mocked earlier, simpler, almost innocent models of liberation from colonial rule or foreign exploitation. Leadership, organization, even ideology are amorphous. The violence that contemporary Western warmaking seeks to minimize and sanitize instead takes center stage, by virtue of its ferocity and its randomness. Analysts who initially spoke of "asymmetric" war increasingly describe "postmodern" war, sometimes even in the context of chaos theory.

So far the "military counterrevolution" has won no clear victories. But neither has it suffered any clear defeats. It may be argued that the protean character making the counterrevolution operationally effective also retards or prevents the development of any result more positive than a Hobbesian model of all against all. That outcome is hardly attractive—especially to armies. Ultimately, viscerally, armies understand themselves as instruments of order. How best to respond to an entropic challenge?

Twentieth-century armies have developed an increasingly comprehensive synergy of technical and human elements. "Postmodern" war is a "polymorphous" exercise, likely to require the simultaneous and effective conduct of high-tech combat, counterinsurgency, peace support, and nation-building. In that context the armies of the twenty-first century may well need their technical mastery and institutional flexibility more than ever. Instead adaptation might better be sought in mentalities.

The armies that set twentieth-century standards have been instruments of decision informed by a dynamic of closure. They have been intended to win wars as quickly as possible, and with minimal suffering to the states and societies that created them. In the twenty-first century military effectiveness may best be achieved by cultivating a sense of the long duration, evaluating results in a context of not merely years but decades. This would be a fundamental attitude adjustment.

But though military cultures have their own rituals and their own ways of doing things—often quite different from the national culture to which they belong—these are not immutable. The frameworks of warmaking are instrumental and customary,

sustained by a mixture of pragmatism, habit, and fear of the consequences of change. Postmodern war will eventually produce postmodern armies whose exteriors might remain familiar, but whose internal dynamics will reflect the new challenges they face.

See also **Cold War; Conscription; Guerrilla Warfare; Gulf Wars; Vietnam War; Warfare; World War I; World War II.**

BIBLIOGRAPHY

Primary Sources

Aron, Raymond. *Peace and War. A Theory of International Relations.* Translated by Robert Howard and Annette Baker Fox. Garden City, N.Y., 1966.

Ludendorff, Erich. *The Nation at War.* Translated by A. S Rappoport. London, 1936.

Trinquier, Roger. *Modern Warfare: A French View of Counterinsurgency.* Translated by Daniel Lee. New York, 1961.

Secondary Sources

Bartov, Omer. *Hitler's Army: Soldiers, Nazis, and War in the Third Reich.* New York, 1992.

Biddle, Stephen. *Military Power: Explaining Victory and Defeat in Modern Battle.* Princeton, N.J., 2004.

Coker, Christopher. *The Future of War: The Re-enchantment of War in the Twenty-First Century.* Malden, Mass., 2004.

———. "The Ethics of Operations on the Cusp." Paper presented at RUSI Conference, "Transformation of Military Operations on the Cusp," March 14, 2005.

Doubler, Michael. *Closing with the Enemy: How GIs Fought the War in Europe, 1944–1945.* Lawrence, Kans., 1994.

Kiesling, Eugenia. *Arming against Hitler: France and the Limits of Military Planning.* Lawrence, Kans., 1996.

Krepinevich, Andrew, Jr. *The Army and Vietnam.* Baltimore, Md., 1986.

Merridale, Catherine. *Ivan's War: Life and Death in the Red Army, 1939–1945.* New York, 2006.

Neiberg, Michael. *Warfare and Society in Europe, 1898 to the Present.* New York, 2004.

Perrett, Geoffrey. *There's a War to Be Won.* New York, 1991.

Pike, Douglas. *Viet Cong: The Organization and Techniques of the National Liberation Front of South Vietnam.* Cambridge, Mass., 1966.

Pollack, Kenneth M. *Arabs at War: Military Effectiveness, 1948–1991.* Lincoln, Neb., 2002.

Reese, Roger. *Stalin's Reluctant Soldiers: A Social History of the Red Army, 1925–1941.* Lawrence, Kans., 1996.

Romjue, John L. *From Active Defense to AirLand Battle: The Development of Army Doctrine, 1973–1982.* Fort Monroe, Va., 1984.

Showalter, Dennis. "Military Innovation and the Whig Perspective of History." In *The Challenge of Change,* edited by Harold R. Winton and David R. Mets, 220–236. Lincoln, Neb., 2000.

———. "It All Goes *Wrong*: German, French, and British Efforts to Master the Western Front." In *Warfare and Belligerence: Perspectives in First World War Studies,* edited by Pierre Purseigle, 39–72. Leiden, Netherlands, 2005.

Van Creveld, Martin. *The Transformation of War.* New York, 1991.

DENNIS E. SHOWALTER

ARMISTICE. *See* Versailles, Treaty of; World War I.

ARMS CONTROL.

As a term, *arms control* only came into vogue at the start of the 1960s, based on theoretical work that had begun in the mid-1950s. Initially it referred to attempts to stabilize Cold War military relations, and in particular the nuclear balance; it was contrasted with disarmament, which was taken literally to mean arms reductions, presented as a measure born out of idealism without thought for strategic stability. Arms control eventually came to refer to any cooperation between potential enemies in the military sphere, just as in practice disarmament had been given a similarly wide definition before that time. After the end of the Cold War, the rather precise focus on regulating types of weapons and military inventories encouraged by both arms control and disarmament tended to give way to a much broader concern with security, and any military measures were considered as part of a wider package designed to influence broad political relationships between countries that were either trying to move away from or getting into antagonistic relations. Because much of the relevant activity has been global in scope, the European element cannot be easily isolated, Europe during the twentieth century was so central to great power war and conflict that its security was at issue in all negotiations.

The initial enthusiasm for disarmament came after World War I as a direct response to the assumption that the catastrophe was the result of the prewar arms race. Not only was it important to avoid such vicious cycles in the future, but there might be a way of securing a virtuous cycle, whereby political relations between antagonistic countries might be improved, if ways could be found to move from arms competition to arms cooperation. Military expenditure was also often castigated as wasteful and designed to line the pockets of arms manufacturers and a diversion from welfare needs. Governments always proclaimed their commitment to disarmament as a principle (as they continue to do into the twenty-first century) and tended to blame others for the lack of progress, but in practice they also were reluctant to take great risks when it came to trusting the word of potentially hostile foreign governments. They rarely accepted the simple notion that fewer arms should mean more peace, and so negotiations for disarmament and then arms control tended to be quite complex in their purposes and their effects.

In the immediate aftermath of World War I, the main negotiations were on naval forces (the Anglo-German naval arms race having been blamed, inaccurately, for the war). The major all-encompassing disarmament negotiations took place in Geneva in 1932–1933 but, after little progress, they collapsed with the rise of Adolf Hitler (1889–1945). There were some agreements but by and large they did not survive World War II, which rather, by its very occurrence, undermined the notion that peaceful gestures were of much value in the face of willful aggression. After World War II the arrival of the atomic bomb prompted activity at the new United Nations, but the developing Cold War between the United States and the Soviet Union reduced the possibilities for progress. Only toward the end of the 1950s did negotiations begin in earnest again. The first agreements were on peripheral matters, but by the end of the 1960s there was an appetite for more substantial negotiations, and during the early 1970s the improvement in East-West relations was reflected in a series of initiatives that began to peter out as relations worsened again, only to pick up in the late 1980s as the Cold War moved to its conclusion. In some respects, the end of the Cold War made arms control in Europe much easier, but it also became unclear what exactly it was supposed to achieve.

CONTAINING WAR

Prior to World War I, the major purpose of disarmament negotiations was to contain war as a social institution. The aim was to limit the effects of war, usually by proscribing certain weapons (or at least their use) as excessively cruel in their effects or apt to extend the destructiveness of war. Though the scale and intensity of twentieth-century "total" war could have hardly been comprehended, this effort reflected anxieties both about the consequences of warfare burgeoning out of the categories in which it had previously been contained, and about the prospect of greater suffering on the battlefield, a greater exposure of commerce and civilian life to military attack, and a greater strain on national resources. The fruits of this interest can first be found in the St. Petersburg Declaration on exploding bullets of December 1868, and then in the Hague Conferences of 1899 and 1907. After World War I, this focus continued but now with heavy bombers, submarines, and poison gases as the main areas of concern. Efforts to control air warfare met with no success, though the problems of banning heavy bombers, and of writing effective conventions to restrict aerial bombardment to a "combat zone" or for use against solely military targets, were discussed during the 1920s and through the international Disarmament Conference of 1932–1933. The major success was with the Geneva Protocol of 1925, which prohibited the use of "asphyxiating, poisonous or other gases, and bacteriological methods of warfare." This did not prevent stockpiling of chemical weapons, so the enforcement mechanism was largely fear of retaliation. As this was a very real fear, the Protocol survived World War II, in part also because of doubts surrounding the military benefits of chemical weapons.

Less successful was the London Protocol of 1936, in which thirty nations agreed to grant the passengers and crew of merchant vessels some protection against submarines. It was too vague in defining when attack became legitimate and failed to acknowledge the structural weaknesses of submarines, which were too small to rescue passengers and crews and too vulnerable to come to the surface to make a visible challenge. Because of its limitations, the code was liable to be unintentionally violated. On the second day of World War II, a German U-30 submarine sank the unarmed British passenger liner *Athenia*, with the loss of 120 lives, in the belief that it was attacking an auxiliary cruiser. The British then ceased to rely on the submarine code and ordered the arming of all merchantmen, which meant that they were, in effect, participating in hostilities. By the end of September, Germany had announced that it would suspend adherence to the code.

After 1945, the atomic bomb was the obvious weapon to be singled out for special treatment. The United States introduced proposals to the United Nations in 1946 that would have put the peaceful exploitation of atomic energy under an international agency and prevented the stockpiling of atomic bombs. In the light of the developing Cold War, these proposals failed to impress the Soviets and thus came to naught. When the two sides began to negotiate again in the 1950s, there were some successes, most notably the partial nuclear test ban of 1963, which dealt with atmospheric testing (widely seen as a health hazard) but still allowed underground testing, and so provided only a minimal impediment to weapons development. In the 1990s, a draft comprehensive test ban treaty was agreed to, but the U.S. Senate refused ratification. The spread of nuclear weapons was restricted to particular areas (Latin America, Antarctica, the seabed, and outer space). These could be agreed upon without too much difficulty because there were few good reasons for putting such weapons there in the first place. The 1970 Seabed Treaty was likened to an agreement not to screw aircraft to the ground. Attempts to control the spread of weapons to new countries (after the United States, the Soviet Union, United Kingdom, France, and China) through the 1970 Nuclear Nonproliferation Treaty can claim modest but not complete success, with India and Pakistan declared nuclear powers by the 1990s, Israel widely presumed to be a covert power, and Iran and North Korea on their way to developing nuclear capability. On the credit side, South Africa and Libya abandoned nuclear plans and Iraq was forcibly disarmed. Following the break-up of the Soviet Union, Belarus, Kazakhstan, and Ukraine were briefly nuclear powers but they were persuaded by western governments not to attempt to retain this status, which would have also been expensive and technically demanding. The record on the abolition of "cruel and unusual" weapons shows a complete blank. Attempts at arms restriction have failed to impede the development of modern weaponry.

FORCE RATIOS

The pressure for disarmament after 1918 was reflected in policies of national demobilization and so did not require international treaties. This was not, however, considered a sufficient guarantee of peace so long as arms races were still possible. What could be demobilized could be remobilized. It was considered desirable that states should renounce the right to be the sole judges of their own armaments and place their trust in the Covenant of the League of Nations. To preserve national security, a formula was developed based on the assumptions that (a) force levels reflected calculations of the external danger and (b) a sharp reduction in absolute levels would not reduce the level of security if the ratio between national forces was maintained.

The first attempt to put this theory into practice came with the Washington Naval Conference of 1922. Here the United States, the British Empire, Japan, France, and Italy reached agreement on capital ships, setting ratios of 5:5:3:1.7:1.7. This more or less reflected the ratios of the time. This treaty demonstrated the problems with this approach to disarmament. To achieve acceptable arms ratios it was necessary to simplify strategic relationships, exclude many militarily relevant factors, and concentrate on a few prestige weapons. The naval parity between the British and Americans soon became irrelevant and the strategic significance of capital ships also declined in comparison with cruisers, carriers, destroyers, and submarines. Shipbuilding efforts were redirected into a race in heavy cruisers.

The attempt in the early 1930s to produce a comprehensive treaty failed because of the deteriorating political situation and the inherent complexity of the exercise. The greater the number of elements and aspects of military strength covered by negotiators, the less chance they have of reaching an agreement, yet simplifying the military balances in order to render them manageable may also render them politically unacceptable. The Germans saw disarmament talks as a way of escaping from the humiliating military inferiority imposed at Versailles; the French saw the same talks as a means of maintaining this inferiority, arguing that there was no satisfactory way of compensating for Germany's industrial resources and manpower except by undermining its capacity for military preparedness in every possible way.

This approach only enjoyed some success in the 1970s with the Strategic Arms Limitation Talks (SALT) between the United States and Soviet Union, which eventually mutated into the Strategic Arms Reduction Talks (START) in the 1980s. In this case, the strategic value of vast quantities of nuclear weapons came to be questioned in view of the diminishing marginal returns on nuclear weapons beyond those required for "assured destruction." In principle this should have meant that disparities in actual numbers, so long as destruction was assured, should not have been of great importance, but in practice neither superpower liked to accept an appearance of even notional inferiority. The guiding principle became that of "parity"—a rough equivalence in military strength between two nations that allowed both to claim they are "second to none." Definitions of parity that required asymmetrical adjustments in force structures were unacceptable. Thus the prior existence of parity became a necessary precondition for the negotiation of an arms agreement seeking to create a formal condition of parity. This was one reason why the attempt in the 1970s to translate the SALT approach to conventional forces in Europe in the talks on mutual force reductions failed. As with those of the 1930s, the problems lay in basic asymmetries, in this case the preponderance of Soviet manpower and tanks in Central Europe. Warsaw Pact proposals preserved the existing balance; North Atlantic Treaty Organization (NATO) proposals sought to create a new one.

ARMS STABILITY

The argument against putting restrictions on the "natural" development of armaments has been that peace depends on a healthy awareness of the costs of war, and that this awareness is helped by the imposing presence of well-stocked arsenals. The problem with this argument is that so long as war-avoidance is not the preeminent policy objective, then, despite the costs, other objectives lead to declarations of war. Furthermore, if war appears unavoidable, then, as the rapid descent into World War I demonstrated, the mobilization of forces and the strategic attraction of getting in the first blow might create their own imperatives before political leaders can fully exhaust diplomatic alternatives to war.

From the mid-1950s, arms control was presented as an approach to arms cooperation based on strategic realism. This approach accepted the continuation of the nuclear age but sought to dissuade political leaders from precipitate military action in the midst of a crisis by reducing the incentives for getting in the first blow. If it was not possible to stop political leaders embarking on war as a "rational" act of policy, then it might still be possible to make sure that they remained the masters rather than the victims of events. The cooperative management of the military sphere would ensure the primacy of the political sphere at times of conflict.

Arguably the origins of this approach can be discerned at the 1932–1933 disarmament conference, where one objective was to render aggressors impotent through the proscription of "offensive" weapons. Unfortunately no weapon readily falls into a strict category of "offensive" or "defensive." In the case of heavy artillery and tanks, designated the key weapons for a land offensive, there would be occasions, such as when it was required to dislodge invaders from a foothold, when the defense might wish to call on these weapons. Yet while these weapons might be useful to the defense, they would be invaluable to the offense. (In ordering German rearmament, Hitler stressed "offensive weapons such as heavy tanks and artillery.") Offensiveness or defensiveness might be considered properties of a total force structure, but does that mean it is necessary to ask whether or not a professional army is more suitable for aggression than a conscript army? At the conference there was intense debate about the point at which a particular weapon developed the qualities necessary for offensive action, for example when a tank moved from

being "light" to "heavy." The British and Americans disliked submarines for their "offensive" role as commerce raiders, while the French and others considered them defensive as the only weapon that, at the time, enabled a nation with few capital ships to defend itself at sea. A sufficiently cunning and resourceful offense can still prosper by making full use of the advantages of surprise, geographic position, and enemy uncertainties, as well as by making inspired use of non-prohibited weapons. It was not, for example, until the German sweep through Europe in 1940 that the tactical uses of aircraft as an offensive instrument were fully appreciated.

There was also the question of what confidence could be shown in such agreements if political relations deteriorated. Until the 1930s, the strategic advantage that might be gained through the violation of an arms treaty was not seriously considered. During the 1920s, with the exception of the control commission to check Germany's compliance with the Treaty of Versailles (and here the problem was not a lack of knowledge of Germany's transgressions but the reluctance to do anything about them), it was assumed by most governments that compliance was not a problem; international law would be respected. With the worsening world climate of the early 1930s, the Americans, British, and Soviets all swung round to the emphatic and total endorsement of international inspection. In 1955, President Dwight Eisenhower (1890–1969) suggested that transparency could be a confidence-building measure in its own right. His "open skies" proposal of October 1955 involved the mutual exchange of blueprints of "military establishments from one end of our countries to the other" and verification of these by reciprocal aerial inspection. This position was maintained by the United States in all arms negotiations with the Soviet Union after the war until 1958. The Soviets were reluctant to give up their high level of military secrecy, considered a great strategic asset, and saw "open skies" as just another form of espionage. Eventually this asset was severely diminished by the advent of reconnaissance satellites, which came to be accepted by both sides as a means of verification.

The open skies idea was discussed during the late 1950s as part of an East-West discourse on the specific question of avoiding surprise attacks. The American approach, which very much informed the original concept of arms control, depended on the need to reduce the possibility of getting caught out by a long-range nuclear strike that would remove the capacity for retaliation. The most deadly surprise attacks in the thermonuclear age, therefore, would be planned and executed within the territory of a superpower and would take the form of a first strike by long-range bombers or intercontinental ballistic missiles (ICBMs). U.S. proposals started from the assumption that before concrete adjustments could be made in force structures, it was necessary to build up confidence in the pacific intentions behind current military dispositions and to develop a system of inspection so as to demonstrate that any agreements could be verified. They led eventually to proposals in the strategic arms limitation talks to remove antiballistic missiles (ABMs) on the grounds not only that these systems encouraged the proliferation of offensive weapons (the offense being always likely to retain the upper hand in any contest) but also, to be sure that the defense would be swamped, that they might give an aggressor confidence in the possibility of defense against any residual retaliation after an attempted first strike against the enemy's means of retaliation. The Soviets needed some persuading of this case before the 1972 ABM Treaty could be agreed to, and later Republican administrations in the United States also wondered about the wisdom of banning "defensive" weapons in this way.

Just as the American proposals were guided by a fear of a "nuclear Pearl Harbor," Soviet proposals reflected their past experiences of surprise attacks. They also reflected a traditional view that to prepare for aggressive war, it was necessary to concentrate forces suitable for an invasion. Therefore, if the forces of NATO and the Warsaw Pact could be prevented from getting too close to each other in the areas of major tension in the center of Europe, then the opportunities to start a war, deliberately or through miscalculation, would be diminished. Soviet proposals therefore involved reducing armaments in Central Europe, establishing a nuclear-free zone, and, in addition, setting up control posts at large ports, railway junctions, highways, and aerodromes to guard against "dangerous concentrations" of forces. The military sterilization of Germany was a recurrent theme, as this was the

country that had launched a surprise attack against the Soviet Union in 1941. During the late 1950s, there was substantial interest in NATO countries in the idea of "disengagement" in Central Europe, but the ideas fell foul of the political realities of the time. There was a familiar problem of equitable concessions. Disarmament in a zone equal in area on both sides of the Iron Curtain would be strategically unfair to NATO in that NATO lacked defense in depth and its zone would contain more installations of strategic significance than the Eastern zone. A nuclear-free zone would also have been comparatively disadvantageous to the West. More seriously, while a zone that took the Iron Curtain as its central line might make military sense, it was diplomatically awkward because it required recognition of the division of Europe and, in particular, of the division of Germany.

This final objection was eased as a result of the move to détente in the early 1970s. By the time of the 1975 Helsinki Conference on Security and Cooperation in Europe, the division of Europe was formally recognized. The new Mutual and Balanced Force Reduction (MBFR) talks involved a central guidelines area; nonetheless, the basic problem of asymmetry in force structures remained. Attempts to develop a compromise based on a trade-off between the prime offensive weapons held by each side—Western "tactical" nuclear weapons for Soviet tanks—did not get anywhere. Helsinki did lead to the introduction of confidence-building measures by the provisions for notification of and attendance at large-scale maneuvers. The experience of these measures, which the Warsaw Pact never took seriously, if anything, reduced confidence in arms control.

AFTER THE COLD WAR

During the darker days of the Cold War, there was debate over whether measures of disarmament or arms control might be the key to an improvement in political relations, or whether they must wait upon such an improvement taking place for other reasons. The manner of the Cold War's conclusion confirmed that cooperative agreements on armed forces are shaped by, rather than shape, core political relations. Agreements were most needed when relations were poor, but the lack of trust made them hard to achieve. Thus the conditions in the

Soviet general secretary Mikhail Gorbachev and U.S. president Ronald Reagan sign the Intermediate Nuclear Forces Reduction Treaty in Washington, D.C., 8 December 1987. AP/WIDE WORLD PHOTOS

late 1980s made traditional arms control more possible to achieve, with regular summits between the superpowers and the winds of political change blowing throughout the communist world, but also rendered the agreements largely irrelevant, though the informal aspects of the negotiating process may at times have provided important opportunities for communication and reassurance. In practice, arms control reinforced the dominant political tendency of the time. When tensions were increasing, it could aggravate the process (for example, through disagreements over compliance or intransigence over apparently trivial points of negotiating detail). When tensions were easing, it could accelerate an improvement in relations. During the last years of the Cold War, there were major breakthroughs with agreements in 1987 on intermediate nuclear forces (INF) that saw cruise

and Pershing nuclear missiles (which had caused massive protests in Western Europe at the start of the decade) and Soviet SS-20 missiles being removed. Even more important was the major Treaty on Conventional Armed Forces in Europe (CFE), which was signed to mark the formal end of the Cold War in November 1990. The CFE framework allocated force levels to individual states. These numbers represented high ceilings rather than realistic floors. As they were to be monitored, this element of transparency was hailed as an important source of confidence-building. But the political shift meant that many of its provisions were irrelevant and sometimes counterproductive as the states of postcommunist Europe started to reassess their strategic interests.

The problem, at least in Europe, shifted away from one of reinforcing stability in relations among great powers to creating stability in the internal and external relationships of medium, small, and in some cases quite tiny powers. The instruments employed by the international community in their attempts to rein in the various conflicts that erupted throughout the former Yugoslavia during the 1990s illustrate the new options: arms embargoes, air-exclusion zones, air and land humanitarian relief corridors, control of artillery pieces, cease-fire lines. All these measures suffered from partiality, in controlling only limited types of military activity, and also in tending to favor one side rather than another in the conflict. There is clearly much to be said for limiting the availability of weapons to the belligerents, but an embargo will tend to penalize the weaker, especially if geographically isolated (so that an embargo is readily enforced) and without an indigenous arms industry. The 1996 Dayton Peace Agreement on Bosnia, which included an arms control element, was turned into an agreement on force levels. Essentially the deal saw the Bosnian Serbs agreeing to cut down their arsenal (largely in the form of more elderly weapons) in return for a cap on the combined Muslim-Croat federation forces, which they could see growing through the combined efforts of the United States and a number of Muslim states. The agreement reflects the expectation of "balance," but of course the balance only exists to the extent that the federation holds together and that it is not upset by external sources in the event that hostilities resume. Stability here really depended on a continuing and strong international presence. The history of arms control warns that it can never be free-standing but is always a function of larger questions concerning the utility of force and security guarantees. It must also reflect the broad political currents of the time.

See also **Cold War; Disarmament; Helsinki Accords; NATO; Nuclear Weapons; Peace Movements; Warsaw Pact.**

BIBLIOGRAPHY

Blacker, Coit D., and Gloria Duffy, eds. *International Arms Control: Issues and Agreements.* 2nd edition. Stanford, Calif., 1984. A good assessment of efforts during the Cold War.

Blackwill, Robert D., and F. Stephen Larrabee, eds. *Conventional Arms Control and East-West Security.* Durham, N.C., 1989. Covers conventional arms control in Europe.

Bunn, George. *Arms Control by Committee: Managing Negotiations with the Russians.* Stanford, Calif., 1992. Another account of the negotiating process.

Graham, Thomas. *Disarmament Sketches: Three Decades of Arms Control and International Law.* An interesting memoir covering many key negotiations.

Madariaga, Salvador de. *Disarmament.* New York, 1929. Reprint, Port Washington, N.Y., 1967. A sharp, classic critique of disarmament over this period.

McKercher, B.J.C., ed. *Arms Limitation and Disarmament: Restraints on War 1899–1939.* Westport, Conn., 1992. On the history of arms control and disarmament up to World War II.

Pelz, Stephen E. *Race to Pearl Harbor: The Failure of the Second London Naval Conference and the Onset of World War II.* Cambridge, Mass., 1974. Covers naval treaties.

SIPRI Yearbooks: World Armaments and Disarmament. Oxford, U.K., 1968–. The best coverage of postwar discussions on arms control and disarmament.

Talbott, Strobe. *Deadly Gambits: The Reagan Administration and the Stalemate in Nuclear Arms Control.* New York, 1984. An inside account of many of the nuclear arms control debates relating to Europe.

Wittner, Lawrence S. *Toward Nuclear Abolition: A History of the World Nuclear Disarmament Movement.* Stanford, Calif., 1971. Fully covers the history of the antinuclear movements pushing for disarmament.

LAWRENCE FREEDMAN

ARON, RAYMOND (1905–1983), French philosopher and political commentator.

Raymond-Claude-Ferdinand Aron was born in Paris and his education was that of a young French bourgeois, son of a law professor. He was a brilliant student, entering the elite École Normale Supérieure in 1924 and placing first in the philosophy *agrégation* in 1928. He was Jewish but had no particular concern with religion. Immanuel Kant presided over his philosophical development, thanks notably to the influence of the neo-Kantian Léon Brunschvicg, though Aron would later feel that this perspective was inadequate. He was introduced to the social sciences by Célestin Bouglé, a social democrat who was the director of the Centre de Documentation Sociale at the École Normale.

In the 1920s Aron felt a certain affinity for Alain, philosopher of "man against [established] powers." This affinity, however, had more to do with Alain the man who fought as a simple private in World War I than Alain the philosopher and moralist, whose pacifism seemed to Aron to lead nowhere. He felt no attraction whatever, meanwhile, for Charles Maurras, the other star in the French conservative intellectual firmament of the time and leader, with his newspaper *L'Action Française,* of the party of reaction. Maurras's desire to restore the ancien régime struck Aron as irrelevant—trapped in the impasse of any traditionalism seeking to reinstate an order that no longer exists; a situation exacerbated in his view by the fact that the "modern" aspects of Maurras's views brought him close to fascism. What Maurras shared with Alain was an antihistorical and anachronistic approach; to Aron the thinking of both men smacked of ideology, and both turned their backs on the resources of critical rationality.

As a young philosopher Aron spent the years 1930–1933 in Germany, first in Cologne and then in Berlin. There he encountered politics in full flood—and there his Jewishness was assaulted by Hitlerism. He also encountered the critical philosophy of history, especially the work of Karl Marx and Max Weber. His discovery of German politics, as of German philosophy and sociology, determined the particular feeling for the relativity and tragedy of history expressed in his doctoral thesis, *Introduction à la philosophie de l'histoire* (1938; *Introduction to the Philosophy of History: An Essay on the Limits of Historical Objectivity,* 1961). His lucidity concerning the political situation was manifest in an article of 1939, "États démocratiques et états totalitaires" (Democratic and totalitarian states). The year 1940 found him in London, where, in the periodical *La France Libre,* independently of Charles de Gaulle and his followers, he honed his talents as an acute analyst of ideas and political situations and began to address international politics and strategy. In this context he was one of the first (in 1944) to evoke what he called "secular religions" to describe ideologies.

At the beginning of the Cold War, Aron was somewhat attracted by social democracy, but he soon moved on. His approach was in part polemical, polemics being for him an essential dimension of thought in general and liberalism in particular. His liberalism was increasingly defined by way of contrast with the French Left, which he engaged in debate around three themes: ideology, totalitarianism, and Soviet imperialism.

For Aron "ideology" meant the kind of distortion of reason that he examined in articles written between 1947 and 1968, many of which were collected in *Polémiques* (1955) and *Marxismes imaginaires* (1970). His main work on the subject appeared in 1955: *L'opium des intellectuels* (*The Opium of the Intellectuals,* 1957). Aron's targets in this book were revolutionary idealists such as Jean-Paul Sartre, who passed directly from the ontology of a free consciousness to total political commitment. The intellectuals he was addressing were less "men of the Church" (i.e., card-carrying Communists) than those "men of faith" in whom he detected not only the search for a secular religion but also the traces of a reason needing to be retrieved. He argued that three myths had to be demystified, namely the Left, the revolution, and the proletariat. Each updated an earlier myth: progress, reason, and the people, respectively. The myth of the Left projected a retrospective illusory unity into the future. Aron distinguished between a "historical left," seeking salvation through Marxism and the Soviet Union, and an "eternal left," to which he claimed allegiance, that refused all orthodoxy (*Opium,* p. 45). The historical Left was fascinated by revolutionary violence and defended the myth of a revolution that had been no more than the violent replacement of one elite by another. The proletariat had fallen victim to its own myth, which had turned it into a new messiah: the epitome of total alienation. History, he argued, was the framework within which these political myths were deployed and reinterpreted by existentialist Marxists—primarily Sartre and Maurice Merleau-Ponty—in accordance with their philosophy and reading of the young Marx's theory of alienation. In this way, for Aron, they abandoned the study of concrete reality for "metaphysical controversies" ("Marxisme et existentialisme," 1948, in *Marxismes imaginaires,* p. 61). Later, in *La révolution introuvable* (1968; *The Elusive Revolution,* 1969), Aron broadened his critique to include the events of May 1968.

The constructive side of Aron's attack on ideological thinking emerged in his opposition to totalitarian regimes and the comparison he drew between totalitarianism and "constitutional-pluralist régimes" in *Démocratie et totalitarisme* (1965). He first tackled this issue on the eve of World

War II in connection with "totalitarian tyrannies" (*Machiavel et les tyrannies modernes*), when he discussed the technique of seizing and retaining power. The Machiavellianism he described was profound, resting on a conception of man that supported the "totalitarian spirit" and eliminated "every obligation with respect to persons" (*Les guerres en chaîne* [Chain-reaction wars], 1951, p. 483; translated from the French). From this time until *Démocratie et totalitarisme*, Aron continued to elaborate upon his theory of totalitarianism, ending up with a model, based mainly on the Soviet Union, which was close to that of Carl J. Friedrich and which stipulated five defining characteristics: a single party monopolizing the political sphere; armed with an absolute ideology; sole proprietor of the means of coercion and persuasion; master of all economic and social life; and capable of wreaking terror by virtue of the politicization of all activities. The "chief variable," however, concerned the presence or absence of parties, the constitutional or unconstitutional exercise of authority: "the institutional mode of transmission of the democratic principle" (*Démocratie*, p. 98; translated from the French). Aron gave an existential primacy to politics that effectively linked his thinking to the international dimension.

Soviet imperialism was indeed asserting itself during this period, which Aron preferred to call a "bellicose peace" rather than a cold war. As he wrote in the French daily newspaper *Le Figaro* for 10 December 1947, "it is henceforth the political parties that wage the battles of worldwide diplomacy." He summed things up in the same year with the title "Paix impossible, guerre improbable" (Peace impossible, war improbable, in *Le grand schisme*, 1948). Although he belonged to the realist tendency in international studies, Aron felt that the clash of national interests was not direct. In his view American policy was defensive, following a period of hesitancy, whereas Soviet policy was offensive, its tactics changing according to the circumstances. He refused to wear blinkers with respect to the weaknesses of American diplomacy, but unlike the pro-communist Left he stressed the duty of free regimes to defend themselves against the two main characteristics of Soviet imperialism, namely its boundless ambitions and its promotion of "permanent war." A strategy of containment

was indispensable to the defense of a free Europe. The adoption of such a strategy by the United States represented a victory over American isolationism. The Korean War was a turning point: Mao Zedong's seizure of power in China had brought the Far East into the arena of world diplomacy and confirmed the necessity of action. At the close of this period of "limited war," Aron enumerated three features of the international standoff in *Paix et guerre entre les nations* (1962; *Peace and War: A Theory of International Relations*, 1966): persuasion (ideological), dissuasion (conventional and nuclear), and subversion (indirect conflict via guerrilla warfare). This summary was precisely, for Aron, what the "historical left" rejected, whether out of ideological fear or because of a partial or complete allegiance to a Soviet regime that negated the very freedoms that it claimed to champion.

Aron's legacy is varied, as is consistent with his thought. His direct or indirect disciples have explored and continue to explore different areas of the social sciences, including political science (Pierre Manent and Philippe Raynaud), philosophy and international relations (Pierre Hassner), history (François Furet), and political economy (Jean-Claude Casanova). At the same time, a rediscovery of Aron's own contribution is under way, both abroad and in France, as a result of a renewed interest in the politics and intellectual debates of the twentieth century and especially in political liberalism. This rediscovery continues to explore the pluralism of Aron's thinking and has found a congenial institutional focus in the Raymond Aron Center for Political Research at the École des Hautes Études en Sciences Sociales in Paris.

See also **Merleau-Ponty, Maurice; Sartre, Jean-Paul.**

BIBLIOGRAPHY

Primary Sources

Aron, Raymond. *Les guerres en chaîne.* Paris, 1951.

———. *L'opium des intellectuels.* Paris, 1955.

———. *Polémiques.* Paris, 1955. Writings from 1949 to 1954.

———. *Démocratie et totalitarisme.* Paris, 1965.

———. *La révolution introuvable.* Paris, 1968.

———. *Marxismes imaginaires: D'une sainte famille à l'autre.* Paris, 1970. Writings from 1948 to 1970.

———. *Penser la guerre, Clausewitz.* 2 vols. Paris, 1976.

———. *Le spectateur engagé*. Paris, 1981.

———. *Mémoires: 50 ans de réflexion politique*. Paris, 1983.

———. *Paix et guerre entre les nations*. 8th ed. Paris, 1984.

———. *La guerre froide*. Edited by Georges-Henri Soutou. Paris, 1990. Articles about international politics published in *Le Figaro* from June 1945 to May 1955.

———. *Machiavel et les tyrannies modernes*. Paris, 1993. Writings from 1938 to 1982.

———. *Introduction à la philosophie politique: Démocratie et révolution*. Paris, 1997.

Secondary Sources

Baverez, Nicolas. *Raymond Aron: Un moraliste au temps des idéologies*. Paris, 1993.

Gremioon, Pierre. *Intelligence de l'anticommunisme: Le congrès pour la liberté de la culture*. Paris, 1995.

Launay, Stephen. *La pensée politique de Raymond Aron*. Préface de Philippe Raynaud. Paris, 1995.

———. "Un regard politique sur le communisme: Remarques sur la pensée de Raymond Aron." *Communisme* (L'Age d'Homme, Paris) 62–63 (2000).

Mahoney, Daniel J. *The Liberal Political Science of Raymond Aron: A Critical Introduction*. Lanham, Md., 1992.

STEPHEN LAUNAY

ARP, JEAN (also known as Hans Arp; 1886–1966), Alsace-born artist and poet.

Moving easily between the French and German languages, Jean Arp developed a cosmopolitan outlook from an early age through his contacts with the European avant-garde. A member of the expressionist generation, he was one of the founders of the Dada movement in Zurich and contributed to surrealism in the interwar years. Arp is considered a pioneer of abstract art and poetry who explored automatic composition through the idea of chance. Born out of an impersonal creative act, abstract art expressed spiritual truths by means of form alone and was thus in search of the absolute and the transcendent.

As a teenager Arp had been part of a Strasbourg avant-garde group, led by the writer René Schickele, that sought to rejuvenate Alsatian culture through international modernist styles. Having attended art schools in Weimar and Paris, Arp moved to Switzerland in 1909 to become a founder-member of the Moderne Bund in Lucerne. Largely drawing on the human figure, his paintings and woodcuts of this period are executed in a swift style, thick colors and black silhouettes giving them an expressive quality. Arp exhibited with the Blaue Reiter (Blue Rider) group in Munich and contributed to Wassily Kandinsky and Franz Marc's *Blaue Reiter* almanac (1913), sharing their interest in primitivism and Romanticism. His view that modern art should reject naturalism and express higher truths by means of form, line, and color alone links him with many expressionists. Like the Blaue Reiter, Arp saw abstract art as holding the key to the spiritual awakening and renewal of humankind. At the same time, influenced also by cubism and futurism, he contributed to the expressionist periodical *Der Sturm* and began to create collages on paper and fabric, some of which he exhibited in Zurich in late 1915. It was at this exhibition that he met the Swiss artist and dancer Sophie Taeuber (1889–1943), who was to become his lifelong partner. Inspired by Taeuber's abstract pictures, he began collaborating with her on collages using cutout squares to create vertical-horizontal compositions modulated only by the nonsymmetrical use of dark colors.

From Dada's beginnings in Zurich in early 1916, Arp became its principal visual artist, producing collages, woodcuts, paintings, lithographs and three-dimensional reliefs. He also participated in performances and contributed artwork and texts to publications. For Arp, Dada was not just "against art" but "for nature and life," suggesting that Dada's nihilistic anti-art stance be transformed into an ethics of creativity.

Arp's typical style emerged during the Dada years. Resolutely abstract, his art continued to be characterized by simple geometrical forms, as in his collage *Squares Arranged According to the Law of Chance* (1917), where Arp dropped pieces of paper onto a mount and fixed them where they landed. For Arp, the law of chance was a creative principle, inscrutable to humans and only to be experienced by completely surrendering to the unconscious. Chance was also closely linked to nature. Hence at the other pole of Arp's creativity was biomorphic abstraction, exemplified by his painted wood reliefs. These incorporate materials and shapes

Coquille Bâillante (Yawning Scallop). Sculpture by Jean Arp, 1964–1965. ART RESOURCE, NY

from nature, while their infinitely variable appearance suggests constant metamorphosis.

From the Dada years onward, Arp wrote poetry attempting to emulate the effects of abstraction in language. His poems, too, follow the "law of chance," integrating in dreamlike fashion contrary styles and meanings. Like his art, Arp's abstract poetry represents a radical break with symbolic language to explore prerational expressiveness.

From 1918, Arp collaborated with other Dada artists such as Max Ernst, Kurt Schwitters, and Raoul Hausmann, as well as forging important links with German-based constructivists such as Lazlo Moholy-Nagy and El Lissitzky. Through Ernst, Arp was introduced to the circle around André Breton, who in 1924 launched the surrealist movement. Arp exhibited and published with the surrealists, but this allegiance did not alter his style or his outlook. While continuing to work in ink, paper, and wood, Arp also explored new materials such as plaster and stone. Moving on from his Dada

biomorphism, he produced distinctive sculptures utilizing more solid curvilinear shapes. Arp's art and poetry came to be seen as an example of surrealist "automatism," although his radical submission to chance had little to do with the psychoanalytic framing of automatism propagated by the surrealists.

Throughout this period, Arp was in contact with artists and groups that preferred geometric abstraction, such as Cercle et Carré (Circle and Square) in Paris, formed around his friend Michel Seuphor. In 1928 Arp, Taeuber, and the Dutch artist Theo van Doesburg collaborated in creating a modernist interior design for the Strasbourg Café de l'Aubette. From the early 1930s onward, Arp produced numerous sculptures he called *Concretions* that suggest a return to the human figure while also incorporating organic forms and resisting facile naturalism.

See also **Avant-Garde; Dada; Modernism; Painting, Avant-Garde.**

BIBLIOGRAPHY

Primary Sources

Arp, Jean. *On My Way*. New York, 1948.

————. *Arp on Arp*. Translated by Joachim Neugroschel. New York, 1972.

————. *Collected French Writings*. Translated by Joachim Neugroschel. London, 1974.

————. *Arp: Line and Form*. Essay by Walburga Krupp. New York, 2000. Exhibition catalog.

Arp, Hans, and El Lissitzky. *Die Kunstismen. Les Ismes d'Art. The Isms of Art*. New York, 1925. Reprint, Baden, 1990.

Secondary Sources

Andreotti, Margherita. *The Early Sculpture of Jean Arp*. Ann Arbor, Mich., 1989.

Fauchereau, Serge. *Arp*. New York, 1988.

Giedion-Welcker, Carola. *Jean Arp*. Translated by Norbert Guterman. New York, 1957.

Hancock, Jane, and Stefanie Poley, curators. *Arp, 1886–1966*. Translated by John Gabriel et al. Cambridge, U.K., 1987. Exhibition catalog.

Last, Rex W. *Hans Arp: The Poet of Dadaism*. London, 1968.

Read, Herbert. *The Art of Jean Arp*. New York, 1968.

Soby, John Thrall, ed. *Arp*. New York, 1958. Exhibition catalog.

ANDREAS KRAMER

ARTAUD, ANTONIN (1896–1948), French writer, actor, director, dramatist, and dramatic theorist.

Along with German dramatist and director Bertolt Brecht, Antonin Artaud was the theorist whose ideas had the most decisive influence on the development of European and American theater in the twentieth century. Born in Marseille, Artaud moved in 1920 to Paris, where he worked as a theater and film actor and published his first texts. From 1924 to 1926 he was a member of the avant-garde surrealist group of artists and writers led by André Breton. Artaud shared the surrealists' fascination with dreams and the unconscious as sources of creativity, as well as their transgressive and defiant spirit of rebellion against middle-class values. However, he disagreed strongly with their decision to align themselves with the Communist Party. Artaud felt that only a spiritual or metaphysical revolution—not a political revolution—was needed in modern Europe. Because of this fundamental disagreement, he was expelled from the surrealist movement in 1926. He then cofounded the Alfred Jarry Theater (named after Alfred Jarry, the provocative author of the 1896 play *King Ubu*, which caused a riot when it opened in Paris). The Alfred Jarry Theater was able to mount only a few productions between 1927 and 1930, when it closed. Later, in 1935, Artaud staged *The Cenci*, a drama of incest and murder. This production failed to incarnate his ideas on theater in a clear way and ended after seventeen days. Following journeys to Mexico and Ireland in 1936 and 1937, Artaud spent almost nine years confined in French insane asylums. In 1946 he returned to Paris, where he gave a last performance at the Vieux Colombier Theater in 1947. During his final years, he produced many volumes of new writings and many drawings.

Artaud is best known for his influential project for a new theater, which he called "The Theater of Cruelty." His 1938 book *The Theater and Its Double* is a visionary manifesto offering powerful metaphors for the theater as a form of plague or alchemy, along with more concrete proposals for renewing theater by returning to its primitive origins. Like the plague or alchemy, theater should bring about a total transformation, Artaud argued. It needed to move beyond its debased status as entertainment. Rather than presenting actors playing characters who discuss their thoughts and feelings on stage, at a remove from the audience, the Theater of Cruelty would abolish the separation between the audience's space and the performance space. Theater would become a collective ritual, like a primitive religious ritual. In this revitalized theater, language would no longer be used as an abstract medium for the exchange of ideas; it would have the same function as lighting, sound, props, and the other basic elements of staging. In the end, through violent sounds, images, and gestures presenting famous myths in a new form, the Theater of Cruelty would propel the audience into an altered state of consciousness, leading them to a spiritual cleansing and enlightenment. Artaud defined "cruelty" not (exclusively) as sadism or

Antonin Artaud (right) in Carl Theodor Dreyer's film *The Passion of Joan of Arc,* 1928. BRIDGEMAN ART LIBRARY

violence but as a cosmic rigor or implacable necessity imposing itself on the bodies of the actors.

Artaud's project for a Theater of Cruelty is generally considered impossible to realize. *The Theater and Its Double* presents no practical blueprint. However, many of the individual suggestions made in the book had an immense impact on the ideas and practices of various major directors, theater groups, and playwrights during the second half of the twentieth century. In particular, a revival of interest in Artaud's thought took place in the 1960s and 1970s. The director Peter Brook of the Royal Shakespeare Company cofounded a troupe called the Theater of Cruelty in the 1960s, and Brook's 1964 production of the German playwright Peter Weiss's play *Marat/Sade* is a celebrated example of Artaudian theater. Similarly, in America, Julian Beck and Judith Malina's Living Theater, Joseph Chaikin's Open Theater, and Richard Schechner's Performance Group incorporated important insights of Artaud into their work. Moreover, critics have discussed Artaudian features in plays written by Fernando Arrabal and Jean Vauthier in France, by Sam Shepard in the United States, and by Peter Shaffer in Britain, among others. Artaud's ideas continue to influence work in the theater in the twenty-first century. For example, DNA Theatre in Toronto undertook a series of performances entitled "Artaud and His Doubles" in the 1990s, including a production of Artaud's own 1923 play *The Spurt of Blood*. The American performance artists Rachel Rosenthal and Diamanda Galas also acknowledge the relevance of his thought for their work.

See also **Brecht, Bertolt; Brook, Peter; Theater.**

BIBLIOGRAPHY

Primary Sources

Artaud, Antonin. *The Theater and Its Double.* Translated by Mary Caroline Richards. New York, 1958.

———. *Antonin Artaud: Selected Writings.* Edited by Susan Sontag and translated by Helen Weaver. New York, 1976.

Secondary Sources

Barber, Stephen. *Antonin Artaud: Blows and Bombs.* London, 1993.

Bermel, Albert. *Artaud's Theater of Cruelty.* New York, 1977.

Plunka, Gene A., ed. *Antonin Artaud and the Modern Theater.* London, 1994.

Scheer, Edward, ed. *Antonin Artaud: A Critical Reader.* London, 2004.

JOHN C. STOUT

ART DECO. The term *art deco* originates from the 1925 International Exhibition of Modern Decorative and Industrial Arts that took place in Paris. Initially planned for 1916 and postponed because of World War I, this exhibition consecrated a style that is often associated with the postwar years but that dates back to the early twentieth-century reaction against the lyrical excesses and flowerings of art nouveau, which is sometimes referred to as noodle style. It was therefore as early as 1910, at the Salon des Artistes Décorateurs, that critics hailed the emergence of a truly modern decorative art, with refined geometrical forms, just when the names of its future great masters in France, such as Maurice Dufrêne and Paul Follot, were emerging. After World War I, the need for change and the desire to create a totally new living environment contributed to the final repudiation of the Belle Epoque style. For Dufrêne, the art of 1900 belonged to the realm of fantasy, whereas the art of 1925 would belong to the realm of reason.

"BE MODERN"

However, the style of 1925 was more than a reaction to art nouveau. It emerged and developed within a social context dominated by the slogan "be modern." Nevertheless, unlike the modernist movement, for which modernism was an ideological concept, this style responded to the aspirations of the middle classes, with their sensitivity to a particular French tradition as well as to speed, the machine age, and the trends of fashion, while also drawing on an amalgam of exotic inspirations originating from Turkey, Russia, Egypt, Africa, and Japan. Space in art deco is also different from the modernist concept of space; it rejects the universal project, internationalism, and the notion of collectivism in the broadest sense, instead combining individual and national values under the common denominator of modernity and contemporaneity. It is realist in accordance with its age—the space is both functional and decorative in the traditional sense of the art of living in this period.

The 1925 International Exhibition in Paris marked the apogee of this movement. The pavilions offered an insight into the prevailing situation, in which innovative standpoints (seen in the Dutch, Danish, and Polish pavilions) alternated with traditional concepts (seen in the Spanish and Greek pavilions). The high point of the exhibition was the plan for a French foreign embassy, organized by the Société des Artistes Décorateurs, which arranged twenty-four spaces in collaboration with interior designers such as Jacques-Émile Ruhlmann, Pierre Patout, Jean Saudé, and Robert Mallet-Stevens. The dominant aesthetic of the embassy was toward luxury, a deliberate choice on the part of these "traditionalist" interior designers, whereas art deco is characterized by a twofold dialectic of tradition and modernity, elite and social art.

Department stores played an important role in the creation, circulation, and democratization of art deco by establishing studios dedicated to the modern decorative arts. The first to appear were the Ateliers Primavera (1912) in the Le Printemps chain of department stores. In 1922, Maurice Dufrêne was appointed to run Maîtrise, the creative studio at the Galeries Lafayette; the following year, Paul Follot took charge of the Pomone line in Bon Marché and Studium in the Le Louvre department stores. Art deco gained mass circulation through these channels, which presented it as the new art of living. Original artwork and personalized architecture were thus replaced by a collection of furniture and ingenious design creations that achieved mass circulation at affordable prices.

Design for the salon of the ambassador's residence. Project for the Exposition Internationale des Arts Décoratifs Modernes in Paris by Henri Rapin, 1925. Bridgeman Art Library

THE ART OF LIVING

In general, architecture, interior décor, and furniture production in art deco were guided by an idea of beauty that was expressed predominantly in ornamentation: they drew inspiration from a sense of refinement and aimed to develop good taste in the general population. Daily living and households were made considerably more pleasant through a profusion of objects created for every budget: the stoneware of René Buthaud, the furniture of Robert Block and Pierre Legrain, the Swedish-manufactured Orrefors vases, the glassware of René Lalique, the wallpapers of Victor Servranckx, the creations of Marcel Wolfers, the jewellery of Dario Viterbo, the fabrics of Atelier Martine and the collections of Duncan Grant and Vanessa Bell. With art deco, fixed household decor could also be changed at will through the addition of new elements: ornamental paneling and sculptures, low-reliefs and friezes, moldings, stucco, mosaics, wrought iron, works in bronze and copper, stained-glass windows, ornamental paintings and frescoes, lacquerware and fabrics.

Among the best-known objects and creators of this period are the furniture of Francis Jourdain and Eileen Gray, who also designed many lacquer screens, having learned the technique from the Japanese artist Sugawara. In 1919, Gray caused a sensation by decorating the apartment of the fashion designer Suzanne Talbot, covering it in black lacquer panels mixed with eggshells. At the other end of the spectrum was Jacques-Émile Ruhlmann, descended from the line of great eighteenth-century cabinetmakers, the quintessence of French genius in the classical tradition. André Groult, who signed the work he had done decorating a bedroom for the embassy at the 1925 exhibition, represented yet another trend, that of the modernizers who revived tradition by combining ancient refined styles, including Louis XV and empire, while also being overtly contemporary in their simple lines and rigorous proportions.

After the 1925 exhibition, the art deco style continued to feature in many buildings, including the spectacular entrance hall of the *Daily Express* (by Robert Atkinson) and the Strand Palace Hotel (by Olivier P. Bernard) in London. The depression of the 1930s brought some decline in the luxury market, as well as in the artistic professions with which art deco was associated. However, the movement continued to develop in the United States, which had been conspicuous by its absence from the 1925 exhibition and which adopted and adapted this style for large symbolic building projects such as the Chrysler Building in New York and for everyday objects created by European émigrés such as the Austrian Paul T. Frankl and the Dane Erik Magnussen.

It is probably in its tremendous capacity for adaptation that the immense success of art deco resides, and the style proved to be highly versatile. Free of all doctrine and difficult to define, this movement continued to be called modern right up to the 1960s and is undoubtedly one of the most protean styles of the twentieth century.

See also **Avant-Garde; Modernism.**

BIBLIOGRAPHY

Art Deco 1910–1939. Exhibition catalog, Victoria and Albert Museum. London, 2003.

Brunhammer, Yvonne, and Suzanne Tise. *The Decorative Arts in France, 1900-1942: La Société des artistes décorateurs.* New York, 1990.

Duncan, Alastair. *Art Deco Furniture: The French Designers.* New York, 1992.

Hillier, Bevis, and Stephen Escritt. *Art Deco Style.* London, 1997.

VIRGINIE DEVILLEZ

ASQUITH, HERBERT HENRY (1852–1928), British politician.

The son of a Yorkshire clothing manufacturer, Herbert Henry Asquith was born on 12 September 1852 in Morley, Yorkshire. Educated at the City of London and Balliol College, Oxford, Asquith became a lawyer in 1876. In the 1886 general election he was elected as the Liberal MP for East Fife. William Gladstone appointed him home secretary after the 1892 general election. He was granted the title Earl of Oxford in 1925. Asquith died on 15 February 1928 at Sutton Courtney, Oxfordshire.

By August 1914 Asquith had established himself as an outstanding figure in British political life. He had been prime minister of the Liberal government since 1908 and had worked efficiently as leader of a ministry with many outstanding figures. Certainly, he had failed so far to resolve some powerful difficulties. But he had presided over the introduction of striking pieces of social legislation and had led a long and successful battle against the powers of the House of Lords.

The collapse of international relations in July–August 1914 did not immediately undermine his position. While country and cabinet were divided about whether war on the Continent required British intervention, Asquith declined to rush to a decision. By 3 August it was evident that, from the British viewpoint, Germany was determined to impose its military hegemony on western Europe, maintain (and increase) its naval challenge to Britain, and crush the unoffending state of Belgium. This placed the issue of Britain's intervention beyond doubt. With only trivial exceptions, government, parliament, and the country followed Asquith's lead.

Asquith instantly brought Lord Kitchener into his Liberal government as war secretary and established a series of dramatic measures to guard national security, ensure the availability of railways for military as well as civilian purposes, and secure alternative sources of sugar.

Yet there was always an aspect of incongruity in this spectacle of a Liberal prime minister leading a government steadily obliged to implement state control. The Liberals were traditionally the party of peace, retrenchment, and reform, the first two of which were inapplicable in wartime and the third, when it occurred, an accidental by-product of war. The expression "business as usual," whereby Britain would just control the seas and meet war costs by developing its peacetime economy, suggested a Liberal position. But it was flatly contradicted by the government's decision to raise a mass (if still voluntary) army to participate in a continental war. The attempt to square this circle, along with problems in the actual conduct of the conflict, rendered Asquith's concluding two years as prime minister painful and ill rewarded.

It is usually claimed that everyone in Britain (excepting Kitchener) expected the war to be over by Christmas 1914. Asquith certainly did not and told the nation later in August that this would be "a protracted struggle." Yet he took little action to create the instruments that would convince the nation that it was being firmly directed. Nor, to all appearances, did he amend his own way of life or enhance his devotion to politics so as to create the impression of a firebrand driving affairs with utter conviction.

In December 1914 he established an eight-man War Council (subsequently the Dardanelles Committee and then the War Committee) as a subcommittee of the cabinet specifically to deal with war matters. But the cabinet retained, and often enough exercised, overall authority, so that the new body seemed rather to extend and even dilute the process of decision-making rather than concentrating it.

The overwhelming problem, of course, was the progress of the war. The small British Expeditionary Force had played a part in putting an end to Germany's bid for quick victory in the West. But Germany retained much of Belgium and France, and the predominance of weapons of defense over offense (at least until 1918) both preserved this situation and extinguished thousands of Allied lives.

So various members of the Liberal government began in early 1915 gestating ideas for a "quick" and even "decisive" victory elsewhere. Only one of these schemes was given serious application, and so was shown to be no improvement on the western front: the naval, and then combined, assault at the Dardanelles. This, it should be noted, was not a scheme imposed on helpless politicians by naval or military chiefs. It was something required of the armed forces by Asquith and other heads of government: a reassuring demonstration that the prime minister retained command of the war, but not, in its outcome, an event that redounded to his credit.

By May 1915 Asquith's difficulties had come sufficiently to a head that, in order to forestall the Conservatives' abandonment of the political truce, he resorted to the formation of a coalition government. His conduct toward some of his Liberal colleagues appeared cavalier, yet the fact remained that he retained many key posts in the government for the Liberals and fobbed off Bonar Law, the Conservative leader, with a quite minor post. In the event, with the course of the war driving politics in a conservative direction, and with the political position of his once principal Liberal colleague David Lloyd George increasingly open to doubt, this did not serve Asquith well.

Lloyd George, plainly, was advancing in the political stakes. As a consequence of a munitions "scandal" severely damaging to Kitchener, Asquith elevated him to the new (and very rewarding) post of minister of munitions. At the same time, Lloyd George was becoming powerfully identified with pressure from Conservative politicians and journalists for the introduction of conscription, a proposal that Asquith clearly disliked but in the end could not resist. Plainly what was keeping Asquith in office was the deep distrust that Lloyd George continued to arouse in the higher ranks of politics, Conservative as well as Liberal. But this meant that Asquith, increasingly, was dependent for his retention of the chief office on a singularly negative factor.

The year 1916 was not a happy one for the prime minister. First Asquith was forced to concede conscription for virtually all male Britons of military age, and then he had to deal with the consequences of the Easter Rebellion in Ireland. Neither event redounded to his credit. Yet it was the Battle of the Somme, commencing on 1 July 1916 and continuing until the outset of winter four and a half months later, that dominated the political landscape. Its huge casualties and failure to take ground left Asquith powerless. People may have recognized that these sorry results were dictated by the nature of warfare in the early twentieth century, but they demanded a leader more visibly devoted to the struggle and more engulfed by hatred of the enemy.

Lloyd George struck in December 1916. He persuaded Bonar Law—aware of the fragility of his own position—to join him in demanding of Asquith the creation of "a small War Committee ... with full powers" of which Asquith, although remaining prime minister, would not be a member. Briefly Asquith contemplated acceptance but recognition of his humiliating position under it, and the appearance of a particularly vicious interpretation in *The Times,* led to his refusal. This was as well, for he would have been an unwelcome fifth wheel on a coach he could not control. So Asquith went, and Lloyd George took power as head of a predominantly Conservative government with an element of Liberals and the qualified support of Labour.

For the rest of the war Asquith remained leader of the Liberal Party, occupying a role of unwavering support for the war and unforgiving, if unexpressed, separation from the government. Only once did he hint at his inner feelings toward Lloyd George, when General Frederick Maurice accused the prime minister in public of concealing his withholding of troops for the western front in the run-up to the Germany offensive of March 1918. The government having proposed an inquiry by judges, Asquith moved instead for a select committee. Lloyd George then realized that any inquiry would cause him great embarrassment and launched against Asquith's motion a withering attack. Asquith needed either to attack or to withdraw his motion but did neither. Lloyd George carried the day. This only mattered because the prime minister was making preparations for his postwar career, which he saw as the leader of a right-wing coalition consisting of the whole Conservative Party and a Liberal splinter group. So in the 1918 general election he selected 150 Liberals, whom he regarded as his particular supporters, and listed them on a "coupon"—a letter to voters cosigned by the unionist chancellor, Andrew Law—thereby guaranteeing a seat in parliament to nearly all of them, as they were unopposed by Conservative candidates. This somewhat disguised the fact that the result was a smashing Conservative victory. Asquith, whose Conservative opponent did not receive the coupon, was nevertheless firmly defeated. And the ruling Liberal Party of four years earlier was now not even an official opposition.

Yet this is not the last word to be said about Asquith. In part thanks to his direction in peace and war, Britain emerged from the conflict a partially welfare and a firmly liberal (if not Liberal) state, in which free trade and free service and freedom of opinion continued (anyway for the moment) unchallenged. It was not a small achievement.

See also **Lloyd George, David; World War I.**

BIBLIOGRAPHY

Primary Sources

Asquith, Henry Herbert. *H. H. Asquith: Letters to Venetia Stanley.* Edited by Michael Brock and Eleanor Brock. Oxford, U.K., 1982.

Secondary Sources

Cassar, George H. *Asquith as War* Leader. London, 1994.

Jenkins, Roy. *Asquith.* London, 1964.

ROBIN PRIOR

ATATÜRK, MUSTAFA KEMAL

(1881–1938), founder and first president of the Turkish Republic.

Although Atatürk ("Father of Turks") left this world behind in 1938, in Turkey his movie hero profile, icy-blue stare, elegant silhouette, and classically tailored suits remain everywhere to be seen. His portrait adorns the walls of teahouses as far flung as Van and Gaziantep. He was the founder of modern Turkey, the new nation-state forged from the ruins of the Ottoman Empire just after World War I. Sensing his death and wishing to secure his role in history for eternity, Mustafa Kemal began calling himself Atatürk in 1934, and it is the name posterity has assigned him as well. His extraordinary destiny captivated his contemporaries and continues to elicit the interest of historians. The "Kemalist Experiment" represented a crucial moment in the twentieth-century history of the Muslim developing countries. The West has yet to comprehend that what was being erected in Turkey during the 1920s and 1930s was a highly original model of nationalism and authoritarianism that continues even in the twenty-first century to function as the glue cementing the Turkish state and society in place. No other entity in the twentieth century, constructed purely of ideology and history, has so effectively preserved its political power.

In Turkey, Atatürk remains an icon and symbol of veneration and celebration. He is both the historical founder of the Republic and its actual and present foundation as well. His life's story, officially codified, written and told by Atatürk himself on multiple occasions (the most famous of which was the "Six Day Speech" in October 1927), is blended with the history of Turkey and constituted a radical break with Ottoman tradition. Atatürk sought to supply the new nation-state with previously unrecognized roots in the more or less mythical past of the Hittites, in order to deemphasize the Ottoman Empire and its inevitable decline. Atatürk conceived this history while he was building the nation-state, thereby laying the definitive groundwork for a national model that was only beginning to be contested at the turn of the twenty-first century, as Turkey opened to the European Union and with the installation of a moderate Islamic government.

A SOLDIER WITH THE YOUNG TURKS

Originally from Macedonia, one of the richest and most strategically important Ottoman provinces, the young Mustafa Kemal entered the military school at Salonica. He quickly stood out and his military career advanced rapidly because of both his aptitude for command and his personal abilities, but also because he fought in diverse campaigns at a time when the Ottoman Empire was forced to fight on numerous fronts. At the same time he became involved in the Young Turk movement, which was active precisely among those functionaries and officers of the European provinces concerned with reforming the empire in order to avoid its dismantlement, particularly in the Balkans. When Sultan Abdul-Hamid II (r. 1876–1909) surrendered to the demands of the Young Turks on 24 July 1907, what was an insurrection that had bubbled up in Macedonia was transformed into a revolution. The liberal constitution of 1876 was restored and general elections were planned. However, as a series of military and diplomatic reversals mounted, a Muslim-dominated conservative counterrevolution sought to regain power in Constantinople. The Young Turks, though, ultimately succeeded in reversing the situation and consolidating their revolution by having the sultan deposed.

During this period, Mustafa Kemal was earning his stripes (he was promoted to lieutenant-colonel after commanding an infantry division during the Balkan Conflict in 1912) and did not take part directly in these political events. He did, however, pay close attention to the Young Turk experiment (and studied their theoreticians of Turkish nationalism, such as Mehmet Ziya Gökalp [1875–1924]), which would prevail in 1913 in a coup d'état carried out by the most authoritarian members of the Committee of Union and Progress (or "Unionists"). The Young Turk Triumvirate that came to power ended the liberal era launched in 1907 and installed a military dictatorship. The desire to exact revenge against Russia and the Balkan states brought the Ottoman Empire into World War I against the Triple Entente powers (the United Kingdom, France, and Russia). Its new rulers wanted not only to preserve its unity but also to realize a project of pan-Turkish expansion into the Caucasus region. The army, even with Germany's powerful support, proved incapable of repelling the Russian onslaughts, however. The humiliation of these defeats, at Sarikamish in particular, and the nationalist propaganda denouncing the presence of minorities in the empire, drove the Unionist leadership to unleash the twentieth century's first genocide, perpetrated against the Armenians.

A GENERAL VICTORIOUS

At the same time, near the end of April 1915, the Ottoman Empire faced an offensive in the Straits of the Dardanelles when French and English forces landed on Gallipoli. Stiff resistance by the Ottoman army and the heroism of certain of its leaders, including Mustafa Kemal, thwarted the operation; Kemal was then sent to fight the Russians on the Caucasus front, where he was promoted to the rank of general. Following this, Kemal assumed various commands in Syria (as part of the prestigious Yildirim Army Corps) and then in Palestine, where victories on the front line prevented, during two years of conflict, the empire's total collapse. At the beginning of October 1918, the Allies were threatening Constantinople; the Triumvirate withdrew from power, and a new government signed an armistice whose conditions were hard on the empire—in particular Article 7, which authorized the Allies to proceed with the occupation of any territory they deemed necessary. The sole concession made to the empire in the armistice was the right to reassemble troops scattered across its territories in the region of Anatolia and allowing them to retain their light weaponry. The Germans evacuated the Unionist ministers, and the Young Turk movement was effectively scuttled. An Allied fleet entered the Dardanelles and Constantinople was occupied. British, French, Russians, Greeks, Armenians, and

Mustafa Kemal Atatürk inspects Turkish troops, 1922. THE GRANGER COLLECTION, NEW YORK

even Italians assumed control over almost the entire empire based on secret accords. Simultaneously, the Liberal Entente government eliminated the last vestiges of Young Turk power, hoping this reaction would avoid the empire's complete dismantlement, and thereby sign the movement's political death warrant. The Allies, however, dashed these hopes when the Treaty of Sèvres, signed 10 August 1920, consecrated the end of Ottoman sovereign rule and the empire's permanent partition.

Anatolia was the only region to avoid Allied occupation. However, this large central province, whose Turkish population had become wholly homogenous following the destruction of the Christian communities formerly residing there, was largely destabilized due to its exposure to pillage by demobilized soldiers, the destruction of its

infrastructure, and the destitution of its population. A national resistance movement found refuge there, but it was divided between outlaw Young Turks, stragglers devoted to the dream of pan-Turanianism, and Ottoman dissidents. Lauded for his military successes and reputation for authority, at just thirty-nine years of age Kemal was sent to Anatolia in 1919 by the Entente government and entrusted with the mission to reorganize the remaining military troops there, as part of an effort to reassert Constantinople's sovereignty. He landed at Samsum, birthplace of the great Kemalist era, and entered Anatolia where he encountered a fierce but fragmented nationalism based on a hatred aimed equally at both the imperial government and the European powers. Kemal immediately understood the opportunity laid out before him to head up the nationalist movement by offering it a plan for a nation-state founded on three primary values: military strength, Turkishness, and modernity.

This program was deeply Young Turk in inspiration, although it also contained a strong nationalist component. From the outset, numerous and prestigious groups supported Kemal in the great design he set out to accomplish under cover of his official mission. On 22 June 1919 in Amasya, he proclaimed the Turkish nation in danger, launched a call to arms to all patriots, and convoked a national congress. The British then demanded his immediate recall; he chose secession instead. "I shall remain in Anatolia until the Nation has regained its complete independence," was his reply to the sultan as he tendered him his resignation. The national Congresses at Erzurum (July 1919) and Sivas (September 1919) laid the groundwork of Kemalism proper. The National Pact, adopted by delegates assembled from throughout the empire, affirmed the fundamental indivisibility of the Turkish people and the mission to engage in a radical struggle for territorial integrity. Following this, a parliament created by empire-wide general elections defied the Allies by siding with the rebels. Kemal had successfully countered threats from both Constantinople and the maneuverings of the former members of the Unionist Triumvirate. He responded to them by forming a Turkish Grand National Assembly in April 1920 and a government he controlled seated at Angora, the future Ankara.

THE "WAR OF NATIONAL INDEPENDENCE"

Possessing a galvanized and well-organized army, Kemal launched his early military offensives, first against the Armenian forces that had proclaimed an independent republic in the Caucasus. Armenia's incorporation into the Soviet Union, and the common interests shared by the Kemalists and the Soviets (formally laid down by the "Treaty of Brotherhood and Friendship" signed in March 1921), allowed Kemal to divert his troops toward the west. France and Italy quickly ceded the battlefield, making it possible for Kemal to mobilize his forces against the Greeks who were occupying a large portion of Asia Minor but whose troops were dispersed over a large swath of territory. The signing of the Treaty of Sèvres strengthened his political hand in a rebellion he did not entirely control, by allowing him to don the cloak of "reluctant savior of the Turkish nation." His initial military

and political successes had already rendered him the title of ghazi, or triumphant commander. The legend of Kemal had begun. Its telling and retelling would erase his earlier ties with the Young Turks, his strivings after a ministerial career in 1919, and his religious leanings that had made it possible for him to refuse the sultan's fatwa in April 1920.

The Kemalists reached the end of winter 1920–1921, and the renewal of the Greek offensives, in a relatively strong position. Kemal managed to resist the first waves of enemy pressure, and in July 1921 the Grand National Assembly accorded him full powers and named him Generalissimo, at which point he issued the famous order: "Soldiers! March! Objective: The Mediterranean Sea!" After a difficult and at times uncertain battle at Sakarya in August 1921, the Grand National Assembly granted him the title of marshal and officially elevated him to the rank of ghazi. The diplomatic isolation relented after the conclusion of the 16 March 1921 treaty with Moscow and the complete surrender of Cilicia by France on 20 October of the same year. The renewal of the Greek offensive in the spring of 1922 was followed by a victorious counteroffensive conducted by Kemal himself. The Greeks, who had agreed to the Armistice of Moudania (Mudanya) on 15 October 1922, chose negotiation, as did the Allies, who were counting on the sultan and the government in Constantinople to deal with the rising Kemalist regime.

THE TREATY OF LAUSANNE AND THE BIRTH OF MODERN TURKEY

In order to counter the maneuverings of the Allies, Kemal directed his offensive against the remainder of the Ottoman Empire and its institutions. He denounced the sultanate before the Grand National Assembly, which led to a vote for its abolition on 2 November 1922. Sultan Mehmed VI (r. 1918–1922) fled Constantinople and the Kemalists proclaimed his downfall. The ghazi then picked up the pace of his transformation of the old empire by creating a sizable political party known as the Republican People's Party, whose lines of support began with his Anatolian clients. The Republican People's Party handily won the general elections organized for the following June, and Kemal himself was elected head of state by the Grand National Assembly.

The extent to which his victory was complete was then measured by the concluding of the Treaty of Lausanne, which ended the War of Independence. Opened at the beginning of 1923, the treaty's negotiations were quickly cut short by Kemalist intransigence. They resumed on 23 April and the Treaty was signed on 23 July, constituting a bitter reversal of the Treaty of Sèvres, but also the concretization of the ghazi's political and military crusade. At that point the National Pact was entirely completed. The young Kemal regime, sole interlocutor with the Allies, was legally recognized and given full sovereignty over the Turkish territories of the former empire up to and including Thrace in the east, excluding the islands bordering Asia Minor. The sole concession granted was for the Armenians, Greeks, and Jews, who obtained official status as "minorities." The Lausanne Treaty emerged out of a series of other treaties delineating the demographic and territorial map of modern day Turkey, most notably involving a large-scale population exchange of 900,000 Orthodox Christians who moved to Greece, and 400,000 Muslims transferred to Turkey.

On 6 October 1923, Kemalist troops entered Constantinople, which would assume the name *Istanbul* and lose its status as capital in favor of Ankara. The Republic of Turkey was officially declared on 29 October 1923. The makeup of the government highlighted a profound shift away from the form of an empire, and by designating the entire country "Turkiye" (ratified by the Constitution of 1924), the Kemalist regime was rejecting Ottoman and pan-nationalist solutions in order to affirm a nationalist Turkish identity that was incorporated into the state institutions and the territory itself.

KEMAL'S AMBITIONS

To achieve the model Turkish nation and to ensure his own dominion as well, Kemal envisioned a national regime and discourse that borrowed equally from both the fascist regimes and the democracies of the West. The radical modernity of the Kemalist program nonetheless revealed deep-rooted ties to the past, including both the Young Turks, to whom he owed the essentials of his political formation, and the Ottoman Empire, whose cloak of conservative notability he donned in Anatolia. His political bases, steeped in tradition, revealed numerous practices put in place in Ankara that detract from Kemalism's revolutionary character.

Pluralism was suppressed after the Kurdish revolt in February 1925, when a single-party system was instituted by the promulgation of a law to "restore public order" and by the reactivation of the "Independence Tribunals" that had been used to condemn to death hundreds of opposition figures during the war. The Progressive Republican Party was banned along with numerous journalists. An assassination attempt against Kemal at Izmir (Smyrna) on 15 June 1926 was followed by a new phase of repression that decimated the ranks of the remaining Young Turks who had escaped capture previously, along with some of their former collaborators.

The new political path being followed led to the construction of a single-party system centered on one man, the Supreme Head of the Nation and State. The similarities to Italian fascism and Russian sovietism, which arose at that time, were real. The only things missing were the ideological underpinnings and the revolutionary credo that Kemal was to proclaim in his Six-Day Speech at Nutuk, at the first congress of the Republican People's Party from 15 to 20 October 1927. Considered the "Sacred Book of the Turks," this event demonstrated the consolidation of the single-party system and the Kemal cult of personality. By rewriting the entire history of the Turkish people from the Golden Age to the Ottoman downfall, and up until the realization of the Republic in 1923 for which he was proclaimed a hero, Kemal conferred upon future generations, the army, and the state the duty to perpetuate this inaugural and definitive story. This grand historiographic plan would not, however, prove sufficient to anchor Kemalism in Turkish society.

The "Six Pillars," elaborated in 1931, encapsulated the bases of Kemal's regime: nationalism, republicanism, populism, statism, secularism, and finally revolutionarism. The invention during these same years of Turkishness, of being Turkish, was not directly contradictory with this universal project because it proclaimed the Turkish origin of humanity itself. At the same time, Turkishness defined a particular ethnicity whose historical birthplace, according to a racializing framework that nourished serious racism and anti-Semitism, was Anatolia.

REFORMER OR DICTATOR?

The experiments conducted in the 1930s made way for Kemal to strengthen his control over the Turkish state and society by considerably increasing the cult of personality surrounding him. Already ghazi and "Eternal Leader," he became Atatürk ("Father of the Turks") in 1934 through a special law that also forbade all other Turks from the use of the same name. A large number of statues and monuments also appeared during this time. The principle of submitting to the decisions of national leaders, and the most preeminent one among them in particular, was diffused throughout all segments of society. Anything that might disturb national unity or threaten Turkey's territorial integrity was violently attacked. Persecution of the Armenians and Greeks remained prevalent even after the Treaty of Lausanne, and Kurdish revolts were suppressed with extreme harshness.

Atatürk, however, was not a presence among his people solely in the guise of a force of repression and coercion. He instituted a series of highly radical social changes, including the introduction of the Swiss Civil Code in 1926, and the renunciation of the Arabic alphabet in favor of the Latin as part of a purification of the Turkish language in 1928. In 1934 women were accorded the right to vote (in the midst of a single-party system), and in 1935 he instigated the "Six Pillars," including secularism.

This last reform was certainly the most emblematic of the nature of Kemal's political project for Turkey—in which conservatism was harnessed to the needs of revolution. Even as the politico-religious institutions associated with the Ottoman Empire were radically suppressed, the Muslim faith acceded in practice to the status of state religion, because true religious liberty could not exist so long as it threatened Turkish unity and identity.

The final years of Atatürk's life and reign were not the most brilliant. He abused alcohol and shut himself off from the outside world, primarily in his Dolmabahce Palace in Istanbul (the former palace of the last sultans), where he died on 10 November 1938. He left behind a stable, economically developed, and highly cultivated country, most notably in the large cities of Istanbul, Ankara, and Izmir, but also in the regions populated by Kurds and saturated with nationalist sentiment. A colossal mausoleum was erected in Ankara, and an outpouring of iconography was put on display in every public place imaginable. Atatürk's death had transfigured him into a symbol that could be used as justification for any act, benign or malign. A critical historiography could not develop as long as his cult was omnipresent, especially in the army, which guaranteed that his role and regime would live on. Contestation of this official version would only arise at the dawn of the twenty-first century, with the rise to power of moderate Islamic governments ready to replace Kemalist nationalism with a different one: one wrapped in the national flag, as emblem for another kind of ethnocentrism, religious fervor, and populism. Having invented Turkey but being unable to adapt to democratic forms, Atatürk and his Kemalism had become barriers to political and social change. However, given the fact that they continue to embody contemporary Turkey, they remain charged with its problems and impasses.

See also **Armenia; Armenian Genocide; Istanbul; Turkey.**

BIBLIOGRAPHY

Copeaux, Étienne. *Espace et temps de la nation turque: Analyse d'une historiographie nationaliste 1931–1993.* Paris, 1977.

Dumont, Paul. *Mustafa Kemal invente la Turquie moderne.* Brussels, 1983.

Feroz, Ahmad. *The Young Turks.* Oxford, U.K., 1969.

Fromkin, David. *A Peace to End All Peace: The Fall of Ottoman Empire and Creation of the Modern Middle East.* New York, 2001.

Hanioglu, M. S. *Preparation for a Revolution: The Young Turks, 1902–1908.* Oxford, U.K., 2001.

Kedouri, Sylvia, ed. *Turkey before and after Atatürk: Internal and External Affairs.* London, 1999.

——. *Seventy-Five Years of the Turkish Republic.* London, 2000.

Kinross, Patrick Balfour, Baron. *The Ottoman Centuries: The Rise and Fall of the Turkish Empire.* New York, 1977.

——. *Atatürk: The Rebirth of a Nation.* London, 1996.

Kuchner, David. *The Rise of Turkish Nationalism, 1876–1908.* London, 1977.

Lewis, Bernard. *The Emergence of Modern Turkey.* London, 1961.

Mango, Andrew. *Atatürk: Biography of the Founder of Modern Turkey.* London, 2002.

Shaw, Standford J., and Ezel Kural Shaw. *History of the Ottoman Empire and Modern Turkey.* Vol. 2: *Reform, Revolution, and Republic: The Rise of Modern Turkey (1808–1975).* Cambridge, U.K., 1977.

Vaner, Semih, ed. *Modernisation autoritaire en Turquie et en Iran.* Paris, 1991.

Zürcher, Erik Jan. *The Unionist Factor: The Role of the Committee Union and Progress in the Turkish National Movement, 1905–1926.* Leiden, Netherlands, 1984.

———. *Turkey: A Modern History.* London, 1998.

VINCENT DUCLERT

ATHENS. Athens became the capital of Greece in 1834. At the time, it was a small town of around twelve thousand people without economic significance, but it was chosen because of its associations with Greece's glorious ancient history. In the nineteenth century Athens was the administrative center of the country but the centers of economic dynamism (such as commerce, manufacturing, shipping) were located either in other Greek cities like Patras and Ermoúpolis (Syros island) or beyond the borders, in cities of the Ottoman Empire where vibrant Greek communities lived. In the beginning of the twentieth century Athens developed rapidly. In the first two decades of the twentieth century, the urban development of Athens (and its port, Piraeus) exceeded that of other Greek cities. Between 1900 and 1920 the population of Athens grew yearly by 5.6 percent, and in 1920 there were 292,991 people living in the capital. The limits of the city extended and the fields around Athens were divided into small plots and houses were built hastily without any planning. The lower classes lived in the center of the city, in very old homes with unhygienic conditions. In 1924 a committee drafted the first comprehensive city plan for Athens, but it was never taken into consideration; for the next decades the city grew through the integration of small areas that had been divided into plots, and building occurred without prior permission from the authorities.

The 1920s represented a turning point in the history of Athens (and of Greece in general) because of the arrival of Greek refugees from Asia Minor (1922) and the compulsory exchange of populations between Greece and Turkey in the wake of World War I. While most of the refugees settled in rural areas in northern Greece, a considerable number of them (130,000) settled in Athens. The settlement of the refugees presented the government with an unprecedented challenge, and it was one of the few instances in which the government worked out and materialized plans for urban and housing development. The Refugee Settlement Commission oversaw the construction of twelve large and thirty-four minor settlement areas in the outskirts of Athens, and the government facilitated the construction of new houses by providing public land and loans to individuals with favorable terms. Most of the refugees (63 percent) were housed in settlement areas. The arrival of the refugees and a growing wave of internal migration nearly doubled the size of the population of the city of Athens and the number of people living in the surrounding areas also rose spectacularly. In 1928 there were 459,211 people living in Athens, or 802,000, if one includes Piraeus and the areas around Athens.

In the 1920s and 1930s Athens was also transformed from being the administrative to the industrial center of Greece. The refugees provided abundant cheap labor that proved to be crucial for the industrial development of Athens. Nearly half of the refugees were employed in the growing industrial sector while some of the refugee settlement areas were turned into industrial sites, especially for textile and carpet factories. The economic development, however, was fragile and the endemic unemployment of a large number of workers would only grow worse with the world economic crisis of the early to mid-1930s. Class differences became apparent in the residential areas of the city: the upper classes lived in the very center of the city and in the new "garden cities" in the north, whereas the lower classes were concentrated in the new suburbs of Piraeus and in the east and northwest of the capital. At the same time the rise of the population extended the city limits geographically, from 3,264 hectares (8,062 acres) in 1920 to 11,400 hectares (28,158 acres) in 1940. Overcrowding in the center of the city and changing trends in architecture opened the way for the construction of apartment blocks and high-rise buildings, which had been rare before World War II.

On 6 April 1941 Nazi Germany invaded Greece and on 27 April German troops entered

Athens. During the winter of 1941–1942 the population of Athens suffered from a terrible famine. The cessation of imports of cereals from overseas, due to the naval blockade, and the economic dislocation that the war and occupation brought deprived the population of the capital of the necessary foodstuffs. About forty thousand people died in Athens from hunger and related causes during the winter months. The situation improved in the following years thanks to the relief aid that the International Red Cross imported and distributed to the population. The distribution of relief in the capital and the destruction in the countryside caused by the occupation forces in campaigns against the resistance forces brought several thousands of destitute people to Athens—it is estimated that about 1.5 million people lived in Athens during the occupation. The leftist resistance organization, the National Liberation Front (EAM), gained a mass following among the population of the capital and often the demonstrations were violently suppressed by the occupation forces. After the liberation of the country (October 1944), Athens became the site of a civil war in December 1944 that broke out between the largely leftist resistance and government troops supported by the British army. After thirty-three days of bitter street fighting the leftist forces evacuated the capital and surrendered their arms.

The economic development in the postwar years accelerated the process of urbanization and contributed to the rapid growth of Athens. The concentration of major industries in greater Athens, and the employment opportunities that the expanding public sector offered, attracted thousands of people from villages and towns to the capital. Between 1951 and 1971 the population of greater Athens almost doubled (from 1.3 million in 1951 to 2.5 million in 1971). Internal migration increased the demand for housing and as a result Athens was once more expanded as plots of land were turned into sites of (unplanned) housing construction. Moreover, in these two decades a large part of Athens was eventually rebuilt and the architectural profile of the capital changed completely. The old houses were demolished and were replaced by apartment blocks that could house a large number of families. The construction of apartment blocks was not undertaken by the state

or real estate developers but by the individuals who owned the plot of land. In this way housing construction became the best investment for the moderate savings of the middle classes. The growth of the housing sector had a positive impact on the economy in general because it contributed to the development of the related industries, like cement factories, metallurgy, chemical plants, and others. However, it was in the postwar years that the growth of Athens underlined the structural problems in the modernization of Greece. Internal migration created an uneven urbanization. Athens concentrated a disproportionately high percentage of the population of Greece, as one out of four inhabitants of the country lived in the capital. The growth of the capital together with the overcentralization of the state bureaucracy led to the demographic decline of other cities (except Salonica, which in a much smaller scale became the center in northern Greece) and the widening of the gap in regional differences between Athens and the rest of the country.

The rapid expansion and the unplanned growth of Athens were accompanied with several housing and environmental problems that became apparent in the 1980s. Air pollution, heavy traffic, and the lack of parks and communal spaces drove many Athenians out of the city center to the suburbs. The population living in the municipality of Athens fell from 885,000 in 1981 to 772,000 in 1991, whereas the population living in greater Athens rose from 2.1 million to 2.3 million in the same period. At the same time the character of economic activities changed. The economic crisis of the 1980s was coupled with de-industrialization, and numerous factories in Athens and Piraeus closed down, while at the same time there was an expansion of the commerce and, most importantly, of the service sector. In the 1990s Athens faced two major challenges. The first was that Athens had been named the host of the 2004 Olympics. There had been major construction and infrastructure projects (peripheral highways, new subway lines, new airport) that eased the transportation and improved the traffic conditions, while there were critical interventions in the city planning of the center. The second change was the arrival of economic migrants, mostly from Albania. In 2005 there were 132,000 immigrants living in the

A soldier stands guard at a sentry station overlooking Athens during the Greek civil war, December 1947.
©HULTON-DEUTSCH COLLECTION

municipality of Athens, and they constituted 17 percent of the local population. Although there is a high concentration of immigrants in some neighborhoods of the center of Athens and there have been instances of xenophobia, in the early twenty-first century there are no signs of "ghettoization" as the immigrants are integrated into the social fabric, thereby adding economic dynamism and cultural diversity to the life of the capital.

See also **Albania; Greece; Olympic Games; Papandreou, Andreas; World War II.**

BIBLIOGRAPHY

Burgel, Guy. *Athina. I anaptyxi mias mesogeiakis proteuousas.* Athens, 1976. Translated as *Croissance urbaine et développement capitaliste: le "miracle" athénien.* Paris, 1981.

Hirschon, Renée. *Heirs of the Greek Catastrophe: The Social Life of Asia Minor Refugees in Piraeus.* Oxford, U.K., and New York, 1989.

Leontidou, Lila. *Mediterranean City in Transition: Social Change and Urban Development.* Cambridge, U.K., and New York, 1990.

POLYMERIS VOGLIS

ATLANTIC CHARTER. From 9 August to 12 August 1941, the U.S. president Franklin Delano Roosevelt and the prime minister of the

THE ATLANTIC CHARTER

The President of the United States of America and the Prime Minister, Mr. Churchill, representing His Majesty's Government in the United Kingdom, being met together, deem it right to make known certain common principles in the national policies of their respective countries on which they base their hopes for a better future for the world.

First, their countries seek no aggrandizement, territorial or other;

Second, they desire to see no territorial changes that do not accord with the freely expressed wishes of the peoples concerned;

Third, they respect the right of all peoples to choose the form of government under which they will live; and they wish to see sovereign rights and self government restored to those who have been forcibly deprived of them;

Fourth, they will endeavor, with due respect for their existing obligations, to further the enjoyment by all States, great or small, victor or vanquished, of access, on equal terms, to the trade and to the raw materials of the world which are needed for their economic prosperity;

Fifth, they desire to bring about the fullest collaboration between all nations in the economic field with the object of securing, for all, improved labor standards, economic advancement and social security;

Sixth, after the final destruction of the Nazi tyranny, they hope to see established a peace which will afford to all nations the means of dwelling in safety within their own boundaries, and which will afford assurance that all the men in all the lands may live out their lives in freedom from fear and want;

Seventh, such a peace should enable all men to traverse the high seas and oceans without hindrance;

Eighth, they believe that all of the nations of the world, for realistic as well as spiritual reasons must come to the abandonment of the use of force. Since no future peace can be maintained if land, sea or air armaments continue to be employed by nations which threaten, or may threaten, aggression outside of their frontiers, they believe, pending the establishment of a wider and permanent system of general security, that the disarmament of such nations is essential. They will likewise aid and encourage all other practicable measures which will lighten for peace-loving peoples the crushing burden of armaments.

Franklin D. Roosevelt

Winston S. Churchill

United Kingdom, Winston Churchill, met secretly aboard U.S. and British warships anchored in Placentia Bay, Newfoundland, Canada. This dramatic encounter, which transpired while the United States was officially neutral, proved the first of many wartime conferences between the two leaders. The Atlantic Conference confirmed Roosevelt's policy of all-out American aid for Britain and the Soviet Union and produced a statement of war and peace aims shortly afterward termed the "Atlantic Charter." The circumstances in which the Atlantic Charter was promulgated ensured that this declaration of principles would be both celebrated as an epochal event in the struggle for individual and group rights and fiercely criticized and subjected to endless analysis and debate.

In one sense, the meeting of President Roosevelt and Prime Minister Churchill was a logical culmination of some fifteen months of ardent wooing of America by the British. As soon as he took office in May 1940, Churchill launched a campaign to bring the United States into the war on Britain's side. Gradually, Roosevelt and the American people responded to Churchill's plea to have the "New World" come to "the rescue of the Old." Via such steps as the destroyer-bases deal, Roosevelt's commitment to make America the "Arsenal of Democracy," and Lend-Lease, the United States adopted a pro-British and anti-Nazi stance. But Churchill and his advisors wanted more—full scale American participation in the war and quickly before the British public's resolve to fight on gave way to despair. The events of spring–summer 1941 revealed that President Roosevelt was not yet prepared to take that epochal decision for war.

Thus, Roosevelt, Churchill, and their respective staffs brought divergent agendas to their meeting off Newfoundland. The British pushed for active American participation in the struggle to block Axis threats to North Africa, the Atlantic islands, and Southeast Asia. Roosevelt's goal was to obtain a statement of "peace aims" to mollify isolationists back home and to get on record a British commitment to such traditional American goals as no secret agreements, self-determination, and multilateral trade. Difficult negotiations during the four-day conference produced an eight-point "declaration of principles." The statement set forth views later incorporated in the "Declaration by the United Nations" of 1 January 1942 as the "common program of purposes and principles . . . known as the Atlantic Charter." Five of its articles (self-determination, freedom from fear, freedom from want, freedom of movement) dealt in some sense with individual and group rights; the remaining clauses espoused political and economic aims (disarmament of aggressors and removal for all of the "crushing burden" of armaments, open access to markets and raw materials, and the establishment of mechanisms to ensure just and lasting peace) that embodied liberal internationalist thinking about the causes of war and the foundations of world peace. The Atlantic Charter reflected American ideals from the "Fourteen Points" of Woodrow Wilson (1856–1924) to Roosevelt's "Four Freedoms" proclamation of January 1941, and the statement strongly implied general applicability.

Long after the circumstances that led to the August 1941 meeting between Roosevelt and Churchill had faded into the mists of memory, the Atlantic Charter remained a live issue. Dismissed by Berlin and such collaborators as Vichy France as "mere propaganda," the unrealistic ravings of advocates of a discredited ideology, the Charter nonetheless fired the imagination of men and women throughout the world. Hitler appears already to have concluded that the United States was in the war, and some scholars go so far as to suggest that his violent reaction against the Atlantic Charter contributed to his executing the final solution of the Jewish problem. He had promised that should the war become a world war, the outcome would be the destruction of European Jewry. He kept his word.

Viewed by its creators as an assertion of aspirations for those nations that fought the Axis, the Charter became the vehicle of Allied Powers war aims and the guiding manifesto that led directly to the establishment of the United Nations. Though the charter was officially no more than a press release by the leader of a belligerent power and the head of a neutral nation, the U.S. Department of State's listing of treaties still in force includes the Atlantic Charter and identifies as its signatories all of the adherents to the Declaration by the United Nations. As a result, the Atlantic Charter is in the early twenty-first century considered a pivotal document in the struggle to achieve acceptance of universal principles of human rights and justice.

See also **NATO; United Nations; Universal Declaration of Human Rights; World War II.**

BIBLIOGRAPHY

Facey-Crowther, David, and Douglas Brinkley, eds. *The Atlantic Charter.* New York, 1994.

Gilbert, Martin. *Churchill and America.* New York, 2005.

Kimball, Warren F. *Forged in War: Roosevelt, Churchill, and the Second World War.* New York, 1997.

Wilson, Theodore A. *The First Summit: Roosevelt and Churchill at Placentia Bay, 1941.* Rev. ed. Lawrence, Kans., 1991.

THEODORE A. WILSON

ATOMIC BOMB. The first atomic bomb was tested in New Mexico in the United States in July 1945, and the second and third were used against the Japanese cities of Hiroshima and Nagasaki the next month, bringing World War II in the Pacific to a ferocious close. By this time Germany had surrendered, yet it was the European war, and the prospect of the Nazis getting the bomb first, that provided the stimulus to the wartime development of the bomb, and it was the demands of European security that continued to influence the development, deployment, and strategic thinking surrounding nuclear weapons.

The remarkable continuity of the Cold War that developed following World War II, and the apparent symmetry, with two alliances each dominated by a superpower owning a formidable nuclear arsenal, provided an unusually stable context. It meant that on the one hand there were always strategic reasons to develop new weapons and explore new strategies, yet on the other there was a limited risk of the weapons actually being used in anger. In part this was because of the caution and circumspection induced by the fear of nuclear war. Memoirs and archives all testify to the anxieties felt by political leaders at times of crisis when there was the slightest risk of having to make decisions that could lead to these weapons being used.

ORIGINS

By the late 1930s, scientific breakthroughs in nuclear physics were coming so quickly that the theoretical possibility of creating massive explosions through splitting the individual atoms (nuclear fission) within a critical mass of material (uranium) and so producing a "chain reaction" was coming to be widely recognized. If Germany had not expelled so many of its top scientists because they were Jews, they would have been well placed to turn the developing science into actual weapons. In the event, émigré scientists, first in Britain and then the United States, fearful of this possibility, played critical roles in the wartime race to build the first weapons. Their work was completed just in time for the end of the war, and it is an interesting question for speculation as to what would have happened if there had not been time for the actual use of these weapons. The secret would not have been withheld from the Soviet Union, which was kept well informed by its spies in the Anglo-American project.

After years of air raids of increasing horror, the destructive impact of the first atomic bombs was not in itself so shocking. The Allied air raids against Hamburg and Tokyo inflicted more death and destruction. In addition to the new, insidious feature of radioactivity, the main difference was in their efficiency. One bomb could achieve what would otherwise require the loads of two hundred heavy bombers. In addition, the new weapons were not of great importance in the onset of the Cold War in Europe. It has been argued that their monopolistic position gave the Americans some confidence in their bargaining over the shape of postwar Europe, but while there may have been some momentary hopes of strategic advantage, the administration of Harry S. Truman (1884–1972) could not actually threaten their use so soon

after World War II (and there were actually very few weapons available for use), and the Soviet advantage lay in the fact that it was their troops and commissars who were actually controlling developments on the ground in Central and Eastern Europe. Although a combination of events, including the Communist Czech coup (1948) and the Berlin blockade and airlift (1948–1949), convinced the Americans that they had to make a renewed commitment to Europe, reflected in the formation of the North Atlantic Treaty Organization (NATO) in April 1949, this was, at first, essentially a political more than a military move.

The limited potential relevance of the weapons to the fate of Europe was apparently confirmed in August 1949 when it was learned that the Soviet Union had tested its own device. Whatever advantages gained by the United States through its nuclear monopoly would eventually be neutralized. The Truman administration accepted that over time it would be necessary to build up conventional forces to counter Soviet strength on the ground if it wished to prevent the sort of push across the Iron Curtain that was witnessed in the summer of 1950 as communist forces invaded South Korea. As a result the United States and Britain began a major rearmament program.

MASSIVE RETALIATION

To buy time, and because he had no confidence that American restraint would be reciprocated by the Soviet Union, President Truman authorized the development of thermonuclear weapons. The move from fission to fusion weapons, based on the energy generated as atoms combined, was almost as important as the original development of atomic bombs. There was now no natural limit on the destructive power of weapons. Their explosive yields could range from the low kilotons (equivalent to thousands of tons of TNT) to the high megatons (equivalent to millions of tons of TNT). In addition, new production facilities meant that there was a move from scarcity to plenty.

The administration of President Dwight Eisenhower (1890–1969), which came to power in January 1953, was sufficiently emboldened by these developments, including the success, after some false starts, of the thermonuclear program, to push nuclear weapons to the center of its strategy. This was in part because of the frustrating experience of the inconclusive conventional war fought in Korea and also because of the developing economic burden of conventional rearmament. So much had now been invested in nuclear weapons that the marginal costs of building up the arsenal made them a relatively cheap option compared with matching the Eastern bloc in conventional weapons. Most importantly, Eisenhower was confident in nuclear deterrence. He did not believe that the Soviet Union was in a rush to go to war and was instead prepared for a long haul, during which both sides might maneuver for strategic advantage and test the other's staying power. In this context he saw the great advantage of nuclear weapons as reminding Moscow just what dangers they would run if they ever tried to break out of the developing Cold War stalemate.

U.S. secretary of state John Foster Dulles (1888–1959) announced the new strategy in January 1954. He declared that in the future, rather than attempting to maintain large conventional forces around the Sino-Soviet periphery (the two communist giants were still treated as a single entity at this time), a U.S. response to aggression would be "at places and with means of our own choosing." This was interpreted as threatening nuclear attack against targets in the Soviet Union and China in response to conventional aggression anywhere in the world, and the doctrine became known as "massive retaliation." This was probably intended to be of more relevance to areas other than Europe. The French were battling it out in Vietnam at the time, and Eisenhower had been influenced by the apparent role of nuclear threats in getting the Soviets to agree to an armistice in the Korean War. The doctrine was widely criticized for placing undue reliance on nuclear threats, which would become less credible as Soviet nuclear strength grew. Few doubted that the United States would respond vigorously to any challenge in Europe, but the concern was that a limited challenge elsewhere would find the United States with few options other than the nuclear with which to respond, leaving it with a dire choice between "suicide or surrender."

Yet while the Eisenhower administration clearly put Europe in a higher category than its other security commitments, and did not remove from the continent the conventional forces that had been sent during the alarms of the early 1950s, the dependence on nuclear deterrence created problems. There was bound to be some doubt as to whether the Americans really would be prepared to sacrifice New York or Chicago for Paris or London. Furthermore, the allies were responsible for the security of the western part of a divided Germany and, much more difficult, the western part of a divided Berlin, stuck well inside East Germany and not obviously defensible by conventional means. Under the conventional buildup set in motion under the Truman administration, the United States always planned to rearm West Germany. So soon after the Nazi era, this was bound to be controversial. It took until 1954 for a formula to be found by which West Germany rearmed but was permitted no chemical or nuclear weapons and was part of NATO's military command. In return, the West German government sought a commitment by its new allies to the concept of "forward defense," so that any aggression would be held at the inner-German border, for so much of its population and industry was concentrated close to this border. The German fear was that otherwise its territory would be used to provide a battleground, to be sacrificed, in extremis, to gain time for reinforcements to arrive from North America. Now that NATO was not going to attempt to match Soviet conventional forces, forward defense meant, in effect, that nuclear deterrence was linked to this border.

European governments came to see great advantages in the Eisenhower approach. It did not rely on a readiness to fight conventional wars, which could be almost as devastating for the continent as a nuclear war. One of the problems with conventional deterrence was that Moscow would not feel that its own territory would be at risk so long as the combat could be confined to the center of Europe. In addition, this arrangement saved the Europeans the expense of sustaining large-scale conventional forces, especially as they were pessimistic as to the possibility of ever matching Warsaw Pact strength. Despite the evident Soviet concern over what it saw to be the anomalous position of West Berlin, NATO countries grew increasingly doubtful that there was a serious risk of a World War III.

People dressed in hydrogen bomb costumes march in an anti-nuclear protest sponsored by the British Communist Party, London, May 1957. ©BETTMANN/CORBIS

NUCLEAR WEAPONS AND EUROPEAN SECURITY

An important shift in American thinking came when John Fitzgerald Kennedy (1917–1963) became president in January 1961. Kennedy was not so sanguine about Soviet intentions, especially when he faced an early and severe crisis over West Berlin, which peaked when the Berlin Wall was constructed in August 1961. Nor did he and his senior aides feel any confidence in nuclear threats given the growing Soviet capacity for retaliation. How could a credible deterrent be fashioned out of an incredible nuclear threat? Kennedy wanted NATO to commit extra forces to raise the nuclear threshold—that is, the point at which nuclear weapons would be necessary to stave off conventional defeat. He was fortified by analyses that suggested that previous intelligence assessments had exaggerated the strength of the Warsaw Pact.

European governments resisted these arguments strongly. They argued that all war had to be deterred, not just nuclear war, and that conventional buildups would be expensive and ineffectual. The Americans kept up the pressure, but after the 1961 Berlin crisis (and the 1962 Cuban missile crisis), concern about a European war subsided. Meanwhile, demands in Vietnam reduced the spare military capacity of the United States. In 1967 a compromise was found in the doctrine of "flexible response." The Europeans recognized the U.S. requirement for an extended conventional stage, so that the first shots across the Iron Curtain would not lead automatically to a nuclear holocaust, and the United States accepted the need for a clear link between a land war in Europe and its own strategic nuclear arsenal. If the alliance looked like it was being overrun as a result of the conventional superiority of the Warsaw Pact, NATO reserved for itself the option of being the first to use nuclear weapons.

This link would be provided by short-range, tactical nuclear weapons (TNWs). These had first been introduced into the NATO inventory during the 1950s as nuclear equivalents to all types of conventional munitions—from mortars and artillery shells to air-delivered bombs and depth-charges, and even mines. There was a hope that this extra firepower would make it possible to take on communists in limited nuclear wars without resorting to incredible threats of massive retaliation. Simulations of their use during the 1950s soon demonstrated that they were not just more powerful conventional weapons, but would lead to great death and destruction, including among the people supposedly being defended. Warsaw Pact forces would obtain comparable weapons of their own and would neutralize any Western advantage. Nor could there be confidence that nuclear use, once begun, would stop with TNWs. There could soon be escalation to strategic—intercontinental—nuclear use.

Though TNWs could not be considered ordinary weapons of war, their close integration with conventional forces meant that they were more likely than strategic forces to get entangled in a land war in Europe. This created an added risk for the Soviet Union. It was hard to demonstrate that under any circumstances nuclear war would be a rational option for NATO leaders, but once a major war was under way the circumstances would not be conducive to rationality and it was possible that, in the heat of the moment, some nuclear use might be authorized. The dynamics of escalation could lead to a potentially catastrophic conclusion. Deterrence did not require certainty that nuclear weapons would be used—only a small possibility. So TNWs provided a demonstration of the extent to which the fate of both superpowers was linked to stability in the center of Europe.

This meant that deterrence would depend less on the implementation of a clear threat but a risk of matters getting out of control, which was an uncomfortable prospect. There was an intense alliance debate in the late 1970s over how to replace the first generation of TNWs. If they were made smaller and more precise, then this would imply a readiness to use them to fight a nuclear war rather than simply deter, and a return to the idea that they were just more powerful forms of conventional weapons. This was the purpose of the so-called "neutron bomb" (actually a thermonuclear missile warhead or artillery shell of enhanced radiation and reduced blast), which was criticized for blurring the boundary between conventional and nuclear weapons and thereby making it much easier to go nuclear.

MUTUAL ASSURED DESTRUCTION

The debate over the neutron bomb, which ended with President Jimmy Carter (b. 1924) deciding not to deploy it, was the first major public discussion of these weapons since the 1950s. During the intervening years, most of the attention had been taken up with the problem of the strategic nuclear balance. The doctrine of massive retaliation had assumed that U.S. nuclear superiority could last for some time, but the Americans were slow off the mark when it came to developing intercontinental ballistic missiles (ICBMs) and were stung when the Soviet Union apparently stole the lead, and undermined its reputation for technological inferiority, when it launched the first artificial Earth satellite (Sputnik 1) in October 1957, not long after it had also tested the first ICBM. Now the fear was of Soviet superiority, and there was talk of a missile gap. Of particular concern was that the Soviets might turn their advantage into a first strike capability, so that they could mount a surprise attack against U.S. air and missile bases and so render retaliation impossible. This would be the

only way to "win" a nuclear war. This possibility would be denied with the development of a second-strike capability, the capacity to launch a devastating riposte even after absorbing an enemy attempt at a first strike. If both sides developed first-strike capabilities then future crises would be very tense, because it would create pressure to gain the advantage by preemption. On the other hand, if both sides enjoyed second-strike capabilities then the situation should be more stable, as there would be no premium attached to striking first.

In the event, technological developments supported the second strike. As ICBMs were deployed by the United States in the early 1960s, they were placed in hardened underground silos, so that an unlikely direct hit would be required to destroy them. Harder to hit because they would be harder to find would be submarine-launched ballistic missiles (SLBMs). In principle, effective defenses might shore up a first-strike capability, but the standards for defense against nuclear weapons had to be much higher than for conventional air raids, because of the impact of just one offensive weapon getting through—and the defensive systems would have to cope with thousands. Any improvements in the radars and anti-missile missiles were countered by even greater improvements in offensive systems—notably multiple independently targeted reentry vehicles (MIRVs) that could swamp any defenses, especially when combined with decoys. Civil defense promised scant protection to civilians: at best, there might be some chance of avoiding exposure to nuclear fallout.

During the 1960s, the U.S. secretary of defense Robert S. McNamara (b. 1916) argued that the situation was one of "mutual assured destruction" (which soon became known by its acronym MAD). This meant that the two superpowers were each able to impose "unacceptable damage" (defined as 25 percent of population and 50 percent of industry). This he considered the source of stability and he urged that all policies, from new weapons procurement to arms control measures, be geared toward this end. Although this approach encountered strong opposition, it was, by and large, followed through the Richard Nixon (1913–1994) and Carter administrations. Opponents warned that if MAD failed to deter, then any war would soon lead to genocide, and also that it suggested that nuclear weapons could only be used to deter other nuclear weapons, thereby adding to the risk of conventional aggression and so undermining the commitments made to allies to use nuclear weapons first on their behalf. Nor, it was argued, was there evidence that the Soviet Union had signed up to this theory. Soviet strategy appeared to envisage using nuclear weapons to obtain a decisive military advantage and reducing the damage that an enemy might do to Soviet territory (if necessary, by launching preemptive strikes).

The main effort to break out of MAD was made by President Ronald Reagan (1911–2004) in the 1980s. Initially, he continued with the search for offensive nuclear operations to allow the United States to "prevail" in a protracted war with the Soviet Union, but his most significant initiative was to call for a true ballistic missile defense system that could protect lives rather than avenge them, thereby rendering nuclear weapons "impotent and obsolete." The science was bound to defeat the ambition, given the diverse means of delivering nuclear weapons. Reagan concluded with increasingly radical arms control proposals developed in dialogue with Soviet leader Mikhail Gorbachev (b. 1931) from 1985. In January 1986, Gorbachev set out a radical disarmament agenda leading toward a nuclear-free world by the end of the century, and Reagan was clearly not unsympathetic to this vision. The only difference was that he saw his strategic defense initiative fitting in with this vision and Gorbachev did not.

BEYOND DETERRENCE

The shared disarmament agenda constituted a formidable challenge to the orthodox view that nuclear weapons were vital to West European security in the face of preponderant Soviet conventional forces. Yet in practice the Europeans tolerated the steady decline in the credibility of threats to use nuclear weapons first. They concluded that deterrence could survive with only the slightest risk of nuclear use, especially when it was so hard to construct a realistic scenario for a European war. In addition, Europe's own populations were unenthusiastic about allowing their security to depend on nuclear threats. This became apparent following NATO's decision in 1979 to modernize its intermediate nuclear forces (INF) with the Pershing II intermediate-range

ballistic missile (IRBM) and the Tomahawk cruise missile. The idea was to convince the Soviet Union that it could be put directly at risk by systems based in Europe in a way that could not be achieved by TNWs. European governments had also expressed concern that during the Strategic Arms Limitation Talks (SALT II, signed in 1979), the United States concentrated on achieving symmetry between the nuclear forces of the two superpowers, while paying little attention to the superiority within the European theater of the Warsaw Pact in both nuclear and conventional weapons. However, after NATO's 1979 decision, large-scale protests sprang up in Europe and North America. Voicing a concern that a new arms race was getting under way in Europe, the protests took on special urgency following the 1979 Soviet invasion of Afghanistan and the election of the hawkish Ronald Reagan.

The protests encouraged NATO to put less public stress on the requirements of flexible response and more on the need to match the deployment of the Soviet intermediate-range SS-20. In November 1981, at a time when there was real doubt that the NATO missiles would ever be deployed, Reagan offered to abandon the program if all SS-20s were removed. This "zero option" was rejected. The measure of the change during that decade was that, once deployment had taken place, Gorbachev agreed to the zero option. In December 1987, Gorbachev and Reagan signed the Intermediate-Range Nuclear Forces (INF) Treaty.

Reagan's interest in a nuclear-free world encouraged discussion about the possibility of a European nuclear force, independent of the United States, based on the French and British capabilities. The United Kingdom had always, officially at least, committed its strategic nuclear forces (which since the late 1960s had been SLBMs) to NATO. Britain's rationale for maintaining a national nuclear force involved a combination of the political influence that could be brought to bear on its allies, especially the United States, and a claim to be contributing to the overall deterrent posture. France, by contrast, had always had a much more nationalistic rationale, although it had claimed that its force de frappe would defend allies. Neither country was eager or really able to take over from the United States the broader deterrent role; nor did their allies see them in that role. The alternative to

Soviet intercontinental ballistic missiles are paraded in Red Square on the anniversary of the Bolshevik Revolution, 7 November 1969. ©JERRY COKE/CORBIS

reinforcing deterrence was to introduce new TNWs, but the Germans could see that these would mean that any nuclear war would be confined to its soil (East and West), and the political climate was now against any new nuclear systems. Soon the whole issue appeared to be irrelevant as European communism collapsed and the Cold War could be declared over. There was nothing left to deter, while the potential targets for NATO's short-range nuclear missiles were embracing liberal democracy and capitalism.

AFTER THE COLD WAR

The traditional calculus of European security was turned upside down. NATO now had conventional superiority—against all comers—and it was Russia that was considering using nuclear first-use threats to shore up its security position. The nuclear danger in Europe was soon seen to be less the traditional threat of a rising and radical great power and

more chronic weakness in a declining great power, leading to questions about the control of the nuclear systems within the former Soviet Union, and the revival of older conflicts and rivalries within Europe, suppressed during the Cold War. Instead of moves to introduce new TNWs, the Americans moved to encourage Russians to eliminate all of their own, to prevent them falling into the wrong hands, and triggered the process by announcing the withdrawal of their systems from land and sea deployments. In the strategic arms reduction talks, both sides agreed to progressive reductions in the size of their arsenals, with the main limiting factor the cost of their decommissioning.

While relations between the old nuclear antagonists had been transformed, new nuclear powers were starting to emerge. After the First Persian Gulf War in 1991, it was revealed just how advanced Iraq had become in its nuclear capability. During the 1990s concerns also grew about Iran and North

Korea, while India and Pakistan actually tested nuclear weapons in 1998. Within Europe the major risk of proliferation came with the breakup of the former Soviet Union, but Ukraine, Belarus, and Kazakhstan accepted that they could not hold on to the systems inherited from the Soviet Union. NATO countries took the view that so long as other states had nuclear arsenals, and even a capacity to inflict death and destruction on a massive scale by other means, then it was only prudent to sustain arsenals of their own. What was less clear was whether they would consider nuclear use in response to the use of chemical or biological weapons. In practice because of conventional superiority, particularly in air power, they would have plenty of alternative means of responding without having to inflict massive destruction themselves.

The attacks on the World Trade Center in New York and the Pentagon in Washington, D.C., on 11 September 2001 raised the specter of superterrorists gaining access to nuclear or, more likely, chemical or biological weapons. This specter was used to justify the U.S.- and U.K.-led war against Iraq beginning in 2003, although the lack of subsequent evidence of these capabilities undermined the rationale. This episode nonetheless illustrated the extent to which nuclear weapons, having first been developed in the context of titanic struggles between great powers, when major centers of population had come to appear as natural and legitimate targets for attack, now had to be understood in a world in which the major powers were at peace, and conventional forces could be used with precision, but where weak powers and sub-state groups might try to gain some artificial strength through gaining access to the most destructive weapons.

See also **Cold War; Disarmament; Gorbachev, Mikhail; NATO; Nuclear Weapons; Soviet Union; World War II.**

BIBLIOGRAPHY

Bundy, McGeorge. *Danger and Survival: Choices about the Bomb in the First Fifty Years.* New York, 1988. An excellent account of the key decisions made by U.S. policymakers, in particular about nuclear weapons, by an academic who had been a key insider.

Freedman, Lawrence. *The Evolution of Nuclear Strategy.* 3rd ed. Houndmills, U.K., 2003. Summarizes the history of strategic thought in this area.

Gaddis, John Lewis, Philip H. Gordon, Ernest R. May, and Jonathan Rosenberg, eds. *Cold War Statesmen Confront the Bomb: Nuclear Diplomacy since 1945.* Oxford, U.K., 1999. Considers the impact on policymakers.

Garthoff, Raymond. *The Great Transition: American Soviet Relations and the End of the Cold War.* Washington, D.C., 1994. An excellent discussion of the interaction of nuclear weapons and foreign policy as the Cold War came to an end.

Heuser, Beatrice. *NATO, Britain, France, and the FRG: Nuclear Strategies and Forces for Europe, 1949–2000.* New York, 1997. Covers the key debates within West European countries.

Holloway, David. *Stalin and the Bomb.* New Haven, Conn., 1994. The history of the early Soviet program.

Rhodes, Richard. *The Making of the Atomic Bomb.* New York, 1986. Author wrote the best books on the development of the first nuclear weapons.

———. *Dark Sun: The Making of the Hydrogen Bomb.* New York, 1995.

Sagan, Scott D., and Kenneth N. Waltz. *The Spread of Nuclear Weapons: A Debate.* New York, 1995. Debates the big issues of post–Cold War nuclear war policy.

Zubok, Vladislav, and Constantine Pleshakov. *Inside the Kremlin's Cold War: From Stalin to Khrushchev.* Cambridge, Mass., 1996.

LAWRENCE FREEDMAN

ATOMIC ENERGY.

The prospect of atomic energy became a matter for widespread speculation at the beginning of the twentieth century. The discovery of radioactivity in 1896 created opportunities for investigating the structure of the atom, giving rise to the possibility that the energy bound up in the atom might one day be released and put to practical use. This aroused great hopes for cheap electric power, as well as apprehension about the atomic bomb. A number of scientific centers, including Cambridge, Copenhagen, Paris, and Rome, contributed in the first decades of the century to rapid progress in atomic and nuclear physics.

EARLY PROSPECTS

It was the discovery of nuclear fission in uranium in Berlin in December 1938 that opened the door to the practical application of atomic (nuclear) energy. Physicists everywhere understood that nuclear fission chain reactions would make it possible to create explosives of enormous power and to build reactors to generate electricity. In 1939–1940 a number of centers in Europe and the United States did intensive research on the conditions under which a nuclear fission chain reaction—whether explosive or controlled—could take place in uranium.

The discovery of nuclear fission on the eve of World War II made it inevitable that attention would focus first on the military uses of atomic energy. Britain, the United States, and the Soviet Union each decided during the war to make an atomic bomb, though only the United States succeeded in doing so before the war was over. Germany did not make a serious effort to build the bomb but focused instead on the construction of an experimental reactor.

The prospect of nuclear power was not forgotten during the war. A small number of scientists fled France to work in England and later in Canada on the development of a heavy water reactor. British interest in nuclear power was clearly indicated by the July 1941 Maud Report, which concluded that a nuclear reactor could be used as a substitute for coal or oil in the production of electric power. The Americans were sufficiently interested in nuclear power to insist, when Anglo-American nuclear cooperation was established by the Quebec Agreement of August 1943, that the British renounce the right to use, in the postwar industrial or commercial exploitation of atomic energy, any of the knowledge gained from wartime collaboration, except on terms specified by the U.S. president.

The military and civilian applications of atomic energy turned out to be more closely intertwined than was understood in 1939–1940, because reactors proved to have a key role in the production of nuclear weapons. It became clear that atomic bombs could use as the active material not only uranium-235, which had to be separated from natural uranium by complex and costly methods, but also the newly discovered element plutonium, which could be produced in reactors. The United States built several reactors during the war to produce plutonium.

FIRST STEPS

The first nuclear power plants in Europe were outgrowths of the military programs. In 1954 the Soviet Union launched a small power reactor in Obninsk, which provided electricity to the local area. In the 1950s the Soviet Union built dual-purpose reactors at Tomsk to produce plutonium and generate electricity. Britain opened a power reactor at Calder Hall in 1956, and this generated electricity for the national grid. France's first power reactor went critical at Marcoule in 1958. Like the British reactor, it was designed to produce electricity as well as plutonium for weapons.

The mid-1950s were a crucial period for nuclear power. The United States had adopted a policy of strict nuclear secrecy after the war—even in relations with Britain, its partner in the Manhattan Project. Once the Soviet Union (1949) and Britain (1952) had tested the bomb, it was clear that secrecy would not prevent other states from developing nuclear weapons of their own. In a radical change of policy, President Dwight Eisenhower announced the Atoms for Peace program in December 1953 with the aim of redirecting atomic energy from military to peaceful applications. In August 1955 the first international conference on the peaceful uses of atomic energy took place in Geneva, with Soviet and East European participation. There was a significant reduction of secrecy in the nuclear field: information could now be published about most elements of the fuel cycle, including reactor design, and about the use of atomic energy in fields such as medicine. This was a period of enormous optimism, bordering on euphoria, about the future of atomic energy. Nuclear power was now a symbol of national status and a focus of technological pride. In February 1955 Britain announced a plan to build twelve nuclear power plants over the next ten years. Britain was not alone in its belief that nuclear power had a bright future. In March 1957 the six founding members of the European Economic Community (France, West Germany, Italy, Belgium, Luxembourg, and the Netherlands) signed a treaty setting up the European Atomic Energy Community (Euratom) to create the conditions necessary for the speedy establishment and growth of nuclear industries. Eastern Europe too was swept by a wave of optimism. The Soviet Union had reacted with skepticism to the "Atoms for Peace" proposal, but it soon adopted a similar program for the socialist countries. It signed agreements in 1955 to help them set up nuclear research programs, and in the following year

Britain's first nuclear power station, Calder Hall, photographed in July 1960. ©BETTMANN/CORBIS

it opened an international nuclear physics institute at Dubna, where scientists from the socialist countries could collaborate.

The first power reactors had their origins in military programs, but it was now understood that barriers were needed between the military and civilian uses of atomic energy. Euratom adopted measures to prevent the development of nuclear power from contributing to military purposes. So too did the Soviet Union in Eastern Europe (its nuclear relations with China were another matter). The International Atomic Energy Agency was established in Vienna in 1957 in order to accelerate and enlarge the contribution of atomic energy to peace, health, and prosperity throughout the world, while ensuring at the same time that such assistance was not diverted to any military uses.

NUCLEAR POWER PROGRAMS

The enthusiasm for nuclear power began to bear fruit in the 1960s, though slowly at first because of construction delays and cost overruns. The technological challenges and economic costs proved to be greater than had been estimated. The choice of reactors was also a difficult problem. Britain and France focused initially on natural uranium, graphite-moderated, gas-cooled reactors. The United States, which had built huge uranium enrichment capacity during the war, emphasized light-water reactors fueled with enriched uranium. The Soviet Union produced a graphite-moderated, light-water, enriched-uranium design, as well as a light water reactor. Gradually light-water reactors came to dominate the market. France adopted them in the late 1960s, and Britain followed suit twenty years later.

By 1964 there were fifteen power reactors in operation (twelve in Europe and three in the United States) and worldwide installed nuclear electrical capacity amounted to about 5,000 megawatts. The rate of growth increased rapidly in the 1970s, as new and more powerful nuclear plants came on line. In the late 1970s worldwide installed capacity passed the 100-gigawatt mark and ten years later it reached 300 gigawatts. Thereafter the rate of growth fell off sharply. By the end of 2003 worldwide installed capacity stood at 360 gigawatts. The modest growth after the late 1980s came from the construction of nuclear plants outside Europe, notably in Asia.

The stagnation in Europe was even greater than the worldwide figures suggest. Nuclear power grew rapidly in both parts of Europe in the 1970s and 1980s, with expansion in the Soviet Union and Eastern Europe coming somewhat later than in Western Europe. After that there was little or no increase in generating capacity in Europe, although existing nuclear power plants produced more electricity as a result of more efficient operation. In 2004 Europe had 204 power reactors in operation (including a small number under construction).

Within this overall pattern, there has been considerable variation among European countries in the share of electricity generated by nuclear power. Britain, for example, obtained 10 percent of its electricity from nuclear power in 1970, a higher proportion than any other country at that time. Britain's nuclear share did not rise rapidly in the 1970s and 1980s, and in 2004 it was about 20 percent. The highest nuclear share was in France, which after starting more slowly than Britain invested heavily in nuclear power in the 1970s. By 1990 it was obtaining more than 70 percent of its electricity from nuclear power; in 2004 the proportion was almost 80 percent. Italy, to take a third example, was generating no electricity from nuclear power by 1990, even though it had imported power reactors from Britain and the United States in the 1960s and, in the 1970s, had had ambitious plans for nuclear power. A referendum in 1987 had led to the shutting down of Italy's nuclear power plants.

Several countries have adopted legislation to phase out nuclear power and to ban the construction of new plants. In 1980 the Swedish parliament decided, following a referendum, to eliminate

nuclear power by 2010 if new energy resources were available and could be introduced without harming social welfare and employment. In 2000 the German government decided to phase out nuclear power in an orderly manner, with the result that by 2020 all nuclear power plants will be shut down. Belgium and the Netherlands have taken similar decisions. The ultimate significance of these decisions is uncertain, because new governments could reverse them in response to altered circumstances. Those decisions do nevertheless reflect the deep antipathy to nuclear power that emerged in Europe in the 1970s. The Finnish decision in 2002 to authorize construction of a new nuclear power plant is significant because it is the first such decision by a European government—other than a postcommunist government—in more than a decade.

The picture is different in the postcommunist world. When the Soviet Union collapsed in 1991 it had forty-five nuclear power reactors in operation, twenty-eight of them on the territory of Russia, fifteen in Ukraine, and two in Lithuania. Soviet-designed power reactors had been built in East Germany, Czechoslovakia, Hungary, and Bulgaria, and were under construction in Romania. There was some contraction after the collapse of Communist rule: the four power reactors in East Germany were shut down after German reunification; Bulgaria shut down two of its six power reactors in 2002; one of the units at the nuclear power plant in Lithuania was shut down in 2004, and the other was due to close in 2009. Alongside this contraction, however, expansion has also been taking place. In 2003 Russia had three power reactors under construction, and Ukraine four, and both governments were planning to increase nuclear generating capacity still further. Slovakia completed two nuclear power reactors in the late 1990s. In the Czech Republic two new power reactors joined the grid in 2000 and 2002. In 2004 Romania was working to complete the second unit of its nuclear power plant at Cernavoda.

In 2004 the nuclear share in electricity generation in Russia was 16 percent; in the Czech Republic, Hungary, and Bulgaria it was more than 30 percent; and in Ukraine, Slovakia, and Lithuania it exceeded 50 percent. In spite of the Chernobyl accident in April 1986, there was at the end of the twentieth century a stronger commitment to nuclear power in the postcommunist world than in Western Europe. After the collapse of communism, Western governments worried about the safety of Soviet-designed reactors and took steps to have them either closed down or upgraded, thereby providing welcome work for the nuclear power industry.

THE CONTEXT OF NUCLEAR POWER

As nuclear power expanded, so too did opposition to it. An antinuclear movement became active in Western Europe in the 1970s. The opposition took different forms in different countries; it was most active in France and West Germany, with demonstrations and clashes with the police at the sites of nuclear power plants. In Eastern Europe the conditions for protest did not exist.

The opposition focused on several features of nuclear power technology. First, the danger of low-level radiation in the areas surrounding nuclear plants was a cause of great anxiety—all the more so because radiation is invisible and its effects very hard to measure. The second focus of opposition was the danger of catastrophic accidents leading to widespread radioactive contamination. The Three Mile Island accident in the United States in 1979 and more especially the Chernobyl accident in the Soviet Union in 1986 reinforced the fear of such accidents. Third, the problem of long-term storage of high-level radioactive waste was a major public concern. Nuclear power produces radioactive wastes that will need to be stored carefully for thousands of years, and no long-term solution for this problem has yet been found. Fourth, in some cases, notably West Germany, the connection to nuclear weapons through the production of plutonium was an important issue for the opposition. Beyond these specific objections, opposition to nuclear power was, for many people, rooted in a broader critique of modern technological society.

The effects of the antinuclear movement varied from one country to another. In France, where the movement was strong, the state remained firmly committed to nuclear power and retained the support of public opinion. In West Germany, where the antinuclear movement was also strong, the government eventually decided to phase out nuclear power. Antinuclear opposition instilled in most European societies a measure of skepticism about nuclear power. Public opinion responded

strongly, therefore, when the explosion at the Chernobyl power plant released a cloud of radioactive materials that spread across Europe. This accident had a considerable impact on the public debate about nuclear power in Italy, Germany, Sweden, the Netherlands, and other countries that decided to renounce nuclear power.

The actual consequences of Chernobyl for public health are still a matter of dispute, but the political impact was undeniably significant. Ironically, that impact may have been stronger in Western than in Eastern Europe. In the Soviet Union, Chernobyl gave a major boost to glasnost—the process of political reform initiated by Mikhail Gorbachev—and brought to light information about past nuclear accidents. Antinuclear movements emerged in different parts of the country, and work on new nuclear power plants was postponed or canceled. These were signs of a long-suppressed civil society seeking to gain control over unaccountable bureaucracies. After the collapse of the Soviet Union, however, attitudes to nuclear power changed. Movements that had once embraced the antinuclear cause in their struggle against Moscow abandoned it when they escaped from Moscow's control. The Ukrainian parliament voted in 1990 for a moratorium on new nuclear power plants; three years later, after Ukraine had become independent, the parliament rescinded the moratorium. For postcommunist states nuclear plants have sometimes served as symbols of independence, not least because they do in fact reduce dependence on energy supplies from other countries.

Important though antinuclear sentiment has been, the history of nuclear power in Europe cannot be understood merely as a clash between its supporters and its opponents. In the first place, countries differ in the energy options they have available to them and in the strategies they adopt. Britain's nuclear power policy in the 1970s and its response to the oil crisis of 1973 cannot be understood without taking North Sea oil and gas into account. Similarly, one reason for the popularity of nuclear power in Ukraine is that it lessens dependence on Russia for oil and gas. Second, the policy choice is not always between one form of energy and another. One response to the 1973 oil crisis was to build nuclear power plants; another was to let prices rise, thereby enabling the market to encourage efficiency and lower demand. In the

1990s the stagnation of the nuclear power industry was not only a response to the antinuclear movement; it was also a consequence of changes in the electricity market in Europe. Deregulation uncovered excess capacity, pushed prices lower, lessened the utilities' revenue, and made investments in nuclear plants more risky. Popular opposition to nuclear power was one of the factors inhibiting investment, but not the only one.

CONCLUSION

The history of nuclear power in Europe has proved to be more complex than its advocates expected in the mid-1950s. The technological euphoria of the time led to the neglect of issues that would later prove to be important for the future of nuclear power: cost, safety, and the storage of radioactive waste. Antinuclear sentiment, sometimes expressed in violent protest, became widespread. The rapid growth of nuclear power in the 1970s and 1980s was followed by stagnation. There was, however, considerable variation among the different countries in their reliance on nuclear energy, and Western Europe and post-communist countries differed in their attitude to nuclear power.

In the coming years European governments will have to decide whether or not to replace aging nuclear power plants. Some have decided not to do so, but those decisions are not irreversible. Other governments remain committed to nuclear power, and still others plan to increase their reliance on it. There are three factors that may improve the prospects of nuclear power in Europe. The first is climate change. European governments are committed, under the Kyoto Protocol, to reducing greenhouse gas emissions. Nuclear power plants could make a contribution to that goal because, unlike fossil-fuel power plants, they do not produce such emissions. (Nor of course do alternative energy sources.) Concern about climate change has grown significantly since the 1990s, and this might increase the attractiveness of nuclear power. Second, if the worldwide demand for energy—especially from China and India—drives up gas and oil prices, then nuclear power will come to look more attractive from an economic point of view. If China and India adopt nuclear power on a large scale, that too might influence policies in Europe. Third, if European states grow more concerned about energy security and seek to reduce their dependence on other countries and regions for energy, that might change the context for nuclear power and make it appear a more attractive option. A return to the euphoria of the 1950s and 1960s is most unlikely, however, and if nuclear power is to expand in Europe it will need to overcome the legacy of skepticism and distrust that has built up since then.

See also **Atomic Bomb; Chernobyl.**

BIBLIOGRAPHY

Dawson, Jane. *Eco-Nationalism: Anti-Nuclear Activism and National Identity in Russia, Lithuania, and Ukraine.* Durham, N.C., 1996.

Fischer, David. *History of the International Atomic Energy Agency: The First Forty Years.* Vienna, 1997.

Goldschmidt, Bertrand. *The Atomic Complex: A Worldwide Political History of Nuclear Energy.* Translated by Bruce M. Adkins. La Grange Park, Ill., 1982.

Gowing, Margaret. *Britain and Atomic Energy, 1939–1945.* London, 1964.

Hecht, Gabrielle. *The Radiance of France: Nuclear Power and National Identity after World War II.* Cambridge, Mass., 1998.

International Atomic Energy Agency. *Country Profiles.* Available at http://www-pub.iaea.org/MTCD/publications/PDF/cnpp2003/CNPP_Webpage/pages/countryprofiles.htm

Jasper, James M. *Nuclear Politics: Energy and the State in the United States, Sweden, and France.* Princeton, N.J., 1990.

Nelkin, Dorothy, and Michael Pollak. *The Atom Besieged: Extraparliamentary Dissent in France and Germany.* Cambridge, Mass., 1981.

Touraine, Alain, Zsuzsa Hegedus, François Dubet, and Michel Wieviorka. *Anti-Nuclear Protest: The Opposition to Nuclear Energy in France.* Translated by Peter Fawcett. Cambridge, U.K., 1983.

Williams, Roger. *The Nuclear Power Decisions: British Policies, 1953–78.* London. 1980.

DAVID HOLLOWAY

ATTLEE, CLEMENT (1883–1967), British politician and statesman.

Clement Richard Attlee was born on 3 January 1883 in Putney, London. Raised in a loving, conventional family, the small, shy Clem was taught at home by his mother until he was nine years old. He then went to preparatory school and thereafter, aged thirteen, to Haileybury College. From there he went to University College, Oxford, in October 1901 to read history, graduating with a good second-class degree in the summer of 1904. He began training that autumn to be a barrister, passed his bar exams in the summer of 1905, and then joined his father in the family firm of city solicitors. He was called to the bar in March 1906.

EARLY CAREER

Up to this point, Attlee was no different than many upper-middle-class British men. Until he left Oxford there was nothing to suggest that his was to be an exceptional life, let alone that he would become the longest-serving (twenty years) leader of a political party in twentieth-century Britain and the first Labour prime minister to form a government with a substantial majority. What provoked the turning of a conventional life into an exceptional one was a chance visit to the Haileybury Club in the poor Stepney borough of dockland London. Like many public schools, Haileybury had established a club to give poor London boys an opportunity to pursue activities that were not provided in their own state schools. Accompanying his brother Laurence to the club in October 1905, Attlee began a deep involvement with the club, becoming its manager in 1907, and living on the premises for seven years and for fourteen years in the East End of London.

Sharing his parents' sense of moral and social responsibility, but not their Christian beliefs, Attlee became increasingly interested in social and economic reform so as to address the causes rather than the symptoms of the poverty and inequality of opportunity that he saw all around him. This preference for making practical improvements to people's lives rather than engaging in the more excitable aspects of political theorizing was to characterize his political career. This he began by joining the Stepney branch of the Independent Labour Party, and when a small inheritance from his father in 1908 ironically enabled him to finally turn his back on a paternally approved legal career at the bar, he became a full-time, if yet unpaid, politician. In 1909 he stood unsuccessfully as the ILP candidate for the Stepney Borough Council.

Too old at thirty-one to join the army on the outbreak of World War I in 1914, he secured a position as lieutenant to the Sixth Battalion of the South Lancashire Regiment. Promoted captain in February 1915, he sailed with the "South Lancs" for Gallipoli in June 1915. This tragically muddled, but potentially important effort to provide an alternative field of conflict to that of the deadlocked western front was to leave Winston Churchill (1874–1965) with many critics for the rest of his life, but Attlee was never among them. Landing in Gallipoli in June 1915, Attlee suffered dysentery and was taken to hospital, missing an assault in which two-thirds of the men in his company were killed. Recovered, he returned to the front line for two months, until the soldiers were evacuated and redirected to the fighting in Mesopotamia, where Attlee was shot in the thigh and sent back to England. In December 1916, now promoted major, he began tank training in Dorset and, seeing action in August 1918 on the front line before Lille, he was injured again. It was not until 16 January 1919 that Attlee was discharged from Wandsworth Hospital.

POLITICAL CAREER

Back in civilian life, Attlee recommenced his political career. Appointed mayor of Stepney at the age of thirty-six, in the general election of 15 November 1922, Attlee became MP for Limehouse with a slim majority of 1,899. He increased his majority to 6,185 in the December 1923 general election, and in the minority Labour government (1924) of James Ramsay MacDonald (1866–1937), he served as undersecretary for war. In November 1927 he was appointed to what became the Simon Committee to examine developments in India since the Government of India Act of 1919 and thereby began a lifetime of increasing familiarity with the complexities of Indian life and politics. He contributed heavily to the writing of the 1930 Simon Commission's report, which favored moves toward a central government embracing the interests of Muslims, Hindus, and the provincial princes under Dominion status. Appointed to succeed Sir Oswald Ernald Mosley (1896–1980) as chancellor of the duchy of Lancaster in the spring of 1930, and then transferred to become postmaster-general, Attlee was well out of the firing line as MacDonald embarked on what Attlee regarded as his "betrayal" of the Labour Party and the British working class.

In the 1931 general election, Attlee held his seat with a narrow majority of 551, but many of his former colleagues did not. The pacifist George Lansbury (1859–1940) was elected as party leader, but he was uneasy in the face of the aggressive fascism of Adolf Hitler (1889–1945) and Benito Mussolini (1883–1945). When Lansbury resigned in October 1935, Baldwin called a snap election, and the Labour Party elected Attlee as a temporary leader. As party leader Attlee refused to support the distrusted government of Neville Chamberlain (1869–1940), and in the subsequent wartime coalition, only Attlee, as deputy prime minister, and Churchill served in the war cabinet for the entire period.

As prime minister from July 1945, Attlee presided over a formidable legislative program, in which the bases for the postwar welfare state were laid and major industries were taken into public ownership. Internationally, probably his greatest contribution was his realization that India should be given its independence as quickly as possible, his appointment of Louis Mountbatten (1900–1979) to effect this, and his reluctant acceptance of the need for a separate Muslim state, Pakistan. Domestically, apart from the legislative program, he performed the difficult task of holding the talented but disparate personalities in government together, aided by his understated but firm insistence on working toward a fairer society, his suspicion of ideological enthusiasts, his mastery of technical detail, and his ability to steer committee meetings toward agreement. Breaches only began to become publicly evident as the younger Aneurin Bevan (1897–1960) and Hugh Todd Naylor Gaitskell (1906–1963) fought for the future leadership of the party, and the older generation fell ill or died. In the 1950 general election, the government's majority was cut to five and then lost the following year. Yet throughout, Attlee remained high in public affection, recognized as an ethical man with a preference for substance over form. Married at the age of thirty-nine to the twenty-two-year-old Violet Millar, Attlee enjoyed a happy and fruitful marriage. Violet predeceased him in 1964; Attlee died on 8 October 1967.

See also **British Empire, End of; India; United Kingdom.**

BIBLIOGRAPHY

Attlee, Clement Richard. *As It Happened*. London, 1954.

Harris, Kenneth. *Attlee*. London, 1982.

MARTIN CHICK

AUDEN, W. H. (1907–1973), British poet.

The leading younger British poet of the 1930s, W. H. Auden became one of the most influential English-language writers of his time. Wystan Hugh Auden was born in York, England, on 21 February 1907, and educated at Gresham's School, Holt, and Christ Church, Oxford. Shaped by modernist experimentalism, and drawing on his time in Weimar Berlin and his reading of Sigmund Freud and Karl Marx, Auden's early work combined a focus on psychosexual disorder with a sense of acute historical anxiety. With striking images of modern industrial landscape and a tone that spoke to readers' anxieties about economic crisis and the rise of fascism, volumes like *Poems* (1930), *The Orators* (1932), and *Look, Stranger!* (1937) made Auden the preeminent figure in a group of young British writers sympathetic with communism, including Christopher Isherwood, Stephen Spender, and Louis MacNeice.

Auden's "Spain, 1937," inspired by his visit to the front during the Spanish civil war, became the most famous English poem to confront the threat of fascism, but it marked the peak of his identification with leftist politics. His most celebrated work of the late 1930s—poems like "September 1, 1939," and "In Memory of W. B. Yeats" (1939)—instead sought to affirm the apolitical value of art in the face of impending world war. Auden's 1939 emigration to the United States marked his disavowal of any voice as a poet of the left; his espousal of existentialist Protestantism and adoption in 1946 of U.S. citizenship distanced him further from the English literary establishment. Auden's major long poems of the 1940s—"New Year Letter" (1941), "The Sea and the Mirror" (1944), and *The Age of Anxiety* (1947)—disappointed those who had valued his more directly political poetry. Nonetheless, his Pulitzer Prize for 1948—one of many such honors over the course of his career—confirmed his stature in the United States. There was no disagreeing about

Auden's importance among contemporary existentialist writers, or about the formal ambition of his poetry, which drew inspiration from texts that ranged from medieval alliterative poetry to the prose of Henry James. At the same time, his work of the 1940s was often strikingly personal in its grappling with faith and love, particularly his relationship with Chester Kallman (1921–1975), whom he had met in 1939 and lived with for the remainder of his life.

The later Auden wrote that he aspired to be "a minor Atlantic Goethe"—a claim of characteristic modesty and self-assurance. Volumes like *Nones* (1951), *The Shield of Achilles* (1955), and *Homage to Clio* (1960) mix masterful light verse with some of his most morally challenging poetry. Present throughout is a deep ambivalence about art and language, which Auden saw as equally capable of honoring the sacred and corrupting civil society in an age of manipulative mass media. His late poetry is often comic and apparently casual, but these qualities mask formal and conceptual subtlety. In "Thanksgiving for a Habitat" (1963), for example, he devoted one poem to every room of his house in Kirchstetten, Austria, dedicating each to a friend, and the sequence playfully undoes distinctions between public and private, serious and trivial. In later years Auden also produced much important literary criticism, most notably on William Shakespeare, and significant achievements as a librettist. He had already worked with Benjamin Britten on *Paul Bunyan* in 1941, but his writing for opera intensified in collaboration with Kallman, on the libretto for Igor Stravinsky's *The Rake's Progress* (1951); Auden and Kallman also wrote libretti for Hans Werner Henze's *Elegy for Young Lovers* (1961) and *The Bassarids* (1966), as well as English versions of Mozart's *The Magic Flute* and *Don Giovanni*.

Auden's significance in literary history has been defined largely by his centrality to British writing of the 1930s, and by his authorship of some of the most famous poems to address the crises of the West in the twentieth century. But his enormously diverse output includes signal achievements in an array of literary genres and modes—not only some of the twentieth century's finest religious verse, but also some of its most memorable love poetry in English, much of it remarkably candid in its concern with Eros and homosexual identity. Auden's most enduring influence on later poets remains his technical virtuosity, which extended from free verse to virtually every available English verse form; in addition to his highly varied longer works, his elegies, odes, and sonnets are among the most accomplished of the twentieth century. Following his death in Vienna on 28 September 1973, Auden was buried near his home in Kirchstetten.

See also **Antifascism; Modernism.**

BIBLIOGRAPHY

Auden, W. H. *The Dyer's Hand and Other Essays.* New York, 1962.

———. *The English Auden: Poems, Essays, and Dramatic Writings 1927–1939.* Edited by Edward Mendelson. London, 1977.

———. *Collected Poems.* Edited by Edward Mendelson. New York, 1991.

Carpenter, Humphrey. *W. H. Auden: A Biography.* London, 1981.

Hynes, Samuel. *The Auden Generation: Literature and Politics in England in the 1930s.* Princeton, N.J., 1976.

Mendelson, Edward. *Early Auden.* New York, 1981.

———. *Later Auden.* New York, 1999.

Smith, Stan, ed. *The Cambridge Companion to W. H. Auden.* Cambridge, U.K., 2004.

RICHARD R. BOZORTH

AUSCHWITZ-BIRKENAU. On 27 January 1945 Soviet troops discovered, almost by chance, seven thousand haggard survivors of the concentration and extermination camp of Auschwitz-Birkenau. Ten days earlier, the Nazis had begun evacuating the fifty-eight thousand survivors in what became known as "death marches." The Soviet soldiers did not at first comprehend what they had just "liberated." The name *Auschwitz* was familiar but what had transpired there was not. Auschwitz-Birkenau was in fact a vast complex with two main camps: Auschwitz 1 was a concentration camp opened by the Nazis in Oświęcim, Poland, in 1940 to imprison Polish victims of the repression; Birkenau, also known as Auschwitz 2, was the extermination camp built in

1942 to kill Jews of the region and later deportees from the whole of Europe. To these may be added Auschwitz 3, which consisted of the IG Farben synthetic rubber factory known as "Buna" and forty-odd smaller labor camps.

INDUSTRIAL EXTERMINATION

Auschwitz-Birkenau began to enter the consciousness of the world only in the last twenty years of the twentieth century. The Cold War, persistent anti-Semitism in Poland and Russia, resistance to survivors' stories, and the greater attention given to accounts by non-Jews long hindered any real acknowledgment of how the Jewish victims had suffered. On 27 January 2005 European leaders gathered at Birkenau, "the largest cemetery in the world," to issue a reminder about the worst atrocity in history. As Primo Levi, a survivor, described it, "At no other place or time has one seen a phenomenon so unexpected and so complex: never have so many human lives been extinguished in so short a time, and with so lucid a combination of technological ingenuity, fanaticism, and cruelty" (Levi, 1988, p. 21).

Adolf Hitler clearly outlined his racist policy in *Mein Kampf* and began to put it into action in 1933, but it was a long road from his maniacal Judeophobia to extermination at Auschwitz. Since he understood the world as a superior race's struggle for survival, he ordered sterilization, internment, and eventually extermination of elements that might "contaminate" German blood. These included the physically and mentally handicapped, who became victims of the T4 euthanasia program, as well as Gypsies, homosexuals, and above all, Jews, since Hitler's biologically based racist ideology was combined with an apocalyptic vision of the world in which Jews were considered demons.

The opening of the Soviet front in June 1941 accelerated and exacerbated the brutality and led to a radicalization of the racial policy of interning, humiliating, and murdering targeted groups that had begun in 1933 and intensified in 1939. Jews and "defective" Germans and Poles were deported to Auschwitz. Meanwhile, during the summer and fall of 1941, the Einsatzgruppen, or mobile killing units, machine-gunned men, women, and children en masse. Later, the Nazis used mobile gassing trucks and gas chambers. Forced ghettoization

and executions were carried out by region. After the Wannsee Conference of 20 January 1942, at which the "Final Solution" was translated into bureaucratic language, Jews were transported thousands of kilometers by train for "industrial extermination" in death centers at Chelmno, Belzec, Sobibor, Treblinka, Majdanek, and finally Birkenau, which would become the central location for the destruction of the European Jews.

In March 1942 the first convoys of Jews arrived, from Silesia, Slovakia, and France, initially for forced labor. On 4 July 1942 Slovakian Jews became the first victims of the gas chambers, where they were sent upon their arrival. Subsequently, the Nazis created a carefully laid-out industrial plant—buildings designed for the extermination process, Zyklon B (a deadly gas that became active when exposed to the air), crematoriums—to perpetrate their crimes against humanity. This system operated like an elaborate conveyor belt. Victims were first sorted out or "selected" on what became known as the "ramp of death": those who were to be immediately killed were separated from those destined to perform slave labor in the camp. These prisoners then underwent industrial "disinfection" for "bacilli" and "vermin." Those with interesting physical peculiarities—dwarfs, giants, twins, and so on—served as guinea pigs in gruesome "medical experiments" before rejoining the others for the "full treatment." Their hair was shaved in a "hygienic" operation and they were exterminated in the "shower room," after which any gold in their teeth was extracted. Personal belongings were appropriated and everything was exploited for profit: victims' hair sometimes went to make blankets, and artificial limbs were recycled for use by the army. To prepare ever more victims for the "Final Solution," four additional buildings were built. Crematoriums 2, 3, 4, and 5 included rooms for undressing, gas chambers, and ovens. But the sheer number of corpses made it difficult to destroy them quickly. For this reason the Nazis resorted to open-air mass graves. The prisoners known as *Sonderkommandos,* who were responsible for disposing of the bodies, were themselves regularly exterminated; photos taken by one of them at unimaginable risk show naked, living women, along with trees, smoke, and masses of burning cadavers.

A guard inspects Jews arriving at Auschwitz, 1944. Those deemed unfit for work or unacceptable for medical experiments were often sent for immediate execution. GETTY IMAGES

LIFE IN THE CAMPS

When the Soviet troops arrived, they found huge mounds of ashes as well as shoes, suitcases, prayer shawls, children's clothes, hair by the ton, and gold teeth not yet melted down. Several thousand survivors remained. These prisoners had suffered every sort of dehumanizing brutality at the hands of guards. At Auschwitz, survivors (or "sub-vivors," in the expression of S. Aaron) became the daily testing ground for acts of barbarism in an upside-down world made not for the living but for the dead. Those judged fit to work and to live for a few more weeks or months were branded, classified, and archived in an atmosphere dedicated to bestializing and reifying prisoners. They were called "pieces" (*Stücke*), "vermin," or "rats." Identities

were erased: numbers replaced names and were tattooed in the flesh of the forearm. Auschwitz prisoners, with dark humor, called the tattoo "heaven's phone number," *Himmlische Telefonnummer*. Numbers were also painted or sewn onto clothes, with triangles in various colors to indicate the category of the prisoner: pink for homosexuals, red for political prisoners, and so on. The camp administration produced endless records, including fingerprints and anthropometric photos, each classified by the prisoner's number. By contrast, all pictures and personal items were taken from prisoners in the same depersonalization process. Survival was an act of daily resistance: to wash, to dress, to eat, to seek another's care and affection was to hold together body and spirit, to maintain one's being, one's individuality. On the traditional fasting day of Yom Kippur in 1944, Hungarian Jews, who had recently arrived by the thousands, refused their meager meal, to the astonishment of the guards.

Prisoners in the camp experienced an assault on all their senses, from shouting SS troops, barking dogs, the smoke from mass graves and crematoriums, the freighted odors of urinary incontinence, dysentery, and decomposing cadavers. On seeing the prisoners' extreme emaciation and smelling their body odor, Imre Kertész, a deportee from Hungary, was reminded of a plague; but the plague was the camp itself. In weeks, sometimes days, teenagers transmuted into old men and old women, the walking dead. Auschwitz looked like a garbage dump; all traces of vegetation had disappeared, having been trampled or eaten, roots included. The parasites and vermin that flourish in filth—lice, scabies, and mosquitoes—infected prisoners, often afflicting them with abscesses and boils. There were overcrowded barracks, too few toilets, an utter lack of hygiene, revolting food, piles of garbage foraged repeatedly for some scrap to eat. Some prisoners, known as *Muselmanen,* or "Muslims," having lost all hope and all human appearance, simply wandered about aimlessly.

All aspects of prisoners' lives at Auschwitz were conducted in the open; it was impossible to be alone. Prisoners were always on view, crowded together, vulnerable to all types of indecency. Any job that carried responsibility, no matter how small, was sought out because it offered a modicum of protection and sometimes additional food, and made various types of barter possible. Guards multiplied humiliations, intentionally spilling soup on the ground, for example, then forcing starving prisoners to crawl on all fours and lick it up, or to use their hand as a spoon. People were thus transformed into things that could be discarded. Weak from the arduous journey and nearly always ill, sometimes further worn down by interrogations and torture, they were forced to work while enduring constant abuse from the guards. They were even victims of the guards' cynical view of culture and civilization. Inmates left for work and even labored to the accompaniment of a prisoners' orchestra performing at the gate, under a sign that proclaimed: *Arbeit macht frei* (Work shall make

you free). The productivity of human beings beaten, starved, and terrorized in such an oppressive environment could hardly be very high. Outdoor work was the hardest and was for the most part pointless and ridiculous: building drainage ditches and earthen embankments with nothing but picks and wheelbarrows, for example. After a time in this ghastly world, a still more horrific fate awaited them in Auschwitz 2, when laborers were sent to the same gas chambers in which, on the day they arrived, their children, wives, and elderly parents had been murdered.

AUSCHWITZ AS MUSEUM

Auschwitz eventually usurped Buchenwald, the concentration camp in Germany, as the principal symbol of Nazi inhumanity. Former prisoners who have returned to visit the camp, however, note that it scarcely resembles the place they knew. Blockhouses and paths have been rebuilt, trees planted. During the war it was the vast factory of death by forced labor, Luger pistol, torture, and Zyklon B. It is now a memorial and, in contemporary museum parlance, the "orientation center" for the entire group of camps collectively known as Auschwitz. The museum is unique in that it presents both the face of the new democratic and Catholic Poland and vestigial relics from the time before 1989, when Poland was a Soviet satellite and the Russians were the "big brothers" who had liberated the camp in January 1945. After 1989 the national exhibitions of countries that no longer exist—the Soviet Union, Yugoslavia, Czechoslovakia—were closed or remodeled by the new nations that replaced them.

By turning the former blockhouses into exhibition centers for various nations, the museum demonstrates the magnitude of the enterprise of destruction, which extended throughout Europe. But so great was the effort to repress the past that for decades the dual reality of Auschwitz-Birkenau was difficult to grasp. There were resistance fighters imprisoned there, adults who made the choice to stand up to fascism. But there were also massive numbers of Jews arrested, deported, and imprisoned in death camps simply because they were Jews, regardless of age or sex. In 1943 Raphael Lemkin coined the term *genocide* for this event, and in the early twenty-first century the words

One of the gates at the camp at Auschwitz bears the phrase "Work Makes One Free." UNITED STATES HOLOCAUST MEMORIAL MUSEUM

Holocaust and *Shoah* are also used to refer to the destruction of the Jews in Europe. The new national exhibitions attempt to compensate for the long years of silence. The French pavilion, for instance, describes the journey of five Jews, children and adults, to Auschwitz; the Hungarian pavilion displays a transparent boxcar on rails, inviting visitors to take a symbolic journey.

The use of Christian icons to evoke the Shoah, in an assimilation of the Poles' suffering to that of European Jews, is characteristic of the way many Poles understand Auschwitz. After a long and painful controversy that began in the 1980s, Carmelite nuns moved five hundred meters away from the camp, where they had created a cloister in a former storage area for the Zyklon B containers; a huge cross erected there was taken down. Polish visitors usually do not go to Birkenau but prefer the shrine of Father Maximilian Kolbe or other martyrs,

whose cells bear Christian inscriptions. And yet the dilemma persists as to how to represent a Jewish catastrophe at this site. Christian symbols are problematic, to say the least.

The reality of the Holocaust is on view in two blockhouses in Auschwitz 1. One room is set aside for a cross-section model of the gas chamber at Birkenau. What no photograph has preserved— and for good reason—has been reconstituted with architectural precision. Also on display are the clandestine photos of the prisoner "selections" at the railhead. Canisters of Zyklon B are piled in a showcase. Victims' belongings, items of daily life sorted into immense heaps, form an overwhelming sight. All the same yet different, they are the confiscated pieces of broken lives and bodies: eyeglasses, prayer shawls, hairbrushes, enameled pots and plates, artificial limbs, corsets, infants' clothing, hair, and suitcases. On view is a blanket with a certificate from a Polish scientific laboratory identifying the fibers as human hair. Millions of destroyed lives appear with great immediacy in this accumulation of objects. There are piles of suitcases with the names and birth dates of their owners painted in white letters, inscriptions made by the deportees themselves; they serve as epitaphs, represent a memorial that rescues the victims from the anonymity of mass murder.

At the railhead in Birkenau stand the ruins of the crematoriums and gas chambers that the Nazis dynamited before fleeing. Four commemorative stelae at the top of the railway have identical inscriptions in Polish, English, Hebrew, and Yiddish: "To the memory of the men, women, and children who fell victim to the Nazi genocide. Here lie their ashes. May their souls rest in peace." Even though most of the victims were Ashkenazic Jews whose native language was Yiddish, the Yiddish texts appeared only fifty years after the fact.

The space occupied by the gas chambers at the end of the selection platform of Birkenau, directly across from the tower and entrance, was chosen as the site for the camp's commemorative monument, which consists of a huge pile of black stones falling over one another. At the summit of the highest section, this abstract sculpture gives way to a recognizable object, the triangle that political prisoners were forced to wear. Polish communist authorities framed this inscription: "Four million persons suffered and died here at the hands of Nazi murderers between the years 1940 to 1945." By 1989 that inaccurate text had been replaced. Four million was the wrong number. Probably 1.1 million died among the 1.3 million deported to Auschwitz: one million Jews, twenty-one thousand Gypsies, seventy-five thousand Poles, fifteen thousand Russian prisoners of war, and fifteen thousand of other nationalities. The new tablets were engraved with the following inscription in twenty-two languages: "For ever let this place be a cry of despair and a warning to humanity, where the Nazis murdered about one and a half million men, women, and children, mainly Jews, from various countries of Europe. Auschwitz/Birkenau 1940–1945."

See also Buchenwald; Concentration Camps; Dachau; Genocide; Holocaust; Zyklon B.

BIBLIOGRAPHY

Browning, Christopher. *The Origins of the Final Solution: The Evolution of Nazi Jewish Policy, September 1939– March 1942.* Lincoln, Neb., 2004.

Des voix sous la cendre, manuscrits des Sonderkommandos d'Auschwitz-Birkenau. Paris, 2005.

Didi-Huberman, Georges. *Images malgré tout.* Paris, 2003.

Gutman, Israel, and Bella Gutterman, eds. *Auschwitz Album: The Story of a Transport.* Translated by Naftali Greenwood and Jerzy Michalovic. Jerusalem, 2002.

Huener, Jonathan. *Auschwitz, Poland, and the Politics of Commemoration, 1945–1979.* Athens, Ohio, 2003.

Kertész, Imre. *Fatelessness.* Translated by Tim Wilkinson. New York, 2004.

Laks, Szymon. *Music of Another World.* Translated by Chester A. Kisiel. Evanston, Ill., 2000.

Levi, Primo. *The Drowned and the Saved.* Translated by Raymond Rosenthal. New York, 1988.

———. *Survival in Auschwitz: The Nazi Assault on Humanity.* Translated by Stuart Woolf. New York, 1993.

"Memorial and Museum: Auschwitz-Birkenau." Available at http://www.auschwitz-muzeum.oswiecim.pl.

Pelt, Robert Jan van, and Déborah Dwork. *Auschwitz, 1270 to the Present.* New York, 1996.

ANNETTE BECKER

AUSTRALIA. In 1914 Australia was racially, politically, economically, and culturally an outpost of Europe. More precisely, it was a British colony, farm, and mine. Nearly all five million Australians were of English, Scottish, Welsh, or Irish stock. The last group, mostly Catholic in religion, was nonetheless essentially British too. Sydney and Melbourne, in which nearly one Australian in four lived, were great cities of the British Empire; Sydney was effectively a British naval base. A self-governing dominion within the empire, Australia had no diplomatic identity beyond it. The prime minister nominally deferred to a governor general who represented Britain's monarch. Most Australian authors were published in London, most of Australia's successful artists and singers worked there, and nearly all loans taken by Australian governments were raised there. Nearly half of Australia's exports went to Britain (principally wool, gold, butter, and meat), and more than half of Australia's imports came from there.

SOME IMPRESSIONS OF AUSTRALIA AND AUSTRALIANS

"The Australian, at present, is little other than a transplanted Briton with the essential characteristics of his British forbears, the desire for freedom from restraint, however, being perhaps somewhat accentuated. The greater opportunity for an open-air existence and the absence of the restrictions of older civilizations may be held to be in the main responsible for this." (*Official Year Book of the Commonwealth of Australia,* 1919)

"They are healthy, and to my thinking almost imbecile. That's what life in a new country does to you: it makes you so material, so outward.... Everything is happy-go-lucky, and one couldn't *fret* about anything if one tried. One just doesn't care. And they are all like that." (D. H. Lawrence, 1922)

"This land belonged to our forefathers 150 years ago, but today we are pushed further and further into the background." (Jack Patten, Australian Aborigine, 1938)

"In short, a people fairly like ourselves have in a relatively short time built a Western-type civilization on a difficult continent in a far corner of the Pacific Basin." (Hartley Grattan, visiting American, 1942)

"It's so empty and featureless, like a newspaper that has been entirely censored. We used to drive for miles, always expecting that around the next corner there'd be something to look at, but there never was. That is the charm of Australia." (Robert Morley, 1949)

"This is one of the most peaceful, well-ordered, prosperous, happy, law-abiding and Christian communities in the whole wide world." (J. J. Cahill, premier of New South Wales, 1959)

"We are a smug, piddling country, blowing our own trumpet for all we are worth, while our achievements are few and mostly material." (Patrick White, 1968)

"I see Australia closer to my vision ... than it has ever been—I no longer stand [to attention] for an imperial [British] anthem, hear people pretending to be English when neither they nor their ancestors were ever there, and, above all ... I can say proudly 'I am a republican of Spanish and Irish background' without causing a riot or provoking an arrest under the Crimes Act." (Al Grassby, former federal politician, 1984)

"Australia the most bewitching, the most endearing, the most fragile, strongest in an innocence still unviolated. You can't appreciate it unless you see the horrors of the rest of the world. In this land there remains a goodness still unsullied." (Marivic Wyndham, immigrant, quoted in Peter Read, *Belonging,* 2000)

Life was better for most British Australians than for their relatives on the other side of the world. Their continent was the least populated on earth, and shortage of labor encouraged high wages. Export sales subsidized tariff walls that encouraged manufacturing and employment. Most men, and most women too, could vote in state and federal elections, and the trade-union-based Labor Party, which claimed to represent the working man, was already winning federal elections. An arbitration court, set up to settle strikes, was spreading a "basic wage" derived more from the cost of supporting a family than from an employer's ability to pay. All this good fortune was imperfectly spread, of course, while the dry, empty landscape made rural life hard. More notable, though, was the effective exclusion of non-Britons from the prevailing prosperity, or even from the country at all. Most of the ninety thousand Aborigines, whose forebears had once possessed Australia, were consigned to mendicancy on the fringes of towns and farms. An Immigration Restriction Act (1901) deterred most Asian immigrants and some Europeans too.

WARS AND DEPRESSION

Australia went to war along with the rest of the British Empire in August 1914. Its militia mobilized to protect the coastline, its little navy was merged into Britain's, and it raised a khaki-clad Australian Imperial Force (AIF) from volunteers to fight in Europe. Brigaded with New Zealanders as an Australian and New Zealand Army Corps (better known by its acronym, Anzac), the AIF joined in the landing on Gallipoli on 25 April 1915. To the delight of most Australians, the AIF fought bravely in its baptism of fire. Later, greatly expanded with new recruits, it helped fill the trenches of the western front, where Germany was eventually beaten, and the ranks of the cavalry that annexed Palestine to the empire.

Australia's war effort exceeded that of comparable British dominions—Canada and South Africa. It added the German portion in New Guinea to the British portion that Australia already administered. It gave Australia a seat in the League of Nations, a legend of military prowess, and a sense of being a nation—though still within the British Empire. But the effort also maimed and divided the hitherto cohesive society that made it. Fifty-nine thousand men, or one in every ten of military age, had been killed. The middle class had embraced the war, but many workers had come to resent it. Two plebiscites (on October 1916 and December 1917) on whether to conscript men to replenish the AIF were bitterly contested and narrowly defeated, alienating many Irish Catholics and splitting the Labor Party. Industrial strikes and the influenza pandemic disfigured the first year of peace.

The 1920s brought uncertain, uneven prosperity to Australia, along with some enduring institutions. Anzac Day (25 April) became a de facto national day, war memorials became civic shrines, and returned soldiers formed a powerful political lobby. The federal government moved to a new capital, Canberra. Voting became compulsory, the Labor Party became the dominant political force in several states, and rural electors turned to a Country Party. Tariffs became steeper, and Japan emerged as a significant buyer of Australian exports. Taking Aboriginal children from their parents and raising them under white supervision became common. A suburban bungalow with a car in the garage became the popular ideal. Saturday afternoons were given over to watching sports, Saturday nights to cinema. Hollywood shaped the mental universe of many ordinary Australians, while Moscow did the same for working-class militants.

The fall in price of primary products that began the Great Depression struck Australia hard. A conservative federal government that tried to cut labor costs by turning on trade unions and the arbitration court was voted out in 1929. Its Labor successor reluctantly joined state governments in cutting spending and wages. In 1932 nearly a third of the male workforce was unemployed. Poor families were evicted from houses they could no longer afford to rent, charities were swamped, and state governments distributed ration vouchers. Australia's few communists and fascists hoped to exploit the crisis. Instead voters turned to a cautious coalition government under Joseph Lyons (who was prime minister from 1931 to 1939). The economy crawled slowly out of the mire, helped by trade with Japan. Yet Japan also seemed to pose a grave military threat to white predominance across Southeast Asia and Australasia.

When World War II began in Europe in 1939, Australian air force crews and part of a second AIF joined the fighting in North Africa, Greece, and the Middle East. Other AIF units went to help garrison Malaya and the Dutch East Indies should Japan strike south; most fell prisoner when Japan did so in December 1941. By February 1942 Japanese airplanes were sporadically bombing Australia's north coast. By July Japanese soldiers were in New Guinea fighting Australian militiamen along the Kokoda Trail.

With the fall of Singapore and Hong Kong, the British shield that had preserved British Australia was smashed forever. A Labor federal government under John Curtin (prime minister from 1941 to 1945) immediately called for American protection. It came anyway, since Australia was the ideal base for striking back at Japanese forces in the southwest Pacific. Australians now mobilized for total war and accepted an industrial and military conscription that put nine working-age men in ten and nearly one working-age woman in three into uniform or onto farms and production lines. The AIF regrouped in Australia and then, with the militia, joined tough but militarily irrelevant campaigns in the jungles of New Guinea and Borneo.

When peace came in 1945, the names of thirty-four thousand dead were added to the war memorials erected after World War I. Nearly a quarter had died as prisoners of the Japanese. The war, and the consequent collapse of the British Empire, changed how most Australians saw the world. Britain remained a sentimental second home for most Australians, especially middle-class ones, and its monarch was as widely revered as ever, but now Southeast Asia and the United States joined Britain as centers for Australia's cultural, strategic, and economic attention. The war also brought political change. Australians wanted wartime full employment for men to continue, though they

Queen Elizabeth and Prince Philip are greeted by enthusiastic crowds in Newcastle on their 1954 tour of Australia. Though Australia became increasingly removed from British political and economic influence during the postwar period, affection for the queen remained strong. ©BETTMANN/CORBIS

voted in 1944 against carrying wartime regimentation of the economy into peacetime. In 1949 they elected a Liberal federal government under Robert Menzies (prime minister from 1949 to 1966) that supported full employment, free enterprise, affection for Britain, and alliance with the United States.

PROSPERITY AND IMMIGRATION

The postwar economic boom brought unrivalled prosperity to a generation of Australians. Virtually every man who wanted a job found one and kept it. After a brief postwar return home, a third of all women went to work again, often for three-quarters the pay a man would have received rather than at the prewar standard of half. Home, car, and television ownership at last became nearly universal. New suburbs sprawled, and some modest skyscrapers rose. The architect Robin Boyd mocked the visual ugliness of the new prosperity. The comedian Barry Humphries ridiculed its beneficiaries as narrow minded. Australians ignored the critics, filled their spare bedrooms with children, and enjoyed their good fortune.

Growing faster at times than that of the United States, the Australian economy easily supported high tariffs, a large public service, subsidized medicines, a dole for the unemployed, and generous pensions for war veterans. The economy also supported, and in part was supported by, mass immigration. Almost two and a half million immigrants settled Australia from 1947 to 1973. Fewer than half were British or Irish. Australia's leaders wanted a sudden injection of people to build up industry and infrastructure, and perhaps deter another lunge south by a hostile Asian power. They knew that Britain and Ireland could not provide the numbers wanted. So they turned, at first, to northern Europe, then from the mid-1950s to the Mediterranean and Middle East, and from 1966, reluctantly, to East Asia.

Together, immigration and births nearly doubled Australia's population between 1947 (7.6 million) and 1976 (13.5 million). About every four years a million new Australians could be counted. The non-British immigrants among them were hailed officially as New Australians. Unofficially they received less flattering names. Still, no social strife accompanied their arrival. Outwardly they assimilated, as other Australians expected. At home, most kept their customs, languages, and cuisines.

The end of the British Empire, and Britain's subsequent turn to Europe, increasingly required Australia to make its own way in the world. The military and cultural predominance of the United States, and the economic revival of a tamed Japan, determined the path Australia would take. In 1951 the wartime alliance with the United States was confirmed by the ANZUS treaty; henceforth American power, not British, protected Australia. In 1966 Australia's currency shifted from British to American denominations. A year later, American imports into Australia began to exceed British imports in value, while the value of Australian exports to Japan began to exceed those to Britain. The new order could also be seen in Australia's contribution to wars waged in East Asia after 1945 against communist and nationalist threats to friendly postcolonial states. The new professional army that replaced Australia's militia and AIF fought in Korea (1950–1953) and in Malaya and Borneo (1950–1966) alongside British troops. But in Vietnam (1962–1972), reinforced by conscripts, it supported an American war effort. Fewer Australians died in these wars (nine hundred) than were killed each year in motor vehicle accidents. But the resort to conscription for Vietnam, along with television reportage of that war's realities and reverses, prompted protests. The largest one (May 1970) put two hundred thousand people onto city streets across Australia.

These protests were also local expressions of the arrival in Australia of the 1960s social revolution. The wilder demands of the revolution were rebuffed; not so the vaguer desires behind it to exploit prosperity, relax old social strictures, question the supposed superiority of European ways, and renounce lingering affection for Britain and its monarch. Thus official censorship of offensive words and images wound down, while public funding for the arts rose. Oral contraception became widespread, and abortion no longer seemed shameful. Unoccupied land was judged more in need of preservation than development. Taking Aboriginal children from their parents fell from favor, and in 1967 Aborigines were symbolically voted full citizenship. In 1972 Australians elected a Labor federal government under Gough Whitlam (prime minister from 1972 to 1975), partly to carry on this new program. It abolished conscription, made medical care and university enrollment free, proclaimed to the world Australia's hitherto quiet abandonment of the Immigration Restriction Act, relinquished Australian rule in New Guinea, and cut tariffs to open up Australian industry to international competition.

RECESSION AND REPUBLICANISM

In 1975 a governor general made a unique intervention into federal politics by dismissing the Whitlam government and calling an election. Australians were divided over the dismissal but overwhelmingly chose a different, conservative government. Their choice largely reflected the impact of tariff reduction and the sudden end of postwar prosperity. Wages and prices were spiraling upward; factories were closing down. By 1983 nearly one Australian in ten who wanted work could not find it. Export sales, tariff protection, and the basic wage no longer created and spread prosperity, yet to the north the economies of East Asia were thriving. The answer seemed to be better integration into the global economy, particularly its Asian component. In 1983 a Labor federal government under Bob Hawke (prime minister from 1983 to 1991) then Paul Keating (treasurer from 1983 to 1991 and prime minister from 1991 to 1996) dismantled the fences that had long protected Australian industries and workers. The dollar's value was no longer fixed and capital was allowed free transfer in and out of the country. Tariffs were cut further and the arbitration court hamstrung.

Keating also called on Australia to make itself a republic by replacing its governor general with a president. The call reflected both the old Irish Catholic distrust of England and a new eagerness to present a less European face to Asia.

While East Asia took an increasing share of Australia's exports, Southeast Asia provided an increasing proportion of its immigrants. The trend began when refugees from Vietnam first arrived in 1976. By 1985 more than half the immigrants who stayed in Australia were Asian. By 1995 one Australian in twenty-five was Asian by birth or descent. An official policy of multiculturalism hailed the new immigrants and the customs they brought with them as a source of national strength. Perhaps this eased what was an uncomfortable adjustment for many of the immigrants, who found their new country's language and laws impenetrable at first. Many lived in the poorest suburbs and worked long hours in low-wage jobs, trusting their sacrifice would lift their children into the professions.

Aborigines, who now made up about three in every two hundred Australians, were also finding official encouragement and everyday hardship. In 1976 the federal government handed Aboriginal reserves in its vast Northern Territory to Aborigines themselves, and allowed them to claim ownership of some other lands they lived on. State governments began to make similar gestures until by 1992 Aborigines owned about a seventh of the nation—effectively the unwanted portions. A high court ruling (*Mabo v. Queensland*) that year paved the way for them to own even more. By declaring that Aborigines had once been the legal owners of Australia, it prompted federal legislation allowing them to claim any otherwise unused land they had long occupied. At the same time, shame was growing among some white Australians, and anger among some black ones, that Aboriginal children had once been taken from their parents. There were calls for some kind of reconciliation between black and white that would morally, and perhaps financially, compensate Aborigines for past wrongs they had suffered. But one compensation already in train—welfare payments—was helping to undermine Aboriginal communities as well as sustain them.

Economic deregulation, the call for a republic, Asian immigration, multiculturalism, and Aboriginal reconciliation were popular among Australians whose incomes came from professional jobs. Many other Australians opposed them. They wanted their own struggles eased, not those of new immigrants and Aborigines, and their jobs protected. Some wanted Asian immigration to cease, and turned to the handful of politicians who agreed with them. Most Australians wanted a republic, but not tied to a political agenda they increasingly disliked. They voted out the Keating government in 1996, and three years later voted against a proposed republican constitution. By then their discontent was easing. The economy was reviving, Asian migrants were proving keen to assimilate, and Aborigines were not being given suburban land.

By the close of the twentieth century inflation and unemployment were beaten and the economy was growing rapidly. Australia ranked among the top ten nations for prosperity, longevity, home ownership, and equality between the sexes. Many of its nineteen million people led a comfortable, perhaps innocent existence. The great Australian heroes from the world wars were, in their eyes, an ambulance worker who carried wounded soldiers under fire and a captured doctor who helped others in a Japanese prison camp. Their iconic national inventions were a winding clothesline and a motor mower. Half their population growth derived from immigration, yet their continent remained the least populated on earth. It was also the most urbanized. Four in every five Australians lived in ten cities on the coast, with five million living in or near Sydney. That city hosted the Olympic games in 2000. The efficient, informal, and friendly arrangements had an Aboriginal athlete at their center. They suggested an Australian genius for practicality and enjoyment and a desire by many Australians to make amends with the Aborigines. On the surface Australia no longer seemed an outpost of Europe, and economically it had long ceased to be one. In language and political system, though, and to a great extent in culture and lifestyle, it remained one.

See also **British Empire; Depression; Immigration and Internal Migration; Minority Rights; New Zealand; World War I; World War II.**

BIBLIOGRAPHY

Blainey, Geoffrey. *A Shorter History of Australia*. Melbourne, 1994.

Cochrane, Peter. *Australians at War*. Sydney, 2001.

Inglis, K. S. *Sacred Places: War Memorials in the Australian Landscape*. Melbourne, 1998. How Australians have commemorated their wars.

Jupp, James, ed. *The Australian People: An Encyclopedia of the Nation, Its People, and Their Origins*. New York, 2001.

Kelly, Paul. *100 Years: The Australian Story*. Crows Nest, Australia, 2001. Charts the changes in twentieth-century Australia's politics and economy.

Lack, John, and Jacqueline Templeton, eds. *Bold Experiment: A Documentary History of Australian Immigration since 1945*. Melbourne, 1994.

Martin, A. W. *Robert Menzies: A Life*. 2 vols. Melbourne, 1993–1999. Biography of twentieth-century Australia's longest-serving prime minister.

Morgan, Sally. *My Place*. Perth, 1987. An influential Aboriginal memoir.

Read, Peter. *Belonging: Australians, Place, and Aboriginal Ownership*. Cambridge, U.K., 2000.

Sang, Ye. *The Year the Dragon Came*. St. Lucia, Australia, 1996. Experiences of recent Chinese immigrants to Australia.

CRAIG WILCOX

AUSTRIA.

The evolution of Austria is exemplary in the way it reflects the extreme experiences of European nations during the "short twentieth century." Once part of the vast Austro-Hungarian Empire, which had a population of fifty two million, Austria in the early twenty-first century was a republic and corporate state of slightly more than eight million; the former centerpiece of *Mitteleuropa* (central Europe) now forms the eastern border of the European Union. An uncommon feature of Austria's development is that in the twentieth century it came into being both as a nation with a unique identity and as a sovereign state.

FROM MULTINATIONAL EMPIRE TO THE FIRST AUSTRIAN REPUBLIC (1890–1918)

Austria-Hungary occupied a unique place in central Europe, and Austria (Cisleithania) constituted the western portion of the Dual Monarchy. Political reorganization in 1867 stirred up the separatist tendencies of nationalist movements, especially among Czechs and Germans, groups that comprised 22 and 35 percent of the population, respectively. The existence of these movements underscored the inability of the imperial system to contend with national identities, particularly since Austria was struggling with democratization. Emperor Francis Joseph I (r. 1848–1916) exercised executive power while sharing legislative power with the Reichstag (parliament). With the establishment of universal male suffrage in 1906, the rule of the country started to catch up to its reality: the influence of the nobility waned in favor of the social democrats, Christian socialists, and *Deutschnationalen* (members of the German National People's Party). The Christlichsoziale Partei, or CSP (Christian Social Party), founded in 1891, presented itself as reformist, supported by the petty bourgeois and the peasantry. The Sozialdemokratische Arbeiterpartei, or SDAP (Social Democratic Workers' Party) was born of an older movement but had only recently organized (1889–1890) as the party of Austro-Marxism, first under Victor Adler, then under Otto Bauer. It mobilized ninety thousand members around three demands—universal suffrage, the eight-hour workday, and social security. The *Deutschnationalen* came together under the leaders Georg Ritter von Schönerer and Karl Lueger and were united around what they rejected, exemplified in the anti-Semitic slogan: "Gegen Juda, Habsburg, Rom / bauen wir den deutschen Dom" (Against Judah, Habsburg, and Rome / we build the German cathedral). The slogan reflected the fact that Austrian Jews, representing 4.5 percent of the population, completely embraced the Habsburgian state and were its most faithful subjects.

While the imperial-appointed governments remained solely under the rule of the kaiser, conflicts grew between new political forces that lacked a track to power and traditional groups that had lost their legitimacy—namely, the bureaucracy headed by the emperor, the nobility, and the clergy. The absence of a democratic culture rendered the parliamentary system ineffective and this led Austrians to be suspicious of parliamentary government. Faced with these divisions, *Kakania* (Robert Musil's pejorative term for the Austrian state) offered as unifiers the Habsburg dynasty, the Catholic Church (which brought together all the major nationalities), and the army (obligatory military service functioned to assimilate the populace). In any event, no genuine Austrian nation existed and the affirmation of its Germanic character served only to associate it with a national entity larger than itself.

On the economic plane, Austria's relatively late industrialization led to rising social discontent. At the same time, the fin de siècle fueled a creative intellectual boom in Vienna: in psychoanalysis (Sigmund Freud), in literature (Arthur Schnitzler and Hugo von Hofmannsthal), in music (Johannes Brahms, Johann Strauss, Gustav Mahler, and Arnold Schoenberg), in painting (Gustav Klimt), and in architecture (Josef Hoffmann and Otto Wagner).

The Habsburg Monarchy tried to overcome the various internal tensions through a risky foreign policy directed against the Slavic nationalists in the Balkans—Bosnia-Herzegovina was annexed in 1908—whose aspirations had been encouraged by Russia. The assassination of Archduke Ferdinand, heir to the Austrian throne, on 28 June 1914 and Austria's alliance with Germany and Italy dragged Europe into World War I. Outmoded ways of thinking about defense in Europe, Austria's economic interests in southwestern Europe, and the socio-imperialist ambitions of its elites all explain why the empire chose war.

After four years, however, the empire was obliged to sign the Armistice on 4 November 1918. The price in human lives was enormous: 180,000–190,000 military dead, with 90,000–95,000 women left widowed and three times as many children orphaned. The death of Emperor Francis Joseph I in 1916 and a food shortage beginning that year, together with decisions by his heir, Charles I (r. 1916–1918), fractured the monarchy. Charles (who was beatified by the Catholic Church in 2004) made peace proposals to the Allies while the *Völkermanifest* (a declaration Charles made on 16 October 1918 calling for the nationalities of Austria to form assemblies [*nationale Räte*]) transformed the monarchy into a federal state. Between 21 and 31 October 1918, the various nationalities one by one proclaimed their independence. For the first time since 1526, Austrian Germans lived in an independent state, the Republic of Austria.

FROM DISAPPOINTMENT WITH THE REPUBLICAN MODEL TO THE *STÄNDESTAAT* (1918–1938)

The provisional social democratic government of Karl Renner consolidated the regime, overcoming the threat by the Austrian republican councils during June and July 1919 while marginalizing the communists. Although agricultural production had dropped by half since 1913, the country avoided famine. Most important, the new government signed the Treaty of Saint-Germain in October 1918. The Austrian republic, one of the seven states created from the old empire, would be compelled to pay reparations. Anschluss (union) with Germany was forbidden.

The government initially engaged in unprecedented social and political reform. It established the eight-hour workday, provided unemployment benefits and paid vacations, granted women the right to vote, and gave organized labor an advisory role in the working environment. To many observers, however, the new republic's economic situation did not appear viable. In 1920, when Austria reorganized its territory, cosmopolitan Vienna was disproportionately large; it contained more than one-third of the population.

The National Constituent Assembly, with a majority of social democrats and Christian socialists and a right-wing coalition led by the latter from 1920 to 1938, broke entirely with old imperial Austria. By according parliament a leading role, the Constitution of October 1920 attempted to reconcile the principle of federation (Austria's division into *Länder*, or autonomous regions) with republicanism and the principle of centralization. Europe's parliamentary crisis in the interwar period would considerably weaken the new republic, which installed twenty-two successive governments from 1918 to 1933.

Political life was dominated by the Sozialdemokratische Arbeiterpartei, or SAP (Socialist worker's party). The majority of its seven hundred thousand members were recruited from the working class and from Vienna, whose mayor, Karl Seitz, developed a social welfare (*Wohlfahrtstaat*) policy in 1919. Opposition grew between "Red" Vienna and the rest of Austria, which was more conservative. Meanwhile, the Christian socialists, backed by civil servants and clerics, were solidly allied with the Bauerbund, or farmer's association, which was anticapitalist and pan-German. Nationalists supported reunification with Germany but, because of inner strife, they lacked political power. Although these movements

Followers of former Austrian chancellor Kurt von Schuschnigg, who opposed annexation by Germany, wait to be transported to concentration camps following the Anschluss, March 1938. ©HULTON-DEUTSCH COLLECTION/CORBIS

supported the new institutions, none was able to offer an "Austrian alternative." Constituting the new republic of Austria had more to do with creating a form of government than with founding a nation-state.

The 1920s were marked by the personality of the chancellor, Monsignor Ignaz Seipel (1876–1932), a Christian socialist who defended independent Catholic Austria against the Prussian Reich, which was under the sway of the Protestant tradition. The Seipel governments improved the economy, controlling hyperinflation and launching the schilling with loans from the League of Nations in 1922. This entailed an austerity policy with heavy social costs, however. From 1924 on, the social democrats took advantage of widespread

dissatisfaction, which forced the chancellor to form a coalition with the Germanophile nationalist parties. It was within this context that paramilitary groups appeared on the scene: the socialist Republikanischer Schutzbund (Republican defense league) in 1920; the far right-wing Mussolini-supported Heimwehr (Home guard) in 1925, which aimed at the destruction of the social democracy; and the Nazi *Marschformationen* (paramilitary groups).

In 1927, when bloody riots pitted Christian socialists, or "Blacks," against social democrats, or "Reds," Chancellor Seipel became the "prelate without mercy" and his actions caused the working-class party to abandon the government; successors continued his get-tough policy. The 1929 world economic crisis hit Austria hard; the failure of the banking giant Creditanstalt was the largest in history, and by 1933 six hundred thousand people were unemployed. In 1932 a new loan negotiated with the League of Nations by Chancellor Engelbert Dollfuss (1892–1934) further compromised the country's sovereignty. The failure of a plan for a customs union with Germany and for government centralization in 1931 only aggravated the economic and political crisis.

It should be added that this was also the heyday of the *Wienerlied* (popular songs in the Viennese dialect) and the apotheosis of the cabaret scene in Vienna, with artists such as Fritz Grünbaum. There was also the circle of logical positivists, including Moritz Schlick and Kurt Gödel, and the macroeconomic school of Joseph Schumpeter, both also centered in the capital. But that did not prevent the rise of regional centers of culture, with events such as the annual Salzburg Festival and the New Realism movement associated with Herbert Reyl-Hanisch.

Faced with political crisis, Dollfuss followed the lead of Italian Fascists by dissolving Parliament, employing the Heimwehren as auxiliary police, and opening internment camps. He remains a controversial figure. Was he democracy's chief undertaker or Hitler's greatest adversary? In any event, his clear aim was to replace the parliamentary system with a corporate and authoritarian state rooted in Christian socialism.

On the extreme right, the Nazis made important gains in elections beginning in 1932 and renewed the demand for Anschluss. Dollfuss banned the Nazi Party, the Communist Party, and the Republikanischen Schutzbund. In 1934 civil strife broke out briefly between right-wing militias supported by the army and left-wing groups, and the battles of 12–15 February ended with a victory for the Heimwehr. All unions and political organizations were banned. Dollfuss called for the formation of a patriotic front (*Vaterländische Front*) and transformed Austria into a Christian *Ständestaat* (corporate state).

Meanwhile, the ascension to power of Adolf Hitler (1889–1945) put an end to any future protection of Austria by Italy. Although Hitler's first attempt at Anschluss on 25 July 1934—during which the Nazis murdered Dollfuss—was a failure, his creation of the Rome-Berlin Axis in 1936, together with Austrian Chancellor Kurt von Schuschnigg's continuation of Dollfuss's policies and the effects of the worldwide economic depression, all conspired to deprive the Austrian government of popular support and threatened the new nation's independence. After 1936, a rapprochement policy with Germany turned Austria into a German satellite and augmented Nazi influence. Those who supported the *Ständestaat,* which gave rise to an Austrian national consciousness, mistakenly focused their propaganda efforts on the concept of a second German nation to such an extent that they essentially imitated the Nazi adversary from which they had hoped to distance themselves.

1938–1945: THE COST OF ANSCHLUSS

Encouraged by his foreign policy successes, Hitler again attempted to achieve Anschluss in March 1938. He demanded that Schuschnigg form a new government with Nazi participation. When the chancellor reacted by organizing a plebiscite, Hitler launched his invasion plan, code-named "Operation Otto," and the Nazi Arthur Seyss-Inquart replaced Schuschnigg; shortly thereafter the German army occupied the country. Annexation was proclaimed by plebiscite, with the Nazis claiming the approval of 99.6 percent of voters.

Austria became "Ostmark," part of the greater German Reich, its territory administered by *Gauleiters,* or Nazi governors, from Germany. *Gleichschaltung,* the Nazi euphemism for totalitarian control, followed immediately, with seventy thousand Austrians arrested and 70 percent of high-ranking public servants removed from office. The first convoys of political prisoners, Jews, and Gypsies were deported to Germany and later to the Mauthausen concentration camp (90 percent of the Gypsies and more than one-third of Austrian Jews were murdered). Germany integrated the Austrian economy into its own, pillaging its gold and natural resources, confiscating private property, and privileging Germans of the *Altreich* (that is, within the borders of the Third Reich as of 1937, as opposed to the territories annexed after that date) for jobs. Full employment and economic modernization also followed, with output in some industries increasing to twenty-five times its

Austrian children, including members of the Vienna Boys Choir, give the Nazi salute. The banner reads "We sing for Adolf Hitler." ©CORBIS

prewar level. Beginning in 1943, Allied bombing took a terrible toll in human lives. In all, Austria suffered some 247,000 military deaths; 25,000 to 30,000 civilians were also killed and 120,000 fell victim to Nazi repression.

By 1939, however, a resistance movement, consisting primarily of communists and conservative Christian socialists, began to operate with limited effectiveness. But about 20 percent of the population joined the Nazi Party; 1.2 million men enlisted in the Wehrmacht, and a number of Austrians, aside from Hitler, such as Ernst Kaltenbrunner and Adolf Eichmann, held high-ranking posts in the Reich. This number vastly exceeded the number of victims and resistance fighters in Austria, unless one is willing to apply the term *Opfer* to victims of the war's aftermath as well as to those of the Nazi persecution.

FROM THE COLD WAR TO EUROPEAN INTEGRATION (1945–2004)

For Austria the postwar period entailed the creation of a viable state separate from Germany and the birth of a national consciousness, founded upon the myth that the country had been a victim of Nazism.

At the conclusion of the Moscow Conference on 1 November 1943, the Big Three declared the Anschluss null and void and decided to reestablish Austria as a free and independent country. A provisional government was set up in April 1944; as in 1918, it was headed by Karl Renner and included the major parties. The Allies divided the country into four occupation zones, while Renner ordered the reinstatement of the 1929 Constitution and totally rejected Anschluss. The Second Republic was at once parliamentary and presidential, organized as a federated state.

The political parties were reconstituted almost exactly as they had been in the past, with the populists (as the Christian Socialists were now called) assembled under the banner of the Österreichische Volkspartei, or ÖVP (Conservative People's Party) and the Sozialistische Partei Österreichs, or SPÖ (Social Democratic Party), which replaced the SDAP. The Kommunistische Partei Österreichs, or KPÖ (Austrian Communist Party) and the far right-wing Verband der Unabhängigen, or VdU (Federation of Independents) remained marginalized over the next four decades. Thus a new political culture emerged, characterized by coalition building among major parties. Shifting alliances among parties were replaced by an interparty concept by which the *Staatspartei* (party in power) assigned posts based on popular elections and a proportional system, or *Proporzsystem*. Legislative compromise through preliminary consensus, or *Junktiemierung,* was common; social partners such as the trade union federation Österreichischer Gewerkschaftsbund (Austrian Trade Federation) joined the consensus. The Grand Coalition (1945–1966) of the ÖVP and the SPÖ was succeeded by a smaller alliance between the Freiheitliche Partei Österreichs, or FPÖ (Austrian Freedom Party), and the SPÖ (1983–1986), and then by the new-style coalition of the SPÖ-ÖVP (1987–1999). This political culture finally led to *versäulte Konkordanzdemokratie* (petrified democratic consensus) characterized by the lack of transparency and an absence of alternative programs or genuine parliamentary debate.

Once the postwar leaders were in place—a People's Party chancellor would remain in power until 1970 and a Socialist president until 1986— the government attended to priorities, which included reconstructing and restructuring the economy, purging the country of its Nazi past, and introducing land reform. Ten percent of all housing had been destroyed and factories reduced to rubble, and the postwar period brought the return of displaced persons. In addition, from 1947 on Austria was a pawn in the Cold War and benefited from the Marshall Plan, which allowed the western parts of the country to rebuild their industry and infrastructure. Vienna and Lower Austria, however, were under Soviet occupation. The USIA (a Russian acronym for "Administration for Soviet Property in Austria") employed 10 percent of the workforce. The Austrian government decided to nationalize German assets in the Soviet occupation zone to avoid their being appropriated. As a consequence, the public sector became enormous, employing one in six workers.

It took much longer to eradicate the political legacy of Nazism. The Allied Occupation Law of 8 May 1945 banned the Nazi Party and instituted "People's Court" tribunals. The failure to distinguish adequately between ordinary followers (*Mitläufer*) of the Nazis and the real criminals, however, together with the huge number of implicated persons (estimated at 537,000), combined to undermine the effectiveness of denazification. About 7.5 percent of the active population was excluded from professional activities. Soon the Cold War put an end to the antifascist spirit of 1945, as anticommunism eclipsed the struggle against the former champions of anti-bolshevism. Amnesty laws were promulgated in 1948 and 1953, while 1949 saw the resurgence of the VdU, made up of former Nazis who rejected an independent Austria. In 1955 the VdU was re-formed as the Freiheitliche Partei Österreichs, or FPÖ.

On the international stage, Austria's leaders managed to ensure the country's independence by taking advantage of events such as the Soviet-Yugoslav split, the death of Joseph Stalin in 1953, and the end of the Korean War. With the 1955 State Treaty and a constitutional law by which Austria declared itself neutral in perpetuity, the country took its place among other nations. Occupation forces withdrew and Austria joined the United Nations (UN), the Council of Europe (COE), and the European Free Trade Association (EFTA). Neutrality, adopted as a condition of Soviet withdrawal, did not stop the country from joining the Western camp in the Cold War. The date on which the Soviets withdrew and neutrality was legally adopted, 26 October, became a national holiday.

The decade that began in 1950 was notable for the remarkable economic recovery known as "Raab-Kamitz-Kurs" (after Chancellor Julius Raab and his finance minister, Reinhard Kamitz). The government reduced expenses, established a new fiscal system, increased industrial capacity and production, and institutionalized the social partnership (*Sozialpartnerschaft*). Repercussions from these reforms and the repositioning of Europe on the world stage after formation of the European Economic Communities (EEC), which rendered the ÖVP more pro-European than the SPÖ, made coalition governments ever more inadequate, however. In 1966, the ÖVP obtained an absolute majority and decided to set up a populist administration. Reemphasizing the distinction between the party in power and the opposition, it launched reforms in radio broadcasting, university education, and social security for private-sector workers. Strategic errors, however, together with a wave of dissatisfaction—such as the scandals of Friedensreich Hundertwasser or the group Wirklichkeiten (Realities) in the arts—paralyzed the administration, allowing the SPÖ to achieve an absolute majority for the first time in 1970.

Over the next thirteen years, Chancellor Bruno Kreisky presided over a vast and historic reform movement that included liberalization of the media, a family policy (including the legalization of abortion), an education system that supported low-income children, and the abandonment of the nuclear power program. Thanks to an "Austro-Keynesian" budgetary policy, he succeeded in reducing unemployment to the range of 1.6–2.5 percent. Vienna also became the United Nations' third headquarters. The chancellor dispatched Austrian UN troops to Cyprus and the Middle East and in 1972 signed the first free trade agreement with the EEC.

The Socialist Fred Sinowatz, Kreisky's successor, set up a limited coalition with the FPÖ to keep the ÖVP from returning to power. It soon had to confront a difficult economic situation, with mounting government debt and growing unemployment as well as political-financial scandals and, finally, the Waldheim affair. After ten years as secretary-general of the United Nations, Kurt Waldheim ran for president of the Republic in 1986. Confronted with documents that implicated his wartime collaboration as a staff lieutenant in the Wehrmacht, against the partisans in the Balkans, Waldheim replied that he had only done his duty. But defense of one's nation regardless of the political system in place was no longer acceptable to many Austrians. Waldheim was nevertheless elected president on 8 June. The next day Sinowatz relinquished his post to Franz Vranitsky (SPÖ), who for the next ten years remained chancellor of a coalition with the ÖVP. Environmentalists from the Green Party were elected to seats in parliament. On the international scene, Austria found itself increasingly isolated, and in this context Vranitsky officially acknowledged Austria's participation in the crimes perpetrated by Nazi Germany. But only in 1995 was a fund established for victims; in 2000 Austria signed an agreement by which it would compensate its former forced laborers.

The end of the Cold War opened the way for integration with other European states. On 1 January 1995 Austria became the thirteenth member of the European Union, and in 2002 it adopted the euro as its monetary currency. Austria also closely watched discussions about expanding NATO, but membership would call into question its identity as a neutral power and further weaken the *Proporzsystem*, already undermined by massive privatization. Meanwhile, the fall of the Berlin Wall in 1989 placed Austria at the heart of a newly unified Europe, in which common values were to replace ethnic affiliation as the basis for one's identity, putting an end to the traditional conception of the Austrian nation.

A new domestic policy was slow in coming. As a result, the electorate mobilized in favor of the FPÖ, the opposition party that from 1986 on was headed by Jörg Haider. Attracting a growing number of voters with antiestablishment and xenophobic speeches, Haider also revived the theme of the country as victim, proposing that, while some Austrians ought to be held responsible for Nazi crimes, others should be compensated as victims of the Allied occupation. In 1999 the FPÖ placed second in the elections, behind the SPÖ. When Wolfgang Schlüssel (ÖVP) established a coalition government with Haider's FPÖ, the European Union decided on a policy to isolate Austria temporarily. As a political strategy, Haider stepped down from the government and ended the coalition. He suffered a major defeat in the 2002 elections and the ÖVP returned to the top spot. This array of forces led Schlüssel to create a second coalition with the FPÖ on 28 February 2003, under the control of President Heinz Fischer (SPÖ, 2004).

In the long run, Austria's political culture evolved toward a European political model: more voters abstained from national elections; fewer people joined the various interest groups; the *Lagermentalität* (camp mentality) came to an end as the electorate became more independent in its voting habits; a consociational democracy replaced more adversarial politics; and the role of parliament underwent a reevaluation.

See also **Denazification; Dolfuss, Engelbert; Germany; Haider, Jörg; Munich Agreement; Reconstruction; Salzburg Festival; Seyss-Inquart, Arthur; Sudetenland; Waldheim, Kurt.**

BIBLIOGRAPHY

Bischof, Günter. *Austria in the First Cold War, 1945–55: The Leverage of the Weak.* London, 1999.

Denscher, Barbara, ed. *Kunst und Kultur in Österreich: Das 20. Jahrhundert.* Vienna, 1999.

Gehler, Michael. *Der lange Weg nach Europa. Österreich vom Ende der Monarchie bis zur EU.* 2 vols. Innsbruck, Austria, 2002.

Goldinger, Walter, and Dieter A. Binder. *Geschichte der Republik Österreich: 1918–1938.* Vienna, 1992.

Mantl, Wolfgang, ed. *Politik in Österreich. Die zweite Republik: Bestand und Wandel.* Vienna, 1992.

Sandgruber, Roman. *Das 20. Jahrhundert. Geschichte Österreichs.* Vol. 6. Vienna, 2003.

Tálos, Emmerich, et al., eds. *NS-Herrschaft in Österreich. Ein Handbuch.* Vienna, 2000.

Williamson, Samuel R., Jr. *Austria-Hungary and the Origins of the First World War.* New York, 1991.

FABIEN THÉOFILAKIS

AUTOMOBILES.

"From 1885 to 1895, men struggled to make the car go," writes Laurence Pomeroy in the 1956 book *From Veteran to Vintage.* "From 1896 to 1905 they contrived to make it go properly. Between 1906 and 1915 they succeeded in making it go beautifully" (Karslake and Pomeroy, p. 3).

THE EARLY YEARS

On the eve of the First World War, the products of the European motor industry had reached a level of mechanical development that would have seemed unthinkable just ten years earlier. "Time was when it was the exception rather than the rule to get home, even on a 20-mile run, without having to do something to the car," commented Henry Sturmey, who had been a key figure both in the birth in 1896 of the British motor industry and editor in 1895 of the country's first motoring magazine, *The Autocar.* "Today, we have vehicles that will take us 'there and back again' with a certainty and a celerity that can be equaled by no other form of conveyance" (*The Motor,* 4 April 1911).

But though the design of the motor car had progressed to a point where reliability could—almost—be taken for granted and the basic mechanical layout had been standardized to such an extent that beneath the skin there would be little discernible change between a popular car of 1914 and its 1939 counterpart, manufacturing methods were still by and large a question of assembling cars on the spot with the components being transported manually from other parts of the factory or delivered by outside suppliers. Labor-intensive hand fitting of those components was a virtual given.

The turning point came in 1914, when the Ford factory that had opened in the United Kingdom at Trafford Park in Manchester in October 1911—the first Ford plant to be established outside North America—installed Europe's first moving assembly line a matter of months after the production chains had started rolling in the company's Highland Park, Michigan, factory. At the time, it was perhaps the most dramatic example of technology transfer from the New World to the Old—Ford inaugurated plant tours so that the public could watch this industrial marvel in action, turning out anything up to twenty-one cars an hour from standardized parts that needed no hand fitting. Yet, this production model was virtually ignored by the rest of the automobile industry, which was still reliant on an abundance of cheap skilled labor.

Nowhere was this truer than in France, the dominant nation in Europe's automotive sector; surprisingly, the British Ford plant, with just 1,500 workers, almost immediately overtook France's leading manufacturer, Renault, where some 4,000 workers built 5,500 cars annually, in terms of output. Output in 1912, the first full year of production, was 3,081 Model Ts and passed 6,100 in 1913.

Despite the outbreak of war in August, in 1914 Ford produced 8,300 cars, outselling the combined total of Britain's next five biggest marques, and the assembly lines operated throughout the hostilities, providing 30,000 Model T troop carriers, water carriers, ambulances, and munitions wagons to the Allied forces. Nimble-footed as a goat, simple to drive and maintain, the Model T was an ideal military vehicle; Lawrence of Arabia (T. E. Lawrence; 1888–1935) declared that the Model T and the Rolls-Royce Silver Ghost—many of which had cast off the patrician coachwork of peacetime in favor of armored carapaces—were the only two cars suitable for desert warfare.

The Model T also ushered in the concept of a global automobile industry: from 1913, Fords were also being assembled in a little plant in Bordeaux, France, and an office had been set up in Paris to coordinate European sales, with its American manager being paid the colossal salary of 24,000 dollars annually.

IMPACT OF THE FIRST WORLD WAR

Despite the stalemate of the trenches, the First World War was the first motorized war. The internal combustion engine provided power for everything from trench electricity generators to dispatch riders' machines and made possible two major new weapons that changed the nature of warfare—flying machines and tanks.

Moreover, the exposure of a generation of young men, previously unused to motoring, to the cars and motorcycles used for military purposes, fueled an immediate postwar demand for motor vehicles and the creation of companies to meet that demand. In Britain, forty new makes of cars came on the market in 1919–1920, and another forty-six appeared between 1921 and 1925. However, the inevitable slump that hit the market in 1922 saw more than eighty motor manufacturers go out of business during the same period. For the most part, these were small firms that attempted to break into the popular car market, most notably Clyno of Wolverhampton, which reached third spot in the industry before crashing spectacularly in 1929. Paradoxically, it was specialist sports-car makers like Aston-Martin and Bentley, though perennially short of cash, that survived, thanks to backing from moneyed enthusiasts. In the late 1920s and early 1930s the brothers William Edward "Billy" Rootes and Reginald Rootes snapped up the failed Humber, Hillman, Singer, Sunbeam, and Talbot companies to make their Rootes Group a major player in the motor industry.

Though they had lost their lead to Ford, some French motor manufacturers also came out of the war well: in 1918 Renault had 22,500 workers and built 14,500 vehicles, Hispano-Suiza employed the technological lessons it had learned in building aircraft engines in the design of luxury cars, and Louis Delage, ever the opportunist, used a military contract to supply staff cars as the testbed for his postwar model. But the only one to follow the Taylorite (efficiency) principles of Fordism was André-Gustave Citroën, who launched his own marque in 1919, mass-producing a single model in his former munitions factory on the Quai du Javel, Paris.

In 1920 the French government, anxious to stimulate a market hindered by high taxes, created a reduced-rate "cyclecar" tax for two-seated vehicles weighing under 350 kilograms, but the concession was short-lived. France at that time had an estimated 350 manufacturers: only a handful would make it through the decade.

Britain, having erected a tariff wall of 33.3 percent in 1915 with the McKenna Duties to discourage the imported American cars that had gained a foothold while domestic production was suspended during the First World War, sought to tackle what it saw as the enemy within with the introduction of a one pound per horsepower tax in its 1920 Finance Act, which charged the large-engined but very cheap Model T Ford—still regarded as "foreign" even though it was British-built—the same rate as a costly 3-liter Bentley. The result was that Ford quickly lost its market lead in favor of the indigenous Morris marque, established in 1912 in Cowley near Oxford, away from the motor industry's traditional Midlands location but in an agricultural area with abundant cheap labor. Curiously, Morris—who overtook Ford as market leader in 1924—did not introduce a moving assembly line until 1934.

Another successful rival for the Model T—on price, at least—was the diminutive Austin Seven. Against the advice of his board, Sir Herbert Austin (1866–1941) introduced the car in 1922 as a rival for the then-popular motorcycle combination. At the time, Austin's American-style one-model

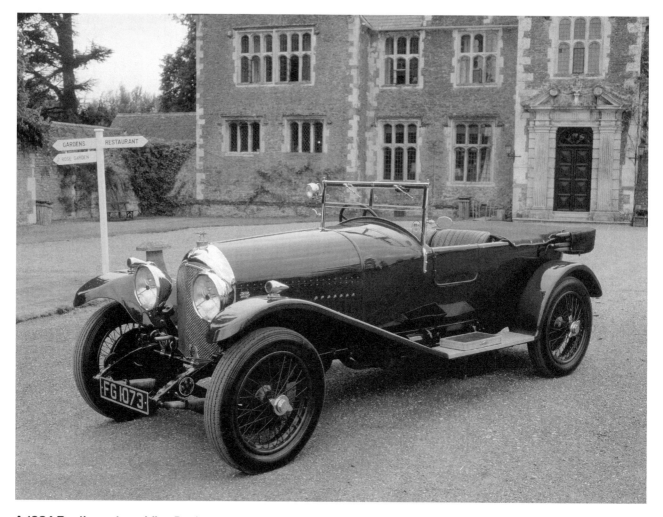

A 1924 Bentley automobile. Due in part to taxes resulting from the 1920 Finance Act in Britain, the three-liter Bentley eclipsed the Ford Model T as the market leader in Europe. ©CHRIS TAYLOR; CORDAIY PHOTO LIBRARY LTD./CORBIS

program had stalled, and a plea to Henry Ford to buy his company had fallen on deaf ears.

Ford had other plans for Europe; in 1917 the company had begun work on the first purpose-built Ford factory in the Old World—a tractor plant at Cork in Ireland—signaling the start of a relentless program of installing assembly plants in every major European market, but offering the same product—Ford's Model T "universal car"—regardless of market conditions or fiscal regimes.

General Motors (GM), however, only operated very low-key assembly operations of its United States products in Europe, gaining a stronger toehold during the 1920s with the acquisition of well-established but financially weak companies—Vauxhall in England and Opel in Germany—which

enabled the corporation to introduce new models more attuned to European tastes.

Production in Britain and France remained roughly on a par in the 1920s, with Germany and Italy trailing a long way behind. For some years after the war, there was a ban in many countries on buying German-built cars; this, coupled with raging inflation, meant that the German industry remained in a generally backward state. The main development was the amalgamation in 1926 of Germany's two oldest companies to form Daimler-Benz—its vehicles were sold under the Mercedes-Benz name. In Italy a plethora of small manufacturers gave way before the relentless march of Fiat of Turin, whose ambitious founder, Giovanni Agnelli (1866–1945), had hitched his wagon to the rising star of Fascist leader Benito

Mussolini (1883–1945). This enabled him to suppress potential rivals, most particularly Ford Italiana, whose factory, opened in 1922 in a Trieste warehouse, had quickly secured 75 percent of a market covering thirty-six countries on three continents. When in 1929 Ford sought to expand by taking over Isotta Fraschini of Milan, Agnelli protested to Mussolini, and Ford's Italian venture was stifled.

Before World War I Belgium and Holland had both had small national motor industries mostly serving national needs, but these faded away in the 1920s as imported models encouraged by liberal tax regimes took over their markets.

THE GREAT DEPRESSION

The European industry took on a new complexion when the manager of Ford's British organization (hereinafter Ford-Britain), Percival Perry, met Henry Ford in Detroit to formulate the "1928 Plan," in which a new Ford Motor Company Limited was incorporated to take over and operate the European assembly plants previously controlled from the United States. Work began in 1929 on a new "Detroit of Europe" factory at Dagenham in Essex, which would be the center of manufacture for Europe, serving assembly plants in Manchester, Cork, Paris, Berlin (replaced by Cologne), Antwerp, Barcelona, Copenhagen, Trieste, Stockholm, Helsinki, Rotterdam, and Constantinople. But the plan was thrown into disarray as depression gripped Europe in the wake of the 1929 Wall Street crash and it was never fully implemented, as France and Germany implemented laws demanding high local content levels.

Moreover, Dagenham itself was threatened with closure as Ford-Britain plunged deep into debt, weighed down by the five-million-pound cost of the new factory and by disastrous sales of the British-built Model A, which plummeted to just five cars in the last quarter of 1931. Henry Ford himself took charge, and within five months a new small Ford with a 933cc 8-hp engine designed specifically for Europe was developed. It proved an immediate success and gave Ford 19 percent of the British market, lifting the onetime market leader to third place behind Morris and Austin.

While in 1934 Britain and France had roughly the same number of vehicles—about 1.87 million—in use, by the end of 1938 Britain had moved well ahead with an increase in the vehicle park of 670,000, almost 300,000 more than France. And while in 1929 France had been the second largest producer in the world, eight years later output had declined by almost 20 percent. British production had more than doubled over the same period. Just as telling was the decline in French exports: in 1924 French companies had represented some 25 percent of world vehicle exports, a figure that plunged to 5 percent by 1937.

After the Nazis came to power in 1933, the moribund German industry was revitalized as a showcase for German technology and as a tool to obtain foreign currency through the medium of export sales. Thus, production rose from 92,200 cars in 1933 to 270,000 in 1938. Of the twenty-one companies engaged in vehicle production that year, Opel was Germany's biggest manufacturer with about 40 percent of the car market and 30 percent of light commercials, with Auto-Union in second place with 25 percent, and Ford (hereinafter Ford-Germany) and Daimler-Benz each with 10 percent. The rise in car production was accompanied by the building of a nationwide network of high-speed motor roads, the so-called autobahns. Despite much anticipation and a saving-stamp scheme for prospective customers that would allegedly secure delivery, few examples of the much-vaunted Volkswagen "Peoples' Car" were seen before the outbreak of war in 1939.

WORLD WAR II AND AFTER

While the German industry had been heavily involved in the buildup to war, British companies had erected so-called shadow factories, which could be switched to war matériel production should hostilities break out. And when war was declared, British companies played a vital role. Austin built airplanes, Vauxhall built tanks, and Rolls-Royce built the Merlin aircraft engines that powered the aircraft that won the Battle of Britain in 1940. The following year Ford-Britain opened a new factory near Manchester that built a further 30,000 Rolls-Royce Merlins to the most exacting standards. Ford also supplied 250,000 V8 engines for fighting vehicles, over 13,000 Bren Gun carriers, and large numbers of trucks. However, the Labour government elected in 1945 placed great restrictions on motoring and the motor industry. Apart from strict material rationing, manufacturers were given an export target of 50 percent of production—and many of its vehicles were ill suited to overseas conditions, earning a reputation for unreliability that would persist for many years. In contrast to its British cousin, Ford-Germany built only some 15,000 trucks annually for the German war machine; some were also assembled in Ford's plants in occupied Europe, but these were subject to ingenious sabotage by disaffected workers.

The German occupation of France devastated the French auto industry. The Germans removed much of its machine tools, and bombing seriously damaged the remaining factories. After the Liberation in 1944, Louis Renault, accused of having collaborated with the Germans, died mysteriously in prison, and his company was nationalized. The industry recovered slowly: output in 1946 was less than one-sixth of the 1938 level and did not pass it until 1949. A degree of rationalization took place under the Monnet Plan of 1947, but the industry fell far short of its targets. The head of the National Planning Council, Jean Monnet had proposed production of 396,800 vehicles in 1947; actual production was 137,400.

Badly affected by Allied bombing, the German industry had few plants capable of resuming production after the Nazi surrender and the division of Occupied Germany. The Bayerische Motoren Werke (BMW) plant at Eisenach in the Russian zone became Eisenacher Motoren Werke (EMW) and was for a while a flagship factory for the Soviets. Of the Daimler-Benz factories, only the Gaggenau truck plant in the French zone was operable, and the badly damaged Volkswagen factory in the British zone only restarted manufacture thanks to the efforts of British Army officer Ivan Hirst. It recovered to such an extent that when Henry Ford II (1917–1987) visited Europe in 1948 he expressed an interest in taking over the business, only to find that its complex ownership made this infeasible. He was unsuccessful, too, in recruiting Volkswagen chief executive Heinz Nordhoff to head Ford's German operations.

Indeed, Ford was to make unsuccessful overtures to most major European motor manufacturers in the years ahead. A proposed merger with Peugeot in 1948 came to nothing, while in the short period between 1958 and 1964 Ford dallied

with Lancia, Fiat, Mercedes-Benz, Auto Union, BMW, Berliet, the Rootes Group, Lotus, and Ferrari, yet failed to consummate a single deal, any one of which could have changed the face of the European motor industry.

The Michelin tire company, which had owned Citroën since 1934, sold the company to Peugeot in 1975, and in 1978 Peugeot acquired Simca (which had itself absorbed Ford's French production arm in 1954) and rebranded it as Talbot—an ancient name with a convoluted history that was also applied to the products of the former British Chrysler that Peugeot had also acquired in the 1978 acquisition.

POSTWAR BOOM

Partnerships could prove dangerous: in 1952 Britain's two leading companies, the Nuffield Group and Austin, merged to create the British Motor Corporation (BMC), with some 40 percent of the market. The company prospered in the booming 1950s and 1960s, but little was done to reorganize the companies into a cohesive unit. Old rivalries were rampant, and financial procedures were inadequate—typically, management had no idea of how much it cost to produce a car! A downward slide in sales ensued.

In strict contrast was the postwar rise of Ford-Britain, guided by the charismatic Sir Patrick Hennessy, with its strict purchasing and costing disciplines. The contrast between BMC and Ford was never more clearly shown than when BMC launched the advanced front-wheel-drive Mini in 1959; Ford bought one, dismantled it, and costed every part, to find that BMC could not possibly be selling the little car at a profit. But when Ford's managing director confronted his BMC counterpart with a proposal that if the Mini's price were raised to an economic level, then Ford would make a matching price increase on its new Anglia, he was politely brushed off.

BMC's off-the-cuff strategy fatally undermined its profitability. In 1966 it merged with the luxury brand Jaguar as British Motor Holdings, and two years later BMH came together with the Leyland Group—which had taken over the ailing Standard Triumph company in 1961—to form British Leyland (BL). In less than a decade BL—plagued by an appalling strike record—was in desperate

The Dagenham automobile factory, Essex, England, 1937. Built in 1929, the plant was intended to serve as the centerpiece of Henry Ford's European operations. ©HULTON-DEUTSCH COLLECTION/CORBIS

financial straits and turned to the government for help. Vast sums of public money were pumped into BL, in which the government's National Enterprise Board now had a 95 percent stake, to little avail.

In 1975 the American Chrysler Corporation, which had taken over Rootes after Ford had turned the company down, threatened to close the loss-making company down unless the government gave financial aid. The government gave in, to the tune of 162.5 million pounds.

Perversely, in view of Henry Ford's vision of the "universal car," Ford-Britain and Ford-Germany had produced completely different models for the same market segments in the years after the war and, indeed, regarded each other as their main rival on the Continent, often with competing dealerships on either side of the same street. It was an insupportable position that ended in 1967, when Henry Ford II set up Ford of Europe as a blanket organization to coordinate development and marketing programs of a single model range. It took far longer for the rival General Motors brands Opel and Vauxhall to coalesce into a single European organization, although common models, differently badged depending on market, had been produced since the mid-1970s.

A new factor in the European marketplace was the arrival of Japanese imports in 1965. The increasing popularity of these models eventually led to the establishment of European production plants, particularly in Britain, where by 2005 Japanese manufacturers were building over 800,000 cars a year.

JOINT VENTURES AND COMMON MARKET

With the increasing liberalization of European trade in the 1970s, transnational joint ventures brought a new look to the motor industry. The Swedish company Volvo, which acquired the last native Dutch manufacturer Van Doorne's Automobiel Fabriek (DAF) in 1975, joined forces with Peugeot and Renault the same year in a new "Douvrin" V6 engine, which the three makers all fitted in their luxury models.

This was a period of expansion despite a fourfold increase in fuel prices following the Arab-Israeli War of 1973. In 1974 Peugeot took over a 30 percent share in Citroën (and took it over completely in 1976); Volkswagen introduced the front-wheel-drive Golf to succeed the perennial Beetle; and Ford opened new plants in Bordeaux (transmission) and Valencia (cars) as part of a program that would see a new front-wheel-drive "supermini," the Fiesta, launched to face off against cars like the Fiat 127 and give the company a far stronger presence in southern European markets.

When it became clear that the industry was moving into a state of overcapacity, "Project Oyster," a plan to open a new Ford car plant at Sines in Portugal, was shelved in 1983. Instead, Ford began a new round of merger and takeover talks. In 1985 "Project Columbus," a merger proposal with Fiat, foundered at the last minute on the question of who would hold overall control, while Ford bids to acquire the failing Alfa Romeo and Rover (late British Leyland) companies were scuppered by high-level political machinations. Alfa Romeo was acquired instead by Fiat, and BL went first to British Aerospace and then to BMW. Moves to acquire luxury and sports marques were more successful. Ford acquired Aston Martin in 1987, the recently privatized Jaguar company in 1989, Volvo in 1999, and Land Rover in 2000, which together formed the new Premier Automobile Group.

Interestingly, Ford had to choose between Jaguar and the Swedish company Saab and had gone for the British marque largely on sentimental grounds because its vice chairman William Clay Ford had owned Jaguars since his college days. General Motors picked up Saab (which had been the Ford accountants' favorite, but by 2005, when Saab shared the common "Epsilon" chassis platform with the Opel/Vauxhall Vectra, it looked as though production of the mainstream Saabs would be transferred from Sweden to the Opel plant in Germany). Jaguar gave Ford much needed class but proved a heavy drain on corporate funds.

That break with traditional national ties was symptomatic of the rapidly changing fortunes of the European industry. By the dawn of the new millennium, the go-it-alone optimism of the mid-1980s had given way to intercompany collaboration—most notably between Fiat and General Motors—and the eastward shift of production to countries like Poland and Hungary in the wake of the fall of the Iron Curtain.

The family-car segment of the market weakened, while the VW-Audi Group—which already owned the Sociedad Española de Automóviles de Turismo (SEAT), a Spanish company from which Fiat had walked away in 1980—acquired the prestigious British brand Bentley in a bidding war that saw its rival BMW take over the Rolls-Royce name, and bought the reborn but struggling Bugatti brand to develop the world's fastest road car as a showcase for its engineering skills.

Long-established Western European plants closed: in 2002 Ford ceased car manufacture at its former flagship Dagenham factory. Only the engine plant remained operative just twenty years after a costly robotization program had transformed production methods and manning levels. And GM stopped making Vauxhall cars in Luton, U.K., its headquarters since 1905. But the most spectacular crash was that of Rover, which had been sold to a management consortium for a nominal ten pounds after BMW had failed to make it profitable (though it retained the Mini brand and its Cowley, Oxford, factory). In 2005 the Rover plant at Longbridge (the old Austin factory, opened in 1905) suspended production, unable to pay its bills because its aging models had failed to meet sales forecasts. Controversially, its assets were acquired by a Chinese group, and some, if not all, production seemed likely to be transferred to Shanghai.

After 120 years since the first Benz car stuttered into life, the European motor industry appears to be in a state of continuous change, with

WORLD WAR I

French postcard, 1914. The phrase "Je suis prêt!" ("I am ready!") reflects the optimism of the belligerents at the beginning of the war. ARCHIVES CHARMET/BRIDGEMAN ART LIBRARY

OPPOSITE PAGE: *La Mitrailleuse.* Painting by Christopher Nevinson, 1915. Nevinson was sent to the front by the British War Propaganda Bureau, but his modernist depictions of the realities of warfare were deemed not suitable for the purpose of enlisting support for the war effort. © TATE, LONDON/ART RESOURCE, NY

TOP: **French soldiers in trenches.** Hand-colored postcard photograph c. 1914–1918. Trench warfare quickly became the structural constant of the war as armies dug in to protect themselves from the mechanized firepower of their opponents. GIRAUDON/BRIDGEMAN ART LIBRARY

MIDDLE: *The Landing at Anzac Bay, 25 April 1915.* Painting by Charles Edward Dixon, 1916. The landing that began the Franco-British attempt to secure the Gallipoli peninsula in Turkey is recreated by a noted British academic painter. The campaign was a complete failure and cost the lives of approximately 252,000 Australian, New Zealand, Irish, British and French troops. IMPERIAL WAR MUSEUM, LONDON/BRIDGEMAN ART LIBRARY

BOTTOM: *The Airship Schutte-Lanz Bombarding Warsaw.* Illustration from *Our Airforce in the World War 1914–1915,* a collection of six color plates by Hans Rudolf Schulze published by the German Air Force Organization, 1916. Air ships were used by Germany for bombing raids during the early part of the war but became susceptible to attack by airplanes as use of the latter increased. THE STAPLETON COLLECTION/BRIDGEMAN ART LIBRARY

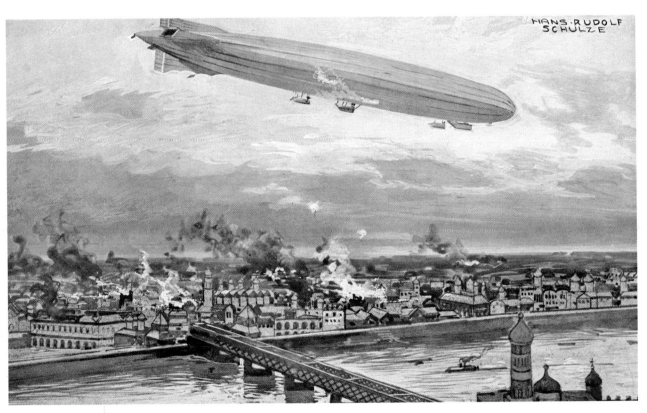

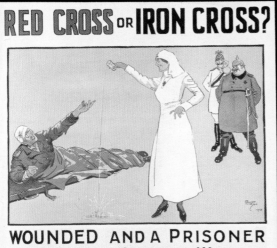

TOP LEFT: Propaganda poster by David Wilson, England, date unknown. Demonization of the enemy was one tactic of war propaganda, deemed crucial in maintaining public support as the conflict dragged on with few discernible gains and overwhelming losses. BRIDGEMAN ART LIBRARY

BOTTOM LEFT: Front cover of the wartime monthly publication *La Guerre Illustrée (The Illustrated War)*, December 1917. *La Guerre Illustrée* was published by the *Illustrated London News* and consisted solely of illustrations reprinted from that periodical for a French audience. This cover celebrates the contributions of women who were enlisted to serve in British munitions factories. ARCHIVES CHARMET/BRIDGEMAN ART LIBRARY

BOTTOM RIGHT: French postcard c. 1914-1918. The exhortation "Affectionate memory! Let your heart keep a place for this sweet flower of Alsace!" reminds the French that one of their primary goals in the war is to recapture the territories lost in the Franco-Prussian War of 1870. GIRAUDON/BRIDGEMAN ART LIBRARY

RIGHT: *The Assault, Verdun.* Painting by Henry de Groux, 1916. Belgian symbolist de Groux drew upon his battlefield experience to create a vision of the Battle of Verdun, the longest battle of the war, lasting from February through July of 1916. Musée des Deux Guerres Mondiales, Paris/Bridgeman Art Library

BELOW: *The Battle of Jutland.* Painting by Claus Bergen, 1916. Bergen, the official marine painter to Kaiser Wilhelm, witnessed the largest and costliest sea battle of the war. At the height of the battle, 250 ships were engaged; 14 British and 11 German ships were sunk. Erich Lessing/Art Resource, NY

TOP LEFT: *Canadian Gunners in the Mud, Passchendaele, 1917.* Painting by Alfred Bastien. During the second half of 1917, the British Expeditionary Force attempted a frontal assault on German positions in Belgium that was severely hampered by torrential rains and mud so deep that equipment was rendered inoperable and soldiers sank and were drowned. CANADIAN WAR MUSEUM, OTTAWA, CANADA/BRIDGEMAN ART LIBRARY

MIDDLE LEFT: *The Menin Road.* Painting by Paul Nash, 1919. The Menin Road was the primary route eastward from the town of Ypres and therefore the object of massive shelling by German forces throughout the war. Official British war artist Paul Nash depicts its appearance in 1919 in one of the most renowned images of the devastation of modern warfare. IMPERIAL WAR MUSEUM, LONDON/BRIDGEMAN ART LIBRARY

BOTTOM LEFT: *The Country Hospital.* Painting by François Flameng, 1916. Flameng, a legendary wartime painter, documents a grim reality of the war: thousands upon thousands of injured soldiers returning from the front. MUSÉE DE L'ARMÉE, PARIS/ARCHIVES CHARMET/BRIDGEMAN ART LIBRARY

BOTTOM RIGHT: *Thiepval Memorial and War Cemetery, Thiepval, France.* Dramatic battlefield memorials such as the ones at Thiepval and Douaumont reflect Europeans' overwhelming sense of grief and loss in the postwar period. RICHARD KLUNE/CORBIS

The War. Painting by Otto Dix, 1932. Dix, who served in the German army during the war, later created some of the most dramatic images of the conflict and its aftermath. In these three panels he depicts soldiers marching to the front, the chaos of the battlefield, and wounded soldiers wearily making their way home.

U.K. output, once the Continent's biggest, down to 18 percent of the British market, niche models playing a growing role in sales, Asian brands taking an ever-increasing share of sales, and the world's oldest marque, Mercedes-Benz, forced to revise its future model plans in the face of falling profitability. Past certainties have vanished, and customer requirements have changed radically in an increasingly complicated market. The motorcar now has to offer more than mere transportation, and the European industry is being forced to respond.

See also **Agnelli, Giovanni; Fordism; Industrial Capitalism; Renault; Taylorism; Volkswagen.**

BIBLIOGRAPHY

Adeney, Martin. *The Motor Makers: The Turbulent History of Britain's Car Industry.* London, 1988.

Burgess-Wise, David. *Ford at Dagenham: The Rise and Fall of Detroit in Europe.* Derby, U.K., 2001.

———. *Century in Motion.* Oxford, U.K., 2003.

Dumont, Pierre. *Peugeot d'Hier et D'Avant-Hier.* Paris, 1983.

Georgano, Nick, Nick Baldwin, Anders Clausager, and Jonathan Wood. *Britain's Motor Industry—The First Hundred Years.* Sparkford, U.K., 1995.

Karslake, Kent, and Laurence Pomeroy. *From Veteran to Vintage: A History of Motoring and Motorcars from 1884 to 1914.* London, 1956.

Montagu of Beaulieu, Lord, and David Burgess-Wise. *Daimler Century: The Full History of Britain's Oldest Car Maker.* Sparkford, U.K., 1995.

Seidler, Edouard. *The Romance of Renault.* Lausanne, Switzerland, 1973.

———. *Let's Call It Fiesta: The Auto-Biography of Ford's Project Bobcat.* Sparkford, U.K., 1976.

Turner, Graham. *The Leyland Papers.* London, 1971.

Wood, Jonathan. *Wheels of Misfortune: The Rise and Fall of the British Motor Industry.* London, 1988.

DAVID BURGESS-WISE

AVANT-GARDE. Although the use of the military term *avant-garde* goes back to medieval times, and it started to be applied to vanguard art long before the nineteenth century, consensus sets the use of this label for those early-twentieth-century art movements that combined artistic innovation with political dissent. Avant-garde artists were activists of progress, both artistic and social.

Avant-garde movements were thriving in metropolitan environments early in the twentieth century, finding their exhibition and publication venues as well as audiences in the midst of urban populations.

The outbreak of World War I in the summer of 1914 was a serious setback for artistic activities in Europe. Italian futurists and German expressionists lost talented members to the war. Among the many artist victims, the Italian futurist sculptor Umberto Boccioni (1882–1916) and architect Antonio Sant'Elia (1888–1916) and the German expressionist painters August Macke (1887–1914) and Franz Marc (1880–1916) died in the trenches, while several artists suffered incurable nervous exhaustion.

During and after World War I art got intensely politicized. Artists felt responsible for the new direction that history would take and acted as public figures. One of the political concepts of the post–World War I avant-gardes was pan-European internationalism. Having learned the catastrophic lesson of war between nations and witnessing the birth of new nation-states after the falling apart of the Habsburg Empire, artists considered the dissolution of national boundaries a token of progress. Progress, a central tenet of modernism, was particularly embraced by the vehemently modernist avant-garde groups, which set out to eliminate all boundaries that had been imposed on artistic expression by academic and bourgeois mentalities. Dada was particularly radical in doing away with everything that had been held sacred before the war, challenging the art world by using garbage and decomposing images and by politically provoking viewers. The Bauhaus proposed the elimination of boundaries between traditional genres and the equal ranking of art and design. The constructivists set out to redesign the entire society. The surrealists sought to find and master the nuts and bolts of the human psyche. The feverish activity of the avant-gardes culminated in the early 1920s, when general optimism and faith in a better future dominated the art scene and the intellectual landscape of Europe. As these expectations turned dim in the late 1920s and Europe turned increasingly conservative, with a Fascist regime rising in Italy and the Nazis gaining ground in Germany, the gleaming images of a new international culture turned out to be utopian.

With the Nazis lampooning and outlawing modernist art in their notorious 1937 Degenerate Art exhibition, the avant-gardes were charged with even more profound political meaning. Abstraction rose in the wake of World War II as the organic continuation of antiwar humanism and intellectual independence, often implying leftist political views. Artists formed the group CoBrA in Copenhagen, Brussels, and Amsterdam in 1948 and its offshoot, the Imaginist Bauhaus, in 1954. American abstract expressionism had a great impact on European art, radicalizing the neo-new avant-garde views and artistic practices.

The increasing wealth of Western societies absorbed criticism, and in the 1950s and 1960s the younger generation considered the avant-gardes the institutionalized culture of the establishment. The neo-avant-gardes emerged: Gruppe Zero, which defied museums and all art institutions, was launched in Germany in 1957, and the Situationist International was founded the same year in Italy. The international Fluxus movement was launched by the Lithuanian American George Maciunas in Wiesbaden in 1962. Fluxus denied the art object, and with this iconoclastic attitude discarded the entire concept of the art object. Pop art, the introduction of mass culture and consumer culture into the field of art, originated in England in the late 1950s and rapidly conquered American art, followed by strictly geometric minimalism, which traced its roots back to 1920s constructivism, and, in the 1970s, by photo realism. The development of the neo-avant-garde implied criticism of both the classic avant-gardes and establishment culture, accelerating the cycles of innovation and obsolescence of the emerging new trends but keeping the function of art as cultural criticism alive.

ZURICH

In February 1916 the German writer Hugo Ball (1886–1927) transformed the former Hollandische Meierei Café in Zurich into the Cabaret Voltaire. He wrote in his diary on April 14: "Our cabaret is a gesture. Every word that is spoken and sung here says at least this one thing: that this humiliating age has not succeeded in winning our respect" (Ball, p. 61). Expatriates from various European countries joined him in staging radically nonsensical shows, sound-poem recitals, and primitivist dances. This is where Dada was launched in 1916. The origin of the name is not clear. According to legend, it was obtained from a dictionary by a blindfolded member of the group. Leading personalities of the Dada movement were the Alsatian poet, painter, and sculptor Hans (Jean) Arp (1887–1966); his wife, the dancer and marionette maker Sophie Taeuber Arp (1889–1943); the German dancer and cabaret singer Emmy Hennings (1885–1948); the German writer Richard Huelsenbeck (1892–1974); the Romanian painter and sculptor Marcel Janco (1895–1984); the German painter Hans Richter (1888–1976); and the Romanian poet Tristan Tzara (1896–1963), who published the magazine *Dada* in Zurich between 1917 and 1920. In 1917 they were joined by the Swedish painter and experimental filmmaker Viking Eggeling (1880–1925), who was also a member of the Radical Artists Group, set up by Richter in Zurich in 1919.

The first Dada exhibition opened in January 1917 at the Galerie Corray, followed by an exhibition in March in the group's new location, Galerie Dada. The French painter Francis Picabia (1879–1953) joined in 1919, publishing the Zurich number of his journal *391*.

A key document of the group, among many to follow, was Tzara's 1918 "Dada Manifesto," where he stated that "Dada does not mean anything." The Dada group protested against the ongoing war with activities pointedly refusing to make sense in order to express their contempt for rational, high-brow Western culture, which had not been capable of helping to avoid the war.

After the Zurich years, which ended in the wake of World War I, Dada was dispersed all over the globe, from Zurich to Paris, Berlin, Cologne, Hanover, Vienna, Budapest, Prague, Warsaw, Poznan, Lviv, Sofia, New York, Tokyo, and other urban centers.

BERLIN

The city of Berlin, officially Greater Berlin after 1920, had 3.8 million inhabitants. After the collapse of the Austro-Hungarian Empire in 1918 and the defeat of the Hungarian Soviet Republic in the summer of 1919, many German-speaking eastern European emigrants set up shop in the accommodating and wildly eventful city. Berlin was crammed with theaters, cabarets, publishers, movies, exhibitions, and cafés, was home to a variety of art movements, and was vibrant with ongoing debates.

In the wake of the war's end in November 1918, which brought the abdication of Emperor William II, the declaration of the Weimar Republic, the organization of right-wing paramilitary troops, and the formation of the German Communist Party, almost all progressive artists living in Germany joined forces in two major societies: the Novembergruppe (November Group) and the Arbeitsrat für Kunst (Work Council of the Arts). Many artists and intellectuals were members of both. The choice of name in both cases reflects the progressive, politically leftist direction of these groups (council being the equivalent of the Russian word soviet).

Berlin emerged as the new cultural capital of Europe. The tremendous energy of artists and intellectuals, fueled by the opportunity to found a new republic, was contagious: artists, writers, and thinkers flocked to Berlin from central Europe, Russia, Holland, Sweden, and other parts of the world.

The passionately critical and rebellious expressionists, who were radicalized during the war and represented a strong antiwar stance in many venues, including the periodicals *Der Sturm* (Storm), *Die Aktion* (Action), and *Der Gegner* (The opponent), as well as in their art, were invigorated after the war. Although lambasted by the establishment, expressionism gained currency and emerged by 1918 as Germany's national modern style. It was, along with Dada, the dominant progressive art current in Germany until international constructivism's geometric abstraction and collectivist ethos occupied center stage in 1922.

The headquarters of expressionist art was Herwarth Walden's Der Sturm gallery, which gave visibility to an international group of artists and was instrumental in turning Berlin into a cosmopolitan art center. The Russian painters Ivan Puni (1892–1956) and Wassily Kandinsky (1866–1944), the Romanian painters Arthur Segal (1875–1944) and Max Hermann Maxy (1895–1971), the Czech sculptor and painter Otakar Kubin (1883–1969), the Polish sculptor Teresa Zarnower (1895–1950),

the Ukrainian sculptor Alexander Archipenko (1887–1964), the Hungarian artists Sándor Bortnyik (1893–1976), László Péri (1899–1967), and László Moholy-Nagy (1895–1946), and the Swiss painters Johannes Itten (1888–1967) and Paul Klee (1879–1940) showed their avant-garde works here along with German artists, which greatly contributed to the wide scope and international vibrancy of the Berlin art life. Progressive artists who set up shop in Berlin regularly gathered in the studios of the German painters Gert Caden (1891–1990) or Erich Buchholz (1891–1972) to discuss art and politics, and visited or participated in the Bauhaus, a factory of ideas as well as modern design, operating in Weimar (1919–1925), Dessau (1926–1932), and, during its last year, in Berlin (1932–1933). The Bauhaus was a magnet for the young and progressive artists and designers and had a great impact on the Berlin art discourse. Founded and directed by the architect Walter Gropius (1883–1969), its international faculty included Johannes Itten, Paul Klee, Wassily Kandinsky, László Moholy-Nagy, the German American painter Lyonel Feininger (1871–1956), and the German painter Oskar Schlemmer (1888–1943); but its student body was also packed with future designers and artists.

In 1917, coincidentally with the first Dada exhibition in Zurich, the leftist publishing house Malik Verlag was opened in Berlin by Wieland Herzfelde (1896–1988) and his brother Helmut, who anglicized his name as John Heartfield (1891–1968) in an antiwar and antipatriotic gesture, as did the painter Georg Gross (1893–1959), who changed the spelling of his first name to George Grosz.

In January 1918 the periodical *Club Dada* was founded by Huelsenbeck, Raoul Hausmann (1886–1971), also known as Dadasopher, and the expressionist writer Franz Jung (1888–1963), who was also active in the circles of the leftist antiwar journal *Die Aktion*. Jung's own periodical *Die freie Strasse* (Free road), which he published between 1915 and 1918, was an important inspiration for Berlin Dada.

While Zurich Dada was mostly literary and theatrical, Berlin Dada was a highly politicized left-wing art movement led by Hausmann, Hanna Höch (1889–1978), and Johannes Baader (1875–1955), alias Oberdada. Walter Mehring (1896–1981), also known as Pipidada, founded the radical left-wing journal *Political Cabaret* in 1920.

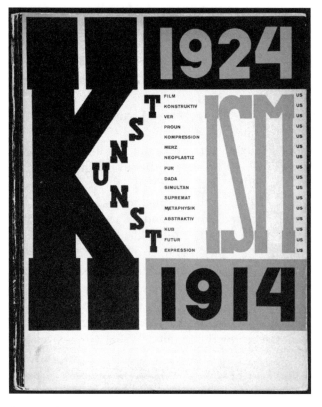

Cover of *Die Kunstismus (The Isms of Art)*, 1925, designed by El Lissitzky. Compiled by El Lissitzky and Hans Arp, this anthology served as a manifesto of avant-garde art of the period. PRIVATE COLLECTION/BRIDGEMAN ART LIBRARY

In June 1920 the Dada exhibition titled The First International Dada Fair opened in the gallery of Dr. Otto Burchard, who sponsored the show and got the name Finanzdada for it. Organized by George Grosz (the Propaganda Marshall), Raoul Hausmann, Johannes Baader, and John Heartfield (Dadamonteur), it was an international exhibition featuring 174 works, including photomontages, collages, effigies, posters, and objects, densely lining the walls. An effigy, *The Prussian Archangel,* made by Rudolf Schlichter (Dadameisterkoch; 1890–1955) and John Heartfield, hung from the ceiling. A slogan of the show was "Art is dead, long live the new machine art of Tatlin!" voicing the intense interest of Berlin artists in the Russian avant-garde, which was manifest also in Hausmann's exhibited collage *Tatlin at Home.*

A wave of émigrés left Russia after the 1917 Bolshevik Revolution. Berlin's Russian population reached a hundred thousand by the end of the war.

More than a dozen daily newspapers were published in Russian, and the city's Charlottenburg district was dubbed Charlottengrad.

The first authentic information about the new Russian art originated from the journalist Konstantin Umansky, who traveled from Russia to Berlin, where he became the correspondent of the Soviet news agency TASS in 1920. In January 1920 he published a series of articles on new Russian art in the Munich journal *Der Ararat* and later that year published his book *Neue Kunst in Russland, 1914–1919* (New art in Russia, 1914–1919). In November he gave a slide-illustrated talk in Vienna for the Hungarian exile avant-garde circle Ma, members of which were in regular contact with their compatriots living in Berlin.

After the end of the civil war in Soviet Russia in 1922, the Soviet ministry of culture adopted a new strategy to cultivate official cultural relations with Germany. In addition to Russian émigré artists like Ivan Puni and the sculptor Naum Gabo (1890–1977), who were active in Berlin in the years 1920–1923 and 1922–1932, respectively, El Lissitzky (1890–1941) arrived from Moscow late in 1921, presumably as a cultural ambassador, to establish personal contacts with Berlin artists. He brought news about the First Working Group of Constructivists, formed in Moscow in March 1921, and constructivism soon became the buzzword in the German capital's modernist art world.

Lissitzky, together with the Russian writer Ilya Ehrenburg (1891–1967), published the trilingual periodical *Veshch, Gegenstand, Objet* (Object) in 1922, which had two issues altogether but was influential nevertheless. The journal's program was to familiarize Berlin artists with the latest developments in the Russian-Soviet avant-garde and inform Soviet artists of the latest in Western art. Its title referred to the Russian constructivists' concept of the irrelevance of painting and their idea that objects, not pictures, were what should be created.

The actual encounter with Russian art happened in the fall of 1922, when the Erste Russische Kunstausstellung (First Russian Art Exhibition), a joint Soviet-German undertaking, opened in the Galerie van Diemen and presented the works of the Russian avant-garde—suprematists, constructivists, productivists—for the first time in the West.

Although many critical reviews expressed disappointment because of the great proportion of traditional (impressionist and postimpressionist) artworks, this show was the breakthrough of the young Soviet-Russian art in Berlin. The exhibition traveled to Amsterdam early in 1923. An important forum for what started to be called international constructivism was the journal *G: Zeitschrift für elementare Gestaltung* (G: Journal for elementary design), edited by Hans Richter and El Lissitzky in 1923–1924.

PARIS

Still a central scene of the arts, Paris continued to play a very important role in the unfolding of new art and remained the city where artists made pilgrimage. Paris Dada, with more of a penchant for the absurd than politically leftist Berlin Dada, morphed into surrealism by the early 1920s.

The French writers Louis Aragon (1897–1982) and André Breton (1896–1966) contributed to Tristan Tzara's *Dada* journal, published in Zurich. In turn, Tzara contributed the Paris journal *Littéraire,* edited by Breton and Aragon. Picabia, having visited New York and cooperated with Alfred Stieglitz and his 291 Gallery there, started to publish the mostly dadaist *391* magazine in 1917.

Paris Dada was mainly literary, featuring manifestos, theater events, short-lived periodicals, and demonstrations. The artists of the movement in Paris—the German painter Max Ernst (1891–1976), Arp, and Picabia—were not in the forefront of these events. Paris Dada split into two factions, headed by Tzara and Breton, and it expired in the congress convoked in 1922. Before the split Breton, Tzara, Picabia, and Marcel Duchamp (1887–1968) regarded Dada as the boldest, most anarchic, and most provocative direction in the arts. Together they published an issue of *Bulletin Dada* in 1920, but by 1922 had Breton turned against Dada, claiming that it had become conformist. He disrupted the Dada congress in Paris, and to break new ground he explored "automatic writing," which artists adopted as "automatic drawing," doodling without conscious intention. By 1924 Breton's group, joined by the poets Paul Éluard (1895–1952), Jean Cocteau (1889–1963), and Ezra Pound (1885–1972), adopted the name *surrealism.* The term was first used by Guillaume Apollinaire (1880–1918) in

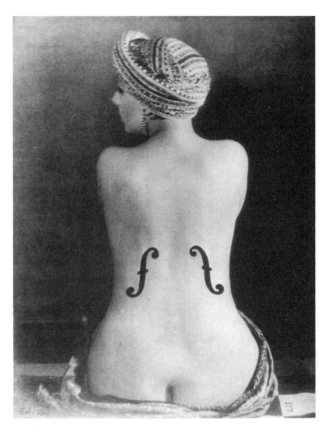

Le violon d'Ingres. This mixed-media work by Man Ray demonstrates avant-garde experimentalism in both subject and medium. ART RESOURCE, NY. ©2000 MAN RAY TRUST/ARTISTS RIGHTS SOCIETY (ARS), NEW YORK/ADAGP, PARIS.

1917, in reference to his own drama *Les mamelles de Tirésias* (The breasts of Tirésias).

The first surrealist group exhibition opened in the Galerie Pierre in 1925. Participants included Arp, Giorgio De Chirico (1888–1978), Ernst, Paul Klee (1879–1940), Man Ray (1890–1976), André Masson (1896–1987), Joan Miró (1893–1983), and Pablo Picasso (1881–1973). In 1927 the Surrealist Gallery was opened, where Yves Tanguy (1900–1955), Duchamp, and Picabia also exhibited. The Belgian painter René Magritte (1898–1967) and the Spanish painter Salvador Dalí (1904–1989) soon joined the group.

The ideas of the surrealists were most clearly articulated by Breton, who thoroughly studied Freud's teachings. He hoped to open up new fields by a new kind of imagery drawn from the subconscious, which was manifested in dreams or by associations. He published the first "Manifesto of

Surrealism" in 1924, the "Second Manifesto of Surrealism" in 1930, and the "Political Position of Surrealism" in 1935. Surrealism inherited Dada's revolt against the establishment and its culture. In the first "Manifesto" Breton declared that "Surrealism, such as I conceive of it, asserts our complete *non-conformism*....Surrealism is the 'invisible ray' which will one day enable us to win out over our opponents" (Breton, p. 47). He pronounced his conviction that by exploiting the vast reservoir of the unconscious, surrealism, "*as a method of creating a collective myth* with the much more general movement involving the liberation of man" (Breton, p. 210), could transcend all previous forms of thought and expression.

Surrealists created cinematic works as well. The first surrealist film was the 1928 collaboration between Dalí and the Spanish film director Luis Buñuel (1900–1983), *Un chien andalou* (An Andalusian dog).

A current of clean forms, purism unfolded parallel with surrealism. The Swiss-born architect Charles-Édouard Jeanneret, known as Le Corbusier (1887–1965), and the French painter Amédée Ozenfant (1886–1966) initiated the movement with the publication of their manifesto *After Cubism* in 1918, going on to publish the journal *Esprit nouveau* (New spirit) from 1918 to 1925. Their friend Fernand Léger (1881–1955) cooperated with them. They celebrated modern machines and new technologies, combining the new possibilites they offered with pure classic forms, rejecting Dada and surrealism: "Purism fears the bizarre and the 'original,'" as they put it in *After Cubism.*

AMSTERDAM

A will to radical innovation and the reinvention of the visual arts pervaded the artistic and theoretical output of the De Stijl (The Style) group, founded in Amsterdam in 1917. The painters Piet Mondrian (1872–1944), Theo van Doesburg (1883–1931), Vilmos Huszar (1884–1960), and Bart van der Leck (1876–1958), the Belgian sculptor George Vantongerloo (1886–1965), and a group of architects including Cornelis van Eesteren (1897–1988) and Johannes Jacobus Pieter Oud (1890–1963) embraced the program of neoplasticism, new architecture, and new design based on total abstraction. The architect and designer Gerrit Rietveld (1888–

1964), who would build the emblematic Schröder House in 1924, joined in 1918.

The De Stijl philosophy was purely spiritual and radical at the same time. The straight line, pure mathematical relations, and the reduction of the palette to the three primary colors and the three "non-colors" (black, white, and gray) served the attainment of spirituality and harmony. Mimesis and representation were unacceptable. Emotional expression in painting was incompatible with lucidity and spirituality. De Stijl's interior design considered a room as a six-sided box, the ceiling and floor of which play as important a part in the overall design as the walls and furniture. To achieve the ideal of "spiritual living," squares or rectangles running across corners were often painted in a color that differed from that of the wall, overwriting the architectural structure.

De Stijl architecture, which was part of the modernist trend labeled "international style" by the American architect Philip Johnson, was the earliest effort to simplify the living space, painting it white and light tones of gray with occasional highlights of one or another of the primary colors, using built-ins and clear outlines to offer the inhabitants an easier, liberated, and rational lifestyle.

Van Doesburg published the trilingual (Dutch, German, French) journal *De Stijl* between 1917 and 1931, which soon became one of the most important venues of the international avant-garde, recruiting authors from all over Europe. Van Doesburg himself was a personal link between the Bauhaus, De Stijl, the Russian avant-garde, international constructivists, and Dada. He secretly doubled as the Dada poet I. K. Bonset and as the editor and publisher Aldo Camini, putting out the short-lived avant-garde journal *Mecano* in 1922–1923.

In Amsterdam, as in Berlin and Paris, modern architecture was a contested field of the avant-garde. In 1918 the architect Hendricus Theodorus Wijdeveld (1885–1987) launched *Wendingen,* a periodical of modern architecture, art, and design that ran until 1931, for which El Lissitzky designed a cover (November 1922 issue).

The anarchist and essayist Arthur Lehning (1899–2000) edited and published a little magazine titled *Internationale revue i 10* between 1927 and 1929 with the intention to integrate art, sciences, philosophy, and sociology into the political reality of the society. Moholy-Nagy did the typography and layout, and among the contributors were Lehning's friends Walter Benjamin and Ernst Bloch, along with Arp, Kurt Schwitters (1887–1948), Wassily Kandinsky, Moholy-Nagy, and others.

See also Arp, Jean; Bauhaus; Constructivism; Dada; De Stijl; Expressionism; Futurism; Kandinsky, Wassily; Le Corbusier; Lissitzky, El; Malevich, Kazimir; Moholy-Nagy, László; Mondrian, Piet; Painting, Avant-Garde; Surrealism.

BIBLIOGRAPHY

Altshuler, Bruce. *The Avant-Garde in Exhibition: New Art in the Twentieth Century.* Berkeley and Los Angeles, 1994.

Ball, Hugo. *Flight Out of Time: A Dada Diary.* Edited by John Elderfield and translated by Ann Raimes. Berkeley, Calif., 1996.

Blotkamp, Carel, et al. *De Stijl: The Formative Years, 1917–1922.* Translated by Charlotte I. Loeb and Arthur L. Loeb. Cambridge, Mass., and London, 1986.

Breton, André. *Manifestoes of Surrealism.* Translated by Richard Seaver and Helen R. Lane. Ann Arbor, Mich., 1972.

Bürger, Peter. *Theory of the Avant-Garde.* Translated by Michael Shaw. Minneapolis, Minn., 1984.

Călinescu, Matei. *Five Faces of Modernity: Modernism, Avant-Garde, Decadence, Kitsch, Postmodernism.* Durham, N.C., 1987.

Foster, Hal, Rosalind Krauss, Yve-Alain Bois, and Benjamin H. D. Buchloh. *Art Since 1900.* New York and London, 2004.

Huelsenbeck, Richard, ed. *The Dada Almanac.* English edition presented by Malcolm Green, translated by Malcolm Green et al. London, 1993.

Lodder, Christina. *Russian Constructivism.* New Haven, Conn., 1981.

Poggioli, Renato. *The Theory of the Avant-Garde.* Translated by Gerald Fitzgerald. Cambridge, Mass., and London, 1968.

EVA FORGACS

AVIATION. As an instrument of war, focus of mass culture, and incubator of technology, powered flight is a defining element of contemporary Europe. Its rapid development was driven by the unique military advantages of aircraft in terms of power, performance, and versatility; its advances required huge long-term investment, making the industry heavily dependent on governments and politics. But aviation also provided the early twentieth century with some of its strongest metaphors of progress, as the architect Le Corbusier acknowledged, proclaiming the airplane "advance guard of the conquering armies of the New Age," capable of arousing "our energies and our faith" (p. 10).

While the Wright brothers' flights of 1903–1905 were American triumphs, the heritage of aviation was European. The word itself was created in 1863 by the French writer Gabriel de la Landelle, combining *avis* (Latin for bird) with *action*. The hot-air balloon (1783), parachute (1797), and airship (1852) all originated in France. The first man-carrying glider, designed by the Englishman George Cayley, flew in 1849. In 1877 the Italian Enrico Forlanini successfully demonstrated a steam-engined model helicopter. The German Otto Lilienthal made almost twenty-five hundred glider flights, crashing to death in 1896 as he was beginning to experiment with powered aircraft. The Brazilian Alberto Santos Dumont eventually made the first powered flight in Europe on 23 October 1906. Within three years, Louis Blériot would fly across the English Channel.

The airplane exceeded two hundred kilometers per hour in 1913, embodying the revolution of speed and influencing art in its every form, from the more sophisticated works to posters destined for popular consumption. In turn, art created the cultural codes of flight, defining enduring interpretive categories. Airplanes were prominent features of avant-garde movements. From 1909 onward, the futurist movement announced its plan to replace museums, women, and the past with speed, war, and machines. Aircraft offered a new viewpoint: not just height, already provided by towers, hilltops, and balloons, but speed. A series of aggressive manifestos theorized its incorporation into everything from theater to poetry to painting. Futurism proposed the use of engines as musical instruments, and the soundtrack of Filippo Masoero's film *Vertigine* (1932) consisted entirely of engine roar. The futurist impact on visual arts would soon be seen, in less radical ways, in popular graphics and advertising but also in the identification of airplanes with technology. This reversed the earlier approach of legitimizing aviation by borrowing established and reassuring imagery.

In 1910 Elise Deroche became the world's first licensed woman pilot, and two years later Melli Beese established a flying school in Germany. Despite this, and the gradual removal of cultural and legal barriers, aviation has remained, with few exceptions, a largely male affair.

THE AIRPLANE GOES TO WAR

The European contribution to aviation included transforming it from sport to weapon. In 1910 the French general Pierre-Auguste Roques foresaw that armies would need airplanes as much as cannon and rifles, and warned that those who refused to accept the fact consciously risked having it forced upon them against their will. Giulio Douhet, the Italian officer and theorist, wrote that fighting in the air had become "inevitable" at the very moment that mankind had learned to fly. The 1911 Turkish-Italian war saw Captain Carlo M. Piazza make the world's first heavier-than-air operational sortie, arguably the single most significant flight after the Wrights' of 17 December 1903.

In 1914 European powers fielded just a few hundred aircraft. World War I provided the demand for an aviation industry. Britain alone accounted for about one-third of the 172,000 aircraft built in Europe, with Germany and France closely behind. The breakneck expansion strained capabilities and resources, sometimes compounded by quality control problems. The unarmed and largely similar wooden-truss, fabric-covered biplanes soon became differentiated by role and performance. In 1915 the Italians deployed the world's first heavy bombers, conceived by Gianni Caproni. Metal construction, supercharged engines, and heavy armament were some of the advanced features introduced by the end of the war.

The conflict also shaped the views of the relationship between man and machine. In the final scene of his 1910 novel *Forse che sì, forse che no* (Maybe yes, maybe no), Gabriele D'Annunzio described an old woman greeting a pilot who just completed a daring flight with the eloquent words "Son, there is no god if you are not the one." This superhuman status is arguably the archetype for the wartime myth of the pilot as modern-day knight engaged in chivalrous duels with similarly noble opponents. The identification was most visible in the emergence of the "ace," the informal title bestowed upon pilots who downed at least five enemy aircraft, exploited for its propaganda value to military, nationalist, and industrial purposes. Its spread was reinforced by the need for individual recognition and skill in a war of masses and industrial output. The names of the leading aces still enjoy greater popular recognition than their commanders in chief: Manfred von Richthofen, the so-called Red Baron, is better known than Erich Ludendorff, and Luigi Cadorna is eclipsed by Francesco Baracca, whose black prancing horse badge adorns Ferrari sports cars.

With their notoriety, aces distort the relative importance of the military applications of airpower. By 1918 aviation had become indispensable in tasks ranging from artillery spotting to antisubmarine patrols and from long-range reconnaissance to bombing. In most countries, short-range reconnaissance accounted for half or more and heavy bombers for less than one-tenth. Only in the British Royal Air Force (RAF) did fighters represent a majority of the frontline strength. The extensive German and Italian use of airships confirmed their vulnerability and unwieldness. Although no battle was decided by airpower, the war led aviators to conclude that its full potential would only be exploited by entrusting its control to airmen. The RAF, the world's first air service independent from both army and navy, came into being on 1 April 1918. Its initial purpose was the improved defense of London against the German bomber offensive.

Aviators soon went beyond this, claiming that future wars would be decided by air attacks on enemy morale and resources. The main proponent of this doctrine was Douhet, who advocated massive bomber fleets to strike enemy population centers with chemical and incendiary weapons, arguing that the resulting shock would lead to rapid surrender and shorter wars, obviating the senseless carnage of the western front. (In fact, Douhet believed that the mere threat of such destruction would serve as deterrent.) It followed that air forces should be independent from surface forces and should receive funding priorities, an idea bitterly contested by armies and navies everywhere: in France their opposition delayed the creation of the Armée de l'Air until 1933, five years after the Air Ministry was created.

A German bi-plane crashed in a field during World War I. ©CORBIS

But airpower theory also ran contrary to immediate needs. The RAF proved its value by controlling internal conflict in Iraq. The Italian Regia Aeronautica, independent from 1923, was employed in tactical roles in the Ethiopian campaign (1935–1936) and Spanish civil war (1936–1939). Ironically, these undesired duties did much to make air forces acceptable to the other services. The German military never believed in strategic airpower, but the Luftwaffe successfully demonstrated its value at the operational level in Spain and in the 1939–1940 Blitzkrieg.

A TROUBLED PEACE

The Versailles treaty severely curtailed German flying, but throughout Europe the armistice challenged aviation to survive without huge military orders. Because abundant war-surplus aircraft, as cheap as they were obsolete, stifled technical development, spectacular sporting feats helped attract capital and promote "air mindedness" in the public. Charles Lindbergh's celebrated 1927 solo Atlantic crossing should not obscure the fact that by 1920 European aircraft and crews had already flown from Canada to Ireland, from Britain to South Africa and Australia, and from Italy to Japan. In 1926 the airship *Norge* overflew the North Pole.

In 1919 thirteen countries, nine of which were European, signed the first international air navigation convention, providing the framework for commercial services. Pilots and industrialists hoped that airlines would sustain aviation, but limited payload and performance made companies dependent on airmail subsidies.

An abundance of courage compensated for the lack of resources; achievements bordered on the legendary. Latécoère (later Aéropostale) inaugurated mail service from France to Algeria in 1919. Ten years later it reached Chile and in 1933 replaced ships with aircraft even on the transatlantic portions of the route. Among its pilots was Antoine de Saint-Exupéry, who drew upon the experience for his celebrated novels. To improve efficiency, in 1933 and 1934 France and Italy concentrated their subsidies into the government-owned flag carriers Air France and Ala Littoria.

All countries seized on the value of aviation to reinforce national identities and promote ideologies. Competitions quickly went beyond the means and goals of individual manufacturers. Massive state support for Schneider Cup seaplanes allowed speeds to climb from four to seven hundred kilometers per hour between 1926 and 1934; other records followed a similar pattern. This progress allowed professionalism to replace luck and talent as the key to success. To signal this change and spread the image of a country thrust into modernity by fascism, Italo Balbo, the Italian minister of aeronautics, led formation flights to Brasil (1930–1931) and the United States (1933). The Soviet Union formed a propaganda squadron, whose aircraft included the giant ANT-20, fitted with a cinema, printing press, photo lab, and powerful broadcasting equipment.

But government involvement in aviation, which frequently included nationalizing industries, was driven by more compelling reasons. By transferring its technologies to develop airlines and aircraft to the Soviet Union, Germany circumvented the Versailles restrictions. Aircraft exports furthered Benito Mussolini's attempt to erode British influence in the Middle East and American influence in China.

Amid mounting international tension, in 1935 Adolf Hitler announced the forming of the Luftwaffe and unleashed international rearmament programs. The simultaneous introduction of all-metal monoplanes with stressed-skin structures, variable-pitch propellers, and retractable landing gear endowed new designs with superior performance. The best aircraft of this period—like the Messerschmitt Bf 109 (first flown in 1935) and Supermarine Spitfire (1936)—would remain in production until 1945, albeit in much evolved variants. In 1937, the destruction of the airship *Hindenburg*, which burst into flames in New Jersey after a commercial flight from Germany, marked the decline of the dirigible.

WORLD WAR II

The Luftwaffe's contribution to the crushing of Poland in September 1939 suggested the pivotal role that aviation would play in the new global conflict. Production expanded dramatically, and organizations grew correspondingly. Germany built close to 118,000 aircraft, and Britain almost 132,000. By 1945 the RAF numbered 1,000,000 men. Italian output was limited to about 12,000 aircraft, but even this required 160,000 air force personnel and as many industry workers.

For the first time, airpower decided the fate of nations. In summer 1940 Germany launched an air offensive designed to soften Britain before the cross-channel amphibious assault. The lonely and defenseless island was widely expected to follow the fate of France. But the RAF prevailed, through a mix of superior technology, superb leadership, and enemy targeting blunders; the invasion was first postponed and then canceled. The Battle of Britain instantly became a defining episode in British history, and the public perception that the country had been saved by Hurricanes and Spitfires still endures.

But the war also linked airplanes to mass destruction, tainting forever their image. Aviation lost its innocence at Guernica, the Basque town destroyed by the Germans in 1937 and immortalized in Pablo Picasso's famous painting. Then came Rotterdam, Coventry, Dresden, and innumerable cities consumed by aerial bombardment. At first, the bomber offensive was the only means available to Britain to strike back at Germany. Under Air Marshal Arthur Harris, commander in chief of Bomber Command, it later became an attempt to win the war single-handedly. With brutal pragmatism, his "area" or "saturation" targeting policy sidestepped the difficulty of pinpointing military or industrial targets at night. Precision daylight bombing was left to the Americans, whose approach was based on a detailed analysis of the German economy and its bottlenecks. Germany was laid waste by 1.5 million tons of bombs, but the anticipated knockout blow never came. The war of aerial attrition cost nearly a hundred thousand aircrew and sixteen thousand bombers and killed up to one million Germans, but its success remains hotly debated.

The war ushered in major advances, including pressurized cabins and gas turbine engines ("jets").

A World War II–era Messerschmitt ME-109 airplane undergoes testing in a wind tunnel at Hermann Goering aviation ministry c. 1940. ©CORBIS

The latter were a peculiarly European affair, achieved separately in 1937 by Frank Whittle in Britain and Hans von Ohain in Germany. Inherently simple and efficient, jet engines brought dramatic performance improvements. Airborne radar signaled the start of the electronic era. Large-scale production allowed some measure of production engineering, conspicuously lacking from the piecemeal prewar purchases.

BUILDING EUROPE THROUGH AVIATION

Chuck Yeager exceeded the speed of sound in 1947, sealing American dominance of the jet age. In Europe, only Britain had emerged from the war with an intact industry. Imperial delusions translated into a flawed postwar development plan, which failed to identify priorities for government support. The attitude was typified by the 1946 decision to build three different jet-engined nuclear bombers to the same requirement.

A flying ban was again imposed on Germany. Its industries lay in ruins but its advanced technologies pollinated the world. While Werner von Braun developed rockets in the United States, Willy Messerschmitt designed jet trainers and supersonic fighters in Spain, and a BMW team launched the French turbojet program. The Soviet Union also preyed on German talent, but its jet program only blossomed after the 1946 transfer of Rolls-Royce technologies by the ideologically motivated British Labour government.

If the Berlin blockade of 1948–1949 signaled the beginning of the Cold War, the ensuing Anglo-American airlift proved the political value of "soft" airpower applications. It also led to the North Atlantic Treaty Organization (NATO) and provided the stimulus to rebuild the aviation industry. It soon was clear that it would be difficult to compete with American technology, particularly when supported by generous financial terms and "offshore procurement" work. But governments could still choose between supporting aviation mainly for its technological benefits, as in France, or to protect employment, as in Italy. Small countries like Sweden produced remarkable aircraft by asking industry to underpin their neutrality.

Wartime progress and experience allowed airlines to offer reliable transatlantic service. European air transport prospered on regulation as much as anything else. Bilateral agreements invariably assigned traffic rights to national carriers, whose commercial practices often included sharing route profits.

The ban lifted, West Germany joined NATO in 1955. Three years later its selection of the American nuclear-capable F-104G Starfighter triggered the largest international aviation program attempted until then. The fifteen hundred fighter-bombers built in Europe paved the way for continental aerospace collaboration.

In 1961 Britain flew the revolutionary P.1127 vertical takeoff jet, later developed into the Harrier, whose commercial success extended to the United States, but the 1965 cancellation of the TSR.2 attack jet signaled the end of British ambitions of independence and quickly multiplied European collaborative programs. In 1967 Britain launched four military programs with France. It then joined with Germany and Italy to develop the Tornado strike aircraft (1974). Its success, expensive as it was, was demonstrated in the 1991 Gulf War and led to the very ambitious Eurofighter (1994). The program now included Spain, while France elected to proceed alone with the broadly similar Dassault Rafale.

While these programs were generally successful, only Germany and France had a long-term strategy to overcome industry fragmentation and build global competitors in terms of technologies, finances, and size. With political support, the vision of industrialists such as Ludwig Bölkow and Henri Ziegler became Airbus, established in 1970 by the French and German governments. Previous European challenges had produced remarkable

jetliners—including the De Havilland Comet (1949) and Sud-Est Caravelle (1955)—and equally significant losses. The Anglo-French Concorde epitomized the "magnificent loser" category: the twenty supersonic transports built showed an operating profit only after the governments wrote off their development and production costs. Airbus, later joined by Britain and Spain, reversed the pattern and eventually became the world's foremost airliner manufacturer, ahead of Boeing. The giant A380 airliner challenged the Boeing 747 on symbolic rather than business grounds. By 2003 Airbus was proclaimed an icon of European unity as great as its common currency, its success being attributed to peculiarly European values and approaches.

The 1977 launch of Freddie Laker's no-reservation, no-frills transatlantic service was a rare challenge, immediately countered by British Airways with strongly anticompetitive measures. When the European Union (EU) undertook to deregulate air transport in the 1990s, it shook the long complacent industry. The new market emphasis bankrupted airlines like Sabena (the Belgian flag carrier that had never turned a profit since its founding in 1923), Swissair, and Olympic. The spread of low-fare air travel quickly stripped the industry of any lingering jet-set mentality. Ryanair, the Irish no-frills airline, asked the EU to exempt its buslike service from expensive airline regulations, including those designed to protect consumers. It lost, but its argument confirmed the new image of mass air transport.

TWILIGHT?

In the 1960s aviation ran out of performance milestones. The frontier moved outside the atmosphere, beyond human gaze (and, largely, interest), in a space contested by the American and Soviet superpowers. Unable to compete individually, early in the decade five European countries joined in the European Launcher Development Organization (ELDO) and European Space Research Organization (ESRO) programs, sowing the seeds of the European Space Agency (1975), whose story lies outside the scope of this entry.

Upon realizing the pioneers' dreams, aviation exchanged heroics for a business approach. Development took less glamorous avenues: safety,

An Airbus A340–600 passenger plane takes off near Toulouse, France, 23 April 2001. ©REUTERS/CORBIS

affordability, professionalism, capabilities, and even environmental impact. Innovative composite materials made possible exceptional airframe weight reductions, but are hardly exciting. Ubiquitous electronics, now the main part of aircraft cost, turned aircraft into "platforms" for "systems." Automated flight—met with universal skepticism when prophesied by Duncan Sandys, the British minister of defense, in his much maligned 1957 White Paper—is now reality, depressing what romanticism remained.

When the Berlin Wall fell in 1989, industry was belatedly forced to reduce chronic overcapacity. Despite a trend to privatize, this reinforced its dependence on political decisions, making "Buy European" an unwritten requirement for EU membership, or even application. In 2000 the French and German governments merged their aviation industries, including Airbus, in the giant European Aeronautic Defence and Space Company (EADS). To balance the Paris-Berlin directorate, Britain and Italy drew closer and allied with American industry. The strategy bore fruit in AgustaWestland, now the world's leading

helicopter manufacturer, selected in January 2005 to supply the American presidential transport helicopter.

When Europe celebrated the Wrights' centennial, aviation had cut travel time, shrunk the world, modified individual lifestyles, cross-contaminated cultures, and made globalization possible. The price for such impressive success and universal acceptance was the loss of its age-old appeal.

See also **Automobiles; Blitzkreig; Britain, Battle of; Futurism; Guernica; Public Transport; Technology; Warfare.**

BIBLIOGRAPHY

Primary Sources

Douhet, Giulio. *The Command of the Air.* Translated by Dino Ferrari. 1942. Reprint, Washington, D.C., 1983. Translation of *Il dominio dell'aria.*

Le Corbusier. *Aircraft.* London, 1935.

Saint-Exupéry, Antoine de. *"Southern Mail" and "Night Flight."* Translated by Curtis Cate. London, 1971. Translation of *Courrier du sud* and *Vol de nuit.*

Secondary Sources

Chadeau, Emmanuel. *L'industrie aéronautique en France, 1900–1950.* Paris, 1987.

Christienne, Charles, and Pierre Lissarrague. *A History of French Military Aviation.* Translated by Frances Kianka. Washington, D.C., 1986.

Corum, James S. *The Luftwaffe: Creating the Operational Air War, 1918–1940.* Lawrence, Kans., 1997.

Davies, R. E. G. *A History of the World's Airlines.* London, 1964.

Fritzsche, Peter. *A Nation of Fliers: German Aviation and the Popular Imagination.* Cambridge, Mass., 1992.

King, Peter. *Knights of the Air.* London, 1989.

Morrow, John H., Jr. *The Great War in the Air.* Washington, D.C., 1993.

Overy, R. J. *The Air War, 1939–1945.* New York, 1980.

Wohl, Robert. *A Passion for Wings: Aviation and the Western Imagination, 1908–1914.* New Haven, Conn., 1994.

GREGORY ALEGI

AXIS. The expression *Axis,* used to designate the enemies of the Allied forces during the Second World War, originated in the interwar period, when it was first employed by the Italian dictator Benito Mussolini (1883–1945) in 1936. The anti-democratic, militaristic, and totalitarian regimes of Nazi Germany and Fascist Italy found common ground for joint activities in the form of the Spanish civil war (1936–1939), which at the time was being waged full-scale, and whose Republican and Nationalist camps were both looking to Europe for support.

Based on the aid they had only recently begun to lend the Spanish Nationalists of Francisco Franco (1892–1975), Italy and Germany formalized a nonmilitary accord on 25 October 1936, which Mussolini characterized as an "axis" around which other European nations would eventually gravitate. Thus was the expression born. The motivations behind the treaty stemmed from Italy's growing international isolation as a result of the Fascist regime's invasion of Ethiopia, and from the desire of the German dictator Adolf Hitler (1889–1945) to find an ally in Europe. After having secured Italy's neutrality in the first phase of its expansion into the Austrian Sudetenland, Germany transformed the nonmilitary accord into a formal alliance with the signing in May of 1939 of the "Pact of Steel," a treaty providing for both military and economic cooperation. However this "Rome-Berlin Axis" was to signal but the first phase in the constitution of a more ambitious alliance whose groundwork the two powers were only beginning to lay, in order to further the enactment of their aggressive and expansionist foreign policies. The founding act of their common policy in this respect was the expansion of the original Pact of Steel into a tripartite alliance with Japan, signed 27 September 1940, which cemented the Rome-Berlin-Tokyo Axis in place.

Once established, however, the tripartite axis was not destined to remain as such. Two months later the three founding powers were joined by the majority of the authoritarian regimes of central Europe, including Hungary (20 November 1940), Romania (23 November 1940), Slovakia (24 November 1940), and finally Bulgaria (1 March 1941). The lone holdouts, Yugoslavia and Greece, were thus earmarked as the first targets of the Germano-Italian alliance in the Balkans.

Although it was highly diverse from a geostrategic perspective, the Axis was nonetheless surprisingly homogeneous as concerns the type of states that joined it. All of its participant regimes were either dictatorships or authoritarian, all echoed the antidemocratic and unyieldingly nationalist chorus, and all pursued expansionist foreign policy goals. The point here is not to compare the Nazi drive for world domination with the relatively modest foreign policy objectives of Bulgaria, but rather to emphasize the degree to which this homogeneity constituted one of the glues holding the alliance together, and how this figured as a favored theme of Allied propaganda, which found it thereby easier to maintain day in and day out that the war was indeed against tyranny itself. Although the question of negotiating the division of one or another specific territory never seriously arose, it was nonetheless clear that the Axis sought a fundamental reshuffling of the global geostrategic deck, and the institution of clearly defined spheres of influence between its three primary players. In this sense the second-tier members of the alliance did not relate to the first-tier powers on an equal footing, although their existence as states did not depend on their Axis membership as such. This was not the case with the third-tier Axis states, whose virtual existences were largely the incidental outcome of actions designed to create breathing room. The ranks of this hodge-podge of Axis members included for example the Central Council of Belarus, a phantom assembly on which the German occupiers bestowed independence just as Russian tanks were encircling Minsk, and Manchukuo, a Japanese puppet regime propped up in February 1932.

In this way the Axis developed into a disparate alliance effectively run by the three great powers and serving primarily to define each of the three countries' spheres of influence. Mussolini's downfall and the founding of the Italian Social Republic in September 1943 profoundly altered the state of relations at the heart of the treaty. From that point forward the Axis became synonymous with Berlin and Tokyo only, and the chronology of its demise went hand in hand with the crumbling of Nazi Germany and imperial Japan themselves.

See also **Fascism; Nazism; World War II.**

BIBLIOGRAPHY

Jacobsen, Hans-Adolf. *Nationalsozialistische Aussenpolitik, 1933–1938*. Frankfurt, 1968. This is the most complete account to date of German foreign policy during the early years of the Axis.

CHRISTIAN INGRAO

AZNAR, JOSÉ MARIA (b. 1953), Spanish politician and prime minister of Spain (1996–2004).

José Maria Aznar was born into a conservative family of journalists and politicians. Both his grandfather and his father had senior state positions during the dictatorship of Francisco Franco. After graduating in law, he passed the official exams to become a tax inspector. As a student in the mid-1970s and a young graduate, he identified himself as a Falangist (a member of the Fascist Party) and opposed the drafting of the 1978 democratic constitution. In 1979 he joined Alianza Popular, then the most conservative force in parliament, becoming a deputy for the province of Ávila in 1982. Alianza Popular's founder, the former Francoist minister Manuel Fraga, was a family friend, helping Aznar to rise in the party. As a result, in 1985 he was elected premier of the region of Castile-Leon. After Fraga retired to become premier of his native Galicia region, the party went through a period of internal crises and electoral defeats against the ruling Socialists (1982–1996), in part because voters perceived Alianza Popular as being too conservative and too closely identified with the previous regime.

In 1992 Aznar became the leader of the organization, renamed the Popular Party (PP) in 1989. Since the late 1980s, the popularity of the Socialists had been affected by a number of scandals and a downturn in the economy. Aznar moved his party decisively to the center while at the same time conducting a very aggressive opposition with the help of large sectors of the media, particularly those close to the Catholic Church. In 1995 his personal popularity was boosted when the Basque terrorist organization ETA attempted to assassinate him with a car bomb. In 1996 the Popular Party defeated the Socialists by a narrower margin than expected, forcing Aznar to govern from a minority position. This led him to look for support among the conservative Catalonian, Basque, and Canary Island nationalist groups, softening what had been until recently a centralist political discourse. In the process he discarded some of his most strident collaborators. In 2000 voters rewarded both his moderation and his government's handling of the economy (under his mandate Spain moved swiftly to meet the requirements to join the new European single currency, the euro) by giving him an absolute majority in that year's general elections.

During his second term Aznar adopted an increasingly arrogant political tone, to the point of dismissing any criticism as a threat to the progress of the nation and even as evidence of disloyalty toward the constitutional order. This approach was closely mirrored by the state's broadcasting system, which often presented strongly biased views. He also embraced a more marked Spanish nationalism and departed from the country's recent foreign policy, which had been centered around increasing cooperation within the European Union, and particularly with France and Germany. Instead, Aznar formed a personal partnership with Britain's Tony Blair and later with Italy's Silvio Berlusconi. The high point of this diplomatic shift came after it became clear that George W. Bush's administration planned to invade Iraq during late 2002 and early 2003. Disregarding strong opposition from the citizens of Spain, of whom around 90 percent opposed the United States' polices on Iraq, Aznar actively supported the invasion.

Aznar had vowed several times that he would not seek a third term in office, a promise that he kept. His appointed successor, and candidate to become the next prime minister, was Mariano Rajoy. Confident that the performance of the economy would maintain electoral support for his party, elections were called for 14 March 2004. In the weeks before the voting, most polls predicted a victory for the Popular Party, even if the Socialists insisted that they were gathering electoral momentum. The campaign was suddenly transformed when, on the early hours of March 11, several bombs placed in commuter trains approaching Madrid killed 192 people. The government was quick to blame ETA for the carnage, a fact that, if confirmed, could only boost its chances of being reelected. However, within hours it became evident to everyone, except the government, PP candidates, and the media close to both, that the terrorist attack was the work of Islamic fundamentalists, not Basque separatists. The government angrily rejected this interpretation, dismissing both the material evidence and critical analysis. On voting day, electoral turnout was much higher than in previous years, with many young people, a traditionally apathetic sector, voting for the first time. The result was the unexpected victory for the Socialists, whose leader had announced several months before his commitment to withdraw Spanish troops from Iraq and from the American-led coalition.

See also **ETA; Islamic Terrorism/Al Qaeda; Spain.**

BIBLIOGRAPHY

Aznar, José Maria. *Ocho años de gobierno.* Barcelona, 2004.

Tusell, Javier. *El gobierno de Aznar: Balance de una gestión, 1996–2000.* Barcelona, 2000.

ANTONIO CAZORLA-SANCHEZ

BAADER-MEINHOF. *See* Red Army Faction; Terrorism.

BABI YAR.

When the Sixth Army of Field Marshal Walther von Reichenau (1884–1942) encircled Kiev in mid-September 1941, the majority of the city's 220,000 Jews had already been evacuated. After the city was captured on 18–19 September, however, an estimated fifty thousand still remained in the Ukrainian capital, mostly women, children, and the elderly. They were unaware that they were in mortal danger.

WEHRMACHT PLANS FOR STARVATION

Works by the historians Christian Gerlach and Aly Götz have revealed that the Wehrmacht (German army) commanders who planned Operation Barbarossa expected that the Ostheer (eastern army) would be able to feed itself almost exclusively off the land and resources of the countries it conquered, which by implication would mean starvation for tens of millions of civilians. Destruction of cities and condemnation of whole populations to die of hunger in the ruins of those cities—such was the aim of the Nazi generals. Russian Jewish communities in the large cities were among the first to be threatened.

After they entered Kiev, the German army's first order of business was security. From the beginning of the Russian campaign, the Jewish communities were everywhere held responsible for numerous incidents of resistance. Shootings by civilians, fires, and various kinds of sabotage—even massacres that had been in fact perpetrated by the Soviet secret police (NKVD) during the panicked evacuations of cities on the Galician border—were all taken as proof of the malignancy and cruelty of Jews. However frequent such attacks, they were also improvised, which was characteristic of the special Soviet forces that conducted them. In Kiev, the planned evacuation had left Soviets enough time to engage in a campaign of sabotage and systematic destruction. Crops were destroyed or spirited away, and public buildings were blown up. Despite intensive measures to stop them, arson and explosions multiplied, and the city's center was devastated by a huge fire. At each new explosion, Ukrainian accounts emphasized the role of the Jewish community in transforming Kiev into a living hell.

These incidents led to discussions between the Wehrmacht occupation authorities and the SS (Schutzstaffel) security factions represented by Paul Blobel, chief of Einsatzgruppe C's Sonderkommando 4a, and his superior, Otto Rasch, who headed the Einsatzgruppe C, one of the mobile killing units that had organized the security operation by locking up all male suspects. On 27 September a crucial meeting took place with the aim of preventing further attacks. It appears that a vast reprisals operation was also planned at this meeting.

MASS MURDER

The next day two thousand posters appeared all over the city, demanding that "All Jews living in

SS soldiers prepare to shoot Jewish prisoners during the Babi Yar massacre, September 1941. GETTY IMAGES

the city and its vicinity must come to the corner of Mel'nikowskaja and Dochturovskaja streets by 8 o'clock tomorrow morning. They are to bring with them documents, valuables and warm clothes." Any civilian who failed to appear would be subject to summary execution.

Some thirty-three thousand Jews who complied with the Nazi demand were escorted to Babi Yar, a natural ravine near the city limits. The method of elimination had been carefully planned. Wehrmacht commandos had supplied significant logistical equipment, including trucks. The Ukrainian militia supervised the victims as they were compelled to disrobe and give up their valuables. They were then led along trails to the ravine, where victims were grabbed by pairs of shooters. One executioner forced the victim to lie face down on the ground with his or her head on the feet of the preceding victim. The second shot the victim in the neck. This highly standardized method presumed that victims would realize their fate only at the last moment. It also reduced the space required for the corpses. On

the evening of the second day, Wehrmacht infantry units exploded the walls of the ravine to cover the corpses.

The men of Sonderkommando 4a had organized the single largest machine-gun killing operation of the whole Holocaust. However, their method had clear limitations. It did not accomplish an exhaustive annihilation of Ukrainian Jews; in addition, mass execution by machine gun placed a heavy burden on the killers' psyches. Finally, it was a secret that could not be kept.

After the German army suffered its first defeats, concern arose among the Nazis about the evidence of genocide. In late 1942 Paul Blobel was placed in charge of exhuming and burning corpses from the mass graves left by the Einsatzgruppen. One of the first such sites he worked on was Babi Yar. Despite Blobel's efforts, no sooner had Kiev been retaken in November 1943, than Soviet authorities inquired about the massacre. Their aims were dubious; they inflated the number of victims to one hundred thousand while concealing the fact that all were Jewish.

When Yevgeny Yevtushenko (b. 1933) wrote his famous poem "Babi Yar" in 1961, put to music by Dmitry Shostakovich (1906–1975), authorities condemned it as a deviation that contaminated the memory of a fascist massacre led against the Soviet republic. The first line of the poem, "No monument stands over Babi Yar" nevertheless led the Soviet government 1966 to contemplate one, which was erected ten years later with no mention that the victims were Jews. This was only rectified after the fall of the Soviet Union, in 1991.

Paul Blobel was sentenced to death at Nuremberg and hanged in 1951. His subordinates were sentenced to heavy jail terms in the mid-1960s. Their trials, which took place in Darmstadt, as well as at Ulm and Frankfurt, brought about among Germans a new awareness of the magnitude of Nazi crimes.

See also **Holocaust; Kiev; Operation Barbarossa.**

BIBLIOGRAPHY

Aly, Götz, and Susanne Heim. *Vordenker der Vernichtung: Auschwitz und die deutschen Pläne für eine neue europäische Ordnung.* Hamburg, Germany, 1990.

Arnold, Klaus Jochen. "Die Eroberung und Behandlung der Stadt Kiew durch ide Wehrmacht im September 1941: Zur Radikalisierung der Besatzungspolitik." *Militärgeschichtliche Mitteilungen* 58, no. 1 (1999): 23–63.

Dempsey, Patrick. *Babi-Yar: A Jewish Catastrophe.* Misham, Pa., 2005.

Gerlach, Christian. *Kalkulierte Morde: Die deutsche Wirtschafts- und Vernichtungspolitik in Weißrußland, 1941 bis 1944.* Hamburg, Germany, 1999.

Krausnick, Helmut, and Hans-Heinrich Wilhelm. *Die Truppedes Weltanschauungskrieges: Die Einsatzgruppen der Sicherheitspolizei und des SD, 1938–1942.* Stuttgart, Germany, 1981.

Pohl, Dieter. "Die Einsatzgruppe C." In *Die Einsatzgruppen in der besetzten Sowjetunion 1941/42: Die Tätigkeits- und Lageberichte des Chefs der Sicherheitspolizei und des SD,* edited by Peter Klein. Berlin, 1997.

Rüß, Hartmut. "Kiev/Babij Jar 1941." In *Orte des Grauens: Verbrechen im Zweiten Weltkrieg,* edited by Gerd R. Ueberschär. Darmstadt, Germany, 2003.

CHRISTIAN INGRAO

BACON, FRANCIS (1909–1992), British painter.

An epigraph that historians of art often use to see and read Francis Bacon's paintings comes from the mouth of the painter himself: If it can be said, why paint it? All of the artist's canvases stage what cannot be put into words. The philosopher and critic Gilles Deleuze notes that Bacon's oeuvre is based on a "logic of sensation," an ordered, often systematic, but also haphazard creative process that brings to the tissue and webbing of the stretched canvas forms and colors that figure monstrous and unnameable events and things. Flayed bodies, avatars of the skinned oxen in the studios of Rembrandt's imagination, are displayed in isolation in garishly colored arenas that could be in the same glance an installation space, the flat surface of a gigantic potter's wheel, or an uncanny "living room" graced with curvilinear walls. The bodies at the center of the canvases of his great creative period (the 1960s and 1970s) exude sensation, where anatomical shapes blend and bleed into the silken fabric of plasma, twisted flesh, or swaths and blobs of pink and rose.

Often these bodies display evidence of biological complexity: from a clump of entwined legs on a table at the center of a diptych there emerges a mandible studded with bicuspids and molars, teeth attesting to different stages of biological development or regression amid forms of flesh that seem to be without integument. Now and again a robust ribcage displays the vertebrae of a spinal column that arches into what could be at once a face and an anus. Rubbery bodies dressed in black shorts or boxers' shoes—immediately recalling pugilists or sturdy peasants in heroic painting—are so bent and contorted that they bear coy resemblance to a painter's palette. In *Study for a Portrait of John Edwards* (1982), a figure seated, shown on the canvas as if it were at once a study for a portrait and the portrait itself, becomes, literally, a standing *cul-de-jatte* (legless person) whose body, a mix of tan and rose, twists into a crown of a Neanderthal's head graced with an elegantly shaped earlobe.

The forms of Bacon's paintings blend into and out of each other, and so also do the paintings themselves in the fifty years of their production.

Three Studies for a Crucifixion. Painting by Francis Bacon, 1962. Solomon R. Guggenheim Museum, New York, USA/Lauros/Giraudon/The Bridgeman Art Library

To describe them as monstrous or fraught with atrocity would not do justice to the pleasures—heady, perverse, polymorphous—they arouse. Insofar as it is scarcely productive to write of "phases" in the evolution of his work for the simple reason that the paintings treat of biogenesis and degeneration (in ways that in literature may have parallels only in Samuel Beckett or Franz Kafka), viewers grasp them through their styles of ocular effect. Haunting portraits mix shock and familiarity when their photographic sources are juxtaposed with the ways the painter literally *defaces* them. The same portraits are often doubled in the paintings themselves, such that a picture or a painted version of the picture of the model, already deformed, becomes the object of the sitter's contemplation. The portraits often recur in triptychs that can be read either as any of the many but simultaneous phases of some kind of disintegration or, in the same glance, "studies" within a highly contrasted field of color that isolates them (such are the *Three Studies for a Crucifixion,* 1962). They can be seen as fields of tension in which geometrical forms—rectangular panels, oval lines—form implicit canvases within the canvases, circles or cubes set upon or enclosing flesh in congress on beds. The mattresses support the action and at once double and mollify the events being depicted,

which might simultaneously include fellatio, copulation, anthropophagia, cunnilingus, ingestion, defecation, such as in *Three Studies for Characters in Bed* (1972). Yet there often exists in these triptychs a "reporter" looking on the scenes, as in the "*Triptych Inspired by T. S. Eliot's Poem 'Sweeney Agonistes'* of 1967, who is not exactly a point of reference for the viewer: holding a telephone and ostensibly "speaking" in silence about the scene, he or she brings forward the fact that what is painted cannot *be spoken.* What we see in the portraits and triptychs is at times a strange geography of solitary life: the triptych of *May-June* (1972) recalls in the sinister panel Auguste Rodin's "thinker" seated on a toilet in a black rectangle of obscure but utterly flat space behind—but also parallel to—the sienna-colored walls of a living room whose beige floor is marked by a broad arrowhead aiming at him. His contorted shape seems to be in harmony with the contractions and inner fluxions of thought as it is shown, arrested, on canvas. In the central panel the face peers across the black space from the other side and, below a pendent lightbulb (the viewer wonders how many of Bacon's figures are needed "to change a lightbulb"), it seems born of itself in the figure seen to the left. The arrowhead gives way to a shadow, pouring onto the floor, that morphs the silhouettes of Batman and Mickey Mouse. And in the dexter panel the figure reposes against a wash-basin whose bent pipe, indicated by the return of the arrow on the beige floor, seems to lead back to the unseen plumbing of the other panels. The observer reporting about or describing this painting and others ventures into unspoken regions of psychic and bodily drive.

Whether in large or small scale Bacon's paintings are crushing and compelling. Crafted to embody nerve and flesh, the paintings are "monstrous" only where they contort inherited shapes, be they those of classical painting from Rembrandt and Velasquez to Van Gogh, or where they seem to be exercises in anatomy gone awry. They are monstrous in their demonstration of the unnameable forces they draw from their viewers.

See also **Painting, Avant-Garde.**

BIBLIOGRAPHY

Primary Sources

Bacon, Francis. *Francis Bacon.* Exhibition catalog, Centre Georges Pompidou. Paris, 1996.

Secondary Sources

Brighton, Andrew. *Francis Bacon.* Princeton, N.J., 2001.

Deleuze, Gilles. *Francis Bacon: The Logic of Sensation.* Translated by Daniel W. Smith and with an afterword by Tom Conley. Minneapolis, Minn., and London, 2003.

Russell, John. *Francis Bacon.* Rev. and updated ed. London, 1993.

TOM CONLEY

BADEN, MAX VON (1867–1929), last chancellor of the German Empire (October 1918–November 1918).

While considered weak and indecisive, the wrong man for the position, Maximilian (known as Max von Baden) was responsible for some of the most consequential political decisions during last days of the empire and set the stage for the Weimar Republic.

Max von Baden was destined for a different world than the one he came to shape. He became heir to the throne in liberal Baden in 1907. He had married Marie Luise of Hanover, royal princess of Great Britain and Ireland and Duchess of Brunswick-Lüneburg in 1900 and was self-consciously a member of the high aristocracy. Due to his disinterest in military matters, he left active military service in 1911. While reentering the military world briefly at the beginning of World War I, he almost instantly resigned and took on the role of the honorary chair of the Baden Red Cross. In this capacity, he became a leading figure in the promotion of the welfare of prisoners of war in Germany and in Allied countries.

The prominent humanitarian role of Max von Baden reinforces his image as a gentlemanly cosmopolitan of considerable moral standing. His comportment rather makes him a quintessential member of the Wilhelmine German elite. His aesthetic inclinations led him to become an avid Wagnerian and also a close correspondent with Houston Stewart Chamberlain (1855–1927), as well as into a free-church pietism that defined his personality. During the war he was part of the elite political culture and avidly corresponded with more moderate elements in the academy, like Alfred Weber (1868–1958); in the German government, like Wilhelm Solf (1862–1936); and the Reichstag, like the liberal deputy Conrad Haußmann (1857–1922). He came out strongly against unrestricted submarine warfare, but was opposed to the peace initiative of the Reichstag in 1917, mostly because he rejected its defeatist tone. Like many others, he exhibited an unbroken sense of German culture and of a distinctly Germanic mission in Europe and the world. This "liberal" world picture neither suffered radical nationalism and militarism, nor certainly an admission of weakness. It was, above all, concerned with preserving honor and with salvaging the moral stature of Germany.

Max von Baden's name came into circulation in consideration for the imperial chancellorship in 1917, a position he also began to pursue actively. He finally became chancellor on 3 October 1918. He entered the chancellorship believing that imperial Germany could yet be saved, but he was rudely undercut when the Supreme Command, Paul von Hindenburg (1847–1934) and Erich Ludendorff (1865–1937), demanded that Max von Baden make the request for an immediate armistice the first and foremost initiative of his chancellorship. This he did after much prevarication in the night of

3–4 October, which set in motion a most remarkable sequence of events.

As chancellor, Max von Baden, who was revolted by the Supreme Command's armistice initiative, came around to recognize that Germany was no longer capable of fighting with any chance of success and that continuing war would invite invasion. Therefore, he insisted on negotiating an armistice at virtually any price in the month-long exchange with U.S. President Woodrow Wilson (1856–1924). In the pursuit of an armistice and peace negotiations, he turned against the Third Supreme Command, which made preparations to prolong war into 1919, and brought about the resignation of Ludendorff, an extraordinary show of determination that brought down military rule. Two days later, on 28 October 1918, the chancellor endorsed and the Reichstag ratified the parliamentarization of government, including the position of the (Prussian) war minister and thus tipped the balance not only between constitutional and extraconstitutional (the monarch, and the military) forces, but also between the states, including his own, and the imperial federation. He declared an amnesty for imprisoned pacifists and communists and appointed an Alsatian as governor of Alsace-Lorraine. Above all, on 9 November 1918, he announced on his own initiative the abdication of the emperor; in renouncing his own chancellorship, he made the leader of the strongest parliamentary party, the Social Democrat Friedrich Ebert (1871–1925), his successor, thus ascertaining the continuation and legitimacy of parliamentary rule.

Max von Baden did none of this on his own, and all of it came too late to save the empire or reverse defeat. Much of it he had not initiated and, indeed, outright opposed when becoming chancellor. But while known to be weak and dithering, he acted with great fortitude. He subsequently suffered the scorn and wrath of the Right. He withdrew from politics and founded Salem School (on his estate in Baden) in 1920 to educate a future German elite dedicated to self-discipline and the spirit of community. He worked in this and other endeavors with his private secretary and confidant throughout this period, Kurt Hahn. The latter went on to found Gordonstoun public school (1934) and Outward Bound (1941), after having been thrown out of Germany by the Nazis both for his Jewishness and his protest against Nazi rule.

See also **Aristocracy; Germany.**

BIBLIOGRAPHY

Baden, Max von. *Erinnerungen und Dokumente.* Edited by Golo Mann and Andreas Burckhardt. Stuttgart, 1968.

Epstein, Klaus. "Wrong Man in the Maelstrom: The Government of Max von Baden." *Review of Politics* 26, no. 2 (1964): 215–43.

Matthias, Erich, and Rudolf Morsey, eds. *Die Regierung des Prinzen Max von Baden.* Düsseldorf, 1962.

MICHAEL GEYER

BADOGLIO, PIETRO (1871–1956), Italian general.

Pietro Badoglio was born in Grazzano Monferrato (now Grazzano Badoglio) in Asti province on 28 September 1871 and died there on 1 November 1956. After completing his lycée studies he attended the Royal Academy of Artillery and Engineering in Turin and in 1892 he received the rank of lieutenant. Badoglio enlisted as a volunteer and served in the Eritrean campaign (1896–1898). Afterward he graduated from the War College and in 1904 was promoted to captain. With this rank he entered the General Staff; he participated in the Italo-Turkish War for the possession of Libya (1911–1912), earning the rank of major for his war record. He was promoted to colonel in February 1915. During World War I he was victorious in the August 1916 battle of Monte Sabotino in the Carso region, for which he became major-general and received the title of Marquis of Sabotino. He was a leading figure in the second battle of the Isonzo and in the famed defeat at Caporetto (24 October 1917), for which he found himself in the middle of a heated controversy that did not, however, prevent him from retaining his post and receiving a decoration. After serving as special military commissioner for the Venezia Giulia region during the Fiume affair (1919–1920), he returned to Rome, where he assumed the position of chief of staff until he resigned in 1921.

In the difficult circumstances that followed the end of World War I and of which Benito Mussolini (1883–1945) took advantage, Badoglio distanced himself from other military leaders in order not to be involved in profascist activities and to be ready to intervene with force against the fascist squads if King Victor Emmanuel III (r. 1900–1946) and the government ordered him to do so. During the fascist regime he accepted Mussolini's offer to head the Italian embassy in Brazil (December 1923–April 1925), which many interpreted as an exile. He later returned to Italy to assume the position of coordinator of the armed forces. Badoglio's malleability, his hostility toward any reform of the military structure, and his vulnerability on the ever-present question of Caporetto were, in Mussolini's opinion, sure guarantees of his total and uncritical subordination. On 4 May 1925 Badoglio thus became chief of staff of the army and simultaneously head of the general staff (until 1940) with vague supervisory powers over the three Armed Forces. In 1926 he was named Field Marshal of Italy. He held various offices, such as governor of Tripolitania and Cirenaica (now Libya) (January 1929–January 1934), High Commissioner for East Africa (November 1935), Viceroy of Ethiopia (1936), and chairman of the National Council for Research (1937–1941). The frequent changes that Mussolini made in high government posts did not harm Badoglio, who always obtained a position, probably because of the support of the king, to whom he had given repeated proofs of his loyalty.

On two occasions he demonstrated his independent professionalism: on the eve of the Ethiopian war (1935–1936) he pointed out the high costs of the operation and proposed a more reasonable plan of preparation; then, before World War II, he wrote a notable report on the state of the Armed Forces in which he denounced the failure to replace and modernize the military matériel lost during the Ethiopian and Spanish wars (1936–1939). He participated in the early phases of World War II, but the differences of opinion between him and Mussolini and the disastrous management of the Greek campaign (1940) led to a rupture and eventually to Badoglio's decision to retire. He returned to the political scene on 25 July 1943 when the king called upon him to replace Mussolini. He constituted an initial government composed of civil servants which—during the forty-five days from the fall of the fascist regime to the armistice with the Allies— attempted a painless disengagement from Germany.

The unrelenting bombardments of the Allies, however, persuaded Badoglio to seek the necessary agreements and to accept surrender. He authorized the armistice, which was signed at Cassibile, near Syracuse, on 3 September 1943 and made public on 8 September. Without leaving any orders for the Armed Forces and without organizing the defense of the capital, Badoglio, along with the king and the highest-ranking military officers, abandoned Rome and transferred to Brindisi, which became the seat of the government in the south. The "flight" of the king and Badoglio, which became the subject of endless debates, was undertaken in order to escape capture and to safeguard the continuity of the state. Beset by the nonmonarchical antifascist forces and by the Committee of National Liberation (Comitato di Liberazione nazionale [CLN]) because of his past and his ambiguous political stances, forced to accept the "long armistice" of 29 September, opposed to the abdication of the king, and having declared war on Germany on 13 October, he nevertheless had to reorganize the government in November 1943. When the leader of the Italian Communist Party (PCI), Palmiro Togliatti (1893–1964), returned from the USSR, he announced the "svolta di Salerno" (Salerno turning point, 31 March 1944), which had been suggested by Joseph Stalin (1879–1953). It opened the way for the first coalition government (22 April 1944) composed of the antifascist parties and led by Badoglio. This government lasted until the liberation of Rome (4 June 1944) and the formation of the first Ivanoe Bonomi (1873–1951) government. Badoglio retired to private life; a senator of the Kingdom since 1919, he was debarred in 1946, but the action was annulled by the Court of Cassation in 1948.

See also **Ethiopia; Italy; Mussolini, Benito; World War I; World War II.**

BIBLIOGRAPHY

Aga-Rossi, Elena. *Una nazione allo sbando. L'armistizio italiano del settembre 1943 e le sue conseguenze.* Bologna, 2003.

Badoglio, Pietra. *Italy in the Second World War: Memories and Documents.* Translated by Muriel Currey. London and New York, 1948; reprint Westport, Conn., 1976. Translation of *L'Italia nella seconda guerra mondiale.* Milan, 1946.

Biagini, Antonello, and Alessandro Gionfrida. *Lo stato maggiore generale tra le due guerre: Verbali delle riunioni presiedute da Badoglio dal 1925 al 1937.* Rome, 1997.

Pieri, Piero, and Giorgio Rochat. *Pietro Badoglio.* Turin, 1974.

Rainero, Roman, ed. *Otto settembre 1943: L'armistizio italiano 40 anni dopo.* Rome, 1985.

Vailati, Vanna. *Badoglio racconta.* Turin, 1955. Memoirs told to a relative.

MARIA TERESA GIUSTI

BAGRATION OPERATION.

The Bagration Operation was a Soviet code name for a multifront strategic offensive operation (23 June–29 August 1944) during World War II on the eastern front that shattered the German Army Group Center. Named after Peter Bagration, a tsarist general of Georgian heritage who fell at Borodino in 1812, and also known as the Byelorussian Operation, it was perhaps the most important of the "ten destructive blows" during 1944 that marked all-out Soviet pursuit of the strategic initiative against Adolf Hitler's Wehrmacht. Despite the recent Allied landing at Normandy, the German army retained over 235 divisions in the East, in comparison with roughly 85 in the West. Even as the Allies slugged their way through French hedgerows, the Bagration Operation initially yielded 57,000 German prisoners for a minor victory parade in Moscow, while continuing to roll back German army defenses in the East by several hundred additional kilometers.

With Leningrad relieved in January 1944, and with nearly half of Ukraine now liberated, Joseph Stalin and his high command began planning in mid-April for a new series of offensive operations that was to ripple across the eastern front from north to south. The intent was to keep Hitler and his generals off-balance, to wrest the remaining occupied Soviet territory from German hands, to exact heavy losses on the Wehrmacht, and to position the Soviet Union favorably in east-central Europe for the closing stages of World War II against Germany. With the opening of a second front in the west now imminent, Stalin resolved to press the advance not only for political purposes, but also to prevent the Germans from shifting troops westward to counter an allied assault on France. Despite unfavorable terrain for mobile operations, the German salient in Byelorussia represented a significant strategic objective, both because of its central location and because of its importance as a military springboard into the heart of Europe.

Although Field Marshal Ernst Busch's Army Group Center lacked significant mobile formations, it occupied defenses in depth that relied heavily on prepared positions and Byelorussia's dense, swampy terrain. Against Busch's (after 28 June, Field Marshal Walter Model's) Third Panzer Army and three field armies, the Soviet intent was to break through German defenses in six sectors, then transform tactical success into operational success. The concept was to pin in the center while destroying German forces on the flanks with encirclement operations at Vitebsk (north) and Bobruysk (south). While these pockets were being reduced and without pause, Soviet armored and mechanized spearheads from both flanks were to close a larger encirclement in the vicinity of Minsk, thereby trapping Army Group Center's main forces east of that city. With assistance from supplementary offensives against German Army Groups North and Northern Ukraine, subsequent Soviet objectives extended to the Vistula, Narew, and Bug Rivers. The plan relied on Soviet air superiority and incorporated extensive partisan attacks against German communications and rear-area objectives. To coordinate the entire complex of front- (army group-) level operations, Stavka, the Headquarters of the Supreme High Command, assigned Marshals Alexander Vasilevsky and Georgy Zhukov to oversee planning and execution.

Soviet preparations were elaborate and highly secret. With Soviet tanks and artillery reserves scattered among many fronts, these and supporting assets had to be concentrated without giving away the plan. Accordingly, the Soviets employed extensive deception and operational security measures, including radio silence, night movements, and rigid camouflage discipline. In consequence, the Soviet high command covertly marshaled against Army Group Center twenty combined arms armies, two tank armies, and five air armies. Altogether, the Soviets counted 2.4 million troops in 172 divisions, 12 corps, 7 fortified regions, and 22 brigades of various types. Their armaments and equipment included 36,400 guns and mortars, 5,200 tanks and self-propelled guns, and 5,300 aircraft. For operational direction, the major front-level command instances were (north to south) the 1st Baltic (Ivan Bagramian), 3rd Byelorussian (Ivan Chernyakhovsky), 2nd Byelorussian (Georgy Zakharov), and the 1st Byelorussian (Konstantin Rokossovsky).

The actual execution of Operation Bagration unfolded over two stages. The first, 23 June–4 July 1944, began with breakthrough attacks rippling across the front from north to south. By 27 June, the 1st Baltic and 3rd Byelorussian Fronts had encircled and annihilated five German divisions at Vitebsk. Meanwhile, the 2nd Byelorussian Front had crossed the Dniester to seize Mogilev on 28 June. Almost simultaneously, the right wing of the 1st Byelorussian Front had encircled and destroyed six German divisions at Bobruysk. On 3 July, advancing mobile groups from the north and south flanking Soviet fronts occupied Minsk, encircling to the east the German Fourth and Ninth Armies (100,000 troops). As Soviet forward detachments pressed ever westward, they managed over the first twelve days of Bagration to reach penetrating depths of 225 to 280 kilometers (140 to 175 miles). These depths, together with the 400-kilometer-wide (250-mile-wide) breach in German defenses, signaled liberation for the majority of Byelorussia. The German defenders, meanwhile, hampered by Hitler's injunction against retreat, by partisan sabotage against railroads, and by the piecemeal commitment of reinforcements, utterly failed to reverse their disintegrating situation.

The second stage of Bagration (5 July–29 August 1944) involved pursuit and liquidation of resisting German pockets. Between 5 and 12 July, the German forces trapped east of Minsk attempted a breakout, but were either destroyed or captured. As the Soviet offensive rolled to the west, the German high command threw in units drawn from the west and other parts of the eastern front, but to no avail. Later coordinated offensives in the north by the 2nd Baltic Front and in the south by the 1st Ukrainian Front only added to German woes. By the end of August, the Red Army had established crossings on the Vistula and the Narew, and had overrun Vilnius and reached the border of East Prussia. German Army Group North was now isolated. But Soviet offensive momentum stopped short of Warsaw, where Stalin apparently chose consciously not to support a rebellion against the German occupiers by Polish patriots beyond his control.

Bagration had enormous military and political-military consequences. It liquidated German Army Group Center and inflicted punishing losses on neighboring groups. It destroyed two thousand German aircraft and twelve German divisions and brigades, while reducing to one-half the strength of an additional fifty divisions. Meanwhile, it opened the way for further Soviet offensives into central Europe and the clearing of the Baltics. The cost to the Soviets was more than 178,000 dead and another half-million wounded. In the realm of military art, Bagration represented a further refinement of breakthrough and encirclement operations and of the ability to insert, after such operations and without pause, mobile groups into the operational depths of enemy defenses.

See also **Kursk, Battle of; Soviet Union; Stalingrad, Battle of; World War II; Zhukov, Georgy.**

BIBLIOGRAPHY

Chaney, Otto Preston. *Zhukov.* Rev. ed. Norman, Okla., 1996.

Erickson, John. *The Road to Berlin.* London, 1983. Reprint, London, 2003.

Glantz, David M., and Jonathan M. House. *When Titans Clashed: How the Red Army Stopped Hitler.* Lawrence, Kans., 1995.

Niepold, Gerd. *The Battle for White Russia: The Destruction of Army Group Centre, June 1944.* Translated by Richard Simpkin. London, 1987.

Vasilevsky, A. M. *A Lifelong Cause.* Translated by Jim Riordan. Moscow, 1981.

Ziemke, Earl F. *Stalingrad to Berlin: The German Defeat in the East.* Washington, D.C., 1968.

BRUCE W. MENNING

BAKER, JOSEPHINE (1906–1975),
African American singer, dancer, and actress.

Josephine Baker took Paris by storm when she first arrived in 1925. She quickly became emblematic of the French fascination with black culture, often

Josephine Baker in the film *Zouzou*, 1934. LE FILMS H. ROUSILLON/THE KOBAL COLLECTION/LIMOT

called negrophilia. She, in turn, was so delighted with the French acceptance of her performances and skin color that she made France her home.

Baker was born in Saint Louis, Missouri, on 3 June 1906, the out-of-wedlock daughter of Carrie McDonald. In a childhood that she remembered as being filled with financial difficulties, Baker was especially disturbed by glimpses she caught of the 1917 East Saint Louis race riot. After a brief marriage at the age of thirteen to a man named Willie Wells, Baker started performing with a number of variety shows. She made her way to New York City, pausing in Philadelphia when she met William Howard Baker, whom she married at the age of fifteen.

Once in New York, Baker started to make a name for herself as the comic relief for chorus lines in Broadway shows such as *Shuffle Along*. In 1925 the first-time producer Caroline Dudley persuaded Baker to join the cast of *La revue nègre,* and in September Baker left for France. Once there, Baker quickly replaced the original leading lady, Maude de Forest, as the star of a show that blended urban scenes of modernity with primitive depictions of savage dances. The public reacted strongly, either loving or hating the show, and Josephine Baker became an instant star.

At first, Baker was praised for her ability to perform the part of a dark savage. She had arrived, after all, in the midst of the Jazz Age. The French had first been introduced to jazz during World War I, when African American jazz bands accompanied the troops. Stunned by the warm welcome they received, many of these musicians chose to stay. The arrival of jazz in France coincided with a fascination for black culture displayed by the artistic avant-garde. This interest, first demonstrated by painters such as Pablo Picasso, became more intense after World War I. Avant-garde artists such as the surrealists reacted to a war marked by technological devastation by turning to what they considered more primitive cultures, which they believed would help to regenerate French society. Baker became a particularly able representative of this French fascination with black culture.

Baker quickly enlisted the help of a number of men, some of whom were also her lovers, in order to market her dark skin to the French. The graphic artist Paul Colin sketched her, often nude or in her famous banana skirt, while Pépito (born Giuseppe) Abatino, an Italian with no fixed profession who haunted Montmartre nightclubs, became her manager. During performances in other parts of Europe and Argentina, Baker became convinced that she far preferred France, where negrophilia made her feel welcome. In five years she learned French, styled herself as an elegant Parisian belle, and trained herself to sing music-hall numbers while dressed in designer gowns. Her transformation did not keep her skin color from being one of her greatest attributes during these early years. Indeed, Baker performed a number of colonial characters in her reviews and films, including a Berber shepherdess and an Indochinese woman. Baker's ability to market race was a great strength. She appeared in films such as *Zouzou* (1934) and *Princesse Tam Tam* (1935), which allowed her to showcase her comedy and singing talents, and even had her own hair product: Bakerfix.

In 1937 Baker married the French millionaire Jean Lion. Although the marriage was short lived, Baker gained French citizenship. Her patriotism became an attribute during World War II. She helped the Resistance in any way she could, joining before most people knew it existed, in 1940. Her prominence made stealth difficult, but her enthusiasm and performances for Free French troops in Africa and the Middle East won her the Croix de Guerre and the Legion of Honor with the rosette of the Resistance.

Baker devoted the last years of her life to adopting twelve children of various origins with the entertainer Joseph Bouillon, whom she had married in 1947. They lived in her chateau at Les Milandes in the Dordogne, and although Bouillon and Baker separated in 1957, they remained on good terms. When Baker lost her chateau to debt in March 1969, she returned to performing. Indeed, it was on 12 April 1975, the morning after a triumphal gala, that Baker died after suffering a cerebral hemorrhage. To this day, her image remains iconic to the French, who continue to celebrate her performances and life.

See also **France; Jazz; Popular Culture.**

BIBLIOGRAPHY

Archer-Straw, Petrine. *Negrophilia: Avant-Garde Paris and Black Culture in the 1920s.* New York, 2000.

Baker, Josephine, and Jo Bouillon. *Josephine.* Translated by Mariana Fitzpatrick. New York, 1977.

Haney, Lynn. *Naked at the Feast: A Biography of Josephine Baker.* New York, 1981.

Rose, Phyllis. *Jazz Cleopatra: Josephine Baker in Her Time.* New York, 1989.

Wood, Ean. *The Josephine Baker Story.* London, 2000.

JENNIFER ANNE BOITTIN

BALDWIN, STANLEY (1867–1947),

British politician and the dominant political figure of the interwar British political scene.

The Conservative Party leader from 1923 to 1937, Baldwin served as British prime minister in 1923, from 1924 to 1929, and from 1935 to 1937. In very marked contrast to the popular support he received upon his retirement as prime minister in May 1937, at the time of his death Baldwin's reputation had been severely tarnished by the "Guilty Men" slur attached to those involved in the "appeasement" of the European dictators in the 1930s.

Baldwin was one of the first British politicians who became a recognizable household figure, both visually and audibly, to the new masselectorate. He skillfully utilized the fledgling media of radio and cinema newsreels to communicate with the increasingly urban electorate. As a consequence, during his fourteen years as Conservative leader he always sustained better relations with the wider electorate than he did with his own party. Baldwin successfully created an illusion of himself among the voters by communicating a sense of "Englishness," provincialism and ordinariness that appealed beyond partisan political lines. Sometimes his appeal for ordinariness backfired, as with the 1929 general election when the campaign slogan of "Safety First" failed to inspire electoral support. As prime minister, Baldwin responded to many of the key crises of the interwar era: the General Strike of 1926 and the abdication crisis of 1936–1937. Although he led his party for fourteen years, his relations with it were strained and he failed to impose his authority and vision upon it. The reason he remained leader for so long was because he chose to, not because his party desired it. At this time there existed no formal rules for disposing of a Conservative Party leader.

After an early period in local Worcestershire politics and involvement with the family business, Baldwin inherited his father's Bewdley House of Commons seat when he ran unopposed in 1908. His early Westminster career suggested little of his potential, but the support of the party leader, Andrew Bonar Law (1858–1923), saw Baldwin climb through the ministerial ranks from 1916 onward. His political break came when he opposed the continuation of the Liberal-Conservative coalition of David Lloyd George (1863–1945) in 1922. His reward was the chancellorship of the exchequer, which gave him vital political exposure.

May 1923, ill health obliged Law to retire as Conservative leader and prime minister and Baldwin was asked to succeed. He foolishly decided to call an unnecessary election over tariff reform that resulted in a short-lived minority Labour government. Baldwin's next administration in 1924–1929 saw the return to the gold standard (April 1925), the Pact of Locarno (December 1925), the General Strike (May 1926), and extensive reforms to local government and social service provision. The General Strike was his high point. He successfully rallied party and middle-class opinion against the strike and forced the collapse of the action within a matter of days. He then encountered difficulties restraining the anti–trade union backlash that many in his party favored, which resulted in the 1927 Trade Disputes Act.

Returned to the opposition position in 1929, Baldwin found his leadership under attack from those who favored tariff reform and who were opposed to self-government for India. Stirring the attacks were the newspaper empires of William Maxwell Aitken, 1st Baron Beaverbrook (1879–1964), and Viscount Edmund Cecil Harmsworth Rothermere (1898–1978). The political-economic crisis of 1931 led to the creation of the National Government. Baldwin sensed it provided an opportunity to exclude Lloyd George and might offer a vehicle for more centrist politics. Willingly he took a subordinate position as lord president under the prime ministership of ex-Labour leader James Ramsay MacDonald (1866–1937).

Baldwin once more became prime minister in June 1935, but virtual civil war among the Conservative Party members over the 1935 India bill again threatened his leadership. The turmoil was initially quelled by the November 1935 general election that enabled Baldwin to secure a mandate for the National Government to commence rearmament. Foreign policy, though, largely dominated this period as various crises—such as the German remilitarization of the Rhineland (March 1936)—again questioned his abilities as leader. Baldwin would most likely have chosen to retire in late 1936 had not the abdication crisis, over the desire of Edward VIII (1894–1972) to marry American divorcee Wallis Simpson (1896–1986), delayed his decision. Many considered Baldwin's handling of this crisis to be his greatest political achievement. He retired to the House of Lords as Lord Bewdley in May 1937. Neville Chamberlain (1869–1940) replaced him as prime minister. Baldwin was a political enigma, who successfully engaged with the middle class but who failed to win the devotion of his political party.

See also **Appeasement; Chamberlain, Neville.**

BIBLIOGRAPHY

Ball, Stuart. *Baldwin and the Conservative Party: The Crisis of 1929–1931.* New Haven, Conn., 1988.

Middlemas, Keith, and John Barnes. *Baldwin: A Biography.* London, 1969.

Williamson, Phillip. *Stanley Baldwin: Conservative Leadership and National Values.* Cambridge, U.K., 1999.

NICK CROWSON

BALFOUR DECLARATION. On 2 November 1917, Arthur J. Balfour, the British Secretary of State for Foreign Affairs, wrote to Lord Rothschild, a leading figure in Anglo-Jewry, and declared that the British government viewed "with favour the establishment in Palestine of a national home for the Jewish people, and will use their best endeavours to facilitate the achievement of this object."

The reasons behind the Balfour Declaration have been hotly debated by historians since its publication. For many years, it was claimed that the declaration derived from a genuine sympathy for the aims of the Zionist movement, which stemmed from a long British tradition of Christian Zionism and philo-Semitism. Following the publication of official documents in the 1960s, however, historians have argued that there were clear political motives behind the government's Zionist policy, though there have been disagreements as to which were of greater significance.

Arguably, the primary purpose of the Balfour Declaration was to foster pro-British sentiment among world Jewry, particularly in the United States and Russia. With so much depending on the financial and military support of the United States, following its entry into the war on 2 April 1917, the British wished to ensure that American society was fully mobilized behind the war effort. In Russia, British officials were desperately trying to fight the pacifism and socialism that had spread since the revolution of February 1917. Due to an erroneous belief in Jewish influence and the misplaced notion that Jews were predominantly Zionist, views that were encouraged by Zionists in London, British policy makers were convinced that a pro-Zionist declaration would help further British objectives in both the United States and Russia. By October the sense of urgency within the government regarding a pro-Zionist statement gathered apace, following incorrect reports that Germany was about to issue its own declaration. Despite some opposition from within the War Cabinet by Lord Curzon, Lord President of the Council, and Edwin Montagu, the Secretary of State for India, the decision was taken on 31 October to issue a declaration. In response to their objections, however, a caveat was included in the text to protect the religious and civil rights of the indigenous population. The Balfour Declaration thus held a dual obligation to support Jewish national aspirations and to protect the interests of the Palestinian Arabs.

Though the propaganda motive was the driving force behind the Balfour Declaration, there was another key reason for publicly supporting Zionism, particularly for Lloyd George. So as to secure the Suez Canal and the path to India after the war, Lloyd George considered it essential that Britain gain control of Palestine. However, the Anglo-French Sykes-Picot agreement of May 1916 had stipulated that the Holy Land would be under international control after the war. In addition, Woodrow Wilson, the president of the increasingly powerful United States, had asserted that he would not accept any annexations at the postwar peace settlement, due to his support for the cause of national self-determination. As a solution, it was considered by Lloyd George and Sir Mark Sykes, the influential war cabinet advisor on the Middle East, that British support for Zionism would help to secure a British protectorate in Palestine after the war. Nevertheless, it is worth noting that a number of those behind the declaration, including Balfour and other members of the Foreign Office, were not interested in using Zionism to this end. Throughout the development of Britain's Zionist policy, the government was heavily influenced by Zionist activists in London, such as Vladimir Jabotinsky, Chaim Weizmann, and Nahum Sokolow. Though some historians have questioned the impact of the Zionists, and the role of Weizmann has been exaggerated, their efforts were of critical significance in prompting and driving British policy.

The effects of the Balfour Declaration were far reaching. By the end of the war, Britain had occupied the entirety of Palestine and was assigned the League of Nations Mandate at the San Remo conference on 24 April 1920. Zionist support for British control of the Holy Land helped to justify the Mandate. As a result, the terms of the Mandate, which were finally confirmed by the League of Nations on 24 July 1922, incorporated the text of the declaration. This commitment to supporting the creation of a Jewish national home remained a key plank of British policy in Palestine for much of the Mandate. Despite tensions between the Zionist leadership and the British authorities, the institutions for eventual Jewish statehood were created during the mandatory period. In this sense, the promise of the declaration was more than fulfilled, and its effects went well beyond the intentions of its makers. However, the attempt to ensure the peaceful coexistence between the Jewish nationalists and Palestinian Arab population failed spectacularly. Almost from the publication of the Balfour Declaration, the Arab leadership feared that the emboldened Zionists were seeking to take the whole country for themselves. That fear never subsided. The Mandate was punctuated with Arab-Jewish violence, culminating in the Arab revolt of 1936–1939, and ultimately war, following the declaration of Israeli independence on 14 May 1948.

See also **Israel; Palestine; Zionism.**

BIBLIOGRAPHY

Friedman, Isaiah. *The Question of Palestine, 1914–1918: British-Jewish-Arab Relations.* Princeton, N.J., 1973. Emphasizes importance of securing British control of Palestine after the war.

Levene, Mark. "The Balfour Declaration: A Case of Mistaken Identity." *English Historical Review* 422 (1992): 54–77. Argues anti-Semitism lay behind the British belief in Jewish power and the Balfour Declaration.

Stein, Leonard. *The Balfour Declaration.* Jerusalem and London, 1961. Classic study of the history of the Balfour Declaration, written before the release of official documents.

Vereté, Mayir. "The Balfour Declaration and Its Makers." *Middle Eastern Studies* 6 (1970): 48–76. Discounts the role of the Zionists in the making of the Balfour Declaration and argues the declaration was to secure a British Palestine.

Vital, David. *Zionism: The Crucial Phase.* Oxford, U.K., 1987. Like Vereté, questions the role of the Zionists and highlights the importance of both imperial and propaganda objectives behind the declaration.

JAMES RENTON

BALKANS. The term *Balkan* has a number of different manifestations that can be roughly grouped into three categories. At its simplest, *Balkan* is a name. A Turkish word meaning "mountain," since its appearance in the fifteenth century, it designated the ancient Haemus (the mountain range crossing Bulgaria from east to west). Then, beginning in the nineteenth century, it was applied to the southeast European peninsula as a whole, and thus became the name of a region. At one point in the nineteenth century it was correctly argued that the peninsula, which had until then been variably designated as "Hellenic," "South-Slavic," "Turkey-in-Europe," and a dozen more different names, was erroneously called "Balkan" because of the geographic mistake assuming that the Balkan mountains represented its northern frontier. By that time, however, the term had gained currency and ascendancy over the earlier used ones. Finally, *Balkan* is used as a personal name (family name in Bulgaria, given name in Turkey).

Balkan is also employed as metaphor. By the beginning of the twentieth century, it became a pejorative, although this was only a gradual process, triggered by the events accompanying the disintegration of the Ottoman Empire and the creation of small, weak, economically backward, and dependent nation-states, which were striving to modernize. The difficulties of this modernization and the accompanying excesses of nationalism made the Balkans a symbol for the aggressive, intolerant, barbarian, savage, semideveloped, semi-civilized, and semi-oriental. The array of stereotypes, although of a relatively recent provenance, added to a deep layer of oppositions between Catholicism and Orthodoxy, Europe and Asia, West and East, and especially between Christianity and Islam. The creation of a specific discourse—*balkanism*—has often shaped attitudes and actions toward the Balkans in the twentieth century. However, *Balkan* can be also used as a positive metaphor, especially in Bulgaria, where the word denotes independence, love of freedom, courage, and dignity.

Balkan is also used as a scholarly category of analysis—a geographic region shaped by specific historical legacies. As a concept, then, the Balkans have a modern—nineteenth or twentieth century—provenance.

GEOGRAPHIC BOUNDARIES

In the early twenty-first century, "the Balkans" most often serves as a synonym for Southeastern Europe. But are they the same category? Southeastern

Europe falls within the range of taxonomical designations such as Eastern Europe, Western Europe, Southern Europe, and Northwestern Europe within the Europe-*cum*-geographical-derivatives family. Most geographers treat it as synonymous with the Balkans. The exception, represented by a minority of German-language academic works and building upon a purist geographical approach, argues that the lands southeast of the Carpathian range form the entity Southeastern Europe, of which the Balkans are but a geographic subregion. Thus, Hungary and occasionally Slovakia would be catalogued as southeast European, but they would not be considered Balkan within this matrix.

"The Balkans," however, as the appellation of a territorial mass, is of the same nature as historical designations like the Iberian and Apennines peninsulas, Scandinavia, or the Alpine and Baltic regions, all following a historical geographic or ethnic name. There is general consensus among geographers about the western, southern, and eastern borders of the Balkans, defined by the Adriatic, Ionian, Mediterranean, Aegean, Marmara, and Black Seas. The northern border is most often considered to begin at the mouth of the river Idria in the Gulf of Trieste, following the southeast foothills of the Julian Alps, and coinciding with the Sava and Danube Rivers. This approach, disregarding history, leaves out Romania (with the exception of Dobrudzha). The best way to define the territorial scope of the Balkans, however, is to employ a combination of geographical, political, historical, cultural, ethnic, religious, and economic criteria. In the narrow sense of the word, and sticking to the Turkish origins of the name *Balkan*, one can posit that the Balkans are this part of Europe, which had been for a long historical period under Ottoman rule or suzerainty and which displays the features of the Ottoman legacy.

More broadly, the Balkans may be regarded as the complex result of the interplay of numerous historical periods, traditions, and legacies, some synchronic or overlapping, others consecutive or completely segregated. They can be classified according to their influence in different spheres of social life—political, economic, demographic, and cultural. One can enumerate many of them: the Roman, the Byzantine, the Ottoman, and the communist are some of the most important political legacies. In the religious sphere, it is the Christian, Muslim, and Judaic traditions with their numerous sects and branches; in the sphere of art and culture, the legacies of pre-Greeks, Greeks, and the numerous ethnic groups that settled the peninsula; in social and demographic terms, the legacies of large and incessant migrations, ethnic diversity, seminomadism, a large and egalitarian agricultural sphere, late urbanization alongside a constant continuity of urban life. For the purposes of this text, the Balkans encompass Albania, Bosnia and Herzegovina, Bulgaria, Croatia, Greece, Macedonia, Romania, Serbia and Montenegro, Slovenia, and, with qualifications, Turkey.

THE BALKAN NATION-STATES

Contrary to received wisdom, the Balkans were not as central to European developments in the twentieth century as they were in the nineteenth, when events in the Ottoman Empire, especially its European possessions, known collectively as the Eastern Question, preoccupied European diplomacy. The states that came to be known as Balkan emerged in the course of the nineteenth and early twentieth centuries: Greece (independence 1830), Serbia (autonomy 1830, independence 1878), Montenegro (independence 1878), Romania (unification 1859, independence 1878), Bulgaria (autonomy 1878, independence 1908), and Albania (independence 1913). The national movements that gave birth to these states were part of the general European drift toward nationalism and espoused programs based on the revival of their medieval states and/or unification of their respective ethnicities.

The frontiers of the new states, however, disregarded these principles without exception and were determined by the interest of the European Great Powers in order to preserve the balance of power and prevent the undue strengthening of any one of the states in the power vacuum created by the shrinking Ottoman Empire. This pattern started with the creation of the small and poor rump Greece, whose inhabitants were less than a quarter of the empire's Greeks and that determined their irredenta—the program of unifying the unredeemed territories inhabited by Greeks—until the 1920s. It was particularly flagrant at the outcome of the Eastern Crisis of 1875–1878, when autonomous Bulgaria, comprising the territories of the

Italian troops in the streets of Tirana, Albania, April 1939. Italian troops occupied Albania in the spring of 1939 and retained control until they were expelled by Albanian resistance groups backed by Allied forces. ©BETTMANN/CORBIS

Bulgarian ethno-religious community, was created by the Treaty of San-Stefano (March 1878). Only three months later the newly formed state was partitioned, with only one-third receiving autonomy, with the sole rationale being that too big a state, suspected to be a Russian client, would upset the balance of power on the peninsula and on the Continent. The result was another troubled irredenta until World War II. Likewise, the occupation of Bosnia by Austria-Hungary (1878) and its annexation (1908) fed the Serbian irredenta, confined to the small Belgrade region.

This is not to pass value judgments about the positive or negative outcome of the way the map of the Balkans was redrawn. Ironically, the creation of Albania could have remained an unrealized national aspiration had it not been for the confluence of Italian and Austrian interests to forestall Serbian expansion to the Adriatic. One can generalize, however, that the particular shape the Balkans took in the

nineteenth century and the roots of inter-Balkan relations were to a large extent, if not predominantly, due to the central position that these states occupied in European affairs. By the early twentieth century the relative importance of the Eastern Question had decreased as other areas of conflict had come to the fore—the Far East, Africa, Latin America—and Europe itself was divided into two hostile camps.

BALKAN WARS AND WORLD WAR I

It is in these circumstances that four of the Balkan nation-states—Greece, Bulgaria, Serbia, and Montenegro—whose expansion was naturally sought at the expense of Macedonia and Thrace, territories still controlled by the Ottomans, entered into an alliance in 1912, known as the Second Balkan League (the First Balkan League dated from the 1860s). Only Romania stayed out, since its unification drive was directed to the north, to the heavily Romanian-populated Habsburg region of Transylvania.

The four allies declared war on the Ottoman Empire (October 1912), and at the Treaty of London (May 1913) the Ottoman Empire ceded all of its territory in Europe with the exception of Istanbul's small hinterland. The disagreements over the division of the newly acquired territories led to the Second Balkan War (1913), a fratricidal conflict in which Bulgaria was catastrophically vanquished by its former allies, now allied with Romania and the Ottomans, and remained, for the next three decades, an embittered revanchist, seeking to retrieve its losses. The cruelties of these wars, in a European climate that believed in the stability of the Belle Epoque, gave rise to the stereotypical images of a particularly harsh and savage region. These persisted, no matter that West European barbarities largely outnumbered and outdid Balkan atrocities only a few years later, during World War I.

So persistent are these stereotypes that despite definitive scholarly verdicts about the roots and causes of World War I, the assassination of Archduke Francis Ferdinand (1863–1914) in Sarajevo (June 1914) by the young Serb Bosnian nationalist Gavrilo Princip (1894–1918) is still often evoked as the principal reason for the global imperialistic conflagration. Accordingly, the sobriquet "powder keg of Europe," coined at that time, can still be heard about the Balkans. In fact, all Balkan states tried to avoid the Great War. It was imposed by Austria-Hungary on a pliant Serbia. Bulgaria committed to the Central Powers only after the Allied failures at the Dardanelles and Gallipoli, in the hope of reversing the humiliation from the Balkan Wars, and occupied Macedonia. Turkey was virtually coaxed to enter the war on Germany's side, and Romania cautiously joined the Allies in 1916. The Albanians had little choice and were partitioned between the warring parties, and the Greeks entered the war on 27 June 1917, even after the United States, which had joined the conflict in April. The Balkans never became a major theater of operation, although the war proved devastating for their populations and their economies.

INTERWAR DEVELOPMENTS AND WORLD WAR II

The end of World War I saw the disintegration of the Habsburg and Romanov empires and the final collapse of the Ottoman. The secession of the Balkan nation-states, however, was already completed during the nineteenth century, and the retreat of the Ottomans from Europe had ended with the Balkan Wars. The formation of the Turkish Republic, therefore, did not affect national frontiers in the Balkans, although it had enormous repercussions for the Middle East. But the huge population exchanges, sanctioned by the Treaty of Lausanne (1923), had deep-reaching legal and demographic consequences in the Balkans. The great expansion of two Balkan states—Serbia and Romania—was effectuated at the expense of Austria-Hungary and Russia. Romania annexed Transylvania (from Hungary), Bukovina (from Austria), and Bessarabia (from Russia). Serbia became the nucleus of the Kingdom of Serbs, Croats, and Slovenes (Yugoslavia after 1929), with acquisitions from Austria and Hungary.

The 1920s marked the diplomatic ascendancy of France and later of Italy in the Balkans. The Great Depression (1919–1933), however, paved the way first for Germany's economic penetration and then political predominance. In the early 1930s the Balkan states made an attempt at a regional alliance, which was meant to withstand great-power pressures. The 1934 Balkan Entente (an alliance between Greece, Yugoslavia, Romania, and Turkey) proved, however, limited and even futile in the face of German and Italian ascendancy, Bulgarian revisionism, and the international collapse of the principle of collective security.

Despite attempts at staying out of the looming conflagration, all Balkan countries with the exception of Turkey were pulled into World War II. Bulgaria and Romania became German satellites and strove to fulfill their irredentist programs. Bulgaria occupied Macedonia and Thrace, although it refused to send troops to the eastern front. Romania, in an attempt to regain Bessarabia, which it had lost to the Soviets in 1940, joined the German army against the Soviet Union. Albania was occupied by Benito Mussolini (1883–1945) as early as 1939, and Yugoslavia and Greece were overrun by Adolf Hitler (1889–1945) in 1941. Both Yugoslavia and Greece staged a remarkable (mostly communist-led) resistance against a particularly brutal occupation, although the fractured character of their resistance movements fed the Greek Civil War (until 1949) and haunted Yugoslavia during its violent breakup in the 1990s.

FROM THE COLD WAR TO THE DISINTEGRATION OF YUGOSLAVIA

After World War II the Balkans were divided along Cold War lines, agreed upon by Winston Churchill (1871–1947) and Joseph Stalin (1879–1953) in the famous percentage deal in Moscow (October 1944). Greece and Turkey became part of the Western alliance, the rest became part of communist Eastern Europe. But even in this respect, the Balkans proved sui generis. Greece and Turkey, both members of NATO, came several times to the brink of war with each other. Yugoslavia under Josip Broz Tito (1892–1980) maneuvered deftly between World Wars I and II and played at being at the helm of a third. Bulgaria was the Soviet Union's most faithful ally, but, ironically, it was politically more liberal than the anti-Russian Nicolae Ceaușescu's (1918–1989) Romania. Albania broke with the Soviet bloc and found protection from China. Most remarkably, the designation *Balkan*, not to speak of the negative stereotypes, all but disappeared, submerged in the bipolar Cold War rhetoric.

The stereotypes resurfaced again in the course of a twofold process that took place after 1989. The first was the disintegration of the socialist system and the issue of European Union expansion to the east. The strategy and costs of this expansion, and the potential competition between the candidates, brought to the fore the differential treat-ment of Eastern Europe's subregions. The Central European ideology of the 1980s (with Poland, Hungary, and Czechoslovakia at its center), which initially was only anti-Soviet, by the 1990s evoked the Balkans as its constituting other. This seemed to be mostly motivated by the initial tendency of the West to treat non-Soviet Eastern Europe as a group, a tendency that slowed Central Europe's prospects for integration. Although the Central European ideology was rhetorically successful, it has remarkably and ironically all but disappeared since its goals were achieved.

The second coinciding process was Yugoslavia's bloody disintegration. Despite the fact that the wars of succession were confined entirely to the territory of the former Yugoslavia, and none of the other Balkan countries was ever involved, the world insisted on naming this a "Balkan" conflict and even the "Third Balkan War." To a great extent this was the result of an attempt not to get involved, to

A Muslim woman clears rubble inside a bombed building, Turanje, Croatia, 1994. Violence between ethnic groups during the breakup of Yugoslavia reinvigorated the stereotype of the Balkans as a region of unresolvable political tensions, although other nations in the region were not involved. ©PETER TURNLEY/CORBIS

restrict the problems to Europe's southeastern corner. Rhetorically, it was based on a number of cultural arguments, particularly the application of the "clash of civilizations" theory positing that henceforth international conflicts would occur not so much between states and ideologies but rather along cultural, especially religious, fault lines. It was the time of the blooming of *balkanism,* a discursive paradigm that described the region as essentially different from the rest of Europe and thus legitimized a policy of relative noninvolvement and isolation.

THE END OF THE BALKANS?

Extending a protective arm around the old centers of the Habsburg Empire after 1989, the West, motivated in part by sentiment, followed neatly the new trench lines outlined by the "clash of civilizations" theory that drew a border not only between Christianity and Islam but also between Eastern (Orthodox) Christianity and Western (Catholic and Protestant) Christianity. This led to predictions that beyond Central Europe "Byzantine Europe" would be left out, too close to Russia, too poor and disorderly to jeopardize "Fortress Europa."

However, the differing American and European visions of NATO produced a series of unintended consequences. The year 1997 saw the beginning of NATO expansion, but since 1989 the question of the raison d'être of the alliance never ceased to be high on both the European and U.S. foreign policy agenda, so much so that in Europe there were plans to build alternative security systems confined only to the Continent and disband NATO. Until 1999 the international community channeled its pressure on and involvement in Yugoslavia exclusively through the United Nations. The 1999 NATO bombing of Yugoslavia, effectively carried out by the United States, was motivated by a host of political and moral considerations, not least among them the desire to revive and make relevant the last organization in which the United States played a leading role in Europe. Whatever the order of motivations, the bombing clearly had unintended consequences. Before the Kosovo war, the dominant paradigm applied to the Balkans translated into the practical ghettoization of the region. The European Union's visa regime absolved Central Europe but not the rest of Eastern Europe and the Balkans and put restrictions on the movement of their populations. This was *balkanism* in action.

But the rhetorical legitimation of 1999—bombing in the service of universal human rights—effectively brought the Balkans back into the sphere of Western politics, and the bombing and its aftermath brought the Europeans and Americans deeper and, it seems, inextricably into involvement with the Balkans. They are running two (Bosnia and Kosovo) and arguably four (with Macedonia and Albania) protectorates. There is also, for the first time, a significant lobby among Eurocrats who believe that it is in Europe's greater interest to bring the Balkans in, instead of ghettoizing them. The unintended result was the early suspension of the visa barriers for Bulgaria and Romania and, more importantly,

the curious but predictable restraining of the balkanist rhetoric: it no longer served power politics, although it is there, conveniently submerged but readily at hand. In the meantime, NATO, which was founded in 1949, and during the Cold War added Greece and Turkey to its ranks (1952), has admitted as full members Bulgaria, Romania, and Slovenia (2004). Albania, Macedonia, and Croatia are partners in NATO's Membership Action Plan. Slovenia is already part of the European Union (2004), the second Balkan state after Greece (1981), and Bulgaria and Romania are scheduled to join in 2007. Turkey, a long-term applicant, does not yet have a firm accession date, and Croatia applied in 2003.

It seems that one can tentatively speak of the end of the Balkans-as-metaphor. The concept is retreating from politics and relegated to nomenclature and scholarship.

See also **Albania; Bosnia-Herzegovina; Bulgaria; Croatia; Greece; Kosovo; Macedonia; Montenegro; Romania; Serbia; Slovenia; Turkey; Yugoslavia.**

BIBLIOGRAPHY

Clogg, Richard. *A Concise History of Greece.* Cambridge, U.K., and New York, 1992.

Crampton, R. J. *A Concise History of Bulgaria.* Cambridge, U.K., and New York, 1997.

———. *The Balkans since the Second World War.* New York, 2002.

Fischer-Galati, Stephen. *Twentieth Century Rumania.* 1970. 2d ed. New York, 1991.

Jelavich, Barbara. *History of the Balkans.* 2 vols. Cambridge, U.K., and New York, 1983.

Lampe, John R. *Yugoslavia as History: Twice There Was a Country.* Cambridge, U.K., and New York, 1996.

Lampe, John R., and Marvin R. Jackson. *Balkan Economic History, 1550–1950: From Imperial Borderlands to Developing Nations.* Bloomington, Ind., 1982.

Mazower, Mark. *The Balkans: A Short History.* New York, 2000.

Pavlowitch, Stevan K. *A History of the Balkans, 1804–1945.* London and New York, 1999.

Stavrianos, L. S. *The Balkans since 1453.* 1958. New York, 2000.

Stoianovich, Traian. *Balkan Worlds: The First and the Last Europe.* Armonk, N.Y., 1994.

Sugar, Peter F., ed. *Eastern European Nationalism in the Twentieth Century*. Lanham, Md., 1995.

Todorova, Maria. *Imagining the Balkans*. New York, 1997.

Todorova, Maria, ed. *Balkan Identities: Nation and Memory*. Washington Square, N.Y., 2004.

Vickers, Miranda. *The Albanians: A Modern History*. London and New York, 1995.

Woodward, Susan L. *Balkan Tragedy: Chaos and Dissolution after the Cold War*. Washington, D.C., 1995.

MARIA TODOROVA

BALL, HUGO (1886–1927), German writer and performer, leading figure in the Dada movement.

After studying German literature, history, and philosophy at the universities of Munich and Heidelberg, Hugo Ball enrolled at the Max Reinhardt (1873–1943) school for stage design and acting at the Deutsches Theater in Berlin. In 1911, he worked briefly at the municipal theater in Plauen before becoming the artistic director of the Munich Kammerspiele in 1912. He also wrote provocative poems, some in collaboration with his friend Hans Leybold, which were published in the expressionist periodicals *Die Aktion* and *Revolution*. In 1913, Ball was charged with obscenity for his violent poem "Der Henker" (The Hangman), but later acquitted on account of its "unintelligibility." In addition to writing, acting, and directing, he was interested in music, dance, and the visual arts. His plans to form with Wassily Kandinsky (1866–1944) an experimental, multimedia theater in Munich were interrupted by the beginning of World War I. Ball volunteered to serve in the German army but was rejected for health reasons. Having briefly witnessed trench warfare action in Belgium, he reacted in horror and became a pacifist, organizing expressionist and antiwar readings in Berlin. In May 1915, he emigrated with the singer and cabaret artist Emmy Hennings (1885–1948), whom he later married, to Zurich.

Ball became a leading figure in the Dada movement. On 5 February 1916, he and Hennings formed the Cabaret Voltaire, which became the main public platform of the Zurich Dada group. Alongside Jean Arp (or Hans Arp), Richard Huelsenbeck, Marcel Janco, and Tristan Tzara, Ball and Hennings engaged in anarchic performances of music and poetry, including deafening recitals of "bruitist" (noise) and "simultaneous" poems. Ball is also credited with inventing the term *Dada,* which makes its first appearance in his diary on 18 April 1916. This word was found by randomly leafing through a dictionary, and its apparent meaninglessness, or rather, its openness to a variety of meanings, testifies to the spontaneity and provocative nihilism of the group. In June 1916, Ball edited one issue of the periodical *Cabaret Voltaire,* which contained work by the Zurich Dadas and, among others, Guillaume Apollinaire, Blaise Cendrars, Kandinsky, Filippo Tommaso Marinetti, Amedeo Modigliani, and Pablo Picasso. In a preface dated 15 May 1916, Ball publicly introduced the term *Dada* to describe the stylistic pluralism and cultural internationalism of artists united against war and nationalism.

Ball's reputation as a poet rests largely on his astonishing *Lautgedichte* (sound poems), some of which he performed at a Dada soirée on 14 July 1916 (Bastille Day). These poems, which include "Karawane" (Caravan) and "gadji beri bimba," were composed from invented words that have no obvious referential meaning, but create an intense emotional power. He intended these poems in part as a protest against the "misuse" of language during the war, and the way in which the languages of art and culture had been perverted in the West to uphold dangerous values and murderous societies. Wearing an exotic costume made of cardboard, with a giant collar suggesting wings, and a cylindrical shaman's hat, Ball recited the sound poems in the style of "priestly lamentations." As a self-styled "magic bishop," Ball sought to convey in language "primeval strata" of experience untouched by reason or logic. Deliberately undermining "meaning," his performance was an attempt to reintegrate body and mind, the physical and the spiritual. For Ball, Dada's mix of "buffoonery and requiem mass" was meant to become a therapeutic creativity with which to heal modernity.

Following a nervous breakdown, Ball broke with Dada in the summer of 1916 and moved to the artist colony of Ascona, and later settled in

Agnuzzo. He wrote many political articles for *Die Freie Zeitung* in Berne between September 1917 and February 1920, and continued to work on several books, including a sharp indictment of the German intellectual tradition from Martin Luther to the twentieth century, and the prose work *Tenderenda*, which is written in a multilayered experimental style. Disappointed with the outcome of the revolution in Germany in 1918–1919, he turned away from politics and his stance became increasingly religious. In 1920, he rejoined the Catholic Church and subsequently wrote on Byzantine Christianity and on the Reformation. In 1924, he stayed in Rome to study psychoanalysis, in particular the works of Carl Gustav Jung. In 1927, shortly before his death, he published *Flight Out of Time*, his autobiography in the form of a diary, which offers much information on Dada. His home city of Pirmasens has established a Hugo Ball archive and publishes, since 1977, an annual almanac devoted to his life and work. Wallstein Verlag is publishing a critical edition of his writings; the first volume appeared in 2003. While Ball's Dada texts and activities continue to attract scholarly attention, recent research has highlighted the wide (and perhaps eclectic) range of his interests across artistic and intellectual boundaries, and suggested ways in which Ball's self-transformations in his life and work betray a male subjectivity attempting to respond to the challenges of modernity.

See also **Apollinaire, Guillaume; Arp, Jean; Cabaret; Dada; Expressionism; Kandinsky, Wassily; Marinetti, F. T.; Picasso, Pablo; Tzara, Tristan.**

BIBLIOGRAPHY

Bähr, Hans-Joachim. *Die Funktion des Theaters im Leben Hugo Balls.* Frankfurt, 1982.

Ball-Hemmings, Emmy. *Hugo Ball: Sein Leben in Briefen und Gedichten.* Berlin, 1930.

———. *Hugo Balls Weg zu Gott: Ein Buch der Erinnerung.* Munich, 1931.

Egger, Eugen. *Hugo Ball: Ein Weg aus dem Chaos.* Olten, Switzerland, 1951.

Last, Rex W. *German Dadaist Literature: Kurt Schwitters, Hugo Ball, Hans Arp.* New York, 1973.

Mann, Philip. *Hugo Ball: An Intellectual Biography.* London, 1987.

Schmidt, Christoph. *Die Apokalypse des Subjekts: Ästhetische Subjektivität und politische Theologie bei Hugo Ball.* Bielefeld, Germany, 2003.

Stein, Gerd. *Die Inflation der Sprache: Dadaistische Rebellion und mystische Versenkung bei Hugo Ball.* Frankfurt, 1975.

Steinbrenner, Manfred. *"Flucht aus der Zeit?": Anarchismus, Kulturkritik, und christliche Mystik—Hugo Balls "Konversionen."* Frankfurt, 1985.

Steinke, Gerhardt Edward. *The Life and Work of Hugo Ball: Founder of Dadaism.* The Hague, Netherlands, 1967.

Süllwold, Erika. *Das gezeichnete und das ausgezeichnete Subjekt: Kritik der Moderne bei Emmy Hennings und Hugo Ball.* Stuttgart, Germany, 1999.

Teubner, Ernst. *Hugo Ball: Eine Bibliographie.* Mainz, Germany, 1992.

Teubner, Ernst, ed. *Hugo Ball (1886–1986): Leben und Werk.* Berlin, 1986. Exhibition catalog.

Wacker, Bernd, ed. *Dionysius DADA Areopagita: Hugo Ball und die Kritik der Moderne.* Paderborn, Germany, 1996.

White, Erdmunde Wenzel. *The Magic Bishop: Hugo Ball, Dada Poet.* Columbia, S.C., 1998.

Wild, Peter. *Hugo Ball, Tenderenda der Phantast: Untersuchungen zu Sprache und Stil.* Bonn, Germany, 1987.

Zehetner, Cornelius. *Hugo Ball: Portrait einer Philosophie.* Vienna, 2000.

ANDREAS KRAMER

BALTIC STATES. *See* Estonia; Latvia; Lithuania.

BANKING. Throughout the twentieth century, banks have played a major role in Europe's economy, society, and politics. As companies banks have counted among the largest, while as financial intermediaries they have contributed decisively, though sometimes controversially, to economic development. Yet banking has displayed different features in each European country. For if a broad definition of a bank can easily be provided (taking deposits on the one hand and granting credit on the other), there have been multiple variations on this theme, in terms of type of banking activity (commercial or investment bank), ownership (private, joint stock, or state-owned), size (small, medium-size, large), and geographical expansion (local, regional, national, multinational). The combination of these different characteristics has varied between countries, contributing to their distinctive banking architecture, as well as over time.

By 1914 national banking systems had adopted their distinctive features, which were not entirely to disappear with the transformations of financial activities occurring in the course of the twentieth century, especially from the 1960s. Despite national idiosyncrasies, two main models have been dominant across Europe: the British model of deposit banking complemented by a more active capital market, and the German model of universal banking, with France combining some elements of the two. This entry will thus mainly concentrate on these three cases, Europe's three leading economies, while paying attention, when necessary, to other national experiences.

THE RISE OF THE BIG BANKS

By the eve of the First World War, the effects of the banking revolution of the nineteenth century—the emergence of the large joint-stock bank—were being fully felt, though in different degrees, in all European countries. The phenomenon was most pronounced in England, where twelve banks, based in London with a national or regional network of branches, controlled two-thirds of the country's deposits. The three largest—Lloyds, Midland, and Westminster—were among the world's top five, together with Crédit Lyonnais of France and Deutsche Bank of Germany (see table 1). Such powerful institutions were the result of an amalgamation movement starting in the mid-nineteenth century and leading to the complete disappearance of the private country banks and of most regional banks. The level of concentration was also high in France, with more than half of the resources of the registered banks in the hands of the four largest. Unlike England, however, over two thousand local banks survived in France, and although their importance cannot be assessed quantitatively, as they did not publish their balance sheet, recent historical research has revealed that they played a

major role in supporting small and medium-size enterprises. The situation was still different in Germany, where the nine big Berlin banks collected barely 12 percent of the country's banking resources. There were still several hundred local and regional joint-stock banks, whose joint resources were more or less equal to those of the big banks, as well as a good thousand private banks that were not included in the Reichsbank's statistics. But the bulk of the deposits lay elsewhere: almost 75 percent was in the hands of savings banks, mortgage banks, banking cooperatives, and other specialized banks. Alongside the big banks, old established private banks—the *haute banque,* to use the evocative French terminology—had managed to retain an influential position, especially in international finance, thanks to their prestige and networks of relationships. Their position was particularly strong in London, then the world's financial center, less so in Paris and Berlin.

NATIONAL BANKING SYSTEMS

The strength of the London merchant banks—the English version of the *haute banque,* with such famous names as N. M. Rothschild, Baring Brothers, Morgan Grenfell, Schroders, or Kleinwort—was partly the result of the highly specialized nature of the English banking system. While German banks were specialized by type of customer (large companies for the big banks, small and medium-size firms for the local and regional banks, and so on), the English banking system was specialized by functions. However, in all countries central banks were starting to establish their role as lenders of last resort in order to ensure the stability of the financial system.

In Britain banking basically meant deposit banking. The golden rule of deposit banks, or clearing banks as they are usually called, was not to tie up in long-term investments the money deposited with them on a short-term basis. Assets thus had to be as liquid as possible, with self-liquidating bills of exchange being especially popular. Investments were in consols—the British national debt—or in other highly liquid securities, not in industrial securities; advances were granted on a short-term basis, whether in the form of loans (granted for a fixed sum and for a given period) or of overdrafts (which customers could use as they required, up to a limit agreed upon beforehand with the bank). For their long-term

TABLE 1

The fifteen largest commercial banks in Europe in 1913	
	Total assets (£ millions)
Crédit Lyonnais (France)	113
Deutsche Bank (Germany)	112
Midland Bank (United Kingdom)	109
Lloyds Bank (United Kingdom)	107
Westminster Bank (United Kingdom)	104
Société Générale (France)	95
Comptoir National d'Escompte de Paris (France)	75
National Provincial Bank (United Kingdom)	74
Dresdner Bank (Germany)	72
Société Générale de Belgique (Belgium)	72
Barclays Bank (United Kingdom)	66
Disconto-Gesellschaft (Germany)	58
Parr's Bank (United Kingdom)	52
Credit-Anstalt (Austria)	50
Union of London and Smiths Bank (United Kingdom)	49

requirements, companies could raise money on the capital markets, traditionally more developed than in continental Europe, though clearing banks did not issue securities on behalf of customers, a task left to company promoters.

International credit was provided by the merchant banks that accepted, or upon which were directly drawn, bills of exchange, generally for three months, which constituted the main instrument for financing international trade. These bills were negotiable instruments, and well before they reached their maturity dates they were discounted by other specialized banking firms, the discount houses, which then resold them to commercial banks. Merchant banks were also specialized in the most prestigious financial activity of the day, issuing loans on behalf of foreign companies and governments. In addition to being specialized by functions, banking was divided between international and national financial activities. Though more involved in the latter, the clearing banks provided the cash credit, in the form of day-to-day loans, to discount houses that discounted the bills of exchange accepted by the merchant banks, thus making the whole wheel of international trade financing turn. Finally, the overseas banks were English banks, insofar as their capital and management were English and their registered office was usually in London, but their sphere of activity was in the British Empire or abroad. Their goal was to finance trade with the regions in which they were established and to obtain exchange facilities.

Among them were the Hong Kong and Shanghai Banking Corporation, the London and River Plate Bank, the Standard Bank of South Africa, and several others, all independent companies and not subsidiaries of big commercial banks.

In Germany, by contrast, universal banks undertook all types of operations: they collected deposits, granted short-term commercial credit as well as medium- and long-term industrial credit, discounted bills of exchange, and acted as brokers and as issuing houses. Bankers were also massively represented on the boards of other, especially industrial, companies. The German big banks were thus involved in both national industrial financing and large international banking and financial transactions, especially in issuing foreign loans. The French banking system is usually seen as standing roughly halfway between the British and German models. On the one hand, the French big commercial banks followed the principles of the English joint-stock banks, while more risky industrial financing was left to another type of bank, the *banque d'affaires* (banks akin to investment banks, mainly dealing in securities and holding controlling stakes in other companies), whose most famous representative was the Banque de Paris et des Pays-Bas. Overseas banks were also part of the German and French banking systems, though they were less numerous and had smaller networks of foreign branches than their British counterparts and, unlike the latter, were often subsidiaries of the large commercial banks. Elsewhere, Belgium, Switzerland, Italy, and Austria were close to the German model, Holland and the Scandinavian countries to the British one.

BANKING AND ECONOMIC DEVELOPMENT

There have been intense debates about the respective merits of these systems, in the first place the British and the German ones, particularly with respect to their contribution to economic development. A long historiographical tradition holds that the financial sector contributed to Britain's relative economic decline in the three or four decades before the First World War. British banks have been criticized for their reluctance to provide long-term industrial finance and the London capital market for directing overseas funds that could have been more beneficially invested in the British economy. A similar criticism has been directed at the French banks, especially as far as their preference for foreign investments is concerned. Such criticisms are not surprising given that Britain and France were the two largest capital exporters (with respectively 18.3 and 8.7 billion dollars of assets in foreign countries in 1913 out of a total of 44 billion dollars, as against 5.6 billion for Germany) and experienced slower economic growth than Germany during the three decades preceding the First World War. The German banking system, for its part, has often been seen as working in the long-term interest of the manufacturing industry, while some authors, most famously Rudolf Hilferding in *Das Finanzkapital,* published in 1910, have stressed the power of the banks, in particular the control they were in a position to exert over industry and, ultimately, over the entire German economy.

Historical evidence reveals a picture often at odds with such analyses. French banks have been absolved from the sin of "failing" industry. Recent research has shown that British banks were more involved in industrial finance than they had been credited for and that large industrial companies were able to make effective use of the flexibility of the capital markets. And German industrial companies have been shown to have been far more independent from the banks than Hilferding and his followers had assumed. As for capital exports, they barely affected the economies of centrally located countries. In the end, finance held a stronger position in Britain, as a result of the international position of the City of London, than in Germany, where the banks' power and prestige ultimately lay in their support of the country's industrialization.

THE FIRST WORLD WAR AND ITS AFTERMATH

Banking prospers in times of peace, not in times of war. Indeed, for most bankers and financiers the First World War meant a marked decrease in their activities owing to disruptions in the trading of goods, services, and capital among countries, as well as to growing state intervention in economic and financial affairs. A large number of services traditionally offered by the banks were henceforth superfluous, like commercial credit or issuing syndicates, since governments at war tend to pay companies up front or borrow directly from savers. The London merchant banks, cornerstone of the international credit mechanism prior to 1914,

suffered from the slump in their accepting and issuing businesses, while the commercial banks had to adjust to the part played from then on by financing the growing needs of the state: the assets of all big European banks mainly comprised Treasury bonds and similar stocks at that time.

However, despite the disruptions caused by war and monetary disorders in the early 1920s, the trend toward the strengthening of the large joint-stock banks and increased banking concentration continued during the 1920s. This trend was particularly strong in Britain, where the amalgamation movement reached its peak in 1918, before the war was over. Five mergers took place in that year, involving the country's ten largest banks and resulting in the formation of five huge banks that immediately came to be known as the "Big Five"—Barclays, Lloyds, Midland, National Provincial, and Westminster—and controlled 90 percent of the country's deposits. The "Big Five" emerged as the largest banks in the world, far ahead of their German and French counterparts (in 1929 the largest British bank was nearly four times larger than the largest German or French one), which encountered more difficulties in the early postwar years. French banks suffered from the devaluation of the franc and the absence of significant mergers. As for German banks, even though they expanded by taking over provincial banks, they were weakened by the devastation of war and hyperinflation: in 1924 the commercial banks' capital was valued at 30 percent of its prewar gold value, their assets at only 21 percent. However, they strengthened their position within the German banking system, with their share of the total assets of all German banks reaching 33 percent in 1929, a level not to be surpassed until the 1980s.

Business conditions somewhat altered in the 1920s. In Britain the clearing banks, with their enormous financial means, increasingly competed with the merchant banks in the accepting and issuing activities. Moreover, the former became involved in long-term industrial finance, though this policy was somewhat forced upon them rather than deliberately chosen. During the boom of 1919–1920 they granted large overdrafts, particularly to heavy industry, which with the downturn of the 1920s often had to be converted into frozen loans and nursed for the remainder of the period.

In France the big banks had to face growing competition from the main provincial banks (Crédit du Nord, Société Nancéienne de Crédit, and others). And as Germany became a capital-importing country (having been stripped of its foreign assets and required to pay reparations by the Treaty of Versailles), the big banks and the leading private banks played an active role in these transfers, borrowing on a short-term basis abroad and then lending on a long-term basis to German companies, a risky strategy in the event of the influx of foreign capital coming to a stop. Furthermore, they had to deal with competition from foreign banks, especially American, which granted credit directly to German companies and took charge of issuing securities on their behalf on the New York market.

THE BANKING CRISIS OF THE 1930S

The Wall Street crash of October 1929 and the ensuing slump soon affected banking. The big Italian banks—Banca Commerciale Italiana, Banca di Roma, and Credito Italiano—went through serious difficulties in 1930 and were rescued in secrecy by the Bank of Italy and the Italian government, which undertook a thorough transformation of the banking system, leading, in particular, to the nationalization of the banks and the end of universal banking. In May 1931 the Credit-Anstalt in Vienna went bankrupt, and the crisis then moved to Berlin. On 13 July 1931 the Danat Bank, weakened by the collapse of the large textile trust company Nordwolle, closed its doors, provoking a run of depositors on the other banks, which decided to only pay 20 percent of the sums that their clients wanted to withdraw, in other words to suspend their payments. The German banks were initially penalized by the interruption, following the crash, of foreign capital inflows into Germany, on which the entire credit mechanism hinged. Then, with the prolongation of the crisis and international tensions, especially surrounding the payment of reparations, they had to contend with massive withdrawals of foreign funds. Finally, in July 1931, they were no longer able to obtain refinancing from the Reichsbank, whose gold and currency reserves shrank below their statutory minimum. The intervention of the German government put an end to the panic. It ordered the immediate closure of all banks for two days, during which the Dresdner Bank also declared itself bankrupt, and introduced exchange controls on 15 July. With state backing, the Reichsbank set up the Akzept- und Garantiebank to obtain credit for commercial banks and savings banks. Furthermore, the government undertook major restructuring of the big banks, resulting in their near nationalization; they were denationalized, however, during the Third Reich.

From Germany, the crisis moved to England. The big banks held out well, with no major English bank having to close its doors during this period. The merchant banks were hit harder by the contraction in international trade and especially the introduction of exchange controls in Germany, and some of the smaller houses had to be wound up. The real crisis was a crisis of the pound sterling, whose convertibility in gold was suspended by the British government on 21 September 1931—a turning point in monetary history, with the end of the gold standard, rather than in banking history.

The French banks were not spared. Between October 1929 and September 1937, 670 French banks became insolvent, the vast majority of them small local and regional banks. Among the big banks, the Banque Nationale de Crédit (BNC), the country's fourth-largest deposit bank, collapsed in 1931 and was built up again the following year, with help from the state, under the name of Banque Nationale pour le Commerce et l'Industrie (BNCI). The Banque de l'Union Parisienne, one of the main *banques d'affaires*, shaken by the crises in Germany and central Europe, experienced very serious difficulties that brought it to the brink of bankruptcy in 1932, but it was saved by the joint intervention of the Banque de France and the main Parisian banks.

Small countries were also affected by the crisis, including safe havens such as Switzerland, then Germany's fourth-largest creditor. The large Swiss banks suffered badly from the effects of German banking crisis, with their assets more than halving between 1930 and 1935. Only the two largest banks—Swiss Bank Corporation and Crédit Suisse—avoided large reductions of capital, while one of them—the Banque d'Escompte Suisse, Geneva—collapsed in 1934 and another—the Schweizerische Volksbank, Berne—was only saved by the intervention of the federal government.

German depositors, fearing a bank failure, wait to withdraw their savings, 5 July 1931. ©MARY EVANS PICTURE LIBRARY/ THE IMAGE WORKS

The depression of the 1930s interrupted the forward march of the big banks that had started fifty years earlier, reinforcing the public and para-public banks. The shift was most spectacular in France, where by the late 1930s the share of the publicly owned institutions, in the first place the savings banks, far outstripped those of the commercial banks: between 1930 and 1937 deposits held by the former rose from 67 to 113 billion francs, while those held by the latter actually fell from 87 to 67 billion. In Germany, the share of the savings banks in the total assets of all banks increased from 31 percent in 1929 to 43 percent in 1938, while those of the commercial banks fell from 33 to 15 percent. Despite their rapid growth,

savings banks and building societies never reached such a dominant position in Britain: by 1933 their assets represented 37 percent of those of the clearing banks, up from 17 percent in 1920.

SUPERVISION AND REGULATION

The bank bankruptcies and the crisis of confidence in financial institutions led governments to intervene in financial affairs, with the aim of ensuring the stability of both the financial system and the economy. Moreover, state regulation was encouraged by the prevailing ideology and growing distrust toward market mechanisms. The main issue was the risks involved in universal banking. Mention must be made here of the United States, the first country to legislate and the one that went the furthest in this field, in particular with the Glass-Steagall Act (from the names of the two promoters of the Banking Act passed in 1933), which decreed the complete separation of commercial banking activities (raising funds and loans) from investment banking activities (issuing, distributing, and trading securities). Similar measures were taken in a number of European countries, notably Belgium, where two decrees passed in 1934 and 1935 (and in fact largely inspired by bankers anxious to restore confidence) abolished universal banking and subjected all institutions having banking status to control by a new body, the Banking Commission. From then on, the Société Générale de Belgique, Europe's oldest universal bank, founded in 1822, concentrated all of its commercial banking activities in a new institution, the Banque de la Société Générale, later known under the name of Générale de Banque.

The universal bank survived in Germany, though its abolition was debated. The banking law of December 1934, enacted under the Nazis, attributed the crisis to individual failings rather than to any shortcoming of the system and made do with strengthening bank supervision and introducing some restrictions on long-term deposits and on banks' representation on the supervisory boards of other companies. But even though universal banking survived, the government considerably strengthened its hold over financial institutions. Other laws, of a more sinister nature, also transformed the banking landscape in Germany by excluding Jews from economic life.

In Switzerland the federal banking law of 1934 did not abolish universal banking, and its only effect was the Swiss Confederation's very mild interference in banking affairs arising from the establishment of a Federal Banking Commission to supervise the system. The law was above all famous for its Article 47 relating to banking secrecy. This article made those who were subject to it—bank employees, managers, directors, auditors, and supervisors—liable to fines or up to six months' imprisonment if they divulged information on the trend of the business market and, above all, the names of a bank's clients.

England, for its part, steered clear of the trend toward greater regulation of the banks, probably because there had not been any bank bankruptcies during the 1930s, and because the financial system was more specialized than elsewhere and effectively monitored by the Bank of England. France too left things as they were until 1941, when the Vichy government introduced a law, upheld and completed in 1944, that controlled and regulated banking activities that until then had been open to any newcomers. Henceforth, banks had to be registered according to their type of activity, with a clear distinction between *banques d'affaires* and deposit banks, as well as between banks and other specialized institutions such finance companies and discount houses.

WARTIME CONTROLS AND RECONSTRUCTION

All banks, in all countries, were affected by the Second World War. As in the First World War, contributing to the war effort meant, as far as their business operations were concerned, a shift from commercial to government lending. Everywhere, including in the neutral countries, their assets became dominated by government securities. In Britain, by August 1945 government paper and cash amounted to over 82 percent of the deposits of the London clearing banks. The figure was just under 50 percent at Deutsche Bank, as well as at the Swiss Bank Corporation.

However, these were but temporary effects, even though banks did not return to fully normal business conditions until the early 1950s. More fundamental changes affected German and French banks. In Germany, the Allies' determination to decentralize the German economy led to the decision to divide each of the three big banks (Deutsche, Dresdner, and Commerz) into regional banks. The Deutsche Bank, for example, was succeeded in 1948 by ten separate institutions. Such measures, inspired by American banking legislation, were clearly at odds with German, and more generally European, banking traditions. They met with strong resistance from the German banking community, which immediately set about working toward reunification. As soon as 1949 bank representatives made proposals for a first regrouping on a wider regional basis, taking advantage of Britain's disagreement with the decentralization projects and the favorable conditions presented by the Cold War. The number of successor banks had already been reduced to three by 1952, and

A 2001 aerial photograph shows London's financial district with the massive Bank of England building at center. ©LONDON AERIAL PHOTO LIBRARY/CORBIS

complete reunification took place in 1957 for Deutsche and Dresdner and the following year for Commerz. During this period the credit banks progressively returned to their traditional business practices, in particular their close links with large industrial companies, through both advances and interlocking directorships.

In France the main transformation was the complete control established by the state over the mechanism of credit. The Banque de France and the major deposit banks (Crédit Lyonnais, Société Générale, Comptoir National d'Escompte, Banque Nationale pour le Commerce et l'Industrie) were nationalized in 1945, to be added to a public sector already including the Caisse des Dépôts et Consignations (the recipient of most of the assets

of the savings banks). However, the nationalized banks did not lose their corporate identity, while the *banques d'affaires,* including the Banque de Paris et des Pays-Bas, remained in private hands. The nationalized banks played only a modest role in the country's economic reconstruction and modernization and contented themselves with collecting short-term deposits and supporting Treasury issues. They hardly extended their network of branches and were happy to avoid competition in a cartelized sector. With the state now in the driving seat, it was the Treasury that financed the first of France's many five-year economic plans and the Caisse des Dépôts that financed local communities.

In Britain, only the Bank of England was nationalized in 1946, though the Big Five were under strict official control. They received precise instructions from the Treasury concerning not only their liquidity ratios but also their lending priorities, especially as far as manufacturing investment and the support of exports were concerned, leading John Maynard Keynes to comment that the clearing banks hardly needed to be nationalized. Official controls also had the effect of curbing competition. Despite their giant size, the Big Five were content to operate a price cartel that set interest rates and to remain strictly within the limits of deposit banking. Merchant banks, for their part, were working in a much less congenial economic environment: New York had become the world's undisputed financial center, the dollar was the main trading and reserve currency, and the pound suffered from not being fully convertible on current account until 1958. While they resumed their traditional activities, merchant banks increasingly turned their attention to domestic issues, preparing the ground for their later dominance of the field of corporate finance.

THE EMERGENCE OF THE EUROMARKETS

In the late 1950s and early 1960s, the emergence of the Euromarkets—Eurodollars, then Eurobonds and syndicated Eurocredits—marked a turning point in the history of international finance. As truly international capital markets, separate from the United States financial system and unregulated, they gave a new impetus to international capital flows.

Eurodollars are dollars deposited outside the United States. From the early 1950s, they started to accumulate in Europe, especially in London, partly because of the Cold War (the Soviet Union and Eastern European countries preferred to deposit their dollars in Europe rather than in the United States for fear of their being blocked in case of international tension) but mainly as a result of the United States' overseas investment—in the first place by multinational companies but also in foreign aid, as well as the country's growing payment deficit. Banking regulations also played their part, in particular the so-called Regulation Q, which dated back to the Banking Act of 1933 and enabled the Federal Reserve System to put a ceiling on the rate of interest that banks paid on domestic bank deposits. As British banks were able to offer a higher rate, funds were attracted to Britain, especially those

earned overseas by American multinationals. With the ban on the use of sterling instruments for financing third-party trade imposed by the British government following the sterling crisis of 1957, London banks, unwilling to lose customers, began to use these dollars instead. The Eurodollar market was born. With the return to external convertibility of European currencies in 1959 and the relaxation of exchange controls on capital account from the early 1960s, the Eurodollar market was soon to provide world credit on an unprecedented scale, with banks as the main operators and deals usually for very large amounts. Eurodollars were mainly used in the interbank market (banks placing funds at other banks), usually, though not exclusively, for short periods. From 1.5 billion dollars in 1959, it reached 25 billion ten years later and over 130 billion in 1973.

The emergence of Eurodollars signaled the rebirth of the City of London, whose standing had been suffering from the pound's decline. The City soon established itself as the home of this new market, taking advantage of its long experience of international finance and its large pool of skilled personnel. The merchant banks' early role in initiating the market also helped to determine its location, together with the Bank of England's flexible system of control. Since the end of the war, major international financial operations could only be undertaken from New York. With the use of the Eurodollar, and to a lesser extent other Euro-currencies, such operations could once again be carried out from London. This was especially the case with one of the City's specialties: international issues.

The Eurodollar market led to the development of the Eurobond market—foreign dollar bonds issued in Europe—which provided longer-term loans than was usual with Eurodollars. The first Eurobond issue took place in London in 1963—a fifteen-million-dollar, 5.5 percent six-year loan to Autostrade Italiane, with the state-owned holding company IRI as guarantor, floated by S. G. Warburg and Co. Eurobonds quickly proved very popular, especially as they were bearer bonds and were not subject to withholding tax. And with the introduction later in 1963 of the Interest Equalization Tax by the American authorities (a tax on purchases of foreign securities by U.S. residents to check the outflow of capital), American multinationals increasingly borrowed outside the United States. From 258 million dollars in 1963, the Eurobond market grew to 4.2 billion dollars in 1973, catching up with the traditional foreign bonds (denominated in the currency of the country where they are issued) and overtaking them in the 1980s.

In addition to short-term Eurodollar deposits and long-term Eurobonds, medium-term loans (three to ten years) were also granted to industrial corporations, as well as to governments and public authorities. They usually took the form of syndicated loans (the funds were made available by a syndicate of thirty to forty international banks organized by a lead institution) with floating interest rates. From a mere two billion dollars in 1968, syndicated loans reached over twenty billion dollars in 1973 and played a major role in the recycling of "petrodollars" (dollars accumulated by oil-producing countries in the wake of the oil price increases of the 1970s) during the rest of the decade.

COOPERATION AND COMPETITION IN INTERNATIONAL BANKING

The emergence of the Euromarkets heralded a new era in multinational banking (banks owning at least one branch in a foreign country). Major changes took place in three main areas: the location of foreign branches, the type of operations undertaken abroad, and the home country of the banks involved. Multinational banks shifted their attention from developing countries, where British overseas banks, in particular, had been active since the mid-nineteenth century, to the world's major financial centers: London, far and above, as home of the Euromarkets; New York, the world's leading financial center; but also Paris, Frankfurt, Luxembourg, Zurich, and others. These banks were much more involved in wholesale banking (transactions with other financial institutions and large companies involving huge deposits) than in retail banking. And the leading players, at least until the mid-1970s, were American banks, with their formidable expansion abroad, especially in Europe, being perceived as an "invasion" by some contemporaries. For if American banks did not pioneer Eurodollar transactions—the first such loans were granted by London merchant banks and British overseas banks—they were quick to join and soon captured the bulk of the market in

dollars traded outside their home country. British multinational banks had to undergo a profound restructuring, and, with the exception of French banks (which had retained a network of foreign branches, mostly in France's colonial empire), other European banks only started to move abroad in the 1970s and did not form major multinational banking groups before the globalization of the 1980s.

International expansion might have been the order of the day, yet it was a costly and risky proposition, especially if it meant entering new markets requiring a large capital basis. In order to face the "American challenge," European banks, including British banks, chose to cooperate. The innovation of the 1960s was the formation of banking "clubs," designed to extend the services of their members throughout Western Europe without the need for direct representation in other countries. Closer collaboration was also encouraged by the formation in 1958 of the European Economic Community and the prospect of rapid monetary integration: there is no doubt that the founders of these "clubs" saw them as a first step toward pan-European mergers. Cooperation also included launching several joint ventures in various parts of the world. By the early 1970s four such clubs had been established: Associated Banks of Europe Corporation (ABECOR), Europartners, European Banks International Company (EBIC), and Inter Alpha. They included most leading European banks, each with no more than one bank per country—for example, Amsterdam-Rotterdam Bank, Deutsche Bank, Société Générale de Banque, and Midland Bank were members of EBIC, later joined by Société Générale and Creditanstalt-Bankverein. Consortium banks represented another form of international cooperation. They were joint ventures that enabled their shareholders to share the risks and the profits involved in operating in the Euromarkets. Most of them were based in London (there were as many as twenty-eight in 1974), some established by members of the banking clubs, several others including American and other non-European banks.

Despite significant achievements, cracks started to appear from the mid-1970s, and the entire cooperative project eventually collapsed in the following decade, usually through one bank buying its partners' share in the joint ventures. This eventual

TABLE 2

The fifteen largest commercial banks in Europe in 2003	Market capitalization ($ millions)
HSBC (United Kingdom)	97,967
Royal Bank of Scotland (United Kingdom)	69,356
UBS (Switzerland)	54,322
HBOS (United Kingdom)	40,013
Barclays (United Kingdom)	38,433
BNP Paribas (France)	36,607
Santander Central Hispano (Spain)	29,872
Lloyds TSB (United Kingdom)	29,194
Banco Bilbao Vizcaya Argentaria (Spain)	27,561
Deutsche Bank (Germany)	26,844
ABN Amro (Netherlands)	24,332
UniCredito Italiano	24,167
Société Générale (France)	23,108
Crédit Suisse (Switzerland)	22,080
Crédit Lyonnais (France)	20,295

failure occurred in part because a pan-European merger was no longer on the agenda, as European monetary union became an increasingly remote prospect in the wake of the monetary upheavals of the 1970s; because conflicts of interest between members increased; and especially because the partners wished to build their own international networks and be represented in their own name in the major financial centers.

TOWARD THE TWENTY-FIRST CENTURY

Five interrelated trends have characterized the course of European banking since the 1970s. The first has been the gradual liberalization and deregulation of financial institutions and markets, leading to the despecialization of banking activities, among other effects. In both Britain and France, commercial banks have become akin to universal banks, offering a variety of services, usually through subsidiary companies. Such services ranged from wholesale banking (competing for the deposits of large customers) to retail banking (credit cards, consumer credit, mortgage financing), as well as those usually associated with investment banks (corporate financial advice, capital issues facilities, etc.). A second trend has been toward increased financial disintermediation (companies raising funds through the capital markets rather than bank borrowing), forcing banks to offer a wider range of products and to combine with nonbank financial institutions. This development has not eradicated the differences

between "bank-based" and "market-based" banking systems, and the debates on their respective merits have been reminiscent of those related to the British and German models in the early twentieth century.

A third trend has been the unprecedented role played by innovation, made possible by the formidable development of information technology and resulting in the continual appearance of ever more sophisticated financial products—derivatives (financial instruments based on dealings in an underlying asset, such as bonds, equities, commodities, currencies, and indices representing financial assets), with futures, options, and swaps being the most important among them. A fourth trend has been toward increased competition. With the relaxation of state regulation, the end of cartel agreements, and the technological revolution in banking, competition intensified or simply resumed, not only within commercial banking but also from outside the traditional world of banking, with savings banks and other public and semipublic institutions beginning to provide their customers with a complete, or near complete, range of banking services. On the other hand, international competition has stiffened in the major international financial centers with the globalization of financial activities, especially in London, where there were 481 foreign banks in 2000, as against 242 in Frankfurt and 187 in Paris. A fifth trend has been a renewed consolidation movement, in other words the domination of the banking system by a handful of giant institutions. Megamergers and acquisitions have played a role in the process: Algemene Bank Nederland (ABN) and Amsterdam-Rotterdam Bank (AMRO) in 1991, Midland and the Hong Kong and Shanghai Banking Corporation (HSBC) in 1993; Union Bank of Switzerland (UBS) and Swiss Bank Corporation (SBC) in 1998; Banque National de Paris (BNP) and Paribas, and Santander and Banco Central Hispanoamerico (BCH), in 1999; National Westminster and the Royal Bank of Scotland in 2000. Interestingly, these mergers have taken place within a national context. So far, and despite the advent of the single European currency in 1999, no merger between major European banks of different countries has yet taken place, even though they have all acquired other banks abroad, in the first place in the United States. In the event, the group of the fifteen largest commercial banks in Europe in 2003 (table 2) looked different than ninety years earlier, especially in the decline of the German banks and the progress of the Spanish and Swiss ones, though not radically so, with most changes being due to mergers rather than the advent of newcomers. The top position held by the HSBC Group (the second-largest bank in the world after Citigroup, of the United States), present in seventy-seven countries, is a reflection of the degree of internationalization of banking and finance at the turn of the twenty-first century.

See also **Capitalism; Euro.**

BIBLIOGRAPHY

Ackrill, Margaret, and Leslie Hannah. *Barclays: The Business of Banking, 1690–1996.* Cambridge, U.K., 2001.

Battilossi, Stefano, and Yousef Cassis, eds. *European Banks and the American Challenge: Competition and Cooperation in International Banking under Bretton Woods.* Oxford, U.K., 2002.

Born, Karl Erich. *International Banking in the Nineteenth and Twentieth Centuries.* Translated by Volker R. Bergham. New York, 1983.

Bussière, Eric. *Paribas 1872–1992: Europe and the World.* Antwerp, Belgium, 1992.

Capie, Forrest, and Michael Collins. *Have the Banks Failed British Industry?: An Historical Survey of Bank/Industry Relations in Britain, 1870–1990.* London, 1992.

Cassis, Youssef. *Capitals of Capital: A History of International Financial Centres, 17802005.* Cambridge, U.K., 2006.

Cassis, Youssef, ed. *Finance and Financiers in European History, 1880–1960.* Cambridge, U.K., 1992.

Cassis, Youssef, Gerald Feldman, and Ulf Olsson, eds. *The Evolution of Financial Institutions and Markets in Twentieth-Century Europe.* Aldershot, U.K., 1995.

Cottrell, P. L., Håkan Lindgren, and Alice Teichova, eds. *European Industry and Banking between the Wars.* Leicester, U.K., 1992.

Edwards, Jeremy, and Klaus Fischer. *Banks, Finance, and Investment in Germany.* Cambridge, U.K., 1994.

Feinstein, Charles H., ed. *Banking, Currency, and Finance in Europe between the Wars.* Oxford, U.K., 1995.

Gall, Lothar, et al. *The Deutsche Bank, 1870–1995.* London, 1995.

Holmes, A. R., and Edwin Green. *Midland: 150 Years of Banking Business.* London, 1986.

Holtfrerich, Carl-Ludwig, Jaime Reis, and Gianni Toniolo, eds. *The Emergence of Modern Central Banking from 1918 to the Present.* Aldershot, U.K., 1999.

James, Harold, Håkan Lindgren, and Alice Teichova, eds. *The Role of Banks in the Interwar Economy.* Cambridge, U.K., 1991.

Jones, Geoffrey. *British Multinational Banking, 1830–1990.* Oxford, U.K., 1993.

Kasuya, Makoto, ed. *Coping with Crisis: International Financial Institutions in the Interwar Period.* Oxford, U.K., 2003.

Kindleberger, Charles P. *A Financial History of Western Europe.* 2nd ed. New York, 1993.

Pohl, Manfred, ed. *Handbook on the History of European Banks.* Aldershot, U.K., 1994.

Pohl, Manfred, Teresa Tortella, and Herman Van der Wee, eds. *A Century of Banking Consolidation in Europe.* Aldershot, U.K., 2001.

Roberts, Richard. *Schroders, Merchants, and Bankers.* London, 1992.

YOUSSEF CASSIS

BARBAROSSA OPERATION. *See* **Operation Barbarossa.**

BARBIE, KLAUS (1913–1991), German Nazi leader.

The son of village schoolteachers, Klaus Barbie was born in Bad Godesberg, Germany, on 25 October 1913. He joined the Nazi youth group in April 1933. A mediocre student, he afterward devoted himself to militant activity. He joined the Schutzstaffel (SS) in September 1935 and was soon appointed to the central department of the Sicherheitsdienst (SD), the intelligence arm of the SS. Working in Berlin, he had the opportunity to develop his skills as an investigator at the expense of Jews, homosexuals, prostitutes, and other "criminals."

In May 1937 Barbie joined the Nazi Party (NSDAP), and, after various training and military instruction, he was promoted to the rank of *Untersturmführer* SS (second lieutenant) on 20 April 1940. Sent to Amsterdam, he hunted Jews and resistance fighters with such brutality and efficiency that he was awarded an Iron Cross.

At the end of May 1942, Barbie, now *Obersturmführer* (first lieutenant), was assigned to head the intelligence service on the Franco-Swiss border. After the Nazis occupied southern France on 11 November 1942, Barbie became chief of section IV of the Sipo-SD, the combined wartime Nazi security force. From his headquarters in the Hotel Terminus in Lyon, he organized the repression and attempted to shut down the Resistance. Known as "the butcher of Lyon" for his ferocity during interrogations, he conducted a merciless campaign not only against the Resistance but also against men who tried to evade the Service du Travail Obligatoire (STO), the forced labor service, and against Jews. The arrest of the Resistance leader Jean Moulin in Caluire on 21 June 1943 was an operation that brought Barbie a First Class Cross with Swords from Hitler's own hands. Barbie also directed the raid on 6 April 1944 on the Children's Home in Izieu, about 80 kilometers from Lyon, where forty-four Jewish children, ages three to thirteen, were being sheltered. Interned first at Drancy, they were subsequently deported to Auschwitz, where all were exterminated. Barbie terrorized the region during the summer of 1944 by ordering numerous executions.

On 27 August 1944, two weeks after deporting a final convoy of several hundred Jewish and non-Jewish citizens of Lyon, Barbie, who now held the rank of captain or *Hauptsturmführer,* returned to Germany. In the early postwar period, from 1945 to 1951, he was protected by the United States Army Counter Intelligence Corps (CIC), which valued him for his fanatic anticommunism and intelligence-gathering skills. The CIC subsequently helped Barbie resettle in Bolivia with his family. There, under the name Klaus Altmann, he led a comfortable life as a businessman while also playing an active role as secret police officer on behalf of that country's military regimes. In 1957 he became a Bolivian citizen.

Meanwhile, Barbie had been sentenced to death in absentia in May 1947 in France, and a military tribunal passed the same judgment in 1954. But Bolivian politics did not favor extradition, and only in February 1983 was Barbie, who had been identified in 1971 by the French lawyer and Nazi-hunter Serge Klarsfeld (b. 1935) and his wife Beate (b. 1939), brought back to France.

On 4 July 1987 Barbie was sentenced to life in prison without parole for crimes against humanity after a two-month trial in the Rhône Court of Assizes. The trial became the first of three—Paul Touvier's in 1992 and Maurice Papon's in 1997–1998 were the others—that fueled a passionate judicial debate on the definition of "crimes against humanity," the only crime, by French law decided 6 December 1964, that carried no statute of limitations. On 20 December 1985 the Court of Appeals, asked to rule, chose to include "war crimes" in the definition of crimes against humanity, to avoid distinguishing two classes of victims, Resistance fighters and Jews. Barbie was judged as a Nazi occupier. His superiors, the SS general Carl-Albrecht Oberg, chief of the SD in France, and his assistant Helmut Knochen, had been sentenced to death in France in 1954, but in 1958 their sentences had been reduced to life in prison without parole, and in 1961 they had been discreetly freed by the president Charles de Gaulle. But by the 1980s times had changed. Barbie's trial provoked great media attention in France and sparked new interest in the "black years" of the occupation. The defense lawyer Jacques Vergès attempted to turn the tables by calling attention to colonial crimes perpetrated by the French government. But the trial also gave many of Barbie's victims the opportunity to testify and to describe the terrifying and sadistic tortures that were his speciality. Barbie died of cancer in prison on 25 September 1991.

See also **Collaboration; France; Gestapo; Nazism; Resistance; War Crimes.**

BIBLIOGRAPHY

Finkielkraut, Alain. *Remembering in Vain: The Klaus Barbie Trial and Crimes against Humanity.* Translated from French by Roxanne Lapidus with Sima Godfrey. Introduction by Alice Y. Kaplan. New York, 1992.

Jean, Jean-Paul, and Denis Salas, eds. *Barbie, Touvier, Papon: Des procès pour la mémoire.* Paris, 2002.

Morgan, Ted. *An Uncertain Hour: The French, the Germans, the Jews, the Barbie Trial, and the City of Lyon, 1940–1945.* New York, 1990.

Truche, Pierre. "Le crime contre l'humanité." *Les Cahiers de la Shoah* 1 (1994).

RENÉE POZNANSKI

BARBUSSE, HENRI (1873–1935), French novelist.

Having already earned a reputation with his naturalistic novel *L'enfer* (1908; *Hell,* 1966), Henri Barbusse was ensured mass popularity during his lifetime and beyond thanks to his war novel *Le feu* (1916; *Under Fire,* 1917), which sold five hundred thousand copies and won the Prix Goncourt in 1916. In this novel he embodies the ideas of the pacifist veteran and of the politically committed intellectual.

Born into a family of the intellectual bourgeoisie on 17 May 1873—his father was a theater critic—Barbusse chose a literary career and married the daughter of Catulle Mendès, one of the most celebrated French poets of the time. His first literary efforts were in a symbolist vein, poetry such as the *Pleureuses* cycle (1895; The hired mourners) and *Les suppliants* (1903; The suppliants), a novel in verse. It was during this time that he began to take an interest in pacifism and socialism.

And yet this "antimilitary socialist" joined the army at the age of forty-one when World War I broke out. On 9 August, a week after enlisting, he explained himself in *L'humanité:* "This war is a social war that will help our cause take the next, and perhaps definitive, step. Its target is the oldest and vilest of our eternal enemies: militarism and imperialism, the Sword, the Boot, and, I would add, the Crown. Our victory will mark the obliteration of this den of Caesars, crowned princes, lords, and ruffians who imprison an entire people and would seek to imprison everyone else" (1920, p. 7; here translated).

Barbusse spent over ten months on the battlefront, first as an infantryman and then as a stretcher-bearer. Twice cited for bravery, he was transferred to military headquarters for health reasons. It was then that he wrote *Le feu,* which was first published in installments, then as a novel in 1916. It achieved enormous success. Even though the novel presents French soldiers as both heroes and victims of the war in a style that shifts between raw realism and apocalyptical mysticism, its overarching message remains ambiguous, since the legitimacy of the war against Germany is never truly questioned. Nevertheless, it was critically received as the paradigmatic and pioneering book of the veterans for peace movement. Indeed, veterans themselves received it enthusiastically.

Clarté, published in French and English translation as *Light* in 1919, was Barbusse's second novel and contained the same pacifist message, which became something of a revolutionary prophecy. The novel gave its name to the journal and international pacifist intellectual group that Barbusse founded that same year. Two years earlier, in November 1917, Barbusse had cofounded, with Raymond Lefèbvre and Paul Vaillant-Couturier, the Association Républicaine des Anciens Combattants (ARAC; Republican veterans association), a clearly leftist group. In Barbusse's ideological battle against the intellectual Right represented by Henri Massis and company, he was joined by Romain Rolland. But in 1921 and 1922, Barbusse began taking his distance from Rolland and becoming more closely associated with the Communist Party, which he finally joined in 1923. Henceforth, he pledged his pacifism to the revolutionary cause and urged intellectuals to support unambiguously the Bolshevik Revolution.

Barbusse wrote many essays: *La lueur dans l'abîme* (1920; The glimmer in the abyss); *Le couteau entre les dents* (1921; Knife in one's teeth); *Paroles d'un combattant* (1920; Words of a soldier), and others. He also worked as a journalist for *L'humanité* and for the weekly journal *Monde,* which he founded in 1928. In the early 1920s Barbusse became an untiring propagandist for the cause of communism, simultaneously pursuing his career as a novelist, with *Les enchaînements* (1925; *Chains,* 1925) and *Faits divers* (1928; Current events). These novels were less inspired than his war novels. The surrealists thoroughly despised his books, though they sometimes shared his ideology.

Barbusse cofounded the Association des Écrivains et Artistes Révolutionnaires (AEAR; Association of revolutionary writers and artists) in 1932 and was one of the principal actors in the antifascist Amsterdam-Pleyel Committee. In 1933 he was named president of the Comité Mondial de Lutte contre la Guerre et le Fascisme (World committee to fight war and fascism) but, despite the backing of the Communist Party in 1934, did not succeed in taking control of the Comité de Vigilance des Intellectuels Antifascistes (CVIA;

Vigilance committee of antifascist intellectuals), which spearheaded intellectual antifascism.

The battle against fascism proved to be his last. Henri Barbusse died in Moscow on 30 August 1935. He had published a biography of Joseph Stalin that year, with an eloquent subtitle: "A New World Seen through a Man." Barbusse was given hero's status. His funeral, attended by several tens of thousands of people, became the pretext for an enormous propaganda campaign by the Communist Party, which was in the midst of its struggle against fascism, just before the rise of the Popular Front. That ceremony also revealed the passion that the author of *Le feu* still inspired in the leftist community.

See also **Pacifism; Rolland, Romain; World War I.**

BIBLIOGRAPHY

Primary Sources

Barbusse, Henri. *Le feu.* Paris, 1916, 1988.

———. *Clarté.* Paris, 1919, 1978.

———. *Paroles d'un combattant.* Paris, 1920.

Secondary Sources

Baudorre, Philippe. *Barbusse.* Paris, 1995.

Lindner-Wirsching, Almut. *Französische Schriftsteller und ihre Nation im Ersten Weltkrieg.* Tübingen, Germany, 2004.

Relinger, Jean. *Henri Barbusse écrivain combattant.* Paris, 1994.

NICOLAS BEAUPRÉ

BARDOT, BRIGITTE (b. 1934), French actress and activist.

The choice of Brigitte Bardot in 1970 as the first real-life model for the bust of the French national emblem Marianne was perhaps more significant than the sculptor Alain Gourdon had intended. Following references to a legendary Marianne in the writings of the French revolutionaries, the image of Marianne, meant to embody the republic's ideal of liberty, entered the realm of visual interpretation in the nineteenth century. Two centuries of idealized iconography later, the conjunction of Marianne and Bardot came as an ingenious—if unintentional—comment on the real woman's own revolutionary role in post–World War II French culture. Only in Bardot's case, the revolution in question was sexual.

Bardot first made her mark at the age of twenty-two in *Et Dieu créa la femme* (1956; And God created woman), directed by her husband at the time, Roger Vadim. Arbiters of morality in the French provinces were shocked by the way in which Vadim's film showcased a brand of female sexuality never before seen in their national cinema. Audiences were accustomed to well-groomed, womanly stars such as Danielle Darrieux, Micheline Presle, and Edwige Feuillère. As for Bardot, it was difficult to tell she had been raised in Paris's posh sixteenth arrondissement. Her wild hair, bare feet, little-girl voice, and disregard for all fashion—including girdles—were a titillating foil for her athletic voluptuousness. Here and in other movies that featured her in orphan and schoolgirl roles, Bardot eroticized the quality of girlishness. Quickly christened "BB" (*bébé,* or baby) in the French media, Bardot obliged by displaying innocent knowingness offscreen as well, claiming in interviews that she had not performed in *Et Dieu,* but simply "was." The unapologetic pleasure in her own body that she exhibited on-screen elicited letters from indignant parents to newspaper editors, politicians, and priests. She was even blamed for episodes of juvenile delinquency. Bardot found an unlikely defender in the person of French philosopher Simone de Beauvoir, who was intrigued by the actress's uncomplicated relationship to her sexuality: amoral rather than immoral. More likely, it was less BB's way of being in the world on- and off-screen than her not-your-mother's-Dior "new look" that appealed to young women at the time.

Bardot would go on to make two more notable films, *Le mépris* (1963; Contempt, directed by Jean-Luc Godard) and *Viva Maria!* (Louis Malle, 1965). Also worth noting are her sultry recordings with the brilliant singer-songwriter Serge Gainsbourg ("Harley-Davidson," "Je t'aime… moi non plus," "Bonnie and Clyde"), and her appearance at the Elysée Palace—invited by Charles de Gaulle—wearing pants.

If Brigitte Bardot is one of the few French actresses of the 1950s and 1960s familiar to the American public, it is less for her acting career, which ended in 1973, than for her status as a sex symbol, which persisted even as she took up the two brands of activism for which she is best known

Brigitte Bardot in a scene from *Et Dieu créa la femme*, 1956. IENA/UCIL/Cocinor/The Kobal Collection/Mirkine

in the early twenty-first century. Animal rights have been her cause célèbre; her campaign to protect baby seals began in 1977, the year before her reign as Marianne ended. She created the Fondation Brigitte Bardot in Saint Tropez in 1986. "Je t'aime... moi non plus," recorded with Gainsbourg in 1967, was only released in 1986 on the condition that all proceeds go to her animal rights foundation. More recently and most troublingly, her 1992 marriage to the National Front politician Bernard D'Oremale coincided with a chain of racist statements and stances. She has faced four convictions from French courts for "inciting racial hatred." In June 2004 she was fined for the first time, for her comparison of Muslims in France to barbaric invaders in her best-selling book *Un cri dans le silence* (A cry in the silence). It is difficult to believe this is the same BB whose frenetic solo dance in the company of Afro-Cuban musicians revealed generous glimpses of her inner thighs to an emasculated

husband, would-be lovers, and the moviegoer in the culminating scene of *Et Dieu créa la femme.*

See also **Cinema; France.**

BIBLIOGRAPHY

Bardot, Brigitte. *Un cri dans le silence.* Paris, 2003.

Beauvoir, Simone de. "Brigitte Bardot and the Lolita Syndrome." *Esquire,* August 1959, 32–38.

Weiner, Susan. *Enfants Terribles: Youth and Femininity in the Mass Media in France, 1945–1968.* Baltimore, 2001.

SUSAN E. WEINER

BARRÈS, MAURICE (1862–1923), French novelist and politician.

Maurice Barrès is best known for his theories of individualism and for his intense nationalism.

Born in the small town of Charmes-sur-Moselle in Lorraine, Barrès was educated at the lycée in Nancy and in 1883 went to Paris to pursue legal studies. After an initial foray into the world of journalism as a contributor to the monthly periodical *Young France,* and then as founder of the short-lived *Spots of Ink,* he traveled to Italy, where he wrote *Under the Eyes of the Barbarians* (1888). This work would become the first volume of a *"trilogie du moi"* (trilogy of the ego) that also included *A Free Man* (1889) and *The Garden of Bérénice* (1891). In these books, Barrès set forth a program of self-analysis, dividing the world into *moi* (myself) and the barbarians, which included anyone who opposed the writer's individuality. The trilogy established Barrès as one of the leading voices of the younger generation and had a profound impact in both literary and political circles of the fin de siècle.

Barrès carried his theory of individualism into politics as an ardent supporter of General Georges Boulanger (1837–1891). Then, at the age of twenty-seven, he ran a successful campaign to become deputy from his native Lorraine on a platform demanding the return to France of Alsace-Lorraine, which had come under Prussian control following France's defeat in 1870. Barrès remained deputy from 1889 to 1893. The anarchic individualism of his earlier works gave way to an intense patriotism rooted in his anger about the loss of France's eastern provinces. The development of Barrès's increasingly intransigent nationalism and his conversion to an almost mystical attachment to the native province, his cult of *la terre et les morts* (the earth and the dead), was duly chronicled in his next trilogy of novels, *The Novel of National Energy.* The series, which began with the publication in 1897 of *The Uprooted,* is an appeal to local patriotism and the distinctive qualities of the French provinces. It tells the story of seven young Lorrainers who set out to make their fortune in Paris but instead encounter disillusionment and failure because they have been uprooted from their native traditions. Six of them survive in the second novel of the trilogy, *The Call to the Soldier* (1900), which recounts the history of Boulangism; the final installment, *Their Faces* (1902), deals with the Panama scandals.

During the controversy surrounding the accused spy Alfred Dreyfus (1859–1935), Barrès was a vocal and articulate representative of the anti-Dreyfus camp, joining other right-wing luminaries such as the monarchist Charles Maurras (1868–1952) and the nationalist Paul Déroulède (1846–1914). Barrès continued to advance his political views, warning the French of the threat posed by a decline in patriotism within and by German military might without in such works as *Scenes and Doctrines of Nationalism* (1902), *In the Service of Germany* (1905), and *Colette Baudoche* (1909), which later earned success as French propaganda during World War I. In 1906 Barrès was admitted to the Académie Française and reelected to the Chamber of Deputies. Barrès was a vocal supporter of World War I when it erupted in 1914, and during the war he promoted the national solidarity of the *union sacrée* (sacred union), a stance most clearly seen in his *Various Spiritual Families of France* (1917). After the war, Barrès was one of the leaders of the nationalist camp in French politics, serving as president, first, of the Ligue de la Patrie Française (League of the French nation) and then of the Ligue des Patriotes (League of patriots).

To the generation that came of age during the Dreyfus affair, Barrès brought a heady combination of racist nativism and integral nationalism. He was a celebrated writer, an insistent right-wing voice, and an intellectual leader for a generation that navigated through the troubled political waters of France's Third Republic. Barrès's calls for cultural and social rootedness, his critique of liberalism, his virulent anti-Semitism and nationalism, his cult of *la terre et les morts,* and his warnings about national decline and decadence found a responsive audience among those who wished to resist disturbing social change by preserving the sanctity of ancestral values and traditions. More recently, scholars have seen in Barrès's particular blend of national socialism, anti-intellectualism, and populist anti-Semitism in the 1890s the intellectual origins of interwar fascism that emerged in France in the 1920s and 1930s.

See also **Action Française; Anti-Semitism; Maurras, Charles.**

BIBLIOGRAPHY

Primary Sources

Barrès, Maurice. *Un homme libre.* Paris, 1889.

———. *Sous l'oeil des barbares.* Paris, 1894.

————. *L'ennemi des lois*. Paris, 1910.

————. *Les diverses familles spirituelles de la France*. Paris, 1917.

————. *Les déracinés*. Paris, 1920.

————. *Scènes et doctrines du nationalisme*. Paris, 1925.

————. *L'appel au soldat*. Paris, 1926.

————. *Mes cahiers: 1896–1923*. Texts selected by Guy Dupré. Paris, 1960.

Barrès, Maurice, and Charles Maurras. *La République ou le roi: Correspondance inédite (1888–1923)*. Paris, 1970.

Secondary Sources

Broche, François. *Maurice Barrès*. Paris, 1987.

Soucy, Robert. *Fascism in France: The Case of Maurice Barrès*. Berkeley, Calif., 1972.

————. *French Fascism: The First Wave, 1924–1933*. New Haven, Conn., 1986.

Sternhell, Zeev. *Maurice Barrès et le nationalisme français*. Brussels, 1985.

KATHLEEN CAMBOR

BARTH, KARL (1886–1968), Swiss theologian.

Karl Barth was a figure of major importance in European history during the interwar period, and not only for his innovative theology in the German Protestant Church and his work as a theologian in the universities in Germany. He influenced many Christians in his stand against Nazism, for which he lost his post, and which led him to be well known and respected in most of Europe and America. His lectures and writings brought Christians to realize the importance of resisting from both a moral and a political point of view. As a historical figure of the twentieth century he deserves a place in any intellectual study of the period.

Barth was born in Basel, Switzerland, the son of a Protestant theology professor specializing in the New Testament. He studied in Berlin, Tübingen, and Marburg, where he met leading members of historical criticism: Adolf von Harnack, the Old Testament scholar Herrman Gunkel, and Martin Rade. Having served a probationary year as a Calvinist pastor in Geneva, during his pastoral life in Safenwil (Aargau) he came to realize that the modernist approach did not satisfy the social and pastoral problems with which he was confronted. Turning to Christian socialism, he befriended Leonhard Ragaz and came to know Christoph Blumhardt. At the latter's retreat house at Bad Bol, the preaching of the Kingdom of God during the early years of the First World War led Barth to question the tenets of his theological training. The war brought another disappointment; all except one of his former professors had signed the manifesto of the ninety-three intellectuals approving the policies of William II.

These disappointments can be seen in Barth's *Römerbrief* (1919; Epistle to the Romans), whose central theme is the sovereignty of God and the fundamental otherness of man. Contrary to the teaching of the liberals, where humanity searches for God, in Barth's work it is God who instigates a moment of crisis in human existence.

Appointed professor of reformed theology at Göttingen University in 1921, Barth restructured the *Römerbrief* for its second edition. That position of leadership in German and Swiss Christian socialist theology gave him the opportunity to make his point: seek what God is doing in the world and follow him. During this period he contributed to a theological journal called *Zwischen den Zeiten* (Between the lines), which he founded with a number of other theologians of repute—Rudolph Bultmann, Friedrich Gogarten, Eduard Thurneysen, and Emil Brunner. For the next ten years, he attempted to purify his ideas, and with the help of St. Anselm he clarified the relationship between faith and reason. In subsequent posts in Münster (1925–1930) and Bonn (1930–1935), he wrote his major work, *Kirchliche Dogmatik* (Church dogmatics). Seeking to free the notion of the Word of God from philosophical determinants, particularly existentialism, Barth refused natural theology too, showing that only God's Word to man could reveal to him the true nature of his depravity. This position brought Barth into conflict with the Nazi belief that the law of God is the same as the *nomos* (law) of the German people. He criticized the German Christians for their acceptance of the synthesis between Nazism and revelation, which claimed that God can and will reveal himself through history, race, the state, or the Führer. Refusing to sign the oath of allegiance to the Führer, Barth was dismissed from his chair by the regime and took refuge in his native Switzerland. The theological and historical repercussions of this act made him famous throughout Europe and North America, where he was invited to lecture and his articles were read, translated, and commented on. From 1935 Barth was a hated figure to the Nazis, but his absence from Germany meant he did not suffer the fate of Dietrich Bonhoeffer or Martin Niemöller.

After the war, Barth was one of the first to speak of reconciliation with Germany, in a book entitled *The Germans and Us,* and during the Cold War he was active in denouncing the stockpiling of nuclear weapons.

See also **Bonhoeffer, Dietrich; Nazism.**

BIBLIOGRAPHY

Busch, Eberhard. *Karl Barth: His Life from Letters and Autobiographical Texts.* Translated by John Bowden. Grand Rapids, Mich., 1994.

Gorringe, Timothy. *Karl Barth: Against Hegemony.* Oxford, U.K., 1999.

Torrance, Thomas F. *Karl Barth: An Introduction to His Early Theology, 1910–1931.* London, 1962.

———. *Karl Barth, Biblical and Evangelical Theologian.* Edinburgh, 1990.

                                    MARTIN BRAY

BARTHES, ROLAND (1915–1980), leading figure of French structuralism and poststructuralism.

Ten years younger than Jean-Paul Sartre, Roland Barthes held a similar representative place for his generation, one that moved beyond Marxism to the study of how meaning is created in sign systems. Barthes's sensibility is detached, cool, witty. He is interested in style, in the ways we make sense of the world, in how we live in culture and language, and in the practice of writing itself.

Barthes's early work, in *Writing Degree Zero* (1953) and *Mythologies* (1957), displays his interest in writing and culture as systems. In particular, he directs attention to how cultural codes, such as advertising, attempt to pass themselves off as natural: nature to Barthes is "the last outrage" since it offers a convenient and often totalitarian cover for propaganda and prejudice of all sorts. In the 1950s and 1960s Barthes also published acute essays on a number of writers important to his understanding of writing, notably Bertolt Brecht and the "new novelist" Alain Robbe-Grillet. His *On Racine* (1963) provoked a defining critical polemic with partisans of traditional (biographical and historical) criticism; it underlined Barthes's repudiation of the notion of "author" in favor of "text." He moved toward a more rigorous engagement with linguistics (derived essentially from the founder of modern structural linguistics, Ferdinand de Saussure) and semiotics, especially in *Elements of Semiology* (1964) and *The Fashion System* (1967). This fledgling "science of signs" was to provide a way to understand all signifying systems invented by human culture on the basis of the linguistic sign.

Barthes's most creative and lasting contributions to literary criticism and theory may come in his work on "narratology" (the analysis of narrative) and the visual image (particularly photography, in *Camera Lucida,* 1980). After an early essay on the structural analysis of narrative (reviving a project begun by the Russian formalists), he offered a book-length demonstration of how to do it in *S/Z* (1970), devoted to the rigorous—and playful—reading of a novella by the nineteenth-century writer Honoré de Balzac. More and more, reading became a focal point for Barthes's thinking and writing: pursued deliberately, with close attention to language and style, to textual surface and connotation, reading should be a radical experience. To read a text only once, he says, is to be condemned to read always the same text: the true richness, the plurality (and indeterminacy) of meanings, comes only with rereading. In the sequel to *S/Z,* called *The Pleasure of the Text* (1973), Barthes analogizes the text (which etymologically evokes the activity of weaving, the making of textiles) to the spider web: "Lost in this weaving—this texture—the subject unmakes itself, like a spider dissolving in the secretions constructing its web" (p. 64). Barthes here displays a certain influence of Jacques Lacan's version of psychoanalysis: the human subject is never quite master of language; he or she is spoken by language as much as speaking it, never quite in control of the elusive process of meaning.

Barthes was a restless thinker who never stayed put in one system for long. He moved from his (only relatively) strict allegiance to structuralism and semiotics to "poststructuralism" with his more overtly playful work of the 1970s. By the time of his inauguration of the first chair of semiology at the Collège de France (the summit of French academia) in 1977, he renounced his earlier search for a "metalanguage," a language outside and above natural language that would enable its scientific analysis. "It is precisely in reflecting on the sign that semiology discovers that every relation of exteriority of one language to another is, *in the long run,* untenable," he claimed in his inaugural lecture. Barthes's later work (still very much in process at the time of his accidental death at age sixty-five) takes a self-reflective and even autobiographical turn in *Roland Barthes by Roland Barthes* (1975) and *A Lover's Discourse: Fragments* (1977); and the posthumous *Incidents* (1987) addresses more openly Barthes's place in gay culture.

Barthes was unabashedly a theorist, though he cared relatively little for system, paradoxical as that may seem—but paradox was one of his favorite forms of thought and expression: he sought to expose its opposite, the *doxa,* the accepted, mindless, self-blinding belief system. He tended to write essays, not treatises, often "an introduction to" or "elements of"; his thought tends toward the fragmentary, the aphoristic, the understated. Ever an elegant and artful writer, Barthes renewed a very old tradition of French writing, reaching back to authors such as La Rochefoucauld and La Bruyère in the seventeenth century: the keen observation of self-deceptive social and cultural practices, and the promotion of lucid observational writing as the antidote.

See also **Lacan, Jacques; Sartre, Jean-Paul.**

BIBLIOGRAPHY

Primary Sources

Barthes, Roland. *The Pleasure of the Text.* Translated by Richard Miller. New York, 1975.

———. *A Barthes Reader.* Edited by Susan Sontag. New York, 1982.

Secondary Sources

"Back to Barthes: Twenty Years After." *Yale Journal of Criticism* 14, no. 2 (2001): 437–543.

Culler, Jonathan. *Barthes.* London, 1983.

Lombardo, Patrizia. *The Three Paradoxes of Roland Barthes.* Athens, Ga., 1989.

Ungar, Steven. *Roland Barthes: The Professor of Desire.* Lincoln, Neb., 1983.

PETER BROOKS

BARTÓK, BÉLA (1881–1945), Hungarian composer, pianist, and ethnomusicologist.

Béla Bartók's art emerged from the search for an inner, spiritual voice in an attempt to confront the anxieties, both personal and communal, that he experienced as an artist living in twentieth-century Europe. As a result of a disease, Bartók was isolated from his peers during the first years of his life. His father died when he was seven, and his mother, an elementary school teacher, could provide for the family only with difficulty. This background— loneliness, isolation, the discomfort of illness, a religious-moral ideal of hard work, and a longing for an ideal "wholeness"—defined Bartók's inner world both as a pianist and as a composer.

After he graduated from the Academy of Music in Budapest, Bartók quickly became known in Hungary for his heroic-nationalistic symphonic compositions, but he soon grew disenchanted with this style and its message. After a compositional crisis, he set out, at Hungarian composer Zoltan Kodály's suggestion, on field trips in mainland Hungary (1906) and Transylvania (1907). These trips were the beginning of a lifelong project, in the course of which Bartók collected, transcribed, and analyzed thousands of folk pieces of various ethnicities (including Hungarian, Rumanian, Slovakian, Ruthenian, Arabic, and Turkish) and published major ethnomusicological collections and studies. The extraordinary energy he devoted to folk music reflected not merely scholarly interest but a deeper artistic need: Bartók regarded all folk music as a spontaneous human expression and believed that its study would lead to an understanding of basic musical techniques. It was these techniques, rather than fragments of folk songs, that he integrated into his compositional style.

More importantly, the encounter with folk music provoked in Bartók a new attitude toward emotional expression. Bartók realized that his artistic goal was to grasp in music complex emotions that reflected the polarity of thoughts and feelings, not only positive emotions but also anxiety, confusion, and ambivalence. The impetus for this aesthetic came partly from folk music (which, as he himself noted, can express complex feelings in simple forms) and partly from the modernist milieu in Budapest that included the era's leading artistic and intellectual personalities, as well as from his readings, particularly the poetry of Endre Ady and the philosophy of Friedrich Nietzsche.

Between 1908 and 1920, each major work explored novel techniques and ideas within this basic aesthetic orientation. The opera *Bluebeard's Castle* (1911) is a Freudian exploration of the soul through the metaphor of folk-inspired nocturnal "landscapes," while the pantomime *The Miraculous Mandarin* (1918–1919; orchestrated 1923–1924) integrates folk music elements into a dissonant style, evoking the clash between primeval or sincere passions and those of the modern city.

In the 1920s and 1930s, European art moved in two sharply contrasting directions: toward neoclassicism, on the one hand, and toward a complete dissolution of forms (abstract art), on the other. Bartók's music from 1920, and even more markedly from 1926, integrates these tendencies. Although it underwent significant stylistic changes (for example, a more explicit use of baroque techniques from 1926), Bartók's music from these two decades shows an underlying emotional and aesthetic basis. There is a return to traditional forms and techniques, but below the surface these pieces are actually more expressionistic than his previous music (their visionary character was noticed already by contemporary critics). As the titles and texts of works from this period suggest (such as "The Music of the Night" and "Chase," from the series *Out of Doors* [1926], or the text of the 1930 *Cantata profana*), the pieces capture an intense emotional "story" whose basis is an imaginary journey through the dark fears of the soul in search for an ideal world that is pure, simple, and positive. This underlying theme is perceivable also in works to which Bartók did not supply words, such as *Music for Strings, Percussion, and Celesta* (1936) or the fifth and sixth string quartets (1934 and 1939). In order to recount this "story," Bartók

used varied means of artistic expression, including irony and playfulness. This hidden story, which is more fundamental to the message of the works than the classical forms that cloak them, expresses both Bartók's childhood memories and a European modernist experience, both a belief in and longing for wholeness and the realization that wholeness is impossible in the modern world.

Fleeing the Nazi regime, Bartók emigrated to the United States in 1940. The trauma of emigration and his advancing illness brought him to a creative crisis; he was not able to compose for more than three years. The last works—Concerto for Orchestra (1943), Piano Concerto no. 3 (1945), Sonata for Violin (Solo Sonata; 1944)—bespeak fantasy but also confusion: each points in a different direction, and it is unclear which one he would have followed had he remained alive. Bartók left behind an unfinished and fragmented oeuvre, a beautiful and intense exploration of the human condition in the twentieth century.

See also **Modernism.**

BIBLIOGRAPHY

Frigyesi, Judit. *Béla Bartók and Turn-of-the-Century Budapest.* Berkeley, Calif., 1998.

Gillies, Malcolm. *Bartók Remembered.* New York and London, 1991.

Leafstedt, Carl S. *Inside Bluebeard's Castle: Music and Drama in Béla Bartók's Opera.* New York and Oxford, U.K., 1999.

Lendvai, Ernő. *Béla Bartók: An Analysis of His Music.* London, 1971.

Somfai, László. *Béla Bartók: Composition, Concepts, and Autograph Sources.* Berkeley, Calif., 1996.

Stevens, Halsey. *The Life and Music of Béla Bartók.* 3rd ed. New York, 1993.

Tallián, Tibor. *Béla Bartók: The Man and His Work.* Translated by Gyula Gulyas. Budapest, 1981.

JUDIT FRIGYESI

BASQUES. The Basques are a people who live in northern Spain and southern France. Most speak French or Spanish, but many also speak Basque, a language totally unrelated to the Romance language family (to which both French and Spanish belong).

No consensus exists on Basque's connections to any other languages. As of 2006, the population of Euzkadi, as the Spanish Basque region is called, was 2.1 million.

HISTORY

For centuries, the Basque Provinces in Spain had their own regional privileges (*fueros*), which reduced the taxes and number of military recruits the region owed the monarchy. Such privileges were common in Europe through the eighteenth century, but following the example of the French Revolution, governments in a number of European countries, including Spain, sought to create a more centralized administration and bring all citizens into an equal relationship with the nation-state. They also sought to impose greater control over the Catholic Church. These developments, along with a disputed succession to the Spanish throne following the death of Ferdinand VII in 1833, gave rise to a civil war known as the Carlist War (1833–1840), whose center of gravity was in the Basque Provinces. A second Carlist War, driven by similar issues, took place in 1875 and 1876. At the end of this conflict, the region lost most of its distinctive privileges.

Favored by rich deposits of iron ore, the Basque Provinces emerged as one of Spain's early industrial powerhouses. Mining, iron production, and shipbuilding drew many thousands of immigrants from other parts of Spain to the burgeoning cities of the region in the decades following the Second Carlist War. For many Basques, these changes were a threat to their culture and way of life, which they saw in idealized terms as bucolic, peaceful, and deeply Catholic. From such concerns emerged a movement devoted to asserting Basque cultural identity and winning political authority for the region.

BASQUE NATIONALISM

The founder of Basque nationalism was Sabino Arana Goiri (1865–1903). Arana's nationalism was profoundly Catholic, almost theocratic, as well as deeply racist, a defense of what he saw as a pure Basque race against defilement by an influx of *maketos,* a pejorative Basque word for other Spaniards. Arana's early death left the Basque nationalist movement with a confused legacy, one that a century later has yet to be entirely clarified. Is Basque nationalism a movement for regional self-government within Spain or for separatism and national independence? Who is a Basque and what is the place of immigrants in Basque society?

The most important institutional embodiment of Basque nationalism was the Basque Nationalist Party (PNV). The party was founded at the beginning of the twentieth century, but it was only during the Second Republic (1931–1939) that it achieved significant success. In elections held in 1933 and 1936, the PNV won more votes in the region than any other party, although it never achieved a majority. In 1932, the Republic granted regional autonomy to Cataluña and Basque nationalists demanded similar treatment. This was not an option under the center-right governments in power between November 1933 and February 1936, but following the electoral victory of the Popular Front, autonomy for the Basque region returned to the political agenda. It was still under discussion in parliament when the Spanish civil war broke out, but the decision of the PNV to support the Republic and not Francisco Franco's Nationalist rebels led to approval of an autonomy statute in October 1936.

The conditions of civil war meant that the Basque regional government, a coalition of Socialists and Republicans dominated by the PNV, enjoyed much broader freedom of action than the statute stipulated. Unlike the rest of the Republican zone, the Basque region did not experience social revolution; indeed, the Basque nationalists, who were social conservatives and strong Catholics, retained political and economic control. The Nationalist offensive in northern Spain led the Basque government to surrender in June 1937. As it became clear that the conquest of their region was inevitable, the Basque authorities chose to surrender, thus sparing Bilbao and its heavily industrialized hinterland from attack and destruction.

Not all Basques supported the Republic. Considerable support existed within the region for Franco's Nationalists, and this manifested itself in the large number of Basques who supported the Carlists, a reactionary, ultra-Catholic movement that harked back to a mythical Catholic monarchy before the installation of liberalism and that was the most fervent civilian support for the military uprising against the Republic. Many Basques joined the Carlist military force, the *requetes.*

THE FRANCO DICTATORSHIP

The Franco dictatorship that was born out of the civil war was rigidly centralist and completely hostile to any expression of regional identity. Basques, as well as Galicians and Catalans, saw their autonomy abolished; they also suffered prohibitions on the public use of their languages, which were officially declared to be dialects. For many Basques, Franco's regime was a Spanish occupation of their region, but in fact, other than in the question of language, the Basques suffered no more heavily than other Spaniards from the severity of the regime. And in some respects, the region can be said to have been favored.

The Basque region did well economically during the Franco years. When the dictatorship ended, the Basque Provinces had a per capita income 11 percent above the national average and two of the provinces, Alava and Guipúzcoa, ranked among the top ten of the country's fifty provinces (at number two and nine, respectively).

Anti-regime politics remained alive during the Franco years, as they did in much of the rest of Spain. Led by the PNV's José Antonio Aguirre (1904–1960) and Jesús María Leizaola (1896–1989), the Basque government from the civil war period continued to exist as a government-in-exile. The PNV also retained an organization inside Spain, which put it in an excellent position when democracy was restored after Franco's death. At least as significant, however, was the emergence in 1959 of Euskadi Ta Askatasuna (ETA), a radical nationalist movement that split off from the PNV's youth wing and is dedicated to using armed struggle to achieve complete independence.

THE POST-FRANCO PERIOD

Following Franco's death in November 1975, Spain began a surprisingly rapid and relatively peaceful transition to democracy. One of the Franco regime's paradoxical legacies was widespread support for regional autonomy among Spanish democrats. The constitution of 1978 established what came to be known as the "state of the autonomies" and recognized seventeen regions that had the right to self-government. The constitution also recognized the existence of three "historical nationalities": Basque, Catalan, and Galician, which had had autonomy statutes before the Franco regime. These regions had a quicker mechanism for establishing their regional government and, initially, a wider range of powers. The constitution also recognized the Basque, Catalan, and Galician languages as co-official with Spanish in their respective regions.

The new constitution received broad support in the referendum held on 6 December 1978: 88 percent of Spaniards who voted, voted in its favor. The Basque Provinces were the significant exception. With the PNV and other nationalists urging abstention, less than half of Basque voters, only 44.5 percent, turned out. This was a marked contrast to Cataluña, where two-thirds of eligible voters turned out and 90 percent favored the constitution.

Since 1978, the PNV has been the dominant political force in the region and has headed the regional government since one was first elected in 1980. At the same time, the nationalist political spectrum has become more complex. On one extreme stands the PNV, essentially a center-right, Christian Democratic–type party; on the other extreme stands ETA, advocating armed struggle for national independence. During the 1980s these groups were joined by Herri Batasuna, radical nationalists connected to ETA. In between were other nationalist parties: Euskadiko Ezkera, with a left-wing agenda, and Eusko Alkartasuna, a centrist party created in 1986 following a schism in the PNV. The Basque wing of the Socialist Party is nationalist but opposed to independence, whereas the Popular Party is antinationalist. By 2000 electoral support was split almost evenly between nationalist and non-nationalist options.

Support for Basque nationalism has varied significantly within the region. Nationalists have dominated the two provinces of Guipúzcoa and Vizcaya but have been less successful in Alava and especially in Navarra, which has its own autonomy statute. Important differences also exist between rural and urban areas; the latter, and especially those which have large numbers of immigrants from other parts of Spain, have tended to give more support to non-nationalist parties.

See also **ETA; Spain.**

A Basque farmer tends his fields in the traditional way, 1985. ©Owen Franken/Corbis

BIBLIOGRAPHY

Gómez Uranga, Mikel. *Basque Economy: From Industrialization to Globalization.* Reno, Nev., 2003.

Juaristi, Jon, *El bucle melancólico: Historias de nacionalistas vascos.* Madrid, 1997.

Mees, Ludger. *Nationalism, Violence, and Democracy: The Basque Clash of Identities.* London, 2003.

Watson, Cameron J. *Modern Basque History: Eighteenth Century to the Present.* Reno, Nev., 2003.

ADRIAN SHUBERT

BATAILLE, GEORGES (1897–1962), French writer.

Georges Bataille was an iconoclastic writer whose literary and nonliterary works ranged across ethnography, sociology, aesthetics, religion, and political economy. Not much is known about Bataille's boyhood. He was born in Billom, France, and grew up in Reims. His father, a syphilitic, was blind and paralyzed; he apparently went mad when Bataille was a teenager. His mother expended herself taking care of her husband and also may have had bouts of madness sometime around his death in 1915, after she and Bataille had abandoned him in Reims as the German army approached during World War I. Around that time Bataille was baptized and became a devout Catholic. He was mobilized for the war in 1916 but did not fight, and he was discharged after one year because of illness. After a year in the seminary with thoughts of becoming a priest, Bataille went to Paris to attend college, where he earned a degree as a paleographic archivist. He lost his faith in the early 1920s, turning to an increasingly dissolute lifestyle and to unpious authors such as Friedrich Nietzsche and Fyodor Dostoyevsky. In 1922 Bataille became a career librarian, beginning with a post at the Bibliothèque Nationale.

In 1924 André Breton and others launched the surrealist movement, to which Bataille was momentarily attracted but with which he would find himself in a tense and sometimes hostile relationship. In the late 1920s Bataille began the literary explorations that would make him one of the most scandalous writers of the twentieth century. In 1928 he published under a pseudonym *Histoire de l'oeil* (*The Story of the Eye*), a shocking tale of martyrdom and ecstasy through the means of violently transgressive adolescent sex and ultimately the cutting out and desecration of an eye. It set forth his signature themes of a fascination with death, ritualized cruelty, the erotic, and the sacred—though not for the sake of themselves but rather for their relationship to the constitution of community. Other texts from this period confirm that although his work was pornographic by any conventional standard, it also represented a serious investigation into the nature of human community. Thus, for example, "La valeur d'usage de DAF de Sade" (1930; "The Use-Value of D. A. F. de Sade") and *L'anus solaire* (1931; *The Solar Anus*) discuss the "surplus" excretions of the human body in terms of Marcel Mauss's claim that some societies give special symbolic value to "unproductive loss" such as luxury, rituals, and war—an idea to which Bataille returned in his more mature work.

By the early 1930s Bataille had been involved in a number of clashes with Breton and the surrealists. He was deeply involved (along with Michel Leiris, Robert Desnos, and Marcel Griaule) in a quasi-ethnographic journal, *Documents,* that mocked the seriousness of the surrealist endeavor. He also signed a particularly violent attack on Breton in 1930, called *Un cadavre* (A corpse), referring to Breton. In 1935, with a drastically different political situation both in France and in Germany, Bataille and Breton briefly reconciled for reasons of counterfascist political solidarity in Bataille's group, Contre-Attaque (1935). They split once again, however, and Bataille then founded two experimental groups, Acéphale (1936–1939) and the Collège de Sociologie (College of Sociology) (1937–1939), each of which collected various ex-surrealists around it. With Acéphale, Bataille attempted to found a community and a religion; he envisioned the collective participating in a ritual human sacrifice, an act he thought to be at the origin of communal and sacred bonds. It is unknown whether or not such a sacrifice actually took place. The Collège de Sociologie, founded with Leiris and Roger Caillois, though neither a college nor a matter of scientific inquiry, attracted some of the most original minds of the twentieth century to its sessions on society and the sacred.

Many commentators have raised the question of whether Bataille's fascination with death and eroticism place him in indirect complicity with fascism, in spite of Bataille's repeated rejection of it. While Bataille certainly scorned the conventions of middle-class morality and of liberal-democratic politics, he also consistently denounced the Nazi attempt at collective ritual experience as superficial and not genuinely representative of the limit-experiences he aimed to explore.

During the Nazi occupation of France, Bataille continued to write, publishing *L'expérience intérieure* (1943; *Inner Experience*), an investigation into the relationships among experience, the sacred, and knowledge. He also founded one of the most important literary and intellectual journals of the postwar era, *Critique* (1946 to the present), and began to rework Mauss's concept of "unproductive loss" for a three-part inquiry into political economy. The first volume, *La part maudite* (1949; *The Accursed Share*) is considered one of Bataille's most important books; the two other projected volumes, *L'histoire de érotisme* (*The History of Eroticism*) and *La souveraineté* (Sovereignty), did not appear in his lifetime.

Bataille's works in the 1950s included an unfinished novel, *Ma mère* (written in 1954–1955; *My Mother*), published in 1966, which recounts the story of a woman who reaches a state of saintliness and sacrifice through increasingly debauched acts that include seducing her son; and *L'érotisme* (1957; *Erotism: Death and Sensuality*). Bataille died in 1962 but continued to be a major influence on writers such as Philippe Sollers and philosophers such as Michel Foucault and Jacques Derrida.

See also **Breton, André; Surrealism.**

BIBLIOGRAPHY

Connor, Peter Tracey. *Georges Bataille and the Mysticism of Sin*. Baltimore, Md., 2003.

Dean, Carolyn J. *The Self and Its Pleasures: Bataille, Lacan, and the History of the Decentered Subject*. Ithaca, N.Y., 1992.

Gill, Carolyn Bailey, ed. *Bataille: Writing the Sacred*. New York, 1995.

Hollier, Denis. *Against Architecture: The Writings of Georges Bataille*. Translated by Betsy Wing. Cambridge, Mass., 1992.

Richman, Michèle H. *Reading Georges Bataille: Beyond the Gift*. Baltimore, Md., 1982.

Surya, Michel. *Georges Bataille: An Intellectual Biography*. Translated by Krzysztof Fijalkowski and Michael Richardson. New York, 2002.

PAIGE ARTHUR

BAUDRILLARD, JEAN (b. 1929), French sociologist.

Jean Baudrillard was born in the cathedral town of Reims, France in 1929. In 1956, he began working as a professor of secondary education in a French high school (lycée) and in the early 1960s did editorial work for the French publisher Seuil. Baudrillard was initially a Germanist who published essays on literature in *Les temps modernes* in 1962–1963 and translated works of Peter Weiss and Bertolt Brecht into French, as well as a book on messianic revolutionary movements by Wilhelm Mühlmann. During this period, he met and studied the works of Henri Lefebvre, whose critiques of everyday life impressed him, and Roland Barthes, whose semiological analyses of contemporary society had lasting influence on his work.

In 1966, Baudrillard entered the University of Paris, Nanterre, and became Lefebvre's assistant, while studying languages, philosophy, sociology, and other disciplines. He defended his "Thèse de Troisième Cycle" in sociology at Nanterre in 1966 with a dissertation on *Le système des objects,* and began teaching sociology in October of that year. Opposing French and U.S. intervention in the Algerian and Vietnamese wars, Baudrillard associated himself with the French Left in the 1960s. Nanterre was a key site of radical politics, and the "22 March movement" associated with Daniel Cohn-Bendit and the *enragés* began in the Nanterre sociology department. Baudrillard said later that he participated in the events of May 1968 that resulted in massive student uprisings and a general strike that almost drove President Charles de Gaulle from power.

During the late 1960s, Baudrillard began publishing a series of books that would eventually make him world famous. Influenced by Lefebvre, Barthes, and a French avant-garde arts and theory tradition, Baudrillard undertook serious work in the field of social theory, semiology, and psychoanalysis in the 1960s and published his first book, *The System of Objects* in 1968, followed by a book on *The Consumer Society* in 1970, and *For a Critique of the Political Economy of the Sign* in 1972. These early publications are attempts, within the framework of critical sociology, to combine the studies of everyday life initiated by Lefebvre with a social semiology that studies the life of signs in social life. Combining semiological studies, Marxian political economy, and sociology of the consumer society, Baudrillard began his lifelong task of exploring the system of objects and signs that forms everyday life.

While Baudrillard's first three works can be read in the framework of a neo-Marxian critique of capitalist societies, in his 1973 provocation, *The Mirror of Production*, Baudrillard carries out a systematic attack on classical Marxism, claiming that Marxism is but a mirror of bourgeois society, placing production at the center of life, thus naturalizing the capitalist organization of society.

Like many on the left, Baudrillard was disappointed that the French Communist Party did not support the radical 1960s movements and he also distrusted the official Marxism of theorists like Louis Althusser, whom he found dogmatic and reductive. Consequently, Baudrillard began a radical critique of Marxism, one that would be repeated by many of his contemporaries who would also take a postmodern turn. In works like *Simulations* (1983) and *Symbolic Exchange and Death* (1976), Baudrillard posits a divide in history as radical as the rupture between premodern societies and modern ones. In the mode of classical social theory, he systematically develops distinctions between premodern societies organized around symbolic exchange, modern societies organized around production, and postmodern societies organized around "simulation" by which he means the cultural modes of representation that "simulate" reality, as in television, computer cyberspace, and virtual reality. Baudrillard argues that in the contemporary era, simulation, or social reproduction (information processing, communication, and knowledge industries, and so on), replaces production as the organizing form of society. Technology replaces capital for Baudrillard and semiurgy (interpreted as proliferation of images, information, and signs) supplants production. His postmodern turn is thus connected to a form of technological determinism and a rejection of political economy as a useful explanatory principle—a move that many of his critics reject.

In his later works, Baudrillard continues reflection on contemporary developments and events, although his work also takes a metaphysical turn in which he develops unique philosophical perspectives around a theory in which the object-world displaces the subject and individuals are subjected to ever more domination and control. While his work on simulation and the postmodern break from the mid-1970s into the 1980s provides a paradigmatic postmodern theory and analysis of postmodernity that has been highly influential, his later post-1980s work is arguably of more literary and philosophical than sociological interest. Baudrillard thus ultimately goes beyond social theory altogether into a novel sphere and mode of writing that provides occasional insights into contemporary social phenomena and provocative critiques of contemporary and classical philosophy and social theory, but does not really provide an adequate theory of the contemporary era.

See also **Postmodernism; Semiotics.**

BIBLIOGRAPHY

Primary Sources

Baudrillard, Jean. *The Mirror of Production.* St. Louis, 1973.

———. *For a Critique of the Political Economy of the Sign.* Translated by Charles Levin. St. Louis, 1981.

———. *Simulations.* Translated by Paul Foss, Paul Patton, and Philip Beitchman. New York, 1983.

———. *Symbolic Exchange and Death.* Translated by Iain Hamilton Grant. London, 1993.

———. *The System of Objects.* Translated by James Benedict. London, 1996.

———. *The Consumer Society.* Paris, 1998.

Secondary Sources

Kellner, Douglas. *Jean Baudrillard: From Marxism to Postmodernism and Beyond.* Stanford, Calif., 1989.

DOUGLAS KELLNER

BAUHAUS. The Bauhaus is widely regarded as the single most influential school of art, architecture, and design in the twentieth century. Founded in Weimar, Germany, in 1919 by the Thuringian state, the school, led by the architect Walter Gropius, featured an all-star faculty that included such luminaries as Wassily Kandinsky, Paul Klee, Johannes Itten, László Moholy-Nagy, Lyonel Feininger, and many others. Gropius, an ambitious school director whom the Belgian artist Henry van de Velde had recommended as his successor upon van de Velde's dismissal in 1915, successfully combined the Weimar Academy of Art and what remained of van de Velde's Weimar School of Applied Arts into a single institution after World War I. Under his leadership, the school quickly broadened its mission to promote a radical fusion of the fine arts, the decorative arts, architecture, and industrial design. The Bauhaus's innovative introductory course, developed initially by Johannes Itten, together with the school's production of numerous formally innovative industrial prototypes, left many aspects of pre–World War I applied-arts teaching far behind. Rising to become the standard bearer of a reformed, modern artistic culture, the Bauhaus, Gropius proclaimed, would lead postwar German society in a process of artistic, social, and cultural renewal.

From its beginning in 1919, however, the school struggled against right-wing political forces that denounced the Bauhaus and its forward-looking, experimental artistic and cultural pedagogy as a menace to traditional German culture. Constantly embattled, underfunded, and forced to leave the cities of Weimar, Dessau, and later Berlin, the school functioned as a kind of crucible for Germany's avant-garde. The Bauhaus drew strength from its affiliations and its affinities to such peer European movements as Russian constructivism, Dada, surrealism, and the Dutch De Stijl movement—precisely the international influences that conservative nationalists, and later

Hitler's National Socialists, saw as such a threat to native German traditions. Aided in part by exhibitions and publicity received after the emigration of Gropius, Moholy-Nagy, Josef Albers, Marcel Breuer, and Ludwig Mies van der Rohe to the United States, the Bauhaus's reputation achieved mythical status, towering over all other modern German schools of design. The dizzying number of historical reinterpretations of the Bauhaus that have accumulated since its dissolution in 1933 have, in fact, functioned as a veritable index of Western cultural trends and preoccupations ever since.

THURINGIA

The Thuringian state initially founded the State Bauhaus in Weimar (Staatliches Bauhaus Weimar) in 1919 for the purpose of reviving the crafts. As the thirty-five-year-old Gropius wrote when he sought budget approval from Thurinigian authorities in 1919, the Bauhaus would promote "a proliferation of the crafts and industry in the state of Weimar as a result of the re-molding of the schools in accordance with a craft-oriented, practical approach" (Wingler, p. 26). This agenda quickly expanded as, in response to the left-wing political ferment that followed World War I, Gropius assembled a broad-based, experimental faculty of artists and designers to facilitate Germany's postwar cultural renewal. Political attacks and controversy soon led Gropius to promote an official school policy of "nonalignment" in political matters. This in no way dampened the experimental nature of the school's broad-based curriculum, however. In addition to a bracing, six-month introductory course (*Vorkurs*) designed to unburden students of historicist thinking and unleash their individual creative potential, the school established practical instructional workshops in woodworking, ceramics, book binding, weaving, metalworking, and sculpture. Leading artists further taught courses in painting, art theory, typography, and set design, and the school collectively explored a variety of performance-based media, including music and experimental theater. Architecture, considered by Gropius to be the "mother of all the arts," after John Ruskin's dictum of half a century earlier, did not become an official Bauhaus department until the school relocated with new energy and funding in Dessau in 1926.

Rather than representing any particular philosophy or defined approach to design, the Bauhaus was, as the architect Ludwig Mies van der Rohe famously characterized it, always "an idea." That is, the school was always the collective product of its faculty, students, and three successive directors, whose experimental inclinations were highlighted by contributions from particular, highly individualistic, and influential instructors. Thus Gropius, the director from 1919 to 1928, presided over the Bauhaus's initial crafts and expressionist phases, which lasted into the early 1920s. By 1923, Gropius felt compelled to dismiss the innovative Swiss painter Johannes Itten, a charismatic instructor and follower of Mazdaznan religious traditions, in order to consolidate his leadership of the school and reconnect its curriculum to resurgent German industry and the product design fields. For this new phase, Gropius adopted a fresh school slogan, "Art and Technology: A New Unity," which became the title of an influential Bauhaus exhibition in Weimar in 1923.

DESSAU, BERLIN, AND BEYOND

Defeated and driven out of Weimar by victorious right-wing nationalist parties in the Thuringian state legislature in early 1925, the Bauhaus found a generous new patron in Fritz Hesse, mayor of Dessau, a town located roughly halfway between Weimar and Berlin. Funding organized by Hesse's administration enabled Gropius to complete an iconic, self-consciously modern industrial school building based on his own designs in 1926. The Dessau Bauhaus's asymmetrical plan and separate wings, containing glass curtain-walled workshops, a dormitory tower, and classrooms—all linked by a dramatic "bridge" that housed the school administration—acted as a visible manifesto of the Bauhaus outlook. In addition, Hesse's patronage made possible the construction of individual "masters' houses" that Gropius designed for himself and senior Bauhaus faculty. Although the school's operating budget was still tight, a newly founded architecture department thrived with such commissions as the experimental Törten housing estate, which used Gropius's methods for serial production of more than three hundred housing units constructed of standardized parts. At the same time, a growing number of Bauhaus posters and specially designed publications helped establish the

The dormitory building of the Bauhaus complex in Dessau, designed by Walter Gropius, 1919. BRIDGEMAN ART LIBRARY

school as a popular center for the German and European avant-garde. Faculty such as Moholy-Nagy and later Albers took the Bauhaus introductory course in new directions, and other courses explored new technologies and utopian design schemes as ways of pushing students to think beyond the range of customary product design and interior design.

By 1928 resurgent local political opposition and a desire to devote more time to his architectural practice prompted Gropius to hand over directorship of the Dessau Bauhaus to the Swiss architect Hannes Meyer. Meyer, an avowed socialist from the Swiss collectivist-constructivist school, emphasized utilitarian, affordable designs of everyday products using industrial materials and scientific design methods. Sacrificing art in favor of technical excellence, individual will in favor of collective purpose, and the luxury product in favor of the useful commodity, Meyer shocked the painters Klee, Kandinsky, and Feininger. Meyer's reorientation of

the school toward a "radical functionalism" further prompted the resignations of Moholy-Nagy and Herbert Bayer. Nevertheless, the school's new cult of scientific reason, socialism, and sober pragmatism enabled Meyer to enlarge the school's connections to German industrial producers, who cooperated in the production of iconic Bauhaus prototypes for light fittings, wallpaper, glassware, and other successful products. Older handcrafts workshops were replaced by new departments of photography and interior design, whose workshops were characterized as laboratories rather than studios.

Meyer's radicalism fired local opposition in Dessau, which led to his resignation in 1930. He was succeeded by Mies van der Rohe. When local Dessau municipal politics led to the closure of the Bauhaus in 1932, Mies van der Rohe moved the school to Berlin. Greatly reduced in size and scope, the curriculum emphasized architecture as a systematic and rigorous practice in accordance with Mies van der Rohe's philosophy. Typical student assignments included spending months perfecting designs for a simple single-family home that was extremely carefully planned in terms of materials, space, and structure. In 1933, Nazi pressures led Mies van der Rohe and his faculty to close the Berlin-based school, but the Bauhaus idea was carried elsewhere. The appointments of Gropius, Mies van der Rohe, Breuer, Albers, and Moholy-Nagy to leading positions at Harvard University, the Illinois Institute of Technology, and other schools in the United States in the late 1930s ensured that various permutations of Bauhaus thinking and methodology would alter the way many Americans and American businesses would come to think about design and modern life. In Germany, the Swiss Bauhaus graduate Max Bill would found and direct the Hochschule für Gestaltung (school of design) in the south German city of Ulm beginning in 1955. The Ulm school operated as Germany's leading post–World War II Bauhaus successor institution until its closure in 1968. Only during the 1960s, when architects such as Robert Venturi and Philip Johnson rebelled against a somewhat caricatured image of Bauhaus dogmatism and perceived modernist universalism, did the Bauhaus's reputation significantly wane. Nevertheless, the school's impact on the design world and the progressive, experimental spirit of much of contemporary architecture and design education continues to be felt.

See also **Architecture; Constructivism; Dada; Gropius, Walter; Kandinsky, Wassily; Klee, Paul; Mies van der Rohe, Ludwig; Moholy-Nagy, László.**

BIBLIOGRAPHY

Betts, Paul. "The Bauhaus as Cold-War Legend: West German Modernism Revisited." *German Politics and Society* 14 (summer 1996): 75–100.

Fiedler, Jeannine, and Peter Feierabend, eds. *Bauhaus.* Cologne, 2000.

Franciscono, Marcel. *Walter Gropius and the Creation of the Bauhaus in Weimar: The Ideals and Artistic Theories of Its Founding Years.* Urbana, Ill., 1971.

Kentgens-Craig, Margret. *The Bauhaus and America: First Contacts, 1919–1936.* Cambridge, Mass., 1999.

Maciuika, John V. *Before the Bauhaus: Architecture, Politics, and the German State, 1890–1920.* Cambridge and New York, 2005.

Naylor, Gillian. *The Bauhaus Reassessed: Sources and Design Theory.* New York, 1985.

Wahl, Volker, and Ute Ackermann, eds. *Die Meisterratsprotokolle des Staatlichen Bauhauses Weimar, 1919 bis 1925.* Weimar, Germany, 2001.

Wick, Rainer K. *Teaching at the Bauhaus.* Ostfildern-Ruit, Germany, 2000.

Wingler, Hans Maria. *The Bauhaus: Weimar, Dessau, Berlin, Chicago.* Translated by W. Jabs and Basil Gilbert. Cambridge, Mass., 1969.

JOHN V. MACIUIKA

BAYREUTH. The music of the composer and festival founder Richard Wagner (1813–1883) and the national myths staged and set to music in his operas make up the fascination surrounding the most famous German festival in the twentieth century. Wagner's conception, developed in the middle of the nineteenth century, of an "artwork of the future" as *Gesamtkunstwerk* (total artwork) bore within it a modern and totalitarian ideology that was politically interpreted and realized in the twentieth century. The Bayreuth Festival thus became a point of crystallization for the cultural and educational policies of National Socialism; even at the turn of the twenty-first century the artistic discussions about the interpretation of Wagner's operas have been partially shaped by Bayreuth: the festival has remained a surface of projection for the German self-image.

In the 1870s, with the support of patrons and in particular of the Bavarian king Louis II, Richard Wagner erected a concert hall reserved exclusively for the presentation of a number of his operas in the small Protestant Prussian town of Bayreuth. This monopoly has been maintained to the present day, as has the tradition that the descendants of Richard Wagner direct the festival and claim for themselves a special "authenticity" in the interpretation of his works. Wagner's wife, Cosima (1837–1930), directed the festival until 1906; she was followed as heir by their son, Siegfried (1869–1930).

By 1914 the festival had become established as one of Europe's leading cultural events, artistically and socially respected the world over. The festival productions were considered the epitome of German national culture. World War I was both an institutional and a spiritual turning point for the

A British travel poster from the 1920s by Austin Cooper advertises rail services to Bayreuth. ©YALE CENTER FOR BRITISH ART, NEW HAVEN, USA/BRIDGEMAN ART LIBRARY

festival. Closed during the war, the festival was able to reopen in 1924 after considerable start-up difficulties. The renewed festival was influenced by a combination of German national resentment, rejection of the Treaty of Versailles, and the ideas of the nineteenth-century French racial determinist Joseph-Arthur, comte de Gobineau, which shaped a group of intellectuals centered around the British publicist Houston Stewart Chamberlain, who disseminated their ideology in the journal *Bayreuther Blätter*. Despite the influence of this ideology, during the Weimar Republic the cosmopolitan conductors Fritz Busch, Karl Elmendorff, and Arturo Toscanini, as well as the stage designer Hans Pfitzner, left their mark on the festival, which, with productions such as *Tristan and Isolde* and *Tannhäuser,* scattered the dust of the imperial era and for the first time allowed non-German artists, though not any Jews, to share in the spotlight.

Faced with the loss of foreign interest in the festival after Adolf Hitler's takeover of power, the wife and heiress of the late festival director Siegfried Wagner, Winifred Wagner (née Williams; 1897–1980), decided as early as the spring of 1933 to accept the help of the National Socialist state and its protagonists. Hitler had been friends with Winifred Wagner from the time of the founding of the Nazi Party; Richard Wagner was his favorite composer. In principle preserving its status as a private enterprise while also presenting itself as a private refuge for Hitler, the festival became the symbol of the National Socialist appropriation of traditional cultural institutions. From an exclusive and international rendezvous of the elite, the festival became in the 1930s a destination for the Nazi travel organization KdF (Kraft durch Freude, "strength through joy"); in wartime, festival productions were continued for armaments workers and the wounded. Mass accommodations, quasi-religious services, and a visiting program were directed toward the ideal of a new National Socialist community. Typical of National Socialism as an amalgam of neoromanticism and progress, modernizing tendencies already began to emerge during the Nazi period. In addition to Winifred Wagner, Heinz Tietjen from Berlin and Wieland Wagner directed operas, and Hans Knappertsbusch, Wilhelm Furtwängler, and Emil Preetorius shaped stage aesthetics. As productions, *The Meistersinger of Nuremberg* (1933/1943), *Lohengrin* (1936) and *The Flying Dutchman* (1939), stand out.

With the end of Nazi Germany, the nationalist transformation of the festival became absurd. Reopening immediately after the war was inconceivable for organizational reasons, but also due to the moral dubiousness of the festival and its director, Winifred Wagner; despite her classification as "less guilty" in denazification proceedings, the public debate over her future participation had not ended.

Only her relinquishing of the directorship cleared the way for her two children, Wolfgang (b. 1919) and Wieland (1917–1966), who managed to reopen the festival in 1951 with the help of state institutions and industry, until the West German government also provided financial support for a new beginning. In the production history after the war, a changed relationship to the concept of a German nation can be traced: through his staging, Wieland Wagner strove to achieve an explicitly psychoanalytical and ancient-mystical interpretation of the Wagner dramas. No longer was the nation important, but the individual. This fundamental shift in emphasis provoked opposition in nationalistic circles but allowed contact with international aesthetic discussions. In contrast to the isolation during National Socialism, Wieland Wagner's productions of *Parsival* (1951), *Meistersinger* (1956), and *Tristan* (1962) became world famous.

After Wieland's death in 1966, the festival direction was taken over by his brother, Wolfgang, who is considered an administrative expert, but whose numerous mise-en-scènes have for the most part not achieved the suggestiveness of Wieland's. In 1973 the relationship between the private festival enterprise and the government was finally regulated officially: Wolfgang and Winifred Wagner agreed to the establishment of a publicly dominated foundation. In the late 1960s, Wolfgang had developed the festival into a "workshop" by inviting internationally renowned directors, hoping in this way to retain the eminence of Bayreuth. Operations have continued to follow this practice of inviting outside directors, which has diminished the Wagner family's artistic control and internationalized the festival. The high point of this practice was the staging of the *Ring of the Nibelungen* by the Frenchman Patrice Chéreau for the centennial of the festival in 1976, followed by Jean-Pierre Ponelle's *Tristan* in 1981.

With Götz Friedrich (*Lohengrin*, 1979), Harry Kupfer (*Flying Dutchman*, 1978), and Heiner Müller, East German artists also directed festival productions. From the 1950s Bayreuth had profited from connections with the other part of Germany, which was reunified with the Federal Republic in 1990. The first decade of the twenty-first century has been marked by the succession debate, pitting Wolfgang Wagner's daughter Katharina (b. 1978) against Nike Wagner (b. 1945), the daughter of Wieland. Would it mean an end to the Bayreuth tradition—which has previously undergone so many transformations—if no family member directed the festival? Even in the twenty-first century the festival poses the question of the approach to music and politicized music in Germany and internationally.

See also **Anti-Semitism; Germany; Hitler, Adolf; Nazism; Opera.**

BIBLIOGRAPHY

Hamann, Brigitte. *Winifred Wagner, oder, Hitlers Bayreuth.* Munich, 2002.

Spotts, Frederic. *Bayreuth: A History of the Wagner Festival.* New Haven, Conn., 1994.

Vaget, Hans Rudolf. "Hitler's Wagner: Musical Discourse as Cultural Space." In *Music and Nazism. Art under Tyranny, 1933–1945,* edited by Michael H. Kater and Albrecht Riethmüller, 15–31. Laaber, Germany, 2003.

Weiner, Marc A. *Richard Wagner and the Anti-Semitic Imagination.* Lincoln, Nebr., 1995.

HOLGER R. STUNZ

BBC. The British Broadcasting Corporation (BBC) is Britain's national broadcasting organization and a pioneer of public service broadcasting. It began life in October 1922 when a consortium of radio manufacturers founded a British Broadcasting Company. In 1927 a government charter transformed this body into a public corporation with a monopoly of the British airwaves. The BBC was funded by a license fee levied on all radio users and overseen by a board of governors drawn from Britain's elite. The board contributed to a socially conservative bias in the corporation's early output. The BBC's first director general, the Scottish-born engineer John Charles Walsham Reith (1889–1971), added his own vision that the BBC had a duty to educate. Britons affectionately nicknamed the new corporation with its prudish style "Auntie."

In 1932, as the government moved to promote British values around the world, the BBC began an *Empire Service* in English. Foreign language broadcasts, funded and guided by the Foreign Office, began in 1938 with an Arabic service, designed to counter Italian propaganda in the Mediterranean. Further services followed as war grew near, and by the outbreak of World War II the BBC was broadcasting in the languages of allies, enemies, and neutral powers alike.

British actor George Robey, performing the role of Falstaff in William Shakespeare's play *Henry IV* for a BBC broadcast, March 1935. ©BBC/Corbis

In some ways the war blocked the development of the BBC. Its small television service, launched in 1936, shut down for the duration. However, the BBC swiftly became central to British wartime life, maintaining morale and political cohesion. The corporation gained a reputation for credibility as a news service at home and abroad. This served as a potent contrast to the totalitarian approach to propaganda.

The war years saw a lightening of the tone of the BBC with more regional accents, comedy, and dance music. In 1941, the BBC even introduced its first soap opera, *Frontline Family,* originally created as a device to win over female listeners in the still-neutral United States. Successful wartime broadcasters included Yorkshire-born writer J[ohn] B[oynton] Priestley (1894–1984), who used the BBC to advance ideas of the war as an opportunity for social reform. Key figures in the European resistance to Adolf Hitler (1889–1945) in exile in London, including Charles de Gaulle of France (1890–1970) and Guido Leo J[ohn] C[hristmas] Møller (1898–1948) of Denmark, broadcast to their occupied homes over the BBC. The agency coordinating radio warfare—the Political Warfare Executive—took care to avoid encouraging useless acts of resistance, fearing that this would result in a damaging backlash against Britain. Famous campaigns included encouraging Belgians to chalk the "V" for victory on walls. In deference to the sensitivities of the Soviet Union about propaganda, the BBC did not create a Russian service at this time.

After the war, the BBC's foreign language services were regrouped into the *World Service* and played a major role in the propaganda Cold War with the communist world. The BBC launched its Russian service in 1946. This service and others drew on script material created by a special propaganda section of the Foreign Office called the Information Research Department, created in 1948. It is a testament to the potency of the BBC that its broadcasts from the spring of 1948 onward were jammed across the Eastern bloc. The cost of blocking the BBC far outstripped the cost of running its foreign language services, and merely served to emphasize that the communist regimes felt that they had something to hide. Other communist countermeasures included the murder in 1978 of a BBC Bulgarian service broadcaster, Georgi Markov (1929–1978). In the long run the BBC, along with other Western broadcasters to the communist bloc, played a key role in undermining communism.

At home, with the end of World War II, the BBC relaunched its television service. The coronation of Elizabeth II (b. 1926) in June 1953 prompted many Britons to embrace the medium for the first time. But the postwar BBC was slow to become a prime forum for political debate. Since 1944, the BBC had been subject to a "fourteen-day rule" requiring the corporation to wait two weeks before carrying political comment on an issue before parliament. The Suez Crisis of 1956 destroyed this rule, and thereafter BBC programming became a key element in British political life. Important and long-running current affairs programs include *Panorama* and *Question Time*. BBC drama has also played a part in raising public consciousness, as with the 1966 docudrama on homelessness directed by Ken Loach (b. 1936), *Cathy Come Home*.

The BBC lost its domestic monopoly in September 1954 with the creation of the

BBC war correspondent Frank Gilliard uses a gramophone to make a recording in the field, 1944. ©HULTON-DEUTSCH COLLECTION/CORBIS

Independent Television Authority (ITA). In 1964 the BBC gained a second channel—BBC Two—by way of compensation. In 1967 the BBC began local radio broadcasting. In the 1990s, the corporation launched international satellite news and entertainment channels, challenging the dominance of American channels such as CNN. By 2004, the BBC offered an array of domestic niche digital channels on television and radio, though critics questioned whether the general license fee should pay for such minority channels. The BBC had also become one of Europe's leading providers of information via the World Wide Web.

As a central institution in British life, the BBC has seldom been distant from controversy. The BBC has been a master of self-censorship. Notorious examples include the suppression of the 1965 film by Peter Watkins (b. 1935), *The War Game*, which used amateur actors to depict the effect of a nuclear attack on Britain. The film circulated theatrically and won an Academy Award. In 1985, Margaret Thatcher (b. 1925) attempted to squash a *Real Lives* documentary: *At the Edge of the Union.* When the board of the BBC demanded changes in the program, broadcast journalists protested with a one-day strike. In 2003, a radio journalist named Andrew Gilligan (b. 1968) accused Prime Minister Tony Blair (b. 1953) of manipulating evidence to justify the invasion of Iraq. A subsequent investigation chaired by Lord James Brian Edward Hutton (b. 1931) vindicated Blair's position and led to the resignation of both the director general and chairman of the BBC. The BBC's international reputation for accuracy suffered as a result.

See also **Popular Culture; Propaganda; Radio; Television.**

BIBLIOGRAPHY

Briggs, Asa. *The BBC: The First Fifty Years.* Oxford, U.K., 1985. A condensed history of the BBC, which has also been documented in a multiple volume series by this author.

Negrine, Ralph, ed. *Television and the Press since 1945.* Manchester, U.K., 1998. A useful collection of documents and commentary introducing the key issues in the postwar British media.

Walker, Andrew. *A Skyful of Freedom: 60 Years of the BBC World Service.* London, 1992. A history of the BBC World Service.

NICHOLAS J. CULL

BEACH, SYLVIA

BEACH, SYLVIA (1887–1962), the owner of Shakespeare and Company bookshop in Paris and the first publisher of James Joyce's *Ulysses.*

Sylvia Beach, born Nancy Woodbridge Beach in Baltimore, Maryland, was the second of three daughters of the Reverend Sylvester Woodbridge Beach, a Presbyterian minister, and Eleanor Orbison Beach. Though she took a name to echo her father's when she was an adolescent, she soon realized she was disinclined toward both religion and formal education. She fled the Presbyterian parsonage of Princeton, New Jersey, for Europe, spending the years 1907–1908 and 1911–1912 in Florence and 1914–1916 in Spain. In midsummer of 1916 she settled in Paris, where her father had served as associate pastor at the American Church from 1902 to 1905. Paris would remain her home until her death forty-six years later.

During World War I Beach met her lifelong companion, Adrienne Monnier, who owned a small but influential French bookshop on the Left Bank, La Maison des Amis des Livres (The House of the Friends of Books). Beach worked as a volunteer farmhand in Touraine (1917) and served with the Red Cross in Serbia (1919) before opening Shakespeare and Company bookshop and lending library, with Monnier's assistance, at 8 rue Dupuytren on 17 November 1919. A year and a half later she moved around the corner to 12 rue de l'Odéon, across the street from Monnier's bookshop. Beach sold only English-language books; Monnier sold only French literature. Together they orchestrated much of the exchange of English and French literature for the first half of the twentieth century.

Beach's single greatest achievement was the publication of James Joyce's *Ulysses,* agreed upon on 1 April 1921, printed by Maurice Darantiere of Dijon, and published on 2 February 1922, in time for Joyce's fortieth birthday. During the months before publication, Beach interceded with the printer to allow Joyce to revise and expand page proofs until he had written a third more of his great novel of Dublin. For a decade, until her relationship with Joyce became strained and Random House took over publication, she reprinted the novel and cared for all of Joyce's literary, financial, and sometimes family needs. She published his second collection of poems, *Pomes Penyeach,* in France (1927) and the United States (1931), and published the early reviews of what was to become his *Finnegans Wake* in a volume called *Our Exagmination Round His Factification for Incamination of Work in Progress* (1929), for which she wrote the introduction.

Shakespeare and Company bookshop, which Joyce called "Stratford-on-Odéon," served as a center for Joyce studies as well as for the exchange of avant-garde twentieth-century literature. Beach's library cards—for she operated chiefly a lending library—afford a valuable index to the reading habits of her famous patrons, from Ernest Hemingway and Gertrude Stein to Simone de Beauvoir and Richard Wright. Beach distributed all the small expatriate publishers' books and periodicals, participating directly in three French journals. Monnier's *Navire d'argent*

Sylvia Beach with James Joyce, Paris, 1920s. ©Bettmann/Corbis

(June 1925–May 1926) published Monnier and Beach's (first) translation of T. S. Eliot's "The Love Song of J. Alfred Prufrock." Beach also assisted *Commerce* (1924–1932) and served on the board of *Mesures* (1935–1940).

She kept her bookshop open during the difficult Depression years through regular donations from Bryher (Annie Winifred Ellerman, the English novelist). But the success and endurance of the bookshop resulted primarily from the force of her personality, which was characterized as much by her hospitality and loyalty (the quality Hemingway most admired) as by her sharp wit and verbal play. Janet Flanner

praised her "vigorous clear mind." In 1935 her French friends, who had been her first customers and would be her last, came to the rescue. Headed by André Gide, who organized the support group, The Friends of Shakespeare and Company sponsored readings by, among others, Eliot, Hemingway, Stephen Spender, Gide, and Paul Valéry. Beach finally had to close the shop at the end of 1941 during the German occupation.

While presiding over this literary crossroads, Beach introduced William Carlos Williams to Valéry Larbaud, F. Scott Fitzgerald to André Chamson, and Eugene Jolas to James Joyce. For a decade Jolas published portions of Joyce's last novel in his *transition* magazines. With Monnier, Beach translated Bryher's *Paris 1900* in 1938. In 1949 she translated Henri Michaux's *A Barbarian in Asia,* for which she won the Denyse Clairouin Award the following year. Her awards included the French Legion of Honor (1938) and an honorary doctor of letters from the University of Buffalo (1959). Most of her Joyce papers are at Lockwood Memorial Library, State University of New York, Buffalo, and her bookshop papers are at the Firestone Library, Princeton University.

See also **Eliot, T. S.; Gide, André; Joyce, James; Pound, Ezra; Stein, Gertrude; Valéry, Paul.**

BIBLIOGRAPHY

Beach, Sylvia. *Shakespeare and Company.* New York, 1959.

Fitch, Noel Riley. *Sylvia Beach and the Lost Generation: A History of Literary Paris in the Twenties and Thirties.* New York, 1983.

Mathews, Jackson, and Maurice Saillet, eds. *Sylvia Beach (1887–1962).* Paris, 1963.

Monnier, Adrienne. *The Very Rich Hours of Adrienne Monnier.* Translated and edited by Richard McDougall. New York, 1976.

Murat, Laure. *Passage de l'Odéon: Sylvia Beach, Adrienne Monnier et la vie littéraure à Paris dans l'entre-deux-guerres.* Paris, 2003.

NOEL RILEY FITCH

BEATLES. The explosion of Beatlemania, in Britain in 1963 and the rest of the world the next year, remains unparalleled. No popular musicians before or since have approached the Beatles' achievement of both unprecedented commercial dominance and near-universal acclaim for their artistry. The group sustained its status as the bellwether of its era until an acrimonious breakup in 1970.

The ascendancy of the Beatles is attributable in large part to the band containing not one but two of the finest singers and songwriters in the history of popular music, John Lennon (1940–1980) and bassist Paul McCartney (b. 1942), who met in 1957 in their native Liverpool, which visiting sailors had exposed to a wide range of music. Guitarist George Harrison (1943–2001) would emerge as a major songwriter as well. But only after a grueling period of constant live performance between 1960 and 1962 in Liverpool and an even more wide-open port city on the continent, Hamburg, did the ensemble's talents jell. At that point, Ringo Starr (née Richard Starkey; b. 1940) replaced drummer Pete Best (b. 1941) for reasons never fully clarified, just before the sessions leading to the group's first British releases.

At a time when rock and roll had very nearly been killed off by manufactured teen idols, the example of this fulsome collective writing its own songs and doing all the singing and playing on them established the very idea of the rock group. The "British invasion" spearheaded by the Beatles in the United States amounted to the resuscitation of rock and roll from its moribund condition in the early 1960s, when the original rock and rollers were dead (Buddy Holly), disgraced (Jerry Lee Lewis), imprisoned (Chuck Berry), retired (Little Richard), or sold-out (Elvis Presley). Along with other self-contained "British beat" groups such as the Rolling Stones, the Kinks, and the Who, the Beatles created a uniquely ebullient rock and roll that the United States supposedly embraced as a tonic after the assassination of John F. Kennedy, though the music was an international success, too.

A further attribute of the Beatles that made them unique and even startling was their musical synthesis, compelled by the arduous Liverpool and Hamburg gigs, of virtually every element in early rock and roll. To the heavy beat of rock and roll and up-tempo rhythm and blues (Little Richard, Larry Williams), the Beatles added early soul (Arthur Alexander), including Motown (the Miracles), and the vocal harmonies of doo-wop and surf music, usually worked out with producer George Martin, whose musical expertise remained crucial throughout their existence. The result was leavened with the sprightliness of girl groups (the Shirelles) and friendly white rockers such as Holly, as well as the jangle of country and western and rockabilly (Carl Perkins). Lennon and McCartney's songwriting was inspired by Brill Building teams such as Gerry Goffin and Carole King, who supplied the cutting-edge producer Phil Spector.

After rejuvenating rock and roll through four albums in this vein by the end of 1964, and achieving a surprising critical success with the film *A*

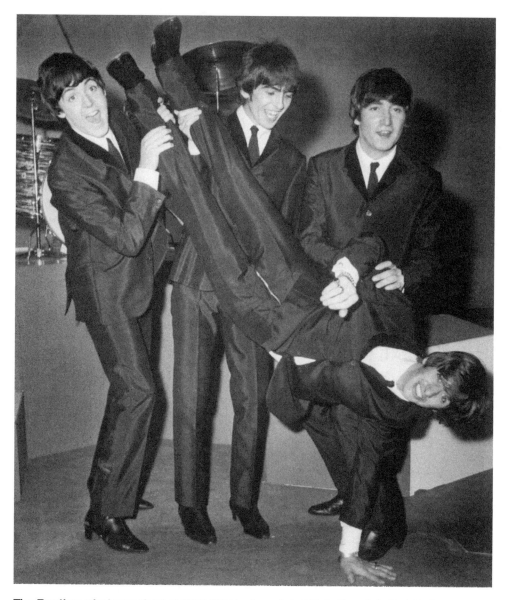

The Beatles, photographed at BBC-TV studios, July 1964. From left: Paul McCartney, George Harrison, John Lennon; Ringo Starr on floor. ©BETTMANN/CORBIS

Hard Day's Night, the Beatles fully established their regnancy by stunningly reinventing themselves with *Rubber Soul* (1965) and *Revolver* (1966), more subtle, complex, experimental albums that essentially reflected their discovery of the drug LSD. (Lennon and McCartney had also diverged as songwriters, taking on the "harder" and "softer" qualities, respectively, attributed to them ever since.) The electronic cacophony of "Tomorrow Never Knows" drew inspiration from psychedelia, a music and culture originating in San Francisco that was likewise inspired by hallucinogenic drugs

and established the classic 1960s package of antimilitarism, free love, and Eastern mysticism. In late 1966 the group abandoned touring and devoted itself entirely to studio work, having wearied of the physical danger posed by hysterical fans whose screaming, moreover, prevented the group from hearing itself onstage.

The first result in 1967, the single "Strawberry Fields Forever," was greeted as a psychedelic masterpiece, and the intense international anticipation of the subsequent album, *Sgt Pepper's Lonely Hearts Club Band,* made the week it was released, the rock

314

critic Langdon Winner wrote, "the closest Western Civilization has come to unity since the Congress of Vienna in 1815." But the Beatles had begun to follow as much as lead; hence they took an already stereotypical turn to the East by consorting with the Maharishi Mahesh Yogi in 1967 and 1968. *Sgt Pepper,* in retrospect, was simply the most elaborately produced manifestation of psychedelia at the time, and its chief impact was to give birth to the pretensions of "art rock" over the next decade. When *The Beatles* appeared in 1968, a collection of clearly individually authored, in some cases individually performed, songs, it was apparent that the tension between Lennon and McCartney, along with Harrison's growth, had caused the band to fragment. They pulled together one last time in 1969 to make one of their finest albums, *Abbey Road,* a testimonial to a collective talent that may never be equaled.

See also **Popular Culture; Rolling Stones.**

BIBLIOGRAPHY

Cohn, Nik. *Awopbopaloobop Alopbamboom: The Golden Age of Rock.* New York, 2001.

Friedman, Robert, and Robert Sullivan, eds. *The Beatles: From Yesterday to Today.* New York, 2001.

Frith, Simon, and Howard Horne. *Art into Pop.* New York, 1987.

Lewisohn, Mark. *The Complete Beatles Chronicle.* London, 2000.

Marcus, Greil. "The Beatles." In *The Rolling Stone Illustrated History of Rock and Roll,* edited by Anthony DeCurtis et al., 209–222. New York, 1992.

NEIL NEHRING

BEAUVOIR, SIMONE DE (1908–1986), French philosopher, author.

Simone de Beauvoir is one of the most significant French existentialist philosophers and authors of the twentieth century. Her writings include fiction and autobiography as well as works on philosophy, feminism, ethics, and politics. Beauvoir's fame is largely attributed to *The Second Sex* (1949), her groundbreaking study of women's oppression, to her post–World War II novel *The Mandarins* (1954), and to her lifelong partnership with philosopher Jean-Paul Sartre.

BEAUVOIR'S LIFE

Beauvoir was born Simone-Ernestine-Lucie-Marie Bertrand de Beauvoir in Paris on 9 January 1908. Her father, Georges Bertrand de Beauvoir, was staunchly conservative and her mother, Françoise (née Brasseur), was a devout Catholic. Beauvoir would spend the greater part of her adult life rebelling against both the political conservatism of her father and the religiosity of her mother. Although she was a pious child, she underwent a crisis of faith as an adolescent and permanently disavowed the existence of God.

Beauvoir's father was unable to provide a dowry for his daughters and thus ambivalently and somewhat inadvertently encouraged Beauvoir's intellectual growth and self-sufficiency. Devoted from an early age to serious learning, Beauvoir attained her baccalaureate in 1925. She passed exams for certificates in history of philosophy, general philosophy, Greek, and logic in 1927, and in 1928 she passed exams in ethics, sociology, and psychology. She studied philosophy further at the Sorbonne and, although not an official student, attended lectures at the École Normale Supérieure in 1928 and 1929. She wrote her graduate dissertation on Gottfried Leibniz under the supervision of Léon Brunschvig.

In 1929 she took second place in the highly competitive philosophy *agrégation* exam, placing ahead of Paul Nizan and Jean Hyppolite and barely losing to Jean-Paul Sartre, who took first (it was his second attempt at the exam). At twenty-one she was the youngest student ever to pass the *agrégation* in philosophy and consequently became the youngest philosophy teacher in France. She completed her practice teaching at the Lycée Janson-de-Sailly in 1929 with fellow students Maurice Merleau-Ponty (another notable existentialist) and Claude Lévi-Strauss (who later became famous for his work in structural anthropology).

Beauvoir first met Sartre at the École Normale Supérieure in 1929, after he invited her to help him and his group of friends to study for the *agrégation*. The two fell in love and agreed to remain committed to each other—or as Sartre referred to it, to be "essential" lovers. They worked closely with each other throughout their time together,

Simone de Beauvoir, 1947. ©HULTON-DEUTSCH COLLECTION/
CORBIS

socializing with many of the same people, diligently reading and commenting on each other's works, and becoming involved in many of the same political struggles. Although the two never lived together, married, or had children, and even though both of them had numerous lovers on the side, they were true to their commitment and remained devoted to each other until Sartre's death in 1980.

Following her teaching apprenticeship, Beauvoir spent a year tutoring students in philosophy and teaching Latin. Afterward, she became a professional philosophy teacher at lycées in Marseille, Rouen, and Paris. In 1943 she was dismissed from her teaching post by a Nazi-controlled administration after a charge of sexual impropriety was leveled against her by one of her female students. Beauvoir never again supported herself by teaching and instead made a permanent career as a writer.

In 1945 Beauvoir and Sartre were instrumental in founding the journal *Les Temps Modernes*. The

original editorial committee of this journal also included Merleau-Ponty, Albert Ollivier, Raymond Aron, Michel Leiris, and Jean Paulhan. The journalist Claude Lanzmann joined the board in 1952. Lanzmann (who is best known for his Holocaust film documentary, *Shoah,* for which Beauvoir composed the preface to the published text) became one of Beauvoir's lovers. They were a couple for seven years (1952–1959) and he was the only man with whom Beauvoir ever lived. Some of her other more famous "contingent" relationships were with the author Jacques-Laurent Bost, the American writer Nelson Algren (author of *Somebody in Boots, The Man with the Golden Arm,* and *A Walk on the Wild Side*), and Olga Kosakiewicz, who formed part of a stormy romantic trio with Beauvoir and Sartre.

World War II fundamentally altered Beauvoir's view of the relationship between the intellectual thought and politics and inaugurated a life of political activism. Whether she was involved in the French Resistance during the 1940s, being escorted around Fidel Castro's Cuba by Che Guevara in 1960, speaking out against the French war in Algeria in 1962, or helping to launch the French women's liberation movement by signing the Manifesto of the 343 advocating abortion rights in 1970, Beauvoir was at the forefront of French politics.

Following the death of Sartre in 1980, Beauvoir officially adopted her companion, Sylvie Le Bon, who became the executor of her literary estate. Beauvoir died on 14 April 1986 of a pulmonary edema.

BEAUVOIR'S WRITING

Paris lived under Nazi occupation from June 1940 to August 1944. The occupation inaugurated what Beauvoir later called the "moral period" of her literary life. In 1944 she published her first philosophical essay, an ethical treatise, *Pyrrhus and Cinéas.* Her novel *The Blood of Others* (1945) was a significant existential novel documenting the French Resistance. This period also saw the writing of her only play, *Who Shall Die?* (1945) and her novel *All Men Are Mortal* (1946). In 1947 Beauvoir wrote *The Ethics of Ambiguity,* which is one of the few published works providing a framework for an atheistic existentialist ethics. In this work, Beauvoir outlines an ethics based on the rejection of any kind of predetermined human nature, or essence. She ties together the dual demands of the individual's radical freedom and responsibility on the one hand, and the ethical obligation humans have to protect and fight for the freedom of others on the other.

In 1949 Beauvoir published her two-volume investigation into the oppression of women, *The Second Sex*. Before the writing of this groundbreaking work, Beauvoir had not considered herself a feminist. After its publication and the worldwide response it generated, she would become one of the most powerful voices of modern feminism in the twentieth century. In *The Second Sex*, Beauvoir argues that women have been historically constructed by men as the "Other" sex. This definition characterizes women as all that men are *not*, thus allowing for men to define themselves positively as subjects. Beauvoir maintains that in order to demarcate one's subjectivity, others are needed to form the limits of the self. For example, a country uses other countries to circumscribe itself as a single nation; members of a religion use other religions to distinguish the parameters of their beliefs; and men use women in order to define themselves as men. The key to Beauvoir's view is that there is nothing essential in the definitions of a country, religion, or male subjectivity. These are arbitrary classifications that can be changed (a country's borders can be altered or a person can choose a different religion, for example). In short, Beauvoir argues that women are socially constructed to be "Women" solely for the benefit of men. They are thus oppressed as Others and never allowed to define themselves as subjects. Beauvoir calls, accordingly, for the end of the oppression of women, who like men need to acknowledge their radical freedom, take total responsibility for their actions, and engage the world as self-determining agents.

Already an accomplished fiction writer, Beauvoir's novel *The Mandarins* received the prestigious Prix Goncourt award in 1954. The story follows the lives of a group of French intellectuals struggling to cope with post-occupation France and the emerging Cold War landscape. In her autobiographies, Beauvoir admits that many aspects of the main characters were loosely based on herself and other members of the French intelligentsia who had been involved in the Resistance, including Sartre, Albert Camus, and Arthur Koestler.

Although most famous for *The Second Sex* and *The Mandarins* (both of which were so controversial in their portrayals of sexuality and in their critiques of traditional femininity that the Vatican put them on the index of prohibited books), Beauvoir was also a prolific autobiographer. Her autobiographies cover her entire life, beginning with the account of her childhood in *Memoirs of a Dutiful Daughter* (1958), followed by her early professional career in *Prime of Life* (1960), the post–World War II years in *Force of Circumstance* (1963), her mother's death to cancer in *A Very Easy Death* (1964), and her reflections on her life as a powerful but aging feminist and intellectual in *All Said and Done* (1972).

Beauvoir traveled around the world as a lecturer, reporter, student, and tourist. Two of her works, *America Day by Day* (1948) and *The Long March* (1957) detail her lecture tour of the United States in 1947 and her visit with Sartre to communist China in 1955, respectively. Her concern with oppression was a lifelong passion and gave rise to *The Coming of Age* (1970). Using the same method as *The Second Sex,* it studies the marginalization of the elderly by societies that fear aging even more than death. Beauvoir's writing and influence spanned the entirety of her adult life and continue to be a source of philosophical and literary influence the world over.

See also **Camus, Albert; Existentialism; Feminism; Koestler, Arthur; Merleau-Ponty, Maurice; Resistance; Sartre, Jean-Paul.**

BIBLIOGRAPHY

Primary Sources

Beauvoir, Simone de. *The Second Sex*. Translated by H. M. Parshley. New York, 1989.

———. *The Mandarins*. Translated by Leonard M. Friedman. New York, 1991.

Secondary Sources

Bair, Deirdre. *Simone de Beauvoir: A Biography.* New York, 1990.

Francis, Claude, and Fernande Gontier. *Simone de Beauvoir: A Life, a Love Story.* Translated by Lisa Nesselson. New York, 1987.

Lundgren-Gothlin, Eva. *Sex and Existence: Simone de Beauvoir's* The Second Sex. Translated by Linda Schenck. Hanover, N.H., 1996.

Scholz, Sally J. *On de Beauvoir.* Belmont, Calif., 2000.

SHANNON M. MUSSETT

BECKETT, SAMUEL (1906–1989), Irish dramatist and novelist.

Samuel Barclay Beckett was born at his parents' house in the prosperous Dublin suburb of Foxrock on Good Friday, 13 April 1906. He was educated locally and in Dublin city before completing his schooling at Portora Royal School in Northern Ireland. In 1923 he entered Trinity College, Dublin, where he studied French and Italian, graduating in 1927 with the award of a gold medal for achieving first among firsts.

He taught school in Belfast for two terms before moving in 1928 to Paris, where his university had an exchange-lecturer arrangement with the École Normale Supérieure. Almost immediately Beckett was introduced to James Joyce (1882–1941), the leading literary artist of the time. The association with Joyce led to Beckett's first publications, a short story and a critical essay on Joyce's "Work in Progress" (published as *Finnegans Wake*, 1939) in the magazine *transition*. Beckett was also writing poetry, and in 1930 his award-winning poem *Whoroscope* was published in book form by the Hours Press in Paris.

He returned to Dublin in 1930 as an assistant lecturer in French at Trinity College. The following year his critical monograph, *Proust,* was published in London. He was, seemingly, launched on a career as a scholar and academic. However, in 1932 he resigned from Trinity and moved to Paris to set up as a full-time writer. Within months he had completed his first novel, *Dream of Fair to Middling Women* (posthumously published, 1992). No publisher took the novel, so Beckett recast his materials as linked short stories, published in 1934 as *More Pricks than Kicks.*

Beckett could not subsist on earnings from his writing and was back living in the family home in 1933 when his father died. The impact of this death, in conjunction with difficulties in his relationship with his mother, propelled Beckett into psychotherapy at the Tavistock Clinic in London. He read widely in psychology while in London and used his reading in the composition of his second novel, *Murphy* (published in 1938). Beckett corrected the proofs for *Murphy* while in hospital recovering from an unprovoked and near-fatal knife

Pen-and-ink portrait of Samuel Beckett by J. P. Donleavy. Bridgeman Art Library

attack on a street in Paris. Joyce was supportive of him at this time, providing his personal physician to care for him and paying the hospital bills.

Beckett decided to leave Ireland in 1937 with only a small annuity from his father's estate—earnings from his writing were negligible. Within a year he had embarked with his friend Alfred Péron on a translation into French of *Murphy*. Beckett saw his future in France but it was not until 1946 that he used French as his language of composition. In 1939 he began cohabiting with Suzanne Deschevaux-Dumesnil. They formalized their relationship by marriage in 1961 and continued to live together until Suzanne predeceased Beckett in July 1989.

Beckett was visiting his mother in Dublin when war broke out in September 1939. He returned to Paris, preferring "France at war to Ireland at peace," as he later said. After the German occupation he was recruited into the French Resistance by his friend Péron. The security of the cell he worked for was breached in 1942, and Beckett fled with Suzanne to refuge in the village of Rousillon in the south. By war's end Beckett had completed another novel in English, *Watt,* which did not appear in print until 1953. By then Beckett had achieved a distinguished reputation as a French author of experimental novels and a puzzling and controversial play, *En attendant Godot* (1952).

His autotranslation, *Waiting for Godot* (1954), established Beckett as a major presence in mid-twentieth-century international theater and was to prove seminal and influential. For the rest of his writing life he continued to produce (in French and English) stage plays notable for bold experimentation and dramatic power—*Fin de partie* (1957; *Endgame,* 1958), *Krapp's Last Tape* (1959), *Happy Days* (1961), *Spiel* (1963; *Play,* 1964), *Not I* (1972)—that increasingly dispense with plot, characterization, movement, and dialogue. A Beckett stage play offers its audience a dramatic experience that is not educible to a single interpretation, to a single meaning. The "outcome" of whatever dramatic action there is takes place in the collective mind of the audience. Thus *Krapp's Last Tape* ends with Krapp still seated by his tape recorder. The audience realizes he has made and discarded his last tape—his death is imminent. *Play* is brought to a conclusion by the failure of the mobile spotlight to continue its interrogation. Beckett also wrote innovative works for radio and television. In 1964 he traveled to New York to participate in the filming of his screenplay, released under the title *Film* (1965), featuring Buster Keaton (1895–1966).

He wrote prose and poetry right up to December 1989, when he died in Paris. While many of his works did not command a popular audience, they have proved to be enduring. He was awarded the Nobel Prize for Literature in 1969 and an honorary doctorate from Trinity College (1959), politely declining all other honors. He is buried in Montparnasse.

See also **Theater.**

BIBLIOGRAPHY

Akerley, Chris J., and Stanley E. Gontarski. *The Grove Companion to Samuel Beckett: A Reader's Guide to His Works, Life, and Thought.* New York, 2004.

Cohn, Ruby. *A Beckett Canon.* Ann Arbor, Mich., 2001.

Knowlson, James. *Damned to Fame: The Life of Samuel Beckett.* London and New York, 1996

GERRY DUKES

BECKMANN, MAX (1884–1950), German painter and graphic artist.

Max Beckmann's paintings and prints are representative of modernist trends in the visual arts in Germany during the Wilhelmine and Weimar periods, yet they transcend national boundaries. Neither aggressively abstract nor classically representational, Beckmann was able during his lifetime to synthesize and distill powerful elements from experimental developments in his native country as well as from France and Italy. His works became a favorite of American collectors after World War II and helped to precipitate a revival of interest in German expressionism.

Beckmann became associated with expressionism after World War I. His oils and his prints, especially his lithographic portfolio *Hell* (1919), were singled out for their power in expressing the terrible turmoil and despair evident in Germany at the beginning of the Weimar Republic. But before 1914 Beckmann had kept his distance from the experimental stylizations and abstractions of the Brücke (Bridge) and the Blaue Reiter (Blue Rider), the groups most connected with prewar expressionism. As a young art student, he attended the Grand Ducal Academy in Weimar and traveled to France, where he became acquainted with the works of Paul Cézanne. He moved to Berlin in 1905 and the following year married Minna Tube; his only son, Peter, was born in 1908. Preferring a painterly naturalistic interpretation of the physical world, he became a member of the Berlin Secession, exhibiting with them during the remainder of the Wilhelmine years. When expressionism became publicly recognized in 1911, Beckmann criticized artists connected with the new trend as too decorative in their depiction of space and form. His experiences in the war as a medical orderly on the front and his involvement with a radical political and artistic group at the

Night. Plate 7 from the series *Hell,* by Max Beckmann, 1919. DIGITAL IMAGE ©THE MUSEUM OF MODERN ART/LICENSED BY SCALA/ART RESOURCE, NY

birth of the republic contributed to his turning away from naturalism. Critics and art historians began to praise his oils and the numerous print portfolios produced during the early 1920s for their expressive form and for their "violent" and dislocated space as effective commentaries on humanity and the chaotic situation of the new republic. Beckmann also revealed his critical view of human nature and of economic inequality in several plays written at that time.

During the mid-1920s, as the republic began to stabilize after numerous rounds of inflation, strikes, and civil conflicts, the critic and museum director Gustav Hartlaub included Beckmann in a major German exhibition that he called *Neue Sachlichkeit* (New concreteness). Believing a new

direction was emerging from figurative rather than abstract expressionism, Hartlaub celebrated a return to concrete imagery that reflected everyday events in a timeless manner. In the 1925 exhibition, he displayed Beckmann, along with other German artists—George Grosz, Otto Dix, Georg Scholz— whose clarity of forms overshadowed their use of ambiguous and sometimes caricatured features and disquieting spatial effects. The exhibition reinforced interest in Beckmann's work among a broader group of patrons. In 1925 he was appointed to teach in the Städel Art School in Frankfurt, and he remarried, this time to Mathilde von Kaulbach, the daughter of a well-known artist, who frequented upper-class circles. He began traveling frequently during the winter months to France and Italy, absorbing new developments in both countries. On occasion, his dealer Alfred Flechtheim promoted him as the German Picasso. Despite these achievements, Beckmann grew increasingly acrid about the need to promote himself and his creative efforts. In an essay of 1927, "The Social Stance of the Artist by the Black Tightrope Walker," Beckmann wrote about patrons, who were unlike his earlier, more liberal ones such as the gallery dealer I. B. Neumann and the publisher Reinhard Piper, and described his new supporters as only concerned with a gauzy, colorful view of the world. He increasingly felt like an outsider in Germany and immersed himself in metaphysical and religious texts.

By 1937, after the opening of the Degenerate Art Exhibition in Munich, where his works—along with other well-known modern artists associated with expressionism and Neue Sachlichkeit—were condemned as depraved by Adolf Hitler and the National Socialists (Nazis), Beckmann left Germany. In exile, first in the Netherlands and, after 1947, in the United States, he continued to paint, producing most of his triptych series. In 1942, while waiting to emigrate to the United States, the Museum of Modern Art in New York purchased the first of his triptychs, *Departure*, begun in 1932 and finished in 1935, three panels that prophetically expressed his fate as an exile. He died in New York at the end of 1950.

See also **Degenerate Art Exhibit; Dix, Otto; Expressionism; Grosz, George.**

BIBLIOGRAPHY

Primary Sources

Beckmann, Max. *Max Beckmann: Self-Portrait in Words: Collected Writings and Statements, 1903–50.* Edited and translated by Barbara Copeland Buenger. Chicago and London, 1997. See especially "Thoughts on Timely and Untimely Art" (1912), text for *Hell* portfolio (1919), and "The Social Stance of the Artist by the Black Tightrope Walker" (1927).

Hartlaub, G. F. Preface to the Catalogue of Neue Sachlichkeit Exhibition (1925). In *German Expressionism: Documents from the End of the Wilhelmine Empire to the Rise of National Socialism,* edited by Rose-Carol Washton Long, 151–153. New York, 1991.

Schmidt, Paul F. "Max Beckmann's *Hell*" (1920). In *German Expressionism: Documents from the End of the Wilhelmine Empire to the Rise of National Socialism,* edited by Rose-Carol Washton Long, 290–292. New York, 1991.

Secondary Sources

Göpel, Erhard, and Barbara Göpel. *Max Beckmann: Katalog der Gemälde.* Bern, 1976.

Hofmaier, James. *Max Beckmann: Catalogue Raisonné of His Prints.* Bern, 1990.

Wiese, Stephan von. *Max Beckmann zeichnerisches Werk 1903–1925.* Dusseldorf, 1978.

ROSE-CAROL WASHTON LONG

BELARUS. For most of the twentieth century (1922–1991) Belarus was a republic of the Soviet Union, the Belarusian Soviet Socialist Republic (SSR). The 1897 census of the Russian Empire revealed that a clear majority of the population of five northwestern imperial provinces was Belarusian speaking. After the Revolution of 1905, Belarusian activists sought to define this largely peasant population as a nation. They treated the medieval Grand Duchy of Lithuania as the font of Belarusian national tradition and recalled the Uniate Church as a Belarusian national confession. That church, established in 1596, combined an Eastern liturgy with subordination to the Vatican. It was banned in most of the Russian Empire in 1839. Henceforth the Belarusian-speaking population was divided among an Orthodox majority and a Roman Catholic minority. These activists hoped that speakers of Belarusian would come to regard themselves as members of a Belarusian nation, deserving of an independent state. City dwellers in the territories considered Belarusian were Jews, Russians, and Poles.

World War I opened the Belarusian question. German occupying authorities created Belarusian-language schools. Under German occupation, Belarusian activists proclaimed a republic in March 1918, with Vilnius its capital. After the German defeat, the Bolsheviks established in February 1919 a Lithuanian-Belarusian SSR, another reference to the old Grand Duchy. In spring 1919 the Polish army advanced eastward, its commander Józef Piłsudski promising self-determination to the inhabitants of "the ancient

Grand Duchy of Lithuania." In 1920 the Red Army drove out the Poles, only to be routed near Warsaw. In fall 1920 the Polish army again occupied Minsk. Poland conceded that city and other Belarusian lands to Bolshevik Russia in the Treaty of Riga in 1921. The city of Vilnius was incorporated by Poland.

The Bolsheviks established their Belarusian SSR, with a capital in Minsk. They enlarged its territory in 1924 and 1926. Thus the Belarusian SSR embraced some five million people, about four-fifths of them Belarusian speakers. In the 1920s the Soviet Union pursued a vigorous policy of Belarusization, founding Belarusian schools and promoting Belarusian communists. This policy was designed to integrate the peasant population and to destabilize neighboring Poland. The Communist Party of Western Belarus, operating in Poland, stressed these achievements in propaganda. Poland closed all Belarusian schools, and social inequality drew Belarusian peasants to left-wing politics. Poland banned the main Belarusian party, the Hromada, for its communist connections in 1927. In the 1930s Soviet authorities began to connect Belarusian culture to internal and external security threats. Peasants were deported for resisting collectivization, and the intelligentsia was decimated during the Great Terror.

After Nazi Germany and the Soviet Union jointly invaded and divided Poland in September 1939, the Belarusian SSR was extended westward to what had been Poland, and tens of thousands of Poles were deported. To the disappointment of Belarusians, the Soviets granted Vilnius to Lithuania. In June 1941 Germany invaded the Soviet Union. German authorities allowed Belarusian schools and Belarusian theater, and the Orthodox Church in Belarus declared its autocephaly. With assistance from local policemen, the Germans killed the vast majority of the Jewish population in shooting actions. Belarus became the center of the Soviet partisan movement that emerged in 1943, and the Red Army returned to Minsk in July 1944. In 1945 the Soviet Union was able to restore the Molotov-Ribbentrop boundaries (although Białystok was granted to Poland) as the Belarusian SSR was extended west again. By war's end some 20 percent of the Belarusian population had been killed, and the major cities were destroyed.

Postwar Belarus was a theater of political Russification and economic industrialization. High party posts were filled by Russians. In 1960 half the books in the republic were published in Belarusian; by 1985 the figure was only 10 percent. By 1980 there were no Belarusian schools in Minsk. Cities were rebuilt, populated by Russian-speaking immigrants and upwardly mobile Belarusians who employed Russian in daily life. Cities that had been Jewish-Russian-Belarusian before the war became largely Russian thereafter. Mikhail Gorbachev's reforms opened national discussions after 1985. The mass graves of tens of thousands of Belarusians killed by Soviet security organs during the Great Terror of the 1930s, discovered at Kuropaty in 1988, became a symbol of the horrors of Soviet rule. Yet the emergence of an independent Belarusian state in 1991 was a consequence of the internal collapse of the Soviet Union, not of Belarusian national strivings. In 1994 Alexander Lukashenko rose to the office of president as an anticorruption crusader. He appealed to Soviet nostalgia while avoiding economic reform. By the early twenty-first century Lukashenko had established a dictatorial system. His regime did not support Belarusian culture but preserved Belarusian state independence.

See also **Lithuania; Poland; Russia; Soviet Union; Ukraine.**

BIBLIOGRAPHY

Snyder, Timothy. *The Reconstruction of Nations: Poland, Ukraine, Lithuania, Belarus, 1569–1999,* New Haven, Conn., 2003.

Vakar, Nicholas. *Belorussia: The Making of a Nation, a Case Study.* Cambridge, Mass., 1956.

Zaprudnik, Jan. *Belarus: At a Crossroads in History.* Boulder, Colo., 1993.

TIMOTHY SNYDER

BELGIUM. On the eve of World War I Belgium was an industrialized and prosperous country that had been ruled for thirty years by the Catholic Party. Three conflicts had affected Belgian society for decades: an ideological conflict between clerical and anticlerical camps; a linguistic and identity-based conflict stemming from the emergence of Flemish claims upon the Francophone state and a nascent Walloon movement that sought to counter them; and finally a social conflict fueled by the socialist and liberal progressivist movement to obtain universal suffrage. These conflicts notwithstanding, all political struggles disappeared into a *union sacrée* (sacred union) around King Albert I (r. 1909–1934) for the duration of the war once German troops invaded the country on 4 August 1914.

Belgium was a small country dragged into the torment despite itself, invaded without having declared war, and a young and relatively untested country where the church continued to play a preponderant role. The country experienced civilian massacres and the destruction of several cities during the invasion, the horror of the trenches on the Yser front, the deportation of civilians beginning in 1916, and the daily misery and systematic pillage of a country under occupation. Indeed, given the fact that the king stayed on the front lines alongside his troops and the government was exiled to France, practically the entire kingdom spent four years under the boots of the Germans.

However, the image Belgium held of itself changed radically over the course of this conflict. Its identity became tied to the emblem of the soldier-king; innocence lost; and undying fidelity to right, courage, honor, heroism, and martyrdom. At the end of the war the country emerged with a new face. Although Belgium lay in ruins it had nevertheless maintained its rank in the eyes of the nations arrayed against the invaders. In the Treaty of Versailles Belgium made several territorial gains on its eastern border and was awarded mandates over the African territories of Rwanda and Urundi. However victory would prove insufficient to quell the immense expectations born in the war. In general terms, the interwar years comprised two contrasting periods lasting one decade each: the 1920s was a time of change, reconstruction, and reform, followed by the Great Depression provoked by the Crash of 1929.

When universal male suffrage and proportional representation were introduced in 1919 the structure of Belgium's political landscape and governmental modes of functioning were radically altered.

The bipartisanship of the war years ended, heralding an era of alternating Catholic versus liberal regimes incapable of governing alone, and required therefore to make concessions to the Belgian Socialist Workers Party. Coalition governments have resulted ever since, with the exception of 1950 to 1954, when a Catholic-only government briefly led the country. During the interwar years the most stable coalitions were composed of Catholics and liberals, but the more frequent and hence short-lived regimes were tripartite in nature, including Catholics, liberals, and socialists. The advent of coalition-style government had a considerable impact on Belgian political discourse, which progressively shed its pre-1914 ideological tone, in particular regarding the confrontation between Catholics and opponents to clericalism, and from groups devoted to the search for a consensus based on mutual concessions and negotiations about the great socioeconomic, linguistic, and educational questions of the day. Furthermore, the king no longer presided over the cabinet after 1918, when he was replaced by the newly created post of prime minister, a position held by a Catholic during this entire period with just two exceptions. Although government instability, particularly due to the language question, was rife during the interwar period (especially between 1918 and 1921 and from 1931 until World War II), certain ministers were seen to maintain their portfolios across different governments.

The first decade after 1918 was a period therefore of reforms, many of which were either being talked about or actively planned as early as 1914. Besides universal suffrage, most of the post-1918 socioeconomic changes, including the eight-hour workday and the right to strike (both legalized in 1921), went hand-in-hand with efforts being made at the international level by the International Labour Organization, which was created by the Treaty of Versailles. Nationalized industries were also founded at this time, including the National Industrial Bank and the Belgian National Railroad Company. The rise of unionism laid the groundwork for a publicly funded social safety net as well. Government-run industry-specific regulatory commissions were erected in 1919, requiring the various social groups to negotiate collective contracts on workers' issues.

The immense destruction wrought by the war called for a difficult reconstruction of the country and its economy. This reconstruction was only completed in 1925–1926 following a drastic devaluation of the Belgian franc. In this reconstruction, which was inspired by the American model, Taylorism and rationalization, as well as a movement favoring the concentration of businesses in fewer enterprises, were de rigueur in business management circles, as witnessed in the takeover by the Société Générale of the National Arms Manufacturers. In 1926 the first regional economic association, the *Vlaams Economisch VerBond* (Flemish Employers Association), also appeared.

The importance of these economic and social questions to national life at the time, and above all their institutionalization according to the liberal model, led the traditional political parties to marry their political activities with social organizations sharing the same tendencies, for example the Christian Workers wing of the Catholic Party. The socialists in the Workers Party of Belgium, largely untroubled by the founding of the Communist Party in 1921, carried out its development in three classic forms of organization: unions, mutualist groups, and cooperatives.

The language question also evolved during this period. The Flemish movement did not make it through World War I unscathed because some of its activists, a clear minority of Flemish speakers who had collaborated with the occupying forces, were immediately condemned by public opinion and later by Belgian tribunals. A newly formed Regional Front Party, composed of Flemish faithful to the Belgian resistance, made it into parliament after 1919 and renewed key Flemish demands. Many activists were gradually pardoned as a series of language laws in their favor were easily adopted, especially between the years 1921 and 1928. These laws testify to the progressive formalization of a bilingual state and state institutions such as schools, the army, the courts, and public administration, accompanied by the identification of Belgian regions according to the language spoken by the majority of its inhabitants. Later this process was accelerated by a 1932 law establishing unilingualism in Flanders and Wallonia and bilingualism in Brussels for administrative matters. Two years earlier an age-old Flemish demand had been satisfied when the University of Gand (Ghent University) was designated solely Flemish-speaking.

After the stock market crash of 1929 and the depreciation of the pound in 1931, Belgium was struck by economic depression, with catastrophically high unemployment rates and severe downward pressure on workers' salaries leading to strikes in 1932, particularly in heavy industries like coal mining and metallurgy. The government responded by giving special budgetary powers normally reserved for the Legislature to technocrats in the finance ministry. Mixed-use banks were banned in 1934 and the franc was devalued in 1935. Henri de Man (1885–1953) and the Belgian Socialists promoted a work plan intended to establish a mixed-economy regime.

The accidental death of Albert I in February 1934 led to the succession of his son Leopold III (r. 1934–1951), whose reign began under difficult political circumstances. In the 1930s the antidemocratic extreme Right was making progress via new movements and political parties, including Verdinaso, founded by the National Front Deputy Joris Van Severen (1894–1940) and the Vlaams Nationaal Verbond (VNV), which brought together Flemish fascists who comprised the majority of the National Front caucus in parliament, as well as the Rex in Wallonia, led by the charismatic Léon Degrelle (1906–1994). Although the Rexists became a worrisome political force after the elections of 1936, the traditional parties banded together to oppose it, and by 1939 Rex was practically nonexistent. Despite circumstances hostile to democracy throughout Europe, Belgium resisted the onslaught of fascism.

During the interwar years the Catholic and Socialist parties alternated between first and second place, with the Liberals occupying the perpetual third position. Regional differences also appeared during this time, with the Parti Ouvrier Belge (POB) being the predominant party in Wallonia and the Catholics occupying this position in Flanders, while the electoral situation in Brussels was more fluid. Federalist state-reform initiatives introduced by respective Flemish and Walloon deputies broke new ground in the process of recognizing regional differences. Although these projects were not rigorously followed up at the time, they

Belgians march in Brussels, opposing a government order to disband the resistance movement, 1944.
©HULTON-DEUTSCH COLLECTION/CORBIS

reassumed its position of political neutrality when confronted with that region's remilitarization. This voluntary neutrality was recognized by all the major European powers, Nazi Germany included, but in vain. On 10 May 1940, without a formal declaration of war, German troops invaded Belgium in a blitzkrieg operation, provoking an ineffectual response from Belgium's British and French alliance partners. After eighteen days of combat Leopold III capitulated and chose to remain at the head of his army, then fallen into German hands, rather than follow his government, led by the prime minister, Hubert Pierlot (1883–1963), into exile. Leopold III was placed under house arrest at the Château de Laeken in Brussels.

During the first period of the occupation Belgian administrative and economic officials attempted to find a modus vivendi with the Germans, so that Belgium might in some way take advantage of the concessions of autonomy while at the same time allowing the military administration led by Alexander von Falkenhausen (1878–1966) to make the occupation satisfactory to the Reich and thus maintain order. But this fool's paradise was quickly exposed for what it was by the exploitation of the country, the demands of occupation, supply shortages, the repression of political dissent, the continued holding of Walloon prisoners of war in captivity, and the anti-Jewish policies implemented in 1940. Furthermore once the Battle for Britain was won public opinion changed—Hitler might just yet lose the war.

The country was divided by a rhythm of conflict that came to be known the world over. Active and passive forms of collaboration with the occupiers emerged, but organized resistance also arose as the application of the Final Solution to the Jews of Belgium progressed and the deportation of Belgian workers began in 1942. The Belgian Resistance assumed many guises, including supporting downed Allied pilots, persecuted Jews, and people who escaped from the Forced Labor Service; providing information and running underground presses; and armed attacks by groups adhering to various tendencies, from communism to ultra-monarchism. In short the usefulness and the intensity of the Belgian Resistance in the war effort would later be fully recognized by the Allies,

nonetheless embodied the first manifestations of federalist political aspirations at the heart of the national legislature.

In the international sphere, after having taken part in the occupation of the Ruhr Valley alongside the French (1923–1925) and having signed the Locarno Accords (1925), in 1936 Belgium at the price of seventeen thousand Belgians dead in the service of freedom.

Collaboration also assumed various forms: economic, political, and even military in the case of the Flemish Nationalists of the VNV and the monarchist Walloons under Léon Degrelle. All told some thirty-one thousand Belgians would fight alongside the Nazi ranks. After the invasions at Normandy the Germans transferred Leopold III to Austria. In September 1944 Belgium was liberated by the Allies and its government-in-exile in London returned to Brussels, although Germany's bomb-equipped rockets and its harsh counteroffensive in the Ardennes placed a temporary halt on the country's complete return to normal.

In keeping with the constitution, as soon as the chamber of deputies returned it declared Leopold III, then whisked away by the Reich, ineligible to rule, and the king's brother Prince Charles (1903–1983) was installed as regent on 20 September 1944. The "royal affair" had just begun, but more urgent questions were then pressing the country as it began to emerge from the war. Following strict monetary policies led by the finance minister, Camille Gutt (1884–1971), and with the help of the Marshall Plan, economic reconstruction was achieved relatively quickly, especially as Belgium had escaped the wholesale destruction of its industrial infrastructure, including the Walloon Basin and the Port d'Anvers. The political landscape did not change dramatically, with the exception of the suppression of Rex and VNV. The Communists received a slight boost in the immediate postwar period, and the other parties were rebaptized as the Christian Socialist Party, the first political force to arrive on the scene as early as February 1945, and the Socialist Party of Belgium. A social-security system still in place today was formally institutionalized after having been laid out in private during the war. Besides this the process of flushing out collaborators was the order of the day, leading to the condemnation of fifty-three thousand Belgians (comprising 0.52 percent of the population of Wallonia and 0.73 percent of that of Flanders). Amnesty was a key theme in the demands raised by Flemish nationalists, and this became a kernel of discord between the country's two communities. Women were at last accorded the right to vote in legislative elections in 1948.

One of the most significant shifts to have occurred after the war was the ending of Belgium's political neutrality, which had twice been swept away. The country was integrated into the Western camp and the institutions of its international partnerships. As early as 1944 Belgium supported the formation of a customs union with the Netherlands and Luxembourg, which culminated in the Benelux alliance. It was also active in the creation of the United Nations and in 1949 became a member of NATO, whose headquarters would be housed in Brussels. A contingent of Belgian volunteers took part in the Korean War. These pro-Western policies, maintained despite internal differences by actors as diverse as the socialist Paul-Henri Spaak (1899–1972) and the Catholic Paul Van Zeeland (1893–1973), made Belgium one of the early architects of the European Coal and Steel Community in 1951, and of Euratom and the European Economic Community in 1957. This earnest and loyal engagement with Europe made Brussels the seat of even more European institutions, and ended with its designation as capital of the European Union.

Belgium's international stature would be tarnished by its handling of the crisis in the Congo beginning in 1960. On 15 November 1908 Congo became a Belgian colony after having first been the Independent State of Congo with Leopold III as its sovereign from 1885 onward. The colony's economic development had only begun to be felt in the 1920s, particularly in Katanga. In certain areas, such as primary school education, health, and communications infrastructure the local population appeared to benefit from colonization, but Belgium carried out strict segregationist policies. When it gained independence, the country had practically no homegrown political, social, and intellectual elites. Belgium was a colonial power until 30 June 1960, the date when the Congo gained its independence under difficult conditions.

Postwar Belgium still had to sort through the poisonous "royal affair." For several years the Christian Socialists, sole supporters of restoring Leopold III (then living in Switzerland), failed to muster a sufficient parliamentary majority because the other parties reproached him for his conduct

Belgians march in protest of the government of King Leopold prior to elections, Brussels, March 1950.
©BETTMANN/CORBIS

during the war. A popular referendum was held on 12 March 1950, and 57.68 percent of voters favored his return to power, but marked regional disparities between Flanders and Wallonia, which was primarily against the king, were indicative of a fracture in Belgian public opinion. The highly significant electoral victory of the Catholics in 1950 allowed them to form a unified government and then make use of the referendum's results. The king was restored amid strikes and urban violence in the heart of industrial Wallonia, leading to the death of four men. In order to avoid civil war and despite his constitutional legitimacy, Leopold III ended up abdicating in favor of his son Baudouin (1930–1993), who became king on 17 July 1951.

Besides the royal affair, the education question was the site of the first great postwar confrontation because the majority Catholic government that

ruled Belgium between 1950 and 1954 was followed by an anticlerical Socialist, Liberal, and Communist coalition that took aim at measures adopted by the previous legislature, which had favored Catholic instruction. A war over education seemingly right out of the nineteenth century led many Belgians to take to the streets. The demonstrations ended with the implementation of an education pact. The effects of this pact can still be observed. Its provisions included free middle-school education, equal treatment for teachers, and freedom of choice for heads of households regarding educational matters.

It was the evolution of the issue of group identity that would ultimately weigh most heavily on the nation's destiny. The Walloon movement and the various elements comprising it across the political spectrum emerged from the war unscathed in moral terms and began to organize its pro-federalist political activities from Liège beginning in 1945, opting for a formula of annual congresses, including one at Charleroi in 1950 notable for its gathering of popular and union forces together under the banner of the charismatic André Renard (1911–1962), secretary-general of the General Federation of Belgian Workers. At the same time deputies of Walloon origins would try in vain to pass state-reform propositions in parliament during the 1950s.

The Flemish movement recovered more slowly from the war because of its having been compromised by collaboration with the Germans, and the subsequent effects of the cleansing process. That being said, its ability to rebound through various cultural associations and the activities of parliamentary deputies united by a newly formed nationalist party in 1954 called the Volksunie was further fueled by the fact that Flanders, already favored by demographics, had become the predominant economic region in Belgium versus Wallonia, whose aging coal and steel industries were marked by deep discontent, most evident in the general strikes that took place in the winters of 1960 and 1961. In fact during these years population growth in Flanders led to a reversal in economic power relations in Belgium in its favor. These disparities led to the establishment of a formal linguistic border in 1962, the drawing up of which was hotly contested, and which today remains the object of considerable controversy. In January 1968 tensions between the Flemish and Walloons brought down the government and the University of Louvain was split in two: the Flemish wing stayed in the Old City and the Francophones were obliged to move to the other side of the language border. In June 1968 a government composed of Socialists and Christian Socialists led by Gaston Eyskens (1905–1988) found itself at a crossroads—institutional changes were inevitable, especially since the three main political parties were about to undergo divisions into Flemish and Walloon factions.

The country was dragged into a lasting economic downturn during this period by the fragility of successive governments, the oil crisis of 1973, regional disparities, and a rise in unemployment and inflation. The influence of Wilfried Martens

(b. 1936), who led eight successive governments, would dominate the 1980s. It was under these conditions that in the latter part of the twentieth century a series of constitutional reforms were undertaken beginning in 1970, continuing in the 1980s (especially in 1988–1989), and ending in 1993 when Belgium became a full-fledged federal state. The first revision, which took place in 1970, established three cultural communities (French-, Flemish-, and German-speaking), and envisioned the creation of three regions: Wallonia, Flanders, and Brussels. In 1980 these communities received additional powers over cultural matters, including health and social welfare. They were also granted regional councils (parliaments) and executive branches, effectively founding the Regions of Wallonia and Flanders at the same time. Soon thereafter the Region and Community of Flanders were fused, and in 1988–1989 the Region of Brussels-Capital was established, even as regional and communal powers were further enhanced, a process completed by the fourth revision of the Constitution in 1993, the year when King Baudouin died and his brother Albert II (b. 1934) succeeded him on the throne.

In the 1990s Belgium remained at the head of efforts to strengthen and expand the European Union, which had been formally established by the ratification of the Maastricht Treaty in 1992. Brussels's status as the Union's capital obviously stimulated this engagement with Europe. However, the 1990s were also years marred by a climate of social and economic transformation. Events in that decade included the assassination of the Socialist leader André Cools (1927–1991), corruption scandals, and the child murders underlying the "Dutroux Affair." Following the electoral decline of the Christian Democrats and Socialists in both the northern and southern regions of the country, identity problems continued to confront Belgium in the 2000s: Flanders, pressured by the far-right populist Vlaams Blok, became more aggressive with respect to Brussels's claims to sovereignty, and has increased its demands for the division of the country's social-security system, widely considered one of the few items still holding Belgium together. Despite all these ordeals, Belgium weathered the twentieth century with a keen sense of adaptation to varying circumstances, defying those who regularly foretold of its imminent disappearance. As the country celebrated its 175th anniversary in 2005, the question remained as to whether this adaptability will persist in the years to come.

See also **Albert I; Brussels; Education; European Union; Flemish Bloc; Flemish National League; Leopold III; World War I; World War II.**

BIBLIOGRAPHY

Baudhuin, Fernand. *Histoire économique de la Belgique 1914–1939.* Brussels, 1946.

———. *Histoire économique de la Belgique 1945–1955.* Brussels, 1958.

Bitsch, Marie-Thérèse. *Histoire de la Belgique, de l'Antiquité à nos jours.* Brussels, 2004.

Chlepner, B.-S. *Cent ans d'histoire sociale en Belgique.* Brussels, 1972.

Delforge, Paul, ed. *Encyclopédie du mouvement wallon.* Charleroi, Belgium, 2000.

de Schaepdrijver, Sophie. *La Belgique et la Première Guerre mondiale.* Brussels, 2004.

Gérad-Libois, Jules, and José Gotovitch. *L'an 40. La Belgique occupée.* Brussels, 1971.

Höjer, Carl Henrik. *Le régime parlementaire belge de 1918 à 1940.* Brussels, 1969.

Mabille, Xavier. *Histoire politique de la Belgique: Facteurs et acteurs de changement.* Brussels, 1992.

Nieuwe Encyclopedie van de Vlaamse Beweging. Tielt, Belgium, 1998.

Witte, Els, and Jan Craeybeckx. *La Belgique politique de 1830 à nos jours: Les tensions d'une démocratie bourgeoise.* Brussels, 1987.

PHILIPPE RAXHON, LAURENCE VAN YPERSELE

BELGRADE. Belgrade, in the early twenty-first century the capital city of Serbia and Montenegro, is situated at the confluence of the Danube and Sava Rivers. Through the course of the twentieth century Belgrade served as the capital of Serbia (until 1918), of the Kingdom of Serbs, Croats, and Slovenes (1918–1929), of the Kingdom of Yugoslavia (1929–1941), of Nazi-occupied Serbia (1941–1944), of socialist Yugoslavia (1945–1991), and of the Federal Republic of Yugoslavia (1992–2003).

WORLD WARS

The first shots of the First World War were fired on Belgrade, which lay on the border of Austria-Hungary and the Kingdom of Serbia, when Austro-Hungarian troops began their fifteen-month battle against the city on 28 July 1914, a battle marked by incessant bombardment. The city fell and was occupied by Austro-Hungarian forces twice during the war—first between 2 and 15 December 1914 and the second time between 9 October 1915 and 1 November 1918. The war had wreaked extensive damage on the city center, including the destruction of government ministry buildings and important cultural institutions, such as Belgrade University, the National Museum, and the National Theater, as well as private homes and businesses. Belgrade's industries, such as the tobacco and sugar factories and the Weifert brewery, suffered severe damage and significant loss of materials, machines, and tools as a result of the bombardment and pillage of the occupying forces. Belgrade's transportation and communication networks also suffered extensive damage. The prewar population of ninety thousand dwindled to between seven and twelve thousand in October 1915, and was reported by occupying authorities to have risen to forty-eight thousand in 1916. During the war, Belgrade was the urban center in Serbia that suffered the most damage.

At the end of the First World War, Belgrade became the political, administrative, economic, and cultural center of the newly proclaimed Kingdom of Serbs, Croats, and Slovenes. Its administrative government faced substantial economic and social challenges and a humanitarian crisis as it entered the postwar period, especially the problem of supplying the city with provisions and dealing with a severe housing shortage. The city not only had to contend with fact that the destruction of the war had deprived former inhabitants of their homes, but also had to accommodate an influx of members of government administration, military and economic, as well as an influx of people from the countryside.

The interwar period was one of expansion for Belgrade. Already by 1921 the population of the city had risen to 112,000 and reached 226,000 by 1929. The area of the city extended to formerly

Austro-Hungarian territory across the Sava River, to include the twin city of Zemun and nearby Pančevo. In 1923 a general plan was proposed for the renovation of the city center, which was ultimately thwarted because of excessive costs, bureaucratic delay, and the inability of the municipal and federal governments to cooperate, leading only to the completion of the Parliament (Skupština) and some government buildings. German reparations and the U.S.-based Carnegie Endowment provided funds for the construction of a library. Belgrade's commercial class grew, and immigrants from across the new state and Europe swelled its ranks. Immigrants, including around thirty thousand Russians, were also key in stimulating cultural and educational development. Belgrade's rapidly growing artistic life was evident in the flourishing of publishing houses, such as Geca Kon, as well as newspapers and periodicals, the appearance of new movie theaters and the Cvijeta Zuzorić Pavilion, a free performance center for exhibits and concerts, and the emergence of a vibrant café culture where authors and artists gathered in Belgrade's seven hundred cafés, especially in the bohemian Skadarlija neighborhood.

In the Second World War, Belgrade once again found itself to be the object of enemy bombs and occupation. The Nazi Luftwaffe bombing of the Yugoslav capital on 6 and 7 April 1941 inflicted extensive physical damage, again destroying the National Library and many government facilities and cutting off all essential services. The bombing also inflicted around twenty-three hundred deaths, wounded many more, and induced a still greater number to flee the city. The invading Nazi troops conducted authorized looting of the city before taking direct control of Belgrade and essentially imposed martial law. The occupying forces imposed anti-Jewish measures and established concentration camps around the city, most notably Banjica and Sajmište, located in the western suburbs of Belgrade, which according to the new boundaries of wartime Yugoslavia was located in the Independent State of Croatia. Toward the end of the war, Belgrade was bombed by Anglo-American planes for several months. It was liberated finally by communist partisan forces and the Red Army on 20 October 1944.

POSTWAR EXPANSION AND THE LATE TWENTIETH CENTURY

After the war, the reconstruction of the now capital of the Federal People's Republic of Yugoslavia (renamed the Socialist Federal Republic of Yugoslavia in 1963) proceeded apace. In 1947 the Belgrade municipal government instituted a five-year plan for the improvement of the city, and a general plan was developed in 1950. The city expanded both physically and demographically. Between 1944 and 1971 the city's population grew from 270,000 to 780,000, and reached 1.6 million by 1985. New neighborhoods and municipalities rapidly developed, most notably Novi Beograd (New Belgrade) in 1952. This municipality was the result of a massive construction project undertaken on the left bank of the Sava River in 1948, which employed work brigades composed primarily of rural workers and student volunteers in constructing large government buildings, residence halls for students of Belgrade University called Studentski grad (Student City), and complexes of urban housing known as "blocks."

By the 1980s, economic crisis had overtaken the Yugoslav capital. It had not received necessary federal funds for the development of urban infrastructure, and its population growth leveled off because of emigration. Conditions worsened after the United Nations imposed sanctions on now the Federal Republic of Yugoslavia in May 1992 during the wars of Yugoslav succession, which led to severe hyperinflation in 1993 and 1994.

Throughout the 1990s, Belgrade was the site of many political demonstrations. On 9 March 1991, estimated tens of thousands of citizens flooded the city's central Republic Square to protest against the regime of Slobodan Milošević. Once again, in winter 1996–1997 tens of thousands of people took to the streets when Milošević's regime annulled the results of local elections, which had resulted in the victory of the opposition coalition, Zajedno (Together). Among the leaders of the coalition was Zoran Djindjić, who consequently became the first democratically elected mayor of Belgrade for a brief period, and ultimately premier of Serbia in 2001, an office he held until his assassination in March 2003. In 1999 Belgrade was targeted by North Atlantic Treaty Organization (NATO) bombs during the Kosovo War, and several government ministries, the presidential residency, the Socialist Party of Serbia headquarters, and several television and radio broadcasting stations, especially Radio Television of Serbia, were damaged or destroyed. After the presidential elections of 2000, there were once again mass demonstrations, which succeeded this time in ousting Milošević from power on 5 October 2000.

Following the fall of Milošević, Belgrade, still a city of 1.6 million, underwent renovation and revitalization, both physically and spiritually as it aimed toward rejoining the European and international communities from which it was isolated for nearly a decade. In 2005 it hosted the Euro-Basket championship of the International Basketball Federation, for which it erected a new sports center. Belgrade's vibrant café culture and nightlife especially have attracted an increasing number of foreign visitors, and the Serbian capital has been featured repeatedly in the Western press.

See also **Milošević, Slobodan; Serbia; Yugoslavia.**

BIBLIOGRAPHY

Blagojević, Ljiljana. *Modernism in Serbia: The Elusive Margins of Belgrade Architecture, 1919–1941.* Cambridge, Mass., 2003.

Djurić, Dubravka, and Miško Suvaković, eds. *Impossible Histories: Historic Avant-Gardes, Neo-Avant-Gardes, and Post-Avant-Gardes in Yugoslavia, 1918–1991.* Cambridge, Mass., 2003.

Howell, Anthony. *Serbian Sturgeon: Journal of a Visit to Belgrade.* Amsterdam, 2000.

Lampe, John. *Yugoslavia as History: Twice There Was a Country.* New York, 1996.

Milojković-Djurić, Jelena. *Tradition and Avant-Garde: The Arts in Serbian Culture between the Two World Wars.* Boulder, Colo., 1984.

JOVANA L. KNEŽEVIĆ

BEN BELLA, AHMED (b. 1916), Algerian political leader.

One of Algeria's "historic chiefs," who is still considered by many as the father of the nation, Mohamed Ahmed Ben Bella was born in 1916 to a Sufi Muslim family in Maghnia, a small village close to the Moroccan border, during the height of the French colonial period. He completed secondary school in Tlemcen, a center of conservative religious thought and influence in western Algeria. At twenty-one, Ben Bella was drafted into the army and, when World War II broke out and Germany occupied France, he served with the Free French forces as a master sergeant, earning the Croix de Guerre and the Médaille Militaire for his bravery.

NATIONALISM

Like many of his generation born and raised under French colonial rule (1830–1962), Ben Bella communicated in French but never felt fully French. His nationalist consciousness was aroused to action when he heard about the bloody massacres of May 1945 in Sétif that left an estimated forty-five thousand Algerian Muslims dead at the hands of French security forces retaliating for the murder of scores of French nationals in the region. He refused a commission in the French army and instead joined the Party of the Algerian People (Parti du Peuple Algérien, or PPA), led by the charismatic and militant nationalist hero, Messali Hadj (1898–1974). When the French authorities banned the PPA, Messali formed the Movement for the Triumph of Democratic Liberties (Mouvement pour le Triomphe des Libertés Démocratiques, or MTLD), a group that attracted political activists like Ben Bella.

As French policies toward the incipient Algerian nationalist movement hardened, a clandestine, violence-prone group was created (Organisation Spéciale, or OS) within the MTLD. Ben Bella joined the OS and led a number of armed attacks against French territorial assets including the robbery of a post office in Oran in 1949. He was captured and imprisoned in 1950 but escaped two years later and reached Cairo. There he joined others of the "historic chiefs." It was in Egypt, led at the time by the young revolutionary leader, Gamal Abdel Nasser (1918–1970), that Ben Bella became inspired by pan-Arabist principles. It was also in Egypt that he finally learned to speak Arabic properly, thereby fusing his militant nationalism with its indigenous idiom and overcoming the sense of inferiority that French socialization had created in him. Like so many of his contemporaries in Algeria and elsewhere, Ben Bella was fascinated by and enthusiastic about pan-Arabism, Nasserism, and other forms of militant Arab nationalism, serving as an ideological template for Algeria's own struggle for national liberation. For his part, Nasser's close ties to Ben Bella and his extensive material, moral, and political support for Algeria's independence struggle was used as an excuse by France to join Britain and Israel in attacking and occupying the Suez Canal in 1956.

Dissatisfied with Messali's nationalist leadership and the slow pace of change, Ben Bella became one of the leading figures of the Revolutionary Committee for Unity and Action (Comité Révolutionnaire pour l'Unité et l'Action, or CRUA), which organized the National Liberation Front (Front de Libération Nationale, or FLN). The FLN launched the Algerian revolution against the French on 1 November 1954. Organizationally the CRUA split up into a group of "internals," involved in organizing Algeria into six separate military regions, and "externals," headed by Ben Bella and headquartered in Cairo, where they worked to gain foreign support for the rebellion. While in Egypt, Ben Bella was assigned the job of collecting funds and material for the newly established National Liberation Army (Armée de Libération Nationale, or ALN), the armed wing of the FLN. Ben Bella was not invited to the historic Soummam Conference of August 1956, when the primacy of the internals was declared over that of the externals. In October 1956 Ben Bella and five other "historic chiefs" (Hocine Ait Ahmed, Mohamed Boudiaf, Abdelkrim Khider, Rabih Bitat, and Mostefa Lacheraf), were skyjacked by the French while en route from Morocco to Tunisia. Ben Bella remained in a French prison until 1962, the year Algeria achieved its independence.

INDEPENDENCE

After the war Ben Bella returned to Algeria, where he teamed up with the powerful external military commander of the ALN, Houari Boumédienne (1927–1978), to form the Political Bureau (Bureau Politique) in opposition to the Provisional Government of the Algerian Republic (Gouvernement Provisoire de la République Algérienne, or GPRA). With the backing of Boumédienne, Ben Bella was able to overcome a brief intra-elite struggle for power and assert his dominance as the premier political figure in Algeria. He became the country's first prime minister, serving from 1962 to 1963, and then its first president in 1963. As president, Ben Bella assumed a militant posture promoting socialism at home and revolutionism abroad. He overtly supported numerous third world national liberation movements and aligned himself ideologically with Nasser's radical brand of Arab nationalism. Despite the heavy legacy of French colonialism and the recent armed conflict, Ben Bella managed to secure a certain bilateral "normalcy" with France while confronting continued French military presence in the Sahara. He also challenged French and Western petroleum interests in southern Algeria by establishing the Société Nationale de Transport et Commercialisation des Hydrocarbures (SONATRACH), a national oil and gas company that eventually assumed complete control of the country's hydrocarbon resources.

Yet these globally oriented efforts failed to secure the kind of political stability and socioeconomic development that the nation assumed would follow with the ousting of the much-hated French. As the country began to experience civil unrest in the Kabyle region, and a brief border war in 1963 with Morocco ended inconclusively, support for Ben Bella among high army officers began to dissipate rapidly. Thus, on 19 June 1965, Colonel Boumédienne overthrew Ben Bella in a military coup d'état and imposed himself as head of a newly formed Council of the Revolution. Ben Bella was placed under house arrest. Following Boumédienne's death in December 1978, Colonel Chadli Benjedid (b. 1929) became president of Algeria (1979). Benjedid ended Ben Bella's detention in July 1979, and all further restrictions were lifted in October 1980, when Ben Bella went into exile in Switzerland.

In May 1984 Ben Bella formed an opposition party called the Movement for Democracy in Algeria (Mouvement pour la Démocratie en Algérie, or MDA) that called for a pluralistic social order and a democratic form of government, yet one that incorporated Islamist religious and moral principles. In 1990 Ben Bella was allowed to return to Algeria when for a brief period it seemed he could serve as a bridge between the ideologically polarized forces that had emerged in the late 1980s between militant Islamists and radical military commanders. In 1991 Ben Bella declared himself a candidate for the presidency, but this came to naught as the country plunged into a violent civil war in the aftermath of a military coup d'état. Staged by high army officers on 11 January 1992, the coup ended all forms of competitive politics in the country.

Ben Bella retreated into the political background, reappearing momentarily as one of numerous opposition groups assembled in Rome in 1994 and 1995 under the sponsorship of the Catholic lay organization, Community of Sant'Egidio, to formulate an end to the civil war. These efforts proved futile. When the Algerian constitution was amended in 1996, it imposed tight restrictions on political parties that led the country's supreme court in 1997 to disband Ben Bella's MDA party.

While he never regained his former political prominence, Ben Bella was viewed as a distinguished figure in Algeria, one of the nine "historic chiefs." In 2004 he participated actively in the country's fiftieth-anniversary commemoration of the beginning of the war of national liberation. In 2005 President Abdelaziz Bouteflika asked Ben Bella to head the campaign to promote an amnesty plan that the Algerian president was advancing as a solution to the country's decade-long civil war.

In the moral, political, and globalized environment of the early twenty-first century, Ahmed Ben Bella defined himself as a mild and peace-loving Islamist. Despite the one-party state that he had once headed, Ben Bella advocated democracy in Algeria and elsewhere. He believed that the rise of militant Islamic fundamentalism was the result of a faulty interpretation of Islam, a topic on which he wrote numerous articles and monographs. He had long ago made peace with his former French enemies and considered France an important supporter of Algerian national interests. Ben Bella came to embody a conflictual mixture of Algeria's colonial and postcolonial legacies, fusing revolutionary idealism with one-party authoritarianism and democratic aspirations with religious principles.

See also **Algeria; Algerian War; Colonialism; Decolonization; French Empire; Partisan Warfare.**

BIBLIOGRAPHY

Bennoune, Mahfoud. *The Making of Contemporary Algeria, 1830–1987: Colonial Upheavals and Post-Independence Development.* Cambridge, U.K., 1988.

Confer, Vincent. *France and Algeria: The Problem of Civil and Political Reform, 1870–1920.* Syracuse, N.Y., 1966.

Connelly, Matthew James. *A Diplomatic Revolution: Algier's Fight for Independence and the Origins of the Post–Cold War Era.* Oxford, U.K., 2002.

Entelis, John P. *Algeria: The Revolution Institutionalized.* Boulder, Colo., 1986.

Gordon, David. *North Africa's French Legacy, 1954–1962.* Cambridge, Mass., 1962.

————. *The Passing of French Algeria.* London, 1966.

Henissart, Paul. *Wolves in the City: The Death of French Algeria.* New York, 1970.

Horne, Alistair. *A Savage War of Peace: Algeria, 1954–1962.* New York, 1987.

Ottaway, David, and Marina. *Algeria: The Politics of a Socialist Revolution.* Berkeley, Calif., 1970.

Quandt, William B. *Revolution and Political Leadership: Algeria, 1954–1968.* Cambridge, Mass., 1969.

JOHN P. ENTELIS

BENELUX ECONOMIC UNION.

The organization of postwar Europe through regional agreements finds its origin in the Benelux accord, the first of its kind, which arose out of World War II and was concluded as a treaty in 1958. Negotiations among Belgian, Dutch, and Luxembourgois delegates began in exile in London during World War II. An economic agreement among them was signed on 21 October 1943, while they were still under German occupation. A transitional bilateral customs convention followed on 5 September 1944, further linking the three countries. The thinking behind these documents was clear. The future Netherlands-Belgium-Luxembourg economic union was intended to contribute to the birth of a stable European and eventually to a stable global monetary system, embodied in the Bretton Woods Conference. In Bretton Woods, New Hampshire, in 1944 the Belgian and Dutch delegations adopted a common standpoint, pointing to a shared future of small European states in international economic affairs.

The Benelux Treaty, signed only in 1958, but there in outline from the time of the customs convention of 1944, did not aim at a complete economic integration of the three signatory countries. The three states joined it to improve their standing in international negotiations, which had hardly been salient before and during the war.

Through the impetus given by the Belgian Minister of Foreign Affairs, Paul-Henri Spaak (1899–1972), the first ministerial conference of the Benelux countries took place on 17 and 18 April 1946, in the Hague, where the ministers decided to bring the institutions of the union immediately into effect. During July 1946 the office of the Secretary-General of the Benelux group began its work in Brussels.

The common customs tariff came into force on 1 January 1948. While customs duties were removed for trade within the Benelux group, all the other protective barriers remained: quantitative restrictions, value-added tax, licenses, monetary and financial regulations, and fixing of quotas. One of the principal tasks of the organs of the Benelux union during postwar years was gradually to remove all the protectionist measures enacted during the 1930s.

The Benelux Economic Union Treaty, signed in the Hague on 3 February 1958, came into force on 1 November 1960. The treaty bore the hallmarks of the experience gained starting in 1946, in the context of a customs convention. Each of the three partners had the right to appoint three members of a Committee of Ministers, thus signaling the continued political independence of the three states.

The model of a customs union, based on older patterns, was adopted to provide the basis for cooperation, rather than to define what common policies would be. More complete economic integration would have required major constitutional change, which in the immediate postwar period was unacceptable to the populations of all three partner states.

In the pre-1958 period the economic and monetary tasks faced by the Benelux countries related to the consequences of the war. The Netherlands, whose entire territory was liberated only in April–May 1945, suffered war damage of a kind much more extensive than did Belgium. In addition, Belgium did not face the monetary problems of the Netherlands, encumbered from 1945 by an expensive colonial war in Indonesia. Both countries could not export to Germany, whose economy was prostrate in the immediate postwar period. The

effects were felt more heavily in the Netherlands, which had a serious deficit in its balance of payments.

The monetary difficulties of the Netherlands were solved gradually at the beginning of the 1950s, thanks to the European Payments Union. The temporary absence of the German market encouraged the three governments to look to joint benefits through the Benelux union, so as to mutually open outlets for trade for their export sectors. Belgian industry, until at least 1952, profited substantially from these agreements through access to Dutch markets, previously dominated by German competition.

Free movement of goods among the three countries did not extend to agricultural goods. That problem was resolved only at the level of the Common Market after 1958. The same was true in other sectors—for example, in the area of tax harmonization (in particular as regards excise duties) and with respect to the opening of national markets to foreign competing companies.

Despite the incomplete and limited nature of the Benelux initiative, the progressive dismantling of trade barriers had positive effects on trade among the three after the war. This presented a strong precedent observed closely by those contemplating joining the process of European economic integration. For this reason, the Benelux group boasted that it was a veritable "laboratory of Europe." The experience accumulated by the Benelux countries with respect to a common tariff policy and a coordinated external marketing policy played a clear role in the negotiations leading to the establishment of a Common Customs Tariff of the European Economic Community. The Benelux experiment thus prepared the ground for the Western European pathway to economic union, one that now extends well beyond the horizons initially envisioned during World War II.

See also **Belgium; Bretton Woods Agreement; European Commission; European Constitution 2004–2005; European Union; Luxembourg; Netherlands.**

BIBLIOGRAPHY

Bloemen, E. S. A., ed. *Het Benelux-effect: België, Nederland en Luxemburg en de Europse integratie, 1945–1957.* Amsterdam, 1992.

Griffiths, Richard T., ed. *The Netherlands and the Integration of Europe 1945–1957*. Amsterdam, 1990.

Karelle, Jacques, and Frans De Kemmeter. *Le Benelux commenté. Textes officiels*. Brussels, 1961.

Postma, A., et al., eds. *Regards sur le Benelux: 50 ans de coopération*. Tielt, 1994.

THIERRY GROSBOIS

BENEŠ, EDUARD (1884–1948), second (1935–1938) and fourth (1945–1948) president of Czechoslovakia.

Born in the village of Kožlany into a family of ten children, Eduard Beneš supported himself during his studies in Prague and abroad (Paris, Berlin, London), receiving a doctorate of laws in 1908. Beneš came to prominence during World War I as one of three founders of Czechoslovakia, along with Tomáš Garrigue Masaryk and the Slovak leader Milan R. Štefánik. Although he first hoped that the multiethnic Austrian Monarchy could be transformed into a modern federation, under the influence of Masaryk he began to work toward breaking up the Habsburg Empire. At the Paris Peace Conference, Beneš excelled as a diplomat in gaining considerable territories for the new republic, especially in its eastern half against the claims of Hungary. However, in addition to absorbing too many ethnic minorities, Czechoslovakia's new borders proved too extenuated to be effectively defended.

Throughout the interwar period Beneš controlled Czechoslovakia's foreign policy. This was true also after his election as the country's second president, replacing the aged Masaryk in 1935. Against the double threat of Hungarian revisionism and Habsburg restoration he prevailed upon Romania and Yugoslavia to join Czechoslovakia in forming in 1919 the Little Entente. Apart from maintaining the Versailles system and very actively promoting the League of Nations, Beneš became one of the leading advocates of collective security, which received a substantial boost through the Franco-Soviet military assistance pact of 1935 and which Czechoslovakia joined. However, other countries refused to participate, and the French, under British influence, decided to appease the fascist powers instead of restraining them. The German annexation of Austria in March 1938 signaled the outbreak of the Sudeten crisis, which was settled at the infamous Munich conference at the end of September.

Facing the threat of military attack by Adolf Hitler, who pledged to rescue the German-speaking population of Czechoslovakia, Beneš and his government succumbed to joint Anglo-French pressure and agreed to German occupation of the Sudetenland. Following Munich, Beneš resigned his presidency and went into exile to London with his wife. In early 1939 the Benešes left for the United States. Heralded as "Europe's most distinguished democrat," Beneš taught at the University of Chicago. Here he experienced the shock of Hitler's invasion of Prague on 15 March 1939 and the disintegration of Czechoslovakia. What followed was arguably Beneš's finest performance as, still a private person, he condemned the German occupation as an act of barbarism and breach of the Munich settlement. On 28 May 1939 Beneš met secretly with Franklin D. Roosevelt and left with the impression that the U.S. president wished to restore Czechoslovakia if the United States entered the war. He returned to London a few weeks before the German assault on Poland. Beneš's activities concentrated on the difficult task of maintaining unity among Czechoslovakia's exiles, boosting through radio broadcasts the morale of those suffering under occupation, and achieving the full recognition of his exile government from the Allied forces. After Hitler's invasion of the Soviet Union in June 1941 the Soviets began to support the restoration of Czechoslovakia within its pre-1938 borders. Beneš saw this erroneously as a confirmation of his theory of convergence, whereby Joseph Stalin's Soviet Union was bound to adopt some democratic reforms because of the close wartime alliance with Britain and the United States. Against British warnings but anxious to secure the best terms, Beneš went to Moscow in December 1943 to sign with Stalin the treaty of assistance and postwar cooperation. What followed was a steady retreat on Beneš's part under the pressure exercised by Moscow and Czechoslovak Communists.

Still deeply traumatized by the betrayal of Western powers in 1938, Beneš argued that he needed common border with the Soviet Union in order to receive military assistance to thwart a future German invasion. With regard to internal changes, Beneš issued a series of decrees ordering the expulsion of Germans and Hungarians, confiscation of their property and that of the Nazi collaborators, and nationalization of banks and heavy industry. He opposed, as in the past, Slovak aspirations for autonomy. His deteriorating health was exploited unscrupulously by Moscow and domestic Communists. Thus he had no strength to resist when Stalin vetoed Czechoslovak participation in the Marshall Plan. When it came to the showdown between Communists and noncommunists in February 1948, Beneš failed to support the latter, and by remaining in office he legalized the Communist takeover. In May 1948, nevertheless, Beneš finally refused to sign a Communist-sponsored constitution and resigned as president. After abdicating, the sick Beneš tried in vain to finish his wartime memoirs. He died of a stroke on 3 September 1948.

See also **Czechoslovakia; Munich Agreement; Sudetenland.**

BIBLIOGRAPHY

Primary Sources

Beneš, Edvard. *Memoirs of Dr. Eduard Beneš: From Munich to New War and New Victory.* Translated by Godfrey Lias. London, 1954.

———. *The Fall and Rise of a Nation: Czechoslovakia 1938–1941.* Edited by Milan Hauner. New York, 2004.

Secondary Sources

Lias, Godfrey. *Beneš of Czechoslovakia.* London, 1939.

Hitchcock, Edward. *"I Built a Temple for Peace": The Life of Eduard Beneš.* New York, 1940.

Zeman, Zbyněk, and Antonín Klimek. *The Life of Edvard Beneš 1884–1948: Czechoslovakia in Peace and War.* Oxford, U.K., 1996.

MILAN HAUNER

BENJAMIN, WALTER (1892–1940), German philosopher.

Walter Benjamin's earliest writings displayed a fascination with the concepts and orientation of German Romanticism. Literature was not merely one form of writing. It possessed a privileged and unique redemptory function. It was a path to divine wisdom, or the Absolute. Science, in the German sense of *Wissenschaft,* offered secular knowledge, but these truths were fundamentally prosaic. They pertained to the inferior sphere of physical causality and as such yielded merely second-order insights. They failed to approximate the higher order of wisdom that was theology's province. For decades German scholarship had labored under the influence of neo-Kantianism, with its stubborn refusal to traverse the realm of "phenomenal knowledge"—the "bounds of sense." For Kant, speculative insight was a species of "nonknowledge," or delusion. In Benjamin's view, the neo-Kantian approach was an intellectually self-defeating rejection of metaphysics and all its fruits. It represented a form of intellectual timorousness that consigned thought to the historical present in its impoverished, empirical state. By renouncing transcendence, it rested content with Being-as-such, rather than—as Plato did—with ultimate reality, or "true Being." From an early age, Benjamin attempted to set forth these ideas in a series of pathbreaking literary and philosophical essays: "On Language as Such and on the Language of Man"; "The Program of the Coming Philosophy"; the "Theologico-Political Fragment"; and "Goethe's *Elective Affinities*"; as well as his dissertation on "The Concept of Art Criticism in German Romanticism." He believed that by refusing to speak the language of science, literature was able to approximate the realm of noumenal or intelligible truth.

Yet there remained something inherently paradoxical about literature's status as a vehicle of supersensible knowing, for its means of expression were, unavoidably, the language of "man": the error-suffused, post-Edenic idiom stemming from the biblical "tree of knowledge"—language after the Fall. As such, there was something futile, even Sisyphean, about literary endeavor. It tried to purvey absolute knowledge via the flawed and limited conceptual mechanisms of the human understanding. As the German Romantics knew well—and in this regard too Benjamin followed their directives carefully—this paradox spoke volumes about the nature of literary form. It accounted for the fact that literature, unlike scholarship or *Wissenschaft*, was forced to proceed via allusion and innuendo. Irony, a standard Romantic trope, accounted for the gap between literature's grandiose aspirations and its prosaic means of expression. Allegory, a form of literary indirection that Benjamin investigated at length in *The Origin of German Tragic Drama* (1925), suggested that literature expressed "absent" rather than "immanent" truths.

Benjamin took a keen interest in the doctrines of art for art's sake. Like the symbolists, he believed that literature was invested with a higher, salvific mission. Most of his early aesthetic and literary writings revolved around the concept of "experience," which would play a large role throughout all phases of his work. Benjamin accepted the view articulated by "critics of modernity" such as George Simmel, George Lukács, and Max Weber that one of the hallmarks of the modern age was the decline or loss of experience in the replete or integral sense. His literary-theological interests aimed at the restoration of an original, prelapsarian context of meaning that, amid the fragmentation of modern life, seemed perceptible only in disparate and faint traces. Whereas profane knowledge, with its scientific biases, contributed to the loss of experience, literature, in Benjamin's view, thematized its disappearance and presaged its ultimate restoration.

Yet by the early 1920s, Benjamin's focus had already begun to shift perceptibly. The Weimar Republic's social and political turbulence influenced his orientation. Increasingly, given the pressing historical concerns at issue, a belletristic concentration on art for art's sake seemed an unconscionable luxury. One turning point was Germany's devastating inflation of 1923, which threatened the nascent republic's survival. The following year, Benjamin encountered Lukács's *History and Class Consciousness* (1923), which opened up possibilities for a philosophically sophisticated, nondogmatic approach to Marxism. More and more, the theological remedies he had flirted with early on seemed out of step with the political demands of the times. At one point he confided in a letter to his friend Gershom Scholem (1897–1982) that his aspiration was to be the greatest German literary critic of his generation. Yet later

on, in his brilliant collection of prose pieces *One-Way Street* (1928), he redescribed himself combatively, echoing Karl Marx, as a "strategist in the literary struggle."

Correspondingly, Benjamin's literary and cultural interests underwent a dramatic alteration. Recent developments in Paris began to attract his attention—above all, the first provocative stirrings of the surrealist movement. As a translator of Marcel Proust and Charles Baudelaire, he was well-positioned to appreciate surrealism's uniqueness. In his "Manifesto of Surrealism" (1924), André Breton made much of surrealism's desire to break with the affirmative pretense of traditional literature. Thereby, surrealism sought to contest the illusions of bourgeois aestheticism: the presupposition that the sublime ideals expressed in art and literature should subsist in a sphere separate from everyday life.

Benjamin's encounter with surrealism coincided with his political radicalization during the 1920s. He had always been fascinated by the allure of "anthropological nihilism": the writings of "dark spirits"—Mikhail Bakunin, Friedrich Nietzsche, Georg Büchner—who believed that wholesale destruction of the existing social order was a necessary precondition for regeneration. In its antipathy to the institution of literature, surrealism satisfied many of Benjamin's desiderata—especially the idea that aesthetic consciousness must infuse the sphere of everyday life.

It was in this spirit that during the late 1920s Benjamin coined one of his most memorable phrases: "profane illuminations." As opposed to religious illuminations, which aimed at transcendence, the profane variety was, Benjamin insisted, exoteric and this-worldly. In a surrealist spirit, they represented a type of transcendence in immanence. He believed that surrealism had been partly successful in shattering bourgeois aestheticism's aura of affirmation. Once the contents were dispersed, they could be generalized instead of accessible solely to an educated elite.

It was around this same time that, after a brief stay in Moscow, Benjamin began following revolutionary developments in Soviet film—including the work of Dziga Vertov and Sergei Eisenstein—which he viewed as a genuinely collective art form capable of advancing the revolutionary conscious-ness of the toiling masses. At a later point, his friendship with Bertolt Brecht, who harbored anal-ogous suspicions of "high culture," helped to further catalyze these interests. Many of these insights would find their way into what would become Benjamin's most-cited essay: "The Work of Art in the Age of Mechanical Reproduction" (1936). At the height of the popular front era, Benjamin praised film for having dissolved the aura of affirmation endemic to bourgeois aestheticism.

Yet the exoteric and critical cinematic tenden-cies Benjamin lauded remained precarious. As Hollywood showed, film as a medium was hardly averse to the spirit of affirmation Benjamin system-atically mistrusted. The just response to his opti-mistic, political reading of film in the "Work of Art" essay was provided by his friend and interloc-utor Theodor Adorno in "The Culture Industry: Enlightenment as Mass Deception," which appeared in *Dialectic of Enlightenment* (written jointly with Max Horkheimer from 1941 to 1944). There Adorno exposed film's regressive side—its role in providing ideological window dressing for industrial capitalism's transition to a consumer society.

Despite his new stress on cultural revolutionary themes, Benjamin never entirely abandoned his love of literature. During the 1930s he wrote a series of pathbreaking essays that helped him consolidate his reputation as one of the twentieth century's premier critics. His reflections on the work of figures such as Proust, Franz Kafka, Baudelaire, and Nikolai Leskov stand out as exem-plars of literary criticism. In all these articles, Benjamin's primary concern was the atrophy of the modern capacity for experience, but also the various literary remedies to redress this loss. In Benjamin's literary pantheon, Proust occupied a privileged niche. *Remembrance of Things Past* sig-nified the level of discipline and dedication it took for a contemporary author to restore, via the alchemy of remembrance, a dimension of experien-tial integrity in an era when experiential wholeness could no longer be taken for granted.

The major work on which Benjamin labored during the last thirteen years of his life was *The Arcades Project*. With this study, Benjamin sought to combine Breton and Marx. Sifting through Marx's juvenilia, he discovered an aside in an 1843 letter that suggested telling affinities between Marxism and the surrealist celebration of dream experience. "The world has long been dreaming of something which it can acquire if it becomes conscious of it," Marx observed. The dialectical interrelationship between these two states, dream-ing and awakening, would become *The Arcades Project*'s methodological signature. In a revealing passage, Benjamin wrote, "The utilization of dream elements upon awaking is the canon of dia-lectics." The *Arcades Project*'s didactic intention was to stir a somnambulant humanity from its capitalism-induced ideological slumber—the mass narcosis that coincided with the universal triumph of the commodity form.

Marx had brilliantly described capitalism's mythological, phantasmagorical side in his discus-sion of "commodity fetishism" in *Capital*. He claimed that commodity production engendered an inverted world in which things (i.e., commod-ities) functioned as the prime movers while men and women were degraded to personifications of economic categories—a process demonstrated in the Orwellian phrase popular among managerial types, "human capital." Whereas a commodity, observed Marx, initially appears as "a very trivial thing [that] is easily understood," upon closer scrutiny, it abounds in "theological subtleties and metaphysical niceties." For under conditions of advanced capitalism, the commodity—the product of labor—assumes the form of a social relation existing not among the workers but among the products themselves. "There," Marx concludes, "it is a definite relation between men, that assumes, in their eyes, *the fantastic form of a relation between things*." In acknowledging the importance of the sphere of circulation, Benjamin recognized that the obstacles to revolution no longer lay with the sphere of production per se but instead with the realm of the "superstructure": the site of commod-ity fetishism as a realm of ideological narcosis or "false consciousness."

But the *Arcades Project* featured some problem-atical methodological aspects that placed Benjamin at loggerheads with his sponsors at the Institute for Social Research, which in 1934 had moved to New York, for the project openly relied on two aspects of German *Lebensphilosophie* to which both Horkheimer and Adorno took exception: Ludwig Klages's idea of "archaic images" and Carl Jung's notion of the "collective unconscious." In Benjamin's view, prehistory embodied a (primitive) classless society that had deposited utopian "wish images" in humanity's collective unconscious. Under conditions of high capitalism, whose revolutionary productive capacities presaged a future society of abundance, these wish images began to resurface in the arcades, the world exhibitions, the iron constructions, and other phenomenal manifestations of the epoch. In Benjamin's view, the advent of a classless society would ideally turn these utopian promissory notes into a vivid reality.

In *The Origin of German Tragic Drama*, Benjamin had lionized inconsummate literary works or fragments. In his view, they expressed the lacerated or unreconciled nature of the reigning social order. It was somehow fitting, therefore, that the *Arcades Project* itself remained unconsummated—a series of suggestive, if fragmentary and disparate, notebook entries.

Among the contradictions in Benjamin's work that were never reconciled was the tension between Marxism and theology. He could never really decide if his ultimate desideratum was a socialist society à la Marx or a redeemed humanity inspired by the model of the Last Judgment. His writings often oscillated between these twin poles, with the hope and expectation that ultimately they would reinforce one another. This paradox found its way into his last work, the "Theses on the Philosophy of History," where Benjamin, despondent over fascism's recent military triumphs, openly declared that Marxism would succeed only if it took theology into its service. As he observed in another context, "Hope is given to us only for the sake of those without hope."

See also **Adorno, Theodor; Frankfurt School; Jung, Carl; Klages, Ludwig; Lukács, György.**

BIBLIOGRAPHY

Primary Sources

Benjamin, Walter. *Illuminations.* Edited by Hannah Arendt. Translated by Harry Zohn. New York, 1969.

——. *One-Way Street and Other Writings.* Translated by Edmund Jephcott and Kingsley Shorter. London, 1985.

——. *The Arcades Project.* Translated by Howard Eiland and Kevin McClaughlin. Cambridge, Mass., 1999.

——. *Selected Writings.* Vol 1: *1913–1926.* Edited by Marcus Bullock. Cambridge, Mass., 2002.

Secondary Sources

Buck-Morss, Susan. *The Dialectics of Seeing: Walter Benjamin's Arcades Project.* Cambridge, Mass., 1989.

Wolin, Richard. *Walter Benjamin: An Aesthetic of Redemption.* 2nd ed. Berkeley and Los Angeles, Calif., 1994.

RICHARD WOLIN

BERG, ALBAN (1885–1935), Austrian composer.

Alban Berg lived in Vienna at a time when his musical mentors, Gustav Mahler and Arnold Schoenberg, changed the course of Western music. Following Mahler, Berg's music reflects his life and contemporary Viennese society in autobiographical "programs" encoded in musical symbols. Following Schoenberg, Berg initially wrote tonal music, then nontonal music from 1908, and twelve-tone music from 1923. Berg's compositional style is related to but also distinct from his colleagues in the "second Viennese school," his teacher Schoenberg and fellow pupil Anton Webern. Berg achieved success in his lifetime, particularly with his first opera, *Wozzeck* (first performed in 1925), but he suffered as others did with the rise of Adolf Hitler. His output is relatively small, with seven numbered opuses and seven additional works, but has had great influence.

In Berg's early songs (to 1908), from which the *Sieben frühe Lieder* (Seven early songs) were orchestrated in 1928, he engaged the German lied tradition. He developed rapidly after studies with Schoenberg commenced in 1904; following preliminary instrumental studies, the Piano Sonata, op. 1 (1907–1908), is a one-movement work that reflects Berg's awareness of contemporary French music. The *Vier Lieder,* op. 2, for voice and piano (1909–1910; Four songs) move to a nontonal language in the fourth song, but the retention of cyclic aspects of tonality, embodied in the "circle of fifths" progression in which voices move in cycles of the same intervals, is a thread that continues throughout Berg's oeuvre, in cycles of not only pitch but rhythm, serial order, and orchestration.

Berg's two-movement string quartet, op. 3 (1910), is an unusual large-scale instrumental nontonal piece; an acclaimed performance in 1923 at the International Society for Contemporary Music Festival in Salzburg was a first success for Berg. It was also the last work written under Schoenberg's tutelage. In his subsequent *Altenberg Lieder* for voice and orchestra, op. 4 (1912), and *Vier Stücke* for clarinet and piano, op. 5 (1913), Berg reflected literary trends from writers Karl Kraus and Peter Altenberg in composing highly condensed, aphoristic pieces. An abbreviated performance of two of the songs at a scandalous concert in March 1913, and a confrontation with Schoenberg over the nature of his recent works, was followed by a return to the more characteristically substantial *Drei Stücke* for orchestra, op. 6 (1914–1915). These pieces are also studies for *Wozzeck*, finished in 1922.

Georg Büchner's fragmentary play *Woyzeck* (1837), adapted by Berg as *Wozzeck*, foreshadowed many of the aspects of expressionism, an artistic movement in Germany in the early twentieth century. The antihero's psychosis, ill-treatment by society, murder of his mistress Marie, suicide, and the life cycle that traps his child are all themes that resonated with the times, as reflected in the contemporary art of the painter Oscar Kokoschka, among others. The story of the downtrodden soldier also reflected Berg's own experiences in World War I. Berg's combining of instrumental forms and drama is described in his lecture on the opera, given before several of the many performances.

The themes of injustice shift in his second opera, *Lulu* (1927–1935)—adapted from Frank Wedekind's controversial plays *Erdgeist* (1895; Earth spirit) and *Die Büchse der Pandora* (1904; Pandora's box)—to the character of Lulu, who starts off as a figure like Eliza Doolittle in Bernard Shaw's *Pygmalion* but becomes a sexual and spiritual force embodying society's fears and desires. Taking inspiration from Kraus's lecture on Wedekind's *Die Büchse der Pandora* in 1905, Berg conceived of Lulu's three husbands, her victims in act 1, returning musically to take revenge in

act 3 as her clients when she has become a prostitute. Berg inserts himself as Dr. Schoen's son, the composer Alwa, who, along with the lesbian Countess Geschwitz and other lovers, falls under Lulu's spell to his ultimate destruction. Lulu dies at the hands of Jack the Ripper in the mixed fiction-realism of the story. Berg sets the drama with musical palindromes, twelve-tone character rows derived from serial cycles, *leitforms* associated with characters, and many corresponding details of tempo and orchestration.

Berg's twelve-tone works follow the neoclassical trends of the time. They include the *Kammerkonzert* (1923–1925) and second string quartet, the *Lyrische Suite* (1925–1926), both partially twelve-tone in language, the commissioned concert aria *Der Wein* (1929), and the violin concerto (1935), composed around the time of *Lulu*. The concerto includes a chorale from J. S. Bach, "Es ist Genug" (It is enough), woven into the twelve-tone fabric of the triadic-based row (G, B-flat, D, F-sharp, A, C, E, G-sharp, B, C-sharp, D-sharp, F), as a public requiem for Alma Mahler's daughter but also a foreshadowing of Berg's own death in December 1935.

Berg's music has undergone censure in the Webern-influenced 1950s and renewed acclaim in later revivals of tonal and Romantic ideals. The unfinished *Lulu* was completed by Friedrich Cerha and premiered in its full form in 1979. Unfolding details of Berg's life, including his daughter, Albine, born in 1902 to a family servant, his marriage to Helene Nahowski in 1910, and an affair with Hanna Fuchs-Robettin in 1925 documented in an annotated score of the *Lyric Suite* discovered by George Perle, await a definitive biography. Berg scholarship begins with his own writings, sketches, letters, and analyses, writings from Theodor Adorno and Hans Redlich, and the work of George Perle.

See also **Opera; Schoenberg, Arnold.**

BIBLIOGRAPHY

Adorno, Theodor W. *Alban Berg: Master of the Smallest Link.* Translated by Juliane Brand and Christopher Hailey. Cambridge, U.K., 1991.

Hall, Patricia. *A View of Berg's "Lulu" through the Autograph Sources.* Berkeley, Calif., 1996.

Headlam, Dave. *The Music of Alban Berg*. New Haven, Conn., 1996.

Jarman, Douglas. *The Music of Alban Berg*. Berkeley, Calif., 1979.

Perle, George. *The Operas of Alban Berg*. 2 vols. Berkeley, Calif., 1980–1985.

Redlich, Hans. *Alban Berg: The Man and His Music*. London, 1957. Abridged translation of *Alban Berg: Versuch einer Würdigung*. Vienna, 1957.

DAVE HEADLAM

BERIA, LAVRENTY

BERIA, LAVRENTY (1899–1953), Soviet political figure under Joseph Stalin and head of the Soviet secret police.

Born to a poor peasant family in 1899, Lavrenty Pavlovich Beria was, like Joseph Stalin, a Georgian by nationality. Joining Vladimir Lenin's Bolshevik Party in March 1917, Beria participated in the 1917 Russian Revolution and the subsequent civil war (1918–1920) in the Red Army and in various revolutionary administrations.

By the end of the civil war Beria was working in Bolshevik intelligence organizations, and during the 1920s he rose through police ranks to become chief of the secret police in Soviet Georgia and Transcaucasia in 1930. This position probably brought him to Stalin's notice during the dictator's holidays in that region, and in 1931 Stalin put the thirty-two-year-old Beria in charge of the entire Georgian Communist Party in the dictator's home region.

In 1938 Stalin brought Beria to Moscow to take over the Soviet secret police (NKVD) from Nikolai Yezhov, who had administered the Great Purges (1936–1938). Blaming the "excesses" of the terror on Yezhov's former administration, Beria released a few thousand purge victims and instituted policies designed to demonstrate an ostensible return to "legality" after the orgy of arrests in 1937–1938, during which millions had been arrested and about 750,000 summarily executed. Beria's liberalism was more apparent than real. He had been an energetic purger back in his Georgian bailiwick, supervising the execution of thousands and the purge of more than two-thirds of the Georgian party leadership. Although the number of executions did fall sharply

under Beria, the remainder of Stalin's rule until his death in 1953 saw a steady increase in the level of arrests. Memoirs from the time, however, remember Beria as a good administrator, who raised salaries for police and rations for prisoners, increased efficiency, and brought systematic and predictable management to what had been a chaotic organization.

Vyacheslav Molotov, another of Stalin's senior lieutenants, noted Beria's "almost inhumanly energetic" capacity for work. Stalin agreed, and at the outbreak of World War II in 1941 he made Beria a member of the all-powerful State Committee of Defense, putting him in charge of evacuating Soviet industry in front of the German advance and organizing forced labor for wartime production as well as heading up state security both at the front and in the rear areas. In 1945, faced with the Cold War challenge of a successful U.S. atomic bomb program, Stalin tapped Beria to head the most important Soviet effort of the day: development of a Soviet atomic bomb, which Beria did with his trademark brutality and energy, combined with a willingness to listen to experts. Igor Kurchatov, the scientist considered the "father of the Soviet atomic bomb," admired Beria's administrative ability, flexibility, and energy.

Stalin trusted Beria. In addition to his talents as a tireless and efficient administrator, Beria was able to read Stalin's moods and to adjust himself instantly to the dictator's shifts. The Soviet leader Nikita Khrushchev described Beria as "chameleon-like," and Beria's obsequious flattery and manipulation of Stalin's vanity led the dictator's wife and daughter to despise him; the wife of another of Stalin's lieutenants called Beria a "rat." In Stalin's last years he too was becoming suspicious of Beria. At that time the dictator authored several political maneuvers against Beria, indicating that Stalin was planning a new purge, with Beria almost certainly on the list of those slated for arrest.

Stalin's death in March 1953 therefore was very convenient for Beria. Although there is no evidence that he procured the dictator's death, Beria later told both Molotov and Khrushchev that he, Beria, had "saved them all." Beria's conduct at Stalin's sickbed, as the dictator lay dying, seemed to demonstrate his cunning and lack of principle. When Stalin was unconscious, Beria made scornful remarks about him, but when Stalin was lucid,

Lavrenty Beria (center) with Georgy Malenkov (right) and V. M. Molotov, 1953. AP PHOTOS

Beria hurried to proclaim his loyalty and kiss the dictator's hand.

After Stalin's death Beria initiated policies that seemed to display an un-Stalinist liberalism. He launched an amnesty for prisoners, favored conciliatory policies toward Yugoslavia and Germany, and began to replace Russian administrators in the provinces with indigenous officials. His bold forays into policy making alarmed his comrades and competitors in the "collective leadership" that governed after Stalin. Their discovery that Beria's police were tapping their telephones and bugging their apartments was probably the last straw. In June 1953 Khrushchev organized a secret conspiracy among the other top leaders to remove Beria, who was arrested at a meeting of the Presidium of the Communist Party. Beria was executed hours after he was convicted in a secret trial in December 1953.

See also **Khrushchev, Nikita; Soviet Union; Stalin, Joseph; Yezhov, Nikolai.**

BIBLIOGRAPHY

Primary Sources

Beria, Sergo. *Beria, My Father: Inside Stalin's Kremlin.* Translated by Brian Pearce. London, 2001. Somewhat laudatory but revealing memoir by Beria's son.

Naumov, V. P., and IU. V. Sigachev, eds. *Lavrentiy Beria, 1953. Stenogramma iiun'skogo iiulskogo plenuma TsK KPSS i drugie dokumenty.* Moscow, 1999. The transcript of the Central Committee meeting that approved Beria's fall, with speeches by the other post-Stalin leaders.

Secondary Sources

Knight, Amy. *Beria: Stalin's First Lieutenant.* Princeton, N.J., 1993. The authoritative scholarly biography of Beria in English.

J. ARCH GETTY

BERLIN. At the beginning of the twentieth century, the city of Berlin and its surrounding municipalities were the largest urban agglomeration in the German-speaking world. Berlin was geographically defined by the plains on both sides of the Spree River around the city center, the upper Spree region with its lakes to the southeast, and the confluence of the Spree into the Havel River to the west. Already in the preceding centuries, waterways had been a central factor of Berlin's development as the commercial and economic core of central Germany, now complemented by its nodal function in the German railway system.

Berlin's population in 1900 was the product of several decades of rapid population growth. Taking into account the creation of Greater Berlin in 1920, about 2.7 million people lived in the region. The population continued to grow, but at a more moderate pace during the first half of the century, reaching about 4.3 million in 1930. It slowly but continuously receded after 1945 to stagnate around 3.4 million in 2000. In 2000, as in 1900, the "typical" Berliner was not born in Berlin. Immigrants continuously arrived from all German regions, but in the first half of the century particularly from the surrounding countryside, the Eastern Prussian provinces, and Poland. In the heyday of Nazi Germany's terror against subjugated populations in Europe, about seven hundred thousand forced laborers (*Zwangsarbeiter*) swelled the city population. After World War II, immigrants from southern and southeastern Europe as well as from Turkey stabilized West Berlin's net population balance. In the postcommunist era, reunified Berlin is marked again by East European (Poland, and the countries of the former Soviet Union) and global migration trends. By contrast, fertility rates throughout the century show the classical features of urban decline, from 26 (1901) to over 17 (1918) to 15 (1938) to fewer than 10 births per 10,000 inhabitants, in all cases a level insufficient for population growth. Regarding age structure, however, a major shift has occurred. Still a city of the young in the first half of the twentieth century, Berlin was not spared the second demographic transition of very low fertility and rising life expectancy during the second half of century. It has tended to be a city of the old in the late twentieth and early twenty-first centuries.

ECONOMIC PROFILE

Berlin has always been and still is the largest industrial city in Germany, despite the overall decline of the industrial sector in the last decades of the twentieth century. As the German capital, the city's labor force engaged in multifold activities in commerce, business, the civil service, education, and culture.

The traditional strength of Berlin's industry lies in the manufacturing sector and is based on advanced technology and the transfer of knowledge from the natural and engineering sciences. Huge conglomerates with international reputations such as Rheinmetall-Borsig (mechanical engineering), Siemens and AEG (electrical industry), and Schering (pharmaceuticals) dominate the picture, complemented by a large segment of small and medium-sized and highly specialized businesses. Already during the late years of the German Empire, however, Berlin had also become an early center of services mainly because of its central functions as a capital, but also because of the increasing relevance of knowledge transfer from universities, of modern marketing coupled with burgeoning consumerism, of the commodification of culture and leisure time on a mass scale, and of the expansion of the interventionist state, a tendency continued under the Nazi dictatorship with its own set of new central administrations. The expansion of the public sector was taken to its extremes in both halves of the divided city during the Cold War: East Berlin became the site of the bloated bureaucracy of central economic planning and political surveillance of state socialism, while West Berlin's public service remained heavily overstaffed thanks to the politically motivated subsidies from West Germany that safeguarded attractive living standards. Only since German reunification have efforts been made to reduce these disproportions. Private services have now established themselves as the dominating sector of the city's economic activities, while the late adaptation to the logics of a globalized economy has led to a dramatic reduction of industrial workplaces.

POLITICAL AND ADMINISTRATIVE STRUCTURE

1900 to 1919 Before the creation of Greater Berlin in 1920, the city of Berlin with its 1.9 million inhabitants was a municipality with restricted autonomy thanks to the prerogatives of the central state in the residence and capital of the Kingdom of Prussia, itself the largest member state of the German Empire. De facto, the police president of Berlin, placed immediately under the Prussian Ministry of Interior, had power over the city's affairs at least as substantial as that of the mayor (*Oberbürgermeister*). The latter was elected by a parliament based on census suffrage. City politics were therefore marked by a double discrimination: The overwhelming majority of the (exclusively male) electorate, consisting of the low income earners from the working class primarily voting for Social Democratic candidates, was grossly underrepresented in the city parliament as well as among the Berlin members of the Prussian House of Commons. City politics were thus dominated by middle-class liberals, but lacked the means of effective municipal autonomy thanks to the semi-absolutist constitution and the governance of the Prussian state. The same is true for the large neighboring cities of several hundred thousands that were later integrated into Greater Berlin, including Charlottenburg, Wilmersdorf, Schöneberg, Neukölln, Spandau, Lichtenberg, and Cöpenick. Left liberals and the Social Democrats were allies in fighting the unequal voting system and established a pragmatic cooperation on the local level in such areas as welfare, urban planning, and public education, prefiguring the coalitions vital for Greater Berlin's politics during the Weimar Republic.

The political profile of the city population found its expression in a much more accurate way in the Reichstag, the empire's house of commons based on equal male suffrage. Starting in the 1890s, Berlin was overwhelmingly represented by the Social Democratic Party, whose candidates always carried between 50 and 80 percent of the votes. In consequence, Berlin's politics were marked by a unique overlapping of three heterogeneous forces: the antidemocratic power center of the Prussian monarchy, an economically influential and in large parts progressively oriented middle-class liberalism, and the absolute hegemony of socialism among the lower middle classes and the working class.

The unresolved tensions among these camps were muted in the name of a domestic "truce" proclaimed at Germany's entry in World War I,

only to break open again with the dramatic deterioration of living conditions and the extremely unequal distribution of the war's burden within society. When the Social Democrats split over the war support issue in 1916, the traditional strength of the left wing among Berlin's Social Democrats made for a particularly strong section of the new Independent Social Democratic Party, which during the 1920s became a recruiting ground for the German Communist Party. The November revolution in 1918 was therefore marked by the direct competition between the project of a socialist republic of workers' and soldiers' councils (*Arbeiter- und Soldatenräte*) as proclaimed by the left-wing leader Karl Liebknecht from a balcony of the imperial castle on 9 November, and a parliamentary republic as proclaimed by Philipp Scheidemann, one of two leaders of the right-wing Social Democrats, from a window of the Reichstag a few hours later. The alliance between parts of the military and the right-wing Social Democrats "to restore order" was met with fierce resistance among Berlin's radicals. During the overthrow of their revolt in January 1919, their famous leaders, Liebknecht and Rosa Luxemburg, were murdered by right-wing paramilitaries on 15 January.

1919 to 1933 The establishment of the Weimar Republic also entailed the thorough reform of Prussia into a democratic legal state. One of the most important projects of the Prussian National Assembly elected in February 1919 was the reorganization of the municipality of Berlin according to exigencies of modern urban planning and administration. A law passed with the majority of both Social Democratic parties, the left liberals, and the Catholic Center Party merged the old city of Berlin with seven independent cities, 59 rural counties, and 27 estates to form a new single municipality with a surface area of 88,000 hectares (217,400 acres). This "Greater Berlin" was divided into twenty city districts with local administration functions and was governed by an *Oberbürgermeister* heading a body of city councillors. Because of the inclusion of large rural areas, forests, and lakesides the new metropolis offered plenty of areas for recreational purposes and modern housing developments. In these regards, as in the realm of public transportation, public education, and social welfare, Greater Berlin saw a process of rapid modernization.

Throughout the 1920s city politics were dominated by Social Democratic–Liberal–Catholic alliances, which, however, came under increasing pressure from both left-wing and right-wing extremist opponents. Berlin's traditional working-class districts quickly developed into strongholds of the young German Communist Party and its vast network of social and cultural mass organizations. From 1926 onward, the emergent Nazi Party waged a fierce "battle for Berlin" spearheaded by the gifted orator and organizer Joseph Goebbels. The Nazis' strategy consisted primarily of waging guerrilla wars in the "enemy's" strongholds through a decidedly provocative and violent style of street politics, to which the communist camp hit back accordingly. Caught in-between, the moderate Social Democrats had to fulfill the role of upholding law and order, eventually making them the prime target of communist "revolutionary" propaganda against "social fascism." The rift between the two camps of organized labor, one of the crucial causes of the failure of the Weimar Republic, thus found its most violent and spectacular manifestations in Berlin, when, for instance, a police force under Social Democratic leadership killed thirty-three demonstrators and other civilians in order to enforce the ban on communist demonstrations on May Day 1929. Although the Berlin electorate remained relatively immune to the Nazi challenge, the city's Nazi votes remaining more than 10 percent below the Reich average of 44 percent in the irregular elections of March 1933, the continuous antagonisms between the Nazi opponents had contributed to a fatal erosion of the social and cultural resources necessary for any effective resistance before and after the Nazis' seizure of power in January 1933.

1933 to 1945   For the city of Greater Berlin, the Nazi policy of *Gleichschaltung* (synchronization) resulted in the loss of its municipal self-administration and the placement into power of a Prussian State commissioner under the direct control of the Prussian minister of the interior, Hermann Goering, who purged the city administration of civil servants with democratic party affiliations or those of Jewish descent. Berlin's schools were affected by this measure. Starting in 1937, principal matters of urban planning and representative architecture in the capital of the Third Reich were placed under the responsibility of Adolf Hitler's personal confidant, the architect Albert Speer. At the same time, the successive waves of political repression and ostracism against minorities hit segments of all the classes of the Berlin population: Among the first to be interned in the makeshift concentration camp set up in 1933 in nearby Oranienburg were activists of both working-class parties, liberal politicians, publicists, and Christian priests of both confessions. Anti-Semitic purges also hit large parts of Berlin's universities, the liberal and artistic professions, and the upper class, triggering off a brain drain to Great Britain and the United States from which the capital's intellectual and cultural life never fully recovered. State terror was moderated for a short period around the Olympic Games of 1936 to provide an opportunity to present Berlin as a modern and highly civilized metropolis to the international public, while the celebration of the (alleged) seven-hundred-year anniversary of Berlin in the following year was extensively used to display the reconcilability between Nazi ideology and Berlin's sense of local pride.

Also in Berlin, the so-called *Kristallnacht* of 9–10 November 1938 marked a first climax of public anti-Semitic terror supported by state authorities. During the years of World War II, the Reich capital acquired an eminent and to some extent ambivalent role in the history of the Holocaust. On the one hand, it was the site of the large administrative staffs designing and organizing the registration, expulsion, exploitation, deportation, and murder of the Jewry in Germany as well as in occupied Europe. Of the 161,000 Jews living in Berlin in 1933, only 1,000 to 2,000 still lived in Berlin at the end of the war. The great majority emigrated, while 56,000 were killed by the Nazi terror, often following long years of increasing discrimination and eventual denunciation by their fellow citizens. On the other hand, no other urban agglomeration in Germany provided comparable possibilities to escape and thereby resist the Gestapo thanks to the anonymity that is typical in large cities. Berlin offered myriad opportunities for going underground, hiding with the help of informal networks, and adopting false identities.

Soviet tanks in the streets of Berlin, April 1945. The graffiti on the wall reads "Berlin remains German." ©CORBIS

Thus, although the last two years of the war were marked by the intensified terror of Berlin Nazi "Gauleiter" Goebbels's "total war" mobilization, by increasing the chaos and the disintegration of the city's vital functions due to bombing raids, mass evacuation, and, in the last weeks of the war, massive westward flight from the approaching Red Army, it was also a site of survival for thousands of individuals persecuted by the Nazi terror machinery.

1945 to 1961 Through the destruction of World War II, Berliners suffered the loss of more than half their living space and about 60 percent of their workplaces. A relevant part of this destruction occurred at very end of the war during the "battle for Berlin," which was launched by the Soviet Army on 16 April 1945 and ended with the surrender of the city to the Soviets on 2 May. The battle cost tens of thousands of Soviet and German lives, both soldiers and civilians, and was

accompanied and followed by contrasting and irreconcilable experiences. The Soviet victory brought the end of life-threatening terror and freedom to several hundred thousand forced laborers, concentration camp inmates, and Nazi opponents, but it was experienced as a wave of retaliatory acts on the part of the triumphant conquerors, notably by tens of thousands of raped women and girls. At the same time the Soviet Army was eager to restore basic services such as provisioning and clearing the debris through a combination of generosity and despotism. In part, these first measures of restoration of public service were designed to install a reliable group of German communists in Soviet exile under the leadership of Walter Ulbricht as officeholders in the new emergent city administration.

But according to a September 1944 agreement between the war allies, not only Germany as a whole was to be divided up in occupation zones, but also its capital, which would serve as the headquarters for the joined bodies of control. For this purpose, the territory of Greater Berlin was divided first into three sectors, and then, after the admission of France, four sectors, which the Western partners took over in June 1945 in order to establish their respective sector administrations. Because of the early and preemptive admission of German political parties and trade unions under the short period of exclusive Soviet control, German politics in Berlin and in the Soviet Occupation Zone were revitalized much earlier than in the three Western zones. Thereby reverberations of the growing tensions between the Allies had already manifested themselves by April 1946, when the Soviets, in their zone of occupation, imposed the unification of the two refounded working-class parties, the Social Democrats and the Communists, and mounted repressive measures against recalcitrant German politicians among the Social Democrats as well as the Christian Democrats and Liberals. In Berlin, however, the Western Allies could secure a fair vote within the Social Democratic Party resulting in a first manifestation of democratic anticommunism, later to become the hallmark of West Berlin's political culture. The four-power consensus secured the coexistence of a Western-oriented Social Democratic Party and the newly founded Socialist Unity Party, the state party of the future East German dictatorship, in all city sectors and also within the structures of the city administration.

The first democratic elections in fall 1946 made it clear that the pro-Soviet forces would never gain a majority among the Berliners. After increasing disputes about the city's administration and in the Soviet refusal to accept the West Berlin Social Democratic leader Ernst Reuter as the new city mayor, it was the issue of all-German currency reform that led to the first Berlin crisis in June 1948. After futile inter-allied negotiations about an all-German currency reform, the Western Allies had replaced the old hyperinflated reichsmark in their West German zones by the deutsche mark and announced to do the same in their West Berlin sectors. On the pretext of preventing a massive influx of devaluated reichsmark, the Soviets closed the official terrestrial transit connections (highways, railways, and waterways) between the Western sectors and the Western zones through

which the Western Allies had maintained all the provisions and goods traffic necessary for their sectors. These "measures" (Soviet rhetoric), or "blockade," as the Western public would quickly term it, were countered by the Western Allies with the logistically and technically unique Berlin airlift, conducted from 26 June 1948 through September 1949, while the Soviet blockade was lifted on 12 May 1949. The airlift was made possible by the tacit understanding that the Soviets would not interfere with the Allied usage of the air corridors and because Greater Berlin by its sheer territorial size offered enough room for three inner-city airports, one of which was constructed during the blockade. Although the airlift was not capable of importing virtually all required goods from the beginning, and West Berliners therefore had to provision themselves through the semi- and unofficial channels they had been using since the last years of the war, it quickly became clear that the proficiency of the airlift could be increased to the point of complete maintenance of the Western sectors. Above all, it was the imagery of the beleaguered but undeterred West Berlin population amicably assisted by its former enemies that brought a moral triumph for the Western cause in the eyes of the international public.

During the blockade the city's joint administration fell apart, engendering the double structure of an East and a West Berlin municipality with their own city parliaments, mayors, and councillors, which remained basically intact until 1990. Nevertheless, Berlin remained the place in the Cold War theater with the most intensive exchanges between the antagonistic power spheres. The two halves of the city were still linked by their economic, technical, and social interactions on an everyday basis, with frequent commuting of workers, integrated public transportation, and even some practical cooperation between the two administrations on the lower level. This became blatantly evident during the popular uprising on 16 and 17 June 1953, the first anticommunist revolt against Soviet hegemony. Initially, East Berlin construction workers went on strike over low wage and endemic supply problems. With the U.S.-sponsored and German-staffed radio station RIAS covering the event, the protest movement grew into to a general, East German–wide protest against Ulbricht's regime, which was suppressed only after the intervention of Soviet troops.

Throughout the 1950s, both city halves were integrated, step by step, into the unfolding political structures of their respective hemispheres: From the Eastern side, Berlin was declared the capital of the German Democratic Republic (GDR) and fully adapted to its administrative and political structures. The Western allies, by contrast, insisted on the provisional status of Berlin, which therefore could not be fully integrated as a federal state into the new Federal Republic of Germany (FRG). Nevertheless, the legal, administrative, and economic structure of West Berlin was completely aligned to the West German system, making it de facto the twelfth federal state of the FRG.

With the Soviet ultimatum that the Western allies should give up their sectors, the second Berlin crisis was under way in 1958. The open traffic between the two parts of the city had meanwhile become the only opening in the otherwise sealed-off East German republic, to the point that it endangered its very existence. The erection of the Berlin Wall on 13 August 1961 therefore marked a point of no return for the city's further development.

1961 to 1989 For both sides, the Berlin Wall brought a consolidation of their middle term development. Each side had already regarded its own half as a showcase in the inner-German conflict and felt compelled to display the attractive aspects of their respective systems to their own populations and to the world at large and undermine the adversary's morale. In the case of East Berlin, the city was given preferred status within the state planning processes when it came to the allocation of resources for industrial investment and construction, a practice that earned the city and its inhabitants persistent unpopularity among the rest of the GDR. This preferential treatment was complemented by the unproportional growth of the huge bureaucracies of the party state, making East Berlin the capital as well of the loyal "service class." According to principles of strict centralism in the communist dictatorship, East Berlin's politics never transcended the status of an executive outpost of the party and the state leadership.

Walled-in West Berlin, by contrast, developed into a highly dynamic factor in West German and international politics. The material existence of its 2.1 million inhabitants was continuously subsidized by the FRG to the point of covering approximately 50 percent of public spending. Subsidies supported both manufacturing enterprises and public institutions of higher education and research, as well as other federal institutions, thus stabilizing but also petrifying the socioeconomic situation. At the same, the need to find some basic practical arrangements with the GDR leadership in the realm of travel permits into the East formed the background for Willy Brandt's new *Ostpolitik* and its strategy of "change by rapprochement," a policy that would gradually distance itself from the aggressive anticommunism of pre-détente times and emphasize dialogue and exchange. This atmospheric shift, under way since the late 1950s, found a peculiar expression in West Berlin because of the growing influx of West German students attracted both by the highly politicized climate per se and, among the males, by the exemption of West Berlin citizens from military service in consequence of West Berlin's status as occupied territory. West Berlin universities were therefore among the most virulent centers of the 1968 German youth rebellion. Although large parts of the West Berlin population at first fiercely resented this resurgence of left-wing radicalism from within, shouting their angry "*Geh och rüber!*" (Just go to the other side), the persistent attractiveness of the student and youth subcultures added much to the city's open and liberal-minded atmosphere during the 1970s and 1980s. This atmosphere did not change when, after nearly thirty years of uninterrupted Social Democratic majorities, a Christian Democratic, Richard von Weizsäcker, was elected governing mayor in 1981.

In the relations between the two city halves, a smooth change began to set in only some years before the fall of the Berlin Wall. Because of the international Berlin treaty of 1972, personal encounters through West Berliners visiting the East were furthered. With inner-German exchanges expanding in the 1980s, direct contacts on the cultural and scientific level also became more frequent, in particular in the aftermath of the double 750th anniversary celebration of Berlin, when an exchange of historical and art exhibits was organized.

1990 to 2000 While there surely was some—mostly unarticulated—skepticism in the West

German public about the rush to German reunification after the collapse of the wall, there was no question that the cities of East and West Berlin should be reunited once the path to reunification was treaded. Even in the months before October 1990, both city governments, the West Berlin Senate, and the East Berlin Magistrate held their sessions together in order to handle the multifold problems emerging from the reintegration of two cities of millions of inhabitants. The Bundestag decision of 20 June 1991 to move the bulk of federal government institutions to Berlin restored the city's unique character among German urban agglomerations and united the functions of an industrial and commercial, political and cultural center of national and international relevance.

Reunified Berlin therefore reflects the political subcultures of reunified Germany in peculiar ways: The legacy of West Berlin alternative culture is expressed in an exceptionally strong Green Party, while the prevalence of loyal state servants in the former capital of the GDR secures an exceptionally strong position to the postcommunist successor of the SED, the "Party of Democratic Socialism" (renamed Left Party/PDS in 2005). The latter being practically excluded from executive functions on the Land level during the first half of the 1990s, a "great coalition" of Christian Democrats and Social Democrats had to form the new governments after the first elections in reunified Berlin on 2 December 1990. This coalition was replaced by a so-called red-red coalition of Social Democrats and the PDS in 2000. The impetus for this remarkable shift of coalition partner for the Social Democrats was the Christian Democrats deep involvement in a scandalous affair of bankruptcy and corruption within the city's investment banking house, which added some 38 billion euros to its deficit. But this was not the only burden on Berlin's finances. In both parts of the city the public sector remained overproportional during the 1990s—a legacy of the Cold War. Instead of readjusting public spending to the new conditions of the free market economy that had been established in both former city halves, unrealistic growth expectations regarding demographic potential and tax revenue accumulated to a de facto insolvency of Berlin in 2000, a burden that it will be able to get rid of only with the help of federal aid.

CULTURAL LIFE AND PRACTICES

Berlin's cultural life throughout the twentieth century was marked by the permanent encounter of heterogeneous and volatile elements: immigrants from all regions of central and eastern Europe, German and non-German, were attracted by a city that offered chances alike not only to unskilled workers and skilled artisans, and to maids and female clerks, but also to career-minded scientists and scholars, and to artists, musicians, and writers of all varieties and orientations. The massive concentration of industry and finance, of central state and large business bureaucracies, and of higher education and high-culture institutions fostered a vast public sphere of cultural activities that developed a particular dynamic until the sudden crackdown on anything deemed un-German by the Nazis. Overcoming the burdens of tradition and living up to the exigencies of the present was the unquestioned self-understanding of these activities. It can be found in the mass enthusiasm for modern sports such as car racing, boxing, and soccer, and for all kinds of industrial fairs and shows at the Funkturm exhibition area, and also in the continuous support shown by Berlin's public and private patrons for avant-garde movements in the arts and architecture, and in theater, dance, literature, and film. Most importantly, Berlin's cultural life stands out for the continuous cross-fertilization between two dimensions of cultural modernity: expressionist architects such as Bruno Taut and Walter Gropius engaged in public housing projects; their playwright and director counterparts such as Max Reinhardt, Erwin Piscator, and Bertolt Brecht drew large audiences to their experimental stage settings and movies; and Berlin's music life combined a supreme position in nineteenth-century classicism with groundbreaking advances in modern music by such notable composers and conductors as Arnold Schoenberg, Richard Strauss, Bruno Walter, Hans Eisler, Kurt Weill, and Wilhelm Furtwängler, to name only a few. The Nazi years clearly put a sudden halt to this dynamic of incessant innovation. Although the spread of modern forms of mass entertainment continued with the popularization of radio and the first experiments with public television, these activities, as with all other sectors of cultural production, stood under strict control of Goebbels's ministry of propaganda.

Although Berlin could never regain its original stature of the years of classical modernity, it remained a crucial focus for cultural life thanks to its double showcase function in divided Germany: both sides invested heavily in the infrastructure of mass and high culture. The 1950s saw an inner-city competition for the future not only of urban planning but also of film, theater, and the arts. Whereas in East Berlin culture policy was often caught between the conventional tastes of party leaders and the reaffirmation of left-wing modernism by practitioners, West Berlin developed into a hub for international cultural trends of the Western world, as embodied in regular events such as the Berlin Film Festival (since 1951) and the Berlin Jazz Festival (since 1964), both notable for their mass audience. Although party censorship always tried to contain autonomous cultural expression in communist East Berlin, its population was never effectively isolated from cultural life in the capitalist world thanks to the accessibility of Western radio and television programs and the remaining personal contacts with the West. As the popularity grew on both sides of the wall for particular new forms of mass entertainment such as rock 'n' roll and beat music and the fashion styles that went with them, as well as for new trends in film and television entertainment, the GDR authorities were eventually forced to offer "homegrown" derivates to their young audiences. This trans-systemic congruence can also be observed, though to a lesser extent, in the realm of high culture. While it was quite natural that East German readers took eager interest in the Western cultural life they were barred from by party interdiction, it is noteworthy that top figures of East German literature such as the playwright Heiner Müller or the writer Christa Wolf gained nationwide and international followings.

It can be argued, however, that everyday culture in both city halves developed in different directions to a point of a mutual alienation that soon became evident once the initial reunification euphoria had worn off. This is pertinent in particular to the cultural effects of the growing presence of non-German migrants in West Berlin, who, although integration policies remained halfhearted at the best, nevertheless found their accepted place within the social fabric of the city. Internationalist rhetoric notwithstanding, the communist regime,

by contrast, had pursued a particularly nationalist identity politics, hindering free exchange with the few foreigners living in the capital. Therefore the territory of reunified Berlin has developed a peculiar geography: downtown districts with condensed immigration populations and their sociocultural infrastructure stand in stark contrast to eastern suburbs with a reputation as no-go areas for anyone looking "un-German," something unknown in the western part of the city. Such phenomena might confirm the pervasive talk about a persistent "wall within the heads," to which other, less harmful examples could be added. Such simplifications, however, tend to overlook the actual social and cultural distances (and antagonisms, if one thinks of the civil war situations before 1933) that always existed inside such a large urban agglomeration, whether divided by world politics or not. They also tend to underrate the forces and effects of continuity of Berlin as an urban public sphere, as the city after 1989 quickly reaffirmed its role as a site of intensive internationally oriented and innovative cultural life, in the realms of both mass and high culture.

See also **Berlin Wall; Brandt, Willy; Germany; Kristallnacht; Ulbricht, Walter; Weizsäcker, Richard von.**

BIBLIOGRAPHY

Borneman, John. *Belonging in the Two Berlins: Kin, State, Nation.* Cambridge, U.K., 1992.

Large, David Clay. *Berlin.* New York, 2000.

Ribbe, Wolfgang, ed. *Geschichte Berlins: Eine Veröffentlichung der Historischen Kommission zu Berlin.* Vol. 2: *Von der Märzrevolution bis zur Gegenwart.* Berlin, 1987.

THOMAS LINDENBERGER

BERLIN, ISAIAH (1909–1997), British political philosopher.

Isaiah Berlin was born in Riga in Latvia in 1909. He was a descendant of the Chabad Hasidim and a distant relative of the Lubavitcher Rebbe. His family lived through the Bolshevik Revolution of 1917 and immigrated to England in 1921. Berlin was educated at Saint Paul's School, London, and at Corpus Christi College, Oxford. Except for a short time spent in New York and Washington, D.C., working for the British government during World War II, he spent virtually his entire adult life at Oxford. Berlin spent a short time in Moscow after the war where he met Boris Pasternak (1890–1960) and the celebrated poet Anna Akhmatova (1888–1966). Berlin was a renowned lecturer, conversationalist, and raconteur, and later became the founding principal of Wolfson College, Oxford. Since his death in 1997, numerous works on his life and work have been published as well as several volumes of previously unpublished lectures and essays. Berlin's will certainly turn out to be one of the most important philosophical voices of the twentieth century.

Berlin never wrote a systematic treatise on political philosophy. With the exception of an early biography of Karl Marx (1818–1883) written in the 1930s, he never in the strict sense of the term wrote another book. In place of the formal treatise, he wrote on a range of different topics employing a variety of literary genres from the history of ideas to philosophical analysis, to a series of wonderful intellectual portraits—*éloges* he called them—of well-known friends and contemporaries. He was capable of using a broad canvas as well as painting in miniature. Among philosophical writers of the last century, he is rivaled only by Michael Oakeshott (1901–1990) as a master of English prose. Berlin once described himself not as a philosopher but as a historian of ideas. This is only partially true. While he trafficked in the history of ideas, writing essays and monographs on thinkers and statesmen like Niccolò Machiavelli, Giambattista Vico, Johann Gottfried von Herder, Leo Tolstoy, Ivan Turgenev, John Stuart Mill, Benjamin Disraeli, Chaim Weizmann, and Winston Churchill, these essays and other writings convey a deep philosophical teaching about the place of freedom in the overall economy of human life.

Berlin's most famous work was his essay entitled "Two Concepts of Liberty," delivered originally as an inaugural address as the Chichele Professor of Social and Political Theory at Oxford in 1958. The core of the essay turns on two different kinds of liberty that he refers to as negative and positive liberty, respectively. Negative liberty means freedom from external impediments or controls. We are free when we are left alone or unattended; that is, when other persons, institutions, or agencies do not interfere with us. Negative liberty concerns itself with the space within which persons are free to act without being coerced by others. Negative liberty presupposes that persons are malleable and underdetermined, that we not only choose between values and ways of life, but that we are also the active makers and shapers of these values and ways of life.

The theory of positive liberty, on the other hand, is ultimately less about will and choice than about human rationality. On the positive theory of liberty, we are said to be free only when we exercise control over our choices. The classic theorists of positive liberty understood that our choices may be constrained by a range of variables—upbringing, education, social conditioning, and the like. We are not free unless and until we exercise control over those determinants that condition our choices. Berlin associates this kind of liberty with a conception of self-mastery.

The distinction between negative and positive liberty may sound innocuous, but it is said to carry major political consequences. Berlin associates negative liberty with the tradition of political liberalism whose great heroes were thinkers like Montesquieu, the *Federalist* authors, Benjamin Constant, and Mill. By contrast, it was the tradition of positive liberty championed by Jean-Jacques Rousseau and his epigones (Johann Gottlieb Fichte, Georg Wilhelm Friedrich Hegel, and Marx) who were responsible for the creation of some of the worst experiments in social control known to history. In its effort to make humans more rational, enlightened, or virtuous, proponents of positive liberty are bound to violate the autonomy of the individual. Positive libertarians are necessarily led to treat individuals as means to the promotion of their goals, however worthy those goals might be. And when such people feel called upon to use the state or other institutional means of coercion and control to achieve those ends, the result can only be despotism masquerading as freedom. The paradox that Berlin never ceased to explore is how political ideas that aimed to liberate people from tyranny could be at the root of even more extensive forms of tyranny, all in the name of political freedom. One reader not inaccurately described "Two Concepts of Liberty" as the "anti-communist manifesto."

Berlin's defense of negative liberty is, however, only one aspect of his teaching and in a curious way perhaps not even the most important aspect. Underlying Berlin's account of both positive and negative liberty is a set of assumptions about human nature and the limits of knowledge that make his views more complex and controversial than would at first sight appear. At the core of Berlinian liberalism is not just a teaching of negative liberty, but a defense of what he calls value pluralism. It is his view that values—the ideals and aspirations that we care most deeply about—are in a condition of permanent and ineradicable conflict. The belief that it is not a peaceful convergence of ultimate ends, but rather a spirited struggle between these ends, that gives Berlinian liberalism a tragic, even heroic, dimension.

Berlin developed his understanding of value pluralism in a number of historical studies beginning in the 1970s, beginning with *Vico and Herder* and *Against the Current*. These studies traced the appreciation of a fundamental conflict of values back to the tradition of what Berlin called the European Counter-Enlightenment. It was this tradition of European Romanticism that most deeply appealed to Berlin's Russian sensibilities. In particular, the Counter-Enlightenment appreciated not only the difference between individual values and choices, but between different cultures and ways of life. Cultures and nations follow no overall pattern of development, whether cyclical or progressive, but constitute unique and irreducible ways of life that can only be understood from within by an act of intellectual and imaginative sympathy.

It was Berlin's later emphasis on the diversity and conflict between ends that led some readers like Leo Strauss and Arnaldo Momigliano to associate the doctrine of value pluralism with a kind of cultural relativism. If values and cultures are unalterably plural, how are people to resolve conflicts between them? Is there any way of ranking cultures or ways of life, or are they simply incommensurable? Berlin's question is how can people (and peoples) with vastly different scales of values live together in a way that does justice to the plurality of ends and yet recognize their common humanity? If the "Platonic" idea of a harmonious reconciliation of interests and beliefs is not just impractical but incoherent because basic values will always collide, what kind of political order is best?

Berlin struggled mightily with this problem, although he came up with no satisfactory answer. This was due in part to his skepticism toward all theoretical solutions to moral and political life. Berlin valued freedom not by offering grand theories or abstract models but by showing how ideas interact with life, by showing the complex ways in which good ideas taken to the extreme can have bad consequences, and how even the love of freedom, if taken in abstraction from all the other goods that human beings can pursue, can end up turning into its opposite. At the core of Berlin's thought is his recognition of a conflict between the claims of moral diversity, pluralism, and openness and the need for order, permanence, and stability. How to achieve some kind of balance between competing goods? He offers no formula for arriving at an answer, but only an awareness that not all good things are compatible and that life is more often a conflict not between good and bad but between competing sets of goods. It is this awareness that life is choice and that not all ends are compatible that forms the basis of Isaiah Berlin's liberal legacy.

See also **Liberalism.**

BIBLIOGRAPHY

Berlin, Isaiah. *The Proper Study of Mankind: An Anthology of Essays.* Edited by Henry Hardy and Roger Hausheer. London, 1998.

Ignatieff, Michael. *Isaiah Berlin: A Life.* New York, 1998.

Mali, Joseph, and Robert Wokler, eds. *Isaiah Berlin's Counter-Enlightenment.* Philadelphia, 2003.

STEVEN B. SMITH

BERLIN BLOCKADE. *See* **Berlin.**

BERLINGUER, ENRICO (1922–1984), Italian politician.

The Italian politician Enrico Berlinguer was born in Sassari on 25 May 1922. He enrolled in the law school of Sassari in 1940 where, in 1943, he intended to graduate with a thesis on "Philosophy and Philosophy of Law from Hegel to Croce and Gentile." In 1943 he joined the Italian Communist Party (PCI). On 7 January 1944 he was arrested for having participated in the "bread riots," an anti-Badoglio demonstration probably organized by the local Communist section (Pietro Badoglio was the head of the government after the fall of Mussolini). He remained in prison until April, then in June he visited his father in Salerno, who introduced him to Palmiro Togliatti (1893–1964). In 1944 Berlinguer settled in Rome, where he began working as a functionary in the youth movement of the PCI. After 25 April 1945 he moved to Milan, the headquarters of the Fronte della gioventù (Youth front). For more than a decade he was a scrupulous interpreter of the Togliatti line in political youth organizations.

When the PCI decided to revive the FGCI (Federazione Giovanile Comunista Italiana; Italian Communist Youth Association), Berlinguer was appointed to head its executive committee, and from 1949 to 1956 he served as its secretary general. The FGCI afforded Berlinguer an excellent experience in political bureaucracy, for which he was ideally suited. His role as the leader of the youth movement and as a member of the executive committee put him in close contact with Togliatti, whose ideological line he followed meticulously. On the eve of the Party Congress (1956), he left the secretariat of the youth organization; he assumed the post of director of the Istituto Centrale di Studi Comunisti (Central Institute of Communist Studies) and in 1957 was sent to Sardinia as regional assistant secretary. In July of 1958 he returned to Rome and entered the national secretariat and the office of the secretariat under the direction of Liugi Longo (1900–1980), then assistant secretary. At the Ninth Party Congress (February 1960), he became a full-fledged member of the executive committee and replaced Giorgio Amendola (1907–1980) as organizational coordinator. His appointment, requested by Longo, seems a clear indicator of Togliatti's centrist line. The new post was not without difficulties: the party was experiencing a steady loss of members, although its support at the electoral polls was growing.

At the Tenth Congress (1962) Berlinguer was elected as a member of the executive committee and of the secretariat and director of the office of the secretariat, a position that he held until 1966; he also became head of the important office of foreign relations.

Although he fell into disfavor with the party in 1966 for not taking sides against the left wing and for being hostile to the official party line, he soon returned to the top ranks of the PCI, becoming assistant secretary in 1969. Having resolved the crisis in the party caused by the expulsion of the "Manifesto" group and by the youth protests (1968–1969), he worked to improve relations with the democratic political forces and to strengthen the independence of the PCI from Moscow, stressing the legitimacy of an "Italian path to socialism." In 1969 during the conference held at the Kremlin, Berlinguer condemned the invasion of Czechoslovakia by Soviet armed forces and the principle that only one kind of communist society could be accepted, the Soviet one. In 1972 he became national secretary general and proposed "a new political direction": "collaboration among the great populist currents: socialist, communist, Catholic." This project, launched in 1973, became known as the "Historic Compromise."

In a speech in Moscow (27 February 1976) Berlinguer defined the structure of socialism in Italy and the historic function of the working class as inseparable from a pluralistic and democratic system. More striking were the statements made in June of that same year in which Berlinguer recognized the North Atlantic Treaty Organization and declared that he felt "safer standing on this side," referring to the West. Such political positions constituted the final touches to the politics of Eurocommunism that Berlinguer had initiated in 1975 with the French and Spanish Communists.

The new role of the PCI, together with the unusual circumstances (electoral success, economic crisis, and terrorism) in which it came about, encouraged Berlinguer to propose a complex strategy focusing on a politics of austerity, which also encompassed rigor, efficiency, and social justice. At the same time he advanced the dialogue with Aldo Moro (1916–1978) on the prospects of a greater involvement of the PCI in the management of the government, an idea that was translated into the direct parliamentary support given to Giulio

Andreotti's (b. 1919) second national unity cabinet (March 1978). In the following months Berlinguer was attacked by the socialists on ideological grounds as well as for his firmness in refusing to deal with the terrorists during the kidnapping of Moro; opposed also by the extreme Left because of the Historic Compromise, Berlinguer concluded that further collaboration with the Christian Democratic Party (DC) was, after the murder of Moro in May 1978, useless and unproductive.

Despite its return to the opposition, the PCI suffered severely in the political elections of June 1979. In November 1980 Berlinguer set forth the "moral question" as a precondition to the renewal of political life, a line maintained in polemics with the DC but in particular with the Socialist Party (PSI) and with the government headed by the socialist leader Bettino Craxi (1934–2000). During this same period he was bringing to completion a final break with the USSR by drawing closer to the Chinese communists (April 1980) and by declaring in December 1981 that the "original progressive thrust" launched by the October revolution "had exhausted itself." Austerity, moral concern, and the possibility of a third way all defined the profile of a politician whose clear and rigorous principles contributed to a popularity that reached beyond the boundaries of the communist world. Berlinguer died on 11 June 1984 of a cerebral hemorrhage suffered during a meeting for the European elections. The presence of enormous crowds at his funeral on 13 June testified to his popularity.

See also **Craxi, Bettino; Eurocommunism; Italy; Togliatti, Palmiro.**

BIBLIOGRAPHY

Fiori, Giuseppe. *Vita di Enrico Berlinguer.* Rome-Bari, 1989.

Urban, Joan Barth. *Moscow and the Italian Communist Party: From Togliatti to Berlinguer.* Ithaca, N.Y., 1986.

MARIA TERESA GIUSTI

BERLIN WALL. In the aftermath of the division of Germany into two states in 1949, the city of Berlin, controlled by the four Allies (France, Great Britain, and the United States on the one side and the Soviet Union on the other side), remained the only place where Germans could freely commute between the Eastern and the Western blocs of the Cold War. The inner German border zone had already been sealed off by the East German state in May 1952. By August 1961, approximately 2.2 million citizens of the German Democratic Republic (GDR) had left their country without official permission via the border separating the West Berlin sectors from the Soviet sector and the surrounding GDR territory. Reacting to the dictatorial transformation of East German society, the curtailing of basic human and civil rights, and a chronically weak economy, members of all classes and social groups, but in particular qualified workers and professionals, opted for a new start in the liberal capitalist part of their country. The impending collapse of the East German state and economy led the communist regime to close the Berlin border completely on 13 August 1961. They thus began to erect a wall, protected by barbed wire and made of concrete bricks and slabs. These barriers were later replaced by large concrete segments approximately 3.6 meters (12 feet) high and 1.2 meters (4 feet) wide (and topped by barbed wire) both inside the city (the "Berlin Wall" in the colloquial sense) and at the border between West Berlin and its rural surrounding regions.

East German plans to close the Berlin border dated back to the early 1950s but had lacked support by the Soviets. In a climate of rising international tension after the 1958 Berlin ultimatum proclaimed by Nikita Khrushchev, the Soviet premier, to get the Western Allies out of their sectors, this seemed to be the only option to prevent a breakdown of the regime, in particular because U.S. president John F. Kennedy had assured the Soviet leadership that the Western powers would not take any military countermeasures as long as their own rights in West Berlin and the free use of the transit ways between West Berlin and the Federal Republic of Germany (West Germany) were guaranteed. The logistic and military preparation by the East German people's police had been under way for several months but successfully hidden from the public, so that the closure of the border and its immediate and effective fortification within a week came as a shock to the German population and the Western political elite. The actual work was done by civilian construction

The Berlin Wall, photographed from the west, August 1962. ©BETTMANN/CORBIS

workers under the close supervision of paramilitary units of the people's police and the voluntary "fighting squads of the working class," a free-time militia recruited from state-owned enterprises. Units of the National People's Army (Nationale Volksarmee) and the Soviet Army were held in reserve in more remote areas, but did not have to intervene.

Even before the construction of the wall, attempting to leave East Germany without formal permission was persecuted under the law as a crime. A system of meticulous regulations prohibited nonresidents from staying in near-border areas. This was now complemented by a system of no-access areas with all vegetation or other objects removed, observation towers, and the continuous patrolling of guards armed with submachine guns who were trained to prevent any illegal trespassing, if necessary by "eliminating" the "violator of the border." From the whole setting it was evident that such persons were expected to come from within the GDR territory rather than, as the communist

propaganda incessantly claimed, from the West. Later on the border installations at the inner German border, though not those around West Berlin, were fortified through the deployment of automatic gunfire devices, mines, and electronic detectors.

EFFECTIVENESS AND DEATH TOLL REASSESSED

As a means to cut short the drain of GDR refugees, the Berlin Wall proved to be effective. Their numbers immediately dwindled from 47,000 in August 1961 to fewer than 30,000 per year. Crossing the Berlin Wall as well as the inner German border became a life-threatening undertaking mostly risked by young single men, while others preferred to accept the assistance of refuge assistants (*Fluchthelfer*) to reach the West either by being smuggled out on one of the official transit ways or by using forged documents and traveling through a third transit country. The death toll at the fortified borders of the GDR after 13 August 1961 is now estimated to number at least 169 following the conservative numbers of the Berlin state prosecutor, while the Central Agency for the Investigation of Government and Unification Crimes at the Berlin Police Department has counted a total of 262. To these numbers, one must add the 159 persons killed at the GDR border before August 1961 to arrive at the total for the period from 1949 to 1989. According to both sources a slight majority of these victims died at the inner German border between East and West Germany. There are still no reliable figures for the much smaller numbers of those drowned or shot in the attempt to leave the GDR via the Baltic Sea, nor for those who were killed while crossing the border to one of the other socialist countries (Czechoslovakia, Poland) or from one of the Soviet bloc countries to the West. The estimate of an overall toll of nearly one thousand victims of the GDR border regime published by the Working Group August 13th must be considered as an exaggeration.

TUMBLING DOWN DURING THE DEMOCRATIC REVOLUTION

During the 1980s the number of GDR citizens being allowed to visit West Germany rose to the hundreds of thousand. In this context, lifting all constraints on traveling abroad quickly became a top issue once the political U-turn came about in the fall of 1989. On the evening of 9 November 1989, Günter Schabowski, a member of the East German Politburo of the ruling Socialist Unity Party (SED), acting as its spokesperson, held a live televised press conference communicating the most recent decisions taken by the SED leadership. One of these decisions he announced was a new decree regulating permission for GDR citizens to travel out of the GDR. Asked by a reporter when the new regulation would come into effect, he replied "immediately, with no delay." Because news agencies and television stations immediately repeated Schabowski's statement, and many East Berliners interpreted his announcement literally, within hours several thousand people had gathered at East Berlin border checkpoints clamoring for the gates to be opened. Because Schabowski's public communication had been coordinated neither with other members of the SED leadership nor with the Ministry of Defense and its border troops, the gatherings at the border, which had been observed and reported on by Western media, went on unhindered, leaving the border guards on-site without any instructions. In a chaotic situation of failing communication, the resignation of top leaders, and the peaceful presence of ever more persons at the checkpoints, permission was given to "flood" the checkpoint areas at 11:30 P.M. With the barriers lifted, some ten thousand East Berliners entered downtown West Berlin to be joined by their Western co-citizens in a spectacular all-night mass party covered live throughout the world.

JURIDICAL AND MEMORIAL AFTERLIFE

The fall of the Berlin Wall marked the point of no return in the breakdown of the Soviet bloc, opening the window of opportunity for Helmut Kohl's policy of immediate German reunification. In the days that followed, a spontaneous reappropriation of the wall by the people set in. Thousands of "wall peckers" dismantled the concrete segments, which, because they had been embellished and decorated by myriads of unknown graffiti and mural artists on their Western side, made nice colorful collector items that could also be sold in Berlin and elsewhere at good prices. Under the continuing pressure of mass demonstrations, additional checkpoints were now opened for free passage. By the end of the year the GDR created additional crossing points by tearing down the wall where old street connections between East and West Berlin had been blocked for twenty-eight years. When both city halves were also united politically, in conjunction with the joining of the two German states in October 1990, one of the first projects of the new city government was to do away with all the remaining sections of the wall. By December, most former border areas had been cleared and were made available again for urban planning and construction. In the meantime, with the construction boom following reunification, it has become rather difficult to identify the last traces of the former borderline in the downtown cityscape. There are only two large stretches of concrete wall segments left: one at Bernauer Straße, where a documentation center on the Berlin Wall run by the Federal Republic is situated, and one south of the city center, where East German artists had used its eastern side to create the East Side Gallery during the democratic revolution.

The criminal dimension of killings at the GDR borders have been dealt with in several trials both

Residents of East Berlin help destroy the Berlin Wall, November 1989. ©DAVID TURNLEY/CORBIS

against rank-and-file members of the border troops and against their superiors and finally the top party functionaries. Whereas most of the lower ranks came away with short prisons sentences or probation, some of the top leaders such as Schabowski and the last SED leader, Egon Krenz, had to serve several years in prison. By the early twenty-first century, a sometimes heated debate had set in regarding how to memorialize properly the Berlin Wall as part of the city's history, and several research projects on the victims and the details of the GDR border regime were under way.

See also **Cold War; 1989.**

BIBLIOGRAPHY

Bundeszentrale für politische Bildung, Deutschlandradio, and Zentrum für Zeithistorische Forschung Potsdam. "Chronik der Mauer, January 1961–1989/90." Available at http://www.chronik-der-mauer.de.

Burkhardt, Heiko. "Berlin Wall Online." Available at http://www.dailysoft.com/berlinwall.

Hertle, Hans-Hermann. "The Fall of the Wall: The Unintended Dissolution of East Germany's Ruling Regime." *Cold War International History Project Bulletin*, no. 12/13 (2001): 131–164.

Klausmeier, Axel, and Leo Schmidt. *Wall Remnants, Wall Traces: The Comprehensive Guide to the Berlin Wall.* Berlin, 2004.

When the Wall Came Tumbling Down: 50 Hours That Changed the World. VHS Directed by Hans Hermann Hertle and Günther Scholz. Northampton, Mass.: Icestorm International, 1999. Originally made for German television.

THOMAS LINDENBERGER

BERLUSCONI, SILVIO (b. 1936), Italian businessman and politician.

Until 2006 businessman and politician Silvio Berlusconi was the Italian prime minister and the leader of his party, Forza Italia. He is the president of AC Milan, a first-division soccer team; the owner of Elmond, parent company of the publishing house Einaudi; and the majority stockholder of the publisher A. Mondadori. According to *Forbes,* he was in 2005 the richest man in Italy. He began his road to fortune in the 1960s in the building sector, constructing many residences in Milan, and later entire residential and commercial complexes, becoming in the process the leading Italian figure in the industry. After the Edilnord Center, he built Milan 2, Milan 3, and the "Sunflower," all residential complexes near Milan. His entrepreneurial activity even won him the honorific *Cavaliere del Lavoro* (Knight of industry) in 1977. In 1974 he launched Telemilano, the cable television affiliate of Milan 2, which was soon diffused throughout all of Lombardy, and created the holding company Fininvest, of which he became president. In 1980 he founded Canale 5 (Channel 5), the first private national television network in Italy, which he followed with Italia 1 (1982) and Rete 4 (1984). His networks benefited from well-known favors (particularly the Mammì Law on television broadcasting, which aimed at regulating radio and television networks, but which allowed one "player" to own three networks) conferred by the ruling Italian Socialist Party, or PSI, which Berlusconi repaid by granting to Bettino Craxi's (1934–2000) party free interviews, bulletins, and commercials on his channels.

His entry into politics occurred in the early 1990s. At the end of 1993 Italy was wracked by the "Clean Hands" (*Mani Pulite*) judicial investigation launched by Judge Antonio Di Pietro (b. 1950) of the Public Prosecutor's Office of Milan on 17 February 1992, which implicated nearly the entire leading class of the political establishment. On 26 January 1994 all the television news programs transmitted a message from Berlusconi, who announced that he was resigning from all active duties related to his conglomerate in order to "take the field" and dedicate himself to politics. He explained his decision as an essential measure aimed at containing the "communist threat" (traced to the center-left coalition challenging him in the polls); while his detractors attributed it to the necessity of protecting his economic interests, then threatened by the loss of Craxi's support. He therefore founded Forza Italia (Go Italy!), a "company-party" with its foundations in Fininvest and the

other colossus among his holdings, Publitalia, an advertising firm. Forza Italia is entirely identifiable with Berlusconi, who presents himself as a liberal and as an entrepreneur in the service of politics.

During his career Berlusconi addressed himself to the Italian public with simple and incisive slogans ("A worker-president," "A million jobs"). Speaking the language of soccer and using a plethora of sports metaphors, he imbued his political endeavors with an aura of a sporting match and proved himself capable of galvanizing the fans. For the elections of 1994 he allied himself with the party of Gianfranco Fini (the Alleanza Nationale, or "National Alliance") to win votes in the South, in the coalition called the "Pole of good government"; while in the North he formed an accord with the Lega Nord (Northern League) of Umberto Bossi (b. 1941), thus engendering the "Pole of liberty." The two coalitions won the elections (Forza Italia garnered 21 percent of the ballots) with a 45.9 percent share, against the 32.9 percent of the progressives. On 10 May 1994 Berlusconi formed his first government (Forza Italia, Alleanza Nationale, Lega Nord, CCD or Center Christian Democrats, UDC or Union of Christian Democrats, and the Democrats of the Center), which ended its short life on 22 December 1994 with the withdrawal of the Lega Nord. After an interim government led by Lamberto Dini (b. 1931) (17 January 1995–11 January 1996), there followed the elections of April 1996, won by the center-left. Under the government of Romano Prodi (b. 1939), first, and then that of Massimo D'Alema (b. 1949), Berlusconi remained with the opposition until the next national elections of 2001, when he returned to government with a new coalition, called the "House of Liberties" (Casa delle Libertà, composed of the Alleanza Nationale, Lega Nord, CCD, and UDC).

The second government of Berlusconi began on 11 June 2001 and to 2006 was the most enduring in the history of the Italian Republic. This success was due to the ability of the leader of Forza Italia to conciliate traditionally opposing forces, such as the Alleanza Nationale and the Lega Nord, and to patch up differences whenever these have menaced the internal coherence of the coalition. Berlusconi has been at the center of numerous accusations of corruption and budgetary falsification; with regard to

Italian judges, he has often expressed himself publicly in a critical manner. The outcome of various cases that include him among the accused (in the SME case, in November 2004, the public prosecutor's office requested a sentence of eight years for kickbacks allegedly given to the financial police, or Guardia di Finanza) has been blocked by a law, approved by the Berlusconi government, which affords immunity to the highest officials of the state.

In foreign policy he was pro-American, and he supported the United States in the decision to attack Iraq in 2003 (although Italy did not send troops during the conflict, but only in the aftermath). In domestic policy, Berlusconi decriminalized budgetary irregularities; offered two amnesties in the fiscal and building sectors; launched reforms of the educational, judicial, and telecommunications systems; and inaugurated various projects to improve highway infrastructure. At the end of November 2004 the houses of the Senate approved a contentious reduction in taxes, which constituted one of Berlusconi's pre-election promises. In the April 2006 elections, Berlusconi was narrowly defeated, with Prodi once again taking over the position of prime minister.

See also **Crime and Justice; Italy; Leisure; Northern League; Television.**

BIBLIOGRAPHY

Andrews, Geoff. *Not a Normal Country: Italy after Berlusconi.* London, 2005.

Bell, Martin, and Paolo Bellucci. *Italian Politics.* Vol. 17: *The Return of Berlusconi.* New York, 2002.

Blondel, Jean, and Paolo Segatti. *Italian Politics: The Second Berlusconi Government.* New York, 2003.

Bufacchi, Vittorio, and Simon Burgess. *Italy since 1989: Events and Interpretations.* New York, 1998.

Ginsborg, Paul. *Silvio Berlusconi: Television, Power, and Patrimony.* London and New York, 2004.

Jones, Tobias. *The Dark Heart of Italy.* New York, 2004.

Ruggeri, Giovanni, and Mario Guarino. *Berlusconi. Inchiesta sul signor TV.* Milan, 1994.

Santarelli, Enzo. *Profilo del berlusconismo.* Rome, 2002.

Stille, Alexander. *The Sack of Rome: How a Beautiful European Country with a Fabled History and a Storied Culture Was Taken Over by a Man Named Silvio Berlusconi.* New York, 2006.

Maria Teresa Giusti

BEUYS, JOSEPH (1921–1986), German artist.

Joseph Beuys is associated with several important twentieth century avant-garde art and political movements in Germany. Among these are installation sculpture, "happenings" performance, Fluxus performance and multiples, and the Student and Green parties. Several common threads connect these activities: the use of found objects, fat, felt, blood, earth, and, occasionally, dead animals as sculptural and performance materials, the frequent appearance of a blood-red cross on objects made of these materials, and a wide range of public actions demonstrating the interrelatedness of museums, art schools, public life, and political parties. Beuys termed his work "social sculpture" linking his thought to his art objects and performances as constitutive of a radically creative relationship to the social domain. One expression of this idea is Beuys's famous phrase "everyman an artist," meaning that all activities can be approached creatively and that the term *artist* need not be reserved for specialists.

Beuys was born in Krefeld, Germany, a small northwestern city near the Dutch border, in 1921. He spent his childhood in nearby towns Rindern and Kleve. As a child, Beuys was interested in both nature and art. In his early life, the interest in nature seemed paramount and Beuys selected a medical career. In 1940, at the age of nineteen, his studies were interrupted when he volunteered to join the military. As a member of the Luftwaffe, Beuys became a combat pilot and radio operator. The mythology that surrounds Beuys at this moment in his life nearly supersedes his actual artistic practice in general cultural relevance. Later, Beuys would attribute his use of fat, felt, blood, dead animals, and the blood-red cross to his rescue by nomadic Tatars in rural Crimea following a plane crash while serving in the German military during World War II. By Beuys's account, he had nearly frozen to death when he was found and wrapped in animal fat and felt, which warmed and healed his hypothermic body. The story now

How to Explain Pictures to a Dead Hare. Performance by Joseph Beuys, 1965. GETTY IMAGES

poetry, conceptual art, and everyday life. Through his relationship to two of Fluxus's many cofounders, George Maciunas (1931–1978) and Nam June Paik (b. 1932), Beuys understood art to have a potentially limitless function to play in the larger society. Like the Fluxus artists who inspired him, he began to produce editions of sculptures called multiples, installation environments, avant-garde graphic material, and politically activist performance. In his later life, Beuys would be involved in the establishment of several activist organizations including the German Student Party (1967), the Organization for Direct Democracy (1971), the Free International University (1972) and the Green Party (1979).

Remarkably charismatic, Beuys fashioned himself as a shaman in the service of healing the wounds of Europe after World War II. Uniformed in a heavy wool coat, safari vest, and gray felt hat, Beuys would pontificate to an audience on the legacy of fascism, the value of Christ independent of official Christianity (Beuys's family had been staunchly Catholic), and the importance of global cooperation and unity. In *How to Explain Pictures to a Dead Hare* (1965), he covered his head with honey and gold leaf and spoke of art to a dead hare. In New York in 1974, Beuys performed *I Like America and America Likes Me* in which he protested American treatment of indigenous people, in this case Native Americans and the Vietnamese. In that work he pretended to live for a week in a gallery with a live coyote, a cane that he used as a shepherd's crook, and piles of felt that he could wrap himself in as he engaged with the wild animal and the audience in a ritualistic encounter incorporating nature, Native American mysticism, and political protest. Finally, in 1982 with the help of a small army of student workers, Beuys created *7000 Oaks* at Dokumenta 7, the enormous fair of contemporary art held in Kassel, Germany, every five years. While the environmentalism and community basis of the work is its most overt reference, the forest is a nationalistic symbol in Germany that extends into deep history and was therefore somewhat problematic in a context that less than thirty years earlier had wielded the symbols of nationalism toward different ends.

Commendable as Beuys's communitarian aims may be, Beuys's attempts to aestheticize the public

appears to have little basis in fact. Nevertheless, the narrative still holds sway among many Beuys enthusiasts and helped the early audiences of Beuys's art come to terms with the unorthodox materials and imagery he used. What is known with certainty is that he was wounded and spent some months as a prisoner of war in a British internment camp, returning to Kleve in 1945. His plans to become a doctor were exchanged for the pursuit of art, and from 1947 to 1952 Beuys studied sculpture at the Düsseldorf Academy of Art.

In the 1950s, Beuys produced thousands of drawings and became a professor at his alma mater in 1959. However, Beuys is best known for the work he made in the 1960s after his contact with the international avant-garde Fluxus movement. In 1962, while on a tour of Europe that included Düsseldorf, Fluxus introduced Beuys to the intermedia arts of performance events that blended boundaries between the visual arts, music, theater, sphere in the form of "social sculpture" bear an eerie resemblance to the aestheticization of political life under Adolf Hitler (1889–1945). There are striking similarities between Beuys's use of public space and student activists and their function under National Socialism. Most overtly, like the Hitler Youth, Beuys's student activists wore armbands to identify their associations with each other and with Beuys. Similarly, the materials in Beuys's work, specifically blood and soil, appear repeatedly in fascist propaganda of the Third Reich in a linking of Aryan blood and German soil. The Final Solution, extermination of the Jews, was justified largely on the grounds of a purification of bloodlines and soil. Thus, even though Beuys made clear his desire to atone for his role in World War II, enthusiasts of Beuys should be cautious as to the nationalistic associations of his images and practice.

See also **Avant-Garde.**

BIBLIOGRAPHY

Götz, Adriani, Winfried Konnertz, and Karin Thomas. *Joseph Beuys: Life and Works.* Translated by Patricia Lech. Woodbury, N.Y., 1979.

Kuoni, Carin, ed. *Joseph Beuys in America: Energy Plan for the Western Man: Writings and Interviews with the Artist.* New York, 1990.

Mennekes, Friedhelm. *Beuys on Christ: A Passion in Dialogue.* Stuttgart, Germany, 1989.

Stachelhaus, Heiner. *Joseph Beuys.* New York, London, and Paris, 1987.

HANNAH HIGGINS

BEVAN, ANEURIN (1897–1960), British politician.

Aneurin Bevin is famous as the instigator of the free National Health Service (NHS), which was formed in July 1948 during the period of the first postwar government of Clement R. Attlee (1883–1967). Bevan was also the center of a loose grouping of left-wing Labour members of Parliament (MPs) known as the Bevanites.

Bevan was born in Tredegar, South Wales, on 15 November 1897 and educated at an elementary school. He became a miner but won a scholarship to the Central Labour College, London, in 1919. From 1921 onward, he was involved in trade union affairs. Yet Bevan was very much a political figure and became member of Parliament for Ebbw Vale in 1929, representing the constituency until his death in 1960.

During the 1930s, Bevan campaigned tirelessly for both the employed and unemployed members of the working class, opposed the Household Means Test (which was introduced in the early 1930s and reduced unemployment benefits as household income rose), and pressed his views forward through the left-wing journal *Tribune*, which was begun in 1937. In 1934, Bevan married Jennie Lee, an influential force in the Left in her own right. Together, and through *Tribune*, they rejected the political truce during World War II, and Bevan continued to attack Winston Churchill (1874–1965), the Tory Party, and the Fascists in the House of Commons, gaining a reputation for being a fine orator.

Bevan's finest hour arrived when Attlee appointed him minister of health and housing in 1945. In this role he attempted to create a nationalized health service, a commitment which went well beyond the 1945 Labour Manifesto. This led to resistance from the doctors and the British Medical Association, who feared that the doctors would become civil servants and be forced to work in "under-doctored" areas. They reacted to Bevan's plans by referring to him as a "squalid nuisance," "the Minister of Disease," and the "Tito from Tonypandy." Bevan's remark that his Conservative opponents were "lower than vermin" led many Conservatives to form themselves into "vermin clubs." Nevertheless, most doctors, dentists, and opticians had joined the NHS by the end of 1948 and it quickly transformed the health provision for the average British citizen. However, the NHS proved very expensive at a time when Britain faced serious financial difficulties, and Attlee and Labour Party leader Herbert Stanley Morrison (1888–1965) sought to curb expenditure and introduce prescription charges. Bevan resisted these until the 1950 general election, but then, on 17 January 1951, was moved to the post of minister of labor and national service. This coincided with the decision of the new chancellor of the exchequer, Hugh

Gaitskell, to impose health charges. Bevan responded by resigning on 24 April, along with Harold Wilson and John Freeman.

Bevan then became the leading figure of the Bevanite left-wing group of MPs in the Labour Party. Along with Barbara Castle, Anthony Crosland, and others, the Bevanites opposed the Parliamentary Labour Party by declaring themselves in favor of unilateral nuclear disarmament and opposing the manufacture of the hydrogen bomb, which almost led to Bevan being expelled from the Labour Party in 1955. However, in December 1955 Gaitskell defeated him in a contest for the Labour leadership, and from 1956 Bevan was patriotic over the Suez Crisis and was treasurer of the party between 1956 and 1960. He effectively divested himself of the title "Leader of the Left" when he attacked British occupation of the canal zone in favor of unilateral disarmament at the 1957 Labour Party Conference, famously asking delegates not to send a future Labour foreign secretary "naked into the Conference chamber." He preferred to negotiate away nuclear weapons rather than abandon them. In 1959, Bevan became deputy leader of the Labour Party and, as a symbol of party unity, adorned Labour's postwar general election alongside Gaitskell and Castle. However, Labour was defeated and, shortly afterward in 1960, Bevan died of cancer.

Bevan's precise political leanings have been subject to some considerable controversy. Biographer Michael Foot has emphasized his traditional trade union and working-class Labour credentials, while John Campbell has referred to his Marxist roots. It is difficult to see Bevan as a Marxist, but what is undisputed is that he was one of the great parliamentary orators of the twentieth century, using his famous stutter to great effect. However, his lasting claim to fame is that he created the NHS.

See also **Attlee, Clement; Public Health; United Kingdom.**

BIBLIOGRAPHY

Campbell, John. *Aneurin Bevan and the Mirage of British Socialism.* London, 1987.

Foot, Michael. *Aneurin Bevan: A Biography.* 2 vols. London, 1962–1973.

KEITH LAYBOURN

BEVERIDGE, WILLIAM (1879–1963), British economist.

William Henry Beveridge is closely associated with the formation of the modern British welfare state, largely through the publication of *Social Insurance and Allied Services,* also called the Beveridge Report. He was deeply involved with the Liberal reforms of 1906–1914, Director of the London School of Economics between 1919 and 1937, and Master of University College, Oxford, from 1937. Beveridge was drawn into the civil service in Winston Churchill's wartime administration in 1940, and was put in charge of a relatively insignificant Ministry of Labour manpower survey. Released from his duties, in June 1941 Arthur Greenwood, Minister without Portfolio, made Beveridge chairman of the proposed inquiry into the reorganization of social insurance and allied services, which was to form part of a plan for postwar reconstruction.

Beveridge's brief was to survey the existing national schemes for social insurance and allied services, to examine how they interrelated, and to make recommendations. When it became clear that the report would be controversial, it was decided that Beveridge would sign the report himself and that the civil services would be regarded as an advisory body. The report was published in December 1942, just after the British military success at El Alamein and at a time when British confidence and expectation was high. It was an immediate bestseller and made three major claims or objectives. First, it claimed to be a break from the past, although in fact it was based very much upon the contributory system adopted by the Liberals before 1914, and Beveridge wrote that "I am sure that it is good Liberal doctrine" (Beveridge Papers, IIb, 42, letter dated 14 January 1943). Secondly, social insurance was to be directed at tackling want, although it was assumed that it would be part of a combined attack upon the "five giant problems of Want, Disease, Ignorance, Squalor and Idleness." Thirdly, it sought to combine state and personal initiative, and assumed that any government would wish to establish a family allowance system (as Beveridge had done for his staff at the London School of Economics), create a comprehensive health service, and establish full employment.

With all these in place, he argued that the attack upon want would work.

The Beveridge scheme was not particularly revolutionary in its form. Much like the pre-1914 Liberal reforms, it suggested that, in return for a single and uniform weekly contribution, a qualified individual would receive standard benefits for sickness, unemployment, widows, orphans, old age, maternity, industrial injuries, and funerals. The system would be based upon a flat-rate contribution, and would provide subsistence benefits for all, although there would be room for adjustment based upon differing circumstances. In principle, however, it was to be universal; this is where it was different from the selective approach adopted by previous social legislation. In addition, the tackling of want was to be connected with the tackling of the other four giants. Therefore, as author Derek Fraser suggests, "Here, in the totality of vision, was the revolutionary element in the Beveridge Report" (p. 216). It would work if governments remained committed to ensuring that there was full employment (unemployment not being more than 3 percent).

The Beveridge Report certainly created a storm in wartime Britain and it sold hundreds of thousands of copies. Nevertheless, Churchill was less than enamored of it. He was suspicious of where it might lead and noted that "Reconstruction was in the air" and that there was "a dangerous optimism … growing about post-war conditions" (Pelling, p. 170). As a result, Churchill refused to accept the recommendations, though Clement R. Attlee (1883–1967) and the Labour Party were supportive, Attlee stating that "Socialism does not admit to an alternative, Social Security to us can only mean Socialism" (Harris, p. 220). As a result, the Labour Party pressed for the government acceptance of the Beveridge Report, although a Labour resolution committing the government to accepting the Beveridge Report was beaten on 18 February 1943 by 335 votes to 119, with ninety-seven Labour MPs—twenty-two of whom were government ministers—voting for the resolution. Churchill's wartime administration was clearly in difficulty. With Labour 11 percent ahead of the Conservatives in the Gallup Poll, Churchill moved, reluctantly, toward setting up a Reconstruction Committee toward the end of 1943 that oversaw moves toward health, educational, and employment reforms during 1944 and 1945—the famous "White Paper Chase" that began to implement the Beveridge Report with, for instance, such documents as the white paper on *Employment Policy* (1944).

The Beveridge Report influenced the Attlee Labour government's postwar welfare state and shaped the domestic policies of postwar governments until the 1970s. Thereafter, the commitment to full employment, to universal provision, and many other aspects of the Beveridge Report was broken, and the Thatcher governments of 1979 to 1990 reintroduced selective social policies on a grand scale. Yet this was predictable given the great opposition the Beveridge scheme faced. Historians, as well as feminists, socialists, and Conservatives, have objected to the Beveridge welfare state for many different reasons. It has been argued that its universalism led to unnecessary expenditure and that there were many anomalies that cut across the provision, not least the continuance of the means test, which reduced benefits as family incomes rose, and the failure to merge the tax and benefit system. Conservative historians such as Correlli Barnett complain of the arrogance of the "Field Marshal Montgomery of social welfare" in imposing upon Britain a system of provision it could not afford; the "New Jerusalem" was not sustainable and was seen as responsible for Britain's industrial decline. This suggestion is debatable, but what is not is that the Beveridge Report shaped Britain's modern welfare state for about thirty years before falling foul of the problems of economic decline and the selective social policies of both Labour and Conservative governments.

See also **United Kingdom; Welfare State.**

BIBLIOGRAPHY

Barnett, Correlli. *The Audit of War: The Illusion and Reality of Britain as a Great Nation.* London, 1986.

Beveridge, William. *Social Insurance and Allied Services* (Beveridge Report). London, 1942.

Fraser, Derek. *The Evolution of the British Welfare State: A History of Social Policy since the Industrial Revolution.* 3rd ed. London, 2003.

Harris, José. *William Beveridge: A Biography.* Oxford, U.K., 1977.

Pelling, H. *Britain and the Second World War*. London, 1970.

Williams, Karel, and John Williams, eds. *A Beveridge Reader*. London, 1987.

KEITH LAYBOURN

BEVIN, ERNEST (1881–1951), British labor leader and statesman.

Ernest Bevin was the greatest British trade union leader of the twentieth century, being a member of the Trades Union Congress from the early 1920s, the organizer of the 1926 general strike, and an influential figure in developing Labour Party policy in the 1930s. Yet he is best known as Winston Churchill's minister of labor during World War II and Clement Attlee's foreign secretary between 1945 and 1951, during which period he helped found the North Atlantic Treaty Organization in 1949.

Bevin was born at Winsford in March 1881, the illegitimate son of an agricultural laborer. First raised by his mother, who died when he was eight, he was then raised by his half sister in Devon. He became a farmworker at the age of eleven but moved to Bristol to live with his half brother when he was thirteen and found a job delivering soft drinks. He became an active lay preacher in the Baptist Church and gained experience in public speaking before moving on to work with the Bristol Socialist Society. At this time he married Florence Townley, with whom he had one child, Queenie, who was born in 1914.

Bevin was drawn into organizing the dockers and carters on the Bristol docks following his involvement in Ramsay MacDonald's "Right to Work" movement in 1908. Asked to organize the carters for the Dock, Wharf, Riverside, and General Labourers' Union, he increased the membership substantially and became one of the three national organizers of the union. Bevin became increasingly convinced of the need for unions to unite against increasingly organized employers and strongly pressed for the amalgamation in 1921, which saw fourteen unions form the Transport and General Workers' Union.

Although Bevin became a member of the general council of the Trades Union Congress in 1925, it was the general strike of May 1926 that shot him to fame, for it was his last-minute organizational activity that prevented the strike from being a complete disaster. However, the general council's decision to end the general strike on 12 May, after only nine days, provoked a storm of fury from the Communist Party of Great Britain, which claimed that the miners' cause had been abandoned. Bevin bore the brunt of much of their criticism, and throughout the rest of the interwar years he was in conflict with Communists, in and outside his own union.

Bevin played a major role in shaping the Labour Party throughout the interwar years and was a member of the second Labour government's Economic Advisory Committee and of the Macmillan Committee. However, his economic policies were largely ignored, leading him to publish his views in a pamphlet entitled *My Plan for 2,000,000 Workless* (1933), which advocated raising the school-leaving age and lowering retirement age in order to create work for the unemployed. After the collapse of MacDonald's second Labour government in 1931 and the expulsion of MacDonald from the Labour Party, Bevin became the dominant figure in the party, helping to remove George Lansbury as leader in 1935 and supporting Clement Attlee's leadership thereafter. He was largely responsible for the Labour Party moving from a pacifist stance in the mid-1930s to openly advocating rearmament by 1937. The need for rearmament was powerfully presented during the Spanish civil war by the German air force's bombing of the Basque town of Guernica in 1937. In other spheres, Bevin was part of the process of socialist planning in the 1930s and contributed significantly to the work of the Amulree Report, which led to the Holidays with Pay Act of 1938.

Bevin never saw himself as a political figure, although he contested and lost parliamentary contests in 1918 and 1931. However, when Winston Churchill formed his wartime administration in May 1940, Bevin was offered the post of minister of labor and national service. This appointment was facilitated by Bevin's unopposed return as member of Parliament for Wandsworth in 1940, a seat he retained until 1951. In his new role Bevin was responsible for the organization of Britain for the war effort. His scheme for directing young men, sometimes boys from private schools, to coal mines gave rise to the term "Bevin's boys."

After the war the Attlee Labour government was returned to power and Bevin was appointed foreign secretary. He was remarkably successful in this role, the Foreign Office particularly enjoying the prominence that Bevin gave it. He supported the Marshall Plan of 1947, whereby the United States gave financial aid to Western Europe, and he pressed for the Washington Treaty of 1949, which led to the formation of the North Atlantic Treaty Organization. He was particularly concerned to preserve Britain's position as a world power and fiercely opposed to the communist regimes of Eastern Europe, being prominent in the defeat of the Soviet Union's air blockade of Berlin in June 1948.

Bevin resigned as foreign secretary on 9 March 1951, owing to continuing ill health, and was given the post of lord privy seal, which carried no departmental responsibilities. He left government less than a month later and died on 14 April 1951.

See also **Labor Movements; MacDonald, Ramsay; United Kingdom.**

BIBLIOGRAPHY

Bullock, Alan. *The Life and Times of Ernest Bevin.* 3 vols. London, 1960–1983.

Weiler, Peter. *Ernest Bevin.* Manchester, U.K., 1983.

KEITH LAYBOURN

BICENTENNIAL OF THE FRENCH REVOLUTION.

The bicentennial celebration of the French Revolution should be seen as part of a cycle initiated by previous commemorations, both during the revolutionary period proper and at a later stage, in 1889 and 1939 respectively.

POLITICAL CONTROVERSIES AND DEBATES

The 1989 celebration inherited the pedagogical and symbolic ambitions of its predecessors—to educate the citizenry and to accomplish such significant gestures as planting liberty trees, holding meetings or republican banquets, and transferring last remains to their ultimate burial place in the Pantheon. In the context of that tradition, two phenomena were particularly noteworthy: a commemoration calendar generally reduced to the year 1789 (with the sole exceptions of the victory of Valmy and the proclamation of the Republic in September 1792) and far-ranging controversies about diverse themes such as the actual meaning of the concept of *revolution,* the contents of social rights—such as the right to work, the right to social protection, and the right to education proclaimed in 1793—and the use of violence during the Revolution.

The Revolution was instrumental in shaping French political culture, and each commemoration has born the mark of important historical and political debates. Needless to say, in the years leading up to the bicentennial celebration in 1989 the fate of the Republic was no longer at stake. Nevertheless, there was a weakening of the economic and social interpretation of the Revolution as a result of social change and progress, which is associated with Marxism. During the period from 1986 to 1989 wide coverage was given to François Furet's thesis, which views the revolutionary course as the by-product of a political game while ruling out the notion that the Terror may have been induced by "compelling circumstances." Critics further to the right in the political spectrum put the French Revolution on trial because of the failure of its Russian counterpart. From this point of view, the French Revolution was seen as the beginning of totalitarianism rather than of democracy. The repression of the Vendée uprising (1793–1796), during which thousands of people died, was even sometimes presented as the first instance of genocide in modern times. It became clear that the legacy of the Revolution as a whole was in need of reassessment regarding its conformity to the Republican doctrine.

From 1986 to 1988 the Right was in power—with the conservative Jacques Chirac serving as prime minister during the presidency of the socialist François Mitterrand—and the Left started mobilizing in the run-up to the bicentennial. Celebrating the Revolution became one way of safeguarding the identity of the Left, fighting to preserve the past as a key to building up the future. Networks were set up, such as CLEF, the network formed by the Ligue des Droits de l'Homme and the Ligue de l'Enseignement, and "Vive 89!," which was an association founded by historian

A huge crowd gathers in the Place de la Bastille to celebrate the bicentennial of the French Revolution, 13 July 1989. ©DAVID TURNLEY/CORBIS

members of the French Communist Party or those sympathetic to the party, although it was not directed by the party itself. Both groups criticized the government's Bicentennial Mission, led by Edgar Faure, for planning a half hearted and too-critical commemoration that failed to present the Revolution as a promise.

The 1988 electoral victory of the Socialist Party as well as Mitterrand's appointment of Jean-Noël Jeanneney as the new president of the Bicentennial Mission after Edgar Faure's death somewhat reduced causes for apprehension. Jeanneney redirected the official sense of the commemoration from a search for a minimal consensus emphasizing human rights toward a message, more in consonance with previous commemorations, exalting the concept of the Revolution as a "rupture" with the past and the "luminous side" of the Revolution in an attempt to understand the process of revolutionary violence rather than reprove it. Still, difficulties continued,

since commemorating a revolution at a time when revolutions were on the ebb provoked irony from the media. The desire for commemoration itself was seen as archaic because it expressed a degree of confidence in the future and in progress that seemed no longer to be the order of the day.

SEEKING NATIONAL SUPPORT

To ensure the success of the bicentennial celebration, the Mission entrusted a well-known advertiser, Jean-Paul Goude, with the task of designing and organizing the 14th of July parade. This parade, which would take place during the G-7 summit, was to be the high point of the commemoration. The artist decided to avoid pure historical evocation and instead, playing with national stereotypes, depicted "globalization on the move" through a planetary musical interbreeding that announced the triumph of human rights. The aesthetic choices, the refusal of a heavily educational bias—quite unexpected in such circumstances, and the dramatic tension produced by the huge black-draped drum opening the parade, symbolizing China's Tiananmen Square repression, which had occurred that same year, convinced the media of the value of such a commemoration.

Although at the national level reluctance about commemorating the bicentennial of the Revolution was widespread—a result of the controversies over its possible interpretations—most regions were proactive in its celebration. In almost all *départements* (counties), towns, and villages, ambitious commemorative programs were put together. In the smallest villages trees of liberty were planted, giving people an opportunity to gather together and celebrate—sometimes the traditional values of the place, rather than revolutionary values as such. In many areas festive traditions, often forgotten, were reactivated and reinvented. All over the country the bicentennial presented an opportunity for communities to present live historical shows and for local assemblies to inaugurate cultural policies. Whereas the Right-Left division was noticeable at the national level (most leaders of the right wing decided not to attend Goude's parade and criticized the government for wasting money on the celebrations), most local communities, whatever their political affiliation, devoted a significant budget to the commemoration. The will to assert a local identity undoubtedly overcame reluctance with respect to the bicentennial commemoration, even if, as was the case in Vendée or in the city of Lyon, the claimed identity was that of a tradition opposed to the Revolution. Thus, national support for the bicentennial commemoration was characterized by local appropriations of the event as an opportunity to create new sociabilities and by a concern for a collective identity linked to the entry into a postnational era.

See also **France.**

BIBLIOGRAPHY

Davallon, Jean, Philippe Dujardin, and Gérard Sabatier, eds. *Politique de la mémoire: Commémorer la Révolution.* Lyon, 1993.

Garcia, Patrick. *Le bicentenaire de la Révolution française: Pratiques sociales d'une commémoration.* Paris, 2000.

Kaplan, Steven Laurence. *Farewell Revolution: Disputed Legacies: France, 1789/1989.* Ithaca, N.Y., 1995.

———. *Farewell Revolution: The Historians' Feud: France, 1789/1989.* Ithaca, N.Y., 1995.

Ory, Pascal. *Une nation pour mémoire: 1889, 1939, 1989, trois jubilés révolutionnaires.* Paris, 1992.

1789: La commémoration. Paris, 1999. A collection of articles from the journal *Le débat.* dedicated to the bicentennial.

PATRICK GARCIA

BICYCLES. *See* **Cycling.**

BIERMANN, WOLF (b. 1936), German songwriter and performer.

Wolf Biermann was born on 15 November 1936 and grew up in a Hamburg working-class milieu during the Nazi dictatorship. His father, a communist of Jewish origin, was murdered by the Nazis in Auschwitz when Wolf was only seven years old. In 1953 Biermann moved to East Berlin to finish grammar school and take up studies in political economy, philosophy, and mathematics. Meanwhile he also worked at the Berlin Ensemble of Bertolt Brecht (1898–1956), encountered the composer Hanns Eisler (1898–1962), and founded a short-lived "Berlin Workers' and Students' Theatre," which was banned in 1962. From about 1960 he began to write lyrics and songs, heavily influenced by the current French chanson tradition as represented by Georges Brassens (1921–1981).

During the short period of cultural liberalization after the construction of the Berlin Wall Biermann established himself as prolific singer-songwriter, combining poignant polemics against the evils of Stalinist bureaucracy and a politicized subjectivism with the entertaining qualities of an astute singer and guitar player. He also gained recognition in such West German left-wing circles as the Sozialistische Deutsche Studentenbund, which invited him to tour in 1965. After the publication of some of his lyrics with the West Berlin publisher Wagenbach and an LP record with the West Berlin satirist Wolfgang Neuss (1923–1989), the East German politburo banned Biermann from any further public appearance in the German

Democratic Republic (GDR). The poems and the recordings of his songs, however, continued to circulate in secret, not least due to his lasting reputation in West Germany, where he was welcomed not only as an accomplished poet and singer but also as the rare case of a leftist opponent to both German states. Although under heavy surveillance by the East German secret service, his apartment in downtown East Berlin Chausseestraße became a hub of communication for political opponents inside the GDR and their contacts with Western artists and intellectuals. In due course the first of a series of five LP records that Biermann published with the American CBS record company was called *Chausseestraße 131*. The recording and smuggling out of the material was well known to the East German leadership, as was the ongoing underground circulation of his works within the GDR. Although the tone of his criticism became more provocative, Biermann was never formally legally prosecuted in the GDR.

Apart from very rare informal performances in church institutions, Biermann did not perform in public until he was invited by the West German metalworkers' union to tour in West Germany. The first concert took place in Cologne on 13 November 1976. When the East German authorities permitted his visit, this was only a part of a detailed plan to get rid of this most irksome and uncompromising East German dissident. Four days after the first concert he was deprived of his GDR citizenship and forced to settle in Hamburg again. The highly symbolic stature Biermann had acquired by now became evident when hundreds of East German artists, intellectuals, and other citizens openly joined in opposition against this measure by petitioning and using West German media channels to publicize their protest. A wave of repressive measures (in particular against the less prominent among such petitioners) was the consequence while at the top level of GDR cultural life the Biermann expatriation was followed by a wave of partly voluntary and partly mandatory emigration to West Germany. This event marked the beginning of a growing and definitive alienation prefiguring the inner erosion of the regime in the second half of the 1980s.

In West Germany Biermann quickly took up engagements as a poet, singer, and commentator on political events, taking part in the fermenting processes of the new social movements of the post-1968 leftism, both in Germany and abroad. With the fall of the Berlin Wall in November 1989 he immediately visited Leipzig and Berlin to perform in East Germany again. In the years to follow, however, he began to fall out with the left-wing mainstream due to his support of the U.S. intervention in the First Gulf War (1991), which reflected the priority he gave to the existence of the state of Israel. Also his uncompromising stance in dealing with the crimes and failures of the GDR did much to further his distance from the socialist cause (or what was left of it). It is in connection with his part in the effort to work through the past of the communist dictatorship that Biermann still appears in public in his old role as a singer-songwriter, poet, and political entertainer on rare occasions.

Looking back on his oeuvre, his early years up to his expatriation stand out in terms of quality through the high-pitched tone of a politically engaged subjectivity articulated to a wide repertoire of poetic forms from politically engaged poetry in German literature. Biermann can thus be seen in the tradition not only of Brecht (as a poet) but above all of Heinrich Heine (1797–1856), to whom he devoted a brilliant actualization of one his most important poems, "Deutschland, ein Wintermärchen" (Germany, a winter tale). Biermann has been presented with several literary prizes and awards, among them the highly prestigious Georg-Büchner-Preis in 1991, and received invitations as a visiting professor in Germany and abroad. His outstanding capacity to adapt poetry from other cultural, temporal, and linguistic contexts—"translation" would be much too weak a term for this—has also become evident in his rendition of poems from the Russian dissident poet Vladimir Vysotsky (1938–1980), William Shakespeare's (1564–1616) sonnets and, more recently, in German adaptations of Yiddish poetry such as the seminal "Dos lied vunem ojsgehargetn jidischn volk" (Song of the murdered Jewish people) by Yitzhak Katznelson (1886–1944).

See also **Berlin; Brecht, Bertolt; Dissidence; Germany; World War II.**

BIBLIOGRAPHY

Primary Sources

Biermann, Wolf. *Alle Lieder.* Cologne, 1991.

———. *Alle Gedichte.* Cologne, 1995.

———. *Wolf Biermann Edition, vols. 1–23.* His complete collection on CD, available through LiederProduktion, Altona.

Secondary Sources

Rosellini, Jay. *Wolf Biermann.* Munich, 1992.

THOMAS LINDENBERGER

BIERUT, BOLESŁAW (1892–1956), Polish Communist leader.

Born in 1892 in a suburb of Lublin, in the Russian-ruled part of Poland, Bierut grew up in a poor, Catholic family. His parents were impoverished peasants who had just moved to the city; of their twelve children only five lived to adulthood. Bierut did not complete elementary school. Although Russian proved most useful in his future political career, during the 1905 Revolution he joined a student strike in demand for instruction in Polish and consequently was dismissed. In the next few years he took various manual jobs but also read widely. Bierut became active in a secret patriotic youth circle, and at the age of sixteen he joined the printers' trade union. Evening classes enabled him to take a clerk position in a grocery cooperative, which began his career in the cooperative movement. In 1910 he met Jan Hempel, a self-taught philosopher and Freemason who greatly influenced young Bierut and in 1912 introduced him to the (illegal) socialist movement. Bierut joined the radical, left splinter of the Polish Socialist Party (PPS-Left). In 1918, as Poland was regaining independence, the PPS-Left merged into the Communist Party; in this way Bierut became a Communist.

In the 1920s Bierut advanced within the Communist Party of Poland (KPP) and in the cooperative movement. He was by no means outstanding, rather a mediocre but diligent and devoted activist. Like many Communist adherents, loyalty to the party and to the USSR ("the fatherland of the world's proletariat") became Bierut's guiding principle. As a party functionary beginning in 1925, he visited the Soviet Union several times and was admitted to Lenin's International School, which combined political instruction with military and intelligence training. In Moscow he met his second wife, Małgorzata Fornalska, a KPP activist. In 1931–1932, under the alias "Iwanow," Bierut became the Comintern envoy to Austria, Bulgaria, and Czechoslovakia. The police interrupted his activity in Poland with repeated arrests and eventually a longer imprisonment from 1933 to 1938. Paradoxically, imprisonment saved his life: during what became known as the Great Purges most of the KPP leaders were summoned to Moscow and executed. Because of alleged infiltration by Polish intelligence, the Comintern disbanded the KPP in 1938.

Following the German-Soviet partition of Poland in 1939, Bierut went to the Soviet zone but did not play any prominent role there. After the German invasion in 1941 he worked in the local administration in Minsk and probably also served in the Soviet intelligence. In 1943 the Soviets moved him to Warsaw, where (as comrade "Tomasz") he entered the executive committee of the new Polish Workers' Party (PPR). In early 1944 he took the chairmanship of the Communist-dominated National Council of the Homeland (KRN), which despite its narrow political base challenged the mainstream underground movement, which was loyal to the Polish government-in-exile.

In the summer of 1944, when the Soviet-backed Polish Committee for National Liberation began to build its administration in territories freed of Germans, KRN was declared the official legislature; Bierut began to act as the head of state and used the title of president. Following the spurious elections of 1947, the Communist-dominated Diet (Sejm) confirmed him in this position. Meanwhile he went to Moscow several times and earned Joseph Stalin's confidence. His membership in the PPR and its Politburo remained secret until 1948 when, along with the Stalin-Tito rift and the tightening of Moscow's grip on its satellites, he replaced Władysław Gomułka as the party's secretary general. He was most eager to eradicate "deviations" inside the party and accelerate the Sovietization of Poland. The latter included completing the process of building a monolithic and monopolist Polish United Workers' Party (PZPR), suppression of all independent organizations, forced collectivization, heavy industrialization, mass political mobilization, and mass repression. He strictly followed Soviet Cold War policies in aggressive anti-Western propaganda, isolating Poland from the West and dramatically increasing military spending during the Korean war.

Quiet, modest, and polite, Bierut was an unlikely tyrant, yet he became one of the "little Stalins" (like Hungary's Rakosi or Albania's Enver Hoxha): head of a gigantic party-state pyramid and object of public worship, with his icons omnipresent, his name given to factories and schools, his sixtieth birthday a national holiday. He personally supervised progress of political trials and rejected thousands of petitions for pardon of death sentence. He continued to be called "Stalin's most faithful student" by Polish communist propaganda, even after the latter's death. Destalinization in the USSR literally killed him: he went to the CPSU Twentieth Congress despite serious illness, and his health deteriorated further after hearing Khrushchev's "secret speech." He died in Moscow in March 1956, opening the struggle for succession inside the Polish Communist Party.

See also **Cold War; Collectivization; Destalinization; Gomułka, Władysław; Hoxha, Enver; Poland; Stalin, Joseph.**

BIBLIOGRAPHY

Kozłowski, Czesław. *Namiestnik Stalina.* Warsaw, 1993.

Lipiński, Piotr. *Bolesław Niejasny. Opowieść o Foreście Gumpie polskiego komunizmu.* Warsaw, 2001.

Paczkowski, Andrzej. *The Spring Will Be Ours: Poland and the Poles from Occupation to Freedom.* University Park, Pa., 2003.

DARIUSZ STOLA

BIRTH CONTROL.

Efforts to control fertility are as old as human society itself. Traditional methods of birth control included abortion, infanticide, late marriage, prolonged sexual abstinence, extended nursing (to prevent ovulation), coitus interruptus (withdrawal), douching, and nonreproductive sexual practices such as masturbation. For hundreds of years, women used substances such as sponges to block conception and herbal potions to kill sperm or to cause miscarriages. Condoms (also known as sheaths), in use since the early modern era, were originally made of sheepskin, then of vulcanized rubber from the 1870s.

Although various birth control technologies and practices had long existed, by the turn of the twentieth century, the most frequently used methods continued to be withdrawal—a method dependent on men—and abortion. But key changes were already underway that would ultimately produce revolutions in both technologies and practice. Between 1870 and 1914, fertility rates throughout Europe had declined dramatically, reflecting a major transformation in values about ideal family size and a stronger motivation to limit it. Although feminist movements did not officially advocate birth control, female emancipation of the late nineteenth century led many women to consider reproductive choice a personal right. At the same time, the science of sexology emerged, which led to new ways of thinking about, regulating, and intervening in sexuality. It also led to the eventual recognition that female sexual pleasure was important to marital happiness. These transformations took place in the broader context of the rise of strong nation-states and international competition, discourses about "racial purity," and governments and professional experts who viewed their populations as a resource whose health needed improvement and whose families needed stabilization. By the turn of the twentieth century, the confluence of these factors led to improved contraceptive devices intended specifically for women and a new ideology—neo-Malthusianism—that spawned movements to distribute them.

Improved methods for women included various types of pessaries, a generic term for blockage methods, which included thimble-shaped cervical caps made of rubber or of cellulose and metal. One version had sharp teeth around the inside edge to adhere better to the relatively insensate cervix. The diaphragm, also made of rubber but wider and shallower than the cap, was (and is) held in place with an encased metal spring and used with spermicide cream. Intrauterine devices (IUDs) also came into use, though they were expensive. One type consisted of a plate placed at the base of the cervix, with a stem that extended into its canal.

Others had a V-shaped spring that extended into the uterus.

Despite the expressed need many women felt for birth control, the widespread adoption of appliance methods required new attitudes toward sexuality and sexual practices, as well as women's knowledge about and comfort with their own bodies, which was uncommon during the Victorian era. Appliance methods also required premeditation prior to the sexual act, a psychological state many women continued to lack in the second half of the twentieth century. For this reason abortion—an act of desperation after the sexual act—seemed more innocent for many women than did conscious actions in advance of coitus to prevent conception. Appliance devices themselves posed difficulties. Placing any object in the vagina unrelated to sex or childbirth seemed unnatural to both women and doctors. Health practitioners sometimes advised patients to keep cervical caps and diaphragms in place for weeks at a time, which produced infections. Not surprisingly, the cervical cap with teeth often caused inflammation of the cervix. Finally, because they required fitting, instruction, and privacy, poor women, especially in the countryside, had little access to them.

BIRTH CONTROL MOVEMENTS

Birth control movements in the early twentieth century originated with "neo-Malthusian" concerns about economic distress and other social evils caused by overpopulation. The eighteenth-century political economist Thomas Malthus, in *An Essay on the Principle of Population* (1798), warned that because food production could not keep pace with population growth, the latter had to be checked. To that end, he preached celibacy and delayed marriage. Neo-Malthusians, however, thought that the sexual instinct could not and should not be suppressed; they hoped to alleviate social ills through the use of contraception. Controlling population growth was not only a matter of food, wages, and prices, but also of the potential for human perfection and freedom. Neo-Malthusian doctrine contributed to eugenicist notions of using birth control for the purposes of improving the quality, not just reducing the quantity, of the population.

Neo-Malthusianism started in Great Britain, and spread to the Netherlands, France, and Italy. The movements mostly concerned themselves with the more prolific working classes—middle classes were already the ones to deliberately limit family size. With their focus on birth control primarily as a panacea for social and economic ills rather than sexual emancipation for women (though movements varied nationally), neo-Malthusian movements were primarily dominated by men. But there were important exceptions. The Dutch physician Aletta Henriëtte Jacobs (1854–1929) opened a birth control clinic in Amsterdam in the 1890s. The French feminist Nelly Roussel (1878–1922) widely campaigned in France for women's access to contraception and argued that reproductive choice was the centerpiece of female emancipation. The American Margaret Louise Sanger (1879–1966) coined the term *birth control* in 1914 as a substitute for the gloomy economic label *neo-Malthusianism* and as a deliberate effort to focus on the well-being of mothers and children. All three particularly reacted to the hardships of working-class women who suffered from repeated childbearing and poverty, but implicit in their work was a belief in women's reproductive autonomy. The Englishwoman Marie Charlotte Carmichael Stopes (1880–1958), through her marriage manual *Married Love* (1918), became famous for her focus on women's sexual pleasure. But readers' responses to the manual stressed how fears of pregnancy interfered with pleasure, so she quickly produced *Wise Parenthood* (1918) in which she provided descriptions of contraceptives and their use. Finding that she could not depend on medical professionals to dispense contraceptives, she opened her own birth control clinic in 1921.

By the 1930s the idea of birth control was widely accepted and practiced, and an increasing number of women sought female contraceptives. Nonetheless, their adoption was slow, and until the last third of the twentieth century, withdrawal continued to be the most commonly used method throughout much of Europe. Everywhere, those who sought to spread contraceptives for women met with resistance from the church, governments, the medical profession, moral reformers, and social activists across the political spectrum. In 1930 Pope Pius XI (r. 1922–1939) issued the encyclical

Casti Connubi (On Christian marriage) to concretize the Church's staunch opposition to any artificial control of fertility and to reinforce Church doctrine regarding women's proper role as mothers. The only method of birth control acceptable to the Church was the rhythm method, made possible when doctors finally discovered the pattern of ovulation in 1929. But this method was dubbed "Vatican roulette" since it had such a high failure rate.

Many others opposed birth control for secular reasons. National defense required large populations, pronatalists argued. Moralists believed that access to female contraceptives would make women into sex objects, render them promiscuous, and destroy the family. Both prostitution and venereal disease would spread. Many feminists believed that contraceptives would rob motherhood of its dignity and deny women their single most important excuse to resist sexual advances. Doctors and other health professionals justifiably thought that appliance methods were unnatural and dangerous to the female body. Although most advocates of birth control came from the left wing—many were anarchists and freethinkers—opposition also came from the Left. Socialists believed birth control was selfishly individualistic and bourgeois. Any improvement in living standards resulting from smaller families would divert the working classes from the only true source of emancipation—the overthrow of capitalism.

GOVERNMENT INTERVENTION AND NATIONAL VARIATIONS, 1920–1960

The massive disruptions of World War I had direct impacts on attitudes toward birth control that varied considerably by nation. Hardships and economic disruptions of everyday life did not end with the war. Everywhere, large families were simply impractical, even though many viewed them as a potential source of national regeneration. But accustomed to rationalized economies from the war years, politicians and health professionals generally came to accept the need to develop population policies and intervene in issues of birth control in order to reduce abortion and stabilize family life. Governments born of war and revolution, such as the Communist Soviet Union and the German Weimar Republic, were more open to sexual reform movements that advocated birth control than were Western democracies.

The Russian Revolution of 1917 brought unprecedented gender equality—at least in principle—and with it a new consciousness about women's double burden of work and motherhood. But the effort to address women's issues did not initially extend to reproductive rights. Official Communist doctrine opposed birth control as a product of Western capitalism, and a source of race suicide in a nation surrounded by anticommunist countries. But relatively backward in even traditional methods of family limitation, the USSR differed from Western countries in the persistence of high birthrates. It also had very high abortion rates. In 1920 the government took the opposite path of other nations: it legalized abortion in order to reduce the mortality and illness resulting from illegal operations. This bold step did not mean that the government favored abortion as a means of birth control. But the effort to regulate abortion led to open discussion about birth control. At the same time, concerns about the health of mothers and children led the government to form the Department for the Protection of Motherhood and Infancy that, in the mid-1920s, formed a commission to research birth control methods. In 1925 the department officially endorsed birth control and its dissemination as a means to reduce abortion. Even before that endorsement, pharmacies openly displayed contraceptive devices and handed out instructions to use them.

What happened in the Soviet Union was crucial for other countries as well. Because of its advances in women's equality and reproductive freedom, numerous women from Europe and the United States visited the Soviet Union in the 1920s and 1930s. German women were particularly influenced by what they learned. The prewar German penal code prohibited abortion and outlawed the discussion, display, and advertisement of contraceptives, though their manufacture and sale continued to be legal. After the war, in the context of national defeat, economic crisis, and a new democratic government, German reformers became deeply worried about the health of families. Communists and Social Democrats, influenced by the Soviet model and by Margaret Sanger, joined representatives of the health professions in the belief that sexuality should be regulated even though birthrates were in decline. Rather than

A group of men dramatically demonstrate their advocacy of birth control, Stratford, England, 1972.
©HULTON-DEUTSCH COLLECTION/CORBIS

trying to raise the birthrate, they focused on the quality of children born. They believed that sex and birth control counseling would stabilize marriage and reduce illegal abortion, infant mortality, and babies born out of wedlock. Weimar Germany was unique in its grassroots birth control movement, and in the early establishment and large number of clinics and sex reform leagues. They also openly fought to legalize abortion. But like the earlier neo-Malthusians, they framed their vision in economic terms with the intent of improving domestic happiness among the working classes, a vision they linked strongly to eugenics.

Western democracies that had neo-Malthusian movements prior to World War I, afterward proved more conservative with regard to reproductive rights. Birth control propaganda had always remained legal in Britain as long as it was not judged "obscene." The church and the medical profession continued to oppose birth control in

the 1920s. Doctors not only feared race suicide and a decline of the British Empire, but they also believed contraception would cause sterility, fibroid tumors, and a number of other gynecological disorders. Despite this resistance, the economic dislocations and the plight of the working classes helped advocates of family limitation prevail. In 1930 the Anglican Church announced its acceptance of birth control, and the Ministry of Health finally approved the distribution of contraceptive devices—but only with the advice of local medical officers, and only to married mothers whose further pregnancies would be harmful to their physical health.

The situations in France and Italy differed markedly from those in other countries where the toleration for birth control grew. Because of France's uniquely low birthrates for more than a hundred years, its government felt particularly threatened by neo-Malthusianism even prior to

World War I. Pronatalists had fervently argued for the legal prohibition of birth control from 1909 and believed that low birthrates made them vulnerable to German aggression. The French, moreover, lost proportionally more of their mobilized soldiers than any other country in World War I and suffered the damages from the war having been fought on their soil. In July 1920 the government passed a law that prohibited the sale, advertisement, and public discussion of birth control devices, though condoms remained legal to prevent venereal disease. A law of 1923 made prosecution for abortion easier. These laws remained in place until 1967 and 1975, respectively.

Legislation prohibiting abortion and birth control became an important aspect of totalitarian doctrines and practices in the 1920s and 1930s and reflected newly conservative views about gender roles. Fathering large families became a sign of masculinity and an important element of Italian dictator Benito Mussolini's fascism after he came to power in 1922, even though he had supported neo-Malthusianism prior to the war. Women were expected to sacrifice themselves through childbearing. Birth control was outlawed as a crime against the state in 1926. In Germany the Nazi takeover in 1933 resulted in the closure of birth control clinics and marriage counseling centers. The Nazis used "birth control" for eugenic ends, forcing abortions and sterilization on Jews, Gypsies, non-Aryans, and others deemed a threat to the German race. In both Germany and Vichy France during World War II, abortion became punishable by death for those who performed it. Soviet policy regarding reproduction reversed direction in the 1930s under Joseph Stalin. Like the right-wing dictators, he too encouraged large families and maternal self-sacrifice; abortion was again prohibited, and birth control information became unavailable.

THE REVOLUTION IN BIRTH CONTROL, 1960 TO THE EARLY TWENTY-FIRST CENTURY

As these examples indicate, government population policies, traditional attitudes about gender and sexuality, and the difficulties contraceptive devices posed hindered their adoption through much of the twentieth century. Only in the 1960s did new technologies begin to change attitudes in fundamental ways. New, presumably safer forms of the IUD became available and relieved women of all the inconveniences of the earlier methods. More important, the oral contraceptive pill became available. At least five scientists contributed to the hormonal research that eventually led to the Pill, though contraception had not been their intent. The irrepressible Margaret Sanger convinced one of them, Gregory Goodwin Pincus, to apply his research to contraceptive purposes and secured funding for him. Having proved that progesterone inhibits ovulation in 1951, he undertook the task of developing a synthetic hormone. In 1960 the American Food and Drug Administration approved the Searle synthetic anovulent, and it quickly spread to Europe. Like the IUD, the Pill offered the obvious advantage that its use was completely separate from the sex act and required no messy, unromantic preparations. But its adoption nonetheless required approval of the medical profession, legal sanction, and attitudinal change among women. By 1970, for example, only 6 percent of French women used the Pill, in part because its distribution required a prescription and because it was initially withheld from unmarried women and minors. Today the oral contraceptive has been followed by other means of injecting hormones such as patches, shots, and suppositories. Other applications of hormones have also come into use, such as the postcoital "morning-after pill" that blocks implantation of a fertilized egg.

The myth most commonly associated with the Pill is that it caused the sexual revolution of the 1960s and 1970s. In fact, that revolution resulted from the complex confluence of other cultural factors beyond the scope of this entry. The Pill, however, remains controversial for other reasons. While for some women it seems like a more "natural" method of contraception than appliance devices such as the diaphragm, others fear it might have long-term effects such as cancer and wonder why only women are subjected to such "biointervention." Such fears led many women in the 1960s and 1970s to choose the IUD. But various versions of this device eventually proved to be damaging to the uterus. Finally, abortion rates remain high despite the wider availability of contraception.

Birth control—especially the availability of female forms of contraception—enabled a separation of reproduction from sexuality and had an enormous influence on the evolution of modern

European society. The few examples of national variation offered here illustrate the complex inter-relationships between technology, sexuality, gender relationships, and the overarching influence of social policy engineered by various national agendas. The Pill fostered dramatic change and resolved many problems women and married couples confronted in the past. It has also raised new questions about sexual and reproductive autonomy. Moreover, large segments of the European population still have little access to safe and effective forms of birth control.

See also **Abortion; Feminism; Sexuality.**

BIBLIOGRAPHY

Primary Sources

Sanger, Margaret. *Margaret Sanger: An Autobiography.* New York, 1938.

Smith, Jessica. *Women in Soviet Russia.* New York, 1928.

Stopes, Marie Carmichael. *Married Love.* London, 1918.

———. *Wise Parenthood: A Practical Sequel to "Married Love"; A Book for Married People.* London, 1919.

———. *Contraception (Birth Control): Its Theory, History, and Practice; A Manual for the Medical and Legal Professions.* London, 1923.

Secondary Sources

"Before the Pill: Preventing Fertility in Western Europe and Quebec." Special issue of *The Journal of Interdisciplinary History* 34, no. 2 (autumn 2003).

Cook, Hera. *The Long Sexual Revolution: English Women, Sex, and Contraception, 1800–1975.* Oxford, U.K., 2004.

Grossmann, Atina. *Reforming Sex: The German Movement for Birth Control and Abortion Reform, 1920–1950.* New York, 1995.

Heims, Norman. *The Medical History of Contraception.* Baltimore, Md., 1936.

Marks, Lara. *Sexual Chemistry: A History of the Contraceptive Pill.* New Haven, Conn., 2001.

McLaren, Angus. *A History of Contraception: From Antiquity to the Present Day.* Oxford, U.K., 1990.

———. *Twentieth-Century Sexuality: A History.* Oxford, U.K., 1999.

Soloway, Richard Allen. *Birth Control and the Population Question in England, 1877–1930.* Chapel Hill, N.C., 1982.

ELINOR ACCAMPO

BLAIR, TONY (b. 1953), British prime minister.

Tony Blair was born in 1953 in Edinburgh but grew up mainly in Durham. He returned to Edinburgh at age fourteen to complete his education at the private Fettes school and went on to read law at Oxford University. He qualified as a barrister and entered Labour Party politics in a by-election at Beaconsfield in 1980. Though ticking all the correct radical boxes for the Labour Party of the 1980s—a party which at that point in its history was committed to unilateral nuclear disarmament, withdrawal from the European Economic Community (EEC), and widespread nationalization—Blair was impatient with the rhetoric and frustrated with continued electoral defeat. He won a safe seat at Sedgefeld in 1983 at the age of thirty, and was given a room at Westminster with Gordon Brown. Brown had deep roots in the party and was initially the senior member of a political double act that led the modernizing wing of the party. Under the patronage of Neil Kinnock and then John Smith, Blair and Brown rose to the Shadow Cabinet, Brown having given Blair his most famous sound bite of these years, "tough on crime, tough on the causes of crime." When John Smith died it looked likely that Brown would take the leadership, but instead, after a meeting with Blair, the modernizers decided that Blair would be the better candidate to continue the process of modernization that had been started by Neil Kinnock's wide-ranging policy review.

Once leader, Blair quickly developed a striking ability to communicate effectively with "middle England"—the suburban middle class—which Labour needed to win over to achieve power. In 1997 Labour won a landslide victory over a discredited Conservative government. This opened the most sustained period of electoral and political success in the history of the Labour Party. Blair developed an ideological approach called the Third Way and branded his party as New Labour. The Third Way owed a great deal to U.S. president Bill Clinton's ideas of triangulation, but it also had a strongly British perspective based around the forging of a new progressive consensus. The basis of Blair's statecraft was presidential rather than prime ministerial and his major policy

Tony Blair (left) with U.S. president George W. Bush at a press conference, 17 July 2003. ©BROOKS KRAFT/CORBIS

achievements—the introduction of a minimum wage, devolution of power, reform of the House of Lords, modernization of the management and running of schools, the incorporation of the European Convention on Human Rights into U.K. law—were all effectively communicated. Brown became chancellor and delivered sustained economic growth, falling unemployment, and low interest rates. Labour was reelected with reduced majorities in 2001 and 2005 and Blair became the longest serving Labour prime minister.

The early part of the new Labour period in office was characterized by radical reforms that had a strong civil liberties content, for example, the European Convention and the passage of a Freedom of Information Act. The momentum for this process of reform was stopped in its tracks by the attacks on New York's World Trade Center. In the aftermath of this attack, as the United States launched its war on terror, Blair's liberal instincts were largely replaced by a realist analysis of

measures necessary to combat international terrorism in the United Kingdom and abroad. This "realism" resulted in the creation of the most draconian set of anti-terrorism legislation in any major democracy. Blair's liberal credentials had already been brought into question by his pursuit of highly populist policies on issues such as asylum and immigration. Most British prime ministers move to the center as their administrations develop. In Blair's case, the impact of world events on his political philosophy transformed what had been a keen populist political instinct for mainstream political positions into a harder edged belief in the use of force, in the need for a coercive police power to combat terrorism, and a broadly illiberal attitude to immigration and asylum.

Major problems during his term of office were protests against the price of fuel by truckers and a sustained confrontation with the pro-hunt lobby when his government made fox hunting illegal. Both issues concerned relatively small and politically isolated groups of voters. The broad coalition that supported Blair in 1997 remained remarkably solid over the first two terms, though Labour's vote and voter turnout dropped sharply. However, while his premiership has been characterized by almost unbroken approval ratings for domestic policy, his foreign policy has been more controversial. Coming to office with virtually no foreign policy experience, Blair advocated and then committed British forces to a series of humanitarian interventions to control or remove unacceptable regimes. British troops were involved in five armed conflicts culminating in the invasion of Iraq. This foreign policy, coupled to an increasing move toward individualism, choice, and private sector involvement in public service delivery made him deeply unpopular with his own party and saw his approval rating decline. Following the 2005 general election he announced that he would retire before the next election.

Blair's record suggests that he will go down in history as one of the most successful British prime ministers of the last one hundred years, but it is a record that is contested. Critics from the Left argue that his period in office was based on the endorsement of the reforms in political economy introduced by Margaret Thatcher and that his foreign policy has been based on appeasing the United States rather than pursing vital British interests. Critics from the Right argue that he failed to solve the problems of the public services but instead massively increased the administrative burden on teachers and doctors with a system of league tables and performance indicators. Both Left and Right characterize Blair's governing style and policy approach as being more akin to management consultancy than socialism. Others criticize Blair's alleged obsessions with message over content. Part of the modernization of the Labour Party introduced by Blair was the professionalization of communications. This continued in government with all communications centralized through a strong communications unit in the prime minister's office. This was heavily criticized, especially when it became clear over time that it was not the cabinet that was the central decision-making body of government but rather the prime minister working through a small group of senior aids and key ministers. Constitutionally the role of these special advisors on policy and communications remained a major issue in Blair's period in office.

Internationally, Blair's record was also contested. Widespread opposition to the Iraq war, along with deep divisions within his own party on the future of the European Union with respect to the single currency and the accession of Turkey, contrasted with a settled advantage over the other parties on a domestic policy that centered on a £42 billion investment program in public services. Blair's premiership coincided with the increasing maturity of the knowledge economy and a broad sense of social and cultural confidence in the United Kingdom. Blair's own confident style of communication, his ability to spot and capitalize on populist issues such as asylum, youth crime, and antisocial behavior, were not matched by the substance of his reforming achievements. Much of the credit for the success of the administration lay with his chancellor Gordon Brown, but Blair retained one virtue that places him in the forefront of British prime ministers: he was the greatest election winner the Labour Party has ever produced.

See also **Thatcher, Margaret; United Kingdom.**

BIBLIOGRAPHY

Brivati Brian, and Tim Bale, eds. *New Labour in Power: Precedents and Prospects.* London and New York, 1997

Brivati Brian, and Richard Heffernan, eds. *The Labour Party: A Centenary History.* New York, 2000.

Seldon, Anthony. *Blair.* London, 2005.

Seldon, Anthony, and Dennis Kavanagh, eds. *The Blair Effect, 2001–2005.* Cambridge, U.K., 2005.

Stephens, Philip. *Tony Blair: The Making of a World Leader.* New York, 2004.

BRIAN BRIVATI

BLITZKRIEG. Blitzkrieg, or "lightning war," is a military strategy devised by the German high command between the two world wars and applied during World War II. It was inspired by the lessons drawn from the strategic impasse of the war of position in the trenches and the experience of the lost battles of the last year of World War I. Blitzkrieg became a kind of legend, and in the years 1939–1942 it buttressed the myth of the

Wehrmacht's invincibility. In the early twenty-first century historians agree that the concept reflected the mind-set of the generals who invented it and the economic and strategic constraints under which Nazi Germany operated.

The blitzkrieg strategy was thus developed on the basis of the last German offensives on the western front in the early spring of 1918—and on the basis too of their failure. The Germans' obsessive fear of reliving the dark hours of 9 November 1918, a fear discernible at every level of the military hierarchy, was surely the main determinant of the doctrine of blitzkrieg.

Blitzkrieg is a set of tactics employing mechanized infantry assault groups, almost indistinguishable from the Stosstruppen (shock troops) of World War I, advancing with cover from massive armored forces and concentrating their attack on the enemy's lines of communication. The attack is a coordinated one, mobilizing ground and air forces, the combination being essential to the fastest possible destabilization of the enemy troops. Thus air power is concentrated on enemy communications, while the task of the armored units is to breach the enemy defenses at their weakest points and pour through the opposing lines before assaulting the more strongly defended positions from behind. In a second phase of such an offensive, classic troop formations are expected to reduce all remaining pockets of resistance and secure the terrain on a permanent basis. The main objective of blitzkrieg is to avoid getting bogged down and any possible regression to a war of position.

These principles were worked out by Generals Erich von Manstein and Heinz Guderian. Von Manstein was interested in the strategic aspects of the plan of attack in the Polish and French campaigns, while Guderian was one of the main champions of rapid armored units concentrated on particular parts of the front with a view to making decisive breakthroughs.

Debate continues about the nature of blitzkrieg: Was it a doctrine framed in advance and applied by the Germans in Poland and France? Or merely a set of "empirical prescriptions," framed after the fact, that had produced brilliant successes but that nevertheless remained somewhat questionable? Karl-Heinz Frieser has argued for this

latter view in a well-documented examination of the question. The fact remains that blitzkrieg made it possible for the Germans to crush Poland, and later France, in just weeks—and this despite the fact, at least in the case of France, that their forces were at a distinct numerical disadvantage.

The possible shortcomings of a strategy of coordinated breakthroughs were already discernible in the Polish campaign, as cumulating losses associated with weaknesses of the German production machine clearly exposed shortages in the supply of matériel. These shortfalls could be partially offset only by great productive efforts, so that the "phony war" was a welcome chance for the Germans to make up some of this leeway. As for the stunningly successful French campaign, it convinced the German generals that their strategy was sound, even though the logistical problems had been considerable, as witness the 250-kilometer-long tie-ups seen in the Ardennes during the early days of the offensive.

It was their faith in blitzkrieg that led the German generals to conceive of Operation Barbarossa as a gigantic instance of the strategy on a subcontinental scale. From the beginning of 1941 their strategic thinking reflected both their ambitions for world domination and their lack of lucidity: some looked forward confidently to a victory over the Soviets within a few weeks; others dreamed of lightning operations that would put Iraq in their grasp and leave them well placed to threaten India from the Caucasus.

Omer Bartov and Christian Gerlach have nevertheless clearly highlighted the structural problems confronting the blitzkrieg approach in the Soviet Union. The immense losses suffered from the outset by the German forces (betraying a structural defect of blitzkrieg already noted with respect to assault troops during the offensives of summer 1918), logistical disorganization, and a desperate but effective in-depth defense on the part of the Soviets combined to defeat a strategy whose main aim was to avoid immobilization. By the end of the summer of 1941 a war of position was the order of the day, and though the Germans managed to escape from this during the offensives of winter 1941–1942, their forces were effectively bogged down. Wrecked, therefore, by logistical constraints, the cost in men, and the Soviets' defensive strategies, blitzkrieg had failed. By an irony of fate it was the Germans themselves who had devised the strategy of in-depth defense alongside that of assault-group offensives in 1917–1918, thus simultaneously developing the most advanced offensive strategy and a defensive response that could counter it. In 1945, as in 1918, victory was vouchsafed to those best supplied in men and matériel, those able to survive the terrible impact of the German armored assault and reply with a more rational, completely conceived, and long-term mobilization.

See also **Armies; World War II.**

BIBLIOGRAPHY

Bartov, Omer. *Hitler's Army: Soldiers, Nazis, and War in the Third Reich.* New York, 1992.

Frieser, Karl-Heinz. *The Blitzkrieg Legend: The 1940 Campaign in the West.* Annapolis, Md., 2004.

Gerlach, Christian. *Kalkulierte Morde: Die deutsche Wirtschafts- und Vernichtungspolitik in Weißrußland.* Hamburg, 1999.

Moser, John. *The Blitzkrieg Myth: How Hitler and the Allies Misread the Strategic Realities of World War II.* New York, 2003.

CHRISTIAN INGRAO

BLOCH, MARC (1886–1944), French historian.

Marc Bloch has cut quite a figure both in the history of his discipline and the history of France in the twentieth century. This double impression that Bloch made, both scientific and political, may explain why in the early twenty-first century he is one of the authors most often cited—as an example to be followed and even as an icon—in the human and historical sciences in France and on the international scene.

LIFE

Marc Bloch was born on 6 July 1886 in Lyon, to a family of Jewish and Alsatian origins. Because his father was a professor of Roman history at the Sorbonne, Bloch received his education entirely in Paris. From 1904 to 1908 he studied history and geography at the École Normale Supérieure, then spent two semesters at the Universities of Berlin

and Leipzig. This "German Year," during which he attended the courses of Gustav Schmoller (1838–1917), Karl Bücher (1847–1930), and Karl Lamprecht (1856–1915), affected him deeply as might be expected. Although Bloch certainly did become one of the top specialists in German history and historiography in France, he never became a Germanophile. All his sympathies tended instead toward England, about which he did not only become an expert as concerns its history, but which he also loved to visit for both professional and personal reasons.

During World War I Bloch served as a soldier on the front and was promoted to the rank of captain. He was wounded and decorated several times. In 1919 he was appointed lecturer at the now-French Strasbourg University. He then proceeded to become associate professor and finally full professor (in 1927). It was also in Strasbourg in 1929 that Bloch founded, along with Lucien Febvre (1878–1956), the journal *Annales d'histoire économique et sociale,* which became one of the most important laboratories for "New History" on both the French and international scenes.

After several unsuccessful attempts Bloch managed to leave Strasbourg in 1936, as Febvre had done three years before. In 1936 he was elected to the Sorbonne as chair in economic history. Although too old to fight in 1939, he served as a volunteer during the "would-be war" ("drôle de guerre"). After the debacle was complete, he pulled no punches in his analysis of the errors committed by France's general staff, as well as the crisis in French society, which had led to defeat (*L'étrange défaite,* 1946; *Strange Defeat,* 1953). Despite an offer from the New School for Social Research to come to New York, he remained in France during the occupation. After having taught in Clermont-Ferrand and Montpellier thanks to a favor from the Vichy government, he joined the active resistance at the moment when German troops invaded the southern zone. Under various pseudonyms, he took part in the direction of the "franc-tireur" resistance movement. On 8 March 1944 Bloch was arrested by the Gestapo in Lyon. On 16 June, just a few days after the landings at Normandy, he was shot along with twenty-nine other prisoners just outside the city.

WORKS

Bloch's professional works primarily concern the economic and social history of the Middle Ages, rural history, and the history of mentalities. Because of its wide intellectual scope and comparative approach, it was held up by numerous historians as the model for "total history," which draws on contributions from all the human sciences, in particular economics, sociology, and anthropology. Furthermore, in the tradition of Émile Durkheim (1858–1917), Bloch never lost interest in the evolution of contemporary societies and their mentalities, so much so in fact that he was able to formulate, based on his own personal experiences, particularly fruitful hypotheses concerning the phenomena of rumors ("Les fausses nouvelles de la guerre [False rumors in wartime]," 1921) and collective memory. In addition, his work on the French defeat of 1940 became a founding text for what is now called "*l'histoire du temps present*" (contemporary history).

On the epistemological level, Bloch initially adopted the scientistic critique of the French sociologist François Simiand (1873–1935) regarding the vulgar positivism of "political historians." But later, after having been deeply impressed by the intellectual revolutions fueled by the discoveries of Albert Einstein (1879–1955) and Werner Heisenberg (1901–1976), he pleaded for a certain "softening" of Durkheimism and a "history that is both enlarged and deepened," a program for which his last book, *Apologie pour l'histoire* (1949; *The Historian's Craft,* 1953), sought to outline. Though it was left incomplete, this book nonetheless represents an important installment in a work that was varied, innovative, and highly rigorous.

See also **Annales School; Braudel, Fernand; Febvre, Lucien; Resistance.**

BIBLIOGRAPHY

Primary Sources

Bloch, Marc, Lucien Febvre, et al. *Annales d'histoire économique et sociale. Correspondance.* 3 vols. Edited by Bertrand Müller. Paris, 1994–2004.

Secondary Sources

Atsma, Hartmut, and André Burguière, eds. *Marc Bloch aujourd'hui: Histoire comparée et sciences sociales.* Paris, 1990.

Dumoulin, Olivier. *Marc Bloch.* Paris, 2000.

Fink, Carole. *Marc Bloch: A Life in History.* Cambridge, U.K., 1989.

Friedman, Susan W. *Marc Bloch, Sociology, and Geography: Encountering Changing Disciplines.* Cambridge, U.K., 1996.

Raulff, Ulrich. *Ein Historiker im 20. Jahrhundert: Marc Bloch.* Frankfurt, 1995.

Schöttler, Peter ed. *Marc Bloch: Historiker und Widerstandskämpfer.* Frankfurt, 1999.

PETER SCHÖTTLER

BLOOMSBURY. The Bloomsbury Group consisted of friends who knew one another mostly through being together at Cambridge University. The name of the group is derived from the Bloomsbury section of London where in October 1904 the four just-orphaned children (all in their twenties) of the eminent Victorian man of letters Sir Leslie Stephen—Thoby, Vanessa (later Vanessa Bell), Virginia (later Virginia Woolf), and Adrian—rented 46 Gordon Square and invited Thoby's Cambridge friends to come by and chat on Thursdays. The group was capable of formidable silences, but it also became notorious, contrary to the conventions of middle-class life at that time, for discussing in mixed company sexual questions and in particular their own unconventional lifestyles. Although they were not activists in any modern sense and believed in keeping private life private among themselves, they nevertheless were an important influence in the growing belief that one had the right to follow one's passions where they might lead. And among themselves, such events provided endless opportunity for discussion. The fact that the Stephen children had moved from the family house in fashionable Kensington to respectable but dull Bloomsbury, close to raffish Soho, suggests the somewhat bohemian style of the group's artists, Vanessa Bell and Duncan Grant. As a result, an informal group of artists and intellectuals emerged of varying talents but who made the most important English intellectual contribution during the twentieth century to the European world in four areas: economics, through John Maynard Keynes; literature through Virginia Woolf;

art criticism through Roger Fry; and biography through Lytton Strachey.

The group owed its social origin to the austere hospitality of Vanessa and Virginia. It owed its intellectual origin to the philosophy of G. E. Moore, who, in his *Principia Ethica* (1903), argued that "by far the most valuable things, which we know or can imagine, are certain states of consciousness which can be roughly described as the pleasure of human intercourse and the enjoyment of beautiful objects" (p. 7). This doctrine was preached at the meetings of a famous Cambridge undergraduate society, the Apostles, to which Strachey, Keynes, and Leonard Woolf belonged. As older members, Fry and E. M. Forster sometimes attended their meetings. The undergraduate members shared their ideas with fellow undergraduates who were not members of the society, such as Clive Bell—later a writer on art and popularizer of Fry's idea of "significant form," a concept that favored a more abstract art—and Thoby Stephen, who introduced Bell and Woolf to his sisters, who subsequently became their husbands.

The year 1910 was of particular importance in the life of the group, although its members would not become well known until after World War I. Virginia Woolf wrote in 1924, somewhat tongue in cheek: "on or about December 1910 human character changed" (*Mr. Bennett and Mrs. Brown*, p. 4). She was mainly referring to Roger Fry's London exhibition "Manet and Post-Impressionism," which introduced Paul Gauguin, Vincent van Gogh, and Paul Cézanne to the British public. Vanessa Bell and Duncan Grant were heavily influenced for a while by this style of painting. In a somewhat muted and rather domestic way, modernism, with its belief in getting beneath the surface to the reality of things, began to manifest itself in English intellectual life. Woolf also was referring to the writings of D. H. Lawrence, James Joyce, T. S. Eliot, and herself. In 1910 Woolf began serious work on her first novel, *The Voyage Out* (1915), and E. M. Forster published *Howards End*. In contrast to the Edwardian novelists, such as Arnold Bennett, H. G. Wells, and John Galsworthy, the Bloomsbury writers attempted, much like a painting by Cézanne, to penetrate to the essence of their characters rather than concentrate on mere externals. Fry also attempted to design objects in a modernized Arts and Crafts

The cover of the first edition of Virginia Woolf's novel *The Waves*, designed by Vanessa Bell. BRIDGEMAN ART LIBRARY

tradition with his Bloomsbury colleagues in the Omega Workshop from 1913 to 1919.

Artistic creation marked the first phase of Bloomsbury. But after the war, when the friends met less as a formal group, although they saw much of one another in London and in the countryside in Sussex, they became increasingly important and well known. In 1918 Lytton Strachey published *Eminent Victorians*, composed of short, sharp studies of Florence Nightingale, Thomas Arnold, General Charles Gordon, and Cardinal Henry Manning that, rather than glorifying them, as had happened in their previous Victorian entombments, exposed them as hypocritical figures who had created a world that had brought on World War I. Strachey started a tradition of debunking biographies and was heavily influenced by Sigmund Freud. (His brother, James Strachey, was Freud's

English translator, and Virginia and Leonard Woolf's Hogarth Press was Freud's English publisher.)

Ultimately Virginia Woolf and John Maynard Keynes were the two most distinguished members of the group. Keynes was the greatest English economist of the twentieth century and his ideas were heavily influenced by the Bloomsbury ethos. He represented its sexual variety in his long affair with Duncan Grant and then his marriage to the ballerina Lydia Lopokova. He represented its left-liberal side in his belief in the positive role for government in spending rather than saving money. This became particularly important in shaping the New Deal in the United States. During World War II he spread Bloomsbury's ideas through intense cultural activities for the population, in part to provide a sense of the values the war was being fought for. His idea that the government should be actively involved in the arts led to the founding of the British Arts Council after the war. His early death in 1946 cut short his career. Strachey had died in 1932, Fry in 1934, and Virginia Woolf committed suicide in 1941, depressed by the war but more importantly determined to avoid going mad again.

She undoubtedly is now the most famous member of the group. She and her sister Vanessa were at its center. Between the two world wars she became an increasingly successful novelist, writing in a more and more experimental way, most notably in *The Waves* (1931). She also became more concerned with feminist issues, as in *A Room of One's Own* (1929) and *Three Guineas* (1938). She was a magnificent essayist and her fame has increased through her posthumously published diaries and letters. She perhaps best exemplified the commitment of the group to fight against what they saw as Victorian pretense and humbug, to penetrate below the surface to what might violate ordinary standards of reality but would nevertheless be something "truer," to follow ideas bravely wherever they might lead, not to forgo their middle-class comforts but to work for a better world economically and artistically for others. The members of the Bloomsbury Group were crucial shapers of modernism in the twentieth century.

See also **Keynes, J. M.; Modernism; Woolf, Virginia.**

BIBLIOGRAPHY

Bell, Quentin. *Bloomsbury*. London, 1968.

———. *Virginia Woolf*. London, 1972.

Lee, Hermione. *Virginia Woolf*. London, 1996.

Moore, G. E. *Principia Ethica*. Cambridge, U.K., 1903.

Palmer, Alan, and Veronica Palmer. *Who's Who in Bloomsbury*. Brighton, U.K., 1987.

Richardson, Elizabeth P. *A Bloomsbury Iconography*. Winchester, U.K., 1987.

Rosenbaum, S. P., ed. *The Bloomsbury Group: A Collection of Memoirs, Commentary, and Criticism*. London, 1975.

Shone, Richard. *Bloomsbury Portraits: Vanessa Bell, Duncan Grant, and Their Circle*. New York, 1976.

Skildelsky, Robert. *John Maynard Keynes*. London, 1983–2000.

Spalding, Frances. *Roger Fry, Art and Life*. London and New York, 1980.

Stansky, Peter. *On or About December 1910: Early Bloomsbury and Its Intimate World*. Cambridge, Mass., 1996.

PETER STANSKY

BLUM, LÉON (1872–1950), French politician.

Léon Blum tends to be identified with the "ray of sunshine" of the Popular Front reforms of 1936, which he gallantly cited before the Supreme Court when the Vichy government brought him to trial in 1942. A Socialist and a Jew, this president of the Council of State (Conseil d'État) was despised on both accounts by the far right. He was born in 1872 into a liberal middle-class Jewish family. After a short stint at the École Normale Supérieure (ENS), he switched to law, joining the Council of State in 1895 and then leaving the judiciary for the legislature when he was elected to the Chamber of Deputies in 1919. A sensitive aesthete and something of a dilettante, he meanwhile remained active as the literary and drama critic for *La Revue blanche,* where he rubbed shoulders with members of the avant-garde. His essays include a penetrating analysis of Stendhal (1904) and the audacious "Marriage" (1907).

Like many intellectuals of his generation, Blum entered politics during the Dreyfus affair, and marshaled his legal skills and contacts during the trial of Émile Zola (1840–1902). Attracted to Jean Jaurès's synthesis of idealism and materialism, the Republic and socialism, he joined the party founded by Jaurès (1859–1914) after the Dreyfus affair, collaborated with him in the venture of *L'Humanité,* and participated in the founding congress of the French Section of the Workers' International (SFIO) in 1905.

The war radically changed Blum's priorities. Minister of Public Works Marcel Sembat (1862–1922) called him to serve as executive secretary in his ministry, where Blum remained until 1916, familiarizing himself with the wheels of government. *La Réforme gouvernementale* (The reform of government), published in 1918, advocated strengthening the role and powers of the president of the Council. It predicted his actions in 1936.

A fierce defender of the policy of national defense, Blum assumed the role of Jaurès's successor, theorized a socialism that would also be "a morality, almost a religion," and drafted the Socialist platform for the 1919 elections. As the brains behind the opposition to joining the Communist International, he tirelessly denounced the fundamental heteronomy between Bolshevism and socialism and asserted himself as one of the main forces in setting right the "old house" after the split. The political editor of *Le Populaire,* and deputy from Paris until 1928 and then from Narbonne, Blum emerged as leader of the party officially headed by Paul Faure and put his talent for political synthesis and compromise into the service of party unity, which was being threatened by participationists, supporters of economic planning, neosocialists, and the far-left Bataille socialists.

The fight for the defense of the Republic and liberties led to his involvement, during the general strike of 12 February 1934, in forms of mass action foreign to his background, and into an alliance with the Communists, whom he mistrusted as much as they execrated him. It ended in a victory that allowed him to size up concretely the distinction between "conquest" and "exercise" of power that he had theorized in 1926. In exercising his new responsibilities, he combined his habitual legalism with a bold spirit of innovation whose limits were quickly revealed by the Spanish civil war. Aligning

himself with Great Britain, Blum resigned himself to nonintervention. Having resumed the editorship of *Le Populaire* after the fall of the government, he took the same stance during the Munich crisis, sacrificing his personal convictions to party unity.

Interned by the Vichy regime in 1940, Blum fought his accusers, forcing the suspension of his trial. From prison he laid the groundwork for a clandestine resurrection of the SFIO and forged links with General Charles de Gaulle (1890–1970). After the occupation of the southern zone, he was deported to the fringes of the camp at Buchenwald, where his status as a potential bargaining chip earned him preferential treatment.

For All Mankind, written during his internment, is a kind of manifesto for the democratic socialism that had always inspired him: a humanist socialism detached from Marxism, capable of reconciling Christianity and socialism. But in 1946 (as in 1920), his reformist advocacy of a French-style labor philosophy was at odds with power relations and their exigencies: the Communist Party had become the foremost party in France, de Gaulle's stature gave him considerable weight, and Blum's partisans within the party were soon defeated by Guy Mollet's neo-Marxists. These reverses did not put an end to his political career. In March 1946 he helped negotiate the preliminary loan under the Marshall Plan and, in counterpoint, the much-decried Blum-Byrne accords on the cinema, which liberalized the entry, previously subject to restrictions, of American films into France. President of a short-lived Socialist government in December 1946, and again approached for political office in the fall of 1947, Blum theorized the need for a Third Force between the Communist coalition and Gaullism, whose constitutionalist tendencies he opposed. Blum died in 1950.

See also **France; Socialism.**

BIBLIOGRAPHY

Greilsammer, Ilan. *Léon Blum.* Paris, 1997.

Sadoun, Marc. *De la démocratie française: Essai sur le socialisme.* Paris, 1993.

DANIELLE TARTAKOWSKY

BOBBIO, NORBERTO (1909–2004), Italian philosopher and historian.

The Italian legal philosopher and cultural historian Norberto Bobbio was born in Turin on 18 November 1909 and died on 9 January 2004. The city of Turin, a leading center of culture and politics, played an important part in his development. At Massimo D'Azeglio High School he met the Italian politician Vittorio Foa (b. 1910), the writer and militant antifascist Leone Ginzburg (1909–1944), and the writer Cesare Pavese (1908–1950). Ginzburg was for Bobbio a first exemplar of the "militant intellectual," drawing him toward contemporary Italian culture, particularly that inspired by Bendetto Croce (1866–1952). In 1931 Bobbio took a degree in jurisprudence with Gioele Solari (1872–1952), and in 1933 another in philosophy under the guidance of Annibale Pastore (1868–1956). Thanks to his association with numerous intellectuals, he participated in the founding of the Einaudi publishing house. The intellectual movement of the day centered on the journal *La Cultura* (Culture); in this atmosphere he published his first scientific works on the philosophy of law and German phenomenology, *Aspetti odierni della filosofia giuridica in Germania* (1934; Present-day aspects of legal philosophy in Germany), *L'indirizzo fenomenologico nella filosofia sociale e giuridica*, (1934; The phenomenological trend in social and legal philosophy), and *Scienza e tecnica del diritto* (1934; Science and practice of law).

The activities of the group of intellectuals connected with Einaudi gradually moved from a predominantly cultural sphere to clandestine political undertakings. When in 1935 there came the arrest of the "Giustizia e Libertà" (Justice and liberty) group, and of the circle associated with *La Cultura* at Einaudi, Bobbio was also briefly arrested as a sympathizer. After his release he began to teach, first philosophy of law at the University of Camerino (1935–1938), then at Siena (1938–1940), where he joined the liberal-socialist group founded in 1937 by Guido Calogero and Aldo Capitini (1899–1968), two philosophers at the Scuola Normale Superiore di Pisa. In 1940 he went to Padua, where he taught until 1948.

Returning thence to Turin, he taught philosophy of law in the Faculty of Jurisprudence from 1948 to 1972, and taught political philosophy in the Faculty of Political Science from 1972 to 1979. In 1960 he became a national member of the Turin Academy of Sciences and in 1966 a national member of the Accademia dei Lincei. Beginning in 1965 he was a corresponding associate of the British Academy. He never assumed political responsibilities until he was named senator for life in 1984 by the president of the republic, Sandro Pertini (1896–1990). Beginning in 1935 he was affiliated with the *Rivista di filosofia* (Review of philosophy), of which he became director. He was co-director of the *Rivista internazionale di filosofia del diritto* (International review of philosophy of law), and director of the international journal *Comprendere* (Understanding), an organ of the Societé européene de culture. He was one of the founders of the journal *Reset* in 1993.

With his support for liberal socialism during the years at Padua, his conception of a rapport between politics and culture became apparent. Bobbio undertook an attentive analysis of existential philosophy, particularly of the role it attributes to the philosopher in the face of society and politics, a theme that would be especially dear to him. In the fall of 1942 at Padua Bobbio participated in the foundation of the Partito d'Azione (Action party), the political wing of the Resistance in which "Giustizia e Libertà" and the liberal-socialist movement came together. His meetings at Padua with Antonio Giuriolo and Luigi Cosattini resulted in a critical appraisal of the proposals of Calogero and Capitini regarding the theme of a rapport between socialism and liberalism, and their synthesis in a greater whole. The "ethical" aspiration of socialism with respect to justice, and that of liberalism with regard to liberty, were not considered antithetical. What Bobbio in fact meant by liberalism was a theory according to which the rights of liberty were the necessary (albeit not sufficient) condition for any potential democracy, even in a socialistic form. In this formulation there appear the three poles of Bobbio's cultural outlook: classical liberalism; the tradition of socialist thought, recast by the perspective of Gobetti; and a connection with European philosophical culture.

The decision to abstain from an active political life did not prevent Bobbio from being present and participating: he was, rather, a point of reference in intellectual and political debate for more than forty years. In 1966 he supported the process of unification between socialists and social democrats.

His preferred interlocutor, however, was the PCI (Italian Communist Party), which he sought to discourage from its unquestioning allegiance to the Soviet Union, which he regarded as a totalitarian regime. He supported Eurocommunism in the PCI and, in a debate with Palmiro Togliatti (1893–1964) in the 1950s foresaw its adoption twenty years before the fact. When in 1974 the PCI announced its complete conversion to the principles of Eurocommunism the way was paved for the favorable reception of Bobbio's ideas on democracy and dictatorship, liberalism and Marxism. Seizing this opportunity, Bobbio wrote two key studies in *Mondoperaio*, the theoretical journal of the PSI (Italian Socialist Party), in 1975: the first on the lack of a real Marxist doctrine of the state, and the second on the absence of any alternative to representative democracy as a political framework for a free society. Regarding the history of Marxism and the history of critiques of Marxism, Bobbio stressed that the desire to reconstruct the theoretical agenda that led Marx to his famous political conclusions had been superseded by a tendency to co-opt theoretical principles into simple instruments of political strategy.

BOBBIO'S WORKS

Bobbio was an extremely prolific author, publishing in the fields of law, philosophy, and history. Within the confines of the general theory of law, he applied himself to the criticism of the Enlightenment concept of natural law and to the construction of juridical science as a coherent system: *L'analogia nella logica del diritto* (1938; Analogy in the logic of law), *Scienza del diritto e analisi del linguaggio* (1950; Science of law and analysis of language), *Studi di teoria generale del diritto* (1955; Studies on the general theory of law), *Teoria della norma giuridica* (1958; Theory of the juridical norm), *Teoria dell'ordinamento giuridico* (1960; Theory of juridical organization), *Giusnaturalismo e positivismo giuridico* (1965; Natural law and juridical positivism), *Dalla struttura alla funzione: Nuovi studi di teoria del diritto*

(1977; From structure to function: new studies on the theory of law).

In works dedicated to philosophical problems Bobbio insisted on the necessity of elaborating a satisfactory liberal democratic framework for the exercise of power, and on the independence of intellectuals and culture from political parties: *Politica e cultura* (1955; Politics and culture), *Saggi sulla scienza politica in Italia* (1969; Studies on political science in Italy), *Quale socialismo?* (1976; What socialism), and *Il futuro della democrazia* (1984; The future of democracy).

His ample historical works are devoted to the critical exposition of the contributions of past thinkers, and of several usually overlooked exponents of the positivistic-empirical tradition in nineteenth- and twentieth-century Italian culture, such as Carlo Cattaneo: *La filosofia del decadentismo* (1944; The philosophy of decadence), *Diritto e stato nel pensiero di Kant* (1957; Law and state in the thought of Kant), *Locke e il diritto naturale* (1963; Locke and Natural Law), *Italia civile* (1964; Civil Italy), *Da Hobbes a Marx* (1965; From Hobbes to Marx), *Una filosofia militante: Studi su Carlo Cattaneo* (1971; A militant philosophy: studies on Carlo Cattaneo), *Pareto e il sistema sociale* (1973; Pareto and the social system), *Gramsci e la concezione della società civile* (1976; Gramsci and the concept of the civil society). Along with Nicola Matteucci (b. 1926), he oversaw the *Dizionario di politica* (1976; Political dictionary; a second edition with Gianfranco Pasquino was published in 1983 and republished in 2004).

See also **Eurocommunism; Italy; Togliatti, Palmiro.**

BIBLIOGRAPHY

Bobbio, Norberto. *Old Age and Other Essays*. Translated and edited by Allan Cameron. Cambridge, U.K., 2001. Translation of *De senectute e altri scritti autobiografici*.

———. *A Political Life*. Edited by Alberto Pupuzzi. Translated by Alan Cameron. Cambridge, U.K., 2002.

Greco, Tommaso. *Norberto Bobbio. Un itinerario intellettuale tra filosofia e politica*. Rome, 2000.

Lanfranchi, Enrico. *Un filosofo militante. Politica e cultura nel pensiero di Norberto Bobbio*. Torino, Italy, 1989.

MARIA TERESA GIUSTI

BODY CULTURE.

In twentieth-century Europe, the culture of the body encompassed a whole range of disparate practices. Vegetarian diets and water cures; nudism and body building; sports and gymnastics; aesthetic surgery, cosmetics, and tattooing were just some of the means by which people changed their bodies and refashioned their selves. These cultural practices centered on the human body in order to transform human subjectivity. This is not surprising, because the body was a locus of social meanings on which people projected their cultural anxieties as well as their social aspirations. European body culture reflected, therefore, the social tensions, culture, and politics of the period. Five areas in particular have caught the attention of scholars in the humanities and social sciences: (1) European body culture reinforced mechanisms of social distinction and reflected assumptions about social class. (2) Female bodies and women's physical activities in particular became invested with anxieties about sexuality and gender roles. (3) The state, the medical profession, employers, and physical educators promoted hygiene and physical exercise in order to create a performance-oriented, productive, and disciplined labor force. (4) The representation of idealized or adorned bodies symbolically delineated social or ethnic communities. (5) The cultivation of the human body allowed people to create a sense of self-fulfillment and personal agency.

SOCIAL DISTINCTION AND CLASS

Practices related to the cultivation of the human body have served as means to symbolically reinforce social distinctions. Body culture was part of a discursive arena in which assumptions about social class were negotiated. In early-twentieth-century Germany, for example, the social standing of males was based on their education (*Bildung*) or their property or both. In the 1920s, pursuing specific sports reinforced such distinctions. A contemporary sports guide, for example, claimed that a successful rowing team was a piece of art that could only be formed by people with the same educational and cultural background who shared a spiritual sense of community. Rowers, therefore, were mostly from the educated middle class and rowing

did not contribute to the leveling of social distinctions, as other sports did.

The cultivated body also served as a way to claim social distinction. In the 1920s, the German physical culture propagator Hans Surén claimed that the nude display of physical prowess would easily silence achievers in other areas of life by making them painfully aware of their physical deficiencies. After 1900, cleanliness and beauty care became status symbols for French bourgeois women who could afford bathtubs, cosmetics, and other expensive beauty products. The sociologist Pierre Bourdieu has pointed out the ways in which cultivation of the body (or the lack thereof) in late twentieth-century France contributed to the formation of a class-specific habitus for different social classes.

SEXUALITY AND GENDER ROLES

Sexual anxieties and concerns about changing gender roles influenced European debates about body culture in important ways. For social conservatives, the image of the sexually promiscuous, economically independent, and androgynous "new woman" of the 1920s was the negative counterpart to a morally superior feminine ideal type who rejected urban amusements in favor of healthy living and ultimately motherhood. While the depraved new woman misrepresented herself by falsifying her appearance through fashion, aesthetic surgery, or cosmetics, the wholesome feminine type cultivated her true self by taking care of her body through healthy living and physical exercise. Such attitudes were a reaction against modernist discourses that defended women's sexual liberation, adoption of masculine habits such as smoking, and participation in late-night pleasures.

Women's reproductive health was a major concern in European societies in the early twentieth century and the promotion of physical activity for women was often justified in terms of the reproductive health of the nation. However, no agreement existed about how women were supposed to exercise their bodies. Should they merely cultivate their feminine graces through rhythmic gymnastics—one of the few forms of physical exercise which conservatives considered suitable for women—or should they, like men, condition their bodies for competitive sports? The answer depended on a person's attitudes toward women's role in society. Advocates of women's social, sexual, and economic emancipation were more likely to advocate competitive sports as part of women's body culture. In their view, women who had to balance careers with domestic duties should not be deprived of the performance-enhancing benefits of strenuous physical exercise.

Discussions about the appropriate forms of exercise for women were widespread in interwar Europe. In fascist Italy, for example, women's participation in sporting events was a subject of disagreement. The fascist state had to balance the cultural sensibilities of Italian Catholicism with its own pro-natalist goals in order to promote physical activities that did not compromise maternity as women's central mission in life.

In the second half of the twentieth century, resistance to women's participation in competitive sports slowly dwindled. This could be seen as a reflection of the growing equality of the sexes in European societies. However, the greater media presence of male competitive sports, along with the different earning potentials of male and female athletes in the same disciplines, suggests a slightly more complicated story that deserves greater scholarly attention.

SOCIAL DISCIPLINE

Scholars have also explored the power of medical discourses to regulate social behavior. Since the late nineteenth century, physicians, employers, and the state promoted hygiene and healthy habits as a way to exert some disciplinary power over women and workers. It would be a mistake to reduce early-twentieth-century concerns with healthy living and exercise to the desire of states or employers to have disciplined citizens and a reliable workforce; nevertheless, European authorities expended a great deal of effort to shape the character of citizens and workers by promoting healthy living and exercise.

Although early-twentieth-century debates about women's body culture reflected concerns about women's changing sexual mores and social roles, contemporaries were equally worried about the postwar reintegration of men as productive members of their communities. In most European nations, the human losses caused by World War I prompted concerns about restoring the health and productivity of the nation-state. The rehabilitation of wounded and shell-shocked soldiers was one of the priorities of physicians and psychiatrists, who worried about the burden that a large number of disabled pensioners would pose for social and health insurance systems. Dependent, unproductive men threatened traditional assumptions about the nexus between economic independence, productivity, and masculinity. These concerns focused on the physical performance levels of males as well as their psychological preparedness to lead productive lives.

After World War I, the male body was discovered as an important economic resource. Work physiologists developed systems of sustainable human resource management that tried to enhance the performance potential of human bodies without overtaxing them. By promoting physical exercise and healthy living, physical educators and physicians hoped to promote self-confidence and a performance-oriented habitus characterized by a will to work. Sports and other forms of physical exercise were seen as crucial for the regeneration of European societies. Promoters of exercise argued that physical activities strengthened the general constitution of individuals, rendering them less susceptible to disease. They claimed that exercise had a powerful impact on the character of individuals, who would become more determined and self-conscious. The high-ranking German sports official and acting director of the German University of Physical Exercise (*Deutsche Hochschule für Leibesübungen*) Carl Diem called for a physical education offensive for the general population in order to promote physical health as well as a general mental and physical performance orientation among Germans.

Employers who introduced sports and leisure activities for their workers often had similar motivations. They hoped that company sports would help create a productive and disciplined workforce. Physical fitness in mass organizations and in schools was an important concern for the fascist regimes of the interwar periods. The promotion of physical exercise for the broad mass of the population was an attempt to make the racial people's body (*Volkskörper*) fit for war. In Nazi Germany the SA (Sturmabteilung) sports medal gave millions of

Members of the Czech Sokol sports and fitness organization exercise together at a stadium in Prague, 1955.
©BETTMANN/CORBIS

German males an incentive to work on their individual fitness as a way of increasing the performance potential of the "racial community" as a whole.

ADORNMENT, INCLUSION, AND EXCLUSION

The cultivation, adornment, or mutilation of the body functioned as a mechanism of inclusion or exclusion from racial, social, and subcultural communities. Debates about the meanings of physical fitness and beauty frequently revolved around the construction of ideal physical norms for a community of people. Already in pre–World War I Germany, some physicians and racial anthropologists claimed that human beauty was the expression of a perfect harmony of body, mind, and soul. People of "good heredity" could achieve this

harmony through physical exercise as well as cultivation of the mind. In some cases, such aesthetic assumptions formed the basis of racial theories that considered the white Nordic race the epitome of human perfection. In the interwar years, this line of thought gained credence. The philologist Hans F. K. Günther, for example, racialized the aesthetic preferences of middle class people with humanistic education (*Bildung*) by claiming that members of the Nordic race embodied the beauty ideals of Greek antiquity. Günther's racial physiognomy fed on a long Western tradition that saw in physical characteristics signifiers of psychological traits.

As Sander Gilman has shown, assumptions about the psychological significance of physical stigma (e.g., a certain type of nose signifying particular character traits) were often essential for the construction of racial and sexual "others." Aesthetic surgery found acceptance in the Western world in part because it allowed people to correct stigmatizing physical features, such as large noses, that had become popularly associated with ethnic or racial otherness. They hoped to find social acceptance and happiness by "normalizing" their bodies.

A popular topos in early-twentieth-century Europe was the notion that physical culture eased class conflicts or leveled social distinctions. Before the Nazis took power in Germany, life reformers (propagators of alternative forms of living) promoted nudism as part of several utopian visions of a classless people's community (*Volksgemeinschaft*). According to this line of thinking, nudity guaranteed authenticity. Stripped of expensive clothes and makeup, people presented their true, unadorned selves and external markers of social distinction became unimportant. The selection of a marriage partner would then be based on mutual attraction instead of social considerations. Some nudists hoped that nudism or physical culture would help erase barriers of race, religion, and nationality, as well as social class. Some of them were socialists and hostile to the rising Nazi movement. Others promoted a people's community based on racial principles from which foreigners and Jews were excluded. Such visions anticipated the racial people's community of the Nazi period, in which Jews and other outsiders were systematically ostracized.

In Britain, the notion of sportsmanship became a starting point for the self-definition of British fascists, which they contrasted with an image of the sporting Jew who rejected British notions of fairness and propriety. In Nazi Germany, the members of the racial people's community were expected to strive for physical beauty and perfect health. The representation of ideal beauty and health in medicine, art, and popular culture exacerbated the social stigmatization of people with disabilities that in turn helped justify the mass murder of the disabled from 1939 onward.

In her movie *Olympia*, Leni Riefenstahl idolized the bodies and performances of male elite athletes. Her heroic representations of athleticism have been interpreted as symbolic reinforcement of the racist policies of the Nazi regime, which aimed at the exclusion of racial outsiders. But the heroic celebration of athletic performances was a widespread twentieth-century phenomenon and should not be reduced to the stigmatizing practices of fascist regimes. Body-centered cultural practices served as discursive mechanisms of inclusion and exclusion in many social and political contexts.

Like other ways of adorning the human body, tattooing or branding could fulfill multiple social functions. In nineteenth-century Russia, for example, authorities employed branding as way to control transient and criminal populations. In the twentieth century, Russian and Soviet prisoners appropriated such stigmatizing practices and signaled their elevated status in the prison hierarchy through tattoos. Such practices also allowed people to voice opposition and place themselves symbolically outside the larger respectable community. One scholar has argued that tattooing and piercing might in themselves transgress or negate something central about the kind of person demanded by late capitalist society. By associating themselves with "savage" practices, people reconfigure their identities as authentic, uncommodified, and pure, in opposition to mainstream society and the discipline demanded by the culture.

IDENTITY, AGENCY, AND SELF-FULFILLMENT

Twentieth-century body culture comprised a wide range of practices that promised to reform people's lives. One need only think of the numerous variants of alternative medicine that emerged. In the first half of the century, natural therapists promoted water cures along with dietetic prescriptions for natural living, promising to restore the health of individuals where orthodox medicine had failed. During the late twentieth century, many Europeans appropriated non-European medical practices, such as traditional Chinese medicine or ayurveda, in a search for health and happiness. Others turned to transforming their bodies and selves through bodybuilding and surgery. These variations of body culture can be described, in Nikolas Rose's term, as "technologies of the self" and understood as instruments for the fashioning of identities, self-knowledge, and self-mastery in a modern world that lacks binding value orientations based on traditions.

By transforming their bodies through diet, exercise, bodybuilding, and plastic surgery, people try to transform their selves as if it were "through the body and in the body that personal identity is to be forged and selfhood sustained" (Susan Benson, quoted in Caplan, p. 236). Although some people have transfigured their bodies through plastic surgery in order to pass as "normal" members of their respective communities, for others body work is a way to find self-fulfillment by standing out from the crowd. By working on their bodies, men and women reconfigure their personal experiences as well as their identities. If people see their career trajectories and life chances as the outcome of their own performances and merit, the body becomes the locus for creating a sense of personal agency. Bodybuilding, dieting, and exercising serve as disciplinary regimes through which people try to condition themselves for success in their careers and personal relationships. In the 1920s, the advertisement of a Weimar fitness institute praised bodybuilding as a way to overcome all personal and professional obstacles in life. Physical culture would help people perform better in life in a double sense: If they were healthier, they could improve their job performance by overcoming nervousness and physical weakness. But a beautiful body also improved the performance of men and women who had to further their careers and personal relationships by impressing others with their personal appearance. Both higher physical and mental performance levels and the ability to perform in the symbolic social exchanges of a modern society with a significant division of labor were considered necessary for professional success.

Those who did not find such success could find solace in the writings of another physical culture propagator of the period: Hans Surén urged his male followers to reflect on what it meant to be really successful. Success in competitive sports or in one's profession should not be idolized, because such superficial success was often not fulfilling. Real success had to be found in the personal self-fulfillment that everyone could achieve by cultivating his or her body. Through body culture, people could escape the alienating tendencies of modern urban society and find their true selves in activities that were divorced from the alienating realities of their work environment.

Twentieth-century European societies exhibited a bewildering array of practices aimed at embellishing, manipulating, and improving human bodies, and their meanings are dependent on particular historical, social, and cultural contexts. Contradictory claims, for example, were made for bodybuilding. Cultivating the body could be a path to social distinction or a way to transcend the barriers of social class. It promised self-fulfillment and was a way to condition the body for better physical and mental performance. In short, European body culture expressed the contradictions as well as the utopian promises of Western modernity.

See also **Diet and Nutrition; Fashion; Popular Culture; Public Health; Sexuality.**

BIBLIOGRAPHY

Bourdieu, Pierre. *Distinction: A Social Critique of the Judgment of Taste.* Translated by Richard Nice. Cambridge, Mass., 1984.

Bourke, Joanna. *Dismembering the Male: Men's Bodies, Britain, and the Great War.* Chicago, 1996.

Caplan, Jane, ed. *Written on the Body: The Tattoo in European and American History.* London, 2000.

De Grazia, Victoria. *How Fascism Ruled Women: Italy, 1922–1945.* Berkeley, Calif., 1992.

Felsch, Philipp. "Volkssport. Zur Ökonomie der körperlichen Leistungsprüfung im Nationalsozialismus." *SportZeit* 1, no. 3 (2001): 5–30.

Gilman, Sander. *Making the Body Beautiful: A Cultural History of Aesthetic Surgery.* Princeton, N.J., 1999.

Hau, Michael. *The Cult of Health and Beauty in Germany: A Social History, 1890–1930.* Chicago, 2003.

Rabinbach, Anson. *The Human Motor: Energy, Fatigue, and the Origins of Modernity.* New York, 1990.

Rose, Nikolas S. *Inventing Our Selves: Psychology, Power, and Personhood.* New York, 1996.

Sarasin, Philipp, and Jaboc Tanner, eds. *Physiologie und industrielle Gesellschaft: Studien zur Verwissenschaftlichung des Körpers im 19. und 20. Jahrhundert.* Frankfurt, Germany, 1998.

Spurr, Michael. "'Playing for Fascism': Sportsmanship, Anti-Semitism, and the British Union of Fascists." *Patterns of Prejudice* 37 no. 4 (2003): 359–376.

Stewart, Mary Lynn. *For Health and for Beauty: Physical Culture for Frenchwomen, 1880s–1930s.* Baltimore, 2001.

MICHAEL HAU

BOHR, NIELS (1885–1962), Danish physicist, philosopher, statesman.

Niels Henrik David Bohr, who ranks with Albert Einstein (1879–1955) in the pantheon of modern physics, was the son of Christian Bohr, professor of physiology at the University of Copenhagen, and Ellen Adler Bohr, the daughter of a civic-minded Jewish banker. Bohr was very close to his younger brother Harald (1887–1951) in both study and play. They learned science and mathematics quickly, read philosophy precociously, and, oddly, were very good at football.

When Bohr began to study at the University of Copenhagen in 1903, physics was an attractive subject for minds, like his, that could tolerate ambiguity. Max Planck's novel quantum postulate dates from 1900 and Ernest Rutherford's discovery of the decay of atoms from 1902. Einstein began to publish his revolutionary ideas about relativity and the quantum in 1905. By 1910, when Bohr was at work on his doctoral degree, physicists knew that the foundations of their subject needed repair. Bohr's doctoral thesis (Copenhagen, 1911) uncovered evidence of the failure of what he called "ordinary physics" in the electron theory of metals.

THE QUANTUM THEORY OF THE ATOM

To develop his ideas further, Bohr began a postdoctoral year at the Cavendish Laboratory in Cambridge, England, whose director, Joseph John Thomson (1856–1940), had pioneered the electron theory of metals. Unfortunately Thomson had lost interest in the theory and had no patience for the long discussions Bohr needed to work out his ideas. In the spring of 1912 Bohr moved to Manchester to learn about radioactivity from Rutherford. He soon developed a deep interest in Rutherford's then-new nuclear atom. It appealed to his dialectical turn of mind. In distinction to all atomic models previously proposed, Rutherford's specified that the hydrogen atom had exactly one electron. Its dialectical value for Bohr resided in its radical instability; the lone electron should radiate its energy quickly and fall into the nucleus. Only a nonmechanical constraint could save it. Early in 1913 Bohr found the key to a mathematical expression for this constraint in an empirical rule for the frequencies of spectral lines in hydrogen (the Balmer formula).

Bohr's constraint limited the electron in the hydrogen atom to orbits in which its angular momentum (mass x orbital radius x velocity) equaled an integral multiple n of Planck's quantum h. When n exceeded 1, the electron could jump orbit(s), radiating a "quantum of energy" as a spectral line; when $n = 1$, the electron circulated in the orbit of lowest energy available to it, and the atom achieved the stability required. From this principle and the concession that in the special or "stationary" states ordinary physics held, apart from the constraint on the angular momentum, Bohr could calculate the frequencies of the Balmer lines from "fundamental constants" (h and the charge and mass of the electron) alone. He published this result and other applications of his constraint in 1913.

By the outbreak of World War I, several important physicists including Einstein had conceded that, despite its mixture of incompatibles, Bohr's atom contained some truth. During the war the professor of physics at the University of Munich, Arnold Sommerfeld, extended the scope of Bohr's principles by introducing several quantum numbers besides n. When physicists demobilized, they faced Sommerfeld's large volume, *Atombau und Spektrallinien* (1919), which would guide their attack on elements beyond hydrogen. They soon discovered that Bohr's theory worked well only for hydrogen-like atoms.

PHILOSOPHY AT THE RESEARCH FRONT

In the early 1920s, from the Institute for Theoretical Physics built for him in Copenhagen, Bohr led the effort to devise a "quantum mechanics" that would free the stationary states from ordinary physics. He relied upon a "correspondence principle" to bootstrap his way toward the unknown quantum mechanics. Correspondence required that at certain limits—for example, an electron far distant from its nucleus—quantities like orbital frequency calculated for the stationary states by ordinary physics should be equal, almost, to quantities like radiated frequencies calculated by quantum jumps.

Following this vague indication, Bohr's one-time assistant Werner Heisenberg invented his matrix mechanics in 1925. Shortly thereafter Erwin Schrödinger, following an entirely different path, invented an easier alternative, wave mechanics.

After Max Born had suggested that Schrödinger's wave described the probabilities of outcomes of experiments, Bohr developed his fertile notion of complementarity (1927). According to it, the physicist must apply both wave and particle concepts to subatomic entities to give a full description of physical reality. Evidently both these concepts cannot hold fully and simultaneously. Their mutual limitation is indicated by Heisenberg's uncertainty principle (also 1927), which complementarity subsumes.

Complementarity requires renunciation of the possibility of chronicling the motions of subatomic entities in space and time. Einstein rejected this renunciation as cowardly. His argument with Bohr, conducted with much light and no heat for many years, revealed that complementarity required stranger ideas than even Bohr had entertained. For example, subatomic entities once coupled should retain a memory of their embrace and accomplish spooky actions at a distance. Experiments conducted after the deaths of the protagonists confirmed the prediction.

From about 1930 Bohr applied complementarity to dissolve the problem of free will. He declared that we must use the concepts of freedom and determination to give a complete account of our experience and behavior. No contradiction need be feared, since we only feel free before we act and constrained afterward, and we cannot simultaneously contemplate an action and retrospectively analyze it. Bohr took on materialism/vitalism in the same democratic way.

THE ALL-TOO-REAL WORLD

Bohr's institute was a Mecca for Jewish physicists fleeing fascist regimes until the German occupation of Denmark began in 1940. Bohr remained in Copenhagen until 1943, when his Jewish ancestry put him in grave danger. He fled to Sweden and thence, via the Royal Air Force, to England. He went on to the United States ostensibly to work at Los Alamos on the atomic bomb. He had inferred the possibility of nuclear weapons almost immediately after Lise Meitner and her nephew Robert Frisch invented the concept of nuclear fission in January 1939. Frisch then had a temporary post at Bohr's institute.

Heisenberg also recognized the possibility. It was as head of the German "Uranium Project" that he visited Copenhagen in 1941 in the train of a "cultural mission" to encourage Danish intellectuals to join the German cause. He sought an interview with Bohr during which he may have hinted at the uranium project, asked Bohr's advice about the morality of working on it, pumped him for information, and/or tried to enlist him in a new sort of renunciation. If Bohr used his influence to persuade Allied physicists not to make an atomic bomb, Heisenberg would ensure that German physicists would not make one either. Whatever Heisenberg said in this exchange, which took place during a walk, Bohr returned home very angry.

After the war Bohr wrote but did not send Heisenberg a letter objecting to his reconstruction of their talk as reported in Robert Jungk's bestseller, *Brighter than a Thousand Suns* (1958). According to Jungk, Heisenberg had asked Bohr to join in an effort to suppress work on the bomb, but Bohr, perhaps mistaking his purpose, broke off the conversation. Bohr's unsent reply, in his measured, tedious style, goes little further than stating that his recollections differed from Heisenberg's. However, Bohr's intention to send a copy of the letter to the Danish Foreign Ministry makes plain the cause of his anger. He thought that Heisenberg, convinced that Germany would win the war, was asking him to try to dissuade the Allies from pursuing the one weapon that might save them. Bohr worried that a suspicion of treason (or madness!) might attach to listening to such a crackpot proposal.

Bohr spent most of his time in Britain and the United States talking to senior politicians cleared to know about the Manhattan Project. Bohr argued that the bomb would transform relations among nations as much as the quantum had changed physics. By internationalizing nuclear energy, including nuclear weapons, the United States and Britain could strengthen the prospective United Nations and head off an arms race with the Soviet Union. He managed to obtain one interview each with Winston Churchill and Franklin Delano Roosevelt to explain his ideas. He need not have bothered. Churchill toyed with locking him up as a communist agent. Through Robert Oppenheimer, Bohr's viewpoint resurfaced in the Acheson-Lilienthal plan, but it too failed. Bohr's last major effort to bring East and West together over the atom was an open letter addressed to the United Nations in 1950. It could not help but fall dead as the Korean War opened and the Cold War deepened.

Bohr received innumerable honors, including the Nobel Prize for physics in 1922. From 1932 until his death he occupied the villa left by the founder of the Carlsberg brewery as accommodation for the greatest living Dane. His death was mourned with trappings usually reserved for royalty.

See also **Einstein, Albert; Science.**

BIBLIOGRAPHY

Primary Sources

Bohr, Niels. *Collected Works.* Edited by Léon Rosenfeld. Amsterdam, 1972–1999. Ten volumes to date; includes correspondence and authoritative essays on Bohr's work.

Secondary Sources

Aaserud, Finn. *Redirecting Science: Niels Bohr, Philanthropy, and the Rise of Nuclear Physics.* Cambridge, U.K., 1990.

French, Anthony P., and P. J. Kennedy, eds. *Niels Bohr: A Centenary Volume.* Cambridge, U.K., 1985. Contains articles by historians, philosophers, and physicists.

Murdoch, Dugald. *Niels Bohr's Philosophy of Physics.* Cambridge, U.K., 1987.

Pais, Abraham. *Niels Bohr's Times, in Physics, Philosophy, and Polity.* Oxford, U.K., 1991. The reigning biography, by a Dutch-American physicist who knew Bohr and the Danish cultural scene.

Rozental, Stefan, ed. *Niels Bohr: His Life and Work as Seen by His Friends and Colleagues.* Amsterdam, 1967.

J. L. Heilbron

BOLSHEVIK REVOLUTION. *See* **Russian Revolutions of 1917.**

BOLSHEVISM. In ideological terms, bolshevism, or Soviet communism, was instituted in Russia after the Bolshevik Party, led by Vladimir Ilyich Lenin, took power in October 1917, an event that came to be known inside Soviet Russia as the Great October Socialist Revolution. It was shaped by a number of factors: belief in the unalterable laws of Marxist economic and social development; antipathy toward the reformist and syndicalist socialism prevalent in Europe in the late nineteenth and early twentieth centuries; the seeming paradox of instituting a Marxist, proletarian revolution in a country without a sizable proletariat of long standing; the vicious context of Russia's civil war between 1918 and 1920; and the perception among leading Bolsheviks that Soviet Russia was encircled by hostile powers bent on their destruction. Bolshevism aspired ultimately to the creation of a "new Soviet man," someone whose life was defined not by the selfish pursuit of personal gain but by collectivist sentiments and aspirations within a modern, mechanistically run and technologically advanced society. It was a militant and iconoclastic ideology that argued for a sharp, violent, and irrevocable break with the past. Its millenarian and internationalist aspirations brought it the admiration and support of many outside of Soviet Russia. In its implacable and violent aspects, and in the avowed irrevocability of its revolutionary transformation, many others saw the seeds of the terroristic policies of Joseph Stalin during and after the 1930s. Still others regarded it less as a coherent ideology per se than as a cynical justification for naked political maneuvering by a small clique of revolutionaries with few real ties to the masses.

In organizational terms bolshevism was synonymous with both the Bolshevik Party, which developed from a faction of the Russian Social Democratic Labor Party (RSDLP), and with the figure of Lenin. In a treatise entitled *What Is to Be Done?* Lenin had argued in 1902 that the RSDLP should be led by an elite group of conspiratorial, professional revolutionaries who would be able to organize and educate the broader masses and thereby foment revolution in Russia. At the Second Congress of the RSDLP in Brussels and London in 1903, he triggered a split in the party over this issue with those socialists, led by Yuli Martov, who argued for a more inclusive policy of open membership on the model of the mass Social Democratic parties of western Europe. Lenin's faction became known as the Bolsheviks (Majority

Group), while his opponents became known as the Mensheviks (Minority Group). Despite persistent and serious efforts by many prominent Russian socialists, including Martov, Fyodor Dan, Georgy Plekhanov, Leon Trotsky, and Pavel Axelrod, to bring the factions together and reunite the RSDLP, Lenin consolidated his faction at a conference of his supporters in Prague in January 1912. Much has been made of Lenin's personal role in forging this faction and, later, in persuading and cajoling his fellow Bolsheviks to take power in October 1917, despite the belief among many of them that Russia was not yet politically mature enough for a socialist revolution.

In cultural terms bolshevism signified the longer-term process of revolutionary transformation that followed the party's takeover in October 1917. The goal of this process was that all citizens of Soviet Russia would ultimately articulate their interests and aspirations, indeed their very identities, within a communist worldview. Guided by the Bolshevik Party, renamed the All-Russian Communist Party (bolsheviks) [VKP(b)] in early 1918, this transformation involved mass campaigns to bring electricity to Russia's rural interior and literacy to its largely uneducated masses. It included campaigns against the relics of the old order, notably religion, using methods ranging from propaganda campaigns to outright persecution of the clergy. It also attempted to create its own secular sacred, including efforts through such organizations as the Proletarian Culture movement (Proletkult) and the constructivist movement in the 1920s to create a new proletarian art and literature accessible to all and beneficial to the new socioeconomic revolution. These efforts eventually gave way in the 1930s to more extreme efforts to break the prerevolutionary modes of production and social relationships through forced collectivization of agriculture, dekulakization, and rapid industrialization.

Variations of bolshevism included millenarian bolshevism and national bolshevism. Millenarian bolshevism aspired to make a new religion of communism with man in the place of God. It was championed by Alexander Bogdanov and Anatoly Lunacharsky, who became known as the God builders (bogostroiteli), and elicited a sharp critique from Lenin in his *Materialism and Empirio-*

Criticism, published in 1909. National bolshevism applied to Soviet Russia's efforts during the 1930s—in preparation for the coming Second World War—to resurrect aspects of Russia's prerevolutionary national past at the expense of the prevailing emphasis on class consciousness and proletarian internationalism.

See also **Bukharin, Nikolai; Communism; Lenin, Vladimir; Russian Revolutions of 1917; Trotsky, Leon.**

BIBLIOGRAPHY

Primary Sources

Kara-Murza, A. A., and L. V. Poliakov, eds. *Russkie o bol'shevizme.* St. Petersburg, 1999.

Secondary Sources

Brandenberger, David. *National Bolshevism: Stalinist Mass Culture and the Formation of Modern Russian National Identity, 1931–1956.* Cambridge, Mass., 2002.

Burbank, Jane. *Intelligentsia and Revolution: Russian Views of Bolshevism, 1917–1922.* Oxford, U.K., 1986.

Fueloep-Miller, René. *The Mind and Face of Bolshevism: An Examination of Cultural Life in Soviet Russia.* New York, 1965.

Gleason, Abbott, Peter Kenez, and Richard Stites, eds. *Bolshevik Culture. Experiment and Order in the Russian Revolution.* Bloomington, Ind., 1985.

Haimson, Leopold H. *The Russian Marxists and the Origins of Bolshevism.* Cambridge, Mass., 1967.

Rowley, David G. *Millenarian Bolshevism, 1900 to 1920.* New York and London, 1987.

FREDERICK C. CORNEY

BONHOEFFER, DIETRICH (1906–1945), German theologian.

If anyone symbolized the struggle against the moral bankruptcy of the German people under the Nazis, it was Dietrich Bonhoeffer. As a Lutheran clergyman, he represented a theological tradition steeped in a culture of respect for secular authorities. As a pacifist, he ruled himself out of direct action in political life. And yet he managed to break all these conventions and join a conspiracy to assassinate Adolf Hitler in July 1944. The failure of that plot led to his arrest and execution a few days before the end of the war.

Bonhoeffer was born to a prominent professional family in the eastern German town of Breslau, now in Poland. His father was a distinguished psychiatrist. Dietrich studied theology, first in Tubingen and then in Berlin, where he completed the two doctoral dissertations needed to qualify for a professorship in German universities. After this period of study, he went to the Union Theological Seminary in New York, and found an entirely different world of spirituality a few blocks to the east in Harlem. He returned to Berlin and taught theology until 1933. The Nazis terminated his employment at the University of Berlin in 1936.

Bonhoeffer was ordained a Lutheran pastor in 1931 and spent his early years in the ministry in part in Berlin and in part in London, where he formed a lifelong friendship with George Bell, bishop of Chichester. In 1936, on his return to Germany, he participated in the work of the Confessional Church, a movement of Lutherans opposed to the Nazis on moral and religious grounds. Bonhoeffer worked with Lutheran clergymen in a theological seminary on the Baltic Sea, later relocated to Finkenwlade in Pomerania.

Bonhoeffer was unique not simply in opposing the Nazis but in turning again and again to the Jewish question. This preoccupation was not his choice. In the 1930s the Jewish problem was simply not a significant matter for him and his family until the Nazis made it so. Their ties with liberal, assimilated Jews were numerous and deep. Among his dearest friends was Franz Hildebrand, a Lutheran pastor whose mother was a Jew. The vulgarity of the Nazi movement was simply from another world. When Hitler came to power in 1933, they were all forced to think about the Jews again.

In 1933, as the machinery of anti-Semitic persecution was being assembled by the new regime, Bonhoeffer wrote an essay titled "The Church and the Jewish Question." At issue were the "Aryan clauses" barring from the Lutheran ministry in Prussia anyone who had been born a Jew and had converted to Christianity. This Bonhoeffer could not accept. He traversed some familiar terrain in the Lutheran tradition as to the limits the church accepts in its critique of the laws of the state, and then threw down the gauntlet. The church has three roles to play at such times: first, it "can ask the state whether its actions are legitimate" in promoting law and order rather than lawlessness; second, "it can aid the victims of state action"; third, it may be moved "not just to bandage the victims under the wheel, but to put a spoke in the wheel itself" (Godsey and Kelly, p. 71).

The context here is the question of the relevance of race to faith, and for this reason Bonhoeffer returned to the writings of Luther to show the absurdity of a Lutheran Church banning converted Jews from acts of Christian worship. In his *Table Talk*, Luther had written that the Jews "nailed the redeemer of the world to the cross" and therefore bore "the curse for its action through a long history of suffering. But the history of the suffering of this people, loved and punished by God, stands under the sign of the final homecoming of the people of Israel to its God. And this homecoming happens in the conversion of Israel to Christ."

Here Bonhoeffer is on conventional grounds as a Lutheran. He is still focusing on converted Jews, rather than on Jews as fellow human beings. That shift happened soon enough. The seeds of this ecumenical position were there in 1933, when in rejecting the Aryan clauses, Bonhoeffer wrote "The people of Israel will remain the people of God, in eternity, the only people who will not perish" (1965, pp. 225–226).

From 1933 on, Bonhoeffer more and more placed the Jewish question at the forefront of his antiregime activities and his Christian teachings. And as time went on, it became apparent that for a Christian, the mission to the Jews was no longer to try to convert them but to share the misery of their predicament. In 1935 the Nazis promulgated the Nuremberg laws, statutes of racial difference. Stupefied that the German churches offered no protest over this set of measures, Bonhoeffer penned this challenge: "Only he who cries out for the Jews may sing Gregorian chants" (Godsey and Kelly, p. 71).

His position as a prominent clergyman with a wide circle of friends both in Britain and abroad suited him perfectly for work as a liaison between the German resistance to Hitler and the Allies. His cover was that he was pursuing such contacts at the instruction of Admiral Wilhelm Canaris, the head of German intelligence. Canaris was part of the conspiracy to assassinate Hitler. When the plot failed in July 1944, these ties were exposed.

Bonhoeffer was sentenced to death. Before his execution on 9 April 1945, he wrote some of his most daring and influential theology, pointing to a doctrineless Christianity and toward a faith in redemption despite the horrors through which he lived. More than his writings, his courage and his ability to stare death in the face make him one of the towering moral figures of the twentieth century.

See also **Antifascism; Germany; July 20th Plot; Nazism.**

BIBLIOGRAPHY

Bethke, Eberhard. *Dietrich Bonhoeffer: Theologian, Christian, Contemporary.* Translated by Eric Mosbacher. London, 1970.

Bonhoeffer, Dietrich. *No Rusty Swords: Letters, Lectures, and Notes, 1928–1936.* Edited and translated by Edwin H. Robertson and John Bowden. London, 1965.

———. *Letters and Papers from Prison.* Edited by Eberhard Bethge. New York, 1971.

———. *Writings.* Selected with an introduction by Robert Coles. Maryknoll, New York, 1998.

Godsey, John D., and Geffrey B. Kelly, eds. *Ethical Responsibility: Bonhoeffer's Legacy to the Churches.* New York, 1982.

Mengus, Raymond. "Dietrich Bonhoeffer and the Decision to Resist." *Journal of Modern History* 64 (1992): 134–146.

JAY WINTER

BORMANN, MARTIN (1900–1945?), German Nazi leader.

Martin Bormann was born on 17 June 1900 in Halberstadt, a small town east of Göttingen, into a family of lower-echelon civil servants. Orphaned at a very young age, he received a secondary education and performed his military service, after which he went on to study agronomy. As early as 1920–1921, he joined the right-wing Völkische movement, where he supported the most virulently anti-Semitic elements. Before long, giving up all vocational ambitions, he dedicated himself full-time to the most militarized and violent tendencies

of the radical Far Right as an executive manager of the veterans' association of the Rossbach Freikorps. Alongside Rudolf Franz Höss, future commandant of the Auschwitz concentration camp, he committed a political murder for which the two men were sentenced in 1924 to a year's imprisonment. Upon his release Bormann made the acquaintance of Ernst Röhm and joined the organization, the Sturmabteilung (SA), that Röhm had created as a stand-in for the National Socialist German Workers Party (NSDAP) after it was banned in the wake of the November 1923 Munich Putsch, led by Adolf Hitler (1889–1945).

Thus when the NSDAP was legalized in 1927, Bormann entered it as a professional political leader and an activist quite prepared to kill if need be. He served at first in his native Thuringia as regional press officer and business administrator. He was attached to the SA's Supreme Command from 1928, worked at Röhm's headquarters, and ran the NSDAP's endowment fund. Henceforward Bormann was a party leader, though less in the political realm than as an administrator; daily paperwork was his preferred sphere of influence. He also built up solid bonds of kinship in Nazi circles, as witness his marriage to the daughter of the party's supreme judge, Walter Buch, with Hitler as best man at the wedding. In July 1933 he became an NSDAP Reichsleiter, the highest rank in the party hierarchy, and a close advisor to Deputy Führer Rudolf Hess. In that same year he was elected to the Reichstag, and before long he was entrusted with the management of the private assets of the führer and chancellor. Between 1933 and 1941, although he was just one of many leaders of the NSDAP and the burgeoning Nazi regime, he was able to carve out a unique place for himself within the (equally unique) state apparatus of the Third Reich.

As Rudolf Hess's right-hand man, Bormann enjoyed direct daily access to the führer from 1933 onward. It is now well understood by historians that the Nazi state apparatus, though it certainly placed the dictator at the center of the decision-making process, also modified that process in a unique way in that the traditional institutions of government were rapidly sidelined through the creation of new, often highly specialized departments vigorously competing among themselves. This was the context in which the day-to-day operations of the chancellery became immensely important. All open files, those awaiting Hitler's signature, were arranged according to priority by the chancellery, a process that determined not only the order of business for the highest authority but also, and more significantly, the role and place of every Nazi institution and every Nazi leader. Even Hess himself, the deputy führer, was marginalized as Bormann gradually made himself the sole master of the paper reaching Hitler, thereby making him indispensable in the führer's eyes. By the time Hess undertook the dangerous journey that was to take him to Great Britain in 1941, Martin Bormann was the sole gatekeeper controlling access to Hitler. His role in the hierarchy of the Third Reich grew ever more important, and thanks to his "chancellery of the party" he came to control the whole NSDAP without ever holding sway, as a Heinrich Himmler or Hermann Goering did, over some particular sector that was strategic from the party's point of view. He protected Hitler from administrative tasks while successfully controlling the distribution of power and the bestowing of the führer's approval throughout the Reich.

The image Bormann projected was that of a stone-faced bureaucrat—brusque, efficient, and unwaveringly loyal to Hitler. There is no doubt that Bormann was an anti-Semite from an early age and a lifelong party loyalist. His undeviating commitment to the NSDAP was rivaled only by his anticlericalism, which led him, beginning in 1942, to champion the brutal repression of the Catholic Church. Like other Nazi chieftains, Bormann proved a fervent last-ditcher as the war's end approached, feeding the self-destructive impulse that took hold of the führer in the final weeks of hostilities. He was a prime mover of the *Volkssturm,* the Nazis' forced call-up, begun in 1944, of all undrafted German males, young and old alike. And he remained by his master's side until the moment of Hitler's suicide. Bormann himself was killed to the north of the chancellery on the second or third of May 1945 as he sought to cross the Russian lines. His demise was not confirmed, however, until his remains were identified in 1973, and his fate was at first such a mystery that he was judged and condemned to death in absentia at Nuremberg. For this reason, no doubt, this faceless administrator, so underestimated by his contemporaries, gained enormous notoriety in the postwar years, as all kinds of legends grew up concerning his alleged survival.

See also **Hess, Rudolf; Hitler, Adolf; Nazism.**

BIBLIOGRAPHY

Kilzer, Louis C. *Hitler's Traitor: Martin Bormann and the Defeat of the Reich.* Novato, Calif., 2000.

Longerich, Peter. *Hitlers Stellvertreter: Führung der Partei und Kontrolle des Staatsapparates durch den Stab Hess und die Parteikanzlei Bormann.* Munich, 1992.

CHRISTIAN INGRAO

BOSNIA-HERZEGOVINA.

BOSNIA-HERZEGOVINA. For a long time Bosnia was the extreme western point of the Ottoman Empire, on the European side. The Muslim population was larger there than anywhere else in the Balkans (38.8 percent in 1879). The Muslims lived side by side with Christians, Orthodox Christians (42.9 percent), and Catholics (18 percent). Religious communities in the Ottoman system were strongly differentiated and judicially unequal. After a long process that ended during the nineteenth century the Orthodox Christians came to identify themselves as "Serbs" and the Catholics as "Croats." They considered themselves different peoples. But the entire population was Slavic and spoke the same language, usually called "Serbo-Croatian."

In 1878 the country (from then on named Bosnia-Herzegovina, Herzegovina being the southern part) passed under the rule of another, equally multinational empire: Austria-Hungary, which first occupied it and then annexed it in 1908. The Austrian power respected the already existing religious diversity and social structure: an aristocracy made up of Muslim landowners; peasants of all three religions; and in the cities, Muslim artisans and merchants, but also a strong Orthodox mercantile presence; and, all over, the heavy influence of the various churches. However, some Muslims migrated to Turkey after 1878 and Catholic merchants and civil servants came to settle in Bosnia-Herzegovina from other parts of the Austro-Hungarian Empire (mostly from Croatia).

Politically, Bosnia-Herzegovina was Reichsland (land of the empire), indivisible between the two parts of the empire, Austria and Hungary, and administered by a common Austro-Hungarian minister of finances.

The empire tried hard to encourage a Bosnian identity and to oppose the demands of the Croats and the Serbs. The former wanted the union of the province with Croatia, which would have replaced the dual structure (Austro-Hungarian) with a triple one (Austro-Hungaro-Croatian), a solution that was flatly refused by the Hungarians. The Serbs, the largest of the three populations, wanted to be annexed to Serbia, a country then very hostile to Austria.

The Austro-Hungarian administration tried as best it could to play up the rivalry between these three local populations. It handled the Muslims with care, respecting their customs and moderating the attempts at conversion made by some Catholic clerics. In doing this the administration sought to rely on an alliance between the Muslims and the Croats to counter the ambitions of the Serbs.

The Austrian government launched a campaign of modernization in what was then a very backward province: railway systems were built, mining and processing industries were developed, and new European-looking neighborhoods were built in the cities. A real administration was created, schools opened, and students were trained in Austrian universities. This modernization allowed for the appearance of associations, political movements, and publications that expressed opinions reflecting, among other things, the divisions among the three ethnic groups. The Landtag (provincial parliament), despite its limited power, operated as a true legislature with parties representing each of the three groups.

Simultaneously, however, more radical political movements developed as well, such as Mlada Bosna (Young Bosnia), which rejected foreign power and wanted either the unification of Serbia or the creation of a large South Slavic state, or "Yugoslavia." The group was made up mostly of young Serbs, but also included a few Croats. They were encouraged by Serbia's victory in the Balkan Wars (1912–1913), and were heavily repressed by the Austrian authorities. Some activists of Young Bosnia were in

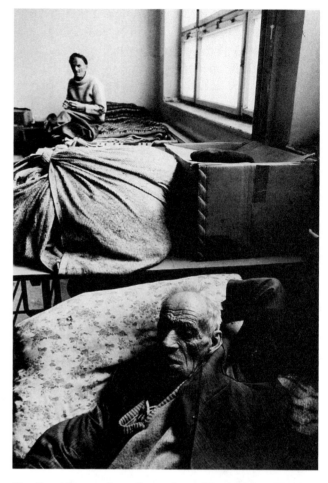

Muslim refugees from Gorazde and Srebrenica, Bosnia, separated from their families, wait for relocation at a sports center in Tuzla, 1994. ©CHRIS RAINIER/CORBIS

contact with a secret Serb terrorist organization called "The Black Hand."

Archduke and heir Francis Ferdinand's (1863–1914) visit to Sarajevo on 28 June 1914 was meant to symbolize Austria's intention to keep Bosnia-Herzegovina in the empire. Activists of Young Bosnia lay in wait, however, and one of them, the very young Gavrilo Princip (1894–1918), shot and killed the archduke.

Locally, the incident provoked violent reactions by both Muslim and Croat mobs against the Serbs. Externally, it engendered the Austro-Serbian and international crisis that led to World War I.

WORLD WAR I
At the beginning of the war, although Serbia was much weaker than Austria, the Serbian army

advanced into eastern Bosnia almost up to Sarajevo. But in November 1914 it was pushed back and during 1915 the Austro-German army occupied all of Serbia. From then on Bosnia was far from the theater of operations. It was affected only by the massive arrests of individuals suspected of being pro-Serbian and by the heavy losses of soldiers fighting on all the battlefronts in the Austrian army.

In 1918 the first Austro-Hungarian defeats strengthened those, even within the Muslim and Croat populations, in favor of a "Yugoslav" solution in Bosnia. On 5 October 1918, after the liberation of Serbia by Serbian and Allied troops, Bosnian delegates participated in the "Council of Slovenes, Croats, and Serbs" in Zagreb. This council proclaimed an independent state reuniting all Southern Slavs who had been until then under the rule of the Habsburgs. The Council also immediately began negotiations to unite the newly created state with Serbia. From then on Bosnian communities with Serb majorities proclaimed their incorporation into Serbia and called on the Serbian army to maintain order. On 1 December 1918 an agreement was signed in Belgrade unifying Serbia and the "State of Slovenes, Croats, and Serbs" under the Karadjordjević dynasty to form the "Kingdom of Serbs, Croats, and Slovenes," later called "Yugoslavia."

MONARCHICAL YUGOSLAVIA

The new kingdom emerged from the Serbian victory and the Serbs therefore became the dominant people. The constitution approved in 1921 was not federal, as the Croats had desired, but was strongly unitarian. Bosnia was no longer a distinct administrative unit.

The land issue was first to come up after the war. Serb farmers working on Muslim-owned lands wanted to take them over. Violence ensued, and many Muslims escaped to Turkey in self-exile. The governing power had promised agrarian reform. The reform it promulgated in 1919 was regarded by the Muslims as a despoilment but it still provided compensation for landowners. The troubles ceased.

Suffrage would henceforward be universal and no longer based on poll tax, as it had been under Austrian rule. Muslims voted in droves for the newly formed "Yugoslavian Muslim Organization" led by

Mehmed Spaho (1883–1939). The royal government needed Muslim voices (and Slovene voices) to counter Croat opposition. Spaho participated in most of the governments under the monarchy, from the constitutional regime of the 1920s to the royal dictatorship established in 1929.

Bosnia enjoyed a period of peace. Lifestyles and dress codes became more European-looking (more quickly in the Christian population than among Muslims) but the economy remained stagnant. However, the government faced a strong Croat opposition. In 1939 Prince-Regent Paul (1893–1976) sought to resolve the matter by creating a "*banovina* [autonomous region] of Croatia," with large powers. In Bosnia the limits of the banovina were traced according to the numerical predominance of either Serbs or Croats in each locality, but without counting the Muslims. Thus was Bosnia divided for the first time. But this regime only lasted for two years: in April 1941 Adolf Hitler's (1889–1945) troops invaded Yugoslavia, whose army collapsed in only a few days.

WORLD WAR II

By decision of the occupying powers, Yugoslavia was divided. All of Bosnia, together with Croatia proper, was subsumed into the "Independent State of Croatia," governed by the *poglavnik* (führer) Ante Pavelić (1889–1959) and his movement the Ustaše (Insurgent), which became the sole authorized party. In this regime Catholics and Muslims were considered "Croats." Serbs, along with Jews and Gypsies, were deemed undesirable and were the victims of mass killings from very early on, either in their villages or later in concentration camps. The numbers of victims of these massacres were often inflated by Serb writers and minimized on the Croatian side. Today's best documented demographic research estimates that approximately one hundred fifty thousand Serbs were killed in Bosnia between 1941 and 1945, and just as many in Croatia (the numbers include all war-related deaths, not only the massacres).

It is no surprise that these acts of violence were answered by armed resistance, first on the part of the Serbs. The rebels were divided into two opposing factions: in eastern and southeastern Bosnia near Serbia and Montenegro, the Chetniks, a Serb nationalist and monarchist movement under the leadership of General Dragoljub Mihajlović (1893–1946) (at least, theoretically) remained loyal to the government exiled in London. The northwest, in contrast, was home mostly to Communist partisans led by Josip Broz (1892–1980), known as Tito, a Croat himself, who stayed in Bosnia for almost the entire duration of the war. The Chetniks engaged in numerous massacres, mostly against Muslims (seventy-five thousand Muslims were killed in Bosnia during the war), but also against Croats. The partisans promoted a policy of openness to all ethnic groups. As the war dragged on and the people's discontentment with the occupiers grew, this openness enabled the partisans to recruit a great many Muslims and Croats for whom they were the only alternative.

Bosnia therefore became the main stage of a triangular war. The Chetniks fought more often against the partisans than against the Germans, and openly collaborated with the Italians. Partisan resistance was much more active militarily. In March 1943 Tito also sought to negotiate with the Germans, but Hitler refused.

In the end, the partisans could pull together many more men and cause many more enemy casualties. They salvaged all the weapons that the Italians had left behind after they capitulated in September 1943, and they had the support of England and America. In October 1944 the Soviet army liberated Serbia. It was therefore Tito who took power over all of Yugoslavia.

COMMUNIST YUGOSLAVIA

As early as 1943 the Antifascist Council for the National Liberation of Yugoslavia meeting at Jajce, Bosnia, had already determined the future organization of the country: it had to be a federal and not an unitarian state, as it had been during the monarchy, and the diversity of its peoples had to be acknowledged. Bosnia-Herzegovina became one of six federated republics and regained its pre-1918 borders. Two peoples were recognized: Serbs and Croats. Muslims had the right to declare themselves as "nationally undetermined," which most of them did. Much later, in 1968, they were recognized as an individual people, called Muslims (with a capital "M," while muslim without the capital referred to the religion). Therefore, Bosnia officially had three peoples.

This recognition of the Muslims as a distinct people (as had been done with Macedonians and Montenegrins twenty-five years earlier) was an answer to the need to develop multiple partnerships within the federation and to avoid confrontation between the two "great" peoples: Serbs and Croats. It also served the state's foreign policy as Yugoslavia became closer with Muslim countries in the framework of the nonaligned countries movement. At the same time, Muslim Bosnian intellectuals celebrated Bosnia's history and traditions, creating nationalist myths that were parallel to those established a century before by Serbs and Croats. Religious Muslim political movements also began appearing, inspired by those in other Islamic countries. Due to diverse migratory currents, it was also during these years that the Muslim population (39.6 percent) outnumbered for the first time the Serb (37.2 percent) and Croat (20.6 percent) populations (according to the 1971 census).

After the fall in 1966 of Serb centralist minister Aleksandar Ranković (1909–1982), Tito started paying greater attention to national characteristics. In 1974 a new constitution implemented a quasi-confederate regime in which each republic was given very large powers. During the whole of the communist regime Bosnia was peaceful and fully enjoyed the progress taking place across the country: universal schooling, improvements in all means of communication, creation of industries, and a higher quality of life. Nevertheless, the gap between it and the northern and more prosperous republics (Serbia, Slovenia, Croatia) continued to grow. Bosnia was an underdeveloped republic that received federal aid. It was politically backward as well: unlike those that broke out in Zagreb in 1971 and Belgrade in 1972, there was no opposition movement in Bosnia in the 1970s. It remained a conservative republic with a particularly inefficient self-management system and very powerful oligarchies. In 1987 the country was shaken by a management scandal involving (Muslim) top executives at Agrokomerc, an agribusiness firm.

THE IMPLOSION

After 1985, Bosnia, along with other Serb-populated areas, saw a rise in Serb nationalist sentiments that collided with an ever-more-present Muslim

400

Aerial photograph showing the location of mass graves in Nova Kasaba, Bosnia, 1995. The bodies are some of an estimated 7800 Muslims killed by Serbian security forces in Srebrenica in July of 1995. ©Corbis Sygma

and Croatian opposition. At the beginning of 1990, when a multiple-party system had been authorized, noncommunist nationalist parties began to form in each of the three communities. These parties went on to win the first free elections in December 1990. They stayed united and shared power. Alija Izetbegović (1925–2003), leader of the Muslim Party of Democratic Action, was unanimously elected president of Bosnia-Herzegovina.

When the crisis worsened in 1991 Bosnia and Macedonia proposed a plan for an "asymmetrical confederation" intended to reconcile the opposing Serb and Croat factions. The plan failed. During the Croatian War despite a few local incidents, Bosnia was never directly affected by military operations. It served only as a remote base for the federal army.

But when Slovenia and Croatia became independent the balance in Yugoslavia shifted. In the truncated federation, the Serbs had an overwhelming preponderance. The Muslim and Croat populations (the majority in Bosnia when put together) could not accept this. On 15 October 1991, the Bosnian parliament, in spite of the opposition of its Serb members, declared Bosnia-Herzegovina's sovereignty. Bosnia's Serbs and their leader, Radovan Karadžić (b. 1945), opposed the decision. They had begun to establish "Autonomous Serb Regions" in the spring of 1991, and in January 1992, they proclaimed a "Serb Republic of Bosnia-Herzegovina" (later called "Republika Srpska"), that would be separate from Bosnia, should Bosnia separate from Yugoslavia. The international community demanded a referendum for Bosnia's independence, which took place on 1 March 1992. The Serbs boycotted the vote. The voters almost unanimously chose independence for Bosnia, which was internationally recognized on 6 and 7 April. War immediately broke out.

THE WAR

The Serbs wanted to include as much territory as possible in the state they had proclaimed. They prepared for this by organizing their party efficiently with the full support of the Yugoslav army. Rather quickly, they managed to establish control over about two-thirds of Bosnia-Herzegovina: all of the north, and all of the east. They sought to eliminate all non-Serb people from these regions: this was called *ethnic cleansing,* complete with massacres, rapes, looting, prisoner camps, and the destruction of places of worship. The majority of these operations took place between April and December 1992. Sarajevo, the capital city, resisted, but it was completely surrounded, besieged, and bombarded for more than three years (April 1992–October 1995).

Armed groups started to organize in the rest of the country also: the Croatian Defense Council, which formed quickly and had the full support of the Croatian army, and, later, the Army of Bosnia-Herzegovina, which supported President Izetbegović and was mostly made up of Muslims. In the territories that these forces controlled, similar violence was exercised against Serbs.

The international community intervened from the very beginning of the conflict. But the United Nations peacekeeping troops were sent on humanitarian missions to relieve the population's suffering, not to stop the war. A series of international peace talks ensued, where, each time, a new plan for the division of Bosnia was proposed to representatives of each of the three communities. And each in turn rejected the plan (the Serbs, twice; the Muslims, once), and nothing was done to impose and enforce it. But the very idea of sharing the country was being legitimized by these talks.

Eventually, relations between Croats and Muslims deteriorated as well, following the same logic that caused the partition of Yugoslavia and then of Bosnia. There were twice as many Muslims as there were Croats, who feared the Muslims would dominate them, although they had a stronger army, at least at the beginning. Basing their actions on the partition plans designed by the UN, the Croats began appropriating certain regions and expulsing not only the army, but also the Muslims that lived there. The Muslims resisted, then took the offensive. This new war lasted for all of 1993 and became particularly violent with mutual massacres, camp imprisonment, the destruction of monuments, and expulsions. The Croatian army destroyed half of the city of Mostar and its famous bridge. It was a war where "everyone was against everyone." From time to time Serb and Croat forces would secretly connive as a result of meetings between their political leaders.

However, starting in 1994 (the second year of Bill Clinton's presidency in the United States), the West became more active. The United States forced Muslim and Croat forces to sign the Washington agreement: together they would found the Federation of Bosnia-Herzegovina. They stopped fighting and became de facto allies against the Serbs, which won them a few military victories and great territorial gain in 1995. In the spring of 1995 (upon the election of Jacques Chirac in France), UN troops were given a quick-reaction force (British and French) that sometimes fired back at the Serbs in Sarajevo. Throughout August and September 1995 NATO airstrikes bombarded Serb positions in Bosnia-Herzegovina. This display of force brought the parties to sign a cease-fire agreement on 12 October 1995, and, under international pressure, to start negotiations at Dayton, Ohio. But in July 1995, a few weeks before all this could happen, Serb forces massacred seven thousand Muslim prisoners at Srebrenica, the largest killing yet. The Dayton negotiations concluded on 21 November 1995, with the understanding that Bosnia-Herzegovina would be a single state, within its original boundaries, but would be—divided into two "entities," the Republika Srpska (Serb), and the Federation of Bosnia-Herzegovina (Croat and Muslim). The two entities would be of approximately equal size (49 percent and 51 percent of the country), and would each enjoy great powers. A UN High Representative would monitor the operations and ensure that the agreements were respected.

AFTER DAYTON

In 1998 Bosnia had a population of 3.2 million people as opposed to 4.3 million before the war. The estimated number of casualties varies from seventy-five to ninety-five thousand to one hundred sixty thousand. There were up to 2.2 million refugees, 1.2 million of whom went abroad, and the others to different regions of Bosnia. The destruction toll was enormous (fifteen to twenty billion dollars, according to the World Bank) and the economy was in shambles. The country was legally divided into two entities, and de facto three geographically intertwined territories, each under the rule of one of the three ethnic groups. The theoretically Croat-Muslim "Federation" was a myth. Each zone became, ethnically, almost homogenous, except for certain cities in the Muslim zone (Sarajevo, Tuzla), where diversity was better preserved.

The international administration succeeded in reestablishing links of communication between the different zones. International aid enabled the reconstruction of destroyed communities and a certain revival of the economy, especially in the "Federation," but the unemployment rate (48 percent in 1997) remained staggeringly high.

The following elections confirmed the dominance of the three nationalist parties, even though the international administration forcefully removed some of the more radical leaders. Only half of the refugees ever returned, and in each zone, the return of these "minorities" caused many problems. Some of the principal war criminals, particularly Radovan Karadzić, had not been arrested as of 2005.

Bosnia-Herzegovina is no longer a multiethnic society, but a collection of small zones, each with a homogenous population, that only holds together because of the international protectorate. The central Bosnian power is nothing now but a fiction. It is a politically and economically fragile country.

See also Croatia; Izetbegović, Alija; Karadžić, Radovan; Mihailović, Dragoljub; Pavelić, Ante; Sarajevo; Serbia; Tito (Josip Broz); World War II; Yugoslavia.

BIBLIOGRAPHY

Primary Sources

Bildt, Carl. *Peace Journey: The Struggle for Peace in Bosnia.* London, 1998. Bosnia before and after Dayton, and international action, as seen by the first High Representative of the United Nations in Bosnia.

Djilas, Milovan. *Wartime.* Translated by Michael B. Petrovich. New York, 1977. Memoirs of war by one of Tito's principal deputies, containing numerous revelations.

Holbrooke, Richard. *To End a War.* New York, 1998. Testimony of the American negotiator of the Dayton agreements.

Secondary Sources

Banac, Ivo. *The National Question in Yugoslavia: Origins, History, Politics.* Ithaca, N.Y., 1984. In-depth study of the national aspirations and policies of various peoples.

Bataković, Dušan. *The Serbs of Bosnia and Herzegovina: History and Politics.* Paris, 1996. A Serbian historian's point of view.

Donia, Robert J. *Islam under the Double Eagle: The Muslims of Bosnia and Herzegovina, 1878–1914.* Boulder, Colo., and New York, 1981. Description of a clash of civilizations at in an era of major changes.

Džaja, Srećko M. *Bosnien-Herzegowina in der österreichisch-ungarischen Epoche (1878–1918). Die Intelligentsia zwischen Tradition und Ideologie.* Munich, 1994. Definitive work on this period.

Krulic, Joseph. *Histoire de la Yugoslavie de 1945 à Nos Jours.* Brussels, 1993. A very fine study of the evolution of the communist regime.

Magaš, Branka. *The Destruction of Yugoslavia: Tracking the Break-Up 1980–92.* London, 1993. This book brings its well-supported answers to the most controversial questions. Bosnia has an important place in it.

Malcolm, Noel. *Bosnia: A Short History.* London, 1994. First systematic history of Bosnia, very complete documentation.

Melčić, Dunja, ed. *Der Jugoslawien-Krieg. Handbuch zu Vorgeschichte, Verlauf und Konsequenzen.* Opladen/Wiesbaden, Germany, 1999. International collective work containing the most complete and critical studies in the field: cultural facts, political history, statistics.

Mudry, Thierry. *Histoire de la Bosnie-Herzégovine. Faits et Controverses.* Paris, 1999. Deeply historical and very well-documented work; the "controversies" section is particularly useful.

Popovic, Alexandre. *L'Islam Balkanique. Les Musulmans du Sud-Est Européen dans la Période Post-ottomane.* Wiesbaden, Germany, 1986. Text by an expert on Islam.

Ramet, Sabrina P. *Nationalism and Federalism in Yugoslavia, 1962–1991.* 2nd ed. Bloomington, Ind., 1992.

———. *Balkan Babel: The Disintegration of Yugoslavia from the Death of Tito to the Fall of Milošević.* 4th ed. Boulder, Colo., 2002. These two books by Ramet cover the region's history since the 1960s and shed light on the cultural and institutional issues.

Tomasevich, Jozo. *The Chetniks.* Stanford, Calif., 1975. Classic text on the Chetnik movement and World War II.

PAUL GARDE

BOULEZ, PIERRE (b. 1925), French composer and influential figure in French avant-garde music.

Much music in France during the first half of the twentieth century suffered from what might be called a "post-Debussy prettiness" (Francis Poulenc, Jean Françaix) or a light, flippant ambience of the cabaret (Darius Milhaud [1892–1974]). That changed when Messiaen and Pierre Boulez brought avant-garde techniques to French music. Boulez enrolled in Messiaen's harmony class in 1944 at the Paris Conservatoire, and with René Leibowitz he studied the twelve-tone (serial) compositional methods of Arnold Schoenberg. Both studies influenced the style of his Piano Sonata No. 1 (1946), a twelve-tone (serial) piece with recurring rhythmic and melodic patterns. Yet the texture, denser than that of Schoenberg or Anton Webern, more closely resembles that of Messiaen. After Messiaen composed *Mode de valeurs et d'intensités* (1949), Boulez took that composer's series of pitches, durations, attacks, and dynamics and added a strict twelve-tone organization, thus integrating all these elements by serialization.

INTEGRAL SERIALISM

Boulez's integral serial style is evident in his Structures for Two Pianos (1951–1952). The first section (Ia) is the most strictly serial movement, with only a few decisions made by the composer. (In the twenty-first century, it could probably be done by a computer.) The third section (Ic), which he wrote next, still contains strict integral serialism, but is more inventive and has greater variety of sound. With Ib, Boulez began to loosen his strict serial style. He then reordered the movements to give what he calls an "anti-evolutionary impression to the whole." Boulez later saw an "absurdity" in this strict serial method and so relaxed this approach even more with *Le Marteau sans maître* (1954), for voice and various instruments. He says that when he began this piece, he was already beginning to go beyond strict serialism, "to try to make the discipline very flexible."

This flexibility then led to his aleatoric works. The word *aléa* literally means chance, but in this context it comes closer to choice. Boulez was influenced by Stéphane Mallarmé's poem "Un coup de dés," which has different typography for different lines. You can read it straight through or follow the same typeface and ignore others. Boulez applies a similar procedure to his Piano Sonata No. 3 (1957), which takes on different forms at different times. It is somewhat like a mobile by Alexander Calder (1898–1976) that has a fixed number of components, but changes its overall form depending on chance movements (e.g., wind direction) or the position of the observer.

One movement, "Trope," has four sections— "Glose," "Commentaire," "Texte," and "Parenthèse"—but because the score is spiral-bound, a performer may begin with any section. "Commentaire" is printed in two different positions, allowing the performer to play it either the first time or wait until the second. Similar situations occur if one starts with one of the other sections. In addition, "Parenthèse" and "Commentaire" contain passages within parentheses, which may either be played or omitted. The second movement, "Constellation-Miroir," consists of many fragments with a certain freedom of order, somewhat like Karlheinz Stockhausen's *Klavierstücke XI.* Aleatoric devices also appear in Structures for Two Pianos, Book 2 (1961); *Éclat-Multiples* (1965); and *Domaines II* (1969).

ELECTRONIC MUSIC

Until the 1970s, Boulez showed little interest in electronic music. *Etude sur un seul son* and *Etude sur sept sons* (1951–1952) were early electronic experiments, produced at about the time as Stockhausen's two electronic *Studien.* He incorporated a tape track with *Poésie pour pouvoir* (1958) but did not continue in this direction due to the limited electronic technology at the time. Then in 1970 President Georges Pompidou asked Boulez to organize a music research center, Institut de Recherche et Coordination Acoustique/Musique (IRCAM). By the time it opened in 1977, electronic technology had improved, especially through advances in computers, and Boulez composed several new works there incorporating the latest electronic sound possibilities, notably . . . *explosante-fixe* . . . (1972–1974, rev. 1991– 1993). *Répons* (1980–1984) employs live manipulation of electronic sounds.

CONDUCTOR, AUTHOR, AND TEACHER

Boulez's compositional output slowed down somewhat when he pursued his interest in conducting. He led concerts of his own music in the 1950s and became principal guest conductor of the Cleveland Orchestra in 1967 and the Chicago Symphony Orchestra in 1995. He was the principal conductor of the BBC Symphony Orchestra in 1971 and music director of the New York Philharmonic from 1971 to 1978. His recordings with various orchestras over the last few decades of the twentieth century received great critical acclaim. He has also written several articles and many of his interviews have been published. In the 1950s and 1960s he taught composition at Darmstadt, Germany, and was visiting professor at Harvard University in 1963. For decades he has been a major force in French music.

See also **Schoenberg, Arnold.**

BIBLIOGRAPHY

Primary Sources

Boulez, Pierre. *Notes of an Apprenticeship.* Translated by Herbert Weinstock. New York, 1968.

———. *Boulez on Music Today.* Translated by Susan Bradshaw and Richard Rodney Bennett. Cambridge, Mass., 1971.

———. *Conversations with Célestin Deliège.* London, 1976.

Secondary Sources

Black, Robert. "Boulez's Third Piano Sonata: Surface and Sensibility." *Perspectives of New Music* 20 (1982): 182–98.

Griffiths, Paul. *Boulez.* London, 1978.

Jameaux, Dominique. *Pierre Boulez.* Translated by Susan Bradshaw. Cambridge, Mass., 1991.

Ligeti, G. "Pierre Boulez: Entscheidung und Automatik in der Structures Ia." *Die Riehe* 4 (1958): 38–63.

Peyser, Joan. *Boulez: Composer, Conductor, Enigma.* Rev. ed. White Plains, N.Y., 1993.

Trenkamp, A. "The Concept of 'Aléa' in Boulez's *Constellation-Miroir*." *Music and Letters* 57 (1976): 1–10.

Wentzel, Wayne C. "Dynamic and Attack Associations in Boulez's *Le Marteau sans maître.*" *Perspectives of New Music* 29 (1991): 142–170.

Winick, Steven D. "Symmetry and Pitch-Duration Association in Boulez's *Le Marteau sans maître.*" *Perspectives of New Music* 24 (1986): 280–321.

WAYNE C. WENTZEL

BOURDIEU, PIERRE (1930–2002), French sociologist.

Best known for developing a sociological framework grounded in the concepts of field, habitus, and capital, Pierre Bourdieu was among the most influential sociologists of the twentieth century. He first came to national attention in France with the publication in 1964 of *Les héritiers* (The inheritors; coauthored with Jean-Claude Passeron), a critique of the French higher educational system. Among his subsequent books were *La distinction* (1979), *Homo academicus* (1984), *La noblesse d'état* (1989; The state nobility), *Les règles de l'art* (1992; The rules of art), and *Les structures sociales de l'économie* (2000; The social structures of the economy). Translated into many languages, Bourdieu's hundreds of articles and dozens of books earned him an international audience and influence within and beyond sociology. A series of books written late in his career and aimed at a broader readership were widely read and discussed in France: *La misère du monde* (1993, with multiple coauthors; The misery of the world), *Sur la télévision* (1996; On television), and *La domination masculine* (1998; Masculine domination). He held the chair in sociology at the Collège de France from 1981 to the time of his death.

Born in a remote village in southwestern France to a father who served in the postal service and a homemaker mother, Bourdieu studied in Paris at elite schools, first at Louis-le-Grand high school and then at the École Normale Supérieure, from which he graduated with a degree in philosophy, at that time the most prestigious of academic disciplines in France. Bourdieu's trajectory from provincial origins to one of the most elite high schools in France had a profound effect on his intellectual development, as did several years spent in war-torn Algeria in the late 1950s. These experiences contributed to his growing dissatisfaction with philosophy and an increasingly strong commitment to anthropological and sociological research.

Influenced by the anthropologist Claude Lévi-Strauss, Bourdieu conducted intensive research on social rituals and family relations in Kabylia (Algeria) that would result in his pathbreaking *Esquisse d'une théorie de la pratique* (1972; published in English as *Outline of a Theory of Practice* in 1977). Nevertheless, deeply discomfited by what he characterized as the paradoxical detachment of Lévi-Straussian anthropology from the social world, Bourdieu turned decisively in the early 1960s to sociology, a discipline that afforded him the freedom to explore, in great empirical detail, the issues of power and inequality that were to become the dominant themes of his life's work. This decision, in turn, would have a major impact on French sociology. When Bourdieu began teaching at the École Pratique des Hautes Études in 1964 (later the École des Hautes Études en Sciences Sociales), sociology was among the least prestigious of academic disciplines. By the end of his career, through his books and articles, the work produced by his research group, and his increasingly visible public profile, Bourdieu had contributed to a dramatic shift in the place of sociology in the hierarchy of academic disciplines in France.

Bourdieu's primary contribution to sociology was his articulation of a theory of social life aimed at overcoming a number of persistent dualisms that dominated sociological theory and research: between subject and object, between structure and agency, and between the micro and macro levels of analysis. Drawing on (but also criticizing) Karl Marx, Émile Durkheim, Max Weber, Lévi-Strauss, and Erving Goffman, Bourdieu developed a sociological research program centered on the concepts of field, habitus, and capital, which he insisted could not be understood in isolation from one another. The concept of field was elaborated to describe and explain the macro-level social contexts in which social actors find themselves. Bourdieu's framework assumes that any given society is composed of multiple, historically specific fields of varying scope or scale; examples of fields Bourdieu himself analyzed in his empirical work include the French literary field in the nineteenth century and the field of French higher education in the 1960s. According to Bourdieu, each individual social actor at any given time is engaged in one or more different fields; one's behavior within a given field is, in

large part, the product of one's past experiences in various social fields, particularly those experienced early in life. Through these experiences, Bourdieu argued, social actors acquire particular dispositions, habits, and patterns of thought that guide, but do not determine, one's relation to and behavior in the social fields encountered later in life. These dispositions, habits, and patterns of thought are, in turn, captured in Bourdieu's framework by the concept of the habitus. The concept of capital, for its part, allows the specific structures of fields and the relative positions of power of given actors in these fields to be mapped out. Bourdieu extended the concept of capital beyond its more common economic sense to include all the resources—for example, cultural, educational, linguistic, literary, political—that social actors draw on, whether consciously or otherwise, in their daily lives. The unequal distribution of these resources and the consequences of this inequality for different social groups was an abiding theme in Bourdieu's work.

In the 1990s this interest in social inequality led him to speak and write with increasing public visibility about what he considered the most pressing political issues of the day. In 1995 he spoke on behalf of striking railroad workers at the Gare de Lyon in Paris; in 1996 he launched a new book series, *Raisons d'agir* (Reasons to take action), in which he and others published strong critiques of neoliberalism and globalization. Bourdieu was criticized in France for his political activities by a number of scholars and journalists who saw a tension between objective scholarship and political engagement, yet he continued to insist until his death that what he termed "scholarship with commitment" was both possible and necessary.

See also **Globalization; Lévi-Strauss, Claude; Neoliberalism.**

BIBLIOGRAPHY

Bourdieu, Pierre. *Outline of a Theory of Practice.* Translated by Richard Nice. Cambridge, U.K., 1977.

———. *Distinction: A Social Critique of the Judgment of Taste.* Translated by Richard Nice. London, 1986.

———. *Homo Academicus.* Translated by Peter Collier. Stanford, Calif., 1988.

———. *The Rules of Art.* Translated by Susan Emanuel. Stanford, Calif., 1996.

———. *The State Nobility: Elite Schools in the Field of Power.* Translated by Lauretta C. Clough. Stanford, Calif., 1996.

———. *On Television and Journalism.* Translated by Priscilla Parkhurst Ferguson. London, 1998.

———. *Masculine Domination.* Translated by Richard Nice. Stanford, Calif., 2001.

Bourdieu, Pierre, and Jean-Claude Passeron. *The Inheritors: French Students and Their Relation to Culture.* Translated by Richard Nice. Chicago, 1979.

VICTORIA JOHNSON

BOURGEOISIE. The long existence of the term *bourgeoisie* in the various European languages and the multiplicity of meanings it took on over time, beginning in the Middle Ages and in different historical and geographic contexts, make a comparative study of this group throughout Europe in the twentieth century particularly problematic. For ease of translation from country to country, we here limit ourselves to a minimalist definition that identifies this group with the upper, nonaristocratic strata of society possessing wealth, income, and/or educational levels that are clearly above average. According to Jürgen Kocka, the bourgeoisie would then represent, depending on the country, from 5 to 15 percent of the population at the beginning of the twentieth century, depending on whether or not we include the petty bourgeoisie and the middle classes. Beyond a definition of the term, three main historiographic debates still remain unresolved.

First, there is the classic debate over the internal unity or diversity of this group: in light of geographic divisions (rural/urban bourgeoisie, capital cities/provinces, etc.), or divisions in terms of education, religion, wealth, and power, can we still speak of a unified class, as in the Marxist vulgate that dominated the social discourse on this topic for a large part of the period? In fact, if one includes in this group, alongside the most important business leaders, the upper echelons of the liberal professions, high-level state employees, and rural notables, the answer becomes dubious at best, given the divergences in lifestyle and standard of living, as well as cultural values and ideological choices, that become increasingly pronounced as one moves southward and eastward into Europe,

where these educated bourgeois groups have a strong foothold and sometimes play an essential political role and enjoy higher prestige than members of the economic bourgeoisie.

The second debate concerns the persistence and relevance of the use of such a definition, a legacy of the nineteenth century, throughout the twentieth century, when the structures of the economy, governments, educational systems, relations between the sexes and family life, political boundaries, ideologies, wars, and political upheavals have radically changed the social situation in Europe by comparison with the eve of World War I. This is why many social historians or specialists in the social sciences have preferred, since 1930–1950, to coin new terms that are more abstract or closer to the specific traditions of each nation, rather than reuse vocabulary that is strongly marked by the legacy of the controversies and representations of the nineteenth century: elites, dominant class, establishment, managers, technocrats, senior management or chief executives, upper middle classes, and high-income groups (or, more banally, the "rich," "nouveaux riches," etc.) are among the many notions proposed as more flexible or less connoted alternatives to the terminology inherited from the previous century.

The third debate is even more political. Because most European countries went through horrendous experiences in the twentieth century, many works of social or political history have been tempted to "bring to trial" and assign responsibility to the privileged groups within the societies involved—and therefore to the most important of these groups, the bourgeoisie, the source of the main elites in power—in connection with the failures, errors, or complicities with the extremist regimes that have left a permanent mark on some European states. This "history-as-trial" is no doubt especially prevalent for the first half of the twentieth century, owing to the magnitude of the catastrophes and the influence of Marxism on a part of European historiography. But it is also present for the second half of the century, when it assumes more sophisticated forms with the emergence of new forms of critical sociology, focused on new forms of domination and on the development of new types of inequality, as a result of the calling into question of the welfare state, globalization, and the neoliberal policies of the last twenty years of the twentieth century, which revived the values and discourse of the nineteenth-century bourgeoisie of free enterprise.

Many of the issues cited above are far from being resolved and will require from historians, especially for the second half of the twentieth century, many more comparative studies to move beyond polemics and simplifications. With such highly charged and recent topics, the social historian cannot completely cut himself off from the world of which he is a part; the interpretation he proposes can thus be only provisional and imperfect.

THE SITUATION ON THE EVE OF 1914

The conventional image of the European bourgeoisie just before World War I goes hand in hand with the retrospectively constructed myth of the Belle Epoque. It is the apogee of this class that is presumed to have gradually gained ascendancy over other privileged groups (in particular the remains of the aristocracy) and imbued societies with its cultural values and ideological goals (liberalism, the national and patriotic ideal, a preoccupation with accumulating wealth, the spirit of enterprise, individual success, the passing on of a family legacy, the ascetic morality of accumulating wealth, etc.). This classic reading, which corresponds primarily to the societies of France and England, northern Italy, northern Europe, and the western part of Germany, was strongly contested by Arno Mayer (1981) in an essay that was controversial but nonetheless provided the impetus for a good deal of research, with its emphasis on "the persistence of the Old Regime" and on the substantial weight that the aristocracy and groups and values associated with it still carries in central and Eastern Europe (and even in England and southern Europe). In these more traditional areas of Europe, such factors influenced even the modern bourgeoisie, which was restricted to the margins of the political domain. We cannot completely concur with all of the analyses and consequences of Arno Mayer's interpretation, but his provocative hypothesis was beneficial in that it forced historians, in particular in Germany and central Europe, to conceptualize the particularities of the bourgeoisies of this region in terms other than those of the model

postulated as being "normal" and "universal" by Marxists and by liberals from the French and English bourgeoisie.

In Germany and Austria-Hungary especially, bourgeois groups remained strongly imbued with the preeminence of hierarchies defined by the monarchical state and by a prestige scale in which service to the state, especially the army, strongly linked to aristocratic values (the code of honor, dueling), remained more influential than the cult of material profit. Even the industrialists, financiers, and members of the liberal professions who in France, England, the Netherlands, and elsewhere were the transmitters of liberal and individualistic values were caught up in this system of older representations. This did not prevent the emergence of a very dynamic economic grand bourgeoisie in the German Empire and in part of the Austro-Hungarian Empire. Its wealth (cf. the Krupp, Thyssen, and Siemens families, the German and Austrian branches of the Rothschilds, the Wittgenstein family, etc.) and successes were on a par with those of its western counterparts, but its specific characteristics explain the particular difficulties of the bourgeoisies of eastern and southern Europe in adapting to the upheavals produced by World War I and the interwar period.

EFFECTS OF THE FIRST WORLD WAR AND THE INTERWAR PERIOD

The effects of the First World War and the interwar years on the bourgeoisies of Europe were eminently contradictory. On the one hand, in those countries where the bourgeoisie was subordinate to nobles who remained influential in political, social, and cultural life, the defeats of monarchies and empires forever ruined the old ruling classes on every level—political, symbolic, economic, and social. This was the case in the Weimar Republic and in the Austrian, Czech, and Hungarian republics. On the other hand, the wartime economy had supported the birth and rapid expansion of new commercial and industrial businesses and had promoted or considerably enriched new bourgeois strata that had profited from government commissions or the new interventionist economic conditions. The topic of the "nouveaux riches" and war profiteers was almost ubiquitous and led to the denunciation of a new plutocracy and to increasingly virulent anti-Semitism with the arrival of the economic crisis of the 1930s (in Germany, Austria, Hungary, and France, for example).

In the defeated countries, the new ruling elites came in part from the recent bourgeoisie, but sometimes, whether in the short or long term, they also came from socialist, communist, or populist parties with antiaristocratic or even antibourgeois ideologies that used the suffering of the people, the errors of former leaders, or the multiple economic and financial disruptions caused by the war and the interwar period to contest the old social order and promote egalitarian measures. Such measures affected not just the former elites but also some bourgeois strata. Even in the victorious countries, where the liberal bourgeoisie was already dominant in every realm (France, Great Britain, and Italy), the economic, monetary, and financial disorder undermined the former certainties of this group. It split into a traditionalist wing, which sought to restore the liberal, pre-1914 situation, and a modernist wing (instead composed of high-level state employees, engineers, technocrats, or managers) that advocated a new approach to managing the economy, government, and social relations, and which sometimes drew its inspiration from the American model. Major social movements (strikes in Great Britain in the 1920s, activism by worker councils and rural strikes in Italy from 1918 to 1920, revolutionary and counterrevolutionary unrest in Germany from 1918 to 1923, mass strikes in France from 1919 to 1920 and then in May–June 1936) challenged the authority of business elites and even the political and social order. An entire pessimistic discourse and a negative or critical image of the bourgeoisie spread throughout Europe; this explains the reactions of fear among the bourgeoisie that led some fractions, including degreed professionals, to form alliances with the fascist extreme Right.

This contrasting picture should not mask the fact that overall, the various bourgeois strata, although they had had to make concessions to challenging forces, had essentially maintained their pre-1914 privileges. New taxes (income tax in France, legislated in 1914; heavier income and estate taxes in England); new social relations in businesses, imposed by collective negotiations instituted by the state (e.g., in France and Germany) or by the power of labor unions (Great Britain); the emergence of the welfare state (social insurance, unemployment compensation); and educational or political reforms (wider access to secondary and university education for the new social classes, the extension of suffrage to women and to social groups previously excluded in some countries) were adopted very gradually and very unevenly. In some cases (the United Kingdom after 1930, Germany after 1931, fascist Italy, Austria under the authoritarian corporatist regime from 1934, and France after the end of the Popular Front in 1938), swings of the political pendulum in the other direction, abetted by the division of the parties of the left and international tensions, allowed these concessions to be called into question or even completely abolished and restored the power of business elites by reining in or suppressing the labor unions. At the same time, the development of new, mass-consumption or high-technology industries and the expansion of the service sector opened the way for new entrepreneurs, managers, or engineers who had become executive-level managers or high-level state employees in the new economic and social administrations to enter the bourgeoisie or the grand bourgeoisie.

Statistical data demonstrate the narrowing of some economic gaps (in income and, to a lesser extent, wealth) by comparison with the prewar period, owing mostly to inflationary phenomena, the collapse of some investments made by prewar investors (Russian loans, war loans, etc.), or the forced liquidation of the legacies of some families affected by wartime losses. Some aspects of the former bourgeois lifestyle were therefore permanently changed: fewer households employed domestic help and fewer people lived off private income; some women and girls from bourgeois families were forced to seek employment; and families became concerned with providing even heirs with training and university degrees, for fear of a loss of social position. The feminization of some professions (teaching, medicine, qualified administrative jobs) aroused antifeminist reactions and even, during the crisis years, discriminatory measures, both in authoritarian or fascist countries and in liberal democracies, where "women's liberation" was identified with the decay of the bourgeois family and blamed for falling

German chancellor Adolf Hitler and Gustav Krupp von Bolen shake hands during Hitler's visit to the Krupp factory in Essen, Germany, September 1940.
Successful bourgeois families who collaborated with fascist regimes in some cases paid a high price for their activities. Gustav's son Alfried, who took control of the firm in 1941, was convicted of war crimes in 1947 and sentenced to a lengthy prison term. ©BETTMANN/CORBIS

birthrates and unemployment among young university graduates.

Other statistics relating to social mobility, the recruitment of various elites, and practices of marital alliances, however, attest to the relative permanence of the old patterns of class reproduction that privileged the various categories from bourgeois backgrounds for access to the higher professions and social positions.

The ascendancy to power of anti-Semitic or Nazi-ideology–inspired regimes did, however, profoundly affect a specific fraction of the bourgeoisie and middle classes that had experienced a spectacular ascent in Europe in the nineteenth century—those of the Jewish faith or tradition. Even before the putting into effect of the "final solution," anarchic or legal "Aryanization" measures allowed for the expropriation of property and businesses held by Jewish businessmen, to the benefit not only of

the new leaders or supporters of Nazi or fascist regimes, but also of members of the bourgeoisie and the middle classes affiliated with the dominant religions. The latter cynically used the persecution of Jews to exact social revenge against competitors, often more prosperous than they, whose success in banking, business, commerce, and the liberal professions created all the more resentment during a period of acute economic difficulties, especially in Germany, Austria, and Hungary, and slightly later in France under the Vichy regime and during the anti-Semitic phase of the fascist regime in Italy. Even those members of the Jewish bourgeoisie who, by paying significant sums to the anti-Semitic states, had been able to escape the worst by emigrating, were rarely or only very belatedly able to recover their property or social standing after 1945.

TRANSFORMATIONS OF THE BOURGEOISIES, 1945–1975

To all appearances, the period after 1945 had certain analogies with the period after 1918 for the bourgeoisies of Europe. The liberal economy and the social categories defending it were even more destabilized than after World War I. More than half the Continent came under Soviet control, and state-run economies replaced liberal capitalism in these areas. Communist Party cadres, often from humble backgrounds, held the leadership positions in all sectors (business, administration, and political and intellectual life). The bourgeoisies in these countries lost their fortunes, their businesses, and sometimes their lives (in purges), and they were forced into exile or had to make do with low-level jobs while their children faced discrimination in gaining access to higher education. In Western Europe, where coalitions on the left, sometimes allied with the Communists, were in power at the end of the 1940s, major structural reforms and postwar shortages gave the state a growing role in the economy while fiscal legislation and social security systems sought to reduce inequalities in income between the bourgeoisie and other groups. Through nationalizations in key sectors, especially in France, Italy, Austria, and the United Kingdom, the former bourgeois dynasties or founding heads of companies were replaced by technocrats and engineers from business or from the administrative and political elites. In the countries affected by fascism, Nazism, and collaboration, some important business leaders with links to the fallen regimes were brought to trial, and some of them were subjected to heavy sanctions: in Germany, Alfried Krupp, the executives of IG Farben, and the financier Friedrich Flick; in France, Louis Renault, Marius Berliet, and so forth.

This antibourgeois and anticapitalist climate was fairly short-lived, however: by 1947–1950 American influence via the Cold War and the Marshall Plan, the return to power of markedly more conservative political coalitions, and the rise of consumerism after years of shortages restored to the foreground a new, American-inspired social model that reached its apogee in the 1960s: the society of mass consumption and free enterprise. Since it coincided with a break in social and sexual mores from patterns inherited from the nineteenth century, many observers have interpreted this juncture as the birth of a new society based on credit instead of savings; a constant rise in the standard of living; the obliteration of the old classes in favor of a vast middle class bounded by a small group of the very wealthy and a small margin of the poor; and the emancipation of women, who were gaining access to new bourgeois professions. In this view, the old bourgeoisie, committed to accruing wealth and to frugality, thus gave way to new groups, mainly salaried workers, oriented toward consumption and short-term enjoyment of their growing incomes, gaining access to high-level positions in big businesses whose individual owners were no longer identifiable due to the dilution of the pool of shareholders. At the same time, mass access to and the standardization of higher education in most European countries beginning in the 1960s seemingly obliterated another of the old bourgeoisie's privileges of cultural standing and opened high-level public- and private-sector jobs to the middle classes.

Of course, the prosperity of the period of full employment did not eliminate wage inequalities (although it tended to reduce them), nor did it eliminate all forms of frustration among workers (as attested to by major labor strikes in the 1960s and 1970s in France, Italy, and England) or in other categories (for example, the student movements that mainly emerged from the middle classes, or the recurring discontent of farmers and small merchants in the face of state intervention). But the new welfare states, increasingly generous thanks to prosperity or because of social pressures, and low unemployment created the illusion that the once very large inequalities between the bourgeoisie and other groups would eventually disappear for good, especially in the countries of northern Europe, which implemented the strongest measures of wealth redistribution and the heaviest tax rates.

In the dominant discourse of the time, merit and competence were the only acknowledged justifications for status, power, or income: a bourgeoisie composed of owners and business executives was succeeded by a group of career managers, selected from within big businesses, or technocrats from the administration or nationalized businesses, depending on how large a role the state played in a given economy (Germany and England vs. France and Italy). At the same time, development of the service sector and urbanization multiplied the number of high-level, qualified, and well-paying jobs seen as the guarantee of social promotion for the middle classes or of the possibility of starting new small and midsize businesses without a large amount of capital.

This optimistic and modernist sociology was very quickly challenged by more critical analyses from the end of the 1960s. They emphasized the persistence of older phenomena and indeed a renaissance of new groups that were more similar to the old forms of the bourgeoisie than to more recent ones. Even in those countries most affected by state control, like France, England, and Italy, some old industrial and financial dynasties were able to survive the upheavals or to redirect their wealth into dynamic new sectors. Out of the one hundred largest Italian businesses from 1950 to 1970, almost half remained under family control. Members of the de Wendel family, after the collapse and subsequent nationalization of the major steel-producing groups in France, pooled their indemnities to establish a holding company that invested in several different sectors. Its main representative, Ernest-Antoine Seillière, even became president of the most important French employers' association in 1997.

At the same time, consumer society encouraged the rise of new sectors and new family firms that grew very large and even expanded internationally: for example, the supermarket chain Carrefour, founded by the Defforey and Fournier families at the end of the 1950s, or clothing businesses in central and northeastern Italy, such as the Benetton firm, founded in the 1960s by four brothers and a sister. In Germany in the 1970s, despite the reconstitution of some giant businesses, small and midsize family-type businesses still employed more than 70 percent of salaried workers. Even if consideration is limited to the largest businesses, family control, which recalls the bourgeoisie of the nineteenth century, endured to a significant degree: 17 percent of the one hundred largest companies in Germany, 46 percent of the largest businesses in the Netherlands, 33 percent of the one hundred largest Swiss companies, and, in France, 50 percent of the two hundred largest companies during the 1970s were family-controlled.

Moreover, the opening of higher education to new, more modest social strata did not erase more subtle class hierarchies between academic tracks (law, commercial studies, engineering training, or medicine vs. letters, sciences, or short vocational-technical courses) where more of the heirs of bourgeois families tended to be concentrated. Such tracks ensured income and markedly more remunerative careers after graduation. In some countries, private schooling, more expensive and socially or culturally elitist, shielded boys and girls from bourgeois families, beginning in adolescence, from the mixed social milieu of standard secondary education (for example, the public schools in England, posh private and/or Catholic schools in France, Belgium, Switzerland, Italy, and Spain). Studies of the elites show that virtually everywhere, one-third of their members come from the upper classes (old bourgeoisie), more than one-third from the middle classes (recent bourgeoisie), and less than one-third from more modest backgrounds.

THE CRISIS OF THE WELFARE STATE

The seeds of new, subtler inequalities and these early signs of a new breed of "bourgeois conquerors" were further confirmed and accentuated during the 1980s and 1990s. Because of the lasting high rates of unemployment that took hold in most European countries after the two "oil crises," with the opening up of economic exchanges (via European unification and free-trade agreements), and the collapse of some old sectors (textiles, steel, shipbuilding, and mining), power relations between wage-earners and management, between salaried executives and shareholders, and between nationalized states and multinational corporations, were inverted. Neoliberal ideology, inspired by Friedrich von Hayek (1899–1992), and the monetarism of the Chicago School, which saw the stagflation of the 1970s as an illustration of their theories on the harmful influence of the state's economic role and of Keynesian policies, gradually gained ascendancy in public discourse. They inspired some governments—in the United Kingdom (the Margaret Thatcher government from 1979), the United States (the administration of Ronald Reagan), and then, increasingly, in continental Europe, with the return of majorities of the right or the influence of the European Commission's directives on free trade: in the Netherlands, Italy, during certain periods in France (1986–1988, 1993–1997), Germany (the Helmut Kohl government from 1982), Spain (the José María Aznar government), and even the countries of central Europe after the fall of the Soviet Union.

This discourse and politics marked a striking return to the values, behaviors, and discourses of the liberal bourgeoisie of the nineteenth century: glorification of enterprise, risk, bosses, and the laws of the market; stigmatization of the weak and those on public assistance; rehabilitation of profit and wealth as signs of social success and renewed emphasis on the efficiency and value of managers. Privatizations, the suppression of state monopolies, cuts in income taxes and taxes on businesses, access to property (housing, secondary residences, financial stocks) for the majority of the middle and upper classes, and the opening of borders were supposed to re-create a market freed from previous constraints and foster a new, enterprise-based bourgeoisie, freed from state control, that employed "flexible" salaried workers as in the nineteenth century.

Socially, this new trend was expressed in the emergence of new, very quickly made fortunes in finance, computers, new technologies, mass distribution, and the media; in increasing inequalities in income, first in the United Kingdom and then on the Continent; in the return of shareholders' interests to the foreground (often, British and U.S. pension funds required very high returns on the capital); and in the loss of prestige associated with political power and the national state. The collusion of this new, financial or industrial bourgeoisie with the highest levels of administration or politics was nonetheless increasingly visible, in the form of lobbies to the European Commission, the co-opting of former high-level state employees onto boards of directors, and appropriation of the mainstream media. To illustrate the latter, one may cite the paradigmatic case of Silvio Berlusconi, in Italy, who built his fortune in real estate and then the media before rising to the height of political power, or that of the Bouygues family in France, which, thanks in part to political backing from the highest levels of government, moved from public works into the media and telecommunications. Increasingly, the careers of the bourgeois elites combined public and private sectors, politics and business, following a norm similar to that of the United States.

The historian of contemporary society, however, must be wary of the illusion of perpetual newness produced by the partial images promulgated by newspapers and the media that influence his view of the most recent period, as well as the illusions created by studies in the social sciences, which always lag behind the current reality because there is no real way to investigate these circles that preserve or have the means to create a manipulated public image of themselves. The most general statistics make it possible to document, although with variations depending on the date of the implementation of neoliberal policies, increases in income gaps and, especially, inheritances over the last twenty years: the phenomenon is more pronounced in the United Kingdom than in the Scandinavian countries, with France, Italy, and Germany in an intermediate position but becoming more similar to the English pattern at the end of the 1990s. Moreover, the figures probably significantly underestimate the realities because it has become increasingly difficult to monitor such statistics with the liberalization and internationalization of financial flows and the proliferation of tax havens.

Measuring the proportion of heirs or monied newcomers (or parvenus) in the contemporary bourgeoisie is also very difficult since, by definition,

the process is always ongoing and everything depends on the definitions adopted of the groups under consideration. The list of the largest fortunes that many European papers have taken to publishing, following the American model, give an exaggerated impression of instability and renewal of the topmost levels of the grand bourgeoisie. When one broadens the scale of analysis, the dazzling successes of some (which may not last more than one generation, or even less, as demonstrated by the resounding fall of men and women presented as models of success a short time earlier) are found in the midst of a far greater number of less visible, but more enduring, family or dynastic fortunes. Like the bourgeoisie of the nineteenth century, which appropriated the status symbols of the old aristocracy, the new grand bourgeoisie of the end of the twentieth century, despite the modernist discourse surrounding it, adopted strategies of distinction and conspicuous consumption quite similar to those of its predecessors from the "leisure class": opulent country houses, hunting, yachts, racing stables, charitable or artistic foundations, luxurious vacations away from the crowds of the ordinary middle classes, rapid and costly means of transportation (private jets and helicopters in the place of the luxury train or top-of-the-line automobile of 1900). Similarly, the desire to pass wealth on to heirs and to provide them with a private and/or elite education, often in an international setting, is a mark of continuity with the old bourgeoisie.

Of course, there are cultural nuances, depending on the country, sector of activity, the oldness of the family, public lifestyle, and religious tradition. The grand bourgeoisie in early-twenty-first-century Germany is markedly less visible and ostentatious than the parvenus and new money in Italy, the United Kingdom, or France, where the influence of the aristocratic model is apparent in marriages and lifestyles. In centralized countries, the concentration of the different types of high-profile elites and bourgeoisies in the capital cities facilitates social mixing and exchanges and media coverage, and thus promotes visibility of the rich and nouveaux riches. The influence of the American model also comes into play to varying degrees, depending on how old the autochthonous bourgeois culture is.

A final problem remains: beyond this highest strata of the bourgeoisie, whose similarities to the grand bourgeoisie of the beginning of the twentieth century (with the addition of internationalization and the increasingly active role of women) outweigh differences between them, is the term *bourgeoisie* still valid to encompass the middle classes with elevated income, educational levels, or jobs, whose importance in the working population obviously has no equivalent in earlier periods because of changes in the structure of jobs and businesses and because of mass access to standardized higher education? Contrary to simplistic theories on middle-class societies, the most recent research shows persistent national characteristics within intermediate groups and increasing internal differentiation within them according to type of capital (economic, cultural, social, or symbolic) or job status (salaried employee, independent contractor, or member of the liberal professions). These differences are also linked to the history of social representations and the social classifications of each country, and to divides across these groups, depending on whether individuals are more closely linked to the state or to the private sector; on whether their current position depends more on their personal trajectory (and their academic or professional success) or on economic and social family heritage; on their religious or political affiliation; or sex or national origin. In phases marked by prosperity and the success of neoliberal policies, the upper middle classes have supported such policies because they seemed to promise increased wealth for all (via stock purchases, individualized benefits packages offered by employers) or new, well-paid jobs in the emerging sectors of the "new economy," services, and finance. However, as soon as a recession or the bursting of a speculative bubble, bankruptcies, or embezzlement exposed the social limits of the advantages to be derived from them or cast doubts on the abilities of managers, these categories learned through experience what separated them from the ruling groups. The latter retained real power over the capital, which produced very high returns and sheltered them, in contrast to the ordinary middle classes, from the risks of unemployment because, thanks to stock options or departure bonuses, they could quickly amass a fortune to be passed down to their heirs. For the majority of high-level salaried employees,

membership in privileged circles was only partial and only valid during their own lifetime; it guaranteed neither the perpetuity of their status nor the family's future, owing to the intensity of each new generation's race for qualifications and the opening up of international competition for jobs.

From this point of view, neoliberalism reinstated in the representations of the upper socioeconomic groups the same incentives and anxieties that had characterized them before World War I: on the one hand, the idea that opportunities are available to all and that the current bourgeois groups remain open, as demonstrated by the highly publicized successes of entrepreneurs, executives, high-level state employees, stars, and so forth, who "started from nothing"; on the other hand, these ascents, even to very high levels, remain precarious without family or political networks, as indicated by some sensational cases in which captains of industry who yesterday were heaped with praise find themselves financially ruined or charged with wrongdoing. At the same time, because of increased life expectancies, both in the upper middle classes and the grand bourgeoisie of inherited wealth, this return of the "bourgeois conquerors" as a societal ideal goes hand in hand with the development of a sort of new ideal of hedonism and living off private income that rivals that of the Belle Epoque. Insofar as the main stockholders of very large companies are often pension funds that require very large returns on their capital, the new capitalism at the start of the twenty-first century has the paradoxical aim of ensuring a certain standard of living or comfortable retirement for a growing fraction not only of holders of revenues from capital, but above all, individuals entitled to full retirement, drawn mainly from the upper middle classes, who are members of these funds. Indirectly, then, pressure from the oldest, most financially secure generations is exerted on ordinary wage-earners and young workers, who are hard hit by the new, increasingly rigid management rules for the businesses (social or fiscal "dumping," flexibility, the intensification of work, globalization, etc.) whose performance provides livelihood, via pension funds, for the growing ranks of those living off interest income.

See also **Aristocracy; Capitalism; Consumption; Economic Miracle; Working Class.**

BIBLIOGRAPHY

Beller, Steven. *Vienna and the Jews, 1867–1938: A Cultural History.* Cambridge, U.K., 1989.

Boltanski, Luc. *The Making of a Class: Cadres in French Society.* Translated by Arthur Goldhammer. Cambridge, U.K., 1987. Translation of *Les cadres* (1982).

Bottomore, Tom, and Robert J. Brym. *The Capitalist Class: An International Study.* New York, 1989.

Bourdieu, Pierre. *Distinction: A Social Critique of the Judgement of Taste.* Cambridge, Mass., 1984. Translation of *La distinction: Critique sociale du jugement de goût* (1979).

Butler, Tim, and Mike Savage, eds. *Social Change and the Middle Classes.* London, 1995.

Cassis, Youssef. *Big Business: The European Experience in the Twentieth Century.* Oxford, U.K., 1997.

Charle, Christophe. *La crise des sociétés impériales (1900–1940), Allemagne, France, Grande-Bretagne, essai d'histoire sociale comparée.* Paris, 2001.

Duby, Georges, and Michelle Perrot, gen. eds. *A History of Women in the West.* Vol. 5: *Toward a Cultural Identity in the Twentieth Century.* Edited by Françoise Thébaud. Cambridge, Mass., 1994. Translation of *Histoire des femmes en Occident* (1992).

Goldthorpe, John, in collaboration with Catriona Llewellyn and Clive Payne. *Social Mobility and Class Structure in Modern Britain.* 2nd ed. Oxford, U.K., 1987.

Joly, Hervé. *Patrons d'Allemagne, sociologie d'une élite industrielle 1933–1989.* Paris, 1996.

Kaelble, Hartmut. *Social Mobility in the 19th and 20th Centuries: Europe and America in Comparative Perspective.* Leamington Spa, U.K., 1985.

Kaelble, Hartmut, ed. *The European Way: European Societies during the Nineteenth and Twentieth Centuries.* New York, 2004.

Kocka, Jürgen. "The Middle Classes in Europe." In *The European Way,* edited by Hartmut Kaelble. New York, 2004.

Kuisel, Richard F. *Capitalism and the State in Modern France: Renovation and Economic Management in the Twentieth Century.* Cambridge, U.K., 1981.

Malatesta, Maria, ed. *Society and the Professions in Italy, 1860–1914.* Cambridge, U.K., 1995.

McKibbin, Ross. *Classes and Cultures: England 1918–1951.* Oxford, U.K., 1998.

Mosse, Werner E. *The German-Jewish Economic Elite, 1820–1935: A Socio-Cultural Profile.* Oxford, U.K., 1989.

Perkin, Harold. *The Rise of Professional Society: England since 1880.* London, 1989.

Piketty, Thomas. *Les hauts revenus en France au XXè siècle: Inégalités et redistribution.* Paris, 2002.

Rubinstein, W. D. *Wealth and Inequality in Britain.* London, 1986.

Zunz, Olivier, Leonard Schoppa, and Nobuhiro Hiwatari, eds. *Social Contracts under Stress: The Middle Classes of America, Europe, and Japan at the Turn of the Century.* New York, 2002.

CHRISTOPHE CHARLE

BRANDT, WILLY (1913–1992), German politician.

The German politician Willy Brandt was born Herbert Frahm on 18 December 1913. The son of an unmarried shop assistant, he was raised in the social-democratic milieu of Lübeck, a port city on the German Baltic coast. Thanks to a grant from the city he was able to attend a local grammar school, from which he graduated in 1932. Already as a youth he was attracted to social democratic politics, joining the ranks of a left-wing splinter group, the Sozialistische Arbeiterpartei (SAP; Socialist Workers Party) in 1931. Known as a journalist and organizer, he was forced to leave Germany after the Nazi seizure of power in 1933. He went to Norway, and soon became one of the leading figures among German exiles in Scandinavia. Adopting his nom de guerre Willy Brandt, he travelled throughout Europe and Nazi Germany in order to organize underground resistance activities and participated in the Spanish civil war as a news reporter on the republican side. As a Norwegian citizen, he was briefly detained as a prisoner of war after the Nazi invasion in June 1940 but fled to Sweden after his release. During the years until the end of World War II he joined the "International Group of Democratic Socialists," an informal network inspired by the Swedish socialist Gunnar Myrdal (1898–1987), and rejoined the mainstream of the German Social Democratic Party and its headquarters-in-exile in London.

Brandt returned to Germany as a press officer at the Norwegian military mission in occupied Berlin. Quickly he engaged himself in the politics of the capital of the Cold War, supporting a strict pro-western position. Within his party, he helped fend off the attempts of the Soviet occupation powers and their East German vassals, the "Socialist Unity Party," to bring the western sector of the city under communist rule. In 1949 Brandt was elected first as a West Berlin delegate to the West German parliament (*Bundestag*) and secondly in 1950, as a member of the West Berlin *Land* or state parliament. In 1957 he reached the most important political office in West Berlin, the Regierende Bürgermeister (governing mayor, equivalent to federal state prime minister), thereby gaining international stature as the leading representative of his party well before he was elected as the party's president in 1963. In several electoral campaigns Brandt ran for the German chancellery but lost twice to the conservatives in 1961 and 1965. He reached the apogee of his political career only after an interval of three years, in the "great coalition," in which he served as foreign minister under the chancellery of the Christian Democrat leader (and ex-Nazi) Kurt-Georg Kiesinger (1904–1988). Despite his party's coming in second after the Christain Democrats in the 1969 parliamentary elections, Brandt was elected federal chancellor by a "small coalition" of Social Democrats and Liberals by the new parliament on 22 October 1969, putting an end to two decades of Christian conservative hegemony in West German national politics. The years as chancellor were most remarkable for Brandt's foreign policy of détente and reconciliation. As a governing mayor of West Berlin, and later as the foreign minister, he inaugurated a strategy of "change by rapprochement," replacing the policy of strict nonrecognition and polarization vis-à-vis the GDR and the Soviet bloc. Within one year treaties of nonaggression and recognition of the postwar borders were reached with Poland and the Soviet Union. Brandt's state visit to Poland in December 1970 not only included the signature of the Warsaw Treaty but also found its symbolic and emotional climax when, during a wreath-laying ceremony at the Warsaw Ghetto memorial, he spontaneously knelt down on his knees for a moment of silent meditation, thus expressing mourning and historical responsibility for the crimes committed in the name of Germany during World War II. It is this spirit and attitude that earned him the Nobel Peace Prize in 1971. In the same years the four victorious

Allied Powers reached an agreement on the status of West Berlin and its permanent relation to the Federal Republic, allowing the negotiation of a series of treaties between the two German states in 1972. Other treaties with Soviet-bloc countries followed, integrating Brandt's foreign policy into the global climate of détente between the rival power blocs. Although he was furiously opposed by many Christian conservatives and some opponents within his own party who represented the irredentist claims of the refugee lobby in West Germany, his détente policy was confirmed by a triumphant re-election in 1972 that showed broad and unequivocal support for this part of his political agenda. By contrast, his standing turned out to be precarious in the field of domestic politics. On the one hand, major and already long-overdue reform projects (liberalization of the penal code on abortion and homosexuality, broader investments in public and higher education, enlarging trade-union participation rights in large enterprises) were realized. On the other hand, an increasing public-spending deficit, a high level of inflation, and the first signs of shrinking growth rates after the oil shock in 1973, and also the harsh treatment of communist ex-1968ers applying for public service work (the so-called *Berufsverbote* policy) revealed him as less adept at the everyday piecemeal work of balancing lobby interests and a political reform program. So when his personal assistant within the SPD board of governors, Günter Guillaume (1927–1995), was unmasked as an East German spy in April 1974, Brandt's immediate resignation from his chancellery also reflected a growing sense of frustration with this office, not the least intensified by rivalries within the Social Democratic leadership.

Still president of the SPD, Brandt focused again on his preferred field of politics, international relations. Elected president of the Socialist International in 1976, he accepted the World Bank's invitation to chair an "Independent Commission for International Developmental Issues," which resulted in the publication of the "North-South" (or Brandt) Report in 1980 on behalf of the United Nations. It was only after a minor intraparty quarrel that he resigned from the party presidency in 1987. The ensuing sense of growing estrangement from the party in his late years was only interrupted by the democratic revolution in the GDR in 1989 and the ensuing German unification, which Brandt supported in an unequivocal way, coining the famous phrase "Now things grow together that belong together" (*Nun wächst zusammen was zusammengehört*) the day after the opening of the Berlin Wall on 9 November 1989. He was held in high esteem by East Germans since a spectacular official visit to Erfurt in 1970, where he had been cheered spontaneously by a large crowd. Brandt had to withdraw from actual politics due to declining health. He died of cancer in 1992.

During his lifetime Brandt was seen by his contemporaries as a radiant personality who aroused veneration and animosity. It was not just his history as a young antifascist resistance fighter that made him decidedly different from the majority of bystanders and ex-Nazis populating the ranks of his peers in the West German political elite. He also represented modernity and change in a broader sense of lifestyle and cultural interests contrasting with the provincial, petit-bourgeois appeal of the Christian conservative "Bonn republic" of the 1950s. Polyglot by virtue of his travels and experience as an exile, he manifested a very individual flair for cosmopolitan intellectualism. As a former journalist, he established firm links to the community of young West German writers and artists, such as Günter Grass (b. 1927), who would later win a Nobel Prize, and writers and artists in other countries. Brandt was one of the most prolific writers among the guild of full-time politicians in Germany, leaving behind a considerable oeuvre with numerous nonfiction books, memoirs, and hundreds of articles. It comes therefore as no surprise that Brandt engages the imagination of playwrights, moviemakers, and novelists, for instance in the play *Democracy* by Michael Frayn (b. 1933), which premiered in London in 2003. Brandt's political and historical legacy is administered by a Bundeskanzler-Willy-Brandt-foundation erected by the SPD and his wife, Brigitte Seebacher-Brandt (b. 1946), in the town hall of Berlin-Schöneberg, where he had worked during his years as mayor.

See also **Berlin Wall; Germany; 1989.**

BIBLIOGRAPHY

Primary Sources

Brandt, Willy. *Berliner Ausgabe.* Edited by Helga Grebing/Bundeskanzler-Willy-Brandt-Stiftung. Bonn, 2000–.

Secondary Sources

Marshall, Barbara. *Willy Brandt: A Political Biography.* Basingstoke, U.K., 1997.

Münkel, Daniela. *Willy Brandt und die "vierte Gewalt": Politik und Massenmedien in den 50er bis 70er Jahren.* Frankfurt and New York, 2005.

Schöllgen, Gregor. *Willy Brandt: Die Biographie.* Berlin and Munich, 2002.

THOMAS LINDENBERGER

BRAQUE, GEORGES (1882–1963), French painter who, together with Pablo Picasso, developed cubism.

Georges Braque was born in Argenteuil-sur-Seine, a small community near Paris, at a time when modern art was associated with Claude Monet and impressionism both in Paris and in Le Havre, where his family took up residence in 1890. Braque left secondary school quite early in order to enter into apprenticeship first with his father, a building painter and amateur artist, and later with a decorative painter named Roney. At the same time he attended courses in the evening at the École des Beaux-Arts in Le Havre and took flute lessons with the brother of Raoul Dufy. In 1900 he moved to Paris where he pursued his apprenticeship with Laberthe and frequented the courses held in the Municipal Studio of Batignolles. After his military service in 1901 in Le Havre, his parents agreed to allow him to devote himself exclusively to painting.

In Paris, Braque enrolled in 1902 at the Académie Humbert before going to the city's École des Beaux-Arts for a while. In 1905 at the Salon d'Automne he discovered fauvism, a technique he perfected with the help of the painter Othon Friesz, also from Le Havre. The following spring he joined forces with his father, Friesz, and Raoul Dufy to found the Cercle de l'Art Moderne du Havre. It was therefore in the "fauvian" manner that he mounted his first show in 1906, at the twenty-third Salon des Indépendents.

One year later however, Braque was captivated by Paul Cézanne's paintings in a retrospective at the Salon d'Automne. Soon thereafter he completed his first version of the *Viaduc de l'Estaque* (1907), which signaled his passage from fauvism to a style more influenced by Cézanne. During this time Guillaume Apollinaire introduced him to Pablo Picasso, who had just finished *Les Demoiselles d'Avignon.* Braque at this time had begun his *Large Nude* (finished in 1908), a work whose Cézannien influence contrasted with *Les Demoiselles d'Avignon,* which was marked more by primitivism.

In 1908 a series of Braque's landscapes rejected by the Salon d'Automne was shown at the Kahnweiler gallery. As a way of disparaging the works, the critic Louis Vauxcelles described them as bunches of "cubes," whence came the term *cubism.* From that year forward, Braque's artistic strivings would develop in tandem with those of Picasso, with whom he forged a lasting friendship. Together they would give birth to cubism.

In 1911 Braque joined Picasso in Céret, where he used stenciled letters for the first time, in his painting *The Portuguese.* The following year he added sand and sawdust to his works, as well as pieces of "faux wood" wallpaper. With Picasso he invented the use of collage in modern art. In 1912 Braque married Marcelle Lapré and took her with him and Picasso to Marseille, where they purchased masks and African statuettes.

In 1914 World War I broke out and Braque was mobilized along with the 224th Infantry Regiment. Picasso accompanied his friend in uniform to the station in Avignon, where their mutual dialogue of many years came to an end. One year later Braque underwent trepanning for serious head wounds and after his convalescence did not return to the front. In December 1917 he published his "Pensées et réflexions sur la peinture" (Thoughts and reflections on painting) in the journal *Nord-Sud,* where he argued that what accounts for artistic progress is more a knowledge of the limits of artistic language than its extension. He began therefore to refashion his previous work by reconciling the geometry of cubism with the curved line, thereby paving the way for his leap into painting the large-scale, classical-style nudes known

The Canephora. Painting by Georges Braque, 1922. Musée National d'Art Moderne, Centre Pompidou, Paris, France/Lauros/Giraudon/The Bridgeman Art Library

as the Canephores and, later on, smaller-scale seascapes. This period would lead him in 1929 to take up partial residence in Varengeville-sur-Mer near Dieppe, where he maintained a house and studio.

During the 1920s Braque took his first steps into the world of the theater by creating the décor for the Ballets Russes production of *Les Fâcheux* (1924), among others. His work received international recognition the following decade with a retrospective at the Kunsthalle in Basel, Switzerland (1933) and another in the United States (1939–1940). During the Occupation, which he spent in Paris, he deepened the themes apparent in his "Interiors," which were to be followed, after the Liberation, by the "Billiards" series.

Additional accolades were to follow in 1948 with the publication of *Cahier de Georges Braque: 1917–1947* and the Grand Prize for Painting at the Venice Biennale. The correspondences between objects in his works became increasingly harmonious and were soon joined by the figure of the bird, as witnessed in the decorative ceiling of the Etruscan Room in the Louvre (1953). In 1961, on the occasion of his eightieth birthday, his studio was taken down and rebuilt in its entirety in the Louvre's Mollien Gallery, a previously unheard-of honor for a living artist. André Malraux accorded him another exceptional privilege upon his death in 1963 by delivering a eulogy in his honor before the colonnade of the Louvre.

See also **Cubism; Picasso, Pablo.**

BIBLIOGRAPHY

Georges Braque: Rétrospective 5 juillet–15 octobre 1994. Exposition et catalogue réalisés par Jean Louis Prat. Saint-Paul, France, 1994.

Rubin, William. *Picasso and Braque: Pioneering Cubism.* New York, 1989.

VIRGINIE DEVILLEZ

BRASILLACH, ROBERT (1909–1945),
French writer and right-wing journalist.

Having completed his studies at the prestigious École Normale Supérieure in 1928, Robert Brasillach began a journalistic career two years later that continued throughout his short life. After a

biography, *Présence de Virgile* (1931), came his first novel, *Le voleur d'étincelles* (1932; The thief of sparks). In 1931 he began his career as a literary critic for the right-wing, monarchist, Catholic newspaper *L'action française,* whose leading spirit was Charles Maurras. Brasillach became one of Maurras's many "disciples," promoting French nationalism for much of his career. In 1932 he produced an adaptation of the trial of Joan of Arc, a heroine whom Brasillach greatly admired. He was also theater critic for the *Revue universelle* and *1933.* A play, *Domrémy* (1933), followed and then a novel, *Le marchand d'oiseaux* (1936; The bird seller). The antigovernment riots and demonstrations of February 1934 (particularly of 6 February) in Paris moved Brasillach to declare that the dawn of fascism had risen over France. The novel *L'enfant de la nuit* (1934; Child of the night) demonstrated the author's mastery of a type of impressionistic urban poetry. In 1935 he coauthored with Maurice Bardèche the seminal *Histoire du cinéma.* A collection of studies of contemporary writers, *Portraits,* also appeared in 1935. In 1936 Brasillach met Léon Degrelle, the Belgian leader of the Rexist (monarchist, Catholic) movement and wrote *Léon Degrelle et l'avenir de "Rex"* (Léon Degrelle and the future of Rex).

In the first year of the Spanish civil war, he published *Les cadets de l'Alcazar* (1936; The cadets of Alcazar). He also coauthored a second account of this event with Henri Massis (*Le siège de l'Alcazar*). His larger *Histoire de la guerre d'Espagne* (1939; History of the Spanish war) covers the entire war with a distinct pro-Franco bias. The novel *Comme le temps passe* (As time passes) appeared in 1937. In the same year, Brasillach went to Italy and wrote enthusiastically about the new fascist regime of Benito Mussolini. He became editor of the weekly fascist newspaper *Je suis partout* (I am everywhere). In September of that year, he attended the Nuremberg Rally, an experience that apparently bewitched him and increased his admiration for National Socialist Germany. In 1938 Brasillach published a study of the seventeenth-century playwright Pierre Corneille. This biography was highly influenced by his commitment to European fascism. His novel *Les sept couleurs* (1939; The seven colors) is his only truly experimental work of fiction. Each chapter adopts a different literary genre (narrative, correspondence, documents, etc.) in order to relate a continuous story about a couple of lovers who are deeply affected by events on the European political stage, in particular by the rise and apparent triumph of fascism.

Like many other Frenchmen, he was mobilized in 1938 at the time of the Munich crisis, only to stand down for a year, before the outbreak of World War II. From 1939 to 1940, he was stationed on the Maginot Line, where, during periods of idleness, he penned his evocative memoirs of Paris (and France) in the interwar years, entitled *Notre avant-guerre* (1941; Before the war). As a prisoner of war in Germany, he wrote *Les captifs* (The captives; his only unfinished novel). Returning to France in March 1941, he resumed his journalism with *Je suis partout*. His articles for this newspaper and for others were of a literary, artistic, and political nature. They were often brilliantly vituperative and scurrilous, promoting fascism, National Socialism, and the Vichy regime. During the German occupation of France he wrote a novel, *La conquérante* (1943; The conqueror), based on his mother's experiences in Morocco in the early years of the twentieth century. Having vainly attempted to persuade Georges Simenon to write a novel set in the murky milieu of collaboration and resistance, he composed *Six heures à perdre* (1944; Six hours to kill). Finding *Je suis partout*'s collaborationism excessive, he quit the newspaper's team in September 1943. When the Allies arrived in Paris in August 1944, Brasillach went into hiding. Obliged to give himself up to the liberation authorities, he was imprisoned at Fresnes, where, among other works, he wrote the poignant *Poèmes de Fresnes* (1946) and completed his sequel to *Notre avant-guerre,* appositely entitled *Journal d'un homme occupé* (Journal of an occupied man). He was tried for treason in January 1945 and found guilty. Despite a petition for clemency, organized by François Mauriac and signed by many of the most famous writers and artists of the day, Brasillach was executed by firing squad on 6 February 1945.

As of 2005, Brasillach was the only collaborationist to remain unpardoned. His controversial collaborationism during the occupation, his status as an unrepentant French fascist, and his anti-Semitism, together with his acerbic journalistic verve, have exercised biographers and historians alike. As a result, the rest of his work is often considered as being of secondary importance. The controversy over his career, his execution, and, more generally, the responsibility of the writer continues to this day.

See also **Anti-Semitism; Camus, Albert; Collaboration; Fascism; Maurras, Charles.**

BIBLIOGRAPHY

Primary Sources

Brasillach, Robert. *Oeuvres complètes de Robert Brasillach.* 12 vols. Paris, 1963–1966.

———. *A Translation of "Notre avant-guerre/Before the War" by Robert Brasillach.* Translated and edited by Peter Tame. Lewiston, N.Y., 2002.

Secondary Sources

George, Bernard. *Robert Brasillach.* Paris, 1968.

Kaplan, Alice. *The Collaborator.* Chicago, 2000.

Tame, Peter D. *La mystique du fascisme dans l'oeuvre de Robert Brasillach.* Paris, 1986.

———. *The Ideological Hero in the Novels of Robert Brasillach, Roger Vailland, and André Malraux.* New York, 1998.

Tucker, William R. *The Fascist Ego: A Political Biography of Robert Brasillach.* Berkeley, Calif., 1975.

PETER TAME

BRAUDEL, FERNAND (1902–1985), French historian.

The French historian Fernand Braudel was the intellectual heir of Marc Bloch (1886–1944) and Lucien Febvre (1878–1956), later becoming their promoter and finally the leader of what became known as the Annales school. Through both his individual work and his institutional power, he profoundly influenced historiography and the organization of historical research during the second half of the twentieth century.

Born into a family of peasant background in Lorraine, Braudel studied history and geography—the two disciplines were linked at the time—at the Sorbonne. Thus, in contrast to many of his mentors and his students, he was not a graduate of the École Normale Supérieure in Paris and did not have the social status of an "heir." During his subsequent tenure as a high school teacher in Algeria, he discovered the geography of the Mediterranean, which from the 1930s was to become the main focus of his research. The result was a massive doctoral thesis, written in part in a German prison camp and defended in 1947: *La Méditerranée et le monde méditerranéen à l'époque de Philippe II* (*The Mediterranean and the Mediterranean World in the Age of Philip II*). As soon as it was published (1949; English trans., 1972–1973), the book caused a sensation and was hailed as "revolutionary," both in France and abroad (in Germany, for example, by Werner Conze).

In this work Braudel first developed his conception of "long-term" history and his now-famous distinction among the different temporal frames characteristic of different levels of historical evolution: (1) a "slow" history of the geographic environment; (2) a more rapid, "conjunctural" history of societies and cultures; and (3) an "immediate" history of political events, culminating, in this case, in the great naval battle of Lepanto in 1571. By thus rewriting the history of the sixteenth century based not on a decisive event or a central figure such as Philip II of Spain (r. 1556–1598), but instead on a constructed subject, the Mediterranean, Braudel opened up new perspectives onto a history that would be both "total," in the sense of Bloch, Febvre, and the Belgian historian Henri Pirenne (1862–1935), but also "global" in a new sense, capable of playing with different scales and combining macro- and micro-history. Even though Braudel's disdain for "political events," which he viewed as surface phenomena concealing deeper structures, may seem outmoded in the early twenty-first century, his discovery of the "ecological" dimension of history and of the Mediterranean as a "historical laboratory," along with his art in "telling" its history, albeit from a "deterministic" vantage point, earned him a worldwide reputation.

First a professor at the Collège de France, Braudel also became head of the "Sixth Section" of the École Pratique des Hautes Études (today, the École des Hautes Études en Sciences Sociales), and eventually the founder, in 1962, of the Maison des Sciences de l'Homme, a social sciences research center in Paris. He was both a brilliant teacher and a shrewd administrator who was able to take full advantage of favorable circumstances and the competition between East and West in the field of the social sciences to establish, with notable support from American foundations, a multidisciplinary history that the founders of the *Annales* had only been able to dream of.

Under these circumstances, it might naturally be expected that Braudel's scientific work would for a time be relegated to the background, the historian essentially limiting himself to the editorship of the *Annales* or producing articles. And indeed, it was only after his retirement that Braudel was able to publish, in quick succession, two major series of works that extended his research in two almost opposite directions: first, a three-volume socioeconomic history of the "world-system" from the sixteenth through the eighteenth century, *Civilisation matérielle, économie et capitalisme* (1967–1979; *Civilization and Capitalism, 15th–18th Century,* 1981–1983), and second a highly idiosyncratic three-volume history of France, *L'identité de la France* (1986; *The Identity of France,* 2 vols., 1989–1990), in which the author rediscovers the nation's geography—and its diversity—from the perspective of a disillusioned, or even melancholy, social historian. The latter project, unfinished at the historian's death, is nonetheless highly revelatory of the thinking of a man who, beyond the influences of the academy and even his own social origins, was strongly marked by the major transformations of French society since World War I.

See also **Annales School; Bloch, Marc; Febvre, Lucien; France.**

BIBLIOGRAPHY

Daix, Pierre. *Braudel.* Paris, 1995.

Gemelli, Giuliana. *Fernand Braudel.* Translated from the Italian by Brigitte Pasquet and Béatrice Propetto Marzi. Paris, 1995.

Marino, John A., ed. *Early Modern History and the Social Sciences: Testing the Limits of Braudel's Mediterranean.* Kirksville, Mo., 2002.

Revel, Jacques, ed. *Fernand Braudel et l'histoire.* Paris, 1999.

PETER SCHÖTTLER

BRAUN, WERNHER VON (1912–1977),
German scientist.

Wernher von Braun was the famous German constructor of the liquid fuel rocket A-4 (Aggregat 4), which took off for the first time on 3 October 1942. Being relabeled by the Nazis as *Vergeltungswaffe* (retaliation weapon) V-2, it was the first missile in history to be used in warfare, when hundreds of missiles hit large towns such as Antwerp and London in late 1944.

Von Braun was born on 23 March 1912 as the second son of an aristocratic family. Protected by his good-natured mother, he developed even in his youth a characteristic style of playing risky games. Inspired by a book by the rocket pioneer Hermann Oberth, von Braun decided to construct the rockets needed to fly to the moon when he was a teenager. After a series of experiments conducted by Oberth, Rudolf Nebel (1894–1978), von Braun, and others with small rockets on the Raketenflugplatz Berlin (Rocket Port) in 1930, the Army Ordnance offered von Braun the opportunity to continue his experiments with the military, which meant better equipment and payment, but also the obligation of secrecy. The twenty-year-old von Braun couldn't resist this offer and joined the military in December 1932. He may have thought that he could play games with the military.

The legends, produced by von Braun and others after 1945, say that the rocket engineers did not think of war and were not affected by the Nazi regime until 1942. Serious historical research conducted by Michael Neufeld and others, however, reveals that there had been a close relationship of Nazi politics and rocket technology since 1933. Von Braun, member of the Nazi Party since 1937 and member of the SS since 1940, had been appointed technical director of the army rocket center in Peenemünde in 1937 with a staff of ninety employees, later numbering up to five thousand. The task of this center, which had been constructed according to his plans, was to construct a military missile and not a space rocket.

It was an enormous achievement to build the world's first liquid fuel missile—able to transport a warhead of one metric ton over a distance of 250 kilometers—within a period of only five years. The reasons for this success were, according to Neufeld, the integration of all research and testing within one plant (a novelty in history, later called "big science"), the generous support of these efforts by the Nazi regime (although raw materials and qualified personnel generally were short, especially after war had begun), and, finally, the charismatic leadership of von Braun, who was able to integrate and to motivate the team even in hard times.

However, the rocket engineers paid a high price for this success. Thousands of prisoners of the concentration camp Mittelbau-Dora, who were forced to work in the underground production plant of the V-2 missile, died of starvation or were killed by brutal SS warders. Von Braun constantly denied having been informed about this, but records reveal several signs that he was much more involved in the program than the legends suggest. He was the top manager and the top promoter of the missile project, and he even visited Adolf Hitler several times in order to secure support from the very top of the Nazi regime.

The moral failure of von Braun during the Nazi era may be explained by his youth and the constraints and the momentum, which arose step-by-step out of the specific constellation of politics and technology. However, it is hard to conceive why von Braun continued this kind of work after 1945 without any scruple. After being captured by the U.S. army in 1945 and transferred to the United States, in 1949 he even proposed to construct a gigantic rocket to contribute to the assembly of a Strategic Defense Initiative (SDI)-like battlestation in orbit. In 1953 he completed his work on the world's first nuclear missile, the Redstone rocket, which was equipped with terminal guidance systems and thus could also hit small military targets and not only large cities (unlike the militarily useless V-2). In the 1950s, von Braun showed himself as an advocate of the arms race, and he heavily resisted his transfer to the civilian U.S. space agency NASA, which had been founded in 1958. However, the launch of the Soviet Sputnik, the first man-made object in space, in 1957 again created an emergency situation in which the United States needed a rescuer. Von Braun helped to recover the self-confidence of the American

One of von Braun's V-2 rockets is launched in Germany during World War II. GETTY IMAGES

nation by launching Explorer, the first U.S. satellite, on 31 January 1958. Within a period of only eight years on the project, in July 1969 von Braun and his team managed to bring a man to the moon and safely back again—another remarkable success, but a very costly and risky endeavor as well. However, after the Apollo mission, neither another emergency situation nor a new risky game to play arose. Frustrated, von Braun withdrew from NASA in 1972. He died from cancer on 16 June 1977.

See also **Space Programs; Sputnik.**

BIBLIOGRAPHY

Primary Sources

Braun, Wernher von. "Reminiscences of German Rocketry." *Journal of the British Interplanetary Society* 15, no. 3 (May–June 1956): 125–145.

Secondary Sources

McDougall, Walter A. *The Heavens and the Earth: A Political History of the Space Age.* New York, 1985.

Neufeld, Michael J. *The Rocket and the Reich: Peenemünde and the Coming of the Ballistic Missile Era.* New York, 1995.

Ordway, Frederick I., III, and Mitchell R. Sharpe. *The Rocket Team: From the V-2 to the Saturn Moon Rocket.* Cambridge, Mass., 1982.

Weyer, Johannes. *Werner von Braun.* Hamburg, 1999.

JOHANNES WEYER

BRECHT, BERTOLT (1898–1956), German author of plays, poetry, and novels.

Bertolt Brecht was born into a well-to-do middle class family in the Bavarian city of Augsburg where he grew up comfortably, like most children of his class. He had nearly finished secondary school, at the Königliches Realgymnasium, when World War I began. Brecht had been writing as well as publishing poetry for two years, and also a one-act drama, *The Bible.* Confident of becoming a German classic—as he assured his friends—he used to sing his rhymes for them, accompanying himself on his guitar. Though in a few poems he first celebrated the war, he soon turned against it and was nearly kicked out of school for an essay mocking Horace's famous praise of dying for the fatherland. After graduating in 1917, Brecht enrolled at Munich University to study medicine and philosophy, but preferred to attend drama courses and performances in the city's theaters. In early summer of 1918, Brecht finished his first major work for the stage, *Baal.*

Drafted into the army six weeks before Germany's capitulation, he served with a medical unit at Augsburg military hospital. During the brief revolutionary period that ended the war, he was elected to the Augsburg Workers and Soldiers Soviet, or so he claimed later. In 1918 he also wrote his famous anti-war poem, "Legend of the Dead Soldier," which the Nazis cited as evidence when they deprived him of German citizenship in 1935. At the age of twenty, Brecht had created his first dramatic masterpiece and a good deal of the poetry that would earn him his place among the greatest of German poets. Young Brecht was a charismatic performer of his poems, inventing melodies for them or singing them to popular tunes. Had he been born fifty years later, he might well have been tempted to make a career as a folk or rock singer.

EARLY SUCCESS AND ADOPTION OF MARXISM

During the Roaring Twenties, Brecht became an award-winning, if controversial, playwright and an acclaimed poet and lyricist. His first-ever produced play, *Drums in the Night*, at Munich in 1922, received the coveted Kleist Prize for Drama. A second play, *In the Jungle*, premiered in Munich the next year, causing a scandal, as did *Baal* at its premiere in Leipzig. Nevertheless, Brecht's adaptation of Christopher Marlowe's *Edward II* opened in Munich in early 1924, staged by Brecht himself, his first stab at the art that eventually would make him world famous. In 1924 he moved to Berlin, and though there were not that many productions of his plays, he was recognized as a major dramatist. Studying the texts of Karl Marx in the later 1920s, he adopted Marxist ideology as a basis and guide for his literary production. The musical *The Threepenny Opera*, written with the composer Kurt Weill, premiered in Berlin in 1928, to become the most popular German play of its time and, eventually, a most popular play worldwide.

By 1930, Brecht had developed a method of collective work; he fashioned his plays with teams of collaborators in an effort to break with the traditional concept of authorship; this has since been criticized as an indirect exploitation of his coworkers. He also evolved his concept of "Epic Theater," citing his and Weill's opera *Rise and Fall of the City of Mahagonny* (1931) as a case in point. The Great Depression and the concomitant rise of the Nazi movement led by Adolf Hitler motivated Brecht's alignment with the Communist Party, whose program corresponded, of course, to his Marxism. Consequently, he experimented with a sequence of *Lehrstücke*, plays that were supposed to not merely teach audiences but foremost their performers, who learn by enacting narratives of social and political conflict, *The Measures Taken* being a prominent and vehemently disputed example.

THE LONG EXILE

When Hitler took power in 1933, Brecht had to fear for his life and quickly left with his family, settling in Denmark where he spent six years before

A poster by Polish artist Franciszek Starowieyski advertises a production of Brecht's *Mother Courage and Her Children* in Wroclaw, Poland, 1976. BRIDGEMAN ART LIBRARY

moving, in 1939, to Sweden, and then to Finland. When an entry visa for the United States finally arrived, the family traveled through the Soviet Union and sailed from Vladivostok to Los Angeles on 13 June 1941, only nine days before Hitler's armies invaded the Soviet Union. In the poem "To Those Born After" he noted: "changing countries more often than our shoes / We moved through the wars of the classes, in despair / When there was injustice only but no outrage about it." Nevertheless, during his Scandinavian years Brecht completed six of his major plays, along with hundreds of poems, a novel, and numerous writings on Epic Theater.

Brecht settled with his family in Hollywood, hoping to write for the motion picture industry in which many of his European friends were employed. Though he devised numerous scenarios, only one resulted in a released film, *Hangmen Also*

Die (1943, directed by Fritz Lang), though the final screenplay differed vastly from Brecht's script. He mainly devoted his energy to projects for the stage, determined to make a career in the American theater since, at least until 1944, there was hardly assurance that he might be able to return to a Germany not ruled by the Nazis. Three of his plays received professional productions, only one of them on Broadway, but they found no commercial success. He had occasion to truly influence only the staging of *Galileo,* with Charles Laughton, whose performance he later described as a model for Epic acting.

RETURN TO BERLIN AND THE BERLINER ENSEMBLE

After Germany's defeat, Brecht immediately revived old contacts and prepared his return to Europe. In 1947, he had to testify before the House Un-American Activities Committee in Washington; the next day he flew to Paris to take residence in Switzerland where, for the first time since he had left Germany, he directed again, his version of *Antigone,* with his wife Helene Weigel (1900–1971) in the lead. In 1948, he was invited to stage his *Mother Courage and Her Children* in East Berlin. After the production's and Weigel's (as Courage) sensational success, Brecht was invited to set up his own company. At last his greatest wish had been fulfilled and he moved to East Berlin, where the newly established (East) German Democratic Republic's politics were in accord with his socialist convictions.

Brecht devoted his remaining seven years entirely to his theater, as playwright and, first of all, as *metteur-en-scène*. His Berliner Ensemble was to become the prototype of an Epic Theater, the model that he hoped would revolutionize the way theater was done in Germany. He based the company's work on concepts he had formulated in texts such as *A Short Organum for the Theatre* and *The Messingkauf Dialogues,* yet he greatly adjusted them in his practice. A given play's narrative in a particular interpretation, what Brecht called "the fable," was at the core of his directorial approach; his work with actors focused on creating with them the appropriate "gestus," the bodily and vocal manifestation of their character's socially conditioned behavior, for each moment and line of text. The staging was expected to "tell the fable" as clearly as possible in visual terms. The smallest details of performance were constantly scrutinized and many times revised to better serve the fable's presentation. Brecht always encouraged his actors to offer their own inventions and solutions, demanding: "Don't tell me, show me!"

The ensemble had been invited to the "Théâtre des Nations" festival in Paris in 1954 and subsequent years (winning the festival's prize several times), and also to London. As a result soon after his death in August 1956, the influence of Brecht's theater became palpable all over Western Europe. By the turn of the twenty-first century, his practice and commitment to a socially active theater that investigates the individual's role and struggles with society has been absorbed and further augmented by theater artists all over the world; he also is the only German playwright who attained a permanent place in the international repertoire. His collected works amount to thirty volumes, texts ranging from plays to poetry, novels, short stories, theoretical writings and numerous letters; he was unquestionably one of the most prolific authors of the twentieth century.

Shortly before his death, Brecht wrote a poem about not needing a gravestone. If people should need one for him, he said, it should be inscribed: "He made suggestions. We / Have accepted them."

See also Theater; Weill, Kurt.

BIBLIOGRAPHY

Primary Sources

Brecht, Bertolt. *Brecht on Theatre: The Development of an Aesthetic.* Edited and translated by John Willett. New York, 1964. Translations of various writings on Epic Theatre, among them "The Short Organum for the Theatre," with editorial notes.

———. *The Messingkauf Dialogues.* Translated by John Willett. London, 1965.

———. *Werke: Grosse kommentierte Berliner und Frankfurter Ausgabe.* 30 volumes. Berlin and Frankfurt, 1988–2000.

Secondary Sources

Hecht, Werner. *Brecht Chronik.* Frankfurt, 1997. The most comprehensive collection of data, professional and personal facts from Brecht's life.

Mews, Siegfried, ed. *A Bertolt Brecht Reference Companion.* Westport, Conn., 1997. A collection of essays that deal with Brecht's work and its reception by the world theater.

Thomson, Peter, and Glendyr Sacks, eds. *The Cambridge Companion to Brecht.* Cambridge, U.K., 1994. A collection of assessments of all aspects of Brecht's work, as a writer as well as a stage director and theoretician of the theater.

Willett, John. *The Theatre of Bertolt Brecht.* London, 1959. The seminal work on Brecht's theater, commenting on plays as well as on his directorial practice as it was observed by the author in Berlin.

CARL WEBER

BREL, JACQUES (1929–1978), Belgian singer-songwriter.

Jacques Brel was born on 8 April 1929 in Brussels, into a bourgeois family. After elementary school, he was enrolled in the renowned Saint-Louis School. He was not a stellar student, but he took advantage of that time to do theater. As a young Belgian Catholic, he spent his spare time with a mob of scouts who nicknamed him "Phoque hilarant" (hilarious seal).

In 1946, Brel joined the Franche Cordée, a mixed philanthropic movement of Catholic youth. He organized concerts and theatrical performances, which led him to discover his taste for singing in public. His future wife, Miche, was also a member of this group. They were married on 1 June 1950 and had three children: Chantal (1951), France (1953), and Isabelle (1958).

In 1953 Brel seriously considered leaving the family cardboard business. Passionate about music, he frequented such local Brussels clubs as Le Grenier de la Rose Noire (The attic of the black rose). Brel's first record was a 78 rpm with two tracks, "La foire" and "Il y a." It was thanks to this record that Brel met Jacques Canetti, the director of the Parisian cabaret Les Trois Baudets (The three donkeys). He encouraged Brel to start a career in Paris and offered him a recording contract with Philips. Brel became one of the noted singers at the "music haunts" of the Left Bank. Starting in 1956 he toured Europe and North Africa; in 1959 he starred at the Bobino theater in Paris. It was

Jacques Brel performs his farewell concert, Paris, January 1966. ©PIERRE VAUTHEY/CORBIS SYGMA

then that he wrote such great classics as: "La valse à mille temps" and "Ne me quitte pas." Tours and recitals around the world multiplied.

In 1966 Brel left the stage. He turned to movies (notably in 1967 with André Cayatte) and became a producer (*Far West*, 1972). He also produced many musical theater shows, such as *L'homme de La Mancha* (*Man of la Mancha*) at the Théâtre Royal de la Monnaie in Brussels in 1968. In 1974 he set sail aboard his sailboat *L'Askoy* and settled down two years later on the island of Hiva Oa in the Marquesas Islands of French Polynesia. He recorded his final record in 1977 and died the following year, on 9 October, of lung cancer.

Jacques Brel's lifework is both one of the best representations of French songwriting—along with that of Georges Braessens (1921–1981) or Jean Ferrat (b. 1930) and that of a poet with whom many generations could identify. His songs express the melancholy or enraged voice of the unloved: they are the echoes of a universe devoid of pleasure or grandeur, transcended by the lyricism of the artist. His accompaniment was often brilliant, and he mastered not only the language of tenderness ("Madeleine") but also the opposite ("Les flamingants"). In addition, it is essentially thanks to him that the accent and imagination of a French-speaking man from Brussels were heard on French stages.

See also **Popular Culture.**

BIBLIOGRAPHY

Primary Sources

Brel, Jacques, and the Fondation internationale Jacques Brel. *Tout Brel*. Paris, 2001. Complete works.

Secondary Sources

Clouzet, Jean, and Angela Clouzet. *Jacques Brel*. Paris, 2003.

Todd, Olivier. *Jacques Brel: Une Vie*. Paris, 2003.

Vandromme, Pol. *Jacques Brel: L'exil du Far West*. Paris, 1998.

PAUL ARON

BREST-LITOVSK. The Peace Treaty of Brest-Litovsk was signed on 3 March 1918 at the headquarters of the German High Command in the east by representatives of the Bolshevik government of Russia and of the four Central Powers. It effectively ended World War I on the eastern front and represented the victory of the Central Powers in the east. By the terms of the treaty the Russian government agreed to cease all hostilities, demobilize its army and navy, and exchange prisoners of war. The Russians also renounced all territorial claims and agreed to evacuate all troops west of a line encompassing the national boundaries of Ukraine, Poland, Belarus, Lithuania, and Finland as well as the districts of Ardahan, Kars, and Batum on the Turkish border. A supplementary treaty of 27 August 1918 added reparations totaling six billion marks and formally removed Estonia and Latvia from Russian rule. The detached states, containing some sixty million inhabitants, claimed national independence but in fact served as German puppets for the remainder of the war. The Bolshevik government thus surrendered approximately 34 percent of the prewar Russian Empire's population, 32 percent of its arable land, 54 percent of its industry, 89 percent of its coal mines, and virtually all of its oil production.

The Peace Treaty of Brest-Litovsk was preceded by the Bolshevik coup of 7 November 1917 that established Vladimir Lenin's Bolsheviks in power in Russia. Lenin's government, pledged to end the war and desperate to acquire popular backing, obtained an armistice effective 15 December and initiated peace negotiations with the Central Powers one week later. The Bolshevik negotiators, led by Leon Trotsky, called for a peace with no annexations or indemnities and hoped to use the peace conference as a forum for spreading Marxist revolution. The Central Powers' civilian delegates—led by the foreign ministers of Germany and Austria-Hungary, Richard von Kühlmann and Ottokar Czernin— sought moderate terms as a step toward a compromise general peace. Their hopes were dashed by the demands of Germany's de facto dictators Paul von Hindenburg and Erich Ludendorff of the German High Command—represented at Brest-Litovsk by General Max Hoffmann—for a victor's peace and extensive annexations. When negotiations stalled, the Central Powers initiated conversations with an anti-Bolshevik Ukrainian delegation. On 9 February 1918 these talks culminated in the signing of the "Bread Peace" between Ukraine and the Central Powers, whereby Ukraine pledged to provide its former enemies with at least one million tons of grain in exchange for recognition and territorial concessions in occupied Poland. This event, and the generally harsh nature of the terms of peace proposed by the Central Powers, prompted a Russian declaration of "no war, no peace" and withdrawal from the negotiations on 10 February. On 18 February the Germans renounced the armistice and initiated an unopposed military offensive deep into Russian-controlled territory. Under intense German pressure, the Bolsheviks agreed to reopen negotiations at Brest-Litovsk on 1 March. The treaty, with stiffer terms than those originally proposed, was signed two days later.

The Peace Treaty of Brest-Litovsk removed Russia from World War I and encouraged the German High Command to conclude that total victory could be achieved through an offensive in the west in spring 1918. It firmly established the dominance of the German High Command not only in German policy making but also over Germany's allies, thereby linking inextricably the fates of all the Central Powers to the success or failure of German arms. The failure of the final German offensive thus precipitated the collapse of Germany and its allies in the autumn. The treaty doomed any lingering chances for a compromise peace between the Central and Entente Powers, and its harsh terms contrasted starkly with Woodrow Wilson's idealistic Fourteen Points of 8 January 1918. The Peace Treaty of Brest-Litovsk thus hardened Entente leaders toward Germany and its allies and set a vindictive tone for the Paris Peace Conference that imposed the Versailles Treaty on defeated Germany on 28 June 1919. By fulfilling the Bolshevik promise of peace, the Peace Treaty of Brest-Litovsk also purchased Lenin's government the breathing space it needed to consolidate its hold on power before the outbreak of the Russian civil war in summer 1918. Its terms were effectively nullified by the collapse of the Central Powers in the autumn and by the Bolshevik victory in the civil war, in the course of which many of the severed western territories, including Ukraine, Belarus, and territory in the Caucasus, were reattached to the Russian state.

See also **Russian Revolutions of 1917; World War I.**

BIBLIOGRAPHY

Primary Source

Scott, James Brown, ed. *Official Statements of War Aims and Peace Proposals: December 1916 to November 1918.* Washington, D.C., 1921.

Secondary Sources

Kennan, George F. *Soviet-American Relations, 1917–1920.* Vol. 1, *Russia Leaves the War.* Princeton, N.J., 1956.

Ritter, Gerhard. *The Sword and the Scepter: The Problem of Militarism in Germany.* Vol. 4, *The Reign of German Militarism and the Disaster of 1918.* Translated by Heinz Norden. Coral Gables, Fla., 1973.

Wargelin, Clifford F. "A High Price for Bread: The First Treaty of Brest-Litovsk and the Break-Up of Austria-Hungary, 1917–1918." *International History Review* 19, no. 4 (1997): 757–788.

Wheeler-Bennett, John W. *Brest-Litovsk: The Forgotten Peace, March 1918.* London, 1938. Classic work, still the definitive study.

CLIFFORD F. WARGELIN

BRETON, ANDRÉ (1896–1966), founder of surrealism.

André Breton, born in Tinchebray sur Orne in Normandy, was truly a Breton, displaying a deep sense of gloom and foreboding and a certain attraction to mysticism. In 1923, having welcomed Dada's founder, Tristan Tzara, to Paris, Breton and Philippe Soupault wrote the first surrealist text, *Les champs magnétiques* (*Magnetic Fields*)—an illustration of automatic writing, a technique aimed at unleashing the unconscious and recognizing repressed desires that have nothing to do with the world of logic. And in 1924, Breton wrote the *Manifeste du surréalisme* (*Surrealist Manifesto*), in which surrealism was defined in terms of its liberating quality. Down with the rational mind—the Celtic atmosphere was making itself felt in other forms. Although surrealism may have officially ended with Breton's death, Breton and surrealism endured together for at least forty-two years. Breton—leonine, massive, sure, rhetorically and visually gifted—was surrealism itself.

The forceful *Surrealist Manifesto* was produced simultaneously with the journal aptly called *La révolution surréaliste* (The surrealist revolution). In addition to continuing the experiment with automatic writing (and drawing), the journal also recounted dreams, considered the pathway to the unconscious. Breton eventually became disappointed with the techniques of automatism; notwithstanding, he was initially excited about them and they continue to be important in literature and art. What these techniques unleashed, apart from a remarkable series of writings and events, was a point of view that was recognizably that of a free spirit.

Breton's first wife, Simone Kahn, joined him in the early surrealist experiments, which included collective games. With his second wife, the artist Jacqueline Lamba, Breton had a baby girl, Aube, who grew up to be an artist known as Aube Elléouët. The Bretons fled France during World War II, thanks to Varian Fry's rescue mission for European intellectuals. They first took refuge in Marseille, then arrived in New York via Martinique.

Breton did not learn any English in America and remained isolated from New York artists and writers, entirely taken up with the affairs of his own group of surrealists. Perhaps his closest contact was with the abstract expressionist Robert Motherwell, whom he met through the Chilean artist Roberto Matta Echaurren and who translated the idea of automatism into the realm of the visual arts.

Breton's desire for political action is attested in *Surréalisme au service de la révolution* (1930; Surrealism at the service of the revolution), the successor journal to *La révolution surréaliste.* But his discussions with the "cell" of gas workers to which he was assigned did not lead to satisfaction on his part or comprehension on the part of the workers. Breton understandably felt the same sense of disappointment he had experienced when his long-desired encounter with Sigmund Freud led to no entrancing discussion of psychoanalysis or the role of dreams.

When Jacqueline left Breton for the American artist David Hare, Breton married a third time.

André Breton (center) with poets Paul Éluard (left) and Robert Desnos, c. 1923. BRIDGEMAN ART LIBRARY

With his new wife, Elisa Bindhoff, he traveled through North America and was particularly taken by Native American customs and art in the Midwest and on the Gaspé Peninsula of Canada. After the war, he returned with Elisa to Paris but found the atmosphere greatly changed. At the Sorbonne, Tzara and Breton argued publicly over politics and art, Tzara claiming that Breton, who had taken refuge in America, had run away from Europe when others were fighting in the Resistance. While others faced real barbed wire, Tzara maintained, the New York surrealist group was playing with the metallic grids of art stretched across their journal *VVV:* "Feel this with your eyes closed," the caption ran.

Surrealism stood accused of irrelevance. But Breton's poems and essays constitute an important legacy. His insuperably poetic prose style informs *Les pas perdus* (1924; *The Lost Steps*), *Point du jour* (1934; *Break of Day*), *L'amour fou* (1937; *Mad Love*), *Arcane 17* (1944), and *La clé des champs* (1953; *Free Rein*). From the poet Pierre Reverdy Breton adapted the idea of the poetic image as that which weds opposites with great force and in a flash. In the poetic image one thing leads to another, day to night, life to death. All communicate their elements with one another, as in Breton's illustrative scientific experiment called *Les vases communicants* (1944; *Communicating Vessels*), the most theoretical of his essays. It was always his hope to reconcile opposites via the conducting wire leading from field to opposing field. This was surrealism's characteristic and optimistic way of dealing with the universe.

What Breton called "convulsive" beauty is a dynamic recognition of the "reciprocal relations linking the object seen in its motion and its repose." It is a point of view diametrically opposed to static perception, readying itself—in a constant state of expectation—for the encounter with the marvelous, an unexpected and splendid outlook and vision where perception and representation converge. Breton died in 1966, soon after many students and disciples of surrealism had gathered at Cerisy-la-Salle in Normandy to celebrate his ideas and his role as the undisputed leader of the movement. The goal of surrealism is to transform life, language, and human understanding, through what Breton called "lyric behavior," in which the observer is part of the scene observed, to liberate people from any limitation or constriction imposed by something outside them. In this respect, surrealism intended and still intends to remake the world.

See also **Dada; Surrealism.**

BIBLIOGRAPHY

Primary Sources

Breton, André. *Mad Love.* Translated by Mary Ann Caws. Lincoln, Neb., 1987. Translation of *L'amour fou* (1937).

———. *Communicating Vessels.* Translated by Mary Ann Caws and Geoffrey T. Harris. Lincoln, Neb., 1990. Translation of *Les vases communicants* (1955).

———. *Free Rein.* Translated by Michel Parmentier and Jacqueline d'Amboise. Lincoln, Neb., 1995. Translation of *La clé des champs* (1953).

———. *The Lost Steps.* Translated by Mark Polizzotti. Lincoln, Neb., 1996. Translation of *Les pas perdus* (1924).

Secondary Sources

Balakian, Anna. *André Breton: Magus of Surrealism.* New York, 1971.

Caws, Mary Ann. *Surrealism and the Literary Imagination, Study of Breton and Bachelard.* The Hague, 1966.

———. *André Breton.* New ed. New York, 1996.

———. *The Surrealist Look: An Erotics of Encounter.* Cambridge, Mass., 1997.

Caws, Mary Ann, ed. *Surrealist Love Poems.* Translated by Mary Ann Caws. London, 2001.

———, ed. *Surrealist Painters and Poets.* Cambridge, Mass., 2001.

———, ed. *Surrealism.* London, 2004.

Foster, Hal. *Compulsive Beauty.* Cambridge, Mass., 1993.

Krauss, Rosalind, Jane Livingston, and Dawn Ades. *L'amour fou: Photography and Surrealism.* Washington, D.C., 1985.

Lomas, David. *The Haunted Self: Surrealism, Psychoanalysis, Subjectivity.* New Haven, Conn., 2000.

Mundy, Jennifer, Vincent Gille, and Dawn Ades, eds. *Surrealism: Desire Unbound.* Princeton, N.J., 2001.

Polizzotti, Mark. *Revolution of the Mind: The Life of André Breton.* New York, 1995.

Sawin, Martica. *Surrealism in Exile and the Beginning of the New York School.* Cambridge, Mass., 1995.

MARY ANN CAWS

BRETTON WOODS AGREEMENT.

The New Hampshire spa of Bretton Woods gave its name to the international economic agreements negotiated there between the United States and the United Kingdom in 1944, subsequently signed by forty-two other countries. The agreements covered a wide range of commercial and monetary purposes, but the name is used to signify the international trade and payments machinery that replaced the gold standard of the interwar period. The regime did not become fully operative until 1958 and underwent many changes before its collapse in 1971. It makes better historical sense to think of Bretton Woods as a broad agreement on the manner in which world trade and payments were to be managed between the capitalist states and on a readiness to make adjustments for that common purpose.

NEED FOR AGREEMENT

The need for agreement was imperative both for the United Kingdom, deeply in debt to the United States by summer 1944, and for the United States, whose postwar policy was to return to unrestricted international trade based on automatic currency convertibility. Nevertheless, agreement was hard to reach. In London financial reasoning suggested that Britain would need a substantial transition period before its overall balance of payments would be strong enough to accept the automatic dollar convertibility of the pound sterling. The terms of the final settlement of all mutual Anglo-American war debts dominated the Bretton Woods meeting, because they determined what seemed possible.

The experience of the failure of the gold standard in the interwar period helped in reaching agreement. Both countries now wished to control capital movements, confining the purpose of convertibility to the settlement of trade and current accounts. The United Kingdom conceded that currency exchange rates should be fixed against the gold value of the U.S. dollar. The United States withdrew its demand that countries would not have the right to alter their exchange rate, although it insisted on setting too high a rate for the pound against the dollar ($4.03 = £1.00). Tariff preferences for British Commonwealth goods exported to the United Kingdom were regarded by the United States as discrimination against American exports of similar agricultural products, but the issue was compromised by both sides accepting a rule that there should be no new preferences in the Bretton Woods trading system, thus leaving the intended process of reduction of tariffs to reduce the degree of advantage given by the existing preferential tariffs. Such movements toward agreement were testimony to the common impact of the war on economic policy and theory in the United States and the United Kingdom, not least in concentrating both policy and theory on the advantages of reflation.

A common standpoint also emerged about the need for international collaborative institutions to make the management of a world trade and payments mechanism possible. The International Monetary Fund (IMF) was created to supervise the exchange rates, and its permission was decreed necessary before any rate could be changed. The ability to create international supervisory institutions that have lasted is the most telling indication of the underlying common purpose of the two countries and of the subsequent signatories. In practice, as well as in its origins, Bretton Woods was to show that consistent intentions were more durable than rules.

CHANGING THE RULES

The history of the rules is full of change. The United Kingdom was unable to win any longer transition period than two years before automatic currency convertibility in trade settlements had to apply. In the first two years of peace Western European economies experienced a vigorous boom with high levels of investment and a high rate of import growth, particularly of capital goods and food, of which in both cases the United States was at first the only available supplier. By summer 1947 not only Britain, as it had feared, but also other Western European countries were running out of dollars. None, however, except Italy, cut back on imports and tightened its monetary policy. All were faced with imperative public demand for goods, jobs, and public welfare provision. Return to interwar conditions seemed politically impossible. This was against the background of relentless competition with the communist political regimes of Eastern and central Europe.

Faced with the emerging threat of the Cold War and of a political division through the center of Europe and of Germany and no prospect of a peace treaty being signed, the United States had to support Western European domestic policies or face isolation. The outcome was the Marshall Plan, officially styled the European Recovery Program. It opened a new stream of dollars to Western Europe for economic reconstruction and additional international agencies to implement Bretton Woods. The European Payments Union (EPU) added to its task of regulating the trade settlements that of directing trade between the European recipients of Marshall Aid toward greater multilateralism. In retrospect the need for the Marshall Plan justified Europe's fears about the inadequacy of Bretton Woods as a viable regime so soon after the war. It was only at the end of December 1958 that automatic convertibility between all Western European currencies and the dollar was achieved.

To mark even more clearly that the Bretton Woods system was not the monolith envisaged in 1944, Canada maintained its decision in 1950 to float its currency, France used multiple exchange rates for much of 1948, and the pound sterling was devalued in 1949 from $4.00 to $2.80, a decision about which the IMF was informed, without prior discussion, only one day in advance.

PROBLEMS AND FAILURES OF THE SYSTEM

Bretton Woods did not break free from the denomination of international settlements in gold. Convertibility was based on the American dollar being tied to a fixed value in gold, to be maintained by the open-market operations of the American monetary authorities. As under the interwar gold standard, therefore, the exchange rates were at the mercy of variations in the supply and demand for gold, not a commodity whose supply could be quickly increased. Earlier reserve currencies, such as sterling, became less used, from the mid-1960s through deliberate policy actions of the British government. The availability of gold was outpaced by the relentless growth in the value of foreign trade over the long boom from 1945 in the Western world. One characteristic of that trade was the persistent increase of manufactured imports into the United States from Western Europe and Japan. Its counterpart was the remorseless flow throughout the Bretton Woods years of gold from the United States to Europe. Monetary economists often conclude that the dollar price of gold was set too low, but the flow of dollars from the United States reflected the reality of the longest recorded economic boom in Europe and the increasing power of European and Japanese manufacturing.

To exacerbate this problem, there were persistent inflationary trends in the American economy, some of them generated by its long, and in foreign eyes doomed, war in Vietnam. Either the United States would be forced to reduce worldwide liquidity, and thus the expansion of foreign trade, and risk a return to international deflation, or new forms of sustaining liquidity would have to be devised. Experiments in alternatives, chiefly the issue of tradable Special Drawing Rights (SDRs), came too late to be effective. The United States had a balance of payments deficit in its own settlements in every year from 1958 to the close of 1967, although in all except one it had a surplus on current account. The deficit was due to capital exports, of which the largest component was private investment, mainly in Western Europe. The fear was that the dollar value of investments might be converted into gold. The rest of the world's gold stock was already in 1959 estimated to exceed that of the United States. If, alternatively, the United States reduced the size of its dollar deficit, the loss of the liquidity that had been backed by that deficit might well also provoke deflation.

The end came in response to British and French intentions to convert dollars into gold. On 15 August 1971 the United States suspended automatic dollar convertibility into gold, ending its efforts to maintain the fixed value of gold, and imposed a surcharge on imports and wage and price controls within the United States.

BRETTON WOODS IN RETROSPECT

In one sense, this only registered the fact that the system had already changed into a dollar, rather than a gold, standard. But that change should have led to a more determined effort by the United States to reduce its own domestic inflation. Bretton Woods will be remembered as ushering in and for a long time safeguarding the longest recorded period of high economic growth in modern history, although for the United States this was much less evident in the 1950s. Its ignominious end demonstrates that all international payments systems are eventually overtaken by the worldwide economic change that their success in stimulating international trade promotes. No single hegemonic power can prevent such an outcome. International settlements agreements facilitate foreign trade. Foreign trade promotes economic growth, notably so in the 1960s, and states must adjust domestic and foreign policies as long as they wish to maintain that advantage.

See also **Marshall Plan.**

BIBLIOGRAPHY

Bordo, Michael D., and Barry Eichengreen, eds. *A Retrospective on the Bretton Woods System: Lessons for International Monetary Reform.* Chicago, 1993.

Gardner, Richard N. *Sterling-Dollar Diplomacy: Anglo-American Collaboration in the Reconstruction of Multilateral Trade.* Oxford, U.K., 1956.

Milward, Alan S. *The Reconstruction of Western Europe, 1945–51.* London, 1984.

Pressnell, Leslie. *External Economic Policy since the War.* Vol. 1: *The Post-War Financial Settlement.* London, 1986.

Triffin, Robert. *Europe and the Money Muddle: From Bilateralism to Near-Convertibility, 1947–1956.* New Haven, Conn., 1957.

ALAN S. MILWARD

BREZHNEV, LEONID (1906–1982), Soviet leader from 1964 to 1982.

Born in Kamenskoye (renamed Dneprodzerzhinsk in 1936) in Ukraine, where his father was a metalworker, Leonid Ilyich Brezhnev entered the Kursk Agricultural Technical Institute in 1923, graduating in 1927. In that year he married Victoria Petrovna Denisova, and together they moved to the Urals, including a spell in 1931 in Sverdlovsk (Yekaterinburg). Returning to Kamenskoye, he joined the Communist Party on 24 October 1931. As members of the old intelligentsia were replaced by newly trained workers (the *vydvizhentsy*) and the purges took their toll on staff, Brezhnev began his swift rise. By 1933 he had become director of the Dneprodzerzhinsk Metallurgical Institute and in 1935 was awarded an engineering degree. Following military service in Chita in 1935, he became deputy head of the Dneprodzerzhinsk city soviet with responsibility for city construction. From 1938 until the beginning of World War II he worked in Dnepropetrovsk, becoming ideological secretary in 1939. During the war he saw action as a political officer in the Caucasus, Ukraine, the Carpathians, and Eastern Europe, as well as participating in the liberation of Novorossysk and the associated region, which later became the subject of one of his books, *Malaya zemlya* (Little land), exaggerating his military achievements.

On 21 November 1947 Brezhnev became first secretary of the Dnepropetrovsk Obkom (regional party committee), and this became his political base for the rest of his career. In the early 1950s he worked briefly in Moldavia as head of the republic before being elected a member of the Central Committee (CC) of the Communist Party of the Soviet Union (CPSU) and a secretary of the CC by the Nineteenth Party Congress in 1952. One of the leaders of Nikita Khrushchev's Virgin Lands Scheme, on 5 February 1954 Brezhnev became second secretary of Kazakhstan, and on 6 August 1955 he was appointed head of the republic as first secretary.

Returning in 1956, Brezhnev was elevated by the Twentieth Congress to candidate membership of the Presidium (as the Politburo was then known) of the CPSU and was once again elected a CC secretary, now assuming responsibility for defense, heavy engineering, and capital construction. He supported Nikita Khrushchev in his struggle with the so-called anti-party group in 1957. He was rewarded by becoming the deputy head of the Russian Soviet Federated Social Republic (RSFSR) bureau of the CC CPSU, and in 1960 he was appointed chair of the Presidium of the USSR

Supreme Soviet (effectively president). By 1963 he had become the second secretary of the CC CPSU. He played an important role in Khrushchev's overthrow, representing a revolt of the party bureaucracy against Khrushchev's "harebrained schemes," and on 14 October 1964 Brezhnev became first secretary of the party.

Brezhnev is usually remembered through the prism of his last years, when he was physically debilitated and the country under his leadership had entered a period of immobility and stagnation. However, commentators like Henry Kissinger in the late 1960s noted Brezhnev's physical magnetism and energy. His rule began with the promise of economic reform, masterminded by Prime Minister Alexei Kosygin, but these plans soon ran into the sands. Brezhnev's rule represented the end of destalinization, and was accompanied by the policy of "stability of cadres" that allowed corruption and the abuse of the *nomenklatura* system of appointments to flourish. In 1968 Brezhnev was complicit in the invasion of Czechoslovakia, and he gave his name to the "Brezhnev Doctrine" of limited sovereignty for the Eastern European "fraternal" socialist countries. That year he suffered the first of his health breakdowns associated with sedatives. Brezhnev lacked all intellectual curiosity, and although the head of the world's leading communist state, he was never seen to have read any of the classics of Marxism-Leninism. He preferred magazines with big color photographs or cartoons.

The early 1970s saw the onset of détente with the West. In 1970 Brezhnev signed the Moscow agreements between the USSR and West Germany, stabilizing their relationship in response to the West German chancellor Willy Brandt's *Ostpolitik*, his effort to normalize relations with Eastern European countries. Détente brought certain fruits, including the first Strategic Arms Limitation Talks (SALT) and the Anti-Ballistic Missile Treaty, both in 1972. The economic benefits of détente allowed Brezhnev to postpone necessary economic reforms. It was during his meeting with U.S. president Gerald Ford in Vladivostok in 1974 that Brezhnev suffered the first collapse of his nervous system. The main triumph of his leadership was the signature of the Helsinki Final Act in August 1975, in which the Soviet regime undertook human rights commitments in exchange for economic and security gains, including the recognition of the postwar borders. Brezhnev had no intention of observing the human rights promises, and instead by the end of the decade the world was plunged into a second Cold War that in some ways was more threatening than the first, bringing the world to the verge of nuclear war. Although the SALT II agreement was signed in Vienna in 1979, in December of that year Brezhnev sanctioned the introduction of Soviet troops into Afghanistan.

Brezhnev's love of awards and honors culminated in his becoming a marshal of the Soviet Union in May 1976. His chest was soon to run out of space on which to pin the various medals and awards that he granted himself, including four "gold star" medals as "Hero of the Soviet Union." From 1977 he combined the posts of first secretary and head of the Supreme Soviet Presidium, thus becoming not only party leader but also head of state (president). The year 1978 saw the publication of his books *Malaya zemlya*, *Vozrozhdenie* (Rebirth), and *Tselina* (Virgin lands), for which he was awarded numerous literary prizes, including, on 31 March 1980, the Lenin Prize for literature.

Brezhnev's long tenure in power saw the Soviet Union achieve strategic parity with the United States, but the country under him became a colossus with feet of clay governed by an introspective, conservative gerontocracy. Mikhail Gorbachev dubbed the later years of his leadership the period of stagnation (*zastoi*). Brezhnev's refusal to tackle the problems facing the country led to declining economic growth rates, social decay, and external hostility. Although his rule is seen as one of peace and stability, in the end the Brezhnevite system proved unsustainable.

See also **Arms Control; Cold War; Gorbachev, Mikhail; Khrushchev, Nikita; Soviet Union.**

BIBLIOGRAPHY

Bacon, Edwin, and Mark Sandle, eds. *Brezhnev Reconsidered.* Basingstoke, U.K., 2002.

Bialer, Seweryn. *Stalin's Successors: Leadership, Stability, and Change in the Soviet Union.* Cambridge, U.K., 1980.

Breslauer, George W. *Khrushchev and Brezhnev as Leaders: Building Authority in Soviet Politics.* London, 1982.

Kelley, Donald R. *Soviet Politics in the Brezhnev Era.* New York, 1980.

Tompson, William. *The Soviet Union under Brezhnev, 1964–1982.* Harlow, U.K., 2003.

RICHARD SAKWA

BRIAND, ARISTIDE (1862–1932), French statesman.

Aristide Briand was born on 28 March 1862, in Nantes, France, into a family of café owners. He attended high school in Nantes. After his baccalaureate, in 1881, he started clerking at a Saint-Nazaire attorney's office. Two years later he went to Paris to study law. He began his career simultaneously as a lawyer (he registered with the bar association of Saint-Nazaire in November 1886) and as a journalist (he published his first article in August of 1884 in *La démocratie de l'ouest*).

Politically involved at an early age (he was a Radical candidate in the 1889 legislative elections), during the 1890s Briand became a revolutionary activist and a supporter of general strikes. Briand founded the first trade union of the workers of Brière on 10 August 1892, and began to be seen as a fervent strike promoter. In collaboration with the anarchist Fernand Pelloutier (1867–1901) he worked on an essay, *De la Révolution par la grève générale* (Revolution by the general strike). From then on, he ran as a Socialist candidate, suffering several failures before being elected deputy in the 1902 parliamentary elections in the Loire region (he would be reelected for the next thirty years). As secretary general of the Socialist Party, he became close with Jean Jaurès (1859–1914), the founder of *L'humanité*, a newspaper for which Briand wrote several articles.

Though he joined the still-young French Section of the Workers' International in 1905, Briand had another ambition: to become a statesman. His first opportunity came during a debate on the law mandating the separation of church and state, for which he was the spokesperson at the Chamber of Deputies. In this debate he showed qualities that would forge the rest of his career: his talent for conciliation and both a sense of and a desire for openness and compromise. The success of that effort enabled him to become the minister of public education and of culture in 1906, in the cabinet of Jean Marie Ferdinand Sarrien. This was a turning point in his career. Henceforth, his revolutionary ideas would fade and be replaced by a concern for realism and pragmatism. His membership in the Socialist Party was revoked because the party forbade members from participating in "bourgeois" governments.

From then on, Briand ran as an independent socialist, straddling the left and the right. Thus he began an impressive ministerial career (he served as minister a total of twenty-two times over the next twenty-five years). When he was elected president of the council for the first time in 1909 (he was reelected ten times), he governed with firmness and pragmatism, repressing the strikes of 1910 and pursuing a policy of conciliation with the Catholics. During the First World War he was the head of the government (1915–1917); he served as prime minister also in 1921–1922, under the ruling majority of the National Bloc, and in 1925–1926, with the Left Wing Cartel.

Briand's grand design concerned foreign policy much more than it did domestic policy. He was appointed minister of foreign affairs fifteen times and served continuously from 1925 to 1932. At the end of World War I, he was at first a supporter of the firm application of the Treaty of Versailles in Germany—but the man who would "collar Germany" soon revised his position, realizing that France did not have the means to police the European continent. Three ideas would guide his politics from then on: closer ties between France and Germany, defending collective peace and security in the framework of the League of Nations, and developing the idea of a united Europe. So, Aristide Briand, along with his German counterpart Gustav Stresemann (1878–1929), negotiated the Locarno Pact (1925) and sponsored Germany's entry into the League of Nations (1926). Briand was also the originator of the Kellogg-Briand Pact "outlawing" war.

Finally, in a famous speech that he delivered before the general assembly of the League of Nations on 5 September 1929, he expressed his support for "a sort of federal link" that would unify "people who are geographically grouped together like those of Europe." A memorandum, presented on 17 May 1930 as an extension of this speech, proposed the political union of Europe in the name of security and closer ties between the European economies. Lionized by some, especially the "realist" youth of the review *Notre temps*, and despised by others of the nationalist, far-right end of the political spectrum who, like *L'action française*, stigmatized the illusions and pipe dreams of the man they called the "bleating pacifist," Briand's future darkened in the early 1930s. His failure in Geneva was compounded, in 1931, by his loss to the moderate Paul Doumer (1857–1932) in the French presidential elections. Briand's time had passed and his own will to continue was gone. He died on 7 March 1932.

See also **Locarno, Treaty of; Stresemann, Gustav.**

BIBLIOGRAPHY

Bariety, Jacques. "Aristide Briand and the Security of France in Europe 1919–1932." In *Germany and France: From Conflict to Reconciliation, Writings of Colloquium 46 of the Historical College*, 117–134. Munich, Germany, 2000.

Fleury, Antoine, and Lubor Jilek, eds. "The Briand Plan for Europe's Federal Union." In *Acts of the International Colloquium Held in Geneva, September 19–21, 1991*. Bern, 1998.

Suarez, Georges. *Briand, sa vie, son oeuvre avec son journal et de nombreux documents inédits*. 6 vols. Paris, 1938–1952.

OLIVIER DARD

BRITAIN, BATTLE OF. In June 1940, having defeated France in one of the most spectacularly decisive land battles in military history, the German Nazi dictator Adolf Hitler (1889–1945) expected his remaining adversary, Great Britain, to make peace. His expectation was reasonable. The British Foreign Minister, Lord Edward Frederick Lindley Wood Halifax (1881–1959), saw no point in continuing the war, and in May had been one of only two candidates to replace Neville Chamberlain (1869–1940) as prime minister. The other candidate was Winston Churchill (1874–1965), who got the job by the narrowest of margins. Churchill regarded Nazism as a malevolent evil that had to be defeated, whatever the cost, in order to safeguard the West.

An aerial view of London shows a German Heinkels 111 plane on a bombing run, July 1940. ©CORBIS

In order to put pressure on Britain to come to terms, Hitler ordered preparations to be made for an invasion. As a necessary precondition, the German Air Force, the Luftwaffe, was to establish air superiority over southeast England. The head of the Luftwaffe, Hermann Göring (1893–1946), did not take the invasion plans seriously, but thought the Luftwaffe alone could bring Britain to the negotiating table. The Luftwaffe was never clear about exactly what it was trying to achieve.

The odds were stacked against the Germans from the outset. Under the leadership of Air Chief Marshal Hugh Dowding (1882–1970), Fighter Command of the Royal Air Force (RAF) had created the most fearsome air-defense system in the

world, designed to foil just such an assault. Its heart was a unique and extremely robust command and control network—the world's first intranet—that made use of radar to locate hostile aircraft. The British Hurricane and Spitfire were the only fighters in the world in 1940 to match the German Messerschmitt Bf 109. At the time, however, the German threat appeared to be overwhelming.

THE BATTLE

As the Luftwaffe moved to improvised bases along the coast of northern France, it began attacking British convoys in the English Channel. Air battles over convoys reached a new level of intensity on 10 July. This date generally marks the beginning of what Churchill called "the Battle of Britain," now identified with the defensive battle fought by Fighter Command. As this battle went on, the rest of the RAF bombed the invasion barges gathering in French ports and the canals that led to them.

The campaign against Britain itself began in earnest on 12 August with attacks on radar stations, followed on 13 August by "Eagle Day," a series of attacks on mainland targets including fighter airfields. They continued until 18 August, after which there was a pause as the Luftwaffe reorganized before beginning again on 24 August. Believing that they were failing to put the radar stations out of action, the Germans concentrated on airfields. However, they were failing to put those out of action as well.

Under the brilliant leadership of the New Zealander Keith Park, Fighter Command's 11 Group, which covered the main battle area, preserved itself and inflicted heavy losses on its assailants. Despite superior tactics in the air, the German fighter force never came close to achieving the kill ratios it needed in order to defeat the RAF. The bombing of the RAF's infrastructure was neither effective nor sustained enough to cripple it, for the system was designed to withstand many isolated blows. Dowding maintained a reserve throughout the battle, and Fighter Command was able to oppose every major raid. British fighter production outstripped Germany's by two to one, and aircraft were always in good supply. The RAF was strengthened by many pilots from the British Commonwealth and Europe, notably Poles and Czechs. Although replacing losses entailed the sending of many vulnerable novices to frontline squadrons, Fighter Command had more pilots in September than in July. The Luftwaffe could not replace all of its losses, and its strength slowly declined.

Some German commanders had always believed that the Luftwaffe should attack London in order to produce a rapid result. Hitler had forbidden this, but in late August the RAF managed to drop a few bombs on Berlin. This demanded a political response, so Hitler publicly announced that British cities would also be attacked. On 7 September the Luftwaffe launched a mass raid on the London docks, and returned that night, beginning what the British call the London "Blitz."

The following week the weather was bad. There was little flying, and when there was, interceptions were scrappy because the raiders were hard to locate in the clouds. Misled by false intelligence estimates of British strength and buoyed by the optimistic claims of their pilots, Luftwaffe commanders concluded that one more big push would make Fighter Command collapse. When Sunday 15 September dawned fine and clear, they launched two large raids on London. The defenders met them in strength, finally revealing that for the previous four weeks the Luftwaffe had been getting nowhere. Two days later, Hitler postponed the invasion preparations until further notice.

Daylight bombing raids continued until the end of September, after which the Luftwaffe restricted itself to fighters. By that time it was all a bluff, and as the year wore on, daylight air activity died down. While the Battle of Britain is usually taken to have ended on 31 October 1940, the night Blitz continued through May 1941. The RAF's strategy of denying the enemy air superiority had succeeded.

SIGNIFICANCE

The consequences of the British victory were far more momentous for the rest of the world than for Britain itself. From June 1941 the war was largely fought out between Germany and the Soviet Union. British belligerence forced Germany to fight in the West, provided a base for American forces from 1942, and was the precondition of the invasion of Normandy in 1944. This meant a Western presence in postwar Europe. Had Britain lost and made peace—a far more likely outcome of defeat than an invasion—it would have survived largely intact, but Europe from the Urals to the Atlantic would eventually have come under either Nazi or Soviet domination. Either result would have meant at best widespread impoverishment and human degradation for decades, or at worst the displacement and slaughter of millions and the descent of Europe into an age of barbarism.

See also **Aviation; Blitzkrieg; World War II.**

Firefighters pump water onto burning buildings after a German air raid, London, 1940. ©CORBIS

BIBLIOGRAPHY

Bungay, Stephen. *The Most Dangerous Enemy: A History of the Battle of Britain*. London, 2001. The author's own full account of the background, events, and consequences of the battle, which has now become a standard work.

Orange, Vincent. *A Biography of Air Chief Marshal Sir Keith Park, G.C.G., K.B.E., M.C., D.F.C., D.C.L.* London, 1984. The authoritative biography of the key operational commander on the British side, of whom it was said, "if ever any one man won the Battle of Britain, he did."

Price, Alfred. *The Hardest Day: Battle of Britain, 18 August 1940*. London, 1979. A brilliantly detailed account of a single day's action that gives new insights into the battle as a whole.

———. *Battle of Britain Day, 15 September 1940*. London, 1999. A companion work to the above covering the events of 15 September 1940, still celebrated as "Battle of Britain Day."

Ray, John. *The Battle of Britain: Dowding and the First Victory, 1940*. London, 2000. A scholarly but readable analysis of Dowding's role that sheds new light on what went on behind the scenes and illuminates some of the more controversial aspects of the battle.

Steinhilper, Ulrich, and Peter Osborne. *Spitfire on My Tail: A View from the Other Side*. Keston, U.K., 1989. The only firsthand account written by a typical German fighter pilot.

Wellum, Geoffrey. *First Light*. London, 2002. One of the best written of the many autobiographies by British pilots, vivid and moving.

Wood, Derek, with Derek Dempster. *The Narrow Margin: The Battle of Britain and the Rise of Air Power*. Washington, D.C., 1990. First published in 1960, this was for many years the standard work and is still valuable for its explanation of the RAF system and its day-by-day account of the fighting.

STEPHEN BUNGAY

BRITISH EMPIRE.

BRITISH EMPIRE. At the beginning of the twentieth century, those countries colored pink in British school atlases made up the largest empire the world had ever known, encompassing nearly one-quarter of the world's landmass and more than 25 percent of its people. By the end of the 1960s, however, the empire upon which "the sun never set" had shattered into more than forty independent nation-states, most of which found a new status of legal equality with Britain in the Commonwealth. The first to fall out of the imperial tree in the 1920s and 1930s were the so-called White Dominions: Australia, Canada, New Zealand, South Africa, and the Irish Free State. After World War II they were followed by Britain's major colonies in Asia and Africa; for example, India and Pakistan (in 1947), Malaya (in 1957; expanded to form Malaysia in 1963), Nigeria (in 1960), and Kenya (in 1963). British power retracted also in those countries where Britain had not exercised complete colonial control. Hence, in China after 1949, the victory of Mao Zedong's (1893–1976) communists in the civil war brought about the end of the special concessions afforded to the "foreign devils" in ports like Shanghai, and British companies were effectively nationalized without compensation during the 1950s. Britain retained a scattering of rocks and islands around the globe, but even Hong Kong was returned to China in 1997. In 2005 there were only 190,000 residents of British colonies, which were restyled "UK Overseas Territories" in 1999. It is tempting, therefore, to regard the twentieth-century history of the empire as one long sad and sorry tale of ruination. However, as John Gallagher has pointed out, the decline and fall of the British imperial system was punctuated by significant periods of revival.

WORLD WAR I AND ITS AFTERMATH

One such era of resurrection, indicating that there was still plenty of life left in the old imperial dog, occurred during World War I, when the extra resources provided by Britain's colonies and Dominions gave Britain a significant edge in the global struggle with Germany and its allies. Canadian flour saved Britain from hunger, and one-third of the British army's munitions in France during 1917–1918 were made in the North American dominion. Concurrent controls on strategic raw materials, such as Malaya's bountiful rubber and tin exports, denied such vital supplies to Britain's enemies. More important still was the manpower contribution from the empire: 1.3 million soldiers from the Dominions, around one million from India, seventy thousand from west and east Africa, and about ten thousand from the Caribbean assisted the imperial war effort, as well as the numberless nurses and Red Cross volunteers from Britain's overseas territories who tended to the wounded. Moreover, as a victor, Britain was a principal benefactor from "the repartition of the colonial world" (Nasson, p. 147), which was a central feature of the peace treaties after 1919. As such, the empire reached its greatest territorial extent in the early 1920s: Britain succeeded to the administration of German colonies in Africa (Tanganyika particularly), but, more importantly, the United Kingdom was confirmed as the paramount power in the Middle East in its internationally recognized role as protector of various ex-Ottoman territories (Palestine and Iraq notably). Thus the Indian "jewel in the crown" was more secure than ever.

IMPERIAL CONSOLIDATION IN THE INTERWAR YEARS

This is not to deny that there were significant nationalist challenges to the empire both during and in the immediate aftermath of World War I in India, Ireland, and Egypt, which resulted in considerable devolution of imperial authority. Hence, Ireland (bar the northern counties of Ulster) emerged as a Dominion in 1921, Egypt regained its independence in 1922, and India received various forms of self-government culminating in the 1935 Government of India Act (which proposed eventual self-government for India as a Dominion). Moreover, the 1931 Statute of Westminster confirmed that all the Dominions were legally independent in all internal and external matters. Constitutional change in Egypt, India, and the Dominions need not be interpreted, however, as symptoms of "imperialism in decline" since, as Darwin ("Imperialism in Decline?") notes, such changes were calculated to provide the empire with a new "streamlined efficiency." Egyptian independence was seriously qualified by ongoing British dominance of the cotton trade and control of Egypt's foreign and military affairs to safeguard the Suez Canal, through which passed Britain's trade to and from India, the Far East, and Australasia. An additional Anglo-Egyptian treaty in 1936 allowed for the stationing of ten thousand troops in Egypt during peacetime. In a similar vein, Iraq's entry into the League of Nations in 1932 was limited by established sovereign British rights over military bases, and the right of Britain to utilize all Iraq's military facilities in time of war. Devolution in India, meanwhile, merely deflected nationalist energies to provincial government as British administrators continued to control what mattered—overall economic and military policy—in Delhi. India did introduce tariffs that severely dented Lancashire's textile exports to the subcontinent, but the territory remained a huge field for British financial interests and an invaluable source of military troops for imperial emergencies. Political independence notwithstanding, Australia, New Zealand, South Africa, and Canada remained reliant on the Royal Navy for their defense and dependent on the City of London for their investments.

The fundamental basis of the United Kingdom's overseas strength—its economy—was undoubtedly tottering in the interwar years. As a consequence of World War I, Britain had emerged as a major debtor to the United States and was unable to resurrect the prewar gold standard, while the global Great Depression after 1929 increasingly exposed a lack of international competitiveness on the part of the British manufacturing industry. However, this relative economic weakness tended to encourage the greater economic integration of the empire. During the 1930s the sterling bloc unified and regulated the empire's financial and monetary affairs as never before, while imperial trade preferences and quotas secured colonial markets for ailing British industrial exports in return for holding open the British market for colonial commodity exports. As such, the empire ensured that British foreign trade just about stayed in the black: at the end of the 1930s Britain's overseas trade balance was just under £2 million thanks to the huge surplus of £150 million that Britain enjoyed with the empire. Links with the white settler territories were further cemented after World War I by an upsurge in imperial emigration from the United

Kingdom: British nationals who journeyed to the colonies between 1900 and 1904 numbered 465,924 (representing 43 percent of all extra-European journeys by Britons), but between 1925 and 1929, 576,146 British émigrés (over three-quarters of the total) ended up in colonial destinations (and overwhelmingly in British North America and Australasia). In metropolitan Britain, meanwhile, imperial propaganda was probably at its height in the interwar years in the form of grand public exhibitions; popular adventure stories for children; the new mass media of radio and the cinema; the annual celebration of Empire Day in most schools; and in the posters of the Empire Marketing Board, which admonished British consumers to purchase Jamaican bananas, Gold Coast cocoa, Australian currants, Burmese rice, Kenyan coffee, Straits Settlements pepper, and Ceylonese tea.

WORLD WAR II—MOBILIZATION AND COLLAPSE?

The empire once again loyally came to Britain's rescue during World War II. Canada, Australia, South Africa, and New Zealand supplied, and paid the costs of, some 2.68 million fighting personnel. Even 43,000 citizens of the Irish Free State enlisted in British or Commonwealth units, despite their government's policy of remaining stubbornly neutral. India confirmed itself as a vital martial source with more than 2.25 million personnel in the imperial armed forces, and as a crucial base for operations in the Middle East and the rest of Asia. In addition, there were some 374,000 Africans serving in all the armed forces and about 6,400 West Indians in the Royal Air Force alone. About 15,000 seamen in the merchant navy were of colonial origin (a staggering one in three of whom died trapped in the engine rooms of sinking ships). Egypt, meanwhile, was effectively reoccupied with the Suez Canal Base—the world's largest military emplacement by the end of the war—playing a vital role in the defeat of Nazi Germany and Fascist Italy through supplying the Middle East, North Africa, and southern Europe. Once again, in time of crisis, the colonies proved invaluable resource assets in other ways too: commodity production was stepped up and colonial governments extended their bulk-buying powers for foodstuffs and raw materials. As such, the new sterling area was more tightly controlled than the prewar bloc. In certain

Anthony Eden, British secretary of state for the Dominions, inspects Indian troops, Egypt, 1940. British control in India proved a great advantage during World War II, providing over two million soldiers and a crucial base of operations in the region. ©HULTON-DEUTSCH COLLECTION/CORBIS

cases, conscripted, forced labor was exploited in Africa to boost production vital for the prosecution of the war effort: in Tanganyika nearly eighty-five thousand workers produced rubber and sisal; in northern Nigeria more than one hundred thousand peasants mined tin.

Such expediencies were resorted to precisely because the Japanese occupation of Southeast Asia after December 1941 had deprived Britain of vital raw materials. The fall of the supposedly impregnable fortress colony of Singapore in February 1942 was regarded by Britain's wartime prime minister Winston Churchill (1874–1965) as a disaster and has often been regarded as a watershed in the history of British imperialism. Defeat by the Japanese exposed a fundamental weakness of the post–World War I empire—Britain's military under-capacity and "imperial overstretch" meant that it could no longer fight a war on two fronts, not least because the Royal Navy no longer ruled all of the waves. As early as the 1920s it was clear that Britain faced major naval competitors in the fleets of the United States and Japan. Moreover, the sinking of the battleships *Prince of Wales* and *Repulse* off the coast of Malaya, following the assault on the U.S. naval base of Pearl Harbor, which preceded the Japanese occupation of Britain's colonies east of India, were ominous indicators that airpower had superseded naval power. At the same time, for an imperial system built upon the alleged superiority of the white race, defeat by an Asian power was a huge psychological blow for the empire's prestige.

DECOLONIZATION AFTER 1945

Nevertheless, after the surrender of Japan in August 1945, the British returned to their colonial possessions in Burma, Malaya, Borneo, Singapore, and Hong Kong. In repetition of 1918, and despite the election of Clement Attlee's (1883–1967)

Labour government, there was a new sense of imperial mission in post-1945 Britain.

Although India and Palestine were given up, British indebtedness (especially to the United States) after World War II led to a new phase of colonial exploitation; under the revitalized sterling area, Malaya's huge sales of rubber and tin to the United States, for example, earned dollars vital for metropolitan recovery, as did to a lesser extent the Gold Coast's cocoa and Nigeria's palm oil. Additionally, fuel oil from the British-protected Middle East propped up the crisis-ridden postwar metropolitan economy through the avoidance of hard-currency expenditure. A revived imperial commitment was also evident in grand British plans, such as the ill-fated East African Groundnuts scheme, to produce dollar-saving foodstuffs, further reducing economic dependence on the United States. The Empire-Commonwealth was probably more important for Britain from an economic standpoint than ever before: in terms of volume, some 48 percent of British imports were derived from the colonies and Dominions in exchange for 58 percent of UK exports between 1946 and 1949 (the corresponding figures for a decade earlier were 40 percent and 49 percent). Before World War II some 50 percent of British capital exports were directed to the colonies and Dominions and by 1950–1954 this figure had leapt to 65 percent. At the same time, a revitalized Empire-Commonwealth held out the prospect of Britain returning to international power—political greatness as an alternative "Third Force" between the United States and the Soviet Union. In exchange for increased exploitation, colonial peoples were offered a new "partnership," a stakeholder role in the imperial enterprise, through (in Africa particularly) the opening up of local government to aspiring nationalist politicians with the prospect of eventual self-government on the prewar Dominions model.

Even so, with swift independence ceremony after even swifter independence ceremony, the population under British colonial rule dramatically contracted one hundred times from 700 million to 7 million in the twenty years after 1945. Why did the empire collapse so rapidly in the wake of World War II? One obvious reason was the force of popular nationalism in the colonies. The real innovator here was Mahatma Gandhi (1869–1948), who transformed the Indian National Congress from an elite talking shop into a mass movement of peasants, industrial workers, and entrepreneurs after World War I and led a series of peaceful noncooperation campaigns against the Raj. These climaxed in the Quit India campaign of 1942 as the Japanese army was threatening India's borders. Hopelessly understaffed, the empire relied on "collaboration" with colonial peoples. Hence, when, by 1945, much of the Indian police and army had gone over to Gandhi, the Attlee government was forced to withdraw. Gandhi's example was followed by other nationalists; in Malaya, for example, Tunku Abdul Rahman (1903–1990) extracted an elected majority from the British in the new federal council of 1955 after the Alliance Party threatened noncooperation. Others, such as the communists in Malaya and the Mau Mau in Kenya, chose violent insurrection as the means to bring the empire down, tying up British military resources in horrific guerrilla warfare and making colonial rule unbearably costly. What often undermined British rule, however, was internecine conflicts and tensions or "competing nationalisms" in the last phase of colonialism. During 1946 and 1947 Hindu and Muslim Indians were more concerned with killing each other than struggling against the retreating British. The result—much to British chagrin—was partition of the subcontinent into a Hindu-dominated India and a Muslim-dominated Pakistan, and the tragic deaths of upward of one million Indians and Pakistanis. In the 1950s and 1960s territorial parochialism disrupted British plans for postcolonial federations in central Africa, the West Indies, South Arabia, and "Greater Malaysia."

But the empire's demise would not have been possible without the British themselves. The 1940s and early 1950s had been a period of integrated sterling-area economic development in which colonies were expected to produce commodities that would either earn or save dollars while simultaneously absorbing ailing British manufactured goods. By the mid-1950s, however, Britain was back on its feet, and Conservative governments appreciated that the big gains in the international economy were to be made through trade and investments with North America, Europe, and Japan, and not with the colonies. Britain was also determined to secure a nuclear weapons capacity via cooperation with the United States. Hence, membership in the European Economic Community (EEC) and the "special relationship" with the United States were perceived as the new paths to greatness. At the same time, the British hoped to maintain friendly relations with nationalists in the colonies by granting swift independence. In other words, Britain's global economic and strategic interests would be maintained in the new multiracial Commonwealth. Malaysia and Singapore, for example, continued to peg their currencies to the pound sterling and retained British military bases into the 1970s.

Yet, preserving global sway through the Commonwealth was a fantasy because the third reason why the empire could not survive was that British economic and military might had been superseded by the superpowers—the United States and the Soviet Union. In contrast to Britain, the Americans and the Soviets had grown much more powerful as a consequence of World War II. In the ensuing Cold War Washington, D.C. came to see the empire as a hindrance in the global struggle with communism. This came to a head during the Suez Crisis of 1956 when Britain attempted to denationalize the Egyptian canal and reassert itself in the Middle East. Fearing that the Arab states would side with the USSR, President Dwight D. Eisenhower (1890–1969) flexed his nation's considerable financial muscle: he would not support the tottering British economy unless Prime Minister Anthony Eden (1897–1977) withdrew British troops from Egypt. Eden was replaced by Harold Macmillan (1894–1986) in 1957. Macmillan accepted Britain's role as a "junior partner" to the United States and, after 1960, the "wind of change" blew through Africa to prevent the continent from falling to the Soviets and/or Red China. The British Empire collapsed, then, because three phenomena coincided and reinforced each other: colonial nationalism, changing British priorities, and the Cold War.

THE POSTCOLONIAL COMMONWEALTH AND THE IMPERIAL REMNANTS

From the 1960s, however, an important worldwide legacy of the British Empire remained through the continued functioning of the Commonwealth. The ex-colonial club was transformed from the exclusive preserve of Britain and the White Dominions to a multiracial institution with the accession of India, Pakistan, and Ceylon (Sri Lanka) to its ranks in the late 1940s; Ghana's election after 1957 as the first Black African member; and the admission of the smaller ex-colonies, such as Cyprus, after 1960. Beginning in the late 1950s, mass immigration from the non-white Commonwealth—the Indian subcontinent and the Caribbean particularly—produced a genuinely multicultural Britain as well. The British had hoped that the multiracial Commonwealth would serve as a surrogate empire, as another pragmatic streamlined adaptation of colonialism to informally bolster the United Kingdom's global position. However, in practice, the Commonwealth emerged more as a force for third world solidarity rather than a neocolonial conserver of British world power, especially after white supremacist South Africa left the Commonwealth in 1961. Despite British hopes, the multiracial Commonwealth never served as a formal military alliance—India, for example, did not allow the stationing of British troops after independence, while Britain's financial difficulties in the 1960s, culminating in the great sterling devaluation of November 1967, led to the British military withdrawal from the postcolonial bases "east of Suez." Britain did retain considerable investments in ex-colonies, and Commonwealth trade remained important to Britain until the 1970s.

However, the main growth areas for both British manufacturing and capital exports tended to be with Western Europe, reflected in Britain's final entry to the EEC in 1973. British dreams of upholding economic influence through decolonization were shattered by a number of other factors during the 1960s: the reduction of sterling balances in London and the loss of British control over Commonwealth currencies; an emphasis on import-substitution industrialization, as well as the extension of state intervention in postcolonial economies; the emergence of more generous international lending agencies, such as the United States, Japan, the International Monetary Fund, and even the Soviet Union and Communist China; and the decline of British industrial performance, compounded by the end of Commonwealth preference. British influence in the Commonwealth suffered another setback with increased restrictions on non-white immigration to the United Kingdom after 1962. Nevertheless,

Britain has continued to exhibit a determination to act in a quasi-imperial manner in Hong Kong before 1997, and most notably in 1982, when a short war with Argentina ensured that the two thousand inhabitants of the Falkland Islands would remain British, and after 2003 in the invasion and occupation of Iraq (albeit in junior partnership with the United States).

See also **Colonialism; Commonwealth; Decolonization; Egypt; Gandhi, Mahatma; India; World War I; World War II.**

BIBLIOGRAPHY

Barratt Brown, Michael. *After Imperialism*. London, 1963. Classic study of the economic aspects of terminal colonialism and its immediate aftermath.

Bickers, Robert A. *Empire Made Me: An Englishman Adrift in Shanghai*. London, 2003. Fascinating and insightful narrative of Britain's "informal empire" in twentieth-century China through the experiences of an "ordinary" Briton.

Brown, Judith M., and William Roger Louis, eds. *The Twentieth Century*. Vol. 4 of *The Oxford History of the British Empire*. Oxford, U.K., 1999. Indispensable collection of high-quality essays, written by experts in their fields, on all aspects of the British imperial experience.

Cain, P. J., and A. G. Hopkins. *British Imperialism, 1688–2000*. 2nd ed. Harlow, U.K., 2001. Magisterial, if contentious, economic interpretation of British imperialism over four centuries.

Darwin, John. "Imperialism in Decline?" *The Historical Journal* 12 (1980). Seminal article that points to the considerable vitality of the interwar imperial system.

———. *Britain and Decolonisation: The Retreat from Empire in the Post war World*. Houndmills, Basingstoke, U.K., 1988. Early comprehensive study of post-1945 decolonization that remains a central work.

———. *The End of the British Empire: The Historical Debate*. Oxford, U.K., 1991. Excellent analysis of the historiographical debate on why the British Empire collapsed so rapidly after 1945.

Dumett, Raymond E., ed. *Gentlemanly Capitalism and British Imperialism: The New Debate on Empire*. London, 1999. A vital companion volume of critical essays for Cain and Hopkins, *British Imperialism*.

Gallagher, John. *The Decline, Revival and Fall of the British Empire: The Ford Lectures and Other Essays*. Cambridge, U.K., 1982. Contains a compelling, and frequently cited, essay on the peaks and troughs of British imperialism during the twentieth century.

Holland, R. F. *European Decolonization, 1918–1981: An Introductory Survey*. Basingstoke, U.K., 1985. Masterful comparative analysis of European imperialism and decolonization in the twentieth century, which, controversially, argues that the main motor behind the end of the European empires was to be found in the changing priorities and strategies of European policy makers.

Nasson, Bill. *Britannia's Empire: Making a British World*. Stroud, Gloucestershire, U.K., 2004. Elegantly and entertainingly written authoritative account of the rise and fall of the empire from the sixteenth century to the present day.

Smith, Simon C. *British Imperialism, 1750–1970*. Cambridge, U.K., 1998. Highly recommended textbook with particularly useful chapters on imperialism and nationalism in India and decolonization in Africa.

White, Nicholas J. *Decolonisation: The British Experience since 1945*. London and New York, 1999. Student-oriented synthesis and analysis of British late-colonial policy, the rise of anticolonial nationalism, and the international aspects of decolonization.

———. "The Survival, Revival and Decline of British Economic Influence in Malaysia, 1957–70." *Twentieth Century British History* 14 (2003): 222–242. Groundbreaking article on the British economic experience in an independent Commonwealth country, with relevance for the postcolonial situation in general.

NICHOLAS J. WHITE

BRITISH EMPIRE, END OF. When was the beginning of the end of the British Empire? One possible answer is 1776, since the loss of the American colonies constituted in some sense the first act of British decolonization. Another answer might be the 1839 Durham Report, which, though muddled and ill conceived, constituted Britain's first step toward granting self-government to its settler colonies within the overarching framework of empire. The report related to Canada and associated dependencies, but the model eventually established was applied also to Australia, New Zealand, and South Africa; as self-governing dominions, all fought alongside Britain in both world wars. Although the Republic of South Africa broke away from direct British rule in 1910, it remained part of the Empire-Commonwealth until 1961, when the contradictions between African decolonization and South African apartheid became overwhelming. (A very different South Africa was readmitted to a very different Commonwealth in 1994.) A central "pillar" of empire crumbled away after World War I, as Home Rule for Ireland was wrested from the imperial inheritors of many centuries of English rule, although six counties remained in what became Northern Ireland, where local majorities were loyal to Britain. Unlike the dominions, Ireland remained neutral in World War II, although many Irishmen enlisted in British forces.

Each of these turning points arguably served to underline the empire's protean capacity for renewal and reinvention. While this capacity drained away during the twentieth century, most decisively from 1939 to 1945, the story of the British Empire from 1914 is one not simply of decline and fall but also of persistent efforts to redefine and indeed modernize the empire. These efforts failed, since they were sustained neither by economic and political realities nor by late-twentieth-century ideological orthodoxies, but in the end, and notwithstanding the legacies of empire, the capacity for reinvention helps explain why postimperial Britain seems strangely unmoved by memories of its imperial past.

FORMS AND LIMITS OF COLONIAL RULE, 1919–1939

On the eve of World War I the British Empire had never been more powerful or extensive, and indeed, formal British colonial rule did not reach its fullest territorial extent until after 1919–1920, when the Versailles and Sèvres treaties shared German colonies and former Ottoman lands among the victorious colonial powers under League of Nations mandate. For a brief period British imperial control was even extended into, but soon retreated from, former tsarist-controlled (and soon to be Soviet) areas of central Asia. There were to be further retreats in this period: in 1922 Britain granted independence to Egypt after a forty-year "protectorate" (only officially called that in 1914), although British forces maintained control of the strategic linchpin of the Suez Canal, and Egyptian independence did not preclude massive military occupation during, and for a while after, World War II. British support for the wartime Arab revolt against Ottoman rule was famously cynical (even discounting T. E. Lawrence's mythmaking). Britain nonetheless engaged in state building across the Middle East, granting nominal independence to the newly created kingdoms of Iraq and

Transjordan in 1931; the British position in the region did not begin to unravel seriously until the Iraqi revolution of 1958. British policy in a third mandate, Palestine, never reconciled the aims of Arab nationalists and advocates of a Jewish homeland; the British foreign secretary in 1917, Sir Arthur Balfour, had expressed support for the latter in 1917. This led to one of Britain's most humiliating imperial failures, when it withdrew from its mandate in 1948, making way for the formation of the state of Israel.

British rule after World War I was shaken in the heart of empire, in India, where a politically innovative campaign of noncooperation united the Indian National Congress, radical peasant movements, and Muslims demanding the restoration of the recently abolished caliphate. At its height in 1919 this movement provoked one of the most notorious imperial atrocities, when troops fired on unarmed demonstrators at Amritsar: according to no doubt conservative official estimates, 379 were killed and a further 1,200 wounded. The figurehead of noncooperation, Mohandas Gandhi, preached a morally unimpeachable doctrine of nonviolence and promised a nebulous *swaraj* (self-rule); twice, after Amritsar and again in 1922, he halted the movement, appalled by its violence. A further campaign of civil disobedience followed in 1930–1931. Aside from the reflex of repression, British policy makers' response, in the 1935 Government of India Act, was a tightly framed constitution that, although never fully implemented because war intervened, provided for Indian ministerial responsibility at the provincial level but forestalled development toward complete self-government. British India in 1935 was a veritable showcase of modern imperial endeavor, with a thriving industrial sector, forty-two thousand miles of railway, and a civil service and police force both staffed and increasingly officered by Indians, but also, crucially for British power, limited suffrage and a 300,000-strong army. Although official policy had partly determined the emergence of divisive Hindu and Muslim "communal" politics, there was little to suggest that this might lead by 1947 to partition between separate states of India and Pakistan. World War II would reveal how rapidly British rule could become vulnerable.

By contrast, British formal colonial rule in Africa was still, relatively speaking, in its infancy in 1914, so the interwar period represented its high-water mark, when the doctrines and methods of rule were refined and rationalized. Two underlying parameters of rule may be identified here, both with important precedents elsewhere in the empire. The first of these was the need to accommodate substantial settler communities in East and Central Africa. In Kenya and Southern Rhodesia (later Rhodesia, present-day Zimbabwe), white farmers occupied the best land and looked to South Africa for a model of white economic and political dominance, often resisted by British officials but bolstered by the support of "kith and kin" back home. Even during the Mau Mau insurrection and with decolonization looming, emigration to Kenya doubled in the 1950s. In Rhodesia a rebellious Unilateral Declaration of Independence in 1964 delayed African majority rule until 1980. Tanganyika, taken over from German rule after 1919, was declared to be "black man's country" and enjoyed a more peaceful transition to independence in consequence (as Tanzania). Across East Africa, a South Asian emigrant community, more numerous than Europeans but still a small minority, occupied the dubious position of commercial middlemen. They weathered the vagaries of "multiracial" politics in the 1950s and the early years of independence only to be expelled en masse, most brutally by the vicious regime of Idi Amin Dada in Uganda, in the 1970s. This substantial diaspora went on to form a mainstay of the Asian community in postimperial Britain.

Secondly, the preference of the British "official mind" for so-called indirect rule left substantial power in the hands of local "traditional" rulers. The archetype for this system was developed in India following the 1857 Sepoy Rebellion (the "Mutiny"), whereby several hundred Indian princes—the rajahs of many an Orientalist fantasy—ruled some two-fifths of Indian territory under the watchful eye of a British Resident. These "British officers in Indian dress," as Gandhi called them, effectively allowed the British to run an "empire on the cheap" in India and more widely. Indirect rule was adopted across British Africa, most notably in northern Nigeria, the Asante kingdoms, the northern territories of the Gold Coast (present-day Ghana), and the kingdom of Buganda, which dominated Uganda. The principle also informed British relations with the Malay sultans—who successfully resisted British efforts to reduce their status after 1945—and with kings, sheikhs, and emirs across the Middle East, disguising the nature of British power and eventually masking its decline.

Even nominally direct rule depended on a "thin white line" of British administrators, largely recruited from a "ruling class" educated in the exclusive so-called public school system and at Oxford or Cambridge ("Oxbridge") or perhaps London but picked on the basis of "character" more than intellectual attainment. The elite Indian Civil Service, for example, numbered less than a thousand. Across Africa also, a very few district officers relied on local chiefs to raise taxes and recruit labor. The idea, developed by Ronald Robinson and John Gallagher, of a "collaborator system" based on the identification of mutual interests has been used to explain not only the workings of colonial rule (though the term *collaboration* brings unwarranted associations with the history of Nazi-occupied Europe), but also the manner of its end, as the need to identify and co-opt reliable collaborators eventually became too difficult to sustain.

Aside from colonial practicalities, indirect rule also meshed with a whole range of invented traditions of monarchy and a hierarchical social order imported from British society, allowing imperial rulers to claim, and perhaps even to believe, as David Cannadine has suggested, that communities of class could transcend those of race. Thus the scions of Asian and African royalty attended the public schools and Oxbridge, and schools imitating illustrious British models were created in Buganda, Khartoum, and Singapore. Meanwhile the pageantry of Empire Day or, especially, the coronations of George VI (in 1937) and Elizabeth II (in 1953) allowed the "official mind" to assert the continuities of empire while also acquiescing in its evolution or, more generally, to fudge the contradictions confronting, say, France's republican imperialists. Thus, while her father's title "emperor of India" lapsed in 1948, Queen Elizabeth II was styled "head of the Commonwealth," a suitably egalitarian title that allowed newly independent states, as India had already done, to join the Commonwealth without accepting the queen as head of state.

In many ways the preferred mode of British imperialism was neither settler imperialism nor formal colonialism, much less the pomp and circumstance of the House of Windsor, but lay in the informal imperialism characterized by trade and overseas investment and by the status of sterling as global "top currency": in short, by the invisible hand of a resilient "gentlemanly capitalism" based in the City of London. British informal empire in its pre-1914 heyday thus extended far wider than the formal empire, for example to South America and China. Here too decline set in from the outset of the period after World War I, both in absolute terms and relative to the emergence of a formidable financial rival in New York: this much was clear in the American-led boom of the late 1920s. However, the Depression brought the beginnings of irreversible change, as Britain abandoned both the gold standard and the principle of free trade. A new, protectionist "Sterling Area" formed after the gold standard was abandoned in 1931, comprising a group of countries, not all of them in the empire, which depended on British trade and on the pound sterling; this protected its members against the worst of the Depression but could not mask the decline of ailing, uncompetitive British industry or prevent the emergence of an economic *pax americana*, even before World War II. After 1945 the Sterling Area was even more essential, buttressing sterling against the strength of the dollar; the dollar-earning capacity of imperial resources, for example Malayan rubber and tin and West African cocoa, thus sustained Britain's postwar recovery. Curiously, in economic terms the empire thus became more "empire-like" as it approached its end.

IMPERIAL DECLINE DURING AND AFTER WORLD WAR II

The diplomatic challenges of the 1930s were enough to put the "official mind" on the defensive, though perhaps not enough to suggest that imperial dissolution was just around the corner. Still, fears of British chiefs of staff were real enough that the emerging powers of Germany, Italy, and Japan might between them straddle imperial lines of communication around the home islands, in the Mediterranean, and in the Far East. Indeed, a large part of the rationale for the despised British policy of "appeasement" was to prevent a disastrous war on three fronts. War when it came could hardly have been more devastating for British imperial power, short of Axis victory. The lowest point came with the fall of Britain's allegedly impregnable Far Eastern fortress at Singapore in February 1942, the climax of a Japanese campaign that eclipsed Western colonialism across Southeast Asia, directly threatened British India, and provoked violent insurrection by the Indian National Congress, backed by Gandhi, seeking to compel the British to "quit India."

The war forced the British Empire to fight for its life and to do so by allying itself with two dangerous rivals, both in different ways radically anticolonial, though the more immediate threat came from Washington, not Moscow. This threat was first manifested, even before Pearl Harbor, by the August 1941 Atlantic Charter signed by the prime minister, Winston Churchill, and U.S. President Franklin D. Roosevelt, which asserted the "right of all peoples to choose the form of government under which they will live"—which Churchill implausibly took to refer only to those suffering under the "Nazi yoke." British policy makers made extensive efforts to reinterpret the imperial idea in ways that might be acceptable to hostile American opinion, though as the tide of the war turned it became clearer that Washington would not interfere unduly in the internal affairs of its ally. This was the start of a lasting ambiguity, only finally resolved after the Suez Crisis of 1956. A succession of British leaders sought to finesse their American allies by equating imperial interests with those of the Western camp in the developing Cold War. Suez, where Britain had in 1954 abandoned its massive military base, seemed a casebook example of how this should work, since the Egyptian leader Colonel Gamal Abdel Nasser's relationship with the Soviet Union was growing close. However, an improbable Anglo-Franco-Israeli collusive attack on the Suez Canal Zone led the United States to threaten Britain at its weakest point, its currency on world markets, meanwhile exposing the uncomfortable truth that Britain was now the submissive partner in the so-called special relationship—whose special nature was barely acknowledged in Washington.

In late 1942, at a moment of renewed confidence, Churchill claimed that he had "not become the King's First Minister in order to preside over the liquidation of the British Empire." However, Pyrrhus-like, by 1945 he had presided over the depletion of imperial power—strategic reserves, manpower (including colonial troops and labor), economic resources, financial credit, and diplomatic capital—to an extent that put its recovery in doubt. As after 1919, Britain initially found itself committed even beyond imperial boundaries: British troops occupied a populous zone of western Germany and assisted French and Dutch authorities returning to their Southeast Asian dependencies—a last, insensitive, and, given the subsequent course of Vietnamese and Indonesian decolonization, fruitless deployment of the Indian Army. Indeed, military overcommitment and near-bankruptcy, as well as the threat of violent disorder and administrative collapse, largely explain the urgency of British policy in India. However, although brilliantly stage-managed by the last viceroy, Lord Louis Mountbatten, as a final act of imperial generosity, the Transfer of Power in August 1947 from Britain to two separate states of India and Pakistan undercut British ambitions to maintain a strategic stake in a friendly and undivided subcontinent, not least because the Indian Army was also divided. More immediately, it was not simply the fact of Partition that overshadowed Britain's retreat, but its hasty implementation and the unprecedented scale of the population transfers, violence, and massacres that ensued. Two further Asian transfers of power followed in 1948, which may be summed up, from the British perspective, by the suggestion that future policy should aim for "more Ceylons and fewer Burmas"—one, now Sri Lanka, a mainstay of the new Commonwealth; the other hostile and rapidly shifting toward military dictatorship outside the Commonwealth.

LATE COLONIAL RULE AND DECOLONIZATION IN AFRICA AND BEYOND

These first steps in Asia, however, were not intended to initiate a wider process of decolonization. Rather, they accompanied a last concerted effort by the British "official mind" to reform the empire, particularly the hitherto neglected dependencies of tropical Africa. The new Labour government in London thus introduced a Colonial Welfare and Development Act in 1945 (superseding a 1940 act scuppered by bad timing) and oversaw a process seen by historians as a "second colonial occupation," whereby a small army of technicians and advisors sought to modernize the African countryside by methods often deeply resented by African producers, who bore the brunt of their efforts—or who, alternatively, were bypassed completely, as in the notorious "Groundnuts Scheme," which sank huge resources into failing to produce the eponymous root crop on barren Tanganyikan scrubland.

Economic development was complemented by cautious constitutional reforms designed to lead—very gradually, over a generation or longer—to a measure of self-government. In Britain's most politically "advanced" West African colonies, the Gold Coast (present-day Ghana) and Nigeria, however, the constitutional process was rapidly overtaken by the rise of dynamic nationalist movements. In 1951 in the Gold Coast, Kwame Nkrumah, in prison at the time, won a "famous victory" for his Convention People's Party, confounding officials, conservative nationalists, and traditional chiefs alike. A level-headed governor accepted Nkrumah's ascendancy, labeled him a moderate, and helped steer Ghana on an accelerated route to independence in 1957. This created a model for other dependencies, earning Britain a somewhat unexpected reputation as a "liberal" decolonizing power. In Nigeria, British policy centered on cementing the three constituent parts of a federal state, which local political forces tended rather to pull apart, in ways that already pointed forward to Nigeria's civil war of the late 1960s; despite British misgivings, Nigeria carried one-fifth of the population of Africa to independence in 1960.

This "late" colonialism was typically violent, and although a series of British colonial "emergencies" nowhere reached the scale of the Franco-Algerian conflict (1954–1962), they sometimes matched its intensity. British troops, including conscripts enduring National Service (which ended in 1960), saw action every year from 1945 until the late 1960s, while police, prison guards, and locally recruited militias and "home guards" had much to occupy them. This was not just diehard colonialism; Britain now faced new enemies and deployed new tactics and doctrines to combat and sometimes defeat them. Two examples must suffice here. First, from 1948 British troops fought and overcame a communist insurgency in the difficult terrain of the Malayan jungle. Their victory may be attributed to military persistence and to the isolation of the insurgents, almost all drawn from the Malayan Chinese minority, more than to an oft-vaunted appeal to colonized "hearts and minds." Nonetheless, containing the insurgency entailed negotiating with "moderate" political forces from all communities, thus paving the way for the independence of Malaya in 1957 (subsequently Malaysia); in 1963, the majority-Chinese city-state of Singapore gained separate independence. Secondly, the Mau Mau movement among the Gikuyu of Kenya was also a new kind of enemy, though officials and settlers depicted them as atavistic savages, performing unspeakable blood-soaked rituals in forest clearings. Part peasant rebels, part urban gangs, part adept proto-nationalists, their own name for themselves, the Land and Freedom Army, reflected their grievances against their own people, though these grievances originated in colonial structures and policies. Defeating Mau Mau turned Kenya into a police state, with judicial executions exceeding those in Algeria, with "fortified villages" cutting off rebels from their supporters (a technique developed in Malaya, used also in Algeria and by the Americans in Vietnam), and with the mass internment of suspected Mau Mau in concentration camps, the so-called Pipeline. Although documented abuses in Kenya never remotely approached the systematic use of torture in Algeria, the revelation, in March 1959, of the deaths of brutalized internees in one of these camps finally brought change. Here too a familiar pattern led to independence, as the Gikuyu elder Jomo Kenyatta, wrongly convicted in 1953 of leading Mau Mau, and still described by the governor in 1960 as "leader unto darkness and death," was transformed into the "moderate" nationalist leader of independent Kenya.

In 1957 a new British prime minister, Harold Macmillan (brought to power by the Suez debacle and conscious of its lessons), asked colonial officials to provide "something like a profit and loss account" of colonial possessions, which suggested that British interests, narrowly defined, might weigh more heavily than British commitment to development goals and constitutional advance in determining the future of empire. By 1960 Macmillan was preaching the "winds of change" to an unconvinced white audience in Cape Town, while his colonial secretary, Ian Macleod, was soon sponsoring "Westminster-style" constitutions for a succession of independent new Commonwealth members in Africa and the West Indies. Although a Labour prime minister in 1964, Harold Wilson, claimed improbably that Britain's frontier was "on the Himalayas," the reality was one of unimpeded imperial retraction; the final retreat from "East of Suez" came in 1971, when the emirates of the Persian Gulf moved to an independence comfortably sustained by oil revenues. The imperial reflex has occasionally resurfaced since the 1960s, most notably during the last gasp of gunboat diplomacy by which the Falkland Islands were recaptured from Argentinian occupation in 1982. Perhaps the last symbolic act of decolonization came in 1997, with the cession of Hong Kong as a Special Administrative Region of the People's Republic of China, although Britain in 2004, like France, maintained a scattering of tiny dependencies.

The end of the British Empire has been treated here largely from a British perspective: a different entry might consider how the colonized endured and resisted colonial rule, affirmed new identities while doing so, and finally liberated themselves—even if, for many in the early twenty-first century, that liberation still seemed imperfectly realized. One final, paradoxical, aspect of the British perspective needs briefly to be touched upon, that of British public opinion. Historians differ in their accounts of how much the empire mattered to ordinary Britons. The evidence of imperial propaganda, or of the proportion of British production or investment feeding imperial markets and development, certainly suggests popular exposure to imperial values, though whether this equates with consent or imperialist enthusiasm is more problematic. Running the empire per se was always a matter of class, since, as we have seen, only a tiny "ruling class" was needed (though Scottish and Irish involvement in empire was more socially inclusive). In any event, the evidence for widespread loss of confidence occasioned by the end of empire is less compelling, and Britain eschewed the upheavals that visited France in the 1950s: Suez brought down a British prime minister, but Algeria toppled a regime and brought tanks and terrorism to the French capital; debates or protests equivalent to those in Paris over, say, colonial abuses or the overseas deployment of conscripts were notable by their absence. Decolonization was accompanied by a more general "decline of deference," perhaps, detectable in television, fashion, pop music, or the satire boom of the early 1960s. None of this precludes the possibility of deeper structural changes wrought by the end of empire and still ongoing in the early twenty-first century, whether reflected in the emergence of a strongly multicultural demographic profile in British cities, popular resistance to full British engagement in the affairs of Europe, or in the sometimes reluctant embrace of postimperial policies in world affairs.

See also **British Empire; Colonialism; Commonwealth; Decolonization; French Empire; India; Pakistan; Suez Crisis; United Kingdom.**

BIBLIOGRAPHY

Antlöv, Hans, and Stein Tønnesson. *Imperial Policy and South-East Asian Nationalism, 1930–1957.* Richmond, U.K., 1995.

Berman, Bruce, and John Lonsdale. *Unhappy Valley: Conflict in Kenya and Africa.* London, 1992.

Boyce, D. George. *Decolonisation and the British Empire, 1775–1997.* Basingstoke, U.K., 1999.

British Documents on the End of Empire. London, 1992– . A 15-volume series presenting copious selections from British records, divided between a general series and a series devoted to individual territories, each with an authoritative introduction by the editor.

Brown, Judith M., and Wm. Roger Louis, eds. *The Oxford History of the British Empire.* Vol. 6, *The Twentieth Century.* Oxford, U.K., 1999.

Cain, A. J., and A. G. Hopkins. *British Imperialism.* Vol. 2, *Crisis and Deconstruction, 1914–1990.* Harlow, U.K., 1993.

Cannadine, David. *Ornamentalism: How the British Saw Their Empire.* London, 2001.

Darwin, John. *Britain and Decolonisation: The Retreat from Empire in the Post-War World.* Basingstoke, U.K., 1988.

Gallagher, John. *The Decline, Revival, and Fall of the British Empire.* Cambridge, U.K., 1983.

Hargreaves, John. *Decolonization in Africa.* 2nd ed. London, 1996.

Hobsbawm, Eric, and Terence Ranger, eds. *The Invention of Tradition.* Cambridge, U.K., 1983.

Howe, Stephen. *Anticolonialism in British Politics: The Left and the End of Empire, 1918–1964.* Oxford, U.K., 1993.

Le Sueur, James D., ed. *A Decolonization Reader.* London, 2003. See especially articles by Lonsdale and by Louis and Robinson.

Louis, Wm. Roger. *Imperialism at Bay, 1941–1945: The United States and the Decolonization of the British Empire.* Oxford, U.K., 1977.

Sarkar, Sumit. *Modern India 1885–1947.* 2nd ed. Delhi, 1989.

MARTIN SHIPWAY

BRITISH UNION OF FASCISTS. The British Union of Fascists (BUF) was the most significant fascist movement in the United Kingdom in the 1930s. That is not saying much, however. At its peak in 1934 it probably had fifty thousand members. For a movement whose ostensible aim was to restructure British society through the "fascist revolution," after two successive general election victories, it was an abject failure. Indeed, it did not have candidates at the 1935 general election, claiming its supporters should wait for "fascism, next time." The three fascists who stood in by-elections in 1940 achieved an average vote of 1 percent against the candidate of the party who had won the seat in the 1935 election.

The mystery about the BUF is why has such a marginal movement excited such interest? There were a number of reasons for this. Firstly, the personality of its leader, Sir Oswald Mosley (1896–1980), provides an alternative version of the drab politics and economic restructuring of British society in the interwar period. His ignoring the "rules of the game" and going "beyond the pale," and the associated connection of the BUF with political violence, anti-Semitism, and Fascist Italy and Nazi Germany in the 1930s, has stimulated interest. Why should a politician who was talented enough to become a potential leader of a mainstream parliamentary party shunt himself into the sidings of British politics? In a sense Mosley was both unlucky and showed poor political judgment. Unfortunately for him, the slow

Oswald Mosley is greeted by members of the BUF as he arrives at the site of a fascist gathering, London, October 1936. ©BETTMANN/CORBIS

recovery of the British economy in the 1930s, beginning in October 1932 when he formed the BUF, blunted whatever potential appeal the movement may have had.

Although the early dynamism of the new movement attracted the support of Lord Rothermere and the *Daily Mail* in the first six months of 1934, the violence associated with fascist stewards at the Olympia rally on 7 June 1934, and the murder of the Sturmabteilung (SA) leadership and some conservative political opponents on the Night of the Long Knives on 30 June 1934, led Rothermere to withdraw his support. The movement collapsed to about five thousand members, although it slowly recovered in the later 1930s to half of its 1934 membership. Mosley revived it somewhat as a result of local campaigns emphasizing regional grievances—the cotton campaign in Lancashire in 1935 and the use of political anti-Semitism in the

East End of London between 1935 and 1938 being the most conspicuous. The latter was the most successful of these, and the East End probably accounted for half the national membership in the later 1930s.

Second, the relationship with German Nazis and Italian Fascists has stimulated research. While the BUF was influenced by several domestic political traditions, particularly the Edwardian radical Right and political anti-Semitism, there was also inspiration from successful continental fascisms. The similarity between the BUF Blackshirt uniform, symbols, and organization and Italian Fascist regalia, and the development of the theory of the corporate state, owe much to Benito Mussolini (1883–1945). Similarly, the alleged role played by anti-Semitism in the rise of the Nazis in Germany encouraged its development in the East End of London. The British Special Branch police and MI5 have uncovered proof that the BUF received substantial funding from Mussolini, and possibly the Nazis, between 1933 and 1937; at no stage did Mosley ever criticize the foreign policies of the fascist dictators in the 1930s. But these perceived influences were also major reasons for the failure of the BUF. British public opinion associated the threat of political violence, anti-Semitism, dictatorship, and paramilitary squads with continental fascism, and these proved alien to British political culture.

Third, new sources have provided important information and perspectives on the BUF. The opening of Home Office and MI5 files, between 1983 and 1986 and after 1997 respectively, on the BUF at the National Archives illuminated state management of public order and the BUF between 1932 and 1940. In particular it has shown the background to the internment of 750 British fascists and the proscription of the BUF in the summer of 1940. Similarly, the deposits of Diana and Nicholas Mosley at the University of Birmingham and the Robert Saunders papers and associated collections at the University of Sheffield have provided the BUF perspective on the controversial history of the BUF.

Fourth, Mosley and his propagandists Alexander Raven Thomson, William Joyce (called Lord Haw-Haw), and A. K. Chesterton were among both the most interesting, sophisticated, and talented and the most obnoxious articulators of fascist political, economic, and cultural ideas in Europe during the 1930s.

See also **Fascism; Joyce, William (Lord Haw-Haw); Nazism; World War II.**

BIBLIOGRAPHY

Gottlieb, Julie V., and Thomas P. Linehan, eds. *The Culture of Fascism: Visions of the Far Right in Britain*. London, 2004. Essays on British fascist views on contemporary artistic expression and the media in the 1930s.

Linehan, Thomas P. *East London for Mosley*. London, 1996. An excellent study of the impact of Mosley and the BUF on London.

———. *British Fascism, 1918–1939: Parties, Ideologies and Culture*. Manchester, U.K., 2000. The most recent general history of the BUF, which is particularly interesting in its discussion of the cultural ideas of the movement.

Pugh, Martin. *Hurrah for the Blackshirts: Fascists and Fascism in Britain between the Wars*. London, 2005. An excellent synthesis of recent research, particularly illuminating on the links with the Conservative Party.

Thurlow, Richard. *Fascism in Britain: A History, 1918–1985*. Oxford, U.K., 1987. New paperback edition, London, 1998. The history of British fascism in its national and international context.

RICHARD C. THURLOW

BRITTEN, BENJAMIN (1913–1976), English composer.

Benjamin Britten was the most prominent and prolific English composer of the mid-twentieth century. He was born in Lowestoft, Suffolk, to a middle-class family. His childhood was infused with music, and he began to compose at an astonishingly early age; some say from the age of five, others from age nine. In 1927 the composer Frank Bridge started to teach him privately. Bridge introduced him to modern tendencies, from Béla Bartók to Arnold Schoenberg; Britten entered the Royal College of Music in London in 1930, studying piano with Arthur Benjamin and composition with John Ireland. His time in the Royal College was not particularly fruitful, partly because of the dislike of "brilliance," or expressive composition, voiced by Ralph Vaughan Williams, then professor of music. Britten's formation as a musician and composer continued despite, rather than because of, his training in the Royal College. In 1933 he completed *A Boy Was Born,* a choral work performed by the BBC Singers. In 1935 he began composing music for documentary films produced by the General Post Office. The documentary movement of these years was a way people with socialist opinions such as Britten could reach out to popular culture and entertainment.

During this period Britten met the tenor Peter Pears, who became his lifelong companion. They gave their first recital together at Balliol College, Oxford, in 1937, as part of a campaign for the relief of victims of the Spanish civil war. At this time Britten worked for BBC Radio and a number of theater groups in London. In this milieu he began to collaborate with the poet W. H. Auden, who wrote lyrics for some of Britten's songs.

When war became unavoidable in 1939, Britten—a conscientious objector—and Pears left Britain for the United States. Auden too had migrated, and together they collaborated on the operetta *Paul Bunyan* (1941), about the American folk figure. Visiting California, Britten read some work by E. M. Forster on the English poet George Crabbe. From this engagement with Crabbe came *Peter Grimes,* Britten's first full opera, completed after Britten and Pears returned to England in 1942. During the war he produced many sacred works, including *Hymn to St. Cecilia* (based on Auden's poetry), *A Ceremony of Carols, Rejoice in the Lamb,* and the *Festival Te Deum.* In 1945 *Peter Grimes* was first performed by the reopened Sadler's Wells Opera in London and received its American premiere a year later at the Berkshire Music Center at Tanglewood. The conductor was Leonard Bernstein. The tenor role of Peter Grimes was written with and for Peter Pears.

During the postwar decade Britten worked on a variety of operas: *The Rape of Lucretia* (1946), *Billy Budd* (1951), *Gloriana* (1953), and *The Turn of the Screw* (1954). He was commissioned to write the music for the reconsecration of Coventry Cathedral, rebuilt in 1962 by Sir Basil Spence. Britten's *War Requiem,* first performed on 30 May 1962, matching his personal style of shattering lyrical power with the war poetry of World War I, required ambulant choirs engaged in antiphonal and echoing responses. In the space of the new cathedral, at right angles to the ruins of the medieval church, Britten found a way to express his personal pacifist views. He had been a conscientious objector during World War II. But he also found a form for the expression in sacred music of English national feeling in the aftermath of the two world wars. Just as T. S. Eliot found a language of Englishness in the *Four Quartets* to express the harsh struggle between the Nazis and a civilization then termed "Christian," so Britten fashioned in his *War Requiem* a musical icon for the century of total war.

Britten's contribution to modern English music is without parallel. He expanded the repertoire of dramatic and operatic music, drawing from medieval tropes as well as from the cadences of Stravinsky, Dmitri Shostakovich (a personal friend), and other modernists. He edited with Pears substantial editions of medieval English vocal music. Britten's legacy is most evident in the Aldeburgh Festival, which he helped found in 1948. It became both a home for their touring opera company, the English Opera Group, and a center for new music and new composers, whose work is performed there every summer. Britten is buried in the parish church of Aldeburgh, alongside Peter Pears, who died in 1986.

See also **Auden, W. H.; Opera; Schoenberg, Arnold; Shostakovich, Dmitri.**

BIBLIOGRAPHY

Blyth, Alan. *Remembering Britten.* London, 1981.

Carpenter, Humphrey. *Benjamin Britten: A Biography.* New York, 1992.

Evans, Peter. *The Music of Benjamin Britten.* Minneapolis, Minn., 1979.

Kennedy, Michael. *Britten.* London, 1981.

Mitchell, Donald. *Britten and Auden in the Thirties: The Year 1936.* London, 1981.

Palmer, Christopher, ed. *The Britten Companion.* Cambridge, U.K., and New York, 1984.

JAY WINTER

BROOK, PETER (b. 1925), British theater director.

Peter Brook has been the world's most influential theater director during the second half of the twentieth century and beyond. He mastered the arts and necessities of directing for the stage, bringing them to a pitch seldom seen before, and then has spent his professional life submitting the very idea of theater itself to the most revolutionary questioning. In internationally visible productions and writings, Brook has transformed the nature and process of theater directing and inspired several generations of younger directors.

Born in London to émigré Latvian Jews, Brook hurried through an Oxford education and burst onto the English theater scene at the age of twenty-one in Stratford-upon-Avon. His first great vehicle was what would later be called a "concept production" of *Love's Labour's Lost,* transferring Shakespeare's late medieval subject matter into the eighteenth-century France of Antoine Watteau's paintings. He was the very model of the wunderkind director—"the youngest earthquake I've known," according to producer Barry Jackson (Kustow, p. 43)—and an acolyte of Edward Gordon Craig (1872–1966), who held that directors must master all the varied theatrical crafts to become creative artists rather than interpretive artisans. In *Love's Labour's Lost* Brook also created exciting theater from a play that was virtually unproduced at the time, a pattern he would repeat with then neglected Shakespeare plays such as *Measure for Measure* (1950, with John Gielgud), *The Winter's Tale* (1951, again with Gielgud), and most famously *Titus Andronicus* (1955–1957, with Laurence Olivier and Vivien Leigh).

Through his twenties and thirties Brook built a career on sensational, high-profile productions in Stratford-upon-Avon, London, Paris, Brussels, and New York. He put his assertive stamp on classics, operas, and much of the most important contemporary drama from France (Jean-Paul Sartre, Jean Anouilh, Jean Genet), England (T. S. Eliot, Christopher Fry), and America (Arthur Miller, Tennessee Williams). This phase of his career came to a triumphant conclusion in 1962 with a Stratford *King Lear* starring Brook's longtime associate Paul Scofield, a production thought by many critics to be the definitive midcentury vision of Shakespeare's great apocalyptic tragedy.

But beginning in the late 1950s, Brook began to question the most fundamental precepts of the art in which he was making such an astonishing success. This period of doubt and reevaluation was stimulated by many sources: French absurdist and German political drama, the writings of Antonin Artaud (1896–1948), French "new wave" cinema theory, exposure to American experimental companies such as the Living Theatre and Open Theater, travels among non-Western peoples such as the Tarahumara Indians of Mexico, and his own experiments in film (*Moderato cantabile*, 1960). So, through the 1960s, Brook progressively abandoned commercial theater altogether and launched a series of experimental theater projects. At the Royal Shakespeare Company he headed an experimental workshop that achieved international fame with Peter Weiss's *Marat/Sade* (1964–1966). At Britain's National Theatre he took such veterans as Gielgud and Irene Worth through the experimental process with Seneca's *Oedipus* (1968). A Paris workshop on *The Tempest* with an international cast resulted in a production at London's Roundhouse (1968) that forecast much of what lay ahead for Brook after 1970. Perhaps most influential of all Brook's activities during the 1960s was his book *The Empty Space* (1968), opening with some of the most famous words of modern theater: "I can take any empty space and call it a bare stage. A man walks across this empty space whilst someone else is watching him, and this is all that is needed for an act of theatre to be engaged" (p. 9).

As if to prove these theories and forecast much of what was to follow, Brook created an international sensation with his last important production for the established theater, *A Midsummer Night's Dream* at the Royal Shakespeare Company (1970). Set in a huge box of white walls with actors on trapezes, stilts, and upper walkways, the production fused the techniques of experimental theater, circus, and Asian performance with the deepest English traditions of Shakespearean entertainment.

As *Dream* played in England and America, Brook's new life was already commencing in Paris, where he occupied an abandoned theater, the Bouffes du Nord, and assembled a permanent company of actors representing many continents and languages. With this group Brook perfected a new minimalist performance style in which "transparency" and "elimination" became his watchwords, traveling to many continents, experimenting with verbal and gestural language, and creating a series of productions based on myths and legends from the most culturally diverse sources: *Orghast, The Ik, The Conference of the Birds, The Mahabharata, The Man Who, Tierno Bokar,* and an assortment of Shakespeare experiments. Brook occasionally ventured beyond this work, to such shows as a star-studded version of *The Cherry Orchard* and three operatic experiments (*The Tragedy of Carmen, Impressions of Pelléas, Don Giovanni*). And he continued to write about theater (*The Shifting Point,* 1987; *There Are No Secrets,* 1993; *Evoking Shakespeare,* 1998) and about his own life (*Threads of Time,* 1998).

See also **Theater.**

BIBLIOGRAPHY

Brook, Peter. *The Empty Space*. New York, 1968.

———. *The Shifting Point: 1946-1987*. New York, 1987.

Kustow, Michael *Peter Brook: A Biography*. New York, 2005.

Trewin, J. C. *Peter Brook: A Biography*. London, 1971.

DAVID RICHARD JONES

BROZ, JOSIP. *See* Tito (Josip Broz).

BRUSILOV OFFENSIVE. Known also as the Brusilov breakthrough, the Brusilov offensive was one of the most successful ground offensive operations in World War I. Undertaken primarily by the Russian Southwestern Front between 4 June and 13 August 1916, this offensive accomplished simultaneous penetrations to depths of 60 to 150 kilometers (35 to 95 miles) across 550 kilometers (340 miles) of frontage, while shattering major elements of the Austro-Hungarian army.

In accordance with Allied negotiations at Chantilly in February 1916, the Russian high command promised summer offensives against the Central Powers to divert attention from northern Italy and to relieve pressure on the hard-pressed western front in France. Although the Russians had suffered severe losses during the withdrawals of 1915, the eastern front was now stabilized, with approximately 1.7 million troops in twelve armies arrayed across 1,200 kilometers (750 miles) in three army groups, or fronts (Northern, Western, and Southwestern). These fronts faced about 1.1 million Germans and Austro-Hungarians, with Russian manpower advantages of 2:1 north of the Pripet Marshes and 1.2:1 south of the Pripet. Russian troop units were largely at strength, but supporting heavy artillery remained inadequate, and shortages persisted in personnel replacements, rifles, and artillery shells. As Stavka, the headquarters of the Russian Supreme Command, began preparations for the summer, the Germans attacked

at Verdun on 21 February, throwing the entire allied timetable into disarray. To relieve pressure in the west, Stavka hurriedly regrouped General Alexei Kuropatkin's Northern Front and General Alexei Evert's Western Front for a combined offensive against the Germans north of the Pripet. Known as the Naroch offensive, this gambit began on 18 March, but soon stalled because of inadequate artillery support, the early onset of the spring thaw, and the piecemeal commitment of reserves. Still, unexpected pressure in the east temporarily halted German operations against Verdun.

Against this backdrop, General Mikhail Alexeyev, the Russian chief of staff, continued to press for a summer offensive, in part to support the allies, and in part to preempt any German shift to the east. Although critics later charged that Stavka "advised much and ordered little," by 14 April it had produced a concept that called for a main offensive effort in the summer by the Western Front, supported on the flanks by its Northern and Southwestern counterparts. In response to Austro-Hungarian pressure against the Italians in the Trentino, Stavka advanced the Southwestern Front's offensive to 4 June, a week before anticipated mutually supporting Russian offensives in the north.

General Alexei Brusilov, commander of the Southwestern Front, insisted on careful preparation for the impending offensive. In contrast with conventional tactical practice, which emphasized massive firepower preparation and the accumulation of large reserves in a few sectors, he stressed surprise and the careful selection of numerous breakthrough sectors. He conducted a thorough reconnaissance, rehearsed, drove many saps (trench extensions) closer to the enemy lines, concentrated his reserves well forward, and limited his artillery to counterbattery fire to protect the assaulting infantry. Initially, he committed more than a half million troops and seventeen hundred guns against Austro-Hungarian forces numbering half his own.

As a result, the Brusilov offensive enjoyed major success before finally stalling from lack of support in the face of stiffening German-reinforced resistance. During the breakthrough phase (4–15 June), four Russian armies penetrated to varying depths, until on 14 June General Alexei Kaledin's 8th Army encountered fierce German counterattacks west of Lutsk. Meanwhile, other Russian armies reached

Tarnopol and the Carpathians. General Evert's Western Front, however, lent ineffectual support, with the result that Brusilov's momentum dropped off, even though he continued to develop the breakthrough during his offensive's second phase, 16 June to 8 July. During the third phase, 9 July to 13 August, Stavka belatedly shifted forces to the southwest to support Brusilov's success, but too little came too late, and the offensive literally died out in a series of slugging matches along the Stokhod River. At the cost of half a million casualties, the Russians had succeeded, with assistance from near-simultaneous allied offensives on the Somme in France, in forcing the Germans to assume the overall strategic defensive. To meet the Russian challenge, they shifted more than twenty-four divisions to the east.

Despite varying degrees of tactical and operational success, the Brusilov offensive failed to produce victory or decisive strategic consequences. True, the Italians won a breathing space, and the Russians had relieved pressure on the western front. Romania now belatedly joined the Allied cause, but soon required reinforcement that further drained Russian resources. Ultimately, the price of Brusilov's offensive came high, in terms of both immediate casualties and the longer-term erosion in morale, manpower, and materiel that probably hastened the disintegration of the Russian army in 1917. In the end, much of the blame lay with Stavka's failure to effectively control multifront operations and to allocate sufficient reserves to support success. Nevertheless, the Brusilov offensive did manage to break the combat effectiveness of the Austro-Hungarian army, a circumstance from which that army never recovered.

See also **World War I.**

BIBLIOGRAPHY

Brusilov, A. A. *A Soldier's Note-Book, 1914–1918.* London, 1930. Reprint, Westport, Conn., 1971.

Schindler, John. "Steamrollered in Galicia: The Austro-Hungarian Army and the Brusilov Offensive, 1916." *War in History* 10, no. 1 (2003): 27–59.

Stone, Norman. *The Eastern Front, 1914–1917.* London, 1975.

BRUCE W. MENNING

BRUSSELS. The name *Brussels* covers three distinct entities. First, it designates the City of Brussels, the constitutional capital of Belgium since 1831. A township of medieval origin, circumscribed by the layout of its ancient battlements, it was enlarged on several occasions in the middle of the nineteenth century and in 1921, at the expense of bordering townships. Second, Brussels is the agglomeration the city became part of when two belts of urbanized townships cropped up around it. Third, it is the Brussels-Capital Region, an administrative entity made up of the City of Brussels and eighteen townships. This region is governed by a parliament and an executive branch, and since 1989 it has been one of the three districts that make up the Belgian state (federalized in 1993), along with the Flemish Region and the Walloon Region.

FUNDAMENTAL CHARACTERISTICS, EARLY TWENTIETH CENTURY

With seven hundred thousand residents in 1910, Brussels (including its agglomeration) was the most populous city in Belgium. It also supplied the largest number of jobs in the country, which is remarkable in a heavily industrialized nation, where the main industry centers were located in Wallonia (coal, glass, metallurgy) or in Flanders (textiles).

Brussels was industrially diverse (metal products, manufacturing, food processing, chemistry, energy production, printing, clothing manufacturing), and this diverse activity was usually represented by small or medium-sized businesses. Their preferred location was the western side of Brussels and its agglomeration, close to a two-canal waterway: the first, the Charleroi Canal, connected Brussels to the important metal mining basin of Wallonia; the second, the Willebroeck Canal, made it possible to sail to the port of Antwerp, the gateway to the North Sea. Several railway hubs supported these industrial neighborhoods. As the seat of government, command center of the country's economic life, its financial hub, and its cultural and educational heart, the City of Brussels also developed service-sector activities, which found a home in the historical center of the city, as well as in its eastern expansion.

Political, administrative, and cultural functions, conducted almost exclusively in French, created a complex linguistic situation. In this originally

Flemish agglomeration, the "frenchifying" of the population rapidly progressed with the arrival of French speakers who populated the service sector. The trend progressed with the declaration of Flemish-French bilingualism, claimed in 1910 as the linguistic choice of 57 percent of Brussels's population, when exclusively French speakers represented only 26 percent and exclusively Flemish (Dutch) speakers only 16 percent of the population. By contrast, in 1866 nearly 40 percent of the population of Brussels declared themselves exclusively Flemish speakers. The desire for upward social mobility and administrative accessibility evidently motivated this linguistic mutation, which, in the eyes of Flemish activists, turned Brussels into an "oil spill," a machine to "frenchify" the population that moved there or to its periphery. The essentially French character of Brussels's public life and the difficulty of enforcing Dutch-speaking educational programs would make the language and culture of Brussels a long-lasting and divisive national political problem. On the political level, the City of Brussels, like most cities in Belgium, was traditionally liberal and secular, though the country was otherwise very Catholic. Because of its leading administrative role, Brussels politicians had particular influence over national liberalism. In the second half of the nineteenth century a radical movement emerged that focused on democratizing the right to vote, as well as a factory workers' movement, rooted in the progressive federation of professional associations and cooperatives. In spite of a large concentration of workers in both Wallonia and Flanders (Ghent), the Belgian Workers' Party—forerunner of the Socialist Party—was founded in Brussels in 1885. Many of the early and most important leaders of this party, like those of the liberal movement, issued from Brussels intellectual circles, whose center was the Brussels Free University. This institution, founded in 1834, was the product of secular liberalism, destined to combat the influence of the church in higher education and to train the future elite of the country. It was a fighting organization, thought of as such by its professors and students. The student life it generated would trigger cultural events and feed the artistic and literary avant-garde. The presence of young creators and of critical, educated consumers explains why Brussels opened up to musical, choreographic, sculptural, and poetic innovations. Between the two world wars, Brussels would become an important axis for surrealism, and after World War II, one of the headquarters of the expressionist CoBrA movement.

ADMINISTRATIVE GROWTH AND INTERNATIONALIZATION

With larger state responsibilities in social and economic matters and with the concentration of industrial and financial groups—two trends that really took off in Europe in the 1920s—the central role of Brussels solidified. By the 1930s half of the City of Brussels's employment was in the service sector. This phenomenon would be strongly accentuated in the 1960s and would combine with deindustrialization. The agglomeration, which had remained industrial on its western side, was heavily hit. From 1970 to 1990 it lost 50 percent of its manufacturing jobs, losing first place in that sector to Antwerp. In 2004 less than 10 percent of employment in the Brussels region was still tied to industrial production. Light industry and construction were predominant. Mechanical construction was essentially represented by a large Volkswagen factory.

One of the important phenomena contributing to the rapid mutation of Brussels and its acceleration during the second half of the twentieth century was the internationalization of the city. This development resulted from the political repositioning that Belgium underwent at the end of World War II. Belgium renounced the status of neutrality it had been forced to adopt when it became an independent state, participated in the preparatory acts of the United Nations Organization beginning in 1944, and partnered with Holland and the Grand Duchy of Luxembourg in a customs organization called the Benelux. Anxious to have a noteworthy place in the community of nations despite the small size of the country, the leaders of Belgium decided to play an active role in the elaboration and realization of the various policies of integration in progress in the West. The Brussels Pact for a Western European Union (1948), the North Atlantic Treaty (1949), the European Coal and Steel Community (ECSC; 1951), the European Economic Community (EEC; 1957), and Euratom (1957) were all the result of discussions and development projects for which many meetings took place in Brussels, where Belgian representatives were in the spotlight. The most significant of these representatives was Paul-Henri Spaak (1899–1972).

Since the year of the signing of the Treaty of Rome (1957), which established the EEC and Euratom, the City of Brussels officially referred to itself as the seat of the European institutions. The organization of the Universal Exposition of 1958 in Brussels, the first exposition since World War II, was part of the city's policy of attracting business. Other cities or countries, including Luxembourg, Strasbourg, and Paris, also referred to themselves as the seat of the EEC, but because of the lack of any agreement between the states, a temporary situation created for Brussels in 1958 became a permanent fact. The city welcomed community executives from the European Commission and the Council of Ministers. Brussels was also home to some parliamentary activities: the commissions, political groups' meetings, and additional assemblies. It was not until the Merger Treaty (1965) that the three temporary locations of European institutions (Brussels, Luxembourg, and Strasbourg) were formally recognized as such and not until the Edinburgh European Council (1992) that Brussels was officially named the seat of the Commission, the Council of Ministers, the Economic and Social Committee, the Regions Committee, and the parliament. Everything regarding the organization of the commissions and the parties and the preparation of plenary assemblies would take place in Strasbourg. These events triggered the concentration in Brussels of the economic and diplomatic delegations related to the European Union and the establishment of all sorts of lobbying offices.

The internationalization of Brussels was not limited to welcoming the European institutions. The city also has been officially, since 1967, the seat of the NATO Council, with its Military Committee and its International Secretariat, thus taking advantage of France's partial disengagement from NATO, as well as of Belgium's decidedly Atlantic political and diplomatic conjuncture.

The last stage in the evolution of Brussels's importance took place in the 1980s and the beginning of the 1990s. During this time, the reform of the Belgian state was completed. The city, already the federal capital, became the capital of the Flemish Region, the seat of the ministry and the executive branch of the French Community of Belgium Wallonia-Brussels (an institution that organizes the cultural sector and education), the seat of parliament, and the seat of the ministries and administrations of the Brussels-Capital Region.

All of these institutions produced an extraordinary concentration of power and services over a single generation, in spite of the physical constraints of the city. Many administrative jobs were created, which generated the mass construction of office buildings that has pushed the population farther out into faraway neighborhoods. The administrative evolution of the eastern neighborhoods of the city contributed to the creation and enlargement of a business district where other urban functions, especially residential real estate, have had trouble surviving. In 1998 (before the enlarging of the European Union to twenty-five member states in 2004) it was calculated that the business of the European institutions alone accounted for 13 percent of the Brussels-Capital Region's gross domestic product and 13 percent of total office-space occupancy.

POPULATION AND SOCIETY

The City of Brussels proper, the historical center of Brussels, began losing population very early on: between 1900 and 1920, when the trend started, the population in the city went from 183,600 to 154,800, but continued to grow in the surrounding townships making up the agglomeration. In 1968 the total population of the Brussels-Capital Region, counting all of its nineteen townships, reached 1,079,181. At that time, an urbanization campaign was well under way in the surrounding townships of the city, which caused the population to further diminish. Between 1968 and 1997 the nineteen townships combined lost 240,000 people, who resettled in the suburban outskirts to escape city life and the soaring cost of real estate fueled by the growing service sector. This migration remains active, but its effect was largely offset by the internationalization of the city, which brought in many European executives, and by the arrival of many workers from the Mediterranean basin, starting at the end of the 1960s. Moroccans, Tunisians, Algerians, and Turks responded massively to official government-to-government agreements that sought to fill the need for unskilled laborers, which was made evident by the large infrastructure developments carried out in the 1960s and 1970s, and for low-skill maintenance and services personnel. By welcoming these migrant

The European Parliament Building, Brussels. ©ROYALTY-FREE/CORBIS

workers, who settled down with their families, Brussels restored its population count. In 2004, 950,000 people lived in the Brussels-Capital Region, 30 percent of whom were immigrants, mostly Moroccans.

The ethnic structure matches the age structure of the population, where the youth under the age of twenty represented 23 percent of the population in 1997, whereas those older than sixty accounted for 27 percent. The large representation of young people is the result of the demographic behavior of the immigrant population while that of the older residents results from older Belgians being trapped in the city or returning to it (whereas young middle-class Belgian families have a tendency to leave).

The significance of these numbers with regard to the history of the city cannot be established without taking spatial and social considerations into account. The North African and Turkish populations found lodging for reasonable prices in old and quasi-abandoned neighborhoods in the central and western parts of the city, where

industrial workers made modest homes in the old industrial zone, and in some communities in the first belt of peripheral towns, where decaying middle-class houses had lost their appeal by the time the immigrants arrived. The other new residents of Brussels—brought in by the internationalization of the city—were mostly French. Even though these new residents embraced city life more than the native Belgians, they chose to settle in the more elegant residential neighborhoods to the east and southeast of the city.

Because many different nationalities are mixed together in most neighborhoods, one cannot speak of the existence of a ghetto in Brussels. Still, a socio-spatial division in the agglomeration distinguishes a poor multiethnic zone from a dense but not very populated administrative business district and from a second crown of affluent, cosmopolitan townships.

Though Brussels offers many employment opportunities, particularly in the service sector, these jobs do not fit the profile of a large part of its population, especially its youth. The employment situation more often benefits workers from outside the region, who make up a huge daily commuting traffic by road or train between the outskirts and the city. Though Brussels is located in the middle of the largest employment hub in the country, the internal unemployment rate for the capital region is up to 21.5 percent, and its median income is the lowest of the three regions of Belgium.

INSTITUTIONAL AND LINGUISTIC STATUS

Since the beginning of the twentieth century, the Flemish movement has demanded an official place for the Flemish language in a city where French has the upper hand. This demand has had two major targets: schools and public administration. Theoretically, the laws of 1932 were to ensure that the language of primary and middle schools would be that of a child's maternal language in order to slow down the process of "frenchification." They also stipulated that administrative services in Brussels must be bilingual. The laws were poorly enforced, which frustrated Flemish activists, who were witnessing the inexorable progress of "french-ification" in the outer neighborhoods of the city. After World War II, the balance of power between French and Flemish speakers changed. The economic changes of the 1950s and 1960s drastically favored the northern region, Flanders. In the context of the exacerbation of community tensions, Belgium was officially divided by a linguistic barrier: in the north was Flanders, with monolingual Dutch speakers; in the south, Wallonia, with monolingual French speakers; and in the middle, nestled in Flanders, Brussels with its eighteen surrounding townships, all recognized as bilingual (laws of 1962 and 1963). The boundary was designed to be permanent. In fact, the suppression of the language census prevented any new sharing of land based on changes in the ratio of Flemish speakers to French speakers in other towns around Brussels.

The laws of 1962–1963 triggered great opposition among the French-speaking population of Brussels. The more radical among them created a new political party in 1964, the Democratic Front of French Speakers of Brussels, which very quickly won several elections. The creation of this party reflected the emergence of regional parties throughout the country that crossed over the

traditional Belgian political divisions. Brussels became marginalized, as unitarian Belgium progressively took a backseat to the intense institutional work that took place in the 1970s, allowing Flanders and Wallonia to become more autonomous. In spite of important political confrontations, no concrete fate ever emerged for Brussels or its agglomeration. It was only in 1988–1989 that the Brussels-Capital Region was established, even though the constitutional amendment of 1970 had already designated the three regions of the Belgian state. Despite its late creation, the Brussels-Capital Region was the first to elect, by universal suffrage, its parliamentary assembly (1989), at the heart of which a minority was guaranteed to the Flemish deputies. The Flemish population was represented, from the beginning, by two ministers out of four and by one secretary of state out of three in the government, due to the fact that Brussels kept its status as capital city of both the region and the newly federalized state (1993).

In order to help the City of Brussels fulfill its responsibilities as a capital, an agreement between the region and the state in 1993 enabled the transfer of resources to Brussels, based on the idea that the Brussels-Capital Region was in a very difficult situation. Income taxes, which constitute a large part of the city's revenue, weigh heavily on the impoverished population. A large portion of the revenue that Brussels generates through its activity and employment escapes city taxation because most of the people who make their living in the region do not reside there. The region is rigorously delineated, and its limits do not include the whole of the city's active economic areas, nor those generated by the central institutions of Brussels, which could otherwise be taxed (peripheral industrial zones, large commercial areas along the beltways surrounding the city, airport facilities, and so on). The Brussels-Capital Region is heavily dependent on the federal state, which makes it the focal point of the permanent conflict that pits Flemish against French in all institutional matters.

THE EVOLVING BRUSSELS SKYLINE: URBANISM, ARCHITECTURE, CULTURE

The landscape of both Brussels and its agglomeration is surprisingly diverse. Because of this lack of unity, a visitor may have trouble reading its personality. In the mosaic of neighborhoods there is one predominant trait: the massive number of individual homes.

This particularity has encouraged architectural expression, especially in the first half of the twentieth century. Art nouveau until 1914, and art deco and modernism between the two world wars, found a well-off clientele in the first and second belts surrounding the City of Brussels. The second belt was mostly urbanized by the end of the 1930s. Among the residential developments in this area are around ten garden cities, all housing projects, erected in the 1920s by socially committed architects. They have become famous and represent a precious part of the country's modern history. With the exception of a few large luxury buildings, built in rich neighborhoods and close to the city's center in the 1920s and 1930s, apartment buildings did not begin spreading in Brussels until the 1960s and 1970s. They replaced the more destitute houses of the popular neighborhoods or, because of intense speculation pressure, occupied some areas of the second belt still not very densely built.

Urbanization in Brussels during the second half of the twentieth century was notoriously bad. Some informed European circles spoke of "Brusselization" to designate the arbitrary destruction of old residential neighborhoods and their replacement, without any concern for their social or aesthetic context, by large-scale office buildings. This phenomenon struck the center of the city quite heavily, as well as its northern and eastern districts, particularly those neighborhoods where the European institutions are located. However, since 1989 the Brussels-Capital Region has been working to change this trend with the help of its Administration for Land Management and Housing. The administration has been planning urban development while gaining better control over real estate promotion. It has also worked to better the conditions in the more dilapidated neighborhoods and to help local municipalities embellish public spaces. The problem it faces in the early twenty-first century is that of rising rents. This increase, which hits hardest the more fragile populations concentrated in the capital-city region, also accentuates the migration of more wealthy households toward the outskirts.

The construction since 1989, which made the center of the city much more pleasant, has attracted a new type of resident and consumer: young, employed singles or childless couples. These city dwellers, a large number of whom are Flemish, actively participate in the multicultural life of Brussels, known for its concerts and its alternative music, theater, and film festivals. There are many cultural establishments, artist groups, and theaters in the center of the city. Brussels is at the heart of an intense rivalry between Flemish and French entities that subsidize culture, which results in the multiplication and diversification of cultural output. This culture is also enriched by the presence of historical and cultural institutions created or subsidized by the state: the Museum of Fine Arts, the Art and History Museum, the Opera (Theatre de la Monnaie), and the Royal Library.

CONCLUSION

The originality and paradoxes of Brussels are the result of the conflicting history of Belgium in the twentieth century. Its central functions have grown, but its political importance is fading; its internationalization is real, and the wealth it produces grows while public finances are more and more meager. Its culture is mixed and cosmopolitan, while the two linguistic communities continue to fight for its control. Despite the contradictions and problems, Brussels remains a lively city, less hectic and more secure than the majority of Europe's great capitals. A possible hypothesis is that despite the socioeconomic threats that weigh on it, the regional institution has thus far managed to maintain a kind of balance in the urban society. It is a balance in which a waxing sense of belonging among its mixed population probably plays a role.

See also **Belgium; Flemish Bloc; Luxembourg.**

BIBLIOGRAPHY

Billen, Claire, and Jean-Marie Duvosquel, eds. *Brussels.* Antwerp, 2000. Contains a synthesis of the history of the city since the Middle Ages. Abundant illustrations, interesting map portfolio.

Dumoulin, Michel, ed. *Bruxelles l'Européenne, regards croisés sur une région capitale.* Brussels, 2001. Abstracts in English.

Govaert, Serge. *Bruxelles en capitales 1958–2000: De l'expo à euro.* Brussels, 2000. Excellent explanation of the linguistic, political, and institutional problems relative to Brussels's status.

Hoozee, Robert, ed. *Bruxelles, carrefour de cultures.* Antwerp, 2000. Study of cosmopolitan art and literature of Brussels in the nineteenth and twentieth centuries.

Smolar-Meynart, Arlette, and Jean Stengers, eds. *La Région de Bruxelles: Des villages d'autrefois à la ville d'aujourd'hui.* Brussels, 1989. Elaborates on specifically social and spatial aspects of the history of the city since the Middle Ages and includes illustrations.

Witte, Els, André Alen, Hugues Dumont, and Rusen Ergec, eds. *Het statuut van Brussel geanalyseerd.* Brussels, 1999. Very specialized study of the institutional problems and of Brussels's relationship with the European Union; abstracts in English.

Witte, Els, André Alen, Hugues Dumont, Pierre Vandernoot, and Roel De Groof, eds. *De Brusselse negentien gemeenten en het Brussels model.* Brussels, 2003. Study of the political and social problems of the agglomeration. The entries are summarized in English and the conclusions are translated.

CLAIRE BILLEN

BUBER, MARTIN (1878–1965), German-Jewish philosopher and theologian.

The life-work of Martin Buber remains one of the most pervasive and multifaceted testaments of German-Jewish thought and culture. Best known, perhaps, for his dialogical "I-Thou" philosophy, Buber wrote extensively on the subjects of the Hebrew Bible, Hasidism, Judaism, Zionism, as well as on aesthetics, literature, education, and political thought. His ideas continue to be a major source of influence for twenty-first-century and contemporary Jewish and Christian theology, both in Europe and in the United States, where his writings became available after World War II. Upon his emigration to Palestine in 1938, Buber also emerged as an outspoken public intellectual whose largely unpopular views on Jewish-Arab rapprochement and politics left him, more than once, controversial, if not marginalized.

Born in 1878 to an assimilated Jewish family in Vienna, Buber spent the better part of his adolescent years at the traditional home of his grandparents in Galicia, then a province of Austria-Hungary and a center of Hasidism. Between the ages of three and fourteen, Buber lived as a fully observant Jew under the tutelage of his grandfather

Salomon Buber (1827–1906), who, in addition to being the president of the Lemberg (Lvóv) chamber of commerce, was also a pioneer in the scholarship of Rabbinics and Midrash literature. Fluent in Yiddish, Polish, Hebrew, German, and French, Buber received impulses from both the spirit of the Haskalah (Jewish Enlightenment) and the ways of eastern European Judaism.

Soon, however, estranged from traditional Judaism, Buber returned to Vienna in 1896 to take up studies at the capital's university in philosophy and art history. After extended visits at the universities of Leipzig (1897–1899), Zurich (1899), and Berlin (1899–1901), Buber graduated in 1904 with a doctoral dissertation on the "History of the Problem of Individuation from Nicolaus of Cusa to Jakob Böhme." Among his most influential teachers during this time period—both, incidentally, at the university of Berlin—were the sociologist Georg Simmel (1858–1918), whose distinction between religion and "religiosity" recurs in Buber's later works, and the historian Wilhelm Dilthey (1833–1911), whose hermeneutic method and appreciation for the Renaissance period is reflected in Buber's writings as well.

By Buber's own account, the truly formative experiences came from his encounters with literature and theater. Buber's very first publication, in fact, was an essay "On Viennese Literature," written in Polish in 1897. His lifelong friendships with Hugo von Hofmannsthal (1874–1929), Fritz Mauthner (1849–1923), and the philosopher-revolutionary Gustav Landauer (1870–1919) connected him intimately with the fin-de-siècle "crisis of language," which attuned the young Buber to the significance of the "spoken word," establishing an early link to his later philosophy of dialogue. Buber himself stressed the early philosophical influences of Arthur Schopenhauer, Plato, Immanuel Kant, Ludwig Feuerbach, and, most importantly, Friedrich Nietzsche.

His sympathy for Nietzsche's ideas placed the young Buber also among some of the leading thinkers of a Jewish national and cultural revival at the turn of the century. Already during his student years, Buber came in contact with the still emerging Zionist movement under the leadership of the Viennese playwright and journalist Theodor Herzl (1860–1904). Most impressed, however, with the writings of the "spiritual" Zionist Asher Ginzberg (pseudonym Achad Haam, 1856–1927), Buber soon developed a form of Zionism that was cultural and ethical in its orientation and that found its first expression in his call for a "Jewish Renaissance" in 1901. After continuous conflicts with the Zionist leadership of Herzl and Max Simon Nordau (1849–1923), Buber withdrew from the movement in 1904 and began working on a series of highly popular German adaptations of Hasidic texts, including *The Tales of Rabbi Nachman* (1906), *The Legend of the Baal-Shem* (1908), and the collection of Hasidic tales (completed in 1946). Though his interpretation of Hasidism was contested by scholars already at his time, Buber succeeded in conveying a lively and unencumbered style of "religiosity," worldliness, and wisdom that resonated widely with an acculturated Jewish and German audience. Responding to a new public interest in nonwestern wisdom and folklore, Buber continued to produce German renditions of a variety of texts, such as the *Ecstatic Confessions* (1909), *Tschuang-Tse* (1910), and the Finnish national epic *Kalewala* (1914). Between 1906 and 1912, he was also the creator of a unique series of "sociopsychological" monographs, *Die Gesellschaft*, among whose contributing authors were Simmel, Landauer, Mauthner, Ferdinand Tönnies, and Lou Andreas-Salomé. As most scholars agree, Buber's interest in cultural sociology at this time would later shape his dialogical conception of the "inter-human" (*Zwischenmenschliche*) and his fully developed social philosophy in *Paths in Utopia* (1947).

In 1913, Buber's first philosophical book appeared, *Daniel: Dialogues on Realization*, whose mythical, ecstatic tone soon rendered it a major work of German literary expressionism. Grounded in the German *Lebensphilosophie* of its time, as well as in Nietzschean aestheticism and the spirit of a new, syncretistic religiosity, Buber's *Daniel* nevertheless anticipated some of the central themes of his dialogical thought. The mythic-messianic overtones in Buber's earlier writings carried on through most of World War I, which Buber—like many of his German Jewish contemporaries—greeted with a certain enthusiasm and redemptive fantasies. During this time, Buber also composed a series of passionate essays calling for a renewal of Judaism

and championing the idea of national-humanism. Between 1916 and 1924, he founded and edited a journal, proudly titled *Der Jude*, offering a powerful pan-Jewish forum for both Zionist and non-Zionist writers.

At almost the same time, Buber's philosophical breakthrough occurred. In his 1922 series of lectures "Religion as Presence," he first articulated his dialogical principle, followed by the publication of *I and Thou* in December of the same year. Between his lectures and the publication of *I and Thou* a fundamental shift in his thinking occurred from religious experience to speech, which was most certainly inspired by Buber's reading of Ferdinand Ebner's (1882–1931) *The Word and the Spiritual Realities* and Franz Rosenzweig's (1886–1929) manuscript of *The Star of Redemption*, which, in turn, was deeply indebted to late work of Hermann Cohen (1842–1918). Rosenzweig also formed a link to the thinkers of the Johannine "Patmos" circle that was active between 1915 and 1923. With members such as Rosenzweig, Eugen Rosenstock-Huessy, and Karl Barth, the Patmos group sought to relocate theology in an extra-denominational realm of revelation as divine-human dialogue, borrowing richly from the thought of Johann Georg Hamann (1730–1788). Though Buber stood only at the periphery of this circle, his dialogical philosophy was undoubtedly informed by its theology of speech and frequent I-Thou language.

The basic conception of Buber's *I and Thou* is the duality of human attitude (*Grundhaltung*) toward the world as one of either distance and objective perception ("I-It") or relation and dialogic acceptance ("I-You"). In choosing our mode of attitude through speech we also choose, ontologically, our mode of being. We are not the same saying "I-It" and saying "I-You." It is only in the mode of "I-You" that we become an "I" in the proper sense, a person with the ability to respond. But this mode is all but a fleeting moment within the continuity of the "I-It" world, an act of "grace" rather than choice. The only "You" that continues to call on us without ever becoming an "It" is the "Eternal Thou," where the lines of all "I-You" moments meet. Adding the dimension of the "We," Buber developed this conception in subsequent writings, *Dialogue* (1929), *The*

Question to the Single One (1936), and *Elements of the Interhuman* (1954).

A similar dialogical approach also guided Buber's and Rosenzweig's collaborative translation of Hebrew scripture that was begun in 1925 and, after Rosenzweig's untimely death, completed by Buber in 1961. The aim of the *Verdeutschung* was not merely a revision of Martin Luther's standard version but a re-creation of the poetic rhythm and "spokenness" of the Hebrew text in German. Accompanied by a lengthy essay on the philosophy of translation, the Buber-Rosenzweig Bible saw itself as both an authentically Jewish reading of scripture and a genuine renewal of language. As such, it combined sensibilities of a German Jewish renaissance during the Weimar years with a Johannine theology of language and a dialogical philosophy of translation.

With the rise of Nazism in Germany, Buber resigned from his lecturing post at the University of Frankfurt, which he had held since 1924, to assume the leadership of the Frankfurt Lehrhaus. Between 1933 and 1938, Buber wrote most of his essays on aspects of the Bible, such as "Biblical Humanism" (1933) or "Biblical Leadership" (1933), which were thinly veiled calls for intellectual resistance. Forced to leave his home in 1938, Buber left Germany for Palestine and—being denied a position in religious thought—assumed an appointment in social philosophy at the Hebrew University of Jerusalem, where he continued to teach until his retirement in 1951. Much of Buber's thought on society and community, and his engagement with Jewish-Palestinian understanding, stems from this time period, though its deeper roots lay in his friendship with Landauer, his admiration for Ferdinand Tönnies (1855–1936) and Aaron David Gordon (1856–1922), and his involvement with the religious socialism of Leonard Ragaz (1868–1945). Together with his social philosophy, Buber also pursued an "integrative anthropology" (*The Problem of Man*, 1943), as well as a clarification of his philosophy of language, which was significantly shaped by his critical response to Martin Heidegger (1889–1976).

Committed to what he once termed "Hebrew humanism," Buber continued to work toward reconciliation between Arab and Jew, Jews and Germans, and Judaism and Christianity, until his death in 1965.

See also **Jews; Zionism.**

BIBLIOGRAPHY

Biemann, Asher D., ed. *The Martin Buber Reader: Essential Writings.* New York, 2002.

Buber, Martin. *Martin Buber Werkausgabe.* Edited by Paul Mendes-Flohr and Peter Schäfer. Gütersloh, Germany, 2001.

Cohn, Margot, and Rafael Buber, eds. *Martin Buber: A Bibliography of His Writings, 1897–1978.* Jerusalem, 1980.

Glatzer, Nahum N., and Paul Mendes-Flohr, eds. *The Letters of Martin Buber: A Life of Dialogue.* New York, 1991.

Kohn, Hans. *Martin Buber und seine Zeit.* Cologne, 1961.

Mendes-Flohr, Paul. *A Land of Two Peoples: Martin Buber on Jews and Arabs.* New York, 1983.

———. *From Mysticism to Dialogue: Martin Buber's Transformation of German Social Thought.* Detroit, Mich., 1989.

Schaeder, Grete. *The Hebrew Humanism of Martin Buber.* Translated by Noah J. Jacobs. Detroit, Mich., 1973.

Schilpp, Paul A., and Maurice Friedman, eds. *The Philosophy of Martin Buber.* LaSalle, Ill., 1967.

Schmidt, Gilya G., ed. *The First Buber: Youthful Zionist Writings of Martin Buber.* Syracuse, N.Y., 1999.

Silberstein, Laurence J. *Martin Buber's Social and Religious Thought.* New York, 1989.

ASHER D. BIEMANN

BUCHAREST. *See* Romania.

BUCHENWALD. Buchenwald was a major National Socialist concentration camp located in Thuringia in central Germany, on the Ettersberg, a mountain eight kilometers north of Weimar. The origins of the camp can be traced back to a request from the Nazi Party gauleiter or district leader of Thuringia, Fritz Sauckel (1894–1946), who wanted to replace a small concentration camp in his realm. The SS (Schutzstaffel) concentration camp administration itself was interested in setting up a new "modern" concentration camp like the one in Sachsenhausen. The camp was opened in July 1937. The Weimar Nazi Cultural Society (NS-Kulturgemeinde) wanted to avoid the name "Ettersberg concentration camp" because the poet Johann Wolfgang von Goethe (1749–1832), who lived in Weimar, had strolled there frequently. Supposedly, the SS chief himself, Heinrich Himmler, chose the rather "neutral" name, which officially read "K.L. Buchenwald/Post Weimar."

The SS-owned territory subsequently was expanded until 1940, to 190 hectares. The camp itself was divided into several sectors, the "big camp," the "small camp," temporarily the "tent camp," and the area for SS personnel and the economic facilities of the SS-owned Deutsche Ausrüstungswerke (DAW, German armament works). A *Kommandantur,* in 1944 consisting of more than three hundred SS functionaries, organized camp life and crimes against prisoners. Karl Otto Koch (1897–1945) served as the first camp commander; he was replaced by Hermann Pister (1885–1948) in January 1942. Guard duties were first carried out by the SS-Totenkopfstandarte Thüringen, then after the beginning of the war by a Wachsturmbann Buchenwald. Its personnel expanded from 1,200 men in 1938 to 6,300 men and women in early 1945, at which point most of the guardsmen were on duty in subcamps.

The first 149 prisoners arrived at Buchenwald on 14 July 1937. Along with several hundred inmates of the recently dissolved Sachsenburg and Lichtenburg camps, they had to build the camp infrastructure. In April 1938 the victims of mass arrests during the so-called action against asocials arrived in the camp, followed by several thousand Jews during the mass arrests in June and in November 1938, the latter connected to *Kristallnacht.* These prisoners were treated especially badly, and as a consequence hundreds soon died. After the beginning of the war, newly arriving Polish and Jewish prisoners were put into the improvised "tent camp," where within months they died en masse from the horrible living conditions. At the end of 1939 nearly twelve thousand prisoners lived in the camp; then this figure decreased to just under eight thousand. Until the end of 1941 the prisoner constituency remained fundamentally the same, despite some deportations

from the Netherlands. In October 1941 a small extra camp for Soviet prisoners of war (POWs) was established; in October 1942 most of the Jewish prisoners were deported to Auschwitz.

During the second half of the war, subcamps were established, especially for the purposes of the armament industries in central Germany. The subcamps were scattered from the Rhineland in the west, in Westphalia, Hanover province, and especially in central Germany, to Silesia in the east. One of the worst was the subcamp Mittelbau-Dora, which in October 1944 was transformed into a separate main camp, taking over other branches. Similarly, Buchenwald integrated all branches of the Ravensbrück camp for women, which were situated in its geographical realm, by September 1944. Thus, some Buchenwald subcamps consisted exclusively of female prisoners. In the largest of those, five thousand women worked for the Hugo Schneider AG in Leipzig. The biggest branches of Buchenwald, like Ellrich or Nordhausen, had grown to almost the same size as the main camp itself before 1942.

Already by spring 1944 more than half of the forty-two thousand inmates were imprisoned in subcamps. More and more civilians from France and from the Soviet Union were brought to Buchenwald, and in summer 1944 even Jews from Hungary were brought there. In autumn 1944, 27 percent of the inmates were non-Jewish Soviet civilians, 20 percent were Poles, 15 percent were French, and 12 percent were Jews from different countries. Especially in the last period of the war, specific small groups such as German politicians from the pre-1933 era, western Allied POWs, Norwegian students, and Danish policemen were deported to the camp. As a consequence of the evacuation of camps in Poland, especially from Auschwitz and Groß-Rosen in January 1945, Buchenwald grew into the biggest concentration camp in the Reich. The number of inmates finally rose to 112,000 persons in February 1945, among them 25,000 women. At that time the majority of prisoners lived in the eighty-seven subcamps.

LIVING CONDITIONS

Living conditions in Buchenwald were as horrible as in the other camps in Germany. A small number of prominent prisoners—such as the three French

The crematorium at Buchenwald, photographed shortly after the camp was liberated, 1945. UNITED STATES HOLOCAUST MEMORIAL MUSEUM

prime ministers Édouard Daladier, Paul Reynaud, and Léon Blum—were kept in separate camp sectors and treated better than average. But in general almost all prisoners suffered from constant undernourishment, and probably every tenth inmate was infected with tuberculosis. In the early camp period, prisoners worked in the camp itself or in the Weimar area—from 1943 on in the armament industry, such as the gun-producing "Wilhelm-Gustloff-Werke" in Weimar. The penal company was forced to work in the stone quarry at the Ettersberg, a horrible working place with extremely high death rates. Later on, Buchenwald inmates were forced to work in arms, ammunition, and airplane production; excavation work for subterranean installations; or clearing blind bombs in cities. Inhuman living and working conditions led to rapidly deteriorating health; SS guards or

guardsmen of the enterprises frequently beat or even killed prisoners. Systematic torture was applied by the camp SS in the "bunker," a specific penal prison cell, or by the political department of the camp, a branch of the Weimar Gestapo. By 1940 the annual death rate had already risen to 20 percent. Until 1942 corpses of the victims were incinerated in the crematorium of a Weimar cemetery, but then Buchenwald obtained its own crematorium.

From 1941 on, systematic killing actions hit Buchenwald prisoners. From July 1941 medical commissions selected weak and old prisoners, preferably Jews, and sent them to "euthanasia" killing centers such as Sonnenstein and Bernburg, where they were killed by gas. Some months later the SS started to shoot Soviet POWs near the camp territory—the Soviets had been selected as "undesirables" in German POW camps. In sum, approximately eight thousand Red Army soldiers were killed that way. More than one thousand prisoners were shot by the Gestapo inside the crematorium, including the former Communist Party leader Ernst Thälmann. From early 1942, SS camp physicians undertook cruel medical experiments on prisoners, which resulted in the death of most of the victims. Finally in 1944, especially Jewish and Romani inmates were sent to Majdanek and Auschwitz and were murdered there.

Despite the extreme conditions in the camp, some prisoners managed to establish improvised underground organizations; the national camp committees that were founded from the end of 1943 served to assist their fellow countrymen or the almost nine hundred imprisoned children. In August 1944 the U.S. Air Force bombed the Wilhelm-Gustloff-Werke, claiming more than three hundred victims among the prisoners. Thus Buchenwald entered the final phase of the war. The camp SS prepared evacuation from the beginning of 1945. In early April twenty-eight thousand inmates of the main camp were driven south either by rail or in death marches; almost twelve thousand died en route or in other camps. On 11 April 1945, U.S. army troops, assisted by an uprising of the prisoners, liberated Buchenwald, which still housed twenty-one thousand inmates. Hundreds of them died immediately after liberation because their state of health had been extremely critical.

The population of the surrounding area—especially Weimar citizens—was by and large informed about the camp and to a certain extent also about the atrocities. The SS personnel had everyday contacts with locals, and the camp infrastructure was tightly connected to the economy of Weimar, as forced laborers worked in town. After liberation, U.S. military authorities forced Weimar inhabitants to visit the camp area, in order to be confronted with a mass of corpses of those prisoners who had died during the final period of the camp.

From 1937 until 1945, 266,000 persons became prisoners in the Buchenwald camp system, among them 27,000 women added during the 1944 reorganization. Thirty-five thousand prisoners died in the camp and all its branches. If the killings of Soviet POWs and those that took place during the evacuation are added, Buchenwald claimed the lives of fifty-six thousand human beings. Only some of the responsible SS men—thirty-one functionaries—were put on trial during the so-called Buchenwald trial at a U.S. military court in Dachau 1947. Individual perpetrators, including the first commander's wife, Ilse Koch, were sentenced by Soviet or German courts.

The Soviet Secret Police, which entered Thuringia in June 1945 after the repartitioning of the occupation zones, already in autumn of that year started to use the camp facilities for its own purposes, installing there Special Camp No. 2. In the beginning, mostly Nazi functionaries and members of Nazi organizations were interned at the camp, but later victims of political persecutions and denunciations were kept there as well. Almost half of the twenty-six thousand inmates died in the camp, especially from undernourishment during the winter 1946–1947. Thousands were deported to camps inside the Soviet Union. In January 1950 the MVD (Ministry of the Interior) camp was dissolved.

COMMEMORATION

Unlike other camps, such as Dachau for Americans or Bergen-Belsen for the British, Buchenwald did not occupy a central place in war memory after 1945. However, in the second half of the 1950s it developed into a major commemoration site of East German politics. Most of the camp installations had been demolished after 1950. In 1958 the Nationale Mahn- und Gedenkstätte Buchenwald was opened, focusing on the fate of Ernst Thälmann. The communist interpretation of the camp history was highly popularized in the novel by the former prisoner Bruno Apitz, *Nackt unter Wölfen* (1958; *Naked among Wolves*, 1960; film version, 1963). The book glorified the communist prisoners' underground and was introduced as compulsory reading in East German schools. Yet the history of the Soviet camp in Buchenwald was completely ignored in the German Democratic Republic (GDR).

In the West, publications on Buchenwald, most of them written by former inmates, gave a much more differentiated picture. Eugen Kogon based his first overall history of Nazi camps, *Der SS-Staat* (1946; *Theory and Practice of Hell*, 1950), on his Buchenwald experience. The individual and human perspective prevailed in the memoirs of the former prisoners, the most important of which were Robert Antelme's *L'espèce humaine* (1947; *The Human Race*, 1992) and especially Jorge Semprún's *Le grand voyage* (1963; *Long Voyage*, 1964) and *Quel beau dimanche* (1980; *What a Beautiful Sunday*, 1982), written after his break with the Communist Party in 1964.

There has been considerable public debate since the mid-1990s on the communist underground, as some of its members as prisoner-functionaries allegedly decided who was put on death lists of the SS. This almost completely devastated the myths surrounding the communist underground in the camp. The double perspective on Buchenwald's history, as a Nazi and as a Soviet camp, also led to fierce discussions. The memorial, now part of the Stiftung Gedenkstätten Buchenwald und Mittelbau-Dora, opened a new exhibition on the Nazi camp in 1995 and a separate one on the MVD camp in 1999.

See also **Auschwitz-Birkenau; Concentration Camps; Gestapo; Holocaust; SS (Schutzstaffel).**

BIBLIOGRAPHY

"Buchenwald Memorial." Internet homepage. Available at http://www.buchenwald.de/.

The Buchenwald Report. Translated, edited, and with an introduction by David A. Hackett. Boulder, Colo., 1995.

Polak, Edmund. *Dziennik buchenwaldzki.* Warsaw, 1983.

Ritscher, Bodo, et al., eds. *Das sowjetische Speziallager Nr. 2, 1945–1950: Katalog zur ständigen historischen Ausstellung.* Göttingen, Germany, 1999.

Stein, Harry, comp. *Buchenwald Concentration Camp 1937–1945: A Guide to the Permanent Historical Exhibition.* Edited by the Gedenkstätte Buchenwald. Göttingen, Germany, 2005.

DIETER POHL

BUDAPEST. At the turn of the twentieth century, this central European capital—a product of the 1873 union between the settlements of Pest, Buda, Óbuda, and the Margit Island—was Hungary's largest city and an important center of culture, commerce, government, and industry within both the Kingdom of Hungary and the Austro-Hungarian Monarchy as a whole.

GROWTH AND DEVELOPMENT

Already a fairly modern city for its time—home of the European continent's first underground transportation line, which was completed in 1896 and is still in operation—Budapest experienced a period of massive expansion and development at the beginning of the twentieth century. In 1900 the number of people living within what would become the city limits reached 861,434, nearly triple what it had been just three decades earlier. The rapid growth was mostly the result of in-migration from other parts of the Austro-Hungarian Monarchy. During World War I, the number of incoming refugees compensated for the number of wartime casualties, so the population of the city did not change significantly. The interwar period was characterized by another period of steady growth until World War II, when Budapest suffered heavy civilian losses (between 1941 and 1949, the population declined by about 7 percent). In 1950 the city was expanded to include several of its suburbs, raising the number of districts from fourteen to twenty-two and resulting in a significant population increase. The number of inhabitants stabilized at around two million in the 1970s, but the period since 1990 has seen a decline; in 2003 Budapest's population was down to 1,719,342.

1900 TO 1918

Compared to most European cities, Budapest was a highly industrialized urban center prior to World War I. In 1910, 40 percent of employed city dwellers worked in industry. For this reason—and the relatively pragmatic cultural scene, centered around a cultural elite made up more of journalists and politicians than of artists and philosophers—the Hungarian historian Péter Hanák described Budapest as a "workshop." Despite the city's industrial character, the period preceding World War I was characterized by intense cultural production. Among Budapest's most notable figures were the leftist poet and journalist Endre Ady, the leftist philosopher György (Georg) Lukács, the rightwing writer Dezső Szabó, the composers Béla Bartók and Zoltán Kodály, and the painters István

Csók and József Rippl-Rónai. All were innovators in their chosen media and many were politically active.

The bulk of the city's most prominent architectural monuments were built around the turn of the century, including the grandiose and stylistically eclectic parliament building, which was the largest in the world when it was completed in 1902. Budapest's stock exchange (1895) and the Erzsébet Bridge (1903) spanning the Danube River were also of record-breaking size at the time they were constructed. The eclecticism of these monumental structures later yielded to Secession-style architecture, which began to appear in the city a few years before the war.

Politically, turn-of-the-century Budapest was at the center of the crisis of European liberalism. The Hungarian Liberal Party—which had negotiated the famous Compromise of 1867, giving the Kingdom of Hungary a kind of autonomous partnership status in the new Dual (Austro-Hungarian) Monarchy—had remained in control of the Hungarian government until just after the turn of the century. Crippled by corruption and scandal, and threatened by both growing nationalism (represented by the Independence Party) and an increasingly influential Social Democratic Party, the Liberals were finally defeated in the elections of January 1905. The period from 1905 to the beginning of World War I was marked by political antagonism between the national minorities and the Hungarian nationalists and rising social unrest resulting from the gross disparity of wealth between rich and poor inhabitants of the city.

In 1900, 79 percent of the city's inhabitants were native speakers of Hungarian, 14 percent spoke German, and just over 3 percent spoke Slovak. Although only about 5 percent of the total population of Hungary in 1910 was Jewish, Jews constituted nearly 23 percent of the total population of Budapest. Many Budapest Jews considered themselves Hungarians by nationality and most spoke Hungarian at home. They were also involved in the modernization of the city on many levels and made up a large part of the new middle and professional classes. Over 40 percent of individuals in certain professions (among them journalism, law, banking, and medicine) were Jewish. Their over-representation in the middle-class professions and in institutions of higher education fueled anti-Semitic sentiment among non-Jewish Hungarians who felt marginalized by the modernization process. The first anti-Jewish law in Europe, the *numerus clausus* of 1920, limited university enrollment of national and ethnic groups to numbers proportionate to their percentage of the overall population and was crafted to reverse this trend.

The character of the city was much changed by the events of World War I. After an initial wave of nationalist enthusiasm for the war, when the Central Powers—and Hungary with them—started losing, it became clear that a reshuffling of territory and the collapse of the monarchy was imminent. Neighboring countries were gradually occupying more and more Hungarian territory, causing a mass flight of civil servants and other refugees to the capital. From among the sizable Hungarian population remaining outside the country's borders, it is estimated that around 208,000 individuals—particularly members of the elite and former state employees whose livelihood was no longer ensured under foreign rule—converged on the city. Due to massive unemployment and the economic crisis that followed the war, however, many of these refugees did not remain in Budapest but moved to other parts of the country or abroad. Nevertheless, their presence and vocal dissatisfaction with the status quo contributed to the political instability out of which the so-called Soviet Republic was born.

1918 TO 1920

The postwar government headed by Mihály Károlyi was unable to stabilize Hungary's borders or to stop domestic social unrest incited by the Communists and Socialists. As a result, Károlyi ceded power to a left-wing coalition on 21 March 1919. That same day, the Communists—under the informal leadership of Béla Kun, a journalist who had been introduced to bolshevism as a prisoner of war in Russia—seized power from the more moderate socialists and proclaimed the Soviet Republic. The Communist leadership immediately set about nationalizing the economy and trying to negotiate a more favorable territorial settlement for Hungary. Its Red Army successfully re-conquered Kassa/Košice and large parts of Slovakia, and the Hungarian-sponsored Slovak Soviet Republic was proclaimed. On 1 May the workers of Budapest celebrated May Day with mass demonstrations. Despite a hopeful beginning, however, the new government's collectivization policies alienated the rural population, while Budapest residents grew anxious as city dwellers continued to suffer shortages of food and other goods resulting from the wartime economic blockade that was still in force against Hungary. Furthermore, by the end of July 1919, the Hungarian Soviet Republic had been defeated by the Romanian army, sponsored and equipped by the French general staff. The Romanians took Budapest on 4 August 1919.

Admiral Miklós Horthy, who commanded an antirevolutionary militia, entered Budapest at the head of his National Army on 16 November 1919. Following the departure of the Romanian troops from Hungary, Horthy established a "white" government, with himself as regent, in March 1920. That same year Hungary signed the Treaty of Trianon, according to which the country lost two-thirds of its territory to the new neighboring states of Czechoslovakia; Romania; the Kingdom of Serbs, Croats, and Slovenes; and Austria.

Following the collapse of the Soviet Republic, the Horthy regime initiated the White Terror, a series of more or less violent reprisals against suspected communists, other leftists, and many Jews. It is estimated that as many as five thousand people were executed and another seventy-five thousand imprisoned or sentenced to hard labor. As a result of the terror, nearly one hundred thousand people fled the country.

1920 TO 1938

In 1921 Horthy appointed István Bethlen prime minister. Bethlen passed a minor land reform, allowed workers to organize and enter into collective bargaining with their employers, gave free reign to the press, and did not completely enforce the *numerus clausus* law, allowing Jewish professionals to remain active members of a growing urban bourgeoisie. Bethlen also reinstated a limited franchise that allowed only 27 percent of the population to vote. He remained prime minister until 1931 and is credited with rebuilding Budapest's industrial capacity, which had been greatly weakened by the war and the postwar settlement.

His fall coincided with the onset of the Great Depression.

From 1931 onward, Hungary's leadership moved increasingly to the right and became periodically pro-German. It was not long before the Hungarian leadership saw Germany as the only power capable of effecting territorial revision in the region; regaining the territories lost with the Treaty of Trianon was a primary objective for all Hungarian governments of the interwar period, regardless of their political orientation.

1938 TO 1945

After receiving territorial gains through Hitler's dissection of Czechoslovakia (1938) and an Axis-mediated agreement with Romania (1940), Hungary formally became an ally of the Axis in November 1940. The wartime economy brought 130 new factories and forty thousand workers to the capital city. Yet apart from mounting anti-Semitism and the implementation of three increasingly harsh Jewish laws barring Jews from public service and the professions and assigning Jewish men to forced labor battalions, Budapest remained relatively unaffected by the war.

This situation changed on 19 March 1944, when Hitler occupied Hungary following neighboring Romania's defection from the Axis camp. The Jews of Hungary were rapidly ghettoized and deported, but Horthy stopped the deportations when it came to the Jews of Budapest—except for those living in suburban Budapest, who were deported in July—for whom he is supposed to have had a special sympathy. On 16 October, the German SS forced Horthy to resign, installing the leader of the fascist Arrow Cross Party, Ferenc Szálasi, in his place. In November, about fifty thousand Budapest Jews were deported to Austria by Adolf Eichmann and the Arrow Cross militia. Although the Red Army had already advanced deep into Hungarian territory, in early December Budapest police and Arrow Cross militiamen, working under the supervision of a handful of Gestapo men, rounded up about seventy thousand of Budapest's Jews and ghettoized them in Pest. During this time, the Swedish emissary Raoul Wallenberg sought by various means—including by forging Red Cross and Swedish government passes, bribing officials, and making appeals to various governments—to save some of Budapest's Jews. About 120,000 of the Jews who ended up in the ghetto or under Swedish protection survived the war.

For Adolf Hitler, Budapest was an important site as both the capital of Hungary (Germany's last remaining ally in Europe) and the last line of defense for Vienna and southern Bavaria. In addition, the Axis's only remaining crude oil plant was in southwest Hungary. Joseph Stalin also had good reason to hasten the fall of the Hungarian capital, believing that the liberation of Budapest and Vienna would increase his bargaining power with the Allies at Yalta. In late October he called on Marshal Rodion Malinovsky, the commander of the Second Ukrainian Front, to seize Budapest within days. In the first week of November, Malinovsky's troops managed to reach Budapest's eastern suburbs and by Christmas his forces had completely surrounded city, leaving the German and Hungarian forces trapped in a cauldron. On that Christmas day, German forces mounted a massive counterattack and the battle for Budapest began.

Although a number of Budapest's civilian inhabitants had fled to western Hungary to escape the siege, the majority had remained, believing that the Soviets would take Budapest quickly. By January civilians and soldiers alike were scrounging for food, relying on melted snow, horsemeat, and meager bread rations. A breakout attempt initiated by the commander of the German forces on 11 February resulted in huge German and Hungarian losses, and by 14 February the siege was over. After Buda was captured, Red Army soldiers plundered the city and terrorized the populace. Already notorious for raping local women, Soviet forces compounded civilian fears by rounding up able-bodied Hungarian men and sending them to do labor service. The city itself was largely devastated, with thousands of buildings partially damaged or left in ruins. None of the city's five bridges over the Danube survived the siege, and nearly forty thousand Hungarian civilians—many of them Jews—had perished or been killed.

1945 TO 1956

The immediate postwar period saw the brief re-emergence of a democratically elected government,

which was edged out by the pro-Soviet communists by 1947. After the war, the reconstruction of Budapest began almost immediately. Over the next several years, the vast majority of the capital's historic buildings were restored. The communist leadership also initiated the construction of new residential buildings—better known as block apartments—around Budapest's periphery. Among the most notable structures from the Stalinist period is the Népstadion (people's stadium) sporting complex, which was constructed entirely by volunteers. Monuments to communist leaders, the Red Army, and Hungarian leftists also began to appear, and street names were changed to glorify revolutionary heroes. In 1950 the suburbs surrounding Budapest were formally incorporated into the capital, significantly increasing its size and population.

The first years of communist rule were typified by reprisals against wartime fascists and people who had collaborated with the Germans, and Stalinist-style show trials and purges of many old-guard Hungarian communists. Following Stalin's death in March 1953, the political atmosphere in the city became more relaxed. In the fall of 1956, following Poland's successful reform negotiations with Soviet leader Nikita Khrushchev, Hungarian reform communists, students, and workers were inspired to push for change in Hungary. On 23 October, a demonstration in support of reform in Poland attracted tens of thousands of students who marched from Pest to Buda. In an unplanned gesture, the students continued on to the parliament building, where they demanded the reinstatement of reform communist Imre Nagy as prime minister. A smaller group of demonstrators gathered in front of the Budapest radio station, where they were fired upon by Hungarian secret police. Shortly thereafter, a large crowd toppled an enormous statue of Stalin, dragging parts of the statue through the city. Units of the Hungarian army, which had been ordered to protect key buildings, ended up giving their weapons to the rebels.

Nagy was made prime minister on 24 October but quickly discovered that the revolt was no longer about reforming the system but about eliminating it. On 25 October the secret police again fired on the demonstrators in front of the parliament building. Two days later, Nagy formed a new reform-oriented government and announced the

Damaged buildings and debris in Baross Strasse, central Budapest, following the 1956 uprising. ©HULTON-DEUTSCH
COLLECTION/CORBIS

withdrawal of the Soviet military from Budapest, the dissolution of the secret police, and Hungary's unilateral withdrawal from the Warsaw Pact, appealing to the West to protect Hungary against Soviet military retaliation. The Soviets nevertheless invaded Budapest, and by 4 November their forces had crushed the "counterrevolution." Budapest was again heavily damaged by the fighting and an estimated two thousand Hungarians—most of them inhabitants of Budapest—died in the conflict and another two hundred thousand fled the country. Nagy and several members of his government were executed on 16 June 1958.

1956 TO 1989

After Nagy's removal, János Kádár was installed as the new head of government, and he remained in that position for the next thirty years. Immediately following the 1956 events, the Kádár regime began arresting—or in some cases executing—those who had participated in the uprising, but Kádár later softened his stance and implemented a series of reforms that became known as "goulash communism." His reforms included the 1968 New Economic Mechanism, which allowed for limited private enterprise and partially decentralized the economy.

Hungary was becoming the most liberal country in the Soviet Bloc, and Budapest began attracting young travelers from other Warsaw Pact countries.

Rising unemployment, high inflation, and mounting national debt resulted in Kádár's removal from leadership in 1988. The reburial of Imre Nagy in Budapest in June 1989 set the tone for the transition to a noncommunist government. The funeral attracted nearly 250,000 people to Budapest's Heroes' Square. The first free elections in over forty years were held in 1990.

1989 AND BEYOND

As it entered the twenty-first century, Hungary was divided between leftist liberals, represented by the socialist coalition, and nationalist conservatives headed by former prime minister Viktor Orbán and his Young Democrats Party, who struggled for control of the government and the ability to interpret Hungary's role in the past and determine its role in the future of Europe.

Several of the city's postwar cultural figures have received international acclaim. Budapest native Imre Kertész won the Nobel Prize for Literature in 2002 for his largely autobiographical novels about the experience of Hungarian Jews during the Holocaust. The work of another Budapest author from the interwar period, Sándor Márai, has been translated into several languages.

The transition did not come without difficulties and challenges, however. The capital city has, since 1989, earned a reputation as a sex capital of Europe, employing sex workers from poorer parts of the former Eastern Bloc, mainly Ukraine. The city is also battling a sizable illegal labor market that brings poor workers from neighboring countries to the city to take construction and other temporary jobs. Further challenges have included cleaning up the environmental damage brought about by careless industrial practices under communism, combating drug abuse, and dealing with extreme right-wing and skinhead groups who harass and sometimes physically attack members of minority groups living within the city, particularly Roma (Gypsies).

Despite these challenges, the city has nevertheless become a major center of international tourism. Many of the houses and other buildings in and around the centers of Buda and Pest have been renovated or rebuilt, and many historic sites, including churches and monuments, have been restored. In the spring of 2004 central eastern Europe's first Holocaust memorial museum opened in a renovated synagogue. Commercial construction has also increased sharply since the 1990s. Massive new shopping centers now line the city's periphery and a number of multinational companies have set up branches in Budapest. On 1 May 2004 inhabitants of the capital celebrated Hungary's entry into the European Union.

See also **Bartók, Béla; Eichmann, Adolf; Horthy, Miklós; Hungary; Kádár, János; Károlyi, Mihály; Khrushchev, Nikita; Kun, Béla; Lukács, György; Nagy, Imre; Stalin, Joseph; Wallenberg, Raoul.**

BIBLIOGRAPHY

Berza, László, et al., eds. *Budapest Lexikon.* 2 vols. Budapest, 1993.

Enyedi, György, and Viktória Szirmai. *Budapest: A Central European Capital.* London, 1992.

Gerlach, Christian, and Götz Aly. *Das letzte Kapitel: Der Mord an den ungarischen Juden 1944/1945.* Stuttgart, Germany, 2002.

Gerő, András, and János Poór, eds. *Budapest: A History from Its Beginnings to 1998.* New York, 1997.

Gyáni, Gábor, and György Kövér. *Magyarország társadalomtörténete: a reformkortól a második világháborúig.* Budapest, 2003.

Lendvai, Paul. *The Hungarians: A Thousand Years of Victory in Defeat.* Princeton, N.J., 2003.

Lukacs, John. *Budapest 1900: A Historical Portrait of a City and Its Culture.* New York 1900.

Ságvári, Ágnes, ed. *Budapest: The History of a Capital.* Translated by Kornél Balás and and Károly Ravasz. Budapest, 1975.

Sugar, Peter F., Péter Hanák, and Tibor Frank, eds. *A History of Hungary.* Bloomington, Ind., 1994.

Ungváry, Krisztián. *Battle for Budapest: One Hundred Days in World War II.* New York, 2003.

Valuch, Tibor. *Magyarország társadalomtörténete: A XX. század második felében.* Budapest, 2001.

HOLLY CASE

BUKHARIN, NIKOLAI (1888–1938), Russian Bolshevik leader.

Born in Moscow into a middle-class intelligentsia family, Nikolai Ivanovich Bukharin joined the Bolshevik Party in 1906 after participating in the revolutionary events of the year before. In 1917 he was one of the leaders of the Bolshevik party organization in Moscow. Shortly after the Bolshevik takeover in October 1917, Bukharin became a spokesman of the "Left communists," who opposed Vladimir Lenin over the role of "bourgeois specialists" in industry and even more over the failure to continue the war with Germany. Bukharin soon returned to the fold and took over the editorship of the party newspaper, *Pravda*, a post he retained throughout the 1920s. Starting in 1918 Bukharin established himself as the Bolshevik Party's leading theorist. The party textbook *ABC of Communism* (coauthored in 1919 with Yevgeny Preobrazhensky) had worldwide sales and remains the best introduction to the aspirations that animated the Bolshevik Party during its first years in power.

In the early 1920s, after the civil war had run its course, the Bolsheviks introduced the New Economic Policy (NEP). NEP was based on the realization that the price mechanism was the only available way of managing economic relations with millions of scattered single-owner peasant farms. Bukharin, who provided the most elaborate theoretical justifications of NEP, did not see it as a repudiation of earlier policy but rather as an adjustment to the new challenge of managing the transition to socialism in a peasant country. Relying on Lenin's 1923 article "On Cooperation," Bukharin argued that the cooperatives could be used to transform peasant agriculture gradually by appealing to the peasant's direct material interest. In this way the market would integrate peasants into the state-run socialist sector of the economy—and thus prepare the ground for its own self-negation. In 1925 he wrote: "How will we be able to draw [the peasant] into our socialist organization?...We will provide him with material incentives as a small property-owner.... On the basis of [the resulting] economic growth, the peasant will be moved along the path of a transformation of both himself and his enterprise into a particle of our general state socialist system."

During the NEP period, Bukharin was a political ally of Joseph Stalin and provided the polemical heavy artillery against the leaders of the opposition within the Bolshevik Party, especially Leon Trotsky, Preobrazhensky, Grigory Zinoviev, and Lev Kamenev. In the late 1920s, when Stalin broke with NEP and moved toward collectivization and breakneck industrialization, Bukharin continued to defend earlier policies. Stalin quickly branded him a "right deviationist." The ensuing struggle was sharp but short and ended in Bukharin's complete political defeat.

Bukharin soon recanted and again provided theoretical justification for government policy, this time for Stalin's "revolution from above." In 1934 he became editor of the government newspaper *Izvestia*. Soon thereafter, however, he fell victim to Stalin's murderous assault on the Bolshevik elite. Bukharin was arrested in February 1937 and spent a year in prison before being condemned to death in one of the last great public show trials of the Stalin era. Bukharin's remarkable achievement during his time in prison only became known after Soviet archives were opened and it was discovered that he had written extensive philosophical notebooks as well as a novel-memoir of his childhood in

Moscow (available in English under the title *How It All Began*). Some analysts have further argued that Bukharin managed to use his courtroom confession of 1938 to deliver a veiled indictment of Stalin.

In the early years of the Gorbachev era (1985–1991), when the reforms were still portrayed as a return to Leninism, Bukharin was regarded by many reform-minded intellectuals almost as the patron saint of perestroika. In 1988 Bukharin was officially cleared of all charges and posthumously readmitted into the party. He became a powerful symbol of supporters of perestroika not only because of his reputation as a defender of NEP but also because he was widely viewed as a representative of the best aspects of the Bolshevik tradition. However, the "Bukharin boom" in Russia was relatively short-lived.

In the early twenty-first century Bukharin is remembered mainly because of his role as a spokesman for the Soviet NEP period, with all its hopes and contradictions. He himself did not view NEP as an alternative model of socialism, since he clearly meant what he said about the market negating itself. He consistently looked forward to a thoroughly organized and centralized socialist society. Nevertheless, Bukharin at his best embodied the vision of an alternative path to socialism—one that avoided the violence and catastrophes of the Stalin era.

See also **Bolshevism; Lenin, Vladimir; New Economic Policy (NEP); Soviet Union; Stalin, Joseph; Trotsky, Leon.**

BIBLIOGRAPHY

Primary Sources

Bukharin, Nikolai. *How It All Began*. Translated by George Shriver. New York, 1998.

——. *The ABC of Communism*. London, 2004.

Secondary Sources

Cohen, Stephen F. *Bukharin and the Bolshevik Revolution: A Political Biography, 1888–1938*. New York, 1971.

Lih, Lars T. "Bukharin's 'Illusion': War Communism and the Meaning of NEP." *Russian History/Histoire Russe* 27, no. 4 (winter 2000): 417–460.

LARS T. LIH

BULGARIA.

BULGARIA. Twentieth-century Bulgarian history can be divided into three main periods marked by some dominant trait, whether political or economic: the national irredenta until the end of World War II (1914–1944), the rule of Soviet-type communism (1944–1989), and the reintroduction of the free market during postcommunism (after 1989).

NATIONAL PROGRAM

Since its secession from the Ottoman Empire (autonomous principality 1878, independent kingdom 1908), Bulgaria pursued its national irredenta—the unification of all Bulgarian populated areas provided by the Treaty of San Stefano (3 March 1878, Bulgaria's national holiday until 1944, and again after 1989). The prime targets were Eastern Rumelia and Macedonia, lost in the Treaty of Berlin (July 1878). After the successful unification with Eastern Rumelia (1885), Macedonia became the centerpiece of the national program. An active member of the Balkan League, Bulgaria together with its allies drove the Ottoman Empire from its European possessions during the First Balkan War (1912–1913). The inability to divide up the territories between the allies led to the Second Balkan War (1913), in which Bulgaria was vanquished and retained only a small part of Macedonia, while losing Southern Dobrudzha to Romania. The desire to reverse this loss, which was known as the First National Catastrophe, brought Bulgaria into World War I on the side of the Central Powers, who promised significant compensations.

WORLD WAR I

In October 1915 Bulgaria entered the war by attacking Serbia and occupied Macedonia. In the north it reached the Danube delta. These military successes were accomplished by enormous exertions: Bulgaria's army mobilized 40 percent of the male population; the absence of male labor cut grain production by one-third; towns suffered from runaway inflation and shortages. News of the Bolshevik Revolution inspired the antiwar and opposition movements, marked by food riots and military unrest. When the strengthened Allied front in Northern Greece broke the Bulgarian lines at Dobro Pole (September 1918), the army dissolved and a spontaneous military uprising headed for Sofia. King Ferdinand (r. 1908–1918) released the agrarian leaders Alexander Stamboliyski (1879–1923) and Raiko Daskalov (1886–1923) from prison, hoping they might contain the rebels. The two instead joined the insurgents and a republic was proclaimed at Radomir (27 September 1918). The republic was short-lived, and the rebellion was brutally put down. At the same time an armistice was signed, and on 3 October Ferdinand abdicated in favor of his son Boris III (r. 1918–1943).

At Neuilly (27 November 1919), Bulgaria signed a humiliating peace treaty, which allotted Southern Dobrudzha to Romania, some western areas to Serbia, and Western Thrace to the Allies, who gave it to Greece in 1920. Bulgaria was burdened with huge reparations. The country was disarmed and could support only a tiny mercenary army. This has been known as the Second National Catastrophe.

AGRARIAN RULE

The radicalization of the political scene swung the electorate dramatically, and in the first postwar elections three left-wing parties—agrarians, communists, and socialists—commanded two-thirds of the vote. They were divided, and the agrarians with Stamboliyski as prime minister ruled first in coalition and, after 1920, independently. The Agrarian Union (formed 1899) introduced a series of remarkable reforms. It provided land for the numerous war refugees by putting a cap on large estates and absentee owners. It encouraged the cooperative movement and established for young men a year's mandatory labor service on public works instead of military service. Stamboliyski introduced a progressive income tax, a cheaper judicial system, and free compulsory secondary education. This was a blow to the wealthy classes. At the same time, by putting down the communist-led general strike of 1919–1920, the agrarians alienated their natural political allies. In foreign policy, Stamboliyski sought friendly relations with Yugoslavia and followed a pro-French orientation. This put him at odds with the old political leaders and the court but mostly with the Military League and the IMRO (Internal Macedonia Revolutionary Organization), who were devoted to the Macedonian

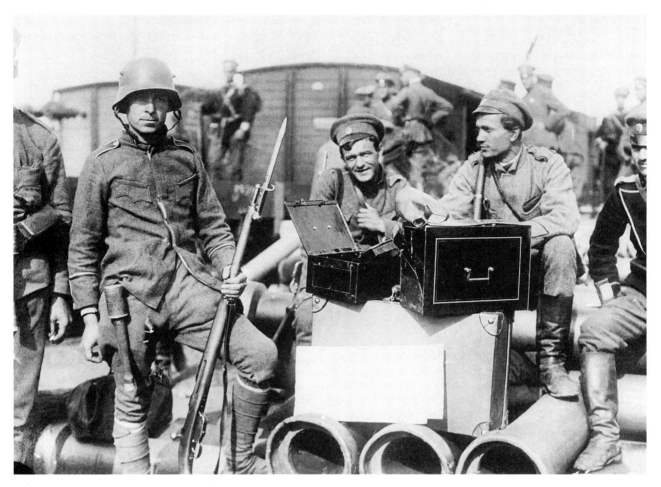

Bulgarian revolutionary soldiers with captured money following overthrow of the Stamboliyski government, July 1923. ©BETTMANN/CORBIS

irredenta. By 1923 they organized a coup d'état, and Stamboliyski was brutally murdered.

INTERWAR POLITICS AND ECONOMY

Bulgaria's recovery from the wars was slow, and after the temporary stabilization (1924–1929), it was hit by the World Economic Crisis (1929–1933), which was particularly devastating to the countryside. Until World War II the country remained a predominantly agrarian backwater, with a small industrial sector focused on food processing, tobacco, and textiles. It was in the political sphere that Bulgaria's development proved most volatile. The coup against Stamboliyski established an extreme right-wing dictatorship. The abortive September Uprising (1923), organized by the communists under Comintern pressure, was ruthlessly suppressed and the Communist Party outlawed. A

terrorist attempt against the tsar and government (1925) provoked bloody reprisals against communists, agrarians, and leftist intellectuals.

The rule of the Democratic Alliance (1926–1931) and the Popular Bloc (1931–1934) marked a moderate return to parliamentarianism. Bulgaria's political scene was extremely fragmented, with dozens of small parties and newly emerging radical right-wing movements, and punctuated by labor unrest and the terrorism of IMRO, which jeopardized the country's foreign relations. On 18–19 May 1934, the Military League and the Zveno group, headed by Damyan Velchev (1883–1954) and Kimon Georgiev (1882–1969), carried out a bloodless coup. Its members espoused a corporatist and elitist centralizing ideology, disbanding political parties for the rule of "competent" specialists. Zveno's great achievement was the suppression of IMRO, but its pro-French orientation, republican sentiments, and relatively meager social base allowed Boris III to stage a counter-coup (January 1935). The Military League was purged, and in the subsequent period the king installed subservient governments, effectively imposing an authoritarian royal regime.

WORLD WAR II

Despite Bulgaria's initial neutrality, Boris III and Bogdan Filov's (1883–1945) pro-German cabinet joined the Axis Powers (1 March 1941). Bulgaria occupied Macedonia and Western Thrace but refused to send troops to the eastern front. The unique episode marking out Bulgaria was the saving of the fifty thousand Bulgarian Jews, due to a timely reaction of MPs, the antiracist stance of the Bulgarian Orthodox church, and broad public protests. Still, some eleven thousand Jews from the occupied territories were deported and perished in concentration camps.

Incomparably smaller than the resistance in occupied Yugoslavia and Greece, Bulgaria's antifascist Resistance was still the largest among Germany's allies. With Germany's retreat and the Soviet declaration of war (5 September 1944), the Fatherland Front (a coalition of communists, left-wing agrarians, social democrats, and independent antifascists) assumed power (9 September) with the help of military forces, organized by Zveno and partisan groups.

THE COMMUNIST TAKEOVER

Although allotted to the Soviet sphere in the percentage deal between Joseph Stalin (1879–1953) and Winston Churchill (1871–1947) in October 1944, Bulgaria took until 1948 to establish an undisputed communist monopoly of power. The Communist Party controlled the most important ministries, and Georgi Dimitrov (1882–1949), exiled since 1923 and with international repute as the hero of the Leipzig trial (1933), returned from Moscow in 1945 to become prime minister. In 1946 a referendum with a 93 percent vote proclaimed Bulgaria a republic, and the nine-year-old Simeon II (b. 1936) left the country and settled in Spain. The elections for the Grand National Assembly (27 October 1946) brought 70 percent to the communist-dominated Fatherland Front.

Through pressure, intimidation, and show trials (the most notorious being the trial against the agrarian leader Nikola Petkov and his execution in September 1947), the communists succeeded in defeating the political opposition and establishing a one-party system. Despite rhetorical protests, both the United States and Great Britain extended recognition to the new regime. Other parties were either absorbed into the Communist Party or disbanded and dissolved into the Fatherland Front, which turned into a broad nonpolitical civil organization. The newly adopted "Dimitrov Constitution" (December 1947) modeled on the 1936 Stalin Constitution, provided the legal basis for the communization of the country.

BULGARIAN STALINISM

By 1948 almost 92 percent of Bulgarian industry was nationalized. This went hand in hand with a broad program of industrialization and electrification, especially creating a heavy industry (mining, metallurgy, construction, and the chemical industry). Industrialization was achieved at the expense of the countryside: 50 percent of state investments went into industry against 10 percent for agriculture. The collectivization of land was accomplished in several repressive waves, and by 1956, 80 percent of the agricultural land was organized in cooperative farms. The combined effects of the extremely rapid industrialization, alongside agricultural collectivization, resulted in a drastic change in the rural/urban ration: from 24.7 percent in 1946, the urban population almost doubled by 1965, to reach close to 70 percent by the 1980s.

The administrative pressures in the economic sphere were accompanied by political ones. By 1949 all religious orders were subject to state supervision, and purges within the Communist Party culminated in the show trial and execution of Traicho Kostov in December 1949. After the death of Dimitrov in 1949, Bulgaria's strongman was Vulko Chervenkov (1900–1980), whose rule followed closely the Soviet model in all spheres of public life, with the building of a ubiquitous repressive apparatus.

The sweeping educational reforms and the introduction of a welfare system remained the incontestable achievements of the communist regime. Compared to 10,000 in 1939, the number

Bulgarians cheer the arrival of Soviet forces in Sofia, September 1944. ©YEVGENY KHALDEI/CORBIS

of people with higher education in the labor force had increased to more than 340,000 in 1989.

THE APRIL LINE AND TODOR ZHIVKOV

Stalin's death (1953) and Nikita Khruschchev's (1894–1971) destalinization course (1956) affected Bulgaria. At the April 1956 Plenum of the BCP Chervenkov was accused of promoting the cult of personality and later removed from the country's premiership. Promoted to party leadership in 1954, Todor Zhivkov (1911–1998) became prime minister (1962–1971) and chairman of the State Council (1971–1989). He managed to purge all potential opposition, deftly maneuvered and played social strata and individuals against each other, and succeeded in staying at the helm of the state until 1989. Raising the population's living standards became the party's priority, and there was a general, though moderate, democratization of life: political prisoners were released, censorship relaxed, a general thaw in cultural life was felt,

foreign relations with neighboring and Western states were improved.

After the 1960s there was a gradual transition from extensive to intensive economic growth. Bulgaria's complete subservience to the Soviet line brought some economic advantages, albeit at the expense of the country's international standing. In the cultural sphere, there was a definite national orientation, culminating with the celebrations of the thirteen-hundredth anniversary of the Bulgarian state (1981). A number of reforms, both in agriculture and industry, aimed at introducing the market principle and achieving greater efficiency. The technological gap with the West, which affected the whole Soviet bloc in the late 1970s, hit Bulgaria in the early 1980s. The economic crisis was compounded by Zhivkov's decision to "solve" the country's Turkish problem. In late 1984 the names of the Turkish population (more than 800,000 individuals) were forcibly changed in an attempt at assimilation. By the summer of 1989, some 300,000 Turks emigrated to Turkey, although roughly half returned. At the same time, the effects of Mikhail Gorbachev's (b. 1931) perestroika were felt, and a fledgling dissident movement was beginning to take shape.

THE "CHANGES" OF 1989

One day after the fall of the Berlin wall and a week before Prague's Velvet Revolution, Zhivkov was deposed in an internal party coup (10 November 1989). The country began its gradual move from one-party rule to pluralist democracy. The rights of the ethnic Turks were restored and a roundtable negotiated the terms of the transition. Although the first free elections (June 1990) brought to power the Bulgarian Socialist Party (the reformed communists), by August 1990 Zhelyu Zhelev (b. 1935), the leader of the newly formed Union of Democratic Forces, was elected president. On 12 July 1991 the Grand National Assembly adopted a new constitution proclaiming Bulgaria a parliamentary republic and guaranteeing political pluralism and private property.

Until 2001 the political spectrum was dominated by the BSP and the UDF, with an arbitrating role for the Movement for Rights and Freedoms (representing the Turkish minority). The year 2001 added also the National Movement for Simeon II, which won the elections and formed a coalition cabinet with the MRF. The political democratization of Bulgaria seemed stable and irreversible. After the 2005 elections won by the BSP, the socialists ruled in a grand coalition with the MRF and the NMSII.

The economic balance sheet is more uneven. The privatization and restructuring on a market basis, hesitant at first, controversial in its mechanism and not yet entirely completed, has created a new wealthy class and introduced social stratification at a tremendous human price, especially at the expense of the elderly. The health and educational systems have all but collapsed. Having lost its traditional export markets, devoid of foreign investments, isolated by the Yugoslav wars, Bulgaria's industry has shrunk enormously and the runaway inflation brought IMF intervention (1997). The gradual economic recovery, Bulgaria's joining of NATO (2004), and prospective entry into the European Union (scheduled for 2007) dominate the country's political agenda.

See also **Balkans; Turkey; World War I; World War II.**

BIBLIOGRAPHY

Bell, John D. *Peasants in Power: Alexander Stamboliski and the Bulgarian Agrarian National Union 1899–1923.* Princeton, N.J., 1977.

———. *The Bulgarian Communist Party from Blagoev to Zhivkov.* Stanford, Calif., 1986.

Bell, John D., ed. *Bulgaria in Transition: Politics, Economics, Society and Culture after Communism.* Boulder, Colo., 1998.

Chary, Frederick B. *The Bulgarian Jews and the Final Solution 1940–1944.* Pittsburgh, Pa., 1972.

Crampton, R. J. *Eastern Europe in the Twentieth Century.* London and New York, 1994.

———. *A Concise History of Bulgaria.* Cambridge, U.K, and New York, 1997.

Creed, Gerald W. *Domesticating Revolution: From Socialist Reform to Ambivalent Transition in a Bulgarian Village.* University Park, Pa., 1998.

Hall, Richard C. *Bulgaria's Road to the First World War.* Boulder, Colo., and New York, 1996.

Kalinova, Evgeniia, and Baeva, Iskra. *Bulgarskite prekhodi 1939–2002.* Sofia, Bulgaria, 2002.

Lampe, John R. *The Bulgarian Economy in the 20th Century.* London, 1986.

Miller, Marshall Lee. *Bulgaria during the Second World War.* Stanford, Calif., 1975.

Oren, Nissan. *Revolution Administered: Agrarianism and Communism in Bulgaria.* Baltimore, Md., 1973.

MARIA TODOROVA

BULGE, BATTLE OF THE. Also known as the Battle of the Ardennes or the von Rundstedt counteroffensive, the Battle of the Bulge, 16 December 1944 to 16 January 1945, allowed the Anglo-American expeditionary armies (under General Dwight D. Eisenhower) to destroy twelve elite mobile divisions of Adolf Hitler's western European army during the latter stages of World War II. The campaign began with Hitler's surprise offensive through the Ardennes region of Belgium and Luxembourg and ended with the elimination of the German salient driven into the heart of the U.S. First Army as far west as the watershed of the Meuse River—this salient resembling a "bulge."

GERMAN PLANS AND PREPARATIONS

The purpose of the German offensive was to disrupt the Allies' logistical lines of communications by taking the key transportation centers of Liege and Antwerp. The desperate offensive, Hitler's personal scheme, was supposed to divide the U.S. Twelfth Army Group (led by General Omar N. Bradley) and the British Twenty-first Army Group (under Field Marshal Bernard L. Montgomery) and throw the Allied advance to the Rhine into confusion. Hitler's ultimate goal (and fantastic hope) was to negotiate a truce with the western Allies so that the German armed forces could concentrate on the eastern front and stop the relentless, vengeful advance of the Soviet armies into central Europe.

Conceived by Hitler during the collapse of the German western armies in France in August 1944, the Ardennes counteroffensive drew its inspiration from the 1940 German offensive in France and the campaigns of King Frederick II of Prussia in the Seven Years' War (1756–1763). Strategic insight, operational excellence, bad weather, and tactical ferocity would overcome Allied superiority in manpower and logistics. Hitler viewed the Allied commanders as weak and their fighting men as even weaker; his senior western commanders, Field Marshals Gerd von Runstedt and Walter Model, were not so optimistic. Hitler argued that the reconstituted mechanized divisions (panzers or panzer grenadiers) would not attack alone. They would be assisted by selective air attacks upon the Allied rear areas by the reconstituted Luftwaffe and the V-1 (a cruise missile) and V-2 (a ballistic missile) vengeance weapons. Special operations groups disguised as American troops would destroy or divert Allied motor convoys with supplies and reinforcements as well as seize key bridges and crossroads for the rampaging panzers. The offensive even had a deceptive code name, *Wacht am Rhein* (watch on the Rhine).

Despite the deep reservations of his senior generals, Hitler withdrew the surviving armored units from France, sent all available replacements (including flak and ground aviation units) to these divisions, reequipped the divisions with the most advanced model tanks (the Mark V "Panther" and Mark VI "Tiger") and self-propelled assault guns (the Stug III G and Jagdpanzer 100), stockpiled ammunition and gasoline, and organized new smaller, more firepower-intensive infantry divisions (*volksgrenadiers* [people's grenadiers]) to commit more support troops and new conscripts, young and old, into the battle. This dramatic reconstitution effort escaped Allied intelligence. The Germans reduced their radio communications and avoided Allied aerial reconnaissance. By mid-December the Germans had organized three field armies (Sixth SS Panzer, Fifth Panzer, and Seventh) of twelve armored-mechanized divisions and special brigades and seventeen infantry divisions along the eastern line of the Ardennes, a forested region of low mountains, many rivers, and few transportation corridors. The three German armies employed 330,000 men and eight hundred tanks and assault guns in the campaign.

THE COURSE OF THE BATTLE

In the first week of the Battle of the Bulge, the three German armies held the operational initiative and drove their armored spearheads through the surprised U.S. VIII Corps (three divisions and a mechanized cavalry group) and advanced 72 kilometers (45 miles) into Belgium on a front 112 kilometers (70 miles) wide. The Germans, however, did not meet their time–distance schedule and lost their short-lived advantage for many reasons, all linked to the stubborn resistance of the U.S. First Army, soon reinforced by the U.S. Third Army to the south in Luxembourg and France. Despite occasional unit disintegrations, the U.S. 99th, 106th, and 28th Infantry Divisions mounted a phased resistance that held the shoulders of the salient and forced the Germans to slide directly west instead of northwest as planned. Within the salient, the U.S. Seventh Armored Division at St. Vith and the U.S. Ninth and Tenth Armored Divisions and U.S. 101st Airborne Division at Bastogne defended key road junctions that forced the Germans to use their scarce elite panzer forces to seize St. Vith and besiege Bastogne. American engineer units destroyed critical bridges, defended key road junctions, and demolished gasoline dumps the panzer divisions needed to maintain their advance. Air attacks and rear area operations proved no substitute for the Wehrmacht's limited success on the ground.

Largely through the key decisions by Eisenhower and General George S. Patton Jr.

(leading the U.S. Third Army) in the first three days of the campaign, the Allies stopped the Germans before they reached the Meuse River, well short of Liège and Antwerp. Three infantry and one armored division of the U.S. V Corps stopped the Sixth SS Panzer Army in the northern part of the salient. Augmented by the U.S. XVIII Airborne Corps (three divisions) and the British XXX Corps (four divisions), directed by Montgomery with his usual caution, the Allied forces also defeated the most advanced western forces of the Fifth Panzer Army. Bradley, distressed that Eisenhower had put about two-thirds of his army group under temporary British control, did not approve a more aggressive Third Army attack against the German Seventh Army at the salient's southern shoulder. Even with the commitment of three corps (nine divisions), Patton had difficulty relieving Bastogne and dealing with the Fifth Panzer Army, too. A plan of greater daring might have bagged all three German armies, not squeezed them back to their initial positions.

In a series of engagements throughout the "bulge," the panzer formations reached the limit of their endurance in firepower and mobility in the last week of December 1944. The infantry divisions found themselves stalled beside and behind the panzer spearheads. The Allies increased their superiority in several critical operational areas: tank numbers, massed artillery, aerial resupply, close air support, and fresh infantry. Much to Hitler's dismay, von Runstedt and other generals reported in carefully phrased messages that in strategic terms Operation *Wacht am Rhein* had failed, but the German armies could still save themselves and inflict crippling casualties on the Allies. The German fighting withdrawal was indeed stubborn, but did not justify the sacrifices of three German armies. By mid-January Hitler's bold stroke had become a forlorn hope, and the Allies had regained the strategic initiative, which they never again surrendered.

LOSSES AND SIGNIFICANCE
The German forces suffered irreparable losses in elite personnel: 30,039 soldiers (14,325 killed or captured) of 159,564 *panzertruppen* and 44,420 of 171,596 *soldaten* in infantry formations (25,966 killed or captured). Tank losses were significant, even if German industry could eventually replace them. New tanks in the hands of new soldiers could

not replace the Ardennes losses. Although the most recent (1943–1944) models of German tanks, assault guns, and tank destroyers enjoyed superior main guns, the six most-heavily engaged panzer divisions could not match the American ability to replace armored losses during the Ardennes campaign. The Germans began their offensive with 713 heavy armored vehicles, but they faced 1,382 armored vehicles (tanks and tank destroyers) in the first five American armored divisions they soon met. As the initiative shifted to the Allies in January 1945, the same five U.S. armored divisions still had 1,298 heavy mechanized vehicles in the field (excluding self-propelled artillery), but the six German panzer divisions could deploy only 332 similar vehicles, their forces cut by combat losses, air attack, breakdowns, and lack of gasoline.

The American losses were serious, 62,439 casualties in all categories and about half lost as killed or captured. The distribution of casualties, however, reveals that only three divisions (the 28th and 106th Infantry Divisions and the 101st Airborne Division) took crippling losses, almost 19,000 soldiers or 6,000-plus per division. All the other American divisions took acceptable losses, an average of 1,300 in each of nine engaged armored divisions and an average of 2,000 in eighteen other infantry divisions. Total British losses were fewer than 2,000.

The Battle of the Bulge probably hastened the end of the European war by ruining the fighting elite of the German army and Waffen-SS in Army Group West. It completed the destruction of Germany's panzer divisions begun in the Normandy campaign (June–August 1944) and on the eastern front in the Soviet victories at Kursk (1943) and in Operation Bagration (1944). Hitler failed to recognize that the Third Reich was not Prussia and that he was not Frederick the Great.

See also **World War II.**

BIBLIOGRAPHY

Cole, Hugh M. *The Ardennes: Battle of the Bulge.* Washington, D.C., 1965.

Dupuy, Trevor N., David L. Bongard, and Richard C. Anderson. *Hitler's Last Gamble: The Battle of the Bulge, December 1944–January 1945.* New York, 1994.

Eisenhower, John S. D. *The Bitter Woods.* New York, 1969.

MacDonald, Charles B. *A Time for Trumpets: The Untold Story of the Battle of the Bulge.* New York, 1985.

ALLAN R. MILLETT

BUÑUEL, LUIS (1900–1983), Spanish filmmaker.

Luis Buñuel was born at the turn of the twentieth century in Aragón, Spain, into a well-to-do middle-class family. Even as a child, he was fascinated by the fantastic, spectral quality of motion pictures; in his autobiography, he relates the delight of watching the shadows cast on a sheet hung up to catch the light of a magic lantern. At seventeen, Buñuel went to Madrid and spent the next seven years studying and living at the Residencia de Estudiantes, where he met the playwright and poet Federico García Lorca, the writer Ramón de la Serna, and the painter Salvador Dalí, among others.

Buñuel moved to Paris in 1925, which opened the world of French intellectual life and, importantly, of movies, to him: the motion picture that inspired him to become a filmmaker was *Destiny* (1921), directed by Fritz Lang. He enrolled in Jean Epstein's acting class and coaxed his way into working on Epstein's films *Mauprat* (1926) and *The Fall of the House of Usher* (1928), for which Buñuel is credited as an assistant. In 1929 Buñuel made his first film with Salvador Dalí (1904–1989). The strange and often disjointed images of *Un chien andalou* (An Andalusian dog) were inspired by Buñuel's and Dalí's dreams, and the seventeen-minute film was a succès de scandale in Paris. Although Buñuel often pointed to Sigmund Freud's theory of the unconscious as a key influence, he rejected the idea that his films were psychoanalytic per se or even rationally analyzable. Nonetheless, Buñuel's cinematic style plays constantly with motifs that resonate with psychoanalytic thought, including repetition, fantasy, dreams, repression, fetishes, and all manner of perversity. In fact, he insistently refused to be characterized as espousing any "school" of thought, referring to himself as a "fanatical antifanatic."

Buñuel's second film, *L'âge d'or* (1930; The golden age), cemented his affinity with the French surrealists and, along with *Un chien andalou*, is the film most readily associated with the surrealist movement. Although Dalí is credited as coauthor of the script, he was much less involved in the making of *L'âge d'or* than he had been with *Un chien andalou*, and we see many elements in it that would come to be known as distinctly "Buñuelian": a sense of gleeful revolution, an effort to épater les bourgeois (shake up middle-class conventions), fantastic, fragmented, dreamlike imagery, and sudden bursts of violence.

After flirting briefly with a career in Hollywood, Buñuel turned to a quasi-documentary style of film with his depiction of the life of poor rural Spaniards in *Land without Bread* (1932). Although it departs in many ways from the fragmented aesthetic of surrealism, it is still satirically tongue-in-cheek (the surrealists called this *black humor*), since the voice-over narration does not match the images, and the viewer is forced to question its authority. Sound and music are extremely important in Buñuel's films—he often pairs canonical classical music with taboo or perverse scenes. He also frequently uses contrapuntal sound, in which sound and image clash, as opposed to direct sound, which matches the action in the image exactly.

Soon after the end of the Spanish civil war, Buñuel returned to the United States, where he worked for the Museum of Modern Art. As word of his previous films reached the States, however, Buñuel found himself a persona non grata, as he was considered too radical for the sensitive U.S. political atmosphere during the 1940s. Buñuel moved on to Mexico, where he formed a partnership with the producer Óscar Dancigers and began making movies again. In 1950 he released *Los olvidados* (*The Young and the Damned*), which trains its eye unswervingly on the poor youth of Mexico City, and which won Buñuel the best director award at the Cannes Film Festival. Like most of Buñuel's films, *Los olvidados* works to break down the binary opposition between oppressor and victim. There are no victims in the pure sense for Buñuel—only people trying desperately to survive in a malevolent and absurd world.

For the rest of the 1950s, Buñuel remained in Mexico making films with Dancigers. Many appear on the surface to be conventional melodramas. Yet even these films contain characteristically

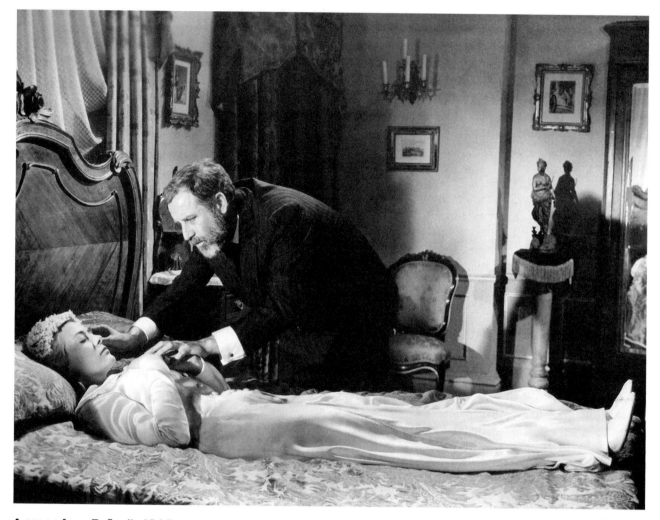

A scene from Buñuel's *Viridiana*, 1961. Eduardo (Fernando Rey) poses his niece Viridiana (Silvia Pinal) as an image of his dead wife in Buñuel's exploration of the nature of purity and sin. FILMS 59/ALATRISTE/UNINCI/THE KOBAL COLLECTION

"Buñuelian" elements: for example, in *The Criminal Life of Archibaldo de la Cruz* (1955), a hilarious send-up of film noirs, we see Buñuel's predilection for putting all the figureheads of authority together—the clergy, the military, and the police—in order to expose their absurdity and thus once again question their authority.

In 1961 Buñuel was invited to return to Spain by General Francisco Franco (1892–1975), who wanted to reinvigorate Spanish art and culture. Rebellious as always, Buñuel took the opportunity to make *Viridiana* (1961), which was subsequently banned in Spain for blasphemy, despite its worldwide success (it won the Palme d'Or at the Cannes Film Festival that year). In *Viridiana*, Buñuel is interested not only in the mysteries and hypocrisies of religion but also in the theatrical nature of

power, whether it is located in the church, the government, or the head of a family. *Viridiana* explores the nature of transgression as well: the patriarch uncle Eduardo kills himself because he believes he has offended Viridiana with his salacious thoughts. This is also the point of *Archibaldo de la Cruz*, in which the police chief finally tells Archie consolingly that the police cannot arrest a person for wishing someone dead, but only for committing the deed of murder.

After his debacle in Spain, Buñuel began a long and intensely productive collaboration with Jean-Claude Carrière (b. 1931), his screenwriter until Buñuel's death in 1983. Together they made *Diary of a Chambermaid* (1964), in which bourgeois "normality" is shown as an oppressive, stultifying force, a fragile container for the roiling perversions of humanity. *Diary* was followed in 1967 by *Belle de Jour* (his biggest commercial success, starring Catherine Deneuve), a film again concerned with the perverse fantasies hidden beneath the surface of staid bourgeois life. Buñuel's filmmaking lends itself to an auteurist approach: as different in style, genre, geography, and time period as the films are, there are virtually always "signatures" that make them recognizable as Buñuel's. He returned to the dreamlike atmosphere of his earliest films, and as such the late 1960s and early 1970s are known as his second surrealist phase. He seemed to alternate between two of his favorite subjects, religion and the bourgeoisie, in *The Milky Way* (1969), *The Discreet Charm of the Bourgeoisie* (1972), and *The Phantom of Liberty* (1974). There is something hilariously free-spirited and at the same time serious about his critique of the religious and socio-cultural edifices that structure our lives, and Buñuel's constant effort to experiment and push the boundaries of what is cinematically possible has made him one of the most influential filmmakers in the history of cinema. In his final film, *That Obscure Object of Desire* (1977), Buñuel uses two different actresses for the same role—he claimed it was a capricious decision on his part, but it brilliantly underlines the ephemeral nature of desire and how difficult it is actually to see another before us.

See also **Cinema; Spain; Surrealism.**

BIBLIOGRAPHY

Acevedo-Muñoz, Ernesto R. *Buñuel and Mexico: The Crisis of National Cinema.* Berkeley, Calif., 2003. The only English-language study to date of Buñuel's underrepresented Mexican films.

Buñuel, Luis, with Jean-Claude Carrière. *My Last Sigh.* Translated by Abigail Israel. New York, 1983. Buñuel's memoir, widely considered one of the finest and most entertaining autobiographies by a filmmaker.

Evans, Peter Williams, and Isabel Santaolalla, eds. *Luis Buñuel: New Readings.* London, 2004. A collection of essays written by contemporary film scholars from the United Kingdom, Europe, and the United States.

ANNE M. KERN

BYELORUSSIA. *See* **Belarus.**

C

CABARET. Friedrich Hollaender, one of the most prolific composers of songs in the Weimar era, noted that cabaret was "engendered in dissolute passion by theater, vaudeville, and the political tribunal." Combining high and low performance art with political engagement, cabaret reached its apogee in Germany and the Soviet Union during the 1920s, before the regimes of Adolf Hitler and Joseph Stalin put an end to its innovative, critical, and entertaining spirit.

PARIS AND ZURICH

Born in Paris in 1881, the *cabaret artistique* spread throughout Europe in the ensuing three decades. With its combination of short numbers—song, dance, monologue, skit—and its satirical tone, the genre parodied the fads and fashions of the day, as well as current events. When war broke out in 1914, this critical spirit dissipated as cabarets adopted the chauvinist and belligerent tones that engulfed all forms of popular entertainment. Those entertainers who would not bark with the dogs of war fell silent—or went to Switzerland. Zurich in particular saw a growing colony of antiwar artists and writers from all corners of Europe, and it was there that the Cabaret Voltaire opened in February 1916. Launched by Hugo Ball and Emmy Hennings, who had emigrated from Munich, its participants included Tristan Tzara and Marcel Janco from Romania, Jean (Hans) Arp from Alsace, and Richard Huelsenbeck from Berlin. They gave the name *Dada* to the radically avant-garde movement that was born on the small stage of the Cabaret Voltaire.

Dada itself was an ambiguous word: Did it mean "father"? "Yes-yes" (from the Russian word "da")? "Hobbyhorse" ("dada" in French)? Or was it derived from pure nonsense syllables? Such absurdity characterized many of the performances, which evoked the absurdity of the European continent, the self-proclaimed epitome of civilization, which was tearing itself apart in a war of unprecedented barbarity. When Janco and Huelsenbeck discordantly declaimed their "simultaneous poems" in English, French, and German, the cacophany replicated not just the jingoism of the day but the breakdown of language itself. The logical outcome was "bruitistic poetry"—a litany of meaningless sounds, first performed by Ball in the form of a "text" that began: "Gadji beri bimba." He did so in a cubist costume, consisting of various cylindrical shapes, designed by Janco.

The Cabaret Voltaire itself lasted a mere six months, but Dada proved to be one of the most innovative and influential artistic movements of the twentieth century. Huelsenbeck brought the Dada spirit to Berlin when he returned in late 1916 and it was quickly adopted by artists such as George Grosz and John Heartfield, who had independently been developing critical graphics and photomontages to express their antiwar attitude. Grosz and Heartfield contributed their designs to a political puppet play at Berlin's first major postwar cabaret, Schall und Rauch (Sound and Smoke), which opened in December 1919. Sound and Smoke's repertory consisted mainly of songs, with lyrics by Walter Mehring, an outstanding dadaist poet, and Kurt Tucholsky, the premier satirist of the Weimar era, while much of the music was composed by Friedrich Hollaender.

WEIMAR-ERA CABARET

Mehring, Tucholsky, and Hollaender were to become stalwarts of Weimar cabaret, as they offered their services to changing venues; the financial insecurity of the genre and the times ensured that cabarets rarely survived more than two years. Two of the most famous cabarets of the early Weimar years were managed by chanteuses: Rosa Valetti's Cabaret Grössenwahn (Megalomania) and Trude Hesterberg's Wilde Bühne (Wild Stage). Like Sound and Smoke, they offered a variety of numbers that sometimes took aim at the crisis-ridden politics and disastrous economic conditions of the time, but most of the pieces dealt with sexual and social foibles and commercial fads—more amusing topics, and ones less likely to alienate potential customers. Songs dealing with Berlin, sung in the local argot, were especially popular. Despite their vivacity, none of these ventures survived the hyperinflation that climaxed in 1923.

The stabilization of the German economy after 1924 allowed more spectacular genres of cabaret-style performance to flourish, which ranged from the topical cabaret-revues of Friedrich Hollaender or the team of Marcellus Schiffer and Mischa Spoliansky to the glitzy revues of Eric Charell or Hermann Haller, which featured the famous kick-line of Tiller Girls. Of the more traditional cabarets, only one—the Kabarett der Komiker (Cabaret of Comedians), directed by Kurt Robitschek—had any longevity. But despite the limited success of individual ventures, cabaret had an impact on a variety of media during the Weimar era. Its format and attitude were reflected in such collaborations of Bertolt Brecht and Kurt Weill as *The Threepenny Opera* (1928); in the theatrical productions of such leftist directors as Erwin Piscator; and in such early sound films as *The Blue Angel* (1930), where Marlene Dietrich, who had performed in the Schiffer-Spoliansky revues, made her screen debut singing chansons by Hollaender.

AGITPROP IN THE USSR

Many cabarets and revues folded after the onset of the Depression in 1929. Simultaneously, mounting political polarization led to a further development of the form on the far left, as the German Communist Party spread its ideas via agitprop (agitation-propaganda) troupes, which were inspired by developments in Russian popular performance. During the three years of civil war that engulfed Russia after the Bolshevik Revolution, numerous impromptu troupes were organized in Russia to spread communist values to workers, peasants, and soldiers. With the consolidation of Bolshevik rule, these ventures acquired more stable backing from institutions like the Komsomol (Communist Youth League), which supported TRAM (Theater of Working-Class Youth) groups, or the trade unions, which sponsored the Blue Blouses, the first of which had been formed at Moscow's Institute of Journalism in 1923. The interest of journalists was appropriate, since one of the major innovations of the agitprop troupes was the performance of "living newspapers"—skits and songs that dramatized current events. Although these numbers were purely political, the performances were leavened with elements of "red cabaret," less overtly political inserts that employed more vaudevillian styles of entertainment; agitprop troupes were well aware that too much propaganda, laid on too thickly, would bore the audience.

In the first years of communist rule, agitprop themes were explicitly economic and political, as the troupes encouraged workers and peasants to increase their output, to support socialization of the means of production, and to join the Red Army. With the stabilization of Bolshevik power, the thematic focus shifted to fostering communist mores. By the mid-1920s, agitprop skits mainly excoriated such holdovers from feudal and capitalist society as alcoholism, sexism, ethnic prejudice, and domestic violence and promoted literacy, hygiene, and sports. Like cabaret in Weimar Germany, the agitprop movement influenced other types of avant-garde theatrical performance: lively episodic elements, such as song, pantomime, dance, and even athletics, appeared in the productions of Vsevolod Meyerhold and the plays of Vladimir Mayakovsky, who occasionally wrote agitprop skits as well. The red cabarets proved to be a versatile medium for spreading communist ideas,

German actress Marlene Dietrich in the role of the cabaret performer Lola Lola in Josef von Sternberg's film *Der blaue Engel (The Blue Angel)*, 1930. Sternberg set his tale of a man's descent into decadence in the context of cabaret life. THE KOBAL COLLECTION

but like so many innovative artistic ventures they began to suffer from Stalin's political and cultural crackdown in the late 1920s and they largely ceased to exist after 1932.

GERMAN CABARET IN EXILE AND AFTER THE WAR

The following year, Hitler's rise to power likewise put an end to cabaret in Germany, as leftist and Jewish performers fled the country or were forbidden to perform. Of the innovative venues, only the Cabaret of Comedians continued to operate until the 1940s, after it divested itself of Robitschek, its director, and its other Jewish performers. Werner Finck's Katakombe (Catacombs), which had exclusively "Aryan" performers, persisted into the Third Reich, even though Finck regularly made fun of

Nazi attitudes. Although some Nazis in the audience found that amusing, Joseph Goebbels did not, and he ordered the Catacombs closed in 1935. Many performers who had fled Germany tried to form cabarets in exile. Erika Mann, the daughter of Thomas Mann, took her Pfeffermühle (Peppermill) cabaret from Munich to Zurich, but in 1935 it was shut down by Swiss authorities under pressure from the Nazi regime. Other émigré entertainers appeared in cabarets in Vienna, Prague, and Amsterdam. The fortunate ones made it as far as London, New York, and Los Angeles. Those who had remained on the European continent were swept up by the expanding Third Reich, beginning with the Anschluss of Austria in 1938. In a tragic denouement, interned Jewish entertainers were "encouraged" to stage cabaret shows in the transit camps of Westerbork and Terezin (Theresienstadt), to provide distraction for both inmates and guards. Almost all of them eventually were murdered in Auschwitz.

After 1945 cabaret lacked the importance that it had enjoyed in the first half of the century. Already in the 1920s, the cabarets of Paris, the birthplace of the genre, were little better than tourist traps; the type of singer that had highlighted turn-of-the-century cabarets had gravitated to the much larger revue stages. After the war, television brought such entertainers to a truly mass audience. Cabarets fared somewhat better in Central and Eastern Europe. In Germany and Austria during the 1950s, they were among the few places where national culpability during the Third Reich was addressed. Helmut Qualtinger's persona, Herr Karl, was an especially bitter and incisive portrayal of the Austrian who bends to every wind, especially if it blows from the far right. During the 1960s and 1970s, stages like Berlin's Reichskabarett contributed significantly to the anti-imperialist movement and the counterculture generally. But Volker Ludwig and other members of the Reichskabarett eventually recognized the limits of cabaret as a political medium; they concluded that satire was unable to change the opinions of adults and refashioned themselves as a progressive theater ensemble for children. Beginning in 1972, their GRIPS-Theater has gained renown as a highly innovative, as well as politicized, stage for children and youths.

EASTERN EUROPE

During the postwar era, the most interesting cabarets were to be found in Soviet-dominated Eastern Europe, inasmuch as they were often the only officially tolerated institutions that allowed a modicum of social and political criticism. In the German Democratic Republic, the Distel (Thistle) was relatively tame, since its location in Berlin placed it directly under the eyes of the nation's rulers. But farther afield, Leipzig's Pfeffermühle (Peppermill) was more audacious, as a result of which its directors were occasionally fired by the communist authorities. Poland likewise enjoyed a vibrant cabaret scene. Its most notable example was the Piwnica Pod Baranami (Cellar under the Rams), founded in Kraków in 1956, which was more devoted to artistic experimentation than were the

English cabaret entertainer Douglas Byng in costume, 1935. ©HULTON-DEUTSCH COLLECTION/CORBIS

cabarets of the German Democratic Republic. Its mainstay was Piotr Skryzynecki, who remained its master of ceremonies until his death in 1997, and it launched the careers of many of Poland's most popular singers, notably Ewa Demarczyk.

With the collapse of the Soviet bloc, the cabarets of Eastern Europe lost their unique critical function. Indeed, the genre resides at the margins of Europe's cultural landscape at the outset of the twenty-first century. Although a number of entertaining troupes and outstanding solo performers can still be found, it is unlikely that cabaret will again play the role that it did in the 1920s, when it was a seedbed of artistic innovation and offered a vivacious combination of critical insight and lively entertainment.

See also **Agitprop; Popular Culture; Theater.**

BIBLIOGRAPHY

Amey, Claude, et al. *Le Théâtre d'agit-prop de 1917 à 1932: Tome I: L'URSS.* Lausanne, Switzerland, 1977.

Appignanesi, Lisa. *The Cabaret.* Revised ed. New Haven, Conn., 2004.

Budzinski, Klaus. *Pfeffer ins Getriebe: So ist und wurde das Kabarett.* Munich, 1982.

Jelavich, Peter. *Berlin Cabaret.* Cambridge, Mass., 1993.

Lareau, Alan. *The Wild Stage: Literary Cabarets of the Weimar Republic.* Columbia, S.C., 1995.

Otto, Rainer, and Walter Rösler. *Kabarettgeschichte: Abris des deutschsprachigen Kabaretts.* Berlin, 1977.

PETER JELAVICH

CALLAS, MARIA (1923–1977), opera singer.

Cecilia Sophia Anna Maria Callas, or Kalogeropoulou, was born in New York on 2 or 4 December 1923 to Greek immigrant parents. The young Maria was an ungainly girl. When she was eleven, she won first place in a national amateur talent contest on the Mutual Radio Network, and her mother began entering her in a seemingly endless cycle of singing competitions. In 1937 Maria and her mother left the United States for Greece. She soon entered the Athens Conservatory (passing for sixteen in order to be admitted) and in 1940 began her studies with the celebrated coloratura soprano Elvira de Hidalgo. The following year she debuted as Tosca and quickly added Santuzza, Marta (in Eugen d'Albert's *Tiefland*), and Ludwig von Beethoven's Leonore to her repertoire.

Acclaim came in 1947 when she appeared under the conductor Tullio Serafin at the Arena in Verona as La Gioconda, and she was soon in demand for many of the heavier soprano roles: Aida, Isolde, Kundry, Turandot, Norma, and Brünnhilde. Controversy about the innate sound of her voice, as well as its occasional unpredictability, began with these early performances. But superstardom arrived in Venice in January 1949 when, to fill in for an indisposed soprano at Serafin's behest, Callas learned and sang the ornate, filigreed, bel canto role of Elvira in Vincenzo Bellini's *I puritani* in a week's time; this feat was all the more remarkable considering that she had just completed a series of performances of the *Walküre* Brünnhilde, a role

entirely at the other end of the soprano spectrum, both vocally and dramatically. Later that year she married Giovanni Battista Meneghini, a wealthy industrialist many years her senior, who acted as her devoted manager and protector, and for the next ten years she sang under the name Maria Meneghini Callas.

She soon dropped the Wagnerian roles and other so-called heavy repertoire and, while keeping Tosca, Elvira, and Norma, eventually added the soprano roles in Gaetano Donizetti's *Lucia di Lammermoor, Anna Bolena,* and *Poliuto;* Giuseppe Verdi's *Macbeth, Nabucco, I vespri Siciliani, Rigoletto, Un ballo in maschera, La traviata,* and *Il trovatore;* Gaspare Spontini's *La vestale;* Christoph Willibald Gluck's *Alceste* and *Iphigénie en Tauride;* Franz Joseph Haydn's *L'anima del filosofo;* Luigi Cherubini's *Medea;* Bellini's *La sonnambula* and *Il pirata;* Giacomo Puccini's *Madama Butterfly;* and Gioachino Rossini's *Il barbiere di Siviglia, Il turco in Italia,* and *Armida.* In 1952 she signed a contract with EMI that resulted in many complete opera recordings and recital albums. Callas insisted on being a "woman of the theater," one to whom movement and physical expression was as important as vocal inflection and loyalty to the music.

In particular, and under Serafin's tutelage, she took Italy—and eventually the world—by storm, breathing new life into the bel canto roles, operas that had been deemed dramatically vacant and relegated to the "songbirds," the high, coloratura sopranos whose main interests were vocal acrobatics and pretty, chirpy sounds. Callas combined remarkable vocal flexibility, accurate runs and scales, and thoughtful, always musically impeccable phrasing with vocal coloration and dramatic thrust the likes of which had not been heard in the twentieth century: one would have to return to Giuditta Pasta (1797–1865) and Maria Malibran (1808–1836), for whom several of the Bellini and Donizetti roles were composed, to experience such depth.

Her feuds with the heads of opera companies (the Metropolitan, La Scala, and Rome), professional jealousies, frequent cancellations, and glamorous jet-setting (in 1959 she began a well-publicized affair with the Greek shipping magnate Aristotle Onassis) became as newsworthy as her singing. The causes of her growing vocal problems—unreliable high notes, a pitch-altering

Maria Callas in the role of Medea, London, 1959.
©HULTON-DEUTSCH COLLECTION/CORBIS

"wobble" on sustained notes, uneven transitions between registers from the top to the bottom of her range, as well as her overly forceful singing, rapid weight loss, insufficient training, and physical problems—were hotly debated and remain so in the twenty-first century. She retired from opera in 1965 after five years of drastically curtailed stage appearances; performed in a nonsinging role in Pier Paolo Pasolini's film *Medea* in 1970; gave master classes at Juilliard in 1971–1972; and took on an ill-advised concert tour with the tenor Giuseppe di Stefano in 1973–1974.

Maria Callas will be remembered for the vocal and physical intensity of her performances, her dedication, her championing of the bel canto operas, and her seemingly instinctive understanding of the stylistic ethos of Italian opera. All sopranos who have attempted her great roles have performed in her shadow; Callas forever altered how people listen to opera and what is expected of an opera singer.

See also **Opera.**

BIBLIOGRAPHY

Ardoin, John, and Gerald Fitzgerald. *Callas.* New York, 1974.

Petsalis-Diomidis, Nicholas. *The Unknown Callas: The Greek Years.* Portland, Ore., 2001.

Sadie, Stanley, ed. *The New Grove Dictionary of Opera.* London, 1992.

Wisneski, Henry. *Maria Callas: The Art behind the Legend.* Garden City, N.Y., 1975.

ROBERT LEVINE

CALVINO, ITALO (1923–1985), Italian writer.

Italo Calvino was born in Santiago de Las Vegas, a suburb near L'Avana in Cuba, where his father Mario (1875–1951), an agronomist, directed an agrarian experimental station and a school of agriculture. His mother, Evelina Mameli, had a degree in natural sciences. His family moved to Sanremo in 1925.

After graduating from the University of Turin with a thesis on Joseph Conrad (1857–1924), Calvino took an active part in the Resistance. He served in the PCI (Italian Communist Party) until 1956. In the postwar period, he contributed to *Politecnico,* a magazine run by Elio Vittorini (1908–1966), with whom he then founded *Il menabò di letteratura* (1959–1967; The literary dummy), a journal of militant culture in which he published his study *Il mare dell'oggettività* (1960; The sea of objectivity). In 1964 Calvino married the Argentine Esther Judit Singer and moved to Rome, returning to Paris in 1967. He was a consultant for the Einaudi publishing house, where from 1971 he directed the series *Centopagine.* He contributed to numerous newspapers and reviews: in 1951 he wrote *I giovani del Po* [written in 1950–1951, serialized in 1957–1958; The young of the Po]), *Il caffè, Il giorno, Le monde, L'espresso, Il corriere della sera,* and *La repubblica.* He moved from Paris to Rome in 1980.

With an introduction from Cesare Pavese (1908–1950), he published his first book, *Il sentiero dei nidi di ragno* (1947; The Path to the Nest of Spiders, 1957), a lengthy account of partisan conflict in Italy. His successive collections of stories ranged from allegorical fables to documentaries—

Ultimo viene il corvo (1949), *L'entrata in Guerra* (1954), *I racconti* (1958; *Adam, One Afternoon, and Other Stories,* 1983)—to which Calvino counterposed his "difficult life" works—*La formica argentina* (1952), *La speculazione edilizia* (1957), and *La nuvola di smog* (1958), translated in one volume as *Difficult Loves; Smog; A Plunge into Real Estate,* 1983—where a recurring topic is the flaws of consumer society, a theme that reappeared in his stories for children, *Marcovaldo; ovvero, Le stagioni in città* (1963; *Marcovaldo; or, The Seasons in the City,* 1983). *Marcovaldo* is a refined attempt to tackle in a fairy-tale idiom the theme, long broached but never definitively treated, of urban alienation.

The brief neorealistic "season" in Calvino's work ended with *Ultimo viene il corvo,* where it becomes evident how Calvino's inclinations to realism and to the fantastic are complementary. *Il visconte dimezzato* (1952; *The Non-Existent Knight & The Cloven Viscount,* 1962) marked an important turning point in Calvino's oeuvre. The "realistic charge" in this novella (the genre that best suited him) is almost completely absent: the work's interest lies in the reinvention of the eighteenth-century *conte philosophique* (philosophical tale), the reinsertion into modern poetics of the artificial Enlightenment narrative, and the potential of the allegorical fable to denounce contemporary reality in a satirical-ironic mien. *Il visconte dimezzato, Il barone rampante* (1957), and *Il cavaliere inesistente* (1959) comprise the trilogy *I nostri antenati* (1960; *Our Ancestors: Three Novels,* 1980). After the novella *La giornata di uno scrutatore* (1963; *The Watcher*), Calvino chose science-fiction themes and episodes for *Le cosmicomiche* (1965; *Cosmicomics,* 1968) and *Ti con zero* (1967; *T zero,* 1969). He attempted an experimental foray into metanarrative with *Le città invisibili* (1972; *Invisible Cities,* 1974), *Il castello dei destini incrociati* (1973; *The Castle of Crossed Destinies,* 1977), and *Se una notte d'inverno un viaggiatore* (1979; *If on a Winter's Night a Traveler,* 1981).

In this phase of his literary studies, the works of the Argentine Jorge Luis Borges (1899–1986) constituted an important point of reference, though not a model. The French novelist, poet, and painter Raymond Queneau (1903–1976) and Paris, a "city-laboratory," were for Calvino a methodological foundation more than a model. In Paris he pursued a line of work all his own, which brought him to a rereading of Honoré de Balzac (1799–1850) and Voltaire (François-Marie Arouet; 1694–1778). What struck him most in Balzac was the sense he first had of the city as language, and as ideology, and his resulting capacity to "make the city become a novel." In his 1974 introduction to Voltaire's *Candide,* Calvino emphasized those themes that recurred in *Le città invisibili:* the ideal of delicacy as a poetic principle but also as a form of thought with something in common with the voice of reason. The allusion that Calvino makes to the idea of a readaptation of the *Milione* of Marco Polo (1254–1324) in the introductory chapter of *Le città* harkens back to a cinematic script about Polo's voyage, written by Calvino in 1960 but never realized on film. In the description of invented cities there is continual allusion to real cities past and present. On the subject of the structure of the novel, the reader encounters a history where the void is juxtaposed with fullness, as Calvino declared. The fullness of invisible cities is represented by the dense dialogue between the founder of the Mongol dynasty in China, Kublai Khan (1215–1294), and the Venetian traveler Marco Polo, while the void is the series of invisible cities that the ambassador Polo describes to the great Khan. These cities do not exist; they are born from Polo's imagination, from his desire to please the hearer and his taste for combining disparate elements in an attempt to construct the ideal city. The friction between the gelid beauty of invisible cities and the chaotic concreteness of the cities humans inhabit forms the theme of the novel, itself defined by three elements: lapidary, crystalline, and delicate prose; the use of the technique of ambiguity; and surrealism.

Calvino did not invent anything merely to invent, he simply concentrated on an actual impression and analyzed it in bits then re-projected on the cosmic void in which fantasy re-creates dreams. His analytical output is also noteworthy (*Una pietra sopra: Discorsi di letteratura e società,* 1980; *The Uses of Literature: Essays,* 1986; *Collezione di sabbia* [1984; Collection of sand]). Pieces written for *Il corriere della sera* are collected in *Palomar,* a volume comprising approximately thirty stories on Mt. Palomar. Posthumous publications include the three stories entitled *Sotto il sole giaguaro* (1986; *Under the Jaguar Sun,* 1988), and *Lezioni americane* (1988; *Six Memos for the Next Millennium,* 1988), which contains five of the six lectures that Calvino was supposed to have delivered at Harvard. He edited an anthology of fairytales, *Fiabe italiane* (1956; *Italian Folktales,* 1980), which he translated from their various dialects. He translated Queneau's *I fiori blu* (1967; The blue flowers, original title *Les fleurs bleues,* 1965).

See also **Italy; Resistance; Surrealism.**

BIBLIOGRAPHY

Calvino, Italo. *Romanzi e racconti.* Vol. 1: *Romanzi e racconti;* Vol. 2: *Romanzi e racconti;* Vol. 3: *Racconti sparsi ed altri scritti di invenzione.* Milan, 1994. See especially Luca Baranelli, ed., "Bibliografia degli scritti di Calvino," Vol. 3, 1351–1516; and Mario Barenghi et al., eds., "Bibliografia della critica," Vol. 3, 1517–1544.

Cannon, JoAnn. *Italo Calvino: Writer and Critic.* Ravenna, Longo, 1981.

Hume, Kathryn. *Calvino's Fictions: Cogito and Cosmos.* Oxford, U.K., 1992.

McLaughlin, Martin L. *Italo Calvino.* Edinburgh, 1998.

Re, Lucia. *Calvino and the Age of Neorealism: Fables of Estrangement.* Stanford, Calif., 1990.

MARIA TERESA GUISTI

CAMPAIGN AGAINST TORTURE.

Torture is violence deliberately inflicted upon another individual with the intention of making him suffer. Its basic psychological mechanism depends on the torturer's manipulation of the idea of the other's death; this manipulation is made possible by the fact that the torturer's power is absolute, that he controls both time and space for his victim. During the Algerian War of independence (1954–1962), torture was widely practiced by the French army in Algerian territory. It was also practiced by the police, both in France and in Algeria. It was considered by some an acceptable means in a struggle where the need for intelligence was regularly stressed, especially to combat terrorism. Others, however, disagreed; as evidence of the regular use of torture became public, a campaign against torture developed throughout France.

HOW THE CAMPAIGN BEGAN

Although French law prohibited the use of torture and characterized it as a crime, repressive institutions regularly resorted to violence of this type. It was perpetrated by agents of the state under the supervision of their direct superiors. Given the ambiguous status of torture as illegal but legitimated violence, it was logical that France officially denied its existence or at best attributed it to the exceptions and excesses of deviant soldiers or policemen. However, study of the punishments inflicted reveals beyond the shadow of a doubt that these men were acting on orders they had received, in spirit if not in letter.

Police use of torture was a recognized reality before the war began, as attested to by precedents in Indochina and Madagascar, but also in Algeria at the beginning of the 1950s. Thus, on 2 November 1954, the writer François Mauriac could write in his weekly column "Bloc-notes": "at all costs, police use of torture must be stopped" (*L'express,* 2 November 1954). News of the fate of militant Algerian nationalists during the first two months of the war reached metropolitan France, giving rise to articles in communist and progressive newspapers such as *L'humanité* and *France-Observateur,* and even the weekly magazine *L'express.*

As yet there was no actual campaign against torture, only individual acts of protest that soon faded from view. Not until the beginning of 1957 did a widespread protest movement emerge, in conjunction with the release of several statements from soldiers on the methods used in Algeria in 1956. Previously, little had been known about violence committed far from metropolitan France, in a territory where censorship was increasingly strict and where, in any case, the military was operating beyond the scrutiny of journalists or other outside observers. Only members of the military were in a position to shape public opinion about crimes committed by the army because only very rarely did the Algerians themselves have access to the media.

Conscripts were thus the source of the first widespread campaign to inform the French public about torture, in the spring of 1957. All of them waited until they had returned to France and left the army to make their experiences known. The first large-scale wave of returning troops took place at the end of 1956, and soldiers' testimonies began to appear in the press early the following year. The accounts varied in format: articles such as the one by Robert Bonnaud in *Esprit,* "La paix des Nementcha" (The peace of the Nementchas), in April 1957; brochures such as the posthumously published letters of Jean Müller, entitled "De la pacification à la répression: Le dossier Jean Müller" (From pacification to repression: The Jean Müller file), published by Les Cahiers du Témoignage Chrétien; or in serial form, as in the case of Jean-Jacques Servan-Schreiber, who in his weekly, *L'express,* published his account of his experiences as a lieutenant in the reserves called up to serve in Algeria. Another important publication came out of more confidential channels close to the Catholic organization Mission de France: the brochure *Des rappelés témoignent* (Recalled reserve officers bear witness), which was published by the Committee for Spiritual Resistance and brought together testimonies from many anonymous soldiers. Such accounts were echoed by the book *Contre la torture* (Against torture), written in protest by the philosopher Pierre-Henri Simon. In it he categorically condemned the use of torture, explicitly referring to the very recent history of the torture of members of the French Resistance by the Nazis and French collaborators.

ETHICAL AND HISTORICAL ARGUMENTS

In France at that time, this reference was by no means rhetorical. It was present in the minds of servicemen charged with "maintaining order" in Algeria and in the stories of some of those who, appalled by what they had seen in Algeria, decided to make these facts known to the public. The reference to World War II thus took on a moral value: Nazism was absolute Evil, and any French action that might be comparable to it was an ethical scandal.

For others, speaking out in public had a more directly political meaning. They wrote or published with the aim of provoking a political reaction from the authorities or influencing public opinion. In this vein, Jean-Jacques Servan-Schreiber asked the French people, By using unworthy methods, was France not simply "handing the enemy the idea of justice, that is, the victory?"

The beginning of 1957 was marked by revelations about the methods used in Algeria, based on soldiers' firsthand accounts, along with symbolic gestures on the part of internationally prominent figures, such as the resistance writer Vercors refusing to accept the Grand Cross of the Legion of Honor, or General Pâris de Bollardière asking to be relieved of his command in Algeria. Although these actions were not concerted, they produced echoes that might have given the impression of an organized campaign to influence public opinion. In fact, there was nothing of the sort. It was simply that the methods used by the French army to win the war and, in particular, to combat terrorism in Algiers since 1957 had by then become a major topic of discussion in French families and at the United Nations alike, and were therefore regularly mentioned in the press. In particular, *Le monde* and its editor, Hubert Beuve-Méry, whose high moral sense was incontestable, participated regularly in questioning the means used and the "demoralization" that might result within the army and within the nation.

It was impossible for a democratic, supposedly law-abiding government to be satisfied with this type of response. The accumulation of damning testimonies led the prime minister to appoint an investigative commission charged with establishing the truth about "the possible reality of the reported abuses." In fact, this commission to "safeguard individual rights and liberties" was charged as much with whitewashing the French army of the accusations made against it as with investigating practices unworthy of France. Initially, it was created above all as a way to gain time: as long as the commission was at work, the critics were relatively silent.

THE AUDIN AFFAIR

Meanwhile, repression and repressive methods continued. The French public was soon made aware of other cases showing that torture was still being practiced, especially in Algiers. The case of members of the clandestine Algerian Communist Party captured public attention. When a group of Christian progressives were arrested and tortured in the spring, Europeans too were affected. One of them disappeared at the hands of the paratroopers who had arrested him. News of the man's disappearance rapidly reached metropolitan France, and it was to become the symbol of the arbitrariness that reigned in Algeria. His name was Maurice Audin.

The public examination of Audin's thesis in mathematics was held in his absence in December 1957, and a committee of intellectuals was formed to discover the truth of his fate and, more generally, to disseminate information about torture. It was headed by the renowned mathematician Laurent Schwartz. Other Audin committees then formed throughout France and served as channels for information obtained by the activists. Among them, the historian Pierre Vidal-Naquet collected all the official documents that would enable him to establish how widespread the practice of torture was and, further, to demonstrate that the official theory of Maurice Audin's escape was a lie to cover up his physical elimination. This patient deconstruction of the official discourse culminated in a book published by the Éditions de Minuit in May 1958: entitled *L'affaire Audin* (The Audin affair), its presentation was modeled on the Dreyfus affair. Pierre Vidal-Naquet's perspective was French: his aim was not to participate in the Algerian struggle for independence but rather to defend France's principles and values, which were being harmed by the actions of its own troops.

THE ALLEG AFFAIR

Other actors in the campaign against torture had different motivations. For the lawyer Jacques Vergès, the issue was first and foremost to support the Algerian National Liberation Front (NLF) in its struggle for independence. Vergès had found a sympathetic listener in the publisher Jérôme Lindon, and the Éditions de Minuit, born out of the resistance to Nazism, had decided to join the campaign against torture in connection with the case of a young Algerian woman arrested in the spring of 1957. *Pour Djamila Bouhired* (On behalf of Djamila Bouhired) was the first in a series of several works denouncing French methods in both Algeria and France. The best known of these was the testimony of Henri Alleg, one of Audin's companions and editor in chief of the Algerian Communist Party organ *Alger Républicain*.

Arrested in June 1957, Alleg had been tortured by paratroopers and then imprisoned. His story was published by Jérôme Lindon under the title *La question* (The question). The fact that the book was published by a press that had no special connections to the Communist Party lent it particular credibility. The French Communist Party nonetheless mounted a public awareness campaign around Alleg's case, and it was not alone in the fight against torture.

Alleg's book immediately became an important vector of mobilization and knowledge. A few weeks after its publication it was banned, but before that it was read in public and distributed by booksellers and activist networks, and clandestine distribution continued after it was seized. The sociologist Edgar Morin was quick to liken its impact to that of war deportees' testimonies. In *France-Observateur* Morin wrote:

> this book is the book of a hero—a hero because he fought, resisted, was subjected to torture, responded, denounced it, and finally, because he wrote this book.... Deportees' accounts hit the complacent full in the face after Nazism. *The Question* is hitting us full in the face during the Algerian war. Each of us must look *The Question* in the face and answer the question it asks. (20 February 1958)

That question besmirched a French government already weakened by the bombing of a Tunisian village on the Algerian border. The book, with a preface by Jean-Paul Sartre, was very quickly translated into several languages. As the Algerian situation became an international concern, questioning of the methods used also became international in scope, and Sartre, together with three other French Nobel Prize winners (François Mauriac, André Malraux, and Roger Martin du Gard) sent a "solemn address" to the president of the republic in April 1958.

A POLITICAL SHIFT: FRESH HOPE?

The accession to power of General Charles de Gaulle led to André Malraux's joining the government. On 24 June 1958 Malraux publicly declared, in a press conference quoted in *Le figaro* the following day, "not a single act of torture has occurred, to my knowledge or yours, since General de Gaulle came to Algiers. Not a single one must occur from now on," and he invited the three other Nobel Prize winners to form an investigative commission in Algeria. This commission never actually came into being; de Gaulle decided instead to reactivate the commission to safeguard individual rights and liberties as the best way to obtain information about and follow up any complaints in this area.

In fact, public opinion at that point seemed willing to grant de Gaulle some time to sort out the tangled situation in Algeria. Testimonies denouncing the practice of torture decreased in number. The censors were also vigilant. To cite just one example, Pierre Leulliette's book *Saint Michel et le dragon* (Saint Michael and the dragon), published by the Éditions de Minuit, was seized. The author, a career paratrooper whose text began with a sentence by Antoine de Saint-Exupéry, "I do not like to see men wrecked," wrote several hundred pages of testimony about an army that had utterly failed to respect the humanity of its enemies, from the very first days of the war in the Aurès Mountains.

Still, accounts of the methods used in Algeria reached public awareness both in France and internationally. Among the activists, meanwhile, a sense that the gangrene was spreading began to outweigh hopes for improvement. Within the government, Minister of Justice Edmond Michelet had clearly reached the same conclusions, because in January 1960 a member of his cabinet arranged to leak to *Le monde* an inspection report by the International Committee of the Red Cross denouncing to French authorities the state of the detention camps for suspects and prisoners.

By this time, developments in French policy in Algeria allowed glimpses of Algerian independence. Antitorture activists began to work both on denouncing acts of violence and on fighting to ensure that such acts, present or future, would not go unpunished. They focused on taking note of official declarations and forcing the French state to adopt a coherent stance.

THE BOUPACHA AFFAIR

The legal arena was the final ground for the campaign, and the last years of the war were dominated by the face of a woman who became the symbol of this form of violence: Djamila Boupacha. This young woman had been arrested in Algiers in 1960, suspected of having planted a bomb. She was tortured and raped. The tactic of Gisèle Halimi, the lawyer for the Algerian militant, was not to focus on general arguments but rather to consistently refer to this particular and concrete case. She thus raised the question of torture as a whole but prevented the authorities from hiding behind general answers: this was a specific case, and specific answers were expected. In the same way that Audin committees had formed, Boupacha committees were organized throughout France and functioned as channels for activist publications and information about the Boupacha case.

Popularized by a portrait by Picasso and supported by Simone de Beauvoir, Boupacha's case was continually pushed into the spotlight by Halimi, who organized press conferences and used the media and public opinion to exert pressure on political and military authorities so that her client's torturers might be brought to justice. These efforts were in vain for Djamila Boupacha, but not for the issue of torture, which from then on figured regularly on the French and international scene, a veritable thorn in de Gaulle's side.

These public awareness campaigns against torture achieved very limited results overall. They cannot be credited with decreasing the practice of torture. Their existence, however, was a problem for the army, which regularly had to respond to them. In the short term, their real consequences may have been both positive and negative for the victims, protecting them from disappearing but exposing them to reprisal. However, these campaigns did help to discredit France within the international community, and they thus played a role in resolving the conflict.

In France there was generally heightened sensitivity around the issues of torture and the war as a whole, but the military resisted any change. In January 1962 three officers who acknowledged having tortured a young Algerian woman to death were acquitted by the military tribunal in Paris. Faced with this independence of military justice from the laws of the state, political authorities filed an appeal in the Court of Appeals, determined to show that the values that had dominated the war could no longer obtain in peacetime. A petition was organized in which a number of prominent figures expressed their indignation:

while we take glory in our civilization and our legal traditions ... and at a time when we are still gripped by the memory of Nazi barbarism, how can we not feel to the highest degree the shame that such a crime could be followed by an acquittal, how can we not feel distressed at the deepest level of our being?

The arguments were the same as at the beginning of the war, except that, within a few weeks of the cease-fire, the focus had shifted from the fight against torture to the struggle against absolving and forgetting it. The amnesty that came with the Evian agreement in March 1962 ending the war in Algeria clearly showed how critical this new focus was.

See also **Algeria; Algerian War.**

BIBLIOGRAPHY

Berchadsky, Alexis. *La question d'Henri Alleg: Un livre-événement dans la France en guerre d'Algérie.* Paris, 1994.

Branche, Raphaëlle. *La torture et l'armée pendant la guerre d'Algérie, 1954–1962.* Paris, 2001.

Evans, Martin. *Memory of Resistance: The French Opposition to the Algerian War.* Oxford, U.K., and New York, 1997.

Le Sueur, James D. *Uncivil War: Intellectuals and Identity Politics during the Decolonization of Algeria.* Philadelphia, 2001.

Simonin, Anne. "La littérature saisie par l'histoire: Nouveau roman et guerre d'Algérie aux Editions de Minuit." *Actes de la Recherche en Sciences Sociales* 111–112 (1996): 59–75.

Vidal-Naquet, Pierre. *La raison d'état.* Paris, 1962.

———. *Torture: Cancer of Democracy, France, and Algeria, 1954–62.* Translated by Barry Richard. Baltimore, Md., 1963.

———. *Les crimes de l'armée française.* Paris, 1975.

———. *Face à la raison d'état.* Paris, 1989.

———. *L'Affaire Audin.* Rev ed. Paris, 1989.

RAPHAËLLE BRANCHE

CAMUS, ALBERT (1913–1960), French writer, playwright, philosopher, and essayist.

Both as a writer and as an intellectual, Albert Camus is a far more complex figure than his reputation as Jean-Paul Sartre's fellow existentialist; a best-selling writer (his works have been translated into more than forty languages); or what the novelist and essayist Jean-Jacques Brochier called a "philosopher for high school seniors" would suggest.

ALGERIA

Camus was born into a very poor family in Mondovi, Algeria. His experience of poverty marked him profoundly. He once wrote that he had "not learned about freedom from reading Marx" but "from poverty." He had lost his father, an agricultural worker-turned-soldier, at the beginning of World War I, and his mother earned a living as a cleaning woman. As much as he was marked by his working-class background, Camus was also marked by his Algerian roots. He and his brother, Lucien, grew up in the working-class district of Belcourt, in Algiers, "half-way between misery and the sun," as he wrote in his first book. He was a brilliant student and was noticed by his schoolteacher, Louis Germain, to whom Camus dedicated his Nobel Prize acceptance speech, published as *Discours de Suède.*

As a "ward of the Nation," Camus received a scholarship that enabled him to continue his studies at the Algiers *lycée* (high school). There he completed the preparatory course for his college entrance examinations. His teacher and mentor was the writer and essayist Jean Grenier, who became a close friend and with whom Camus corresponded throughout his life. During his time in the *lycée*, his contact with middle-class students at the school made Camus conscious of his family's poverty; he had tuberculosis; and his uncle and teachers introduced him to both sports (especially soccer) and literature.

In 1932 he published his first articles in the journal *Sud.* During this period he also met Simone Hié, and the two became what his biographer and friend, Roger Grenier, called a "Fitzgeraldian couple." They married in 1934, but the marriage quickly became a disaster, notably during the trip to central Europe that he later recounted in his first book, *L'envers et l'endroit* (1937; *Betwixt and Between*). Camus joined the Communist Party in 1935, at the time of the antifascist Popular Front government, but he was considered excessively anticonformist and was expelled from the party in 1937. In 1936 and 1937 he came into contact with the theater and with the utopian spirit of the Théâtre du Travail (Workers' Theater) company. He performed with it as Don Juan and wrote stage adaptations for it. The troupe renamed itself the Théâtre de l'équipe (Team Theater), and he began writing the play *Caligula*, a "tragedy of the intelligence" in which "Caligula accepts death because he has understood that no one can save himself all alone and that one cannot be free at the expense of others" (p. vi).

During the same period, he wrote *Noces* (*Nuptials*), which was published in 1938. This short poetic essay is a love song for his country, a land that "contains no lessons. It neither promises nor reveals. It is content to give, but does so profusely" ("Summer in Algiers," p. 62).

This was also when Camus wrote his first novels: *La mort heureuse* (*A Happy Death*), followed by *L'étranger* (*The Stranger*), which took up themes from his first book. *La mort heureuse* was published only posthumously, in 1971. *L'étranger*, on the other hand, brought Camus success, and recognition in literary and intellectual circles. As Roger Grenier wrote, the power of the text lies in the appropriateness of the style—often described as blank or dry—to the subject, an absurd murder followed by a death sentence. Completed in May 1940, the novel was published in 1942.

FRANCE

In 1940 Camus married a second time, to Francine Faure, and they had twins, Catherine and Jean, in 1945. The year of their marriage he left Algiers, where he was working as a journalist, and moved to Paris, where he got a job at *Paris-Soir* magazine with the help of his friend Pascal Pia, whom he had met when he worked at the *Alger-Républicain*. Once he had completed *L'étranger*, he began work on "Le mythe de Sisyphe" ("The Myth of Sisyphus"), an essay that shows the development of his thinking about the absurd, which he described as being "born of [the] confrontation between the human need and the unreasonable silence of the world" (p. 20). The essay was published in 1943 and is often considered devoid of hope. In 1941 he began work on *La peste* (*The Plague*). The execution on 19 December 1941 of journalist Gabriel Péri, a communist member of the Resistance, by the Germans who had taken him

Albert Camus, January 1959. ©BETTMANN/CORBIS

hostage was an existential shock and a turning point for Camus. He became involved in the Resistance and in 1943 joined the Combat resistance network. From August 1944 to June 1947, he was editor-in-chief of the paper *Combat*, one of the main organs of the Resistance.

At the end of 1943, he met Sartre. Looking back on their meeting two years later, surprised that he was being associated with existentialism, he wrote, "When we met, it was to note our differences."

CELEBRITY

After the war, he engaged in a polemic with the writer François Mauriac over the purges of Nazi collaborators, contrasting Mauriac's "charity" toward the collaborators with the need for justice. However, he was opposed to capital punishment—he later wrote about this opposition in "Réflexions sur la guillotine" (1957; "Reflections on the Guillotine")—and, appalled by purges that affected intellectuals more than other groups of people, he signed a petition asking for clemency for the collaborationist writer Robert Brasillach.

In September 1945 *Caligula,* which gave exposure to the young actor Gérard Philippe, was a theatrical triumph, but Camus seemed dissatisfied with the reviews, both good and bad, believing that the critics had failed to grasp the crux of the play. His renown as a multitalented writer was by then solidly established and the publishing house Gallimard hired him to be the editor of a series. In 1947 he left *Combat* and finished *La peste,* which was highly successful. Perhaps fleeing the temptations of success, he left for the small city of Saint-Brieuc with Jean Grenier. There he met Louis Guilloux. Camus's play *L'état de siège* (*State of Siege*), a play protesting Franco's rule in Spain, was produced in 1948 without much success, followed by *Les justes* (*The Just Assassins*), about terrorism and resistance, in 1949.

Around the same time, the differences between Camus and Sartre culminated in a rupture that was triggered by an attack on Camus's *L'homme révolté* (1951; *The Rebel,* in which Camus denounced Soviet totalitarianism) in *Les temps modernes,* of which Sartre was the editor. The many attacks (by André Breton and others) on his book deeply wounded Camus, who commented that he would thereafter "prefer the company of theater people." He redoubled his efforts in the theater, producing a succession of plays and stage adaptations (of Pedro Calderón de la Barca, Félix Lope de Vega, Pierre de Larievy, Dino Buzatti, William Faulkner, Fyodor Dostoyevsky) and publishing articles, talks, and chronicles in the series *Actuelles* (1950, 1953, 1958) as well as *L'été* (*Summer*), a collection of lyrical essays that return to what he called the solar tradition of his earliest works. He remained active in the political arena, voicing his indignation at the repression of an Algerian demonstration in Paris that caused seven deaths (1953) and at communist repression in Berlin (1953), Hungary, and Poland (1956). His independence of mind was hailed by Eastern European dissidents and his outspokenness made him one of the leading figures of the antitotalitarian Left.

DESPAIR

In 1957 Camus was awarded the Nobel Prize in literature, and in his acceptance he thanked the academy for "having been willing to distinguish first [his] country and second a Frenchman from Algeria." If Algeria had illuminated the beginnings of Camus's life, it cast a shadow over the end of it. His sense of despair is reflected in *La chute* (*The Fall*) of 1956.

As early as 1945, he had investigated the colonial massacres in Sétif, Algeria, but beginning in 1954, at the start, with the murder of a French teacher, of the "events in Algeria," as the war for decolonization was then called, Camus grew increasingly heartbroken at what was happening in his native land. He returned to journalism (at *L'express*), no doubt hoping to influence events in some way. The hopes he placed in Prime Minister Pierre Mendès-France (1954–1955) and his policy of appeasement in the matter of decolonization quickly disappeared after the fall of the government and the inexorable escalation of violence in Algeria. He became an advocate for what he called "the path of truce," but his appeal was heard only by a minority of the most liberal colonists, French politicians, and Algerian combatants. Prime Minister Guy Mollet (1956–1957) was intent upon a course of repression, which Camus condemned, but he balanced this position with a refusal to condone the violence of the Algerian National Liberation Front, which he condemned as terrorism.

Camus did not live to see the end of Algerian war. He died in an automobile accident on 4 January 1960. The manuscript of an unfinished novel, *Le premier homme* (*The First Man*), was found in his car; it was published posthumously in 1994.

According to the writer Jacques Julliard, Camus was one of the few intellectuals of his time who was able to uphold "both the need for the fight against oppression and the need for critical rigor," and was "one of the few intellectuals of his generation whom history will prove to have been right."

See also **Algeria; Algerian War; Cold War; Existentialism; Koestler, Arthur; Sartre, Jean-Paul.**

BIBLIOGRAPHY

Primary Sources

Camus, Albert. "The Myth of Sisyphus." In *The Myth of Sisyphus and Other Essays,* translated by Justin O'Brien. New York, 1959.

———. "Author's Preface." *Caligula and Three Other Plays,* translated by Stuart Gilbert. New York, 1962.

———. *Théâtre, récits, nouvelles.* Paris, 1962.

———. *Essais.* Paris, 1965.

———. "Summer in Algiers." In *Nuptials,* collected in *Lyrical and Critical,* selected and translated by Philip Thody. London, 1967.

Secondary Sources

Grenier, Roger, ed. *Album Camus: Iconographie.* Paris, 1982.

Julliard, Jacques. "Albert Camus." In *Dictionnaire des intellectuels français: Les personnes, les lieux, les moment,* edited by Jacques Julliard and Michel Winock. Paris, 1996.

Lottman, Herbert. *Albert Camus: A Biography.* Garden City, N.Y., 1979.

Todd, Olivier. *Albert Camus: A Life.* Translated by Benjamin Ivry. New York, 1997.

NICOLAS BEAUPRÉ

CANETTI, ELIAS (1905–1994), Bulgarian-born British philosopher and writer in German.

A sizable portion of Canetti's work is autobiographical. His writing derives its energy from its status as a grammar of Europe at the crossroads—north and south, east and west, in both halves of the tragic twentieth century. He was born on 25 July 1905 in Bulgaria, the eldest of three brothers in a family of Sephardic Jews. His first languages were Bulgarian and Spanish, which he spoke especially with his mother, with whom he maintained a close and conflictual relationship that was heightened by his father's death in 1912 at the age of thirty-one. It was from his mother that he inherited his love and mastery of the German language. As a child he learned English and French while his family was staying in Manchester on business in 1911–1912. After her husband's death, Mathilde Canetti and her children moved to Vienna following a long stay in Switzerland. Always an excellent student, Elias enrolled in five schools in four different countries, following his family's migrations from Manchester to Vienna, Zurich, and finally Frankfurt. The crowds that filled the streets of Vienna in 1914 left a deep impression on him as a child, and the crowd question would later become a central theme in his work.

In 1924 he left his family in Frankfurt and enrolled in the University of Vienna, where he received his doctorate in chemistry in 1929. He frequented the Viennese intellectual circles of the day, in particular that surrounding the Austrian satirist, critic, and poet Karl Kraus (1874–1936). It was there that he met his wife, Veza Taubner-Calderon (d. 1963). In 1927 he saw the burning of the Vienna courthouse by an angry mob and the police repression that ensued. This encounter further reinforced his interest in the problem of crowds.

In 1928, during his first visit to Berlin, he met many important figures in the literary and art worlds including the Russian writer Isaac Babel (1894–1941), the American artist George Grosz (1893–1959), and the German playwright and poet Bertolt Brecht (1898–1956). Canetti published his first text, a biographical essay on the American writer and social reformer Upton Sinclair (1876–1956) for the journal *Der Querschnitt.* Following this he translated some of Sinclair's novels, which were published by Wieland Herzfelde's avant-garde press Malik Verlag. The next year he finished a draft of his sole, monumental, highly experimental and bizarre novel *Die Blendung* (The glare; completed in 1931 and published in 1935), a grotesque work about the divorce between mind and reality. At the end of the book its antihero Kien is burned alive along with his library of twenty-five thousand volumes, gripped by an enormous fit of laughter. In 1932 Canetti published the play *Hochzeit* (The marriage), a sarcastic social satire that also ends in collapse—this time of a house. That same year he met the Austrian writer Hermann Broch (1886–1951), with whom he formed a lasting bond of friendship.

After being forced into exile by the 1938 Anschluss (annexation) of Austria by Germany, Canetti moved to London and established his new residence there. In 1942 he began writing his internationally acclaimed memoirs, published in three volumes from 1971 to 1985, as a way to relax from the back-breaking work of researching his essay *Masse und Macht* (Crowds and power). This essay, published in 1960, as well as his plays *Komödie der Eitelkeit* (Comedy of vanity; written during the Nazi rise to power in 1933–1934) and

Die Befristeten (1956; Their days are numbered), are testaments to the anxiety of a thinker and intellectual confronted by the power of the masses, at once both alienated and alienating. Through a series of juxtapositions between mythological, symbolic, and ethnological material and the present day, Canetti simultaneously unveiled the blindness, power, and potential for self-alienation possessed by crowds and deplored the powerlessness and voluntary resignation of intellectuals when faced by them.

During this period he also produced travel writing, including *Stimmen von Marrakesch* (1967; The Voices of Marrakesh), published a monograph dedicated to his friend the Austrian sculptor Fritz Wotruba (1907–1975), and was able to attend the premiers of several of his plays. He received literary awards (*Prix International,* 1948; Award of the City of Vienna, 1966; etc.), before being handed the most important of them all, the Nobel Prize for Literature in 1981.

After the publication of *Masse und Macht* he collected and published a number of essays and aphorisms that in essence dealt with the theme of language in its relation to the crowd phenomenon. In the view of his biographer Sven Hanuschek, these short texts or aphoristic notes—*Die Provinz des Menschen: Aufzeichnungen, 1942–1972* (The human province)—constitute Canetti's "major work." Canetti remained active until the end of his life. He died on the night of 13 August 1994 in his sleep.

See also **Brecht, Bertolt; Vienna.**

BIBLIOGRAPHY

Falk, Thomas F. *Elias Canetti.* New York, 1993.

Hanuschek, Sven. *Elias Canetti.* Munich, 2005.

Petersen, Carol. *Elias Canetti.* Berlin, 1990.

NICOLAS BEAUPRÉ

ČAPEK, KAREL (1890–1938), Czech writer.

In 1921 Karel Čapek's scientific drama *R.U.R.* introduced the word *robot* to the world—although the word was actually coined by his brother Josef. Then, fifteen years later, on the brink of World War II, his dystopian novelistic satire *War with the Newts* (1936) presciently warned of runaway technology and militarism. Besides these two works, however, few Westerners are aware that Čapek was a prolific and versatile novelist, short story writer, dramatist, travel writer, poet, and even biographer of Czechoslovakia's first president, Tomáš Garrigue Masaryk (1850–1937).

Čapek studied philosophy at Charles University as well as attended lectures on art and aesthetics. In 1915 he defended his doctoral dissertation entitled *Objective Methods in Aesthetics.* It was a long article he composed on American Pragmatism, however, that seems to have most influenced his later writing and thinking. After a brief stint as a tutor, Čapek assumed the post on the editorial board of the daily *Národní listy* and remained a journalist for the rest of his life. Čapek began writing short fiction with his brother Josef, and their collaborative work is collected in two volumes, *Luminous Depths* (1916) and *The Garden of Krakonoš* (1918). Here we find a curious mixture of burlesque tales, anecdotes, and feuilletons, many of them parodic of symbolist and decadent literature. The overall tone is lyric, eccentric, and above all erotic. Thereafter Karel and Josef parted ways, with Josef going on to become a well-known avant-garde poet and painter, and Karel continuing in a more somber and philosophic vein. Čapek's subsequent collection of stories, *Wayside Crosses* (1917), considers epistemological and metaphysical questions and the stories usually hinge on an inexplicable mystery such as a solitary footprint. In 1921 Čapek published the short story collection *Painful Tales*. Here the mystery has disappeared and is replaced with something painful, embarrassing, or disturbing. Many critics claimed the book was nihilistic. As he was working on these stories, Čapek published his own translations of French avant-garde poetry, including poems by Guillaume Apollinaire and Charles Baudelaire. The impact on postwar avant-garde Czech poets such as Jaroslav Seifert and Vítěslav Nezval was profound.

In 1921 Čapek achieved worldwide fame with his drama *R.U.R.* (written in 1920). The play presents artificial beings used as slaves, who ultimately revolt against their masters. The play was immediately translated and performed in dozens of languages throughout the world and introduced the world not only to Čapek, but Czech literature as well. Other dystopian works followed hard upon, such as the scientific fantasy novels *Factory for the Absolute* (1922) and *Krakatit* (1924). Čapek's drama *The Makropulos Affair* (1922) considers the effect of an elixir of life and inspired Leoš Janáček's opera of the same name in 1926.

In the 1920s Čapek also published several lighter works more in line with his journalistic vocation, volumes on gardening, everyday objects, and words. Each of his trips abroad resulted in a book—*Letters from Italy* (1929), *Letters from England* (1925), *Letters from Spain* (1930), which were quite well received. Čapek also delved into the detective genre with *Tales from One Pocket* and *Tales from the Other Pocket,* both published in 1929 and then collected in *Tales from Two Pockets* (1932).

When Czechoslovakia achieved its independence following World War I, Čapek was heavily involved in its cultural and public life, and his career is intimately linked to the First Czechoslovak Republic. His "Friday-Men Club" functioned as a sort of weekly debating society, which gathered together men of all political backgrounds, including President Masaryk. Čapek's friendship with Masaryk was close, and from 1928 to 1935 he published three biographical volumes of the president. Also in the 1930s during the rise to power of Adolf Hitler (1889–1945), Čapek wrote a series of essays critical of fascism and communism and expounding the public duty of intellectuals. It was at this time that Čapek's creative work reached its zenith with his trilogy of novels *Hordubal* (1933), *Meteor* (1934), and *An Ordinary Life* (1934), investigations into epistemology and identity. As Hitler's power grew next door in Germany, Čapek's warnings against war and the nature of totalitarian power continued with his novel *War with the Newts* (1936) and the dramas *The White Plague* (1937) and *The Mother* (1938). A group of French writers repeatedly asked the Nobel committee to award the prize for literature to Čapek, but the Swedes refused for fear of offending neighboring Nazi Germany. When the committee asked Čapek to write something that would offend no one, he replied, "I've already written my doctoral dissertation." Čapek died on Christmas Day 1938, shortly after the western powers' appeasement of Hitler with the Munich agreement, which ceded the Czechoslovak border regions to Germany, and shortly before Hitler's invasion and dismemberment of the country.

See also **Orwell, George; Zamyatin, Yevgeny.**

BIBLIOGRAPHY

Primary Sources

Čapek, Karel. *Three Novels: Hordubal; Meteor; An Ordinary Life.* Translated by M. and R. Weatherall. Highland Park, N.J., 1990.

————. *War with the Newts.* Translated by Ewald Osers. Highland Park, N.J., 1990.

————. *Tales from Two Pockets.* Translated by Norma Comrada. North Haven, Conn., 1994.

————. *Talks With T. G. Masaryk.* Translated and edited by Michael Henry Heim. North Haven, Conn., 1995.

————. *Apocryphal Tales.* Translated by Norma Comrada. North Haven, Conn., 1997.

————. *Cross Roads.* Translated by Norma Comrada. North Haven, Conn., 2002.

Secondary Sources

Bradbrook, Bohuslava R. *Karel Čapek: In Pursuit of Truth, Tolerance, and Trust.* Brighton, U.K., 1998.

Harkins, William E. *Karel Čapek.* New York, 1962.

Klíma, Ivan. *Karel Čapek, Life and Work.* Translated by Norma Comrada. North Haven, Conn., 2002.

CRAIG CRAVENS

CAPITALISM. During the twentieth century, Western Europe's gross domestic product (GDP) grew at the annual average rate of 2.5 percent. Put another way, it increased more than ninefold in real terms between 1914 and 2004. Measured per capita, income levels increased nearly fivefold during the same period, at an annual rate of 1.7 percent. This general trend, however, conceals major differences between periods (table 1) and between countries, with Britain on the whole lagging behind its main competitors though starting from a higher level of income.

The rhythm of economic change is a reflection of the dynamics of European capitalism, of the interplay of economic, social, and political factors—war and peace, international cooperation and competition, monetary regimes, technological innovation, levels of industrialization, corporate structures, social relations of production, state intervention, and regulation. This entry will examine how these various factors have influenced Western Europe's economic development in the course of the twentieth century. One recurring theme will be the convergence and divergence between European economies and societies, and the extent to which various types of capitalism have coexisted in Europe. Although most countries will be referred to at some point or another, the discussion will be primarily concerned with Europe's three leading economies: Britain, France, and Germany.

EUROPE ON THE EVE OF THE FIRST WORLD WAR

When war broke out in August 1914, European capitalism had been partly reshaped by the effects of a profound economic and social transformation, usually known as the second industrial revolution. A deepening of the industrialization process and a number of technological innovations led to the emergence of new industries, which were to form Europe's industrial base for most of the twentieth century—steel, electricity, chemicals, motor cars, oil, rubber, aerospace, and synthetic fibers, as well as consumer durables in food, drink, and tobacco. These industries were characterized by a more systematic application of science to industry, greater capital requirements, and the rise of large firms.

Big business, which had hitherto been mostly confined to railway companies, thus became one of the major institutions of European capitalism in the twentieth century—without, however, ever reaching the same proportions as in the United States. Large firms came to dominate the new industries because of the economies of scale or of scope made possible by significant progress in production techniques, in particular continuous-process production (in the refining and distilling industries, as well as in the chemical and metallurgical industries) and the assembly of interchangeable parts (more characteristic of the machine industry, including electrical engineering); and because of their increasing need for backward (mostly into raw materials) and forward (semifinished products or distribution) integration.

Big business in Europe displayed both common features and national specificities, reflecting in large measure national patterns of capitalist

TABLE 1

Economic growth in Europe: Percentage increase of Gross Domestic Product per year

	GDP	GDP/head	GDP/hour worked
1890–1993	2.5	1.9	2.6
1890–1913	2.6	1.7	1.6
1913–1950	1.4	1.0	1.9
1959–1973	4.6	3.8	4.7
1973–1993	2.0	1.7	2.7

SOURCE: A. Maddison, *Monitoring the World Economy, 1820–1992*, Paris, 1995.

organization. Truly large firms (with say a workforce of five thousand people or more and market capitalization of $20 million or more) were hardly to be found outside Europe's three largest economies (Britain, France, and Germany), even though the perception of big business, in terms of political as much as economic power, existed in all countries. Similarly, family ownership and control persisted everywhere, including in Europe's largest companies, such as Krupp and Siemens in Germany, Schneider and de Wendel in France, and Vickers and Barclays Bank in Britain, to give but a few examples. State ownership was still limited, though not insignificant with, for example, the nationalization of the Prussian railway network in 1879, the British government share in the Suez Canal Company and the Anglo-Persian Oil Company and, everywhere, the public ownership of the newly established telephone companies.

Even though the frontiers of big business tended to be limited to the unit of the firm, alternative forms of organization included business groups, mostly found in France and based on crossed ownerships and interlocking directorships; and cartels were present everywhere but particularly popular in Germany, a form of horizontal concentration where firms retained their independence while agreeing on prices and quotas of production.

In the financial sector, British, French, and German commercial banks had become giant firms. Moreover, huge financial transactions were also undertaken by family partnerships in the city of London, the world's financial center in the age of the first globalization—a type of big business organization different from its traditional embodiment in a large or giant firm and more typical of the

British economy, where markets played a more important role than in Continental Europe.

Finance was indeed triumphant in Britain, even though the concept of "finance capital," coined in 1911 by the German statesman Rudolf Hilferding, has been used to describe a German phenomenon, the "merger" between banking and industrial capital under the leadership of the big banks. Europe was the world's banker in 1914, above all Britain, with some $18 billion invested abroad in 1914, representing 42 percent of the world's total, well ahead of France (20 percent), Germany (13 percent), Belgium, the Netherlands, and Switzerland (together 12 percent), and the United States (8 percent), which was also the largest importer of capital. Nevertheless, capital mainly flowed toward less developed countries, leading to heated debates between both contemporaries and generations of historians about the links between capital exports and imperialism, characterized by Vladimir Lenin (Vladimir Ilyich Ulyanov; 1870–1924) as the "highest stage of capitalism"—though such analyses have lost a great deal of their impact since the mid-1980s or so.

To what extent had different types of capitalism emerged in Europe at the eve of World War I? The issue has been widely debated, from different perspectives. The notions of "personal capitalism" (for Britain) and "managerial cooperative capitalism" (for Germany) have been applied by the economic and business historian Alfred Chandler (b. 1918) and his followers, mainly on the basis of big business organizational structures and forms of ownership—though no real differences existed in this respect between the two countries, even allowing for the prevalence of cartels in Germany. The same could be said of the concept of "organized capitalism," often applied to Germany past and present. Projecting contemporary analyses to the pre-1914 period, early forms of a "bank oriented capitalism" have been detected in Germany, and of a "market oriented capitalism" in Britain—a contrast that points to the longer-term commitment of German banks to industry, and to the greater development of the British capital market, but overestimates the effective differences between the two countries.

Similarly, any talk of "winners" and "losers" of the second industrial revolution seems misplaced.

The winners are commonly assumed to be the United States and Germany, the losers Britain and France. As far as Europe is concerned, economic growth was indeed faster in Germany than in Britain and France during the Belle Epoque, the years spanning from turn of the twentieth century to World War I. Real GDP grew at the annual average rate of 3 percent in Germany, 1.5 percent in Britain, and 1.7 percent in France, and GDP per head at respectively 1.2 percent, 0.7 percent and 1.0 percent—prompting talk of a relative economic decline in Britain, while the gap between France and Germany was narrower when measured per capita, because of France's weaker demographic growth.

These differences have often been attributed to the greater success of Germany in the new industries. The assumption might seem right when considering electrical engineering, where American and German firms established an early dominance. On the other hand, Germany had a near monopoly, with Switzerland, in dyestuffs, where the United States did not do much better than Britain and France. Things look different again when looking at motor cars, where France was the world's number one until 1904 and only second to the United States thereafter; while in oil, synthetic fibers, and consumer durables, British firms were far more competitive than their European rivals. The dynamism of German capitalism should not be questioned when accounting for the country's economic performance before World War I. However, the fact that Germany was catching up with Britain, the leading economy of the day, goes a long way to explain the difference in the growth rates between the two countries.

In the end, differences rather than divergence best describe the diversity in European capitalism on the eve of World War I. Differences between predominantly "industrial" societies—the proportion of the workforce employed in the secondary sector (50 percent in Britain, 41 percent in Germany, 34 percent in France) was higher in Western Europe in 1910 than anywhere else in the world, including the United States (30 percent). Differences between welfare states, which had emerged in all European countries—a politically motivated early start in the 1880s under the German chancellor Otto von Bismarck (1815–1898), with social insurances mainly targeted toward skilled workers; and a more universal and redistributive system in Britain (and in the Scandinavian countries) following the Liberal reforms of 1906–1911. Different strategies, besides a common paternalism, were followed by employers facing a rising and more militant unionism—early recognition of trade unions by British employers, with increasing determination to preserve the "right to manage" compared to an authoritative stance and refusal of collective bargaining by German and French employers, especially in the heavy industries.

WARS AND DEPRESSION

The period described by Eric Hobsbawm as the "age of catastrophe," marked by two world wars and the most severe depression of the twentieth century, had profound repercussions on capitalism in Europe. At the international level, the balance of power shifted with the transfer of world leadership from Britain to the United States; while in Continental Europe, Germany's rise was temporarily halted, whereas France was initially given a boost before having its momentum slowed by the Great Depression and then the rout of 1940 and the occupation.

Economic growth slowed down dramatically, with real GDP and GDP per head increasing at an average annual rate of respectively 1.4 percent and 1 percent, well below the secular trend (table 1). There were, however, differences, between periods—the 1920s were on the whole more dynamic than the 1930s—and between countries—which fared unevenly and responded more or less adequately to changing economic conditions.

World War I brought about two major developments, which were to mark in varying degrees the functioning of European capitalism for the rest of the twentieth century: one was the greater involvement of the state in economic affairs, the other was recurring monetary instability, in particular inflationary pressures.

State intervention in the economy was a logical consequence of the constraints of a total war fought during four years between highly industrialized countries, with the home front playing a decisive role in the eventual outcome. The supply of raw materials and the production of armaments, in particular, required government coordination and control. In all countries, these tasks were often entrusted to businessmen who, as experts, were called to fulfill senior administrative and sometimes ministerial functions—Walther Rathenau in Germany (in charge of the raw materials department in 1914) and Louis Loucheur in France (as minister of armaments in 1917) are two of the best-known cases.

State intervention receded after World War I, as a result of both the gradual return to normal economic conditions and the wishes of political and economic leaders. Nevertheless, in all countries, a number of measures had to be taken in the field of industrial organization, not only to face the disruptions caused by the war, but also to answer the calls for nationalizations voiced by a politically more powerful labor movement. Hardly any nationalization took place in the interwar years. But industry and public services became more regulated—in Britain, for example, the Railways Act of 1921 reorganized the country's network into four large regional companies, while the Electricity Act of 1926 established a national grid to connect all generating stations, which were overseen by a newly created Central Electricity Board.

Economic policy also became more active, in particular in monetary matters. The gold standard, which had underpinned the international monetary system since the 1880s, stopped functioning at the beginning of World War I. Restoring it, however, came up against numerous obstacles. The United States was the first to reestablish the convertibility of the dollar from 1919, but a widespread return to prewar parities seemed difficult. Inflation was rampant in all the belligerent countries as well as in the neutral countries, but the scale of price increases varied considerably from one country to another. And the differences became more pronounced in subsequent years among the countries that managed to bring inflation under control (the United States, Britain, and the former neutrals), the more inflationist victorious countries (France, Belgium) and the defeated countries ravaged by hyperinflation (Germany, Austria).

The gold standard was finally restored between 1924 and 1926 in conditions that affected economic performance during the whole decade. Britain suffered from an overvalued currency following the pound's return to gold at its prewar

TABLE 2

Level Industrial Production 1920–1929 compared to 1913 (1913 = 100)			
	1920	1924	1929
Britain	100	111	128
France	62	110	142
Germany	64	82	120
Belgium	84	114	140
Netherlands	127	136	187

SOURCE: C. H. Feinstein, P. Temin, and G. Toniolo, *The European Economies between the Wars*, Oxford, U.K., 1997.

parity in April 1925, a decision deemed necessary to restore the country's position in the world economy. France, by contrast, was helped by an undervalued currency after the de facto stabilization of the franc in December 1926—and de jure in June 1928—at only a fifth of its prewar parity after two crises (in January 1924 and July 1926) had taken it to a much lower level. The contrast is clearly visible in the two countries' level of industrial production in the 1920s (table 2). Britain was further handicapped by the structural crisis of its old export industries (coal, iron and steel, textiles, shipbuilding) coming up against competition from newly industrialized countries, while France's industrial expansion, which had been interrupted during the war (not least because of the loss of the northern and northeastern frontier areas) resumed with renewed vigor. Like France, Belgium also benefited from an ever more devalued currency; while the Netherlands, which like Switzerland and the Scandinavian countries had restored its currency at its prewar parity in 1924, took full advantage of its neutrality during the war, in particular in terms of industrial capacity and export markets. In Germany, where the Reichsmark replaced the mark at a trillionth of its prewar value, a number of constraints held down industrial growth, including the ravages of hyperinflation and the loss of territories and industrial capacity, as well as structural imbalances in the economy.

Reorganizing capitalism was envisaged and debated in the 1920s. This was the heyday of the "rationalization" movement, whose basic principle revolved around producing more efficiently, and hence generating more profits, a portion of which could be redistributed to employees in order to improve industrial relations. The notion of rationalization was fairly vague, with both a microeconomic (primarily scientific management) and a macroeconomic (improving economic conditions) meaning—though the two went hand in hand in modernizing circles, as the benefits gained by individual firms by the introduction of advanced methods of production, most often inspired by the American model, should in turn extend to the economy as a whole.

Mergers and acquisitions were seen as one of the best ways of modernizing equipment—by eliminating excessive capacity, closing down inefficient units, and increasing financial capacity to undertake new investment. A number of wide-ranging amalgamations did indeed take place in the 1920s, the most notable being the formation of IG Farben (in chemicals) in 1924, of the Vereinigte Stahlwerke (United Steel) in 1926 in Germany, and of Imperial Chemical Industries (ICI) in 1926 in Britain. However, large-scale operations and the rationalization of production could also be achieved through internal growth, as happened most spectacularly in motor cars, one of the fastest growing industries of the period and a potent symbol of modern capitalism. The French manufacturer André Citroën, for example, increased his production from 2,500 cars in 1919—the year he started applying American methods of mass production, in particular with the introduction of assembly lines—to nearly 100,000 ten years later.

The rationalization movement was not an outright success, at least in the short term. Investment in new machinery often resulted in overcapacity, while the rigidities of new organizational structures could prove to be a handicap rather than an advantage. Citroën went into liquidation in 1934, three years after deciding to entirely rebuild his Javel plant; while the Vereinigte Stahlwerke had to be saved from bankruptcy by the German government in 1932, as its integrated vertical structure lacked flexibility in a dramatically changing business environment. Moreover, at the national level, rationalization had created overcapacity in the old industries in Germany, in particular in textiles and the heavy industries.

Success was also limited in the timid attempts at altering the social relations of production. In France, trade unions were not recognized as negotiating partners until 1936. In Germany, war and, especially, demobilization amid a revolutionary climate led to significant changes: the recognition of trade unions by employers, collective bargaining, and the eight-hour day were the main outcomes of the Stinnes-Legien agreement of 15 November 1918, together with the establishment of a "working community" to implement the agreement. However, relationships between capital and labor soon became very strained, with employers eager to put an end to the labor legislation of the Weimar Republic. In Britain, a number of initiatives were taken to bring together employers and unions, culminating in the Mond-Turner talks of 1928, which however fell short of achieving long-term consultation and cooperation.

In any case, any hopes of modernization that might have been entertained in the 1920s were swept aside by the depression of the 1930s, which shook the very foundations of capitalism. Industrial production in Europe slumped by 28 percent between 1929 and 1932 (and by as much as 39 percent in Germany) and exports by 40 percent, while unemployment soared to between 15 percent (France) and 44 percent (Germany) of the working industrial population in 1932.

The crisis was at first met by deflationary policies (as no other options were available within the constraints of the gold standard if exchange parity was to be maintained), with little success and sometimes devastating effects, as in Germany under Heinrich Brüning, the Reich's chancellor from March 1930 to May 1932. Brüning's drastic measures, including budgetary cuts and tax increases, intended to lower German prices in order to boost exports, only made matters worse.

Reflationary measures were first taken in Britain after the pound left, somewhat unwillingly, the gold standard in September 1931 and was devalued by some 30 percent, thus making British exports more competitive. With a floating currency, though maintained at a competitive rate by the Bank of England through the Exchange Equalization Account, interest rates could be substantially lowered. This policy of cheap money was a the root of the economic recovery of the 1930s, stimulated by the boom in the building industry and the growth of the consumer goods industry, mainly based in London and the southeast of the country, in contrast to the countries that remained in the gold standard, the so-called "gold bloc,"

TABLE 3

Level Industrial Production 1932–1937 compared to 1929 (1929 = 100)			
	1932	1935	1937
Britain	89	113	130
France	74	72	81
Germany	61	100	127
Belgium	85	99	101
Netherlands	84	91	113

SOURCE: C. H. Feinstein, P. Temin, and G. Toniolo, *The European Economies between the Wars*, Oxford, U.K., 1997.

which included France, Belgium, the Netherlands, and Switzerland (table 3).

Recovery in Germany took place within a different economic and political context. The economic policy of the Nazi regime, in power since January 1933, was mainly based on autarky (a policy of establishing a self-sufficient and independent national economy); the growth of capital goods industries, in the first place armaments; and the state's authoritarian and direct intervention in economic affairs (45 percent of gross investment in industry between 1933 and 1938).

France's attempts at reflating its economy came much later, with the electoral victory of the Popular Front in May 1936. The new left-wing coalition did not seek to alter the structure of French capitalism (only the armament industries came into public ownership, while the state took a 51 percent stake in the newly created SNCF, the national railway company), but tried to stimulate demand by increasing purchasing power. Salaries were increased by 7 percent to 15 percent (amid of a wave of sit-down strikes), together with the introduction of paid holidays and the forty-hour week, at the Matignon Accords of June 1936, and the franc was finally devalued in September. These measures, however, failed to revive the French economy.

World War II at first boosted the economies of the belligerent countries (especially Britain, which engaged in a total war effort from an early stage and, unlike Germany and Italy, did not end up defeated and in a state of total devastation), as well as the neutral countries (in particular Sweden and Switzerland); while the occupied countries (in particular France, Belgium, and the Netherlands)

TABLE 4

Level of Gross Domestic Product (GDP) in 1945, compared to 1938 (1938 = 100)	
Britain	115
France	54
Netherlands	52
Germany	57
Italy	49
United States	172

suffered from systematic economic exploitation (table 4). By the end of World War II, the gap between Europe and America had reached an all time high: in 1950 Western Europe's per capita GDP was just over half that of the United States, whereas it had never fallen below two-thirds in previous decades. Even more than the World War I, World War II intensified state intervention in the economy. This time, the effects were to be longer lasting.

GROWTH AND REGULATION

The thirty years following World War II were the golden age of economic growth in Europe. Following postwar reconstruction, real GNP and GNP per head increased at an average annual rate of respectively 4.6 percent and 3.8 percent between 1950 and 1973, twice as fast as the secular trend. In the words of Andrew Shonfield, "capitalism converted from the cataclysmic failure which it appeared to be in the 1930s into the great engine of prosperity of the postwar Western world" (Shonfield, p. 3).

Several explanations have been given for this outstanding postwar expansion. In the first place, it took place in a far more stable and collaborative international context, despite the Cold War, with the founding of the United Nations in 1945 and the setting up of a series of multilateral organizations; the opening up of borders, especially in the field of international trade once the General Agreement on Tariffs and Trade (GATT) had come into force in 1947; and by introducing a more flexible fixed exchange rate system and international monetary cooperation with the foundation of the International Monetary Fund at the Bretton Woods Conference in July 1944.

European integration was another favorable factor, starting with the formation of the Organisation

for European Economic Cooperation (OEEC) in 1948 to organize the distribution of the American aid through the Marshall Plan; then with the setting up of the European Coal and Steel Community (ECSC) in 1952 between France, Germany, Italy, Belgium, the Netherlands, and Luxembourg; and finally, and especially, with the creation of the European Economic Community (EEC) through the signing of the Treaty of Rome by the same six countries in March 1957. Greater European openness provided a competitive business and economic environment, while the establishment of an enlarged common market offered further incentive for investment, one of the main determinants of economic growth during the period.

Yet in the final analysis, the golden age of economic growth can best be explained by the dilapidated state in which Europe found itself after the war, which gave it a huge potential for catching up with the world leader, namely the United States. Catch-up and convergence theories also help to explain the differences between European countries, in particular between Britain and Continental Europe, as countries with levels of income and productivity closer to those of the United States grew at a slower rate, leading to a far greater degree of convergence between European countries by the early 1970s (table 5).

Catching up with the United States was mainly done through technology transfers, starting with the Marshall Plan, which provided not only for the delivery of machinery, but also for the visit of "productivity missions" to the United States, in order to enable groups of business executives, civil servants, trade unionists, and others to observe on the spot American production and management techniques. More generally, European capitalism embraced during the 1950s and 1960s the type of society that had developed in the United States since the 1920s, based on mass production and mass consumption, as witnessed, for example, by the growth of the automobile industry (the United States produced eight times as many cars as Britain, France, Germany, and Italy together in 1929, but only twice as many in 1957), household appliances, and other consumer durables. European businesses also adopted American managerial practices. They grew larger, became more diversified, and, in order to face up to new challenges, increasingly turned to

TABLE 5

GDP per head and growth

	GDP per head 1950 (in 1990 dollars)	GDP per head 1973 (in 1990 dollars)	Growth per year of GDP/head 1950–1973 (percent)
Britain	6,847	11,992	2.5
Netherlands	5,880	12,763	3.4
Belgium	5,346	11,905	3.5
Germany	4,281	13,152	5.0
Italy	3,425	10,409	5.0
United States	9,573	16,607	2.4

SOURCE: A. Maddison, *Monitoring the World Economy, 1820–1992*, Paris, 1995.

the multidivisional structure (a decentralized form of organization consisting of autonomous divisions, each of them corresponding to the firm's main product lines), often on the advice of the American consulting firm McKinsey. To be sure, this "Americanization" was a complex and in many respects hybrid process, with specific forms of adaptation depending on countries and industries, but it undoubtedly played a role in Europe's postwar revival.

Changes in the structure of employment were both a cause and a reflection of economic growth and European convergence in the postwar years. The share of agriculture in total employment fell drastically, not only in Italy and France, but also in Germany; the share of industry grew closer between European countries; while the highest increase was that of the tertiary sector (table 6). Interestingly, the major gains in productivity vis-à-vis the United States, which in the last analysis are at the root of Europe's faster economic growth, appear to have been made not so much in industry, as on the one hand in services, and on the other hand through the massive transfer of labor from agriculture to industry.

European capitalism was far more state oriented during the third quarter of the twentieth century than ever before (except in wartime) or after. In 1945, unlike 1918, there was no wish to return to the prewar order: laissez-faire and deflationary policies had proved unable to solve the Depression, especially mass unemployment. Moreover, a theoretical framework for a new approach was provided by John Maynard Keynes's *General Theory of Employment, Interest, and Money*, published in 1936.

For Keynes, governments should intervene, through a contracyclical policy, in order to make up for the failure of market mechanisms, raising aggregate demand during the recession phase of the business cycle, and decreasing it during the expansion phase, using fiscal policy and monetary policy as its main instruments for intervention. Budgetary deficit, public investment, and social policy (with the development of the welfare state) were also part of a set of economic policies that came to be known as Keynesianism.

Beyond contracyclical policies, a system of "mixed-economy" was set up in European countries, combining government intervention with state ownership of a significant chunk of business activities and enterprises. A series of nationalizations took place after the war, in particular in Britain and France. The move was essentially political, with the Labour Party coming to power in 1945 in Britain, and a more general consensus toward state control in France, reinforced by the weight of the Communist Party and more generally the Resistance in French politics. In 1945 and 1946, in both countries, coal mining, electricity, gas, air transport, railway companies (already nationalized in 1936 in France), and the central bank were transferred to state ownership, in addition to the iron and steel industry in Britain, and the main commercial banks and insurance companies, as well as the car manufacturer Renault in France.

State ownership was even greater in Italy, with the formation of the Instituto per la Ricostruzione Industriale (IRI) in 1933, which controlled most of iron and steel, mechanical and electrical engineering, and shipbuilding as well as the country's three largest banks. And it should not be underestimated in Germany, where part of the manufacturing industry, besides public utilities, transport, and communication, was already in state hands, with 50 percent of the automobile industry (through Volkswagen direct ownership) and 20 percent of coal, iron and steel, shipbuilding, and chemicals (through state holding companies such as VEBA or VIAG).

A degree of economic planning was another characteristic of European capitalism in the postwar years. This was particularly the case in France, where the quadrennial economic plan, starting with the Monnet Plan in 1946, became the principal

TABLE 6

Structure of employment (figures are percentages)

	Agriculture		Industry		Services	
	1950	1973	1950	1973	1950	1973
Britain	5.1	2.9	46.5	41.8	48.4	55.3
France	28.5	11.0	34.8	38.4	36.7	50.6
Germany	22.2	7.2	43.0	46.6	34.8	46.2
Italy	45.4	17.8	28.6	38.1	26.0	44.1
Belgium	10.1	3.8	46.8	39.5	43.1	56.7
Netherlands	13.9	5.7	40.2	35.7	45.9	58.6

SOURCE: A. Maddison, *Dynamic Forces in Capitalist Development*, Oxford, U.K., 1991, p. 248–249.

tool of government intervention. Based on a wide consultation of the various economic interests, the plans established a series of indicative industrial priorities, which the government was nonetheless able to implement through a combination of budgetary measures and fiscal incentives. In Britain, attempts at emulating French economic planning in order to improve economic growth in the early 1960s remained elusive. In Germany, the heritage of organized capitalism survived in the social market economy that developed after the war, based on the long-term relationship between banks and industry and, unlike Britain and France, an independent central bank and codetermination (*Mitbestimmung*) in enterprises, in other words the representation of labor on the supervisory board of large enterprises.

Though a German institution, codetermination points to the greater integration of labor into European capitalism that occurred during the period. The social relations of production came to be organized, at the firm level through a works council, established, in most European countries, in large and medium-sized enterprises, and at the industry or national level, through collective bargaining. Industrial conflicts, however, in particular strikes, differed both quantitatively and qualitatively between countries, being less numerous but longer in northern and central Europe, and more frequent and often politically motivated, though shorter, in southern Europe (France and Italy).

Did the European economies converge during the golden age? There is no clear-cut answer to the question. There was a clear convergence in levels of income and productivity, in the structure of employment, and in the overall influence of the state in economic affairs. On the other hand, the

movement was less evident as far as socioeconomic structures are concerned. Business organization is a case in point. Corporate structures, for example, retained their national characteristics despite the widespread adoption of American management techniques with, for example, a dual board of directors (executive board and supervisory board) in Germany and a single one in Britain and France. Small and middle-sized companies played a greater role in Germany (the *Mittelstand*) and Italy (industrial districts) and are often considered to have contributed more significantly to the two countries' economic performance than large corporations. Differences were also strong in the recruitment of business executives (mostly from the corporate sector in Britain and Germany, and from the state administration in France); and more generally in business cultures and value systems (internal hierarchy, sociability, and so on) within corporations.

GLOBALIZATION AND DEREGULATION

Economic growth slowed down after 1973, returning to its secular trend (table 1), mainly as a result of the weakening of Europe's catch-up potential, whatever the role played at the same time by other factors, including the two oil crises of 1973 and 1978. At the same time the end of the fixed exchange rate system in 1973 gave a new impetus to international capital flows—the first clear signs of a globalization of the world economy, which picked up in the 1980s and especially the 1990s.

As during the period prior to 1914, it was international capital flows that formed the heart of globalization, though other phenomena, such as enhanced transport facilities, faster communications, and increased trade should not be discounted. Recent estimates put the supply of capital invested abroad at some $29,000 billion in 2000, a tenfold increase in twenty years. This upsurge in capital exports was directly linked to the progressive liberalization of the financial markets, which was part of a much broader trend: the growing influence, firstly in the Anglo-Saxon countries, and then elsewhere in the world, of a neoliberal view of the economy and of society.

In this respect, at least symbolically, the coming to power of Margaret Thatcher (b. 1925) in the United Kingdom in 1979 and Ronald Reagan (1911–2004) in the United States in 1981 marked the beginning of this new vogue. Some resistance has certainly been encountered, attitudes have shifted and policies have changed over the following decades; but the fundamental economic dispensation—the smaller state and the strengthening of market mechanisms—has not really been challenged.

Market liberalization meant first of all the free movement of capital: exchange controls and other measures aimed at curbing both capital outflows (in Britain, France, and the United States) and capital inflows (Germany, Switzerland, Japan) were mostly dismantled during the 1980s. It also meant the deregulation of the financial markets, with increased internationalization and competition, epitomized in the "Big Bang" that took place in the city of London in October 1986.

The 1980s were also the years when corporate finance, that is to say all of the activities relating to organizing and financing mergers and acquisitions, really took off. Underlying this trend was the conviction, widespread in the United States by the late 1970s, that the interests of company shareholders were not always well served by their salaried managers. From this viewpoint, a takeover bid, if necessary unfriendly and addressed directly to shareholders, seemed to be the best penalty for poor management and the threat of such an action the best way of compelling management to remain vigilant. A wave of buying and selling businesses and of mergers and demergers followed, first in the United States, then in Britain, thus giving rise to the term "Anglo-Saxon capitalism," meaning dominated by market forces.

But it was the Thatcher government's privatizations that more than anything characterized the 1980s in England. Assets in excess of 40 billion pounds (75 billion dollars) were put on the market between 1981 and 1991, more than half of which belonged to public utilities (telephone, gas, water, and electricity), ushering in a new form of popular capitalism—by the end of the process, Great Britain had more than 8.5 million individual investors, that is to say one fifth of the adult population. Privatizations were more limited in France (they brought the state some 70 billion francs [approximately 13 billion dollars] between 1986 and 1988) and affected enterprises in the competitive sector, mostly nationalized in 1982, and over which the authorities continued to exert a degree of control.

The wave of mergers became even more intense during the 1990s, with hostile takeovers and stock-market battles beginning to hit continental Europe, as exemplified by the takeover in 2000 of Mannesmann, Germany's second industrial group, by the British mobile telephone operator Vodafone after a battle that shook the very foundations of the Rhineland model of capitalism, distinguished by the dominating role of the banks and the preeminence of management over shareholders.

At the turn of the twenty-first century, European capitalism was facing a number of new challenges. Firstly, while firmly engaged in the third industrial revolution (information technologies, biotechnologies), Europe was still lagging behind the United States both in terms of innovative capacities and the development of large and competitive business enterprises. Interestingly, there were no significant differences between European countries even though, and contrary to the second industrial revolution, Britain appeared somewhat more in the vanguard than Germany. Secondly, while still one of the richest regions of the world, and in some respects the most pleasant one in which to live, Europe appeared to be struggling to combine international competitiveness and social welfare. The contradiction might have been more apparent than real and the outcome still uncertain, yet the process of globalization, competition from newly industrialized or industrializing countries, with delocalization and high unemployment in several countries as its most obvious effects, strained the welfare state in Europe. Thirdly, though

European economies had been brought closer together by further integration (and a common currency for those that adopted the euro in 1999), a European model of capitalism, combining the competitiveness of a knowledge-based economy with a socially inclusive society, seemed elusive, not only because of the effects of globalization, but also because diverging types of capitalism—Anglo-Saxon and Germanic—appeared to be at loggerheads. In 2004 uncertainty remained as to which type would, and should, prevail. The outcome is not for the historian to predict, though it is unlikely that the fate of European capitalism in the twenty-first century will lie so much in overcoming this tension as in solving new and unexpected problems with which it will undoubtedly be confronted.

See also **Automobiles; Economic Miracle; European Coal and Steel Community (ECSC); European Free Trade Association.**

BIBLIOGRAPHY

Albert, Michel. *Capitalism against Capitalism.* Translated by Paul Haviland. London, 1993.

Broadberry, Stephen. *The Productivity Race: British Manufacturing in International Perspective, 1850–1990.* Cambridge, U.K., 1997.

Cassis, Youssef. *Big Business: The European Experience in the Twentieth Century.* Oxford, U.K., 1997.

Chandler, Alfred D., Jr. *Scale and Scope: The Dynamics of Industrial Capitalism.* Cambridge, Mass., 1990.

Chandler, Alfred D., Jr., Franco Amatori, and Takashi Hikino. *Big Business and the Wealth of Nations.* Cambridge, U.K., 1997.

Crafts, Nicholas, and Gianni Toniolo, eds. *Economic Growth in Europe since 1945.* Cambridge, U.K., 1996.

Eichengreen, Barry. *Golden Fetters: The Gold Standard and the Great Depression, 1919–1939.* New York, 1996.

Feinstein, Charles H., Peter Termin, and Gianni Toniolo. *The European Economy between the Wars.* Oxford, U.K., 1997.

Hall, Peter A., and David Soskice, eds. *Varieties of Capitalism: The Institutional Foundations of Comparative Advantage.* Oxford, U.K., 2001.

Hardach, Gerd. *The First World War, 1914–1918.* Berkeley, Calif., 1977.

Kaelble, Hartmut. *A Social History of Western Europe, 1880–1980.* Dublin, 1989.

Kindleberger, Charles Poor. *The World in Depression, 1929–1939.* Berkeley, Calif., 1973.

Maddison, Angus. *Dynamic Forces in Capitalist Development: A Long-Run Comparative View.* Oxford, U.K., 1991.

———. *Monitoring the World Economy, 1820–1992.* Paris, 1995.

Milward, Alan S. *War, Economy, and Society: 1939–1945.* Berkeley, Calif., 1977.

———. *The Reconstruction of Western Europe, 1945–51.* Berkeley, Calif., 1984.

Pollard, Sidney. *Britain's Prime and Britain's Decline. The British Economy, 1870–1914.* London, 1989.

Shonfield, Andrew. *Modern Capitalism.* London and New York, 1966.

Van der Wee, Herman. *The World Economy, 1945–1980.* Harmondsworth, U.K., and New York, 1986.

Zeitlin, Jonathan, and Gary Herrigel, eds. *Americanization and Its Limits: Reworking US Technology and Management in Post-War Europe and Japan.* Oxford, U.K., 2000.

YOUSSEF CASSIS

CASEMENT, ROGER (1864–1916), British consul and Irish rebel.

Roger Casement is remembered for exposing the abuse of native people in the Congo and the Amazon, as an Ulsterman and a British consul who became an Irish revolutionary, and (by some) as a gay icon. He first came to prominence in 1903, with his report on the atrocities perpetrated on the native population in the Congo by those who were exploiting the region's valuable rubber resources. The Berlin Congress of 1884 had ceded control of the Congo territory to King Leopold of the Belgians. Casement's exposure of the systematic abuse of the native population, together with the ongoing pressure from the Congo Reform Association, founded in 1904 by Casement and E. D. Morel, ultimately led to the Belgian state taking control of the Congo in 1908. When Casement wrote his report he had spent almost twenty years in Africa, as a member of survey parties and later as British consul. In 1910, when Casement was consul in Rio de Janeiro, the British Foreign Office asked him to investigate reports of comparable brutalities carried out by rubber barons in the upper Amazon basin. Britain appointed a parliamentary select committee as a result of this report, and Casement was knighted for his work.

Casement was from a Protestant gentry background. Following the early death of both parents, he was raised in the Casement family home at Magherintemple, in the Ulster county of Antrim, an area where Irish still survived as a spoken language, as did lore about Gaelic resistance to English conquest. As a teenager he wrote poems that identified with the conquered Gaels. However, like others from modest Irish gentry families, he found his career in the colonial service, and he supported Britain in the Boer War. Casement himself claimed that it was his investigations in the Congo that led him to identify with the underdog and with Irish separatism.

During a long home leave in 1904–1906 he became involved in advanced nationalist causes, such as the Gaelic League and Sinn Féin, and he became acquainted with many leading nationalist intellectuals. He resigned from the consular service in 1913, the year that the Ulster Volunteers were formed to resist Home Rule. As an Ulsterman, Casement was committed a united sovereign Ireland. He became a leader of the pro–Home Rule Irish Volunteers, addressing recruiting meetings throughout Ireland in increasingly militant language. When the Ulster Volunteers successfully landed guns in the spring of 1914, he turned his attention to fundraising for guns for the Irish Volunteers. In July 1914 he traveled to the United States, but his plans were altered by the outbreak of World War I and Britain's decision to postpone the introduction of Irish Home Rule. Casement traveled to Germany in order to raise support for an Irish rising, but Germany showed little interest in Irish independence, and his efforts to attract recruits among Irish prisoners of war proved disastrous. When he returned to Ireland by German submarine in the hope of preventing the rising planned for Easter 1916, he was arrested, brought to London, convicted of his treason, and sentenced to death—the only leader of the rebellion who was put on trial (all the others were court-martialed). His case attracted international attention, and in order to prevent a campaign to commute the death sentence, the British authorities released copies of his private diaries, which contained graphic accounts of homosexual encounters. On the eve of his execution he was received into the Catholic Church.

The posthumous Casement remained important to nationalist Ireland, not least because, as an Ulsterman of Protestant background, he reaffirmed the image of an all-Ireland nationalist open to all traditions. Plans for his reburial in Antrim were linked with the antipartition campaign. In 1965 the British authorities eventually released his body on condition that he be reinterred in Dublin; the state funeral attracted a huge attendance. Allegations that the "black diaries" were forged by British intelligence were another running sore in Anglo-Irish relations; forensic research indicates that they are genuine, but this debate is not over. Casement is now the best known of the 1916 leaders, perhaps because these ambiguities and his international career are more in tune with contemporary Ireland than more conventional heroes.

See also **Colonialism; Easter Rising; Ireland.**

BIBLIOGRAPHY

Daly, Mary E., ed. *Roger Casement in Irish and World History.* Dublin, 2005. Includes a copy of the forensic report on the Casement diaries.

McCormack, W. J. *Roger Casement in Death, or, Haunting the Free State.* Dublin, 2002.

Mitchell, Angus. *Sir Roger Casement's Heart of Darkness: The 1911 Documents.* Dublin, 2003.

Mitchell, Angus, ed. *The Amazon Journal of Roger Casement.* London, 1997.

ó Síocháin, Seamas, and Michael O'Sullivan, eds. *The Eyes of Another Race: Roger Casement's Congo Report and 1903 Diary.* Dublin, 2003.

Reid, B. L. *The Lives of Roger Casement.* New Haven, Conn., and London, 1976.

Sawyer, Roger. *Casement: The Flawed Hero.* London, 1984.

Sawyer, Roger, ed. *Roger Casement's Diaries: 1910, the Black and the White.* London, 1997.

MARY E. DALY

CASSIN, RENÉ (1887–1976), French jurist.

René-Samuel Cassin helped establish human rights as the foundation on which the post-1945 European order was rebuilt. He was born in 1887 in the southwestern French city of Bayonne to a prominent Jewish family. He trained in law, but his professional work was interrupted by the outbreak of World War I in 1914. He joined the 311th Infantry regiment, was promoted to the rank of corporal, and served in the French sector to the east of Verdun at Saint-Mihiel. On 12 October 1914 he was severely wounded. Because of the chaotic medical system at the time, he had to be treated at his original garrison in the south of France. Somehow he managed to survive the four-hundred-mile journey by road and rail despite a stomach wound and endured surgery without an anesthetic.

While in convalescence, Cassin decided to work with and on behalf of fellow soldiers who had been wounded in active service. This led to the creation of a series of veterans organizations, which demanded better treatment and better pensions as a right, not a privilege. He also created an association for the benefit of war orphans, so that the sons of farmers or workers who had not survived the war would have the chance for a good start in life. These activities brought Cassin up against the recalcitrance and indifference of the French bureaucracy.

This struggle for natural justice created something new in European affairs—a pacifist veterans movement. French Republicans such as Cassin saw it as their life's work to ensure that their sons would not have to enter *la boucherie*—the slaughterhouse—of modern warfare.

From 1924 to 1938, Cassin represented the largest French veterans movement, the Union Fédérale, with two million members, in the French delegation to the League of Nations. At the same time, he took the initiative in establishing an international veterans organization, which met for the first time at Geneva in September 1926.

While serving in Geneva, Cassin had a front-row view of the fragility of an international political institution that challenged the supremacy of state sovereignty. He saw how entrenched were conventional approaches to unbridled state power as the *ultima ratio* of international affairs. His patriotism was beyond question, but he had no time at all for what he termed "the ordinary obstinacy of old ideas which, in the name of the absolute sovereignty of states flow directly into the construction of armaments, to the politics of prestige, and then to war" (Agi, p. 188).

In May 1940 he was the legal advisor to the Ministry of Information in the besieged French government under Prime Minister Paul Reynaud. After the fall of France, Cassin escaped to England. There he met Charles de Gaulle (1890–1970), who embraced him as his legal advisor. Cassin drew up an indictment of the new Vichy regime as illegitimate, a rogue state whose writ was legally null and void. Marshal Philippe Pétain's government was de facto, not de jure; therefore, the Republic had not died, it had been usurped by the traitors who had signed the armistice with the Nazis. This document de Gaulle presented to Winston Churchill forty-eight hours after his first meeting with his new jurist colleague. Then de Gaulle asked Cassin to sketch out the structure of a shadow Republic, an administration in exile. This body claimed the legitimate authority to speak for France and to continue the traditions of the French Revolution and the Republic betrayed by the collaborators of Vichy.

In this organization, Cassin was everywhere, and his role was dignified further by the decision of a Vichy court to convict him of treason and sentence him to death in absentia. On 29 July 1940 Cassin started broadcasting for the BBC. He was responsible for the publication of the *Journal officiel de la France libre*, the congressional record of the government in exile. In November 1940 he was named permanent secretary of the new French Council of Defense and in that capacity attended many meetings on the future shape and reconstruction of Europe. He was the architect of the Administrative Conference of Free France, the group planning for the return of the "true" Republic to the European continent. He was responsible for maintaining ties with France's colonies and dominions overseas. In 1944 he held three portfolios in the new French national committee, that of Justice, Law, and Public Instruction, all essential agencies for restoring French political culture after the nightmare of defeat, occupation, and collaboration.

Through these posts he joined inter-Allied discussions on war crimes trials and on the future of the postwar world. Here is where the subject of human rights came to the fore as the sole basis of a future durable peace. The precise form such new commitments to human rights would take was unclear, but it was evident that the newly formed

United Nations recognized the need for such an affirmation.

Three years later, at the Palais de Chaillot in Paris, Cassin provided it. In collaboration with the former First Lady Eleanor Roosevelt and others, he reformulated one of the central foundational texts of the French Revolution, the Universal Declaration of Human Rights. On 9 December 1948 he read this document to the United Nations assembled in Paris, which accepted it the following day.

The form of the commitment was limited. It was a declaration and not a convention, and thereby avoided the risk of colliding with claims to state sovereignty still strong in 1948. But over the next few decades, those claims were muted by other developments. The European Union came into being, and, to breathe life into his project, Cassin helped to institutionalize it within the new European order. From 1965 to 1968, he presided over the new European Court of Human Rights. At the end of his term, he was awarded the Nobel Peace Prize. He died in 1976 and, seven years later, his remains were removed to the Parthenon to lie in state with other heroes of the French Republic.

See also **Pétain, Philippe; Universal Declaration of Human Rights.**

BIBLIOGRAPHY

Agi, Marc. *René Cassin, prix Nobel de la Paix, 1887–1976: Père de la Déclaration universelle des droits de l'homme.* Paris, 1998.

Cassin, Gérard. *René Cassin, prix Nobel de la Paix, 1968: Rédacteur de la Déclaration universelle des droits de l'homme.* Marseilles, 1998.

Glendon, Mary Ann. *A World Made New: Eleanor Roosevelt and the Universal Declaration of Human Rights.* New York, 2001.

Israël, Gérard. *René Cassin, 1887–1976: La guerre hors la loi, avec de Gaulle, les droits de l'homme.* Paris, 1990.

Long, Marceau, and François Monnier, eds. *René Cassin 1887–1976: Une pensée ouverte sur le monde moderne: Hommage au prix Nobel de la paix 1968: Actes du colloque organisé par l'Association René-Cassin et le Collège de France, le 22 octobre 1998.* Paris, 2001.

Morsink, Johannes. *The Universal Declaration of Human Rights: Origins, Drafting, and Intent.* Philadelphia, 1999.

JAY WINTER

CATALONIA. Catalonia in the twentieth century remained one of the most economically dynamic Spanish regions and the site of a powerful nationalist movement. The economic foundations of Catalan industrialization had been laid in the previous century. Catalonia's endogenous development had been led by the production and trade of consumer goods such as textiles. This development from within facilitated a smooth transition to modernity and the emergence of a large local bourgeoisie.

However, industrial growth and the international competitiveness of Catalan industry were hampered by lack of cheap sources of energy, by the weakness of a largely underdeveloped Spanish market, and by state economic policy dominated by the interests of the Spanish land aristocracy. The Catalan bourgeoisie was weak because it had no access to the ruling political elite and because of its inability to meet the growing economic and social demands of an emerging working class. In 1901, economically shaken by Spain's loss of its imperial possessions in Cuba and the Philippines, and tired of failed attempts to influence state policy through the dominant Spanish political parties, the Catalan bourgeoisie turned to nationalism. This turn took the form of a political coalition, the Lliga Regionalista (Regionalist League), forged with conservative segments of the intelligentsia, who for decades had mobilized against political centralization and for the defense of the Catalan language.

PRE–CIVIL WAR PERIOD

In the period before the Spanish civil war (1936–1939), Catalonia increased its weight in the Spanish economy. Economic prosperity and the concomitant accumulation of wealth propitiated a blossoming of the arts, as rich members of the bourgeoisie sponsored major urban development plans and ambitious architectonic projects. Modernismo in particular—as expressed in the unfinished Sagrada Familia cathedral by Antonio Gaudi y Cornet (1852–1926)—stands as the main artistic legacy of this period. The foundations of Catalonia's economic growth remained trade and textile production, but the region also became a national leader in electricity production. In 1922, for instance, average capital assets in the water, gas, and electricity sector were almost five times greater than those in the textile sector. The opportunities offered by rapid economic growth attracted thousands of immigrants from poorer Spanish regions, at rates only matched in the 1950s and 1960s.

Economic development in Catalonia during the first third of the twentieth century was matched by increasing levels of social conflict. Catalan industrial workers were heavily influenced by anarchism, under the leadership of the National Confederation of Labor (Confederación Nacional de Trabajadores, or CNT), and by republicanism. In the aftermath of World War I, the rising cost of living caused by shortages of basic foodstuffs exacerbated social unrest. The CNT reached a peak number of affiliates and sponsored several general strikes that triggered a violent response from the state and from employers themselves. Terror reigned in Barcelona as both employers and CNT members were assassinated by hired gunmen. The final outcome of this escalation of violence was the military coup of Miguel Primo de Rivera y Orbaneja (1870–1930) in 1923.

Electoral politics in Catalonia before Primo de Rivera's dictatorship (1923–1930) were dominated by the rivalry between the dominant Lliga Regionalista and the Unión Republicana (Republican Union, later renamed as Partido Radical) led by Alejandro Lerroux García (1864–1949). The Lliga Regionalista was a conservative party whose supporters came from the industrial and commercial bourgeoisie. Its main political goals were to end political corruption and to establish a more decentralized state structure. Its main political achievement was the creation of the Mancomunitat Catalana (1914), a supraprovincial organization with the power to coordinate the administration of the four provinces of the Catalan region. Unión Republicana was the main opposition party to the Lliga Regionalista. The organizational and logistic talents of Lerroux, who perfectly integrated a revolutionary discourse, anticlericalism, and anti-Catalanism made this party extremely popular among both the Catalan and the immigrant working classes.

Eager to capitalize on the enrichment opportunities created by World War I and deeply concerned with restoring social order, the Lliga Regionalista dilapidated its well-earned political capital by agreeing to participate in statewide coalition governments and then by tolerating Primo de Rivera's dictatorial regime. Months before Primo de Rivera's coup, the Lliga lost an election, and thus its hegemony over Catalan politics, to a more progressive nationalist group, Acció Catalana (Catalonian Action). The long-term meaning of this defeat, however, was only felt in 1931, when Spain's Second Republic was proclaimed.

Although the Lliga retained some of its protagonism in the years that preceded the Spanish civil war, hegemony in the nationalist camp now belonged to the progressive party Esquerra Republicana (Republican Left of Catalonia). This political party, heir to a long tradition of Catalanist republican parties, owed its rise to prominence to the Lliga's political mistakes and to the conservative shift of Lerroux's Partido Radical. These two developments afforded Esquerra Republicana the decisive electoral support of the anarchist CNT and of the rural laborers' organization, Unió de Rabaissaires. Esquerra Republicana's main achievement was the Statute of Autonomy for Catalonia, obtained in 1932.

A detailing of the convoluted political dynamics that characterized Catalonia during the years preceding the Spanish civil war is beyond the scope of this short synopsis. Suffice it to say, however, that Esquerra Republicana's hold on power was short-lived, as it was unable to tame its anarchist electoral base and resist the pressure of socialist- and then communist-leaning political organizations. As the Spanish republican government retreated from Madrid to Valencia (November 1936) and then to Barcelona (November 1937), the power of Catalonia's autonomous institutions diminished and the central state asserted itself. In the end, when Francoist troops gained control over most of Spain, Barcelona found itself in the paradoxical situation of being the last capital of the Spanish Republic.

POST–CIVIL WAR PERIOD

The Spanish civil war had tragic consequences in Catalonia because of the combination of peripheral nationalism, revolutionary class mobilization, and radical anticlericalism, the three main sources of conflict leading to the war. Economically speaking, however, Catalonia emerged relatively unscathed from the civil war. In the following decades, its economic and demographic evolution mirrored that of the rest of Spain. There was stagnation in the 1940s, recovery in the 1950s, and rapid growth in the 1960s.

Nonetheless, both its economic and demographic growth rates were faster than those of other Spanish regions. Catalonia, together with the Basque Country and Madrid, were at the forefront of Spanish development. Development also meant change in Catalonia's economic and demographic structures. Economically, Catalonia became slightly less dependent than before on the evolution of its textile industry because of the growth of the service sector. Meanwhile, the population grew in heterogeneity as a new wave of immigration from Spain's poorer regions arrived in Catalonia. Migration rates to Catalonia, at 158 per thousand in the 1960s, well surpassed the highest levels reached in the pre–civil war years. In the early twenty-first century Catalonia, one of the wealthiest regions in the European Union (EU), was a modern postindustrial society struggling to compete in a global world and confronting the challenge posed by yet a new immigration wave, this time from less developed countries in Latin America and northern Africa. For some nationalists, this immigration wave represented a threat to the survival of Catalan language and culture.

Despite the changes listed above, Catalonia's economic structure under Francisco Franco (1892–1975) retained features that had conditioned political developments in prewar times. Foremost of all, Catalonia remained heavily dependent on the Spanish market, while its economic elites were largely excluded from the Francoist power circle. Not surprisingly, this context was conducive to the engagement of segments of the Catalan bourgeoisie in anti-Franco political activities. Catalan mobilization against the dictatorship proceeded almost without interruption since shortly after the end of the civil war.

What began as a mostly exogenous affair, as leading political exiles sought support from the Allies to topple Franco's government, turned gradually into insidious inner resistance in factories, at the university, and on the occasion of major festivities. This resistance encompassed all social

segments of Catalan society, from workers to members of the bourgeoisie, from secular to Catholic organizations. Early on, from 1947 to 1956, the leading opposition movements were the communist Partit Socialista Unificat de Catalunya (Unified Socialist Party of Catalonia, or PSUC) and the ideologically heterogeneous Catalanist Catholic organizations. In the late 1950s and the 1960s, however, Catalan opposition to Francoism broadened and intensified, as democratic political organizations took advantage of greater opportunities for mobilization. The Nova Cançó, a folk musical movement that vindicated singing in the Catalan language, was the cultural face of this opposition movement.

The social and political heterogeneity of the Catalan opposition to Franco, which contrasted with ETA's monopoly over resistance to Franco in the Basque Country, had long-term implications for the character of Catalan nationalist culture, for it prevented the rise to hegemony of a violent and anticapitalist form of nationalism in Catalonia. Nothing exemplifies better the moderate character of Catalan nationalism in the last stages of Franco's dictatorship than the main demands proclaimed in 1971 by the Catalan Assembly, a movement that virtually represented every sector in Catalan society. These demands were: (1) amnesty for political prisoners and exiles; (2) democratic freedoms; and (3) the reestablishment of the institutions and rights promulgated in the 1932 Statute of Autonomy. One of these rights was the right to speak the Catalan language.

TOWARD REGIONAL AUTONOMY

After Franco's death in November 1975, much of the earlier political consensus in Catalonia broke down. Despite political disagreements, however, based primarily on different ideological conceptions of Catalonia's role in Spain, and of the way Spanish society ought to be organized, consensus generally prevailed on the issue of a statute of autonomy for Catalonia. In the late 1970s the Catalan nationalist movement's two main demands were met: the 1978 Spanish Constitution established both Spanish and Catalan as co-official languages in Catalonia, and the 1979 Statute of Autonomy granted Catalonia a great deal of self-government.

Political hegemony in Catalonia since the restoration of democracy in the late 1970s has corresponded to Convergencia I Unió (Convergence and Unity, CiU), a centrist nationalist coalition with strong Christian-democratic influence. Its leader, Jordi Pujol (b. 1930), a representative member of the Catalan middle class, had been involved in mobilization against Franco since the mid-1950s. In power as president of the Catalan autonomous region from 1980 to 2003, Pujol fought for the implementation of the Catalan Statute of Autonomy and the extension of Catalonia's exclusive competences. He achieved a number of programmatic goals by skillfully playing on the occasional parliamentary weakness of Spain's ruling parties, be it the Spanish Socialist Workers' Party (Partido Socialista Obrero Español, or PSOE) or the Partido Popular (Popular Party). Convergencia I Unió's main rival in Catalonia was the PSOE, represented by its Catalan branch, the Partit Socialista Catalá (PSC), whom it easily defeated in regional elections but which threatened its hegemony in statewide ones. In 2003, however, the PSC, led by Pasqual Maragall (another leading member of the movement of opposition to Franco), succeeded in winning the regional elections. Lacking a large majority, however, the PSC was bound to form a coalition government with either CiU or with the two leading left-oriented political parties, Esquerra Republicana and Iniciativa per Catalunya (Initiative for Catalonia, or IC). Maragall chose the latter.

The most relevant political transformation in Catalonia has been the reemergence of Esquerra Republicana as a major political player, and with it, of a progressive nationalist tradition with aspirations to regional self-determination. Esquerra Republicana was not active in opposing the Franco regime. Led by Josep Tarradellas, Esquerra's president in exile since 1954, it led a low-profile existence. Back in Spain after Franco's death, under the auspices of Spain's first elected prime minister, Adolfo Suárez González, Tarradellas played a key role in negotiating Catalonia's Statute of Autonomy. After this short period of political prominence, Esquerra Republicana returned to relative obscurity as Pujol's CiU cashed in on its leaders' more active engagement in the movement of opposition to Franco.

In the 1990s a rejuvenated Esquerra benefited from part of the nationalist electorate's frustration with CiU's perceived connivance with the Spanish state and from part of the Left's disenchantment with Spain's ruling Socialist Party. With a program that caters to a broad range of social segments, from supporters of self-determination to supporters of the antiglobalization movement, Esquerra Republicana gradually gained in public visibility. This greater public visibility eventually generated sufficient electoral support in the 2003 regional election to turn Esquerra Republicana into a key junior coalition partner of the PSC. Only a year into the regional legislature, Esquerra's presence in Catalonia's government had already led to a radicalization of nationalist demands, a turning point in Catalonia's recent history. On 30 March 2006, the Spanish Congress approved a reformed, more ambitious statute of automony for Catalonia.

See also **Franco, Francisco; Spain; Spanish Civil War.**

BIBLIOGRAPHY

Barbagallo, Francisco, et al. *Franquisme: Sobre resistencia i consens a Catalunya (1938–1959).* Barcelona, 1990.

Benet, Josep. *Catalunya sota el regim franquista.* Barcelona, 1978.

Colomer, Josep M. *Espanyolisme i catalanisme: La idea de nació en el pensament pollític català (1939–1979).* Barcelona, 1984.

Culla i Clarà, Joan. *El republicanisme Lerrouxista a Catalunya (1901–1923).* Barcelona, 1986.

Díez Medrano, Juan. *Divided Nations: Class, Politics, and Nationalism in the Basque Country and Catalonia.* Ithaca, N.Y., 1995.

González Portilla, Manuel, Jordi Maluquer de Motes, and Borja de Riquer Permanyer, eds. *Industrialización y nacionalismo: Análisis comparativos: Actas del I Coloquio Vasco-Catalán de Historia, celebrado en Sitges, 20–22 de diciembre de 1982.* Bellaterra, Spain, 1985.

Guibernau, Montserrat. *Catalan Nationalism: Francoism, Transition, and Democracy.* New York, 2004.

Ivern i Salvà, Maria Dolors. *Esquerra Republicana de Catalunya: 1931–1936.* Barcelona, 1988–1989.

Johnston, Hank. *Tales of Nationalism: Catalonia, 1939–1979.* New Brunswick, N.J., 1991.

Lladonosa I Vall-Llebrera, Manuel. *Catalanisme i moviment obrer: El CADCI entre 1903 i 1923.* Barcelona, 1988.

Miguélez Lobo, F., and Carlota Solé. *Classes socials i poder polític en Catalunya*. Barcelona, 1987.

Nadal, J., and Albert Carreras, eds. *Pautas regionales de la industrialización española (siglos XIX y XX)*. Barcelona, 1990.

Pinilla de las Heras, E. *Estudios sobre cambio social y estructuras sociales en Cataluña*. Madrid, 1979.

JUAN DÍEZ MEDRANO

CATHOLIC ACTION.

Although it was originally used in a rather vague way, the term *Catholic Action* took on a more precise and restricted meaning during the pontificate of Pius XI (1922–1939). Its meaning would be broadened again by Pius XII (1939–1958) before the term disappeared almost entirely from official discourse.

BEFORE CATHOLIC ACTION

In the nineteenth century, in the aftermath of an age of revolution, the laity created associations to defend the church and collaborate in the reestablishment of a Catholic society. These associations were often youth movements, such as the Kartellverbände (Federation) of German students, which was federated in 1868; the Società della Gioventù Cattolica Italiana (Society of Italian Catholic youth), formed in Bologna in 1868; l'Action Catholique de la Jeunesse Française (ACJF; Catholic Action of French youth), founded by Albert de Mun in 1886; and the Federazione Universitaria Cattolica Italiana (FUCI; Italian Catholic university federation), founded in 1892, in which the future Paul VI served as an ecclesiastical assistant. Their method was deductive: "prayer—study—action." But they already insisted on "an apostolate of one's fellow man, by one's fellow man." They were encouraged by Leo XIII, who noted in *Sapientiae christianae* (1890; On Christians as citizens) that laypeople must act in accordance with the voice of church authority. In the encyclical *Il fermo proposito* (1905; The constant purpose), Pius X emphasized that the role of the laity could only be an extension of that of the clergy and must be under the strict control of the hierarchy.

PIUS XI AND CATHOLIC ACTION

After the upheavals of World War I and the Russian Revolution of 1917, the Catholic hierarchy concluded that it was no longer sufficient simply to defend its positions; it had to reconquer the world as it had developed outside of the church. From this perspective, the role of the laity was indispensable. Pius XI gave a strong impetus to Catholic Action as the "participation of the laity in the apostolic hierarchy" with the role of "propagating the reign of Christ as king" in the lives of individuals and society. In 1922 he created a central council for Catholic Action in Italy, which soon turned the movement into a single national organization that included four branches, for men, women, boys, and girls. In 1929 the Lateran Treaty with the Italian Fascist state attempted to preserve the independence of Catholic Action and limit its role to spiritual guidance and apostolate. Catholic Action was encouraged to develop in this direction to the exclusion of any political or union activity. This type of organization served as a model in Poland in 1925, Spain in 1926, Yugoslavia and Czechoslovakia in 1927, and Austria in 1928.

This model was first developed in 1919 in Belgium by l'Action Catholique de la Jeunesse Belge (ACJB; Catholic Action of Belgian youth). In 1925 the future Cardinal Joseph Cardijn founded, out of the Jeunesse Syndicaliste (Young trade unionists), the Jeunesse Ouvrière Chrétienne (JOC; young Christian workers), which was intended exclusively for workers, acting "in them, through them, and for them." The creation of this group produced tension with the ACJB, but it was supported by Pius XI. The JOC promoted an inductive method, "see—judge—act," that prefigured the liberation theology movement. Other movements were addressed to farmers, middle-class youth, and students. The same path was followed in France, starting in 1926. In the Netherlands and in francophone Switzerland, Catholic Action brought together quite diverse groups. But Catholic Action did not make inroads into Germany, the German-speaking parts of Switzerland, or the English-speaking world, countries that already possessed numerous lay movements that were independent of the church's hierarchy and were not limited to apostolate. In 1938 Pius XI created a central office for

Catholic Action, but its activities were interrupted by the war.

FROM PIUS XII TO VATICAN II

In his apostolic constitution *Bis saeculari* of 1948, Pius XII expanded Catholic Action in a new way by making the Marian congregations one of its promoters. He used the name for the entire range of lay organizations with a spiritual and ministerial vocation. Certain associations, however, tried to preserve their monopoly. In a number of countries, the older Catholic Action kept its former vitality, but tensions between progressive and conservative tendencies, especially within the JOC, led to the dissolution of the ACJF in 1956, while the JOC developed into an international organization. The older members of the youth movements went on to create associations for adults. Others became influential in the men's, and especially the women's, branches of the groups to which they still belonged. Still others became active in politics, the unions, or society.

In 1951 the president of the Italian Catholic Action organized a world congress of lay ministries. Its success led the pope to create a committee that organized a second congress in 1957, which was perhaps the high point of the lay movement. As soldiers for the foundation of a new Christian realm, the militants transformed themselves into evangelists and immersed themselves in the world like yeast in dough, with the intention of bringing about a worldwide transformation. The Dominican Yves Congar published his *Lay People in the Church: A Study of the Theology of the Laity* in 1953. But a few years later, in 1961, Joseph Comblin wrote a book with the premonitory title *The Failure of Catholic Action?* In it he argued that Christian movements had very little influence on society.

VATICAN II AND LATER DEVELOPMENTS

In its document on the church, *Lumen gentium* (1964), the Second Vatican Council emphasized the fundamental identity of all baptized persons and the responsibility of all Christians as full members of the "people of God." This perspective reversed the traditional view of the church as an institution centered on its hierarchy, a transformation that sparked a profound change in the responsibility of all Christians to the church's mission. In the decree *Apostolicam actuositatem* (1965; Decree on the apostolate of the laity) on the lay apostolate, the members of the council made apostolate a duty of all the faithful. *Catholic Action* was no longer used as a term to describe cooperation of the laity with the church hierarchy, and this kind of cooperation constituted only one form of the laity's mission.

In the 1960s the church entered into a new world, symbolized by the changes brought about by the protests and civil disturbances of May 1968. The church itself was shaken by the tensions that followed the council and the crisis brought about by *Humanae vitae* (1968), which reemphasized the ban on birth control. Real-life situations threw the directives of the hierarchy into question. The use of Marxian discourse as a tool of analysis by certain agrarian and workers' movements led to the French bishops' renunciation in 1975 of any idea of a special mandate, which officially committed the church authorities, and to splits such as that of the International JOC in 1985. Other spiritual and charitable organizations and new prospects for charismatic renewal now have the wind at their back and the support of the hierarchy.

See also **Catholicism; John XXIII; Vatican II.**

BIBLIOGRAPHY

Achille ratti, pape Pie XI. Rome, 1996.

Aubert, Roger, et al. *The Church in a Secularised Society.* Translated by Janet Sondheimer. London, 1978.

De Haan, Petrus. *Van volgzame elitestrijder tot kritische gelovige: Geschiedenis van de Katholieke Actie in Nederland (1934–1966).* Nijmegen, Netherlands, 1994.

Geaney, D. J. "Catholic Action." In *New Catholic Encyclopedia.* 2nd ed. Vol. 3. Detroit, Mich., and Washington, D.C., 2002.

IYCW: International Young Christian Workers, 75 Years of Action. Strasbourg, France, 2000.

Laloux, Ludovic. "L'apostolat des laïcs en France. D'une politique hexagonale aux impulsions romaines ou le ralliement au décret conciliaire de Vatican II." *Nouvelle revue théologique* 122, no. 2 (2000): 211–237.

Mayeur, Jean-Marie, et al., eds. *Histoire du Christianisme.* Vols. 11–13. Paris, 1990–2000.

Minvielle, Bernard. *L'apostolat des laïcs à la veille du concile (1949–1959): Histoire des congrès mondiaux de 1951 et 1957.* Fribourg, France, 2001.

Tihon, André. "Les mouvements de laïcs dans les Églises aux XIXe et XXe siècles: Rapport general." In *Miscellanea historiae ecclesiasticae VII. Congrès de Bucarest, août 1980,* 143–177. Brussels, 1985.

ANDRÉ TIHON

CATHOLICISM. The twentieth century was a period of profound change for the Roman Catholic Church. Perhaps the most significant change to take place during that time was the globalization of Catholicism, which made it increasingly less European in every respect. A second momentous change came shortly after midcentury, when the Second Vatican Council brought about wholesale renewal. Developments in the world at large also brought multifaceted change. The church had to contend with two world wars, astonishing advances in science and technology, and a constant increase in the secularization of the West, especially Europe. Yet despite all these changes, the Roman Catholic Church managed to remain vigorously committed to its ancient traditions. At the very top of the hierarchy of the Catholic Church, the papacy grew stronger, despite serious challenges. When it comes to writing the history of the church in the twentieth century, one must begin and end with the popes, for their place in it is comparable to that of the kings and emperors of the old absolute monarchies, who had the power to guide the course of events.

PIUS X (1903–1914)

At the dawn of the century, in 1903, when Pope Pius X succeeded Leo XIII (r. 1898–1903), Catholicism was a faith deeply focused on tradition, and the leadership of the Catholic Church was keenly interested in maintaining the status quo, not just with regard to theology and ritual but also with respect to the church's authority structure and its relation to the world at large. Despite its global reach, the Roman Catholic Church was very closely tied to Europe, its leadership still dominated by European clerics, especially by the overwhelmingly Italian curia of the papal court in Rome. The popes were still claiming sovereignty over Rome and remained adamantly fixed on the idea that the Italian republic had turned them into "prisoners of the Vatican."

The pontificate of Pius X (Giuseppe Sarto) was marked by continuous tension with the social, political, and intellectual changes sweeping across Europe. From the very start, Pius X committed himself to fighting "modernism," the name given to a broad spectrum of ideas and attitudes that were viewed as incompatible with traditional Catholic teachings. Two papal decrees issued in 1907 condemned modernism and clearly spelled out what it was: *Lamentabili Sane Exitu* ("On a Deplorable Outcome") and *Pascendi Dominici Gregis* ("Feeding the Lord's Flocks"). That same year, a number of supposedly modernist books were also placed on the Index of Forbidden Books. Chief among the trends labeled modernist was the historical/critical method of biblical scholarship pioneered by German Protestant scholars, which approached the sacred texts of the Bible with exactly the same critical eye it turned on any other ancient document. In 1910 Pius X ordered all Roman Catholic clergy and all teachers in Catholic seminaries to adhere to these two decrees and to take an oath denouncing modernism.

Pius X also committed himself to struggling against political movements that challenged papal supremacy and the rights and privileges of the Catholic Church over and against the state. He thus took aim at Christian democrats in Italy and Europe, and against all other political action groups that fomented change independent of the Catholic hierarchy. Instead, he favored social action groups that accepted the leadership of the clergy and he fostered the creation of such associations. He also constantly denounced the principle of the separation of church and state, and focused intensely on France, where the state had confiscated all church property in 1905, forcing the Catholic Church to pay rent to the French Republic.

As tensions mounted between European states in 1914, European Catholics were thus placed in an embattled position vis-à-vis "the world," a situation that was similar to that of the soldiers who would find themselves waging trench warfare during World War I, which broke out in 1914, during the last month of Pius X's papacy.

BENEDICT XV (1914–1922)

Pius X's successor, Pope Benedict XV (Giacomo della Chiesa), was wholly committed to restoring the peace in Europe but found himself unable to stop the war, which he called "the suicide of Europe." From his call for a Christmas truce in 1914 to his seven-point Papal Peace proposal in August 1917, Pope Benedict's pleas fell on deaf ears. Adopting a policy of pacifism and strict neutrality, the pope steadfastly refused to condemn any of the nations involved in the war. Instead, he repeatedly condemned war itself, associating it with Satan. At war's end, the papacy's neutrality may have cost it inclusion in the Paris Peace Conference and the deliberations that led to the Treaty of Versailles.

On other fronts, the Catholic Church continued to wage a war of its own against modernism and the social and political ills of the age, though Benedict XV had a softer approach to this issue than his predecessor. With the rise of communism after the triumph of the 1917 Bolshevik Revolution in Russia, the Catholic Church stepped up its efforts to address the needs and concerns of workers and the poor. Pope Benedict XV seemed fully conscious of the church's need to address questions of social and economic justice, and urged his clergy to become more active in this area, saying: "It is precisely in this field that the eternal salvation of souls is imperiled" (John, p. 463).

The Catholic laity in Europe continued to engage in social and political action of all sorts and to follow the dictates of their faith, sometimes with surprising results. At the bottom of the social scale, three peasant children in Portugal began to claim in 1917 that they were being visited repeatedly by the Virgin Mary. These reports of apparitions at Fatima drew tens of thousands of the faithful to the site and culminated in the issuance of a number of very political prophecies by the children regarding World War I and the rise of communism in Russia—prophecies that were eventually sanctioned by the papacy. The apparitions themselves were also deemed authentic, and the shrine established at Fatima continued in the twenty-first century to draw millions of pilgrims, laypersons as well as clergy.

PIUS XI (1922–1939)

Embracing the motto, "the peace of Christ in the Kingdom of Christ," Pius XI (Ambrogio Ratti) could no more ignore the upheavals of his day than could any of the clergy or laity that he shepherded. Close to home, in Italy, the rise to power of Benito Mussolini brought an end to the political impasse that had been in place since 1870. In 1929 Pius XI signed the Lateran Treaty with Mussolini's government, creating an independent Vatican State within Rome and supposedly freeing him from his "prisoner" status. Instead of having no territory to call his own, the pope now found himself ruling the smallest independent nation-state in the world, a state composed of no more than a dozen or so buildings. He also found himself wholly surrounded by a Fascist nation that espoused an intensely secularist and even anti-Christian ideology. And across the Alps, even worse regimes were gaining power and momentum day by day.

Pius XI was helpless in the face of a civil war in Spain (1936–1939) that erupted between a conservative coalition led by Fascists (Nationalists) and a coalition of communists, anarchists, and liberals (Republicans), in which the Catholic Church became both a battleground and a weapon. In areas controlled by the Republicans, rabid anticlericalism led to the deaths of thousands of priests and nuns, and to the destruction of many churches and their belongings. In Nationalist areas, the Fascists committed many atrocities in the name of Catholicism, and when they finally triumphed, their leader, Francisco Franco (1892–1975), set up a repressive Fascist state that continually used the Catholic Church for its own purposes, even to the point of naming Saint Teresa of Avila (1515–1582) an honorary general in his army.

In Germany, the postwar economic depression led to the rise in power of Adolf Hitler (1889–1945) and the Nazi Party. Pope Pius XI found himself unable to do more than secure guarantees for the safety and survival of the Catholic Church through the *Reichskonkordat,* an agreement signed in 1933. But this treaty between the Vatican and Berlin, like all others signed by the Nazis, was never fully honored. Hitler boasted of having duped the pope into helping him, saying to his cabinet: "An opportunity has been given to Germany in the *Reichskonkordat* and a sphere of influence has been

Nurses and patients are among the pilgrims at the Shrine of Fatima, Portugal, c. 1949. ©Bettmann/Corbis

created that will be especially significant in the urgent struggle against international Jewry" (Hochhuth, p. 298). At the Vatican, Secretary of State Eugenio Pacelli (the future Pope Pius XII) denounced Hitler's duplicity as well as his virulent racism, but to no avail.

As attacks on Jews and the church mounted, Pope Pius XI found it necessary to issue an encyclical that condemned both Nazi ideology and violations of the concordat of 1933. Written by the Vatican's secretary of state, Pacelli, the encyclical *Mit Brennender Sorge* ("With Burning Sorrow") was smuggled into Germany and read from the pulpit of every Catholic Church on Palm Sunday 1937. In it, the Vatican boldly and clearly spelled out the Catholic Church's opposition to the racist and nationalist thinking of the Nazis, arguing that it was fundamentally wrong for anyone to exalt "race, or the people, or the State" above all else, or to "divinize them to an idolatrous level"

(Carlen, vol. 3, p. 527). A year before the outbreak of war, in September 1938, Pius XI carefully articulated once more the church's stand against anti-Semitism, in a pronouncement that was banned by the Fascist press in Germany: "Anti-Semitism is . . . a movement with which we Christians can have nothing to do. No, no, I say to you it is impossible for a Christian to take part in anti-Semitism" (*New York Times,* 12 December 1938, p. 1).

Although the ghost of modernism continued to haunt Catholic scholarship and learning at this time, fear of it lessened somewhat in Rome. To foster learning, Pope Pius XI established papally sanctioned research institutions such as the Pontifical Institute of Christian Archaeology (1925) and the Pontifical Academy of Sciences (1936). Still deeply conservative, these foundations nonetheless paved the way for a greater rapprochement between Catholicism and modern scholarship.

The most enduring legacy of Pius XI's pontificate may not lie in Europe, however, but in its former colonies. Nineteenth-century imperialism had made Europe master of much of the globe, and the Catholic Church had expanded its reach tremendously as a result of this development. Yet, as late as the 1920s, the vast majority of Europe's colonized subjects remained unconverted to the Christian faith. Pius XI made it his business to remedy this situation by encouraging the development of overseas missions, requiring every religious order to pursue this calling. As a result, by 1939 there were twice as many Catholic missionaries in the field as there had been in 1922. Pius XI initiated another significant change in the mission field by insisting that seminaries abroad train and ordain native clergy, who would eventually make European missionaries unnecessary. In 1926 the consecration of the first three native Chinese bishops was one of the initial steps taken toward the globalization of the Catholic Church, a process that continued into the twenty-first century, producing reverse missionaries, that is, priests from the Third World who serve in Europe and North America as the shortage of priestly vocations there continues to worsen.

PIUS XII (1939–1958)

As Pope Pius XI was preparing to issue yet another public condemnation of Nazism and Fascism in February 1939, he died unexpectedly and was succeeded by the Vatican's secretary of state, Eugenio Pacelli, who took the papal name Pius XII (1939–1958). No other pope in modern history is wrapped in as much controversy as Pius XII, because he seemed so helpless in the face of World War II and the Holocaust. Debate continues to rage. In the minds of some detractors, he seems to have been a willing collaborator, or perhaps an unwilling but uncaring accomplice in the extermination of six million Jews. According to his defenders, he was a brave opponent of consummate evil and a prudent shepherd who did all he could in the worst of circumstances.

As Europe plunged into total war in the fall of 1939, Pius XII assumed a stance of public neutrality similar to that taken by Benedict XV in World War I. But having made public his views of the Nazis and Fascists long before the outbreak of the

war, Pius XII's neutrality was much less convincing. On 25 December 1941, for instance, *The New York Times* praised Pius XII in an editorial, saying his was "a lonely voice in the silence and darkness enveloping Europe this Christmas," and that he was "about the only ruler left on the Continent of Europe who dares to raise his voice at all." Yet the fact that he lived in the capital city of one of the Axis Powers, surrounded by their armies, made his position much more precarious than that of Benedict XV. Moreover, the Nazis were well-known for their brutal reprisals against all opponents, and as a result, the pope was under severe constraints when it came to accomplishing anything within Germany itself. The same was true for every Catholic bishop and priest who lived in Axis-controlled areas. Any protest could incite a reprisal. And indeed, such reprisals routinely occurred on the local level, as in the Netherlands when Dutch bishops protested against the deportation of the country's Jews.

Hitler barely tolerated Pius XII, saying that he was "the only human being who has always contradicted me and who has never obeyed me" (Jansen, p. 429). Pope Pius XII was well aware of his precarious situation yet chose to encourage or engage in clandestine acts of defiance, such as providing hiding places for Jews in churches, monasteries, and convents, or facilitating the escape of Jews from Axis-occupied areas to other countries. It is estimated that about three hundred thousand to eight hundred thousand Jews were saved by such means, at great risk for all involved. Nonetheless, detractors of Pius XII not only challenge the accuracy of these figures but also point out that any such number—no matter how high—is insignificant when compared to the enormity of the Holocaust.

As the Cold War developed in the postwar period and the threat of nuclear annihilation increased, Pius XII began to speak out more forcefully against modern warfare and especially against the concept of deterrence and the stockpiling of atomic weapons, which, as he saw it, served only to make the horror of nuclear war a more imminent possibility. This did not keep him from taking sides, however. A staunch anticommunist and an outspoken critic of the Soviet ruler Joseph Stalin, Pius XII made it clear to the faithful that communism was as incompatible with Catholicism as Nazism had been.

Regarding questions of faith and the relationship of Catholics to the world at large, Pius XII proved to be less conservative than his predecessors, at least in two very important areas. In 1943, Pius XII issued what many consider to be his most important encyclical, *Divino Afflante Spiritu* ("With the Help of the Divine Spirit"), which removed the barriers that earlier popes had erected against modernism in biblical studies and finally allowed Catholic scholars to apply new techniques of historical criticism in their research. In 1947 he issued another highly influential encyclical, *Mediator Dei* ("Mediator of God"), which set into motion a renewal of liturgical studies. Unbeknownst to Pius XII and all his contemporaries, this encyclical would eventually lead to a total revamping of Roman Catholic ritual sixteen years later, at the Second Vatican Council.

JOHN XXIII (1958–1963)

When Pius XII died in October 1958, Angelo Roncalli, the patriarch of Venice, was chosen to succeed him under the name John XXIII. Elected under the assumption that he would accomplish little, because of his age and his prior lack of intimacy with the Vatican, the seventy-one-year-old pope stunned the curia and the world by immediately convening an ecumenical council for the express purpose of renewing the church. *Aggiornamento* is what Pope John XXIII said the church needed: to be brought up to date, put in step with the world rather than in conflict with it. It was to be a "New Pentecost," he proclaimed, an era of renewal and of reconciliation, inspired by the Holy Spirit.

Despite resistance from some in the curia, Pope John XXIII's council assembled for its first meeting in October 1962. This council was unlike any other in the history of the Roman Catholic Church, not only because it had more representatives from nations outside Europe than ever before but also because it was genuinely ecumenical in spirit, allowing the presence of observers from other Christian churches. Its agenda seemed daunting at first and fraught with controversy, but in a mere three years the Second Vatican Council managed to

bring about more change than many in the Catholic Church had ever thought possible.

Sixteen documents produced by the council fathers transformed Catholicism from top to bottom. Of these sixteen, six were most instrumental in bringing about tremendous changes.

In its "Dogmatic Constitution on the Church," *Lumen Gentium,* the council reinterpreted the nature of the church itself and of its hierarchical structure, placing greater emphasis on the role of the bishops within the church hierarchy and softening the rigid monarchical model of the papacy that had accompanied the First Vatican Council's decree on papal infallibility (1870). It also called for much greater participation by laypersons in the work of the church and broadened the meaning of a Christian calling, or vocation, to include the laity as much as the clergy. This emphasis on increased participation by the laity in the church's mission was further reinforced by a separate "Decree on the Apostolate of the Laity," *Apostolicae Actuositatem.*

The "Dogmatic Constitution on Divine Revelation," *Dei Verbum,* not only reassessed the place of the Bible in Catholic teaching, placing it clearly at the center of all theological and moral affirmations, but also encouraged the laity to read and study Holy Scripture in their own languages and called on scholars to approach the sacred texts with modern methodologies. In this respect, Catholicism moved closer to Protestantism.

In its "Constitution on the Sacred Liturgy," *Sacrosanctum Concilium,* the council called for a total transformation of the ritual life of the church, drawing on the work that had been spurred by Pius XII's encyclical *Mediator Dei* in 1947. At the heart of this document stood the theory that the church's ritual, while led by the clergy, is incomplete without the full participation of the laity. This meant that rituals that had not been altered since they had been set in place by the Council of Trent (1563) and the *Roman Missal* (1580), rituals that had seemed frozen for eternity, were to be changed overnight. The most profound and most noticeable change was the rejection of Latin as the sole language of Catholic ritual and its replacement by the vernacular. Given the Catholic Church's global

A missionary listens to the confession of a young woman in Kinshasa, Democratic Republic of the Congo, 1970s. ©Paul Almasy/Corbis

reach, this meant that the ritual had to be translated from Latin into hundreds of other languages.

Two decrees marked a great change in Catholic thinking on questions of the relationship between the church and the world. The council's "Pastoral Constitution on the Church in the World of Today," *Gaudium et Spes,* openly admitted that, as human culture develops, it is the church's responsibility to address itself to change, to adapt itself and to find ways of proclaiming unchanging truths through the constantly evolving means placed at its disposal. With this document, the Second Vatican Council laid to rest the fears of modernism that had so dominated its discourse and behavior at the dawn of the twentieth century. The "Declaration on Human Freedom," *Dignitatis Humanae,* while extremely controversial for conservative and traditionalist Catholics, proved to be

the one decree most warmly received by those outside the church. Its message was clear: "All persons must be free to seek the truth without coercion." Of course, by professing freedom of religion as a basic human right, the council also defended in principle the separation of church and state and every government's duty to protect freedom of religion.

The council also opened the Catholic Church to friendly dialogue with Protestant and Orthodox Christian churches in its "Decree on Ecumenism," *Unitatis Redintegratio.* Similar ecumenist sentiments were voiced by the council in its "Declaration on Relations with Non-Christian Religions," *Nostra Aetate,* which said, among other things, that "the Catholic Church rejects nothing that is true and holy in these religions" and that they should be regarded with "sincere reverence."

In sum, the changes brought about by Vatican II, as this council came to be known, were not only numerous but profound. Suddenly, or so it seemed, many of the customs that had been at the core of Catholic identity were gone: Latin liturgies, veils on women's heads at church, rules for fasting at Lent or for abstaining from meat on Fridays all became a thing of the past, along with nuns who always wore distinctive habits and stayed in their cloisters and priests who always wore cassocks and Roman collars. As could be expected, these reforms could not please all Catholics. Although most of the faithful adapted quickly or even welcomed the reforms of Vatican II after its closing session in December 1965, some disparaged the council for having gone too far, others for not having gone far enough. Among the traditionalists who rejected the council's reforms as too radical, none gained more prominence than Archbishop Marcel Lefebvre, founder of the Society of Saint Pius X, who was excommunicated in 1988 for consecrating four bishops without the pope's approval.

PAUL VI (1963–1978)

The daunting task of guiding the Second Vatican Council and of shepherding the Catholic Church through these momentous changes was not carried out by John XXIII, who died after the council's first session in June 1963, but by his successor, Cardinal Giovanni Battista Montini, archbishop of Milan, who took the name Paul VI. Since his pontificate was so closely linked to the Second Vatican Council, Paul VI quickly drew fire along with praise.

Without a doubt, Paul VI presided over the most intense reform that the Catholic Church had undergone in its long history, and he also redefined the role of the papacy in significant ways. He was the first pope to engage actively in ecumenical dialogue with other Christian churches, meeting with the archbishop of Canterbury, Michael Ramsey, and with the Greek Orthodox patriarch of Constantinople, Athenagoras I. Pope and patriarch also took a significant step toward healing the Great Schism between Catholic and Orthodox Christians by lifting the mutual excommunication that the two churches had leveled against each other in the year 1054.

Paul VI was also the first pope in history to travel extensively, visiting every continent but Antarctica, addressing all of humanity, not just his Catholic flock, preaching brotherhood and toleration, promoting world peace, social justice, and international cooperation, calling for an end to poverty, hunger, and illiteracy.

Yet in spite of these accomplishments, Paul VI came to be viewed as something of a failure by many within the Catholic Church and outside it. Such judgments stem in part from Paul VI's inability to arrest the mass defections of priests and nuns and the sharp decline in clerical vocations that began to plague the Catholic Church in the 1960s and continued unabated into the next century.

But by far the loudest and most biting criticism of Paul VI came from those who disagreed with his stand on the issue of birth control. In 1968, much to the surprise of many Catholics and non-Catholics, Paul VI rejected the recommendations of a commission that John XXIII had established to review the issue of contraception, issuing the encyclical *Humanae Vitae* ("Of Human Life"), which declared all forms of birth control a sin, save for the so-called rhythm or natural method, in which couples abstain from sexual activity during the few days each month when the woman is fertile. The shock waves caused by this encyclical within the Catholic Church and in the world at large were enormous, in great part because this was an issue that affected all Catholic married couples intimately and also had implications for world population growth. To many, it seemed a reversal in the church's recent wave of renewal, even a return to the days of the modernist crisis. It also struck many inside and outside the church as socially irresponsible, given the unprecedented population explosion, especially in poorer nations, many of which were heavily Catholic. Paul VI responded to the firestorm of criticism by standing firm on the issue, but he never fully recovered from the disappointment and grief that this resistance caused him. The last ten years of his papacy were active, but even by his own account, they seemed tinged with gloomy disillusionment. In a sermon preached in 1972, he went as far as to say: "We believed that after the Council would come a day of sunshine in the history of the Church. But instead there has come a day of clouds and storms, and of darkness ..." (Paul VI, Internet site).

One of the post–Vatican II developments that Paul VI surely saw as a cloud was the creation of liberation theology in Latin America in the mid-1960s. A form of socialism dressed in gospel rhetoric, liberation theology began as the anguished response of Catholic clergy who worked with the poor and struggled for justice on their behalf, usually in countries with subsistence economies and an uneven distribution of wealth. Proclaiming Jesus a revolutionary liberator not just in the world to come but in the here and now, liberation theologians called upon the church in Latin America to do more than change the liturgy and to engage itself directly in the transformation of society.

Liberation theology was as much a political movement as an ideology, and its leaders could never separate theory from praxis. Although it had gathered momentum for several years, it seemed to burst into existence in Medellín, Colombia, in 1968, at the second Latin American Bishops' Conference, which openly condemned the industrialized nations for their exploitation of the Third World and also defended the notion that the pursuit of social justice on earth is at the very heart of the gospel message. Liberation theology quickly gained many followers in the 1970s, even among the hierarchy of the Catholic Church in Latin America. One of its chief assumptions was that economic conditions in Latin America made it necessary for the Catholic Church in the Third World to be totally dedicated to the poor and their needs. Mixing Gospel citations, the texts of the Second Vatican Council, and rhetoric about class struggle—some of it openly Marxist—liberation theologians engaged with the poor, dispensing medicine and practical advice along with the sacraments, challenging the status quo on a daily basis. As the movement spread through the creation of small groups known as *bases de comunidad* (community bases), lay leadership increased, making it less clerical and hierarchical, and making liberation theology less and less appealing to many at the Vatican. Occasionally, some liberationists would openly praise the communist revolution in Cuba or turn their revolutionary rhetoric into action. Occasionally, too, some would become martyrs to their cause, as happened with Archbishop Oscar Romero of El Salvador, who was murdered in 1980 by soldiers while he was saying mass.

JOHN PAUL I (1978) AND JOHN PAUL II (1978–2005)

When the weary Paul VI died in August 1978, as liberation theology was gaining momentum far from Rome, he was succeeded by Cardinal Albino Luciani, who, in turn, died unexpectedly after only thirty-three days as Pope John Paul I. The churchman chosen as the next pope in October was as much a surprise as the heart attack that had felled John Paul I. Cardinal Karol Wojtyła, from Kraków, Poland, was so far off every expert's radar screen that he elicited responses of "Cardinal who?" when his name was announced. Yet, by the time of his death in April 2005, this pontiff, who took the name John Paul II, would be well known by billions around the world, Catholic and non-Catholic alike, and would be credited not only with redefining the papacy and the reforms of Vatican II but also with bringing about the demise of the Soviet Union and the end of the Cold War.

The first non-Italian pope to be elected since 1522 and the first ever to hail from a Slavic country, John Paul II defied the odds and baffled the so-called experts from the very start. At fifty-eight, he was one of the youngest popes in well over a century, and this allowed him to serve twenty-seven years in office—the third longest pontificate in history, according to the records of the Catholic Church. There is no denying that this pope is regarded by many as a major figure in the history of the Catholic Church and the world at large.

Having lived under Nazi rule and then under Soviet-style communism in Poland, and having confronted evil with a deep faith based on traditional Catholic values, John Paul II was unlikely to fit any existing mold or any previously devised definition of "conservative" or "liberal." Above all, he was wholly committed to grounding the Catholic Church in its two thousand years of tradition. Yet at the same time, he seemed intent on unflinchingly meeting the contemporary world head-on. At the core of his message lay the conviction that all humans had a "universal call to holiness," and that this call, like the cross itself, was "a sign of contradiction" to the world.

John Paul II baffled all experts by claiming a high moral ground and reveling in apparent contradictions. Resolutely committed to moral absolutes, he condemned both the ethical relativism of the wealthier Western nations and the single-minded absolutism of fascists, communists, and racists. A deeply spiritual man, he assailed all materialistic and hedonistic impulses with equal ferocity, be they grounded in the teachings of Karl Marx and Mao Zedong or in the mindless, insatiable capitalist consumerism of the West. A pacifist and a shrewd politician, he condemned violence while doing his utmost to undermine abusive regimes. Deeply aware of the plight of the poor in the Third World and just as deeply concerned with environmental issues, he called on the wealthier nations to restructure their priorities, aim for greater justice in the distribution of the earth's resources, and promote a greater respect for nature. A mystic at heart, he defended even the smallest points of traditional Catholic belief with dogged tenacity and at the same time publicly approached other faiths with reverence and humility, even to the point of publicly apologizing for past instances of Catholic intolerance.

Had he remained ensconced in the Vatican, much of this might have made little difference. But John Paul II was a very visible and public pope, "the people's pope" as some in the news media dubbed him. An untiring traveler and mingler—even after a would-be assassin in Saint Peter's Square shot and nearly killed him in 1981—John Paul II expanded the reach of the Catholic Church and of the papacy itself in unprecedented ways. During his pontificate, he made more than one hundred trips, more than all the previous popes in Christian history put together, logging more than 1.1 million kilometers, or 725,000 miles (nearly three times the distance to the moon), attracting millions of people to see and hear him in the flesh. It is estimated that some of the crowds he drew were the largest to have assembled in human history.

When he died in the spring of 2005, John Paul II was repeatedly praised for having brought down the Soviet Union and its empire. His first pastoral visit to Poland in 1979 and his support of the Solidarity movement in his native land were often cited as the first step toward the eventual undoing

of that Marxist state and all others in Europe. He never did visit Russia, even after the fall of communism, or China, which he earnestly desired to do. But he did take a swipe at Marxism in Latin America, not through his visit to Cuba, which had no adverse effect on Fidel Castro's long dictatorship, but rather through his condemnation of certain Marxist tendencies in liberation theology. Early in his pontificate, while visiting Mexico in 1979, he began to challenge liberation theologians by warning that "this conception of Christ as a political figure, a revolutionary, as the subversive of Nazareth, does not tally with the Church's teachings" (John Paul II, paragraph 1.4)

By the 1990s, John Paul II made it abundantly clear through the Congregation for the Doctrine of the Faith—formerly known as the Holy Office, or Inquisition—that no matter how much liberation theology squared with Catholic social teachings, especially in regard to the responsibility that all Catholics have toward the poor, all talk of a class struggle and the need for revolution was totally unacceptable. Moreover, by appointing many conservative bishops over a twenty-seven-year period, Pope John Paul II made sure that the hierarchy of the Latin American church would keep a tight lid on liberationists.

Although popular around the globe, especially with traditionalist Catholics, John Paul II was the bane of liberals and progressives in the wealthier nations, who tended to see him as unforgivably retrograde, or worse, as a Grand Inquisitor of sorts. On virtually every issue that was of concern to them, he struck them as being in the wrong. He silenced liberation theologians and ordered all Catholic clergy not to involve themselves directly in politics. He dismissed feminism outright, decried abortion, and denied women access to the priesthood. He also denied priests the right to marry and condemned all forms of artificial contraception, including the use of condoms as a means of halting the spread of the AIDS epidemic. Worse yet—as liberals saw it—he was totally inflexible when it came to sex, branding extra- and premarital relations, homosexuality, and pornography inherently wrong and sinful. On questions of medical ethics he seemed just as obstinate, challenging advances in science at every turn, damning those who favored euthanasia, embryonic stem cell research, and cloning.

But that is only one side of the story. Conservatives, too, were sometimes irked and confused by John Paul II. Ironically, his consistent emphasis on the sacredness of life, which made him seem hopelessly conservative to liberals, also led him to condemn some things that were dear or acceptable to conservatives, such as capital punishment, war, violence, and bare-knuckle laissez-faire capitalism. And his peacemaking efforts also sometimes seemed like useless meddling to them.

John Paul II's long tenure in office allowed him to leave a significant legacy that will last at least a generation: a conservative leadership in the episcopacy and in the college of cardinals. Another of his legacies is the change he effected in the complexion of the ruling elite of the church hierarchy, which at the time of his death was no longer dominated by Europeans, even less by Italians, but was instead more truly representative of the Catholic Church's global reach.

These bishops and cardinals appointed by John Paul II, along with his successor, Pope Benedict XVI (Joseph Ratzinger), will need to confront various problems that surfaced in the final two decades of the twentieth century. First and foremost, they will need to deal with the shortage of vocations to the priesthood that has plagued most of the wealthier nations for nearly two decades. In Western Europe particularly, they will have to contend with a growing secularism and a sharp decline in church attendance. In those countries that were once the epicenter of Roman Catholicism—Italy, France, Spain, Belgium, and Austria—the percentage of the population that attended church regularly or even cared to consider themselves Catholic in the year 2000 was only a fraction of what it had been in 1900. Although great gains were made elsewhere, especially in the Third World, the shifting balance in membership will obviously lead to readjustments in the leadership of the Catholic Church and to other changes. In addition, as at the dawn of the twentieth century, but at a faster pace, the leadership of the Catholic Church will have to contend with unprecedented change in virtually every sphere of life.

But when all is said and done, Catholicism remains vibrant in its twenty-first century and as ready to take on the world as ever.

See also **Abortion; Catholic Action; John Paul II; John XXIII; Lateran Pacts; Paul VI; Vatican II.**

BIBLIOGRAPHY

Atkin, Nicholas. *Priests, Prelates, and People: A History of European Catholicism since 1750.* London, 2003.

Bottum, Joseph, and David G. Dalin, eds. *The Pius War: Responses to the Critics of Pius XII.* Lanham, Md., 2004.

Cahill, Thomas. *Pope John XXIII.* New York, 2002.

Carlen, Claudia. *The Papal Encyclicals.* 5 vols. Ann Arbor, Mich., 1990.

Cornwell, John. *Hitler's Pope: The Secret History of Pius XII.* New York, 1999.

Greeley, Andrew M. *The Catholic Revolution: New Wine, Old Wineskins, and the Second Vatican Council.* Berkeley, Calif., 2004.

Hebblethwaite, Peter. *Paul VI: The First Modern Pope.* New York, 1993.

Hochhuth, Rolf. "Sidelights on History." In *The Deputy (Der Stellvertreter).* New York, 1964.

Holland, Joe. *Modern Catholic Social Teaching: The Popes Confront the Industrial Age, 1740–1958.* New York, 2003.

Jansen, Hans. *De zwijgende paus?: protest van Pius Xii en zijn medewerkers tegen de jodenvervolging in Europa.* Kampen, Netherlands, 2000.

Jodock, Darrell, ed. *Catholicism Contending with Modernity: Roman Catholic Modernism and Anti-modernism in Historical Context.* Cambridge, U.K., 2000.

John, Eric, ed. *The Popes: A Concise Biographical History.* New York, 1964.

John Paul II. Opening Address at the Puebla Conference, 28 January 1979. Available at http://www.ewtn.com/library/PAPALDOC/JP791228.htm

Kent, Peter C. *The Pope and the Duce: The International Impact of the Lateran Agreements.* New York, 1981.

———. *The Lonely Cold War of Pope Pius XII: The Roman Catholic Church and the Division of Europe, 1943–1950.* Montreal, 2002.

Kwitny, Jonathan. *Man of the Century: The Life and Times of Pope John Paul II.* New York, 1997.

Lampomarda, Vincent A. "Reckoning with Daniel J. Goldhagen's Views on the Roman Catholic Church, the Holocaust, and Pope Pius XII." *The Journal of The Historical Society* 3, no. 3–4 (2003): 493–502.

McCarthy, Timothy G. *The Catholic Tradition: The Church in the Twentieth Century.* 2nd ed. Chicago, 1998.

Paul VI. Homily, 29 June 1972. Available at http://www.vatican.va/holy_father/paul_vi/homilies/1972/documents/hf_p-vi_hom_19720629_it.html.

Rhodes, Anthony. *The Vatican in the Age of the Dictators, 1922–1945.* London, 1973.

Szulc, Tad. *Pope John Paul II: the Biography.* New York, 1995.

Tombs, David. *Latin American Liberation Theology.* Boston, 2002.

Twomey, Gerald S. *The "Preferential Option for the Poor" in Catholic Social Thought from John XXIII to John Paul II.* Lewiston, N.Y., 2005.

Wills, Garry. *Papal Sin: Structures of Deceit.* New York, 2000.

Wynn, Wilton. *Keepers of the Keys: John XXIII, Paul VI, and John Paul II, Three Who Changed the Church.* New York, 1988.

Carlos M. N. Eire

EDITH CAVELL (1865–1915), nurse, resistance worker.

Edith Cavell was born on 4 December 1865, the eldest daughter of a family of four children (three girls, one boy). Her father, the Reverend Frederick Cavell, was a pastor in Swardeston, Norfolk. Edith was given a rigid and austere education, first at home, and subsequently in several boarding schools, where she distinguished herself by her proficiency in French. At the age of eighteen, she was employed as a governess in an Essex family. She traveled to Switzerland, Bavaria, and Saxony, where she became acquainted with modern German methods of hygiene and medicine. She subsequently spent six years in Brussels as a governess and returned to England in 1895 to care for her ailing father. This experience convinced her to take up nursing at the age of thirty. She began a training course at Tredegar House in Bow and then moved on to work at the London Fever Hospital, at Saint Pancras' Infirmary, and at the Queen's District in Manchester.

Assigned to different posts and responsibilities, Cavell acquired considerable experience of hospital work. At that time, in Belgium, Dr. Antoine Depage was looking for an experienced nurse to take the direction of the new school for qualified

Edith Cavell, photographed in the year of her death, 1915. ©Bettmann/Corbis

---

nurses, the first of its kind, which he had founded with his wife Marie as an alternative to the monopoly of confessional training and in accordance with their project to introduce modern forms of nursing in Belgium. Fascinated by the English model developed by Florence Nightingale, Antoine Depage contacted Edith Cavell, who had maintained numerous contacts in the Belgian capital. Edith Cavell accepted the charge, and thus laid the first foundations of non-confessional nursing in Belgium. Cavell's beginnings were difficult, as the school was loudly decried in Catholic circles, but her competence was soon to receive due acknowledgement. In 1910 she was offered the post of head nurse at the hospital in the Brussels borough of Saint Gilles. The hospital was soon to host all of Edith Cavell's students, who acquired their hospital experience on the spot. In early 1914 Edith Cavell headed a team of no less than ninety nurses. A reserved and even introverted character according to some, Edith appreciated solitude but had two passions in life: her profession and dogs, on whom she was to write a book. "People may look upon me as a lonely old maid," she once confessed to a friend, "but with my work in the world which I love, I am such a happy old maid that everyone would feel envious of me if they only knew" (Hill, Ch. 4, from Internet site).

When in August 1914 the German troops entered Brussels and Dr. Depage and his wife left for the front to supervise the Ocean Ambulance base hospital at La Panne, Cavell bravely held on to her post at the head of the school and joined the teams in the scores of ambulances transporting the wounded in Brussels. When the many English nurses living in Brussels were ordered to return to Britain, Cavell ignored the order and kept working. When the German troops entered Brussels, her school came to function as a Red Cross hospital, where she was soon to accept and dispense care to wounded German soldiers. In November 1914 two wounded English soldiers found their way into the school. Edith took the risk of nursing and hiding them and subsequently to help them escape toward the Netherlands. Thus she became a resistance worker, involved in a network assisting the escape of Allied soldiers, but was arrested on 5 August 1915 by the Germans and incarcerated at Saint Gilles prison. Together with twenty-seven other members of her network, Cavell was charged with treason by a military tribunal, condemned to death, and executed at the Tir National on 12 October 1915. Shortly before her execution, she uttered the sentence that was to become famous: "I realize that patriotism is not enough. I must have no hatred or bitterness toward anyone."

The execution of a woman, and moreover of a nurse, raised a wave of indignation throughout the world. Edith Cavell became the symbol of innocence at grips with German barbarity, an image that came to be gratefully exploited by the Allied propaganda. An American journalist wrote, "Emperor William would have done better to lose an entire army corps than to butcher Miss Cavell"; the bishop of London pointed out that Britain had now no need for a recruiting campaign: the execution of Edith Cavell was enough. And thus a myth was born amid the conflict. Recruitment stands were set up in Trafalgar Square in front of portraits of Edith Cavell. Her picture could be seen everywhere, and a staggering number of postcards were printed and distributed in her honor. After the war, in 1919, her body was unearthed and solemnly transported to England. Both in Belgium and in England, the ceremony took on the dimensions of a national event. The press reported: "It looks as if all of Brussels wanted to pay a tribute to Miss Cavell's remains." Throughout the city, throngs of people were crowded behind rows of schoolchildren, lined up behind the flags along the streets. A religious service was celebrated in Westminster Abbey, after which the body was buried near Norwich Cathedral in Norfolk. Monuments were erected in her memory in many places, poems and songs were written to celebrate her patriotic acts; her name was given to a rose, to streets, squares, and of course hospitals throughout the world, as far as Australia. A mountain and a lake were named after her in Canada. In 1939, a film was made retracing her career, with Anna Neagle in the lead role. The nursing school that she headed was named both after her and after Marie Depage—the Edith Cavell–Marie Depage Institute—who disappeared in the wreck of the *Lusitania*.

See also **World War I.**

BIBLIOGRAPHY

Barney, Shane M. "The Mythic Matters of Edith Cavell: Propaganda, Legend, Myth and Memory." *Historical Reflections* 31, no. 2 (2005): 217–233.

Grey, Elizabeth. *Friend within the Gates: The Story of Nurse Edith Cavell*. Boston, 1961.

Hill, William Thompson. *The Martyrdom of Nurse Cavell*. London, 1915. Text available at http://www.greatwardifferent.com/Great_War/Cavell/Cavell_10.htm.

Hughes, Anne-Marie Claire. "War, Gender and National Mourning: The Significance of the Death and Commemoration of Edith Cavell in Britain." *European Review of History* 12, no. 3 (2005): 425–444.

Lefèvre, Patrick, and and Jean Lorette. *La Belgique et la première Guerre mondiale. Bibliographie*, 429–431. Brussels, 1987.

VALÉRIE PIETTE

CEAUȘESCU, NICOLAE. *See* **Romania.**

CELAN, PAUL (1920–1970), poet writing in the German language.

Paul Celan's poetry is unquestionably difficult. It is also lively, despite a muted quality, with an inspiration or a form of lyricism that is highly personal but that makes it uniquely identifiable and universally comprehensible. For Celan, in fact, poetry was a communicative act, one of these "gifts, which bring destiny with them"; he also stated that he saw "no basic difference between a handshake and a poem" (Celan, 1986, p. 25).

Paul Celan was born within the former Austro-Hungarian Empire, in Bukovina, "a region inhabited by people and books" (Celan, quoted in Chalfen, p. 4) in Czernowitz (now Chernovtsy, Ukraine); along with the poetess Rosa Ausländer (1901–1988), he is one of this town's major literary figures. Czernowitz with a linguistically varied population, situated at the foot of the Carpathian mountains, was part of Romania after World War I. Paul Celan was therefore born a Romanian citizen. His real name was Paul Antschel and he was of Jewish origin. Almost half of the town's population was Jewish. Otherwise, the region itself was highly multiethnic: Romanians, Ukrainians, Ruthenians, Germans, Hungarians, and Poles lived side by side, sometimes for better and at other times for worse.

Paul's father, a former soldier, was a wood merchant and the family lived modestly. Paul, the only son, received "a conventional middle-class education, in which Judaism served as a moral structure rather than as a religion" (Chalfen, p. 37), although his parents were believers and respected the traditions. At home, the family spoke German, according to the custom in "good" families. After an initial schooling in German Celan's father moved him to a Zionist Hebrew school. He also had to learn Romanian. He always preferred German, even after the Holocaust, when he continued to write his poems in German, thereby addressing "his poems written in a counterlanguage to a counterpublic," as Bertrand Badiou commented (Celan, 2001, vol. 2, p. 9; translated from the French).

In 1930 he entered secondary school, where he proved a highly able pupil. In 1934 he changed school because of the increasingly virulent anti-Semitism of the teachers. At around fifteen to sixteen years old he began to write poems and associated with a "circle" of young and antifascist enthusiasts of the arts and literature. He started to teach himself English in 1937 in order to read Shakespeare in the original. In 1938 he passed his baccalaureate and enrolled as a medical student. The agreements between Romania and France enabled him to go and study in Tours. On his way he stopped in Paris and visited its museums and theatres.

He returned to Czernowitz in June 1939 when, caught unawares by the war that started in September, he was then unable to return to France. He then enrolled to study Romance philology in Czernowitz. The Red Army occupied the town in June 1940 and the occupying forces sovietized the university. It was at this time that Celan learned Russian in a matter of weeks in order to act as an interpreter. That year he met the actress Ruth Lackner, his first great love and the inspiration for many of his poems. In June 1941 the Soviets deported four thousand people from Czernowitz to Siberia, including some of Celan's friends. The following month, the Romanians, soon followed by the Germans, took control of Czernowitz. The Nazi night then fell upon the city. The first systematic massacres of Jews—after pillaging and pogroms—carried out by the deployment group Einsatzgruppe D and the SS under Otto Ohlendorf's (1907–1951) command, began two days after the town was captured. In October 1941 a ghetto was established. Deportations then followed. Paul's parents were deported to a camp in the Bug River region and in 1942 his father probably died of typhus and his mother was murdered. Paul himself was sent to a labor camp. From then on his poetry was haunted by the tragic fate of the Jews and by death. In 1944 he returned to Czernowitz, where he rejoined his friend Ruth, but their romantic relationship dwindled as it mutated into deep friendship. That year he also made the acquaintance of Ausländer. The Soviets occupied the town again.

Celan assembled his poems with a view to their publication. A first selection was in fact published in 1947, when he took "Celan" as his pseudonym. In 1945 he left his town, which was now part of Soviet Ukraine, for Bucharest, where he worked as a translator. There he associated with poets and artists and, in particular, Gherasim Luca (1913–1994) and the Romanian surrealists.

At the end of 1947 he finally carried out his plan to travel to Vienna. He secretly left Romania, going through Budapest, and stayed in Vienna for about six months. There he met the poetess Ingeborg Bachmann (1926–1973), with whom he was to have a romantic relationship, which started again in 1950 and then in 1957. In 1948 he settled permanently in Paris. His first collection, *Der Sand aus den Urnen* (The sand from the urns), with a print run of five hundred, has since disappeared. He embarked on some studies and lived on grants and various jobs. He also began to translate to commission (for example, Georges Simenon's [1903–1989] Maigret novels) and to earn his living from translation. Translation then came to represent a very important dimension of his work. He turned his hand to translating the greatest French poets. They included Arthur Rimbaud (1854–1891), Guillaume Apollinaire (1880–1918), Paul Valéry (1871–1945), Henri Michaux (1899–1984) and others, some of whom—such as René Char and André du Bouchet—became his friends. He also translated from other languages: English (particularly Emily Dickinson [1830–1886] and William Shakespeare [1564–1616]), Russian (particularly Osip Mandelstam [1891–1938]), Romanian, Hebrew, Italian, and Portuguese.

His next volume, *Mohn und Gedächtnis* (1952; Poppy and memory), won him serious acclaim in the literary circles where he was beginning to build a reputation and where he already had many friends. Unfortunately, he also had some enemies, such as anti-Semitic critics. Also, Claire Goll (1891–1977), Yvan Goll's (1891–1950) widow, following a dispute about a translation, seems never to have tired of slandering Celan and accusing him of plagiarism. This was a baseless accusation that left a severe and enduring mark on Celan. It is in *Mohn und Gedächtnis* that some of the poet's most frequently quoted lines appear—those of the *Todesfugue* (Death fugue) written in May 1945 in Bucharest: "a man lives in the house your golden hair Margarete / your ashen hair Shulamith he plays with the serpents / He calls out more sweetly play death death is a master from Germany" (Celan, 1995, pp. 63–65).

Some critics at the time compared these lines to Pablo Picasso's 1937 painting *Guernica*. What is certainly true, as Celan's friend Jean Bollack observes, is that from then on "the murder camps are rarely the object of reference in the poems; more indirectly and more powerfully, they bring a 'meaning,' their shadow, to every altered significance and to every word" (p. 7; translated from the French). In a sense, Celan's work is a response to Theodor Adorno's (1903–1969) statement that writing poetry is impossible after Auschwitz.

Celan was then regularly invited to Germany—he once participated in a meeting of the Gruppe 47—and to German-speaking countries, for literary conferences or lectures. He also received many prizes.

In 1952 he married Gisèle Lestrange (1927–1991), a twenty-five-year-old artist and engraver whom he had met one year earlier. The two artists often collaborated. The following year, the couple lost their first child, François, following a difficult labor. Their second son, Eric, was born in 1955.

In 1956 Celan was working as a substitute teacher at the École Normale Supérieure. In the same year Alain Resnais's film about the concentration camps, *Night and Fog*, for which Celan translated the text, was shown in Germany. Three years later Celan obtained the post of German lecturer at the École Normale Supérieure, which he held until his death. In 1959, he published a further collection, *Sprachgitter*. In 1960, he won the Georg Büchner Prize, one of the most important German literary prizes. From the 1960s onward he suffered from psychiatric disorders and murderous or suicidal impulses that forced him to have himself committed on several occasions. This did not prevent him from writing and publishing some collections that are among his finest: *Die Niemandsrose* (1963; No one's rose), *Atemkristall* (1965; Breathcrystal), *Atemwende* (1967; Breathturn), and *Lichtzwang* (published posthumously in 1970; Lightduress).

On the night of 19 April 1970 Paul Celan threw himself into the Seine, probably from the Pont Mirabeau. His body was not found until 1 May. His wife, Gisèle, disappeared in 1991.

See also **Germany; Guernica; Holocaust.**

GRAPHY

Jean. *Poésie contre poésie: Celan et la littérature.*
Paris, 2001.

Celan, Paul. *Collected Prose.* Translated by Rosemary
Waldrop. Manchester, U.K., 1986.

———. *Werke.* 14 vols. Frankfurt am Main, 1990–2005.

———. *Selected Poems.* Translated with an introduction by
Michael Hamburger. London, 1995.

Celan, Paul, and Celan-Lestrange, G. *Correspondance,*
edited with a commentary by Bertand Badiou and
Eric Celan. 2 vols. Paris, 2001.

Chalfen, I. *Paul Celan: A Biography of His Youth.*
Translated by Maximilian Bleyleben with an introduction by John Felstiner. New York, 1991.

NICOLAS BEAUPRÉ

CÉLINE, LOUIS-FERDINAND (1894–1961), French writer.

Louis-Ferdinand Céline, originally named
Louis-Ferdinand Auguste Destouches, was born
into a lower-middle-class family in Courbevoie, a
Paris suburb. The aristocratic "des" in his family
name was a distant memory: his father was a low-
level employee at an insurance company and his
mother was a milliner. Céline spent his youth in
Paris, where his parents had moved. He also spent
part of his school years in Germany and England.
Before World War I he tried his hand at selling
fabric and then jewelry. In 1912 he joined the
cavalry. On 27 October 1914 he was seriously
wounded in the arm. His convalescence lasted several months, and he was declared permanently unfit
for service. During the war he spent time in
London and Africa. After the war he took advantage of a special dispensations for veterans that
allowed him to earn his *baccalauréat* degree and
study medicine. His first written work, on the life
of the physician Ignaz Phillipp Semmelweis (1818–
1865), was his doctorial thesis in medicine. From
1924 to 1927 he worked for the public health
division of the League of Nations, traveling
throughout the world to spread the gospel of
hygiene. At the end of his assignments he established a practice in Clichy, in northern Paris. In
1929 he began work on a novel. That book,
Voyage au bout de la nuit (1932; *Journey to the
End of the Night,* 1934) immediately established

his reputation as a great and innovative novelist,
an anarchist by virtue of both the violently antimi-
litaristic and anticolonialist positions he endorsed
and his destructured use of language, marked by
his original use of slang. His hero-narrator,
Bardamu, who owed a great deal to Céline's own
experiences in the Great War and in Britain, Africa,
and the United States, became as famous as his
creator.

The novel was followed by a literary scandal
when it failed to win the Prix Goncourt after being
considered the front-runner. It was supported in
particular by a number of leftist writers, such as
Louis Aragon (1897–1982), who misjudged the
author's politics. Céline's true colors were revealed
to the Left in 1936 with the publication of *Mea
Culpa,* a critical essay on his travels in the Soviet
Union. That same year he published his second
novel, *Mort à crédit* (1938; *Death on the
Installment Plan*), whose story chronologically
precedes *Voyage au bout de la nuit* but did not
enjoy the same success. In 1933 he tried his hand
at theater with *L'Eglise* (The church), a satirical
play based on his experiences with the League of
Nations.

Success returned in 1937 with *Bagatelles pour
un massacre* (Trifles for a massacre), a pamphlet-
essay in which Céline used his rich and ever more
hallucinatory style in the service of an extremely
virulent racism and anti-Semitism. This was not an
isolated act of provocation, since Céline committed
the same offense twice more with *L'école des
cadavres* (1938; School of corpses) and *Les beaux
draps* (The fine mess) in the midst of the
Occupation, in 1941. Céline frequented the most
violently anti-Semitic circles of the times and published thirty-five articles in the collaborationist
press. His unbridled anti-Semitism appalled even
the German writer Ernst Jünger (1895–1998),
whom he met while the latter was in occupied Paris.

In 1944 he published a new novel, *Guignol's
Band.* After the Allied landing he fled to Germany
in the hope of reaching Denmark, where he had
savings. He arrived there in March 1945, having
passed through Baden-Baden and Sigmaringen,
where the elites of collaborationist Paris and of
the Vichy government, including Philippe Pétain
(1856–1951) and Pierre Laval (1883–1945), had
taken refuge. He was arrested in Copenhagen on

17 December 1945. From prison, and later from the hospitals where he was detained, he prepared his defense, wrote a voluminous correspondence, and began work on *Féerie pour une autre fois* (1952–1954; Fable for another time). In 1948 he published a violent response to Sartre entitled "A l'agité du bocal" (To the shit-disturber). In 1950 Céline was tried in absentia. He was declared a national disgrace and sentenced to a year in prison and a fine of fifty thousand francs. He was ultimately pardoned the following year and was able to return to France. He settled in Meudon and took refuge in his writing, pursuing his stylistic explorations. *Féerie pour une autre fois* did not attract a wide readership but interest revived somewhat with *D'un château l'autre* (1957; *Castle to Castle*, 1968), an autobiographical novel recounting his flight from France in 1944–1945 to escape justice. He went on to publish *Nord* (North) in 1960 and finished *Rigodon* (Rigadoon) in 1961, just before his death on 1 July 1961.

In a certain sense Céline wrote his own epitaph with the opening of *D'un château l'autre*: "Frankly, just between you and me, I'm ending up even worse than I started" (1997, p. 1). A brilliant and acclaimed stylist, a fanatical anti-Semite, and a raging misanthrope, Céline is at once one of the greatest French writers of the twentieth century and one of its most unpleasant and controversial personalities.

See also **Anti-Semitism; Fascism; France; Jünger, Ernst.**

BIBLIOGRAPHY

Primary Sources

Céline, Louis-Ferdinand. *Romans.* 4 vols. Paris, 1978–1993.

———. *Castle to Castle.* Normal, Ill., 1997.

Secondary Sources

Gibault, François. *Céline.* 2nd ed. 3 vols. Paris, 1985.

Milton, Hindus. *The Crippled Giant: A Literary Relationship with Louis-Ferdinand Céline.* 1950. London, 1986.

NICOLAS BEAUPRÉ

CHAGALL, MARC (1887–1985), painter.

Marc Chagall was born Moishe Shagal in Vitebsk, Byelorussia. He was the eldest of nine brothers and sisters and throughout his life was profoundly influenced by the Yiddish culture of his childhood. Marc Chagall drew inspiration from the mores, traditional costumes, fables, and Russian and Jewish folklore of his native land. In 1906 he began his training as a painter at the studio of Yehuda Pen in Vitebsk. The following year he left for St. Petersburg, where he became the protégé of a lawyer who covered his expenses, which allowed him to develop his talents at several art schools.

In late 1910 he discovered the impressionists at Paul Durand-Ruel's gallery and met Robert Delaunay in Montparnasse, and in 1911 he moved into La Ruche (The hive), a cluster of studios where he and other painters and poets of the Paris School worked and exchanged ideas. Through his association with Pablo Picasso, Georges Braque, Fernand Léger, Amedeo Modigliani, and many others, Chagall became acquainted with the successive phases of the avant-garde. He painted *To Russia, Donkeys and Others* (1911–1912, title provided by his friend the poet Blaise Cendrars), *Homage to Apollinaire* (1911–1912), and *Russian Village under the Moon* (1911), using cubist construction in combination with his own pictorial language. Spaces with displaced elements subvert the rational order of planes, dimensions, figures, and objects. Chagall drew from the lessons of the avant-garde and let the human figures in his art completely break free from the laws of gravitation. They float in the air, heads sometimes detached from bodies, alongside cows, bulls, or goats. Chagall added to Delaunay's "Orphic" spaces a rich range of colors that diffuse light into space. His sojourn in Paris led him to the definitive avant-garde form of his art: the decomposition of elements coexists with the painter-poet's personal universe, dominated by an atmosphere of fable, a symbolic visual language derived from folk art.

When he returned to Russia in 1914, on the eve of World War I, the colors and forms in his paintings changed and their poetic and religious aspects became increasingly evident. Chagall returned to Vitebsk and painted numerous self-portraits and portraits of those around him, juxtaposed with or holding in their hands objects from daily life, which appear as recurrent motifs. Transformed or in a state of levitation, violins,

---

SELECTED WORKS OF MARC CHAGALL

To Russia, Donkeys and Others. 1911–1912. Oil on canvas. 157 x 122 cm. Musée National d'Art Moderne, Paris.

Homage to Apollinaire. 1911–1912. Oil, gold dust, and silver on canvas. 200 x 189.5 cm. Stedelijk van Abbemuseum, Eindhoven, Netherlands.

The Russian Village under the Moon. 1911. Oil on canvas. 126 x 104 cm. Staatsgalerie moderner Kunst, Munich, Germany.

The Lovers series. 1914–1916.

"Chagall's box": Paintings for the Moscow State Yiddish Theater (GOSET). Alexei Granovsky, director. Seven monumental paintings remain (the curtain and ceiling have been lost). Paintings for all walls on sewn sheeting (2.84 m x 7.87 m, left wall); on the right-hand wall four images of arts pertaining to theater: *Music, Dance, Theater,* and *Literature,* surmounted by a long frieze, *The Wedding Feast.* Facing the stage, square image *Love on Stage.*

---

lamps, samovars, chairs, and pendulum clocks are depicted alongside elements typical of the Russian countryside: wooden houses, Orthodox churches, peasants, soldiers, livestock, and poultry. Within this universe Chagall portrayed Jewish elders, sometimes suspended in space; these figures allude either to the Jewish *luftmensch* (someone who lives in the air and subsists entirely on air, and buys and sells dreams) or to the Wandering Jew hovering over the town. In 1915, in response to his marriage to Bella Rosenfeld, Chagall painted the *Lovers* series.

In 1917, following the October Revolution in Russia, Chagall was named commissar of fine arts in the Vitebsk regional department of education by Anatoly Vasilyevich Lunacharsky, then people's commissar of education and culture for the entire country. Chagall dedicated himself completely to creating a school of folk art and a community studio, which opened in 1919. The suprematist concepts of Kazimir Malevich, then teaching at the painting school alongside El Lissitzky and Jean Pougny, conflicted with the pedagogical precepts of Chagall, however, who resigned and left Vitebsk, moving to Moscow. There he undertook work for the Moscow State Yiddish Theater (GOSET), where he painted a group of panels known as "Chagall's box" (two of the panels are now missing). Chagall later left Russia again for Paris.

During the 1920s and 1930s Marc Chagall added more outlining to his shapes, combined different media (oil, pastel, gouache), and produced paintings with Christian themes. The primary colors he preferred are set off by intense whites, his figures now haloed in light. He made greater use of the impasto technique and began to play with multiple planes. In 1926 a series of one-man shows in Paris and New York made Chagall famous. Viewers discovered a body of work that was universal in scope and open to different interpretations but that always incorporated a poetic semantics and elements that were autobiographical, often drawn from the many trips he had taken at the beginning of the 1930s (to Palestine, Holland, Spain, and Italy). Like those of many other artists—all the more so because Chagall was Jewish—his paintings were taken down and destroyed by the Nazis. In 1933, on Joseph Goebbels's orders, a burning of Chagall's works was organized in Mannheim. Marc Chagall became a naturalized French citizen in 1937, then left for the United States in 1941. When he was not doing commissions, he displayed in his works horrendous motifs in response to the barbarism of the war and the Holocaust. His figures became scattered signs within a space that was increasingly imaginary and spiritual, devoid of any reference to natural laws. Apart from exhibits in New York and Chicago, the

To Russia, Asses, and Others. Painting by Marc Chagall, 1911–1912. ALINARI/ART RESOURCE, NY

first retrospective of the painter's works was held in 1947 at the Musée National d'Art Moderne in Paris. The following year Chagall returned to France, where an edition of Nikolai Gogol's *Dead Souls* (1842), illustrated with 107 engraved plates by the artist, was published, having been commissioned by the art dealer and publisher Ambroise Vollard, whom Chagall had met in Paris in 1923. In 1930 Vollard had commissioned him to illustrate the Bible; that commission was not completed until 1952, and the work was published only in 1956. Chagall produced an extremely large and varied body of graphic work, inspired by his unique personal outlook. The lithographs (accentuated with black outlines); the drawings in black and white or in color, with reds, blues, and yellows dominating; the etchings; the pastel drawings; and the watercolors constitute proper exhibitions.

Chagall eventually settled in Saint-Paul-de-Vence, France, where he devoted himself to lithography and ceramics. In 1957, again wishing to diversify his media, he began work on a series of stained-glass windows for sites in Plateau d'Assy, Metz, Jerusalem, New York, London, Zurich, Reims, and Nice.

A multidisciplinary artist, Chagall always infused his work with music, theater, and dance. As early as 1910 he was attending performances of Sergei Diaghilev's Ballets Russes in Paris. Moreover, he always painted expressly for the theater. Beginning in 1942 he did paintings for established theaters in the United States and Mexico, and he designed the sets and costumes for Igor Stravinksy's *Firebird* in 1945. In 1964, commissioned by André Malraux, he painted the ceiling of the Paris Opera; his frescoes are adorned with colorful muses, centaurs, angels, cellos, and houses, and allowed him once again to explore the concept of levitating figures and objects. In 1966 he began work on the mural paintings at the Metropolitan Opera at Lincoln Center in New York City, and in 1967, also for the Met, he designed the sets for Wolfgang Amadeus Mozart's *Magic Flute*. From this point on the themes of his multifigure works included the circus, religious subjects, and universal mythologies, which were always linked to more personal myths. Chagall had achieved international recognition. In 1973 the Chagall Museum was inaugurated in Nice, and the artist embarked on a final trip to the Soviet Union. Chagall died in Saint-Paul-de-Vence in 1985. Two years later, a major Chagall exhibit opened in Moscow.

See also **Braque, Georges; Cubism; Léger, Fernand; Painting, Avant-Garde; Picasso, Pablo; Surrealism.**

BIBLIOGRAPHY

Primary Sources

Chagall, Marc. *My Life.* Translated by Elisabeth Abbott. New York, 1994. Translation of *Mein Leben.*

Secondary Sources

Alexander, Sidney. *Marc Chagall: A Biography.* New York, 1978.

Bohn-Duchen, Monica. *Chagall.* London, 1998.

Cassou, Jean. *Chagall.* Paris, 1966.

Guerman, Mikhail Iourevitch. *Le pays qui se trouve en mon âme la Russie.* Translated by Jean-Louis Chavarot. St. Petersburg, 1995.

Marc Chagall: Les années russes, 1907–1922. Exhibition catalog. Musée d'Art Moderne de la Ville de Paris, 13 April–17 September 1995. Paris, 1995.

Marc Chagall: L'oeuvre gravé. Exhibition catalog. Musée National Message Biblique Marc Chagall, Nice, 4 July–5 October 1987. Paris, 1987.

Meyer, Franz. *Marc Chagall.* Translated by Philippe Jacottet. Paris, 1962.

Schneider, Pierre. *Chagall à travers le siècle.* Paris, 1995.

CAROLINE TRON-CARROZ

CHAMBERLAIN, NEVILLE (1869–1940), British politician, served as prime minister from 1937 to 1940.

Born on 18 March 1869, Neville Chamberlain was the second son of the prominent politician Joseph Chamberlain (1836–1914). His elder half-brother, Austen (1863–1937), was groomed for a political career; Neville was intended to look after the family fortunes in commerce. After seven difficult years managing a plantation in the Bahamas, he had a more successful business career in Birmingham. He entered local government, and was lord mayor of Birmingham in 1915–1916. In December 1916, Chamberlain accepted a national role as director-general of National Service, but after seven months was dropped by the Liberal prime minister David Lloyd George (1863–1945), whom he thereafter detested.

In 1918 Chamberlain was elected to the House of Commons, at the age of forty-nine. He welcomed the downfall of Lloyd George in October 1922, although this also ended Austen Chamberlain's leadership of the Conservative Party. However, Austen did not stand in his brother's way when Chamberlain was offered a post in the new Conservative government. His competence and vigor led to a swift progress: Chamberlain entered the cabinet in March 1923 as minister of health, and was promoted in August 1923 to chancellor of the exchequer. Although the Conservative government was defeated in January 1924, he had arrived in the front rank of British politics.

Neville Chamberlain inspects Nazi troops during his 1938 trip to Munich. ©CORBIS

When the Conservatives returned to power in November 1924, Chamberlain declined the offer of leading the treasury and instead requested the ministry of health. He believed this had greater scope for creative work, and had already prepared an ambitious legislative program that drew on his expertise in local government. By the general election of 1929, Chamberlain had achieved nearly all of his planned reforms, and had emerged as a driving force within the government as a whole. However, his relations with the opposition Labour Party were poor, as in debate he tended to dismiss their arguments contemptuously.

Chamberlain took on key roles while the Conservatives were in opposition in 1929–1931, and emerged as Stanley Baldwin's (1867–1947) undisputed heir as party leader. Chamberlain played an important part in the creation of the National Government in August 1931, and after its landslide election victory became chancellor of

the exchequer on 5 November 1931. He held this office until 1937, and was crucial to the government's durability and success. His orthodox economic approach was severely criticized after 1945, but it was the only acceptable method at the time. Stability and confidence were slowly restored, and in the 1935 general election the government's record secured a comfortable victory. Chamberlain's growing authority led to his taking wider roles, including influencing foreign policy, on which he was forming strong views.

He eventually succeeded Baldwin as prime minister on 28 May 1937. Although sixty-eight years old, he was physically robust and had a tremendous appetite for work. Chamberlain dominated his cabinet with an authority based upon his command of detail and certainty in his views. He was reserved in manner and many considered him to be narrow and humorless. Tackling the problems in international affairs was Chamberlain's

priority as prime mini... ...es with his foreign secretary, A... ...n (1897–1977), led to
the latter's...erlain in February 1938, after
which... was firmly in charge. His policy
of...easement" was a quest for peaceful compromise, intended to open a reasoned dialogue
with the dictators Adolf Hitler (1889–1945) and
Benito Mussolini (1883–1945) and meet their
grievances.

In the 1938 Czech crisis, Chamberlain sought
to avoid war over a distant country where no British
interests were involved. He conceived a dramatic
plan to fly to Germany and negotiate with Hitler
directly. This led to the Munich agreement of
September 1938, which resolved the crisis on
Hitler's terms, but without war and with a promise
of future goodwill; Chamberlain returned in triumph
to an atmosphere of euphoric relief. However,
Hitler's occupation of Prague in March 1939 discredited appeasement and made Chamberlain look
weak and foolish. He continued the quest for
peace, and when Germany invaded Poland in
September 1939, Chamberlain held back from
declaring war until a revolt of senior cabinet
ministers forced his hand.

After war broke out, Chamberlain broadened
his government to include Winston Churchill
(1874–1965) and Eden. Although a capable
administrator, Chamberlain was not temperamen-
tally suited to war leadership, appearing to be
unimaginative and complacent. Loss of support in
the House of Commons after defeat in Norway
forced him step down on 10 May 1940. His successor, Churchill, valued him as a colleague, and
Chamberlain moved to the post of lord president
and was effectively in charge of the Home Front.
After the Dunkirk Evacuation in 1940, the popular
mood turned against the former appeasers, but
Churchill resisted the pressure to dismiss him.
However, in the late summer Chamberlain's health
swiftly failed and he resigned as Conservative Party
leader in September, dying from cancer on 9
November 1940.

See also **Appeasement; Churchill, Winston; Hitler, Adolf;
World War II.**

BIBLIOGRAPHY

Charmley, John. *Chamberlain and the Lost Peace.* London,
1989. Revisionist account favorable to Chamberlain's
policy.

Dilks, David. *Neville Chamberlain.* Cambridge, U.K.,
1984. Only volume yet published of major official life.

Fuchser, Larry William. *Neville Chamberlain and Appeasement: A Study in the Politics of History.* London, 1982.

Parker, R. A. C. *Chamberlain and Appeasement: British
Policy and the Coming of the Second World War.* New
York, 1993.

STUART BALL

CHANEL, COCO (1883–1971), French
fashion designer.

Coco Chanel was probably the best-known,
most widely copied, and longest-lived fashion icon
of the twentieth century. The world cherished the
fragile pink silhouette of Jackie Kennedy wearing
her Chanel suit throughout that tragic day of
23 November 1963 in Dallas as she became a symbol of grace, dignity, and indomitable femininity.

Coco Chanel, too, was a survivor. Nothing in
her modest background—carefully shrouded in
mystery, if not in myth—prepared her to become
a leading figure in the world of fashion. Born
Gabrielle Chanel, Chanel was a small-town girl
from Saumur, raised in a French provincial convent
as an orphan and tried to escape her circumstances
with the help of men of financial means and social
standing. She became in her lifetime a symbol of a
culture that she absorbed, mastered, and interpreted in her own domain. For all the worldwide
recognition that she won, la Grande Mademoiselle
insisted on being known as a *couturière*—a seam-
stress, rather than a couturier—because she envisioned her trade as simply a trade, not highbrow
art. She nevertheless attained a form of perfection
in her craft.

During World War I she waged a fight of her
own against the cumbersome feminine fashion of
the turn of the twentieth century. Always attuned
with her time, she readily understood that women
could not live through those terrible war years
wearing the long, overdecorated garments and
extravagant headgear that the couturier Paul
Poiret had designed before the war. She favored
simplicity, freedom of movement, and practicality,
which were to become the standard fare of the

Coco Chanel wearing an early version of her signature suit, Paris, 1929. GETTY IMAGES

modern woman: it amounted then to nothing less than a revolution in dress.

She borrowed shapes and materials from heavily codified visual universes foreign to traditional feminine elegance: she adapted sailor's outfits, introduced menswear like trousers and ties, used materials of lowly status like wool jerseys, and convinced women that sportswear, comfortable as it was, could become everyday fare. The new silhouette that she launched—by being herself her first and foremost promoter—had the allure of freedom, modernity, and femininity. A garment just had to let a woman go with ease through the motions of everyday life. Chanel saw to it that she could move about, walk, work, run, climb stairs, sit, get up, and go: the elaborate cut of sleeves, the shape and length of the skirts, had to adjust to that need to live in the fast lane.

Her instincts for cultural trends did not translate in politics. Her *maison de couture* remained closed from 1939 to 1954, long enough to let her affair with a Nazi officer fade in the postwar landscape, while the revenues from the Chanel perfumes—Chanel No. 5, the first and foremost, Marilyn Monroe's favorite, which was launched in 1921—secured her financial independence.

In spite of the icy reception her 1954 comeback elicited in the press and the profession, a steady and growing flow of women found again their way to 31, rue Cambon in Paris. She was past seventy then, but managed to sustain a rhythm of work and social life of someone much younger. The classic Chanel "total look" then blossomed fully in all its faultless rigor. Again, the timing was right: after the fascination for youth ubiquitous in the 1960s and the experiments in space-age apparel and hippy attire, women were ready for elegance again, to slip into little black lace dresses and be ready for all occasions in a braided Chanel suit with matching blouse. Accessories became her trademark: boater hats, camellias, two-tone shoes, strings of (faux) pearls, chains around the waist—all concurred to create that unmistakably "Chanel look."

With her unerring feel for the spirit of the times, she set her mind to reach a wider clientele than the socialites she had clad in luxurious silks and tweeds in the 1920s. She did not mind being copied—knowing that her craftsmanship was unique—and never joined the Chambre Syndicale de la Couture Parisienne that tried to protect French creativity against piracy. Her style blossomed again, this time on a much wider scale. The Chanel revolution had turned into classicism.

In 1983, twelve years after her death, Karl Lagerfeld, set up as her heir by the Wertheimer brothers, her long-term business partners, managed to revisit Chanel's classic designs in his own flamboyant way and gave them a truly modern aura that appealed to the younger generations. The spirit of the House of Chanel lives on.

See also **Fashion.**

BIBLIOGRAPHY

Charles-Roux, Edmonde. *Chanel and Her World.* New York, 2005.

De La Haye, Amy, and Shelley Tobin. *Chanel, the Couturière at Work.* London, 1994.

Laver, James. *Costume and Fashion.* London, 1995.

MICHÈLE RUFFAT

CHANNEL ISLANDS. The four larger inhabited islands off the coast of Normandy, known collectively as the Channel Islands, were part of the Duchy of Normandy from 933 C.E. and have been held individually by the English Crown since the Norman conquest of 1066 C.E. Each island has its own system of government. Jersey, Guernsey, and Alderney have their own parliaments, known as the States, with deputies from the constituent parishes. Leading officials are appointed by the Crown: the bailiff, attorney-general, and solicitor general in Jersey and Guernsey, the judge on Alderney. The fourth island, Sark, remains a hereditary seigneurie with a working feudal constitution governed by a seigneur.

Traditionally, the language of the islands was a form of Norman French, but this was gradually replaced by English in the twentieth century as contacts with the United Kingdom increased. The islands' economies had been based on fishing and subsistence agriculture for many centuries, but this changed in the early twentieth century as improvements in transport allowed seasonal produce such as tomatoes and potatoes, grown earlier in the milder climate, to be shipped quickly to the mainland and then sold at premium prices. A second economic change was the development of tourism from the mainland and an increasing trend for the wealthy to retire to the islands. All these activities brought more money into the islands and improved the standard of living for many producers, tradesmen, and artisans. This economic growth also brought seasonal workers to the islands to augment the labor supply during the harvest and tourist periods.

World War II interrupted this gradual economic development and closer relationship with the United Kingdom mainland. On 19 June 1940, the British government decided the islands were indefensible and were to be demilitarized. Civilian evacuations took place, but were very uneven: 17,000 out of 41,000 from Guernsey,

British soldiers in formation wait to greet residents returning to Alderney following the German occupation, January 1946. GETTY IMAGES

6,500 out of 50,000 from Jersey, 1,382 of 1,400 from Alderney, and 129 out of 600 from Sark. These differences were attributed to confusion, both in Whitehall and among the islands' authorities. Evacuees were billeted across the United Kingdom and many men of military age served in the armed forces. The demilitarization did not prevent the bombing of St. Peter Port and St. Helier on 28 June 1940 and the loss of forty-four lives. The German occupation that began on 30 June lasted almost five years and brought about a gradual worsening of material conditions on the islands, as supplies from the European mainland were sporadic and all contact with the United Kingdom was lost. This led to increasing shortages as the occupying Germans requisitioned more and more of the islands' produce. By the last six months of occupation, there were cases of starvation among the civilian population.

The major German project on the islands was the building of a huge fortification on Alderney and substantial defense works on the other islands. With little available local labor, the Todt Organization used around 16,000 slave laborers (usually Russian and some African POWs, but encompassing at least twenty-seven nationalities). They were generally in a wretched condition on arrival, and up to a thousand died or were killed during construction work. Resistance activity by these laborers or by the civilian population was limited by German hostage-taking, the use of deportations, and the difficulties of escape and hiding. Sabotage was rare and most acts against the occupiers were confined to various forms of protest and the hiding of foodstuffs and other confiscated goods.

The islands' administrators, under orders from London, adopted a policy of passive cooperation with the German occupiers in order to protect the islanders' interests. This meant passing on German demands to the population and outward conformity. However, it also left them in office and able to maintain their position and status. The debate about the morality of their behavior remains an issue, but there were also other more obvious forms of outright collaboration such as profiteering, denunciations, and prostitution. These were probably on a scale comparable with other German occupied territories.

The islands were liberated on 9 May 1945 and returned to their prewar status. Some reforms were made in the political system to increase representation and make officials more answerable. Economies were also rebuilt and tourism remains important, but as traditional activities such as market gardening have declined, they have been replaced by reliance on financial activities, aided by the islands' special fiscal regime and their position outside the European Union.

See also **Occupation, Military; United Kingdom; World War II.**

BIBLIOGRAPHY

Bunting, Madeleine. *The Model Occupation: The Channel Islands under German Rule.* London, 1995.

Cruikshank, Charles. *The German Occupation of the Channel Islands: The Official History of the Occupation.* London, 1975.

King, Peter. *The Channel Islands War, 1940–1945.* London, 1991.

BOB MOORE

Charlie Chaplin in a scene from *The Great Dictator*, 1940. ©BETTMANN/CORBIS

CHAPLIN, CHARLIE (Sir Charles Spencer; 1889–1977), English actor, director, and producer.

Charles Chaplin is one of the most famous artists of the twentieth century and remains well known by subsequent generations. Most of his films have been given a new wide release in theaters since 2002, especially in Europe.

Born in the suburbs of London, Chaplin entered professional theater in 1898 as one of the Eight Lancashire Lads, a juvenile music hall act. In 1910, with Fred Karno's London Comedians, he embarked on a tour of the United States. He returned to the United States in 1912 and stayed there until the early 1950s. After working with Mack Sennett's Keystone Company (for $150 a week) in 1913, then with Mutual Film Corporation (for $670,000 a year) in 1916, Chaplin signed a million-dollar contract with First National in 1917. He became his own producer in 1919, with United Artists, the company he formed with Douglas Fairbanks, Mary Pickford, and D. W. Griffith. *The Kid* (1921) was the first feature film that he starred in and directed; *The Gold Rush* (1925), *The Circus* (1928), and *City Lights* (1931) were box office smashes.

Chaplin created a universal character, the Little Tramp. He could convey an experience of the world thanks to the language of pantomime, and because he embodied no national identity and spoke no mother tongue, he touched the hearts of spectators everywhere. Charlie, the Little Tramp, often finds himself on the wrong side of Law, facing the police, big business, the church—all those who hold power in an organized society. His immense success rested on popular acclaim but also on the recognition of intellectuals, especially in France in the 1920s, where many artists and authors praised his genius. In the eyes of the crowd, Charles Chaplin and Charlie the Tramp were the one and same citizen of the world. However, there was certainly a tension between the artist and his character, one that cannot be resolved in the too simple opposition between the "upstart" filmmaker's wealth and Hollywood respectability and the Tramp's voluntarily "outcast" status.

An American soldier in *Shoulder Arms* (1918), Chaplin became a German Jewish soldier in *The Great Dictator* (1940). In the 1920s a Jewish encyclopedia published in Berlin mentioned that Chaplin was the son of an eastern Jewish family that had probably emigrated to England during the middle of the nineteenth century and whose original name was Thonstein. This erroneous information was, predictably, used by Nazi propaganda. If the legend of Chaplin's Jewishness reemerged when he portrayed a Jewish barber in 1940, it was because his tramp character had already been compared to that of the schlemiel, a type found in the literature of the Jewish ghetto. As early as 1928, Joseph Roth compared Chaplin to the fictional double created by Siegfried Kracauer in his autobiographical novel *Ginster:* "Faced with department stores, wars, tailors, nations, Chaplin and Ginster are disconcerted and yellow, curious and awkward, ridiculous and tragicomical. At last, we have found a literary Chaplin: *Ginster.*" The most powerful description of the Tramp comes from Hannah Arendt: "In *The Great Dictator*," she wrote in 1944, "Chaplin attempted to play the monstrous and bestial character of Superman, by confronting 'the little man' with 'the big man' through his twin character. When at the end of the film he threw off his mask to reveal the real-life Chaplin behind the little man whose eminently desirable wisdom and simplicity he sought to represent to the world with seriousness tinged with despair, he, once the idol of the inhabited world, was barely understood."

The Great Dictator, said Chaplin, was his "first picture in which the story is bigger than the Little Tramp." He hesitated between a false happy ending and an open conclusion. He certainly saw the daily news catching up with him as, at the age of fifty, he made ready to give a last breath of life to his character, the Little Tramp, already weakened by the coming of talking movies. His reluctance to resort to derision or, conversely, to strike the pose of the political artist, indicates his belief in the power of conviction and in the sincerity and naïveté of his humanism. In *Modern Times* (1936), when he mimes being dragged into the cogs of the machine, the grace of his movements and of his body is not only preserved but also heightened, in spite of his subjection to a brutal mechanical logic. By constantly playing on the comedy or pathos of his character, Chaplin releases the tension that exists within the social world.

Chaplin always refused to accept American citizenship. During the era of McCarthyism, he was accused of "un-American activities" as a suspected communist, and J. Edgar Hoover, who had instructed the FBI to keep extensive files on him, tried to remove his residency rights. In 1947 he was verbally assaulted at a hostile press conference for *Monsieur Verdoux.* In 1952 he sailed for England to attend the London premiere of *Limelight.* Two days later the U.S. State Department rescinded his permit to reenter the country. Finally, he decided to leave Los Angeles and move to Europe, settling in Switzerland. He directed two more films, *A King in New York* (1957) and *A Countess from Hong Kong* (1967). The worldwide recognition of his genius was now a time long past. With his wife, Oona, he was enjoying fatherhood, raising eight children. In 1972 he returned to the United States to receive an honorary Academy Award and got a standing ovation from a repentant Hollywood. He was knighted by Queen Elizabeth II in 1975.

The Chaplin Association, located in Paris, the municipal archives of Montreux, Switzerland, and the Film Library of Bologna, Italy, preserve the legacy of his work and provide access to his personal archives.

See also **Cinema; Popular Culture.**

BIBLIOGRAPHY

Arendt, Hannah. "Charlie Chaplin: The Suspect." In *The Jew as Pariah.* New York, 1978.

Barthes, Roland. *Mythologies.* Selected and translated by Annette Lavers. New York, 1972.

Bazin, André. *Essays on Chaplin.* Edited and translated by Jean Bodon. New Haven, Conn., 1985. Contributions by François Truffaut, Jean Renoir, and Eric Rohmer.

Chaplin, Charlie. *My Autobiography.* New ed. London, 2003.

Delage, Christian. *Chaplin, la grande histoire.* Paris, 1998.

Maland, Charles J. *Chaplin and American Culture: The Evolution of a Star Image.* Princeton, N.J., 1989.

Nysenholc, Adolphe, ed. *Charlie Chaplin: His Reflection in Modern Times.* Berlin and New York, 1991.

Robinson, David. *Chaplin: His Life and Art.* New York, 1985.

CHRISTIAN DELAGE

CHARTER 77.

Charter 77 was both Czechoslovakia's most important and best-known dissident group and the eponymous document that announced the group's inception. Founded on 1 January 1977, the group brought to light the Czechoslovak communist regime's failures to uphold its international commitments to human rights and its repression of the Charter's signatories, and issued documents on issues of contemporary Czechoslovak and European importance. Several of its signatories also played large roles in the postcommunist Czechoslovak government and legislature.

ORIGINS

The creation of Charter 77 should be seen in the context of changes in the international and domestic environments. Internationally, the Czechoslovak communist government had signed the Helsinki Final Act (1975) and had ratified the two United Nations covenants on rights (1976). The initiation of human rights groups in the Soviet Union (1975) and Poland (1976) also form an important backdrop. Domestically, in the years after the Warsaw Pact invasion that signaled the end of the Prague Spring of 1968, communist reformers from 1968 and noncommunists alike had become convinced of the unreformability of the system and increasingly prepared to act. The immediate catalyst that triggered the formation of Charter 77, however, lay in the trials of members of the rock band "The Plastic People of the Universe" and others in 1976. Many future signatories viewed the prosecution as an unwarranted attack on creative expression and on the alternative lifestyles of many young people. In the wake of the sentencing of the young musicians, discussions continued between former communists and noncommunists, focused on creating a broad program based on the one value they all shared: the defense of human rights. In a series of discussions in December of 1976 the text of the Charter was agreed on, then smuggled into West Germany and published there on 6 January 1977.

PARTICIPANTS

While, as the Charter's declaration explicitly noted, Charter 77 was not a formal organization, it did authorize three spokespeople to represent it. The

EXCERPTS FROM THE CHARTER 77 DECLARATION

Responsibility for the maintenance of civic rights in our country naturally devolves in the first place on the political and state authorities. Yet, not only on them: everyone bears his share of responsibility for the conditions that prevail and accordingly also for the observance of legally enshrined agreements, binding on all citizens as well as upon governments. It is this sense of co-responsibility, our belief in the meaning of voluntary citizens' involvement and the general need to give it new and more effective expression that led us to the idea of creating Charter 77, whose inception we today publicly announce. Charter 77 is a free, informal open community of people with different convictions, different faiths and different professions united by the will to strive, individually and collectively, for the respect of civic and human rights in our own country and throughout the world—rights accorded to all men by the two mentioned international covenants, by the Final Act of the Helsinki Conference and by numerous other international documents. . . . Charter 77 is not an organization; it has no rules, permanent bodies or formal membership. It embraces everyone who agrees with its ideas, participates in its work, and supports it. It does not form the basis for any oppositional political activity.

"Charter 77—Declaration." Quoted in Skilling, pp. 211–212.

initial trio was composed of Jiří Hájek (foreign minister during the Prague Spring), Václav Havel (internationally known playwright), and Jan Patočka (renowned philosopher). Other luminaries who served as spokespeople included the philosopher Václav Benda, the journalist Jiří Dienstbier, and the singer Marta Kubišová. Generally, the triad included a former Communist, a "nonparty" person, and one person from the world of culture. The spokespeople were not conceived as representing these spheres, but served to indicate that Charter 77 was composed of people holding a wide range of beliefs, yet committed to consensus. Women served as spokespeople on over 70 percent of the slates from 1977 to 1989, and individuals from the religious communities also played a prominent role. This diversity also applied to the signatories as a whole, although Slovaks were clearly underrepresented. From its initial 242 signatories, Charter 77 eventually came to encompass some 2,000 individuals from all walks of life. The vast majority of the members of the Committee to Defend the Unjustly Persecuted (Výbor na obranu nespravidlivě stihaných; VONS, founded 1978), a group that aided victims of state prosecution and their families, were drawn from the ranks of the Chartists. While their numbers, given the levels of repression at the time in Czechoslovakia, bear witness to the courage of many Czechs and Slovaks, one cannot say that the Charter gained the allegiance of large sections of the population.

ACTIVITIES

Charter 77's main sphere of activity lay in the creation of documents, more than 570 of them between its inception and the beginning of the "Velvet Revolution" of 1989. While half of these dealt with the repression of the signatories and internal Charter business, the other half addressed such diverse topics as reform of the political system, freedom of travel, the deteriorating state of the environment, the economy, Czechoslovak history, minority issues, the ongoing discussions of the Conference on Security and Cooperation in Europe and other peace issues, developments in other Eastern European countries and, especially, the regime's violations of human rights, including creative freedom and the freedom of religion. In 1978 a group of signatories began publishing these documents and others relating to VONS and underground publication in *Information On Charter 77* (Informace o chartě 77). Charter signatories also supported underground publishing of both fiction and nonfiction, and although these latter writings are not official Charter documents they shed much light on the Charter's underlying philosophy. The most famous of these is Václav Havel's "The Power of the Powerless," which is widely held to be the most influential theoretical work produced by Eastern European dissidency.

SIGNIFICANCE

Charter 77 is notable for many things, but especially for calling attention to the plight of Czechs and Slovaks and revealing the injustices perpetrated by their government. In some sense, the risks the Chartists took, and the harassment and jail sentences they suffered, both served as a badge of honor for the Czech and Slovak peoples and provided visibility for their nations. Further, although the theoretical and analytical value of the Chartists' works may have diminished with the fall of communism, they were exciting and important for their times. Finally, Charter 77 provided a group of people with clean hands when the communist regime fell and new, uncompromised leaders were needed. Several members of the first postcommunist Czechoslovak parliament were Charter signatories, and Jiří Dienstbier and Václav Havel became the state's first postcommunist foreign minister and president, respectively.

See also **Czechoslovakia; Dissidence; Havel, Václav; Velvet Revolution.**

BIBLIOGRAPHY

Primary Sources

Havel, Václav, et al. *The Power of the Powerless: Citizens against the State in Central-Eastern Europe.* Edited by John Keane. Armonk, N.Y., 1985. Contains Havel's seminal essay and ten other important essays by Chartists.

Prečan, Vilém. *Charta 77: 1977–1989: Od morální k demokratické revoluci. Dokumentace.* Prague and Bratislava, 1990. Almost eighty documents about and by the Charter, annotated list of all Charter documents, short biographies of the spokespeople, and a list of signatories.

Secondary Sources

Falk, Barbara. *The Dilemmas of Dissidence in East-Central Europe.* Budapest, 2003. Sets Charter 77 in the context of other similar regional movements.

Skilling, H. Gordon. *Charter 77 and Human Rights in Czechoslovakia.* London, 1981. The standard work. Includes translations of forty Charter-related documents.

Tucker, Aviezer. *The Philosophy and Politics of Czech Dissidence from Patocka to Havel.* Pittsburgh, Pa., 2000. Exploration of the philosophical underpinnings of the Chartists' ideas.

BRADLEY ABRAMS

CHECHNYA.

CHECHNYA. Chechnya is a small, mountainous, land-locked republic in the North Caucasus region of the Russian Federation, somewhat smaller than the U.S. state of New Jersey. Its population of about one million has been decimated by years of warfare as the Russian government, centered in Moscow, deployed tens of thousands of troops in two unsuccessful attempts to eradicate a separatist movement that had declared Chechnya's sovereignty. Russia and Chechnya share a long history, from military rule during the tsarist era through mass deportations and repression under the Soviet dictator Joseph Stalin (1879–1953), to an uneasy resettlement and reintegration in the last decades of the Soviet period. That shared history did not predetermine the outbreak of war in the mid-1990s, but it does go some way toward explaining the Chechens' desire for greater independence. There is also, however, a long history of Russian-Chechen cooperation. During the Soviet era large numbers of Chechens received higher education, loosened their ties to Muslim tradition in favor of secularism, joined professions, and moved to urban centers outside their homeland. If not for the economic and political collapse of the USSR, many Chechens might have continued along this trajectory to a modern cosmopolitan lifestyle, leaving the ways of the guerrilla fighter in the distant past. Instead, the demise of Soviet order and the policies of Russian and Chechen leaders brought about the renewal of violent conflict.

Post-Soviet Russia has fought two wars in Chechnya. The first was waged from 1994 to 1996; the second resumed in autumn 1999 and by 2006 had yet to end. The wars have entailed massive indiscriminate bombing of cities and villages, with high civilian casualties, sweep operations, herding of people into so-called filtration camps, extrajudicial killings, torture, and disappearances. Some one hundred thousand or more people are estimated to have died in the wars—mostly civilians—and several hundred thousand remained refugees.

Russia's military campaigns in Chechnya violated many international and European laws and agreements, including the Geneva Conventions, the European Convention on Human Rights, the European Convention for the Prevention of Torture and Inhuman or Degrading Treatment or Punishment, and, arguably, the Genocide Convention.

THE TSARIST AND SOVIET LEGACIES

Russia's first military encounter with Chechnya came in 1722, when Chechen fighters routed a cavalry force sent there by Peter the Great (r. 1682–1725). Later Chechen resistance to Russian tsarist influence was led by Islamic leaders such as Sheikh Mansur, Kazi Mullah, and Shamil. Typical of European colonial powers of that era, Russia pursued a strategy of economic warfare against the recalcitrant mountaineers, destroying their crops and burning their villages, and perpetrating massacres and deportations.

Some of the mountain peoples of the North Caucasus had opposed the reimposition of Russian rule during the civil war that followed the Bolshevik Revolution, and in subsequent decades resisted Soviet policies of collectivization of agriculture—as did peasants throughout the Soviet Union. Perceiving the Chechens as particularly rebellious, the Stalinist regime undertook a mass deportation of the entire population. Starting in the middle of the night of 22–23 February 1944, about five hundred thousand people were rounded up and packed into trains. Between the deportation itself and the conditions of exile, about a quarter of the population had perished within five years of their departure, according to official statistics.

In 1956–1957, Stalin's successors, led by Nikita Khrushchev (1894–1971), officially permitted the deported groups to return from exile. In Chechnya, a program of industrialization, based on oil refining, led to modernization, urbanization, and a large influx of Russians, especially to the capital city of Grozny. In the next few decades, many Chechens, including the sizable diaspora still spread throughout the Soviet Union, integrated into Soviet society, entered mixed marriages, adopted the Russian language, and pursued higher education and urban lifestyles.

THE END OF THE SOVIET ERA

Although it is fashionable to link the Russo-Chechen war that broke out in the 1990s to previous centuries of conflict, doing so risks overlooking the more immediate and relevant context. The

Chechen drive for independence was part of a broad movement throughout the Soviet Union for greater autonomy from the hypercentralized communist system ruled from Moscow. The economic and political reforms launched by the Soviet leader Mikhail Gorbachev (b. 1931) under the banner of perestroika emboldened activists throughout the multiethnic Soviet Union to speak out and organize for more autonomy. Ultimately it was the de facto secession of Russia itself, under the leadership of Gorbachev's rival Boris Yeltsin (b. 1931), that brought the Soviet Union to an end in December 1991.

With the advent of perestroika, residents of Chechnya mobilized to support political and economic change. Some of them seized on nationalist symbols and chose Dzhokhar Dudayev (1944–1996), a recently retired Soviet air force general, to head their movement. When the local communist authorities in Chechnya failed to condemn the coup against Gorbachev in August 1991, they discredited themselves in the eyes of increasingly nationalist and anticommunist Chechens as well as among the supporters of Yelstin, whose symbolic role in defeating the coup had made him a hero. Demonstrations in Grozny convinced Yeltsin's circle to support Dudayev as an alternative to the Soviet-era leader.

Yeltsin realized his mistake too late. The mercurial Dudayev and his supporters seized government buildings, the radio and television center, and an arsenal of weapons. He was elected president under disputed circumstances and immediately issued a declaration of sovereignty of the Chechen Republic. Yeltsin declared a state of emergency and dispatched twenty-five hundred interior ministry troops. Dudayev responded by declaring martial law and mobilizing forces for Chechnya's defense. Under threat of Russian invasion, most of Dudayev's erstwhile opponents rallied to his side—a phenomenon that was repeated under his successor when Russia invaded again in 1999.

INDEPENDENT CHECHNYA

Post-Soviet Chechnya suffered an unemployment rate of some 40 percent. Its main source of wealth—oil—saw a steady decline from peak production in 1971 of twenty-one million tons to a low of four million in 1991, with further declines projected. Three-fourths of the goods produced in Chechnya, including oil products, were dependent on deliveries from Russia and other countries of the former Soviet Union. In focusing on what he knew best—war—Dudayev neglected everything else that Chechnya would need to become a viable political and economic entity, including good relations with Russia.

Through bribery and intimidation, Dudayev's forces inherited a sizable arsenal of weapons, including some forty thousand automatic weapons and machine guns. Because Chechnya did not possess a formal army, many of the weapons were dispersed throughout the population. They ended up in the hands of rival gangs, many of them oriented more toward crime than national defense. As criminal activity spread beyond Chechnya's borders into other parts of Russia, Moscow authorities became increasingly determined to crush Dudayev's regime.

THE FIRST WAR

The path to war was cleared by Yeltsin's hawkish advisors, who presented one-sided views of the Chechen conflict, and by the Chechen president's suspicious nature, bordering on paranoia. Doubts emerged within the Russian General Staff about the wisdom of an invasion and the inadequacy of planning. Many Russian officers resigned rather than attempt to carry out such an implausible and morally dubious action, and others were fired for refusal to do so—more than five hundred, by some estimates. Chechnya received some support from foreign Islamist groups sympathetic to its plight, but most came in the wake of the Russian invasion in December 1994.

In some respects Russia could have won the war in Chechnya. Its armed forces destroyed the capital and gained nominal control of all other major population centers. Chechen troops retreated to the mountains to conduct a guerrilla campaign. Moscow might have used economic aid to win over the civilian population and police methods to deal with the remaining rebel forces. Instead the Russian forces treated the residents of Chechnya—including thousands of ethnic Russians who lived in Grozny—indiscriminately as enemies. The occupying Russian army—with drunken and drugged soldiers robbing, harassing, and otherwise

Relief workers distribute food to hungry Chechens in the city of Grozny during the Russian–Chechen war, 1995.
©PETER TURNLEY/CORBIS

maltreating civilians—did little to win over hearts and minds.

The Chechen resistance forces turned the tide of the war and put an end to Russian occupation by becoming what Moscow had always branded them: terrorists. The two most notorious attacks took place in June 1995 in the Russian town of Budennovsk and in January 1996 in Kizliar, Dagestan. In both cases Chechen forces seized hospitals and kept hundreds of hostages, executing some of them to keep Russian troops at bay.

Popular opposition to the war was widespread in Russia, led by organizations such as the Committee of Soldiers' Mothers, which supported efforts of parents to travel to Chechnya and rescue their sons or recover their bodies. The presidential election campaign of 1996 also played an important role, as Yeltsin acknowledged that he could not be reelected if he did not try to end the war. In August 1996, after another costly and senseless

attack on Grozny, Yeltsin finally faced reality and gave General Alexander Lebed (1950–2002), an erstwhile rival presidential candidate, authority to negotiate the Russian withdrawal. Four months earlier, the Russian army had assassinated Dudayev, thereby removing an unpredictable and unreliable negotiating partner. Aslan Maskhadov (1951–2005), Dudayev's successor as commander-in-chief, worked with Lebed to craft the so-called Khasavyurt Accord. It formally left the status of Chechnya's relationship to Russia undecided until 31 December 2001, by which date subsequent negotiations were supposed to resolve the two sides' differences.

THE SECOND WAR

Following the Russian troop withdrawal, Chechnya enjoyed a short-lived de facto independence, although "suffered" would be a more accurate characterization. Maskhadov won the Chechen presidency in January 1997, in an election

552

universally acknowledged as free and fair, but he never succeeded in establishing control over the country. Adversaries, including self-styled Islamist revolutionaries, commanded their own armed gangs and challenged Maskhadov's authority and his commitment to a secular state. They carried out kidnappings and murders of foreign workers to disrupt Maskhadov's plans to revive the Chechen economy through oil exports, and they ran a lucrative slave trade, whose victims included Chechens. The lawless nature of independent Chechnya gave Russia ample reason to develop contingency plans for a renewal of military conflict, even though a May 1997 peace treaty signed by presidents Yeltsin and Maskhadov committed both sides "forever to repudiate the use and the threat to use military force to resolve whatever disputes may arise."

Moscow's second war with Chechnya began during the first days of August 1999, when a force of Chechens, Dagestani Wahhabis, and others launched an attack across the Chechen border into Dagestan. They were led by Shamil Basaev (b. 1965) and Khattab (1969–2002), an Arab fighter married to a Dagestani woman. Local Dagestani forces resisted the invasion and were soon joined by regular Russian troops. Even after repelling the attack into Dagestan, Russian forces continued military operations against Chechnya, with massive aerial attacks in early September followed by a ground invasion. Unlike the first Chechen war— which nearly led to Yeltsin's impeachment—this one was popular, owing to its apparent defensive origins and the fact that the attack coincided with a series of terrorist bombings on Russian territory. During the first half of September four apartment buildings were blown up in Dagestan, Moscow, and Volgodonsk. Suspicion naturally fell on Chechens.

Vladimir Putin (b. 1952), appointed prime minister and heir apparent by Yeltsin days after the attack on Dagestan, seized the opportunity to prosecute the war while it still enjoyed public support. Four months into the war Yeltsin resigned his presidency, putting Putin in a position to move from acting president to the real thing with elections in March 2000. Renewal of the war against Chechnya, supported by an increasingly docile Russian press, secured Putin's victory.

The war itself dragged on for years. Even after most of Chechnya was bombed into rubble, and thousands of its citizens killed or driven away, the country remained a dangerously insecure place, with frequent guerrilla attacks, assassinations, and abductions. In autumn 2003, a Russian newspaper, drawing on official sources, estimated a death toll of about twelve thousand troops for both wars, with civilian deaths approaching a hundred thousand.

Moscow's attempts to "normalize" the situation in Chechnya proved futile. Troops alienated the local population with their brutal tactics and gave rise to a wave of terrorist attacks increasingly perpetrated outside Chechnya, including in Moscow. Putin branded Maskhadov an international terrorist and refused to negotiate anything but the terms of his surrender. Holding new presidential elections in Chechnya failed to induce popular support for the pro-Moscow regime. The October 2003 elections, widely denounced as fraudulent, yielded victory for the Kremlin's choice, Akhmad Kadyrov (1951–2004), but his assassination seven months later necessitated yet another round. No one was surprised at the August 2004 victory of Putin's candidate, General Alu Alkhanov (b. 1947), the Moscow-appointed interior minister.

By most accounts, the war-weary Chechen population would gladly trade its short-lived and costly independence for peace, stability, and a return to the status quo ante (of the Soviet era, if that were possible). But by the mid 2000s, the brutal character of the Russian occupation seemed destined only to stoke the embers of resentment and breed further violence.

See also **Al Qaeda; Guerrilla Warfare; Islamic Terrorism; Russia; Soviet Union; Terrorism.**

BIBLIOGRAPHY

Primary Sources

Gall, Carlotta, and Thomas de Waal. *Chechnya: Calamity in the Caucasus.* New York, 1998. An excellent journalists' account of the first war.

Nivat, Anne. *Chienne de Guerre: A Woman Reporter behind the Lines of the War in Chechnya.* Translated by Susan Darnton. New York, 2001. A French journalist's first-hand reporting from inside war-torn Chechnya.

Politkovskaya, Anna. *A Dirty War: A Russian Reporter in Chechnya.* Translated from the Russian and edited by John Crowfoot; with an introduction by Thomas de Waal. London, 2001.

————. *A Small Corner of Hell: Dispatches from Chechnya.* Translated by Alexander Burry and Tatiana Tulchinsky; with an introduction by Georgi Derluguian. Chicago, 2003.

Secondary Sources

Dunlop, John B. *Russia Confronts Chechnya: Roots of a Separatist Conflict.* Cambridge, U.K., 1998.

Evangelista, Matthew. *The Chechen Wars: Will Russia Go the Way of the Soviet Union?* Washington, D.C., 2002.

Lieven, Anatol. *Chechnya: Tombstone of Russian Power.* New Haven, Conn., 1998.

Tishkov, Valery. *Chechnya: Life in a War-Torn Society.* Berkeley, Calif., 2004.

Trenin, Dmitri V., and Aleksei V. Malashenko, with Anatol Lieven. *Russia's Restless Frontier: The Chechnya Factor in Post-Soviet Russia.* Washington, D.C., 2004.

MATTHEW EVANGELISTA

CHEMIN DES DAMES/MUTINIES.

The mutinies of 1917 began in the wake of the failed offensive along the Chemin des Dames, in northeastern France, the last great attempt of the French to achieve a complete rupture of the German lines. Military historians still disagree about many of the great battles of World War I—whether their outcome was inevitable and whether the generals plotting them were fools, rogues, or heroes. Not so for the Chemin des Dames offensive, which military historians condemn unanimously as employing the wrong tactics in the wrong place at the wrong time. There were problems with the scheme from the outset. Any pretense of surprise was forsaken. It was generally known on both sides of the western front well before April 1917 that the French were planning a major offensive along the Aisne River. General Robert Nivelle (1856–1924), an artilleryman by training, had hit upon a genuine tactical innovation, the *barrage roulant* or "rolling barrage." The artillery and the infantry would simply move forward at the same predetermined speed, thereby guaranteeing cover for the men advancing on foot. But the Germans quickly learned to recognize an artillery feint and that they could simply withhold their counter-barrage until the creeping barrage began. The War Minister General Hubert Lyautey (1854–1934) considered Nivelle's plan worthy of light opera. Yet it was allowed to proceed because of the gathering confusion of French politics.

The French made small and irregular gains, and in the first two weeks of the offensive suffered some one hundred forty-seven thousand men killed, wounded, or missing. As early as 22 April 1917, Nivelle scaled down his objectives, now limited to taking the Chemin des Dames plateau—precisely the sort of "tactical gains" at high casualties that he had scorned in his rise to the top. Nivelle was removed on 15 May and replaced by General Philippe Pétain (1856–1951), the hero of Verdun and the apostle of the defensive. But by then, the situation on the ground could not be resolved simply. In the short run, Pétain could not handle affairs much differently from Nivelle. The irregular gains of the offensive had either to be consolidated or abandoned. Abandoning the partial gains would have amounted to a resounding admission of failure, a risky choice given the rising discontent both at the front and in the interior. But consolidating the gains meant, in effect, continuing the offensive in its scaled-down form. Blood would continue to be shed for tactical rather than strategic gains. The point in connecting the Chemin des Dames offensive to the 1917 mutinies is not so much that this particular effort was any more militarily disastrous than the French offensives that preceded it, but that this pattern of heavy casualties and falling expectations had become unacceptable to many French soldiers.

The most common form of mutiny involved soldiers' collective refusal to take up positions in the front lines when ordered to do so. They would then depart to open areas and hold demonstrations airing their myriad demands. No demonstrations took place in the front lines themselves. Incidents of collective indiscipline occurred in nearly half of all of the divisions in the French army. The total number of "mutineers" is most reliably estimated at twenty-five thousand to thirty thousand. But such estimates are intrinsically misleading and perhaps a bit beside the point, because the French army mutinies comprised hundreds of thousands of individual decisions made and remade over a period of several weeks. An essential fluidity characterized events. Any estimate of the number of soldiers involved in a

German troops advance along the Chemin des Dames on their way to the Aisne battlefields, France, c. 1915. ©HULTON-DEUTSCH COLLECTION/CORBIS

particular demonstration is necessarily a mental snapshot, representing a guess as to how many soldiers passed into open defiance at a specific moment in time. The command structure lacked the means to resolve the matter in its favor if it resorted to violence. The mutinies largely displaced the formal authority structure in the French army. Consequently, an understanding of the mutinies must focus on the discontented soldiers themselves. For a brief moment in time, they were essentially free to decide what to do next.

No noteworthy links have ever been established between the mutinies and pacifist movements in the interior of France. Nothing is more surprising about the demands of the discontented soldiers of the spring of 1917 than their diversity. Soldiers moved effortlessly from relatively mundane matters such as the quality of their food, to great concern for their

families behind the lines, to issues as abstract as "injustice." The worry that "blacks" were mistreating soldiers' wives referred to widespread (but apparently untrue) reports that colonial troops had been used to suppress women's strikes. Soldiers sought very traditional male roles as protectors of and providers for their families. Above all, soldiers wanted "peace." But, when pressed, they plainly did not mean peace on any terms, or even on terms inconsistent with the war aims of the national community for the preceding three years. They sought *both* immediate peace and a reformed leave policy, although the former presumably would render the latter irrelevant. Through working out their complicated choices largely in the absence of formal command authority, the discontented soldiers made the mutinies an anguished affirmation of the war effort and the Third Republic that governed it. Paradoxically, the French army mutinies of 1917 became one of World War I's most extraordinary exercises in patriotism. They ended when soldiers chose to resume their duties. Suppression of the mutinies took place only after they had ended.

From a certain point of view, the command structure exercised considerable prudence. The French historian Guy Pedroncini arrived at numbers of 3,427 soldiers tried as a result of the mutinies, with 554 death sentences, and 49 soldiers actually shot. Yet the numbers told only part of the story. Remobilizing the French army in 1917 seemed to require victims. The courts martial were as much about identifying a group of "leaders" as punishing them. This relatively small population could accept blame for the disturbances, and in a very real sense pay the price for the reassertion of command authority.

See also **France; Pétain, Philippe; World War I.**

BIBLIOGRAPHY

Pedroncini, Guy. *Les Mutineries de 1917.* Paris, 1967.

Smith, Leonard V. *Between Mutiny and Obedience: The Case of the French Fifth Infantry Division during World War I.* Princeton, N.J., 1994.

Smith, Leonard V., Stéphane Audoin-Rouzeau, and Annette Becker. *France and the Great War, 1914–1918.* Cambridge, U.K, and New York, 2003.

LEONARD V. SMITH

CHERNOBYL. On 26 April 1986 one of the four nuclear reactors at the Chernobyl nuclear power plant near Kiev, Ukraine, exploded. The explosion generated a huge fire that spewed tons of radioactive material into the atmosphere and made the surrounding towns of Chernobyl and Pripyat uninhabitable. The explosion released four hundred times more radiation than the atom bombs dropped on Hiroshima and Nagasaki during World War II. Most of the radioactive material fell in Ukraine and the surrounding countries of Belarus and Russia, while lighter contaminated material blew as far away as Scandinavia and other parts of Europe, as far south as Greece and Yugoslavia.

The implications of the Chernobyl explosion lie not only in the fact that it was the worst nuclear accident of the modern age but also that it was a significant trigger for the collapse of the Soviet Empire and the communist bloc. Mikhail Gorbachev, the Soviet general secretary at the time of the accident, came to power in 1985 at a time when the world was still dominated by a bipolar geopolitical structure led by the United States and the Soviet Union. For centuries the Russians, during the tsarist monarchies and later under the Soviets, had a tradition of intense secrecy and lack of transparency in their governing bodies. Gorbachev announced a new policy of openness (glasnost) and restructuring (perestroika) soon after he came to power. But old habits die hard, and Chernobyl was a test of Gorbachev's ability to follow through on his promise to be more progressive. Despite the goals for a more open, democratic society, the Chernobyl accident revealed the extremely conservative and rigid nature of the Soviet government. Gorbachev had made a powerful impression on the Soviet people when he first came to office. He was by far the most accessible leader they had ever known. Chernobyl threw Gorbachev off course and he was never able to fully recover.

Firefighters and volunteers were not able to bring the fire and meltdown under control for nine days, and Gorbachev waited for eighteen days before publicly addressing the catastrophe. On 27 April, thirty-six hours after the accident, residents of Pripyat, a town four kilometers away and closest to the reactors, were evacuated. Residents in other surrounding villages were not informed of the accident and continued to go about their daily lives unaware of the fatal levels of exposure. Forty-eight hours after the accident Moscow authorities admitted there had been an explosion but insisted that the radiation situation was not harmful to inhabitants in the area. May Day festivities with parades and speeches in the surrounding villages (except Pripyat) went on as if nothing had happened. Not until after the May Day celebrations, from 2 to 4 May, were more than 100,000 people living in villages within a thirty-kilometer radius informed of the contamination and forced to leave their homes immediately and resettle. On 14 May, in a speech that revealed nothing about the causes or the impact of the accident, Gorbachev slid back into an anti-Western diatribe that claimed the United States used the accident as a launching point for an anti-Soviet campaign. This speech,

Reactor 4, Chernobyl nuclear power plant, photographed in May 1988. The lighter areas of the building are part of the original structure; the larger, darker section is the covering constructed to contain radioactive particles after the explosion.
©REUTERS/CORBIS

the lack of transparency in revealing the true extent of the radiation poisoning, the denial and delay in evacuating residents and alerting the world, all added to the Soviet public's deep distrust and suspicion of its leaders.

CAUSE OF THE ACCIDENT

The official explanation for the accident is that it was the result of a flawed reactor design that was operated by inadequately trained personnel. The less publicized explanation for the catastrophe is far more complex and dates back to the Soviet Union's rush to industrialize the nation in the 1920s and 1930s after the Bolshevik Revolution. Dozens of giant hydroelectric plants, factories, and later, nuclear plants were rushed prematurely into service. Historically the Soviet Union's occupational accident rate was the worst of any industrialized nation.

The reactor that exploded was known to have a problematic design structure; there were many of this same model in use and scheduled to be built all over the Soviet Union. The inadequacies and deficiencies of the reactor design were ignored and hidden by managers of the plant in order to fulfill the demands of the nation's economic plans for more nuclear energy. Following the accident, these design problems were acknowledged and no more of this model were built.

HEALTH CONSEQUENCES

The terrible environmental contamination resulted in the forced resettlement of hundreds of thousands of people and the loss of crops and cropland in the rich area of the Belarusian and Ukrainian black earth region known as the breadbasket of the Soviet Union. Over the next year another 300,000 inhabitants were forced to leave their omes and resettle. More than two thousand villages and towns were razed and covered over to prevent further radiation exposure. Hundreds of other villages were abandoned and still lie empty in 2006. Billions of rubles have been spent on the cleanup, decontamination efforts, and the resettlement and health care costs of the hundreds of thousands of people who suffered radiation poisoning.

The long-term health effects of such high radiation exposure are still a subject of intense debate. In 1986 and 1987 an estimated 200,000 "liquidators" from all over the Soviet Union came to help control the fire and clean up the area so the remaining reactors could continue to operate. The workers who were either forced or volunteered to help with the immediate cleanup operation in the early days before the fire was contained either died soon after the accident or died prematurely, primarily from cancer. The other liquidators also suffered high rates of cancers, but there is no conclusive data on all of them. In 2005, a report by a group of experts called the Chernobyl Forum attributed a total of fifty-six deaths directly to the explosion and the immediate aftermath. The Forum also greatly reduced the estimate of subsequent deaths related to radiation poisoning to 4,000 from previous estimates as high as 100,000. Children are disproportionately affected by radiation poisoning because they are more physically vulnerable. Although there have been extremely high rates of thyroid and other cancers among children exposed to the Chernobyl fallout, and very high rates of congenital birth defects and mental retardation, the link between radiation and these health consequences is still debated by nuclear experts in Russia, Ukraine, Belarus, and other countries. As the Chernobyl Forum report reveals, debates about death rates and the effects of radiation poisoning remain inconclusive and will continue for decades after the disaster.

HISTORICAL LEGACY

Because there were many signs of decay in the Soviet economy and society even before the Chernobyl accident, the explosion acted as a catalyst that propelled the Soviet Union toward collapse by 1991. Imminent signs of the breakup

included rising national consciousness in the fifteen republics of the Soviet Union, a failing war in Afghanistan that had caused deep-seated anger among the populace, and an economy that had been stagnating and declining for at least twenty years. Environmental damage and its impact on human health were hidden under Soviet rule and never publicly discussed nor acknowledged. For seventy years Soviet policies had wantonly destroyed the environment through the overuse of pesticides and chemicals for agriculture, the rush to industrialize, and the buildup of a military-industrial complex to compete with the United States in the Cold War. The nuclear accident at Chernobyl sent shock waves through the country that were irreparable. Chernobyl forced the issue into the public sphere and led to a widespread civil awakening. After the accident, for the first time in Soviet history, civil society spoke up, protesting and forming environmental associations to protect the Soviet Union's remaining natural resources. No peaceful civil gatherings of this nature were allowed before.

CHERNOBYL TWENTY YEARS LATER

After the fire was contained, a concrete sarcophagus was constructed to keep the radioactive material from leaking out. The sarcophagus was supposed to last for twenty to thirty years, but began to show dangerous signs of decay in the 1990s. A new shelter was scheduled to be completed by 2009, which is supposed to contain the reactor and the hazardous material for another hundred years. The remaining three reactors continue to operate. Concerns about possible leaks from leftover nuclear fuel in these three reactors remain.

After the Chernobyl accident the world became far more cautious about the use of nuclear energy and the design of nuclear power plants. International nuclear commissions were formed not only to research and examine the accident and the mechanisms for cleanup but also to ensure that this kind of accident never happens again. Globally, public trust in nuclear energy as an alternate source of power declined dramatically after Chernobyl, and that faith in the potential for nuclear power to solve the world's energy needs has never been fully restored.

See also **Atomic Energy; Gorbachev, Mikhail; Soviet Union.**

BIBLIOGRAPHY

"Chernobyl Children's Project International." Available from http://www.chernobyl-international.org.

"Chernobyl Information." Available from http://www.chernobyl.info/.

Coleman, Fred. *The Decline and Fall of the Soviet Empire: Forty Years That Shook the World, from Stalin to Yeltsin.* New York, 1996.

Feshbach, Murray, and Alfred Friendly Jr. *Ecocide in the USSR: Health and Nature under Siege.* New York, 1992.

Gale, Peter, and Thomas Hauser. *Final Warning: The Legacy of Chernobyl.* New York, 1988.

"International Atomic Energy Agency." Available from www.iaea.org.

Kaiser, Robert G. *Why Gorbachev Happened: His Triumphs and His Failure.* New York, 1991.

Medvedev, Zhores. *The Legacy of Chernobyl.* New York, 1990.

Volkogonov, Dmitri. *Autopsy for an Empire: The Seven Leaders Who Built the Soviet Regime.* New York, 1998.

KATE SCHECTER

CHETNIKS. *See* **Yugoslavia.**

DATE DUE